E15-9

Developing and Training Human Resources in Organizations

Developing and Training Human Resources in Organizations

Second Edition

Kenneth N. Wexley
Michigan State University
East Lansing, Michigan

Gary P. Latham
University of Toronto
Toronto, Ontario

HarperCollins*Publishers*

Sponsoring Editor: Debra Riegert
Project Editor: Claire M. Caterer
Art Direction: Teresa Delgado
Cover Design: Delgado Design, Inc.
Production Administrator: Paula Keller
Compositor: TCSystems, Inc.
Printer and Binder: R. R. Donnelley & Sons Company
Cover Printer: Lynn Art Offset Corporation

Developing and Training Human Resources in Organizations, Second Edition

Library of Congress Cataloging-in-Publication Data

Wexley, Kenneth N., 1943–
Developing and training human resources in organizations / Kenneth N. Wexley, Gary P. Latham.—2nd ed.
p. cm.
Includes bibliographical references and index.
ISBN 0-673-46160-2
1. Employees—Training of. I. Latham, Gary P. II. Title.
HF5549.5.T7W46 1991
658.3′124—dc20 90-23044
CIP

91 92 93 94 9 8 7 6 5 4 3

To the best trainers we know:
Ruth Wexley and Sherry Latham

and in memory of two people
who greatly influenced our lives
in our formative years:
Ruth Sherman and Louise Margaret Marshall

Contents

Preface

Training and development systems in North America must be strengthened if its human resources are to be prepared adequately for the future. Slower labor force growth will offer an opportunity for people to get better and higher-paying jobs. But those opportunities will be available only to those people who have the requisite skills. Thus it is not surprising that many organizations now see the need to equip their people, from managers to factory hands, with effective and efficient skills. Holiday Inns Inc., for example, is boosting training outlays by 25 percent, focusing on training supervisors in how to cope with a fast-changing, diverse work force.

As we enter the twenty-first century, managers will have to handle an increase in cultural diversity with subtle human relations skills. They will have to understand that employees don't necessarily think alike about such issues as handling confrontation or even such basics as what constitutes a good day's work. Thus it is not surprising that nearly one in four major companies, double the number in the early 1980s, now requires upper-middle and senior executives to participate in continuing education programs. With skilled technical and professional employees likely to be in short supply, tomorrow's managers will have to share more authority with their subordinates.

With all this in mind, *Developing and Training Human Resources in Organizations* is intended for human resource specialists in industry and teachers in academia. Thus the language and writing style is straightforward. References are provided throughout the book to substantiate key findings and to provide an exhaustive resource base for those readers who wish to investigate a topic further.

CONTENT AND CHANGES IN THE SECOND EDITION

Since the publication of our first edition (1981), each of us has been honored by a request to write the chapter on training and development for the prestigious *Annual Review of Psychology* (Wexley, 1984; Latham, 1988). Thus this new edition reflects our intimate knowledge of the training field over the past decade.

The second edition is similar to the first in the number and organization of the chapters. The significantly increased length reflects the growth in both theory and practice in the training and development field.

Chapter 1 provides an overview of training and development. We have added a Final Comments section that brings a historical perspective to this subject. The title of Chapter 2 has been upgraded from "The Training Director's Job" to "Organizational Factors Affecting Training and Development." Included in this chapter are the roles that strategy, structure, technology, and the legal environment play in affecting training. We focus on ways that the training staff can secure senior management support for its activities. A special feature of this chapter is making human resource specialists aware of how training can abuse the rights of the individual.

Chapter 3 describes ways of identifying training needs. New to this chapter is the importance of linking training to corporate strategy and the significance of future-oriented job analysis. The latter is a response to the dynamic environment in which organizations now operate. Content validity procedures are explained as a way of ensuring that the needs analysis is complete.

In Chapter 4, we shift our attention to ways of maximizing the trainee's learning of the requisite knowledge, skills, and abilities. The traditional topics of feedback, practice, and overlearning are covered. We emphasize advances in our knowledge on ways to "transfer learning." New to this chapter is the research on training concerning demographic differences regarding age, race, and sex and the need to take into account aptitude-treatment interactions. The Final Comments section stresses how essential it is to view training within a systems framework.

Once the training strategies for maximizing learning have been implemented, it is incumbent on human resource specialists to determine whether the strategies were effective or whether they should be modified or discarded. Hence Chapter 5 focuses on evaluation. It explains the different criteria that can be used in making these decisions, and the various measurement designs available to human resource specialists. New to this chapter is a discussion of the pros and cons of utility analysis. For the reader interested in statistics, we include a brief discussion of their use in detecting change. The chapter ends with suggestions on how to get senior management's appreciation for rigorous evaluation of training strategies. Their recognition of the need for evaluation is key to the prevention or minimization of training fads, which in turn hurt the reputation of human resource departments.

With an understanding of organizational factors affecting training and development systems, ways of identifying training needs in an organization, strategies for maximizing trainee learning, and methods of measuring training effectiveness established, we shift to an examination of the different training approaches for bringing about a relatively permanent change in a person's self-awareness, job skills, and motivation.

Chapter 6 describes on-site training methods. New topics include the role of mentoring and the importance of career development. Chapter 7 describes off-site training methods. The information in this chapter has been updated but is basically unchanged. Emphasis is given to computer-assisted instruction.

Theoretical advances in developing and training leaders resulted in a significant expansion of Chapter 8. Work by Mintzberg, Argyris, Fiedler, Vroom, Blake and Mouton, Miner, McClelland, Likert, Skinner, and Bandura is updated and elaborated upon. In addition, Graen's work on steps that leaders can take to minimize out-groups is described. We reorganized Chapter 9 to focus on management and executive development. In this chapter is a discussion of the role that corporate colleges play in the field of training and development and how universities such as Harvard are evaluating and modifying their programs in the face of this challenge.

Finally, Chapter 10 examines societal concerns in the field of training and development. In this chapter are discussions of illiteracy, sexual and racial harassment, team skills, customer service, and corporate wellness training.

The goal of this book is straightforward: to make human resource specialists aware of advances in the field of training and development that can be used to increase the effectiveness of an organization's work force. It was our intention to do so in an interesting and informative manner.

In closing we would like to thank Willard Young for his help in reviewing the literature and our families for their patience during the writing of these chapters.

K. N. W.
G. P. L.

Foreword

Ten years ago, I wrote the foreword for the first edition of this book. In the original writing, I described upheaval and disruption in the world of business resulting from government regulation, environmental requirements, lack of capital formation, and lagging worker productivity. Finally, I suggested that training was the common denominator associated with all the solutions. Well, here we are a decade later approaching the same subject. We have new issues, but the same problem—training the work force.

We have been buried in a blizzard of technology. We have entered the age of global competition and have experienced the unhappy results in North America as tough foreign competitors have invaded and conquered our traditional markets. Manufacturing remains, for many companies, the elusive frontier of competitive advantage. And U.S. business has spent in excess of $2 trillion over the past ten years attempting to train its workers with varying degrees of success.

Training is still the issue—job skills, safety, process control, sales and marketing, communications, participation. . . . The list is endless and the task is infinitely more difficult as work has become more and more complex. To paraphrase a headline in a recent *Wall Street Journal Report,*[1] we have smarter jobs and dumber workers. As the job markets threaten to expand by the millions, the number of workers with even basic skills grows smaller and smaller. It falls to industry, in the absence of other immediate solutions, to provide the training.

---

[1] *The Wall Street Journal Report,* The Wall Street Journal, February 9, 1990.

Training will improve our productivity, our product quality, and our competitive position. What is required in a world of "smart jobs" is smart workers. Training was a need ten years ago and still is. Now, as then, this is a book that fills a critical need. It is a source book of corporate training. The authors are professionals—training is their business. I recommend both the authors and their work.

Stephen J. Conway
Senior Vice President
Scott Paper Company

Developing and Training Human Resources in Organizations

Chapter 1

Introduction

Wayne Starr has been a research chemist for the past ten years. Both Wayne and his supervisor know all too well that Wayne has not kept up with new developments in the field. His professional obsolescence is beginning to seriously affect his performance in the company.

Roy Davis, a black 19-year-old mechanic's helper in a North Carolina pulp mill, desires to become a first-class maintenance mechanic or machinist.

Mrs. Pat Baker is 55 years old and has been out of the work force for 20 years while raising her children. She was once a bookkeeper. She would like to work in an organization for the next 15 years.

Gene Harvest is a military officer and is looking forward to retiring in two years. He would like to start a new career in the construction trade but is unsure how exactly to go about it.

Bryan Marshall is a white electrician who is upset because he has not been admitted to a training program that would have led directly to a higher paying job. He is threatening his employer with a lawsuit because he believes he has evidence that blacks and females who are less qualified than he have been admitted into the program.

All these people have one thing in common; they are all in need of ways to increase their knowledge and skills. Currently, they are experiencing feelings ranging from frustration due to professional obsolescence and alleged discrimination to anxiety over how to reenter the labor market and to increase their levels of expertise. They have the motivation to change their behavior, but they lack the knowledge and skill to do it. All of them are in need of training and development. Let us look at a few more examples:

George Hancock, the executive director of a medium-sized midwestern medical center, is concerned because the department heads and supervisors at his hospital not only exhibit poor interpersonal skills with their employees but seem to have little idea what their roles should be as managers. This problem has been increasing recently as the medical center has been growing rapidly in size.

Mason Smith, vice president of manufacturing of a large U.S. electronics company, plans on starting foreign plant operations in several underdeveloped nations in Central America and Africa. One of the major challenges ahead for him will be the training and development of the local labor force.

Claire Obreza is training director of a medium-sized factory that manufactures two brands of soap using an extrusion process. Recently, a decision was made to put three additional soap products on line which require another kind of manufacturing process called milling. In addition, corporate headquarters decided to begin production of a liquid detergent product. Claire and her training staff are currently developing new hires and upgrading present employees so that they will be able to handle these technological changes.

A diesel engine company and a large farm-equipment company have recently merged. The diesel company has had a long tradition of manufacturing engines for trucks, commercial fishing boats, and construction machinery. With the new merger, the engine company will also be involved with the production of diesel engines for tractors, combines, and self-propelled sprayers.

These four training needs sketches illustrate the need for training from a systems rather than an individual perspective. Whenever organizations grow in size, anticipate a merger, adjust to new plants coming on line, introduce new products and services, and so on, an organization-wide training effort is often needed.

Our purpose here is to describe how training and development can provide solutions to such problems. Before providing answers to these issues, a brief review of the role of training and development in organizations is in order. Accordingly, we begin with a discussion of the purpose served by training and development in organizations, and then progress to a consideration of the popularity of this approach for increasing both the individual's and the organization's effectiveness. Next, we consider how training and development is related to other human resource systems such as job analysis, personnel selection, performance appraisals, and organization development. When you complete this chapter, you should understand what constitutes training and development. You will then be ready to learn the technical aspects of this field.

PURPOSES OF TRAINING AND DEVELOPMENT

We used the phrase training and development several times in the preceding section. *Training and development* refers to a planned effort by an organization to facilitate the learning of job-related behavior on the part of its employees. The term *behavior* is used in the broad sense to include any knowledge and skill acquired by an employee through practice. Three examples of acquiring knowledge and skill are discussed here.

Margaret Knopf has been working as a salesperson in a large housewares store for six months. Her dollar sales volume has been evaluated by the store's sales manager as only "adequate" despite the fact that Margaret has been repeatedly told by the sales manager that customers find her pleasant, vivacious, and knowledgeable about store products and services. Unfortunately, Margaret has been told by the sales manager that she has a problem with her spoken grammar. Margaret was raised in a rural area and tends to use such phrases as "when we was talking" and "I'm goin' to find me a customer." Although her friends have become accustomed to Margaret's way of speaking, some of the store's customers have complained that her speech is unprofessional. This has affected Margaret's sales performance negatively because many customers approach other salespeople rather than her. It hurts Margaret to learn of her deficiency at this point in her life. Nevertheless, she wants to be a successful salesperson in this store and realizes that she needs training in grammar. Moreover, the sales manager does not want to lose Margaret. Consequently, the company has hired a trainer to teach Margaret the essentials of correct grammar.

Bob Anderson sells life insurance for a small independent insurance firm. As an independent agent, Bob is free to sell different kinds of life insurance for various nationally known life insurance companies. Unfortunately, with the current rate of inflation, Bob's business has been declining. It seems to him that fewer and fewer people want to invest their excess capital (if they have any) in life insurance. Bob has suddenly had to compete with alternative sources of investments such as cash funds, stocks, bonds, and home mortgages. He and his colleagues must learn about the relative advantages and disadvantages of different types of life insurance (e.g., whole vs. term) compared to other avenues of investment. Only in this way can Bob answer the questions and deal with the objections of potential customers. Thus Bob has decided to enroll in a company-sponsored six-week investment course.

Ivan Blum is attending a three-week floral arranging course stressing skills acquisition. During the course, Ivan will be learning how to take telephone orders, work with dry flowers, and care for and handle live flowers. In addition, he will be trained to create bouquets, baskets, corsages, and set pieces for weddings, graduations, funerals, and everyday work.

Jayne Long is a middle-level manager at a large midwestern insurance company. During Jayne's yearly performance review meeting with her boss, Jayne learned that she needs to work on improving her managerial skills, especially delegating work to her subordinates and managing her own time better. Consequently, Jayne and her boss have agreed that she will attend several management development workshops during the upcoming year that focus on improving her weak areas.

As you can see, the general purpose of training and development involves knowledge and skill acquisition. Now let us talk about the specific goals or objectives of such programs. Any training and development effort can have one or more of the following three goals: (1) to improve an individual's level of self-awareness; (2) to increase an individual's skill in one or more areas of expertise; and/or (3) to increase an individual's motivation to perform his or her job well.

Self-awareness involves learning about oneself. It includes understanding one's roles and responsibilities in the organization, recognizing differences between one's actual and espoused managerial philosophy, understanding how one is viewed by others, and learning how one's actions affect other people's actions. Later on in this book, you will see that certain training and development techniques have as their objective giving trainees increased self-awareness.

Most of what is traditionally considered to be training and development deals with increasing an individual's skill. This skill may involve electrical wiring, painting, blueprint reading, using a computerized cash register, following safety procedures, setting priorities, delegating or handling employee grievances, or increasing one's effectiveness as a leader. Obviously, these are just a few of the many different kinds of skills that can be learned during training and development programs. Regardless of the type of knowledge and skill involved, the training program is based on the assumption that it will increase an employee's ability to perform effectively on the job. You will see in chapters 6 through 9 that many training and development methods have as their goal improving an employee's knowledge and skill in the areas of decision making and problem solving.

Often, people possess the skill and knowledge to perform the job, but they lack the motivation to exhibit their abilities. For this reason, the goal of some training and development programs is to maximize the employee's desire to perform the job well. These programs, admittedly, are relatively few in number. Also, most of these programs do not have employee motivation as their sole objective. For example, job rotation (see Chapter 6) involves giving trainees an opportunity to work on a series of jobs in various parts of the organization in order to sharpen their career aspirations and commitment to the organization and, in addition, help them to develop their managerial skills in the process. On the other hand, there are training and development methods where the sole objective is to increase a person's managerial motivation. These programs are discussed in Chapter 8, where the focus is on the developing and training of leaders who will be able to cope effectively with the demands of the twenty-first century. Chapter 9 broadens this emphasis to a discussion of executive and management development.

These three broad goals—namely, increasing employee self-awareness, skill (including decision making/problem solving), and motivation are attained by using one or more training strategies. There are at least three basic strategies that are available to a training specialist: The specialist can try to improve an employee's performance by directing his or her efforts toward (1) cognition (i.e., thoughts and ideas), (2) behavior, or (3) the environment in which the person is working. A few examples might help us to distinguish between these three strategies.

Company orientation programs (see Chapter 6) provide new hires with information about work schedules, vacations, grievance procedures, pay scales, overtime, holidays, benefits, and so on. The intervention strategy used here is one that focuses on the individual's thoughts and ideas. Chapter 8 describes a leadership program that teaches managers how to ask themselves a prescribed series of questions before deciding on how much participation they should allow their employees to have in the decision-making process. Once again, the strategy is cognitive in nature in determining an appropriate leadership style.

Behavioral modeling (see Chapter 8) has its roots in cognitive psychology, but focuses primarily on the trainee's overt behavior. With this training approach, trainees view videotapes showing models who behave appropriately in a particular situation. Supervisors, for instance, might be taught how to take effective discipline action, delegate responsibility to employees, motivate the average performer, and handle customer complaints. Prior to and after viewing each videotape, the trainees review a list of learning points (e.g., greet the irate customer in a friendly manner, listen to the customer's complaints without interrupting him or her) that specifically spell out the effective behaviors that are to be learned. The trainees are also given an opportunity to practice their newly acquired behaviors during role-play exercises, and they receive feedback from both the trainer and fellow trainees on the effectiveness with which they demonstrate these behaviors. As you can see, this training method uses a behavioral strategy in that it focuses primarily on modifying the trainee's behaviors rather than transmitting a large amount of cognitive or factual information.

Sometimes the improvement in an employee's job performance can be brought about by means of planned environmental changes. As noted earlier, job rotation involves training people by moving them systematically from department to department. During the course of training, the trainees are exposed to a well-planned sequence of environmental changes (i.e., jobs, supervisors, co-workers). Another way of affecting environmental change is to change the consequences that take place immediately after the behavior has occurred. For example, a tire manufacturing company reduced excessive employee tardiness in several of its plants. For years, it mattered little if employees came to work as much as 15 minutes late because supervisors ignored all but excessive cases. Recently, the company decided to change this behavior by instituting a program that rewarded punctual behavior. The training and development staff developed a lottery sytem whereby employees who had not been tardy for an entire month would be eligible to enter their name in a lottery drawing for cash prizes. In addition, supervisors were instructed to praise an employee periodically for continued punctual behavior. In this situation, the tire company changed its employees' tardiness record by making the consequences for punctuality positive.

At this point, we have described three goals and three strategies for

Figure 1.1 Goals and strategies for training and development

STRATEGIES	GOALS: Self-Awareness	Job Skills	Motivation
Cognitive	Career development Management role theory Need for achievement Double-loop learning Sensitivity training Self-directed management development Transactional analysis	Orientation training and socialization of new employees Lecture Audiovisual Vroom-Yetton model Case study The incident process Job aids Computer-based training Teleconferencing Corporate classrooms/colleges Seminars and workshops	Role motivation theory Need for achievement Training Survey feedback
Behavioral	Interactive skills training	On-the-job training Apprenticeship Programmed instruction Equipment simulators Computer-assisted instruction Rational manager training Conference discussion Assessment centers Role playing Management games Grid seminars Leader-member exchange Juniors boards Understudy assignments Mentoring	Coaching Behavior modeling
Environmental	Leader match		Job rotation Behavior modification

training and development. Figure 1.1 presents a nine-cell scheme that is useful for categorizing the training and development methods that are currently being used by organizations. It is important to note that these nine categories are not discrete entities because some training methods can be classified properly into more than one cell. This classification was made for convenience and clarity of discussion purposes only. This figure is referred to again in chapters 6, 7, 8, and 9, where the specific training approaches are presented.

POPULARITY OF TRAINING AND DEVELOPMENT

Almost all private and public organizations have formal training and development programs. Some organizations we work with spend as much as 15 percent of their total payroll on these activities. In the late 1970s, the average expenditure per employee ran between $75 and $100 a year (*Employee Training*, 1979). In the 1990s, larger organizations are spending even more. For example, it has been reported that IBM in the mid-1980s had an annual training and development budget that exceeded $700 million per year. That amounted to about $2000 per employee (Heneman, Schwab, Fossum, and Dwyer, 1986). As of 1990, IBM's annual training costs exceeded $1.5 billion (*Wall Street Journal*, February 9, 1990).

There are many dramatic changes occurring in our society that will demand the training and retraining of North American workers. First, as organizations experience more and more pressure to hire and promote women, minorities, individuals over age 40, and the handicapped, this area of personnel activity will become even more critical than it is now for the efficient management of an organization's human resources. Second, many workers are being left to fend for themselves when shifts in the economy or foreign competition have affected or eliminated their jobs. From now on, traditional manufacturing industries such as steel, autos, and rubber will provide a smaller share of the nation's jobs. In these and other blue-collar industries, more than 1 million jobs have disappeared since 1978, and these are jobs that will never come back (Karmin and Sheler, 1982). Instead, employment opportunities are growing in the high technology, service, and information sectors. Feeling most of the brunt and terribly in need of retraining are the mechanics, assemblers, welders, semiskilled and unskilled laborers who work in the factories of the northern industrial belt (Wexley, 1984). Third, new technology is also steadily increasing the need for retraining. For instance, it has been estimated that by 2000, 4 million factory jobs will be replaced by robots (Carnegie-Mellon Report, 1982). Some of the employees who worked on these factory jobs will need to be retrained on tasks such as how to maintain and repair complex robotic equipment or be retrained to perform other, less physical types of work. The continual evolution of new office equipment (e.g., personal computers, FAX machines, duplicating machines) is another example of the effects of new technology. It has been estimated that employers will have to retrain office workers five to eight times during their careers in the near future (Wexley, 1984). Finally, through mergers and acquisitions, some American employees are finding that they are now being managed differently than they were before. Perhaps they are now expected to take on more responsibility in their work, to be supervised less closely, and to make more decisions for themselves. Changes such as these are not easy for many employees; they therefore need training to help them to adapt and accept these changes. Finally, as individuals change jobs because of promotion, layoffs, or mid-career frustration, they want and need training and development.

Unfortunately, the necessity for training and development programs has fostered many fads. The popularity of a program, as indicated by trainee satisfaction, has frequently overshadowed the importance of examining whether the training is bringing about a relatively permanent change in the employee's self-awareness, decision-making/problem-solving skills, or motivation. The fad cycle often occurs in the following sequence: A new technique appears with a group of followers who announce its success. A second group develops modifications of the technique. Empirical studies may appear supporting the technique. Then there is a backlash. Critics question the usefulness of the new technique, but rarely produce any data to support their contention. The technique survives until a new technique appears. Then the whole procedure is repeated (Campbell, 1971). For example, in the early 1960s, T-group (sensitivity) training was the fad (see Chapter 9). Many organizations required their managers to receive sensitivity training in the hope of enhancing their self-awareness and sensitivity to others.

Today, there is no reason to be complacent over the quality of the scientific research on training and development, nor is there reason for despair. A recent Annual Review of Psychology chapter on training (Latham, 1988) showed that fads do not dominate the scientific literature on training; advancement in theory and empirical research is ongoing.

Why did faddism occur? For one thing, few organizations ascertained their training needs systematically. Instead, they purchased packaged programs because someone in another organization told them they were good. Also, organizations seldom rigorously evaluated the effects of the programs they purchased. They simply went by how much the participants liked the session, and how much they "felt" it would benefit them. Little or no attempt was made to see if the training increased employee productivity on the job. For this reason, Chapter 5 explains ways of determining whether a training program is indeed worthwhile. This chapter precedes the discussion of training techniques for three reasons. First, the danger of faddism is always present. Only systematic evaluation of training effectiveness can prevent its return. Second, the way or ways effectiveness will be defined and measured must be decided on at the time the training program is selected or designed, and before it is implemented. Third, an understanding of the criteria for evaluating training and the procedures to be followed in making the evaluation will allow you to appreciate the strengths and weaknesses of the training approaches we described in chapters 6 through 9.

In summary, we hope that the information in this book will help minimize, if not eliminate, all fads in training. People must systematically identify training needs, build content into programs based on job information, and evaluate training in terms of the objectives for which it was designed. Only then will the field of training and development cease to be an art form that is dependent on the persuasiveness of its advocates, and instead be a science that is replicable by others.

THE RELATIONSHIP OF TRAINING AND DEVELOPMENT TO OTHER HUMAN RESOURCE FUNCTIONS

Training and development is only one of several functions usually performed by an organization's human resource department. In order to better understand the nature of training and development in organizations, it is worthwhile to examine how the training function relates to other human resource activities carried out by the personnel department. Specifically, we look at how training and development relates to task analysis, staffing, performance appraisal, and organization development.

The purpose of task analysis is to provide information about the duties involved in performing a job and the skills and knowledge required to do the job well. Task analysis information serves as the foundation for most training and development programs because it answers the important question, "What must a trainee be taught in order to perform a job effectively?" Chapter 3 describes how task analysis information provides a way of systematically determining the appropriate content of training and development programs.

Staffing also has a direct relationship to training. The better an organization's personnel selection procedures, the more likely it is that the people it hires will already possess some of the skill and knowledge needed to perform their jobs effectively. Because these people have been carefully selected, they may not need an extensive training and development program. Conversely, if a company has a weak selection program and hires people who have fewer skills and less knowledge, more training and development will be needed to give these new hires the expertise they lack. Moreover, the emphasis by government agencies on having organizations establish affirmative action programs (i.e., actively recruiting and hiring minority group members and women) to redress an imbalance in the existing employee composition makes the use of sound training programs more and more important.

Measures of employee proficiency (e.g., ratings, behavioral observations, units produced, dollars earned, scrappage) serve many different purposes within an organization. For instance, performance appraisal measures are used as a basis for making decisions regarding promotions, layoffs, separations, and transfers. They can also be used as a method of administering wages and bonuses so that these are contingent on the "goodness" or appropriateness of an employee's performance. Performance appraisal measures affect training and development in four basic ways: (1) as a means of determining the training needs for various organizational units; (2) as a basis for evaluating the worth of training programs; (3) as a means of identifying employee weaknesses that might be alleviated through additional formal training and development; and (4) as a means of improving proficiency of employees by providing each of them with feedback regarding their performance during periodic appraisal interviews with their supervisors (Latham and Wexley, 1991; Wexley and Yukl, 1984).

Organization development (OD) is concerned with increasing the competence and health of an entire organizational system or subsystem. It typically involves a systematic diagnosis of an organization by one or more change agents who then attempt to bring about meaningful and lasting organizational change. In the course of stimulating organizational change, OD specialists may call on different intervention strategies such as team building, career planning, process consultation, and role analysis (see French, Bell, and Zawacki, 1989). OD differs from training and development in that the latter is concerned primarily with improving the self-awareness, skills, and motivation of individual organizational members. Although an OD effort might involve employee development, it would do so only as a part of its larger objective of improving the competence of the units comprising the total organization (Beckhard, 1969). Some of the intervention techniques that are used by OD specialists (e.g., Grid OD, survey feedback, management by objectives) are also used by trainers for developing individual managers (see chapters 8 and 9).

OVERVIEW OF THE BOOK

Now that you have a general understanding of the nature of the training and development function within organizations, you are ready to begin learning more technical subject matter. During the 1980s, we were asked to write the third (Wexley, 1984) and fourth (Latham, 1988) chapters to appear in the *Annual Review of Psychology* on training and development. This book's content reflects these reviews plus our knowledge gained over the past two years from psychological journals, business magazines, management journals, and a large volume of training materials sent to us by different organizations (e.g., hospitals, banks, unions, retail, and manufacturing). We compiled and integrated these materials to describe what is currently happening in the field of training and, at the same time, present our views on how training should be done. This apparent tension between the "ideal" and the "typical" training program surfaces frequently throughout the remaining chapters.

Chapter 2 covers the functions of the training staff within an organization. Once the training staff is established, these people need to determine the training needs of the organization systematically. This process involves analyzing both the short- and long-term goals of the organization, developing training content to teach employees how to attain these goals, and identifying people in need of this training. Chapter 3 examines these issues with special attention given to task analysis, which should be used to determine the content of training programs.

Chapter 4 deals with what the training staff needs to know to maximize learning by the trainees. This chapter considers such important issues as the trainability (i.e., capacity to learn) of the trainees, how the training program should be arranged to facilitate trainee learning, and what can be done to ensure that what is learned during training will be transferred by trainees to their jobs.

Chapter 5 describes approaches to be used for evaluating training program effectiveness. The evaluation of training is mandatory so that the organization, not to mention the training staff itself, can see whether a specific program truly leads to the attainment of the objectives for which it was designed. Only in this way will the organization be able to assess rigorously whether a training program should be continued, modified, or discarded.

Chapters 6 through 9 are concerned with specific approaches to employee development. In reviewing these different methods, we have grouped them according to whether they are typically conducted on the job (Chapter 6) or off the job (Chapter 7). Of course, some of the methods are used in both circumstances.

Management development is the main topic of discussion in chapters 8 and 9. Chapter 8 explains the ideas of several prominent leadership theorists and discusses their prescriptions for developing effective leaders in today's dynamic environment. In Chapter 9 we discuss approaches to management and executive development.

We describe each of the training and development methods covered in chapters 6 through 9 in terms of its advantages and limitations. The research evidence bearing on its effectiveness is reviewed. Where there is little or no research data supporting a method, we point out the need for evaluative research.

Chapter 10 focuses on societal issues that can be influenced positively by appropriate training and development techniques. In the 1990s we can expect to see the increased training of people in society who, in the past, have had limited opportunities to realize their potential. Accordingly, the first part of the chapter discusses people who are illiterate, the handicapped, the aging work force, and displaced workers. The second part discusses six concerns that pertain to the training of managers and /or professionals—namely, training to improve accurate evaluations of employees, cross-cultural training, training to minimize professional obsolescence, company-sponsored employee assistance programs (e.g., substance abuse), as well as ways to manage stress and time. The final section discusses training issues that concern most employees: sexual and racial harassment, corporate wellness training, safety training, team playing, the personal computer, and training to maximize customer service.

FINAL COMMENTS

We might have expected that advances in training and development in Euro-American countries would have progressed at approximately the same rate as industrial growth since the Industrial Revolution. That it did not, explained Downs (1983), was because of the eighteenth- and nineteenth-century views of the work force. The prevalent view of that time was that "the lower orders are innately idle and depraved except when they are goaded by the spur." This philosophy influenced social legislation in England from the reign of Elizabeth I to the revival of liberalism in England in 1906.

Such ingrained attitudes, which discouraged formal training activities, noted Downs, might have changed faster if there had been any prolonged labor shortage. However, the Enclosure movement in England from 1760 to the Act of 1845 accelerated population movements from rural communities to cities. Consequently, labor costs were low because workers were plentiful. High employee turnover reinforced the attitude that any expenditure on training workers would be wasteful.

An additional factor that contributed to an attitude of indifference toward training, according to Downs, was the efficiency of new machinery, with which the labor force was compared to its discredit. However, this view of workers changed rapidly with the advent of scientific management. Taylor (1911) advocated the selection of the best workers for each task, followed by extensive training. Training was viewed as critical for breaking the practice of allowing employees to acquire inappropriate work habits.

Paralleling Taylor was the research of Munsterberg (1913). His work promoted a range of activity in selection and training of both military and civilian personnel during World War I. Between the wars, research was conducted in the United Kingdom by organizations such as the Industrial Health Research Board and the National Institute of Industrial Psychology. The outbreak of World War II again accelerated research on both selection and training.

The continuing need in England after the war for systematic training was recognized by the Industrial Training Act of 1964 and 1973. The government felt that both skill shortages and lack of adaptability to change would arise as a result of insufficient training (Downs, 1983).

Training was defined by the UK Department of Employment (1971) as the systematic development of attitude-knowledge-skill behavior patterns required by an individual in order to perform adequately a given task or job.

Parallel developments in North America during the past 50 years have resulted in a push-pull philosophy between selection and training (Hinrichs, 1970). The selection or early identification philosophy stresses identifying individuals with strong potential and grooming them for positions to which they are likely to be promoted. In the case of a training philosophy, the organization is primarily interested in identifying and overcoming existing performance deficiencies for employees on their present jobs. In a survey of Canadian organizations, Mealia and Duffy (1985) found that regardless of size of the organization, the primary emphasis today is on the latter philosophy.

In the United States, training (which is now a multibillion-dollar activity) is inextricably tied to selection through Title VII of the 1964 Civil Rights Act. Admission into training, as well as promotions, demotions, transfers, and the like, that are based on training performance, are considered employment decisions. Apprenticeship training programs are specifically covered in section 703d of the act. Thus before training is conducted in the United States, understanding of Title VII is required (see Chapter 2).

The tying of training to Title VII reflects the fact that from now until the end of the century, 88 percent of the work-force growth in the United States will come from women, blacks, and people of Hispanic or Asian origin, including immigrants (*Wall Street Journal,* February 9, 1990). White males, meanwhile, will account for most retirees; they will leave the work force in record numbers.

Computer technology (see chapters 7 and 10) and automation have taken, and will continue to take, the sweat and tedium out of many jobs, from coal mining to clerical work. The jobs of the 1990s will involve wrenching adjustments for both managers and their subordinates. Many managers, as they delegate more decision making, will feel threatened about relinquishing their power. Among their subordinates, frustration will be felt as their jobs require problem solving, analytical skills, and teamwork that exceed their current abilities. These final chapters focus on the steps that can be taken to deal with this fear and frustration.

Chapter 2

Organizational Factors Affecting Training and Development

We now turn our attention to the role of training specialists. In small companies, these individuals are usually in charge of all "people" issues and, therefore, find themselves involved in such diverse matters as hiring, benefits, safety, counseling, and possibly even labor relations. These individuals function primarily as training program developers, presenters, and in some instances, evaluators. Their job description includes discovering the training needs of specific groups, planning new programs and revising old programs to meet those needs, analyzing jobs and operations for teaching purposes, preparing course outlines, writing training manuals, furnishing and equipping classrooms, publicizing and selling training within the company, counseling individual employees on problems that might be solved through training, and measuring and maintaining employee productivity and job satisfaction (Planty, McCord, and Efferson, 1948). As the size of the organization increases, so does the number of operating problems and the number of people in need of training. To meet this need, the human resource department usually establishes a training unit consisting of a training manager, an assistant training manager, and one or more full-time trainers. As the training function expands and its activities multiply, the role of the training manager becomes less that of a program developer and implementer and more that of a line manager (Johnson, 1976). Now the training manager must direct and control diverse activities. He or she must structure the training operation for maximum productivity, budget skillfully, employ cost control and cost reduction techniques, be aware of costs versus benefits of each training effort, select and train the staff, secure managerial support for the training unit, and ensure that the training programs satisfy legal requirements. In this chapter six important aspects of the training manager's job are discussed:

- Considerations in organizing the training department
- A financial approach to training
- Selecting the training staff
- Training the trainer
- Maintaining ongoing managerial support
- Legal aspects of training and development

CONSIDERATIONS IN ORGANIZING THE TRAINING DEPARTMENT

Large variations exist in the scope and organization of the training function across companies. For instance, some organizations have one-person training units; others may have as many as 150 or more professional staff people. Some training staffs report locally to the line organization; others operate out of corporate headquarters and report to the vice-presidential level. Some training staffs are involved with training employees ranging from unskilled laborers to company presidents; others are restricted solely to middle management or hourly employee development. Some training staffs act primarily as purchasers of commercially available training programs; in other organizations the emphasis is on the design of tailor-made in-house programs. Finally, in some organizations the training staff acts primarily as instructors; in others it performs largely a coordinating or administrative function.

As you can see, these variations make it difficult to make general statements regarding the organization of typical training units. However, we can examine variables that organizations take into consideration when organizing training staffs.

The Organization's Corporate Strategy

Unfortunately, many organizations still exist that view training traditionally, that is, as merely a staff function whose services might or might not be used by individual line managers. In these organizations, training has no real linkage to the company's business strategy. In fact, the training manager seemingly has no influence on the formation of the corporate strategy, since training is seen by high-level executives as being peripheral to the real work of the organization (Rosow and Zager, 1988). Conversely, in more progressive organizations, the training manager participates in the formation of the business's strategic planning (Latham, 1988). As such, the training manager understands the short- and long-term business objectives of the company and, therefore, is in a position to formulate a training plan that can support the company's business strategy. Sometimes, however, the training manager knows that he or she does not have sufficient training resources to do so. In this case, top management must decide to either increase the training department's budget so that it can support the strategic plan or else modify its plan to meet what the department can accomplish using current resources. In either case, when a strong linkage exists between business operations and training, the appropriate organizational structure of the training function will be clear. Its size and form will be determined by whatever it can get in the way of resources to contribute to its company's strategic plan (Campbell, 1990; Pittam, 1987). Rosow and Zager (1988) provide two excellent examples of a healthy linkage between the training function and corporate strategy. At Travelers Insurance, top management set as one of its goals the changing over from an old-line insurance company to a preeminent financial services company. To accomplish this, the goals of the training department were that all Travelers' employees had to learn how to make the best use of data-processing technology in their jobs, and that Travelers' managers had to be taught how to manage a company in continual change as a result of the onset of high technology. But only when the training manager took the initiative to explain what support the training function needed to accomplish these goals did it receive the necessary resources. A state-of-the-art training center has been built; 5000 of Travelers' employees have gone through the company's computer literacy program; a management redevelopment program is being prepared; the training department itself is gradually being automated; individual computer work stations for managers are being designed; and all of the training materials now incorporate the main themes (e.g., customer service, low cost, innovation) of the company's corporate strategy. At Ebasco Services, what appeared to be a reasonable corporate strategic plan was tentatively decided on. However, when the training manager estimated the costs of retraining Ebasco's employees in the new skills, top management decided that its strategies could not be adequately met. Rather than going ahead and implementing mediocre training programs, as some other organizations would do, Ebasco's top management chose to adopt a more affordable set of business strategies.

Organization Structure

Some organizations have a centralized group that controls all training programs; other organizations place trainers in key locations who are free to operate independently of corporate headquarters. We have found that in organizations with several large divisions it is advisable to have both a corporate and a regional training staff. The role of the corporate people should be primarily one of advising and coordinating the training activities of the various plants or regions and informing the regions of new or revised corporate objectives. Occasionally, the central training staff can be used to develop special training programs to be conducted by trainers at the divisional level. Anything more will usually be viewed by the regions as autocratic and paternalistic. Consequently, they resist corporate training policies. Typical of the many comments heard in these circumstances are "The training doesn't give the grass-roots people what they need," "The training fails to meet the current needs of our people," and "Corporate doesn't realize that we know what we need." Thus, in these situations, the role of the regional training staff people should be one of developing, implementing, and objectively evaluating their own programs. They must continually interact with the corporate staff so that successes in one region can be communicated to other regions.

In organizations where many small locations exist, no one location may be able to support a full-time training person. In these situations, a centralized staff is typically needed to either travel from location to location or else have trainees assemble at one place. For example, a specialty food chain with numerous stores scattered throughout the country develops master programs at its corporate headquarters on topics such as cheese preparation, cash control, and product ordering. Since no one store can support its own trainer, individuals from various stores receive training at the company's training center in Dayton, Ohio.

Other organizations have one location with many employees performing essentially the same types of jobs. For example, a large insurance company has the majority of its clerical employees and underwriters located in Milwaukee, Wisconsin, where there is a central group of five training people who control all training activities.

Technology

Some organizations are involved in rapidly changing technologies; others find themselves in a stable environment. Organizations with highly changing technologies require continual retraining of both employees and managers. These organizations have difficulty finding persons in the job market to meet their needs. They have no choice but to continually upgrade their people via specialized training programs. It is in these kinds of organizations, in particular, that a training staff is essential. For example, an electronics company at one time manufactured, sold, and serviced only manually operated cash registers. Today, its business is rapidly switching to computerized cash registers for large supermarkets and other retail operations. This change requires the continual upgrading and retraining of its manufacturing, sales, and maintenance personnel.

The number and complexity of the products and services provided by an organization also influence the size of its training staff. Training needs will not be as great where there is one simple product or service involved as compared with several complex products or services. For instance, we would expect a greater need for in-service training in a large metropolitan medical center than in a small country hospital. Finally, products that are mass produced using highly automated processes require employees with less training than products made in small batches following customer specifications. For example, individuals on American automobile assembly lines require less training than their counterparts in Scandinavian auto factories where jobs are less automated.

Attitude Toward Training

Some organizations have had training programs for years and are convinced of the benefits. Others are oriented primarily toward the valid selection and placement of experienced applicants and, therefore, deemphasize the training function. The organization's emphasis on personnel selection versus employee training depends a great deal on the attitude of key persons within the company. Specifically, the attitudes of the chief executive officer and the executives in charge of the various divisions or locations are the main source of company training philosophy. Quite often, their attitudes toward training depend on their own past experiences with it. Also important are their perceptions of the labor market; that is, are there prospective employees who have the necessary skills and experiences, or must unskilled people be hired and trained? A third factor that influences their attitude is their philosophy of promoting from within versus hiring from the outside. Organizations that promote from within typically provide their people more opportunities to prepare themselves for future advancements than organizations who hire primarily experienced individuals.

A FINANCIAL APPROACH TO TRAINING

Organizations spend about $210 billion annually on formal and informal training programs (*Wall Street Journal*, February 9, 1990). Approximately one in every eight American workers participates in a formal training course each year (Carnevale, 1986). In 1979 nearly $100 billion was spent annually on training by industrial and governmental organizations (Lien, 1979). Certainly these expenditures are significantly higher now. So we would think that organizations would closely monitor the benefits of their training efforts. However, many companies do not know what benefits they receive from their expenditures on training and development.

Unless training specialists can show the contribution of their efforts to profits in relation to costs, training budgets are likely to get slashed whenever there is a downturn in business. This may be especially problematic in the 1990s, as it was in the 1980s. In order for training to be seen by management as an integral part of an organization's operating plan, it must be viewed like any other business activity. This entails sound budgeting, cost control, and cost/benefit analyses by the training director and his or her staff.

Ideally, the training budget should contain both training and financial objectives and, basically, should include the following (Jenness, 1976):

1. The training programs that the staff plans to conduct during this coming year to meet specific organizational needs that have been systematically determined. For example, the training staff may want to conduct programs for managers in successful delegation, management by objectives, planning cash flow, effective letter writing, and time management.
2. The direct and indirect costs of each of these programs broken down into the finest detail possible. Direct costs are those involved in operating particular programs. They include such things as wages and/or salaries of the participants and trainers, costs for travel, meals, and lodging, supplies and materials, and cost of the facilities. Indirect costs include the costs of operating the entire training unit (e.g., secretarial and clerical help, telephones, audiovisual equipment) and developing new training programs.
3. The estimated savings, or increased profits, that will likely result from this training. This should be calculated in terms of increased productivity, reduced waste, reduced expenditures for equipment breakage, increased attendance, and punctuality.

The budget needs to be supplemented with details about each program's intended length, space requirements, number of trainees per session, audiovisual equipment and materials required, and development and administrative costs.

Once the budget is accepted by management and training begins, the training unit should receive a monthly summary of its actual expenditures compared with budgeted expenditures. This summary from the accounting department should be detailed enough to allow for easy identification of problem areas. Continual cost comparisons against the financial plan are necessary to ensure cost control and, hopefully, bring about cost reduction.

Finally, a utility or cost/benefit analysis of each training program is desirable. This analysis, discussed in detail in Chapter 5, involves a comparison of the actual total costs of the program against all profit improvements. It is important to realize that certain training programs can be expected to affect the organization sooner than others. For example, a sales training course intended to cut selling expenses or a manufacturing course focused on productivity improvement should produce results within the immediate accounting period. In these cases, utility analyses can be conducted soon after training is completed. The rotation of junior executives through various organizational units in preparation for key positions several years hence, or the sending of top-level managers to residential programs offered by various colleges and universities may be expected to enhance profits or recover costs within five to ten years. In these instances, utility analyses cannot be done as quickly, nor as easily. Admittedly, cost/benefit analyses are more difficult to conduct with higher level management development programs than traditional lower level skills training programs because of the intangible nature of much of their work.

Various approaches have been suggested for determining the utility of a training or development program (e.g., Cascio, 1989; Dahl, 1987; Godkewitsch, 1987; Paquet, Kasl, Weinstein, and Waite, 1987). In Chapter 5, we describe an approach that estimates the dollar value of a training and development program to the organization. As you will see, the utility formula includes important factors affecting a program's usefulness such as the number of years the training program has affected an employee's job performance, the number of employees trained, the strength of the impact of the training on their job performance, the dollar value of the training program's impact, the company's marginal tax rate, the effects of variable costs, as well as the direct and indirect costs of designing and implementing the training.

SELECTING THE TRAINING STAFF

The selection of qualified people for corporate and regional training positions is obviously a critical decision for the life of any training department. Unfortunately, this hiring process is frequently treated too lightly by many organizations. Their attitude seems to be that anyone who has adequate verbal skills and is enthusiastic about speaking in front of groups can be a trainer. Often, employees from sales, engineering, and marketing who could not perform adequately in line functions are transferred to the training department. Sometimes, certain employees decide that they want to "work with people" and manage to find their way into the role of a trainer when perhaps they are not qualified to do the job.

We see the trainer's job as requiring extensive skill. The position of corporate or regional trainer requires someone who is a learning specialist, that is, someone skilled in the ability to use learning theory and methods to meet organizational training needs (Lippitt and Nadler, 1967). There is more to the trainer's job than just instructing. The trainer must be able to determine the organization's training needs, design and implement appropriate programs, present them in such a way as to maximize trainee learning, and rigorously evaluate these programs. Only a person who meets the following basic requirements can adequately fill this staff position.

1. *The individual must be expert in the skills and knowledge to be imparted.* A good instructor is expected to be skillful in the crafts and technology that he or she is passing on to others. If instructors are perceived by trainees as not knowing enough about the job being taught or the organization, trainees will quickly lose their desire to learn.

2. *The individual should have knowledge of, and ability to use, various learning principles and training methods.* Each trainee is an individual with strengths and weaknesses, and a certain potential for learning. The instructor's role requires that he or she recognize each trainee as an individual and use those specific training methods (e.g., programmed instruction, role playing, case study) and learning principles (e.g., feedback, active practice, overlearning) that maximize each person's performance.
3. *The individual must be well grounded in organization, task, and person analyses as well as experimental design, criterion development, and statistics.* These skills are essential for systematically determining an organization's training needs and evaluating the organizational effects of training and development programs.
4. *The individual must possess certain personal qualities that facilitate learning.* The individual should be an organized person. This entails being adept at preparing ahead of time and anticipating questions and problems that trainees are likely to encounter. The person must be flexible enough to deal with each training situation so as to choose the best possible learning strategy. He or she must be flexible enough to cope with the diverse personalities among the trainees and their differences in speed of learning. The person must be amenable to change, regardless of whether an emergency arises during the conduct of a training session, a modification is indicated in the program by management, or constructive suggestions are provided by the trainees themselves.

   The individual must be someone from whom the trainees want to learn. Trainers must be able to display, or "model," the very characteristics that they are teaching such as being friendly toward others, observing safety rules, using tools and equipment correctly, having a sense of humor, and keeping calm under pressure. It's also important for trainers to be enthusiastic about their training products and be able to convey this enthusiasm to the trainees. It's difficult for trainees to be motivated if the trainer presents the program as an imposed chore. Finally, trainers must be capable of treating all trainees fairly (e.g., play no favorites) and be firm enough to hold them all to their performance responsibilities (Cenci, 1966).

From where should these trainers be recruited? Actually, this is a controversial issue. Some organizations choose to recruit from the ranks and to encourage these individuals to remain in the training function. For example, Cosmair Inc., a New York City-based cosmetics and fragrance firm, recruits its trainers from its sales force. These salespeople have the opportunity to return to the field if they feel, after a while, that they do not like training. Otherwise, the position is permanent. Becoming a trainer is considered a promotion into management, accompanied by a significant increase in salary. Other organizations use a *pass-through* philosophy when it comes to selecting trainers. At companies such as Pitney Bowes Inc., salespeople receive several years of sales training experience in the training department; then they are usually promoted to a management job. At Lederle Laboratories, young promotables spend two years in the training department rotating through various activities such as management, hospital oncology, and communications training (Geber, 1987). In our opinion, the career trainer approach is superior to the pass-through approach because it selects individuals from the ranks who are committed to a career in employee training. Moreover, their promotion and salary adjustment give them the status they need to be taken seriously by the employees whom they are expected to teach. Realizing their long-term commitment as trainers, their organizations are usually willing to give them the training that they will need to do their job effectively.

TRAINING THE TRAINER

If an organization is to be effective, supervisors should be held responsible for the overall training of the employees who report directly to them. Moreover, many supervisors want to train their subordinates because they are in the best position to teach new employees what is expected of them. Other supervisors may delegate the responsibility for training to their most experienced employees. These individuals are expected to provide on-the-job training to new hires and, occasionally, classroom instruction as well. Where, then, does the training department fit into all this? The training department is typically responsible for planning and conducting training sessions for supervisors and staff personnel (e.g., quality control, research and development, engineering). It either conducts the program using training materials that it has developed, or else it uses materials that have been purchased from outside vendors. Often, the training department assists supervisors in the planning and organizing of special programs for their own work units.

The need to give instruction to supervisors, employees, and training department members in the best methods of training is an important one. This is true even when these individuals possess the abilities mentioned in the previous section. These people must be made aware of the knowledge and skills necessary to make training highly effective and not just a "nice thing to do" when time and money happen to be available to the organization.

What, then, should trainers be taught in order to make the training process work? It is important to realize, first of all, that there is no universal course for all those who instruct others. A review of 37 train-the-trainer programs found that they vary from one to nine days, from $195 to $1035 per trainee, and from general topics (e.g., communications, career transitions) to specific instructional skills and techniques (DiPaolo and Patterson, 1983). Thus it would appear that the length and specific content of a train-the-trainer course must depend on a needs assessment (see Chapter 3) of the particular participants involved. For instance, a consulting firm recently implemented a training-for-trainers course for about a hundred first-line supervisors in a paper mill. The initial step in the project involved a needs assessment to determine exactly what the foremen needed to learn to conduct their own technical training classes for their crews. Based on the needs assessment, a four-day workshop was developed that included such topics as how adults learn, audiovisuals, questioning techniques, individualized learning problems, use of different methods of instruction, and proper instructional design.

We believe that there are common elements that should exist in all train-the-trainer programs. First, trainers must be taught to establish specific training objectives (e.g., to point out fire hazards in a chemical plant, to be familiar with the common terms used by state troopers, to design and lay out newspaper ads). Trainers must learn how these objectives can be used to influence the planning and execution of their training sessions. They need to understand the importance of communicating these objectives clearly, so that the trainees understand the program's purposes at the outset (Randall, 1978).

Second, the trainers need to be taught basic principles of how adults learn. They must understand the factors that facilitate and interfere with the learning process and what they as trainers can do about them (Downs and Perry, 1986). For instance, it is important that trainers understand that their own level of expectations about a trainee affects the nature of their social interactions with the trainee which, in turn, affects how well the trainee learns (Eden, 1984). This phenomenon, known as the *Pygmalion effect,* was demonstrated in the Israeli army by Eden and Shani (1982). One hundred and five trainees in a 15-week combat command course were matched on aptitude and randomly assigned to high, regular, and unknown trainer-expectancy conditions. Trainees from whom trainers had been induced to expect better performance (i.e., "likely to move quickly into a command position") scored significantly higher on objective achievement tests, exhibited more positive attitudes, and perceived more positive trainer leadership behavior than those trainees labeled trainees in the "regular expectations" (average movement), or "unknown" conditions.

Third, the trainers must be taught how to communicate more effectively. This should involve the actual presentation of lessons during training, and receiving feedback from other participants as to the adequacy of their oral, written, and nonverbal (e.g., facial expressions, tone of voice, eye contact) communications. Ideally, the lessons should be videotaped so that trainees can also critique their own performances. In addition, the trainers should be made aware of various visual and audio devices (e.g., overhead transparency projector, videotape recorder, tape recorder, slide and filmstrip projector, flip chart) that can facilitate effective communication. For instance, trainers need to learn that their communication style plays an important role in creating either an "adaptable" trainee, who has accepted responsibility for his or her own learning, or a "trainer-dependent" trainee, who has greater difficulty in transferring his or her learning from the specific instance in which it occurred (Downs, Petford, and McHale, 1982).

Fourth, the trainers must be taught how to plan each training session so that the material is presented clearly. It is also important that the trainers learn to sequence their training sessions and decide on the length and the time interval between them.

Fifth, the trainers should be taught how to choose the most effective method(s) of instruction (e.g., behavior modeling, T-group training, on-the-job training) depending on the particular type(s) of learning involved. They should be given an opportunity to develop their skills in those particular training methods they will eventually be using (e.g., role-playing exercises, lectures, and/or case studies). In addition, they should be shown how to pose questions so as to arouse interest and curiosity, stimulate discussion, channel the trainees' thinking, and determine how well trainees understand the material.

Sixth, trainers must be taught how to deal with individual trainees. They must learn how to get appropriate participation by drawing out the underinvolved and toning down the overinvolved. They must understand resistance to change and anxiety on the part of certain trainees, and what they as trainers can do about it. They need to be shown how to use feedback techniques, praise, and goal setting to motivate certain individuals.

Finally, it is important for trainers to be aware of certain behaviors that are considered improper or unethical for training professionals. Table 2.1 presents the major categories of behavior considered unethical by a nationwide sample of members of the American Society for Training and Development (Clement, Pinto, and Walker, 1978). Incidents such as those shown in the table should be discussed during the training of trainers.

MAINTAINING ONGOING MANAGERIAL SUPPORT

It is important for training managers and their staff not only to develop effective training and development programs but also to ensure that these programs are adopted where they are needed in the organization. Unless the training unit is able to maintain training and development programs, even effective programs may quickly fade away. What, then, can a training staff do to make certain that its training and development programs have staying power?

As pointed out by both Hinrichs (1978) and Latham and Wexley (1991), there must be significant senior management support for the training program, as opposed to passive tolerance. Such support is essen-

Table 2.1 MAJOR CATEGORIES OF BEHAVIOR CONSIDERED IMPROPER OR UNETHICAL FOR TRAINING AND DEVELOPMENT PROFESSIONALS

Major Categories of Behavior Considered Unethical	Typical Response
Lack of Professional Development	1. "Not 'keeping up'—expanding their own knowledge." 2. "I've seen lots of 'good ol' boys' who are not educated in the training profession transferred into training." 3. "Application of 'technology' without understanding concepts, theory, etc."
Violation of Confidences	4. "Breaking the trust of classroom participants." 5. "Relating information gathered in the classroom back to the organization." 6. "Identifying client deficiencies to others." 7. "Reporting information given in confidence."
Use of "Cure All" Programs	8. "Consultants selling programs without any effort to even estimate the needs of the client." 9. "Continuing use of 'sacred cow' type programs when need for them is no longer valid." 10. "Continuation of programs long after they have served their purpose."
Dishonesty Regarding Program Outcomes	11. "Concealing truth on program results." 12. "The assurance that a training program produced results when in fact it was only a good 'show.' " 13. "Falsifying training records to make results look better than they are."
Failure to Give Credit	14. "Failure to give credit for work done by others (includes materials, instruments, and even whole courses)." 15. "Not giving credit when using another's research." 16. "Illegal copies of printed and taped matter from existing suppliers' programs." 17. "Copyright violations."

(continued)

Table 2.1 *(Continued)*

Major Categories of Behavior Considered Unethical	Typical Response
Abuse of Trainees	18. "Treating course participants as children." 19. "Treating training participants as 'lesser' individuals of little importance." 20. "Racist and sexist remarks." 21. "Use of profanity." 22. "Unwillingness to obtain input from the trainees." 23. "Using trainees to practice training techniques and exercises to meet trainer rather than group needs." 24. "Using sexual relations with seminar participants as a portion of training."
Other Improper Behavior	25. "Consultants designing programs that give people what they want rather than what they need." 26. "Acting as entertainers rather than trainers." 27. "Lack of follow-up in order to see that programs are properly implemented after the classroom training."

From "Unethical and Improper Behavior by Training and Development Professionals" by Ronald W. Clement, Patrick R. Pinto, and James W. Walker. Reproduced by special permission from the December 1978 *Training and Development Journal.*

tial as an umbrella under which new norms and expectations can flourish without constant pressures to revert back to the more comfortable and known ways of operating. Active senior management support is necessary for ensuring a high level of commitment by middle managers to the program.

A critical mass must be reached in order for a program to be sustained. In other words, the training must be diffused throughout a significant portion of the organization so as to become a way of life for employees. For these reasons, a new program must be installed on key fronts within an organization simultaneously, rather than implemented in only one area. Change has to spread throughout a substantial segment of the organization and be backed by the managers and employees if it is to remain.

The initial strategy should be to "go with the winners." That is, one must be careful to ensure that the system is implemented in several parts of the organization where there is a good chance of achieving positive results, so that success can be demonstrated early. Once the concepts become widely accepted, it will be easier to tackle the more complex and resistant segments of the organization.

The implementation of the training system should be reviewed quarterly with the vice presidents of operations and human resources. A major topic of each meeting should be the cooperation and active efforts exerted by the managers reporting to these vice presidents in making the training a way of life with the people whom these managers supervise. These managers should know that they run the risk of transfer, demotion, or even termination if they receive poor evaluations from the vice presidents in meeting this objective.

It is important to start thinking of training and development as part of the business (Yeomans, 1982). To gain managerial support, the training department must identify its customers and consumers and begin doing first those programs that satisfy these two constituencies. The customers for the training department include all critical members of the client base *within* the organization. Ultimately, the training department's client is the highest member of management who is impacted by the training activities. For example, the sales trainers within a large operating unit should consider the regional sales vice president as their primary customer. To satisfy this customer, the sales trainers must talk with this individual to understand the unit's business objectives as well as its specific short- and long-term needs. It is imperative that they can see the direct and immediate relevance of the training on their sales behaviors and on sales results. By satisfying consumers, the training department will get the support it needs to be effective. Top management (i.e., customers) will start hearing throughout the organization that the training is useful and realistic (Yeomans, 1982).

Many problems in organizations (e.g., low morale, poor employee motivation, employee dissatisfaction) cannot be solved through training and development efforts. In these cases, training managers have to say no to requests by managers for training. Instead, they need to recommend to management alternative solutions to their problems (e.g., motivational interventions). To secure top management support, it is better to say "sorry, no" than to implement an expensive and time-consuming training program that ultimately fails.

Finally, to maintain ongoing managerial support, it is advisable to get away from a program orientation. Rather than always trying to solve every new problem with another training program, it is better to think more of ongoing learning. For example, Buick-Oldsmobile-Cadillac (BOC) recently trained all of their managers and supervisors in ways of improving their ongoing communication and coaching skills with their employees. Providing ongoing communication and coaching to employees is the key to "continuous improvement and development," one of BOC's most cherished philosophical concepts.

LEGAL ASPECTS OF TRAINING AND DEVELOPMENT

We now turn to a very important topic: the impact of federal fair employment regulations and issues of workers' rights on training practices. It might be helpful for us to begin by briefly reviewing the history of these regulations.

Although the federal requirement of equal treatment under the law dates back to the Bill of Rights and the Thirteenth and Fourteenth amendments of the Constitution, it was the 1964 Civil Rights Act that specifically brought employment practices under the jurisdiction of the courts. Title VII of this act specifically states that "it shall be an unlawful employment practice for an employer to . . . discriminate against any individual with respect to compensation, terms, conditions, or privileges of employment, because of the individual's race, color, religion, sex, or national origin" (Sec. 703). Furthermore, Title VII established the Equal Employment Opportunity Commission (EEOC) as an enforcement agency of fair employment practices. In 1978 the EEOC and three other federal agencies (i.e., the Civil Service Commission, Department of Justice, and Department of Labor) issued the Uniform Guidelines. The guidelines concern themselves primarily with an organization's selection procedure, but they have important implications for training as well.

Often, certain kinds of training are required before an employee can be considered for entry into a particular job. For example, a clerk in a retail store might be required by the personnel department to have a college degree in order to be admitted into a training program for buyers. Or, a person may be expected to pass a pole-climbing course prior to becoming a telephone installer or repair technician. In such cases, the potential for discrimination exists. It can be especially problematic in those situations where women or nonwhites are less likely to pass a training course than white males, and the company has no proof that the training requirements are relevant to later job proficiency.

Any company which intends to use the successful completion of training as a job prerequisite should attempt to show that their training program has no negative (i.e., adverse) impact on women and minorities. In other words, women and minority group members must have as much chance of successfully completing the training as white males. If the training does have a negative impact, however, the organization must stand ready to demonstrate the validity (i.e., job relatedness) of its training requirements in the event of a lawsuit or a government compliance review. That is, the company must be able to show that persons with this training perform the job better than persons without the training. To carry out such a study, it is necessary for the company to permit persons without this prerequisite training to be placed on jobs in order to measure their later performance. The performance of the trained and untrained groups should not only show statistically significant differences, but the differences must be great enough to be of practical significance as well.

If for some reason the strategy just described is not technically feasible, another strategy known as *content validation* may be used. Content validation of training requirements would first necessitate an analysis of the skills and knowledge needed on the job (see Chapter 3), and then a systematic documentation that the training content covers these things. For example, we might find through a careful job analysis that building maintenance mechanics must understand advanced heating systems and refrigeration absorption systems. Therefore, a content valid training program would deal with the electrical and mechanical maintenance, operation, and wiring of common heating plant components. In addition it would cover common absorption principles and specific differences between the major manufacturers' systems. The course also would allow trainees to gain hands-on experience with various maintenance routines and troubleshooting procedures. The objective, then, is to document that the training content is representative of the skills and knowledge that will be required in doing the job.

Admission into a training program is another situation where potential discrimination exists. Selection of trainees is almost always based on some informal or formal selection procedure such as testing, interviewing, reference checking, and/or supervisory recommendation. Where negative impact exists against females and nonwhites, the selection procedure may be discriminatory and should not be used unless it can be demonstrated to possess *criterion-related validity*. That is, it must be shown statistically that an applicant's level of performance on the selection procedure will, on the average, be indicative of his or her level of performance on the job. The advisability of validating selection procedures by correlating them with measures of success taken during training (e.g., scores on achievement tests and trainer's ratings) is open to question. In our opinion, a relationship should always be established between measures of trainees' success and actual job performance before training measures are used in criterion-related validity studies.

Several years ago, we established a skilled-trades training program to provide an opportunity for disadvantaged employees to receive on-the-job work experience and off-the-job training to qualify eventually for skilled maintenance job openings. The program involved a three-year training period during which selected applicants were given direct learning opportunities in a designated maintenance skill area. Each trainee was under the immediate supervision of the maintenance supervisor in the department (e.g., electrical, mechanical, instrumentation) in which he or she was being trained. The supervisor assigned the responsibility of instructing the trainee to one or more qualified tradespeople. Each trainee was assigned to certain departments (e.g., curing, calendaring, extruding, final finish) for three months during which time he or she became familiar with and knowledgeable about the maintenance assignments in the respective departments. Each trainee was exposed to the most troublesome and frequent maintenance-related breakdowns within the trainee's skill designation while in each department. The training also consisted of correspondence schoolwork during the first two years of the program.

Based on the skilled-trades training program, a battery of tests were assembled to choose objectively those employees who had the necessary learning capabilities for this training program. The test battery measured such things as mental alertness, mechanical reasoning ability, tool knowledge, ability to visualize and mentally manipulate objects in space, skill in using ordinary mechanics tools, and fine eye-hand coordination. It was found that the tests had no negative impact on the selection of minority employees. Moreover, each test was shown to have criterion-related validity, in that there was a relationship between scores on the selection tests and appraisals of job performance subsequent to the completion of training.

Sometimes women and members of minority groups may allege that the training process itself has shown disparate treatment toward them. According to the Uniform Guidelines (1978), "disparate treatment occurs where (members of a minority) have been denied the same employment opportunities as have been available to other employees or applicants" (p. 38300). For example, female plaintiffs might testify that the training equipment was designed primarily for males, thereby making it difficult for some females to use because of their shorter legs and arm reach than most males. Hispanic plaintiffs might maintain that the vocabulary level in their company's training manuals requires reading ability in English far above that which is required for performing the job adequately.

Proof of disparate treatment by plaintiffs in such court cases normally follows a three-step procedure: (1) the plaintiffs must establish a prima facie case of discrimination by demonstrating that they belong to a minority group, are qualified for the employment opportunity, and were denied the employment opportunity while others in nonprotected classes were not; (2) the employer must either specify that the actions were taken for legitimate, nondiscriminatory reasons, or the actions were required by business necessity; and (3) the plaintiff must then either prove that the employer's reasons cannot be substantiated by the facts of the case, or prove that the employer was more likely to have been motivated by discriminatory reasons (Russell, 1984).

What should training managers do to prevent court cases where disparate treatment is alleged by plaintiffs? If the training process consistently results in inferior performance by women or minorities, a redesign of the training program may be required unless such differential performance is reflected in similar on-the-job performance by nonminorities. For example, in the early 1970s a demand for smaller pole-climbing gear began to develop in the Bell System as a result of the entry of women into outside craft positions. In 1974 AT&T formally requested the Western Electric Company to develop smaller equipment for use by employees of slight stature. Size and strength data on the male and female adult population of the United States was obtained by Western Electric in its design effort. It also prepared a questionnaire to obtain data from women who used climbers as part of their assignments and from short men who had difficulty using full-size climbers. By 1976 Western Electric had completed its small climber design. Some of the design changes were as follows: (1) the stirrup width was made about one-half inch narrower than the standard climber to accommodate the narrower work boot of the smaller individual; (2) the stirrup depth was decreased to produce a snug fit in front of the work boot heel for the smaller size boot; and (3) the stirrup end was modified to permit the foot strap to firmly hold the smaller size work boot. Based on the results of a questionnaire study, AT&T found that the new design met the needs of 98.6 percent of the female employees (Smith, 1978).

Another example of the need for redesign of training content that takes into account the unintentional effect of adverse impact comes from a chemical company that examined the reading difficulty of its training materials compared to that required on the job by chemical operators. The company used a readability index that took into account both the number of syllables per 100 words as well as average sentence length. It learned that the training manuals were excessively difficult to comprehend, which partially explained why some Spanish-surnamed trainees were dropping out of the program. Based on this information, the training department revised the training manuals by shortening words and sentences.

A potential source of discrimination related to training occurs when measures collected during training are used in certain career decisions about trainees. These measures might be used for making decisions about a trainee's retention in the program. Or they may be used to give those who performed better in training the preferred job assignments after training is completed. In these two situations as well as others, if there is a differential performance for minority groups, then the training performance measures must be validated. For example, a large banking firm used paper-and-pencil quizzes, work sample tests, and trainer's ratings to evaluate trainee performance during an 18-day training class for bank tellers. Trainees were assessed on how effectively they could issue new bonds, open new accounts, and record deposits and withdrawals on computer terminals. A validation study was conducted which showed that performance on each of these measures correlated substantially with the trainees' performance six months later as tellers. Performance ratings were obtained from each teller's bank manager, who had no knowledge at all of the individual's performance during training. The bank showed that there was no differential performance for minority group trainees on any of the measures used during training.

Another aspect of legislation that training specialists must be sensitive to is the Equal Pay Act, passed by Congress in 1963. This act prohibits pay discrimination between males and females whose jobs require equal skill, effort, and responsibility and who work under similar conditions (Holley and Jennings, 1987). The courts will not tolerate pay differentials between males and females due to "flaws" in the training provided. The courts' standards were laid down in *First Victoria Bank* when the Fifth Circuit Court ruled that the bank's training program was fatally flawed because (Russell, 1984)

1. Employees were not hired with the understanding that they were to be in a training program.
2. The training program was not in writing.
3. Employees were not rotated to predetermined jobs and, moreover, assignments were apparently based on the employer's needs.
4. No formal instruction was given to the "trainees."
5. The training program had historically excluded women.
6. Advancement from the training program to fully qualified employment was sporadic.

Since the bank violated all six of the court's training standards, it was ordered to grant equal pay to its female employees. To prevent future litigation of this kind, training managers should obviously take steps to ensure that these types of training flaws do not exist.

Recently, there have been lawsuits concerning two additional training issues. First, the growing popularity of so-called New Age training programs is creating legal challenges by employees who claim that these programs violate their religious or philosophical beliefs. These New Age programs vary widely, but may include such controversial things as Eastern mysticism, emotional confessions, positive thinking, and hypnosis (Brannigan, 1989). The groups that promote these programs all have a common aim—to alter people and their corporation by unleashing in them energies that purportedly remain unused in most people. They seek to liberate the mind by allegedly breaking the chains of habit and passivity.

In an article in *Fortune* magazine that is highly critical of this training (Main, 1987), Carl Raschke, an expert in religion and society at the University of Denver, was cited as describing these techniques as an attempt by its advocates to transplant culturism and mysticism from the counterculture of the 1960s and 1970s to the corporate world. Robert Tucker, head of the Council of Mind Abuse in Toronto, an organization which helps people break from cults, was quoted as stating, "It's one thing if an individual walks in off the street and signs up for a course, but quite another if your boss sends you. Then there is a level of coercion. Does my boss have the right to put me through training that conflicts with my religion and any worldview?"

The *Fortune* article argues that corporations are building an enormous potential liability. That the number of known lawsuits is currently small in number reflects the fact that many cases are shrouded in medical and legal confidentiality. Moreover, many employees are understandably reluctant to publicly criticize training that is strongly endorsed by their bosses.

The best documented case of employees in revolt, stated *Fortune*, is that of Pacific Bell. *Fortune*'s description of the event is quoted here:

> After the breakup of AT&T, Pacific Bell, a subsidiary of Pacific Telesis, decided that it needed to overhaul its corporate culture, which had been standard Bell. To help, it hired two associates of Charles Krone, a trainer who for years has served the likes of Scott Paper and Du Pont. Krone, who often veils his ideas in impenetrable language, claims to make people rethink the way they think and hence arrive at new ways of solving problems. The Krone consultants worked with Pacific Bell for two years and obviously made an impression on corporate culture: This year's corporate statement of principles was worked in a manner even Krone might find indecipherable. It defined interaction, for example, as the "continuous ability to engage with the correctedness and relatedness that exists and potentially exists, which is essential for the creations necessary to maintain and enhance viability of ourselves and the organization of which we are a part."
>
> When the mounting resentment inside Pac Bell was revealed by the San Francisco *Chronicle* in March, the California Public Utilities Commission investigated and asked a consulting firm, the Merdian Group, to survey the utility's employees. Guaranteed anonymity, employees by the hundred complained furiously. They hated the jargon and obscure language, the perceived threats that those who didn't adopt the new-think would have no future at Pac Bell, the "facilitators" who sat in as "thought police" at meetings to make sure the Krone procedures about agendas and note-taking were followed, and the implication that anyone who didn't get the new routine was stupid. There were, admittedly, also some pluses. Company meetings became more purposeful, and managers got to know each other better.
>
> The commission found, too, that the Kroning of Pac Bell was enormously expensive. It is recommended that $25 million of the $40 million cost of the program in 1987 be charged to the stockholders, not the rate payers. Pac Bell suspended further training and ordered its own study. The company's president, Theodore Saenger, took early retirement, and his heir apparent, Executive Vice President Lee Cox, the chief supporter of the Krone program, was demoted to the presidency of a subsidiary, PacTel Corp. (Main, 1987, p. 100)

The need to guard the rights of the individual is discussed in Chapter 10. Suffice it to say here that Title VII of the Civil Rights Act of 1964 requires an employer to "reasonably accommodate" a worker's religious beliefs unless it creates undue hardship. To prevent these kinds of lawsuits, we recommend that employees be informed of the training techniques beforehand and be allowed to truly choose whether to attend.

Second, the issue of stress on the job has gathered more and more attention by the media and the courts. Recent court decisions clearly suggest that employers will sometimes be held financially liable for stress created on the job. In response, Ivancevich et al. (1985) have counseled that managers learn to identify the potential stress trouble spots in their organizations (i.e., training programs), try to relieve these where possible, and document their efforts.

From 1973 to 1982, the major law regulating the training of the disadvantaged was the Comprehensive Employment and Training Act (CETA). In 1983 CETA was replaced by the Job Training Partnership Act (JTPA). Like CETA, the JTPA was directed at providing training and job search assistance to economically disadvantaged youths, adults, and displaced workers. Unlike CETA, the JTPA puts the private sector employer as an equal partner with local government in planning, designing, and implementing local training programs (Guttman, 1983). According to Scarpello and Ledvinka (1988), here is how JTPA establishes a network by which training needs within a state are systematically addressed at the state and local levels:

> Title I of JTPA specifies that the governor must prepare a statement of the state's job training and placement programs, goals, and objectives. The governor also must appoint a state job training coordinating council whose job it is to propose statewide training delivery areas. Based on the distribution of the population across the state, the governor then designates the state's delivery areas. In each area, a private industry council is established. Representatives from industry chair the council and make up the majority of its members. The remaining council members are from unions, rehabilitation agencies, economic development agencies, community organizations, and the state employment service. (Guttman, 1983)
>
> Title I also specifies that the council's role is to
>
> 1. Set policy.
> 2. Oversee training activities conducted within the training delivery area.
> 3. Determine the procedures for the development of the training plan.
> 4. Select the plan's administrator.

The private council is required to submit a two-year job training plan to the governor for approval. The law specifies the content areas that must be covered in the plan. Other JTPA Title I provisions deal with training plan reviews, program performance standards, administrative cost ceilings, financial assistance to educational agencies, and financial assistance for older worker retraining programs (Guttman, 1983). "The significance of JTPA to organizational training is that many of the joint labor-management training programs and other cooperative efforts are coordinated through JTPA" (Scarpello and Ledvinka, 1988, pp. 476–477).

As you can see, the legal aspects of training and development should not be underestimated. They will continue to be an important aspect of this field in the years to come.

FINAL COMMENTS

The underlying theme of this and the subsequent two chapters is that training cannot be viewed as an isolated process. It is affected by a wide variety of organizational factors that can enhance or reduce its value.

These include the organization's corporate strategy, structure, technology, and attitude toward selecting the most effective employees versus training to develop their capability.

The company's financial health obviously affects the company's training department. A financial downturn usually is the direct cause of a reduction in training staff and budget. Tying the training budget to the company's financial health, however, may sometimes be a mistake, especially if the company is experiencing the results of an economic recession.

Haveman and Saks (1985) wrote an essay on transatlantic lessons for training policy. The Swedish government has argued that training should be emphasized rather than deemphasized during an economic recession so that skilled workers will be available during a recovery to relieve inflationary pressures and rapidly expand the industries. Thus training is expanded to include some 5 percent of the labor force during peaks of recessions by paying companies to expand in-house training.

To ensure ongoing managerial support for training departments, the training staff must be selected on the basis of their knowledge, skill, and ability as trainers. They must receive ongoing training of trainers to ensure that they maintain their knowledge, skills, and ability. In addition, the training staff needs to take it upon themselves to stay abreast of the organization's short- and long-term goals so that they can show upper management how the various training processes are playing a key role in the effective implementation of the corporate strategy. Organization analysis is the subject of the next chapter. The steps to maximizing trainee learning is the subject of Chapter 4. The ways of determining whether the training accomplished the objectives for which it was designed is discussed in Chapter 5.

Another step that training staffs can take to ensure senior management support is to keep abreast of legal issues which affect the way organizations develop the capability of their people. More than one leader has reached a plateau or, even worse, ended his or her career because of ignorance of Title VII implications that led to a class action lawsuit against the company in question. Ensuring that managerial decisions and training processes are in compliance with the law is a vital service that training staffs can perform for the organization. We discuss this subject further in Chapter 10.

Chapter 3

Identifying Training Needs

Too often training and development programs get their start in organizations simply because the program was well advertised and marketed, or because "other organizations are using it." It makes little sense for any organization to adopt an expensive and time-consuming training effort simply to "keep up with the Joneses." However, because organizations often imitate one another, training techniques (as pointed out in Chapter 1) can be faddish. This faddish nature of training can be minimized by systematically determining training needs. In this way, organizations will use training and development interventions only for the people and the situations where needed. In this chapter we discuss the most comprehensive and sophisticated system of determining an organization's training needs. This approach consists of three kinds of analyses: organization, task, and person (McGehee and Thayer, 1961). These analyses provide answers to the following three questions: Where is training needed in the organization? What must a trainee learn in order to perform the job effectively? Who needs training and of what kind?

Before proceeding, it is important to keep several things in mind about this approach to training needs. First, these analyses require time and human resources to be conducted properly. It is clearly not something that a few individuals in an organization can complete overnight. Second, it is a process that needs repeating when the organization's products, services, or technology changes. Third, the three analyses are usually performed simultaneously since they interrelate so highly with one another. Even if an organization cannot afford financially to carry out each step mentioned in this chapter, it should attempt to do whatever it can to approach this ideal.

ORGANIZATION ANALYSIS

Organization analysis looks at the organization as a whole. This involves examining its interface with the external environment in which it operates, the attainment of its stated objectives, its human resources, and its climate. The primary purpose of an organization analysis is to determine where in the organization training activities should be conducted (i.e., "Are they needed?") and could be conducted (i.e., "Will they be successful?"). It is unusual for all units within an organization to have the same training and development needs. To implement an organization-wide training program without assessing where the training is needed makes little sense from a cost/benefit standpoint. Nevertheless, we have seen organizations adopt expensive "organization-wide" programs with little or no regard to where the training was actually required.

The environment in which an organization operates can be a critical factor in determining whether training and development should be conducted. For one thing, if a training function is to survive it must be supported financially by the organization. The amount of support the organization gives can be affected by its overall profitability or vitality in the competitive market, as well as by the resources available (i.e., labor, raw materials, capital, technology, markets) for its continued success (Hinrichs, 1976). Further, the larger environment in which an organization operates can affect the organization itself which, in turn, can affect training needs. For one thing, the environment can affect the way the organization's managers design jobs, supervise their employees, and make decisions (Schneider, 1976). The environment may also influence the structural nature of the organization itself. Those organizations operating in dynamic, uncertain environments where there are frequent scientific discoveries, technical inventions, and changes in market conditions (e.g., electronics firms) need structural features (e.g., flexible roles, open communications that cut across hierarchical levels, coordination by committees) that will allow them to adapt rapidly to changing environmental conditions. On the other hand, those organizations functioning within relatively stable commercial and technological environments (e.g., banks, insurance companies) can function well using a more bureaucratic or mechanistic structure (Burns and Stalker, 1961). Designing a bureaucratic structure may involve clearly defining roles and responsibilities, instituting a one-way chain of command from the top to the bottom of the authority hierarchy, and delegating sufficient authority to each manager to carry out his or her responsibilities.

Unless it is known what the organization and its subunits are trying to accomplish, there is little basis for determining where training is needed. Knowing, for example, that an organization's 90 retail stores had a net profit of $1 million last year tells us little unless we can evaluate this outcome in relation to store objectives. Once we know the objectives, we can examine how closely these goals are being achieved.

An organization's overall objectives should first be stated in broad terms and then stated more specifically for the organization's various divisions, departments, and sections. In this way, training programs can be directed toward the improvement of those organizational units that are currently the weakest.

Furthermore, both short- and long-term goals must be established. Programs should not focus solely on solving immediate problems to the extent that long-term, preventive training is completely forgotten. For example, Table 3.1 presents a few of the short- and long-term objectives established by the medical records department and housekeeping department of a small midwestern hospital. Suppose that the medical charts of some patients had been misplaced in the past and that some members of the medical staff had voiced their complaints regarding the operation of the medical records department. Suppose, also, that the housekeeping department had been meeting or exceeding its stated objectives. All of this may suggest that members of the medical records department, but not the housekeeping department, need training of some kind.

It is important to remember, however, that not all inefficient operations can be dealt with by means of training. It could be that such nontraining factors as boredom with the work itself, low wages, inefficient work procedures, and poor physical working conditions are causing the problems. Furthermore, if employees know how to engage in certain behaviors but do not want to engage in those behaviors, the problem may be one of motivation rather than training. The important point here is that the individuals performing the organization analysis must ultimately decide why a particular organizational unit is not meeting its stated objectives (i.e., training vs. nontraining causes).

Another aspect of organization analysis is the estimation of how many people need to be trained immediately and in the future. This can be determined by conducting a process called employment planning or human resource analysis.

Every organization performs employment planning, either on an intuitive or a formal basis. Formal planning is especially necessary for large organizations with high growth rates, high employee turnover, and rapid changes in technology and product lines. The techniques used in forecasting vary from guesses by experts to sophisticated mathematical approaches.

Table 3.2 presents hypothetical information to illustrate how human resource analyses can be used to shed light on a department's training needs. Items 1 and 2 indicate that there is an immediate need to train one new employee. Item 3 shows that two employees will be retiring within the next year. Their replacements will require training and development. Items 4 and 5 indicate that as many as nine present employees are either "questionable" or "unsatisfactory" in skill and knowledge about their jobs. This suggests that they may need retraining to improve their current performance levels.

Table 3.1 SHORT- AND LONG-TERM OBJECTIVES OF THE MEDICAL RECORDS AND HOUSEKEEPING DEPARTMENTS OF A SMALL HOSPITAL

Medical records department	Housekeeping department
• Develop 5-year capital and manpower plan in accordance with long-range plan for hospital • No more than 1 complaint per month as to the organization, operation, or attitude of personnel in department from members of medical staff • No more than 3 formal grievances per year from members of the department • Written and current policies and procedures for the operations of the medical records department will be maintained, "current" being defined as semi-annual • No medical record shall ever be lost • Medical records shall be completed within time frames set up in Medical Staff Bylaws (a) All charts will be assembled and deficiency slips made out and put in physician's box within 48 hours of discharge (b) If chart is still incomplete 1 week later, physician will be notified that he or she has 8 days to complete the chart • All registered and professional employees will maintain continuing education requirements • All other employees to receive some form of continuing education at a minimum of 1 hour per month	• Compliance with WisPRO and JCAH requirements for audit activities (a) No deficiences on audit cited by survey (b) Be in compliance within current standards • Maintain all necessary records for (a) Infection control (b) State license (c) Legal documents • Annual operating budget will be prepared according to timetable presented by the director of finance. Year-end variance will not exceed ± 5% • Monthly status report will be turned in to administrative head by the 10th of each month • Develop 5-year capital and manpower plan in accordance with long-range plan for hospital • No more than 4 complaints per month as to the organization, operation, or attitude of personnel in department from members of medical staff • No more than 5 formal grievances per year from members of the department • All employees to receive some form of continuing education at a minimum of 1 hour per month • Educational activities to include at least 12 hours of management education per year for the housekeeping supervisor • Written and current policies and procedures for the operations of the housekeeping department will be updated during the next 5 years in accordance with the hospital's projected expansion

It is evident from item 6 that the problem with these employees cannot be solved simply by transferring them to other jobs, since so few of the employees in this department have the skill and knowledge levels for other company jobs. Items 7 and 8 show that most replacements will have to come from outside the company and that their training time will take 12

Table 3.2 A HUMAN RESOURCE ANALYSIS OF ONE HYPOTHETICAL DEPARTMENT

1. Number of employees in the job classification: 37
2. Number of employees needed: 38

3. Age levels:	29	33	45	47	50	51	53	55	69
No. per age group:	2	8	7	10	3	2	2	1	2

Factors	Satisfactory	Questionable	Unsatisfactory
4. Skill	32	2	3
5. Knowledge	33	3	1

6. Skill and knowledge for other jobs within the company:

Classification	Number	Jobs
No other jobs	35	none
One other job	1	Job Z, Dept. Y
Two or more other jobs	1	Job Z, Dept. Y; Job A, Dept. B

7. Potential replacements and training time:

Outside company	Within company	Training time
0	1	Less than 1 week
0	1	3 weeks to 6 weeks
10	0	12 weeks to 16 weeks

8. Training time on job for novice: 12 to 16 weeks
9. Turnover (two-year period): 5 employees; 13.5%

to 16 weeks. Finally, item 9 indicates that, assuming the current rate of turnover, five new employees will have to be trained within a two-year period.

A final aspect of organization analysis sometimes involves an organizational climate survey. A climate survey is used to determine the way employees perceive specific aspects of their work (e.g., compensations, opportunities for advancement, supervision received) and their membership in the organization (e.g., policies, goals, procedures, benefits, concern for human resources). If a group of employees perceive the company and their jobs as congruent with their own personal needs, goals, and aspirations, then the environment within their organizational unit will be one of trust and willingness to cooperate. On the other hand, if employees see the company and their jobs as being antagonistic to their personal needs, goals, and aspirations, then the environment in their unit will be characterized by mistrust and resistance to change.

Why would we want to assess an organization's climate? First, the environment may affect whether training can produce changes in behavior which will contribute to organizational effectiveness. Often, if the environment is very poor, employees will resist any kind of training given by the company. We have witnessed excellent training and development programs doomed to failure because the social-psychological environment basically made employees say to themselves, "I refuse to change." Second, a careful examination of an organization's climate using a technically sound attitude survey can help pinpoint problem areas within the organization.

An organizational climate survey is typically conducted by using a questionnaire that is completed by all employees. One such organizational diagnosis questionnaire is known as Perspectives, a computer-scored 82-item instrument that yields the following subdimension scores:

- Overall Job Satisfaction
  - Satisfaction with the Work Itself
  - Satisfaction with Co-workers
  - Satisfaction with Compensation and Advancement
  - Satisfaction with Pay
  - Satisfaction with Benefits
  - Satisfaction with Promotions
- Overall Attitude Toward Leadership and Supervision
  - Considerateness
  - Promotes Teamwork
  - Supervision of the Work Itself
- Evaluation of Communication
- Attitudes Toward the Organization
  - Policies
  - Concern for Human Resources
  - Physical Working Conditions
- Individual's Relation to the Job
  - Job/Person Match
  - Identification with Work
  - Organizational Stress
  - Job Contribution to Quality of Life
- Relative Importance of Various Job Aspects

Table 3.3 shows some of the items found in this questionnaire. As you can see, all of the questions employ a multiple-choice answer format. Table

Table 3.3 SAMPLE CONTENT OF AN ORGANIZATIONAL CLIMATE QUESTIONNAIRE

The following questions are to be answered using the number associated with the choice that comes closest to your own feelings:

1 = not at all, or none
2 = very little
3 = somewhat
4 = quite a bit
5 = a great deal, or to a great extent

1. Does your job make the best of your own particular skills and abilities?
   1 2 3 4 5
2. Are the people in your work group encouraged to work together as a team?
   1 2 3 4 5

In this section several aspects of your job are listed. Please indicate the importance of each of these for your overall job satisfaction by selecting one of the five choices below:

1 = very unimportant
2 = unimportant
3 = neither important nor unimportant
4 = important
5 = very important

1. Promotions 1 2 3 4 5
2. Benefits 1 2 3 4 5

The following questions are to be answered using the number associated with the choice that comes closest to your own feelings.

1 = almost never
2 = seldom
3 = sometimes
4 = often
5 = almost always

1. How often do you leave work with a good feeling of accomplishment about the work you did that day?
   1 2 3 4 5
2. Do you get conflicting orders or instructions and, as a result, don't know what you are supposed to do?
   1 2 3 4 5

3.4 presents some of the data obtained after computer scoring of the questionnaire. The table gives summary data for all 879 respondents from one organization as to their satisfaction with pay, benefits, and opportunities for promotions. The table also compares the attitudes of the office clerical employees with those of all 879 respondents.

In summary, an organization analysis prevents training from being viewed as an isolated activity or series of activities by training specialists. As we go through the 1990s, two themes should be kept in mind in order for training departments to be considered effective by senior-level management. First, training needs must be linked strongly to corporate strategy. Second, organizations have an ethical responsibility for developing training programs that minimize the technical obsolescence of their employees.

Table 3.4 SAMPLE DATA FROM AN ORGANIZATIONAL CLIMATE QUESTIONNAIRE

Summary Data for All 879 Respondents from Consolidated Corporation

Attitude dimension	Percentage responding LO 1	2	3	4	HI 5
SATISFACTION WITH					
Pay	9	11	34	32	14
Benefits	3	3	11	34	49
Promotions	13	28	28	24	8

Comparative Summary of
136 Office Clerical (C)
879 Overall Company (O)

Attitude dimension		Percentage responding LO 1	2	3	4	HI 5
SATISFACTION WITH						
Pay	C	14	33	25	25	3
	O	9	11	34	32	14
Benefits	C	3	0	3	39	56
	O	3	3	11	34	49
Promotions	C	16	38	25	18	3
	O	13	28	28	24	8

With regard to the first theme, Brown and Read (1984) concluded that the productivity gap between UK and Japanese companies can be closed by taking a strategic view of training policies. This should be done by ensuring that the training plan is constructed in the same context and by the same process as the business plan, and more importantly, that it is viewed in direct relationship to it. Thus achievement of training goals should be regularly monitored and subjected to a thorough annual review alongside the business plan.

Hussey (1985), too, argued that training objectives, especially for management development, should be reviewed by top management whenever a major switch in strategic emphasis is planned. However, his survey of UK companies revealed that only one-third of the respondents saw the necessity for doing so. Most managers felt that training objectives should be tailored to the individual rather than to corporate needs. Hussey argued for a shift in thinking regarding the purpose of training. Training should not be solely for the improvement of the individual with the hope that it will benefit the organization; training should be for the benefit of the firm, knowing that this, in turn, will benefit the individual.

Such training should ensure that strategy is communicated and implemented effectively throughout the organization.

The second theme in organizational analysis is a relatively new one: the objective of minimizing technical obsolescence. The plight of displaced workers in the United States has exposed business to considerable political attack in the past few years. For example, Congress nearly passed a law regulating plant shutdowns. In a *Business Week* (1986) editorial, Randolph Hale, vice president of the National Association of Manufacturers, was quoted as stating that retraining workers is one way for business to cool down this issue. In addition to reducing political pressure, retraining workers should foster corporate loyalty and make the work force more flexible and adaptable. The *Business Week* editorial, sympathetic to this viewpoint, pointed out that Ford Motor Company and General Motors Corporation even train displaced workers who must seek jobs elsewhere. Hansen (1984) provided an excellent description of a Ford-UAW approach to retraining that included adult basic education, vocational training, and job-search skills training. For more information on this subject, see Chapter 10.

To repeat, organization analysis focuses on the organization as a whole, including the external environment in which it operates. It attempts to answer the question, "*Where* is training and development needed and where is it likely to be successful within an organization?" It consists of an analysis of the following:

1. How the organization relates to its external environment, in order to assess how these external variables influence the need for training and development
2. How well the organization and its various subunits are achieving their stated objectives
3. What are the short- and long-range training and development needs of its employees
4. What factors in the internal and external environment are likely to present problems and to what extent can they be dealt with through the training and development of the organization's human resources

Once questions of *where* and *why* training is needed have been answered, the design or content of the program itself can be considered. This is done through a systematic task analysis.

TASK ANALYSIS

As shown in Figure 3.1, there are five steps in conducting a task analysis, as follows: (1) Obtain a copy of the company's job description; (2) identify the tasks involved in performing the job for which the training program is being designed; (3) identify the knowledge (K), skills (S), and abilities (A) needed for performing these tasks; (4) develop course objectives; and (5) design the training program.

Figure 3.1 Steps in course development using task analysis

Job Description → Task Identification → KSA Identification → Course Objectives → Design of Program

Suppose we wanted to develop a training program for newly hired Tire Store Managers. Figure 3.2 shows the types of information that would be generated at each step of the task analysis.

Job Description

The first step in determining the content of a training and development program is to develop a description of the target job. A job description is essentially a narrative statement about what a person does on the job, including the conditions (e.g., cold weather, excessive time pressures, dealing with irate customers) under which the job is performed.

Figure 3.2 An example of the information collected at each step of the task analysis

Job Description

Supervises and coordinates activities of the workers engaged in servicing and repairing automobiles and truck tires and tubes. Examines damaged, defective, or flat tires to determine feasibility of repair and assigns workers to tasks.

Task Identification

Attends meetings with district manager.
Communicates Occupational Safety and Health Administration (OSHA) regulations to employers.
Selects employees to train a new worker.
Schedules overtime as needed.

KSA Identification

Oral communication skills.
Tolerance of stress.
Numerical ability.
Persuasiveness.

Course Objectives

To be knowledgeable about company overtime policies and procedures.
To be knowledgeable about store return policies.
To handle customer complaints on the phone and in person.
To maintain the security of the tire store building.
To know and be able to communicate OSHA regulations to employees.

Design of Program

Methods: lecture, behavioral modeling, computer-assisted instruction, and on-the-job training (OJT)
Length: 15 days
Place: Corporate Training Center
Trainers: HRD, Inc. + 3 in-house trainers
Trainees: 75 new hires per year

Some organizations already have written job descriptions that are filed in the personnel department. Often, however, these descriptions are not comprehensive enough for course preparation purposes. Thus the training staff must frequently rewrite them. This entails observing current employees performing their jobs and questioning them about what they are doing. In some instances, the training analyst may perform some of the job duties him- or herself in order to obtain firsthand knowledge of exactly what is involved in doing the work. More often than not, this cannot be done because the work is either too complex or dangerous for a novice to perform.

Two examples of job descriptions are presented in Figures 3.3 and 3.4. The first one, a description of an investment specialist, comes from the securities department of a large life insurance company. The second one describes the job of a medical librarian in a small hospital. In writing these two descriptions, the training specialists tried to include those things that are critical to performing these jobs satisfactorily, no matter how infrequently or briefly they occur. Moreover, the training specialists took care to describe these jobs as they exist now, not as the training specialists or the supervisors would like them to be in the future.

Task Identification

As you saw in the last section, a job description portrays the job in some detail, but it does not give us enough specific information to put together a training and development course. This is where task identification comes in.

Task identification focuses on the overt, observable behaviors that are involved in performing a job. A task listing of a home telephone installer might include the following behavioral statements:

1. Reads and interprets service orders
2. Climbs pole to hook up the drop wire
3. Runs drop wire from pole to house
4. Checks protector to make sure it is functioning correctly
5. Uses ladder on side of house to hook up drop wire

Several different approaches can be used for identifying tasks. Although the procedures differ somewhat from one another, they all break down human work into task units that can then be used for determining the content of a training and development program. In this section, the following six procedures are described:

1. Stimulus-response-feedback
2. Time sampling
3. Linear sequencing
4. Critical incident technique
5. Job inventories
6. Future-oriented job analysis

Figure 3.3 An example of a job description for the job of investment specialist

The incumbent reports to a manager of investments and an investment officer. The manager, along with three other managers, an assistant manager, the investment research officer, the investment officer (markets), and the assistant treasurer-assistant secretary, reports to the vice president—securities and treasurer.

The incumbent frequently accompanies the manager or investment officer on trips made to the site of borrowing corporations, and may occasionally make such trips alone. She or he actively participates in negotiation conferences both in the home office and in the field between JMW and potential borrowers and/or their investment banking representatives. After mutually satisfactory terms have been reached and the investment has been finally approved, the incumbent works closely with the law department to review the loan agreement and assure that it conforms to the conditions and stipulations approved by the finance committee.

The incumbent spends much of his or her time performing various necessary service and analytical functions for JMW's offshore oil and gas project. She or he is required to maintain liaison with joint venture partners for the purpose of acquiring and updating information. He or she is further responsible for authorizing the disbursement of funds, updating the project budget periodically, and projecting future expenditures. Finally, the incumbent performs various research activities for the project such as computing the probable rate of return on JMW's investment.

The incumbent also has major responsibility for evaluating consent requests for changes in existing investment loan agreements. She or he pursues the financial and legal aspects of the requested changes to assess their investment consequences. The incumbent then presents oral and/or written recommendations concerning the requested changes to a manager of investments and/or an investment officer for approval.

The incumbent occasionally prepares special projects related to portfolio analysis, securities department procedures and activities, and so on. He or she is generally expected to be knowledgeable about the portfolio, and to monitor its status periodically in order to identify and anticipate problem areas.

The incumbent assists a manager of investments and an investment officer in the analysis of new investment opportunities. This involves an appraisal of the credit worthiness of potential borrowers, including the general state of the borrower's industry, a thorough understanding of the terms of the loan agreement, and analysis of the yield required to make the deal attractive to JMW. The incumbent is expected to research and analyze these investment offerings with minimum supervision, developing and incorporating meaningful data on her or his own initiative. Based on this research, the incumbent's recommendation on a proposed investment is presented orally and in a detailed written memorandum to the manager and investment officer for approval. They direct any necessary revisions, and accompanied by the incumbent, present the proposal to the vice president—securities. Investment proposals approved by the vice president are subsequently presented to the finance committee by the manager and/or investment officer.

Figure 3.4 An example of a job description for the job of medical librarian

GENERAL RESPONSIBILITIES

Under general, but limited, supervision the librarian assumes responsibility for the administration, operation, organization, and expansion of a professional hospital library providing document delivery, bibliographic and reference services, and containing current books, serials, other appropriate print material, audiovisual material and bibliographic tools necessary for the use of the medical staff, medical and nursing students, and employees serving the hospital.

SPECIFIC RESPONSIBILITIES

1. Works with and makes recommendations to the library committee in the selection of appropriate books, serials, and audiovisual material for acquisition through purchase, gift, and/or exchange and in the establishment of library policies and procedures.
2. Classifies, catalogs, and indexes books, serials, and audiovisual material.
3. Issues materials to qualified library users and keeps pertinent records of lending in order to locate material when necessary or prevent material from remaining outside of the library for undue periods of time.
4. Performs reference services for library users including requests for factual information and for subject or bibliographic searches to be done manually and/or with MEDLINE terminal.
5. Provides document reproduction/delivery services as requested consistent with the Copyright Law of the United States (Title 17, U.S. Code).
6. Contacts other medical libraries and/or intertype library networks with shared services arrangements for material requested but not available in the hospital library.
7. Performs routine library clerical procedures including taking care of the library mail and correspondence, recording acquisitions, and checking in journals.
8. Coordinates through all medical center departments the purchase and/or subscription of reference materials or journals.
9. Develops annual departmental budget recommendations.
10. Develops annual plan of short-term and long-range departmental objectives.
11. Develops and establishes coordinated program of library service with the director of staff development and the hospital education council for in-house and community education.
12. Keeps all staff aware of library services and materials and orients the new medical staff, students, and employees to use of the library, its services, and materials to assure that effective use is made of the library.
13. When possible, participates in the professional organization, medical library consortia, and intertype library networks for the purpose of continuing education in librarianship and to be aware of and/or influence legislation, activities, and programs that may affect the hospital library.

The stimulus-response-feedback method was developed by Miller (1962). He argued that each task activity consists of the following components. An indicator may be any object that provides the cue for making a response. It may be an aircraft instrument, a pressure gauge, a millivolt meter, a circuit tester, or even a written message. The indicator cue that triggers the response may appear all at once, or it may have to be pieced together by the worker from recall through periods of time. In its broadest sense, it is an out-of-tolerance signal that there is a difference between present conditions and how conditions ought to be. Examples here might include the excessive vibrations of a piece of machinery, exhaust sounds from an automobile, or a clock that runs too slowly. The control object refers to any means the employee uses to correct the out-of-tolerance situation. It may require the use of a tool, a piece of machinery, or even another worker. The activation or manipulation deals with the employee's actual use of the control object. Here, Miller recommends describing the actual use of the tool or machinery or even the message conveyed by one employee to another regarding the situation. The indication of response adequacy is the feedback that the employees receive regarding the adequacy of their behaviors. The indication of response adequacy may be proximal (as by the feel of a switch when a machine is being adjusted), or distal (as when one hears the machine starting up again). In short, Miller's approach basically calls for the analysis of each task in terms of a stimulus-response-feedback framework. This paradox is illustrated here for two different tasks.

This approach to task identification is of value when describing simple structural tasks that are amenable to a stimulus-response-feedback dissection. However, the method is limited with complex tasks (e.g., executive management) because of the difficulties in specifying cues, responses, and/or feedback involved (Cunningham and Duncan, 1967). Nevertheless, the approach can be particularly useful in training where equipment simulators need to be developed. Imagine how much easier it would be to design a truck simulator or a punch press simulator after identifying the exact stimuli and responses involved in each aspect of the truck driver's or press operator's job.

A second task identification approach is called time sampling. Here, direct observations of work activities are made by trained observers. Time sampling enables trainers to determine through direct observation exactly what employees do on the job and how frequently they do it. By making randomized observations of employee behavior, trainers can learn in a relatively short time how employees perform their jobs. For example, in an analysis of entry-level clerical jobs, 37 clerical workers representing 10 clerical positions were selected for observation (Blood, 1975). At 25-minute intervals, an observer made "rounds" of observations that took him or her past the work stations of each of the 37 persons being observed. As the observer passed each work station, he or she simply noted the job duty (e.g., filing, checking, typing, receiving information, giving information) the worker was performing. Each observer's "rounds" were begun at random times throughout the workday. Over 1900 individual observations were made in all. This information enabled the organization to identify the tasks performed in each of these clerical positions.

In another organization, four observers were trained to monitor customer contacts of telephone company service representatives for a three-day period (Wexley, 1975). Well over a hundred service representatives in two district offices were monitored while handling almost a thousand telephone calls. The monitoring procedure required the observer to follow a "new" call through to completion (a new call was signaled by a light on a switchboard in an observation room). When the contact was completed, the observer switched off that representative, recorded the behavior(s) engaged in by the service representative, and waited for the next call. Randomization of service representative positions was ensured because the positions were connected to the central switchboard on a rotary number basis; that is, the next call was automatically connected to the next service representative available. Several interobserver agreement checks were conducted to assess the consistency of their task identification procedure. Correspondence between pairs of observers listening to the same 30 telephone calls was found to be quite high, ranging from 90 percent to 100 percent agreement.

The third task identification procedure, called linear sequencing, was designed expressly for specifying training content (Dean and Jud, 1965). The method is applicable for trainers who want to analyze the basic steps of any job so that they can successfully teach these steps to someone else. To do this, the task description must be sufficiently detailed so that trainees who know nothing about the procedure to be performed can read the analysis and perform the job correctly without guidance. This approach can be illustrated by using another telephone example and asking you to imagine for a moment a person who has never seen or used one. The trainer would use the following procedure:

1. Write each step on a card, with each card containing a stimulus and a response.
   Stimulus: When the phone rings.
   Response: Pick up the receiver (that part of the telephone that is attached to the base by a wire).
   Stimulus: If you hear nothing.
   Response: Say "hello."
2. Make certain that the response portion of the card begins with an imperative verb telling the reader to do something. For example, when taking an outgoing call some of the response cards could read: Press the buttons corresponding to the seven-digit telephone number of the person you are calling. Next, listen for a series of long tones interspersed with long pauses.

3. Technical terms commonly used by subject-matter experts should be included in the write-up and defined.
   Example: If you do not hear a DIAL TONE (Steady buzzing signal), HANG UP (replace the receiver on the phone as you found it).
4. If it seems desirable to record the rationale for a step (i.e., the reason why the step is performed) for future reference, the rationale should be recorded on the back of the card.
5. The trainer places the cards in the proper sequence. A series of steps that follow one another without any alternatives is called a linear sequence. If the steps are not always followed in exactly the same manner, and the trainees are required to make procedural decisions, the procedure is known as branching. The following are examples of these two types of sequences:
   Linear: (5) Next, insert the letter in the envelope. (6) Next, close the envelope. (7) Next, moisten the stamp. (8) Next, affix the stamp to the envelope.
   Branching: (5) Next, insert the letter in the envelope. (6) Next, close the envelope. (7) Next, determine if there is a postage meter in the office. (8) If there is a postage meter, . . . (instructions telling how to use it). (8a) If there is no postage meter, moisten a stamp.

As you can imagine, branching sequences occur more frequently as jobs become more complicated. This is an excellent method for determining training content with any job involving certain prescribed procedures (e.g., orthopedic surgery, dentistry, pipe fitting) since it specifies the exact things to be taught.

A fourth approach to task identification is known as the *critical incident technique* or CIT (Fivars, 1975; Flanagan, 1954). The CIT requires observers who are aware of the aims and objectives of a given job and who frequently (e.g., daily) see people perform the job, to describe to a task analyst incidents of effective and ineffective job behavior that they have observed over the past 6 to 12 months. This means that supervisors, peers, subordinates, and clients may be interviewed about the critical requirements of a specific job. The specific steps in conducting a task identification based on the critical incident technique are listed here (Latham and Wexley, 1991):

1. (Introduction): "I am conducting a job analysis to determine what makes the difference between an effective and an ineffective ______ (e.g., foreman, pipe fitter, secretary). By effective performance, I mean behavior you have seen in the past that you wished all employees would do under similar circumstances. By ineffective performance I mean behavior which, if it occurred repeatedly or even once under certain circumstances, would make you doubt the competency of the individual.

"I am asking you to do this because you are aware of the aims and objectives of the job, you frequently observe people in this job, and you are able to discern competent from incompetent performance. Please do not tell me the names of any individual to whom you are referring."

Job incumbents are not interviewed concerning their own behavior. This is because incumbents are usually objective in describing their effective behavior, but there is sometimes a tendency for them to attribute their ineffective behavior to factors that were beyond their control.

2. (Interview): "I would like you to think of specific incidents that you yourself have seen occur over the past 6 to 12 months." The emphasis on the past 12 months is to ensure that the information is currently applicable. For example, behaviors that were critical for a salesperson in the 1950s may no longer be critical in the 1990s. Moreover, memory loss may distort the facts if the analysis is not restricted to recent incidents. The requirements that the interviewer report only firsthand information maximizes the objectivity or factual nature of the information to be reported.

For each incident that is recalled, the same three questions are asked, namely:

a. "What were the circumstances surrounding this incident?" In other words, what was the background? What was the situation? This question is important because it establishes when a given behavior is appropriate.

b. "What exactly did the individual do that was either effective or ineffective?" The purpose of this second question is to elicit information concerning observable behavior.

c. "How is the incident an example of effective or ineffective behavior?" In other words, how did this affect the task(s) the individual was performing?

Generally, an interviewee is asked to report five effective and five ineffective incidents. Attention is given to both types of incidents because an effective incident is not necessarily the opposite of an ineffective incident. For example, setting a specific goal has been found to be effective for increasing productivity in many jobs, but not setting goals does not necessarily decrease productivity (Latham, 1969).

A total of 10 incidents are collected because they can usually be collected within one hour. This is the maximum time period that many employees can be away from the job without disrupting their workday. No more than 10 incidents are collected from any one individual so that the data are not biased by talkative people. In order to obtain a comprehensive sample of incidents, it is recommended that at least 30 people be interviewed for a total of roughly 300 incidents (Latham and Wexley, 1991).

The interviewer must be skilled in collecting information describing observable behaviors. If the interviewee responds to question b with the answer, ". . . the employee really showed initiative in solving the problem," the interviewer must ask, "What exactly did the individual do that indicated initiative?"

This procedure has particular utility where training specialists want to develop programs that concentrate on critical tasks. For example, a restaurant's waiters and waitresses may know how to set up tables and clean them after customers have left. The same waiters and waitresses may have difficulty, however, taking customer orders and relaying these orders accurately to the kitchen. Therefore, the training program should be concerned with these critical tasks.

The fifth approach to task identification involves the development of a job inventory (sometimes referred to as a task inventory). A job inventory is a structured questionnaire that consists of a listing of tasks comprising a particular job. Once the questionnaire is constructed, it is administered to employees who currently perform the job since they are considered to be among the most knowledgeable about it. In many cases, supervisors are asked to describe the job as well.

In brief, one or more small groups of persons (8 to 12 in a group) are initially selected to generate an exhaustive list of job tasks necessary to perform a particular job adequately. The individuals in these groups are not randomly selected, but are chosen on the basis of their exhaustive knowledge of the job. A technique known as group brainstorming is used by the training specialist during the meetings to encourage the group members to list as many tasks as possible. Employees and supervisors usually participate in separate meetings, as the presence of a supervisor may inhibit the employees from speaking openly. Listed here are several tasks that were generated during group sessions we held with tire store managers:

- Takes a physical inventory monthly
- Reviews salespersons' expense reports
- Arranges for outside collection of bills through independent agencies
- Holds safety meetings with store personnel
- Informs employees of all company benefits
- Assigns sales quotas to sales and service personnel
- Makes certain that customers are informed of all warranties and guarantees

Following the group meetings, a job inventory is constructed by the training specialist and mailed to a random sample of employees. These employees are asked to rate each task in terms of both importance and amount of time spent. An example of a typical job inventory is presented in Figure 3.5. Both low and high performers can be used to complete job inventories, since both groups of employees provide similar ratings of importance and time spent on tasks (Wexley and Silverman, 1978).

Figure 3.5 An example of a job inventory used with tire store managers

	Importance					Amount of Time Spent					
INSTRUCTIONS: For each task activity, *circle* the number corresponding to its importance for *your* job and the amount of time you spend on it.	1 - *Not at all* important 2 - *Slightly* important 3 - *Moderately* important 4 - *Very* important 5 - *Extremely* important					0 - *Never* do this task 1 - *Very little time* compared to other tasks 2 - *Somewhat less time* compared to other tasks 3 - *Same amount of time* as other tasks 4 - *More time* compared to other tasks 5 - *A great deal more time* compared to other tasks					
1. Assign and define duties to *all* new store employees.	1	2	3	4	5	0	1	2	3	4	5
2. Take a physical inventory monthly.	1	2	3	4	5	0	1	2	3	4	5
3. Assign accounts to salespeople for collection.	1	2	3	4	5	0	1	2	3	4	5
4. Monitor overtime payments to employees.	1	2	3	4	5	0	1	2	3	4	5
5. Make sure the inside and outside of building is maintained in a presentable condition.	1	2	3	4	5	0	1	2	3	4	5
6. Schedule and place advertisements in newspapers and on radio.	1	2	3	4	5	0	1	2	3	4	5
7. Make certain customers are greeted when coming into store and properly handled upon leaving.	1	2	3	4	5	0	1	2	3	4	5
8. Establish a probationary period for new hires and review their performance periodically.	1	2	3	4	5	0	1	2	3	4	5
9. Advise staff accountant of store claims.	1	2	3	4	5	0	1	2	3	4	5
10. Arrange promissory notes payable at customer's bank if deemed necessary.	1	2	3	4	5	0	1	2	3	4	5
11. Ensure that trucks are routed profitably.	1	2	3	4	5	0	1	2	3	4	5
12. Hold safety meetings with store personnel.	1	2	3	4	5	0	1	2	3	4	5
13. Make telephone solicitations to customers.	1	2	3	4	5	0	1	2	3	4	5
14. Ensure that advertised products are available to customers.	1	2	3	4	5	0	1	2	3	4	5
15. Discuss career goals with employees.	1	2	3	4	5	0	1	2	3	4	5

After the questionnaire is completed by a number of employees, the training specialist calculates the mean (i.e., average) rating for each task for both importance and time spent. The end product of this analysis is a comprehensive picture of the job's tasks as seen by not just one person or a few people, but by many knowledgeable employees currently working on the job.

A sixth and final approach to task analysis anticipates the dynamic environment in which organizations will be operating throughout the 1990s. It is called future-oriented task analysis. This concept at the present time is admittedly a fuzzy one. It is based on research such as Downs (1985) which has indicated that the jobs of the future will require less memorizing of facts and procedures, fewer physical skills, and far more conceptual ability than is true at the present time.

Consistent with these findings, Hall (1986) argued that an organizational analysis must focus on future objectives of the organization rather than only present ones. Only in this way can the development and training of senior executives be effective (see chapters 8 and 9).

The purpose of future-oriented task analysis is to link the management succession process, individual executive learning with the business strategy. In this way, future executive requirements are defined in terms of the future strategic organizational objectives. To do this, the organization's executives speculate on the future mission and future goals of the organization. This is followed by an updating process (Arvey, 1984; Fossum and Arvey, 1986).

In updating, the critical incident technique we described earlier can be used to develop behavioral observation scales (also discussed in this chapter) that specify what a person must do to engage in updating behaviors (e.g., keep abreast of technical journals, periodicals, and in-house publications; allocate working time for developmental purposes; volunteer for special assignments and tasks that represent a change in present job assignments).

Summary We have described six different task analysis procedures. Any of these methods can be recommended for determining job tasks. The stimulus-response-feedback and linear sequencing methods are extremely time consuming and microanalytic. With these methods, the training specialist essentially observes employees at work and records stimulus-response links. Of the two methods, stimulus-response-feedback is more microanalytic, since tasks are broken down even further than in linear sequencing. Time sampling is a sound method of ascertaining what employees do and how frequently they do it simply by making direct observations of their behavior. The soundness of this approach, however, depends on the randomness of the "rounds" and the comprehensiveness of the checklist on which job duties are noted. The CIT involves interviewing individuals who have themselves made direct observations. This method is particularly useful when we are interested in identifying critical aspects of the job. The use of job inventories is quite appealing, because employees participate in the construction of the inventory. The inventory is mailed to a large sample of employees who report their opinions about the importance and the relative amount of time they spend on each task. The end result is their averaged view of the job. Finally, the use of future-oriented task analysis captures the dynamic environment in which organizations find themselves in the 1990s.

KSA Identification

Once the tasks involved in performing the job have been identified, the training specialist must identify the knowledge, skill, and ability needed to perform these tasks. A *K* (Knowledge) refers to factual material that an employee needs to learn (e.g., marketing strategies, company overtime policies and procedures, store return policies). An *S* (Skills) pertains to the hands-on, overt doing of things (e.g., delegating responsibility to subordinates, handling irate customers, operating the cash register, operating car lifts). An *A* refers to basic abilities that new hires are typically expected to possess, but that can be developed through training (e.g., multilimb coordination, deductive reasoning, selective attention).

The identification of K, S, and A's can be accomplished using a panel of about ten people who are very familiar with the particular job. Typically, a combination of one's best job incumbents and supervisors of the job constitute an appropriate panel. Once the panel members understand the meaning of KSAs, they should be asked to brainstorm the K's, S's, and/or A's for each and every job task.

Course Objectives

The information obtained from KSA identification is used to construct the course objectives, which consist of statements that specify the desired behavior of the trainee at the end of training. That is, these statements explicate what the training specialist expects the trainee to know and to do after participating in the training program. Following are examples of the many course objectives that participants are expected to achieve upon completion of a four-week tire store manager training and development program:

1. Set down conditions of employment for new hires (i.e., spell out exactly what their jobs are)
2. Maximize one's employees through efficient scheduling and use of part-time people
3. Critique the appearance of different stores, and offer cost-effective solutions to any problems discovered
4. Fill out a customer invoice
5. Be familiar with the proper use of safety cages for safely dismounting and mounting split run truck tires

6. Handle customer complaints effectively
7. Make a complete diagnosis of any car malfunctions in order to deal with customer service questions
8. Handle radio advertisements, newspaper ads, and direct mailings
9. Be familiar with some of the more critical OSHA guidelines affecting store operations (e.g., proper stocking of aisles, storage of flammable materials, use of safety equipment in service area)
10. Be familiar with all types of store inventory (i.e., truck tires, passenger tires, brake and mechanical parts, and paperwork).

Although course objectives are based on the KSA identification, they differ in two important ways. First, KSA identification describes all of the personal characteristics involved in performing a job. Course objectives do not include those things that trainees are expected to know or be able to do before entering a course. For example, if prospective store managers already know how to complete a monthly inventory, there would be no need to include this task as a course objective.

Course objectives also do not include those KSAs called for in performing a job that are impractical to teach during a training course and are better left to learn on the job. For example, the handling of certain store operations may not be taught during a four-week store manager program since the training specialist may feel that it can be learned better on the job. Second, the KSAs describe the job as it is performed by an experienced employee. Course objectives need only describe the KSAs we can reasonably expect at the end of a training program. For example, an experienced store manager may be totally knowledgeable about all safety regulations affecting his or her store operations. It would be unrealistic to expect a trainee to know all of this upon course completion. It is far more realistic to expect the graduate to know the more critical regulations and learn the remainder through managerial experience (Mager and Beach, 1967).

It is important to remember that course objectives are tailored to people who will take the training course. Their level of motivation and their abilities (see Chapter 4) will influence the quality of terminal performance that can reasonably be expected at the conclusion of the course. Finally, although the course objectives are expressed in terms of the KSAs, the actual material taught during the training pertains to the job's tasks. Only in this way can we expect to maintain the trainee's level of motivation and positive transfer (see Chapter 4).

Design of Program

The final step in task analysis involves making decisions about the actual design of the training program. Of course, these decisions must be based on the particular set of course objectives. The first decision that needs to be made is whether to "make" or "buy." The answer, of course, depends on whether there exists a ready-made program that meets one's objectives as well as the program's quality and costs. If the training staff decides that it is advisable to make their own program, decisions must be made about its length, the techniques and methods to be used, where and when it will be conducted, who the trainers should be, the type of training the trainers will be given, who will train the trainers and, finally, who the trainees will be. If the decision is to buy, then the trainers must take steps to ensure that the program teaches the critical knowledge, skills, and abilities identified in the task analysis. This is done by examining the content validity of the training.

Content Validity

A training program can be judged as possessing *content validity* if (1) it trains individuals on the skills, knowledge, and/or abilities that have been identified previously through the task analysis as being important for performing the particular job, and (2) it does *not* train individuals on KSAs that are irrelevant for the particular job. If we should find, after designing a certain training program, that it lacks content validity, then we must revise it.

For example, Ford and Wroten (1984) assessed the content validity of an existing police officer training program. Several panels of experts (i.e., training staff members, instructors, members of the most recently graduated recruit class) were asked to generate a list of KSAs that were currently taught in the training program. These panels defined the content domain of the training program as consisting of 383 KSAs. Next, the training content domain was evaluated for job relatedness by 114 experts—64 experienced patrol officers who trained recruits on the job, 31 patrol sergeants from the target city, and 20 police personnel from similar-sized communities outside the target city. These experts independently rated the importance of each KSA to job performance. They used a seven-point rating scale ranging from "no importance" to "extreme importance." Ford and Wroten used a decision rule where KSAs with rating above average importance or high (i.e., 5, 6, or 7) were considered important; KSAs with ratings of average importance or below (i.e., 4, 3, 2, 1) were considered to be unimportant. The degree of consensus was determined by calculating a Content Validity Ratio (CVR) for each KSA. A CVR was determined by taking the number of experts who stated that a KSA was important (Ni), minus the number of experts who stated that a KSA was unimportant (Nu), divided by the total number of experts (i.e., 114) involved (Nt). Finally, the job relatedness of the total police officer training program was determined by calculating the average value of all the CVRs—the Content Validity Index (CVI). Their CVR and CVI values supported the conclusion that the content of this training program had a substantial degree of job relatedness. Specifically, they found that of the

383 KSAs defining the training content domain, 62 percent of them had statistically significant CVR values. In addition, the CVIs for both the target city sample of officers and sergeants and the outside city sample were statistically significant, as was the CVI for the total combined sample of 114 experts.

Even though these findings confirmed the content validity of the training program, Ford and Wroten proceeded to improve the program's content validity by trying to eliminate two types of misses: "deficiencies" and "excesses." Training deficiences are KSAs that are important for job success, but are not matched by a high degree of emphasis in the training program. The most extreme example of a deficiency would be a K, S, or A that is omitted from the training. On the other hand, training excesses are KSAs receiving an excessive amount of emphasis in the training relative to their importance on the job. The most extreme example of an excess would be a K, S, or A that is being covered in training, but is not needed at all on the job.

Before leaving the subject of content validity, an important point needs to be made. Just because a training program possesses content validity does *not* necessarily guarantee that the trainees learned the material taught, *nor* does it mean that the trainees were able to transfer what they were taught back to their jobs (Goldstein, 1986). Checking to see that a training program possesses content validity is important simply to ensure that it is, in fact, teaching what it should be teaching. But, content validity, by itself, is not sufficient. One must also use the various criteria (i.e., reaction, learning, behavior, and results), experimental designs, and quasi-experimental designs discussed in Chapter 5 to make certain that the trainees both learned the material and were able to apply this knowledge to their jobs.

PERSON ANALYSIS

Person analysis focuses on the individual employee. It deals with the question, "Who needs training and of what kind?" For example, one company found that its salespeople spent, on the average, only three hours a day with genuine sales prospects. The rest of their time was spent on various nonsales activities such as joking with one another and making personal telephone calls. The vice president of marketing decided that the entire sales force needed a course teaching them how to make more productive use of their work time. Although the one-day workshop on time management was effective for most people, it was obvious to the trainer that not every salesperson needed this type of training.

What is involved in doing person analysis? Step 1 is concerned with how well a specific employee is performing his or her job. The term *performance appraisal* is used to refer to the techniques employed by training specialists to measure an employee's job proficiency. The results of the performance appraisal determine whether or not step 2 (referred to here as diagnosis) is needed. If the appraisal indicates that an employee's work performance is acceptable, there is no need for step 2. If, on the other hand, the employee's performance is found to be below standard, this is a signal that diagnosis is needed. The diagnosis involves carefully determining what specific skills and knowledge must be developed if the employee is to improve his or her job performance.

Step 1

Since step 1 involves employee performance appraisal, let us turn to an overview of some of the methods that are available for evaluating whether an employee is performing a job adequately. These methods can be conveniently categorized into three general areas: (1) behavioral measures, (2) economic measures, and (3) proficiency tests.

Behavioral Measures Behavioral measures involve ratings based on observations of an employee's on-the-job behaviors by superiors, peers, subordinates, and/or outside evaluators. A major characteristic of behavioral measures is that they are dependent on human observation, and accuracy in reporting observations is often affected by factors irrelevant to job performance. For example, an individual's physical attractiveness, race, seniority in the organization, personality, and level of education may contaminate the performance appraisal. Simply warning or lecturing raters about judgmental errors does not reduce them to any appreciable degree (Wexley, Sanders, and Yukl, 1973).

Fortunately, managers and supervisors can be taught to eliminate certain errors when observing and evaluating their employees (see Chapter 10). For example, in one program, corporate managers were trained to eliminate the following judgmental errors: halo error (the tendency to rate an employee either high, average, or low on many factors simply because the rater believes the employee is high, average, or low on one single factor); similarity effect (the tendency on the part of a rater to judge more favorably individuals perceived as similar to him- or herself); first impressions (the tendency to evaluate another person on the basis of a judgment made primarily after an initial meeting); and contrast effect (the tendency to evaluate subordinates in comparison to one another rather than against preestablished job requirements).

During the one-day workshop, trainees saw videotapes of hypothetical employees being appraised by a manager. The trainees estimated how the manager in the videotape evaluated the employee, and how they themselves would rate the individual. The program provides an opportunity for trainees to actively participate in discovering the degree to which they themselves are prone to making judgmental errors, to receive immediate feedback as to the accuracy of their own ratings, and to practice job-related tasks so as to minimize any errors being committed (Fay and Latham, 1982; Latham, Wexley, and Pursell, 1975).

The training specialist has a number of behavioral procedures available for appraising employee proficiency. Two of the better ones are known as behavioral expectation scales (Smith and Kendall, 1963) and behavioral observation scales (Latham and Wexley, 1977, 1991). Figures 3.6 and 3.7 provide examples of BES and BOS rating scales. The two procedures are similar in that both are variations of the critical incident technique, both are based on observable job behaviors that are viewed by others as critical to job success, and both take into account the multifaceted nature of job performance. The BES and BOS methods differ, however, in at least one important way. Behavioral expectation scales require that each dimension be arranged on a continuous vertical rating scale with a behavioral anchor listed near each of the seven points ranging from ineffective to effective behavior. Raters simply examine the respective dimension and place a check mark beside the one behavioral anchor that they believe best describes the behavior that the employee could be expected to demonstrate. This expectation is based on what the rater has seen the employee do over a period of time. Thus the manager is required to extrapolate from actual behaviors observed to those that could be "expected" as defined by the scale anchors. The BOS is different in this respect, in that it requires no such extrapolation. With BOS, each critical behavior is listed in a questionnaire format and the rater indicates the frequency with which he or she has observed each behavior. An employee's total score on each dimension or criterion of job performance is then determined by totaling his or her scores on the five-point BOS scales. Although the example in Figure 3.7 contains only effective behaviors, in practice ineffective ones are listed as well. As can be seen from the two formats, BOS allows a more comprehensive analysis than does the BES.

The frequently heard complaints of managers and supervisors that the items on performance appraisal instruments are either sufficiently vague to defy understanding or completely inappropriate can be minimized with BES and BOS. The behavioral statements used are expressed in the rater's own terminology. In addition, by actively participating in the construction of the scales, the raters are more inclined to complete the ratings carefully and candidly.

Economic Measures Here, someone in the organization simply records the number of units produced in a given amount of time, sales volume, number of injuries, scrappage weight, and so on. In general, economic measures can be broken down into two subcategories: those dealing with production (e.g., units produced, number of rejects, dollars earned) and those dealing with personnel information (e.g., attendance, tardiness, grievances, training time needed to reach an acceptable standard of performance).

These variables may serve as excellent indicators of an organization's effectiveness, but they often present problems as measures of an individual's job performance. First they cannot be meaningfully applied to many

Figure 3.6 Example of a behavioral expectation scale (BES)

DIRECTIONS: First read the name of the behavioral dimension and its definition. Then notice the examples that illustrate various points on the rating scale. These examples are included to give you clear anchor points to help you make more accurate evaluations. Don't worry about whether or not your employee has actually exhibited the behavior described in the example. By knowing your employee, you should be able to judge whether he or she "could be expected" to display the type of behavior described in the example. After reading all the examples on a dimension, decide where on the rating scale the individual belongs by making a checkmark in the appropriate box. The box you check can range anywhere from the bottom of the scale, which represents low or poor performance, to the top of the scale, which represents high or good performance. Finally, on the next page, describe actual behaviors you have observed that support your rating. This same procedure should be followed for each dimension.

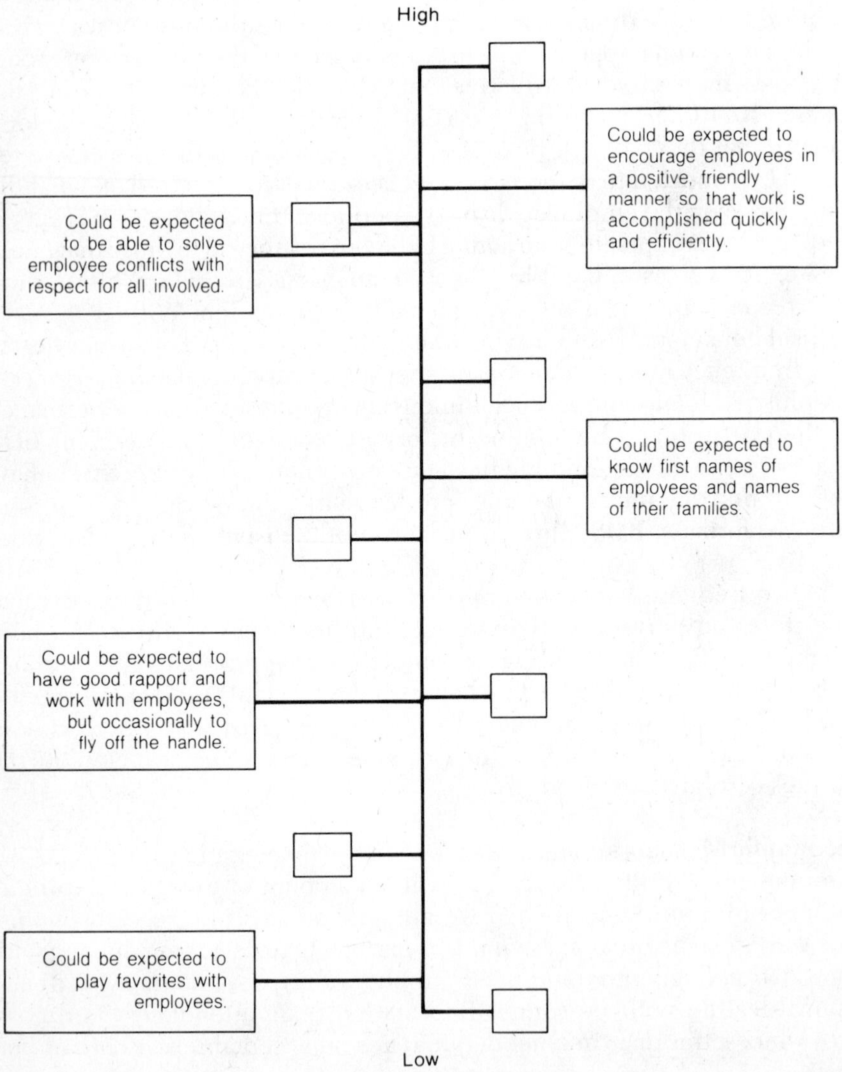

Describe actual behaviors you have observed that support your rating:

____

____

____

____

Figure 3.7 Example of behavioral observation scale (BOS)

DIRECTIONS: This checklist contains performance-related job behaviors that foremen, their supervisors, and their subordinates have reported as critical to the foreman's job success. Please consider the above-named individual's behavior on the job for the past three months. Do not consider other foremen or this individual's behavior at other times in the past in making your ratings.

Read each statement carefully. On the basis of your actual observations or on dependable knowledge (e.g., hard evidence or reliable reports from others), circle the number that indicates the extent to which this particular foreman actually demonstrated each of the following behaviors. For each behavior, a 4 represents "Almost Always" or 95 through 100% of the time. A 3 represents "Frequently" or 85 through 94% of the time. A 2 represents "Sometimes" or 75 through 84% of the time. A 1 represents "Seldom" or 65 through 74% of the time. And a 0 represents "Almost Never" or 0 through 64% of the time.

DIMENSION I. INTERACTIONS WITH SUBORDINATES

1. Asks an employee to do a job rather than tells him or her.
   Almost Never 0 1 2 3 4 Almost Always
2. Tells workers that if they ever have questions or problems with their jobs to feel free to ask him or her.
   Almost Never 0 1 2 3 4 Almost Always
3. Gives employees suggestions on how to do the job more easily.
   Almost Never 0 1 2 3 4 Almost Always
4. After assigning a difficult job, checks back to see if the worker is having any problem.
   Almost Never 0 1 2 3 4 Almost Always
5. When there is conflict (e.g., between two employees, between foremen and worker), takes the time to sit down and discuss the causes and potential solutions.
   Almost Never 0 1 2 3 4 Almost Always

Total = ________

Below Adequate	Adequate	Full	Excellent	Superior
0–4	5–8	9–12	13–16	17–20

In the space below, record observations to support your rating.

____

____

____

____

organizational positions. They are usually appropriate for such jobs as assembly line worker or press operator, where an employee's performance can be evaluated by recording the number of units produced in a given time period, the number of rejectable items produced, or the scrappage weight. However, on such nonproduction jobs as manager or chemist, neither quantitative measures of output nor job-related personal information are typically available (Latham, 1986; Latham and Wexley, 1991; Wexley, 1979). For such jobs, behavioral measures should be used.

Proficiency Tests An entirely different approach to measuring employee proficiency is to use proficiency tests. One variant of this approach is to take a work sample whereby, in either the actual work setting or a simulation of it, the employee is asked to perform the duties required in a job. Examples of this approach would include simulated telephone calls to operators, typing tests for secretarial personnel, and flight simulators for pilots. The assessment center (discussed in Chapter 9) illustrates the use of simulation devices for evaluating the proficiency of managerial personnel. For example, 36 managers at a Wisconsin plant that manufactures wooden doors were put through an assessment center, six managers at a time, by two industrial/organizational psychologists. Each of the managers was observed for two days while participating in the assessment center exercises, and then evaluated in terms of 14 management dimensions needed for managerial success at this particular plant (e.g., delegation, decision making, innovativeness, written communications). Each manager also received a written and oral report detailing his or her strengths and areas for improvement.

Another variant of this approach involves the use of written job-knowledge tests to assess employees. For example, pipe fitters might be given a battery of tests measuring such things as knowledge of fittings, accessories, and tools.

The major advantage of using proficiency tests is that they permit the employee's skills and knowledge to be compared to known standards under controlled and uniform conditions. Their main drawback is that the employee's performance during testing may not accurately reflect daily performance on the job.

We have now reviewed different performance appraisal methods that can be used in carrying out step 1 of person analysis. This step involves determining whether each employee in the organization is adequately performing his or her job. By using a combination of behavioral, economic, and proficiency measures, the training specialist can make an astute assessment of who is not fulfilling job requirements. If an individual is performing satisfactorily, there is no need for training. However, if an individual is not performing satisfactorily, then the next step in person analysis is warranted.

Step 2

Step 2 in person analysis involves determining the specific skills and knowledge that an employee needs to acquire in order to perform the job acceptably. This step requires a systematic diagnosis of each employee's strengths and weaknesses using the performance appraisal information collected during step 1.

Let us consider two examples of how diagnosis can help pinpoint the kind of training and development that an employee may need. Betty is employed as a copy editor for a medium-sized southwestern newspaper. Her job involves writing headlines, editing copy, selecting stories and other news material, laying out pages, and managing production flow. Betty's performance has been below standard ever since she was hired six months ago from another newspaper. Her performance has been evaluated using BOS by both her city editor and the paper's managing editor. Their evaluations indicate that Betty's weaknesses are primarily in the area of writing headlines. Specifically, she often writes inaccurate headlines, misses the point of a story with her headlines, occasionally misses deadlines, and uses poor grammar in headlines. As a result of this diagnosis, Betty is currently being coached by one of her department's most capable copy editors on headline writing. She is also taking a grammar course several nights per week at a community college.

The second example involves Bill who went through the two-day assessment center conducted at the door plant mentioned previously. Besides getting feedback on his strengths and areas for improvement, Bill was told that he should (1) attend a course or seminar on using different types of motivational techniques with his employees, as well as when and how to use them; (2) attend a course on time management to improve his organizing and planning skills; and (3) attend a training course to enable him to give constructive individual feedback to his people and to deal with difficult employees. A written copy of Bill's feedback report was sent to his manager and the plant's training coordinator so they could each help Bill to follow through on his developmental plan.

An alternative way of performing step 2 is to simply ask employees to self-assess their own individual training needs. Many organizations use self-reports as an important source of training needs information (Ford and Noe, 1987). For example, one organization asks all their supervisors and managers to complete a Need-for-Training Questionnaire. Each respondent is asked to review a list of 100 skills (e.g., "confronting unsafe behaviors," "resolving conflicts among employees") that are normally used by supervisors and managers in their daily jobs. Respondents are asked the extent to which they feel that they personally need training in each of the skill areas.

The use of self-ratings with respect to person analysis has its strengths and limitations. On the one hand, this approach prevents the problem of forcing employees to attend training programs that they believe do not address their needs. In these cases, individuals become dissatisfied with the training and do not have the motivation to learn or to transfer skills back to their jobs (Hicks and Klimoski, 1984; Noe and Schmitt, 1986). On the other hand, what employees report they "need" in the way of training may be more an expression of preference or demand, and not an observable discrepancy in performance produced by a lack of skill (Latham, 1988; Mitchell and Hyde, 1979). Further, what they feel they need is also influenced by their attitudes toward training utility. Specifically, it has been shown that managers who have negative attitudes toward training will report less need for training than managers with favorable attitudes (Ford and Noe, 1987). Finally, more research is clearly needed on the interobserver reliability and construct validity of self-ratings with regard to person analysis (Latham, 1988). For instance, several studies have found that employee and supervisor needs assessments do not correlate highly with one another (McEnery and McEnery, 1987; Staley and Shockley-Zalabak, 1980).

THE FINAL PRODUCT: A TRAINING PLAN

The end result of this systematic process of identifying an organization's training needs is a training plan. This plan is constructed by the training department and is used to strategically plan what kinds of training will be conducted in the near future.

For each training program to be implemented in the future (e.g., five years) certain key information should be included in the training plan. Consider this information for the tire store manager program as an example.

Course Title:	Tire Store Manager Training I
Classification:	Management Development
Needs Analyses:	Organization (employment planning, store diagnoses) Task (job inventory) Person (self-report)
Course Objectives:	Effectively handle customer complaints Handle radio advertisements, newspaper ads, and direct mailings
Length:	15 days (3 days/week for 5 weeks)
Trainees:	75 new hires per year 15 trainees per class

Trainers:	HRD, Inc. + 3 in-house trainers
Place:	Corporate Training Center (Toronto, Ontario)
When:	Classes will start the first week of February, April, June, August, October
Training Methods:	Lecture, Behavioral Modeling, Computer-Assisted Instruction, OJT
Measures of Achievement	
During Training:	Weekly paper-and-pencil achievement tests Weekly proficiency testing
Evaluation Reaction:	End of training and 6 months later
Learning:	End of training + 6 and 12 months later
Behavior:	6 and 12 months later
Store Results:	6 and 12 months later
Utility Analysis:	18 months later
Transfer:	Immediate supervisor
Job Follow-up:	Relapse prevention Weekly meetings with trainer
Estimated Cost to Develop:	$80,500
Estimated Cost to Implement:	$37,500 per year

FINAL COMMENTS

We have presented several approaches that organizations can use for determining training and development needs systematically. Obviously, not all organizations will be able to afford the time and money to do every phase of organization, task, and person analyses as presented here. Yet we offer these approaches as an ideal to strive for. Even a reduced application of these approaches is better than what many organizations are doing today to determine training and development needs.

Let us look for a moment at a few current organizational practices. Some organizations break down each of their jobs into a list of detailed parts or steps arranged in a logical sequence. A copy of this list is given to those employees whose opinions are valued. The employees check off those items for which they would like to have more skill. Lists of all kinds are assembled. The one for salespeople might include prospecting for new business, conducting a fact-finding interview, sales closing, and sales follow-through. The list for retail store managers might include credit management, inventory control, building maintenance and security, sales management, customer relations, expense control, and community relations. One for industrial truck mechanics might include assembling distributors, changing generator brushes, replacing contacts and coils, reading blueprints, and so on.

Other organizations have a committee established for each special area of training such as orientation, sales, clerical, technical, supervisory, and executive. Each committee advises the training staff as to what particular training and development programs they think are needed. Sometimes the advisory committees also get involved in constructing the content of the courses and even evaluating course results.

Still other organizations purchase canned training and development programs from vendors who call on them periodically. The salesperson may be promoting programs on effective reading, improved human relations skills, or increased assertiveness. A vice president of manufacturing, marketing, or personnel may decide that this type of program is needed and purchase it on the spot or after giving it a short trial run.

Although these methods of determining training needs have their merit, it should be obvious that they are not as rigorous as the approaches presented in this chapter. Their biggest drawback, in our opinion, is that they are based solely on the assumption that someone can simply look at a list of training needs and accurately indicate what they themselves need or someone else needs in the way of personal development. Further, these methods tell us nothing about where within the organization a particular type of training is needed or who needs it. The end result is the indiscriminate use of a training and development program across company locations and people. It is no wonder that employees are often heard making statements such as, "I have no idea why I've been told to go to that training course," "I know just about everything they taught me in this program," and "Why doesn't the company just leave me alone and let me get on with my work!"

Chapter 4

Maximizing the Trainee's Learning

This chapter focuses on what the trainer needs to do to maximize learning on the part of trainees. Here, three main questions are of interest:

1. Is the individual trainable?
2. How should the training program be arranged to facilitate learning?
3. What can be done to ensure that what was learned during training will be retained and transferred to the job?

Since there are no well-developed and tested theories of learning to answer these questions, trainers must rely on two main sources for guidance. First, there are principles of learning that have been derived over the years by psychologists in their study of human and animal behavior. These principles are useful in maximizing learning if they are regarded as guiding principles and not as immutable laws. Second, there are theories of motivation that are very helpful in inculcating in the trainee the desire to learn and apply the skills and concepts being taught during training.

The present chapter is divided into three main sections: (1) trainability, (2) arrangement of the training environment, and (3) retention and transfer of learning. Let's first examine the issue of trainability.

TRAINABILITY

The largest component of training costs is the labor cost of the trainee. When large numbers of trainees are involved, course development and administrative costs become only a fraction of trainee labor costs (Ross,

1974). This clearly suggests that substantial cost savings in training are possible through a reduction in training time. Such a reduction is best accomplished by selecting and retaining in training only those individuals who are clearly trainable.

Trainability is a function of the individual's ability and motivation. Ability refers to the extent to which the individual possesses the aptitude or skills to perform the tasks at hand. For example, does the individual possess the muscular coordination to perform the motor tasks required of him? Does she have the visual acuity needed for learning watchmaking, radar monitoring, or surgery? Does he possess personality characteristics such as self-confidence, persuasiveness, sociability, decisiveness, and assertiveness needed to perform the job effectively? Does she have the mental ability to learn complex concepts and rules for computer programming, financial planning, or electronics?

Motivation is concerned with those variables which influence the trainee's effort, persistence, and choices. Such variables as the individual's need for achievement or competence are included here. Included here, too, are an individual's feeling of job involvement as well as their level of career interest (Noe, 1986). Trainees' involvement in their jobs and careers are important antecedents of learning during training and behavior change after training. Research shows that if trainees personally agree with the assessment of their skill weaknesses on which their training assignments were based, they are then more likely to be satisfied with the training program's content as compared to trainees who disagree with the assessment of their weaknesses (Noe and Schmitt, 1986). Also important is the individual's expectancy that participation in training will lead to desired outcomes such as feelings of accomplishment, greater responsibility, opportunity for advancement, higher pay, job security, status, stimulating colleagues, or a good geographical location (Latham and Crandall, 1991). Another crucial motivational variable worth noting here is anxiety. Anxiety has been shown to facilitate performance in relatively simple types of learning (e.g., assembly line operations), but to interfere with learning complex tasks. It is reasonable to expect that anxiety will interfere with most classroom-type learning, which generally consists of teaching concepts of a fairly complex nature. One possible way of reducing anxiety and thereby increasing motivation to learn the material is to give trainees a choice of whether to attend training. In making this choice, they should be provided detailed and accurate information about the program. Hicks and Klimoski (1984) found that managers who were given complete freedom to participate in a two-day workshop on performance appraisal–related issues had higher self-assessed mastery of the workshop content and achievement test performance than managers who were given little freedom of choice. They also found the same positive effects when managers were given detailed and accurate information about the workshop as opposed to a traditional (brief, overly positive) announcement.

The relationship between ability and motivation is expressed by the following formula:

Performance = Ability × Motivation

According to this formula, a trainee's performance will have a value of zero if either ability or motivation is absent, and it increases as each factor rises in value (Maier, 1973). The objective, then, is to train individuals who possess both the ability and motivation to perform what is taught in training.

Ability and motivation can be assessed by various measurement instruments in order to predict performance of prospective trainees. For example, the Navy School for Divers has used a motivational instrument to predict success in their ten-week training program in SCUBA and Deep Sea Air (DSA) procedures (Ryman and Biersner, 1975). Briefly, SCUBA training consists of instruction in diving medicine and physics, as well as the use of the neoprene wet suit and SCUBA breathing equipment. It concludes with ocean dives to a depth of 60 feet. DSA training involves learning to dive in a canvas suit and metal helmet. The training includes underwater communication and the use of underwater tools. DSA concludes with ocean dives to a depth of 180 feet. Research has shown that a trainee confidence measure is significantly related to eventual graduation from the program. Each of the following questions are answered on a six-point scale ranging from disagree strongly (score of 1) to agree strongly (score of 6):

- I have a better chance of passing this training than most others.
- I volunteered for this training program as soon as I could.
- The knowledge and experience that I gain in this training may advance my career.
- Even if I fail, this training will be a valuable experience.
- I will get more from this training than most people.
- If I have trouble during training, I will try harder.
- I am more physically fit for the training than most people.

Another example of the value of predicting trainability involves a welding program to train unemployed and underemployed individuals from east Tennessee for entry-level work in various vocational fields (Gordon and Cohen, 1973). The plate welding section of the training program consists of 14 separate welding tasks ordered in terms of increasing complexity. The last three welding positions are used as test positions to decide whether a trainee should receive certification. It was found that the time required by a trainee to complete the first four welding tasks was an excellent predictor of the time the trainee required to complete the entire training course. The importance of this study is that it demonstrates that a sampling of a trainee's ability level can be used as a valid predictor of subsequent success in training. The research also supports the widely accepted truism in psychology that an excellent predictor of future behavior is past behavior.

Another excellent approach for assessing trainability is known as the "miniature job training and evaluation approach" (Siegel, 1975, 1983). For example, suppose we wanted to use this approach for selecting applicants for a machinist training program for the navy. First, we would isolate a sample of tasks typically performed by naval machinists using task analytic procedures (Chapter 3). Second, we would build short training sessions (15 to 30 minutes) around each of these identified tasks. Once the training was completed, the evaluation phase would begin. The evaluation, of course, involves administering performance tests which measure the amount learned by each applicant during training. For example, a machinist task might be, "Ability to start up and shut down a motor and pump apparatus." The miniature training session might teach applicants how to follow a 33-step procedure, including safety precautions. After training, each applicant would be rated by knowledgeable judges on how well he or she started and shut down the apparatus. Reilly and Manese (1979) used this approach for selecting telephone company switching technicians. Applicants were given a minicourse that was designed to be a self-paced content valid sample of a lengthy and complex Electronic Switching Systems (ESS) training program. They found that a combination of time to complete the minicourse and performance on several objective tests was predictive of the time it took trainees to complete the self-paced ESS training.

Excellent research on trainability testing was conducted by Robertson and Downs (1989) in the United Kingdom. Trainability tests are used to improve the selection process of untrained applicants for training programs. Most trainability tests take the following form: (1) Using a standardized form of instruction and demonstration, the instructor teaches the applicant a task; (2) the applicant is asked to perform the task unaided; (3) the instructor records the applicant's performance by noting errors on a standardized error checklist (prepared and different for each trade) and by making a rating of the applicant's likely performance in training, usually on a 5-point scale (Robertson and Downs, 1979). For example, Downs (1968) developed trainability tests for welding and carpentry. The carpentry test involved making a half-lap T joint; the welding test involved making several straight runs along chalk lines on mild steel. Both tests took 30 to 45 minutes to administer and score. Robertson and Downs (1989) completed a meta-analysis of trainability tests in which they concluded that these tests produce a worthwhile level of validity. More specifically, they found that these tests are quite useful for predicting an untrained applicant's subsequent success in training and job performance. They also concluded that in order to attain a high level of trainability test validity, it is essential that the instructional procedures used during the tests simulate those involved subsequently during actual training and later learning on the job itself. For instance, to predict success in a sewing machine operator training program, we might decide to teach and test the following tasks to be encountered by operators: joining pieces of cloth, joining two pieces to make an open bag, and operating a lockstitch machine. Robertson and Downs also found that the greater the length of the training program, the smaller the size of the validity coefficient. In fact, attempts to predict success in training over a one-year period resulted in considerably smaller validities. Apparently, more complex jobs and longer training periods may expose trainees to a wider variety of instructional processes and call for a greater range of learning abilities from trainees, some of which may not have been captured in the initial learning period during the trainability test.

ARRANGEMENT OF THE TRAINING ENVIRONMENT

In the previous section we discussed the importance of measuring ability and motivation levels that exist in the individual before training occurs. These are the *internal* conditions necessary for learning to occur by an individual.

A second major category of learning conditions is *external* to the learner (Gagné, 1977). These are the environmental arrangements that the trainer can control so as to facilitate learning. Before examining these external conditions and how they can be arranged to enhance learning, it is important to agree on a definition of what is meant by learning.

Learning is defined as a relatively permanent change in behavior that occurs as a result of practice. *Behavior* includes the knowledge and skills acquired by people. When we say that an individual has learned something, we are not referring to temporary changes in behavior. Instead, we are referring to enduring behavioral changes.

In order to arrange the training program to facilitate learning, the following variables need to be taken into account:

1. Conditions of Practice
   a. Active practice
   b. Overlearning
   c. Massed versus distributed practice sessions
   d. Size of the unit to be learned
2. Feedback
3. Meaningfulness of the Material
4. Individual Differences
5. Behavior Modeling
6. Maintaining Motivation

Conditions of Practice

Active Practice Whether a trainee is learning a new skill or acquiring knowledge of a given subject, the individual should be given the opportunity to practice what is being taught. During the early stages of learning skills, the trainer should be available to guide the trainee's practice. This minimizes the risk of the individual developing inappropriate behaviors. The trainer might tell the novice cab driver to "return your cab to the home base location on 'weekends only' "or "turn your wheels in the direction in which you are skidding." It is not enough during skills learning for the trainees to merely verbalize what they are expected to do, nor to listen to the trainer or to other trainees repeat the directions again and again. Rather, the trainee must actively practice the skill. Only by actually repeating the essential movements can the trainee be provided with the internal or proprioceptive cues that regulate motor performance. As practice continues, internal cues leading to errors are progressively discarded, and internal cues associated with smooth and precise performance are retained.

Overlearning Closely related to the principle of active practice is that of overlearning: providing trainees with continued practice far beyond the point when the task has been performed correctly several times. It is relevant to those activities that must be practiced under simulated conditions (e.g., missile firing) because the real situation is either too expensive and/or too dangerous. It is even more crucial in those tasks which are designed so that individuals cannot rely on lifelong habit patterns, as, for example, in certain emergency procedures. It pertains less to those types of work (e.g., press operators, pipe fitting, carpentry) where individuals practice their skills on a daily basis (Fitts, 1965).

An actual example of overlearning can be found in the U.S. Air Force training school:

> Boldface Emergency Procedures are procedures that must be accomplished immediately and in the proper sequence after an indication of a specific system malfunction. Failure to initiate these procedures promptly or in sequence could result in loss of aircraft and/or pilot injury or death. Therefore, all procedures that are printed in bold type in the aircraft flight manual must be committed to memory. The pilot must also be familiar with all other emergency procedures discussed in the emergency procedures section of the flight manual. During Undergraduate Pilot Training (UPT), student pilots must write or orally recite the Boldface Emergency Procedures for the aircraft he or she is flying. Unsatisfactory performance on the daily quiz usually results in counseling, remedial instruction, and grounding from flying that day. Pilots in operational squadrons must indicate their knowledge of Boldface Emergency Procedures weekly and before training flights.*

Overlearning is important for several reasons. First, it increases the length of time that training material will be retained. By continually pairing a response with a particular stimulus, the bonds between the two will be strengthened, thereby making the response less likely to be

* Personal communication with Captain Frank Tetreault, United States Air Force.

forgotten (Schendel and Hagman, 1982). Second, it makes the learning more reflexive, that is, the trainee will have to concentrate less strongly on the task as it becomes "automatic" with practice. Third, trainees will be more likely to maintain the quality of their performance on their jobs during periods of emergency and added stress. For example, those professional athletes who have thoroughly mastered their sport are more likely to perform effectively despite such factors as unfavorable weather conditions and large crowds of spectators. Finally, overlearning helps trainees transfer what they have learned during training to their job settings.

Massed Versus Distributed Practice Sessions Another consideration in designing a training program is the problem of whether to divide the practice period into segments or plan one continuous session. For example, if you decided to give trainees eight hours of practice, which of the following schedules would be best to follow?

One eight-hour nonstop session

Four hours a day for two days

Two hours a day for four days

The answer depends on the nature of the task being trained. For years, psychologists have known that distributed practice sessions interspersed with reasonable periods of rest permit more efficient learning of skills than continuous practice (McGehee and Thayer, 1961). Therefore, in the case of training someone to operate a sewing machine or a printing press, it would be advisable to schedule practice sessions for two hours a day for four days.

Unfortunately, this principle of spreading the effort of the trainee over a period of time is often ignored in organizations. Management is frequently anxious to get the individual trained to standard as quickly as possible. The result is often inadequately trained employees.

Some organizations have used ingenious ways to obtain the advantages of distributed practice and, at the same time, make efficient use of the trainee's time. For example, a supermarket chain trains its checkout clerks on using computerized cash registers by having each of them work two hours on the new equipment and the remainder of the day on their former equipment. A large furniture retail chain trains its salespeople by alternating their time on the floor with performing other beneficial activities such as reading decorator catalogs, studying fabrics, telephoning customers, and rearranging store merchandise.

Why, we might ask, is distributed practice better for learning motor skills than massed practice? The answer seems to be that the rest periods between practice sessions allow for dissipation of the fatigue that builds up when we continually perform the same set of responses over and over (Hull, 1943).

The effectiveness of massed versus distributed practice becomes less clear-cut when it comes to learning factual information. Should the learning be massed, as in cramming for an exam, or distributed over time? The less meaningful the material to be learned and the greater its length or difficulty, the better distributed practice becomes relative to massed practice. Moreover, the less trainability the trainee possesses, the more that person will benefit from distributed practice.

Size of the Unit to Be Learned When designing any training program, the following questions naturally arise: What is the optimum size of the unit to be learned? Should you attempt to teach the entire task at each practice session, or is it more efficient in the long run to teach individual subtasks initially and as the trainee starts mastering each subtask begin the process of combining them?

Many different approaches can be used in scheduling a training program, but all seem to be derivations of three basic strategies. Suppose you have a task that can be divided into three distinct parts or subtasks: A, B, and C. The three basic strategies would proceed as shown in the diagram.

	Phase I	Phase II	Phase III	Phase IV
Whole Training	A + B + C	A + B + C	A + B + C	A + B + C
Pure-Part Training	A	B	C	A + B + C
Progressive-Part Training	A	A + B	A + B + C	A + B + C

As you can see, whole training consists of practicing all subtasks during all phases of training. In pure-part training, successive subtasks are practiced separately in successive phases of training. Progressive-art training involves practicing the first subtask in the first phase of training: the first and second subtasks in the second phase; the first, second, and third subtasks in the third phase, and so on.

Which strategy is superior? There are some writers who mean well, but incorrectly advocate a one best way of training. For example, Strauch (1984) advocates using a so-called holistic approach to employee training which always makes the object of attention the whole activity and never an isolated piece. More accurately, which strategy to use depends on two components of the task itself: *task complexity* and *task organization.* Task complexity refers to the difficulty of each of the subtasks comprising the total task. Task organization refers to the degree of interrelationship among the set of subtasks. For highly organized tasks, the whole method seems to be more efficient than the part methods. Both part methods, however, are superior to the whole method when task organization is low. These two statements are especially true as task complexity increases (Naylor and Briggs, 1963).

For example, when learning to operate a bulldozer (a task of high organization), a person must learn skills like starting the engine, steering, braking, backing up, and shifting. It makes little sense to learn each of these subtasks individually because all of them are so highly interrelated. In contrast, secretarial work often consists of a number of subtasks that are largely independent of one another (i.e., low task organization). Secretaries typically type letters, answer telephone calls, take dictation, photocopy reports, greet visitors, and so on. Each of these subtasks can be learned and practiced separately. Indeed, it would be impractical to teach all of these subtasks at every training session.

The examples just described offer situations which are relatively clear-cut. In many situations, however, a combination of whole and part training is used to optimize the benefits of both approaches. For example, suppose you wanted to train someone to be a pipe fitter. Certain training sessions would be devoted to specific topics such as valves, gaskets, traps, and strainers. Other sessions would concern themselves with larger chunks of the job such as cutting, bending, and threading pipe. Suppose for a moment that a politician is memorizing a speech to be given at a fund-raising dinner. Where the different parts of the material are logically related, the whole method should be employed. Where the material is very complex and long, it should be broken down into parts and learned progressively, one section at a time.

Feedback: Knowledge of Results

Practice Without Evaluative Feedback Retards Learning Feedback or knowledge of results is critical for both learning and motivation (Ammons, 1954; Arnett, 1961). Trainees should be informed when and how they have done something correctly. Feedback, whether in the form of verbal praise, test scores, productivity reports, or performance measurement, serves three functions in promoting learning and motivation: (1) It tells trainees whether their responses were correct, thereby allowing them to make the necessary adjustments in their subsequent behavior; (2) it makes the learning process more interesting for the trainees, thereby maximizing their willingness to learn; and (3) it leads to the setting of specific goals for maintaining or improving performance (Locke and Latham, 1990).

Imagine, for a moment, how difficult and frustrating it would be for people to learn a job such as assembling television sets or building radial tires if they received little or no feedback. Without the trainer's specific comments about what they are doing right and wrong, supplemented with reasons and explanations, it would not be long before trainees would discontinue learning.

To be effective, feedback should be provided as soon as possible after the trainee's behavior. It is not necessary that feedback be instantaneous, only that the relationship between behavior and feedback be clearly evident to the learner. For example, Wexley and Thornton (1972) showed that college students learn better when their instructors give them verbal feedback on the correctness of their test answers. The beneficial effect of this verbal feedback occurred even when a delay of 30 minutes ensued between the students' test taking and the feedback session.

The specificity or amount of feedback provided must be appropriate to the particular capabilities and stage of development of the learner. Too much feedback at one time, or too early in the learning process, can be confusing and lead to a decline in trainee performance. Likewise, too little information at critical stages can lead to similar consequences. It appears that, for each trainee and each stage of learning, there is an optimum level of feedback which should be given. It is important that trainers be cognizant of this inverted-U relationship when designing training programs (see Figure 4.1).

Praise can be a powerful source of positive feedback. For example, a trainer may look at certain indices of trainee performance (e.g., sales records, attendance, production figures) and compliment the positive aspects of the individual's performance as it relates to established goals or to the trainee's previous level of performance. Making praise the consequence of behavior will usually strengthen that behavior (Latham, 1989; Latham and Wexley, 1991).

Should trainers provide negative feedback? Positive feedback is per-

Figure 4.1 Hypothesized relationship between specificity of feedback and amount of learning

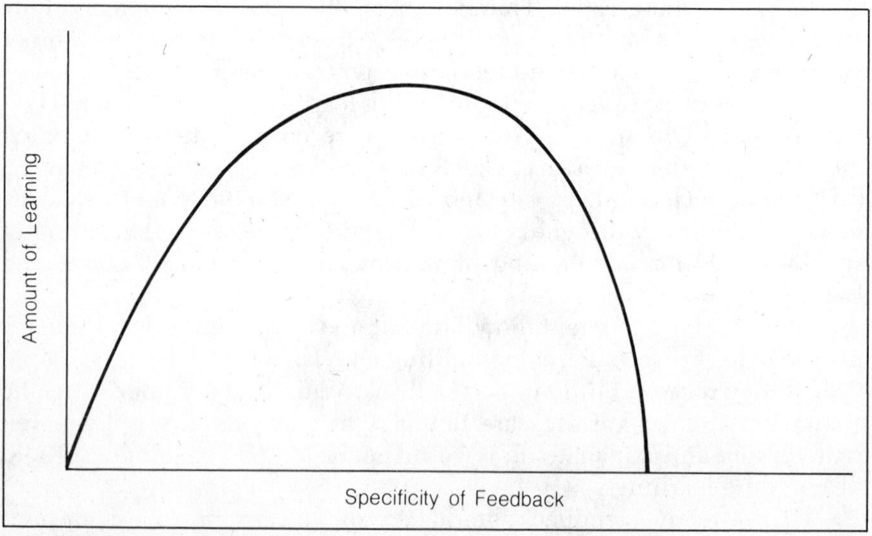

Adapted from Blum and Naylor, 1968.

ceived and recalled more accurately and accepted more readily than negative feedback. Negative feedback is often denied, especially by trainees with low self-esteem, due to their unwillingness to accept critical comments about themselves. However, most trainees will accept and respond to negative feedback from trainers whom they view as trustworthy, knowledgeable about the subject matter being taught, and powerful enough to influence the trainee's receipt of certain valued outcomes such as pay increases, promotions, and retention in training (Ilgen, Fisher, and Taylor, 1979). Similarly, other researchers have found that negative feedback is more effective when the supervisor who gives it has a relatively close and friendly relationship with the employee than when the relationship is distant and unfriendly (Arvey and Ivancevich, 1980). Perhaps counter to common sense is their finding that punishment is more effective when it is given on a continuous rather than on an intermittent schedule. Finally, the effect of punishment is enhanced if the employee is made aware of alternative acceptable behaviors. Thus trainers should provide both positive feedback (e.g., "Now you're igniting that acetylene torch correctly," "Your sales presentation this morning was perfect," "Your auditing report was submitted on time") and negative feedback (e.g., "You've got too much amperage on that torch," "You spoke down to the prospective customers during your sales presentation," "Your report was two days late"), so long as the negative feedback does not become punitive for the trainee. Of course, what will be experienced as punitive will depend on the particular interpersonal relationship (i.e., trust, respect, liking) between the trainer and trainee.

It is interesting to note that in the behavioristic tradition (Skinner, 1953), error feedback was conceptualized as being a form of punishment, and punishment was to be avoided. Erroneous performance was thought of as being disruptive to learning. Programmed instruction (Chapter 7), which strives to prevent trainees from making errors, grew out of this Skinnerian tradition. Frese and Altmann (1988), however, have argued that error training can have positive effects because one has to learn to deal efficiently with errors on both a strategic and an emotional level. They contend that training programs need to be designed so that trainees have an opportunity to make errors, receive immediate feedback on these, and be encouraged by the trainer to solve these problems by themselves, thereby enhancing their error management skills. Research on error training is still too new to make definitive statements about its advisability.

Another important issue for training specialists concerns the effects of *intrinsic feedback* on learning. Obviously, a trainee can derive knowledge of results from the trainer (extrinsic) as well as from the task itself (intrinsic). An example of feedback emanating from the task itself would include a tailor looking at a finished suit that he or she has made and realizing the workmanship is perfect. In certain situations, individuals may be able to judge their own performances and thereby generate their own intrinsic feedback. How much these individuals rely on this self-generated intrinsic feedback depends on their experience in the job being taught and their particular level of self-esteem (Ilgen et al., 1979).

An effective learning strategy should include both intrinsic and extrinsic feedback. For example, in a large midwestern telephone company, employees performing service-type jobs (i.e., building equipment mechanic, motor mechanic, building servicer, cleaner, stocker) received intrinsic and extrinsic feedback. Each Friday, the employees rated themselves in terms of the number of days absent, accidents, amount of money spent compared to the amount budgeted, and their subjective evaluation of their service quality (intrinsic feedback). Every Monday, the supervisors met with the people they supervised to establish goals for the coming week and to tell how many employees had met the previously determined weekly goals (extrinsic feedback). The results of this project showed that the combination of intrinsic and extrinsic feedback (in conjunction with goal setting) was successful in reducing actual dollar expenditures and number of accidents (Kim and Hamner, 1976).

Finally, feedback is effective only when it affects a person's goals. Further, feedback works best when it involves simultaneously both behavioral feedback (e.g., "Joe, as a salesperson, you need to smile when greeting our customers") and end-results (e.g., "Joe, your level of sales volume has fallen 10 percent during the past month") feedback (Kim, 1984).

Meaningfulness of the Material

Factual material is more easily learned and remembered better when it is meaningful to the trainees (McGehee and Thayer, 1961). Meaningfulness refers to material that is rich in associations for the trainees and is thus easily understood by them. Material can be structured to maximize its meaningfulness in the following ways:

1. At the outset of training, trainees should be provided with an overview of the material to be presented. Seeing the overall picture allows the trainees to understand how each unit of the program fits together as well as the objective of the program. An excellent illustration of this would be the instructor who provides a detailed course outline during the first day of a new semester or quarter.
2. The material should be presented using examples, terms, and concepts familiar to the trainees in order to clarify key learning points. For instance, a supervisory development program for head nurses in a medical center should employ examples concerning patient care. Visual aids can be used to augment abstract concepts. For example, one vocational training program teaches its educable mentally retarded students the concepts of city, county, state, and

country by having them play darts using a board similar to the one shown in Figure 4.2.

3. Meaningfulness is also facilitated when the material is sequenced in a logical order. For instance, it has been shown that trainees learn best when they are told the function of a piece of machinery (i.e., what is it used for and when will they need to use it) before they learn its operations or its structure.
4. Complex intellectual skills are invariably composed of simpler skills, and the attainment of these subordinated skills is necessary before the complex skills can be assimilated (Gagné, 1977). For instance, a mechanical trainee must first learn to discriminate successfully among various machine components before being able to understand such concepts as gears, sprockets, bushings, and couplings. Once these discriminations and concepts are ab-

Figure 4.2 An example of a visual aid for teaching the handicapped

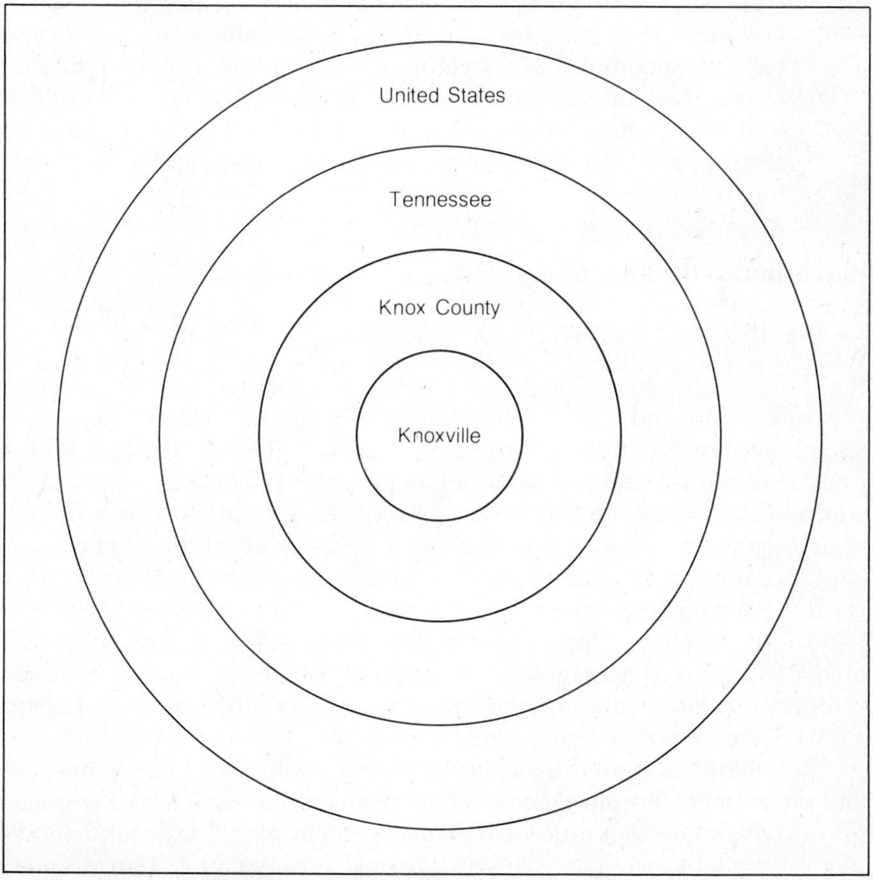

Figure 4.3 Prerequisites in the learning of intellectual skills

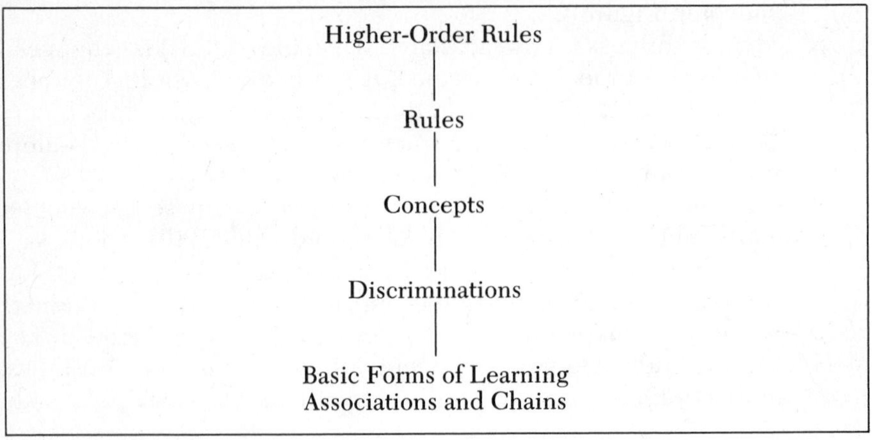

Adapted from Gagné, 1977.

sorbed, the trainee is ready to learn sample rules (e.g., how a reduction gear operates) and higher-order rules (e.g., how to put together a complex set of reduction gears to solve a specific mechanical application problem). Figure 4.3 suggests the most meaningful sequence for learning intellectual skills. Each level of learning requires as a prerequisite that one learn all levels underneath it.

Individual Differences

In the coming decade, there is likely to be an increase in interest in providing alternative modes of instruction for the needs and aptitudes of the individual trainee. This concern can be attributed to governmental pressure to hire and train members of minority groups, including women and older employees. It can also be attributed to the capacity of sophisticated computer-based instructional techniques (see chapters 6 and 7) to adapt to the unique characteristics of individual trainees. For example, regarding age, Tucker (1985) conducted a survey which focused on perceptions of workers age 40 and older in order to determine their training needs in the technological and management areas within the U.S. Geological Agency of the Department of the Interior. The younger age group, 40 to 49, preferred management training; the upper age group, 50 to 59, preferred training in technological areas; the age 60-and-above group showed little interest in any kind of training.

Bernick et al. (1984) used management hierarchy to determine the audience to which training courses should be directed. Through the use of a correlational technique called factor analysis, 28 training courses were reduced to six factors. First-line supervisors had as their highest need technical factors (e.g., record keeping, written communications), mid-level managers rated human resource courses as most important for meeting their needs (e.g., leadership skills, performance appraisal), and upper management rated conceptual courses (e.g., goal setting, planning skills) as most important for their development.

Gordon et al. (1986) found that trainees with greater seniority tended to require more time than standard to complete training than people with less seniority. Interjob similarity, not surprisingly, was a strong predictor of training time.

Berryman-Fink (1985) focused on male and female managers' views of the communication needs and training needs of women in management. Both male and female managers identified four communication skills for which women managers need training: assertiveness, confidence building, public speaking, and dealing with males. Male managers need training in listening, verbal skills, nonverbal communication, empathy, and sensitivity. However, in her survey of government workers, Tucker (1985) found no significant difference between women's and men's expressions of training needs. Nevertheless, her study demonstrated the need for human resource planning with regard to organizational analysis. Such planning, she showed, reveals the necessity for discouraging the early retirement of older workers from the U.S. Department of Interior because fewer people are entering the work force.

Streker-Seeborg et al. (1984) investigated whether training economically disadvantaged women for male-dominated occupations increases the probability of their achieving employment. The results showed that despite training, they were much less likely than their male counterparts to become employed in male-dominated occupations.

Because of projections of a lack of qualified personnel in male-dominated technical jobs, the West German Ministry of Science instigated a large-scale study of the apprenticeship of women in mechanical-technical occupations. Schuler (1986) found that the training could develop job-relevant aptitudes for women, but could not diminish the initial differences that existed between males and females prior to training.

The studies just cited are demographic in nature. In contrast, learning curves are used to depict an *individual's* rate of learning as a function of continued practice. Figure 4.4 illustrates the unique patterns of learning of four trainees. It can be seen from the slope of the curves that some trainees learn faster (e.g., trainee A learns fastest), some begin learning at higher initial levels of expertise (trainee B), others are capable of higher terminal levels of performance (trainee C), and still others improve very little despite their continued practice (trainee D). These variations in learning patterns are the result of individual differences in levels of motivation and ability among trainees. The effective trainer is flexible enough to modify his or her training strategies to accommodate these differences in learning patterns among trainees.

Figure 4.4 Four learning curves of four trainees

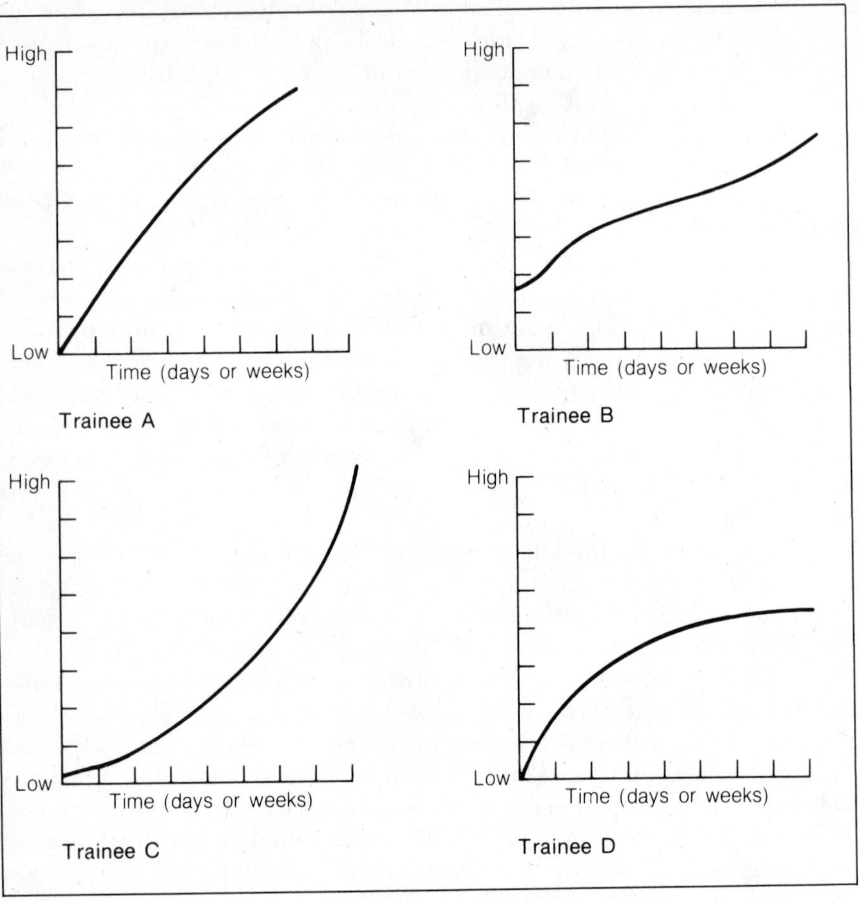

Most graphs of learning progress usually follow the S-shaped pattern depicted in Figure 4.5. Rapid improvement comes during the early practice trials, but then the curve levels off, or plateaus, and may remain level for quite a while. There are several reasons for the plateau: The trainee may have reached the level of his or her capability, the trainee's interest may have waned temporarily, the person may be in the process of integrating levels of different skills, or the individual may need a different method of instruction. Regardless of the cause, the trainer should recognize that this leveling process is normal for most trainees, and that it is essential to provide encouragement to the learner at this time. Unless this encouragement is present, the learning process may be stopped prematurely.

One of the more interesting developments in the past few years is called *Aptitude-Treatment Interaction* (ATI). ATI is concerned with

Figure 4.5 An S-shaped learning curve with a plateau

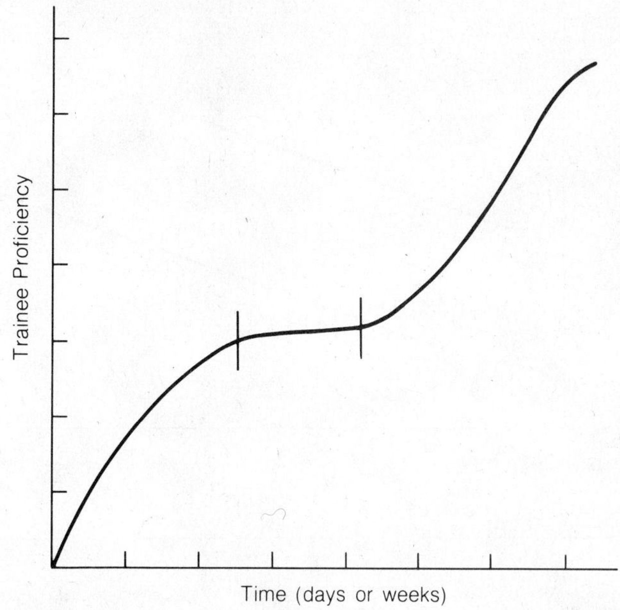

providing each trainee with the most appropriate model of instruction based on the trainee's aptitude level (Cronbach and Snow, 1977; Lohman and Snow, 1984; Snow and Yallow, 1982). An aptitude refers to any characteristic of the trainee that may affect his or her capability to learn. Figures 4.6 and 4.7 illustrate two types of ATI relationships. In both figures, performance has been plotted for each training group with payoff on one axis and aptitude on the other. Figure 4.6 depicts the case where the treatment lines do not cross. This indicates that one method (treatment A) is best for all trainees regardless of their aptitude level. A *disordinal aptitude-treatment interaction* (see Figure 4.7) occurs when the treatment lines cross, and can be interpreted as evidence for a meaningful aptitude-treatment interaction; that is, trainees should be assigned differentially to alternative training methods in order to maximize instruction payoff. Specifically, trainees with high aptitude levels (those to the right of the cutoff line) will learn best with treatment A; persons with lower aptitude levels (those to the left of the cutoff line) will learn best with treatment B. For example, entry-level auditors conduct financial analyses of an organization's plants, stores, and/or distribution centers. One company found that trainees with high aptitude as measured by an accounting test, a numerical reasoning test, and a bookkeeping test learned most

Figure 4.6 Illustration of no aptitude-treatment interaction

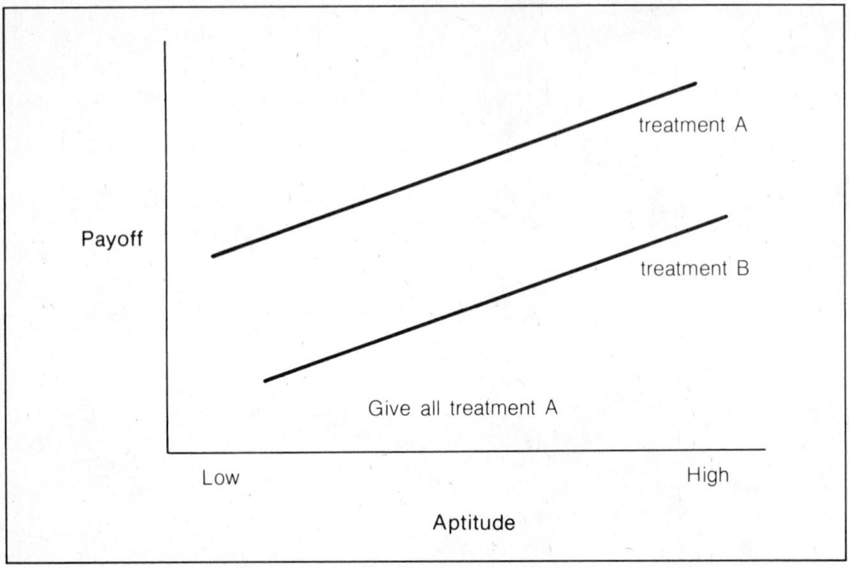

From Cronbach, L. J. "The Two Disciplines of Scientific Psychology." *American Psychologist,* 1957, *12,* 671–684. Copyright 1957 by the American Psychological Association. Reproduced by permission.

effectively by means of on-the-job coaching conducted by senior auditors. Those trainees with less aptitude learned best when their on-the-job coaching was supplemented with special lectures and programmed levels.

What else is known about the effect of individual differences on learning? First, there are a number of studies indicating that differences among trainees in abilities, motivation level, interests, and prior history will affect performance and attrition in training programs (Christal, 1974; Ghiselli, 1973; Mumford, Weeks, Harding, and Fleishman, 1988). By measuring applicants' individual differences by means of various aptitude and personality tests, we can select applicants for training programs who possess trainability. Second, individual differences in trainee abilities (e.g., memorization, deductive reasoning, multilimb coordination, static strength) have been found to relate to a number of different learning phenomena such as performance during massed versus distributed practice sessions, whole versus part training, as well as retention and transfer (Fleishman, 1965; Fleishman and Ellison, 1969; Fleishman and Parker, 1962). These individual differences have enormous implications for training design. For instance, a shorter training program may be possible if trainees are experienced and possess high levels of task-related abilities. On the other hand, longer training programs are advisa-

Figure 4.7 Illustration of a disordinal aptitude-treatment interaction

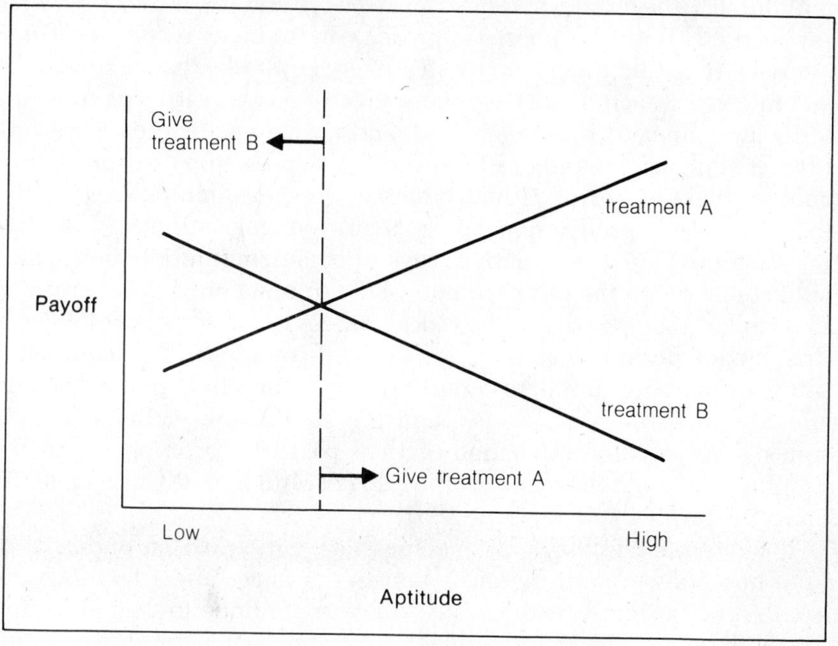

From Cronbach, L. J. "The Two Disciplines of Scientific Psychology." *American Psychologist,* 1957, *12,* 671–684. Copyright 1957 by the American Psychological Association. Reproduced by permission.

ble for relatively inexperienced trainees, since they need to focus on fact acquisition, knowledge-structure development, and certain basic abilities (Fleishman and Mumford, 1989). Third, we know that trainees differ in the kinds of "mental models" that they formulate, and that these mental models affect how well they learn what is being taught. Mental models are similar to schemata in that they are descriptions of a trainee's conceptualizations of physical devices or systems, and they are used by the trainee to explain and predict the system's behaviors (Fleishman and Mumford, 1989). Frese et al. (1988) were interested in comparing alternative training approaches for teaching the word-processing program Wordstar. They found that the training approach which encouraged trainee exploration and the active development of an integrated mental model led to better performance as compared to the approach that did not help trainees to actively develop a mental model. With the better approach, the trainees did not get any written material on the computer, since they were supposed to develop their own coherent mental model. Before beginning to work on the computer, they received a hard copy of the flawed text and were asked to develop hypotheses about the commands to be used to correct these mistakes. They were encouraged to try out all solutions that came to mind. After a while, the correct command was mentioned by the trainer, and the trainees were asked to write down what they learned. With the poorer approach, the trainees received written material which told them step by step every keystroke that needed to be used to correct each flaw. They were given no explanation as to *why* a particular command had to be used, and no mnemonic aids were provided. As long as the trainees followed the step-by-step directions, they could not make any errors. Finally, on the average, older trainees require longer to reach proficiency levels than younger trainees, and they may have developed alternative ways of organizing information which could conflict with the requirements of the training program (Sterns and Doverspike, 1989). Perhaps, the older trainees need slower presentation rates, longer periods for study, greater self-confidence by sequencing their learning from simple to complex tasks, greater help in their organizational and memory processes, and the greater use of training techniques that provide active (rather than passive) participation in the learning process (Belbin and Belbin, 1972; Mullen and Gorman, 1972; Schmidt, Murphy, and Sanders, 1981).

It is important in the years to come that we increase our understanding of how individual differences between trainees affect learning and also training design. It is imperative that we continue to deal more and more with trainees on an individual basis through such training methods as computer-based training (Chapter 6) and computer-assisted training Chapter 7). Training practitioners must be on the lookout for differences among trainees as well as disordinal interactions. This will require measuring various trainee characteristics prior to training and using more than one training method, if deemed necessary. For example, Snow's (1986) work has shown that less able learners do better when instruction is tightly structured and lessons are broken down into a sequence of simplified units. Because they are structured, computer-based training and computer-assisted instruction result in better learning in highly anxious trainees.

Behavior Modeling

Learning would be exceedingly laborious and hazardous if everything we learned resulted from our actually performing the behaviors involved. Fortunately, a large majority of our behavioral repertoire can be acquired through observing others. That is, we can learn by imitating those actions of others that we see as leading to desirable outcomes. If the consequences of their actions are positive, the models' actions come to function as a cue to what constitutes appropriate behavior (Bandura, 1986). For example, the head nurse in a hospital's cardiac care unit had a reputation for being a demanding, hard-working manager. She received a great deal of admiration and loyalty from her floor nurses and took a lot of pride in developing them for supervisory positions in other departments. When her nurses eventually got promoted to supervisory positions, they tended to exhibit the same hard-hitting managerial style as their mentor.

Despite the fact that each day people observe hundreds of behaviors by other people, they only choose to imitate some of them. What are some of the factors that cause people to model others?

Modeling occurs when the person who is imitated is seen as being competent, powerful, friendly, and of high status within an organization. This identification occurs because the model's behavior is seen as desirable and appropriate by the observer. Modeling is increased when the person to be imitated is seen as being rewarded for how he or she acts, and when the rewards received by the model (e.g., status, influence, friendship) are things that the observers would like for themselves. However, in a training context, observer identification with the model is maximized when the model is similar to the observer. If the observer sees little similarity between him- or herself and the model, it is very unlikely that the model's behaviors will be imitated (Goldstein and Sorcher, 1974).

Greater modeling also occurs when the modeling "display" (either a live physical demonstration or a pictorial representation) portrays the behaviors in a clear and detailed manner. Clarity is enhanced by presenting trainees with a list of specific key behaviors (commonly referred to as *learning points*) that the trainer wants the trainees to attend to when observing the model. Following are examples of four learning points which were used in training supervisors to improve their interpersonal skills while orienting new employees (Johnson and Sorcher, 1976; Latham and Saari, 1979).

1. Welcome the employee to her or his area in a warm and friendly manner.
2. Put the employee at ease by getting the person to talk about him- or herself.
3. Tell the employee you are confident that she or he is going to do well on the job.
4. Tell the employee you're going to do everything you can to help him or her succeed.

Mann and Decker (1984) found that when creating a behavior-modeling display, attaching learning points closely to the key behavior performed (especially for key behaviors that are not naturally distinctive) enhances both the acquisition and the recall of these behaviors. Trainees were unable to identify key behaviors from simply observing the model. As was found in Latham and Saari (1979), giving trainees the learning points in the absence of the model did not affect trainee behavior.

That the absence of learning points can have unintended and undesirable effects on trainees was discovered serendipitously by Manz and Sims (1986). The exposure to a reprimanding model inadvertently led to a decrease in both goal setting and positively reinforcing behaviors.

Hogan et al. (1986) showed that trainees should not be restricted to the use of learning points written by trainers, even if trainer-generated points are assessed by subject-matter experts to be of higher quality than trainee-generated learning points. Their study revealed that when trainees developed their own mnemonics in organizing the material presented via modeling and displays, better performance occurred on a generalization test one week later than was the case when trainees were restricted to learning trainer-generated rules.

Finally, the effectiveness of the modeling process can also be aided by sequencing the behaviors to be modeled from least to most difficult. For example, if we were training supervisors how to coach their employees, the first modeled performance should be with an employee who has a minor performance problem, the second modeled performance with an employee whose problem is more severe, and so on. It is also important to show the modeled behaviors with enough repetition to make overlearning possible as well as to have the behaviors portrayed by several models rather than just one (Decker and Nathan, 1985; Goldstein and Sorcher, 1974). There is research suggesting that the inclusion of a negative model (i.e., showing a trainee the incorrect way of doing something) together with a positive model appears to facilitate transfer of learning to other situations (Baldwin, 1987). See Chapter 8 for additional information on the application of behavior modeling for training and developing leaders.

Motivation

No one doubts the importance of trainee motivation for facilitating the effectiveness of any training program. If you think back over your own experiences, you will remember how much more readily you learned ideas and skills that you believed were relevant for you. Conversely, when you were disinterested in what was being taught, often little progress was made, despite your ability to learn what was being taught. What ways are there to motivate trainees? To answer the question, we need to examine three theories of motivation which are particularly relevant to trainee motivation: goal setting, reinforcement theory, and expectancy theory.

Goal setting as formulated by Locke and Latham (1984, 1990) states that an individual's conscious goals or intentions regulate one's behavior. A goal is anything an individual is consciously trying to achieve. Given that the goal is accepted, hard goals result in higher levels of performance than do easy goals, and specific hard goals result in higher performance levels than do no goals or even a generalized goal such as "do your best." Numerous laboratory experiments and field studies conducted in a wide variety of organizational settings have demonstrated the practical feasibility of goal-setting programs as means of increasing employee performance (Latham and Lee, 1986).

The research findings on goal setting have three important implications for motivating trainees. First, the learning objectives of the training program should be conveyed clearly to the participants at the outset of training and at various strategic points throughout the training process. Second, training goals should be difficult enough so that trainees are adequately challenged and thus are able to derive satisfaction from the achievement of objectives. However, the goals should not be perceived as being of such difficulty that trainees feel they are unable to reach them. Third, the distal goal of "finishing the program" should be supplemented with periodic subgoals during training such as trainer evaluations, work sample tests, and periodic quizzes. In this way, the trainee can derive a feeling of goal accomplishment and, consequently, look forward to tackling the next hurdle. For example, department heads from large urban hospitals participated in an effective management development program designed to improve their human relations skills in dealing with their employees (Wexley and Nemeroff, 1975). The department heads actively took part in a series of role-playing exercises. The trainer assigned specific and moderately difficult performance goals to the trainees prior to each exercise. The trainer also met with each trainee on his or her job to review performance and to assign specific performance goals for their subsequent meeting. The results were an improvement in the interpersonal skills of the department heads and a reduction in the absenteeism of their employees.

Trainers need to be aware that high levels of anxiety may debilitate one's feelings of self-efficacy. *Self-efficacy* refers to the person's conviction that he or she can master a given task (Bandura, 1986). Low self-efficacy can result in a decreased level of performance.

In a training program, goal setting can be a two-edged sword. For example, goal setting is important for increasing self-efficacy because without specific goals people have little basis for judging how they are doing, or for gauging their capabilities. Self-motivation is sustained by adopting specific attainable subgoals that lead to large future ones (Bandura, 1982; Locke and Latham, 1990). Subgoal attainment provides clear markers of progress which, in turn, verifies a person's sense of self-efficacy. Thus it is important that a trainer coach trainees to set specific goals that are difficult, but attainable, for the trainee.

Trainers must realize that the trainee's perception of their adequacy of performance is measured against their personal standards. Depressive reactions often arise from stringent standards of self-evaluation. Trainees who are prone to giving up are often people who impose high performance demands and then devalue their accomplishments because they fall short of their exacting goals. Thus it cannot be overemphasized that trainers must help trainees to set specific goals that are difficult, but attainable.

Finally, trainers must distinguish between process (i.e., behavioral) and outcomes goals. The latter can be detrimental to the learning process.

For example, learning theorists describe skill acquisition as a three-phase process: (1) declarative knowledge, (2) knowledge compilation, and (3) procedural knowledge (Adams, 1987; Anderson, 1982, 1983). Kanfer and Ackerman (1989) found that the effectiveness of goals set with regard to performance outcomes are moderated by the attentional demands of each specific learning stage. The higher the attentional demands of the learning stage, the less effective the goal-setting intervention.

In the first phase of learning, declarative knowledge, the trainee acquires a basic understanding of what is required to perform the task. During this phase, the training content often includes a lecture on the general principles of the task, observation of task performance, and strategies on how to perform the task. The declarative knowledge phase involves high attentional demands, which makes it difficult for trainees to concentrate on additional information-processing demands.

During the second phase of learning, knowledge compilation, trainees integrate the sequence of cognitive and motive processes required to perform the task. Performance improvement results from task practice and trying out various methods of simplifying or reducing each task component. As performance stabilizes during this phase, attentional demands are reduced and attention may be diverted to other areas without substantial decrements in performance.

In the third phase of skill acquisition, procedural knowledge occurs when the learner has essentially automatized the skill. After sufficient practice, performance becomes rapid and accurate; thus it can usually be performed with minimum attention devoted to the learned task.

Based on the attentional demands of each acquisition phase, Kanfer and Ackerman (1989) derived and tested hypotheses on the effectiveness of performance outcome goals. Since the self-regulation required in attaining a specific performance outcome requires attentional demands, the researchers hypothesized that attentional resources would be diverted from the learning task.

Kanfer and Ackerman tested this hypothesis using U.S. Air Force trainees who were learning an air traffic control computer simulation task. The task involved accepting and landing planes on appropriate runways based on specific rules (e.g., weather conditions, amount of fuel) over ten trials. In a series of experiments, subjects received either no goal ("do your best") or an outcome goal on early trials ("achieve score of 2200 during trials 5, 6, and 7"). The results showed that only outcome goals assigned late in the skill acquisition process exerted a significant positive effect on task performance.

With regard to goal commitment, there is evidence to suggest that trainees should make their goals known to peers. For example, Hayes et al. (1985) had students set goals on a number of questions they would answer correctly on reading passages of the Graduate Record Examination. Students in the "public condition" handed their goals to the experimenter, who then read them aloud. Students in the "private condition" deposited their goals into an anonymous box. Although the goal difficulty levels of the public and private conditions were not significantly different, the public goal group did perform better than the private goal group.

In a second study by the same researchers, students read a series of modules on improving their study skills. They set goals on both the number of modules that they would read, and on their posttest performance. Students in the public condition read their goals aloud to the group; those in the private condition placed their goals anonymously in the box. Similar to the results of the first study, students in the public condition significantly outperformed students in the private condition. Again, this result occurred in spite of the fact that the two groups did not differ greatly in the difficulty level of the goals they set.

In another study investigating the effects of public commitment, Hollenbeck et al. (1989) had subjects set goals for the grade point average (GPA) they would obtain the following term. Subjects were randomly assigned to either a public goal or a private goal condition. In the public goal condition, students' GPA goals were distributed to other individuals within that condition, and a copy of their respective goals was sent to a self-determined significant other person. The results of this study revealed that subjects in the public goal condition had higher goal commitment than those in the private goal condition. Further, there was a significant effect for commitment on performance that was independent of goal level.

Reinforcement theory, otherwise known as behavior modification or operant conditioning, is another approach for stimulating a trainee's desire to learn. One of its major principles is that "the frequency of behavior is influenced by its consequences." If the consequence is positive for the individual, the likelihood that the behavior will be repeated is increased. Rapid behavior change results when the consequence follows immediately or shortly after a behavior being taught in training is demonstrated by the trainee.

The consequences of behavior can be categorized into two major types: positive reinforcers (rewards) and punishers. The use of positive reinforcement is generally more effective for modifying behavior than punishment (Skinner, 1953, 1969). Punishment often has unfortunate side effects such as anxiety, hostility, and withdrawal. More important than the magnitude of a reinforcer is the schedule with which reinforcers occur. A continuous schedule involves administering a reinforcer after every correct response; a partial or intermittent schedule entails administering reinforcers only after a certain number of correct responses have been emitted or to the first correct response after a specified period of time has elapsed.

In applying reinforcement theory, it is crucial that the trainer define precisely the target behaviors that the trainee is expected to learn. Answers such as "improving attitudes," "providing job knowledge," and "increasing performance" are much too general. The key question for the trainer to ask is, "What should the trainee be able to do at the end of training that will enable that person to become an effective employee?" This is why task analysis, particularly the critical incident technique discussed in Chapter 3, is so important. Examples of appropriate course objectives would include: "Punch in at 7:30 A.M. every workday"; "Produce an error-free typed letter"; and "Be familiar with terms commonly used by operating room technicians." Unless the desired behaviors are specified in advance, it is difficult for the trainer to know what to reward during the training program.

Just as the target behaviors (Latham, 1989) and ideas must be identified, so must the positive reinforcers to be used. It is important for the trainer to make certain that the most powerful positive consequences are used for each trainee. Again, individual differences must be taken into account because the same reinforcers are not effective with all trainees (Latham, 1990; Wexley and Yukl, 1984).

Once the effective reinforcers for an individual have been identified, it is important that they are administered as soon as possible after the desired behavior. Delay of reinforcement can strengthen irrelevant behavior in lieu of the appropriate behavior. For example, a trainee learning to make an electrical assembly will perform considerably better if the trainer rewards correct behaviors immediately after they occur rather than informing the individual about them weeks after. If the trainer waits too long, there is an increased possibility that the trainee will develop bad habits.

It is best to provide continuous reinforcement when the trainee begins the learning of new behaviors. As the behaviors become better established, the schedule of reinforcement should be stretched. In other words, a partial schedule should be used, since it not only makes the new behaviors more stable or resistant to extinction, but it can also lead to an increase in the rate of desired behavior (Latham and Dossett, 1978; Yukl, Wexley, and Seymore, 1972). An example of a partial schedule would be the trainer who occasionally drops by a trainee's work station without prior notice to formally recognize appropriate behavior.

Rather than frustrating trainees by forcing them to perform behaviors that they are presently incapable and/or unwilling to exhibit, the trainer can use a process called *shaping:* the procedure of reinforcing any behavior that approximates the terminal behavior desired by the trainer while refraining from rewarding all other behaviors. As time proceeds, closer and closer approximations to the terminal behavior are required of the trainee before any reinforcement is given. For example, suppose a particular trainee gets to work 15 minutes late each day, and the trainer wants to teach him to be punctual. At first the trainer praises any attempt by the individual to show up more punctually, even if this may mean rewarding him for being only 14 minutes late. After a while, the trainer demands more and more by praising only closer approximations to the desired response of being on time. Finally, the trainee is praised only when he or she is truly punctual.

Expectancy theory also has important implications for motivating trainees. Although a number of versions of expectancy (also called *instrumentality*) theory have been proposed (see Ilgen and Klein, 1989), they all share certain common features. Each version proposes that an individual will be motivated to choose a behavior alternative that is most likely to have favorable consequences. When deciding whether to expend effort on a given activity, the individual asks, "What am I going to get out of that?" A decision to put forth effort is made if it is perceived that there is a good chance it will result in obtaining something of value. The key concepts in the theory are (1) outcome, (2) valence, (3) E (effort) → P (performance) expectancy, and (4) P (performance) → O (outcome) expectancy. Outcomes in a work context include such things as salary increase, promotion, dismissal, illness, injury, peer acceptance, recognition, and achievement. Valence refers to the desirability or attractiveness of an outcome to the individual. For instance, one worker may value pay more than recognition; another may feel just the opposite. The "E → P expectancy" concerns itself with the employee's perceived probability that a given amount of effort will result in improved performance (i.e., quantity and/or quality of work). The perceived probability that improved performance will lead in turn to the attainment of valued outcomes (e.g., bonus, pay increase, promotion) is called the "P → O expectancy." The theory assumes that, before deciding how much effort to exert, employees ask themselves whether or not (1) the action has a high probability of leading to better performance (E → P); (2) improved performance will yield certain need-related outcomes (P → O); and (3) those need-related outcomes or organizational rewards are of value (valence). The two expectancies are affected by different conditions. The E → P expectancy depends in part on relatively stable characteristics of the worker such as intelligence, motor abilities, and personality traits. In addition, the individual's perception of what makes for a successful employee will influence whether effort can be transformed into effective performance. The P → O expectancy depends on a person's perceptions of the reward contingencies presently found in the organization.

Expectancy theory has several important implications for motivating trainees. First, for any program to be successful, the trainee must believe that "there's something in it for me." The individual must perceive that his or her participation in training will lead to more desirable rewards than not being in training. Unless trainees can expect the program to lead to valued outcomes (e.g., higher wages, opportunities for advancement, skill acquisition, less fatiguing and safer work), it will be viewed as merely a waste of time. Trainees will either expend minimal effort or simply drop out. This is precisely the problem that has been encountered in training underprivileged individuals. These individuals often do not expect these behavior-reward contingencies and, consequently, see their training as just another futile exercise leading them nowhere.

Second, trainers should not assume that their trainees have accurate perceptions of reward contingencies. Trainers should explain the contingencies in a manner that will ensure accurate $P \rightarrow O$ expectancies. Trainees must be told exactly what outstanding performance during training will mean to their careers.

Third, the organization should ensure that each trainee has a high $E \rightarrow P$ expectancy by providing effective instructors, eliminating obstacles to effective performance, providing accurate role perceptions, and selecting trainees with requisite ability and motivation. Finally, the valence attached by an individual to potential need-related outcomes should be investigated by the organization, since this will differ among trainees and even within the same trainee over time. Only high valence outcomes should be used as incentives for superior trainee performance.

The practical implications of goal theory, reinforcement theory, and expectancy theory are compatible with one another. These theories can all be applied for motivating learning by making certain that trainees see the value *for them* of participating in the training, understanding the goals or target behaviors of the program, and clearly perceiving the link between their actions during training and their receipt of valued rewards.

Most training programs are based on the assumption that what is taught in training will be used by trainees when they complete the training program. For example, astronauts are taught complex procedures using simulated space capsules on the assumption that these procedures will carry over to their actual flights into space. Medical students are taught surgical procedures on cadavers in the hope that this instruction will transfer someday to their live patients. Supervisors are shown films about handling employee complaints and grievances with the expectation that this new knowledge will be applied by them to their jobs. In the section that follows, we attempt to answer the question. "What can be done to ensure that what is learned in training will be retained and transferred to the job?"

RETENTION AND TRANSFER OF LEARNING

Transfer refers to the extent to which what was learned during training is used on the job. Three transfer possibilities exist:

Positive transfer: Learning in the training situation results in better performance on the job.

Negative transfer: Learning in the training situation results in poorer performance on the job.

Zero transfer: Learning in the training situation has no effect on job performance.

Training that results in negative or zero transfer is either detrimental or of no value to an organization from a cost/benefit viewpoint. Nevertheless, instances of negative and zero transfer occur frequently in organizations. For example, one organization followed the practice of fostering competition among its trainees in the hope of increasing their motivation to learn. Trainers provided special monetary awards for those trainees who showed the highest rates of production at the end of each two-week period. The organization found that the quantity of production of their fiberglass auto bumpers did, in fact, increase during the two-month training period. Unfortunately, the organization also found that, after the training was completed, the individuals involved had considerably more scrappage and waste than comparable employees who had not been exposed to this training strategy. Management soon realized that they were teaching their fiberglass production employees the wrong thing, that is, to maximize quantity of production at the expense of quality.

In a large-sized insurance company, newly appointed department managers were exposed to a week-long lecture series designed to help them plan and organize by maximum output, manage their own time more effectively, set realistic departmental objectives, and develop their employees to their fullest potential. A rigorous evaluative study of the program revealed that the training had no effect whatsoever on the managers' behaviors back in their home departments.

The critical need to increase positive transfer and retention becomes apparent in light of the scope of industrial training in North America and the estimated relapse rate of trainees (Newstrom, 1984). Published estimates indicate that more than $100 billion is spent each year on training and development programs (Kelley, 1982). It is also estimated that merely 10 percent of these training dollars results in actual and lasting behavioral change back on the trainees' jobs (Georgenson, 1982; Wexley and Baldwin, 1986).

How can we optimize the possibility of getting positive transfer? In discussing various strategies for maximizing retention and transfer, we separate our recommendations into three time periods—before, during, and after training (Hagman and Rose, 1983; Leifer and Newstrom, 1980).

Before

• **Conduct a needs analysis that includes multiple constituencies.** A training needs analysis procedure that includes representatives from the training department, the customer (i.e., the people who initially requested some sort of training), as well as the potential participants and their managers, is appropriate if the training is really going to be taken and applied seriously (Trost, 1985).

• **Seek out supervisory support for training.** Supervisory support for training is considered to be a key work variable affecting the transfer process (Baldwin and Ford, 1988). Clearly, when employees perceive that the training is important to their supervisor they will be more motivated to attend, learn, as well as retain and transfer what was learned to their jobs (Huczynski and Lewis, 1980). In light of this, an advance letter to the trainee's supervisor stressing the expected benefits of the training for his or her unit and asking for the manager's help in supporting the behavior changes is a good idea (Leifer and Newstrom, 1980). Better yet, this could be accomplished face to face at a briefing session conducted by the training department for the supervisors.

• **Inform the trainees regarding the nature of the training.** Trainees should be informed ahead of time regarding such things as the training program's purpose, specific behavioral objectives, methods, length, location, trainers, successful graduates, and examples of potential skill applications back on their jobs. According to expectancy theory, it is important that trainees believe that they are capable of performing well in training and that completion of the training will lead to valued rewards (Jackson, 1985).

• **Assign tasks prior to the training sessions.** To stimulate interest, trainers will sometimes assign advanced readings, provide a realistic case study that is to be analyzed, or else ask trainees to fill out various self-analysis materials in advance (Leifer and Newstrom, 1980).

During

• **Maximize the similarity between the training situation and the job situation.** Positive transfer will be maximized to the degree that there are identical stimulus and response elements in the learning and job situations (Wexley and McCellin, 1987). Suppose, for example, that an individual is to be trained as a typist. The job involves typing auto and homeowner insurance policies in a noisy, fast-paced work environment using an electric typewriter. In this case, the training should involve typing alphanumeric symbols accurately and quickly in a noisy setting using a typewriter identical to that found on the job.

• **Provide as much experience as possible with the task being taught.** Positive transfer increases, and negative transfer decreases, with more and more practice on the original task. For example, operator packers in a soap plant spent most of their shift time packing four-bar bundles of soap into shipping cartons. The more practice and feedback that these employees were given during their initial training, the better they were able to adjust to occasional defects—caused by the wrapping machines, fluctuations in the speed of the bundling machines, changes in the size of the cartons, and variations in the sizes of the soap bars.

• **Have the trainees practice their newly learned skills in actual situations that they will encounter back on their jobs.** To help transfer newly learned skills to the trainees' own work environment, each trainee should choose an actual work situation from his or her own unique job environment. It is advisable to videotape the trainee practicing the skill during a role play with one or more other trainees. Immediately after taping, the trainee should critique his or her performance with the help of the trainer and other trainees (Green, Knippen, and Vincelette, 1985).

• **Provide for a variety of examples when teaching concepts or skills.** Provide several examples of instances that do and do not represent the concept being taught. For instance, investment counselors are taught about different tax shelters for their clients. During training, they are given examples of shelters and nonshelters depending on a customer's particular income tax bracket. In skill training, the individual should be given adequate opportunity to practice the skill under a wide range of conditions. A powerhouse trainee, for example, might be taught to fire a boiler under varying temperature and pressure conditions.

• **Label or identify important features of a task.** Labeling helps the trainee to distinguish important features of the task being taught. In training someone to operate a piece of machinery, for example, give a label to each step involved in its operation. In addition, place a label on the various parts of the machine. For instance, in one organization, building maintenance mechanics were shown several types of boilers, each painted various colors to signify their parts (i.e., firebox, compressor, gas cock, water pump). This teaching aid enabled the trainees to detect unique as well as common features across the various types of boilers.

• **Make sure that general principles are understood before expecting much transfer.** Transfer is facilitated when the trainee truly understands the general rules and principles that are needed in solving new problems. For example, the newly trained polymer chemist can only apply her knowledge to tire development if she understands the basic principles and has not merely memorized facts.

• **Provide trainees with the knowledge, skills, and feelings of self-efficacy to self-regulate their own behaviors back on their jobs.** Research has shown that, without the benefit of training, employees do little in the way of self-regulating their own job performance (Brief and Hollenbeck, 1985). Self-regulating entails goal setting, self-monitoring, as well as self-reward and self-punishment depending on the discrepancy between one's behavior and one's goal (Latham, 1988). Recent research has shown that employees can be successfully trained to set goals, formulate written behavioral contracts, self-monitor their own behavior, and self-administer rewards and punishments. For instance, Latham and Frayne (1989) found that unionized state government employees trained in self-management skills increased the work attendance and their feelings of self-efficacy significantly more than employees in a control group. Most importantly, this increase in job attendance continued over 12 months.

• **Design the training content so that the trainees can see its applicability.** It has been shown that individuals who feel that the training course they attended helped them learn skills and ideas directly related to their job situations are more likely to transfer their learning on return to their companies. Positive transfer is also facilitated when trainees feel that the trainers understand their unique job problems. Conversely, training programs felt to be too difficult and poorly organized have been found to generate less positive transfer.

• **Use adjunct questions to guide the trainee's attention.** Research in factual learning has found that questions inserted in instructional materials can influence trainees' retention (Wittrock and Lumsdaine, 1977). Questions in a text that precede the material containing the answers often facilitate the trainee's learning and retention of the information which the questions asked about, but reduce the learning and retention of other information presented. These results suggest that, if adjunct prequestions are to be used, they should be broad enough in scope to cover the entire content domain being taught (see, for example, the three broad questions posed at the beginning of this chapter).

After

• After completing a training program, trainees should be assigned specific behavioral goals. In addition, the trainees and/or their supervisors should complete behavioral progress reports to monitor the extent of the goal achievement back on the job. Wexley and Baldwin (1986b) investigated the effectiveness of three posttraining strategies for facilitating transfer of transfer: (1) assigned goal setting, (2) participative goal setting, and (3) a behavioral self-management approach. Their results showed that both the assigned and participative goal-setting conditions were superior to behavioral self-management and control conditions in inducing maintenance of behavioral change over a two-month period. In another study, Wexley and Nemeroff (1975) incorporated assigned goal setting and behavioral checklists as an element of their management development program for hospital supervisors. Trainees completed a two-day workshop intended to improve their leadership and interpersonal skills. After finishing training, but before returning to their jobs, trainees received a set of behavioral checklists and instructions in monitoring and recording their own on-the-job use of their new skills. The trainees expected to fill out the behavioral checklists three times per week in order to record their progress in achieving the program's behavioral goals. The specific items on the checklists were derived directly from the learning points of the training program. Their results indicated

can help develop appraisal instruments that reflect the organization's values and the behaviors that must be engaged in to implement the corporate strategy for achieving the business's objectives. It is a sad commentary that many organizations often spend too much time developing vision statements and strategy, but spend too little time on the systems that need to be put into place to ensure that people can and will implement the mission.

It was Chandler (1962) who originally pointed out that structure usually follows strategy or, more precisely, that a strategy of diversity fosters a decentralized structure. A decentralized structure characterizes many organizations of the 1990s. The result could be fragmented training programs and an inflation of training budgets to meet the needs of relatively autonomous businesses within the organization. Training departments can bring unity to such situations by retaining a focus on the overall cultural values and vision of the organization. This can be done by getting the key managers from each business to reach consensus on the communalities, ensuring that the appraisal and reward systems reinforce the organizational demonstration of this knowledge and skill, and removing barriers in the environment to this demonstration. In Chapter 5, we discuss the criteria and measurement designs for determining training success.

Chapter 5

Evaluating Training Programs

Once the organizational analysis has been completed and steps have been taken to maximize trainees' learning, the training specialist's attention should shift to the way or ways the actual effectiveness of the training will be discerned. Typically, the training and development is reviewed with one or two vice presidents at the corporate office, various managers in the field, and perhaps a group of prospective trainees. If the program looks good, the organization uses it. In fact, the program may be used again and again until it becomes all but institutionalized. It continues to be used until someone in a position of authority decides that the program has outlived its usefulness. All of this is done on the basis of opinion and judgment. In the end, no one really knows whether the training attained the objective(s) for which it was designed. The result can be an ineffective training program that is perpetuated or an effective program that is terminated or modified inappropriately.

The objective of this chapter is to answer the question, "How can training programs be evaluated?" First, we discuss the various criteria or measures that can be used in evaluating training programs. Then, we review the various ways of designing the evaluation procedures. Finally, we describe the measurement process itself.

MEASURES OF TRAINING EFFECTIVENESS

The effectiveness of a training program can be evaluated in terms of reaction, learning, behavioral, and/or results criteria (Kirkpatrick, 1987).

Reactions

Reaction criteria measure how well the participants liked the program, including its content, the trainer, the methods used, and the surroundings in which the training took place. The specific trainee reactions the organization is interested in examining should be decided on at the time the training program is being developed. Unless reaction objectives are established, irrelevant data are likely to be gathered from the trainees (Hamblin, 1974). One might, for instance, gather information about how much trainees enjoyed the training, when enjoyment per se was not a primary objective of the program.

Once specific reaction objectives are formulated, a comment sheet similar to the one presented in Figure 5.1 can be designed. It should elicit reactions to training objectives, permit anonymous answers, and allow the trainees to write additional comments not covered by the questions. In addition, two or three items that have no relationship to the training program might be included on the reaction questionnaire to determine whether the trainees are responding thoughtfully or blindly (e.g., everything was great or the converse). For example, suppose a training program was designed to teach finance and accounting to nonfinancial managers. We would not expect the responses to items dealing with basic accounting, budgeting, and inventory valuation (assuming that the training program was a good one) to be the same as responses to irrelevant items dealing with data processing techniques or the cost effectiveness of various computer storage systems. If there are no significant differences between the responses to the two sets of items (e.g., relevant vs. irrelevant ones), we know that the reaction measures are somehow contaminated.

The form shown in Figure 5.1 has been used by the training staff of an electric company for gathering trainee reactions to a supervisory training program. As you can see, the training staff was interested in reactions to the utility of the training, the relative value of different components of the program, and the effectiveness of the head lecturer and the case leaders. A few items irrelevant to the program were included within questions 6 and 9.

A somewhat different approach for collecting trainee reactions is used by the Life Office Management Association (LOMA), a nonprofit organization supported by insurance companies. By using the type of form shown in Figure 5.2, LOMA gives its trainees an opportunity to select at the beginning of the program the course objectives that specially apply to them, a means of expressing the relative importance of each objective selected, and a way of expressing how well each objective has been fulfilled (Fast, 1974).

Favorable reactions to a training program do not guarantee that learning has taken place or that the behavior of the trainees has changed

(text continues on page 113)

Figure 5.1 An example of a trainee reaction questionnaire

Evaluation Questionnaire

(Please return this form unsigned to the Training and Development Group)

1. Considering everything, how would you rate this program? (Check one)
Unsatisfactory ____ Satisfactory ____ Good ____ Outstanding ____

Please explain briefly the reasons for the rating you have given:

2. Were your expectations exceeded ____ matched ____ fallen below ____ ? (Check one)

3. Are you going to recommend this training program to other members of your department? Yes ____ No ____. If you checked "yes," please describe the job titles held by the people to whom you would recommend this program.

____

____

4. Please rate the relative value (1 = very valuable; 2 = worthwhile; 3 = negligible) of the following components of the training program to you:

Videocassettes	____	Role-playing exercises	____
Workbooks	____	Small group discussions	____
Small group discussions	____	Lectures	____
Cases	____	Readings: Articles	____

5. Please rate the main lecturer's presentation (1 = not effective; 2 = somewhat effective; 3 = effective) in terms of:

Ability to communicate	____
Emphasis on key points	____
Visual aids	____
Handout materials	____

6. Please rate the following cases, readings, and videocassettes by placing a check mark in the appropriate column:

	Excellent	Good	Fair	Poor
Overcoming Resistance to Change				
Reviewing Performance Goals				
Setting Performance Goals				
Handling Employee Complaints				
Improving Employee Performance				
Slade Co.				
Superior Slate Quarry				
McGregor's Theory X and Y				
Henry Manufacturing				
First Federal Savings				
Claremont Industries				

7. Was the ratio of lectures to cases (check one): High ____ OK ____ Low ____ ?

8. Were the videocassettes pertinent to your work? (check one)

   To most of my work? ____
   To some of my work? ____
   To none of my work? ____

9. To help the training director and the staff provide further improvements in future programs, please give us your frank opinion of each case discussion leader's contribution to your learning. (Place your check marks in the appropriate boxes.)

	Excellent	Above Average	Average	Below Average	Poor
DAVIS					
GLEASON					
LAIRD					
MARTIN					
PONTELLO					
SHALL					
SOMMERS					
WILSON					
ZIMMER					

10. How would you evaluate *your* participation in the program? (check)

Overall workload:	Too heavy	_____	Just right	_____	Too light	_____
Case preparation:	Too much	_____	Just right	_____	Too little	_____
Homework assignments:	Too heavy	_____	Just right	_____	Too little	_____

11. What suggestions do you have for improving the program?

____

____

____

12. Please add any additional comments, criticisms, or suggestions that you think might be helpful for the training group to know before scheduling future programs.

____

____

____

Figure 5.2 A reaction form used by the Life Office Management Association (LOMA)

Systems Design Workshop

Your Name ________ OBJECTIVES Check those that are important to you. (Ignore those that are not.)	✔	DEGREE OF IMPORTANCE × *Weight each checked objective for its importance to you, allocating exactly 100 points *among* all of those checked. A total of 100 points *must* be assigned.	DEGREE OF FULFILLMENT = **Rate *each* objective you checked (from 0–10) to indicate how well it was fulfilled.	INDEX OF OBJECTIVE FULFILLMENT
Be able to				
1. Identify and describe the various elements in the systems development process and understand their significance.				
2. Understand the use and value of systems feasibility studies.				
3. Identify essential considerations (critical factors) in a systems design problem.				
4. Design a management report.				
5. Design an input form.				
6. Develop an overall systems flow.				
7. Understand the objectives and techniques of designing input/output controls.				
8. Select among and be able to use basic data base structures.				

9. Prepare an oral presentation of design recommendations for management.				
10. Exchange ideas with other participants.				
		100	TOTAL =	

*If you checked only one objective, assign all 100 points to it; if you checked two objectives, spread the 100 points between them, etc.

**0 is unsatisfactory; 1–2 poor; 3–4 below average; 5 average; 6 above average; 7 good; 8 very good; 9–10 excellent.

From Fast, D. "A New Approach to Quantifying Training Program Effectiveness," *Training and Development Journal* 28:9 (1974), 8–14. Reproduced by special permission from the September 1974 *Training and Development Journal.*

as a result of the program. Nevertheless, reaction measures are important to collect for several reasons.

First, positive reactions help ensure organizational support for a program. Many programs have been cancelled prematurely by top management because a few participants told them, "This program was a waste of time."

Second, these measures can be used by the training staff to assess the success of their efforts, and to provide them with information that may help them plan future programs. In addition, a comment sheet should be obtained on each trainer as well as on each subject taught. In this way, program weaknesses as perceived by trainees can be pinpointed. Figure 5.3 shows a form that has been used for obtaining trainee reactions to various instructors.

Third, favorable reactions can enhance trainee motivation to learn. That is, trainees are likely to be motivated to learn material when they believe the program is useful to them and they perceive the learning experience to be a positive one.

Fourth, it is sometimes useful to take the reactions of particular groups of trainees and analyze them separately (Warr, Bird, and Rackham, 1970). For example, it may be informative to compare the assessments of trainees from the maintenance department with those given by trainees from production. The trainers may also want to compare the responses of older versus younger, line versus staff, or unionized versus nonunionized employees to particular facets of the program or to the program as a whole.

Fifth, it is important to collect reaction measures again several months after the training program has taken place. This allows the trainee to assess realistically the effectiveness of the training for his or her job. It also permits the training staff to see if the ratings collected immediately

Figure 5.3 An example of a form for evaluating trainers

Rating Scale for Instruction

TRAINING COURSE: ______________________________

DATE STARTED: ______________________________

LOCATION: ______________________________

TRAINER: ______________________________

NOTE TO TRAINERS: To keep conditions as nearly uniform as possible, it is important that *no instructions* be given to the trainees. The rating scale should be passed out without comment.

NOTE TO TRAINEES: Following is a list of qualities that tend to determine if the trainer (instructor) is effective or ineffective. Of course, nobody approaches the ideal in all of these qualities, but some do so more than others. You can provide information that will be used in improving subsequent training programs by rating your trainer on the qualities shown below. Please circle one of the ten numbers along the line at the point which most nearly describes him or her with reference to the quality you are considering.

This rating is entirely confidential. Do not sign your name or make any other mark on the paper that could serve to identify yourself.

	10 9 8	7 6 5 4	3 2 1
Interest in Subject........................	Always appears full of his subject.	Seems mildly interested.	Subject seems irksome to him.
Considerate Attitude Toward Trainees...........	Always courteous and considerate	Tries to be considerate, but finds this difficult at times.	Entirely unsympathetic and inconsiderate.
Stimulating Intellectual Curiosity........................	Inspires students to independent effort; creates desire for investigation.	Occasionally inspiring; creates mild interest.	Destroys interest in subject; makes work repulsive.
Presentation of Subject Matter..........................	Clear, definite, and forceful.	Sometimes mechanical and monotonous.	Indefinite, uninvolved, and monotonous.
Relevance....................	Ties ideas and facts back to the job.	Occasionally goes off onto irrelevant tangents.	Is too academic and school-like.
Depth of Knowledge.....	Knows the area thoroughly.	Sometimes has to look things up to answer questions.	Knows little more than trainees.

after training were inflated due to enthusiasm for the trainers, or the enjoyment derived from sharing experiences with new and old acquaintances. Nevertheless, collecting reaction measures immediately after training is important for two reasons. First, memory distortion can affect measures taken at a later point. Second, there is often a low return rate for questionnaires mailed to people long after they have completed the training.

A different type of reaction measure is the *self-report*. Here, trainees are asked to evaluate themselves on variables related to the purpose of the training such as skill in conference leadership, budgeting, or time management. Research suggests that valid self-report measures for evaluating training programs can be collected as follows (Howard et al., 1979): At the end of the training program, ask each participant to complete a self-report questionnaire, answering each item as viewed at this time (i.e., "Post" rating) and as viewed at the start of training (i.e., "Then" rating).

For example, in evaluating a training program to improve interviewing skills, each workshop participant was asked to rate twice (i.e., "Post" and "Then") the degree to which he or she possessed the following six interviewing skills: questioning techniques, interviewing structure, interviewer supportiveness, techniques of rapport building, active listening, and attention to relevant material (Howard and Dailey, 1979). The difference between the two sets of self-report measures serves as a way of assessing the trainees' reactions to the usefulness of the program. Later on in this chapter we discuss problems that might be encountered when using self-report measures of change.

Learning

Learning criteria assess the knowledge gained by the trainees. Knowledge is typically measured by paper-and-pencil tests. The following multiple-choice items are examples of those that might be used in a test of electrical knowledge at the conclusion of a skilled trades training program:

1. On a D.C. motor starter, what is the function of a field accelerating delay? (a) to prevent excessive current from damaging the armature; (b) to protect the field coils; (c) to prevent the motor from starting if the field current is open; (d) to stabilize motor R.P.M.
2. To phase two three-phase feeders together, you would use a (a) tachometer; (b) pyrometer; (c) oscilloscope; (d) voltmeter.

Quite often, true-false questions are used because they are relatively easy to compose. Multiple-choice and true-false questions assess the trainee's capacity to recognize information or misinformation put before them rather than using their memory to recall the answers. For this reason, we prefer the completion of fill-in type items like those shown in Figure 5.4.

Performance tests are used to determine if trainees have mastered a particular skill. Figure 5.5 presents the instructions for two different performance tests. One performance test is used to determine whether a mechanical trainee has acquired the skills necessary to assemble a reduction gear properly. The other test is used to assess whether a painter apprentice can use a boatsman chair and a spray gun. Similarly, at the managerial level, trainees might be asked to participate in various role-playing exercises or business games to measure their human relations skill after attending a management development program.

Regardless of the type of learning test used, it is essential that it be tied directly to the program's learning objectives. As we discussed in Chapter 3, these learning objectives should be based on the knowledge that has been determined through the task analysis to be truly necessary prerequisites for performing satisfactorily on the job. For example, there

Figure 5.4 An example of a completion or fill-in item

Instructions: Notice that there are seven circles on the print. Notice that there is a list of answers numbered 1 through 12 on the right-hand side of the print. Seven answers are correct, five answers are wrong and do not apply. Write one of these seven correct answers in each of these seven white circles. Use the numbers. Use each number only once.

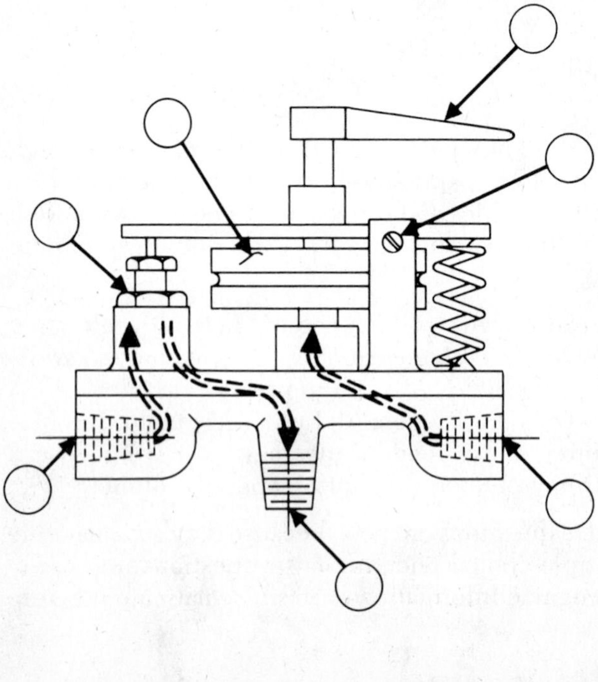

1. Instrument Air Connection
2. Pressure Capsule
3. Set Pointer
4. Metering Needle Valve
5. Orifice
6. Capillary Tube
7. Connection to Control Valve
8. Pilot Valve
9. Chart Plate
10. Nozzle
11. Pressure Connection
12. Fulcrum

Figure 5.5 Instructions to performance tests for mechanics and painters

MECHANICS:	"You have in front of you a gear reducer, a line shaft, bearings, and coupling. I want you to assemble and adjust the proper alignment so that the finished assembly is a right-hand (or left-hand) driven assembly. Set the coupling gap $\frac{1}{8}$" apart. You do not have to put the grid member in place or fasten the coupling covers. After you are finished, I will ask you where and how the grid member should go in. You will have 45 minutes to complete this job."
PAINTERS:	"I want you to boost yourself up about 10 feet off the floor using this boatsman chair, and then tie yourself off so that you don't fall. After that, I would like you to hook this spray gun to the air supply, set the regulator to the correct pressure, and then spray this wall."

is nothing wrong with an electrician learning about Ohm's law, but this knowledge may not be essential for functioning effectively as a skilled craftsman. If it is not strictly necessary, then learning Ohm's law should neither be a learning objective nor a test item.

Behavior on the Job

The importance of collecting behavioral measures of training effectiveness is illustrated by the following story:

> During the week I was particularly impressed by a foreman named Herman from a Milwaukee company. Whenever a conference leader asked a question requiring a good understanding of human relations principles and techniques, Herman was the first one who raised his hand. He had all the answers in terms of good human relations approaches. I was very impressed and I said to myself, "If I were in industry, I would like to work for a man like Herman." It so happened that I had a first cousin who was working for that company. And oddly enough Herman was his boss. At my first opportunity, I talked with my cousin, Jim, and asked him about Herman. Jim told me that Herman might know all the principles and techniques of human relations, but he certainly did not practice them on the job. He performed like the typical "bull-of-the-woods" who had little consideration for the feelings and ideas of his subordinates. At this time I began to realize there may be a big difference between knowing principles and techniques and using them on the job. (Kirkpatrick, 1976, p. 18/16)

This example illustrates how training programs can effectively disseminate knowledge without providing the skill to do the job effectively. It shows clearly the need for assessing changes in a trainee's overt behavior in addition to the knowledge that was acquired. There may be a large gap between knowing facts or principles and demonstrating them on the job. Likewise, it is possible for trainees to do well on performance tests administered during training, yet not be able and/or willing to exhibit these same skills on their jobs (i.e., zero transfer of learning). It is therefore important that measures be gathered on how a trainee behaves in the actual job environment.

The following examples illustrate how behavioral measures have been used to evaluate training. First, a program designed to train managers to conduct better appraisal feedback interviews with employees was implemented in an engineering section of the General Electric Company (Moon and Hariton, 1958). Two years after the adoption of the program, a questionnaire was used to obtain the employees' views about changes in their managers. The questions shown in Figure 5.6 asked the respondents to compare present conditions with what they were two years ago.

A more behaviorally oriented questionnaire was used to evaluate the effectiveness of a two-month training program for tire store managers. Figure 5.7 presents a portion of this BOS (Behavioral Observation Scales) questionnaire, which was completed by each store manager's district supervisor one year after the program.

The appraisal of on-the-job behavior can be collected from various sources such as supervisors, co-workers, and/or subordinates (Latham and Wexley, 1981). The appraisal can take place soon after training, but it should also be done several months later, so that the trainee is given adequate opportunity to put into practice what has been learned during training. Quite often, there is a *sleeper effect;* that is, it takes time for trainees to exhibit on the job what they have acquired during training.

Figure 5.6 An example of a behavioral questionnaire completed by subordinates

Compared to two years ago:

	(CHECK ONE) YES	NO	?
1. Does your manager have a better understanding of how you perform your job?			
2. Does he have a better understanding of you as an individual?			
3. Does he better indicate recognition of your good work?			
4. Does he better utilize your particular skills?			
5. Do you have a better picture of what he expects from you in terms of job performance?			
6. Do you have a better picture of how you stand with him overall?			
7. Does he discuss your job performance with you more frequently?			
8. Do you have a greater opportunity to present your side of a story during those discussions?			
9. Does he take a greater personal interest in you and your future?			
10. Does he make a greater effort to help you develop yourself?			

Adapted from C. G. Moon and T. Hariton, "Evaluating an Appraisal and Feedback Training Program," *Personnel,* November–December (1958), New York: American Management Association, Inc., p. 40.

Figure 5.7 An example of a behavioral observation questionnaire completed by supervisors

Store Manager ______________________________

District Supervisor ______________________________

Date ______________________________

INSTRUCTIONS: Please consider the above-named individual's behavior on the job for the past 12 months. Read each statement carefully, and on the basis of your actual observation or on dependable knowledge, circle the number that best indicates the extent to which this particular store manager actually demonstrated each of the following behaviors. For each behavior, a "5" represents "Almost Always" or 95 to 100% of the time. A "4" represents "Frequently" or 85 to 94% of the time. A "3" represents "Sometimes" or 75 to 84% of the time. A "2" represents "Seldom" or 65 to 74% of the time. A "1" represents "Almost Never" or 0 to 64% of the time.

An example of an item is shown below. If the store manager comes to work 95 to 100% of the time you should circle "5."

Example: Comes to work
Almost Never 1 2 3 4 ⑤ Almost Always

1. Holds weekly credit collection meetings with his/her sales personnel and credit manager.

   Almost Never 1 2 3 4 5 Almost Always

2. Keeps his or her salespeople informed of competitive conditions in the local market.

   Almost Never 1 2 3 4 5 Almost Always

3. Personally reviews all invoices for correct billing and merchandise received.

   Almost Never 1 2 3 4 5 Almost Always

4. Takes inventory monthly, checks discrepancies, and promptly corrects any items requiring correction

   Almost Never 1 2 3 4 5 Almost Always

5. When there is a conflict among employees, takes the time to sit down and discuss the causes and resolution.

   Almost Never 1 2 3 4 5 Almost Always

Results

The objectives of many training programs can be stated in terms of cost-related results or behavioral outcomes rather than the behaviors themselves, for example, a reduction in turnover, an increase in attendance, an increase in quantity and quality of units produced, an increase in sales, and a reduction in accidents. At General Electric, a training program for supervisors was instituted in a manufacturing plant. The cost-related measure used to evaluate the program was an index that reflected the effective utilization of employee and equipment resources by a foreman, calculated by the following formula:

$$\text{Performance} = \frac{\text{Actual Productivity}}{\text{Standard Productivity}}$$

Actual productivity was the production level achieved by a foreman's work group within a production cycle or period. Standard productivity referred to the production level that management had estimated through time and motion study that employees were expected to achieve during a given production period (Goldstein and Sorcher, 1974).

To determine the actual dollar value of the training, a utility analysis can be conducted. The concept of utility is synonymous with evaluating a training program in terms of its costs versus its benefits in financial terms (Cascio, 1989). A utility analysis is important because it is possible for a training program to bring about favorable reactions, increase trainee learning, change employee behavior on the job, and improve cost-related results. However, it is also possible that this same training program is *not* worth implementing in an organization because it is not cost effective; its monetary costs outweigh its monetary benefits to the organization.

In order to estimate the utility of any training program, the following formula has been recommended (Boudreau, 1983a, 1983b, 1988; Schmidt, Hunter, and Pearlman, 1982):

$$U = (T')(N')(d_t)(SD_y)(1+V)(1-TAX) - NC\,(1-TAX)$$

where U = the dollar value of some training program.

T' = T (the number of years' duration of the training effect on performance) reduced by the Discount Factor (see Table 5.1).

N' = number of people trained who are still employed by the organization in the particular job.

d_t = the true difference in job performance between the average trained and untrained employee expressed in standard deviation (SD) units. Preferably, this should be calculated empirically by using one of the recommended evaluation designs employing a control group discussed later in this chapter. Alternately, it can be estimated from published research literature evaluating the particular training method (see, for example, Burke and Day, 1986).

SD_y = the standard deviation of job performance in dollars of the untrained (i.e., control) group. It can be estimated by asking a group of people knowledgeable about the particular job to estimate the dollar value of job performance of an employee who falls

Table 5.1 VALUES OF THE DISCOUNT FACTOR (DF) ADJUSTMENT COMPUTED USING ILLUSTRATIVE COMBINATIONS OF VALUES FOR THE DISCOUNT RATE (i) AND THE DURATION OF THE PROGRAM'S EFFECTS (T)

	T				
i	1	2	5	7	10
.00	1.00	2.00	5.00	7.00	10.00
.05	.95	1.86	4.33	5.79	7.72
.10	.91	1.74	3.79	4.87	6.14
.15	.87	1.62	3.35	4.16	5.02

Note: Table values are computed using the formula

$$DF = \sum_{t=1}^{T} [1/(1 + i)^t].$$

Reprinted by permission of the publisher, from "Economic Considerations in Estimating the Utility of Human Resource Productivity Improvement Programs," by J. W. Boudreau, *Personnel Psychology,* 36, 1983, © Personnel Psychology, Inc., p. 567.

at the 15th, 50th, and 85th percentile. The dollar difference between the 85th and 50th percentiles or between the 50th and 15th percentiles reveals a measure of the variability (standard deviation) of job performance in dollars of an untrained group of people. An alternative approach is to simply calculate 40 percent of the average salary level on the particular job.

(1 + V) = the effects of variable costs (V) on SD_y (see Table 5.2).

(1 − TAX) = the effects of the organization's marginal tax rate on SD_y and on NC (see Table 5.1).

N = the number of people initially trained, regardless of whether they stayed or left the job.

C = the costs of training for each trainee, including all direct and indirect expenses.

Now, let us apply this formula to estimate the utility of a five-day program used to improve the selling skills of route salespeople who drive around in trucks to promote the company's products to supermarkets and grocery stores.

T = 3 Suppose it is estimated by management that the effects of this training program last about three years on a typical route salesperson job performance.

T′ = 2.2 By entering Table 5.1, where T = 3 and i (interest rate) = .15, T is discounted to a T′ of 2.2.

Table 5.2 ILLUSTRATIVE ADJUSTMENTS TO CORRECT UTILITY ESTIMATES FOR THE COMBINED EFFECTS OF VARIABLE COSTS (V) AND TAXES (TAX)

	TAX					
V	0	.05	.10	.30	.45	.55
.33	1.33	1.26	1.20	.93	.73	.60
.10	1.10	1.04	.99	.77	.60	.50
.05	1.05	1.00	.94	.74	.58	.47
.00	1.00	.95	.90	.70	.55	.45
−.05	.95	.90	.86	.68	.52	.43
−.10	.90	.86	.81	.63	.50	.40
−.20	.80	.76	.72	.56	.44	.36
−.30	.70	.67	.63	.49	.39	.32
−.40	.60	.57	.54	.42	.33	.27
−.50	.50	.48	.45	.35	.28	.22

Note: Table values equal (1 + V) (1 − TAX). These values would be multiplied by the sales value of increased productivity to adjust for variable costs and taxes.

Remember, all of the money that the company has invested in designing and implementing this training program could have been otherwise invested in other ways such as stocks and bonds. Assuming that this company could have gotten an annual yield of 15 percent on these monetary investments, i = .15.

$N' = 954$ This is the total number of route salespeople who have gone through the training program and are still employed by the company.

$dt = +1.00$ Suppose we use a Pretest-Posttest Control Group Design (see Figure 5.8 on page 126) and find that the true difference in job performance between the average trained and untrained route salesperson in standard deviation units is +1.00.

$SD_y = \$14,500$ Suppose that the average annual salary of route salespeople in the company is $36,250. Forty percent of this figure is $14,500.

$(1 + V) = 1 + (-.05) = +.95$ In this case, the effects of the training improved the job performance of the route salespeople. This increase in sales performance, in turn, increased variable costs (V) by 5 percent. Thus the company will derive only +.95, or 95 percent, of the dollar value of this improvement in job performance. Why? Because the route salespeople will receive higher pay in the form of sales commissions.

Conversely, in other training situations, an increase in job performance might reduce variable costs (V) by some percentage. For example, well-trained programmers may produce better programs and also help the company train other programmers who are new and less experienced. In this case, variable costs might be lowered by 5 percent. Now, (1+V) equals +1.05. Thus the company will derive 105 percent of the dollar value of the improvement in job performance.

(1 − TAX) = 43 percent Suppose the company's marginal tax rate is 57 percent. So, 1 − TAX equals .43. A company's marginal tax rate is a function of its level of profitability in the past.

N = 1,200 Suppose this many route salespeople have been trained in the past. As you can see from N′, 246 route salespeople have either left the company or else been transferred to other jobs.

C = $1,083 Suppose that a panel of training specialists and company accountants estimated that the total cost of the training program is $1,083 per trainee.

Substituting all of these values into the formula just described tells us that this training program is worth $11,955,530 to the company over a period of 2.2 years with 954 route salespeople trained. This also means that the training program is worth $5,429,331.80 per year and $5,691.12 per trainee.

What kind of a return is the company getting on their training investment? This can easily be calculated be figuring out the benefits/costs per trainee. Thus $5,691.12/$1,083 = 525 percent. Simply stated, this training program is yielding in benefits over five times its costs!

There is often a temptation for training specialists to sell the benefits of a proposed training program solely on the basis of anticipated increases in cost-related measures. This is a mistake for at least two reasons (Latham, 1986; Latham and Wexley, 1991). First, although these measures usually serve as excellent indicators of an organization's effectiveness, they are generally inadequate indicators by themselves of a trainee's job effectiveness because they are almost always deficient. That is, they often omit important factors for which a person should be held accountable (e.g., team playing as defined by a manager in one district loaning equipment to a manager in another district of the same company). This deficiency is a major criticism of management by objectives (MBO) where the performance standards or goals are usually set in terms of cost-related targets. Emphasis is placed primarily on tangible results that are perceived to be easily measurable. Consequently, many employees feel that there is an overemphasis on quantitative goals because they are not measured on nor do they receive credit for important aspects of their jobs which cannot be spelled out in quantitative terms. For example, a marketing manager might specify that a major objective of the forthcoming year is to increase the number of accounts by 10 percent in the Vancouver area. A human resources manager, however, would have difficulty expressing the desired end results of a new career development program in percentage figures.

Second, cost-related measures are affected positively as well as adversely by factors beyond the trainee's control. A senior-level manager who returns from an executive development program (see Chapter 9) may find that his or her performance is either lavishly praised or criticized severely even though the obtained results were due more to the relation of the dollar to the yen rather than to his or her own behaviors (e.g., sales based on log exports to Japan).

Even utility analysis, despite its current level of sophistication, needs to be viewed with caution. Researchers such as Boudreau (1988) and Cascio (1987) are among those who advocate utility analysis as a way of developing credible bottom line estimates of the value of training programs that may soften the criticisms of those executives who view training as little more than the source of burdensome overhead expenses. A critical flaw in utility analysis models, however, is that the standard deviation of job performance in terms of dollars (i.e., SDy) is estimated simply by asking the opinion of supervisory employees. According to Dreher and Sackett (1983), (1) there is no evidence that a rational estimate approach to assessing the standard deviation of job performance approximates the true value, (2) agreement among job experts (i.e., supervisors) is not a guarantee that the estimates are valid, and (3) the procedure lacks credibility in that the basis of each supervisor's judgment is unknown. Tenopyr (1987) reported that utility analysis has little effect on the decision making of executives at AT&T. Thus utility analysis may eventually be discarded along with its predecessors of the 1950s and 1960s, namely, the dollar criterion (Brogden and Taylor, 1950) and human resource accounting (Brummet, Flanholtz, and Pyle, 1969).

The appropriate question to ask is, "What do executives take into account when determining whether training programs should continue?" As noted in Chapter 3, a major impediment to upper-management support for training may be the failure of managers to see how training has had a positive impact on employee behavior with regard to the attainment of organizational objectives. Seeing a positive behavior change on the part of employees may result in upper management treating training more seriously than if presented with dollar estimates that justify time spent on training. Research in the 1990s is needed on managerial decisions regarding the continuation of training programs as a result of seeing observable job-related behavior change versus utility estimates.

In the interim, it would appear prudent to use all four criteria, namely, reactions, learning, behavioral, and cost-related measures as a way of showing the program's construct validity. The construct of interest is on-the-job effectiveness. Each measure supplements the others by providing information on why the training worked or failed to work in improving trainees' performance on their jobs. Each measure provides the trainers with information on the steps that can be taken to strengthen and improve training effectiveness.

Summary

Measures of training success fall into four categories: (1) Reaction—how do the trainees feel about the program they attend? (2) Learning—to what extent have the trainees absorbed the knowledge and skills that have been taught? (3) Behavior—to what extent can the trainees apply what they have learned during training to their job settings? (4) Results—to what extent have cost-related behavioral outcomes been affected by the training? Do these cost-related benefits outweigh the costs of developing and implementing the training?

HOW SHOULD A TRAINING EVALUATION STUDY BE DESIGNED?

Once the measures or criteria of training effectiveness are selected, attention must be given to choosing the proper design, or experimental procedure, in which to do the measurement. Unfortunately, the two designs most frequently used in the training literature are also the most absurd for evaluation purposes. These two designs, commonly referred to as *case study* and *pretest-posttest* are as follows:

Case Study

Training → Measures Taken After Training

Pretest-Posttest Design

Measures Taken Before Training → Training → Measures Taken After Training

In the case study, employees are trained and measures of trainee effectiveness are then taken (e.g., reaction, learning, behavior, and/or results). For instance, one company evaluated a two-day assertiveness training course by asking each manager who had participated to fill out a short assertiveness quiz. The primary problem with this design is that there are no measures taken prior to training. Consequently, there is no way to know whether the assertiveness training brought about any change. The person might have known the answers to the questions prior to receiving the training.

The pretest-posttest design assesses such changes because measures are taken before and after training. Nevertheless, this design also is of little value, because a multitude of unknown factors could be the real cause of a change in performance. For example, if a posttraining measure of performance showed that safety improved (i.e., fewer accidents) after a safety training program had been conducted, there would be no way of knowing whether the training program in any way contributed to this result. If the trainees consisted of newly hired applicants, it could be that the trainees had simply become more experienced by the time the posttraining measure of performance was taken. If new equipment and better lighting had been installed, if management suddenly emphasized safety over production, if the workday were shortened, or if any other of a host of factors occurred at the time the training program took place, it would be impossible to identify what variable or variables were responsible for the change and what variable or variables were a waste of time, money, and energy on the part of the organization.

Two designs that do permit a stringent evaluation of training programs are (1) the pretest-posttest design with a control group (see Figure 5.8), and (2) the after-only design with a control group.

In the pretest-posttest control group design, individuals are randomly assigned to either a group that receives training or a group that does not receive training until after the program has been evaluated. Random assignment ensures that a positive change in performance in Group A relative to Group B cannot be attributed to the fact that the Group A people were more intelligent, experienced, or motivated prior to training than the Group B people. The advantages of a pretest are at least twofold. First, they tell us whether the groups are truly equal prior to training. Second, they allow us to use statistical techniques to correct for imbalance between groups. In short, they minimize the probability we will conclude erroneously that the training was effective or ineffective.

The key factor in this design is the control group (Group B). Any change in equipment, lighting, management policy, hours worked, and the like, are exactly the same for both groups. The only difference between the two groups is that one received training. Therefore, any improvement in learning, behavior, and/or result measures can only be

Figure 5.8 The pretest-posttest control group design

Group A (Trained)	Measures taken before training	Training	Measures taken after training
Group B (Not Trained)	Measures taken before training	—	Measures taken after training

attributed to the training. If the training was of value, the trained group should perform significantly better in learning, behavior, and/or results than the control (i.e., untrained) group. The use of a control group allows us to say with more assurance that the changes in the trained group were due to the instructional treatment per se, and were not brought about by extraneous factors such as the passage of time, maturational changes in the trainees themselves, or certain events happening within the organization. Thus a fairly strong case can be made when using this design for continuing, modifying, or even discarding the training program.

Consider the use of this design as used for an evaluation of a training program on self-management conducted with state government unionized workers in Washington State. In this study, people were randomly assigned to an experimental (i.e., training) or a control group, and several measures of training effectiveness were taken (Frayne and Latham, 1986; Latham and Frayne, 1989).

Assessing employee reactions to the training was important because many trainees had argued that sick leave is a personal privilege. Moreover, in the initial session, the trainees in the original trained group expressed hostile reactions to the training in the form of self-deprecating and aggressive comments (e.g., "I guess we are the delinquent bunch"; "The trainer is a spy for management"). A fistfight occurred in the first class as a result of name calling between two trainees. Thus it was important to determine what, if anything, the trainees perceived was especially effective or ineffective about the program.

Data were collected 3, 6, 9, and 12 months after the training program was completed. Favorable reactions were maintained over time because the trainees reported that the training they had received enabled them to identify obstacles preventing them from coming to work, helped them overcome these obstacles, led them to set specific goals for increasing their job attendance, and increased their self-confidence in their ability to control their own behavior.

An important issue was to understand in what other ways the training was effective. A second criterion was *learning*. Did the trainees learn ways of responding to attendance-related issues? Did they acquire problem-solving principles that enabled them to deal effectively with coming to work? To answer these questions, a learning test was developed on the basis of interviews with the supervisors of the employees. The learning test consisted of 12 situational items with a scoring guide. Here is a sample item: "The reason I can't come to work is that I do not get along with a particular person with whom I work. Whenever she is on shift, I call in sick. I noted that when I do have contact with her on the job, we get into arguments. I decided to set a goal of getting along with her, but it does not seem to be working. What should I do?" The data analysis revealed that the trained group learned significantly more problem-solving skills than the individuals assigned to the control group.

To determine whether people retained the information presented during the training program, the learning test was administered and scored 6 months and again 9 months later. The trainees had not been informed of their scores. Again, the performance of the trained group was significantly higher than that of the control group. Thus any decrease in job attendance could not be blamed on lack or loss of knowledge.

Of crucial importance to the evaluation of training effectiveness is whether the training truly changed the trainees' behavior. The behavioral measures of job attendance of those people who received training in self-management was significantly superior to that of the control group. Later, when the control group people were trained, it was found that their reaction measures were as positive, their learning test scores were as high, and their job attendance was as good as that of the people who were in the original trained group.

In the after-only control group design (see Figure 5.9), individuals available for training are randomly assigned to either a training group or a control group. The control group consists of individuals who will not receive training until after the program has been evaluated. No pretest measures are necessary prior to training because random assignment ensures that the two groups have been equalized prior to training (especially when a large number of individuals are involved). This is particularly true when a process known as *matching* is used. With matching, pairs of workers are found who are alike on relevant variables such as age, sex, experience, and ability. One member of each pair is randomly assigned to the training group while the other is assigned to the control group.

This design is particularly useful where the time required to collect pretest measures is not available, or it is believed that the pretesting of trainees may in some way facilitate their learning and thus contaminate (inflate) the measures of training effectiveness. If this were the case, we would not know whether the same positive effects would have been obtained without giving the pretest.

An example of the use of this design is found in the evaluation of a behavioral modeling program, known as Supervisory Relationships Training (SRT), designed by AT&T to help line supervisors interact more effectively with their subordinates. Two months after the experimental group completed SRT, each supervisor from the trained and the untrained group was given a series of three simulated problem-solving discussions by a staff of assessors. Only the posttest measures of the

Figure 5.9 The after-only control group design

Group A (Trained)	Training	Measure performance after training
Group B (Not Trained)	—	Measure performance after training

trained and untrained supervisors were compared (Moses and Ritchie, 1976).

A minor disadvantage of using either of these two designs is that it is highly desirable to have a minimum of 20 employees for an adequate statistical evaluation of a training program; that is, 10 individuals would need to be randomly assigned to training; the remaining 10 individuals would form the control group. If the number of employees involved in these designs are too small, then the statistical power of detecting any difference between the training and control groups is so low that trainers attempting to evaluate their programs will seldom find any positive results. This is a minor problem, because most employers are interested in training a large number of employees. However, where the number of employees is inadequate for either one of these designs, at least two alternatives may be considered.

The first alternative is called a time-series design (see Figure 5.10), where a series of measures are taken prior and subsequent to training. The logic of this design is that if performance was consistently hovering at a given level before training was introduced, and performance suddenly increased and remained high following training, we can conclude that the training program brought about the change in performance. The important feature of this design is that there must be a sufficient number of pretest data points covering a sufficiently extended period of time so that all possible patterns of variation can be ascertained (Cook and Campbell, 1979). Shown in Figure 5.11 is a hypothetical example of a successful training program. In this example, the purpose of training was to increase employee attendance. Attendance was expressed in terms of the percentage of scheduled work-hours actually worked. As you can see, attendance data were collected for 15 weeks prior to training and 12 weeks after training.

A major drawback of this design is the chance that some fortuitous event will occur at the same time that training is initiated, and that the event (and not the training) is the cause of the increase in performance. The result is even worse if, instead of an increase, a decrease occurs. Training may indeed have improved performance, but this improvement will not show up, because some extraneous negative variable occurred when the posttest measures were taken. The effects of weather and season can be particularly bothersome. For example, five monthly measures of production were taken on several logging operations. The loggers were then given training in goal setting, and five more monthly measures were taken. The results are shown in Figure 5.12.

Figure 5.10 The time-series design

M_1 M_2 M_3 M_4 M_5 M_6 M_7 M_8 M_9 M_{10} TRAINING M_1 M_2 M_3 M_4 M_5 M_6 M_7 M_8 M_9 M_{10}

M = daily or weekly measures

Figure 5.11 Mean attendance data for the 15 weeks before and 12 weeks after a hypothetical training program to increase attendance

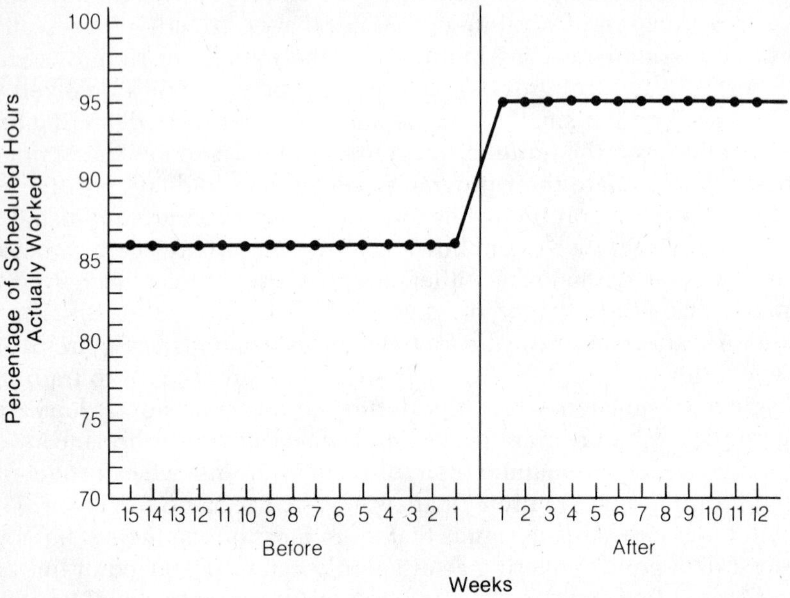

Figure 5.12 Time-series line for loggers who received goal-setting training

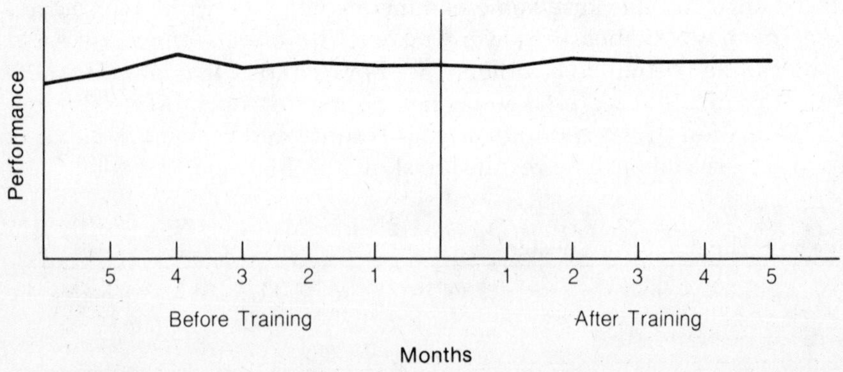

It might be concluded that training neither helped nor hurt production. However, there was heavy rainfall in the months after training occurred. It may be that, without training, performance would have decreased. The point is, we do not know the answer because there is no control group against which performance can be compared.

The time-series design can be vastly improved by adding a control group. Unlike the pretest-posttest control group and the after-only designs, employees are not randomly assigned to the group that receives training or to the group that does not. This design, commonly known as the multiple time-series design (portrayed in Figure 5.13), is used frequently in applied settings where naturally occurring groups must be used (e.g., department A and department B; individuals from the East Lansing plant and the Seattle plant). If the design had been used in evaluating the effects of training loggers to set goals, the effects of heavy rainfall following training might have led to the drawing shown in Figure 5.14.

In this hypothetical situation, the control group's performance dropped significantly while the training group maintained production despite the rain. The employees' performance across the two groups was approximately the same prior to training. Moreover, both groups were exposed to the same factors prior to and during training, except that the control group did not receive training. The only logical conclusion we can draw is that training maintained production by counteracting the negative effects of the heavy rainfall.

More Sophisticated Evaluation Designs

Because of its increased complexity, the Solomon Four-Group design is ideal for ascertaining whether a training intervention had a desired effect on trainees' behavior. Unlike the designs discussed so far, this design involves the use of more than one control group.

Solomon (1949) argued that the very act of taking pretest measures prior to training may reduce the possibility of observing the training effect as it would have occurred naturally (i.e., in the absence of training). That is, there is a possibility that merely taking pretest measures changes the trainees' attitudes and behaviors toward the training procedures. Or, it may conceivably alter the set or attentional factors important to the effectiveness of training. For instance, if a group of supervisory trainees were given a pretest on leadership ability and the test contained a lot of

Figure 5.13 The multiple time-series design

M_1 M_2 M_3 M_4 M_5 M_6 M_7 M_8 M_9 M_{10}	TRAINING	M_1 M_2 M_3 M_4 M_5 M_6 M_7 M_8 M_9 M_{10}
M_1 M_2 M_3 M_4 M_5 M_6 M_7 M_8 M_9 M_{10}		M_1 M_2 M_3 M_4 M_5 M_6 M_7 M_8 M_9 M_{10}

M = daily or weekly measures

Figure 5.14 Multiple time-series lines for loggers who received and did not receive goal-setting training

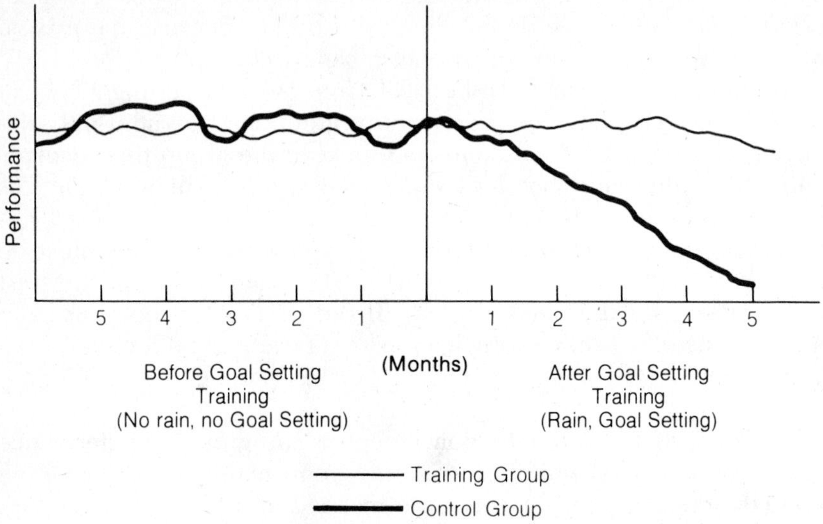

items on participative decision making, it is quite conceivable that the trainees would pay attention to certain relevant portions of the training program in a manner different than if they had not received the pretest at all. This source of contamination is called *pretest sensitization,* and it cannot be adequately measured or controlled using the traditional two-group designs. Solomon, therefore, suggested extending the two-group model to include two additional control groups.

The Solomon Four-Group design is illustrated in Figure 5.15. Note that the first two groups are treated in the same way as in the pretest-posttest control group design. However, two additional non-pretested control groups have been added. Notice that the effects of training can be assessed in four different ways in this design: Measure B should be larger than (>) Measure A, Measure B > Measure D, Measure E > Measure F, and Measure E > Measure C. Also, if there is no pretest sensitization, then Measure E should be the same as Measure B.

Although the Solomon Four-Group is an excellent design, it is rarely used in organizations. It requires a sizable number of employees (e.g., 80 or more) and their random assignment into four, instead of two, groups.

The Solomon Four-Group design was used to evaluate the effectiveness of a training program for telephone installer-repairmen (Bunker and Cohen, 1977). The training program involved a combination of text reading, audiovisual presentations, and hands-on exposure to the basic

Figure 5.15 Solomon Four-Group design

Group 1 (Trained)	**A** Measure performance before training	Training	**B** Measure performance after training
Group 2 (Untrained)	**C** Measure performance before training	—	**D** Measure performance after training
Group 3 (Trained)	—	Training	**E** Measure performance after training
Group 4 (Untrained)	—	—	**F** Measure performance after training

AC/DC characteristics of electronic and telephone systems. As part of the evaluation study, 131 employees were randomly selected from the employee pool and assigned to one of the following conditions:

1. Pretested, Trained, Posttested
2. Pretested, Untrained, Posttested
3. Non-Pretested, Trained, Posttested
4. Non-Pretested, Untrained, Posttested

The pretest and posttests used were equivalent forms of a 50-item multiple-choice examination developed by an electronics expert. Of special significance is the fact that the added costs associated with incorporating the two non-pretested control groups into the design were quite small compared to the expenses associated with the training program itself and the traditional two-group evaluation model. In fact, total expenditures for the evaluation (i.e., employee costs, lost work time, data analysis, etc.) were estimated to be about 10 percent of the amount invested in training program development and implementation. As for the total evaluation costs, 25 percent could be attributed to the extension of the design.

Within-group designs have been embraced by some training specialists because of the difficulty often encountered in obtaining control groups in organizational settings. A within-group design useful for evaluating training programs is the multiple-baseline design (Cook and

Campbell, 1979). This design does not require having more than one group. Rather, comparisons are made between individuals or groups. That is, each person or group serves as his or her own control. Therefore, there is no need to have any separate control groups to infer cause-effect relationships between training and its outcomes. It is often difficult to arrange a suitable group that is similar to the experiment group in every way except for exposure to training. With the multiple-baseline design, the trainer can evaluate the effectiveness of training without using a control group.

This design includes two basic components: (1) concurrent baselines—baseline data taken repeatedly over a period of time across either multiple behaviors or groups of people, and (2) staggered interventions—the treatment is first introduced with one behavior or group of people. When the desired change occurs (or after some predetermined number of training sessions), the treatment is then introduced with a second behavior or group of people. Again following an observed change, the training is introduced with the next behavior or group of people. Again following an observed change, the training is introduced with the next behavior or group, and so on, until the training has been introduced with all behaviors or groups.

To evaluate the effects of the training, comparisons are made between baseline and intervention phases to determine whether the effects of training are replicated at different times. If performance improves after, but not before, the training phase and this happens each time the training is introduced (in its staggered fashion), then it can be concluded with a great deal of confidence that the training itself was responsible for the favorable results.

Let us look at a few examples. A multiple-baseline design across behaviors was used to evaluate whether a training program was effective with clerks in a small grocery store (Komaki et al., 1977). The objective of the training was to improve performance on three desired behaviors: (1) remaining in the store, (2) assisting customers, and (3) stocking merchandise. The training was introduced initially with the first behavior. The training involved clarifying the desired behavior and its rationale during an initial half-hour session. Trainees were also given time off with pay whenever they attained at least 90 percent or more of the desired behaviors. In addition, they were given feedback on their progress in the form of a graph posted regularly on a bulletin board by the trainer. The clerks also learned to give themselves feedback by recording on a specially designed checklist whether or not they had engaged in any of the desired behaviors.

When improvements were noted in the percentage of time spent in the store (after 24 observational sessions), the training approach was reintroduced with the second behavior. When the clerks had begun to assist customers regularly and had continued to remain in the store (after 30 observational sessions), they were given training for the third behavior. Figure 5.16 shows the percentage of time the three target behaviors were performed across the 12 weeks of the study. The mean performance level of the three behaviors improved from 53, 35, and 57 percent to 86, 87, and 86 percent, respectively. Based on these data, it was concluded that the improvements in behavior were due to the training, since performance increased only after, and never prior to, the introduction of each training intervention.

Sometimes, instead of examining the effects of training across behaviors, we are interested in evaluating its effectiveness across groups of people. The groups may consist of different units within a single organization (e.g., sales, quality control, product development), different shifts within a department (e.g., nurses on the 8 to 4, 4 to 12, 12 to 8 shifts), or different branches within a statewide organization (e.g., Flint, Lansing, and Saginaw). For instance, an industrial safety program was instituted in a wholesale bakery that makes up, wraps, and transports pastry to retail outlets throughout the United States. The groups, selected because of their high number of accidents during the previous year, consisted of

Figure 5.16 Example of multiple-baseline design across behaviors; percentage of time the three target behaviors were performed by the grocery personnel during a 12-week period

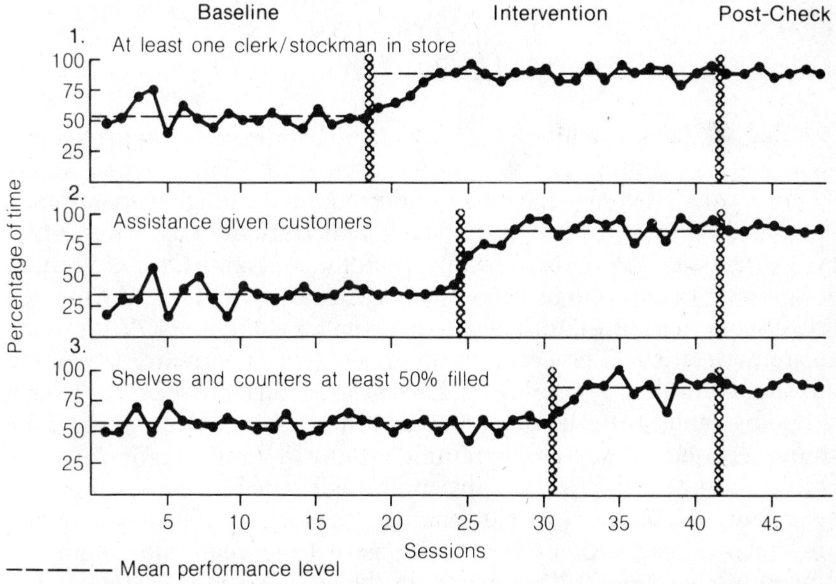

The first intervention took place after 18 sessions (3 weeks), the second after 24 sessions (4 weeks), and the third after 30 sessions (3 weeks).

Source: From J. Komaki, W. M. Waddell, and M. G. Pearce, "The Applied Behavior Analysis Approach and Individual Employees: Improving Performance in Two Small Businesses," *Organizational Behavior and Human Performance*, 1977, *19*, p. 342.

personnel in the second-shift wrapping and makeup departments. Employees in the makeup department measure and mix ingredients, prepare dough, and manually depan and package pastries as they come out of the ovens. Employees in the wrapping department bag, seal, and label the packages and then stack them on skids to be shipped. After collecting baseline data on the percentage of incidents performed safely in both departments, a training intervention was introduced in the wrapping department. During this training, employees were presented with safety information and rewarded for desired behaviors. Following continued improvement by personnel in the wrapping department, the intervention was implemented in the makeup department (Komaki, Barwick, and Scott, 1978).

The multiple-baseline design across groups is a particularly powerful approach for evaluating training programs. Unlike the designs we have discussed thus far, it allows us to determine to what degree the beneficial effects of training can generalize to other organizational settings. In other words, the multiple-baseline design goes beyond merely measuring how well learning transfers from the training setting to the job setting for one group of people. Instead, it concerns itself with the intraorganizational generalizability of the effects of the training program. This, of course, is an important issue within any organization where the training is going to be implemented across groups of people.

HOW SHOULD EVALUATION DESIGNS BE ANALYZED STATISTICALLY?

Now that we have examined the various measures and designs used to evaluate training programs, we briefly discuss the statistics that can detect any *change* that may have resulted from the training intervention.

According to Arvey, Cole, Hazucha, and Hartanto (1985) as well as Arvey and Cole (1989), the best approach for analyzing a training intervention statistically is to use analysis of covariance (ANCOVA) using the pretest score as a covariate. The main reason for using ANCOVA is that it has greater statistical power than other procedures. An alternative, but equivalent, method of performing covariance analysis can be accomplished by using multiple regression procedures whereby the pretest and a dummy-coded variable (e.g., training group = 1; control group = 2) are entered as independent variables predicting posttest scores (i.e., the dependent variable). Another alternative to covariance analysis is the use of hierarchical regression. Here, we construct two regression models, a reduced model and a full model. With the reduced model, the posttest variable is regression onto the pretest variable. The full model involves regressing the posttest variable on *both* the pretest variable as well as the dummy-coded variable. Then, we examine the R^2 values for each of these models. If the R^2 for the full model is significantly larger than the R^2 for the reduced model, we can conclude that group membership (i.e., training versus control groups) predicts the posttest variable, over and above the pretest variable. However, according to Arvey and his associates, all that has been presented here is based on the assumption that the training and control groups are equivalent at pretest. Usually, this situation is arranged via random assignment of employees to the two groups. The existence of nonequivalent groups at pretest can produce biased, misleading results (Latham, 1988; Linn and Slinde, 1977).

In many evaluations of training studies, there is relatively little difficulty in measuring change because the variables of interest are straightforward and reliable (e.g., amount of scrap produced, incidents of customer complaints, amount of productivity). Recent research suggests that, particularly with regard to self-report data (e.g., questionnaires, interviews, personality tests), the measurement of change is far more difficult than just discussed (Wexley, 1984). Self-report measures greatly complicate the measurement of change due to training, not so much because of the statistical procedures we have described but because of problems involved in the definition of change itself (Arvey and Cole, 1989). Specifically, there are three types of change that can occur with self-report data: alpha, beta, and gamma (Golembiewski, Billingsley, and Yeager, 1976).

Alpha change occurs when the observed difference between the pretest and posttest measures represents a true change due to the training intervention.

Beta change occurs when the alpha change is confounded by a recalibration of the scale(s) used to measure the variable of interest. Arvey and Cole (1989) provide an excellent example of beta change. During pretest, a supervisor rates herself as being of "average" supervisory competence. After the training is completed, two things happen: She is now a more competent supervisor, and she now understands how much more there is to being a good supervisor than she previously realized. Consequently, after training, she rates herself again as being "average," thereby giving the erroneous impression that the training had no impact.

Gamma change refers to a trainee's reconceptualization of the variable being measured. For instance, the individual's personal understanding of, say, job satisfaction might change from the pretest to the posttest period.

The best way of measuring these three measures has been suggested by Terborg, Howard, and Maxwell (1980). They recommend using a *then* (otherwise known as a *retrospective pretest*) measure after a training intervention, in addition to the usual pre- and postmeasures. Respondents are asked how they perceive themselves to have been just before the training was conducted (Wexley, 1984). To assess beta change, the average of each respondent's self-reported answers to the items on the pretest measure is compared to his or her own average on the then measure. If no beta change exists, then these averages should be approximately the same for each of the respondents. Terborg et al. recommend using a t-test to assess the degree of beta change for each individual. In a similar manner, alpha change can be assessed by comparing posttest scores to then scores. Finally, to measure each person's degree to gamma change, we compute the correlation as well as the change in variance between pretest and then pretest items (Arvey and Cole, 1989). Of course, our hope is that the self-reported improvement from the training intervention is caused by alpha change, not by beta or gamma changes.

FINAL COMMENTS

It is difficult to understand why the rigorous evaluation of training programs is the exception rather than the rule in North American business and industry. Grove and Ostroff (1990) described four barriers that discourage training evaluation:

1. *Top Management does not usually require evaluation.* Frequently, top management seems ready to take on faith that certain training programs are valuable. Moreover, some top managers reward their training staff for merely staying current with the latest training fads. When sales and profits are good, top management appears to have no problem embracing the value of most training efforts. Further, when a needs analysis implies that training in certain areas is "good to do," it appears to be especially easy for top management to rest assured that things are being done properly by the training department.

2. *Most senior-level training managers do not know how to go about evaluating training programs.* Evaluation of training is a complex procedure. Most people simply do not know how to evaluate training programs properly.

3. *Senior-level training managers do not know what to evaluate.* Many people are not clear on what questions should be answered by an evaluation. Should they focus on the number of key people who want to attend the program? The costs per trainee? The degree of enjoyment expressed by trainees? Changes back on the job? Grove and Ostroff (1990) argued that the major contributor to this problem is a lack of clear training objectives. A review of a sample of corporate training catalogs substantiates their point. They described one manager of a corporate learning center who cut out of his own company's training catalog all of the different stated course objectives. Then, he tried to match these objectives to the various course descriptions. He was not able to do this because the objectives were so vague! This problem can be corrected by tying the training to the organizational analysis (see Chapter 2) where the corporate objectives and strategies for attaining them are identified.

4. *Evaluation is perceived as costly and risky.* There at least two forces acting on training specialists that work against evaluation: cost and risk taking. Many training specialists would rather spend their limited funds on developing new and highly visible training offerings that hopefully will be seen favorably by top management rather than spending scarce dollars on evaluation. The risk with evaluation is that the results may show that a training program which top management and others like is not attaining the objectives for which it was designed.

To counteract these four barriers, we recommend the following actions:

1. Top-level management needs to be educated on the importance of rigorous evaluation and the dangers of taking on faith that a certain training and development strategy is worthwhile.
2. Training managers and their staffs need to be taught the how to's of training evaluation. They need to be given hands-on training where they are shown how to design questionnaires, use the correct experimental design, statistically analyze data, and calculate utility.
3. Training managers and top-level management need to discuss what exactly needs to be evaluated. Training needs to be incorporated into the business strategy (see Chapter 3). It is important that the organization's overall strategy and the human resource management's strategy are aligned.
4. If top management really wants to reinforce rigorous evaluation, it needs to make it clear to the training director that a certain proportion of the training budget should be targeted to evaluation.
5. The risk-taking component of evaluation needs to be minimized by rethinking the purpose of evaluation. Rather than thinking of evaluation as a live or die decision for a training program, evaluation needs to be thought of as a way of finding out if there's anything wrong with the program and, if there is, correcting it.

As stated in Chapter 1, systematic measurement is the key to the prevention or minimization of training fads. It enhances training effectiveness by showing the trainer where and why the training was effective or ineffective. Unfortunately, we have seen too many programs evaluated inappropriately. Here are two actual incidents which illustrate our experiences:

> A medium-sized banking firm develops its managers by presenting a monthly series of lectures by prestigious outside speakers on such topics as participative management, mutual goal setting, and employee motivation. The effectiveness of these training sessions are evaluated ritualistically by the loudness of the audience's clapping and cheerfulness at the end of the session. Used also is a short two-item comment sheet that can be voluntarily filled out by any of the participants and mailed to the training department. The questionnaires received by the training department are largely favorable, thereby demonstrating that the fees paid to the speaker were worth it, and that the training staff is succeeding in its mission.

An office equipment manufacturer and distributor was considering whether to purchase a sales training program from a consulting firm specializing in the development of such programs. The vice president of marketing of the office equipment company wanted to evaluate the sales program before purchasing it. He therefore asked the consultants to demonstrate the two-day program on a trial basis for himself and his staff. They immediately liked the program and adopted it for training over 300 of the company's salespeople.

Although not all evaluations are this bad, there is often a sizable gap between the practice of training and the science of training evaluation as we have presented it in this chapter. Frequently, students ask us how we cope with this discrepancy in our dual roles as both teacher (i.e., telling how it should be done) and practitioner (i.e., experiencing how it is actually done). As practitioners we persuade management to implement the most sophisticated training evaluation possible. For example, a printing company wanted to have its secretarial training program evaluated in terms of reaction, learning, behavior, and results measures. We decided that the Solomon Four-Group design would be the best approach to follow and, therefore, presented it to the company's management. Their position immediately was that the current company situation could not tolerate the training of only one-half of the current secretarial force. They agreed, however, that it would be reasonable to choose half of the secretaries randomly for training now and use the remaining secretaries as a control group. This arrangement was agreed to on the stipulation that, if the training proved to be successful, the control group of secretaries would later be trained. Management also opposed the use of any pretest measures since they would take too long to collect. Management admitted that they were impatient to get the training started. The final result was the use of an after-only control group design.

As you can see from this example, organizational constraints often preclude the use of the most sophisticated designs. However, the training specialists should not throw up their hands in despair. It means essentially that, at times, something less than the ideal must be used. This is acceptable within limits. We feel strongly that the case study and the pretest-posttest without control designs are not acceptable for training program evaluation. In other words, flexibility is good, but there must be limits to anyone's level of flexibility.

With an understanding of the four criteria for evaluating training effectiveness, and the different approaches that can be used in conjunction with them, we now examine the training strategies and procedures that can bring about a relatively permanent change in a person's self-awareness, job skill, and/or motivation.

Chapter 6

On-Site Training Methods

To this point, we have discussed four main areas of training and development: how the training staff fits in with the rest of the organization, how to determine an organization's training needs, how to maximize a trainee's learning, and how to evaluate training and development programs. After the training staff describes the job in general terms (job description), lists each of the specific tasks comprising the job (task identification), and prepares a blueprint of trainee performance desired at the completion of training (course objectives), they must decide which techniques to use to optimize trainee learning.

There are numerous techniques available for presenting information and transmitting skills, in fact, more than can be discussed here. We have chosen to review the major training techniques currently used by both small and large organizations. For convenience of presentation, these techniques are grouped into four main categories: On-Site Training Methods (Chapter 6), Off-Site Training Methods (Chapter 7), Developing and Training Leaders: Theoretical Approaches (Chapter 8), and Management and Executive Development (Chapter 9). As you will see, Chapters 6 and 7 cover those on- and off-site approaches that are used primarily for developing nonexempt (i.e., hourly) employees. Chapters 8 and 9 review those approaches employed primarily for developing managers.

In this chapter, the following on-site approaches are reviewed: orientation training and the socialization of new employees, on-the-job training (OJT), apprenticeship training, job aids, coaching, mentoring, computer-based training, job rotation, and career development. Before proceeding further, let us briefly discuss the advantages and disadvantages of using on-site methods. The main advantages are that the problems of transfer of learning (see Chapter 4) and training costs are minimized because the trainees learn the skills and knowledge in the same physical and social environment in which they will work once training is completed. Moreover, with certain of these techniques (e.g., apprenticeship training, on-the-job training, job rotation) the trainees contribute to the organization while they are learning, thus defraying training costs. A limitation of on-site training is that sometimes co-workers or supervisors acting as trainers do not have the motivation or the capability to provide trainees with worthwhile learning experiences. This can occasionally be a problem for some employees who are asked to train females and members of minority groups. They may believe that their job security is threatened by having women and minorities in their department, especially if these individuals possess more seniority than they do.

In discussing on-site techniques, we use the nine-cell framework presented in Figure 1.1, which shows that any training technique can be conceptualized in terms of its goals (i.e., purposes) and its strategies (i.e., how these goals are to be achieved). A training effort can have one or more of the following goals: (1) to improve an individual's level of self-awareness, (2) to increase an individual's skill in one or more areas of expertise, and (3) to increase an individual's motivation to perform the job well. These broad goals can be attained by directing training efforts at the trainees' cognitions (i.e., thoughts and ideas), behaviors, or the environment in which the trainees work. Figure 6.1 presents six on-site methods cross-tabulated for both goals and strategies. We begin where a new employee would—in orientation.

Figure 6.1 On-site methods classified according to goals and strategies

STRATEGIES	GOALS: Self-Awareness	GOALS: Job Skills	GOALS: Motivation
Cognitive	Career development	Orientation Training and socialization of new employees Job aids	
Behavioral		On-the-job training Apprenticeship training Monitoring computer-based training	Coaching
Environmental			Job rotation

ORIENTATION TRAINING AND THE SOCIALIZATION OF NEW EMPLOYEES

There's an old saying, "Well begun is half done." This is an important concept for any organization to follow after an employee is hired. Getting new employees started in the right way is important, in order to reduce their feelings of anxiety and to increase their subsequent job satisfaction and commitment (Louis, Posner, and Powell, 1983). Poor orientation programs can be financially damaging to the organization because they reduce effectiveness for the first few weeks on the job and may contribute to dissatisfaction and turnover (Gomersall and Myers, 1966).

Orientation training should be the joint responsibility of the training staff and the line supervisor. There must be a clear understanding of the specific obligations of each, so that nothing is left to chance. Too often, we witness situations where both the training staff and the supervisor believe that the other is or should be responsible for orientation. The result is an inadequately trained employee. Generally, the training staff should provide information on matters that are organization-wide in nature and relevant to all new employees. The line supervisor should concentrate on those items unique to the employee's workplace. Although the content of the training will vary from organization to organization and from department to department, the items shown in Table 6.1 are typically included in any orientation (Hollmann, 1976). As you can see, the orientation process has as its goal the development of new employee skills. It attempts to accomplish this objective by transmitting factual (i.e., cognitive) information about the company and the employee's new job. Regardless of what is handled by the training staff versus supervision, every orientation program should accomplish at least the following ten tasks: (1) introduction to the company, (2) review of important policy and practice, (3) review of benefits and services, (4) benefit plan enrollment, (5) completion of employment documents, (6) review of employer expectations, (7) setting of employee expectations, (8) introduction to fellow workers, (9) introduction to the facilities, and (10) introduction to the job (Smith, 1984).

New employees often go through a process known as *organizational socialization* (Nelson, 1987; Schein, 1968). This involves learning the attitudes, standards, and patterns of behavior that are expected by the organization and its various subunits. Although the process of learning the ropes is a continuous one, it is highly intensified whenever we change organizations and/or jobs. It is important that orientation programs facilitate this socialization process by conveying to new employees the expected standards of behavior within the organization.

For example, in one Wisconsin hospital, newly appointed registered nurses and licensed practical nurses are given a one-week basic orientation program. At the end of this program, the nurses (1) recognize their

Table 6.1 ITEMS TYPICALLY COVERED BY ORGANIZATIONS DURING ORIENTATION TRAINING

General company orientation	Specific departmental orientation
The following items are among those typically included in this first phase: 1. Overview of the organization—brief history, what the organization does (products/services), where it does it (branches, etc.), how it does it (nature of operations), structure (organization chart), etc. 2. Policies and procedures—work schedules, vacations, holidays, grievances, identification badges, uniforms, leaves of absence (sickness, educational, military, maternity/paternity, personal), promotion, transfers, training, etc. 3. Compensation—pay scale, overtime, holiday pay, shift differentials, when and how paid, time clock, etc. 4. Benefits—insurance, retirement, tax sheltered annuities, credit union, employee discounts, suggestion system, recreational activities, etc. 5. Safety information—relevant policies and procedures, fire protection, first aid facilities, safety committee, etc. 6. Union—name, affiliation, officials, joining procedure, contract, etc. 7. Physical facilities—plant/office layout, employee entrance, parking, cafeteria, etc.	The following items are typically covered in this phase: 1. Department functions—explanation of the objectives, activities, and structure of the department, along with a description of how the department's activities relate to those of other departments and the overall company. 2. Job duties—a detailed explanation of the duties of the new employee's job (give him or her a copy of the job description) and how the job relates to the activities of the department. 3. Policies and procedures—those that are unique to the department, such as breaks, rest periods, lunch hour, use of time sheets, safety, etc. 4. Department tour—a complete familiarization with the departmental facilities, including lockers, equipment, emergency exits, supply room, etc. 5. Introduction to departmental employees.

From "Let's Not Forget About New Employee Orientation," by R. W. Hollman, copyright May, 1976. Reprinted with the permission from *Personnel Journal*, Costa Mesa, California; all rights reserved.

own position within the structure of the nursing department and the hospital, and can use appropriate channels of communication; (2) understand the philosophy and objectives of the nursing department and use these as a basis for giving quality patient care; (3) are acquainted with key hospital personnel in order to establish positive working relationships, and are aware of proper resource persons available for assistance; (4) are familiar with procedures and policy manuals and other written resource materials available as aids in giving patient care; (5) know their role and legal responsibilities concerning administration of medications as outlined in the hospital's pharmacy policies; and (6) are familiar with the hospital's unique forms and its policies regarding nurses' responsibilities for documenting patient care.

Another example of good socialization by an organization involves a radial tire manufacturing plant in southwestern Ohio. Their new employees receive an eight-hour orientation program. During the program, employees learn the plant's philosophy regarding such things as work rules, safety practices, quality control, and the importance of following engineering specifications. In addition, orientation sessions for spouses of newly hired employees are conducted. Besides providing a tour of plant facilities, the spouse program covers such items as filling out insurance claim forms; the company's policies on attendance, vacations, retirement, holidays, and employee discounts; a full explanation of all fringe benefits; and a discussion of the services provided by the company's credit union.

New employees often have unrealistically high expectations about the amount of challenge and responsibility they will find in their first job (Bray, Campbell, and Grant, 1974). They are often assigned fairly undemanding entry-level positions and consequently experience discouragement and disillusionment. The result is job dissatisfaction, turnover, and low productivity. One solution to this problem is making entry-level jobs more challenging by giving new employees increased responsibility and authority, and assigning them to supervisors who will set high standards. That is, instead of putting a new employee in any open job, some organizations are beginning to give careful thought to job placement. These organizations realize that making first-year jobs more challenging not only reduces turnover but also improves long-term career performance. Some organizations are currently training supervisors of new employees in the skills of job enrichment as a way of making initial assignments more challenging. These supervisors are trained to allow their new employees to deal directly with customers and clients (not just through them), do special projects and make recommendations, follow through and implement their recommendations, and continually assume added responsibility (Hall and Hall, 1976).

Where it is not possible to upgrade the demands of the first job, an alternative strategy is to provide realistic job previews (RJPs) (Wanous, 1980). Recently, several organizations (e.g., Prudential Insurance Company, Texas Instruments, Southern New England Telephone, U.S. Military Academy) employed realistic rather than traditional job previews to recruit outside individuals. The typical approach of most organizations is to make their organization appear very attractive. In doing this, companies draw a lot of applicants and make the most efficient use of their selection systems, which have their maximum utility when the number of applicants exceeds the number of job openings. The realistic job preview represents a different philosophy for recruiting new employees. It involves increasing the amount and accuracy of information given to job candidates in an attempt to maximize the quality of their organizational choices. Booklets, films, plant visits, or talks are used to convey to the new employee not only the positive aspects of the job and the company but the negative features as well (e.g., long hours, time pressures, excessive travel, limited upward mobility). The findings to date show that RJPs appear to lower new employee's expectations about the job and the organization, to increase the number of applicants who self-select themselves out from further consideration for a job, to increase initial levels of organizational commitment and job satisfaction slightly, to increase job survival, and to improve job performance when audiovisual rather than written (booklet) training aids are used (Premack and Wanous, 1985).

The socialization of new employees can be difficult because of their anxiety ("Will I be able to handle it?" "How will I get along with my boss?" "Where do I start?"). With these issues in mind, Texas Instruments conducted a classic experiment in which one group of new workers (control group) were given the normal first-day orientation, consisting of a two-hour briefing by the personnel department on hours of work, insurance, parking, and the like (Gomersall and Myers, 1966). Then, as was customary, the new employee met a friendly but very busy supervisor, who provided further orientation and job instruction. A second (experimental) group received the same two-hour personnel department orientation followed by a six-hour anxiety reduction session. These individuals were told that there would be no work the first day, that they should relax, sit back, and use this time to get acquainted with the organization and each other and to ask questions. The following points were emphasized during this phase: (1) the high probability of success on the job as evidenced by statistics disclosing that 99.6 percent of all new employees are successful on the job; (2) what new employees should expect in the way of hazing and unfounded rumors from older employees designed to intimidate them about their chances of success; (3) encouragement of new employees to take the initiative in asking their supervisors questions about their jobs; and (4) information about the specific personality of the supervisor to whom they would be assigned. This innovative orientation program had a remarkable impact: The experimental group exceeded the control group in terms of learning rate, units produced per hour, absentee rate, and tardiness. Although this research was conducted years ago, it clearly shows the beneficial effects of reducing the anxiety of new workers. Certainly this research suggests that anxiety reduction of some sort should be included in all organizational orientation programs.

Since the supervisor is an extremely important component of the socialization process, everything that this person expects of the new employee should be discussed openly during the orientation process: rest breaks, housekeeping, standards of performance, attendance, and so on. The better the supervisor is trained to explicate goals and expectations, the more confidence the employee will experience, and the quicker the employee will adapt to the organization (McShane and Beal, 1984). Supervisors must be aware of the necessity of following the new employee's work progress by periodically checking how he or she is doing. Supervisors must know how important it is that the new employee has enough to do. Nothing is more frustrating to an individual full of enthusiasm about a new job than sitting around "stacking paper clips." We are happy to report that more and more organizations are beginning to train their supervisors in the subtle management of employee adjustment to jobs. For instance, in a survey of the ways in which 85 of British Columbia's largest private and public sector companies handle employee socialization, over one-half provide training to supervisors on the subject of orientation (McShane and Beal, 1984). Once orientation is completed, the employee is usually exposed to on-the-job training (OJT).

ON-THE-JOB TRAINING (OJT)

The most widely used training and development method involves assigning new employees to experienced workers or supervisors. Often, the experienced employee is told by a superior to "teach Chris your job" or "break Pat in." The trainee is expected to learn the job by observing the experienced employee and by working with the actual materials, personnel, and/or machinery that will comprise the job once formal training is completed. The experienced employee is expected to provide a favorable role model with whom the trainee can identify, and to take time from regular job duties to provide instruction and guidance. In many cases, supervisors themselves assume responsibility for the on-the-job training of their new employees.

OJT has several positive features, one of which is its economy. Trainees learn while producing, thereby partially offsetting the cost of their instruction. For example, individuals in an automobile plant function as maintenance helpers while serving their two-year term as repair mechanic trainees. Moreover, there is no need to establish expensive off-site facilities such as classroom or equipment simulators, nor is there any need for outside trainers or members of the company's training staff. The method facilitates positive transfer of training (see Chapter 4), because the learning and actual job situations are identical. Ideally, the trainees learn by doing and receive immediate feedback regarding the correctness of their behaviors. This feedback can come from their performance on the job itself (i.e., intrinsic) as well as from their co-workers and supervisors (i.e., extrinsic).

Figure 6.1 shows that the major goal of OJT is to improve the job-related skills of employees by using primarily a behavioral (though also a cognitive) strategy. Although OJT can and often does work, it can also turn out to be a failure. This happens when organizations use it haphazardly. In these organizations, OJT is instituted simply by telling an individual to "train Pat," with little or no regard for the trainer's willingness or ability to do so. With these concerns in mind, we offer suggestions here for implementing effective OJT programs.

First, employees functioning as trainers must be convinced that training new employees in no way jeopardizes their own job security, pay level, seniority, or shift status. If for some reason they feel threatened, they will strongly resist training new people. For example, a large manufacturer of industrial boilers decided to institute a skilled trades program for developing their own first-class repair mechanics. Twenty-five experienced production workers were carefully chosen by the training staff to enter a three-year program that involved OJT and evening classes on such topics as blueprint reading, hydraulics, and safety procedures. Soon after the program began, it became evident that the tradesmen resented training the production workers. The tradesmen were concerned that many of the production workers had more plant seniority than they did and could, therefore, "bump them" if the company needed to lay off people. As one repair mechanic said, "Why should I spend my time training someone who could lay me off or bump me to the night shift if things get tight around here?" In order to get the program started, the company and the union had to agree that bumping would be based strictly upon seniority within the mechanical department.

Second, the individuals serving as trainers should realize that their added responsibility would be instrumental in obtaining rewards for them. If they do not, resistance will be encountered. For example, certain chicken producers employ nine-man work crews who are paid on a piece-rate basis as a group, based on the number of chickens they catch and load onto trucks each night. The crews catch the chickens by using special black lights in the chicken houses. Certain crew members bend down and grab seven chickens by their legs (three in one hand, four in the other) at one time. The chickens are then handed to someone at the door, who then passes them to other crew members stationed on the truck. These individuals place anywhere from 10 to 15 chickens into hauling cases. For years, the chicken catchers have been reluctant to train new people. They argue that this requires them to work too hard. They also resent the fact that the group makes less money for about four months during OJT since it cuts down on their crew's performance. They also feel inequity when they look at catchers on other crews making more money and not working as hard. One obvious solution to this problem is to provide special monetary bonuses to those crews who consent to provide OJT to new crew members.

Third, trainers and trainees should be carefully paired so as to minimize any differences in background, language, personality, attitudes, or age that may inhibit communication and understanding. For example, an older bookkeeper/secretary in a truck dealership was having difficulty keeping up with the pressures of her job. Management agreed to hire an assistant for her, whom she could train to assume some of her responsibilities. The trainee, an 18-year-old high school graduate, began learning the job. Within a few weeks, tension developed between these two individuals. One day, the office manager saw that the young woman was crying, and approached the experienced employee to ask what had happened. She replied that she resented the younger person and refused to teach her what it had taken her 40 years to learn.

Fourth, the choice of trainers should be based on their ability to teach and their desire to take on this added responsibility. Trainers will not necessarily be the most competent and experienced employees. Job experience does not ensure that people have the ability to teach the job to somebody else. For instance, in a textile factory, management needed to identify those sewing machine operators who could function best as trainers. A questionnaire was mailed to all factory operators inquiring about their willingness to serve in this role for three months. Next, this list of volunteers was sent out to all operators asking them to nominate the five operators who they expected would be the best teachers. Those individuals who received the highest number of peer nominations were chosen.

Fifth, those skilled workers chosen as trainers should be rigorously trained in the proper methods of instruction (i.e., use of reinforcement, knowledge of results, distributed practice). Too often organizations rely solely on what is known as Job Instruction Training (JIT) for training supervisors and employees to instruct others. JIT was originally developed during World War II as an approach for helping supervisors feel confident in training employees. As shown in Figure 6.2, the approach consists of two major elements (i.e., how to get ready to instruct; how to instruct) and four basic steps (i.e., prepare the worker; present the operation; try out performance; follow-up). The information is usually printed on a wallet-sized card and carried about by prospective trainers. It is unlikely that this oversimplified cookbook approach to training trainers has much benefit (McGehee and Thayer, 1961). JIT does, however, serve as a reminder to trainers on how they can handle training situations more effectively than if they had been completely left on their own.

Sixth, it must be made clear to employees serving as trainers that their new assignment is by no means a chance to exploit others. For instance, a maintenance painter working in a large office building required his trainees to perform only those tasks that he disliked doing (e.g., cleaning paintbrushes, removing rust from metals, cleaning grease and dirt from surfaces). He often said that he enjoyed being a trainer because he liked having his own helper! Unfortunately, those who worked with him learned little about constructing and repairing structural woodwork and equipment because of his abuse of his role as a trainer.

Seventh, the trainees should be rotated to compensate for weaker instruction by some trainers and to expose each trainee to the specific know-hows of various workers. For instance, many home realtors give their prospective real estate agents three months of OJT immediately

Figure 6.2 Job Instruction Training (JIT)

HOW TO GET READY TO INSTRUCT

1. Have a timetable.
   —How much skill you expect and when.
2. Break down the job.
   —List the important steps.
   —Pick out the key points.
3. Have everything ready.
   —The right equipment, material, and supplies.
4. Have the workplace properly arranged.
   —As you would expect the worker to maintain it.

HOW TO INSTRUCT

STEP 1: *Prepare the Worker*
a. Put the worker at ease.
b. Find out what he or she knows.
c. Arouse interest.
d. Place the worker correctly.
(Ensure a learning situation.)

STEP 2: *Present the Operation*
a. Tell.
b. Show.
c. Explain.
d. Demonstrate.
(One point at a time. Stress key points.)

STEP 3: *Try Out Performance*
a. Have the worker perform the operation.
b. Have the worker explain the key points.
c. Correct errors.
d. Reinstruct as needed.
(Be sure he or she knows.)

STEP 4: *Follow-up*
a. Put the worker on his or her own.
b. Encourage questioning.
c. Check frequently.
d. Taper off assistance.
(Practice—key to performance.)

after they pass their state examinations. Trainees are rotated from agent to agent every three to four weeks. This is done because some real estate agents are better at showing homes, others at writing contracts, and others at securing home listings.

Eighth, the organization must realize that there is a possibility that production may be slowed down, equipment damaged, and some defective products made. Learning must take precedence over production, especially during the early stages of training.

Ninth, the trainer must realize the importance of close supervision in order to avoid trainee injuries and the learning of incorrect procedures. Adequate evaluation of the trainee's progress needs to be secured periodically and fed back to the trainee using reliable and valid measures. For example, a cheese and specialty food retailing chain uses film cartridges to train their store salespeople. They offer slide presentations on such topics as customer relations, gift order forms, checkstand selling, cheddar cheese cutting, citation swiss cutting, sampling and selling cheeses, and beefstick sampling and selling. After each film cartridge, trainees are asked to complete a review test similar to the one presented here for the gift order form segment of the program:

What sales step is missing?
1. customer awareness
2. greeting

3.
4. qualifying
5. closing

What is the guarantee delivery card?
What information must go on the back of the gift enclosure card?
When showing a customer our gift pack line, always start with the lowest price pack. True ( ) False ( )
Check the proper gift pack sales approach.
_____ May I help you?
_____ What do you want?
_____ Is there a particular gift pack I can help you with today?
_____ You're just looking, aren't you?

Finally, OJT should be used in conjunction with other training approaches such as programmed instruction, lectures, operating manuals, and films. It is good practice to supplement the skill learning derived on the job with factual (i.e., cognitive) knowledge. In this way, trainees can develop a better understanding of the principles, rationale, or theory underlying what they are being taught each day.

Sullivan and Miklas (1985) described the design of an OJT program in a bank that is generic and useful for a wide range of training situations. For six months, assistant office manager trainees were given OJT in 13 distinct areas of the bank. Seven major steps were followed in the design of this highly successful program. First, the rationale and goals of the OJT program were presented to upper-level executives who, in turn, communicated their support for the program downward to their respective managers whose involvement and support would be essential to the program's success. The second step involved identifying the areas of the bank in which an assistant office manager needs training such as loans, customer credit, and collections. Next, job tasks were analyzed (see Chapter 3) so that lists of performance competencies (i.e., knowledge and skills) for each OJT area could be compiled and then rewritten as course objectives. Fourth, the training staff in collaboration with SMEs (subject-matter experts) began the task of scheduling trainees for their six-month OJT experience. This involved deciding on the length of time each trainee should spend in each OJT area. Next, before the management trainees arrived, they were each assigned to a mentor, an experienced office manager who volunteered to guide the trainee through the program. Sixth, a training manual was developed by the training staff and the SMEs that included such essential information as a description of each OJT area and the OJT manager, the schedule to be followed, the training specifications for each OJT area, and forms for trainees to report on their own performance in each area upon completion. The final step in the design of this OJT program involved the development of a reporting system. Upon a trainee's completion of each OJT area, the OJT manager submitted an assessment of the trainee's performance after discussing it with the trainee.

Closely related to OJT is the subject of apprenticeship training. Here, organizations are concerned with developing journeymen from various skilled trades. A large part of this training involves on-site instruction.

APPRENTICESHIP TRAINING

Organizations that employ skilled tradespeople such as carpenters, plumbers, pipe fitters, electricians, cement masons, bricklayers, painters, roofers, sheet metal workers, and printers develop journeymen by instituting approved apprenticeship programs. Apprenticeship programs are typically initiated by a committee composed of representatives from management and labor. The joint committee works together with the Department of Labor's Bureau of Apprenticeship and Training (BAT) in formulating a set of standards that specify the features of the particular program being established (e.g., curriculum, number of hours of classroom and workshop instruction, number of hours of on-the-job experience, affirmative action goals, schedule of wage advancements).

The official function of BAT, established by the National Apprenticeship Act of 1937, is to formulate and promote labor standards necessary to safeguard the welfare of apprentices, to bring together employers and labor for the formulation of programs, and to cooperate with state agencies engaged in the formulation and promotion of standards of apprenticeship. Once the joint apprenticeship committee and BAT formulate standards, they are sent to a State Apprentice Council for review, possible modification, and eventual approval. This council serves primarily as a regulatory and certification agency. It gives the joint apprenticeship committee official approval to register their apprentices, and it issues certificates to trainees upon completion of their program.

Apprenticeship programs last anywhere from two to five years, with four years being the average length. They combine on-the-job instruction together with a minimum of 144 hours per year of classroom and shop instruction (a mixture of on-site and off-site training). The apprentice method involves the organization's delegating the responsibility for socialization of new employees to several of its skilled journeymen. Thus the journeymen trainers are a critical component of this socialization process in that they serve as a model to be emulated by the apprentices. Like OJT, apprenticeship training has skill development as its major goal. It, too, uses mainly a behavioral (in addition to a cognitive) change strategy.

The classroom and shop instruction is either held in the evenings at local high schools or community colleges, or during regular working hours. Many large organizations send their apprentices to special half-day classes conducted by local trade schools specializing in apprenticeship instruction. Sometimes, it is advantageous for these large companies to hire instructors from these trade schools on a part-time basis to conduct their courses on company premises. Small companies located away from metropolitan areas often have to resort to correspondence courses in order to provide their apprentices with the requisite number of hours of "classroom" training.

During classroom and shop training, each apprentice is typically given a workbook consisting of materials to be read, problems to be solved, short tests to be taken, and reading assignments in other books. The workshop permits the trainees to work at their own individual pace. Many instructors use part of their class time for presenting lectures, giving demonstrations, conducting group discussions of actual work experiences, presenting films, inviting outside speakers, or providing skills practice. An example of what apprentices might be taught in this setting is as follows: A local of the Plumbers and Steamfitters Union established jointly with a manufacturer's association a four-year apprenticeship program for developing plumber-pipe fitters. Trainees are required to work 40 hours per week while attending evening classes six nights per month (four hours per evening). Their curriculum consists of the following topics:

First Year:
- Basic math related to pipework
- Beginning course in isometric drawing and blueprint reading
- Use and care of tools

Second Year:
- City, state, and national plumbing codes
- Advanced blueprint reading and drawing
- (Shop) small piping projects

Third Year:
- (Shop) Heating work on heating equipment

Fourth Year:
- Occupational Safety and Health Regulations
- Theory of refrigeration and air conditioning
- (Shop) Welding

Apprenticeship training has been criticized from both civil rights groups and human resource experts. The major objections are that the unions controlling apprenticeship training restrict entry. In doing so, they not only create labor shortages and high wage rates but also discriminate against women and minority group members (Strauss, 1971).

As a result of affirmative action requirements by the Equal Employment Opportunity Commission (EEOC) and the Office of Federal Contract Compliance Program (OFCCP), some progress has been made in reducing favoritism and alleged discrimination in apprentice admission procedures. Apprenticeship committees are required to set forth affirmative action standards regarding the selection of women and minorities.

According to the Department of Labor's Bureau of Apprenticeship and Training there were 263,023 registered apprentices at the end of fiscal year 1989. Minorities represented 21.6 percent (as compared with 16.3 percent in 1978) and females 7.2 percent (as compared with 1.7 percent in 1978) of the total number, excluding uniform military apprentices.

The amount of apprenticeship training has varied over the past 30 years. For instance, between 1952 and 1965 fewer than 30,000 people each year completed apprenticeship programs in the United States. Since 1965, the numbers have generally increased, reaching an all-time high of approximately 320,000 people in 1980.

What are some of the factors that influence the number of apprentices trained each year? A major consideration is the amount of building construction in the country. Since the building trades are by far the largest employers of apprentices, their prosperity directly influences the need for such training. A second factor is labor and management attitudes toward the bureaucracy and paperwork involved in establishing formal apprenticeship programs to produce qualified journeymen. Organizations can use other channels to develop skilled tradespeople. These include the completion of informal, unregistered apprenticeship without an indenture and with little or no formal classroom training; learning the trade in a nonunion sector of the industry or a related industry; completion of a full-time course in a vocational school; and working one's way up from an unskilled or helper classification.

If organizations do not have to use apprenticeship programs, why then do they continue? Part of the reason is that they have had the support of unions. Union members look upon apprenticeship as a way of controlling entry into their trade, thereby preventing undue displacement of incumbents by trainees. Also, apprenticeships prevent poorly trained individuals from entering the craft and threatening the trade's sense of pride and status.

An on-site learning technique that is sometimes used in collaboration with on-the-job training and apprenticeship training is commonly referred to as a job aid. In the next section, we discuss the benefits of job aids and give a few examples of their usefulness.

JOB AIDS

A *job aid* can be described as instructional material that is located on the job to assist an employee in recalling information that was presented during training, or else it may be used in lieu of formal training. Job aids have a number of benefits: assisting employees in remembering precise or complex procedures and rules, helping to ensure that employees avoid committing critical errors, and guiding employees during a time when operating procedures are in the process of being changed (Pursell and Russell, 1990). They have been used since an early study conducted by the Air Force and Navy showed that they are capable of facilitating the learning process as well as reducing training time (Duncan, 1986). The goal of job aids is to teach job skills, and to accomplish this by using a behavioral strategy (see Figure 6.1).

Job aids are particularly valuable when integrated into a training program, and then later used by employees to recall learning after they return to their jobs. For example, the Buick-Oldsmobile-Cadillac Division of General Motors is committed to the concept of achieving continuous improvements through the ongoing development of B-O-C's greatest assets—its people. Consequently, the company developed and implemented a new personal development process called PDP (Personal Development Plan). All managers and supervisors within B-O-C are given extensive PDP training targeted on teaching each of them how to work with their people on bringing about continuous development and improvement. The job aid shown in Figure 6.3 is used to remind all man-

Figure 6.3 B-O-C's PDP process schedule (introductory year)

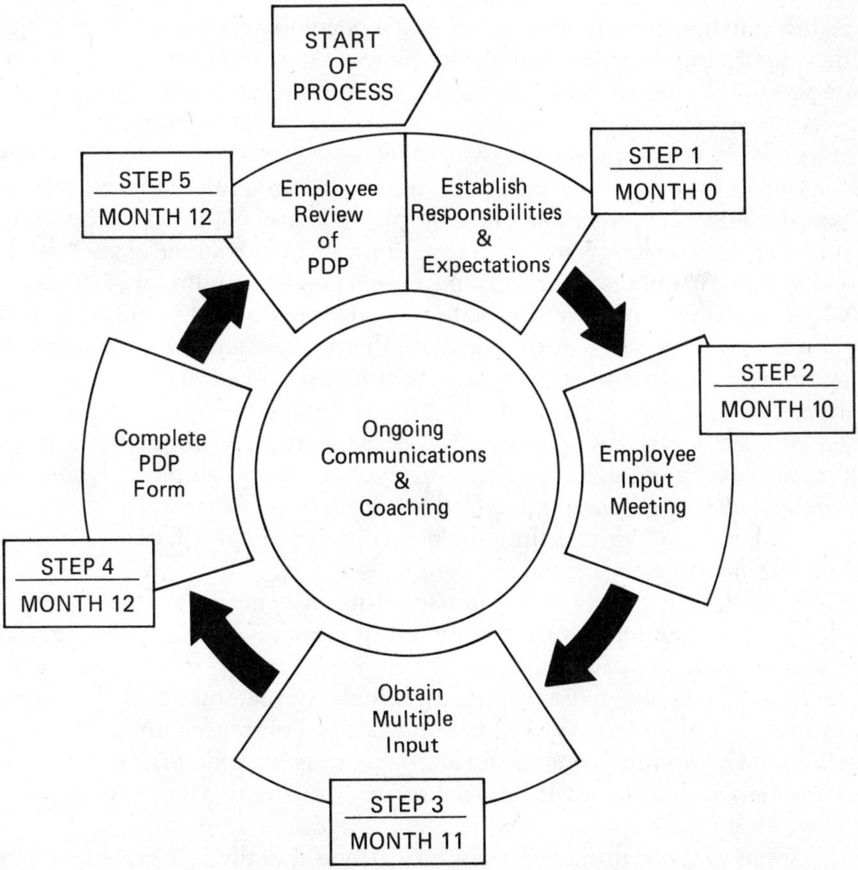

agers, supervisors, and employees about the overall PDP process. It specifies the five PDP steps as well as when during the introductory year each step should be implemented.

Like B-O-C, Domino's Pizza also makes good use of job aids. Directly above the pizza makeline, which is a sort of assembly line, pizzas are made with sauce, cheese, and additional toppings. There are large glossy pictures of exactly what the pizza should look like at successive stages along the pizza makeline. So, if an employee isn't sure whether he or she has added too much cheese, or whether the sausage and pepperoni were spread evenly enough, all the employee needs to do is compare the pie with a photo on the wall. The office tender, who is responsible for slicing and boxing finished pizzas, also uses job aids. This employee uses two photos, one of the "perfect pizza," the other showing ten common flaws, one in each slice. These imperfections include such things as bald spots, burned vegetables, bubbles, and soup bowl edges (Feur, 1987).

COACHING

A different approach to on-site training is coaching the employee through the use of periodic reviews of performance. Coaching serves a number of important functions within an organization. It (1) lets subordinates know what their supervisors think about how they do their jobs, (2) enables supervisors and employees to work together on ways in which employees can improve their performance, (3) improves communication and collaboration between supervisors and employees, and (4) provides a framework for establishing short- and long-term personal career goals. Unfortunately, in many organizations, problems may arise with these sessions which minimize or even eliminate their developmental benefits. Let us look first at some of the problems with this approach to employee development, and then discuss the ways that organizations can deal with them effectively.

Managers and supervisors often resist communicating appraisal information to their employees because they feel uncomfortable when put in the position of "playing God." This is especially true when they lack the skills needed for handling the coaching session itself, and are reluctant to challenge or criticize the employee.

The manager's reluctance to use criticism is not completely unwarranted. In a seminal study conducted at General Electric, managerial attempts to develop an employee by pointing out performance deficiencies were often perceived by the individual as threatening to self-esteem, and resulted in defensive behavior (e.g., denial of shortcomings, blaming others). This defensiveness, in turn, produced unfavorable attitudes toward the coaching program, and a decline in subsequent job performance (Kay, Meyer, and French, 1965).

Some of these difficulties can be attributed to the fact that managers are fulfilling two conflicting roles: judge and helper. The manager is a judge when he or she is observing an employee's performance. As a helper, the manager attempts to work closely with the employee in order to improve the person's job performance.

The following suggestions should be used when conducting coaching sessions for motivational (see Figure 6.1) purposes.

First, employees should have substantial participation in the developmental process (Wexley, Singh, and Yukl, 1973). Supervisors should do more listening than talking, ask questions which evoke lengthy rather than "yes" and "no" responses, and probe the employee's feelings and ideas. In general, the more the employee participates in the process, the more satisfied he or she will be with the coaching session, and the more likely it is that performance improvement goals will be accepted and met (Latham and Yukl, 1975b; Locke and Latham, 1984). An exception to this suggestion is the finding that nonparticipative coaching works well with inexperienced or new employees who seem to have a need for a more directive approach (Hillery and Wexley, 1974).

Second, subsequent performance improves most when specific goals are established during the session (Latham, Mitchell, and Dossett, 1978; Locke and Latham, 1990). Setting specific performance improvement goals in the coaching session results in twice as much improvement in performance than does a discussion of general goals, or criticisms without reference to specific goals (Burke, Weitzel, and Weir, 1978). An improvement plan should always be established that specifies areas in which the individual intends to change, the priority of areas needing change, and how the change will be accomplished.

Third, specific improvement goals should be mutually set by the supervisor and the employee. This leads to higher goals being set than when the supervisor sets them unilaterally (Latham et al., 1978). As mentioned in Chapter 4, hard goals result in higher levels of performance than easy goals.

Fourth, a helpful and constructive attitude on the part of the supervisor is important. The more the supervisor displays supportive coaching behavior (e.g., giving recognition for good performance, assuming the role of helper, treating the employee as a fellow human being, showing tolerance), the more satisfied the employee will be with the session and with the supervisor (Nemeroff and Wexley, 1979), and higher goals will be set (Latham and Saari, 1979b).

Fifth, criticism should be avoided unless it is used to justify disciplinary action. The key to effective coaching is to focus on what the trainee is doing right and, with the trainee, focus on the steps that need to be taken to advance the trainee's growth. The maxim is to emphasize the desired behavior (e.g., when making a forehand shot in tennis, keep your wrist stiff) rather than the undesired behavior (e.g., you are bending your wrist).

Sixth, a supervisor should provide feedback to the trainee on both behavior and results information (Kim, 1984; Porter, Lawler, and Hackman, 1975). If, for example, the employee were a salesperson, the supervisor should tell her she is behaving effectively when dealing with customers and the effect of this in terms of dollar sales. This approach motivates the employee to engage in the appropriate behaviors that lead to the attainment of organizational outcomes (Latham and Wexley, 1991).

Seventh, from a motivational standpoint, coaching sessions conducted on a fixed-interval schedule (e.g., once or twice a year) are not as effective as those conducted on a variable-interval schedule (Latham, 1989). Here, coaching takes the form of a pop quiz. However, daily coaching is more effective than a variable-interval schedule when the trainee has yet to learn the requisite knowledge or skill.

Eighth, coaching is highly effective when the supervisor models the correct behaviors expected. When trainers fail to practice what they preach, the likelihood increases that the trainees will do what was done rather than what was said.

Finally, effective coaches are alert to situational constraints that might be interfering with the trainee's job performance (Latham and Crandall, 1991). For example, trainees who return to the job may find it difficult to demonstrate their newly acquired knowledge and skill due to inadequate tools, equipment, materials, and supplies, or budgeting support. Trainees might also encounter a work environment that is adversely affected by too much noise, too little light, as well as too much or too little heat.

Behavioral criteria have been used by a division of Weyerhaeuser Company, a wood products business, to assist managers in improving the performance and potential for advancement of employees (Latham and Wexley, 1991). Weyerhaeuser's system incorporates many of the suggestions just described and, for this reason, we briefly describe it here. Essentially, the system has three parts: appraisal instrument development, rater training, and goal setting. The system provides a step-by-step process for supervisors to follow when coaching their employees. This process consists of the following three steps:

1. The supervisor describes the employee's behavior by completing a Behavioral Observation Scale (BOS) questionnaire (see Chapter 3). The supervisor is asked to indicate on a five-point scale the degree to which she or he has observed the employee behave in ways similar to those described in the questionnaire.

   Taken together, the items represent a comprehensive picture of effective and ineffective performance in a given position at Weyerhaeuser (e.g., foreman, superintendent). In order to ensure that the evaluations are fair and accurate, the supervisors are given a four-to-six hour training program (a shortened version of the one described in Chapter 10) to eliminate rating errors.

2. After reviewing an employee's performance, the supervisor prepares for the coaching session by identifying the specific behavioral ratings that led to a low rating on a dimension, indicating an area of weakness. Some supervisors ask employees to complete the appraisal on themselves in order to promote open and nondefensive discussion of their performance.
3. The supervisor and subordinate jointly formulate developmental plans and objectives. This process includes setting specific goals that the employee will seek to attain within a three- to six-month interval.

Before leaving this topic, it is important to note that many organizations today train their managers and supervisors to conduct effective coaching sessions with their employees. The goal of such training is to increase employee motivation by giving them more open lines of communication with their boss, concrete feedback on areas needing improvement, positive reinforcement for what they do well, and specific goals for change. The strategy of this training is to ensure the effectiveness of the supervisor or manager who conducts coaching sessions. For example, Weyerhaeuser Company's training incorporates a series of modeling films, role-playing activities, and/or workbook exercises designed to teach such things as how to clarify the employee's job responsibilities, set mutually agreed upon goals, compare actual with targeted performance, analyze performance discrepancies, diagnose employee strengths and weaknesses, and pinpoint needed developmental efforts.

Another example of a systematic approach to coaching has been used successfully by such companies as Goodyear Tire & Rubber, Allstate Insurance, Ohio Edison, Houston General Insurance Company, Sparrow Hospital, and the Lansing Board of Water & Light and is worth describing in some detail. Known as ADEPT, this two-day training program has five steps (Silverman, 1990): clarifying the employee's major job responsibilities, developing performance standards, giving periodic performance feedback, diagnosing and coaching employee performance, and reviewing overall performance.

Now, let's look briefly at the seven learning modules that train managers and supervisors how to implement ADEPT (Silverman, 1990):

Module A: The Performance Appraisal

This video-based module shows a manager conducting a typical coaching session with an employee. The manager makes many of the common mistakes associated with employee coaching. After the video, the trainees are asked to evaluate and discuss this manager's coaching skills.

Module B: Understanding Major Responsibilities (MR) and Performance Standards (PS)

This skill-building module teaches the participants how to establish performance expectations with their employees. Specifically, participants learn how to work with their employees on clarifying the 5 to 10 key functions of their employee's job. They also clarify the way the manager expects the work to be done and the bottom-line results that are be attained.

Module C: Clarifying Program Concepts with Employees

This video-based module teaches the participants how to install ADEPT back in their own departments. Role plays give the participants practice in developing these skills.

Module D: Clarifying the Employee's MR's and PS's

Video scenes are used to teach the participants how to sit down with their employees and generate MR's and PS's in a participatory manner. The object of this module is to eliminate role ambiguity on the part of employees (i.e., employees are not sure what their managers expect of them in their jobs). Vague job descriptions and weak communication between managers and employees often cause role ambiguity. It results in frustrated employees who are putting effort into doing things in their jobs that are relatively unimportant.

Module E: Observing and Documenting Employee Performance

The participants are given instruction and practice on the do's and don'ts of accurately observing and documenting (i.e., recording) employee job performance. They also learn how to eliminate various judgment errors (e.g., the tendency to be too lenient, stereotyping, prejudices) when coaching their employees (Latham, Wexley, and Pursell, 1975).

Module F: Diagnosing and Coaching Employee Performance

Research has shown that most managers and supervisors make incorrect attributions when diagnosing why an employee is having a performance problem, and that these incorrect diagnoses hurt subsequent manager-subordinate communications (Dugan, 1989; Freedman, 1984; Snell and Wexley, 1985). Thus this module focuses on teaching participants how to diagnose the causes of an employee's performance problems, and how to reach agreement on the steps to be taken to solve these problems. The module also teaches participants how to give positive reinforcement to outstanding employees who deserve recognition for superior performance.

Module G: Reviewing Overall Performance

This module teaches participants how to feed back performance information (e.g., quarterly or semiannually) in a manner that motivates their employee to improve as well as how to establish an action plan for the next three- or six-month period.

MENTORING

Related to the teaching of coaching is mentoring. The term dates back to Greek mythology where Odysseus asked his friend Mentor to teach his son Telemachus what could be learned from books as well as the wiles of the world. Teaching newer and younger employees the wiles of the business world is what makes mentors so valuable and helpful. Mentors are typically people two or three levels higher in the organization than the trainee who want to help less experienced employees learn the ropes in a nonthreatening, supportive relationship (Wilson and Danes, 1988). The goal of mentoring is the teaching of job skills (see Figure 6.1), and this is accomplished by means of a behavioral strategy.

According to Kram (1985), a mentor is a manager who is experienced, productive, and able to relate well to a less experienced employee. The manager facilitates the personal development of the employee for the benefit of both the individual and the organization. Typically, the mentor is about 8 to 15 years older than the protégé who is an up-and-coming professional with high career ambitions (Hunt and Michael, 1983). This mentoring relationship can be initiated by either party. Sometimes, the protégé attracts the attention of the experienced manager by being an outstanding performer who shares common interests and values with the older manager. Other times, the protégé may seek an experienced manager who is able and willing to spend time answering questions about the organization and the protégé's job.

Most mentorships are informal, in that both people are interested in establishing and maintaining this relationship. However, formal mentoring programs in which organizations match up mentors and protégés are becoming prevalent in both the private and public sectors (Noe, 1988a; Roche, 1979). One reason for their increased popularity is probably the increasing number of women seeking management positions in the labor force and needing support from a mentor for understanding the culture of male-dominated business organizations.

What can training specialists do to make certain that all employees in an organization derive benefit from having a formal mentor? The purpose and goals of the mentoring program need to be clearly defined. Mentors also must be carefully selected based on their interpersonal skills and interest in developing employees (Phillips-Jones, 1983). The organization should provide mentor training so that mentors know how to apply the principles of learning, engender trust, share information openly, and exhibit interpersonal skills tempered with a professional orientation (Kram, 1985). Finally, steps should be taken to ensure that mentors are accessible to protégés. For maximum effectiveness, mentoring should occur on a weekly basis (Noe, 1988a, 1988b).

A technique that can be used in conjunction with coaching and mentoring is computer-based training. This training is becoming so sophisticated that it lends itself to self-coaching.

COMPUTER-BASED TRAINING

Computer-based training (CBT), also referred to as interactive videos and videodiscs, provides instruction by using the computer terminal on an employee's desk or in his or her office. For instance, a widely distributed training course in CBT's short history is called, "Exploring the IBM Personal Computer." The course is on an IBM floppy disk that has been packaged with each of the more than four million IBM PCs sold. Each lesson presents information on the computer terminal and asks the learner to practice typing in commands for various operations. A correct answer is positively reinforced immediately with a statement such as: "GOOD! You now have identical files on each disk." An incorrect answer generates additional training information followed by another chance to practice the correct response (Hassett and Dukes, 1986). The instructional principles underlying CBT are similar to the reinforcement principles discussed previously in Chapter 4. CBT's training goal is to improve job skills. It accomplishes this goal via a behavioral strategy (see Figure 6.1).

CBT is now being used to teach efficiently many different types of job skills to employees. For example, interactive videos are used to help service technicians learn how to repair defective equipment faster and better, train clerks how to analyze insurance applications, teach salespeople how to make sales calls, improve the diagnostic skills of medical students, train managers how to handle touchy situations by making them more aware of the losses and lawsuits that mismanagement can bring, and boost performance at critical jobs in factories and offices (Boudette, 1989; *Business Week*, September 7, 1987).

The popularity of CBT in industry stems in part from the fact that it can reduce costs by cutting down on trainee travel and training time. For instance, a large company can simply mail computer disks to several thousand trainees rather than flying these people to a centralized training center and then paying for hotel rooms and meals for several days. Furthermore, it is widely alleged that CBT can result in a 30 percent (sometimes, as high as 50 percent) reduction in training time, and an 80 percent increase in retention of training content (*Business Week*, September 7, 1987; Hassett and Dukes, 1986).

Why might this training method be as good as its proponents claim? One answer is that the computer is sensitive to individual differences (see Chapter 4) in learning rates among trainees. Unlike human trainers, the computer terminal cannot become impatient or irritated with a slow learner. Equally important, the computer does not slow down the fast learner because of the presence of slow learners or a plodding trainer.

JOB ROTATION

Job rotation involves giving trainees a series of job assignments in various parts of the organization for a specific period of time. Trainers may spend several days, months, or even years in different locations. The idea is to expose individuals to a number of environmental changes (see Figure 6.1) by rotating them through various key departments. In each department, trainees may assume an observational role, or, preferably, take responsibility for training specified results (Proctor and Thornton, 1961). It is important that they become personally involved in departmental operations. The best way to do this is to assign them full functional responsibility with ample opportunity to exercise judgment and make decisions. This responsibility should be supplemented with supportive coaching from an immediate supervisor in each job assignment.

With job rotation, trainees gain an overall perspective of the organization and an understanding of the interrelationships among its various parts. In this way, trainees can become clearer about their career aspirations and their commitment to the organization (i.e., motivation: see Figure 6.1). Of course, at the same time, trainees increase their problem-solving and decision-making skills as well as their self-awareness.

Job rotation is an excellent method for preparing high-potential specialists for future general executive responsibilities (Farnsworth, 1975). It compels people to broaden their perspective by acquainting them with various people, processes, and technologies. The method is also often used with college graduates and MBAs who have only a vague notion of where they want to be placed in the organization. Job rotation helps them crystallize their career plans before they commit themselves to any one career.

In order to be effective, however, job rotation must be tailored to the needs and capabilities of the individual trainee (Bass and Vaughn, 1966). It should not be a lockstep system in which all trainees proceed through the same departments in a standardized sequence. Instead, trainees' aptitude profiles and interest patterns should determine their particular pattern of assignments. The length of time trainees stay in a job should be determined by how fast they are learning, rather than how much time they have left to put in. Moreover, the trainees should only be placed in company locations where they will receive feedback, reinforcement, and monitoring of their performance by interested and competent supervisors.

An excellent example of the use of job rotation is the Squadron Program that has been used at Goodyear Tire and Rubber Company for training college graduates. Most college hires at Goodyear choose to become squadron members, as participants in job rotation are called. The objective of squadron training is to provide people with a wide range of experience in either technical, sales, production, or business management operations before they take their initial position in production or staff departments.

Each trainee's squadron program is individually tailored to match his or her experience, education, and vocational preference. Programs vary in length from 6 to 15 months with trainees being rotated through various departments. When trainees complete their programs, they have a clearer notion of what they want to do. Also, the organization knows what each trainee can do. Specifically, the technical training program prepares college graduates for careers in such areas as research, development, machine design, project engineering, and plant planning methods.

Trainees begin their program with three weeks in company orientation, becoming thoroughly acquainted with Goodyear. They study the organization's structure, company objectives, basic manufacturing processes, and business communications. They also participate in a series of informal meetings with top company officials.

After an additional month of factory orientation, trainees discuss their career interests with the manager in charge of research and development squadrons. Each trainee selects up to six assignments to specific departments. These assignments, each approximately one month in length, help to clarify the individual's career objectives. A chemical engineer graduate might choose to work in fabric development, chemical materials development, research, central process engineering, process development, or chemical production. A mechanical engineer might choose tire development, industrial rubber products development, central staff engineering, research, or special products development. Ultimately, trainees select a specific job assignment as the starting point of their careers. This decision may be reached as early as the first departmental assignment or after experiencing several different departments.

Goodyear's domestic tire sales division has used job rotation for sales training. Sales trainees begin their training by spending two months at a company-owned tire store where they are exposed to basic selling practices at the retail level. They are then sent to corporate headquarters for three weeks of company orientation during which they learn about the production of auto, truck, farm and earth-moving tires, curing, and final inspection operations. Following this are eight weeks of rotating assignments among corporate sales departments (e.g., budget sales, car and home merchandising, retail merchandising, petroleum sales, sales planning and promotion, retread tire sales and service, auto and truck tire sales). During this period of rotation, trainees study principles of accounting, sales orientation, decision making, and computer concepts. They are asked to make written reports on each phase of their training, and their work is evaluated by training and sales department supervision. Field assignments are then provided. They include two months of training as a TBA (tires, batteries, accessories) merchandiser and two months as a credit sales manager trainee in a company retail store.

The whole area of career development is important both to the individual employee and to the organization. An employee's career represents an entire lifetime of work-related experiences and activities (Hall, 1986). The final section of this chapter deals with what organizations can do to aid their employees in handling career decisions.

CAREER DEVELOPMENT

In today's world of work, it is unlikely that a person will remain with one job or organization for an entire lifetime. This widespread career mobility results from individuals' needs to "gain more responsibility," "find jobs in the same location as their working spouses," and so on. Related to this tendency toward greater mobility is a growing desire by employees for guidance in managing their career paths. Organizations, too, have become aware that effective management of human resource problems (e.g., minimizing turnover among recently hired employees, developing high-potential candidates for managerial positions) can be maximized through career planning activities (Hall, 1986). In this section, we examine ways in which organizations are (or should be) attempting to improve the management of their employees' careers.

The primary goal of career development is to increase employees' awareness about themselves and their career goals by employing an information-based (i.e., cognitive) strategy (see Figure 6.1). Although career development workshops are sometimes conducted away from company premises, most career planning is conducted on site by the employees' supervisors or by members of the organization's training staff.

Certain organizations have designated a portion of their training staff as *career-planning specialists*. These individuals are often given special training in diagnostic testing in order to help employees understand their interests and abilities. Career specialists should be knowledgeable about jobs available in the organization as well as the skills required for successful performance in these positions. In this way, they can develop career paths that fit individual needs.

A career specialist can help an individual set realistic career objectives, plan a sequence of steps for obtaining them, and brainstorm ways of overcoming personal problems that may block goal attainment. For example, career-planning specialists at one of the nation's largest banks use Holland's (1966, 1973) theory of vocational choice when giving career guidance to employees. This theory states that people fit into one of six categories: realistic, investigative, artistic, social, enterprising, or conventional. The realistic person prefers activities involving the systematic manipulation of machinery, tools, or animals. Investigative individuals tend to be analytical, curious, methodical, and precise. Artistic people tend to be expressive, nonconforming, original, and introspective. Individuals who are social enjoy working with and helping others but avoid ordered, systematic activities involving tools and machinery. Enterprising individuals enjoy those activities that entail manipulating others to attain organizational goals or economic gain, but they tend to avoid symbolic and systematic activities. Enterprising people often lack scientific ability. Finally, conventional individuals enjoy the systematic manipulation of data, filing records, or reproducing materials. They tend to avoid artistic activities (Weinrach, 1979). Listed here are typical occupations held by each of these six types of people:

1. Realistic: machinist, mechanic, electrician
2. Investigative: biologist, chemist, physicist
3. Artistic: decorator, musician, sculptor
4. Social: bartender, counselor, funeral director
5. Enterprising: lawyer, office manager, salesperson
6. Conventional: secretary, file clerk, financial expert

According to Holland's theory, there are also six environments (realistic, investigative, artistic, social, enterprising, conventional) and, for the most part, each environment is populated by individuals of the corresponding personality type. Further, individuals are more satisfied and work best in environments that will let them exercise their skills and abilities, express their attitudes and values, and take on agreeable problems and roles.

Congruence occurs when individuals work or live in an environment identical or similar to their personality type. The hexagon shown in Figure 6.4 is used by career specialists to portray the degree of congruence between an employee's personality type and environment. For instance, a perfect fit would occur in the case of a social type and a social environment. The next best fit would be represented by a personality type that is adjacent to an environment type, for example, an artistic person in a social environment. The least degree of congruence between person and environment occurs when a person's type and environment are at opposite points of the hexagon, for example, a social type in a realistic environment.

The career development staff at the bank we mentioned earlier also uses Holland's Vocational Preference Inventory (VPI) and Self-Directed Search (SDS). These instruments identify employees' preference for a

Figure 6.4 The psychological resemblance among types

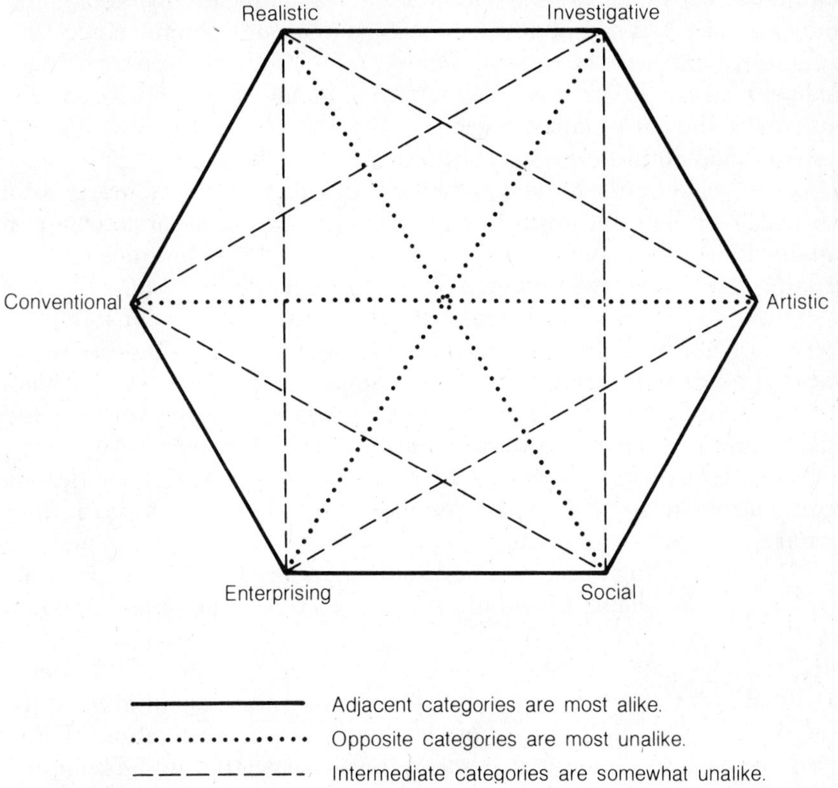
Realistic
Investigative
Conventional
Artistic
Enterprising
Social
Adjacent categories are most alike.
Opposite categories are most unalike.
Intermediate categories are somewhat unalike.

Adapted from Weinrach, S. G. *Career Counseling: Theoretical and Practical Perspectives.* New York: McGraw-Hill, 1979. Reprinted by permission.

particular environment and several occupational alternatives they might consider when making an initial occupational choice, changing jobs, or considering added training. In addition to these two measures, the career development staff uses the Strong-Campbell Vocational Interest Blank (Campbell, D.P., 1977), which provides bank employees with a computer printout of their interests, with appropriate job titles. Employees are also given an aptitude test battery that measures their potential in many areas (e.g., mechanical comprehension, spatial visualization, vocabulary, perceptual speed and accuracy, manual and finger dexterity, administrative, interpersonal).

For managers to become effective career counselors, they must be trained in conducting coaching sessions, establishing challenging work goals, helping employees plan for their next job in the organization, and obtaining and conveying up-to-date occupational information. It is also important that subordinate development be established by the organization as a bona fide aspect of the manager's job. For example, since 1970, General Electric has been successful in motivating its more than 26,000 managers to aid the career development of female and minority employees by linking each manager's compensation to his or her attainment of annual equal employment goals (Purcell, 1974).

In order to better understand career development systems, it is important to explain that even though programs vary from organization to organization, there is a set of common tools and techniques that are usually used in most programs. As listed in Table 6.2, some of these techniques, such as self-assessment tools and individual counseling, are directed toward the employee and are designed to help the individual decide on a career strategy. Other techniques, such as career ladders and replacement/succession planning, focus more on organizational career management activities (Gutteridge, 1986).

Now, let us briefly examine the current practices of three additional organizations to see how they apply some of these techniques in their career development programs.

The first setting is an IBM research laboratory employing about 400 scientists, technicians, and administrative people. A career development workshop, based on an assessment center approach (see Chapter 9) is used to help managers and potential managers discover the challenge involved in interpersonal relations, leadership skills, and administrative complexities, as well as to provide them with an evaluation of their strengths and weaknesses in each of these areas (Hart and Thompson, 1979). Each workshop is limited to six participants and six staff members and requires four days of each participant's time (three days for assessment and one for career planning) and five-and-a-half days for the staff's time. The workshop includes a variety of activities designed to detect the participants' talents (e.g., in-basket exercises, leaderless group problem-solving discussions, psychological tests, personal interviews, peer evaluations).

During the final day, the participants are introduced to several career-planning concepts, given time to contemplate where they are now in their lives and careers, and encouraged to set career goals and test them on their workshop colleagues. Within two weeks of the workshop, each participant receives a comprehensive written report summarizing his or her strengths and weaknesses as judged by the staff, as well as a number of constructive recommendations for improvement. For instance, an individual who displays weak oral communication skills might be encouraged to take a public speaking course and/or join a local Toastmasters Club. Each participant is given complete control over the decision to share the information in the report with his or her manager (about half of the participants choose to share their reports with management). Finally, each participant is encouraged to choose a mentor who will be responsi-

Table 6.2 ORGANIZATIONAL CAREER DEVELOPMENT TECHNIQUES

A. Self-assessment tools
   1. Career-planning workshops
   2. Career workbooks
   3. Preretirement workshops
B. Individual counseling
   1. Personnel staff
   2. Professional counselor (internal or external)
   3. Outplacement
   4. Supervisor or line manager
C. Internal labor market information/placement exchanges
   1. Job posting
   2. Skills inventories
   3. Career ladders/career path planning
   4. Career resource center
   5. Other career communication formats
D. Organizational potential assessment processes
   1. Assessment centers
   2. Promotability forecasts
   3. Replacement/succession planning
   4. Psychological testing
E. Development programs
   1. Job rotation
   2. In-house human resource development programs
   3. External seminars/workshops
   4. Tuition reimbursement/educational assistance
   5. Supervisory training in career counseling
   6. Dual-career programs
   7. Mentoring systems

From T.G. Gutteridge, "Organizational Career Development Systems: The State of the Practice," in D.T. Hall and associates (eds.), *Career Development in Organizations.* San Francisco: Jossey-Bass, 1986.

ble for facilitating follow-through on the career goal setting and planning of the participants. Typically, immediate managers, workshop staff members, or senior members of the research laboratory are asked to serve as mentors.

The National Aeronautics and Space Administration (NASA) has established a Career Development Center (CDC) to help its employees deal with the question, "Where do I go from here?" Most of their employees are specialists and recognized as such, but they are perplexed about what direction to go in order to enhance their careers. Some are locked into dead-end positions and would like the chance to explore other options. To further complicate things, some are confused about what jobs are available and what kinds of skills and knowledge they require. To deal with this need, CDC has established a program called Career Counseling and Work Experience (CCWE), whereby employees are given the opportunity to function in short-term job assignments outside of their normal working area. In this way, they are given a mechanism for testing a new environment before making a career choice. Following is a description of one employee who participated in CCWE:

> This employee was a Grade 13 Mathematician who applied for the work experience entitled "Development of improved computerized configuration change request status reporting system." The tasks performed included reviewing present configuration management systems, comparing their capabilities and making a recommendation for adaptation of a particular system. After completion of the work experience she was reassigned to a new area which makes use of her newly acquired skills and abilities. (Career Development Center, Goddard Space Flight Center)

In addition, CDC employs career specialists who are prepared to examine with employees the experience and education required to move through various career paths. They help the employees integrate these data into a realistic career plan. CDC also provides self-assessment techniques such as interest inventories, values clarification, and skills identification in order to aid the employees in carrying out their plans.

Another example of an approach to career development is used by Disneyland, the well-known entertainment and recreational facility located in Anaheim, California. Disneyland employs, on the average, 4,500 hourly employees and 500 salaried employees. The career development program includes the following services (Gutteridge, 1986):

- Disneyland Intern Program: nonmanagerial employees selected for the program participate in a six-month development program involving weekly classes and on-the-job training. Upon completion of this program, employees are considered ready for promotion into managerial openings.
- Employee Career Counseling: Disneyland employs a full-time professional career counselor who offers counseling services to employees on request.
- Career Planning Workshops: The company offers a series of workshops intended to help employees formulate their career objectives and an individual career plan.
- Career Resource Library: This library includes such things as job descriptions, organizational charts, descriptions of available training programs, reports on occupational trends, and books on career and retirement planning.
- Job Posting: As positions become available, they are posted for all employees to see. This allows the company to fill about 85 percent of its salaried openings through its promotion-from-within policy.
- Skills Inventory: Disneyland has a computerized skills inventory system that contains valuable information (e.g., educational background, previous work experience, desired career interests, relocation preferences) on each employee who has used the services of the career planning department. When a job opening occurs, the skills inventory system generates the names of all employees who

have been recommended by their manager for such positions and/or have expressed an interest in this functional area. These individuals are then interviewed.
- Career Forum: Disneyland schedules monthly forums in which interested employees hear company representatives discuss career opportunities within their area of expertise.

Before ending this topic, we should pinpoint three groups of employees where career development is especially important: employees experiencing "career success/personal failure" (Korman, 1988; Korman and Korman, 1980), employees whose careers have "plateaued" (Ference, Stoner, and Warren, 1977; Hall, 1985), and employees whose "career motivation" has declined (London, 1983; London, 1987; London, 1990; London and Bray, 1984).

Research on career success/personal failure is within the domain of career development, since it pinpoints possible conditions associated with career dissatisfaction and frustration. Korman (1988) states that a key feature of modern society has been an emphasis on career achievement and so-called success. Most of us believe, either explicitly or implicitly, that success will lead to a better life. Yet, sometimes all is not as it should be. Successful people appear to be more satisfied in life than those who are not, but this relationship seems to be increasingly breaking down. Korman found that "career-successful" people are often unhappy with and alienated from others and from themselves. He attributed the emotional depression experienced by many successful people as being due to the fact that the so-called "success" these people have achieved does not meet the expectations they had for a better life (e.g., time for family life, good health, feelings of self-control and self-direction). In fact, many so-called successful people reported that they have *less* of what they had hoped for! One way of preventing this syndrome is to give new employees realistic expectations regarding the personal costs of striving for career success.

Many people are uncomfortable when they find themselves in the middle of their careers and simultaneously in the middle of their organization's hierarchy. They find that they are no longer receiving promotions. Their careers have plateaued. Unless managed correctly, these individuals can resist change and exhibit lowered performance, which can create problems for their organizations. Ways of dealing effectively with these people have been suggested by Bardwick (1986) and London (1990):

1. Exchange individuals laterally between existing jobs for varying time periods.
2. Redesign current jobs so that the new jobs require learning new knowledge and skills.
3. Create temporary work units to solve specific problems.
4. Reward such activities as the mentoring of younger employees and participating in community relations.

5. Use these people as internal consultants in other parts of the organization.

These steps maintain and enhance career motivation (London and Bassman, 1989). *Career motivation* has three principal components: career resilience, career insight, and career identity. Career resilience is the extent to which an individual resists career barriers or disruptions affecting their work. People high in career resilience see themselves as competent people who are able to control what happens to them. Career resilience influences a person's *persistence* in pursuing their career goals. Career insight is how realistic people are about themselves and their careers as well as how well they relate these perceptions to their career goals. They look for feedback about how well they are doing, use this information to set specific career goals, and formulate plans to achieve their goals. Their career insight affects the *degree* to which they pursue their career goals. Career identity is the extent to which people identify and define themselves in terms of their work. Individuals high in career identity are involved in their jobs and careers. Career identity reflects the *direction* of career goals—whether the individual wants to obtain a position of leadership, make a lot of money, have high status or, perhaps, advance in their company (London and Mone, 1987).

How can career development techniques increase an individual's level of career motivation? Although career resilience starts early in life it, nevertheless, can be changed. Supervisors can increase an employee's career resilience by giving them performance feedback, reinforcing them for what they do well, rewarding innovative behavior, and providing training to enhance their skills and knowledge and, thereby, build their self-confidence and desire to achieve.

Career insight can be increased by allowing employees to gain a better understanding of their strengths, weaknesses, and interests. This can be done through self-assessment tools, individual counseling, assessment centers, and psychological testing (see Table 6.2).

Career identity can be increased by giving employees an understanding of the rewards derived from alternative career pursuits. This can be accomplished through job rotation, external seminars/workshops, a career resource center, or other career communication formats (see Table 6.2). Organizations such as IBM, Xerox, and Polaroid offer their employees time off, with pay, to get involved in such things as community action projects, research projects, and government programs (London and Bassman, 1989).

FINAL COMMENTS

There is a lack of formal evaluation studies in the professional literature concerning on-site training techniques. First, most of what is called evaluation is based on logical analysis and common sense. Training directors and their staffs are almost expected to take on faith the effectiveness of such techniques as OJT, apprenticeship training, and job rotation. Probably because these techniques are so closely linked to the job, there has been little empirical evaluation of their value with regard to improving employee learning, behavior, and results.

Second, very little is known at the present time about the factors that will ensure that our orientation, OJT, apprenticeship, job aids, coaching, mentoring, computer-based training, job rotation, or career development efforts will be successful. We need to know more about the proper design of these kinds of programs.

Third, although learning researchers have been at work for decades, there is not yet any science-based guide to tell us how to make accurate decisions about what training technique or combination of techniques to use in a particular organizational situation. Psychological research has provided a start in this direction. We do know, for example, that OJT can be an excellent method for teaching job-related skills because it allows for active practice, immediate feedback, positive transfer of learning, and so on. Until more evaluative research is conducted, however, Figure 6.1 should serve as a guide to the selection of on-site instructional techniques.

Finally, we feel that there is more potential in on-site training approaches than anywhere else in the training and development area. If more of an effort was made by managers and supervisors to develop their employees correctly on the job, organizations would not need to spend so much money on many of the off-site approaches we discuss in the next few chapters.

Chapter 7

Off-Site Training Methods

In the previous chapter, we discussed on-site training methods that are frequently used in organizational settings. In this chapter, we review off-site training approaches. An obvious advantage of off-site training is that it allows the trainee to acquire skills and knowledge away from the day-to-day job pressures in settings such as company-operated training centers, hotels, conference centers, university/college facilities, or resorts (Zemke, 1986a). For instance, the building mechanic, assembly line worker, chemical plant operator, and senior vice president can each learn their jobs without worrying about a boiler explosion, the stoppage of an entire assembly line, the faulty generation of toxic gases, or the continual ringing of the telephone.

Another benefit of off-site training is the use of competent outside resource people who are trained trainers. Such people may include technicians, university faculty, and consultants. Trainees are thus exposed to individuals who not only have expertise in subject-matter areas, but who also are expert teachers. For instance, one manufacturer of conventional and nuclear boilers periodically sends its design engineers to special conferences held in hotels in New York City and Chicago. At these meetings, lectures are given by well known power plant design engineers to familiarize conferees with the newest developments in fossil-generated power boiler design.

A potential limitation of off-site training can be the transfer of learning from the "classroom" to the job. Too often, trainees learn new facts and principles at lectures and special conferences with no idea about how to apply what they learn on the job. As you will see in this chapter, highly effective off-site procedures include those which simulate essential characteristics of the actual job, so that trainees learn to behave during training the way they will have to behave on the job.

In discussing off-site training methods, we again refer you back to the nine-cell framework (three goals x three strategies) presented originally in Figure 1.1. Specifically, seven off-site methods are presented in this chapter: lecture, audiovisual techniques, teleconferencing, corporate classrooms, programmed instruction, computer-assisted instruction, and equipment simulators. Figure 7.1 shows these seven methods classified by their particular goals (i.e., self-awareness, job skills, motivation) and strategies (i.e., cognitive, behavioral, environmental). All of the off-site techniques we discuss attempt to improve trainee skills. These skills may involve effective interviewing, active listening, more tactful handling of customer complaints, or the proper operation of machinery. Many of these skills are relevant to managerial as well as nonmanagerial employees. The strategy used for teaching these skills varies depending on the particular technique chosen.

Lectures, audiovisual techniques, teleconferencing, and corporate classrooms attempt to train employees by focusing primarily on their cognitions (i.e., thoughts and ideas). For instance, trainees may be informed about special features of products to be sold, safety procedures to be followed, more efficient ways to manage their time, or revised quality control standards. Even though lectures and audiovisuals can be equally useful in on-site situations, they are usually conducted in classrooms away from the workplace. Therefore, they are discussed here. Although equipment simulators also involve the presentation of cognitive information, they have been classified as a behavioral strategy because trainees are given considerable opportunity to practice their newly acquired behaviors in simulated, off-the-job settings.

The proper placement of programmed instruction (PI) and computer-assisted instruction (CAI) in Figure 7.1 is arguable in that they can be viewed as using either a cognitive or a behavioral strategy depending on

Figure 7.1 Off-site methods classified according to goals and strategies

STRATEGIES \ GOALS	Self-Awareness	Job Skills	Motivation
Cognitive		Lecture Audiovisual techniques Programmed instruction Teleconferencing Corporate classrooms	
Behavioral		Computer-assisted instruction Equipment simulators	
Environmental			

what is being taught. If trainees are learning to operate or repair a piece of machinery via PI or CAI, then the strategy is clearly a behavioral one. If, on the other hand, trainees are learning about life insurance premiums and mortality rates using PI or CAI, then a cognitive strategy is being used. Since most PI and CAI training programs in industry involve cognitive and behavioral interventions, respectively, we categorize them in this manner in Figure 7.1.

LECTURE

A most innovative use of the lecture method was once used in Adelphi University's Classroom on Wheels program. On the average, commuters spend the equivalent of over 400 hours a year commuting in New York City. Adelphi decided to take advantage of these captive hours by offering commuters a two-year MBA program on the Long Island Railroad! Classroom cars were equipped with a lectern, a chalkboard, and a microphone. Lecture classes were scheduled to run for one hour unless, of course, the train was delayed for some reason. In such cases, classes were extended by increasing class discussions and using additional practical illustrations (Edson, 1979).

Despite such innovative uses, the lecture method has been frequently criticized as a training and development technique (e.g., Bass and Vaughn, 1966; Korman, 1977). First, its format emphasizes a one-way flow of communication from trainer to trainee. The learner is a passive participant in the learning process. Second, the lecture is felt to be deficient for teaching job-related skills that can be transferred from the learning situation to the actual work situation. What can be transferred from the lecture to the job must almost always be limited to cognitive principles, rules, and factual information. Third, the method's stress on verbal and symbolic understanding is not always appropriate for teaching individuals from culturally impoverished backgrounds because they frequently lack the educational tools necessary to grasp what is being taught in the lecture.

Fourth, the lecture ignores differences among trainees' abilities, interests, backgrounds, and personalities. Since it proceeds at a single rate, the slow learner is forced to keep pace or fall behind while simultaneously the fast learner is being held back. In addition, the method often prevents individualized feedback and reinforcement to trainees.

A survey was conducted with 200 training directors who worked for organizations with the largest number of employees, as indicated on *Fortune*'s list of 500 top corporations (Carroll, Paine, and Ivancevich, 1972). The purpose was to determine how these training directors rated the relative effectiveness of nine different training techniques for achieving six training objectives using the following scale: highly effective (5), quite effective (4), moderately effective (3), limited effectiveness (2), and not effective (1).

The training methods evaluated by the training directors were programmed instruction, case study, lecture method (with questions), conference or discussion method, role playing, sensitivity training (T-group), TV lecture (lecture given to large audiences via TV), movie films, and business gaming (using computer or hand calculator).

The training objectives used in the survey were knowledge acquisition, changing attitudes, problem-solving skills, interpersonal skills, participant acceptance, and knowledge retention. Table 7.1 summarizes the major results of this study, indicating the mean effectiveness rating for each training method with each objective, as well as the relative ranking of the nine training methods for each of the training objectives.

Inspection of the means and mean rankings clearly indicates that the lecture (with questions) was very poorly regarded by this sample of training directors. This negativism toward the lecture method, however, may not be completely warranted. In general, the evidence shows that the lecture is more effective for knowledge acquisition and participant acceptance than training directors believe (Carroll et al., 1972). Specifically, when the basic instructional task involves the dissemination of information, the lecture method is as good as instructional methods such as programmed instruction, TV courses, and group discussions (Nash, Muczyk, and Vettori, 1971; Schramm, 1962; Stovall, 1958). Its effectiveness is maximized when it is augmented by other training techniques that provide for learner participation and individualized feedback and reinforcement. For example, a one-day Effective Listening Program for salespeople, secretaries, and office staff might combine lectures on such topics as factors facilitating and impeding listening with audiotaped listening exercises.

A lecture can also be particularly beneficial when it introduces some new area of content (e.g., the special features of some new product to be sold), provides oral directions for learning a task that will eventually be developed through other instructional methods (e.g., the procedures for operating a machine), employs highly skilled lecturers, and when the training materials are neither too abstract nor too complex for the trainees involved (Verner and Dickinson, 1967). In fact, Burke and Day (1986) integrated the findings from 70 different managerial training research studies by using a sophisticated statistical technique known as meta-analysis. They examined the effectiveness of seven different training methods, three of which involved some lecturing: the lecture, lecture plus group discussion, and lecture plus group discussion plus role playing or practice. They found that each of these three lecturing approaches was surprisingly effective in improving on-the-job behavior as perceived by the trainees themselves, peers, and supervisors. Furthermore, these findings indicated that training that employs the lecture method is likely to generalize across situations.

Table 7.1 RATINGS OF TRAINING DIRECTORS ON EFFECTIVENESS OF ALTERNATIVE METHODS FOR VARIOUS TRAINING OBJECTIVES

Training Method	Knowledge acquisition		Changing attitudes		Problem-solving skills		Interpersonal skills		Participant acceptance		Knowledge retention	
	Mean	Mean Rank	Mean	Mean Rank	Mean	Mean Rank	Mean	Mean Rank	Mean	Mean Rank	Mean	Mean Rank
Case study	3.56	2	3.43	4	3.69	1	3.02	4	3.80	2	3.48	2
Conference (discussion) method	3.33	3	3.54	3	3.26	4	3.21	3	4.16	1	3.32	5
Lecture (with questions)	2.53	9	2.20	8	2.00	9	1.90	8	2.74	8	2.49	8
Business games	3.00	6	2.73	5	3.58	2	2.50	5	3.78	3	3.26	6
Movie films	3.16	4	2.50	6	2.24	7	2.19	6	3.44	5	2.67	7
Programmed instruction	4.03	1	2.22	7	2.56	6	2.11	7	3.28	7	3.74	1
Role playing	2.93	7	3.56	2	3.27	3	3.68	2	3.56	4	3.37	3
Sensitivity training (T- group)	2.77	8	3.96	1	2.98	5	3.95	1	3.33	6	3.44	9
Television lecture	3.10	5	1.99	9	2.01	8	1.81	9	2.74	9	2.47	

From Carroll, S. J., Paine, F. T., and Ivancevich, M. M. "The Relative Effectiveness of Training Methods: Expert Opinion and Research," *Personnel Psychology*, 25, (1972), pp. 495–509. Reprinted by permission.

On the other hand, the research evidence clearly indicates that the lecture is not as appropriate as role playing or the case study method (see Chapter 9) for modifying attitudes, developing problem-solving skills, or improving interpersonal competence (Carroll et al., 1972). Furthermore, comparisons of the lecture and the conference discussion methods (see Chapter 9) for behavior change consistently favor the discussion approach (Levine and Butler, 1952; Lewin, 1958). Finally, it would not make sense to expect the lecture to promote skill development as effectively as techniques that provide the trainee with an opportunity for active participation, knowledge of results, and practice. For instance, we would obviously want to train new sewing machine operators using on-the-job training or equipment simulators, rather than merely lecturing to them about the correct procedures to be followed.

In summary, the training objectives determine whether the lecture is an appropriate training technique. If the primary goal is to convey information, the lecture approach is an effective and economical method for training large groups of trainees. The lecture method is quite useful for orienting new employees, giving realistic job previews (see Chapter 6), summarizing material developed by another training technique, and reducing trainee anxiety about upcoming training programs and job changes.

With the rapid increase in the size of organizations and the continual technological changes affecting them, the live lecture may not be adequate to handle the number of people requiring training and retraining. New methods are needed to increase the efficiency of instruction and to accelerate the learning process. In an attempt to deal with this problem, many organizations (e.g., Boeing Company, AT&T) have begun to use audiovisual techniques such as films, closed-circuit television, audiotapes, and videotape recording. These methods allow an instructor's message to be given in a uniform manner to several organizational locations at one time and to be reused as often as needed.

AUDIOVISUAL TECHNIQUES

Audiovisuals can be used in almost any training and development situation, ranging from orienting new employees to upgrading present ones. For example, Harvard University's Graduate School of Business has been conducting experiments to discover whether MBA students learn more if case studies are presented on film rather than read (Zemke, 1986b). Other Harvard experiments include the use of films to simulate pressures on students engaged in in-basket exercises. In addition to the usual written papers, letters, and memoranda found in a typical in-basket, trainees are expected to deal with various distractions that typically exist in busy offices.

At Weyerhaeuser Company, portions of entertainment films such as

Bridge on the River Kwai and *Twelve O'Clock High* have been used as a basis for discussing interpersonal and social relationships in the organization's management school. These films were chosen because they convey particular messages about effective ways of managing and handling other people (Rigg, 1969).

The Ford Motor Company has used a film technique in automobile dealer training sessions in order to simulate problems and reactions a dealer might face in handling various customer complaints. The technique involves filming the action as seen through the eyes of the central character in the role-playing situation, in this case the dealer, who is played by the trainee (Rigg, 1969).

The federal government has used closed-circuit TV instruction in a number of fields, such as secretarial practices and income-tax law. In one of their studies, a TV course for secretaries entitled "From Nine to Five" led to a 59 percent reduction in the need for training as judged by supervisors' evaluations. This training program was especially relevant for entry-level secretaries, since it emphasized basic secretarial practices (Goldstein, 1986).

Films and videotapes have also been used successfully for improving employment interviewing skills. The camera captures the responses of either a real or simulated applicant, as seen through the interviewer's eyes (Latham, Wexley, and Pursell, 1975; Wexley, Sanders, and Yukl, 1973). The training helps participants eliminate judgmental errors (e.g., first impressions, stereotyping, leniency) which often result in poor hiring and appraisal decisions.

Videotapes are used extensively at AT&T's Building Technical Training Center for training Bell System building mechanics. Among the many topics presented on videotape are starting up and shutting down steam boilers, using common hand tools, soldering and brazing, keeping boiler logs, and maintaining traps, strainers, and air vents.

One of the more interesting uses of videotape today is in communications training. Numerous companies are sending their salespeople, junior executives, and chief executive officers to communication specialists with the hope that they will return as more confident, relaxed, and articulate speakers. By using videotape, trainees see themselves as others see them. They can pinpoint what they like and dislike about the way they speak far better than any trainer can tell them. People who think that they are dramatic speakers may learn that they are too soft-spoken and somewhat boring. Others who consider themselves powerful speakers may realize that they are really loud and boisterous. Most trainees react to their videotaped image with the same "do I really come off like that?" incredulity that they experience after hearing their recorded voice for the first time (Gibbons, 1980). The videotapes not only give the trainees excellent feedback, but also help them become aware of their training needs.

An additional use of videotapes has enjoyed widespread popularity in recent years. They are used as an integral part of behavior-modeling training (see Chapter 4). Numerous organizations are now using behavior-modeling videotapes to teach their managers, supervisors, and employees how to improve their interactive skills. Sometimes these videos are developed by the company's own training department or by outside consultants who specialize in the construction of video-based training materials. For example, we have used videos focusing on such skills as orienting a new employee, delegating responsibility, terminating an employee, reducing tardiness, handling grievances, utilizing effective disciplinary action, and handling a suspected substance abuse problem.

There is substantial evidence that the amount of knowledge gained through audiovisual devices such as TV, videotape, and film is as good as that acquired through conventional live lectures (Chu and Schramm, 1967; Schramm, 1962). In fact, in well over 80 percent of the comparisons, the audiovisual approach was found to be as good or better than the conventional live lecture approach.

Audiovisual techniques offer unique advantages over conventional lectures and therefore should be seriously considered in the following situations:

1. When there is a need to illustrate how certain procedures should be followed over time. For instance, demonstrations of wire soldering, telephone repair, and welding can be facilitated with the use of TV or films. Stop action, instant replay, fast or slow motion, close-ups of equipment and manual techniques, and use of arrows to point out fine details are just a few options that are not available in live lectures.

2. When there is a need to expose trainees to events not easily demonstrable in live lectures (e.g., a visual tour of a factory, open heart surgery, childbirth). In training building mechanics, for instance, trainees can be shown a boiler gauge and a valve simultaneously by superimposing them both on videotape. The trainees can clearly see that as the gauge increases, steam begins to seep from the valve.

3. When the training is going to be used organization-wide and it is far too costly to ask the same trainers to travel from place to place or assemble everyone in one location. Instead, copies of the audiovisuals are mailed to all organizational units at one time and administered by local training staff members.

4. When audiovisual training is supplemented with live lectures or discussions before and after the session. Discussions and lectures cue the trainees as to what should be learned from the session. Summaries of the important points after the session let trainees know what is important to remember (Bass and Vaughn, 1966).

Miller (1957) integrated the findings from audiovisual research into a theory of learning. He hypothesized four fundamental factors in training and learning: (1) drive (motivation)—the trainee must want to learn something; (2) cue (stimulus)—the trainee must notice something;

(3) response (participation)—the trainee must do something; and (4) reward (reinforcement)—the trainee must obtain something she or he wants.

Well-developed audiovisuals can arouse strong drive-producing responses, especially when effective instructors are employed. Audiovisuals also cue or attract trainees' attention by using their unique features like instant replay, slow motion, animated cartoons, time-lapse photography, and close-ups. As for response, Miller argued for the necessity of following audiovisuals with such training techniques as group discussions and role-playing exercises. Finally, concerning reward, he advocated giving tests immediately after the audiovisual, and of providing immediate knowledge of test results to trainees.

In the next section, we discuss a particular audiovisual technique that has been used by a few universities and associations since the 1960s, but has only recently been rediscovered by the business community. It is commonly referred to as teleconferencing. It is a $150-million-a-year business and has an annual growth rate of 30 percent (Zemke, 1986b).

TELECONFERENCING

Video teleconferencing is a method for simultaneously training individuals at multiple sites. A teleconferencing network consists of a central broadcasting facility (e.g., at a TV studio, hotel, corporate office, convention center), a satellite service whose signal is delivered to satellite-receiving stations which, in turn, transmit the signal to television projectors in either hotel ballrooms, meeting rooms, convention centers, civic auditoriums, or corporate headquarters. Figure 7.1 shows that teleconferencing trains job skills by using a cognitive strategy.

Let us take a look at some actual examples of its training uses (Zemke, 1986b):

- Allstate Insurance Company links its headquarters in Barrington, Illinois, with its 28 regional offices throughout the company. The company contends that any material that can be presented in a classroom setting is appropriate for their two-way video, two-way audio, 24-hour teleconferencing system. If a trainer wants to pass out some instructional materials to the trainees, she puts it into a facsimile terminal, presses a button, and it shows up in the teleconferencing rooms. If the trainer wants to show an object to the trainees, she puts it on a graphics table and it is projected on the screen. If trainees have questions, they press a button on a console in the room, their questions cue up in order of calls, and the trainer can answer them.
- ComputerLand's major reason for using teleconferencing is that the store managers have a difficult time freeing their technical people

to go to the Los Angeles or Boca Raton development centers for training on servicing new equipment. It is quicker and easier to use teleconferencing.

- Chase Manhattan Bank linked 2500 of its employees in eight countries for a live interactive discussion of the bank's future global strategy.
- Hewlett-Packard Company used teleconferencing to introduce a new business computer to most of its 84,000 employees all at once in 86 North American and 18 European offices.

The costs of airtime and equipment have fallen as much as 70 percent since 1982 and are continuing to drop. For instance, a coast-to-coast video link that would have cost $2000 in 1982 would probably cost less than $700 today. Even so, there are many companies that do not want to build their own facilities. Instead, they can rent facilities from hotel chains such as Holiday Inn, Inc., and Hilton Hotel Corporation (Zemke, 1986b). When should an organization seriously consider either buying or renting a video teleconferencing network? According to Zemke (1986b), a system is worth thinking about when (1) the employees need to receive training immediately, (2) the company does not have enough trainers to do the job, (3) the company does not have sufficient facilities to accommodate all the trainees, or (4) the company does not want to spend a large amount of money bringing people together.

CORPORATE CLASSROOMS

According to a special report issued by the Carnegie Foundation (Eurich, 1985), more and more large corporations have begun to build their own colleges and universities dedicated to the continuing education of their employees. It is estimated that about 400 business sites currently have one or more buildings or else a corporate campus labeled "college, university, institute, or learning center." The goal of corporate classrooms is to teach employees job skills, and to accomplish this by using a cognitive strategy (see Figure 7.1).

These corporate campuses have features similar to traditional college campuses (e.g., classrooms, libraries, laboratories, residence halls). Moreover, these corporate learning centers are modern in that they use the most up-to-date instructional technology (e.g., teleconferencing).

The ambience is very different from the typical collegiate setting because the students are older and hold full-time jobs in the company. The courses are company-oriented, practical, with a time length that varies from a few days to a year depending on the concepts being taught. Despite the use of modern audiovisual equipment and computer technology, the training technique includes live lectures and discussion as well as seminars for small groups.

Among the best-known corporate campuses are Holiday Inn University in Olive Branch, Mississippi; McDonald's Hamburger University in Oak Brook, Illinois; Xerox's Learning Center in Leesburg, Virginia; ARCO's campus in Santa Barbara, California, for top executives; Sun Institute's Learning Center near its corporate headquarters in Radnor, Pennsylvania; and Western Electric's Corporate Education Center in Princeton, New Jersey. According to Eurich (1985), corporations are spending more than $40 billion to educate nearly 8 million employees each year. This cost figure approaches the total annual expenditures of all of the four-year and graduate colleges and universities in the United States!

In order to better understand this off-site training method, let us look at Hamburger University (S.S. Anderson, 1981; Heneman, Schwab, Fossum, and Dyer, 1986). It was originated in 1961 by Ray Kroc, founder of the McDonald's chain of fast-food restaurants. It is used to teach a wide range of subjects to the company's managers and franchise owners. Specifically, it offers 18 courses of study (e.g., market evaluation, advanced operations, employee motivation) ranging in length from one day to two weeks. Besides skills training, students learn about the company's espoused values, namely, quality, service, cleanliness, value, pride, and loyalty. Students learn in a modern three-story building equipped with large classrooms, several small laboratories equipped with actual equipment found in the restaurants, closed-circuit television, and a recording studio.

PROGRAMMED INSTRUCTION

Immediate knowledge of results is one of the major characteristics of a training approach known as *programmed instruction*. In the mid-1960s, great promises were made about the benefits of programmed instruction (PI), or programmed learning as it is sometimes called. It was perceived by many authorities as a major advance in educational methodology for overcoming the motivational frustrations which trainees have experienced when attending organization-sponsored training activities.

Programmed learning is a self-instructional method consisting of the following features:

1. *Objectives:* The process of developing the program involves several critical steps. Programmers must first study the characteristics of the group of trainees for whom the program is intended (i.e., their interests and abilities), as well as their job environments (i.e., whether or not it is conducive to the application of skills to be taught by the program). The next step is a careful analysis of the subject matter or job for which training is to be done in order to identify its elements. When this has been done, programmers

develop clearly defined instructional goals or learning objectives. That is, they must specify what it is they want the trainees to know or do differently after the training is completed. In addition, they specify what will be regarded as acceptable standards of performance. Based on these objectives, programmers must decide on the type of programming (e.g., simple or complex) and the mode of presentation (e.g., programmed textbooks, cassette video playback units, audiotape cassette, rear-screen projectors) to be used.

2. *Own Pace:* Most of us are familiar with the problem of the slow learner who needs to have things explained several times while others sail ahead. Programmed instruction takes into account individual differences in learning ability by allowing each trainee to proceed at her or his own pace.
3. *Logical Sequence:* The training material is broken into discrete steps, or *frames*. Each frame typically consists of information followed by a question requiring a response on the part of the trainee. The frames are carefully ordered in a logical sequence called a *program*. Trainees grasp the subject matter as they are led gradually by reasonable-sized steps through some logical order.
4. *Active Responding:* At the end of each frame, the trainee is asked to make some response that measures comprehension of the material in that frame. The trainee may be asked to solve a problem, operate a piece of machinery, or interpret a blueprint. Rather than sitting passively as in a lecture, the trainee is called upon to do something.
5. *Knowledge of Results:* Trainees receive information immediately on whether their response was correct (see diagram).

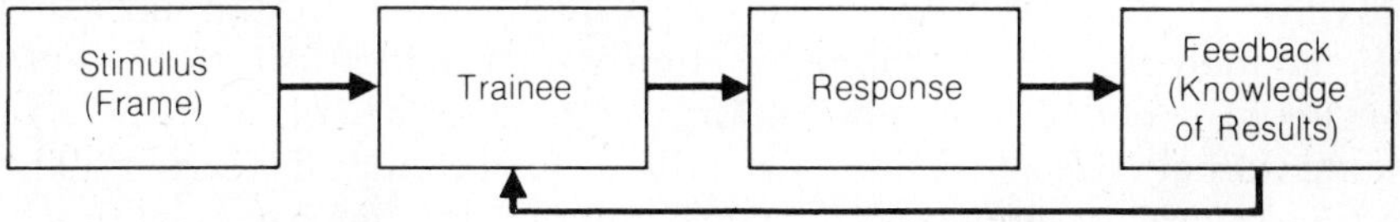

If the correct response is made, the trainee is allowed to proceed to the next frame. If the response is incorrect, the trainee's progress through the program is delayed until the desired behavior is emitted. The object of PI is to maximize the trainees' motivation to learn. This is done in large part by providing feedback that is not only immediate but also primarily positive in nature. Because the program is structured in terms of a logical sequence, the trainees exhibit mostly correct responses.

Several varieties of PI methods that have been used in organizational settings include teaching machines and programmed textbooks. Our example, presented in Figure 7.2, comes from a supervisory course designed to teach management principles such as planning, organizing, controlling, and supervision.

Programmed learning is currently used in organizational settings for a variety of training purposes such as sales training, machine operator training, and safety training. For example, the Life Insurance Marketing and Research Association (LIMRA) has provided self-instructional programs for new life insurance agents of their member companies. One program, Steps into Life Insurance, uses a set of four programmed texts to instruct new agents in insurance fundamentals including the functions and purposes of life insurance; the establishment of rates, mortality tables, and premiums; reserves, cash surrender values, and nonforfeiture options; types of policies; annuities; and legal and ethical situations. *Steps in Prospecting*, consisting of three texts, is designed to give new agents a realistic picture of prospecting and to develop the knowledge and skills necessary for sales success. It covers such areas as obtaining referred leads, using published sources for prospects, qualifying prospects, telephone and personal approaches, preapproach, direct mailings, scheduling, and record keeping.

Another example involves a gift shop retail chain that uses programmed instruction to train their Christmas rush sales force. The training uses self-paced texts and includes diagnostic pretests that allow sales trainees to skip any parts of the program that they already know, since many of them return from year to year. The program consists of the following topics: customer relations, accident prevention, store security, sales slips, check cashing, handling mail, handling refunds, operating cash registers, coding merchandise, merchandise display, breakage, deliveries, and stock storage. As a result, the retail chain has 98 percent of their trainees on the floor and selling within six hours.

Entry-level packers in a disposable diaper plant are trained using programmed instruction in conjunction with machine practice. These packers inspect diapers coming off a large rotating wheel, stuff stacks of them into poly bags, and then place the bags into shipping cartons. The packer training program includes many guides on proper manual procedures, safety precautions, housekeeping, quality control standards, unjamming procedures, and the packer's role in relationship to machine operators. These guides are then used by the packers during one week of practice on the packing machine, closely monitored by their supervisor and three fellow packers.

What can generally be concluded about the effectiveness of PI? The results of over 100 studies using PI in industrial and academic situations suggest that the major advantage of PI is that it almost always decreases the amount of time required for training. Specifically, it appears that trainees can be taught about the same amount of information as other methods in about one-third the time. However, contrary to the claims of its proponents, PI does not seem to improve the acquisition of knowledge

Figure 7.2 Example of programmed materials

1. The principle of *coordination* states that every job must have clearly identified, official channels of communication. These official channels of communication are shown graphically on an organization chart by the lines between positions.

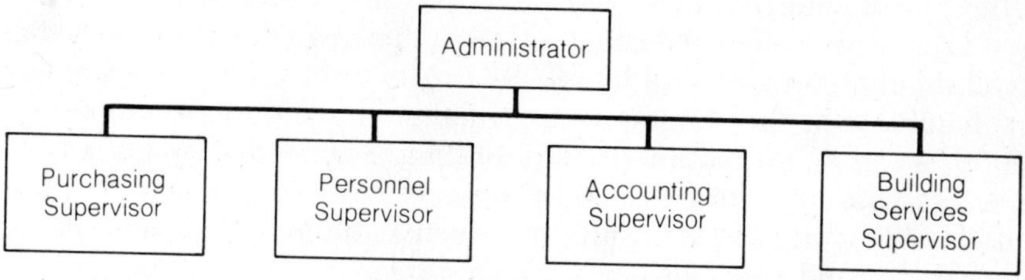

On the chart above, with whom can the accounting supervisor officially communicate? ______

Answer:
Administrator

2. When the accounting supervisor directs communication to the administrator, in what direction is the communication flowing? ______

Answer:
Up or upward

3. With whom can the administrator officially communicate? ______

Answer:
Purchasing supervisor
Personnel supervisor
Accounting supervisor
Building services supervisor

4. Can the four supervisors officially communicate directly with each other through the organization? ______

Answer:
No

5. From the list below, select those communications which are official.
   a. ____ Accounting supervisor asks the purchasing supervisor to close his department 15 minutes early.
   b. ____ Administrator asks all supervisors to turn in their time reports on Thursday.
   c. ____ Purchasing supervisor requests the administrator to have the building service department employees assist in the annual inventory.
   d. ____ Building services supervisor fires a purchasing department employee for being late.

Answer:
b and c

Adapted from "Multimedia In-House Training Program." Supervisory Management Course: Management Principles. *American Management Association,* 1974. Reprinted by permission.

or its retention over time as compared to conventional lecture methods (Nash, Muczyk, and Vettori, 1971).

This latter conclusion misses a fundamental point, namely, the precision of programmed instruction (Latham, 1989). The trainer is required to specify the stimulus, the desired response, the immediate outcome that will be presented to reinforce this response, as well as the schedule and method for administering it. This level of specification not only lends itself to measurement and evaluation, but it increases the probability that a well-thought-out plan will be effective. Measurement provides objective feedback to the trainer about whether the training intervention should be continued, modified, or discontinued. Objective feedback is far superior to the subjective reaction of trainees and upper management. It is the latter which often results in effective training programs being discontinued and new fads being adopted.

The crucial question for any organization contemplating the use of PI is whether the benefits derived from reduced training time exceed the costs involved in developing and implementing programmed learning. This return-on-investment will depend on such factors as the number of people to be trained, the type of PI installation proposed, the cost and effectiveness of alternative training strategies, and the probable organizational outcomes that will be derived from the improved performance of the trainees upon completion of the training.

COMPUTER-ASSISTED INSTRUCTION

One of the newer developments in programmed instruction methodology is computer-assisted learning (CAI). Unlike computer-based training (CBT) that we discussed in Chapter 6, CAI is classified as an off-site training approach because it is often used as a supplement to conventional instruction. Trainees typically interact directly with the computer at a training facility located away from their office. The training is often combined with learners' exercise manuals, equipment simulators, job aids, live instruction, and/or hands-on practice (Schleger, 1984; Thomas and Thomas, 1984). The computer's role in such a training system typically involves administering the training program to the trainees and possibly testing their performance after learning (Patrick and Stammers, 1977). The computer is capable of assessing the trainee's progress continuously and adapting the method and/or material presented to fit the trainee's particular needs, by virtue of its storage and memory capabilities (Goldstein, 1986; Parsons, 1986). Looking across various surveys conducted on using computers in some way in employee training programs, we find that somewhere between 23 to 42 percent of organizations with 50 or more employees have discovered this training technique (Gordon, 1985b; Kearsley and Hillelsohn, 1984; Schaaf, 1987).

Recently, there has been increasing use of computer-assisted instruction in occupational settings for teaching administrative tasks, technical information, perceptual motor tasks, and problem diagnosis. Let us examine a few examples of CAI applications in organizational settings. When British Airways transferred their worldwide reservation system to a computer-based system using visual terminal displays, they needed to train their reservation agents in new procedures. A training program using the system itself was developed that put the trainees through a series of exercises (e.g., cancellations, reservation changes, ticket transfers), depending on each trainee's unique learning capability. In addition, it provided each trainee with prompt knowledge of results. The airline found that using CAI resulted in substantial savings in both training time and speed of customer reservations (Patrick and Stammers, 1977).

IBM Corporation has trained their newly hired electronic technicians in basic data-processing principles using a keyboard-operated terminal device linked remotely to an IBM 1040 computer system. The course deals with data-processing concepts, primary storage and data coding, magnetic tape, stored programs and data flow, logic operations, and console and systems checking. Since time can be directly translatable into economic factors, IBM felt that any savings in time would be significant. They found that CAI resulted in a 10 percent reduction in training time, compared with the programmed texts that had been their standard method for presenting this subject matter. CAI took approximately 22 hours of instruction, compared with 25 hours for the PI technique. This difference was both statistically and financially significant, considering the large number of technicians trained annually by IBM.

The city of Dallas has put CAI to excellent use. It started a program offered through El Centro College called Computer Programmer Training for the Physically Handicapped (CPTPC). The aim is to help disabled people learn programming skills as a way to achieve a fulfilling career. Some of the graduates of CPTPC have been given the opportunity to live independently; for others it has provided the chance to rebuild their lives crushed by a disabling accident; and for others, the opportunity to enter the work force for the first time (West, 1987).

Adaptive training can be considered a form of computer-assisted instruction. The term has come to refer specifically to the automatic adjustment of the stimuli, problems, or tasks presented to a trainee in response to the trainee's performance. Specifically, the system is sufficiently flexible so that the trainee is receiving stimuli commensurate with his or her current level of ability. Thus the trainee is required to handle more and more tasks simultaneously as a function of his or her immediately preceding performance. New and different tasks are introduced as former tasks are learned (Willigies, Roscoe, and Willigies, 1973).

Adaptive training has three basic elements: (1) Trainee performance is continuously measured, (2) the problem or task can be changed in difficulty for the trainee (i.e., the adaptive variable), and (3) the adaptive logic automatically changes the adaptive variable as a function of the trainee's performance (Kelley, 1969). This approach can best be thought of as a closed-loop system, with a feedback loop, so that the problem can be varied in relation to how well the trainee is currently performing (see Figure 7.3).

The major use of adaptive training has been in the area of motor skills training. It was noted anecdotally several years ago that much of a trainee's early training time while learning to fly a helicopter is spent waiting for the instructor to bring the helicopter back under control after the trainee's turn. It was reasoned that this training time would be better spent if the stability of the aircraft could be changed adaptively to adjust to the current level of expertise of the trainee. This should, hopefully, reduce training time and the risk of losing control of the helicopter (Hudson, 1962). Thus the first formal application of automatically adaptive logic was in the training of helicopter pilots by the U.S. Army's Naval Training Device Center. In their Synthetic Flight Training System (SFTS), one central digital computer operates four cockpit simulators in which pilots learn to fly simultaneously under the direction of only one instructor. The difficulty of certain flight tasks can be adapted to each of the four trainees' continuously monitored performance (Willigies and Willigies, 1978).

The results of research thus far suggest that CAI requires less time to learn the same amount of information than more conventional training methods (Goldstein, 1986). Studies also indicate that trainee reaction to CAI is largely positive. The benefits derived from computer-assisted learning must, however, be weighed against its relatively high costs. For example, if the cost of development and use of the computer for training is high while the relative effectiveness is marginal, then the computer should not be used in the instructional process. However, if the computer poses a unique solution to an important problem in the training process and the cost of using it is reasonable, then by all means it should be used (Seltzer, 1971).

Figure 7.3 Adaptive training

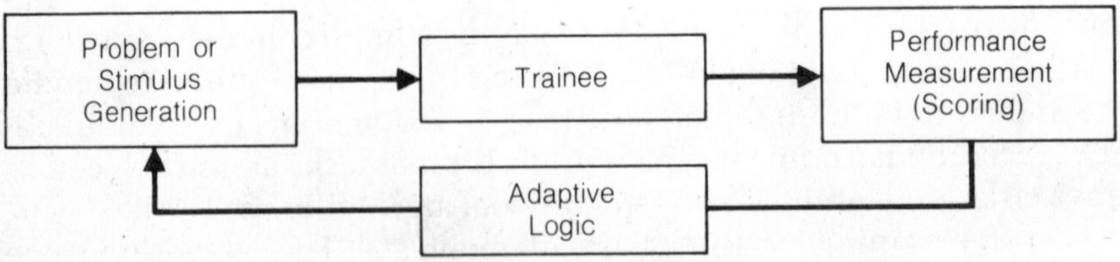

From Kelley, C. R., *Human Factors*, 1969, *11*, pp. 547–556. Reprinted by permission.

EQUIPMENT SIMULATORS

Simulation is an excellent way to bring realism to off-site training situations. For some jobs (e.g., pilot and machine operator) it is either too costly, inefficient, or dangerous to train workers on the equipment used to perform the job. In these cases, facsimiles or simulators of the equipment are designed and set up away from the actual work situation. Here, safety hazards are removed, time pressures for productivity are minimized, individualized feedback is increased, and opportunities for repeated practice are provided.

Simulators can be used in many different training situations. They have generally been designed to represent tasks within the following categories:

1. *Procedures.* In this category are the simulators designed primarily to represent such things as cockpit procedures for pilots, as well as procedures for adjusting and calibrating complex electronic equipment.
2. *Motor skills.* A simulator may be used for teaching a motor skill such as climbing telephone poles, operating presses and lathes, and driving a truck.
3. *Conceptual tasks.* Activities requiring conceptual reasoning may be represented in simulators for equipment trouble-shooting, aerial photo interpretation, and navigation.
4. *Identifications.* Simulators may represent such activities as the identification of safety hazards, terrain features, and radar signals.
5. *Team functions.* Some complex simulators emphasize the coordination of effort among team members toward the achievement of a common goal (e.g., air defense system crews, missile launch teams, air traffic control tower operators, and astronauts).

In designing simulators, it is important to maximize positive transfer of learning from the simulator to the actual work situation. This is accomplished by making certain that the simulator possesses both physical fidelity (representation of the essential physical components of the job) and, more importantly, psychological fidelity (representation of the essential behavioral and cognitive processes necessary to do the job).

Among the important responsibilities of the simulator designer is the careful analysis of the tasks involved in the job and the decision concerning which tasks should be simulated. This decision will depend on the purpose of the simulator. Certain tasks will be omitted since the interactions between person and machine or between person and environment is relatively unimportant to the training objectives.

A survey shows the large impact of flight simulators on U.S. airlines. A survey questionnaire was mailed to all 23 scheduled airlines, 18 of which responded. Of these, 2 reported purchasing simulator time; 16 reported owning one or more flight simulators (Killian, 1976).

A flight simulator is a facsimile of the cockpit of a modern airliner, with functioning controls, lights, and instruments. The flight controls, instruments, lights, and warning signals are controlled by a computer that is programmed to respond to the pilot trainee's actions just as a regular airplane would. Not only can the trainee go through all the procedures involved in a number of normal flight maneuvers, but his or her trainer can call for all types of problems for the trainee to cope with (e.g., a 20-knot crosswind on landing, a fire in an engine, an emergency landing).

Although the simulator cockpit is a fixed installation, it can move to imitate the effect of different aircraft maneuvers. Simulators differ in the number of movements they can reproduce, but some of the newest machines have 60 degrees of motion, and require that the crew use seat belts while performing some of the more turbulent maneuvers (Condon, 1984a).

Visual attachments to flight simulators allow the pilot trainee to see the airport and runway through the windshield. This makes it possible to provide simulator training in takeoff, landing, and instrument approach under widely different weather conditions and flight regimes (Air Transport Association, 1969).

Because people learn best by doing, the training curricula at American Airlines' Flight Academy have been designed to emphasize hands-on experience. They use equipment that enables a trainee to progress from the classroom to the cockpit through cost-effective stages. Here is their own description of the training process:

> First in the order is the systems trainer, a device which duplicates the controls of an aircraft system and displays the system's operation by using logic circuits to activate color-coded schematic diagrams, mechanical movements, indicator lights, etc., in response to the operation of the controls. It demonstrates cause and effect, and it permits problem solving exercises. Once a student masters each system, he advances to the Cockpit Procedures Trainer (CPT) to put his newly acquired skills all together.
>
> The CPT is a reproduction of the total cockpit. It provides a cost-effective means of easing the transition from the classroom and systems trainer to the simulator. It also provides students with their first real-world contact with actual aircraft hardware in the cockpit environment. Here, they become better acquainted with component, switch, and control locations. They also become involved with checklist activities, normal and abnormal procedures, and the development of crew coordination skills. Time spent in the CPT is an invaluable preliminary step toward the experience of flying the flight simulator.
>
> Once they have mastered systems operation in the classroom and at the systems trainers, and after they have become proficient on procedures in the CPT, students are ready for the machine that will give them the initial flying experience in the "new" aircraft. At the Flight Academy, we have digital-computerized flight simulators for the Cessna Citation B-707 (-100 and -300 series), B-727 (-100 and -200 series), B-747 and DC-10 aircraft, all equipped with the most effective motion and rigid-model TV visual systems currently

available. Each flight simulator is capable of precisely reproducing all required performance and handling characteristics. Their unparalleled realism and fidelity provides maximum transfer of training to the actual aircraft. (American Airlines Flight Academy, Fort Worth, Texas)

Why do the airlines use expensive flight simulators in pilot training? American Airlines, for one, reported the following advantages:

Safety: Crews can practice hazardous flight maneuvers in a safe, controlled environment, without endangering personnel and multimillion dollar aircraft.

Learning Efficiency: The absence of conflicting air traffic and radio chatter that exists in real flight situations enables total concentration on the business of learning. The ability to freeze a situation for an instant review of performance, or the added ability to quickly recycle or repeat key exercises, greatly enhances the learning impact.

Money: The cost of flying a flight simulator is only a fraction of the cost of flying an aircraft. Maintenance costs are also significantly lower. Furthermore, since the flight simulator eliminates the requirement for full-time "pilot trainer" aircraft, those that would otherwise be assigned to such an activity are freed to operate for profit as intended.

Fuel: The saving of this very costly and critical commodity is a factor that takes on ever-increasing importance. We might add that, in terms of community relations, the flight simulator permits significant reductions in noise and air pollution. Further benefits are derived from the fact that through substantial reductions in actual flight training time, simulators are providing important reductions in airspace congestion.

Since the energy shortage is so important in all of our lives, let us focus in on this particular advantage for a moment. American Airlines reports that it has now improved its efficiency in the use of simulators to the point that simulator time offsets more than an hour of aircraft time for each hour in the flight simulator. Assuming that American accounts for approximately 14 percent of the total savings due to the use of simulators, it can be estimated that about 204 million gallons of fuel were saved in 1976 through the use of flight simulation in the airline industry (Killian, 1976).

The airlines have a stated goal of "total training through simulation." One key to meeting this goal will be the programming of flight simulators to reproduce all regimes of operational flight. The other key will involve overcoming the major problem area in flight simulator fidelity, namely, the lack of data concerning ground-effect during takeoffs and landings. These problems are not unexpected in view of the lack of performance data for the landing and takeoff regimes made available for the programming of simulators prior to about 1970. Nevertheless, several airlines have already expressed the opinion that their flight simulators are quite adequate to provide all training without additional time in the aircraft.

Remember that simulators are used in many other training settings besides the airline industry. We have seen the use of simulators for teaching employees how to operate automobiles, trains, forklifts, boilers, hydraulic equipment, and maintenance machinery. We have also observed the use of simulators for teaching operators what to do in case of fires, explosions, and accidents.

FINAL COMMENTS

What can we conclude about the various off-site training methods? First, the conventional live lecture has been unduly criticized. It can be a cost-effective technique for transmitting factual information to large groups of trainees. Further, positive results can be expected when dynamic, knowledgeable individuals are chosen as lecturers.

Second, we predict that the future belongs to audiovisual techniques. More and more organizations are realizing that films, videotapes, and audiocassettes can put the nation's best trainers in the classroom with their trainees. This "classroom" can be at work or even in the trainee's automobile and home. Difficult concepts can be illustrated using such techniques as instant replay, slow motion, and microscopic close-ups. Trainees can be shown actual situations (e.g., accidents, sales meetings, grievance sessions, labor negotiations) in the comfort of their homes.

The variety of business skills and concepts that the audiovisual medium is capable of teaching at relatively low cost is wide ranging. A warning, however, is in order. It is essential that training staffs determine their organization's specific training needs systematically prior to ordering audiovisuals. Furthermore, the long-term impact of these audiovisuals on employee learning, behavior, and/or results must be carefully evaluated.

Self-paced techniques such as programmed instruction and computer-assisted instruction are especially important for less experienced or less educated trainees. These people require a learning approach that not only gives them individual attention but also allows each of them to progress through the program at their own speed. If they have a particular problem understanding something, they can spend more time on it as well as get special tutoring from the trainers. It is recommended, of course, that this off-site learning be augmented with periodic hands-on experience during training since, without it, there is a distinct possibility of limited transfer of learning to the job setting.

Although equipment simulators are expensive to implement, there is something quite appealing about training people on a replica of the real thing, so as to ensure maximum positive transfer of learning. When the number of trainees is large enough to warrant the expense, organizations should construct high-fidelity simulators.

Teleconferencing and corporate classrooms have also become popular as off-site training methods. Teleconferencing is an excellent way of providing first-rate training to large numbers of individuals at multiple sites at relatively low cost.

Chapter
8

Developing and Training Leaders: Theoretical Approaches

Peter Drucker (1987) made the observation that in over 40 years of work as a consultant in a wide variety of organizations, he has never met a single "natural"—an executive who was born effective. The underlying theme of this chapter supports that observation, namely, that people learn how to be effective leaders.

In this chapter, we present training methods that can be used to ensure quality leadership in our nation's organizations. These approaches are well grounded in theories of leadership and/or behavior change. In describing each training method, we explain what is done, how it is done, and why it is done.

Finally, we examine evidence to see if the program brings about a positive change in a manager's behavior. We answer the question, "Does the training attain the objectives for which it was designed?" As in previous chapters, we again use the nine-cell conceptual scheme presented originally in Figure 1.1. Figure 8.1 displays the 11 theoretically based approaches discussed in this chapter. We begin our examination with a description of programs designed to promote managers' self-awareness of their leadership style.

SELF-AWARENESS

Training programs designed to increase understanding of ourselves focus on role responsibility in the organization, recognizing differences between our managerial style versus our philosophy and practice, and improving interpersonal skills through awareness of how we are viewed by

Figure 8.1 Goals and strategies of theoretically based approaches for management development

STRATEGIES	GOALS: Self-Awareness	GOALS: Job Skills	GOALS: Motivation
Cognitive	Managerial role theory Double-loop learning	Vroom-Yetton model	Role motivation theory Need for achievement Survey feedback
Behavioral	Leader match	Grid seminars Leader-member exchange	Social learning theory (behavior modeling)
Environmental			Behavior modification

others. Two training approaches that use a cognitive strategy are managerial role theory and double-loop learning. Another approach, called leader match, uses primarily a behavioral strategy to teach people how to change the work environment in order to improve their managerial self-awareness.

Managerial Role Theory: Henry Mintzberg

Management theorists have traditionally been content to point out that the primary job of a manager is to plan, organize, coordinate, and control resources (e.g., technological, capital, human). But these four functions, first introduced by the French industrialist Fayol in the early 1900s, tell us little about what managers actually do in their jobs. Henry Mintzberg (1983) stated that before we can develop effective managers, we must have a clear-cut description of the nature of managerial work. This position is similar to that of advocates of the critical incident technique (Flanagan, 1954; Latham and Wexley, 1991), a method of task analysis we described in Chapter 3.

Mintzberg developed a theoretical perspective of what managers (e.g., first-line supervisors, middle managers, chief executive officers) do in their jobs. Based on interviews and observations of managers, he argued that managers do not have sufficient time to carefully plan, organize, coordinate, and control both their activities and those of their subordinates. Because of the open-end nature of the manager's job, Mintzberg (1975) argued that the manager today must perform a large quantity of work at an unrelenting pace. This work may be best described by such words as brevity, variety, and discontinuity. Half of the manager's activities are completed in less than nine minutes, and only one-tenth of them take more than an hour to complete (Mintzberg, 1973; Yukl, 1989). Because the variety of activities to be performed is so great, and because of a lack of pattern or structure among subsequent activities, the manager is required to shift moods quickly and frequently. In short, the job of managing is often not conducive for reflective, systematic planning. Rather, a manager must be a full-time responder to stimuli and must prefer "live" rather than delayed action.

In order to fully appreciate the implications of Mintzberg's writings for developing effective managers, it is important to understand the concept of role, since the crux of Mintzberg's theory is the notion of managerial roles. A *role* is an organized set of behaviors belonging to an identifiable office or position. An individual manager's personality can affect how, but not whether, a role is performed.

Based on systematic observations of five chief executives, Mintzberg concluded that all managerial positions can be defined in terms of ten roles. A manager's formal authority gives rise to three interpersonal roles which, in turn, give rise to three informational roles; the information input is then used by the manager in performing four decisional roles (see Table 8.1 for a description of each role). These ten roles are highly interrelated and can form an integrated description of the manager's job. Any differences that exist in managerial work, according to Mintzberg, deal with the relative importance of these ten roles within different functions of organizations and at different managerial levels.

Management training based on role theory requires that the trainee become aware of a "contingency theory of managerial work." That is, we must realize that the work of a particular manager at a particular point in time is contingent on four basic variables. These variables influence the relative importance given to each of the ten managerial roles.

First, and most broadly, the manager's job is influenced by the organization, the type of industry, the technology, and other factors in the environment. Second, there are work variations caused by the type of job itself, namely, its level in the organization and the function (e.g., marketing, quality control, or production) which the manager oversees. Third, there are differences in the job stemming from the person in that job, that is, the effects of his or her personality and leadership style. Finally, there are variations in the person's job caused by the situation, such as seasonal variations and temporary threats.

Managerial effectiveness is influenced when people examine their own work. One must study the job and focus consciously on one's own actions in order to understand what is done and why it is done. To stimulate this type of thinking, Mintzberg offers 14 sets of self-study questions. In addition, he suggested that a neutral third party be asked to observe the manager's behavior on the job, record the details of day-to-day activities, analyze the results, and feed back the results to the manager.

After self-study, there are several areas where managers can concentrate their attention to improve their effectiveness. These areas include

Table 8.1 STUDY OF TEN ROLES

Role	Description
Interpersonal	
Figurehead	Symbolic head; obliged to perform a number of routine duties of a legal or social nature.
Leader	Responsible for the motivation and activation of subordinates; responsible for staffing, training, and associated duties.
Liaison	Maintains self-developed network of outside contacts and informers who provide favors and information.
Informational	
Monitor	Seeks and receives wide variety of special information (much of it current) to develop thorough understanding of organization and environment; emerges as nerve center of internal and external information of the organization.
Disseminator	Transmits information received from outsiders or from other subordinates to members of the organization; some information factual, some involving interpretation and integration of diverse value positions of organizational influencers.
Spokesman	Transmits information to outsiders on organization's plans, policies, actions, results, etc.; serves as expert on organization's industry.
Decisional	
Entrepreneur	Searches organization and its environment for opportunities and initiates "improvement projects" to bring about change; supervises design of certain projects as well.
Disturbance Handler	Responsible for corrective action when organization faces important, unexpected disturbances.
Resource Allocator	Responsible for the allocation of organizational resources of all kinds—in effect the making or approval of all significant organizational decisions.
Negotiator	Responsible for representing the organization at major negotiations.

1. *Sharing information:* The manager must give conscious attention to the dissemination of information to subordinates. The manager must realize that subordinates cannot tap many of the informational sources to which the manager has access, and that subordinates need this information for effective decision making.

2. *Dealing consciously with superficiality:* The manager must deal consciously with the pressures that drive her or him to handle problems superficially. A balance must be struck whereby certain issues are delegated, others are dealt with in a marginal way, while others receive the direct attention of the manager.

3. *Sharing the job if information can be shared:* One way to deal with the heavy managerial workload, particularly at top corporate levels, is to share the job. Where feasible, a management team or task force should be formulated to share project assignments.

4. *Making the most of obligations:* Managers should make a conscious effort to turn certain ceremonial duties and routine responsibilities to their own advantage. For example, a ceremonial duty may be an opportunity to lobby for a cause. The need to attend a routine meeting may present a chance to tap a new source of information.

5. *Freeing self from obligations:* Managers must free themselves from obligations that detract them from important issues. The manager must force contemplation time into his or her schedule.

6. *Emphasizing the role that fits the situation:* Although required to perform all ten basic managerial roles, managers must give special attention to certain roles in certain situations. The choice of which roles to emphasize must reflect factors such as the situation of the moment, the level in the hierarchy, the industry, and so on.

7. *Seeing a comprehensive picture in terms of its details:* Though always working with small pieces of information, the manager must never forget to think about the whole organizational picture.

8. *Recognizing own influence in the organization:* Subordinates are highly sensitive to the actions of their manager. Strange things filter down an organizational hierarchy. What may be trivial to a manager—a hasty comment, a bit of careless information, or a sullen mood—can have a profound effect on the behavior of subordinates. Managers must act with conscious recognition of the effects of their actions on employees.

9. *Dealing with a growing coalition:* Any organizational unit exists because certain people ("influencers") created it and are prepared to support it. One of the most important tasks of the effective manager is keeping this coalition of influencers together. This involves ensuring that the benefits received by each of them is commensurate with their support of the unit.

10. *Using the behavioral scientist:* Clearly, the complexity of the problems that managers face, especially those at upper levels, will require that they turn more and more to the behavioral scientist for help in understanding the nature of managerial work and problems.

The question that must be asked is, "What do we know now that we didn't know earlier?" First, from Mintzberg's observational analysis, it appears that training programs are needed to teach people how to shift their cognitive processes quickly, as they encounter different problems that need resolution. Second, from a personnel selection standpoint, we know that we need to identify people who prefer live rather than delayed action. Third, a primary purpose of a management training program should be to stimulate trainees to recognize the actual nature of their managerial work. This is done by introspection; i.e., asking oneself a series of 14 questions and/or receiving feedback from an objective third party who has spent days or weeks collecting answers to these questions.

1. Where do I get my information, and how? Can I make greater use of my contacts to get information? Can other people do some of my scanning for me? In what areas is my knowledge weakest, and how can I get others to provide me with the information I need? Do I have powerful enough mental models of those things I must understand within the organization and its environment?
2. What information do I disseminate in my organization? How important is it that my subordinates get my information? Do I keep too much information to myself because dissemination of it is time consuming or inconvenient? How can I get more information to others so they can make better decisions?
3. Do I balance information-collecting with action-taking? Do I tend to act before information is in? Or do I wait so long for all the information that opportunities pass me by and I become a bottleneck in my organization?
4. What pace of change am I asking my organization to tolerate? Is this change balanced so that our operations are neither excessively static nor overly disrupted? Have we sufficiently analyzed the impact of this change on the future of our organization?
5. Am I sufficiently well informed to pass judgment on the proposals that my subordinates make? Is it possible to leave final authorization for more of the proposals with subordinates? Do we have problems of coordination because subordinates in fact now make too many of these decisions independently?
6. What is my vision of direction for this organization? Are these plans primarily in my own mind in loose form? Should I make them explicit in order to guide the decisions of others in the organization better? Or do I need flexibility to change them at will?
7. How do my subordinates react to my managerial style? Am I sufficiently sensitive to the powerful influence my actions have on them? Do I fully understand their reactions to my actions? Do I find an appropriate balance between encouragement and pressure? Do I stifle their initiative?
8. What kind of external relationships do I maintain, and how? Do I spend too much of my time maintaining these relationships? Are there certain people whom I should get to know better?
9. Is there any system to my time scheduling, or am I just reacting to the pressures of the moment? Do I find the appropriate mix of activities, or do I tend to concentrate on one particular function or one type of problem just because I find it interesting? Am I more

efficient with particular kinds of work at special times of the day or week? Does my schedule reflect this? Can someone else (in addition to my secretary) take responsibility for much of my scheduling and do it more automatically?

10. Do I overwork? What effect does my work load have on my efficiency? Should I force myself to take breaks or to reduce the pace of my activity?

11. Am I too superficial in what I do? Can I really shift moods as quickly and frequently as my work patterns require? Should I attempt to decrease the amount of fragmentation and interruption in my work?

12. Do I orient myself too much toward current, tangible activities? Am I a slave to the action and excitement of my work, so that I am no longer able to concentrate on issues? Do key problems receive the attention they deserve? Should I spend more time reading and probing deeply into certain issues? Could I be more reflective? Should I be?

13. Do I use the different media appropriately? Do I know how to make the most of written communication? Do I rely excessively on face-to-face communication, thereby putting all but a few of my subordinates at an informational disadvantage? Do I schedule enough time touring my organization to observe activity at first hand? Am I too detached from the heart of my organization's activities, seeing things only in an abstract way?

14. How do I blend my personal right and duties? Do my obligations consume all my time? How can I free myself sufficiently from obligations to ensure that I am taking this organization where I want it to go? How can I turn my obligations to my advantage?*

Research involving a survey of nearly 3000 managers supports Mintzberg's role framework by showing that six of his ten roles (i.e., entrepreneur, monitor, liaison, leader, spokesman, resource allocator) are, in fact, measurable and meaningful for managers (McCall and Segrist, 1980). In addition, managers' perceptions of relative role importance across managerial levels and functions were found to be sufficiently similar to support Mintzberg's contention that managerial jobs are essentially alike. Systematic variation was also found that supports Mintzberg's contention that there are differences in role emphasis among levels and functions. Unfortunately, there is currently no evidence that this self-study program increases a person's self-awareness or effectiveness on the job. Much of the previous information can be categorized as platitudes. However, from the standpoint of a realistic job preview, the description may prove effective for reducing training costs. Research suggests that telling people the

---

* Questions reprinted by permission of *Harvard Business Review.* Excerpted from "The Manager's Job: Folklore and Fact" by Henry Mintzberg, March/April 1990. Copyright © 1990 by the President and Fellows of Harvard College; all rights reserved.

drawbacks as well as the strengths of a job significantly reduces turnover and job dissatisfaction, because people have more information other than salary and glowing reports from others (e.g., recruiters, interviewers, job incumbents) on which to make an intelligent decision to enter a job (Premack and Wanous, 1985; Wanous, 1980). Thus Mintzberg's descriptions and questions may stop people from entering managerial training programs for jobs for which they are ill-suited.

Feedback, too, can be a powerful tool for changing behavior (see Chapter 4). To reduce the cost of employing one person to observe systematically another person, peer and/or subordinate ratings can be collected. These ratings should be made anonymously to ensure candid responses. Feedback from peers can be especially useful because, generally, they see how we act with superiors, subordinates, clients, and peers themselves. They frequently have more information than anyone else regarding the job behavior of a particular manager (Latham and Wexley, 1991). The rating scale in Table 8.2 can be modified so that the rater can simply make a check mark beside the appropriate answer. An alternate approach is to do team building (see Chapter 10). In brief, a neutral party interviews each subordinate confidentially about the subordinate's perceptions regarding answers to these questions, interprets the information, feeds back the information to the manager and the subordinates together as a team, and solicits information from the group as a whole on ways that managers and subordinates can work together to improve the group's effectiveness (see Latham and Wexley, 1991).

Further support for Mintzberg's theory is provided in a study of over 1000 managers at IBM (Kraut, Pedigo, McKenna, and Dunnette, 1989). The results suggested that a common approach to training and developing senior-level managers is both feasible and desirable. This is because the leadership positions in an organization involve essentially the same managerial roles. However, the relative emphasis that should be placed on training content for supervisors versus middle managers versus executives should differ.

For supervisors, the IBM study suggested that training should focus on one-to-one skills such as motivation, career planning, and performance feedback. Training at the level of middle managers should focus on the skills needed for designing and implementing effective groups and intergroup work and information systems; defining and monitoring group-level performance indicators; diagnosing and resolving problems within and among work groups; negotiating with peers and supervisors; and, designing and implementing reward systems that support cooperative behavior.

"As these topics suggest, the psychology of the individual, so important to the first-level manager, gives way to social psychology and sociology when one reaches middle management" (Kraut et al., 1989, p. 291). Since the latter topics are less well known and more abstract than the former, the transition from supervisor to middle manager can sometimes be confusing and disorienting.

Training for executive positions, IBM found, should emphasize the external environment. The curriculum should focus on broadening the executive's understanding of the organization's competition, world economics, politics, and social trends. This approach to executive development is elaborated on in Chapter 9.

Double-Loop Learning: Chris Argyris

In a survey of the supervisory training programs conducted in Fortune 500 companies, Alpander (1986) discovered a paradox. Most of the organizations surveyed espoused a participative management philosophy, but about two-thirds of the companies trained their supervisors more in technical skills than in interactive and conceptual ones. Resolving such paradoxes is a primary objective of double-loop learning (Argyris, 1987).

A central theme of Argyris's training program is to overcome the need to defend against embarrassment or threat, be it at the individual, small group, intergroup, or organizational level. Such defensive reactions prevent learning and are not productive (Argyris and Schon, 1986). The thrust of the double-loop learning training program is to make people aware of the discrepancy between their espoused theories and their actions so that they can reduce it.

Consequently, double-loop learning trains leaders to move from one set of behavioral strategies (termed Model 1) to a presumably "better" set of behaviors (termed Model II). This is accomplished by making leaders aware cognitively of the difference between what they do and what they think they should do in managing others.

According to Argyris (1976a), the vast majority (i.e., over 95 percent) of managers today are programmed with "Model I theories-in-use." These people strive to attain four primary values: (1) achieve purposes which they have defined for themselves, (2) win rather than lose, (3) suppress negative feelings, and (4) maximize rationality and minimize emotionality. To satisfy these values, people learn a set of action strategies which maximize their control over others. These action strategies result in other people becoming defensive and secretive about their activities. Problem solving in organizations tends to become ineffective, because the public testing of ideas (especially those issues that may be difficult and threatening) is all but forgotten, since everyone begins to "play it safe." Further, individuals are implicitly taught not to question the fundamental design, values, or goals of their organization. This phenomenon is called *single-loop* learning.

Argyris (1982) has argued that when single-loop learning exists in an organization, people have a tendency to deal with problems that are both difficult and threatening by compounding them instead of trying to truly solve them. In fact, these people create conditions within their organizations that inhibit the effective solution of these kinds of problems, and they also help to create an organizational culture that reinforces these limitations. Given this culture, over a period of time people begin to accept the idea that their organization is not a place for learning and, consequently, they cease learning. In these kinds of organizations, people may accomplish their everyday jobs at increasing cost and organizational rigidity. The only way out, Argyris argued, is for top executives to first address these difficult underlying issues, and then work on converting from Model I (single-loop learning) to Model II behavior.

Model II strategies encourage the sharing of valid information, free and informed choice, and internal commitment among people. Like Model I, the action strategies required to satisfy these values emphasize that individuals articulate their goals and ideas, and openly attempt to influence their environment. Model II, however, couples openness with an invitation to others to confront one's views and possibly alter them using valid information. That is, individuals who understand Model II become skilled at inviting double-loop learning (i.e., knowing how to articulate what one believes in, and encouraging healthy inquiry and questioning of one's beliefs).

Argyris's training is designed to teach people to become aware of their espoused theories of action versus their theories-in-use (Argyris and Schon, 1974). Espoused theories are those that people are aware of and would like to believe are the basis for their actions. Theories-in-use, on the other hand, are determined by observing an individual's actual behavior. Most people are not aware that the theories they espouse are incongruent with how they actually behave when dealing with others. This is true for two reasons. First, most people with Model I theories-in-use are so busy trying to win and control others, they do not have the ability to reflect accurately on their own behavior. Second, other people with Model I theories-in-use have been conditioned not to tell us when our behavior is incongruent with what we espouse.

The ultimate objective of double-loop training is to increase openness of communication and feedback among organizational members, increase willingness to openly communicate errors and failures, so that people will learn from this feedback, and consequently increase decision-making and policy-making effectiveness. The training program involves eight steps. First, the trainees read literature describing Models I and II in detail. Second, a group leader moderates discussion to ensure that trainees have mastered the key concepts in both models. Third, the trainees read or write a case study (see Chapter 9) and propose a solution to the problem (Argyris and Schon, 1986). The solution must include statements of what the trainees would do, plus their feelings and thoughts about their behavior. Fourth, a trainer analyzes the solutions to infer the degree to which they approximate Model I or Model II. Fifth, a trainer divides the trainees into small groups. Each group examines one strategy or solution to the case that was typical of Model I solutions given by the trainees in step 3. Their task is to develop a Model II alternative strategy for the problem. Sixth, after 30 minutes of small group discussion, the groups come together again. Each subgroup describes the intervention or solution that they developed. Seventh, one representative from each subgroup role plays the solution with a trainer. Eighth, the group provides feedback on the effectiveness of the feedback in adhering to Model II and solving the problem.

These steps are based on two basic principles of learning, namely, active participation and knowledge of results. However, a third variable, practice, apparently is not sufficiently provided during the training. Argyris reports that, despite these eight steps, people can only develop Model II solutions; they cannot behave in a manner congruent with Model II. Moreover, at the time that they are engaging in the behavior, they are unaware that they are still adhering to Model I. Thus the training program appears to do well as defined by learning criteria (see Chapter 4), but it fails to do well on behavioral measures. Moreover, the program is extremely costly. Argyris (1976b) illustrated this by describing that it took three years to help presidents of only six organizations move part way from Model I to Model II. As you will see later, this outcome is not surprising when the problem is viewed from an environmental rather than a cognitive strategy. When other people in the trainee's environment fail to reinforce Model II behavior on the job, it is unlikely that the newly acquired behavior will be maintained. The behavior that Argyris wishes to shape is especially difficult to approximate because Model I behavior has been well conditioned in most of us from an early age.

Argyris has continued to prod the scientific community with regard to his views on evaluating training programs. An example of Model I behavior in science is to take steps to minimize threats to internal and external validity, which may result, he stated (Argyris, 1987) in generalizations that have the features of mixed messages and defensive routines. To overcome this dilemma, his prescription is for researchers to combine description with intervention. The intervention becomes the context for testing the prescription. This clearly is not in alignment with the concepts and procedures discussed throughout Chapter 5. For example, in one study (Argyris, 1986), organization development (OD) professionals wrote case studies of the problems they encounter with clients, including the solutions they should employ. The cases were analyzed within subgroups to see if their theory-in-use matched their espoused theory. The next step was for the OD practitioner to use their new ideas and skills in actual client situations. This approach to evaluation is not unlike the case study or the pretest-posttest designs that lack a control group.

The Leader Match Concept: Fred E. Fiedler

Leader match training teaches people how to change the situation so that it is favorable to them. It is classified here as a behavioral strategy because the training is accomplished through programmed instruction (see Chapter 7). The theory on which this training is based could just as easily have it classified under the environmental cell in Figure 8.1, as the emphasis is on changing the situation to fit the leader's basic personality.

Leader match (Fiedler, Chemers, and Mahar, 1976) is a training program based on a contingency model which has been developed over the past 30 years by Fred E. Fiedler and his associates (e.g., Fiedler, 1964, 1967; Fiedler and Chemers, 1974). The theory states that the effectiveness of a leader depends on a proper match between the leader's primary motivational structure or style and the degree to which the situation in which the leader is working enables him or her to have control and influence over subordinates as well as the task itself. The training program is classified under the category of increasing one's self-awareness because it is designed to teach people how to become aware of their primary motivation style, to diagnose the situation in which they are working, and to change the situation to fit their personality rather than the converse. Thus the training differs from that designed by Argyris. Rather than focusing on the inadequacies of the leader and how these inadequacies must be corrected to overcome various situations, Leader Match focuses on teaching managers to understand the nature of the situation and how it can be changed so as to assist them in performing their jobs effectively. Managers become effective leaders when they change their situations to fit their leadership styles (Fiedler, 1967).

The leader's primary motivational structure or style is measured by the Least Preferred Co-Worker (LPC) scale (see Table 8.2). Trainees are asked to think of the one person (e.g., supervisor, peer, subordinate) with whom they least preferred working. This person may be someone with whom the trainee works now or with whom the trainee has worked in the past. It does not have to be the person the trainee liked least well, but should be the person with whom the trainee had the most difficulty getting a job done. Each trainee describes this person on the LPC scale by placing an "X" in the appropriate space. The scale consists of pairs of words that are opposite in meaning, such as pleasant and unpleasant. A score of 64 or above is considered a high score, and a score of 57 or below is defined as a low score.

Fiedler contends that a high LPC score identifies leaders who are motivated primarily by the goal of having close interpersonal relations and group support. These high LPC leaders are said to be primarily *relationship-motivated.* Those who desire more tangible evidence of their accomplishments, as indicated by successful task performance, are said to be primarily *task-motivated* and are identified by low LPC scores. This is not to imply that some people are concerned only with satisfying task requirements or only with getting along with others. Everyone is concerned with the attainment of both goals. The theory states that, for some people, the concern for task accomplishment is dominant over the concern for good relations with others. As soon as the primary need is satisfied, the individual immediately becomes concerned with satisfying the secondary need.

Table 8.2 THE LEAST PREFERRED CO-WORKER SCALE (LPC)

										Scoring
Pleasant	8	7	6	5	4	3	2	1	Unpleasant	______
Friendly	8	7	6	5	4	3	2	1	Unfriendly	______
Rejecting	1	2	3	4	5	6	7	8	Accepting	______
Tense	1	2	3	4	5	6	7	8	Relaxed	______
Distant	1	2	3	4	5	6	7	8	Close	______
Cold	1	2	3	4	5	6	7	8	Warm	______
Supportive	8	7	6	5	4	3	2	1	Hostile	______
Boring	1	2	3	4	5	6	7	8	Interesting	______
Quarrelsome	1	2	3	4	5	6	7	8	Harmonious	______
Gloomy	1	2	3	4	5	6	7	8	Cheerful	______
Open	8	7	6	5	4	3	2	1	Guarded	______
Backbiting	1	2	3	4	5	6	7	8	Loyal	______
Untrustworthy	1	2	3	4	5	6	7	8	Trustworthy	______
Considerate	8	7	6	5	4	3	2	1	Inconsiderate	______
Nasty	1	2	3	4	5	6	7	8	Nice	______
Agreeable	8	7	6	5	4	3	2	1	Disagreeable	______
Insincere	1	2	3	4	5	6	7	8	Sincere	______
Kind	8	7	6	5	4	3	2	1	Unkind	______
									Total	______

From F. E. Fiedler, M. M. Chemers, and L. Mahar, *Improving Leadership Effectiveness: The Leader Match Concept.* New York: Wiley, 1976. Reprinted by permission of John Wiley and Sons, Inc.

A leader's situational control is determined by describing his or her organizational context in terms of the following dimensions: (1) leader-member relations, (2) the degree of task structure, and (3) the leader's position power. Leader-member relations measure the manager's perception of the amount of loyalty, dependability, and support that he or she receives from subordinates; it is a measure of how well the manager perceives that he or she and the group get along with one another. Task structure measures how clearly the procedures, goals, and evaluation of the task are spelled out in the eyes of the manager. Position power measures how much power or authority the manager perceives the organization has given him or her for the purpose of directing, rewarding, and punishing subordinates.

To the extent that a leader has good leader-member relations, the task is highly structured, and she or he can easily reward and punish subordinates, the situation is considered to be highly favorable. Some examples of leaders in highly favorable situations include the well-liked commander of a military crew and the supervisor of an automobile transmission repair shop who is liked by her subordinates. On the other hand, to the extent that there are poor leader-member relations, the task to be performed is highly unstructured, and the leader possesses limited authority, the situation is considered to be unfavorable according to Fiedler's theory. Some examples of leaders in an unfavorable situation include the disliked chairperson of a volunteer committee with an ambiguous problem-solving task, and the unpopular chairperson of the board of directors in a small, cooperatively owned company.

Research based on the contingency model has shown that task-motivated (low LPC) leaders perform well in situations that offer either a high or low degree of situational control (Fiedler, 1972). This is because, in highly unfavorable situations (e.g., the sinking *Titanic*), a take-charge person who is not concerned with the feelings or bruised egos of others is frequently effective in fulfilling job requirements (e.g., getting people immediately into lifeboats). Once the situation becomes highly favorable (i.e., people are rescued), this same person does not need to be concerned with the task because things are going well. Therefore, that person's attention can be turned to showing concern and giving support to others.

Relationship-motivated (high LPC) leaders tend to perform well in situations of moderate control (Chemers and Skrzypek, 1972). In highly favorable situations, their concern for others is no longer dominant and they turn their attention to task accomplishment. Such concern is inappropriate here because things are already running smoothly. The high LPC person is often dubbed the "little colonel" in such instances, whereas low LPC people in a moderately favorable situation may be referred to as a "crisis maker" because they know they do well in unfavorable situations.

These findings suggest two major options for improving the quality of a leader's performance. In order to match the leader's motivational pattern with the situation, one can either attempt to change the leader's personality or the leader's situational control. Attempting to change an individual's personality or motivational structure is an extremely difficult and uncertain undertaking for most managers (e.g., see the previous section on double-loop learning). Leader match focuses on training managers to modify their situational control to fit their personality structure in order to increase their job performance.

Leader match is presented in the form of a self-administered programmed instruction workbook that trainees can complete in approximately 5 to 12 hours. It is recommended that the learning be spaced over two or three days in order to derive maximum benefit from the program. Sometimes the workbook is augmented by lectures, discussions, and films.

The workbook is divided into several major sections. The first section is concerned with helping trainees to identify their leadership style by completing the LPC scale. The second section shows trainees how to diagnose their situational control and influence by filling out scales measuring their perceptions of leader-member relations, task structure, and position power. Part three teaches trainees how to change the situation to maximize their effectiveness. They are given specific suggestions on how to change leader-member relations, task structure, and position power.

For example, leader-member relations can be affected by increasing (favorable) or decreasing (unfavorable) one's accessibility to subordinates; task structure can be affected by spelling out in detail (favorable) what is required of subordinates; and position power can be affected by taking away (favorable) or increasing (unfavorable) the decision-making power of subordinates. Remember, the word *favorable* is not to be confused with the words *good* or *appropriate*. What is good or appropriate for the low LPC person is not necessarily good or appropriate for the high LPC person.

Each chapter of the workbook begins with a short essay that explains the basic concepts of Fiedler's contingency model and its application. The essays are followed by several short problems, or leadership episodes (called *probes*), for which the trainees select the best answer or solution. They are then given feedback on the correct response. An incorrect answer requires a review of the probe or chapter in order to assure that the material is comprehended. Each chapter ends with a short summary. There are also several review sections and self-tests that permit trainees to assess their own progress.

How well does the program work? There is considerable debate on the validity of the LPC scale (e.g., Chemers and Fiedler, 1986; Jago and Ragan, 1986a, 1986b; Schriesheim, Bannister, and Money, 1979; Schriesheim and Kerr, 1977). However, Rice (1978, 1979) has responded to criticisms of Leader Match with an exhaustive review of the literature indicating that the reliability and validity of the scale is satisfactory. Moreover, Fiedler and his associates have provided more empirical evidence than any other training specialists which satisfy the requirements set forth in Chapter 5 for evaluating training effectiveness (e.g., the use of a control group, multiple criteria, longitudinal measures, etc.). For example, Fiedler and Mahar (1979) described 12 studies testing the effectiveness of Leader Match. Five studies were conducted in civilian organizations and seven were conducted in military settings. The performance evaluations were collected from two to six months after training. The evaluations of 423 trained leaders were compared with those of 484 leaders who had been randomly assigned to control groups. All 12 studies yielded statistically significant results supporting Leader Match training.

Frost (1986) used a pretest-posttest control group design (see Chapter 5) and showed that experienced managers who receive the training not only changed their situational control but also were able to do so in accordance with Leader Match prescriptions. Frost also compared the Leader Match training against an alternative training method and a control group. In the alternative training method, trainees were not informed of their LPC scores, but they were taught ways of changing their level of situational control. On-the-job behavior of the trainees was measured using BOS (see Chapter 5). Unfortunately, the results showed that performance in *both* training groups was basically the same as that of the control group. In commenting on these discouraging results, Frost reminded readers that most earlier evaluative studies on Leader Match involved supervisors who either joined new groups or else were new to their positions at the time of training. Based on these findings, Frost concluded that for experienced leaders in established situations, behavior modeling (Chapter 4) may be more effective than Leader Match for improving their performance.

Fiedler and his colleagues (Fiedler, Bell, Chemers, and Patrick, 1984) found that Leader Match training combined with behavior-modeling training was effective in decreasing accidents in silver mining and increasing productivity. A five-year follow-up evaluation showed that the combination of both types of training continued to have a beneficial effect on safety and productivity (Fiedler, Wheeler, Chemers, and Patrick, 1987).

In the Fiedler et al. (1984) study, a comparison was made between "structured management training" (Leader Match + critical supervisory skills + motivation + action planning) versus an "organization development" intervention (team building + problem solving). This aspect of the research was conducted over a 42-month period in soda ash and silver-lead-zinc mines. The results indicated improvements in safety and productivity using either one of the interventions, compared with those mines where no training interventions had taken place. Unfortunately, none of this research tells us how much of the improvements in safety and productivity were due to Leader Match training by itself, the other training methods by themselves or, perhaps, some combination. Future research should certainly be directed at ascertaining these additive and interactive effects.

Burke and Day (1986) conducted a meta-analysis to examine the effectiveness of various managerial training methods. They concluded that, with respect to behavioral criteria (see Chapter 5), Leader Match is indeed effective.

Finally, it should be noted that Leader Match is cost effective. Most leadership training programs require weeks, months, or even years without providing empirical evidence from controlled field experimentation that they actually improve the leader's performance on the job. Leader Match, however, requires no more than 4 to 12 hours of training time. It represents an inexpensive and promising development in an area that has, until now, been frustrating and unsatisfactory. The program has recently been translated into Japanese and German. It has been used in such organizations as the U.S. Civil Service Commission, U.S. Military Academy at West Point, United Biscuits, Ltd. of Great Britain, Chase Manhattan Bank of Hong Kong, and various hotel chains (e.g., Western International Hotels).

MANAGERIAL SKILLS

There are at least three theoretically based training approaches that have as their primary goal the improvement of managerial job skills. The Vroom-Yetton model employs a cognitive strategy to decision making. Specifically, it provides managers with a normative or prescriptive model to help them determine the extent to which they should share their decision-making power with their subordinates in different situations.

Grid seminars, popularized by Blake and Mouton, attempt to increase managerial skills by improving two basic components of a manager's behavior, namely, concern for production and concern for people. These two behavioral categories were originally identified during an extensive program of research on leadership behavior at Ohio State University during the 1950s, and were labeled "initiating structure" and "consideration" (Fleishman, 1957; Halpin and Winer, 1957; Hemphill and Coons, 1957).

Graen's Leader-Member Exchange (LMX) training focuses on improving managers' one-on-one relationships with their subordinates. LMX training improves managers' skills in such areas as active listening, exchanging mutual expectations, and practicing one-on-one interactions.

Vroom-Yetton Model

The training program developed by Vroom and Yetton (1973) focuses on a key aspect of leadership behavior, namely, the extent to which managers should involve subordinates in decision making. The underlying assumption of this training is that a manager should not always be autocratic nor should the person always adopt a participative style of leadership. Rather, a manager should be taught to diagnose a problem and determine how to approach the decision-making process appropriately. The model has been updated by Vroom and Jago (1988). Moreover, user-friendly computer software is now available for training purposes.

The validity of the model on which the training program is based was investigated in a study (Vroom and Jago, 1978) in which managers who were unfamiliar with the model reported one successful and one unsuccessful decision made in their managerial jobs. These managers then described the decision method they employed to solve each problem and the overall effectiveness, quality, and acceptance of the solution by subordinates. The results provided support for the model.

To use the model (see Figure 8.2), the managers ask themselves a series of seven key questions (i.e., A through G) about the problem, following the path developed, to determine the decision processes that are appropriate for that particular problem situation. These five decision processes vary in the degree to which subordinates participate in the decision-making process: AI and AII are variants of an autocratic process, whereby the manager makes the decision; CI and CII are variants of the consultative process, in which the manager obtains suggestions from subordinates; and GII designates a process whereby the manager acts as a chairperson at a meeting with his or her subordinates aimed at reaching a group consensus on how to solve the problem. Each of these decision procedures is defined in detail in Table 8.3. Note that the procedures are arranged in two columns corresponding to their applicability to problems that involve the entire group of employees (i.e., group problems) or a single subordinate (i.e., individual problems).

The training program teaches people to assess situations correctly, in order to choose the appropriate level of subordinate participation in the decision-making process, and thus make a greater percentage of effective decisions. Unlike programs that teach only one approach to managing by urging trainees to always apply the approach despite the situation and the trainee's own ability to conform to the approach, this program emphasizes the need for flexibility in leadership behavior. It recognizes that the search for one correct way to manage subordinates is futile, because people and situations are constantly changing. The training program typically lasts from two to three days. Prior to training, each participant reviews a set of cases that describe a manager confronted with an organizational problem. These cases vary along the situational dimensions specified in the model. The manager must select the decision process that describes what he or she would do in the situation.

Forty to 50 people are then trained at one time. The first four or five hours of training are spent in six- to eight-person teams discussing the cases they had responded to prior to training. The groups analyze the cases, attempt to reach consensus on the appropriate decision strategy, and give one another feedback on their predictions of each other's style for choosing among the various decision processes.

Following this, each trainee receives a computer printout of how he

Figure 8.2 The Vroom-Yetton contingency model of leadership behavior

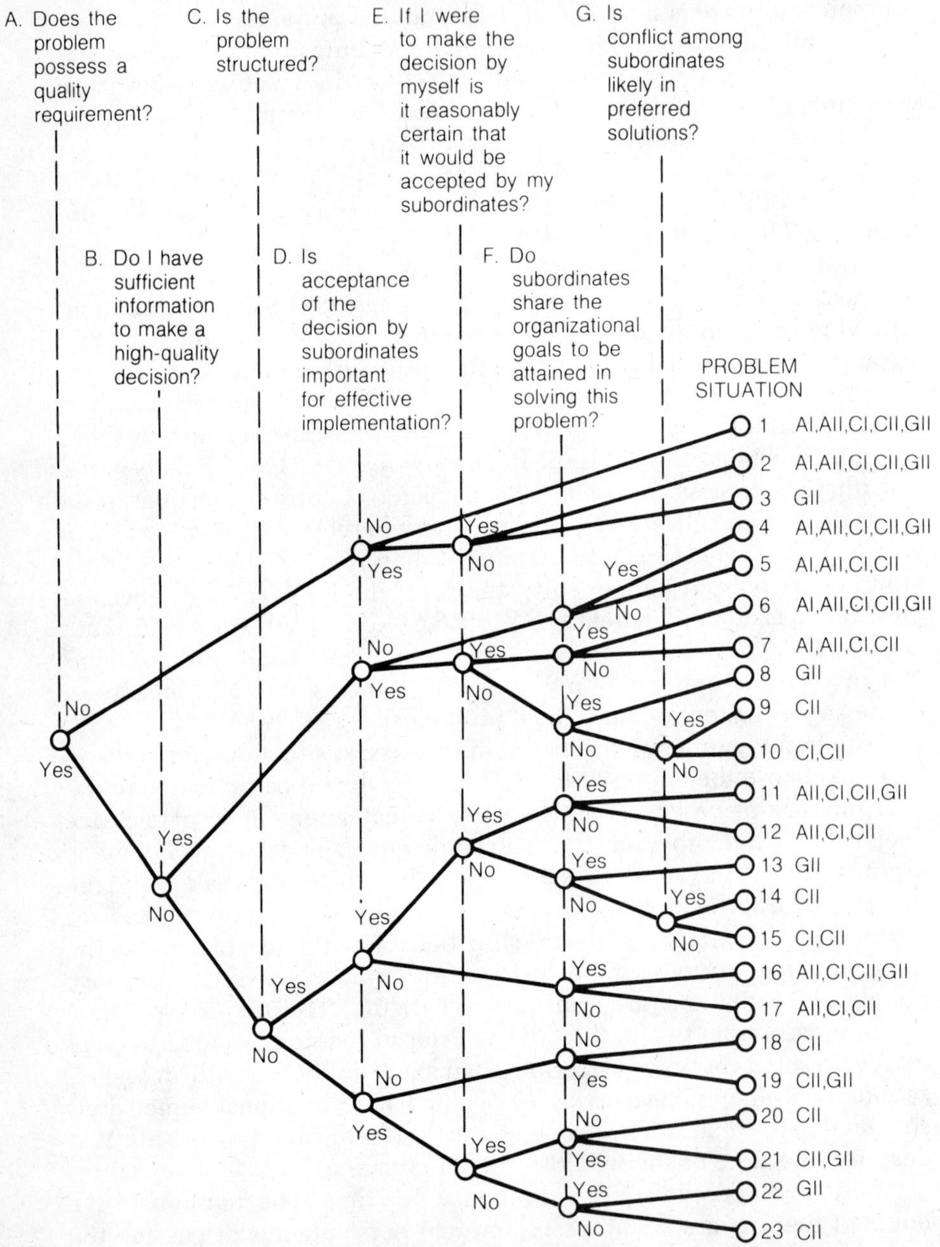
A. Does the problem possess a quality requirement?
B. Do I have sufficient information to make a high-quality decision?
C. Is the problem structured?
D. Is acceptance of the decision by subordinates important for effective implementation?
E. If I were to make the decision by myself is it reasonably certain that it would be accepted by my subordinates?
F. Do subordinates share the organizational goals to be attained in solving this problem?
G. Is conflict among subordinates likely in preferred solutions?
PROBLEM SITUATION
1 AI,AII,CI,CII,GII
2 AI,AII,CI,CII,GII
3 GII
4 AI,AII,CI,CII,GII
5 AI,AII,CI,CII
6 AI,AII,CI,CII,GII
7 AI,AII,CI,CII
8 GII
9 CII
10 CI,CII
11 AII,CI,CII,GII
12 AII,CI,CII
13 GII
14 CII
15 CI,CII
16 AII,CI,CII,GII
17 AII,CI,CII
18 CII
19 CII,GII
20 CII
21 CII,GII
22 GII
23 CII
Yes
No

Table 8.3 DECISION PROCEDURES FOR GROUP AND INDIVIDUAL PROBLEMS

Group problems	Individual problems
AI. You solve the problem or make the decision yourself, using information available to you at the time.	AI. You solve the problem or make the decision by yourself, using information available to you at the time.
AII. You obtain the necessary information from your subordinates, then decide the solution to the problem yourself. You may or may not tell your subordinates what the problem is in getting the information from them. The role played by your subordinates in making the decision is clearly one of providing the necessary information to you, rather than generating or evaluating alternative solutions.	AII. You obtain the necessary information from your subordinate, then decide on the solution to the problem yourself. You may or may not tell the subordinate what the problem is in getting the information from him. His role in making the decision is clearly one of providing the necessary information to you, rather than generating or evaluating alternative solutions.
CI. You share the problem with the relevant subordinates individually, getting their ideas and suggestions without bringing them together as a group. Then *you* make the decision, which may or may not reflect your subordinates' influence.	CI. You share the problem with your subordinate, getting his ideas and suggestions. Then you make a decision, which may or may not reflect his influence.
CII. You share the problem with your subordinates as a group, obtaining their collective ideas and suggestions. Then you make the decision, which may or may not reflect your subordinates' influence.	GI. You share the problem with your subordinate, and together you analyze the problem and arrive at a mutually agreeable solution.
GII. You share the problem with your subordinates as a group. Together you generate and evaluate alternatives and attempt to reach agreement (consensus) on a solution. Your role is much like that of chairman. You do not try to influence the group to adopt "your" solution, and you are willing to accept and implement any solution which has the support of the group.	DI. You delegate the problem to your subordinate, providing him with any relevant information that you possess, but giving him responsibility for solving the problem by himself. You may or may not request him to tell you what solution he has reached.

or she responded to the pretraining cases. The printout includes (1) the proportion of cases he or she chose to handle using each decision process (e.g., AI, CII, GII) and the average use of these decision processes by the training group as a whole; (2) the degree to which the participant chose an authoritarian versus a consultative decision process; (3) the frequency with which his or her decision choices agreed with those specified as appropriate by the model; and (4) the extent to which the individual did not answer each of the seven key questions appropriately. The group members compare their feedback with one another, discuss the accuracy of their prior predictions of each other's style, and share with one another what they have learned and how they plan to change their behavior back on the job.

Since the theory was introduced, there has been little substantive research on it (Landy, 1985). The research that has been done suggests that managers and students who have been trained to use the model are better able to choose the appropriate participation level for their decision-making strategy than those who have not been trained (Hill and Schmitt, 1977; Jago and Vroom, 1977). More importantly, there is some evidence that training increases the overall effectiveness of managers on the job. For instance, a program called TELOS, based entirely on the Vroom-Yetton model of leadership, was presented to 37 different organizations throughout the world involving 1600 managers (Smith, 1979). This program was evaluated at three levels of analysis: participant reactions, learning, and behavior change (see Chapter 5). Two hundred and sixteen managers from 13 different organizations used a self-report questionnaire to report the following benefits of the training:

- 72 percent said they found some specific things they would do differently
- 67 percent reported the program should help them generally in their current job
- 35 percent said the course should significantly increase their current job effectiveness
- 51 percent reported that the course should help in their career development
- 2 percent reported that the course was interesting, but no real value on the current job
- No one reported that the course was a waste of time

What happened on the job as a result of TELOS training? Table 8.4 presents the results obtained from 91 participants 6 to 12 months after they had completed the course. These findings suggest that the course did affect the participants' subsequent job behavior (Smith, 1981).

The revised 1988 Vroom-Jago model includes five additional problem attributes, bringing the total number to 12. Subordinate information, geographical dispersion of subordinates, severe time constraints, subor-

Table 8.4 6- to 12-MONTH FOLLOW-UP OF TELOS TRAINING

1. Which of the following skills are needed by managers in the organization?				2. How effectively does TELOS teach the following skills?		
% Needed	% Not Needed	% No Comment		% Good	% Fair	% Not Applicable
89	2	9	a. More effective leadership techniques	56	42	2
88	1	11	b. Lead differently in different situations	78	20	2
85	3	10	c. Identify elements within a situation	58	38	4
84	2	14	d. Increase input from others to increase probability of success	71	29	0
84	6	10	e. Make decisions alone when information is adequate	70	28	2
90	1	9	f. Use participation as a development tool	58	39	3

From Smith, B. B., "Evaluating a Leadership Training Program," Kepner-Tregoe, Inc., Princeton, New Jersey, 1980. Reprinted by permission.

dinate development, and opportunity costs associated with time have been added as problem attributes.

No training approach is without criticism. Field (1979) pointed out that the evidence supporting the validity of the Vroom-Yetton model is based primarily on self-report data. For example, a major test of the model's effectiveness requested managers to list the details of one successful and one unsuccessful decision-making situation that they had experienced (Vroom and Jago, 1978). The case writing occurred after the managers had been exposed to the five decision processes and after they had received practice in choosing decision processes for 30 cases. After writing the two cases, the managers reported the decision process they used for each case along with a self-reported rating of its effectiveness, quality, and acceptance. According to Field, it is possible that managers report that successful decisions reflect a rational process appropriate to the situation, regardless of their actual behavior back on the job. Thus self-reported rational behavior would tend to match the rational model, thereby validating the model.

To his credit, Field (1982) took it upon himself to test Vroom and Yetton's model by means of a procedure that manipulated decision-process and situation attributes, but he did *not* rely on self-reports as the criterion for assessing training effectiveness. Business students were randomly formed into four-person decision-making groups, and each group was asked to solve five decision-making problems using different decision-making processes prescribed in the model. Field found evidence for the validity of the model. Specifically, he found that decisions made in line with the model were significantly more effective than decisions that were out of line with the model. Decision effectiveness was measured by asking an independent judge to rate the quality of each decision. In addition, two subordinates of each leader independently rated their degree of acceptance with their leader's decisions. Of the 105 decisions that were in line with the model, 51 were effective whereas only 31 of the 87 out-of-line decisions were effective. Regarding the seven key questions, one of three quality questions and three of four acceptance questions worked as predicted by the model.

Heilman and her colleagues evaluated this management development approach without relying on self-report data (Heilman, Hornstein, Cage, and Herschlag, 1984). Their findings showed that the role of the person viewing the leader influences the way that person evaluates the effectiveness of the leader's decision-making style. Specifically, they found that when subjects were cast in the role of *subordinate*, they never rated an autocratic leader's behavior as being more effective than a participative leader's behavior, even when the situation was one in which the Vroom-Yetton model prescribed autocratic decision making. This casts serious doubt on the validity of this training. However, when other groups of subjects were cast in the role of *manager*, they evaluated leader effectiveness in total accordance with the contingency prescriptions of the model.

In their review of Vroom and Jago's (1988) book, Konovsky and Freeman (1990) made the following observations. First, the evidence cited from the six studies that Vroom and Jago cited in support of the Vroom-Yetton model primarily support the model in the aggregate. However, there is little validity evidence isolating and evaluating the problem attributes contained in the model. Second, the revised decision-making model includes precise mathematical functions describing the relationships among the problem attribute configurations, the model's effectiveness criteria, and decision-making methods. Some of the assumptions and hypotheses underlying the derivations, however, are questionable in that they contradict extant empirical research.

From our point of view, this approach to management development is a milestone because it resulted in empirical research that struck at one of organizational psychology's post–World War II's most cherished beliefs: Participative decision making is always good; anything less than participative decision making is not good. Vroom and his colleagues Yetton and Jago have made it clear that it is a mistake to assume that an effective leader always uses participative decision-making techniques. Rather, a manager must learn to diagnose a problem situation and determine which approach is best.

Grid® Seminars: Robert R. Blake and Jane S. Mouton

Blake and Mouton designed a six-phase program for organizations that lasts anywhere from three to five years. It begins by examining managerial behavior and style, and then systematically widens its focus to team and intergroup development, and finally to the total organization. Here we only describe Phase 1 of their intervention strategy, the Managerial Grid Seminar, which focuses its attention on the development of individual managers.

Basic to the Managerial Grid Seminar is Blake and Mouton's (1985) concept of effective leadership as the *managerial grid.* As shown in Figure 8.3, there are two basic dimensions for describing managerial style: concern for production and concern for people. The horizontal axis of the Grid reflects a manager's concern for production. This may include such considerations as the number of units of output, quality of service offered to customers, amount of scrap and waste produced, and the number of innovative suggestions developed. The vertical axis represents a manager's concern for people. This, too, can be exhibited in a number of ways, for example, concern for each subordinate's personal worth, establishment of good personal relationships with bosses and peers, and the promotion of friendly and cohesive work groups. Figure 8.3 shows that concern for production and concern for people can range from low (1) to high (9), thereby yielding 81 (i.e., 9 × 9) possible managerial styles or orientations. For Blake and Mouton, the upper-right corner, the 9,9 position, is the soundest way to achieve leadership excellence. It is important to point out that Blake and Mouton (1982) clearly recognize the need for 9,9 managers to choose specific forms of behavior appropriate for the particular situation in which they find themselves. Although Blake and Mouton advocate a 9,9 pattern of leadership, they do not believe that a manager needs to respond reflexively with the same 9,9 behaviors in every situation. According to Yukl (1989), the universal aspect of their theory is the value orientation of a 9,9 manager that should guide the person's behavior rather than a fixed pattern automatically used in all situations.

There are two basic Grid Seminars available for management development. *Executive Grid Seminars* are for individuals engaged in the policy-making and planning functions at the top of their respective organizations. This seminar brings together persons whose position level permits them to exchange common interests and problems not shared by persons whose managerial job responsibilities are specialized. Typical attendees include presidents, directors, executive vice presidents, and managing partners. *Managerial Grid Seminars* are for persons from the middle and upper range of business and industry, government, and ser-

Figure 8.3 The managerial grid®

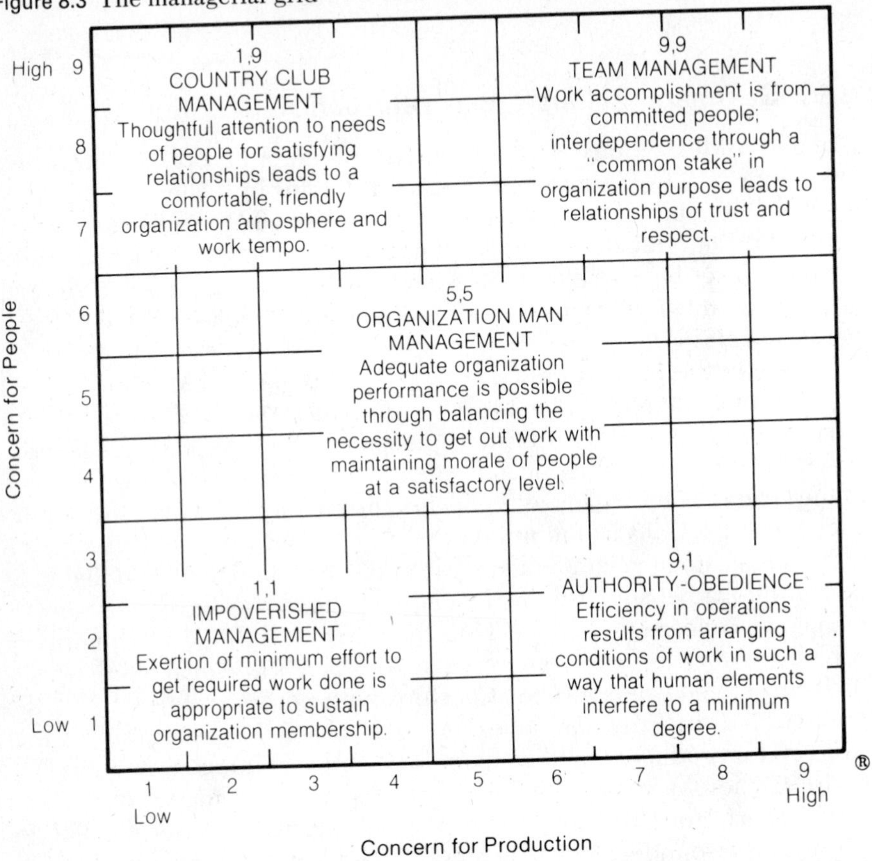

The Managerial Grid Figure from *The Managerial Grid III: The Key to Leadership Excellence,* by Robert R. Blake and Jane Srygley Mouton. Houston: Gulf Publishing Company, Copyright 1985, page 12. Reproduced by permission.

vice organizations. Typical attendees include regional managers, plant managers, project managers, operations managers, and sales managers.

Since 1964, more than 400,000 individuals from companies such as Exxon, Procter & Gamble, and TRW have attended these seminars. In addition, executives from key branches of government including Congress, departments of Defense and Agriculture, and the Internal Revenue Service have utilized Grid Seminars. Each seminar lasts a week and is conducted either away from the organization by outside consultants or on an in-house basis by the organization's own top-level managers who have been trained in grid methodology. Six or more study teams are formed, each consisting of five to nine managers. Ideally, each team consists of members representing different departments, divisions, and levels within the organization. The teams participate in a series of team-learning activities during the week. Each team has an opportunity to work on a problem, score its own performance, compare its effectiveness with that of other teams at the seminar and, finally, to critique its own members' behavior and group performance. While solving problems, it is hoped that team members gain insight into their own leadership style and its impact on others, improve cooperation between themselves and their colleagues, increase their skill in using teamwork for planning and problem solving, use criticism to learn faster from their own experiences, develop skills essential for solving conflicts between groups, learn how their own past practices may work against standards of excellence and how to change their practices, and understand important differences between contingent (i.e., situational) management and 9,9 versatility. The main objective of the seminar is to teach all managers in an organization to become 9,9 managers.

No evaluative studies of the effectiveness of Phase I (the Managerial Grid Seminar) have been published. The limited evidence cited in support of grid ideology comes from a study evaluating the entire six-phase organization development intervention (Blake, Mouton, Barnes, and Greiner, 1964). That study involved 800 managers and technicians in a 4000-member division of a large petroleum firm. The organization reported a considerable increase in profits, cost savings, and productivity per worker-hour while the grid program was in effect. In addition, a number of individual attitudinal and behavioral changes consistent with 9,9 values were also attributed to the program.

The results of this research, however, must be treated with caution. Since no control group was used, we have no way of knowing whether these improvements were due to the grid program itself, or whether they resulted from extraneous factors (e.g., an improvement in the economy). Further, much of the information obtained was anecdotal and subjective in nature, with individuals being asked to describe changes that had occurred more than a year earlier. Finally, we cannot be certain what portion(s) of the program were responsible for the reported changes in organizational outcomes. Therefore, considerably more evidence is needed before any definitive statements can be made about the effectiveness of Grid Seminars.

On the positive side, attendees' comments about what happened in their organizations after Grid training are encouraging. Sixty-two percent reported better communication between themselves and their subordinates, 61 percent reported improvements in working with other groups, 55 percent reported better relationships with colleagues, and 20 percent reported more openness to the ideas of others.

Blake and Mouton have argued that Grid Seminars have the same positive impact on organizational profitability. For instance, Figure 8.4 presents their comparison of the profitability of two matched organiza-

Figure 8.4 Comparision of the profitability of two matched corporations

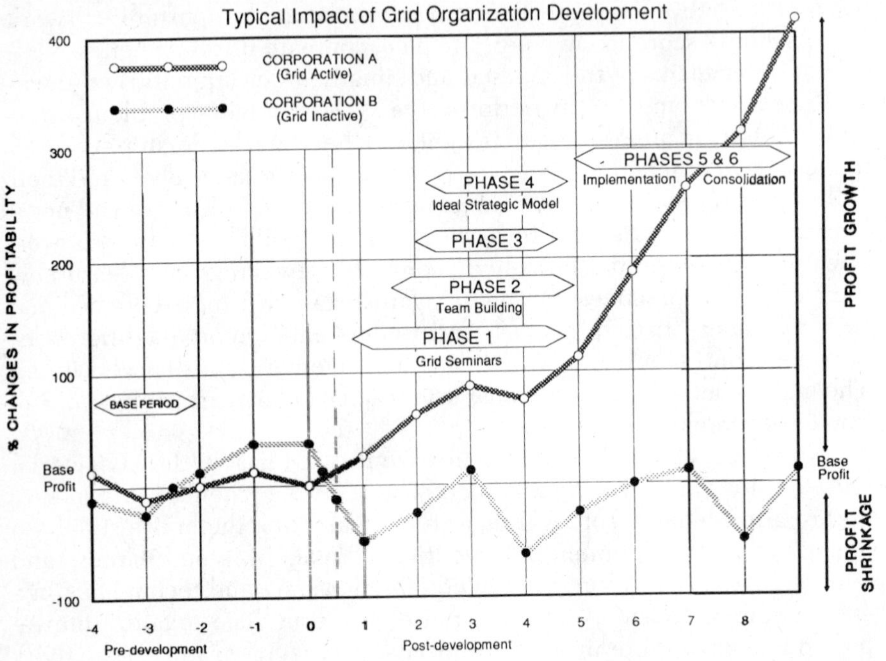

"Typical Impact of Grid Organization Development" figure from *The Versatile Manager: A Grid Profile,* by Robert R. Blake and Jane Srygley Mouton. Homewood, Ill.: Dow Jones-Irwin, Copyright © 1980, page 194. Reproduced by permission.

tions, Corporation A, which was involved in Grid training, and Corporation B, where people did not receive Grid training. The figure reflects the profits of these two corporations. The products of both corporations are identical, yet the profits of the corporation that received Grid training are four times greater than those of Corporation B.

Leader-Member Exchange: George B. Graen

Another approach to dealing with the performance of subordinates is Graen's training in leader-member exchange (LMX). The training is based on Graen's (Graen, 1976; Liden and Graen, 1980) research on role-making in leader-member dyads. This research has shown that there is a consistent pattern to leader-member subordinate transactions. In exchange for positional resources from the leader, the subordinate commits him- or herself to a high level of involvement in the unit's functioning.

This source of influence can result in highly valued outcomes for both the leader and the subordinate. For example, the leader can offer outcomes of increased job latitude, influence in decision making, open communications, support of the subordinate's actions, and confidence in and consideration for the subordinate. A subordinate can reciprocate with greater availability and commitment to the success of the entire unit or organization.

Research on what Graen calls the vertical dyad (i.e., leader-subordinate) linkage model shows that a differentiation process occurs in a predictable manner over time, namely, the formation of low and high LMX relationships (Dansereau, Graen, and Haga, 1975). The consequence of this is the formation of in-groups and out-groups.

LMX training is designed to enable and encourage leaders to correct situations where out-groups exist by teaching leaders to analyze and act on major positive and negative elements of their relationship with each subordinate. This training typically takes place in a seminar setting. It includes lectures, group discussions, and role playing where trainees alternate taking the role of leader and subordinate. The training usually takes place in six weekly two-hour sessions. The topics covered include an understanding of LMX theory and how to use it (two hours), active listening skills (two hours), exchanging resources (two hours), and practicing one-on-one interactions (four hours).

The objective of the training is to get each leader to analyze thoroughly and be prepared to act on major positive and negative components of his or her relationship with each subordinate. During the training sessions, the general structure of the conversations as well as the specific questions and techniques to facilitate the conversation are devised by the managers with the help of the trainer. For example, (1) the manager is to spend time asking about and discussing each person's gripes, concerns, and job expectations about the member's job, the leader's job, and their working relationship; (2) using active listening skills learned in the training, the leader is to be particularly attentive and sensitive to what issues are raised and how they were formulated by each subordinate; (3) the leader is to refrain from imposing his or her frame of reference on the issues raised; (4) the leader is to share his or her own job expectations about his or her own job, his or her member's job, and their working relationship.

The actual treatment, following this training, usually involves a series of 20- to 30-minute conversations between the leader and their subordinates. The goal of this follow-up treatment is to increase the level of reciprocal understanding and helpfulness within dyads regarding job issues and behaviors.

There has been a great deal of research in support of this training that meet the requirements we outlined in Chapter 5. The quality of leader-member relations has been shown to directly affect both productivity and satisfaction (Graen, Novak, and Sommerkamp, 1982), as well as employee turnover (Graen, Liden, and Hoel, 1982).

Scandura and Graen (1984) compared the effectiveness of this training with a placebo control condition. The placebo training consisted of three two-hour sessions of general input on decision making, communicating performance evaluations, and job enrichment. The experimental design was the pretest-posttest discussed in Chapter 5 with random assignment of people to the training and control groups.

The Leader-Member Exchange (LMX) scale (Graen and Cashman, 1975; Liden and Graen, 1980) was employed to measure the quality of exchange between supervisors and subordinates. The member form of the LMX contained seven items such as "How well do you feel your immediate supervisor understands your problems and needs" and "I have enough confidence in my immediate supervisor that I would defend and justify his or her decisions if he or she were not present to do so." The seven items were summed for each participant, resulting in a possible range of scores from 7 to 28.

The LMX training method resulted in significant increases in the degree of supervisor support and member availability perceived by the initial LMX out-group compared to the in-group. The outcome was an increase in both productivity (weekly output records) and job satisfaction.

Graen and Scandura (1986) argued that managers and subordinates can be expected to collaborate on tasks that allow growth opportunities for the subordinate if gain is desired by both parties. This is because the LMX model states that interdependence between a manager and a subordinate is necessary for both the offer and the acceptance of opportunities of growth on the job. To test this assertion, Graen et al. (1986) manipulated growth opportunities by a vertical collaboration offer based on the LMX model. As predicted, only employees high in growth need strength (GNS) responded to the growth opportunity as defined behaviorally by actual collaboration over time on tasks by the subordinate with the manager. The result was an increase in quantity and quality of output on the part of high-GNS people. This was not true of low-GNS people. It would be interesting in subsequent studies to see whether trainers in Miner's role motivation theory (discussed later in this chapter) would significantly affect GNS.

The major criticism of this training program is similar to the criticism of Fiedler's Leader Match training. Both training approaches use a questionnaire to explain their effectiveness (e.g., Fiedler's LPC scale), and both questionnaires have been attacked on psychometric grounds. Specifically, Dienesch and Liden (1986) argued that the LMX scale should be treated as a multidimensional construct. Measurement issues aside, training theorists such as Graen are to be commended for not being content with simply showing that their training process is effective, but rather exploring the psychological variables that explain why training is effective.

MOTIVATION

Five training techniques deal with increasing the motivation level of managers: Role motivation theory, training in need for achievement, and survey feedback employ cognitive strategies; behavior modification employs an environmental strategy; and social learning theory (or behavior modeling) uses cognitive, behavioral, and environmental strategies. The latter is classified in Figure 8.1 as a behavioral strategy because of its emphasis on changing behavior through practice. However, as we will see, it could easily have been designated as a cognitive and/or environmental approach to behavior change.

Role Motivation Theory: John Miner

John Miner (1975) found that certain key attitudes and motives affect an individual's choice of a managerial career, the success achieved in a given managerial position at any organizational level, and the speed of advancement up the managerial hierarchy. These key attitudes are described as follows:

1. *Favorable attitude toward authority*: Managers are expected to maintain a good relationship between themselves and their superiors. Managers should generally have a positive attitude toward individuals who hold positions of authority over them.
2. *Desire to compete*: With regard to peers, managerial work has a competitive element. Managers must be able to compete for available rewards for themselves and their work group, and be favorably disposed toward engaging in such competition.
3. *Assertive motivation*: An individual in a managerial role should derive pleasure from taking charge, making decisions, taking disciplinary action as may be necessary, and protecting members of their work group.
4. *Desire to exercise power*: A manager must exercise power over subordinates and direct their behavior through the use of positive and negative sanctions. The manager should feel comfortable using such power and not find such behavior difficult.
5. *Desire for a distinctive position*: The managerial role requires that an individual act differently from the immediate subordinate group, and do things that inevitably invite attention, discussion, and perhaps even criticism from subordinates.
6. *A sense of responsibility*: The individual should have a positive outlook toward routine administrative chores, such as serving on

committees, filing out forms, and constructing budget estimates. The manager should gain some satisfaction from accomplishing these demands and not regard them with apprehension or dislike.

These six motives comprise what Miner calls "motivation to manage." The concept of motivation to manage applies primarily to bureaucratic organizations. These organizations are typically large and use hierarchical control. The theory is likely to have less applicability in small organizational settings where there is little or no hierarchical or bureaucratic control. In one study, Berman and Miner (1985) found that top executives who had risen up the managerial hierarchy in large, bureaucratic organizations had higher levels of managerial motivation than top executives in small family-owned businesses.

Managers who associate positive rather than negative feelings with the various role prescriptions just described will tend to meet existing organizational criteria of effectiveness. Those with predominantly negative reactions will be relatively ineffective. You must realize, of course, that these motivational factors are not the only ones affecting managerial performance. Factors such as job knowledge, verbal ability, and resistance to stress, among others, are also important. Nevertheless, the six motives of managerial role motivation theory have been found to be related to various criteria of managerial effectiveness (Miner, 1978). And of these six motives, Miner (1985) identified three that correlate most consistently with managerial success, namely, favorable attitude toward authority figures, desire to exercise power, and desire to compete with others. Desire for distinctive position and a sense of responsibility are less frequently associated with managerial success and are, therefore, slightly less important components of managerial motivation. Assertive motivation is the least useful key attitude for predicting success as a manager.

According to Miner's theory, organizations should develop managers by increasing their motivation to manage others. The training program utilizes conventional lecture and lecture-discussion teaching methods. These lectures are often supplemented with special guest lecturers, cases created by the trainees, videotaped scenes role-played by trainees, and selected books and articles. The two primary objectives of training are, first, to help managers deal more effectively with deficiencies in the work behavior of their subordinates; and, second, to develop all six components of managerial motivation. The training sessions are typically held once a week, with each session lasting approximately one hour. The program extends over a period of several months. Ten to 100 people can be trained at one time. The lectures focus on reasons why a subordinate might perform ineffectively, and what a manager can do in such situations. The participants are requested to think of themselves as being in the managerial role and to feel the emotions associated with it. Toward the end of the training these emotions are discussed, along with their implications for managerial effectiveness (Miner, 1974).

The results obtained with this training approach are encouraging. Seventeen experimental (i.e., trained) groups and 9 control (i.e., untrained) groups have been involved in evaluative studies of this program. Significant experimental group changes occurred in 16 out of 17 cases, and in all instances where a control was used, the changes were shown to be due to the training.

Interestingly, not all of these motives are influenced equally by the management development program. The strongest effects occur with assertive and power motivation. Further, increased favorable attitudes toward authority and willingness to perform administrative duties appear in over half of the studies. The desire to compete and the desire for a distinctive position are much less frequently influenced by the training. Nevertheless, all of the motives seem to be sufficiently affected by training to warrant their continued retention in the theory.

Thus far, the data suggest that people who are active and independent are more responsive to this training than those who are passive and dependent. Significant changes have been found among both female and male trainees (Miner, 1978).

What are the implications of this theory for management education in business schools? Since the early 1960s, Miner has found a steady decline in the motivation-to-manage scores of representative samples of business and other students. In particular, there has been a shift toward more unfavorable attitudes toward authority, lessening assertiveness, and lowering sense of responsibility (Miner, 1977). If this trend continues, and it looks to him as though it will, there will be a massive managerial talent shortage in the next decade. The logic of the current situation argues for the addition of courses in business and business schools designed to develop the motivation to manage.

Achievement Motivation Theory: David McClelland

For over 25 years David McClelland (1961, 1965) and his associates have been studying *need for achievement* (abbreviated NAch), a distinct human motive which can be defined as an "urge to improve" or as a "desire to exceed some standard of behavior." Thus the overall objective of this program is to increase one's motivation level to excel in the job. This is done primarily by teaching people to think through the situations in which they are placed, and to develop action plans to increase their effectiveness on the job. A unique aspect of the program is that it is designed primarily for entrepreneurs in small business settings.

People with high NAch seek challenging tasks, assume responsibility for individual achievement, persist in the attainment of achievement goals, enjoy surpassing previous achievements and, generally, find goal attainment to be a satisfying experience. They function most successfully in situations where there is moderate risk, where they receive knowledge of their progress, and where they have individual responsibility for the attainment of the goal (McClelland, 1961). Since these kinds of situations are most frequently found in small business settings, achievement-motivated individuals tend to be attracted to entrepreneurial work situations. They have a burning desire to get things done, and they shun bureaucratic situations where they are plagued by red tape. They make decisions, solve problems, and strive to accomplish the objectives of their organization. Simply put, they are doers; they are motivated to obtain results. It is important to point out that high need for achievement is not always the most important motivator for managers in large organizations. Instead, NAch should be moderately high and supported with a strong need for power, so that a manager will express it to facilitate team performance rather than use it solely for their own success (Yukl, 1989). According to McClelland and Burnham (1976), if a manager were to have a very high level of NAch, she or he would try to accomplish everything alone, be reluctant to delegate responsibility to others, and not be able to develop a strong sense of commitment and responsibility among their subordinates.

McClelland estimated that only about 10 percent of the population is sufficiently high in achievement motivation. These individuals seem to be this way because of their early childhood experiences. Their parents expected and reinforced them to show independence between the ages of 6 and 8 with respect to making their own decisions and accomplishing things without help from others. Despite the importance of childhood experiences, McClelland is convinced that this motivation can be acquired by businesspeople. Consequently, he designed a training course intended to increase achievement motivation.

McClelland's training approach is based on certain theoretical propositions that have evolved gradually over the years while he developed NAch among businesspeople of various cultural backgrounds. For convenience, we summarize these propositions under four main headings: the achievement syndrome, self-study, goal setting, and interpersonal support (McClelland and Winter, 1969).

The Achievement Syndrome The course participants are first taught how to recognize and produce achievement-related fantasies. They take the Thematic Apperception Test (TAT) in which they are asked to write imaginative stories about a series of ambiguous pictures that are shown to them. They then learn how to score what they have written according to a standard coding system for identifying NAch. With practice, they learn how to produce stories heavily loaded with achievement imagery. The object here is to strengthen their associative network or motive by eliciting and reinforcing it. This emphasis is primarily a cognitive strategy.

The next step in the course is to tie thought (i.e., cognitions) to action. As mentioned previously, high NAch individuals behave in certain characteristic ways. They prefer work situations where there is challenge (moderate risk), specific feedback, individual responsibility, and the chance to try new things. These action patterns are taught to the participants in connection with a business game. The game provides an opportunity to learn these action characteristics through practice and through observing other participants. Thus the program incorporates two key principles of learning: active participation and practice.

So far, the course instruction has been abstract and removed from everyday life. The next step is to illustrate how NAch thought and action can be applied to business activities. The training strategy used here is the case study method (cognitive), popularized by the Harvard Business School (see Chapter 9). Participants analyze and discuss actual examples of the development of the careers or firms of business leaders. They are also encouraged to bring in examples from their own business activities for analysis (cognitive) in motivational terms.

Self-Study Through outside reading, lectures, group discussion, and films, the participants develop a clear understanding (cognitive) of the role that high NAch persons must play in a business setting. By doing this, participants can decide for themselves whether they want to be that kind of person, and whether being more entrepreneurial is relevant to their career aspirations. During the course, participants are continually encouraged to think carefully about what information acquired during training means with respect to their own self-image and current job responsibilities.

Next, the course focuses on an examination of the participants' value system. A value analysis of the participants' culture is conducted by analyzing children's stories, myths, popular religion, customs, and so on. The objective here is to identify possible conflicts between high NAch and an individual's prevailing values. This is particularly important when facilitating entrepreneurship among culturally disadvantaged people (Timmons, 1971) or accelerating economic development in countries such as India and Pakistan.

Goal Setting A mainstay of this training is goal setting, namely, inculcating a trainee's NAch through "prestige suggestion." This means that reasons are given to trainees suggesting that each trainee's achievement-oriented behavior should and can change as a result of taking the course. This sales technique makes participants confident before entering the program that they will change their behavior to become more achievement-oriented.

Toward the end of the course, each participant is asked to complete an achievement plan for the next two years. This is tantamount to setting specific performance goals. In addition, the trainees are asked every six months to report back to the trainers how well they are progressing toward attaining these goals.

Interpersonal Support The attitude assumed by the course instructors can best be described as supportive, honest, and noncritical. The program is held in a retreat setting, away from everyday work, so that total concentration on the course objectives is possible.

The course attempts to heighten the participants' feelings that they are joining a new reference group. The new NAch coding system becomes almost a secret language that only those who have gone through the program can use intelligently. The retreat setting also fosters the feelings of alumni who have gone through it together and can thus look to one another for understanding and support.

The effects of achievement development courses on entrepreneurial performance in several small cities in India were reported by McClelland and Winter (1969). Course participants showed significant improvement in several aspects of entrepreneurial performance, both as compared with themselves prior to training, and as compared with several matched control groups. Specifically, trainees worked longer hours, made more definite attempts to start new business ventures, and actually succeeded in starting more such ventures than people without this training. They also made more investments in productive capital, employed more workers, and tended to have relatively larger percentage increases in the gross income of their organizations. Other studies, involving executives in a large corporation in Bombay, suggest that NAch courses increase the subsequent activity levels of businesspeople who received this training. Further, NAch training has been useful for stimulating economic development among small businesspeople and managers from a depressed economic area of Washington, D.C., and from a similarly depressed rural community in Oklahoma (Timmons, 1971). The course participants not only became more active in their businesses but also assumed more leadership positions in solving community development problems.

Additional evidence on the impact of achievement motivation training in three separate programs was reported by Miron and McClelland (1979). The first program was conducted at the Business School of Southern Methodist University (SMU). Through existing minority entrepreneur associations, 36 persons interested in business were recruited for the course; 23 were Mexican American and 13 were black. A second program was sponsored by the Small Business Administration (SBA) in eight cities. In all, 197 people attended the first weekend of the training and 133 attended both weekends. One hundred and seven of the former trainees and 86 of the latter were businesspeople. The third program was a special effort to aid mostly black business firms in Seattle that were not succeeding. This program, called Pep Up, involved 16 businesses.

For the SMU and SBA programs, financial data were available for both 18 months prior to and after the training. In the case of Pep Up, the data covered the 12 months before training and 12 months after training. The results showed that all three programs significantly improved small business profitability. Moreover, no one type of business (i.e., manufacturing, retail, or service) seemed to benefit more than any other from the training.

General Conclusions Taken together, studies on achievement motivation training suggest the following:

1. This development approach has mainly been implemented in small business (sales ranging from as low as $1,000/month up to $10,000 to 20,000/month in 1973 dollars). Thus its effectiveness has clearly been shown in small business firms.
2. The type of business within this range does not seem to matter, since the training appears to be equally effective for all kinds of small organizations.
3. Businesspeople with power motivation higher than achievement motivation benefit less well from this training. High need for power among small businesspeople appears to interfere with their success (McClelland & Winter, 1969), most likely because it results in too much risk taking (McClelland & Teague, 1975).
4. The training has been shown to work not only with disadvantaged minorities in the United States but also with small businesses in other countries as well.
5. Small business entrepreneurs appear to benefit from this type of training in the early stages of their careers.

Survey Feedback: Rensis Likert

Survey feedback begins with a rigorous measurement of the way the total organization is presently functioning. Perceptions of behaviors and conditions related to organizational effectiveness are gathered by administering anonymous questionnaires to all organizational members. This information is carefully tabulated for every work group in the organization, for each combination of groups having responsibility of some sort, and for the total organization. Each supervisor and manager receives a tabulation of this information, based on the responses of her or his own immediate subordinates. A change agent, either from an outside consulting agency or from the organization's own staff, counsels the manager-recipient privately in order to maximize the individual's understanding of the survey feedback information. Afterward, the change agent attends a meeting between the manager and the subordinates for the purpose of examining the survey findings and discussing implications for corrective action. The agent's role is to help group members better understand the feedback information, set goals, and formulate action plans for the change effort (Bowers and Franklin, 1972).

This survey-guided technique was originated in 1947 by Mann and his colleagues at the University of Michigan. Today, Michigan's Institute for Social Research (ISR) is the largest provider of the survey feedback method. Their Survey of Organizations (SOQ) questionnaire is administered to all organizational members. The instrument was developed to tap certain constructs contained in Rensis Likert's (1961, 1967, 1976) system theory of organizational functioning.

Likert postulated three broad classes of organizational variables: causal, intervening, and end result. The *causal* variables are independent variables that influence the course of events within an organization and the results achieved. They include such things as the structure of the organization, managerial or supervisory leadership behavior, the flow of communication, and the decision-making practices. *Intervening* variables reflect the internal state of health of the organization, for example, motivation, attitudes, and loyalties of subordinates. The *end-result* variables are the dependent variables that reflect organizational results such as productivity, satisfaction, and earnings. The 1980 edition of the SOQ yields the measures presented in Figure 8.5. Also included in the 125-item questionnaire are questions measuring demographic characteristics, as well as several questions dealing with supervisory needs. Moreover, space is provided for an organization to add its own questions. Shown in Figure 8.6 are two items from the SOQ. Although the survey admittedly does not tap all aspects of Likert's theory, it is reasonable to conclude that the content is representative of Likert's formulation (Taylor and Bowers, 1972).

The effectiveness of the survey feedback method is supported by a large-scale study involving nearly 15,000 white- and blue-collar employees in 23 organizations. Survey feedback was compared to three other intervention strategies (T-group training and two varieties of process consultation) and two control groups in which there was no systematic change attempt. In general, the results showed survey feedback to be

Figure 8.5 Measures found on the Survey of Organizations Questionnaire

Organizational Climate
- Organization of work
- Communication flow
- Emphasis on human resources
- Decision-making practices
- Influence and control
- Absence of bureaucracy
- Coordination
- Job challenge
- Job reward
- Job clarity
- Work interdependence
- Emphasis of cooperation

Supervisory Explanatory Indexes
- Interpersonal competence
- Involvement
- Administrative scope

Supervisory Leadership
- Managerial support
- Managerial goal emphasis
- Managerial work facilitation
- Managerial team building
- Encouragement of participation

Peer Relationships
- Peer support
- Peer goal emphasis
- Peer work facilitation
- Peer team building

End Results
- Group functioning
- Satisfaction
- Goal integration

Figure 8.6 Sample items from the Survey of Organizations Questionnaire

In this organization to what extent are decisions made at those levels where the most adequate and accurate information is available?
1. To a very little extent
2. To a little extent
3. To some extent
4. To a great extent
5. To a very great extent

How satisfied do you feel with your chances for getting ahead in this organization in the future?
1. Very dissatisfied
2. Somewhat dissatisfied
3. Neither satisfied nor dissatisfied
4. Fairly satisfied
5. Very satisfied

*The interested reader is referred to Schein (1969) for a discussion of process consultation. T-group training, commonly referred to as sensitivity training, is discussed in Chapter 9.

better than the other methods for improving organizational climate, leadership behavior, and job satisfaction (Bowers, 1973).

Additional research suggests that there are 17 distinct work group types common to both civilian and navy organizations, as measured by the respondents' answers on the SOQ. The impact of five intervention strategies (survey feedback, data handbook, T-group training, talk process consultation, interpersonal process consultation) on the different work group types was compared to determine the positive and negative effects (Bowers and Hausser, 1977). Survey feedback appears to have been the most positive across work group types, compared to the other four interventions.

Behavior Modification: B.F. Skinner

Two theories underlie behaviorally based training programs, namely, behaviorism (Watson, 1913; Skinner, 1938, 1987) and social learning theory (Bandura, 1977, 1986). The latter theory is discussed in the next section of this chapter. At least two training techniques are based directly on the work of Skinner, namely, the teaching machine that was presented in the form of programmed learning textbooks (Skinner, 1958), and a set of procedures for shaping and modifying a person's behavior. This latter procedure is referred to by the scientific community as *operant conditioning* in recognition that the environment shapes the behaviors that operate on it. The more popular name given to these procedures is behavior modification. Programmed learning textbooks were discussed in Chapter 7. Here, we focus on behavior modification as a training tool.

Behavior modification (also discussed in Chapter 4) is based on the fundamental assumption that "behavior is a function of its consequences." This means that, if the consequences of behavior are aversive to an individual, the chances are reduced that the individual will repeat the behavior under similar conditions in the future. Conversely, if the outcomes are positive, the probability that the behavior will be repeated at some later time under similar conditions is increased. The process of inducing changes in frequency of behavior by changing the consequences of behavior is known variously among trainers as contingency management or behavior modification.

To better understand how this procedure works, let us briefly examine five strategies by which behavior can be strengthened, maintained, or weakened by making specific consequences contingent on specific behavior. The strategies include positive reinforcement, escape and avoidance learning, punishment, and extinction. The different strategies can be used singly or in various combinations.

According to Skinner (1953, 1987), a positive reinforcer is any stimulus which, when added to a situation, strengthens the probability that the behavior will be repeated. An organizational example includes the aspiring young executive who remains in the office at night because the outcome is immediate attention and praise from the boss. In using positive reinforcement, it is important to keep three things in mind.

First, any consequence of behavior (e.g., verbal praise, feelings of accomplishment, money) may be a positive reinforcer for one person, but not for another. One must make a careful evaluation of what is reinforcing for a given individual before beginning a program of positive reinforcement. Certain self-report paper-and-pencil instruments offer a means of measuring the role of various outcomes for motivating each individual employee. One example is the Job Orientation Inventory (JOI) Scale, which provides a ranking of ten work rewards (e.g., pay, security, recognition, job or company status, opportunity for personal growth) which an individual employee may feel that the job should provide (Blood, 1973). However, the best way to determine whether an agent is a positive reinforcer is to make its presentation immediately contingent upon engaging in a given behavior and seeing whether the response rates increase in frequency.

Second, it is necessary to design the reinforcement contingencies in such a way that the reinforcer follows directly from the desired behavior. This is a rule of reinforcement that is often violated. For example, too often in organizations, managers see little relationship between how much effort they expend on their jobs (performance) and how much money they earn. Regardless of the type of reinforcement used, it is essential that it be tied directly to effective performance.

Third, often an emitted behavior may not measure up to the behavior desired. For example, a subordinate may be submitting technical reports on time, but they are not clearly written. By systematically reinforcing closer and closer approximations to the desired product, the manager can shape the subordinate's writing behavior until it becomes acceptable.

This process, known as *shaping*, is necessary whenever the response to be learned is either extremely complex or not within the trainee's immediate repertoire.

Two additional strategies for strengthening a desired behavior are called escape and avoidance learning. *Escape learning* refers to a contingency arrangement in which a desired response can terminate an already noxious stimuli impinging on the individual. For example, an engineer may learn to perform an unpleasant task assignment efficiently, so that he can move (escape) quickly to other assignments that he finds enjoyable.

When an individual's behavior can prevent the onset of a noxious stimulus, the procedure is called *avoidance learning*. For example, a research chemist may remember to wear safety glasses when entering the research and development laboratory in order to avoid severe criticism from superiors. The important point to remember here is that both escape and avoidance learning increase the frequency of a response through the contingent termination or avoidance of an aversive condition by demonstrating a specific behavior.

One approach for reducing the occurrence of undesired behavior is punishment. In one type of punishment, an aversive or noxious consequence is presented immediately after an undesired response. Numerous examples of this pervade organizational life, such as being reprimanded by a supervisor after engaging in some unsafe behavior. A second type of punishment involves the removal of a positive consequence after an undesired response. Examples include being demoted or even fired after performing one's job poorly. Interestingly, punishment is the most widely used method of behavior control in our society. Its widespread popularity may be due to the immediate effects it has in stopping or preventing undesired behavior. In this sense, the person administering the punishment is positively reinforced for punishing (Nord, 1969). An example of this might be a trainer who screams at a trainee who seems disinterested in learning.

Despite its wide use, punishment can have unfortunate side effects. First, there is a high probability that the response will be reduced only when the punishment agent is present. Thus the response may reoccur at its initial rate whenever the trainer is away. Second, punishment may result in avoidance, hostility, or even counteraggression toward the punishing agent. This effect can be detrimental to the trainer, who also wants to verbally praise the trainees' behavior when it is effective.

When positive reinforcement for a previously learned response is withheld, the behavior will eventually disappear. This decline in the probability of an undesired response by means of ignoring it is called *extinction*. The final strategy, when combined with positive reinforcement, is the procedure recommended by Skinner (1953). From a training viewpoint, the combination allows for the elimination of undesired behavior without the unfortunate side effects of punishment or the use of any noxious stimuli, and it rewards trainees for their performance improvements in a positive way.

The effectiveness of positive reinforcement depends primarily on its scheduling. The two primary reinforcement schedules are continuous and intermittent. The continuous schedule is just that: Reinforcement follows every correct response. If a management trainee is praised every time she completes an assignment on time, that response is being continuously reinforced. With this schedule, behavior improves very rapidly and is maintained as long as reinforcement follows every response. However, the behavior stops being emitted shortly after the reinforcement ceases (extinction). With intermittent or variable ratio reinforcement schedules, the reinforcer is not presented after every response, but rather varies the ratio of reinforcers to responses. Thus, from a training standpoint, trainers should initially provide trainees with continuous reinforcement. Once the desired response has been learned, an intermittent schedule should be used. An intermittent schedule of reinforcement can lead to higher performance levels than a continuous schedule (Lewis, 1963).

There are organizations that have used behavior modification programs in the area of employee training and performance improvement, for example, Emery Air Freight, Weyerhaeuser, General Electric, Michigan Bell, and Standard Oil of Ohio. These programs have been successful in improving attendance, safety, and production (Hamner and Hamner, 1976).

With regard to measurement, Watson (1913), the father of behaviorism, made systematic evaluation a cornerstone of behavioral interventions. No behaviorist, to our knowledge, has taken issue with this emphasis. The only controversy with regard to evaluation has been generated by Skinner.

Skinner (1957) criticized the use of inferential statistics. Specifically, he charged that statistical techniques are often used as a surrogate for good experimental controls. As a result, he advocated the sole use of experimental controls in the study of a single subject. When large numbers of data from a single subject are collected under stringent controls, he argued, the results should be both clearly observable and replicable.

One positive outcome of Skinner's advocacy for studying a single subject has been the development of within-group designs (see Chapter 5). This approach to measurement has been embraced by many others because of the difficulty of obtaining control groups in organizational settings.

Behavior modification has been labeled one of seven milestones in industrial/organizational psychology (Dunnette, 1976). This is primarily because of the emphasis it places on operationalizing both the treatment or the intervention, as well as the criterion or dependent variable. This emphasis on careful description in concrete terms, of the behaviors that a trainee should demonstrate after training, is what has made this behaviorally based approach to training so susceptible to measurement (Latham, 1989).

The simplicity and effectiveness of basic operant principles prompted Porter (1973) to advocate their use in training marginal workers, those whose performance in general is considered well below industry standards. Consequently, two field studies (Yukl and Latham, 1975; Yukl, Latham, and Pursell, 1976) were conducted with women employed to plant trees in a rural area of South Carolina. Research on animals (Honig, 1966) and an organizational simulation (Yukl, Wexley, and Seymore, 1972) led to the hypothesis that high response rates would occur with a variable-ratio schedule, but cognitive factors explain why the resulting data did not support this hypothesis. Money administered on a variable-ratio schedule was interpreted by the women as a form of gambling; thus the women did not approve of the program. The continuous schedule, however, was interpreted by the employees as piecework pay, rather than as a form of gambling; thus it was perceived as morally acceptable.

In a subsequent study in the state of Washington, Latham and Dossett (1978) repeated the study with high school- and college-educated unionized workers. Consistent with laboratory research, employees who were learning the job performed better on a continuous than on a variable-ratio schedule; employees who had already learned the job performed better on a variable-ratio schedule than on a continuous one.

A follow-up study four years later showed that all of these employees had higher performance on the variable-ratio schedule than on the continuous schedule (Saari and Latham, 1982). Questionnaire responses indicated that the variable-ratio schedule was perceived by the employees as including job enrichment variables such as recognition, task variety, and task accomplishment whereas this was not the case when the monetary incentive was paid on a continuous schedule.

Komacki, Waddell, and Pearce (1977) collected data on store clerks daily for twelve weeks, on three different behaviors: remaining in the grocery store, assisting customers, and stocking merchandise. After 18 baseline observations, reinforcing consequences were administered for remaining in the grocery store. When this behavior increased (demonstrated over 24 observations), an intervention was made with regard to the second behavior (asking customers if they would like assistance). After the clerks were consistently in the store and consistently helping customers (demonstrated over 30 observations), an intervention was made with regard to the third behavior (stocking merchandise). Through this use of the multiple baseline design, the researchers were able to conclude that changes in the three behaviors were a function of the training intervention. The clerks' performance improved only after, and not before, the introduction of each intervention.

The criticisms of this approach to training are at least twofold. The first is philosophical. Behavior modification is based on the philosophy of positivism, namely, that only social, objectively observable knowledge is valid. Thus scientific data are restricted to the objective report of muscular movements or glandular secretions in time and space. Mental processes are said to be of little or no importance for scientific inquiry. This position has been attacked vehemently (e.g., Locke, 1977, 1980).

Mitchell (1975) has argued that although radical behaviorism increases the ability to predict behavior, it does not permit an adequate explanation of why the behavior occurs. This is because of the failure to take into account the interaction of environmental and cognitive influences as causes of behavior. Numerous disciplines, Mitchell pointed out, refer to unobservables as causal variables (e.g., physics, astronomy).

These unobservables can be indirectly measured through their effects on other variables and eventually on observables. Through what is called a "logic of theoretical networks" (Cronbach and Meehl, 1955), we can ascribe meaning to these constructs and through a process of empirical confirmation provide support for this meaning. Thus a logical positivist position is both an unnecessary limitation on scientific inquiry and a poor representation of current thought in the philosophy of science (Kaplan, 1964; Mitchell, 1975).

The second criticism of the use of behavior modification has to do with application. Wexley (1984) pointed out that some people are reluctant to use behavior modification procedures. Specifically, they do not feel comfortable giving subordinates praise (Komacki, 1982). One way to overcome this reluctance is for higher level management to model the use of praise and specific feedback. We discuss the subject of modeling next.

Social Learning Theory: Albert Bandura

Social learning theory is a social cognitive theory (Bandura, 1986). It explains human behavior in terms of continuous interplay among cognitive, behavioral, and environmental determinants. In the social learning view, people are neither driven by inner forces nor buffeted by environmental stimuli. Rather, psychological functioning is explained in terms of a continuous reciprocal interaction of personal and environmental determinants (Bandura, 1977, p. 11). Implicit in this statement is the view that behavior is neither determined solely by its environmental consequences (i.e., reinforcer and punishers) nor by an individual's cognitions (i.e., conscious intentions and goals). Instead, social learning theory provides a theoretical structure that incorporates the views of both the behaviorists and the cognitivists. Thus this theoretical approach to training managers is listed toward the end of the chapter, because it encompasses cognitive, behavioral, and environmental strategies for increasing the motivation level of managers, and for improving their interpersonal skills in dealing with subordinates.

Social learning theory specifically acknowledges that most human behavior is learned observationally through modeling (see Chapter 4). Through the process of observing others, an individual forms an idea of how behaviors are performed and the effects they produce. This coded information serves as a guide for action. Because people can learn from example before actually performing the behaviors themselves, they are spared needless trial and error. This conception of the learning process is quite different from the Skinnerian viewpoint, where learning by reinforcement is portrayed as a mechanistic process in which behaviors are shaped automatically and unconsciously by their immediate consequences. Social learning theory holds that people do not merely react to external influences, as if they were unthinking organisms, but actually select, organize, and transform stimuli that impinge upon them.

Both behavioristic (Skinner, 1938) and social learning theories agree that behavior is affected by its consequences, but the two theories differ with respect to the specific role of reinforcement. According to behaviorism, a reinforcer strengthens preceding responses, even without awareness by the person of what is being reinforced. Social learning theorists argue that anticipatory capabilities enable individuals to be motivated by prospective consequences of their behavior (Bandura, 1986; Latham, 1989).

Laboratory experiments have shown that more effective learning is achieved when individuals are informed in advance of the consequences of performing a specific behavior, rather than waiting until the behavior is demonstrated and then receiving a reinforcer. This process is particularly true in observational learning, where anticipation of reinforcement influences what is attended to and how well it is remembered. Observer attention and retention processes are increased when the trainee knows that the consequences of a model's behavior will be effective in producing valued outcomes or in averting punishing ones. Unlike behaviorism, social learning theory also acknowledges that people can regulate their own actions by self-produced consequences. Examples and goals impart standards of conduct that form the basis for self-reinforcing reactions. This process gives humans a capacity for self-direction.

Impressive empirical support for social learning theory has been obtained in well-controlled studies in experimental and clinical settings (see Bandura, 1986, for a review of this literature). In addition, the theory has been embraced as a vehicle for changing employee behavior in organizations. Goldstein and Sorcher (1974) were among the first to explain the potential value of behavior modeling procedures for improving the interpersonal skills of first-line supervisors. More recently, several studies have presented results on the application of behavior modeling procedures to industrial training programs (Burke and Day, 1986; Davis and Mount, 1984; Gist, Rosen, and Schwoerer, 1988; Gist, Schwoerer, and Rosen, 1987; Meyer and Raich, 1983; Porras and Anderson, 1981; Sorcher and Spence, 1982). These studies show that behavior modeling training can be useful for improving the interpersonal and communications skills of managers and supervisors with subordinates.

Behavior Modeling Training Latham and Saari (1979) used behavior modeling to train supervisors how to interact effectively with their employees. Their nine training modules focused on the following topics: (1) orienting a new employee, (2) giving recognition, (3) motivating a poor performer, (4) discussing poor work habits, (5) discussing potential disciplinary action, (6) reducing absenteeism, (7) handling a complaining employee, (8) reducing turnover, and (9) overcoming resistance to change. The training program was designed to include the components of effective modeling, namely, attentional processes, retentive processes, motor reproduction processes, and motivational processes.

The trainees met for two hours each week for nine weeks. Each training session followed a similar format:

1. Introduction of the topic by the trainers (attentional processes);
2. Presentation of a film that depicts a supervisor modeling effectively a situation based on a set of three to six learning points that were shown in a film immediately before and after the model was presented (retention processes);
3. Group discussion of the effectiveness of the model in exhibiting the desired behaviors (retention processes);
4. Actual practice in role-playing the desired behaviors in front of the training class (retention processes; motor reproduction processes); and
5. Feedback from the training class on the effectiveness of each trainee in demonstrating the desired behaviors (motivational processes).

In each practice session, one trainee took the role of supervisor and the other trainee assumed the role of an employee. No set scripts were used. Instead, the two trainees were asked to recreate an incident relevant to the film topic for that week which had occurred to at least one of them within the past year.

The learning points in the film were posted in front of the trainee playing the role of supervisor. For example, the learning points for handling a complaining employee included (1) avoid responding with hostility or defensiveness, (2) ask for and listen openly to the employee's complaint, (3) restate the complaint for thorough understanding, (4) recognize and acknowledge his or her viewpoint, (5) if necessary, state your position nondefensively, and (6) set a specific date for a follow-up meeting. These learning points provided one of the key components of coding and retention.

At the end of each of the nine training sessions, the supervisors were given copies of the learning points for that session. They were asked to use the supervisory skills they had learned in class with one or more employees on the job within a week's time period. In this way, transfer of training from the classroom to the job was maximized. The supervisors were also asked to report their successes and failure to the training class the following week.

To further ensure that the supervisors would be reinforced for demonstrating on-the-job behaviors that were taught in class, their superintendents attended an accelerated program designed to teach them the importance of praising a supervisor, regardless of whether he or she was in the training or control group, whenever they saw him or her demonstrate a designated behavior. This procedure enhanced the motivational processes of the training.

An evaluation of this behavior modeling training included four types of measures: reaction, learning, behavior, and performance criteria (see Chapter 5 for a complete discussion of these evaluation measures). The training program produced highly favorable trainee reactions, which were maintained over an eight-month period. Moreover, the performance of the trainees was significantly better than that of supervisors in a control group on a learning test administered six months after training, and on performance ratings collected on the job one year after training.

The practical significance of this study is that it supports earlier applications of behavior modeling for training first-line supervisors. These studies taken together indicate that certain leadership skills can be taught, provided that the trainee is given a model to follow, is given a specific set of goals or learning points, is given an opportunity to perfect the skills, is given feedback about the effectiveness of his or her behavior, and is reinforced with verbal praise for applying the acquired skill on the job (Latham and Saari, 1979).

Meyer and Raich (1983) evaluated the outcome of behavior modeling training in terms of sales performance. Those who received the training increased their sales by an average of 7 percent during the ensuing six-month period; their counterparts in the control group showed a 3 percent decrease in average sales.

Davis and Mount (1984) compared the effectiveness in the teaching of appraisal skills of (1) using computer-assisted instruction (CAI) and (2) using CAI plus behavior modeling. The CAI training alone was as effective as the CAI plus modeling in terms of performance on a multiple-choice test. However, the CAI plus modeling was found to improve significantly employee satisfaction with the way their managers conducted the appraisal discussion. The CAI training was no more effective than the control group in this regard.

A meta-analysis of 70 studies on the effectiveness of management training found that behavior modeling was among the most effective of all training techniques (Burke and Day, 1986). One reason for this superiority is that modeling affects self-efficacy as an intervening variable affecting performance. However, different training methods may be needed for persons with high and low self-efficacy. In a study involving the use of computer software, Gist et al. (1987) found that modeling increased performance for people whose pretest self-efficacy was in the moderate-to-high range. For those with low self-efficacy, a one-on-one tutorial was more effective. This is why a person analysis, discussed in Chapter 3, is so important. A person analysis takes into account individual differences among trainees.

Bandura (1982, 1986) identified four informational cues which trainers can use to enhance a trainee's self-efficacy beliefs. In descending order of influence, they are enactive mastery, vicarious experience, persuasion, and emotional arousal.

The first strategy trainers can use to increase self-efficacy is to focus on the trainee's experiences with the particular task. Positive experiences and success with the task tend to increase self-efficacy; failures lead to a lowering of efficacy. For example, Bandura (1982) found that self-efficacy increases when one's experiences fail to validate one's fears, and when the skills one acquires allow mastery over situations that the person once felt threatening. But, in the process of completing a task, if trainees encounter something that is unexpected and intimidating, or the experience highlights limitations in their present skills, self-efficacy decreases even if the person's performance was "successful." Only as people increase their ability to predict and manage threats do they develop a robust self-assurance that enables them to master subsequent challenges. It would appear imperative that trainers arrange subject matter in such a way that trainees know in advance what they will be taught and that they experience success in that arena through active participation with the subject matter.

A second way self-efficacy can be increased is through vicarious experience, namely, modeling others' behavior. Observing others exhibit successful performance increases one's own self-efficacy, particularly when the model is someone with whom the trainee can identify (Bandura, 1986).

A third approach trainers can use to increase a trainee's self-efficacy is through verbal persuasion. This involves convincing the trainee of his or her competence on a particular task. For example, Gist (1990) has argued that self-censorship can stifle creativity through the cognitive process of self-judgments (e.g., "my idea is no good"). Thus she argued that cognitive modeling may be more appropriate than behavior modeling when the performance deficiency is due to inappropriate thought rather than overt behavior or skill.

Cognitive modeling is a self-instruction technique that involves visualizing one's thoughts as one performs an activity. The results of Gist's study in a federal research and development agency showed that subjects in the cognitive modeling condition had significantly higher self-efficacy than their lecture-trained counterparts following training (Gist, 1990). In addition, the cognitive-modeling subjects were superior to the lecture/practice group in generating divergent (i.e., creative) ideas.

The persuasive effect the trainer can have directly or indirectly on a trainee's self-efficacy and, hence, behavior has recently been documented under the rubric of the Pygmalion effect (Eden, 1990). For example, Eden and Shani (1982) conducted a field experiment to investigate the Pygmalion effect on Israeli Defense Force trainees. Boot camp trainees were randomly assigned to one of three conditions where they were described respectively to their instructors as having high, regular, or unknown command potential. The results showed that those trainees who were designated as having high command potential performed significantly higher than the control group on an objective achievement test. Moreover, the trainees in the high potential condition reported greater satisfaction with the course and more motivation to continue with the next training course than did their peers in the control group.

A follow-up study by Eden and Ravid (1982) replicated these results and provided further insight into the nature of the Pygmalion effect. Specifically, the researchers wanted to test the influence of the Pygmalion effect when manipulated independently on the trainee as well as the trainer. Trainees in a clerical course in the Israeli Defense Force were randomly assigned to one of three conditions where the instructors were informed that trainees had either high potential for success, regular potential for success, or that insufficient information prevented prediction of trainee success. The trainees in the insufficient information group, unbeknown to the trainers, were then randomly assigned to two groups. Specifically, one group was told they had high potential for success; the other was told they had regular potential for success. Success in training was subsequently measured by instructor ratings as well as by an objective performance examination.

The results of this study demonstrated significant Pygmalion effects for both the instructor-expectancy and trainee-expectancy conditions. Instructor expectancy accounted for 52 percent of the variance in mean ratings; trainee expectancy accounted for 35 percent of the variance. As for the objective performance exam, instructor expectancy accounted for 27 percent of the variance in scores; trainee expectancy accounted for 30 percent of the variance. Interestingly, these results persisted despite a change midway through the training course to instructors who were unaware of the Pygmalion manipulation. Thus the effects of the initial expectancy condition carried over to the relief instructors whose expectations had not been experimentally manipulated.

The results of these two studies show the effects of trainer beliefs on trainee behavior. Trainers who have high expectations of trainees can communicate these expectations in a myriad of ways (e.g., attention). A trainee who believes that others think highly of his or her capabilities develops a strong sense of self-efficacy and thus exhibits high performance. However, taking steps to persuade trainees that they have the capability to perform well would appear to serve as an antidote to a trainer who does not think highly of a trainee's performance potential.

A fourth method of increasing self-efficacy is emotional arousal. Goal setting, discussed in Chapter 4, is an excellent way of accomplishing this.

Self-Management is a second area of social learning theory that is only now beginning to be studied empirically in organizational settings. This training teaches people skills in self-management or self-regulation. The training has proven to be especially effective in increasing one's self-efficacy. The core of the training is goal setting.

Perhaps the most rigorously developed self-management program is that of Fred Kanfer, a clinical psychologist. Kanfer's training program (1974, 1975, 1980) was designed for obtaining commitment to, and the attainment of, self-generated goals. In brief, the training teaches people to assess problems, to set specific hard goals in relation to those problems, to monitor ways in which the environment facilitates or hinders goal attainment, and to identify and administer reinforcers for working toward, and punishers for failing to work toward, goal attainment. In essence, this training teaches people skills in self-observation, how to compare their behavior with the goals they set, and how to administer reinforcers and punishers to bring about and sustain goal commitment (Karoly and Kanfer, 1982). The reinforcer or punisher is made contingent on the degree to which the behavior approximates the goal. Reinforcers and punishers are viewed in terms of informational as well as emotional feedback in order to take into account cognitive as well as motoric and autonomic effects. This training has proven to be especially effective in teaching people coping skills for overcoming alcoholism and substance abuse (Kanfer, 1974).

Brief and Hollenbeck (1985) surveyed salespersons to identify the extent to which self-regulatory activities take place in the absence of training. Self-regulation was operationalized in terms of three components: goal setting, self-monitoring, and self-rewarding and self-punishing contingent upon the magnitude of the discrepancy between one's behavior and one's goal. The data revealed that the salespeople did not regulate their own job performance. The benefit of such training in self-management in an organizational setting was shown in two field experiments.

Using Kanfer's (1980) methodology, Frayne and Latham (1987) trained unionized state government employees to increase their attendance at the work site. The training consisted of goal setting, writing a behavioral contract, self-monitoring, and the selection and self-administration of rewards and punishments. Compared to a control condition, training in self-management gave employees the skills to manage personal and social obstacles to job attendance, and it increased their perceived self-efficacy. As a result, employee attendance was significantly higher in the training than in the control group. The higher the perceived self-efficacy, the better the subsequent job attendance. A follow-up study (Latham and Frayne, 1989) shows that this increase in job attendance continued over nine months. The control group was then given the same training. Both self-efficacy and job attendance increased relative to that of the original experimental group.

Today, downsizing is occurring across industries with emphasis on fewer rather than more managers and supervisors (Latham, 1988; Wexley, 1984). Concomitant with this deemphasis on formal supervision is an emphasis in industry on employee self-management. Thus we predict the need for this training will increase during this decade.

FINAL COMMENTS

Related to the topic of organizational analysis (see Chapter 3) is the value, if any, that organizations place on psychological theory in developing training programs. The emphasis on theory is the theme here.

To the extent that theory is absent, there is a lack of understanding about why a training approach worked or failed to work. Consequently, the steps that can be taken to increase training effectiveness are often difficult to discern. Thus, in the absence of theory, it is not surprising that only an estimated 10 percent of the $100 billion spent annually on training and development programs results in an enduring behavior change (Georgenson, 1982; Kelly, 1982).

Chapter 1 expressed the need to minimize fads in the field of training and explained why a reliance on systematic evaluation of training effectiveness is a forceful way of doing this. The present chapter has illustrated the following points:

1. The scientific leadership literature is no longer dominated by fads. For example, applications of self-regulation techniques, Leader Match, role-motivation theory, LMX, and double-loop learning have been systematically evaluated for more than a decade, and their evaluation is ongoing. The importance of this sentence is threefold. First, these leadership training programs are grounded in theory; the training programs have been subjected to repeated investigation; and the training has been evaluated empirically. Many of the evaluations included follow-up data collected from three months to five years subsequent to the training. Moreover, the measures for evaluating the training programs included observable job behaviors.

2. Investigators have not been content simply to show the causal relationship between training and performance. Intervening variables such as self-efficacy, leadership style, motivation to manage, leader-member exchange, growth need strength, and a reduction in defensiveness have been studied to determine why these programs are effective. Miner (1988) may be right in his belief that what all five of these training programs have in common is a process of sensitization to the leadership role that can interact with the basic personalities of people to increase their motivation to manage. The conditions that can make for change in motivation to manage, he might argue, appear to exist within four of these five training procedures. Double-loop learning, the exception, should increase the learning potential of people regardless of their desire to manage others.

3. Like Campbell (1977) in the United States, Stewart (1984) in the United Kingdom has argued the need to understand what leaders do. She concluded that the background of academicians in business schools may have led to an overrating of management as a "knowing" rather than a "doing" occupation. The theories of training we reviewed in this chapter focus on what leaders do to be successful, and on the psychological processes that make this "doing" a reality. For example, role motivation focuses on what people need to do to increase their motivation to manage others. Self-management training focuses on what people need to do to regulate their own behavior. LMX focuses on what people need to do to prevent "we-they" behavioral patterns in dyadic situations. Leader Match focuses on what people need to do to change the situation in which they are operating so that it is favorable to them. Double-loop learning teaches people what they need to do to minimize defensiveness.

4. Researchers are beginning to use combinations of training programs to form a treatment package to affect change (e.g., Fiedler et al., 1984, 1988). A treatment-package approach analogous to what is done in clinical psychological settings (Azrin, 1977) may be more appropriate than trying to tease out the additive or interactive effects of each, especially in light of the difficulty in making fair comparisons (Cooper and Richardson, 1986). The latter is especially problematic if the components of the treatment package are designed to change different rather than the same target behaviors.

5. We predict that as we move into the twenty-first century, social learning theory (Bandura, 1986) will become increasingly useful as a theoretical framework for understanding and increasing training effectiveness. This theory posits reciprocal determinism among the person's cognitions, the environment, and overt behavior. In other words, behavior influences and is influenced by both cognitive thought processes and environmental (e.g., organizational) contingencies.

Training programs are often ineffective because they fail to take into account each of these three variables, or they fail to understand the interactions among them. Self-regulation plays an important role in social learning theory. Individuals regulate their behavior based on their performance goals, their belief about their ability to achieve these goals (self-efficacy), and their beliefs about the environmental consequences of their behavior (outcome expectancies). This self-regulation should be an important aspect of the training process. Training effectiveness is enhanced when the organization takes steps to ensure that trainees (1) are clear about the organization's goals, (2) develop a strong sense of self-efficacy regarding training content, (3) believe that effective performance on their part will lead to desired outcomes, and (4) believe their mastery of training content will enable them to overcome perceived environmental obstacles. Social learning theory takes these four considerations into account.

At the present time, the diversity in these different management development approaches allows trainers a wide selection from which to choose. Reference to Figure 8.1 shows that these techniques differ not only in terms of the goals they are trying to achieve but also in the strategies they use to attain these goals.

It might be helpful at this point to discuss where these approaches agree and disagree from one another by asking several key questions:

1. *Do the theorists mentioned in this chapter view effective leadership as being contingent upon the nature of the situation*? Clearly, Mintzberg, Fiedler, and Vroom and Yetton would answer yes. Although Mintzberg holds that all managerial positions can be described in terms of ten roles, he points out that the relative importance given to each of these roles should depend on the job itself, the environment, the person, and the situation. Fiedler argued that leadership effectiveness is contingent upon a proper match between a manager's motivational structure or style (i.e., LPC) and the favorableness of the situation. According to Fiedler, certain situations call for relationship-motivated leaders. Vroom and Yetton's model takes into account a number of situational variables that a manager should take into consideration before deciding whether to permit subordinates to participate in a specific decision.

Argyris (Model II), Blake and Mouton (9,9 management), Miner (six motives), and McClelland (high need for achievement) seem to advocate leadership prescriptions that would be good in all situations. Finally, it appears as though Likert, Bandura, and Skinner are not espousing a theory of leadership per se. Their theoretical approaches are concerned more with prescribing ways and means of getting leaders to behave effectively.

2. *Can managers learn to behave effectively*? Everyone would say yes. Fiedler contends, however, that it is easier to train managers to diagnose the particular leadership situation in which they find themselves, and then teach them to alter the situation to match their own individual leadership style.

3. *What are the costs in using each approach to improve a manager's effectiveness*? It seems as though the approaches of Argyris (Model II), Blake and Mouton (9,9 management), McClelland (high need for achievement), and Likert (survey feedback) involve relatively high costs. Argyris confirmed this by describing how three years of time and effort were required to help only six company presidents. Grid seminars last a week and are either conducted away from the company by outside consultants or on an in-house basis by high-level executives who must be given training in grid methodology. Need for achievement training is a relatively long process involving achievement-related fantasizing, self-study, the use of interpersonal supports, goal setting, and follow-up of participants. With survey feedback, a consultant feeds back information to individual managers, typically starting at the top of the organization and proceeding down. Each manager then meets with his or her subordinates to interpret the information and decide on corrective action plans.

The approaches advocated by Mintzberg (self-study questions), Fiedler (self-teaching guide), Miner (lectures), and Skinner (the strategic scheduling of positive reinforcement) involve fewer costs compared to the other approaches. The costs involved in the careful construction of behavior modeling videotapes or films make Bandura's approach moderately priced.

4. *What benefits can be obtained from using these approaches*? This last question returns us to our remarks at the beginning of this chapter regarding the decline in productivity in the United States. What can these approaches do to help this dire situation? This, of course, is a difficult question to answer. However, some of the evaluative research conducted on these management development approaches allows us to make some speculative conclusions.

Despite the continued controversy over Fiedler's contingency model and the validity of his LPC scale, the Leader Match program appears to bring about significant improvements in the performance ratings of managers in a variety of organizational settings. The major contribution of Fiedler's approach is the idea that, since it is extremely difficult to change an individual's leadership style, we should train managers to either adapt the situation to match their style or else choose to lead only in situations that fit their style. The main limitation of this notion, however, is that it may not be feasible for a manager to either change or avoid certain leadership situations.

Vroom and Yetton's approach deals with a more limited aspect of leadership than Fiedler's. However, like Fiedler, this model takes into account a number of situational variables that must be considered by a manager. Too often we have seen managers who are either "too participative" or "too autocratic" in dealing with their subordinates. The Vroom and Yetton model trains managers to decide whether to employ subordinate participation in decision making. Most of the evaluative research to date involves self-reported ratings; the results that do not do so are somewhat discouraging.

Finally, all of the motivation approaches we discussed have enormous potential for increasing the effectiveness of managers and the productivity of their work groups. Before ending this chapter, two points should be made. First, Miner's suggestion to install courses in business schools designed to develop "motivation to manage" is most provocative and should be implemented. Second, need for achievement training for stimulating economic development among small businesspeople and managers should be encouraged in light of the recent trends in Eastern Europe.

Chapter 9

Management and Executive Development

This chapter discusses management and executive development methods. We have chosen those techniques that are most prevalent and represent the range of training methods currently being used. In reviewing these techniques, we have again categorized them according to the scheme presented in Figure 1.1 (see Figure 9.1).

Each technique is described together with its advantages and disadvantages and any research evidence bearing on its effectiveness. Unlike the training methods reviewed in Chapter 8, rigorous evaluation is still lacking in this area. At the present time, we know little about which management development technique is best for which purpose. We begin by discussing those techniques designed to increase a manager's self-awareness.

SELF-AWARENESS

Self-awareness involves learning about ourselves. It involves understanding how our behavior is viewed by others, identifying the interpersonal games being played around us and the ones we are playing ourselves, and understanding our own managerial capabilities and limitations. Those training techniques which embrace one or more of these objectives by changing the way managers think include sensitivity training, transactional analysis, and self-directed management development. Another technique, which uses a behavioral rather than a cognitive strategy to increase managerial self-awareness, is called interactive skills training.

re 9.1 Goals and strategies of additional management development techniques

STRATEGIES	GOALS: Self-Awareness	Job Skills	Motivation
Cognitive	Sensitivity training Transactional analysis Self-Directed management development	Seminars and workshops Corporate classrooms The incident process Case study	
Behavioral	Interactive skills training	Rational manager training Conference (discussion) Assessment centers Role playing Management games Junior board Understudy assignments	
Environmental			

Sensitivity Training

A unique approach to increasing people's awareness of how they behave as viewed by others is sensitivity training. Despite repeated criticism concerning the effectiveness of this approach (e.g., Dunnette and Campbell, 1968) and the potential psychological dangers of the experience (e.g., Odiorne, 1970), sensitivity training (or T-group education as it is frequently called) continues to be a method of management development. Its popularity stems largely from the discouragement many organizations have experienced when attempting to improve the interpersonal skills of their managers by more conventional informational presentation techniques such as lectures and conferences. These organizations often send their supervisory personnel to either the National Training Laboratories (NTL), university institutes, or consulting firms for sensitivity training.

Sensitivity training is usually conducted with small groups of 8 to 14 individuals. During training, each individual examines how they are perceived by others in terms of their interpersonal skills. The goals can be summarized as follows (Campbell, Dunnette, Lawler, and Weick, 1970):

Goal 1: To give trainees an understanding of how and why they act as they do toward other people and how their actions affect others.

Goal 2: To provide insight into why other people act the way they do.

Goal 3: To teach the participants how to *listen,* that is, to truly hear what other people are saying.

Goal 4: To provide insight concerning how groups operate and the processes groups go through under different conditions.

Goal 5: To foster an increased tolerance and understanding of the behavior of others.

Goal 6: To provide a setting in which an individual can try new ways of interacting with people and receive feedback as to how these new ways affect them.

Some programs emphasize the trainee's need for self-awareness and sensitivity to others; other programs emphasize the trainee's understanding of group processes. In some instances, sensitivity training is unstructured and the trainer's role is passive (Campbell and Dunnette, 1968); in other instances, the leader's behavior is often prominent (Smith, 1975). Despite variations among T-groups, they have similar basic processes and structural characteristics. The following excerpt provides a good description of the procedures followed in a typical T-group session:

> At the fifth meeting the group's feelings about its own progress became the initial focus of discussion. The "talkers" participated as usual, conversation shifting rapidly from one point to another. Dissatisfaction was mounting, expressed through loud, snide remarks by some and through apathy by others.
>
> George Franklin appeared particularly disturbed. Finally pounding the table, he exclaimed, "I don't know what is going on here! I should be paid for listening to this drivel! I'm getting just a bit sick of wasting my time here. If the profs don't put out—I quit!" George was pleased; he was angry, and he had said so. As he sat back in his chair, he felt he had the group behind him. He felt he had the guts to say what most of the others were thinking! Some members of the group applauded loudly, but others showed obvious disapproval. They wondered why George was excited over so insignificant an issue, why he hadn't done something constructive rather than just sounding off as usual. Why, they wondered, did he say their comments were "drivel?"
>
> George Franklin became the focus of discussion. "What do you mean, George, by saying this nonsense?" "What do you expect, a neat set of rules to meet all your problems?" George was getting uncomfortable. These were questions difficult for him to answer. Gradually he began to realize that a large part of the group disagreed with him; then he began to wonder why. He was learning something about people he hadn't known before. . . . "How does it feel, George, to have people disagree with you when you thought you had them behind you? . . ."
>
> Bob White was first annoyed with George and now with the discussion. He was getting tense, a bit shaky perhaps. Bob didn't like anybody to get a raw deal, and he felt that George was getting it. At first Bob tried to minimize George's outburst, and then he suggested that the group get on to the real

> issues, but the group continued to focus on George. Finally Bob said, "Why don't you leave George alone and stop picking on him. We're not getting anywhere this way."
>
> With the help of the leaders, the group focused on Bob. "What do you mean, 'picking' on him?" "Why, Bob, have you tried to change the discussion?" "Why are you so protective of George?" Bob began to realize that the group wanted to focus on George; he also saw that George didn't think he was being picked on, but felt he was learning something about himself and how others reacted to him. "Why do I always get upset," Bob began to wonder, "when people start to look at each other? Why do I feel sort of sick when people get angry at each other?" . . . Now Bob was learning something about how people saw him, while gaining some insight into his own behavior. (Tannenbaum, Weschler, and Massarik, 1961, p. 123)

What conclusions can be reached about the effectiveness of sensitivity training? Burke and Day (1986) were encouraged that the training was effective on the basis of reaction criteria. Most trainees reported that they enjoyed it and found it helpful. There was little or no evidence, however, of changes in actual job performance. Where there was evidence, the trainees had selected their own observers to report on the trainees' behavior changes, or worse, the trainees' own self-reports were used.

A major problem with sensitivity training, however, is the lack of an adequate theory behind the process of individual change. For this reason, it is uncertain why it affects certain people in certain ways and not others. Because of this lack of theory, there are no selection standards for determining who needs the training, no standardized procedures for the trainers to follow during training, and no clearly agreed upon behavioral objectives for the training. The objectives of certain T-group programs are often stated in such vague terminology as developing the manager "to be more sensitive" or "relate better to others." It is not clear what the trainee is supposed to do differently as a result of this training experience.

Another problem with sensitivity training is that there is no convincing evidence to date that any resulting behavioral change is job related. There simply is very little evidence that it increases the ability of the person to fulfill critical requirements of the job.

Another important issue concerning sensitivity training is that it may be psychologically dangerous for some people. A few individuals have had serious emotional problems needing psychiatric care as a result of participating in T-groups (Odiorne, 1970). However, Cooper (1975) reviewed the research in this area and tentatively concluded that the psychologically disturbing consequences for participants may not be as bad as some people claim. Wexley and Yukl (1984) recommend the following safeguards when using sensitivity training:

1. Encourage voluntary participation and withdrawal from the program.
2. Carefully select trainers who are qualified to conduct T-groups. Here we strongly recommend that the trainer be required to pro-

duce evidence consistent with the principles described in Chapter 5 that demonstrate training effectiveness.

3. Screen participants by means of psychometric instruments measuring a person's level of adjustment. These tests should be administered by a trained psychologist.

The openness movement that started in the 1960s with the advent of sensitivity (T-group) training has apparently lost much of its momentum (Kaplan, 1986). We know of very few organizations that are currently using this method of management development as it was originally developed. However, as we discuss in Chapter 10, variations of it are used in cross-cultural training and to teach team play.

Transactional Analysis

Transactional analysis (TA) was developed in the 1950s by Eric Berne. Berne (1964) analyzed the daily transactions that take place between people, and described these transactions using simple, nontechnical language.

The book *I'm OK—You're OK* by Thomas A. Harris (1969) has almost become synonymous with TA. What makes a person feel "OK" or "not OK" is the amount of stroking they receive. The term *stroking* comes from the physical contact infants receive from the time they are born. Positive stroking is analogous to the concept of positive reinforcement in behavior modification; negative stroking is analogous to punishment. The important thing about negative strokes, according to TA, is that they are better than no strokes at all (a notion totally contrary to behavior modification; see Chapter 8). Besides positive and negative strokes, people often give "plastic" strokes. Plastic strokes are, essentially, artificial strokes. Saying, "My, how persuasive you are with our customers" to a disliked salesperson caught in an embarrassing situation with one of the company's biggest clients is an example of a plastic stroke. Further, all transactions entail two strokes: the stimulus and the response to that stimulus.

The behavior observed during transactions fall into three categories or ego states: Parent, Adult, and Child. The Parent is that aspect of our personality which we have learned from our own parents. It is not the same as our conscience. Rather, it is that part of our parents which we carry about with us. For example, in a work setting, it might include our attitudes about how hard we should work or how we should treat our co-workers and subordinates. The Adult is the observable behaviors that we emit when adjusting to the world, processing data, or estimating our chances for success. The Child involves the behavioral patterns that we learned to use in adapting to our own parents. It very much determines how we will react whenever another person treats us as a Child. The reactions may take various forms: submission, rebellion, withdrawal, outward aggression, or pleasure.

The important point is that everyone possesses these three ego states. Through a process known as *structural analysis*, transactional analysts describe the ego states that occur during a given transaction. Certain transactions are described as being complementary because the two people involved are responding reciprocally. Here are two examples:

ADULT MANAGER
(TO ADULT EMPLOYEE): What time will you have the final draft of that report ready for me?

ADULT EMPLOYEE
(TO ADULT MANAGER): At 4:30 today.

PARENT MANAGER
(TO CHILD EMPLOYEE): You're late again for work!

CHILD EMPLOYEE
(TO PARENT MANAGER): Stop picking on me; other people are late too.

"Cross transactions" occur when people are not interacting reciprocally. For example:

ADULT MANAGER
(TO ADULT EMPLOYEE): What time will you have the final draft of that report ready for me?

PARENT EMPLOYEE
(TO CHILD MANAGER): It's your fault that I'm having difficulty getting along with co-workers!

PARENT MANAGER
(TO CHILD EMPLOYEE): You're late again for work!

ADULT EMPLOYEE
(TO ADULT EMPLOYER): There was a big accident on the interstate.

Another important aspect of TA is its emphasis on identifying the games that people play. According to Berne, games consume a great deal of time and energy that could be spent on productive activities. One example of a game is what Berne calls "Yes, but." In "Yes, but," a manager might explain that she has tentatively decided on a solution to a problem, but wants to get input from her subordinates before making a final decision. Her subordinates, in turn, all offer reasonable solutions to the problem. Each suggestion by a subordinate is automatically countered with "Yes, but . . ."

Another game is called If It Weren't For You I Could. For instance, an employee might tell his manager that he cannot work overtime this evening because of a previous commitment. The manager responds angrily with "All right, leave early, but if it weren't for you, we could get this project finished by tomorrow morning."

Organizations such as American Airlines, Texas Instruments, Polaroid, Bank of America, Quality Inns International, and Lufthansa Airlines have used TA programs. Although TA was once a widely used management development approach, there is little research on its effectiveness as a training approach. One exception is a study conducted in the home office of a national company (Nykodym, 1978). One work group received six half days of TA designed to increase Adult-Adult transactions between supervisors and employees. Attention also focused on increased listening and approachability by supervisors. The program covered TA concepts of Parent, Adult, and Child transactions combined with role playing.

A second group served as a control group. Both groups were matched for age, experience, education, and job complexity. A statistically significant difference was found between the TA and control groups in terms of employees' perceptions of their managers' supervisory behavior as measured by the Survey of Organizations Questionnaire (see Chapter 8).

Self-Directed Management Development

The underlying assumption of self-directed management development is that the best way to help supervisors and managers improve themselves is to encourage them to become actively involved in thinking about and setting goals for their own development and career growth. The starting point in this process is for them to assess their own supervisory and managerial capabilities and gain an understanding of the skills they must acquire to become effective managers. Through self-assessment, individuals decide for themselves whether they possess the motivation and potential to manage others effectively. Further, individuals are taught that they must assume primary responsibility for their own development. This entails preparing personal development plans to acquire the experience, knowledge, and skills needed to increase their supervisory or managerial talents, or to pursue another career of their choice.

Careers in Management is an example of a management development system incorporating the concepts of self-assessment and self-directed development. This system is comprised of three series. Each series is designed to meet the needs of employees at different levels within the organization. Series 1 is directed at premanagement employees, that is, those individuals interested in a possible career in supervision or management. Series 2 is designed to assist current supervisors and managers assume primary responsibilities for their own development. The third series is intended to help upper-level managers increase their effectiveness in developing the supervisors and managers who report to them. Although these programs have been designed as an integrated system, they can be used independently for personnel in each of these three hierarchical levels. Table 9.1 lists the program objectives for the participants in each of the three series. The instructional technique used in all three series is called the situation-response method. With this method, a group watches a series of typical supervisory situations on videocassettes.

Table 9.1 PROGRAM OBJECTIVES FOR "CAREERS IN MANAGEMENT" SERIES

Series 1 (premanagement employees)

Assess their supervisory and managerial capabilities and potential;
Evaluate the amount of satisfaction they would get from supervising the work of others;
Decide whether they really want to pursue a career in management or supervision;
Identify the capabilities they need in order to become effective supervisors or managers; and
Prepare personal development plans.

Series 2 (supervisors and managers)

Assess their capabilities and supervisory practices;
Identify the knowledge and skills they need to acquire to improve their performance on the job and to increase their potential for future assignments;
Define the development objectives they wish to achieve in order to attain their performance objectives and career goals; and
Prepare "Action Plans" that identify the steps they must take to achieve their development objectives and to increase their supervisory or managerial effectiveness.

Series 3 (upper-level managers)

Identify and evaluate their developmental practices and their development "styles";
Identify opportunities to increase their skill in helping others to develop their capabilities;
Increase their effectiveness in coaching and counseling their subordinates; and
Prepare "Action Plans" to improve the productivity of their organizations by assisting the supervisors and managers who report to them to develop the capabilities they, in turn, need to improve their performance and potential for future assignments.

Adapted from "Careers in Management: A Video-Based Self-Directed Management Development System," Sterling Institute, Washington, DC, 1976.

Each cassette is stopped at a critical point where the supervisor or manager on the videocassette must decide how to handle a particular problem. However, before the participant is shown what happens, a trainer interrupts the program to ask each participant to describe how she or he would handle that particular situation. After each participant indicates his or her intended course of action in a Viewer's Guide, a group discussion takes place. Each member of the group has an opportunity to interact with other participants and defend his or her point of view. After the group discussion, the participants view the video program to learn how the supervisor in the program actually handled the situation. The group is then shown another situation. A module is made up of several situations. At the end of each module, the participants use the materials in the Viewer's Guide to evaluate their own effectiveness, reassess their own capabilities and development needs, and think about their motivation to manage.

When the modules in the series have been completed, the participants analyze their supervisory style profiles, compare their style with that of other members of their discussion group, and consider ways to change their style to improve their managerial effectiveness. In the final segment of the program, each participant generates a developmental action plan and then "reality-tests" his or her plan with the other trainees.

At the present time, there is no scientific evidence on the effectiveness of this training. However, it is based on four key learning principles that have been shown to be effective in bringing about desirable behavior change: observing a model handle interpersonal situations, active participation, feedback, and group discussion on action steps. Because of this, self-directed management development has become quite popular. It has been used by such organizations as General Motors, Ford Motor Company, Coca-Cola, General Tire, and the U.S. Department of Health, Education, and Welfare.

Before ending this section, however, a word of caution is in order: Those organizations using Series 1 should be careful about generating unrealistically high expectations on the part of premanagement trainees. Participants in this series should be informed if there are not enough supervisory positions open to satisfy all those who may want to be supervisors.

Interactive Skills Training

Rackham and Morgan (1977) designed a five-day interactive skills course for managers and supervisors at all organizational levels. As a result of attending the course, it is claimed that participants are able to

1. Identify any differences between the way they perceive their own behavior and the way others see it.
2. Meaningfully interpret the behavior of others.
3. Plan to use behavior that is appropriate to specific situations and the people involved.
4. Control and adapt their behavior according to changing circumstances.
5. Relate what they have learned in the course to situations and problems encountered at work.

It is because of the emphasis given to the first objective that this program has been classified under self-awareness. The content of the course consists of a series of modules, each of which deals with a particular interactive situation that is important for managers and supervisors to handle effectively. The major themes brought out by the situational exercises are persuading, briefing, participating in meetings, handling disciplinary matters and grievances, and fact finding for problem solving or decision making. Typically, the course involves 16 trainees who split up into subgroups to undertake the one-half or two-and-a-half hour exercises.

The unique characteristic of this training approach, originally developed in England for British Airways (BOAC), is the review session that follows every exercise. Each trainee receives feedback from the trainers as well as from fellow course participants. This feedback is provided as quickly as possible after the interactive situation in which it took place. It is expressed in terms of 13 behavioral categories that essentially form the special "language" of the course (see Table 9.2). The trainer maximizes the meaningfulness of this behavioral feedback by helping the trainee to compare this information with the trainee's self-perceptions. Moreover, each individual's behavior is discussed in relation to the other trainees' behaviors, as well as the behaviors of effective performers. On the last day of training, course members are provided feedback on their behavior patterns during the entire week. After this summary feedback session, emphasis is placed on relating the lessons learned during training to the job situation. Specifically, the participants must state how they intend to change their managerial behavior on the job.

Rackham and Morgan present several evaluative studies that they conducted at BOAC. They conclude that these studies produce evidence

Table 9.2 THE CATEGORIES, WITH DEFINITIONS, OF THE CURRENT GENERAL PURPOSE BEHAVIOR ANALYSIS INSTRUMENT

Proposing Behavior which puts forward a new concept, suggestion, or course of action.

Building Behavior which extends or develops a proposal that has been made by another person.

Supporting Behavior which involves a conscious and direct declaration of support or agreement with another person or his or her concepts.

Disagreeing Behavior which involves a conscious, direct, and reasoned declaration of difference of opinion, or criticism of another person's concepts.

Defending/attacking Behavior which attacks another person or defensively strengthens an individual's own position. Defending/attacking behaviors usually involve overt value judgments and often contain emotional overtones.

Blocking/difficulty stating Behavior which places a difficulty or block in the path of a proposal or concept without offering any alternative proposal and without offering a reasoned statement of disagreement. Blocking/difficulty stating behavior therefore tends to be rather bald; e.g., "It won't work," or "We couldn't possibly accept that."

Open Behavior which exposes the individual to possible ridicule or loss of status. This behavior may be considered as the opposite of defending/attacking, including within this category admissions of mistakes or inadequacies provided that these are made in a nondefensive manner.

Testing understanding Behavior which seeks to establish whether or not an earlier contribution has been understood.

Summarizing Behavior which summarizes, or otherwise restates in a compact form, the content of previous discussions or considerations.

Seeking information Behavior which seeks facts, opinions, or clarification from another individual or individuals.

Giving information Behavior which offers facts, opinions, or clarification to other individuals.

Shutting out Behavior which excludes, or attempts to exclude, another group member (e.g., interrupting, talking over).

Bringing in Behavior which is a direct and positive attempt to involve another group member.

From N. Rackham and T. Morgan, *Behavior Analysis in Training.* Maidenhead. © McGraw-Hill Book Co. (UK) Limited, 1977. Reprinted by permission.

for a variety of changes in job performance following interactive skills training. Listed here are some of the changes in performance following the course, according to Rackham and Morgan:

1. More willing to accept responsibility for subordinates' mistakes.
2. Appraises own performance more accurately.
3. Puts across own point of view more clearly.
4. More sensitive to the feelings of subordinates.
5. More effective in dealing with unusual situations.
6. More inclined to work in collaboration with other people.
7. More likely to show subordinates ways to improve their job performance.
8. More effective in anticipating problems.

This managerial development approach incorporates several key learning principles, such as active participation, knowledge of results, and practice. However, the evaluative studies are based on a pretest-posttest design with no control group (see Chapter 5).

JOB SKILLS

Eleven training approaches are designed to increase managerial and executive skills. Seminars and workshops, corporate colleges, case study, and the incident process employ cognitive strategies; rational manager training, conference (discussion) method, assessment centers, role playing, management games, junior boards, and understudy assignments use behavioral strategies to increase managerial effectiveness.

Seminars and Workshops

In a recent survey of management training and education practices in U.S. companies, Saari et al. (1988) found that 90 percent of the 610 responding companies reported using external short-course programs, and that these programs are utilized by small as well as by large companies. A plethora of seminars and workshops are advertised by such organizations as the American Management Association (AMA), Michigan State University's Office of Executive Programs, the University of Washington Business School, the Michigan Business School, the American Productivity Center, the Harvard Business School, NTL Institute, and the Center for Creative Leadership. The following list is a sampling of the diversity of topics that are covered in these seminars and workshops:

- Management of managers
- Basic management for the newly appointed manager
- Negotiating with the Japanese
- Eliminating drugs in the workplace
- Excellence in service management

- Effective communication: improving speaking and writing skills
- Financial analysis, planning, and control
- Information technology for nontechnical managers
- Assertiveness training for managers
- Strategic planning
- Eliminating sexual harassment in the workplace
- Designing effective work teams

These seminars and workshops typically last anywhere from one to five days. They are held at a local hotel, the company's conference room or training facility, or at a college or university's executive education center. These programs are typically conducted by either well-known consultants, writers, or faculty members.

In-house seminars and workshops are preferred by organizations that have a large enough training department and trainee population to make them cost effective (Rynes and Milkovich, 1986). These programs are developed by in-house training specialists, conducted by company trainers (possibly supplemented by outside speakers), and tailor-made to fit the company's needs. Frequently, however, it makes more sense for an organization to simply purchase commercially available programs. The effectiveness of these seminars and workshops vary enormously, depending on the particular program leader(s) as well as the organizational relevance of the content for the attendees. Sometimes these seminars and workshops are enjoyed by the participants with little or no positive transfer of learning (see Chapter 4) back to their jobs.

One way of increasing positive transfer is to make certain that individual managers are attending those particular seminars and workshops that they really need. Conducting a careful person analysis (see Chapter 3) will certainly help identify each manager's unique training needs. In addition, we also recommend taking into consideration the organizational level of the manager involved. For instance, Kraut et al. (1989) found that first-level managers interact primarily on an individual basis with their subordinates. To improve their interpersonal skills, first-level managers need training in such areas as career planning, coaching, motivating, and giving constructive performance feedback. Middle-level managers, on the other hand, are mainly concerned with managing and linking groups. Consequently, training at their level should focus on building a team effort, resolving intergroup conflict, and negotiating effectively with other middle-level managers. In considering the executive's role, training should focus on broadening the executive's understanding of the competition, world economies, politics, and social trends.

Evaluation has been notably absent regarding executive education. In an attempt to fill this void, Hollenbeck (1989) conducted a study of Harvard's Advanced Management Program (AMP) to determine what was actually learned and whether that knowledge brought about an enduring change in the attendee's behavior.

The data were collected through questionnaires and interviews with people who had attended the program two to six years earlier. In addition, spouses completed a questionnaire. Through the use of two different methodologies, the questionnaire and the interview, and through the use of two different respondent populations, the results were shown to have convergent validity (i.e., consensus).

Specifically, attendance at Harvard's AMP brought about the following lasting changes in behavior: broader perspective, strategic thinking, self-confidence, ability to make executive decisions, and interpersonal skill. These five factors were identified through a factor analysis which identified the intercorrelations among the responses to the different items on the questionnaire. The responses from spouses corroborated the findings regarding an increase in self-confidence and taking a broader perspective.

Corporate Classrooms

As we mentioned in Chapter 6, some companies have taken it upon themselves to educate their own managers via corporate classrooms (e.g., ARCO's campus in Santa Barbara for their top-level executives). These corporate colleges have one main feature in common—a dedication to delivering knowledge and skills that their company's managers and executives can apply immediately on their jobs (Wilcox, 1987). Other than this, they have little in common in that they differ from one another in the courses offered, degrees that can be obtained, and training methods. Time will tell whether this is merely another training fad or whether corporate classrooms are here to stay.

Case Study

The use of the case study method as an aid to management development was pioneered at the Harvard Business School. It involves presenting a trainee with a written description of an organizational problem. Each trainee is given an opportunity to read the case in private, diagnose the underlying issues, and exercise judgment in deciding what should be done in the situation described. Then the individual meets with other trainees and, as a small group, they discuss the various diagnoses and proposed solutions.

The trainer's role is primarily that of a catalyst. The trainer provides information sources when appropriate, maintains the direction of the discussion by posing appropriate questions, and encourages the participation of trainees who have difficulty expressing themselves (Simmons, 1975). Thus the primary purpose of the trainer is to facilitate the group's learning process by providing a climate for group discussion. No attempt is made to lecture to the participants; the trainer merely helps them discover for themselves the managerial concepts and principles underlying the case, how the problem might have been avoided, what can be done to prevent this problem from recurring, and so on.

The problems described in the cases vary in length and complexity, depending on the experience level of the trainees involved and the purpose of the case. Most cases deal with solving specific organizational problems, rather than examining theoretical issues.

Advocates of the case method contend that it teaches managers to identify and analyze complex problems and to formulate their own decisions. It exposes trainees to a wide variety of approaches, interpretations, and personalities. In doing so, it shows them that there is seldom a pat solution to most business problems. It also allows managers to derive principles from the cases that they can later apply in solving on-the-job problems (Berger, 1983; Miner and Miner, 1973).

Critics of the method point to its inability to teach general principles and its lack of control over the inferences that trainees draw from their case discussions (Campbell et al., 1970). Advocates argue that this lack of structure is precisely its strong point; trainees learn better and retain more of what they have learned when they discover general principles for themselves. Unfortunately, the research evidence on the effectiveness of the case method as a management development approach is minimal.

One study (Argyris, 1980), based on observations and tape recordings taken during a three-week management development program, uncovered certain limitations of the case study method. First, most trainers dominate the classroom interactions by advocating positions, asking questions, and making connections between responses so as to maintain control of the learning process. This often increases participants' dependence on the trainer and ignores issues that might be important to the participants. Second, trainers often act to save face for the participants as well as for themselves, thus discouraging a confrontational atmosphere and the candid generation of ideas and approaches. Third, participants observe that the trainers' behavior is often incongruent with what they espouse. Some examples of this inconsistency include

1a. There are no right or wrong answers; yet
1b. Some trainers do take positions and give answers.
2a. There are many different views possible; yet
2b. Trainers seem to select viewpoints and organize them on the board in a way to suggest that they have a preferred route.

Finally, very few trainers attempt to relate the participants' behavior in the classroom to their behavior on the job. To improve this method, Argyris argued that participants should read cases from their own organizations (if possible), and that trainers should be less dominating and more willing to allow participants to discuss how to apply their new ideas to their situations back home.

For the case method to be beneficial, it must simulate as closely as possible situations that trainees are likely to encounter on the job. If the case is fabricated, the trainers are likely to find themselves in the uncomfortable position of having to "invent" facts. As soon as the trainees realize that this is happening, they will lose confidence in the trainer's credibility and integrity (Pigors and Pigors, 1987). Moveover, since most management situations are extremely complex, cases cannot be abbreviated reports. Trainees must have an opportunity to see how the problem looked in its early stages, what organizational factors might alleviate or aggravate the situation, and what alternatives are present to prevent further complications.

The Incident Process

The incident process is a variation of traditional approaches to the case study. It attempts to move the training closer to reality by simulating the way managers actually go about making decisions. Unlike the case study, where trainees are given all the facts concerning a situation, the incident process provides only a brief statement of the problem. Trainees must gather additional information by means of a question-and-answer period with a team leader, who supplies only information that is specifically requested.

The originators of this approach (Pigors and Pigors, 1955) believe that this fact finding process parallels the way managers must actually make decisions. No one gives managers all the facts; they have to determine the facts for themselves. "What has the organization done in the past?" "What does the union contract say about this?" "How will this affect our competitive position?" These are just a few of the many questions a manager needs to pose before making decisions.

The incident process has recently been described as a five-step procedure by Pigors and Pigors (1987), as follows:

1. *Starting with an incident.* Trainees begin a case by reading a page or less that depicts some point. They are asked to imagine that the incident has just occurred and to take the role of a manager responsible for coping with it promptly and effectively.
2. *Getting and organizing factual information on the case as a whole.* Trainees now question the trainer (i.e., the person with the facts) for about 20 to 30 minutes. Then they need to reduce these facts to manageable proportions.
3. *Visualizing key facts as interrelated factors and formulating an action issue.* The group at large typically breaks up in subcommittees. At this point, each subcommittee highlights the key elements of the case and creates diagrams that attempt to portray the interrelationships among the elements.
4. *Making, presenting, and testing reasoned opinions.* Next comes the subcommittee presentations to the reconstituted group at large. After the full range of opinions has been presented, the

various subcommittee opinions are compared and appraised during group discussion, and final solutions are generated.

5. *Reflecting on the case as a whole.*The trainees are now invited by the trainer to promote themselves to the role of a senior executive and to engage in long-term, high-level thinking. Specifically, they are asked to examine their solution carefully from this perspective. By doing this, they get to see opportunities that were overlooked, important information that was ignored, and so on.

The incident process is often supplemented by various role-playing and conference leadership techniques that the team leader believes are appropriate to the situation. This training has been widely adopted in the United States and overseas for developing managers in industry, government, and hospitals. In the United States, it has been employed in all three branches of the armed services (Pigors and Myers, 1973). Reports on practical experience with the incident process have been presented in several articles (e.g., Centner, 1956; Marshall, 1954; Schoen and French, 1959). Comments from participants are extremely positive. For instance, Table 9.3 presents the reported effectiveness of the incident process as rated by 60 managerial trainees at a midwestern chemical company. However, there is as yet no evidence that this training actually improves managerial decision-making behavior on the job.

Rational Manager Training

Rational manager training and all the techniques that follow in this chapter are described as behavioral because the employee must actually perform job-related tasks in a simulated setting. Rational manager training, like Vroom and Yetton's program (see Chapter 8), is designed to improve a manager's skill in problem analysis and decision making. The program distinguishes between concepts underlying problem analysis versus those underlying decision making (Kepner and Tregoe, 1975). Problem analysis involves recognizing problem areas, specifying what the problems are by describing them in detail, and, finally, determining their cause. Once the cause of a problem has been identified, its correction requires decision making. Here, the manager is called upon to make a choice between various ways of correcting a problem. This involves establishing goals or objectives (i.e., what one is trying to accomplish), classifying the objectives according to their importance, developing several alternative ways of getting the task done, evaluating each of the alternatives against the objectives, making a tentative choice, exploring the possible adverse consequences of this choice and, lastly, controlling the decision made by taking any actions necessary to prevent these adverse effects.

Another function of the effective manager is taking action before a particular problem develops. The systematic analysis of potential prob-

Table 9.3 EFFECTIVENESS OF THE INCIDENT PROCESS TECHNIQUE

Question	Number of responses			
How well did the Incident Process series	Don't know	Not at all or insignificantly	To a worthwhile extent	A great deal
Improve your ability to be a conference leader?	3	3	41	13
Contribute to the development of general principles that can be used in working with people?	4	4	36	16
Improve your efficiency in conference participation?	2	2	31	29
Improve your ability to get facts?	4	3	24	29
Improve your ability to organize facts?	4	6	33	17
Improve your ability to determine the issues in a problem?	3	6	31	20
Improve the quality of your decisions?	3	7	35	15
Increase your insight into the feelings and motivations of people?	4	8	37	11
Increase your understanding of the points of view of other members of management?	3	3	21	33
Contribute (now or potentially) to improved communications on the job among members who participated?	2	6	26	26
Improve your ability to generalize from specific situations to broader aspects?	3	14	36	7

lems requires a different approach from that used in ordinary problem analysis. In problem analysis, the cause of the problem has already occurred, and the manager is trying to detect it, in order to know what corrective action to take. In potential problem analysis, both the problems and causes are only possibilities, and the manager must decide what actions will prevent these possibilities from occurring. Kepner and Tregoe (1975) offer an orderly set of concepts for accomplishing this process.

The primary purpose of this training is to make managers aware of aids to good decision making and problem solving, give them practice in applying these aids, and then provide them with feedback as to the results of their performance. The program lasts anywhere from two to five days, depending on the target population (i.e., top executives, senior and middle managers, marketing and sales managers, or manufacturing personnel and their immediate supervisors). In this time period, a group of approximately 15 managers grapple with the problems and decisions of a simulated organization. Before each session, the managers and the course instructor discuss the concepts and methods involved. The managers receive materials explaining what has happened recently in this hypothetical company with respect to a given problem. Data are provided in the form of memos, policy directives, financial statements, production and sales records, and so on. During each exercise, each manager is assigned a specific role (e.g., production manager, sales manager). Trainees have their own offices, talk to one another on the telephone, and conduct group meetings to solve the problems at hand (this is why we classify the program with those that use a behavioral strategy).

When the group of trainees has used the time allotted (regardless of whether they solved the problem), they return to the conference room for a critical evaluation of their performance. In this time period, they examine any assumptions they made and the manner in which they used the information available to them. These feedback sessions try to make them aware of inadequate methods of problem analysis and decision making, and to show them where they could have improved if they had followed the systematic procedures prescribed by the course instructor.

In summary, course participants should become aware of (1) the assumptions they make, (2) the procedures they employ for arriving at the cause of a problem, and (3) the decisions they make about it. Although this method of training incorporates many useful learning constructs (e.g., active participation, feedback, practice, simulation), there has been only one systematic examination of its effectiveness. This study, conducted by the NASA-Manned Spacecraft Center, involved the use of self-report questionnaires completed by 125 participants (Goldstein, Gorman, and Smith, 1973). The results indicated that 85 percent of the NASA-MSC managers felt that the course was valuable to them for performing thorough analyses, planning and asking better questions, and making and evaluating recommendations. The average increase in job performance attributed to the course by the NASA managers was 10 percent, with no managers reporting any negative effect on their performance. Almost 40 percent of the managers, however, felt that the most frequent barriers for applying the concepts to their jobs were "not enough time" and "other people not familiar with the course of concepts."

Conference (Discussion) Method

The conference method is basically a small group meeting in which a highly qualified leader helps a group in identifying and defining a problem, guides the discussion so that it is constantly directed toward the problem, and summarizes the principles or explanations that reflect the consensus of the group in dealing with the problem (Lerda, 1967). The conference leader plays a neutral role in the discussion by refraining from manipulating the group or by expressing the ideas he or she favors. To achieve maximum results, the conference leader is often given special training in group decision methods (Maier, 1963). Some of the basic skills that Maier (1973) claims are essential for an effective participative conference leader are outlined here. The leader should:

1. State a problem in such a way that the group does not become defensive, but instead approaches the issue in a constructive way.
2. Supply essential facts and clarify the questions without suggesting a solution.
3. Draw persons out so that all members participate.
4. Wait out pauses; don't jump in with comments.
5. Restate the ideas and feelings expressed in an abbreviated, pointed, and clear form.
6. Ask questions that will stimulate problem-solving behavior.
7. Summarize as the need arises.

Each participant takes an active role in the discussion and obtains feedback from the other participants as well as the leader. The participants pool their ideas, test assumptions, share facts, and reach conclusions. The participants either have some experience related to the problem at hand, or else are capable of dealing with the problem as a result of information provided by the conference leader (Lerda, 1967).

The learning objectives of the conference method are to (1) improve the decision-making and problem-solving skills of supervisors and managers, (2) present new and often complicated conceptual and cognitive information, and (3) change or modify employee behaviors (Hinrichs, 1976). The method is currently used in some organizations to teach such things as supervisory human relations, safety education, effective customer and community communications, and sales training (Utgaard and Davis, 1970). Despite its continued use, there is no evidence to show that this method improves understanding of complex information, problem-solving, or decision-making skills. Several studies have been done, however, which show that the conference method is more effective than lectures in changing employee behaviors (Bond, 1956; Butler, 1967; Levine and Butler, 1952; Lewin, 1958). For example, it was found that it is easier to train interviewers to eliminate judgmental errors during their interviews by using a group discussion method rather than lectures (Wexley, Sanders, and Yukl, 1973).

Assessment Centers

The term *assessment center* refers to a standardized off-the-job simulation of managerial role requirements. It has become common practice for organizations to combine assessment and development activities in one program (Bray, 1976). At IBM, for example, participants spend the first two days being assessed and the next three days going through developmental exercises. Before discussing the benefits of assessment centers, let us take a closer look at this developmental approach.

Assessment center participants are brought to a facility where, for periods ranging from one to seven days, they are observed as a group by several assessors across a wide variety of simulated situations (e.g., business games, in-basket exercises, leaderless group discussions). Other procedures include personal interviews, peer evaluations, and paper-and-pencil tests.

Assessment decisions reflect the combined judgments of several line managers two or more organizational levels above the candidates. The staff is trained to administer the different assessment techniques and, more importantly, to observe and record the candidates' behavior accurately during each of the exercises.

Typically, the candidates are assessed in groups of six or seven. The staff-to-candidate ratio is usually about 1:2 or 1:3. Candidates are evaluated on anywhere from 10 to 15 measurable qualities or dimensions that are considered important for managerial success. Of course, the qualities considered for inclusion in any program will depend on the level and type of management position involved. The following are examples of these qualities:

oral communication skill

written communication skill

personal impact

flexibility

work involvement

career ambition

sensitivity

independence

decisiveness

resistance to stress

energy

organization and planning ability

decision making

An assessment center may have a beneficial training effect on both the participants (assessees) as well as the staff members (assessors). Through formal assessor training and participation as an assessor in the center, staff members may derive the following developmental benefits (Thornton and Byham, 1982): improved interviewing skills; broadened observation skills; increased appreciation of group dynamics and leadership styles; new insights into behavior; strengthened management skills (through repeatedly working with in-basket case problems and other simulations); a broadened repertoire of responses to problems; established normative standards by which to evaluate performance; and a more precise vocabulary with which to describe behavior.

The developmental impact on the assessees is a function of the amount of feedback candidates are provided about their performance at the center. For instance, after taking part in a series of group exercises, assessees at the Ford Motor Company participate in professionally led critique sessions of their performance. After completing individual in-basket exercises, they meet again in groups to share and evaluate their decisions and actions with one another (Byham, 1973).

General Electric had a Talent Development Program (TDP) where participants received performance feedback during a brief counseling session held with one of the staff members just before they leave for home. Within four to six weeks, another staff member conducts an intensive feedback and goal-setting interview with the participant at his or her place of work. This one- to two-hour session reviews all the information obtained at TDP as well as the evaluations given by the staff and co-participants. The TDP representative also confers with the participant's immediate manager. This discussion again concerns the developmental needs and growth potential of the participant. Specifically, it focuses on how the manager could help alleviate the assessee's managerial deficiencies. Figure 9.2 illustrates a typical final written report on an individual who participated in a developmental assessment center.

How worthwhile are assessment centers for developing managers? In one study, Teel and DuBois (1983) interviewed recent candidates to determine their reactions to being evaluated by the assessment center. The researchers found differences of opinion between high and low scorers with respect to the accuracy of the assessors' evaluations, the value of the developmental recommendations they received, and the benefits to their careers of participating in it. As you might expect, the low scorers were more negative on each of these points (Cascio, 1986). Based on their interviews, Teel and DuBois offered the following recommendations for maximizing the developmental value of the assessment center process: (1) feedback interviews should be conducted within two weeks after assessment, (2) assessors should explain fully the bases for their evaluations, (3) a follow-up interview should be held between the immediate manager and the individual to review the strengths and weaknesses identified at the center, and (4) the immediate manager and the individid-

Figure 9.2 Example of a final report from a developmental assessment center

This report is based upon observation of Wilford D's performance in a two-day Developmental Center. Wil was placed in a variety of situations where he had to handle problems similar to the ones with which he would have to deal in most management positions. The exercises upon which observations are based are (1) a background interview where actual past behavior is appraised; (2) a leaderless group discussion with nonassigned roles where a group of participants must organize to recommend solutions to three difficult management problems; (3) a leaderless group discussion (Metropolitan Council) with assigned roles where the group of participants work together in a competitive setting to solve a problem where the solution must be acceptable to all; and (4) an in-basket exercise where each participant must handle the accumulated letters, notes, requests, etc., found in the in-basket of a job to which he or she has just been appointed. In the in-basket exercise, the participant must make decisions, delegate responsibility, write letters and reports, assign work, and plan, organize and schedule his or her activities and those of subordinates.

Overall evaluation

Wil's evaluation reveals an above average prospect for future development and growth at Consolidated or another large corporate property. He ranked above average in 13 of the 14 observable dimensions, with average ratings in flexibility and written communication skills. He is an intelligent, hard working, personable, and persuasive young man. He makes a very positive first impression, is energetic and conveys an air of self-confidence. His peers ranked him as the number two most effective participant in Metropolitan Council and number one in management problems. Wil's performance in the center was excellent, with the exception of the in-basket exercise. His most apparent weakness is written communication skills, plus a lack of experience in management outside of a highly technical environment. These shortcomings are easily subject to improvement as will later be discussed in "Recommended Developmental Actions." Overall, the observers were quite impressed with Wil as a person and with his potential as a candidate for a higher level management position.

Potential

The observers believe Wil to be an above-average candidate for a higher level position in Consolidated management. His technical competency is unquestionable and his general management skills appear to be in order. Several major concerns remain unresolved. Wil indicated no desire to progress upward in any capacity outside his present field. He states on his personal history form that five years from now he wants to be involved in work "similar to what I'm doing now, but on a larger scale." This leaves the observers with the distinct impression that Wil's technical background may work to his disadvantage in gaining a greater understanding of Consolidated's overall operation. Wil's style of management is one compatible with a skilled worker environment. If he is removed from this type of environment, his self-confidence and effectiveness may become shaky. Other concerns are Wil's dislike of paperwork and dealing with people problems. He states that he avoids employee confrontations at all costs. These characteristics are not uncommon for a technically oriented person, but they pose a threat to Wil's career in an expanded management role.

Recommended developmental actions

Wil appears to enjoy his work thoroughly, as long as it involves the intrigue of electronics and/or mechanics. He has not gained an adequate appreciation for written communication skills, interpersonal relationships, or the necessity of accurate preparation of reports, budgets, etc., as directly related to a department head (or higher) position. The observers recommended that Wil engage in writing skills improvement courses at college. Wil should read *The Elements of Style* by Strunk and White. He could also benefit from

"Financial Management for Non-Financial Managers." The observers see Wil as a very sensitive individual, and feel that he may overidentify with subordinates when dealing with their personal problems. He should develop an objective, but concerned and sincere, approach in handling these matters. We recommend he participate in "Effective Human Relations" to gain a better prospective of a manager's role. We also recommend that Wil be delegated additional responsibilities in the day-by-day management of the systems engineering department. This should include budget preparation and maintenance, and reports to higher levels of management. He might also benefit from exposure to any task force or committee activities. A closer association with personalities from other divisions could help shape his organizational perceptions. Career counseling is vital at this point in Wil's life. He must be firmly convinced and accept the fact that upward career movement will intensify his involvement in those areas where he has expressed dislike. Wil is a responsible individual with a bright future. He needs to reevaluate his goals and adjust his management philosophy accordingly.

---

ual should discuss and agree on future actions to capitalize on the individual's strengths and correct weaknesses (Cascio, 1986). In another study, Schmitt et al. (1986) evaluated changes in self-perceived ability as a result of performance in an assessment center. Over 1600 candidates for supervisory positions provided self-ratings on eight ability dimensions (e.g., planning, organizing) before and immediately after their assessment center experience. The researchers found significant increases of self-perceived ability on five of the eight dimensions. This research clearly shows that participation in the assessment center process can improve participants' feelings of self-efficacy.

Before we move on to the next topic, it is important to point out two additional developmental benefits of assessment centers. Through assessment centers, organizations are able to identify people with managerial talent early, thus allowing them a longer period of time for developing individuals prior to putting them in key managerial positions. Further, we highly recommend the use of assessment centers for accurately diagnosing each manager's training needs. This will prevent putting managers in programs to develop strengths they already have, and not getting them the kind of training they need (Thornton and Byham, 1982).

Role Playing

Instead of simply presenting a problem for discussion, as is done in the case study and incident techniques, role playing requires trainees to actually respond to specific problems that they encounter in their everyday organizational roles. The technique makes it possible for them to learn by doing, rather than by merely talking about ways to handle a problem.

Role playing is frequently used in management development for teaching such skills as interviewing, handling grievances, performance reviews, leadership styles and their impact on others, conference leadership, team problem solving, and effective communication. Role playing incorporates the following four theoretical approaches to learning (Shaw, 1967):

1. *Active participation*: Role playing provides the opportunity for practice, experimentation, and trial-and-error learning.
2. *Modeling*: Trainees can observe how others handle problems, and imitate their successful behavior.
3. *Knowledge of results*: Participants can learn about their personal strengths and weaknesses; they receive feedback from trainees who are observing their behavior.
4. *Practice*: Repeated experience with a series of role-play problems allows participants to begin to conceptualize the principles being taught.

Participants are told to imagine themselves in the situations presented by the trainer. The situation may be imaginary and designed solely for training purposes, or it may be an actual organizational problem. Trainees are free to try out different behaviors and reactions as long as they stay "in role" throughout the session. Typically, not all members of a training group role play at the same time. Instead, part of the group acts as observers while others act as participants. Before the session ends, all the trainees role-play at least once. In this way, persons not only receive the benefits of the role-playing exercise, but they also obtain practice in observing and analyzing the behavior of others (Maier, 1952). A discussion follows immediately after each role play. Here, the issues and problems that developed during the enactment are examined, so that both the role players and the observers understand the underlying principles that were demonstrated and their organizational implications.

The appropriateness of role playing depends on the training objectives. For instance, to give participants greater insight into their own behavior and the behavior of others, a role reversal may be used. Here trainees who are experiencing interpersonal conflict are asked to exchange roles. For example, managers from quality control and production might change roles, in order to give them a feel for experiencing and solving problems from the other person's point of view. Hopefully, differences of opinion will be minimized as a result of each person acquiring an understanding of the other person's perspective.

Multiple role playing is a method that is particularly appropriate when the trainer desires to demonstrate the effects of varying organizational factors on the conclusions and decisions reached by groups. With this method, a large number of participants (e.g., 20 to 30) are divided into smaller groups of five or six people. The trainer presents a problem which each group is asked to role-play. After the role playing has taken place within each subgroup, the entire group of trainees reassembles to share their experiences (Maier and Zerfoss, 1952). Often, the various subgroups are given different instructions (not known to them) so that the effects of these factors can be dramatically demonstrated during the final discussion session. For example, different leadership styles (i.e., autocratic, democratic, consultative) might be established in each of the subgroups, resulting in salient differences in member satisfaction and performance effectiveness between the different groups.

Finally, if the training objective is skill development (e.g., sales strategies, interviews involving discipline), videotape playback may be useful for demonstrating to the trainee certain effective and ineffective behaviors that were exhibited during the role play. *Role rotation* can also be useful for teaching interpersonal skills. One trainee plays a role, usually that of an employee who has a problem or is somehow responsible for creating one. Several participants attempt, one by one, to apply their skills in handling the situation. During the final discussion session, the participants can compare the relative effectiveness of their individual approaches. An excellent presentation of other forms of role playing is presented by Wohlking (1976) and Cooke (1987).

Despite the popularity of role playing, there is very little evaluative information available. This is because role playing is rarely used by itself. It is typically employed in conjunction with other methods of management development such as lectures and behavioral modeling (see Chapter 8). In a cumulative study of the effectiveness of managerial training, Burke and Day (1986) applied meta-analysis procedures to the results of 70 evaluative studies of managerial training. Some of these evaluate studies using a lecture/group discussion with role playing or practice. Based on their statistical results, Burke and Day concluded that the lecture/group discussion with either role playing or practice was effective in terms of reaction, learning, and behavioral measures (see Chapter 5). Few evaluative studies using measures of "results" have been conducted.

Management Games

Unlike role playing, where participants are assigned roles and are asked to react to one another in terms of their roles in the exercise, management games ask participants to play themselves. This approach to training is currently enjoying a great deal of popularity in both management development programs and business school courses. Most games concentrate on general management principles such as financial policy, long-range planning, decision making, communications, and marketing. These general systems games are often computer based. They are quite complex, because they attempt to model the major components of a total organizational system (e.g., a company, a city, or a medical center). Other games are directed at teaching very specific skills and techniques, particularly those concerned with production, planning, and control functions (Craft, 1967).

The popularity of management games can be traced to several sources. One of the more important is the increasing expertise and sophistication in the computer simulation area. Today, programmers are able to duplicate various aspects of real-life organizational situations with much of their complex interrelationships. Second, in recent years, there has been an increasing interest in understanding organizations from a systems viewpoint. A gaming simulation allows trainees to manipulate various components of a system, to understand how the components interrelate, as well as the system's relationship with its external environment. Third, the development of decision making as a science has supported gaming because games tend to focus attention on the decision-making processes of managers and the effects of these decisions on the organization's effectiveness (Coppard, 1976). Imperial Oil of Canada, for example, has a game for training the managers of their service stations. The Pillsbury Company has one to develop high-level managers in new divisionalization and decentralization policies. Business students at universities are developing managerial skills by learning from experience without paying the consequences that would result from making wrong decisions in real life.

It might be helpful at this point to provide an example of a typical management game. The following example is based on the Remington Rand Univac Marketing Game:

> The game session begins with a briefing. At this time, the instructor describes for the participants the type of company they are about to manage, the economic environment, the general nature of the products, and the competitive forces they will face. The scope of their authority, the functions to be filled, the decisions to be made, and the information they will receive are all discussed. In addition the mechanics of play, the purpose of the exercise, and the manner in which it relates to the entire educational program are covered.
>
> After the briefing the participants meet with the other members of their management team. In a typical game, involving perhaps forty to fifty executives, there might be six teams each with seven or eight members. The management teams determine their organization, set objectives, decide on the short- and long-range plans necessary to achieve these objectives, and introduce necessary controls and procedures. Typical organizational structures evolve, with presidents, vice presidents, etc. In addition to the obvious desire to maximize net profit, other objectives will be set concerning share of market, stabilized production, inventory control, and personnel policies.
>
> Games are played in periods, each period being a day, week, month, quarter, or year, depending on the particular game. The Univac Marketing Game takes place in months. The participants have already received operating reports for December and begin by making decisions for January. A variety of other pertinent information, such as a case history, sales forecast,

> and reference material on operating costs, production facilities and shipping times is provided. Usually all companies begin in the same condition.
>
> The teams make decisions for January, these are processed by the computer, and operating reports for January are then returned. In most game sessions, management has about a half hour in which to make decisions. Play continues for a simulated year.
>
> In the Univac Marketing Game, each company manufactures one product. All are competing in three regions comprising a common market. The managers set price, spend money on advertising, hire and fire salesmen, set salesmen compensation rate, set production level, engage in special market research projects, etc. The operating reports show the sales obtained, the net profit achieved, and an accumulated year-to-date net profit.
>
> Management is trying to achieve the largest possible net profit, and the team that obtains the greatest accumulated profit is often called the "winner." Good performance in a management game, however, as in a real business, is dependent on many factors such as return on investment, share of market, personnel policies, and the numerous aspects of the company that determine whether it will continue to succeed.
>
> While the participants are busily engaged in operating their companies, other people are observing their performance. Some of these may be guests or visitors, but others may have been specifically selected to follow the proceedings so as to be able later to provide feedback on the human interactions evidenced. These observers may themselves be members of the training course, or may be specially invited social scientists. In some cases elaborate facilities are available for observing and recording the actions of the participants.
>
> At the end of the game play, which may well simulate from six to sixteen months, a discussion session takes place. This "critique" session is held to focus attention on the lessons which were to be taught. The participants have the opportunity of reviewing their performance, discussing management principles with other members of the group, and receiving feedback from the game administrator and observers. Very often the critique takes the form of a report to the "board of directors" and is guided along specific channels by a previously prepared checklist. (*Management Games: A New Technique for Executive Development*, J. M. Kibbee, C. J. Craft, and B. Nanus, New York: Reinhold Publishing Corporation, 1961, pp. 4–6)

Management games can be classified as simple or complex, computer-based or manually operated, media- or player-dependent, or rigidly programmed or flexible (Coppard, 1976). They can also be categorized on the basis of their functional purposes (e.g., marketing, finance, production management). The important point is that there are numerous games available today for purchase. Thus it is essential that a training specialist choose the game that comes closest to satisfying the organization's needs. This requires a systematic determination of training objectives and a rigorous review of available games in light of these specific objectives.

Management games have several advantages. They compress time, so that participants can derive years of on-the-job managerial experience in just a few days. The games are intrinsically interesting for trainees, because of their realism, competitive nature, and the immediacy and objectivity of the feedback. The method is also particularly useful for understanding complex interrelationships among organizational units. For example, one of the most popular management games used today is called "Looking Glass, Inc." There are two versions of Looking Glass that are offered by the Center for Creative Leadership located in Greensboro, North Carolina. There is an eight-hour version developed for managers and executives, as well as a three- to four-hour simulation for students. Looking Glass recreates a day in the lives of the top 20 managers of a mid-sized manufacturing corporation. Participants run the company in any manner that they choose. They can call meetings, write memos, and make decisions. Like most organizations, Looking Glass has its share of problems that need solving. Some are trivial; others are critical. There are about a hundred problems that the 20 participants must deal with as they see fit. These problems impact many areas, including finance, personnel, legal, production, sales, research and development, and safety.

The technique also has its limitations. Sometimes participants become so engrossed in beating the system that they fail to grasp the underlying management principles being taught. This problem can sometimes be minimized by combining games with lectures and discussion periods. Some people claim that the method stifles creative approaches to problem solving. In other words, the highly innovative manager might be penalized financially during the game as a result of his unorthodox strategies.

Finally, and most importantly, very little evaluation of management games has been done. The existing research has been limited primarily to showing that games increase students' enthusiasm and enjoyment for the learning process (Ernest, 1986; Wesson, Wilson, and Mandlebau, 1988). Consequently, it is not possible to say today with any assurance exactly what gaming simulations accomplish regarding on-the-job performance. In fact, based on a review of 39 fairly rigorous studies conducted between 1973 and 1983, it was concluded that it is still difficult to make clear statements about the positive effects, if any, of games regarding performance on the job (Gordon, 1985a). Most of its appeal stems from its face validity and the persuasiveness of its advocates (e.g., Taylor, 1986; Wehrenberg, 1985, 1986). However, Bazerman and Neale (1982) showed that it is possible to improve arbitration skills by means of a laboratory bargaining simulation.

Junior Boards

The purpose of the *junior board of directors*, or *multiple management* as it is sometimes called, is to permit promising young middle-level managers to experience problems and responsibilities faced by high-level executives in their company. Junior managers are exposed to critical aspects of their organization's business, thus enabling them to develop the capacity to identify and explore broad issues. The conceptual ability required to do this assumes more and more importance as the middle-level manager advances in the organization. This is because work becomes more unstructured, unspecialized, long range, complex, intertwined, and less focused than in lower positions (Mintzberg, 1973).

A junior board is generally composed of a dozen or so young executives from diverse functions within the organization, selected for periods of six months or longer. The board is ordinarily permitted to study any problem faced by the organization and make recommendations to the senior board of directors (i.e., the official board elected by the stockholders). Typical problems tackled by junior boards include personnel policies, organization design, interdepartmental conflicts, executive compensation, and communication processes. The following paragraph describes how one organization used a junior board to solve an important problem:

> A company had tentatively considered opening a factory in France or Germany to produce a health drink based on certain soft fruit. There were a number of important matters to be explored before a decision could be made: the market potential, the availability of the right kind of fruit, the effect of cultural differences on the product's acceptability, the costs of production and marketing. It asked the junior board to put up a plan on how it would go about investigating the problem in order to produce a recommendation. This plan was accepted and the board was given the further task of completing the investigations and recommending appropriate action. (Roberts, 1974, pp. 93–94)

In summary, junior board members get experience in grappling with broad-range problems extending beyond the confines of their own current specialty, as well as gain practical experience in problem analysis, group decision making, and teamwork. The major advantage of this approach to development is that it involves learning on the job via real-life experiences. Its biggest drawback is that it can accommodate only a limited number of participants at any one time. Finally, to our knowledge, there is no scientific evidence that this training attains the objectives for which it was developed.

Understudy Assignments

Some organizations develop their future managers by putting them in the role of understudies to senior executives. Unlike mentoring, the understudy relieves the executive of certain responsibilities, thereby giving the manager an opportunity to learn certain aspects of the job and the executive's style of handling it. The benefits that the manager derives from this training depends greatly on the executive's ability to teach effectively via oral communication and behavior modeling. It is also important that the executive and manager understand each other's role, and that they perceive themselves (Pulakos and Wexley, 1983; Wexley et al., 1980; Wexley and Pulakos, 1983).

Understudy assignments ensure that the organization has trained managers to assume key high-level positions in the event that they are vacated due to retirement, promotions, transfers, or terminations. This approach also guarantees the long-range development of homegrown top corporate executives.

The understudy approach is not without its problems. First, understudies who must wait a long time for vacancies to open often become frustrated and leave for positions in other organizations. Second, aspirants for promotions who have not been assigned as understudies may feel that their chances for advancement are diminished and, consequently, stop trying.

Understudy assignments are similar in concept to formalized mentoring programs, which many organizations such as AT&T, Johnson and Johnson, Merrill Lynch, Federal Express, the Internal Revenue Service, and the U.S. Army have initiated (Zey, 1985). Despite the perceived importance of mentoring programs for management development, they have shown mixed results, with programs sometimes resulting in less than expected levels of learning and/or trainee satisfaction (Klauss, 1981; Kram, 1985). Based on this body of research and our experience, we believe that understudy assignments can only function successfully if (1) the executive is recognized in some way for taking the time and effort to train an understudy; (2) there is enough time allotted for the executive and understudy to meet regularly; and (3) people are paired up carefully so that there is mutual trust and open communication between them.

FINAL COMMENTS

Most evaluations of management development programs ask participants if they thought the program was beneficial. With this approach, few participants will indicate that the program was a waste of time, even though they may privately think so. The reason for this is that, in many organizations, program participation is a sign that the trainees are "fast trackers" or "comers" who will soon be promoted. Thus these people are not likely to criticize publicly a program that will help them move upward in the organization. This is why the evaluation procedures presented in Chapter 5 must be thoroughly understood by trainers.

Among the most prevalent management development techniques is coaching. Because it was described in Chapter 7, we did not repeat it here. It is our belief that coaching is one of the most important ways to stimulate the development of managerial talent. The challenge to specialists in management development and to organizations is to overcome the resistance of many managers to improve their coaching practices. Too often executives do not see coaching as an important part of their responsibilities. In our opinion, organizations should make coaching an integral part of all managers' jobs. They should identify good and poor coaches, reward the good ones monetarily, and provide periodic instruction on coaching techniques for the poor ones. The manager who coaches an employee well, that is, models the correct behaviors being taught, assigns specific and challenging goals, and provides employees with frequent and immediate feedback concerning how they are performing their duties, can be an extremely powerful change agent for nurturing and developing employee growth.

Obviously, not all management development programs use just one technique to improve managerial effectiveness. On the contrary, organizations frequently embark on long-term management development efforts that involve several techniques. Today, evaluative research comparing the combined effects of two or more techniques are too few to warrant any conclusions. Hopefully, we will see more effort in this direction in the near future.

Most of the management development techniques we presented in chapters 8 and 9 were aimed at the individual manager. Yet an organization's competence depends greatly on the ability of its managers to work effectively with one another. This is particularly true today as organizations deal with more complex technological problems that cannot be handled by an individual manager. Thus we see the need more and more for establishing special groups of managers (i.e., task forces, ad hoc committees) to tackle specific problems. Consequently, team building programs are being used by certain organizations to clarify role expectations and obligations of team members; improve problem solving, decision making, and planning activities; and reduce interpersonal conflict. For instance, phases 2 and 3 of grid seminars (see Chapter 8) are employed by some organizations to improve team as well as intergroup relations. Other organizations have involved key management teams in variations of sensitivity training to instill in people the desire and skill to be effective team players. Training in team building is among the subjects we discuss in Chapter 10.

We now turn our attention to societal concerns of the training and development staff. This final chapter illustrates how many of the ideas and strategies described in the first nine chapters can be brought to bear on challenging contemporary issues.

Chapter 10

Societal Concerns

In the four previous chapters, we discussed training and development methods for improving the performance of both managers and their employees. This chapter reviews recent efforts aimed at dealing with special concerns within our society requiring training and development.

The distinguishing feature of this chapter is its contemporariness. The topics covered reflect not only current social issues affecting society, but issues that will likely receive significant emphasis in coming years. The first part of the chapter is concerned with the training of disadvantaged people (e.g., the illiterate, the handicapped, and displaced workers). The second part focuses on training managers to improve their skills in evaluating subordinates, working effectively in foreign cultures, preventing managerial and professional obsolescence, dealing with substance abuse, and finally, managing their own stress and time effectively.

The final section focuses on concerns that pertain to all employees in an organization. We highlight issues confronting employees in the 1990s: training for the disadvantaged, wellness training, safety, customer service training, team skills training, and personal computer (PC) training.

THE DISADVANTAGED

Fighting Illiteracy

The *Wall Street Journal* (February 9, 1990) reported that American organizations spend about $210 billion a year on employee training and development. Besides teaching people job skills, companies have been forced to take on the added responsibility of teaching such basic skills as reading, writing, arithmetic, and logical reasoning. Although experts disagree on the number of employees who cannot read, write, compute, do basic arithmetic, solve problems, and/or communicate well enough to perform their jobs, a conservative estimate is that more than 20 to 23 million people fall into this category (Ropp, 1989). Some experts estimate that up to 65 percent of the work force is literate, meaning that this group can read at between grade 5 and grade 9 reading levels (*Wall Street Journal*, February 9, 1990).

Remedial education programs have begun to appear in collective bargaining agreements where the company and the union jointly sponsor the training. An excellent example is the United Auto Workers (UAW)-Ford-Eastern Michigan Academy located in Ypsilanti, Michigan. This academy was established by the UAW and the big three automakers to retrain auto workers. Each year about 300 Ford employees at the Ypsilanti plant, a manufacturer of small parts, are given classes in reading, writing, speaking, and listening. The training is funded through contributions from workers' wages matched by the company. The classes are open to all employees; they are permitted to take any class they wish before and after their shift. The students are recognized at award ceremonies twice a year that are attended by the plant manager, the union president, and Ford supervisors (McGee, 1989). The UAW and Chrysler alone currently train about 75,000 employees at 14 separate training centers (Ropp, 1989). The United Steelworkers of America has enrolled 27,000 employees in 50 centers offering remedial training.

Individual unions often work together to overcome the problem of illiteracy. For example, eight unions in New York formed a Consortium for Worker Literacy. It has received funds from the New York Board of Education, the New York State Department of Education, and the Municipal Assistance Corporation. The consortium estimates that about 450,000 employees (i.e., union members and their spouses and children) are eligible for upgrading their literacy skills (Ropp, 1989).

Organizations such as The Philadelphia Newspapers Inc. (PNI) and Travelers Insurance Company have also taken on the problem of illiteracy. For instance, PNI provides nine hours of training for people inside and outside the *Philadelphia Inquirer* and the *Philadelphia Daily News* who are willing to serve as tutors. Employees at both newspapers can call a confidential hot line or the Center for Literacy to obtain the services of a tutor.

The illiteracy crisis is also being fought through federal and state funding. For instance, part of the 1982 Job Training Partnership Act's (JTPA) multibillion dollar budget can be used by the states for remedial education. Started in 1990, the Job Opportunities and Basic Skills (JOBS) program, authorized by the Family Support Act of 1988, is also providing remedial education, training, and necessary support services. Finally, Employee-Specific Skill Training (ESST) is funded at the state level and is normally associated with state economic development efforts directed at attracting new firms and plants to the state (Ropp, 1989).

The Handicapped

About 12 to 15 percent of adult workers are handicapped either physically and/or mentally. As noted previously, the Vocational Rehabilitation Act requires employers holding federal contracts over $2500 to take affirmative action in hiring qualified handicapped individuals. The act requires organizations to take proactive steps (e.g., special training programs, redesign of tools and machinery, wheelchair ramps) to accommodate workers with disabilities. A *handicapped person* is defined broadly as any person who has a physical or mental impairment that substantially limits one or more major life activities. This classification includes not only those individuals traditionally classified as handicapped (e.g., paraplegic, deaf, blind) but also those with high blood pressure, arthritis, epilepsy, or diabetes. It also includes people with a former history of severe illness (e.g., cancer, emotional breakdown, heart attack) who are no longer suffering from their disability (Arvey, 1979). Although the act applies primarily to those organizations doing business with the federal government, the courts have allowed handicapped individuals to use this law as a basis for suing employers in the private sector as well.

As a result of this legislation, employers should review their personnel processes to determine whether their present procedures assure careful and thorough consideration of the job qualifications of known handicapped applicants and employees for training opportunities. Further, employers should make reasonable accommodations to the physical and mental limitations of employees or applicants during training unless the employers can show that such an accommodation (e.g., modified equipment, special help from co-workers, extra supervision) would impose an undue hardship on the conduct of the business. Employers are also encouraged to arrange for career counseling for known handicapped employees. Lastly, all personnel involved in recruitment, selection, promotion, disciplinary, and related processes should be trained to ensure their commitment and understanding of the organization's affirmative action efforts.

Examples of what constitutes reasonable accommodations for handicapped individuals include the following: A wheelchair-bound multiple sclerosis victim was hired by an engineering firm to be trained in drafting. The firm not only lowered their drafting tables, but installed special ramps so that the employee had access to the other departments within the building. A mentally retarded individual was hired and trained to feed and care for the animals at a pet store. The instructions from the training manuals were rewritten in the form of easy-to-understand checklists. An insurance company had no difficulty training deaf people for positions as data entry operators. Written, rather than oral, instructions were provided during the two-month period of on-the-job training. A bank provided amplified telephones for hard-of-hearing bank teller trainees.

Employees 40 to 70 Years of Age

In the 1980s, increasing numbers of older individuals entered or reentered the work force. It is estimated that the total proportion of the work force between the ages of 45 and 64 will increase by the year 2000 to over 25 percent (Goldstein, 1989). Because the relative proportion of young people entering the work force is expected to decline in the next decade, society will not be able to afford to lose this population of older employees from the world of work. In addition, the Age Discrimination in Employment Act of 1967 (ADEA) now protects individuals ages 40 and older against discrimination with respect to hiring, training, compensation, and other terms of employment.

As with other groups who have experienced discrimination, there are a number of stereotypes that limit the participation of these people in the labor force. Employers and workers alike need to be made aware of research findings in order to change their current attitudes and practices. The following is a summary of pertinent findings on older workers (Meier and Kerr, 1976):

1. It is often assumed that as a worker's age increases, the capacity to perform physical tasks declines so much as to seriously impede the person's ability to perform a job. Actually, in most jobs today, the physical demands are well below the abilities of most normal aging workers.
2. The major obstacle for some older workers is not the physical heaviness of the work, but rather the stresses of a machine or work group to maintain a high rate of productivity. If job performance is being affected, a small change in the design of the task can usually return it to the capability of the older worker.
3. For over 50 years, there has been sufficient research evidence to argue that anyone under 60 can learn about as well as they ever could. Although I.Q. declines with age, it occurs much later than most people have thought. When it does become critical to work performance, most people are already retired and in their late 70s or 80s.
4. Several large-scale studies conducted by the National Council on Aging and the Department of Labor have shown that differences in output rates among age groups are insignificant. In addition, it appears as though supervisors consider a majority of their workers aged 60 and over to be as good as, or better than, younger employees with respect to such job dimensions as absenteeism, dependability, work quality, and work volume.

5. Older workers are generally more satisfied with their jobs, have longer job tenure, and have fewer psychiatric symptoms than younger workers.

In light of these facts, organizations should do seven things when designing training programs for these people (Sterns and Doverspike, 1989). First, a critical feature of successful training programs for older workers is that basic skills are mastered before training progresses to more complex components. By lowering the chances of failure, older trainees' feelings of self-confidence can be enhanced (Latham and Crandall, 1991). The most direct way to do this is to establish performance criteria so that progression can be regulated from one level of training to the next (Sanders, Sanders, Mayers, and Seilski, 1976). When this is not done, any gains at one level can be compromised by the premature introduction of information from higher levels.

For example, underground train guards in London are given six weeks of training before entering passenger service. The program has been sequenced so as to reduce the resignation rates of older trainees, who are less likely to leave their jobs once they have passed the training period (Downs and Roberts, 1977). In the first week of service, the trainee studies the basic operation of the railway, the signaling system, and emergency procedures. Practical experience is gained through three days of actual work as a stationman. During the second week, the trainee learns about the rules governing railway operations, safety, emergency procedures, and the guard's responsibilities. A tour of several train stations provides the practical component. In the third week, the trainee studies the equipment found on a train, the brakes, safety devices, procedures in the event of mechanical or electrical failure, door operation, and so on. For practical experience, there is a visit to the main depot to examine a train and its equipment with a trainman's inspector. The remaining three weeks involve primarily on-the-job training. A trainee must show satisfactory performance before moving on to the next step in the training sequence.

Second, it is important that the pace of training be relaxed. If the pressure to produce is lowered somewhat during training, older workers will be able to learn the tasks correctly, and subsequently be able to cope with time pressures on their jobs (Belbin and Belbin, 1972). For instance, electronics firms have reduced training difficulties on jobs requiring operators to keep up with conveyor belts and machines by slowing down the process during training and/or extending the training period for older individuals.

Third, older adults in particular learn better when the training involves activity rather than rote memorization and passive listening (Mullen and Gorman, 1972). Conventional means of instruction such as lectures, dictation of notes, and question-and-answer sessions need to be deemphasized and replaced by more active learning methods. For example, memorization cannot be completely eliminated in the learning demands of the underground train guard. A detailed knowledge of the braking system, for instance, is important. Rather than using lectures and traditional manuals, the training uses a realistic diagram of the equipment, a series of transparencies showing colored air flows, and a written program. The program guides the trainee to correct solutions, which are readily found in conjunction with the transparencies. Memorization is also aided by means of self-testing cards, consisting of typical problems on one side and answers on the other (Downs and Roberts, 1977).

Fourth, older workers sometimes develop their own unique methods of organizing information, which can clash with the requirements of the training program (Sterns and Doverspike, 1989). To avoid this problem, older trainees can be given strategy training in organizational and memory processes that can lead to improved performance (Schmidt, Murphy, and Sanders, 1981).

Fifth, the training should be built upon the past knowledge, skills, and abilities of older trainees. Rather than presenting material that is unfamiliar to them, the training materials should be designed so that it contains materials from their perspective. For instance, examples of concepts can call upon events that happened, perhaps, 20 or 30 years ago.

Sixth, it is important during training that the future transferability of the training experience be emphasized (Mullen and Gorman, 1972). Most older workers want to be assured that their efforts are not a waste of time, and that it is worthwhile.

Finally, older employees need financial information long before retirement. Although preretirement seminars are becoming more and more prevalent, less than 25 percent of U.S. companies offer this form of training for their older employees. One exception is Coca-Cola USA that has been conducting three-day preretirement training sessions for its employees, 45 years old and above, since the 1970s. The program focuses on various psychosocial issues surrounding retirement as well as estate and financial planning (Odenwald, 1986).

Displaced Workers

Among the most common causes of displacement are plant closings; labor-saving technological advances (e.g., robotics); mass layoffs caused by shifts in consumer preferences, foreign competition, or economic recession; corporate downsizing; and mergers (Condon, 1984b). The most visible population of displaced workers are former employees of the auto and steel industries as well as people from middle-level managerial and professional jobs (O'Boyle, 1985). Many organizations help their displaced employees find new jobs through *outplacement*—a set of activities authorized and paid for by the current or former employer to help displaced employees find new jobs as quickly as possible (Cascio, 1986). Outplacement activities for lower level workers are usually administered directly by the organization's human resources department; outplacement activities for terminated managers and executives are typically handled by outplacement firms (Newman, 1989). These firms teach separated individuals how to deal with an executive recruiter, how to use recruiters to their own advantage, and general job-searching information and resources (Anderson, 1990).

Title III of the Job Training Partnership Act (JTPA) of 1983 was designed to offer training and retraining to displaced workers. This law provided federal funds to authorized training contractors to train unemployed persons in new, employable skills. Unlike its predecessor, the Comprehensive Education and Training Act (CETA), the JTPA mandated coordination between private industry and government contractors (i.e., city and state government agencies). One-quarter of the JTPA funds were earmarked for areas of the country where unemployment is high due to massive layoffs. For instance, the UAW/GM Tri-County Displaced Workers Assistance Program is federally funded through the Michigan Department of Labor, the Governor's Office for Job Training, and the National UAW/GM Human Resource Center. The purpose of the project is to retrain and assist in the reemployment of UAW/GM displaced workers from the Tri-Counties of Saginaw/Bay/Midland in occupations that are in demand. Companies that hire JTPA persons through this UAW/GM Tri-County Program get their training costs reimbursed for a specified rate percentage and training period.

Although the JTPA was effective in training and placing many displaced workers in private sector jobs, only 48 percent of displaced persons under JTPA actually received some form of retraining (London and Bassman, 1989). Consequently, in 1988, Congress replaced Title III with the Economic Dislocation and Workers Adjustment Act, which increases the funding for training and placing dislocated workers (London and Bassman, 1989).

THE MANAGER AND PROFESSIONAL

We now turn our attention to six concerns affecting today's managers and professionals and some of the training efforts designed to alleviate them. First, the current trend to improve the accuracy of managers' evaluations of their subordinates stems largely from governmental pressures to increase fairness in personnel decisions such as promotions, transfers, and layoffs. Second, the fact that more and more organizations are building their offices and plants in foreign countries and transferring their managers to these locations has necessitated the smooth assimilation of these people into other cultures. Third, the rapid and dynamic knowledge explosion in our modern technological society has accelerated the problem of obsolescence. Fourth, problems of substance abuse continue to plague North American industry. Finally, the abilities to handle stress and to manage time remain as two areas of vital concern to today's managers and professionals.

Training to Improve Ratings

Accuracy in evaluating others is critical to effective selection and performance appraisal systems. For example, in one of the first known attempts at changing the rating practices of supervisors, Levine and Butler (1952) worked with 29 supervisors in a large manufacturing plant, where it had been determined that the supervisors overrated those working in higher job grades and underrated those in the lower grades. This rating error resulted in the workers in lower job grades receiving the lowest of their respective wage rates while the more highly skilled workers consistently received the highest of their respective wage rates. This was unfair, because the supervisors were obviously not rating the individual's performance as much as they were rating the job that was held by the individual.

These supervisors were randomly assigned to a control, a lecture, or a conference (discussion) group. Supervisors in the control condition were given no training or information. Supervisors in the lecture condition were given a detailed lecture on the theory and technique of performance ratings. The lecturer explained to the supervisors the problem caused by their previous ratings, and what each supervisor needed to do to correct the problem. In the discussion group, the supervisors met together to discuss the nature of the problem and how it could be solved. The discussion leader merely acted as a moderator, avoiding interjections of his own opinions. After generating a number of ideas, the group arrived at one solution acceptable to all.

The results showed that the lecture method had practically no influence on changing the supervisor's method of rating. The same was true for the control group, who received no training. Only the group discussion method, where the members participated in arriving at solutions to the problem, was successful in overcoming the rating errors.

Similarly, in a later study (Wexley, Sanders, and Yukl, 1973), it was found that simply warning (i.e., lecturing) individuals to recognize and avoid making judgmental errors in their ratings was not successful. Only an intensive workshop resulted in a behavior change. The workshop was based on psychological principles of learning, namely, active participation, knowledge of results or feedback, and practice (see Chapter 4). Specifically, the workshop gave trainees a chance to practice observing and rating actual videotaped individuals. In addition, the trainees were given immediate feedback regarding the accuracy of their ratings.

Two different training approaches to help people minimize rating errors when observing and evaluating others were developed by Latham, Wexley, and Pursell (1975). These were the workshop approach, similar to what was originally used by Wexley et al., and the group discussion method used by Levine and Butler. Both methods were selected because they had previously been effective in reducing at least one type of rating error. Their workshop (also mentioned in Chapter 3) consisted of videotapes of individuals being evaluated. The trainees rated the manager who had evaluated the employee in the videotape, and how they themselves would rate the individual. Group discussions concerning the reasons for each trainee's rating of the individual followed. In this way, the trainees had an opportunity to observe other managers making errors, to participate actively in discovering the degree to which they were or were not prone to making the error, to receive knowledge of results regarding their own behavior, and to practice job-related tasks to reduce the errors they were making. The relationship between the training content and the actual job was similar in principle, so as to facilitate transfer of learning back to the job.

The format for the group discussion method was as follows: Each error was defined by the trainer. An example of each error was given for the performance appraisal, a selection interview, and an off-the-job situation. This was done to ensure that the trainees thoroughly understood the error. The trainees were then divided into groups to discuss personal examples that they had experienced in each situation. The trainees then generated solutions to the problem. Finally, the trainer provided the suggestions that were given in the workshop.

The results of the two training programs were evaluated six months after training on the basis of two criteria, namely, reaction measures and actual behavioral samples. The reaction measures consisted of the trainees' rating of the extent to which they believed that they benefited from the program after they returned to their jobs. The average ratings given to the workshop and the group discussion methods were both favorable and were not significantly different from one another. Further, the researchers found that the workshop approach was slightly more effective than the group discussion in eliminating rating errors, but that both training approaches were successful.

Bernardin and Pence (1980) found that not all rater error training programs are equally effective. In a program they evaluated, trainees were instructed to avoid using the extreme ends of a rating scale (i.e., positive and negative leniency error), and they were taught that the ratings across the different scales should not correlate highly with one another (i.e., halo error). The outcome of this training was a decrease rather than an increase in rating accuracy.

This training was inappropriate in that it replaced one response set or tendency with another. The authors concluded, "Emphasis should be placed on training raters to observe behaviors more accurately and fairly rather than on providing specific illustrations of 'how to rate or not rate' with regard to response distributions" (Bernardin and Pence, 1980, p. 65).

The following year, Bernardin and Buckley (1981) recommended a further elaboration of their training content, namely, frame of reference training (FOR). "This training is similar to that used by Latham, Wexley, and Pursell (1975) and should be effective in 'creating' a common frame of reference for those found to rate on the basis of idiosyncratic standards" (Bernardin and Buckley, 1981, p. 209). The two training approaches are similar in that both Latham et al. (1975) and Bernardin give participants practice in rating vignettes showing important and unimportant job behaviors. This is done after giving the participants job descriptions. Trainees individually rate each vignette and must justify the rating. The raters are then given feedback concerning the accuracy of their ratings (see Bernardin and Buckley, 1981; Latham and Wexley, 1991). An area in which the two programs differ is that Bernardin uses behaviorally based rating scales. To make the training more difficult, Latham et al. use graphic rating scales. The training program, however, results in the trainees developing behaviorally based scales as a means of overcoming rating errors when observing people on videotape.

A field test of FOR showed an increase in interrater agreement (Bernardin, 1980). Similarly, a field study showed that the rater error training developed by Latham, Wexley, and Pursell (1975) significantly increased the validity of selection tests used to hire electricians (Pursell, Dossett; and Latham, 1980).

Like Pursell et al. (1980), Dickinson and Silverhart (1986) argued that accuracy criteria used in most rater training programs are not a substitute for examining rater validity. They compared four training programs and a control group within the context of a multi-trait-multi-method design using behaviorally anchored rating scales (BARS) (discussed in Chapter 3) and another type of rating scale known as Mixed Standard Scales (Blanz and Ghiselli, 1972). The results showed that regardless of training method or rating scale, training resulted in rating with both convergent and discriminant validity.

Fay and Latham (1982) found that in the absence of training, rating errors occur regardless of whether the scale format is based on traits or observable behavior. However, subsequent to training, there were no appreciable differences between behavioral observation (BOS) and behaviorally anchored rating (BARS) scales with regard to rating errors; both were superior to trait scales. The training principles stressed that performance-related dimensions of behavior are, in reality, often correlated. Skewed distributions of ratings are not necessarily an indication of leniency error. Ratings should by no means always form a normal, bell-shaped distribution. Ratings at about the same level across dimensions and within ratees are not necessarily an indication of halo error. Raters should be trained simply to record accurately what they see.

Pulakos (1984) argued that training should be tailored to the rating scale. BOS require the reporting of the occurrence of specific behaviors; BARS require extracting evaluative judgments from observed behaviors. Consequently, FOR training should increase accuracy with the use of BARS as opposed to BOS because it provides an understanding of the performance dimensions and the behaviors representative of different effectiveness levels within each. Training raters to use common standards for evaluating behavioral effectiveness would not be an optimal strategy for increasing training accuracy with BOS. Rather, training with the use of BOS should focus on ensuring that the behaviors of interest are recognized quickly and reported efficiently. Again, true scores were developed as criterion measures.

Pulakos's hypotheses were supported. Accuracy was greater for congruent instrument and training combinations than for incongruent and controlled training conditions. Considering the observational task alone, only observational training was effective for increasing accuracy. Use of an evaluative training strategy with the observational instrument had no effect whatsoever on any of the accuracy components. For those required to make evaluative judgments, evaluative training produced greater accuracy than observational training.

Cross-Cultural Training

As more and more managers are working overseas for multinational organizations, the training they receive in adjusting to their host culture will increase in importance (Bogorya, 1985; Dotlich, 1982; Ronen, 1986).

Despite the importance of cross-cultural training, a survey of 105 American organizations operating abroad revealed that only 32 percent of them had formal training programs to prepare their managers for overseas work. The remaining 68 percent reported having no formal training programs for this purpose (Tung, 1981; Wexley and Baldwin, 1986). Fortunately, some American organizations have become aware that managers who work in a different culture require a cultural orientation prior to assuming their foreign assignments. These organizations realize that the principles of management taught in American business schools are not universal. Concepts of decision making, authority, communication, span of control, and delegation (to name just a few) differ across cultural environments.

One promising approach to preparing managers for work abroad is known as the *culture assimilator.* The assimilator is a programmed learning experience designed to expose members of one culture to the basic attitudes, customs, and values of another culture in the span of two to five hours. Different assimilators have been prepared for North Americans going to India, Greece, and Thailand. Basically, the method requires a trainee to read short descriptions of intercultural incidents, and give an interpretation of each incident by choosing one of four plausible alternative answers. The program then gives the trainee an explanation of why an answer was correct or incorrect. If incorrect, the trainee is asked to reread the material, and to choose again. Typically, 75 to 100 incidents are contained in a culture assimilator. The examples are usually developed by asking Americans and host nationals to describe specific intercultural incidents that made a difference in their understanding of members of the other culture. Figure 10.1 gives an example of an assimilator.

The ideal incident in an assimilator describes a situation that the manager would find puzzling and easy to misinterpret, though it could be explained clearly if the manager had sufficient knowledge about the culture. Moreover, the incident should be relevant to the trainee's managerial job (Fiedler, Mitchell, and Triandis, 1971).

Field studies indicate that culture assimilator-trained individuals see themselves as significantly better adjusted and as having distinctly better interpersonal relations and higher productivity than individuals without this training (Worchel and Mitchell, 1972). There is also evidence that trained individuals perform better in heterocultural situations than persons who have not received this training (Albert, 1983; O'Brien, Fiedler, and Hewitt, 1971; O'Brien and Plooij, 1977).

Two alternatives to the culture assimilator are *didactic-informational training* and *intercultural experiential workshops* (Ronen, 1989). In a study by Earley (1987), managers employed by a U.S. manufacturer of electronic products were given intercultural training in preparation for their assignments in Seoul, Korea, for three months. Some of these managers received didactic-information training in the form of written materials that compared the United States and South Korea in terms of such general areas as politics, economics, religion, and history as well as specific aspects of Korea such as food, relationships between males and females, and culturally appropriate gestures. Other managers were given an intercultural experiential workshop which involved several role-playing and experiential exercises designed to increase their awareness of the South Korean culture, and their openness to unfamiliar modes of behavior and value systems. It was found that both methods were effective in preparing managers to work in a different culture. Specifically, before the trainees returned to the United States, they were rated by their supervisors in South Korea. These ratings were significantly higher than those received by a nontrained (i.e., control) group of managers with respect to job performance and getting along with others.

Another approach to intercultural training is an adaptation of sensitivity training (see Chapter 9). The purpose here is to give trainees an opportunity to explore their own interpersonal styles and their basic values and attributions (Ronen, 1989). An example of this approach is a two-week program, developed in Great Britain, that combines a multicultural group of participants, an international group of trainers, and multinational training materials (de Bettignies, 1975). The program is designed to generate a true cross-cultural situation, in which participants can directly experience cultural differences and learn through them. The participants are confronted with actual organizational cases involving intercultural conflicts and decision making. The trainers serve as resource persons for the trainees in their process of discovering for themselves alternative ways to deal with themselves and others in intercul-

Figure 10.1 An example of a culture assimilator incident

Page X-1

Sharon Hatfield, a school teacher in Athens, was amazed at the questions that were asked her by Greeks whom she considered to be only casual acquaintances. When she entered or left her apartment, people would ask her where she was going or where she had been. If she stopped to talk she was asked questions like, "How much do you make a month?" or "Where did you get that dress you are wearing?" She thought the Greeks were very rude.

Page X-2

Why did the Greeks ask Sharon such "personal" questions?

1. The casual acquaintances were acting like friends do in Greece, although Sharon did not realize it.

Go to page X-3

2. The Greeks asked Sharon the questions in order to determine whether she belonged to the Greek Orthodox Church.

Go to page X-4

3. The Greeks were unhappy about the way in which she lived and they were trying to get Sharon to change her habits.

Go to page X-5

4. In Greece such questions are perfectly proper when asked of women, but improper when asked of men.

Go to page X-6

Page X-3

You selected 1: The casual acquaintances were acting like friends do in Greece, although Sharon did not realize it.

Correct. It is not improper for in-group members to ask these questions of one another. Furthermore, these questions reflect the fact that friendships (even "casual" ones) tend to be more intimate in Greece than in America. As a result, friends are generally free to ask questions which would seem too personal in America.

Go to page X-7

Page X-4

You selected 2: The Greeks asked Sharon the question in order to determine whether or not she belonged to the Greek Orthodox Church.

No. This is not why the Greeks asked Sharon such questions. Remember, whether or not some information is "personal" depends upon the culture. In this case, the Greeks did not consider these questions too "personal." Why? Try again.

Go to page X-1

Page X-5

You selected 3: The Greeks were unhappy about the way in which she lived and they were trying to get Sharon to change her habits.

No. There was no information given to lead you to believe that the Greeks were unhappy with Sharon's way of living. The episode states that the Greeks were acquaintances of Sharon.

Go to page X-1

Page X-6

You selected 4: In Greece such questions are perfectly proper when asked of women, but improper when asked of men.

No. Such questions are indeed proper under certain situations. However, sex has nothing to do with it. When are these questions proper? Try to apply what you have learned about proper behavior between friends in Greece. Was Sharon regarded as a friend by these Greeks?

Go to page X-1

---

tural situations. Unlike other cross-cultural training techniques which involve the imparting of technical knowledge, this approach attempts to increase a trainee's awareness of the cultural bases of behavior and, through this awareness, to improve trainee sensitivity to self and to the environment.

At a minimum, many companies such as Amoco, Bechtel, General Electric, IBM, Coca-Cola, Xerox, and Hewlett-Packard provide an orientation program to new cultures. The orientation may be as extensive as teaching a basic level of proficiency in the host country's language, allowing managers and their spouses to visit the prospective country for a few weeks, plus encouraging them to talk with managers and their families who have already lived in the host country (Copeland, 1985; Ronen, 1989).

Training at Diamond-Star Motors, a joint venture between Mitsubishi and Chrysler, exemplifies an innovative use of cross-cultural training. Diamond-Star developed a cross-cultural training program for its Japanese managers who are being transferred to the United States. The purpose of the program is to provide insight and information on American employee attitudes, values, work-setting needs, and related subjects relevant to the Diamond-Star setting. The program is designed to enable Japanese to work effectively with Americans by providing them understanding and knowledge about what motivates and demotivates Americans. Among the topics covered are motivational influences, work-related values, factors that promote trust and cooperation, educational influences, as well as American views on working with the Japanese (Anderson, 1990).

Professional Obsolescence

Today's professional (e.g., engineer, manager, chemist, physician, accountant) faces the danger of becoming obsolete. *Obsolescence* is described as a reduction in one's professional competence resulting from a lack of knowledge of new techniques and technologies that have developed since the acquisition of the individual's education (Dubin, 1972). Technological changes such as computer-aided design, "just in time" manufacturing, electronic mail, and self-managing work teams have created dramatic changes in people's jobs and, therefore, in the need for continual retraining during their careers (London and Bassman, 1989). A useful measure for estimating the extent of obsolescence in various professions is the concept of half-life, a term borrowed from nuclear physics. For instance, it has been asserted that an engineer's education today has a half-life of five years (i.e., half of what he or she learns in college becomes obsolete in five years) as compared with a half-life of 12 years in 1940. Due to the rapid addition of data and knowledge in many professions, organizations are finding that the performance of their "knowledge workers" (those who apply ideas, concepts, and information) tends to peak in their middle to late thirties and falls steadily thereafter until retirement (Dalton and Thompson, 1971).

An important part of the process of successful updating of knowledge is to increase the professional's own desire for continued lifelong education. A person's decision to expend a certain amount of effort for self-development is a function of the individual's perceptions of the organizational rewards that will accrue from engaging in such behavior (Porter, 1971). Thus organizations must reward (e.g., better salaries and assignments) their people equitably for expending effort to prevent professional obsolescence.

Organizations should make updating behavior an important component of their performance review system, and remove constraints from employees (e.g., bad supervisors, outdated equipment) that keep them from advancing their knowledge and skills. For instance, organizations concerned with avoiding professional obsolescence should encourage their managers to formulate mutually agreed upon updating goals with their subordinates, and make pay increases contingent on the accomplishment of these goals. These organizations should also encourage their employees to attend professional meetings, read technical journals and reports, publish their own findings, and so on.

Several professions take proactive steps to cope with obsolescence. For example, in the medical profession, the American Board of Internal Medicine has accepted the recommendation that periodic recertification of its diplomas be undertaken. The board administers examinations dealing with significant new developments in internal medicine and subspecialties at 10-year intervals (Hickam, 1970).

Research has shown that the degree of technical challenge experienced by engineers early in their careers relates positively to their professional competence in subsequent years (Kaufman, 1978). If an engineer's early work is extremely challenging in terms of using knowledge and skills to the fullest, the individual is stimulated to demonstrate good performance and competence throughout his or her career. Results from a number of other studies clearly show that early challenge is very important to the way a person's career develops. Specifically, the more challenging a person's job is during the first year with an organization, the more effective the individual tends to be years later (Berlew and Hall, 1966). Organizations should capitalize on these consistent findings by providing maximum challenge and stimulation during the professional's early years, so as to encourage later professional development.

The *updating panel* is another approach that can be used to cope with professional obsolescence (Dubin, 1972). This is basically a technique for determining systematically the training needs of professional and nonprofessional people working in organizations. It involves formulating a panel of experts in an occupational area to explore the changes, both theoretical and practical, to be expected in the next five years. From their discussions, recommended areas of training emerge for present and long-term development.

A final approach for coping with obsolescence involves the establishment of *centers*. For example, the Japanese first formulated what they call Science Education Centers in 1960 to remedy the educational obsolescence of science teachers in their schools. These centers have been so successful that the Japanese have broadened their scope and now offer classes in languages, social studies, and other subject areas (Glass, 1970). Similarly, Great Britain has Teachers' Centers, where special self-improvement programs are conducted by the teachers themselves for upgrading their current knowledge (Bailey, 1971).

More research on the effectiveness of continuing education is needed, both in terms of quantity and quality. The vast majority of continuing education programs never test their participants' learning or behavior change back on their jobs (see Chapter 5). They are evaluated only in terms of trainee reactions to the program (e.g., interesting, helpful, worthwhile).

Employee Assistance Programs

In recent years, many organizations have established special programs to aid employees at all job levels who have alcohol-related, drug-related, or emotional problems that affect their job performance. In fact, about 8000 Employee Assistance Programs (EAPs) exist in American work organizations, including 80 percent of the Fortune 500 companies (Maiden and Hardcastle, 1986).

How do these EAPs work? The vast majority involve an independent agency that provides counseling services to one or more client organizations. Usually, training sessions are given by this agency to all employees, labor representatives, and managers of their client organizations to inform them about the service and how they might take advantage of it. They are told that they and their family members may use the service as often as needed. There is no charge since the service is typically paid for by their company. Most often, employees and their family members contact the service on their own because of marital problems, emotional stress, financial difficulties, alcoholism, or drug abuse. Sometimes, however, an employee's supervisor or union representative might refer the employee to the program due to a documentable decline in job performance. To do this, supervisors must receive training in their approach to subordinates whose job performance, attendance, or relationship with other employees has recently deteriorated for some unknown reason. Managers and supervisors are taught to be alert to changes in the work patterns of their subordinates. They are trained to interview the troubled employee and present all the facts regarding declining performance. Their role is simply to advise the employee that outside professional services are available on a confidential basis.

There is no need for the supervisor to know the causes of the employee's problems. The supervisors are taught that they are not qualified to give advice on how to deal with the problem. They are not to be judgmental or moralistic, but simply to show concern and firmness about the employee's declining performance. If the employee refuses help, and performance continues to decline, the supervisors are instructed to give the individual a choice between seeking professional assistance or accepting dismissal. For example, at the Kemper Insurance Company, managers and supervisors are taught the following approach for dealing with employees with declining job performance:

> Make it clear that the company is concerned only with job performance. Unless job performance improves, the job is in jeopardy.
>
> Point out that the Personal Assistance Program is available for assistance to any employee who wants to resolve a personal health problem that may be affecting job performance.
>
> Explain that only the employee can decide whether to accept assistance.
>
> Emphasize that all aspects of the Personal Assistance Program are completely confidential.
>
> Don't try to diagnose the problem.
>
> Don't discuss drinking or drug abuse, unless it occurs on the job or the employee reports to work after having drunk excessively.
>
> Don't moralize. Restrict comments to job performance or attendance.
>
> Don't be misled by sympathy-evoking tactics, at which the alcoholic or drug abuser may have become expert.
>
> Don't discuss the employee's problem with anyone except the personnel in the Personal Assistance Program or those in direct line of authority above you.
>
> Don't "cover up" for a friend. A misguided "kindness" can lead to a serious delay in real help reaching him or her. Many employees have literally been killed by this kind of kindness. (From Rouse, R.A., "What to Do About the Employee with a Drinking Problem." Kemper Insurance Companies, 1964. Reprinted by permission.)

How well do EAPs work? Those organizations that use progressive techniques to deal with alcoholism, drug dependency, and emotional problems report positive outcomes. Typical of the results with problem drinkers are the following reported by the National Council on Alcoholism:

DETROIT EDISON:	"Absenteeism reduced from twice company average to one-half company average."
CONSOLIDATED EDISON:	"Sixty percent successfully rehabilitated. Absenteeism reduced from 14 days to 4 days per annum."
ALLIS-CHALMERS:	"Absentee rate slashed from 8 percent to 3 percent and discharge rate from 95 percent to

	8 percent. Savings to company of some $80,000 per year estimated."
DU PONT:	"Nine hundred and fifty alcoholics—1.09 percent of employees—66 percent successfully rehabilitated.
MINNESOTA MINING:	"Eighty percent are either recovered or controlled to the point where noticeable and marked improvement in attendance, productivity, and family and community relationships now exists."

Evaluation studies of EAPs have clearly shown their effectiveness. Kimberly-Clarke reported a 70 percent reduction in on-the-job accidents as a result of their EAP (Dedmon, 1980). In addition, Detroit Edison Company found an improvement in five measures of productivity (Nadolski and Sandonato, 1987): lost time (which included instances and number of days); health insurance claims; discipline (which included written warnings, suspensions, demotions, and discharges); accidents; and work productivity (which included quality of work, quantity of work, peer relationships on the job, relationship with supervisor, and supervisory performance). General Motors reported a 40 percent decrease in lost time and a 60 percent decrease in sickness and accident benefits. They also reported a 50 percent decrease in on-the-job accidents as well as grievances. All of this resulted in a three to one return on the dollar (Stessin, 1977). Similarly, Equitable Life Assurance Society estimated $5.52 saved for every dollar invested on its EAP; Kenecott Copper estimated a $6 savings (Berry, 1981; Manuso, 1984; Rosch and Pelletier, 1987).

Stress Management

Job stress has been estimated to cost American industry about $150 billion each year when we consider its effect on absenteeism, lowered productivity, employee compensation claims, health insurance, and medical expenses (Manuso, 1984). The Metropolitan Life Insurance Company estimated in 1984 that an average of 1 million American workers are absent from work on any given workday as a result of stress-related disorders (Rosch and Pelletier, 1987).

What are most organizations doing with respect to stress management training programs offered to workers? Based on a review of company practices, Rosch and Pelletier (1987) concluded the following:

1. Most efforts consist primarily of educational programs designed to acquaint employees with the role of stress in health and illness, sources of stress, and the nature of stress-related symptoms.
2. Most commercial programs provide trainees with individual stress profiles based on their answers to self-report questionnaires or standardized psychological instruments.
3. Most stress management programs teach participants one or more physiologic techniques (e.g., muscular relaxation, deep breathing, meditation).
4. Various behavioral techniques such as assertiveness training, time management, and reduction of Type A coronary-prone behaviors are used in programs to reduce inappropriate or exaggerated responses to stress.
5. Physical fitness is definitely the most popular method used to cope with stress in the workplace. This includes a wide variety of activities such as company-sponsored exercise and aerobic classes, weight reduction programs, in-house fitness facilities, and programs to help employees quit smoking.

One of the most effective stress management training programs was developed by Ronald Smith of the University of Washington. It has been applied to such diverse population members as social welfare case workers, university administrators, bankers, business executives, test-anxious college students, heavy social drinkers, and athletes (Smith, 1980). The program has been evaluated using both time-series designs and pre- and postmeasure designs with random assignment of individuals to either the control group or the group to whom the training is given. The conceptual model of stress that underlies the training is similar to Bandura's (1986) social learning theory discussed in Chapter 8 in that it emphasizes reciprocal relationships among the situation, the individual's cognitive appraisal processes of what is occurring to him or her, affective arousal, and instrumental behaviors.

The program involves the five following phases: First, there is pretreatment assessment. Interviews and questionnaires are used for identifying the trainee's behavioral and cognitive skills as well as deficiencies so that the program can be tailored to the person's special needs. For example, the trainer determines how well the person can voluntarily relax, and how aware the person is of the cognitive processes that elicit emotional responses and impair performance or, conversely, reduce stress and improve behavioral efficiency.

In short, the trainer tries to build on the trainee's strengths and help him or her acquire new coping skills in deficit areas. Thus the training program for a person who already has fairly good relaxation skills, but who has little control over self-defeating thought processes, will tend to focus on developing stress-reducing, stress-preventing, and performance-enhancing cognitive skills. Conversely, a primary focus on the development of relaxation and self-instructional skills may be the preferred approach for an intellectually dull and chronically tense person.

Second is the treatment rationale or conceptualization phase designed to help trainees understand the nature of their stress response. This step is of crucial importance in obtaining trainee commitment. Thus care is taken to ensure that the conceptualization is understandable and plausible. The person is asked to describe his or her stress responses. Questions such as "When did it happen?" "What was it like?" and, "What were your thoughts at the time?" are usually sufficient to elicit descriptions of situational, physiological, and cognitive elements. Answers to these questions provide an entrée to the necessity for training that will allow the person to acquire specific cognitive and behavioral coping skills.

Two important points are made during the conceptualization phase. One is that the program is not psychotherapy; it is an educational program. It is emphasized that the basic difference between people who are negatively affected by stress and those who cope successfully is that the latter group has been fortunate in having previous life experiences that enable them to learn the kinds of coping skills taught in this program. The second point is that it is a program in self-control, and the coping abilities that result from the training are a function of how much effort the person devotes to the acquisition of them. This point cannot be overemphasized.

Skill acquisition, the third phase, is directed toward the development of an integrated coping response having both relaxation and cognitive elements. The skill acquisition phase consists of the learning of muscular relaxation and a concomitant analysis of thought processes. Stress-eliciting self-statements are replaced with specific cognitions designed to reduce stress and improve performance.

Training in voluntary muscle relaxation begins immediately. Individual muscle groups are tensed, slowly relaxed halfway, and then slowly relaxed completely. The procedure is designed to enhance discrimination of slight changes in muscle tension. The written training exercises are presented elsewhere (Smith, Sarason, and Sarason, 1978, pp. 258–260).

As training proceeds, increasingly larger groups of muscles are combined until the entire body is relaxed as a unit. Although some of the relaxation is led by the trainer, much of it is accomplished on a daily basis in the form of homework assignments.

Special emphasis is placed on the use of deep breathing to facilitate relaxation. The person is asked to breathe slowly and deeply and to say repeatedly the mental command "Relax" during exhalation. The command is thus repeatedly paired with the relaxation that occurs with exhalation, so that in time the command becomes an eliciting cue for inducing relaxation.

Training in cognitive coping skills begins with a didactic description and the reading of written materials on the manner in which emotional responses are elicited by internal sentences. The trainees are given daily homework forms on which they list a situation that upset them, the emotion they experienced, what they must have told themselves about the situation in order to have been upset, and what they might have told themselves instead in order to have prevented their distress. These exercises, discussions with the trainer, and written materials form the basis for an antistress log in which the trainees list their habitual stress-producing self-statements (usually five or fewer) and an antistress substitute for each. The latter form the basis for further practice and rehearsal.

In analyzing their stress-eliciting thoughts, trainees are shown how the beliefs underlying their self-statements are often irrational (e.g., "I must always be successful in order to be worthwhile"). Replacing irrational statements with comments such as "I can do no more than give 100 percent and I'm still the same person whether I succeed or not" provides the person with a potential tool for preventing or reducing self-induced stress responses.

The approach just described is a form of cognitive restructuring because its objective is to evaluate and replace irrational beliefs that cause stress. However, in addition to cognitive restructuring is self-instructional training. The focus of this approach, as the name implies, is on the development of specific task-relevant self-commands. Examples of such commands are "One step at a time; develop a plan to deal with it." "Take a deep breath and relax." A number of studies have shown that self-instructional training in itself is valuable in enhancing performance and in reducing emotional arousal under stressful conditions (Meichenbaum, 1977).

Skill rehearsal is the fourth phase of this training. Stress coping skills are no different than any other kind of skill. To be most effective they must be rehearsed and practiced under conditions that approximate the real-life situations in which they will eventually be employed. The feature that most clearly differentiates this training from other stress-management programs is the use of *induced affect* during the rehearsal phase after the development of cognitive and physical coping skills.

Induced affect, the fifth phase, is used to generate high levels of emotional arousal, which are then reduced by the trainee, using the coping responses acquired in the preceding phase of training. The trainee is asked to imagine as vividly as possible a stressful situation. The person is then asked to focus on the feeling that the situation elicited. The trainer states that as the trainee focuses on it, it will begin to grow and to become stronger and stronger. The suggestions continue as the trainee begins to respond to them with increasing emotional arousal. Physical indications of arousal are verbally reinforced by the trainer ("That's good, that's fine . . . Let that feeling grow . . . Just let it come . . . It's OK to let it come, because in a minute you'll see how easily you can turn it off"). At intervals during the arousal phase, the trainer asks the trainee what kinds of thoughts are occurring, and this information is used to elaborate on the arousal. It also provides information on the nature of the cognitions that accompany the arousal.

After a high level of arousal is achieved, the trainee is told to "turn it off" with his or her coping responses. Initially relaxation alone is used as the coping skill. Then self-statements alone are used. Finally, the two types of coping responses are combined into an integrated coping response that ties both the self-statements and the relaxation response into the breathing cycle. As the trainee inhales, she or he emits a stress-reducing self-statement. At the peak of inhalation, the trainee says the word "so" and while slowly exhaling gives the command to "relax" and induces muscular relaxation.

It should be noted that during relaxation training, exhalation, the mental command to relax, and voluntarily relaxing are repeatedly combined with one another. The introduction of the self-statement during inhalation results in the integration of cognitive and physiological coping responses within the breathing cycle.

What can be concluded about the impact of other stress management programs? Due to their heterogeneity, the imprecise measures of efficacy used, and the lack of control groups, proof of the success of these programs is difficult to obtain (Rosch and Pelletier, 1987). However, there are stress management training programs that have been evaluated carefully. For example, Johnson and Johnson's "Live for Life" program has been found to affect various health screen measures significantly (e.g., weight, blood pressure, smoking, aerobic calories) as well as various employee attitudes (e.g., self-reported sick days, satisfaction with personal relations at work and working conditions, ability to handle job strain, job self-esteem) (Arnold, 1981; Rosch and Pelletier, 1987).

One approach to minimizing stress in the workplace is to manage one's time effectively. We discuss this important topic next.

Time Management

The underlying theme of time management is goal setting. As noted in Chapter 4, goal-setting theory (Locke and Latham, 1990) states that specific hard goals lead to higher productivity than generalized goals or the setting of no goals at all. Hard goals lead to higher performance than easy goals. Time limits increase productivity to the extent that they lead to the setting of specific hard goals. Support for this contention has been found in both laboratory studies (Bryan and Locke, 1967) and field settings (Latham and Locke, 1975).

In a well-controlled laboratory study, Bryan and Locke found that if the time available to complete a task is longer than needed, the pace will be slowed to fill the allotted time. On the other hand, if the time allotted is minimal, the pace will be adjusted in order to complete the task before the deadline. This occurred because people with shorter time limits set harder goals than those with longer time limits.

In field settings, Latham and Locke (1975) found that logging crews showed a significantly higher rate of output when they were allowed to sell wood to forest products companies only one or two days a week rather than five. Since the crews were paid on a piece-rate basis, there was an incentive for them to maximize production early when the buying restrictions were operative. When the mills restricted the amount of wood they purchased to fewer days per week, they were implicitly urging a higher production goal (per employee hour) on the logging crews. To minimize income loss, the crews tried to harvest as much wood in one or two days as they formerly harvested in five days.

In summary, time limits can affect one's work pace through goal setting—hence the growing interest in the management of time through goal setting. Although the number of books written on time management are too numerous to mention, a synthesis of their ideas is given in the following goal-setting steps.

1. Establish a daily "things to do" list.
2. Categorize your things to do as either (a) top priority, (b) medium priority, or (c) low priority.
3. Rank order the items that fall in the category of top priority.
    a. Tackle only top priority items. An item of top priority that will require an extensive amount of time should be broken down into meaningful subparts. Rank order the subparts and work on the most important first.
    b. Ignore items that are of medium priority until there is a follow-up request.
    c. Ignore items of low priority until all top priority and medium priority items are completed. Do not work on items that fall in these latter two categories because your time limits are such that you can complete one of them more easily than you can complete a top priority item. The principle of setting subgoals by breaking a top priority item into a number of different tasks is to keep you working on top priority items. Adherence to this principle is also necessary to keep you from feeling reinforced for the successful completion of many low priority tasks while top priority items remain untouched.
4. Don't overschedule. The goals set for the day should be difficult but attainable.

Drucker (1987) offers a slightly different approach to mastering time management. Step 1 is the admonishment that planning does not come first. This is because even the best-intentioned plan is doomed unless managers first diagnose exactly how they are spending their time. Only when they take an audit of where their time is going can they hope to cut back on all the unproductive demands that inevitably interfere with their ability to accomplish their high-priority tasks. To uncover time wasters, Drucker suggests the following question: "What would be happening if I didn't do this, or if someone else did it?" If the answer is "nothing," then discard or reassign the task.

Step 2 is to consolidate blocks of time. Larger blocks of time should be assigned to major tasks. Trying to cope with projects in dribs and drabs is a sheer waste of time. Nowhere is the need for continuous and uninterrupted time blocks more vital, contends Drucker, than in dealing with people issues. Managers who attempt to direct or improve the performance of a subordinate in 20 minutes are deceiving themselves and doing a disservice to their employees. It pays to invest time in those things that matter.

Step 3 is to concentrate one's effort. Too many executives and managers try to do several things at once. As a result, they dissipate their powers of concentration. Single-minded concentration on one task at a time is as close to a "secret" of effectiveness as you will find, contends Drucker.

ISSUES CONFRONTING EMPLOYEES IN THE 1990s

In the remainder of this chapter, we discuss six issues that are relevant to all employees in the 1990s: (1) training for the prevention of sexual and racial harassment, (2) wellness training, (3) safety training, (4) customer service training, (5) team skills training, and (6) personal computer training.

Training for the Prevention of Sexual and Racial Harassment

Whether it occurs because of someone's sex or race, harassment is a form of discrimination and is therefore prohibited by federal law in both the United States and Canada. Most human resource departments develop a strongly worded statement against harassment in their employee handbooks. Even better are those companies that supplement these written statements with comprehensive training programs so that everyone in the organization clearly understands the legal basis preventing harassment, how to differentiate illegal and legal behaviors, whose conduct creates liability, additional situations creating liability (e.g., unequal conditions of employment, style of dress, making jokes), as well as recommendations for preventing harassment and avoiding liability. Typical training approaches to this subject use the following training techniques: lectures, behavior modeling, and role playing.

Wellness Training

Organizations are beginning to realize that it is less costly to prevent the onset of disease and injury than it is to allow their occurrence and subsequent treatment. By spending modest amounts of money on teaching their employees ways of reducing health risks for major diseases, these organizations can expect to spend less in the future on corporate health care expenses (Sloan and Gruman, 1988). Let us take, for example, the case of cardiovascular disease (CVD) which is responsible for the largest part of the nation's health care expenses (over $60 billion in 1985). The known risk factors for CVD are smoking, high levels of serum cholesterol, family history of CVD, sedentary life-style, the type A behavior pattern, high blood pressure, and obesity. Note that all of these risk factors, with the exception of family history, have behavioral components. For this reason, wellness programs have focused on teaching employees the importance of health-oriented behaviors such as eating properly, getting regular exercise, and keeping one's weight down (Sloan and Gruman, 1988).

Johnson and Johnson's "Live for Life" (LFL) is an example of an excellent corporate wellness program. It includes a complete health examination, including a risk appraisal; a seminar on the importance of maintaining a healthy life-style; and numerous programs on such topics as smoking cessation, physical fitness, and proper nutrition. In 1986 the LFL program was evaluated by comparing, over a five-year period, two groups of Johnson and Johnson companies who had implemented LFL with one group of companies that had not (Sloan and Gruman, 1988). The researchers found that the LFL groups had a lower rate of increase of inpatient costs, hospital days, and hospital admissions (Bly, Jones, and Richardson, 1986).

With the advancing age of the post–World War II baby boom generation, we predict that the overall health of employees will become a major issue. Training in self-management, discussed in Chapter 8, is ideally suited to teaching self-maintenance of one's health. This training may also be enhanced by computer-assisted instruction.

For example, Schneider (1984), a clinician, has developed a computer program that is supported by the National Heart, Lung and Blood Institute to stop smoking. The program is on CompuServe, a collection of computerized information which is available to 360,000 people, each with a computer and a modem. Once the smoker answers questions about the bonuses of the habit, the computer responds accordingly. One light smoker, after responding to 18 questions, received the following advice:

COMPUTER: Your answers on the questionnaire suggest that you smoke to accentuate pleasure. Soon you'll see you don't really need to smoke.

Schneider's program employs mental restructuring, now a traditional tool in self-management training, in advising smokers who may call into CompuServe when they feel an overwhelming urge for a cigarette.

COMPUTER: Now imagine a giant neon sign brightly lit up saying DON'T SMOKE!!! Do that now. This technique is called "thought stopping" because it makes you focus on an image that counteracts the thought that smoking is desirable. Once you stop the thought that you should smoke, the urge will pass.

Smokers record their progress in a diary and get feedback on their screens in the form of a graph of their tobacco consumption. Some of Schneider's subscribers can even log in and leave messages in order to share their experiences.

Another example of trainee-computer interaction is a training system developed to teach cardiopulmonary resuscitation (CPR). The system uses a video disc player, video monitors, a random-access videotape player, and a mannequin, all of which are controlled by a microcomputer. The system will ". . . answer questions upon request, instantaneously gather information about each student's hands-on performance, respond with appropriate spoken or video demonstration, gather data on the student's next attempt, respond with appropriate instruction or demonstration, provide performance feedback, give repeated drill and practice, and be cost effective" (Huber and Gay, 1984, p. 102). Evaluation of this system indicates that training time is reduced from several hours to 20 minutes. It allows precise coaching, providing exact feedback and individualized responses.

Safety Training

Since the early 1970s, the government has been working to ensure safe and healthful working conditions. As part of its program, it has established certain training standards that various industries are required to follow.

In 1970 the Occupational Safety and Health Administration (OSHA) was established as a federal agency to ensure the safe and healthy working conditions of American workers. Violations of standards may result in citations, fines, or court cases initiated by OSHA personnel who conduct compliance visits to workplaces.

Although OHSA does not certify or approve training programs per se, its compliance officers look for evidence that employers have met certain "training standards" related to their industry. The following is an example of the training standards for pulpwood logging.

> Chain saw operators shall be instructed to daily inspect the saws . . . follow manufacturer's instructions as to operation and adjustment . . . fuel the saw only in safe areas and not under conditions conducive to fire . . . hold the saw

> with both hands during operation . . . start the saw at least 10 feet from fueling areas . . . start the saw only on the ground or when otherwise firmly supported. (Training Requirements of the Occupational Safety and Health Standards, U.S. Department of Labor, Occupational Safety and Health Administration)

Employers must be able to produce records indicating that their employees have received training in the areas identified in the standards. Moreover, the employers must be able to show the compliance officer that the training program is based on an analysis of the tasks performed by the employee. The task analysis must identify, at a minimum, the actual and potential hazards the employee will encounter on the job, and the equipment and practices the employee should follow to minimize the risk of injury to self or others. Finally, employers must be able to demonstrate that the training gives special attention to the conditions and practices most likely to result in injury and illness.

Goodyear Tire and Rubber Company, in accordance with OSHA standards, has established special programs in their tire plants to inform employees of possible health hazards due to carcinogens (e.g., vinylchloride, benzene, acrylonitrile). During these sessions, trainees are informed of such things as the atmospheric monitoring devices that have been used in the plant and the results obtained; possible consequences if one exceeds the action level (i.e., one-half the permissible exposure level); possible diseases that might occur and their symptoms; and the medical examinations associated with the particular job.

The vehicle maintenance division of a large western city's department of public works is responsible for equipment repair and maintenance of the city's rolling stock. This division had one of the highest accident rates of any department in the city prior to implementing a highly successful training program, consisting of information plus performance feedback (Komaki, Heinzman, and Lawson, 1980). The safety sessions begin by showing trainees a series of slides portraying unsafe conditions or practices. The trainees are encouraged to discuss the hazards portrayed and suggest safety rules that have been followed. These unsafe scenes are then shown again, followed by scenes that picture the condition corrected or the act performed safely. As each vignette is shown, the safety rule that has been observed is stated (e.g., the employee under the vehicle now wore eye protection). Next, the trainees are given a copy of all the safety rules, which are also posted in their respective section areas. The trainees are then told by their section supervisors that random daily safety observations will be conducted, with the results posted on a graph in their section areas. The graph displays how the section performed in relation to realistic goals that had been previously set by the division's superintendent, based on each section's previous safety performance.

A different approach, accident simulation, is gaining popularity in safety training programs. It involves the use of devices that duplicate particular dangers while allowing trainees to act safely or unsafely (Rubinsky and Smith, 1973). The most obvious example, of course, is the use of flight simulators for pilot training. Other examples include Aetna Life & Casualty Company's driver education program, which involves automobile simulators used in conjunction with films to portray various highway conditions. This program stresses safe driving procedures, and covers such topics as timing maneuvers to the actions of other highway users, coping with emergencies resulting from vehicle malfunctions, encountering motorcycles in traffic, and executing appropriate evasive actions when only split seconds are available. Goodyear has established Performance-Based Training Centers in their tire plants for new hires and transfers. These centers consist of equipment simulators (e.g., mills, fabric cutting units, tire building machines) as well as permanent training staffs. Trainees are shown the potential hazards that can result from performing each step of their jobs incorrectly, as well as how to do it correctly. The company has found that at their Danville Center in Virginia, for instance, there has been a substantial reduction in the total number of OSHA reportable accidents and lost-time days. Babcock & Wilcox, an organization that manufactures nuclear boilers, uses simulators in Lynchburg, Virginia. Their equipment simulates the operation of nuclear power plants similar to the one located at Three Mile Island in Pennsylvania. It trains nuclear power operators by simulating temperature, pressure, and flow readings on their instruments, allowing them to react, and providing them with immediate feedback regarding the consequences of their actions.

To our knowledge, no effort to address the problems of safety and health equals that of General Motors. Since the UAW-GM Health and Safety Training Center opened in 1985, more than 1400 trainers have received training in safety programs at their home plants designed to reduce the number of accidents and injuries on the job. Located in Madison Heights, Michigan, the center offers numerous training programs on fork truck safety, robotic safety, rigging safety, mobile crane safety, and the potential hazards of handling six categories of chemicals used by General Motors. All of these training programs use state-of-the-art training methods. For instance, the hands-on workshop for the mobile crane safety program involves an obstacle course that has been set up at the center. Working in pairs (i.e., an operator and a signalman), trainees navigate their way through the obstacle course using techniques that they learned through computer-based training.

Besides using training to ensure safe work habits, some progressive organizations have begun to give their employees training in the prevention of ill health and disease. Some organizations call their efforts wellness programs; others refer to them as workplace health promotion programs.

Customer Service Training

"Focus on the customer" has become a corporate mandate in organizations striving for excellence. This is because customer satisfaction results in repeat business and enduring business relationships which increase profitability (Peters and Austin 1985; Peters and Waterman, 1982).

One company that has been using employee training to increase the satisfaction level of their customers is the Radisson Hotel Corporation. Their training program, known as "Yes I Can," is the direct result of a 1985 Radisson study demonstrating that a friendly, helpful staff is the most important element of their customers' hotel experience. The Yes I Can training consists of two parts. Part I teaches Radisson employees about the corporation's commitment to the finest in customer service, the various components of top-quality service, how to better understand guests and their needs, as well as techniques based on a positive attitude that can enhance a guest's experience. The first part of the program also consists of an "Inform and Explore Session" in which new ideas and skills are introduced and examined and a "Review and Practice Session," where the newly acquired skills are perfected and applied. The second part of the training follows graduation from Part I. During follow-up sessions, supervisors encourage employees to review what they have learned, apply their new skills on their jobs, and look for new ways of improving customer service. Monthly meetings help maintain the flow of ideas and innovations.

The Educational Institute of the American Hotel and Motel Association has a guest relations training program known as "The Spirit of Hospitality" available for its members. Thousands of hospitality industry employees have already been through this program which was designed to sensitize all employees to guests' needs and expectations, increase communications (between staff and guests, staff and staff, staff and management), create a spirit of teamwork, promote positive guest relations, provide opportunities for recognition, and motivate employees to take pride in their jobs (The Spirit of Hospitality, 1987).

Numerous service organizations in the energy (i.e., electric and gas utilities), financial (banks and savings and loans), and telecommunications (telephone companies) industries have instituted training programs to enhance, at all levels, employees' skills and attitudes toward serving customers. These service organizations will frequently hire a customer service improvement company (e.g., Kaset, Inc., of Tampa, Florida) that will first help senior executives in establishing a plan and timetable which recognizes their company's situation, the extent of their team's commitment to becoming customer focused, and their visions for the future of their organization. Once senior-level management is committed to cultivating service excellence, everyone in the company is trained in creating satisfied customers. It makes no difference whether the employee interacts with external customers (i.e., the public) or internal customers (i.e., employees in other departments which one's department services). Trainees are taught how to recognize the difficult customer, manage customer expectations, reduce stress, build rapport, and create positive outcomes.

The single most effective training approach to a customer focus is the modeling of that focus by senior-level management. Sam Walton, the founder of the Wal-Mart retail chain, exemplifies this approach to training. His personal attention to merchandising and customer service models what he expects from subordinates. Failure to maintain these standards is considered both a personal defeat as well as a shortfall in mutual obligations between upper management and the Wal-Mart employees.

Team Skills Training

More than ever before, there is a concern in organizations with improving the effectiveness of its work teams (i.e., departments, committees, management teams, task forces, project teams). Improving team functioning can result in (1) the effective management of complexity caused by advancing technologies, (2) rapid response to ever-changing environments and work demands, (3) higher levels of motivation for individuals within the team, (4) higher quality decisions and commitment to carrying out the decisions by individuals on the team, and (5) increased collective strength or synergism that occurs when a group participates in effective team building training (Lawler, 1988).

Let us take a brief look at what companies are currently doing in the way of team skills training.

S.B. Thomas, Inc., has become the largest producer of English muffins in the United States, capturing half of the national market by 1985. At one of their new plants in Schaumburg, Illinois, workers (or, as they are called, associates) are organized into teams, or action groups, according to their function. For instance, associates assigned to muffin production are members of the process action group; those working in the packaging area belong to the pack action group. Once the applicants are hired and appear on the bakery's production floor, they receive weekly reports during their 60-day probationary period which give them specific feedback on both their interpersonal behavior as a team member as well as on technical aspects of their work performance. Moreover, at the Schaumburg plant, traditional supervisory responsibilities are broken down into specific roles that are now handled by the team members themselves (e.g., discussion leader, work assigner, safety facilitator). By serving in these various roles for a period of weeks or months, the employees gain an understanding and appreciation of their entire team, act as nonthreatening mentors of one another, and develop a sense of pride about their contribution to their team's performance (Rubin, 1988).

Some organizations approach team skills training by using an exercise which helps team members gain a better understanding of their own personal behavioral styles, and how their styles are compatible or incompatible with other styles. For example, the Lansing Board of Water and Light, a Mid-Michigan utility company, uses the Myers-Briggs Type Indicator (MBTI) (Briggs and Myers, 1977) to help team members understand themselves and others. The MBTI is primarily concerned with important differences between people that result from where they focus their attention (i.e., on the outer world—extrovert, or inner world—introvert), the way they take in information (i.e., through one's sensing or through one's intuition), the way they decide (i.e., through one's thinking or through one's feelings), and the kind of life-style they adopt in dealing with the outer world (i.e., take primarily a judging attitude by means of thinking or feeling or else take a perceptive attitude by means of sensing or intuition). Each team member learns his or her "type." Imagine, for example, that Betty takes the MBTI and realizes that she is an introvert who likes to process information through sensing, prefers to use thinking to make decisions, and mainly takes a judging attitude toward the outer world. Imagine, also, that Betty feels that she has been having a difficult time understanding and getting along with Fred, another team member. Fred's MBTI indicates that he is an extrovert who prefers intuition for perceiving, feeling for making decisions, and who takes a perceptive attitude toward the outer world. With the help of a skillful trainer, Betty and Fred can be guided toward a better understanding of the causes of one another's behavior and, consequently, improve their working relationships (Myers, 1987).

A variation of sensitivity training, namely, interpersonal team building, is also useful in teaching people how to become effective team members. A primary goal of sensitivity training, as noted in Chapter 9, is to teach people to become aware of or sensitive to how they are perceived by others. The training is often ineffective because it is conducted in a group setting where the members of the group are strangers to one another. Consequently, positive behavior changes that may take place during training are not reinforced by colleagues when the trainee returns to the job. Sensitivity training is generally ineffective even when the training takes place with people from the same work area because the feedback is usually not job related. Finally, specific goals for achieving and/or maintaining the behavior change, in most instances, are not set.

To correct these limitations, job analyses were conducted for a group of first-line supervisors, and for a vice president and his immediate staff (Latham, 1983). Two behavioral observation scales (BOS) were developed for each respective group (see Chapter 3). Each person was then evaluated anonymously on the BOS by his or her peers.

The performance problem in both instances was that the group members were not committed to attaining common goals. Instead, each individual was working to impact favorably the bottom line criteria (e.g., costs) of the department in which he or she was accountable.

The advantage of using BOS, within the context of sensitivity training, is that the individual employee is involved in the job analysis that is the basis for developing the yardstick (BOS) on which he or she is assessed. Thus the BOS are developed by the employee for the employee. Moreover, the items are job related. They represent what the employee and colleagues have observed to be the critical behaviors a person must demonstrate on a given job or set of jobs to be successful. Finally, the items on the BOS facilitate recognition and recall for the team member as to what each is doing correctly/incorrectly on the job. Two open-ended questions at the end of the BOS request each team member to summarize what the person should (1) continue doing on the job, and (2) start doing, stop doing, or do differently.

The arithmetic average of the ratings for each item for each employee is calculated prior to the appraisal session. The appraisal process is then conducted in a group setting. Each person's appraisal is given in typically a one- to two-hour time period. An industrial/organizational psychologist or a person skilled in group processes facilitates the feedback by first asking the individual if he or she has any questions regarding his or her colleagues' evaluations. Peers are coached by the facilitator on how to emphasize, in giving feedback, what the person is to do differently in the future. The listener is then asked to summarize what was "heard" and to set specific goals as to what he or she will do differently as a result of this feedback. The team then discusses how they can help the person achieve the goals. Discussion then focuses on another individual in the group until every individual has received and has set goals.

The results have proven to be highly beneficial in terms of inducing and sustaining behavior change. The mechanisms are straightforward. The feedback is based on job-related items, and specific goals are set regarding job-related items. It is difficult for an employee to downplay the importance of these job-related items because the items were identified as important to job success by the employee and his or her peers. It is difficult for the employee to say that the BOS do not provide a comprehensive measure of what is required of him or her as a team player because everyone in the group participated in the development of the BOS. More importantly, it is more difficult to discredit the observations of a group of people, namely, one's peers than it is to discredit the observations of one person, namely, the boss. The employee cannot risk the condemnation of the group for failing to work toward the attainment of the goals agreed upon during the appraisal, but can enjoy the reinforcement for working toward and attaining these goals on an ongoing basis on the job.

In summary, the focus on team playing is to teach people how to move away from narrow self-interest toward a sense of mutual obligations and responsibilities. Corporations, however, must maintain a proper balance in their emphasis on the team relative to the individual.

Zalesnik (1990) wrote a critical essay on the dangers of corporations placing a premium on the team over the individual. He argued that many organizations have adopted a management mystique that inadvertently encourages people to relinquish their ability to think in favor of adopting slogans and formulas, and management process. The result is that people become so bound up in process that they are no longer free to overcome it to establish creative ideas, actions, and programs. Zalesnik concluded that leadership must be based on compacts that bind those who lead and those who follow into the same moral, intellectual, and emotional commitment rather than on slogans and esoteric vocabulary understood only by those within the team.

In a similar vein, Scott and Hart (1989) have warned against the "organizational imperative," namely, the belief that what is good for the individual can only come from alignment with the organization and, therefore, everything that an individual values must reflect the values of the company.

The solution to this problem is to maintain a proper balance regarding the focus on the team relative to the individual. For corporate leaders, Zalesnik advocated developing the art of self-examination that stimulates the person's imagination as well as toughens analytic thinking.

The problems in this approach have been described by Kaplan, Drath, and Kofodimos (1987). Their hypothesis was that executives avoid coming to terms with their limitations, and that the people who work with them are reluctant, because of the executive's power, to give them constructive feedback. Further, executives are often unable to accept criticism because of their need to appear highly competent. Thus there is often an adamant refusal to admit weakness or acknowledge any need for improvement. The opportune time to encourage self-analysis, they concluded, is in response to a specific need: a setback at work, repeated difficulties at one's job, a career impasse, and a buildup of health-threatening stress. Systematic experiments are needed to test these hypotheses.

Two additional things must occur, from the viewpoint of Scott and Hart, before the proper focus is again placed on the individual. First, organizational leaders must become cognizant of one of the major objectives of the founding fathers of the United States, namely, to keep oppressive governments off the backs of the people so that individualism and personal growth can flourish. Scott and Hart contend that today's corporate leaders must take steps to protect the individual's dignity and personal autonomy in the context of the organization as well as government.

Second, Scott and Hart argue that employees must be empowered to make changes in organizations and be protected for trying to do so. If they do not, companies may become tyrannies ruled with velvet gloves instead of iron hands. Thus the structure of corporate governance must allow the employee to have a voice and encourage him or her to use it. Only then, Scott and Hart contend, will individual moral judgment begin to inform organizational ethics instead of being subservient to them.

Personal Computer (PC) Training

Computers have moved from the domain of the data-processing department into the offices of most employees. In the following section, we discuss what organizations are doing with respect to computer training.

To address the popularity of personal computers (PCs), training specialists in organizations have had to concern themselves with finding the optimum way of teaching people how to use their PCs effectively in their jobs. Effective PC training has presented a challenge to training practitioners because it often involves a fear of technology, resistance to change, long learning curves, and the need to learn a completely new language with unfamiliar concepts (Armstrong and McElhone, 1987).

What do we know today about facilitating the effectiveness of any in-house PC training program? First, either prior to or during the installation of PCs in a company or department, it is advisable to provide groups of employees with a well-rounded introduction to microcomputers so as to allay their misconceptions. The trainers need to answer questions, laugh with employees when they find that their fears are groundless, and give encouragement to tentative beginners (Coppolino, 1986). Second, since trainees differ drastically with respect to their level of trainability, it is important that designers and selectors of PC training programs make certain to provide curricula that allow trainees to move at their own pace consistent with their learning, motivation, and abilities. Third, trainers need to be present during the learning experience to provide immediate feedback as well as a human element for those who are afraid of the technology. A training strategy that combines short lectures with hands-on practice in the presence of a trainer is highly recommended (Armstrong and McElhone, 1987). Finally, some companies allow their employees to train themselves by using a variety of methods such as diskettes, manufacturer's manuals, and tutorial books.

FINAL COMMENTS

There is no reason to be complacent over the quality of scientific research on training and development, nor is there reason for despair. Fads do not dominate the scientific literature on training and development; advancement in theory and empirical research is ongoing. What troubles some people is the extent to which practitioners and practitioner journals appear to be unaffected by these advancements. Overcoming this problem is certainly an area for research. One solution may be simply to translate scientific articles for a lay audience. This has been one of the main objectives of this book.

The success of any training and development program in organizations depends on three basic elements: (1) systematic determination of training needs, (2) careful design to facilitate learning and transfer back to the job, and (3) systematic evaluation of the training program.

If training is to become respected as a science of behavior, we cannot retreat from the crucial task of specifying what it is that trainees are supposed to learn. We need to specify exactly what trainees are expected to know and do differently as a result of participating in the training program. Course objectives cannot be properly generated through armchair speculation and wishful thinking. Instead, they must be determined through a painstaking identification of each of the tasks involved in performing a job.

Unfortunately, at the present time, not enough is known about the principles of learning to ensure that learning will take place with every trainee. However, there are aptitude measuring instruments today to select individuals who have the ability to learn what is being taught. Also, enough is now known about human motivation to design programs so that individuals will remain interested in learning. Further, it is clear that psychomotor learning should include some combination of goal setting + modeling + practice + feedback, whereas, for factual learning, goal setting + meaningfulness + practice + feedback are important components of learning and transfer.

Evaluation should not be viewed as a simple yes/no decision about continuing training. Programs are seldom all good or all bad. Rather, evaluation studies should be part of a continuous feedback process for the training staff. When an evaluation study has been completed, the training staff needs to consider whether and/or how the training should be modified. It is a costly mistake for trainers to let their emotional reactions cloud their thinking about improving their programs. It is important that they carefully think through why certain course objectives were not attained, and how they can improve their program the next time it is administered.

In conclusion, note the following three important suggestions for future efforts in the field of training:

1. It is important to further understand how differences among trainees moderate the effectiveness of different training techniques. More research is needed to examine aptitude-treatment interactions (see Chapter 4). If this is done, instructional programs will be designed that best suit each trainee.
2. It is important to understand how different organizational variables (e.g., technology, motivational conditions, unionization) affect training efforts. Training specialists have to become more cognizant of, and knowledgeable about, the "macro" variables that affect trainees in their organizations. It is no longer appropriate to assume that training exists independent of its organizational context.
3. There is a need for rigorous evaluation studies that examine the usefulness of individual training approaches (e.g., Latham and Saari, 1979) as well as different combinations of training and development approaches (e.g., Wexley and Nemeroff, 1975). Too many of the training methods currently in use fall far short of the standards we have discussed in this book.

References

Adams, J. A., "Historical Review and Appraisal of Research on the Learning Retention and Transfer of Human Motor Skills," *Psychological Bulletin, 101* (1987), 41–74.

Air Transport Association of America. Washington, DC, 1969.

Albert, D., "Intercultural Sensitizer or Culture Assimilator: A Cognitive Approach," in D. Landis and R. W. Brislin (eds.), *Handbook of Intercultural Trainings*. Elmsford, NY: Pergamon Press, 1983, 186–217.

Alpander, G. G., "Conceptual Analysis of Supervisory Training Programs in Major U.S. Corporations." Paper presented at the annual meeting of the Academy of Management, Chicago, 1986.

American Airlines Flight Academy. Fort Worth, TX.

Ammons, R. B., *Knowledge of Performance, Survey of Literature, Some Possible Applications and Suggested Experimentation*. WADC Technical Report 54–14, Wright Air Development Center, 1954.

Anastasi, A., *Psychological Testing*. New York: Macmillan, 1976.

Anderson, J. G., "When Leaders Develop Themselves," *Training and Development Journal, 38* (1984), 18–22.

Anderson, J. G., *Winning to Recruiters: A Professional's Advice on Finding Employment*. Management Services & Resource Corp., Okemos, MI, 1990.

Anderson, J. G., and Wexley, K. N., "Applications-Based Management Development," *Personnel Administrator, 28* (1983), 39–43.

Anderson, J. R., "Acquisition of a Cognitive Skill," *Psychological Review, 89* (1982), 369–406.

Anderson, J. R., *The Architecture of Cognition*. Cambridge: Harvard University Press, 1983.

Anderson, S. S., "Hamburger U. Offers a Break," Survey of Continuing Education, *New York Times*, August 30 (1981), pp. 27–28.

Andrasik, F., "Organizational Behavior Modification in Business Settings: A Methodological and Content Review," *Journal of Organizational Behavior Management*, 2 (1979), 85–102.

Argyris, C., "Theories of Action That Inhibit Individual Learning," *American Psychologist, 31*, (1976a), 638–654.

Argyris, C., *Six Presidents: Increasing Leadership Effectiveness*. New York: Wiley, 1976b.

Argyris C., "Some Limitations of the Case Method: Experiences in a Management Development Program," *Academy of Management Review*, 5 (1980), 291–298.

Argyris, C., "The Executive Mind and Double-Loop Learning," *Organizational Dynamics, 11* (1982), 5–22.

Argyris, C., "Reasoning, Action Strategies and Defensive Routines: The Case of OD Practitioners," in W. Pasmore and R. Woodman (eds.), *Research in Organizational Change*. Greenwich, CT: 1986.

Argyris, C., "Crafting a Theory of Practice: The Case of Organizational Paradoxes" in R. Quinn and K. Cameron (eds.), *Paradox and Transformation: Towards a Theory of Change in Organization and Management*. Boston: Pitman, 1987.

Argyris, C., and Schon, D., *Theory in Practice*. San Francisco: Jossey-Bass, 1974.

Argyris, C., and Schon, D. A., "Reciprocal Integrity." Paper presented at the symposium on functioning of executive integrity. Weatherhand School of Management, Case Western Reserve University, October 1986.

Armstrong, A. W., and McElhone, A., "Computer Skills," in R. L. Craig (ed.), *Training and Development Handbook: A Guide to Human Resource Development*. New York: McGraw-Hill, 1987, 697–716.

Arnett, J., "The Role of Knowledge of Results in Learning: A Survey," *U.S. NAVTRADEVCEN Technical Document Report* 342–3, May 1961.

Arnold, W. B., "Employee Fitness in Today's Workplace," in L. K. Y. Ng and D. L. Davis (eds.), *Strategies for Public Health*. New York: Van Nostrand Reinhold, 1981, 342–355.

Arvey, R. D., *Fairness in Selecting Employees*. Reading, MA: Addison-Wesley, 1979.

Arvey, R. D., and Cole, D. A., "Evaluating Change Due to Training," in I. L. Goldstein and associates (eds.), *Training and Development in Organizations*. San Francisco: Jossey-Bass, 1989.

Arvey, R. D., Cole, D. A., Hazucha, J. F., and Hartanto, F. M., "Statistical Power of Training Evaluation Designs," *Personnel Psychology, 38* (1985), 493–508.

Arvey, R. D., Fossum, J. A., Robbins, N., and Paradise, C., "Skills Obsolescence: Psychological and Economic Perspectives." Unpublished manuscript, 1984.

Arvey, R. D., and Ivancevich, J. M., "Punishment in Organizations: A Review, Propositions and Research Suggestions." *Academy of Management Review*, 5 (1980), 123–132.

Azrin, N. H., "A Strategy for Applied Research: Learning Based Outcome Oriented." *American Psychologist, 32* (1977), 140–149.

Bailey, S. K., "Teachers' Centers: A British First," *Phi Delta Kappan*, November 1971.

Baldwin, T. T., "Effects of Stimulus Variability on Trainee Outcomes," Ph.D. dissertation, Michigan State University, East Lansing, MI (1987).

Baldwin, T. T., and Ford, J. K. "Transfer of Training: A Review and Directions for Future Research," *Personnel Psychology, 41* (1988), 63–105.

Bandura, A., *Social Learning Theory*. Englewood Cliffs, NJ: Prentice-Hall, 1977.

Bandura, A., "Self-Efficacy Mechanism in Human Agency," *American Psychologist, 37* (1982), 122–147.

Bandura, A., *Social Foundations of Thought and Action*. Englewood Cliffs, NJ: Prentice-Hall, 1986.

Banks, C. G., and Murphy, K. R., "Toward Narrowing the Research-Practice Gap in Performance Appraisal," *Personnel Psychology, 38* (1985), 335–345.

Bardwick, J., *The Plateauing Trap*. New York: Amacon, 1986.

Bass, B. M., and Vaughn, J. A., *Training in Industry: The Management of Learning*. Belmont, CA: Wadsworth, 1966.

Bazerman, M. H., and Neale, M. A., "Improving Negotiation Effectiveness Under Final Offer Arbitration: The Role of Selection and Training," *Journal of Applied Psychology, 67* (1982), 543–548.

Beckhard, D. E., and Hall, D. T., "The Socialization of Managers: Effects of Expectations on Performance," *Administrative Science Quarterly, 11* (1966), 207–223.

Beckhard, R., *Organization Development: Strategies and Models*. Reading, MA: Addison-Wesley, 1969.

Belbin, E., and Belbin, R. M., *Problems in Adult Retraining*. London, England: Heineman, 1972.

Berger, M. A., "In Defense of the Case Method: A Reply to Argyris," *Academy of Management Review, 8* (1983), 329–333.

Berlew, D. E., and Hall, D. T., "The Socialization of Managers: Effects of Expectations on Performance," *Administrative Science Quarterly, 11* (1966), 207–223.

Berman, F. E., and Miner, J. B., "Motivation to Manage at the Top Executive Level: A Test of the Hierarchic Rule–Motivation Theory." *Personnel Psychology, 38* (1985), 377–391.

Bernardin, H. J., and Buckley, M. R., "Strategies in Rates Training," *Academy of Management Review, 6* (1981), 205–212.

Bernardin, H. J., and Pence, E. C., "Effects of Rate Training: Creating New Response Sets and Decreasing Accuracy," *Journal of Applied Psychology, 65* (1980), 60–66.

Berne, E., *Games People Play*. New York: Grove Press, 1964.

Bernick, E. L., Kindley, R., and Pettit, K. K., "The Structure of Training Courses and the Effects of Hierarchy," *Public Personnel Management, 13* (1984), 109–119.

Berry, C. A., *Good Health for Employees and Reduced Health Care Costs for Industry,* Health Insurance Associations of America, Washington, DC, 1981.

Berryman-Fink, C., "Male and Female Managers' Views of the Communication Skills and Training Needs of Women in Management," *Public Personnel Management, 14* (1985), 307–313.

Blake, R. R., and Mouton, J. S., *The New Managerial Grid.* Houston, TX: Gulf, 1978.

Blake, R. R., and Mouton, J. S., "Management by Grid Principles or Situationalism: Which?" *Group and Organization Studies,* 7 (1982), 207–210.

Blake, R. R., Mouton, J. S., Barnes, L. B., and Greiner, L. E., "Breakthrough in Organization Development," *Harvard Business Review, 42* (1964), 133–155.

Blanz, F., and Ghiselli, E. E., "The Mixed Standard Scale: A New Rating System," *Personnel Psychology, 25* (1972), 185–199.

Blood, M. R., "Intergroup Comparisons of Intraperson Differences: Rewards from the Job," *Personal Psychology, 26* (1973), 1–9.

Blood, M. R., *Job Analysis of Entry-Level Clerical Jobs in the South Central Bell Company.* American Telephone and Telegraph Company, 1975.

Blum, M. L., and Naylor, J. C., *Industrial Psychology.* New York: Harper & Row, 1968.

Bly, J. L., Jones, R. C., and Richardson, J. E., "Impact of Worksite Health Promotion on Health Care Costs and Utilization," *JAMA, 256* (1986), 2335–3240.

Bogorya, Y., "Intercultural Training for Managers Involved in International Businesses," *Journal of Management Development, 4* (1985), 17–25.

Bond, B. W., "The Group Discussion-Decision Approach: An Appraisal of Its Use in Health Education," *Dissertation Abstracts, 16* (1956), 903.

Boudette, N. E., "High-Risk Actions—with No Real Risk," *Industry Week,* September 18 (1989), 59–61.

Boudreau, J. W., "Economic Considerations in Estimating the Utility of Human Resource Popularity Programs," *Personnel Psychology, 36* (1983a), 551–576.

Boudreau, J. W., "Effects of Employee Flows on Utility Analysis of Human Resource Productivity Improvement Programs," *Journal of Applied Psychology, 68* (1983b), 396–406.

Boudreau, J. W., "Utility Analysis for Decisions in Human Resource Management," Cornell University, School of Industrial Relations, Working Paper 88–21, 1988.

Bowers, D. G., "OD Techniques and Their Results in 23 Organizations: The Michigan ICL Study," *Journal of Applied Behavioral Science,* 9 (1973), 21–43.

Bowers, D. G., and Franklin, J. L., "Survey-Guided Development Using Human Resources Measurement in Organizational Change," *Journal of Contemporary Business, 1* (1972), 43–55.

Bowers, D. G., and Hausser, D. L., "Work Group Types and Intervention Effects in Organizational Development," *Administrative Science Quarterly*, 22 (1977), 76–94.

Brannigan, M., "Employers' 'New Age' Training Programs Lead to Lawsuits over Workers' Rights," *Wall Street Journal*, January 9 (1989).

Bray, D. W., "The Assessment Center Method," in R. L. Craig (ed.), *Training and Development Handbook: A Guide to Human Resource Development*. New York: McGraw-Hill, 1976, 6-1–16-15.

Bray, D. W., Campbell, R. J., and Grant, D. L., *Formative Years in Business: A Long-Term AT&T Study of Managerial Lives*. New York: Wiley, 1974.

Brief, A. P., and Hollenbeck, J. R., "An Exploratory Study of Self-Regulating Activities and Their Effect on Job Performance," *Journal of Occupational Behavior*, 6 (1985), 197–208.

Briggs, K. C., and Myers, I. B., *Myers-Briggs Type Indicator*. Palo Alto, CA: Consulting Psychologists Press, 1977.

Brinkerhoff, D. W., "Recruiting and Selecting the Human Resource Department Staff," in R. L. Craig (ed.), *Training and Development Handbook: A Guide to Human Resource Development*. New York: McGraw-Hill, 1987.

Brislin, R. W., and Hulgns, J. F., "Attributional Training Versus Contact in Acculturative Learning: A Laboratory Study," *Journal of Applied Social Psychology, 15* (1985), 466–482.

Brogden, H. E., and Taylor, E. K., "The Dollar Criterion–Applying the Cost Accounting Concept to Criterion Construction," *Personnel Psychology, 3* (1950), 133–154.

Brown, G. F., and Read, A. K., "Personnel and Training Policies—Some Lessons for Western Companies," *Long Range Planning, 17* (1984), 48–57.

Brownell, K. D., Marlatt, G. A., Lichtenstein, E., and Wilson, G. T., "Understanding and Preventing Relapse." *American Psychologist, 41* (1986), 765–782.

Brummet, R. L., Flamholtz, E., and Pyle, W. C., "Human Resource Accounting in Industry," *Personnel Administration* (1969), July-Aug., 34–46.

Bruwelheide, L. R., and Duncan, P. K., "A Method for Evaluating Corporation Training Seminars," *Journal of Organizational Behavior Management, 7* (1985), 65–94.

Bryan, J. F., and Locke, E. A., "Parkinson's Law as a Goal-Setting Phenomenon," *Organizational Behavior and Human Performance*, 2, (1967), 258–275.

Bunker, K. A., and Cohen, S. L., "The Rigors of Training Evaluation: A Discussion and Field Demonstration," *Personnel Psychology, 30* (1977), 525–541.

Burke, M. J., and Day, R. R., "A Cumulative Study of the Effectiveness of Managerial Training," *Journal of Applied Psychology, 71* (1986), 232–245.

Burke, R. J., Weitzel, W., and Weir, T., "Characteristics of Effective Employee Performance Review and Development Interviews: Replication and Extension," *Personnel Psychology, 31* (1978), 903–919.

Burns, T., and Stalker, G. M., *The Management of Innovation*. London: Tavistock, 1961.

Business Week, editorial. "Automation Needs a Speedup and So Does Retraining," September 29 (1986), 132.

Butler, E. D., "An Experimental Study of the Case Method in Teaching the Social Foundations of Education," *Dissertation Abstracts*, 27 (1967), 2912.

Byham, W. C., "The Assessment Center as an Aid in Management Development," *Training and Development Journal*, 25:12 (1971), 10–22.

Campbell, D. P., *Manual for the Strong-Campbell Interest Inventory*. Stanford, CA: Stanford University Press, 1977.

Campbell, J. P., "Personnel Training and Development," *Annual Review of Psychology*, 22 (1971), 565–602.

Campbell, J. P., "The Cutting Edge of Leadership: An Overview," in J. G. Hunt and L. L. Lawson (eds.), *Leadership: The Cutting Edge*. Carbondale, IL: Southern Illinois Press, 1977.

Campbell, J. P., and Dunnette, M. D., "Effectiveness of T-Group Experiences in Managerial Training and Development," *Psychological Bulletin, 70* (1968), 73–104.

Campbell, J. P., Dunnette, M. D., Lawler, E. E., III, and Weick, K. R., Jr., *Managerial Behavior, Performance and Effectiveness*. New York: McGraw-Hill, 1970.

Campbell, R. J., "Implementing Human Resource Development Strategies," in K. N. Wexley and J. R. Hinrichs (eds.), *Developing Human Resources*. ASPA/BNA Handbook for Human Resources. Washington, DC: BNA Books, 1990.

Caplow, T., *Managing an Organization*. New York: Holt, 1983.

Careers in Management: A Video-Based Self-Directed Management Development System. Sterling Institute, Washington, DC.

Carnegie-Mellon Report, "Retraining Displaced Workers: Too Little Too Late," *Business Week*, July 19 (1982), 178, 181, 183, 185.

Carnevale, A. P., "The Learning Enterprise," *Training and Development Journal, 40* (1986), 18–26.

Carroll, S. J., Jr., Paine, F. T., and Ivancevich, J. J., "The Relative Effectiveness of Training Methods—Expert Opinion and Research," *Personnel Psychology*, 25 (1972), 495–510.

Cascio, W. F., *Managing Human Resources*. New York: McGraw-Hill, 1986.

Cascio, W. F., *The Financial Importance of Behavior in Organization* (2nd ed.). Boston: Kent, 1987.

Cascio, W. F., "Using Utility Analysis to Assess Training Outcomes," in I. L. Goldstein and associates (eds.), *Training and Development in Organizations*. San Francisco: Jossey-Bass, 1989, 63–88.

Cenci, L., *Skill Training for the Job*. New York: Pitman, 1966.

Centner, J. L., "The Incident Process," *Advanced Management, 21*:12 (1956), 15–20.

Chancey, L., "An Orientation System for New Employees: Seven-Phase Process at LTV Missiles and Space Division," *Training and Development Journal*, 22 (1968), 52–56.

Chandler, A. D., *Strategy and Structure: Chapters and the History of the American Industrial Enterprise*. Cambridge, MA: MIT Press, 1962.

Chemers, M. M., and Fiedler, F. E., "The Trouble with Assumptions: A Reply to Jago and Ragan," *Journal of Applied Psychology, 71* (1986), 560–563.

Chemers, M. M., and Skrzypek, G. J., "An Experimental Test of the Contingency Model of Leadership Effectiveness," *Journal of Personality and Social Psychology, 24* (1972), 172–177.

Christal, R. E., The United States Air Force Occupational Research Project (AFHRL-TR-73-75). Lackland Air Force Base, TX: Air Force Human Resource Laboratory, 1974.

Chu, G. C., and Schramm, W., *Learning from Television: What the Research Says*. Washington, DC: National Association of Educational Broadcasters, 1967.

Clark, B. S., "Are Disabled Trainees Handicapped by Our Designs?" *Training and Development Journal, 36* (1982), 56–61.

Clement, R. W., Pinto, P. R., and Walker, J. W., "How Do I Hurt Thee? Let Me Count the Ways: Unethical and Improper Behavior by Training and Development Professionals," *Training and Development Journal, 32* (1978), 10–12.

Condon, M., "Fly the Safe Skies, and Thank Training," *Training and Development Journal, 38* (1984a), 25–32.

Condon, M., "The Ins and Outs of Displacement," *Training and Development Journal, 38* (1984b), 60–65.

Cook, T. D., and Campbell, D. T., "The Design and Conduct of Quasi-Experiments and True Experiments in Field Settings," in M. D. Dunnette (ed.), *Handbook of Industrial and Organizational Psychology*. Chicago: Rand McNally, 1976.

Cook, T. D., and Campbell, D. T., *Quan-experimentation: Design and Analysis Issues for Field Settings*. Chicago: Rand McNally, 1979.

Cooke, P., "Role Playing," in R. L. Craig (ed.), *Training and Development Handbook*. New York: McGraw-Hill, 1987, 430–441.

Cooper, C. L., "How Psychologically Dangerous Are T-Groups and Encounter Groups?" *Human Relations, 28* (1975), 249–260.

Cooper, W. H., and Richardson, A. J., "Unfair Comparisons," *Journal of Applied Psychology, 71* (1986), 179–184.

Copeland, L., "Cross-Cultural Training: The Competitive Edge," *Training, 22* (1985), 49–53.

Coppard, L. C., "Gaming Simulation and the Training Process," in R. L. Craig (ed.), *Training and Development Handbook: A Guide to Human Resource Development*. New York: McGraw-Hill, 1976, 40-1–40-14.

Coppolino, M. J., "PC Training: Giving Users What They Need," *Training, 23* (1986), 59–62.

Craft, C. J., "Management Games," in R. L. Craig and L. R. Bittel (eds.), *Training and Development Handbook*. New York: McGraw-Hill, 1967, 267–284.

Cronbach, L. J., "The Two Disciplines of Scientific Psychology," *American Psychologist, 12* (1957), 671–684.

Cronbach, L. J., and Meehl, P. R., "Construct Validity in Psychological Tests," *Psychological Bulletin, 52* (1955), 581–602.

Cronbach, L. J., and Snow, R. E., *Aptitude and Instructional Methods.* New York: Wiley, 1977.

Cunningham, D. J., and Duncan, K. D., "Describing Non-Repetitive Tasks for Training Purposes," *Occupational Psychology, 41* (1967), 203–210.

Dahl, H. L., Jr., "Return on Investment," in R. L. Craig (ed.), *Training and Development Handbook: A Guide to Human Resource Development.* New York: McGraw-Hill, 1987, 343–348.

Dalton, G. W., and Thompson, P. H., "Accelerating Obsolescence of Older Engineers," *Harvard Business Review, 49* (1971), 57–67.

Dansereau, F., Graen, G., and Haga, B., "A Vertical Dyad Linkage Approach to Leadership Within Formal Organizations: A Longitudinal Investigation of the Role Making Process," *Organizational Behavior and Human Performance, 131* (1975), 46–78.

Davis, B. L., and Mount, M. K., "Effectiveness of Performance Appraisal Training Using Computer-assisted Instruction and Behavior Modeling," *Personnel Psychology, 37* (1984), 439–452.

Dean, E. C., and Jud, R. A., "How to Write a Task Analysis," *Training Directors' Journal, 19* (1965), 9–22.

de Bettignies, H. C., "Management Development: The International Perspective," in B. Taylor and G. L. Lippitt (eds.), *Management Development and Training Handbook.* London: McGraw-Hill, 1975.

Decker, P. J., "Effects of Symbolic Coding and Rehearsal in Behavior-Modeling Trainings," *Journal of Applied Psychology, 65* (1980), 627–634.

Decker, P. J., "The Enhancement of Behavior Modeling Training of Supervisory Skills by the Inclusion of Retention Process," *Personnel Psychology, 32* (1982), 323–332.

Decker, P. J., and Nathan, B. R., *Behavior Modeling Training: Principles and Applications.* New York: Praeger, 1985.

Dedmon, R. E., "Employees as Health Educators: A Reality at Kimberly-Clark," *Occupational Health and Safety, 25* (1980), 18–24.

Dickinson, T. L., and Silverhart, T. A., "Training to Improve the Accuracy and Validity of Performance Ratings." Paper presented at the annual meeting of the American Psychological Association, Washington, DC, 1986.

Dienesch, R. M., and Liden, R. C., "Leader Member Exchange Model of Leadership: A Critique and Further Development," *Academy of Management Review, 11* (1986), 618–634.

DiPaolo, A. J., and Patterson, A. C., "Selecting a Training Program for New Trainers," *Training and Development Journal, 37* (1983), 96–101.

Dotlich, D., "International and Intracultural Management Development," *Training and Development Journal, 36* (1982), 26–31.

Downs, S., "Selecting the Older Trainee: A Pilot Study of Trainability Tests," *National Institute of Industrial Psychology Bulletin* (1968), 19–26.

Downs, S., "Industrial Training," in A.P.O. Williams (ed.), *In Using Personnel Research.* Hants, England: Gower, 1983.

Downs, S., "Retraining for New Shifts," *Ergonomics, 28* (1985), 1205–1211.

Downs, S., and Perry, P., "Can Trainers Learn to Take a Back Seat?" *Personnel Management, 18* (1986), 42–45.

Downs, S., Petford, J., and McHale, J., "Learning Techniques for Driver Training," *International Review of Applied Psychology, 31* (1982), 511–522.

Downs, S., and Roberts, A., "The Training of Underground Train Guards—A Case Study with a Field Experiment," *Journal of Occupational Psychology, 50* (1977), 111–120.

Dreher, G. F., and Sachett, P. R., *Perspectives on Employee Staffing and Selection.* Homewood, IL: Irwin, 1983.

Drucker, P. "Timeless Truths About Performing at Your Best," *Working Smart* '87, 1987, 8–9.

Dubin, S. S.,"Obsolescence or Lifelong Education: A Choice for the Professional," *American Psychologist*, May (1972), 486–498.

Dugan, K. W., "Ability and Effort Attributions: Do They Affect How Managers Communicate Performance Feedback Information?" *Academy of Management Journal, 32* (1989), 87–114.

Duncan, C. S., "The Job Aid Has a Future" in *Introduction to Performance Technology.* Washington, DC: National Society for Performance Instruction, 1986, 125–128.

Dunnette, M. D., "Mishmash, Mush, and Milestones in Organizational Psychology," in H. Meltzer and F. R. Wickert (eds.), *Humanizing Organizational Behavior.* Springfield, IL: Chas. C. Thomas, 1976, 86–102.

Dunnette, M. D., and Campbell, J. P., "Laboratory Education: Impact on People and Organizations," *Industrial Relations, 8* (1968), 1–44.

Earley, C., "Intercultural Training for Managers: A Comparison of Documentary and Interpersonal Methods," *Academy of Management Journal, 30* (1987), 685–698.

Eden, D., "Self-Fulfilling Prophecy as a Management Tool: Harnessing Pygmalion," *Academy of Management Review, 9* (1984), 64–73.

Eden, D. *Pygmalion in Management: Productivity as a Self-Fulfilling Prophecy.* Lexington, MA: Lexington Books, 1990.

Eden, D., and Ravid, G., "Pygmalion v. Self-Expectancy Effects of Instructor and Self-Expectancy on Trainee Performance," *Organizational Behavior and Human Performance, 30* (1982), 351–364.

Eden, D., and Shani, A. B., "Pygmalion Goes to Boot Camp: Expectancy, Leadership, and Trainee Performance," *Journal of Applied Psychology, 67* (1982), 194–199.

Edson, A. S., "Commuting to an M.B.A.," *Scene Magazine* (1979), September, 64–65.

Ernest, P., "Games: A Rationale for Their Use in the Teaching of Mathematics in School," *Mathematics in School*, *8* (1986), 2–5.

Eurich, N. P., *Corporate Classroom: The Learning Process*. Princeton, NJ: The Carnegie Foundation for the Advancement of Teaching, 1985.

Evan, W. M. "Peer-Group Interaction and Organizational Socialization: A Study of Employee Turnover," *American Sociological Review*, *28* (1963), 436–440.

Farnsworth, T., *Developing Executive Talent: A Practical Guide*. London: McGraw-Hill, 1975.

Fast, D., "A New Approach to Quantifying Training Program Effectiveness," *Training and Development Journal*, *28*:9 (1974), 8–14.

Fay, C. H., and Latham, G. P., "Effects of Training and Rating Scales on Rating Errors," *Personnel Psychology*, *35* (1982), 105–116.

Ference, T., Stoner, T., and Warren, F., "Managing the Career Plateau," *Academy of Management Review*, *2* (1977), 602–612.

Feur, D., "Domino's Pizza: Training for Fast Times," *Training*, *24*, July (1987), 25–30.

Fiedler, F. E., "A Contingency Model of Leadership Effectiveness," in L. Berkowitz (ed.), *Advances in Experimental Social Psychology*. New York: Academic Press, 1964, 149–190.

Fiedler, F. E., *A Theory of Leadership Effectiveness*. New York: McGraw-Hill, 1967.

Fiedler, F. E., "Personality, Motivational Systems, and Behavior of High and Low LPC Persons," *Human Relations*, *25* (1972), 391–412.

Fiedler, F. E., "Personality, Motivational Systems, and Behavior of High and Low LPC Persons," *Human Relations*, *25* (1975), 391–412.

Fiedler, F. E., Bell, C. H., Chemers, M., and Patrick, D., "Increasing Mine Productivity and Safety Through Management Training and Organization Development: A Comparative Study," *Basic and Applied Social Psychology*, *5* (1984), 1–18.

Fiedler, F. E., and Chemers, M. M., *Leadership and Effective Management*. New York: Scott, Foresman, 1974.

Fiedler, F. E., Chemers, M. M., and Mahar, L., *Improving Leadership Effectiveness: The Leader Match Concept*. New York: Wiley, 1976.

Fiedler, F. E., and Mahar, L., "The Effectiveness of Contingency Model Training: A Review of the Validation of Leaders Match," *Personnel Psychology*, *32* (1979), 95–102.

Fiedler, F. E., Mitchell, T., and Triandis, H. C., "The Culture Assimilator: An Approach to Cross-Cultural Training," *Journal of Applied Psychology*, *55* (1971), 95–102.

Fiedler, F. E., Wheeler, W. A., Chemers, M. M., and Patrick, D. P., "Managing for Mine Safety," *Training and Development Journal*, *41*:9 (1987), 40–43.

Fiedler, F. E., Wheeler, W. A., Chemers, M. M., and Patrick, D. P., "Structured Management Training in Underground Mining: Five Years Later." Technology Transfer Seminar, July 1987. *Bureau of Mines Information Circular No. 9145*, 149–153.

Field, G. R., "A Critique of the Vroom-Yetton Contingency Model of Leadership Behavior," *Academy of Management Review, 4*:2 (1979), 249–257.

Field, G. R., "A Test of the Vroom-Yetton Normative Model of Leadership," *Journal of Applied Psychology, 67* (1982), 523–532.

Fitts, P. M., "Factors in Complex Skill Training," in R. Glaser (ed.), *Training Research and Education*. New York: Wiley, 1965, 177–197.

Fivars, G., "The Critical Incident Technique: A Bibliography," *JSAS Catalog of Selected Documents in Psychology, 5* (1975), 210.

Flanagan, J. C., "The Critical Incident Technique," *Psychological Bulletin, 51* (1954), 327–358.

Fleishman, E. A., "Factor Structure in Relation to Task Difficulty in Psychomotor Performance," *Educational and Psychological Measurement, 17* (1957), 522–532.

Fleishman, E. A., "The Production of Total Task Performance from Prior Practice on Talk Components," *Human Factors, 7* (1965), 18–27.

Fleishman, E. A., and Ellison, G. D., "Prediction of Transfer and Other Learning Phenomena from Ability and Personality Measures," *Journal of Educational Psychology, 60* (1969), 300–314.

Fleishman, E. A., and Mumford, M. D., "Individual Attributes and Training Performance," in I. L. Goldstein and associates (eds.), *Training and Development in Organizations*. San Francisco: Jossey-Bass, 1989.

Fleishman, E. A., and Parker, J. R., "Factors in Retention of Perceptual-Motor Skill," *Journal of Experimental Psychology, 64* (1962), 215–226.

Ford, J. K., and Noe, R. A., "Self-Assessed Training Needs: The Effects of Attitudes Toward Training, Managerial Level, and Function," *Personnel Psychology, 40* (1987), 39–53.

Ford, J. K., and Wroten, S. P., "Introducing New Methods for Conducting Training Evaluation and for Linking Training Evaluation to Program Design," *Personnel Psychology, 37* (1984), 651–665.

Fossum, J. A., Arvey, R. D., Paradise, C. A., and Robbins, N. E., "Modeling the Skills Obsolescence Process: A Psychological/Economic Integration," *Academy of Management Review, 11* (1986), 362–374.

Francis, D., and Young, D., *Improving Work Groups: A Practical Manual for Team Building*. San Diego: University Associates, 1979.

Frayne, C. A., and Latham, G. P., "Application of Social Learning Theory to Employee Self-Management of Attendance," *Journal of Applied Psychology, 72* (1987), 387–392.

Freedman, S. C., "Attribution Theory and Management Education," *Training and Development Journal, 38* (1984), 95–99.

Freedman, S. M., and Keller, R. T., "The Handicapped Worker in the Workforce," *Academy of Management Review, 6* (1981), 449–458.

French, W. L., and Bell, C. H., Jr., *Organization Development: Behavioral Science Interventions for Organization Improvement.* Englewood Cliffs, NJ: Prentice-Hall, 1978.

French, W. L., Bell, C. H., Jr., and Zawacki, R. (eds.), *Organization Development.* Plano, TX: Business Publications, 1989.

Frese, M., Albrecht, K., and Altmann, A., "The Effects of an Active Development of the Mental Model in the Training Process: Experimental Results in a Word Processing System," *Behavior and Information Technology, 7* (1988), 295–304.

Frese, M., and Altmann, A., "The Treatment of Errors in Learning and Training," in L. Bainbridge and R. Quintanilla (eds.), *Developing Skills in Information Technology.* Chichester, England: Wiley, 1988.

Frost, D. E., "A Test of Situational Engineering for Training Leaders," *Psychological Reports, 59* (1986), 771–782.

Gagné, R. M., *The Conditions of Learning.* New York: Holt, 1977.

Geber, B., "Who Should Do the Sales Training?" *Training* (1987), 69–76.

Georgenson, D. L., "The Problem of Transfer Calls for Partnership," *Training and Development Journal, 36* (1982), 75–78.

Ghiselli, E. E., "The Validity of Aptitude Tests in Personnel Selection," *Personnel Psychology, 26* (1973), 461–477.

Gibbons, T., "Beat the Press," *Passages*, February (1980), 13–15.

Gioia, D. A., and Manz, C. C., "Linking Cognition and Behavior: A Script Processing Interpretation of Vicarious Learning," *Academy of Management Review, 10* (1985), 527–539.

Gist, M. E., "The Influence of Training Method on Self-Efficacy and Idea Generation Among Managers," *Personnel Psychology, 42* (1989), 787–805.

Gist, M., Rosen, B., and Schwoerer, C., "The Influence of Training Method and Trainee Age in the Acquisition of Computer Skills," *Personnel Psychology, 41* (1988), 255–265.

Gist, M. E., Schwoerer, C., and Rosen, B., "Modeling Versus Non-Modelings: The Impact of Self-Efficiency and Performance in Computer Training for Managers," *Academy of Management Best Paper Proceeding, 47* (1987), 122–126.

Gist, M. E., Schwoerer, C., and Rosen, B., "Effects of Alternative Training Methods on Self-Efficacy and Performance in Computer Software Training," *Journal of Applied Psychology, 74*, 1989, 884–891.

Glass, B., *The Timely and the Timeless: The Interrelationships of Science, Education, and Society.* New York: Basic Books, 1970.

Godkewitsch, M., "The Dollars and Sense of Corporate Training," *Training, 24* (1987), 79–81.

Goldstein, A. P., and Sorcher, M., *Changing Supervisor Behavior.* New York: Pergamon Press, 1974.

Goldstein, I. L., *Training in Organizations: Needs Assessment, Development, and Evaluation.* Monterey, CA: Brooks/Cole, 1986.

Goldstein, S., Gorman, J., and Smith, B. B., "A Partnership in Evaluation," *Training and Development Journal*, 27:4 (1973), 10–14.

Golembiewski, R. T., Billingsley, K. R., and Yeager, S., "Measuring Change and Persistence in Human Affairs: Types of Change Generated by OD Designs," *Journal of Applied Behavioral Science, 12* (1976), 133–157.

Gomersall, E. R., and Myers, M. S., "Breakthrough in On-The-Job Training," *Harvard Business Review, 44* (1966), 62–72.

Gordon, J., "Games Managers Play," *Training, 22* (1985a), 30–47.

Gordon, J., "Computers in Training," *Training, 22* (1985b), 54–66.

Gordon, M. E., Cofer, J. L., McCullough, P., "Relationships Among Seniority, Past Performance, Interjob Similarity, and Trainability," *Journal of Applied Psychology, 71* (1986), 518–521.

Gordon, M. E., and Cohen, S. L., "Training Behavior as a Predictor of Trainability," *Personnel Psychology, 26* (1973), 261–272.

Graen, G., "Role-Making Processes Within Complex Organizations," in M. D. Dunnette (ed.), *Handbook of Industrial and Organizational Psychology.* Chicago: Rand McNally, 1976, 1201–1245.

Graen, G., Linden, R., and Hoel, W., "Role of Leadership in the Employee Withdrawal Process," *Journal of Applied Psychology, 67* (1982), 868–872.

Graen, G., Novak, M., and Sommerkamp, P., "The Effects of Leader-Member Exchange and Job Design of Productivity and Satisfaction: Testing Manual Attachment Mode," *Organizational Behavior and Human Performance, 30* (1982), 109–131.

Graen, G. B., and Scandura, T. A., "Toward a Psychology of Dyadic Organizing," in B. M. Staw and L. L. Cummings (eds.), *Research in Organizational Behavior*, Greenwich, CT: JAI Press, 1987, 175–208.

Graen, G. B., Scandura, T. A., and Graen, M. R., "A Field Experimental Test of the Moderating Effects of Growth Need Strength on Productivity," *Journal of Applied Psychology, 71* (1986), 484–491.

Green, T. B., Knippen, J. T., and Vincelette, J. P., "The Practice of Management: Knowledge Versus Skills," *Training and Development Journal, 39* (1985), 56–58.

Grove, D. A., and Ostroff, C., "Training Program Evaluation," in K. N. Wexley and J. R. Hinrichs (eds.), *Developing Human Resources*. ASPA/BNA Series. Washington, DC: Bureau of National Affairs, 1990.

Guest, R. H., "Of Time and the Foreman," *Personnel, 32* (1956), 478–486.

Guion, R. M., *Personnel Testing.* New York: McGraw-Hill, 1965.

Gutteridge, T. G., "Organizational Career Development Systems: The State of the Practice," in D. T. Hall and associates (eds.), *Career Development in Organizations*. San Francisco: Jossey-Bass, 1986, 50–94.

Guttman, R., "Job Training Partnership Act: New Help for the Unemployed," *Monthly Labor Review, 106* (1983), 3–10.

Hagman, J. D., and Rose, A. M., "Retention of Military Tasks: A Review," *Human Factors, 25* (1983), 199–213.

Hall, D. T., "Project Work as an Antidote to Career Plateauing in a Declining Organization," *Human Resource Management, 24* (1985), 271–292.

Hall, D. T., "Dilemmas in Linking Succession Planning to Individual Executive Learning," *Human Resource Management, 25* (1986), 235–236.

Hall, D. T., and associates, *Career Development in Organizations.* San Francisco: Jossey-Bass, 1986.

Hall, D. T., and Hall, F. S., "What's New in Career Management," *Organizational Dynamics, 5* (1976), 17–33.

Halpin, A., and Winer, B., "A Factorial Study of the Leader Behavior Descriptions," in A. Coons (ed.), *Leader Behavior: Its Description and Measurement.* Columbus: Ohio State University, 1957.

Hamblin, A. C., *Evaluation and Control of Training.* London: McGraw-Hill, 1974.

Hamner, W. C., and Hamner, E. P., "Behavior Modification on the Bottom Line," *Organizational Dynamics, 4* (1976), 3–21.

Hand, H. H., and Slocum, J. W., Jr., "A Longitudinal Study of the Effects of a Human Relations Training Program on Managerial Effectiveness," *Journal of Applied Psychology, 56* (1972), 412–417.

Hanlon, M. D., Review of Dyer, L. (ed.), "Human Resource Management—Evolving Roles and Responsibilities." Washington, DC: BNA Books, 1988. *Personnel Psychology, 43* (1990), 166–168.

Hansen, G. B., "Ford and the UAW Have a Better Idea: A Joint Labor Management Approach to Plant Closings and Worker Retraining," *Annual American Academy of Political Sociological Science, 475* (1984), 158–174.

Harris, T. A., *I'm OK, You're OK.* New York: Harper & Row, 1969.

Hart, G. L., and Thompson, P. H., "Assessment Centers: For Selection or Development?" *Organizational Dynamics, 8*:4 (1979), 63–77.

Hassett, J., and Dukes, S., "The New Employee Trainer: A Floppy Disk," *Psychology Today*, September (1986), 30–36.

Haveman, R. H., and Saks, D. H., "Transatlantic Lessons for Employment and Training Policy," *Industrial Relations, 24* (1985), 20–36.

Hayes, S. C., Rosenfarb, I., Wulfert, E., Munt, E. D., Korn, Z., and Zettle, R. D., "Self-Reinforcement Effects: An Artifact of Social Standard Setting?" *Journal of Behavior Analysis, 18* (1985), 201–214.

"Health and Safety Training Center Has Impact at Plants Throughout GM," *UAW-GM Human Resource Center Newsletter*, Fall 1987, 1–7.

Heilman, M. E., Hornstein, H. A., Cage, J. H., and Herschlag, J. K., "Reactions to Prescribed Leader Behavior as a Function of Role Perspective: The Case of the Vroom-Yetton Model," *Journal of Applied Psychology*, 69 (1984), 50–60.

Hemphill, J. K., and Coons, A. E., "Development of the Leader Behavior Description Questionnaire," in R. M. Stogdill and A. E. Coons (eds.), *Leader Behavior: Its Description and Measurement.* Columbus: Bureau of Business Research, Ohio State University, 1957.

Heneman, H. G., III, Schwab, D. P., Fossum, J. A., and Dyer, L. D., *Personnel Human Resource Management*, Homewood, IL: Irwin, 1986.

Hickam, J. B., "Periodic Recertification," *Journal of the American Medical Association, 213* (1970), 1651–1657.

Hicks, W. D., and Klimoski, R. J., "The Process of Entering Training Programs and Its Effects on Training Outcomes." Paper presented at the 44th annual meeting of the Academy of Management. Boston, 1984.

Hill, T. E., and Schmitt, N., "Individual Differences in Leadership Decision Making," *Organizational Behavior and Human Performance, 19*:2 (1977), 353–367.

Hillery, J. M., and Wexley, K. N., "Participation in Appraisal Interviews Conducted in a Training Situation," *Journal of Applied Psychology, 59* (1974), 168–171.

Hinrichs, J. R., "Two Approaches to Filling the Management Gap." *Personnel Journal, 49* (1970), 1004–1014.

Hinrichs, J. R., "Personnel Training," in M. D. Dunnette (ed.), *Handbook of Industrial and Organizational Psychology*. Chicago: Rand McNally, 1976, 829–860.

Hinrichs, J. R., *Practical Management for Productivity*. New York: Van Nostrand Reinhold, 1978.

Hogan, P. M., Hakel, M. D., and Decker, P. J., "Effects of Trainee-Generated Versus Trainer-Provided Rule Codes on Generalization in Behavior-Modeling Training," *Journal of Applied Psychology, 71* (1986), 469–473.

Holland, J. L., *The Psychology of Vocational Choice*. Waltham, MA: Blaisdell, 1966.

Holland, J. L., *Making Vocational Choices: A Theory of Careers*. Englewood Cliffs, NJ: Prentice-Hall, 1973.

Hollenbeck, G., "What Did You Learn in School? Studies of the Advanced Management Program." Unpublished manuscript, Harvard Business School, 1989.

Hollenbeck, J. R., William, C. R., and Klein, H. J., "An Empirical Examination of the Antecedents to Commitment to Difficult Goals," *Journal of Applied Psychology, 74* (1989), 18–28.

Holley, W. H., and Jennings, K. M., *Personnel/Human Resource Management: Contributions and Activities*. Chicago: Dryden Press, 1987.

Hollmann, R. W., "Let's Not Forget About New Employee Orientation," *Personnel Journal, 53* (1976), 244–250.

Honig, W. K., *Operant Behavior*. New York: Appleton-Century Crofts, 1966.

Howard, G. S., and Dailey, P. R., "Response-Shift Bias: A Source of Contamination of Self-Report Measures," *Journal of Applied Psychology, 64*:2 (1979), 144–150.

Howard, G. S., Ralph, K. M., Gulanik, N., Maxwell, S. E., Nonce, D. W., and Gerber, S. R., "Internal Invalidity in Pretest-Posttest Self-Report Evaluations and Reevaluation of Retrospective Pretests," *Applied Psychological Measurement, 3* (1979), 1–23.

Huber, V. L., and Gay, G., "Uses of Educational Technology for Formative Evaluation," *Education for Program Improvement, 24* (1984), 55–64.

Huczynski, A. A., and Lewis, J. W., "An Empirical Study into the Learning-Transfer Process in Management Training," *Journal of Management Studies, 17* (1980), 227–240.

Hudson, E. M., "An Adaptive Tracking Simulator." Paper presented at the IRE International Congress of Human Factors in Electronics, Long Beach, California, May 1962.

Hull, C. L., *Principles of Behavior.* New York: Appleton-Century Crofts, 1943.

Hunt, D. M., and Michael, C., "Mentorship: A Career Training and Development Tool," *Academy of Management Review, 8* (1983), 475–485.

Hussey, D. E., "Implementing Corporate Strategy: Using Management Education and Training," *Long Range Planning, 18* (1985), 28–37.

Ilgen, D. R., Fisher, C. D., and Taylor, M. S., "Consequences of Individual Feedback on Behavior in Organizations," *Journal of Applied Psychology, 64* (1979), 349–371.

Ilgen, D. R., and Klein, H. G., 1989. "Organizational Behavior," *Annual Review of Psychology, 40*, 327–351.

Ivancevich, J. M., Matteson, M. T., and Richards, E. P., III, "Who's Liable for Stress on the Job?" *Harvard Business Review, 63* (1985), 60–65.

Jackson, C. N., "Training's Role in the Process of Planned Change," *Training and Development Journal, 39* (1985), 70–74.

Jago, A. G., and Ragan, J. W., "The Trouble with Leader Match Is That It Doesn't Match Fiedler's Contingency Model," *Journal of Applied Psychology, 71* (1986a), 555–559.

Jago, A. G., and Ragan, J. W., "Some Assumptions Are More Troubling Than Others: Rejoinder to Chemers and Fiedler," *Journal of Applied Psychology, 71* (1986b), 564–565.

Jago, A. G., and Vroom, V. H., "A Hierarchical Level and Leadership Style," *Organizational Behavior and Human Performance, 18* (1977), 131–145.

Jenness, J. S., "Budgeting and Controlling Training Costs," in R. L. Craig (ed.), *Training and Development Handbook: A Guide to Human Resource Development.* New York: McGraw-Hill, 1976, 4-1–4-12.

Johnson, P. D., and Sorcher, M., "Behavior Modeling Training: Why, How, and What Results," *Journal of European Training,* 5:1 (1976), 62–70.

Johnson, R. B., "Organization and Management of Training," in R. L. Craig (ed.), *Training and Development Handbook: A Guide to Human Resource Development.* New York: McGraw-Hill, 1976, 2-1–2-17.

Kanfer, F. H., "Self-Regulation: Research, Issues, and Speculations," in C. Neuringer and J. Michael (eds.), *Behavior Modification in Clinical Psychology.* New York: Appleton-Century-Crofts, 1974, 178–220.

Kanfer, F. H., "Self-Management Methods," in F. H. Kanfer (ed.), *Helping People Change.* New York: Wiley, 1975, 309–355.

Kanfer, F. H., "Self-Management Methods," in F. H. Kanfer and A. P. Goldstein (eds.), *Helping People Change: A Textbook of Methods* (2nd ed.). New York: Pergamon Press, 1980, 334–389.

Kanfer, R., "Motivation Theory of Industrial/Organizational Psychology," in M. D. Dunnette (ed.), *Handbook of Industrial/Organizational Psychology*, Vol. 1. Palo Alto, CA: Consulting Psychologists Press, 1990.

Kanfer, R., and Ackerman, P., "Motivation and Cognitive Abilities: An Integrative Aptitude-Treatment Interaction Approach to Skill Acquisition," *Journal of Applied Psychology Monograph, 74* (1989), 657–690.

Kaplan, A., *The Conduct of Inquiry*. Scranton, PA: Chandler, 1964.

Kaplan, R. E., "Is Openness Passé?" *Human Relations, 39* (1986), 229–243.

Kaplan, R. E., Drath, W. H., and Kofodimos, J. R., "High Hurdles: The Challenge of Executive Self-Development," *Academy of Management Executive, 1* (1987), 195–206.

Karmin, M. W., and Sheler, J. L., "Jobs: A Million That Will Never Come Back," *U.S. News & World Report*, September 13 (1982), 53–56.

Karoly, P., and Kanfer, F. H. (eds.), *Self-Management and Behavior Change*. New York: Pergamon Press, 1982.

Kaufman, H. G., "Continuing Education and Job Performance: A Longitudinal Study," *Journal of Applied Psychology, 613* (1978), 248–251.

Kay, E., Meyer, H. H., and French, J. R. P., Jr., "Effects of Threat in a Performance Appraisal Interview," *Journal of Applied Psychology, 49*:5 (1965), 311–317.

Kearsley, G., and Hillelsohn, M. J., "How and Why (and Why Not) We Use Computer-based Training," *Training and Development Journal, 38* (1984), 21–24.

Kelley, C. R., "What Is Adaptive Training?" *Human Factors, 11* (1969), 547–556.

Kelley, J. B., "A Primer on Transfer of Training," *Training and Development Journal, 36* (1982), 102–106.

Kelly, H. B., "The Problem of Transfer Calls for Partnership," *Training and Development Journal, 36* (1982), 102–106.

Kepner, C. H., and Tregoe, B. B., *The Rational Manager: A Systematic Approach to Problem Solving and Decision Making*. New York: McGraw-Hill, 1975.

Kibbee, J. M., Craft, C. J., and Nanus, B., *Management Games: A New Technique for Executive Development*. New York: Reinhold, 1961.

Killian, D. C., "The Impact of Flight Simulators of U.S. Airlines," American Airlines Flight Academy, Fort Worth, TX, 1976.

Kim, J. S., "Effect of Behavior Versus Outcome Goal-Setting and Feedback on Employee Satisfaction and Performance," *Academy of Management Journal, 27* (1984), 139–149.

Kim, J. S., and Hamner, W. C., "Effect of Performance Feedback and Goal Setting on Productivity and Satisfaction in an Organizational Setting," *Journal of Applied Psychology, 61*:1 (1976), 48–57.

Kirkpatrick, D. L., "Evaluation of Training," in R. L. Craig (ed.), *Training and Development Handbook: A Guide to Human Resource Development*. New York: McGraw-Hill, 1976.

Kirkpatrick, D. L., "Evaluation of Training," in R. L. Craig (ed.), *Training and Development Handbook: A Guide to Human Resource Development*. New York: McGraw-Hill, 1987.

Klauss, R., "Formalized Mentor Relationships for Management and Executive Development Programs in the Federal Government," *Public Administration Review, 41* (1981), 489–496.

Komaki, J., "Alternative Evaluation Strategies in Work Settings: Reversal and Multiple-Baseline Designs," *Journal of Organizational Behavior Management, 1*:1 (1977), 53–77.

Komaki, J., Barwick, K. D., and Scott, L. R., "A Behavioral Approach to Occupational Safety: Pinpointing and Reinforcing Safe Performance in a Food Manufacturing Plant," *Journal of Applied Psychology, 63*:4 (1978), 434–445.

Komaki, J., Heinzman, A. T., and Lawson, L., "Effect of Training and Feedback: Component Analysis of Behavioral Safety Program," *Journal of Applied Psychology, 65* (1980), 261–270.

Konovsky, M. A., and Freeman, A. B., Review of Vroom, V. H., and Jago, A. G., "The New Leadership: Managing Participation in Organizations," *Academy of Management Review, 15* (1990), 337–339.

Korman, A. K., *Organizational Behavior.* Englewood Cliffs, NJ: Prentice-Hall, 1977.

Korman, A. K., "Career Success and Personal Failure: Mid-to-Late-Career Feelings and Events," in M. London and E. M. Mone (eds.), *Career Growth and Human Resource Strategies.* Westport, CT: Quorum, 1988, 81–94.

Korman, A. K, and Korman, R. W., *Career Success/Personal Failure.* Englewood Cliffs, NJ: Prentice-Hall, 1980.

Kram, K. E., *Mentoring at Work: Developmental Relationships in Organizational Life.* Glenview, IL: Scott, Foresman, 1985.

Kraut, A. I., Pedigo, P. R., McKenna, D. D., and Dunnette, M. D., "The Role of the Manager: What's Really Important in Different Management Jobs," *The Academy of Management Executive, 4* (1989), 286–293.

Landy, F. J., *Pschology of Work Behavior.* Homewood, IL: The Dorsey Press, 1985.

Langer, E. J. "The Illusion of Incompetence," in E. Perlmuter and R. A. Monty (eds.), *Choice and Perceived Control.* Hillsdale, NJ: Erlbaum, 1979.

Latham, G. P., "The Development of Job Performance Criteria for Pulpwood Producers in the Southeastern United States." Unpublished master's thesis, Georgia Institute of Technology, 1969.

Latham, G. P., "The Role of Goal Setting in Human Resources Management," in K. Roland and G. Ferris (eds.), *Research in Personnel and Human Resources Management.* Greenwich, CT: JAI Press, 1983.

Latham, G. P., "Job Performance and Appraisal," in C. L. Cooper and I. Robertson (eds.), *Review of Industrial and Organizational Psychology.* Chichester, England: Wiley, 1986.

Latham, G. P., "Job Performance and Appraisal," in C. L. Cooper and I. Robertson (eds.), *International Review of Industrial and Organizational Psychology.* Chichester, England: Wiley, 1986.

Latham, G. P., "Human Resource Training and Development," *Annual Review of Psychology, 39* (1988), 545–582.

Latham, G. P., "Behavioral Approaches to the Training Process," in I. L. Goldstein and associates (eds.), *Training and Development in Organizations*. San Francisco: Jossey-Bass, 1989, 256–295.

Latham, G. P., and Crandall, S. R., "Organizational and Social Influences Affecting Training Effectiveness," in J. E. Morrison (ed.), *Training for Performance*. Chichester, England: Wiley, in press.

Latham, G. P., and Dossett, D. L., "Designing Incentive Plans for Unionized Employees: A Comparison of Continuous and Variable Ratio Reinforcement Schedules," *Personnel Psychology, 31* (1978), 47–61.

Latham, G. P., and Frayne, C. A., "Increasing Job Attendance Through Training in Self-Management: A Review of Two Studies," *Journal of Applied Psychology, 74* (1989), 411–416.

Latham, G. P., and Huber, V. L. "Problems Encountered in Pay Research," *Journal of Organization Behavior Management*, in press.

Latham, G. P., and Locke, E. A., "Goal Setting: A Motivational Technique That Works," *Organizational Dynamics* (1969), Autumn 68–80.

Latham, G. P., and Locke, E. A., "Increasing Productivity with Decreasing Time Limits: A Field Replication of Parkinson's Law," *Journal of Applied Psychology, 60* (1975), 524–526.

Latham, G. P., Mitchell, T. R., and Dossett, D. L., "Importance of Participative Goal Setting and Anticipated Rewards on Goal Difficulty and Job Performance," *Journal of Applied Psychology, 63* (1978), 163–171.

Latham, G. P., and Saari, L. M., "The Application of Social Learning Theory to Training Supervisors Through Behavior Modeling," *Journal of Applied Psychology, 64* (1979a), 239–246.

Latham, G. P., and Saari, L. M., "The Effects of Holding Goal Difficulty Constant on Assigned and Participatively Set Goals," *Academy of Management Journal, 22* (1979b), 163–168.

Latham, G. P., and Wexley, K. N., "Behavioral Observation Scales for Performance Appraisal Purposes," *Personnel Psychology, 30* (1977), 255–268.

Latham, G. P., and Wexley, K. N., *Increasing Productivity Through Performance Appraisal*. Reading, MA: Addison-Wesley, in press.

Latham, G. P., Wexley, K. N., and Pursell, E. D., "Training Managers to Minimize Rating Errors in the Observation of Behavior," *Journal of Applied Psychology, 60* (1975), 550–555.

Latham, G. P., and Yukl, G. A., "A Review of Research on the Application of Goal Setting in Organizations," *Academy of Management Journal, 18* (1975a), 824–845.

Latham, G. P., and Yukl, G. A., "Assigned Versus Participative Goal Setting and Educated and Uneducated Wood Workers," *Journal of Applied Psychology*, 69 (1975b), 299–302.

Latuck, J. C., and Dotier, J. B., "After the Ax Falls: Job Loss as a Career Transition," *Academy of Management Review, 11* (1986), 375–392.

Lawler, E. E., III, *High-Involvement: Participative Strategies for Improving Organizational Effectiveness*. San Francisco: Jossey-Bass, 1988.

Leifer, M. S., and Newstrom, J. W., "Solving the Transfer of Training Problems," *Training and Development Journal*, August (1980), 34–46.

Lerda, L. W., "Conference Methods," in R. L. Craig and L. R. Bittel (eds.), *Training and Development Handbook*. New York: McGraw-Hill, 1967, 154–173.

Levine, J., and Butler, J., "Lecture Versus Group Decision in Changing Behavior," *Journal of Applied Psychology, 36* (1952), 29–33.

Lewin, K., "Group Decision and Social Change," in E. E., Maccoby, T. M. Newcombe, and E. L. Hartley (eds.), *Readings in Social Psychology*. New York: Henry Holt, 1958, 197–211.

Lewis, D. J., *Scientific Principles of Psychology*. Englewood Cliffs, NJ: Prentice-Hall, 1963.

Liden, R., and Graen, G., "Generalizability of the Vertical Dyad Linkage Model of Leadership," *Academy of Management Journal, 23* (1980), 451–465.

Lien, L., "Reviewing Your Training and Development Activities," *Personnel Journal, 58*:1 (1979), 791–807.

Likert, R., *New Patterns of Management*. New York: McGraw-Hill, 1961.

Likert, R., *The Human Organization*. New York: McGraw-Hill, 1967.

Likert, R., *New Ways of Managing Conflict*. New York: McGraw-Hill, 1976.

Linn, R. L., and Slinde, J. A., "The Determination of the Significance of Change Between Pre- and Posttesting Periods," *Review of Educational Research, 47* (1977), 121–150.

Lippitt, G. L., and Nadler, L., "Emerging Roles of the Training Director," *Training and Development Journal, 21* (1967), 2–10.

Locke, E. A., "Toward a Theory of Task Motivation and Incentives," *Organizational Behavior and Human Performance, 3* (1968), 157–189.

Locke, E. A., "The Myths of Behavior Modification in Organizations," *Academy of Management Review, 2* (1977), 543–553.

Locke, E. A., "Latham versus Komaki: A Tale of Two Paradigms," *Journal of Applied Psychology, 65* (1980), 16–23.

Locke, E. A., and Latham, G. P., *A Theory of Goal Setting and Task Performance*. Englewood Cliffs, NJ: Prentice-Hall, 1984.

Lohman, D. F., and Snow, R. E., "Toward a Theory of Cognitive Aptitude for Learning from Instruction," *Journal of Educational Psychology, 76* (1984), 347–376.

London, M., "Toward a Theory of Career Motivation," *Academy of Management Review, 9* (1983), 620–630.

London, M., "Employee Development in a Downsizing Environment," *Journal of Business and Psychology, 2* (1987), 60–73.

London, M., "Career Development," in K. N. Wexley and J. R. Hinrichs (eds.), *Developing Human Resources*. ASPA/BNA Series. Washington, DC: Bureau of National Affairs, 1990.

London, M., and Bassman, E., "Retraining Midcareer Workers for the Future Workplace," in I. L. Goldstein and associates (eds.), *Training and Development in Organizations*. San Francisco: Jossey-Bass, 1989, 333–375.

London, M., and Bray, D. W., "Measuring and Developing Young Manager's Career Motivation," *Journal of Management, 3* (1984), 3–25.

London, M., and Mone, E. M., *Career Growth and Survival in the Workplace.* San Francisco: Jossey-Bass, 1987.

Louis, M. R., Posner, B. F., and Powell, G. N., "The Availability and Helpfulness of Socialization Practices," *Personnel Psychology, 36* (1983), 857–866.

Mager, R. F., and Beach, K. M., Jr., *Developing Vocational Instruction.* Belmont, CA: Fearon, 1967.

Maiden, R., and Hardcastle, D., "Social Work Education: Professionalizing EAP's," *EAP Digest,* Nov./Dec. (1986), 63–66.

Maier, N. R. F., *Principles of Human Relations.* New York: Wiley, 1952.

Maier, N. R. F., *Problem-Solving Discussions and Conferences.* New York: McGraw-Hill, 1963.

Maier, N. R. F., *Psychology in Industrial Organizations* (4th ed.). Boston: Houghton Mifflin, 1973.

Maier, N. R. F., and Zerfoss, L. F., "MRP: A Technique for Training Large Groups of Supervisors and Its Potential Use in Social Psychology," *Human Relations, 5* (1952), 177–186.

Main, J., "Trying to Bend Managers' Minds," *Fortune,* November 23 (1987), pp. 95–108.

Mann, R. B., and Decker, P. J., "The Effect of Key Behavior Distinctiveness on Generalization and Recall in Behavior Modeling Training," *Academy of Management Journal, 27* (1984), 900–910.

Manuso, J. S. J., "Stress Management of Individual Stressors," in M. P. O'Donnell and T. Ainsworth (eds.), *Health Promotion in the Workplace.* New York: Wiley, 1984, 362–390.

Manz, C. C., and Sims, H. P., "Beyond Imitation: Complex Behavioral and Affective Linkages Resulting from Exposure to Leadership Training Models," *Journal of Applied Psychology, 71* (1986), 571–578.

Marshall, D. L., "The Incident Process of Supervisory Training: Case Study of Experience in a Small Plant," *Personnel, 31*:2 (1954) 134–139.

Marx, R. D., "Relapse Prevention for Managerial Training: A Model for Maintenance of Behavior Change," *Academy of Management Review,* 7 (1982), 433–441.

McCall, M. W., Jr., and Segrist, C. A., "In Pursuit of the Manager's Job: Building on Mintzberg," Technical Report No. 14, Center for Creative Leadership. Greensboro, NC, 1980.

McClelland, D.C., *The Achieving Society.* New York: Van Nostrand, 1961.

McClelland, D. C., "Toward a Theory of Motive Acquisition," *American Psychologist, 20*:5 (1965), 321–333.

McClelland, D. C., and Burnham, D. H., "Power Is the Great Motivator," *Harvard Business Review, 54* (1976), 100–110.

McClelland, D. C., and Teague, G. B., "Predicting Risk Preferences Among Power-related Risks," *Journal of Personality, 43*:2 (1975), 266–285.

McClelland, D. C., and Winter, D. G., *Motivating Economic Achievement*. New York: Free Press, 1969.

McEnery, J., and McEnery, J. M., "Self-Rating in Management Training Needs Assessment: A Neglected Opportunity," *Journal of Occupational Psychology, 60* (1987), 49–60.

McGee, L. F., "Teaching Basic Skills to Workers," *Personnel Administrator, 34* (1989), 42–47.

McGehee, W., and Thayer, P. W., *Training in Business and Industry*. New York: Wiley, 1961.

McShane, S. L., and Beal, T., "Employee Socialization Practices on Canada's West Coast: A Management Report," Simon Fraser University, December 1984.

Mealia, L. W., and Duffy, J., "Contemporary Training and Development Practices in Canadian Firms." Paper presented at the annual meeting of the Atlantic Schools of Business, Halifax, Nova Scotia, 1985.

Meichenbaum, D., *Cognitive-Behavior Modification*. New York: Plenum, 1977.

Meier, E. L., and Kerr, E. A., "Capabilities of Middle-Aged and Older Workers: A Survey of the Literature," *Industrial Gerontology, 3*:3 (1976), 147–156.

Meyer, H. H., and Raich, M. S., "An Objective Evaluation of a Behavior Modeling Training Program," *Personnel Psychology, 36* (1983), 755–762.

Miller, N. E., "Scientific Principles of Maximum Learning from Motion Pictures," *A. V. Communication Review*, 5 (1957), 3.

Miller, R. B., "Task Description and Analysis," in R. M. Gagné (ed.), *Psychological Principles in System Development*. New York: Holt, 1962.

Miner, J. B., *The Management of Ineffective Performance*. New York: McGraw-Hill, 1963.

Miner, J. B., *The Human Constraint: The Coming Shortage of Managerial Talent*. Washington, DC: BNA Books, 1974.

Miner, J. B., *The Challenge of Managing*. Philadelphia: W. B. Saunders, 1975.

Miner, J. B., *Motivation to Manage*. Atlanta, GA: Organizational Measurement Systems Press, 1977.

Miner, J. B., *The Management Process: Theory, Research, and Practice*. New York: Macmillan, 1978.

Miner, J. B., "Sentence Completion Measures in Personnel Research: The Development and Validation of the Miner Sentence Completion Scales," in H. J. Bernardin and D. A. Bownas (eds.), *Personality Assessment in Organizations*. New York: Praeger, 1985, 145–176.

Miner, J. B., "Managerial Role Motivation Training," *Journal of Management Psychology*, in press.

Miner, J. B., and Miner, M. G., *Personnel and Industrial Relations*. New York: Macmillan, 1973.

Mintzberg, H., *The Nature of Managerial Work*. New York: Harper & Row, 1973.

Mintzberg, H., "The Manager's Job: Folklore and Fact," *Harvard Business Review, 53*:4 (1975), 49–61.

Mintzberg, H., *Power in and Around Organizations*. Englewood Cliffs, NJ: Prentice-Hall, 1983.

Miron, D., and McClelland, D. C., "The Impact of Achievement Motivation Training on Small Businesses," *California Management Review, 21* (1979), 13–28.

Mitchell, E., and Hyde, A., "Training Demand Assessment: Three Cases in Planning Training Programs," *Public Personnel Management, 12* (1979), 360–373.

Mitchell, T. R., "Expectancy Models of Job Satisfaction, Occupational Preference and Effort: A Theoretical, Methodological, and Empirical Appraisal," *Psychological Bulletin, 81* (1974), 1096–1112.

Mitchell, T. R., "Cognitions and Skinner: Some Questions About Behavioral Determinism," *Organization and Administrative Sciences, 6* (1975), 63–72.

Moon, C. G., and Hariton, T., "Evaluating an Appraisal and Feedback Training Program," *Personnel, 35*:3 (1958), 36–41.

Moses, J. L., and Ritchie, R. J., "Supervisory Relationships Training: A Behavioral Evaluation of a Behavior Modeling Program," *Personnel Psychology, 29* (1976), 337–343.

Mullen, C., and Gorman, L., "Facilitating Adaptation to Change: A Case Study in Retraining Middle-Aged and Older Workers at Aer Lingus," *Industrial Psychology, 15* (1972), 23–29.

Mumford, M. D., Weeks, J. L., Harding, F. D., and Fleishman, E. A., "Relations Between Student Characteristics, Course Content, and Training Outcomes: An Integrative Modeling Effort," *Journal of Applied Psychology, 73* (1988), 443–456.

Munsterberg, H., *Psychology and Industrial Efficiency*. Boston: Houghton Mifflin, 1913.

Murphy, K. R., Martin, C., and Garcia, M., "Do Behavioral Observation Sides Measure Observation," *Journal of Applied Psychology, 67* (1982), 562–567.

Myers, I. B., *A Description of the Theory and Applications of the Myers-Briggs Type Indicator*. Palo Alto, CA: Consulting Psychologists Press, 1987.

Nadolski, H. N., and Sandonato, C. E., "Evaluation of an Employee Assistance Program," *Journal of Occupational Medicine, 29* (1987), 32–37.

Nash, A. N., Muczyk, J. P., and Vettori, F. L., "The Relative Practical Effectiveness of Programmed Instruction," *Personnel Psychology, 24* (1971), 397–418.

Naylor, J. C., and Briggs, G. D., "The Effect of Task Complexity and Task Organization on the Relative Efficiency of Part and Whole Training Methods," *Journal of Experimental Psychology, 65* (1963), 217–224.

Nealey, S. M., and Fiedler, F. E., "Leadership Functions of Middle Managers," *Psychological Bulletin, 70* (1968), 313–329.

Nelson, D. L., "Organizational Socialization: A Street Perspective," *Journal of Occupational Behavior, 8* (1987), 311–324.

Nemeroff, W. F., and Wexley, K. N., "An Explanation of the Relationships Between Performance Feedback Interview Characteristics and Interview Outcomes as Perceived by Managers and Subordinates," *Journal of Occupational Psychology, 52* (1979), 25–34.

The New Grid Seminar, Scientific Methods, Inc., Austin, TX, 1980.

Newman, L., "Outplacement the Right Way," *Personnel Administration, 34* (1989), 83–86.

Newstrom, J. W., "A Role-Taker/Time Differential Integration of Transfer Strategies." Paper presented at the annual convention of the American Psychological Association, Toronto, 1984.

Newsweek, "How Practice Makes Perfect," January 7 (1980), p. 39.

Noe, R. A., "Trainees' Attributes and Attitudes: Neglected Influences on Training Effectiveness," *Academy of Management Review, 11* (1986), 736–749.

Noe, R. A., "Women and Mentoring: A Review and Research Agenda," *Academy of Management Review, 13* (1988a), 65–78.

Noe, R. A., "An Investigation of the Determinants of Successful Assigned Mentoring Relationships," *Personnel Psychology, 41* (1988b), 457–479.

Noe, R. A., and Schmitt, N., "The Influence of Trainer Attitudes on Training Effectiveness: Test of a Model," *Personnel Psychology, 39* (1986), 497–523.

Nord, W. R., "Beyond the Teaching Machine: The Neglected Area of Operant Conditioning in the Theory and Practice of Management," *Organizational Behavior and Human Performance, 4*:4 (1969), 375–401.

Nykodym, N., "Transactional Analysis: A Strategy for the Improvement of Supervisory Behavior," *Transaction Analysis Journal, 8* (1978), 254–258.

O'Boyle, T. F., "Loyalty Ebbs at Many Companies as Employees Grow Disillusioned," *Wall Street Journal*, July 11 (1985), 27.

O'Brien, G. E., Fiedler, F. E., and Hewitt, T. T., "The Effects of Programmed Culture Training upon the Performance of Volunteer Medical Teams in Central America," *Human Relations 24* (1971), 209–231.

O'Brien, G. E., and Plooij, D., "Comparison of Programmed and Prose Culture Training upon Attitudes and Knowledge," *Journal of Applied Psychology, 62* (1977), 499–505.

Odenwald, S., "Pre-Retirement Planning Gathers Steam," *Training and Development Journal, 40* (1986), 62–63.

Odiorne, G. S., *Training by Objectives: An Economic Approach to Management Training*. New York: Macmillan, 1970.

Paquet, B., Kasl, E., Weinstein, L., and Waite, W., "The Bottom Line," *Training and Development Journal, 41* (1987), 27–33.

Parsons, F. W., "Inexpensive Interactive Training," *Training and Development Journal, 40* (1986), 38–39.

Patrick, J., and Stammers, R., "Computer Assisted Learning and Occupational Training," *British Journal of Educational Technology, 8*:3 (1977), 253–267.

Peters, L. H., Chassie, M. B., Lindholm, H. R., O'Connor, E. J., and Kline, C. R., "The Joint Influence of Situational Constraints and Goal Settings of Performance and Affective Outcomes," *Journal of Management, 8* (1982), 7–20.

Peters, L. H., and O'Connor, E. J., "Situational Constraints and Work Outcomes: The Influences of a Frequently Overlooked Construct," *Academy of Management Review, 5* (1980), 391–397.

Peters, L. H., O'Connor, E. J., and Eulberg, J. R., "Situational Constraints: Sources, Consequences, and Future Considerations," in J. Ferris and K. Rowland (eds.), *Research in Personnel and Human Resources Management, 3* (1985), 79–114.

Peters, T., and Austin, N., *A Passion for Excellence: The Leadership Difference.* New York: Random House, 1985.

Peters, T. J., and Waterman, R. H., Jr., *In Search of Excellence.* New York: Harper & Row, 1982.

Phillips-Jones, L., "Establishing a Formalized Mentoring Program," *Training and Development Journal, 37*:2 (1983), 38–42.

Pigors, P., and Myers, C. A., *Personnel Administration: A Point of View and a Method.* New York: McGraw-Hill, 1973.

Pigors, P., and Pigors, F., *The Incident Process: Case Studies in Management Development.* Washington, DC: Bureau of National Affairs, 1955.

Pigors, P., and Pigors, F., "Case Method," in R. L. Craig (ed.), *Training and Development Handbook: A Guide to Human Resource Development.* New York: McGraw-Hill, 1987, 414–429.

Pittman, J. L., "Organization and Management of the Training Function," in R. L. Craig (ed.), *Training and Development Handbook: A Guide to Human Resource Development.* New York: McGraw-Hill, 1987, 19–24.

Planty, E. G., McCord, W. S., and Efferson, C. A., *Training Employees and Managers.* New York: Ronald Press, 1948.

Porras, J. I., and Anderson, B., "Improving Managerial Effectiveness Through Modeling-Based Training," *Organizational Dynamics, 9* (1981), 60–77.

Porter, L. W., "A Motivational Theory for Updating," in S. S. Dubin (Chm.), *Motivation for Professional Updating.* Symposium presented at the XVII International Congress of Applied Psychology, Liege, Belgium, July 1971.

Porter, L. W., "Turning Work into Nonwork: The Rewarding Environment," in M. D. Dunnette (ed.), *Work and Nonwork in the Year 2001.* Monterey, CA: Brooks/Cole, 1973, 113–173.

Porter, L. W., "Leadership Symposium: Introduction," *Organizational Dynamics, 4*:3 (1976), 2–5.

Porter, L. W., Lawler, E. E., III, and Hackman, J. R., *Behavior in Organizations.* New York: McGraw-Hill, 1975.

Premack, S. L., and Wanous, J. P., "A Meta-Analysis of Realistic Job Preview Experiments," *Journal of Applied Psychology, 70* (1985), 706–719.

Prentice-Hall Editorial Staff, *Employee Training,* Personnel Management: Policies and Practices Series. Englewood Cliffs, NJ: Prentice-Hall, 1979.

Proctor, J. H., and Thornton, W. M., *Training: A Handbook for Line Managers.* New York: American Management Association, 1971.

Pulakos, E. D., "A Comparison of Rates Training Programs: Error Training and Accuracy Training," *Journal of Applied Psychology, 69* (1984), 581–588.

Pulakos, E. D., and Wexley, K. N., "The Relationship Among Perceptual Similarity, Sex, and Performance Ratings in Manager-Subordinate Dyads," *Academy of Management Journal, 26* (1983), 129–139.

Purcell, T. V., "How GE Measures Managers in Fair Employment," *Harvard Business Review*, 52 (1974), 99–104.

Pursell, E. D., Dossett, D. L., and Latham, G. P., "Obtaining Validated Predictors by Minimizing Rating Errors in the Criterion," *Personnel Psychology*, 33 (1980), 91–96.

Pursell, E. D., and Russell, J. S., "Employee Development," in K. N. Wexley (ed.), *Developing Human Resources*. ASPA/BNA Series. Washington, DC: Bureau of National Affairs, 1990.

Rackham, N., and Morgan, T., *Behavior Analysis in Training*. Maidenhead, Great Britain: McGraw-Hill, 1977.

Randall, J. S., "You and Effective Training: Part 1," *Training and Development Journal*, 32:5 (1978), 10–14.

Reilly, R. R., and Manese, W. R., "The Validation of a Minicourse for Telephone Company Switching Technicians," *Personnel Psychology*, 32 (1979), 83–90.

Rice, R. W., "Construct Validity of the Least Preferred Co-Worker (LPC) Score," *Psychological Bulletin*, 85 (1978), 1199–1237.

Rice, R. W., "Reliability and Validity of the LPC Scale: A Reply," *Academy of Management Review*, 4 (1979), 291–294.

Rigg, R. P., *Audiovisual Aids and Techniques*. London: Hamish Hamilton Ltd., 1969.

Roberts, T., *Developing Effective Managers*. Stratford-upon-Avon, Great Britain: Edward Fox and Son, 1974.

Robertson, I. T., and Downs, S., "Learning and the Prediction of Performance: Development of Trainability Testing in the United Kingdom," *Journal of Applied Psychology*, 64 (1979), 42–50.

Robertson, I. T., and Downs, S., "Work-Sample Tests of Trainability: A Meta-Analysis," *Journal of Applied Psychology*, 74(1989), 402–407.

Robinson, D. G., and Robinson, J. C., "Breaking Barriers to Skill Transfer," *Training and Development Journal*, 39 (1985), 82–83.

Roches, G. R., "Much Ado About Mentors," *Harvard Business Review*, 57:1(1979), 14–31.

Ronen, S., *Comparative and Multinational Management*. New York: Wiley, 1986.

Ronen, S., "Training the International Assignee," in I. L. Goldstein and associates (eds.), *Training and Development in Organizations*. San Francisco: Jossey-Bass, 1989, 417–454.

Ropp, K., "A Reform Movement for Education," *Personnel Administrator*, 34 (1989), 39–41.

Rosch, P. J., and Pelletier, K. R., "Designing Worksite Stress Management Programs," in *Stress Management in Work Settings*, U.S. Department of Health and Human Services, 1987, 69–91.

Rosow, J. M., and Zager, R., *Training—The Competitive Edge*. San Francisco: Jossey-Bass, 1988.

Ross, P. C., "A Relationship Between Training Efficiency and Employee Selection," *Improving Human Performance*, 3 (1974), 108–117.

Rubin, N., "Training in a Team Environment: S. B. Thomas, Inc.," in J. Casner-Lotto and associates (eds.), *Successful Training Strategies*. San Francisco: Jossey-Bass, 1988, 142–156.

Rubinsky, S., and Smith, N., "Safety Training by Accident Simulation," *Journal of Applied Psychology*, 57:1(1973), 68–73.

Russell, J. S., "A Review of Fair Employment Cases in the Field of Training," *Personnel Psychology, 17* (1984), 261–274.

Russell, J. S., and Wexley, K. N., "Improving Managerial Performance in Assessing Needs and Transferring Training," in G. R. Ferris and K. M. Rowland (eds.), *Research in Personnel and Human Resource Management*, Greenwich, CT: JAI Press, 1988, 289–323.

Ryman, D. H., and Biersner, R. J., "Attitudes Predictive of Diving Training Success," *Personnel Psychology, 28* (1975), 181–188.

Rynes, S. L., and Milkovich, G. T., *Current Issues in Human Resource Management: Commentary and Readings*. Plano, TX: Business Publications, Inc., 1986.

Saari, L., Johnson, T. R., McLaughlin, S. D., and Fimmerle, D. M., "A Survey of Management Training and Education Practices in U.S. Companies," *Personnel Psychology, 41*(1988), 731–744.

Saari, L. M., and Latham, G. P., "Employee Reactions to Continuous and Variable Metro Reinforcement Schedules Involving a Monetary Incentive," *Journal of Applied Psychology, 67* (1982), 506–508.

Sanders, R. E., Sanders, J. C., Mayers, G. J., and Seilski, K. A., "Enhancement of Conjunctive Concept Attainment in Older Adults," *Developmental Psychology, 12* (1976), 484–486.

Scarpello, V. G., and Ledvinka, J., *Personnel Human Resource Management: Environments and Functions*. Boston: PWS-Kent, 1988.

Schaaf, D., "Computer-based Training: The Question Is When, Not If," *Training, 24* (1987), 3–8.

Schein, E. H., "Organizational Socialization and the Profession of Management," *Industrial Management Review*, 9:19 (1968), 1–16.

Schein, E. H., *Process Consultation: Its Role in Organization Development*. Reading, MA: Addison-Wesley, 1969.

Schendel, J. D., and Hagman, J. D., "On Sustaining Procedural Skills over a Prolonged Retention Interval," *Journal of Applied Psychology*, 67 (1982), 605–610.

Schleger, P. R., "A Guide for People Who Use Your Video Program," *Training and Development Journal, 38* (1984), 32–34.

Schmidt, F. A., Murphy, M. D., and Sanders, R., "Training Older Adults' Free-Recall Rehearsal Strategies," *Journal of Gerontology, 36* (1981), 329–337.

Schmidt, F. L., Hunter, J. E., and Pearlman, K., "Assessing the Economic Impact of Personnel Programs on Workforce Productivity," *Personnel Psychology, 35* (1982), 333–347.

Schmitt, N., Ford, J. K., and Stults, D. M., "Changes in Self-Perceived Ability as a Function of Performance in an Assessment Centre," *Journal of Occupational Psychology, 59* (1986), 327–335.

Schneider, B., *Staffing Organizations.* Santa Monica, CA: Goodyear, 1976.

Schneider, S. J., "Who Quits Smoking in a Behavioral Treatment Program?" *Addictive Behaviors, 9* (1984), 373–381.

Schoen, S. H., and French, W. L., "Experience with the Incident Process of Management Training," *Personnel, 36*:4 (1959), 54–61.

Schramm, W., "Mass Communication," *Annual Review of Psychology, 1* (1962), 251–284.

Schriesheim, C. A., Bannister, B. D, and Money, W. H., "Psychometric Properties of the LPC Scale: An Extension of Rice's Review," *Academy of Management Review, 4* (1979), 287–290.

Schriesheim, C. A., and Kerr, S., "Theories and Measures of Leadership: A Critical Appraisal of Current and Future Directions," in J. G. Hunt and L. L. Larson (eds.), *Leadership: The Cutting Edge.* Carbondale, IL: Southern Illinois University Press, 1977.

Schuler, H., "Females in Technical Apprenticeship: Development of Aptitudes, Performance and Self-Concept," in S. E. Newstead, S. H. Irvine, and P. L. Dann (eds.), *Human Assessment: Cognition and Motivation.* The Hague: Nijhoff, 1986.

Scott, W. G., and Hart, D. K., *Organizational Values in America.* New Brunswick, NJ: Transition, 1989.

Seltzer, R. A., "Computer-assisted Instruction—What It Can and Cannot Do," *American Psychologist, 26* (1971), 373–377.

Shaw, M. E., "Role Playing," in R. L. Craig and L. R. Bittel (eds.), *Training and Development Handbook.* New York: McGraw-Hill, 1967, 206–224.

Siegel, A. I., "A Job Learning Approach to Performance Prediction," *Personnel Psychology, 28* (1975), 325–339.

Siegel, A. I., "The Miniature Job Training and Evaluation Approach: Additional Finding," *Personnel Psychology, 36* (1983), 41–56.

Siegel, L., and Lane, I. M., *Personnel and Organizational Psychology.* Homewood, IL: Irwin, 1987.

Silverman, S. B., "Increasing Individual Development Through Performance Appraisal," in K. N. Wexley and J. R. Hinrichs (eds.), *Developing Human Resources.* ASPA/BNA Series. Washington, DC: Bureau of National Affairs, 1990.

Simmons, D. D., "The Case Method in Management Training," in B. Taylor and G. L. Lippitt (eds.), *Management Development and Training Handbook.* London: McGraw-Hill, 1975, 182–190.

Skinner, B. F., *The Behavior of Organisms.* New York: Appleton, 1938.

Skinner, B. F., *Science and Human Behavior.* New York: Free Press, 1953.

Skinner, B. F., *Science and Human Behavior.* New York: Macmillan, 1953.

Skinner, B. F., "Are Theories of Learning Necessary?" *Psychological Review, 19* (1957), 193–216.

Skinner, B. F., "Teaching Machines," *Science, 128* (1958), 969–977.

Skinner, B. F., *Contingencies of Reinforcement.* New York: Appleton-Century-Crofts, 1969.

Skinner, B. F., "What Ever Happened to Psychology as the Science of Behavior?" *American Psychologist, 42* (1987), 780–786.

Sloan, R. P., and Gruman, J. C., "Does Wellness in the Workplace Work?" *Personnel Administrator, 33* (1988), 42–48.

Smith, B. B., *Evaluating a Leaderless Training Program.* Princeton, NJ: Kepner-Tregoe, 1979.

Smith, E. I., *Small Climber Development.* Basking Ridge, NJ: AT&T Co., November 1978.

Smith, P. B., "Controlled Studies of the Outcome of Sensitivity Training," *Psychological Bulletin, 82*:4 (1975), 597–622.

Smith, P. C., and Kendall, L. M., "Retranslation of Expectations: An Approach to the Construction of Unambiguous Anchors for Rating Scales," *Journal of Applied Psychology, 47* (1963), 149–155.

Smith, R. E., "A Cognitive-Affective Approach to Stress Management Training for Athletes," in C. H. Hadeau, W. Holliwell, K. M. Newell, and G. C. Roberts (eds.), *Skillfulness in Movement: Psychology of Motor Behavior and Sport.* Champaign, IL: Human Kinetics, 1980.

Smith, R. E., "Employee Orientation: 10 Steps to Success," *Personnel Journal, 63*:12 (1984), 46–48.

Smith, R. E., Sarason, I. G., and Sarason, B. R., *Psychology: The Frontiers of Behavior.* New York: Harper & Row, 1978.

Snell, S. A., and Wexley, K. N., "Performance Diagnosis: Identifying the Causes for Poor Performance," *Personnel Administrator, 30* (1985), 117–118, 123–125.

Snow, R. E., "Individual Differences and the Design of Educational Programs," *American Psychologist, 41* (1986), 1029–1039.

Snow, R. E., and Yallow, E., "Education and Intelligence," in R. J. Sternberg (ed.), *Handbook of Human Intelligence.* New York: Cambridge University Press, 1982.

Solomon, R. L., "An Extension of Control Group Design," *Psychological Bulletin, 46* (1949), 137–150.

Sorcher, M., and Goldstein, A. P., "A Behavior Modeling Approach in Training," *Personnel Administration, 35*:2 (1972), 35–41.

Sorcher, M., and Spence, R., "The Interface Project: Behavior Modeling as Social Technology in South Africa," *Personnel Psychology, 35* (1982), 557–581.

"The Spirit of Hospitality," *EI Solutions,* The Educational Institute of the American Hotel and Motel Association, September 1987, 8–9.

Staley, C. C., and Shockley-Zalabak, P., "Communication Proficiency and Future Training Needs of the Female Professional: Self-Assessment Versus Supervisors' Evaluations," *Human Relations, 39* (1986), 891–902.

Stark, C., "Ensuring Skills Transfer: A Sensitive Approach," *Training and Development Journal, 40* (1986), 50–51.

Starr, A., and Byram, G., "Cost Benefit Analysis for Employee Assistance Programs," *Personnel Administrator, 8* (1985), 55–60.

Sterns, H. L., and Doverspike, D., "Aging and the Training and Learning Process," in I. L. Goldstein and associates (eds.), *Training and Development in Organizations.* San Francisco: Jossey-Bass, 1989, 229–329.

Stessin, L., "When an Employer Insists," *New York Times*, April 3 (1977), p. 9.

Stewart, R., "The Nature of Management?" *Journal of Management Studies, 21* (1984), 323–330.

Stovall, T. F., "Lecture Versus Discussion," *Phi Delta Kappan, 39* (1958), 225–258.

Strauch, R., "Training the Whole Person," *Training and Development Journal, 38* (1984), 82–86.

Strauss, G., "Union Policies Toward the Admission of Apprentices," Berkeley: University of California, 1971, Reprint No. 357.

Streker-Seeborg, I., Seeborg, M. C., and Zegeye, A., "The Impact of Nontraditional Training on the Occupational Attainment of Women," *Journal of Human Resources, 19* (1984), 452–471.

Sullivan, R. F., and Miklas, D. C., "On-the-Job Training That Works," *Training and Development Journal, 39*:5 (1985), 118–120.

Survey of Organizations. See Taylor, J. C., and Bowers, D. G., 1972.

Tannenbaum, R., Weschler, I. R., and Massarik, F., *Leadership and Organization: A Behavioral Science Approach*. New York: McGraw-Hill, 1961.

Taylor, B. L., "Around the World 80," *Training and Development Journal, 40* (1986), 66–67.

Taylor, F. W., *The Principles of Scientific Management*. New York: Harper, 1911.

Taylor, J. C., and Bowers, D. G., *Survey of Organizations*. Ann Arbor, MI: Institute for Social Research, 1972.

Teel, K. S., and DuBois, H., "Participants' Reactions to Assessment Centers," *Personnel Administrator, 28* (1983), 85–91.

Tenopyr, M. L., "Policies and Strategies Underlying a Personnel Research Operation." Paper presented at the annual meeting of the Society of Industrial-Organizational Psychology, Atlanta, 1987.

Terborg, J. R., Howard, G. S., and Maxwell, S. E., "Evaluating Planned Organizational Change: A Method for Assessing Alpha, Beta, and Gamma Change," *Academy of Management Review, 5* (1980), 109–121.

Thomas, W., and Thomas, C., "The Payoffs and Pitfalls of Video-Based Training," *Training and Development Journal, 38* (1984), 28–29.

Thornton, G. C., and Byham, W. C., *Assessment Centers and Managerial Performance*. New York: Academic Press, 1982.

Timmons, J. A., "Black Is Beautiful—Is It Bountiful?" *Harvard Business Review, 49* (1971), 81–92.

Trost, A., "They May Love It But Will They Use It?" *Training and Development Journal, 39* (1985), 78–81.

Tucker, F. D., "A Study of the Training Needs of Older Workers: Implications for Human Resources Development Planning," *Public Personnel Management, 14* (1985), 85–95.

Tung, R. L., "Selection and Training of Personnel for Overseas Assignments," *Columbia Journal of World Business, 16* (1981), 68–78.

UK Department of Employment, *Glossary of Training Terms*. London: HMSO, 1971.

Uniform Guidelines on Employer Selection Procedures. Federal Register, 43, No. 166, August 25, 1978.

Utgaard, S. B., and Davis, R. V., "The Most Frequently Used Training Techniques," *Training and Development Journal, 24* (1970), 40–43.

"Videos Are Starring in More and More Training Programs," *Business Week*, September 7 (1987), p. 108.

Verner, C., and Dickinson, G., "The Lecture: An Analysis and Review of Research," *Adult Education, 17* (1967), 85–100.

Vroom, V. H., "Can Leaders Learn to Lead?" *Organizational Dynamics, 4*: 3 (1976), 17–28.

Vroom, V. H., and Jago, A. G., "On the Validity of the Vroom-Yetton Model," *Journal of Applied Psychology, 63*:2 (1978), 151–162.

Vroom, V. H., and Jago, A. G., *The New Leadership: Managing Participation in Organizations*. Englewood Cliffs, NJ: Prentice-Hall, 1988.

Vroom, V. H., and Yetton, P. W., *Leadership and Decision-Making*. Pittsburg: University of Pittsburgh Press, 1973.

Walker, C. R., Guest, R. H., and Turner, A. N., *The Foreman on the Assembly Line*. Cambridge: Harvard University Press, 1956.

Wanous, J. P., *Organizational Entry: Recruitment, Selection, and Socialization of Newcomers*. Reading, MA: Addison-Wesley, 1980.

Warr, P., Bird, M., and Rackham, N., *Evaluation of Management Training*. London: Gower Press Ltd., 1970.

Watson, J. B., "Psychology as the Behaviorist Views It," *Psychology Review, 20* (1913), 158–177.

Wehrenberg, S. B., "Management Training Games: The Play's the Thing," *Personnel Journal, 64* (1985), 88–91.

Wehrenberg, S. B., "Simulations: Capturing the Experience of the Real Thing," *Personnel Journal, 65* (1986), 101–103.

Weinrach, S. G., *Career Counseling: Theoretical and Practical Perspective*. New York: McGraw-Hill, 1979.

Wesson, C., Wilson, R., and Mandlebau, L. H., "Learning Games for Active Student Responding," *Teaching Exceptional Children, 5* (1988), 12–14.

West, B., "Training for the Physically Challenged," *Directions, 15* (1987), 4–5.

Wexley, K. N., *A Job Analysis Study of the Position of Residential Service Representative*. American Telephone and Telegraph Company, 1975.

Wexley, K. N., "Performance Appraisal and Feedback," in S. Kerr (ed.), *Organizational Behavior*. Columbus, OH: Grid Publishing, 1979, 241–259.

Wexley, K. N., "Personnel Training," *Annual Review of Psychology, 35* (1984), 519–551.

Wexley, K. N., Alexander, R. A., Greenawalt, J. P., and Couch, M. A., "Attitudinal Congruence and Similarity as Related to Interpersonal Evaluations in Manager-Subordinate Dyads," *Academy of Management Journal, 23* (1980), 320–330.

Wexley, K. N., and Baldwin, T. T., "Management Development," *Journal of Management, 12* (1986a), 277–294.

Wexley, K. N., and Baldwin, T. T., "Posttraining Strategies for Facilitating Positive Transfer: An Empirical Investigation," *Academy of Management Journal, 29* (1986b), 503–520.

Wexley, K. N., and McCellin, D. G., "The Effects of Varying Training Task Difficulty on Training Transfer." Paper presented at the 95th Annual Convention of the American Psychological Association, New York, 1987.

Wexley, K. N., and Nemeroff, W. F., "Effectiveness of Positive Reinforcement and Goal Setting as Methods of Management Development," *Journal of Applied Psychology, 60* (1975), 446–450.

Wexley, K. N., and Pulakos, E. D., "The Effects of Perceptual Congruence and Sex on Subordinates' Performance Appraisals of Their Managers," *Academy of Management Journal, 26* (1983), 666–676.

Wexley, K. N., Sanders, R. E., and Yukl, G. A., "Training Interviewers to Eliminate Contrast Effects in Employment Interviews," *Journal of Applied Psychology, 57* (1973), 233–236.

Wexley, K. N., and Silverman, S. B., "An Examination of Differences Between Managerial Effectiveness and Response Patterns on a Structured Job Analysis Questionnaire," *Journal of Applied Psychology, 63*:5 (1978), 646–649.

Wexley, K. N., Singh, J. P., and Yukl, G. A., "Subordinate Personality as a Moderator of the Effects of Participation in Three Types of Appraisal Interviews," *Journal of Applied Psychology, 58* (1973), 543–560.

Wexley, K. N., and Thornton, C. L., "Effect of Verbal Feedback of Test Results upon Learning," *Journal of Educational Research, 66*:3 (1972), 119–121.

Wexley, K. N., and Yukl, G. A., *Organizational Behavior and Personnel Psychology.* Homewood, IL: Irwin, 1984.

Wilcox, J., "A Campus Tour of Corporate Colleges," *Training and Development Journal, 41* (1987), 51–56.

Willigies, B. H., Roscoe, S. N., and Willigies, R. C., "Synthetic Flight Training Revisited," *Human Factors, 15*:6 (1973), 543–560.

Willigies, R. C., and Willigies, B. H., "Critical Variables in Adaptive Motor Skills Training," *Human Factors, 20*:2 (1978), 201–214.

Wilson, J. A., and Danes, L. M., "Is Mentoring Only for the Chosen Few?" *Executive Excellence, 5* (1988), 8–9.

Wittrock, M. C., and Lumsdaine, A. A., "Instructional Psychology," *Annual Review of Psychology, 28* (1977), 417–459.

Wohlking, W., "Role Playing," in R. L. Craig (ed.), *Training and Development Handbook: A Guide to Human Resource Development.* New York: McGraw-Hill, 1976, 36-1–36-14.

Worchel, S., and Mitchell, T., "An Evaluation of the Effectiveness of the Culture Assimilator in Thailand and Greece," *Journal of Applied Psychology, 56* (1972), 472–479.

Yeomans, W. N., "How to Get Top Management Support," *Training and Development Journal, 36* (1982), 38–40.

Yukl, G. A., *Leadership in Organizations*. Englewood Cliffs, NJ: Prentice-Hall, 1989.

Yukl, G. A., and Latham, G. P., "Consequences of Reinforcement Schedules and Incentive Magnitudes for Employee Performance: Problems Encountered in an Industrial Setting," *Journal of Applied Psychology, 60* (1975), 294–298.

Yukl, G. A., Latham, G. P., and Pursell, E. D., "The Effectiveness of Performance Incentives Under Continuous and Variable Ratio Schedules of Reinforcement," *Personnel Psychology, 29* (1976), 221–231.

Yukl, G., Wexley, K. N., and Seymore, J. D., "Effectiveness of Pay Incentives Under Variable Ratio and Continuous Reinforcement Schedules," *Journal of Applied Psychology, 56* (1972), 19–23.

Zalesnik, A., "The Leadership Gap," *Academy of Management Executive, 4* (1990), 7–22.

Zemke, R., "Off-Site Training," *Training, 23* (1986a), 56–66.

Zemke, R., "The Rediscovery of Video Teleconferencing," *Training, 23* (1986b), 28–34, 38–39, 42–43.

Zey, M. G., "Mentor Programs: Making the Right Moves," *Personnel Journal, 64* (1985), 53–57.

Name Index

Subject Index

Praise for *China*

'Bravo; this is a big, complex and utterly involving portrait of 19th-century China'
The Times

'Takes an entertaining, educational journey through China's rich and complex history, geography, art, and diverse cultures during a tumultuous epoch'
Booklist

'It's a bravura performance, fizzing with incident, excitement and energy'
Daily Mail

'The unparalleled master of the historical saga returns, this time, with an eye on China. Beginning with the First Opium War in 1839 and continuing through the present day, Rutherfurd tells a sweeping tale that brings to life a nation's history, traditions and the people who lived through it as if by magic'
Newsweek

'A spectacularly glorious epic! . . . This barnstormer of a book can take its rightful place as a true historical epic'
On-Magazine

'Rutherfurd's thorough research shows again here in his descriptions of China and other places in Asia like Hong Kong and Macao . . . Besides place, Rutherfurd also has thoroughly researched the many complexities of Chinese culture . . . *China* can perhaps be placed in the same basket as the James Clavell novels of *Tai-Pan* and *Noble House*'
Asian Review of Books

ALSO BY EDWARD RUTHERFURD

Russka

Sarum

The Princes of Ireland

The Rebels of Ireland

Paris

New York

London

The Forest

EDWARD RUTHERFURD

CHINA

HODDER

First published in Great Britain in 2021 by Hodder & Stoughton
An Hachette UK company

This paperback edition published in 2022

1

Map by Rodney Paull

A CIP catalogue record for this title is available from the British Library

Paperback ISBN 978 1 444 78780 1

Typeset in Adobe Garamond Pro by Palimpsest Book Production Ltd, Falkirk, Stirlingshire

Printed and bound in Great Britain by Clays Ltd, Elcograf S.p.A.

Hodder & Stoughton policy is to use papers that are natural, renewable and recyclable products and made from wood grown in sustainable forests. The logging and manufacturing processes are expected to conform to the environmental regulations of the country of origin.

Hodder & Stoughton Ltd
Carmelite House
50 Victoria Embankment
London EC4Y 0DZ

www.hodder.co.uk

In respectful memory of

ARTHUR WALEY, CH,

Poet and Scholar,

whose translations of the Chinese classics
have been an inspiration to me for fifty years

CONTENTS

Forbidden City

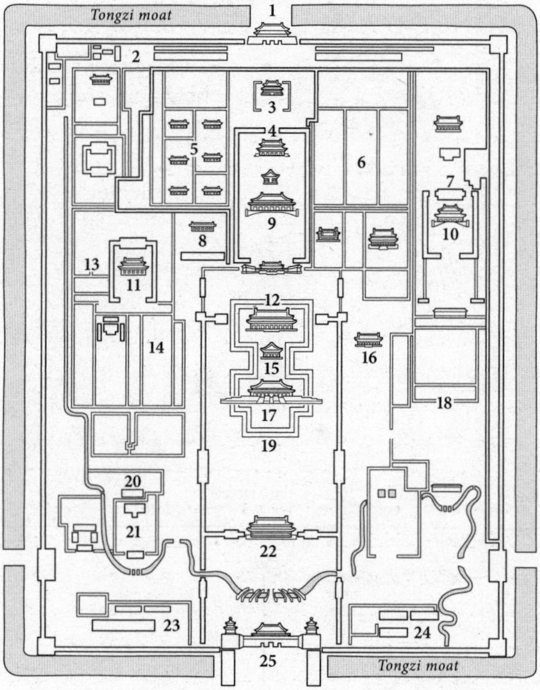

1 Gate of Divine Military Genius
2 Palace kitchens and gardens
3 Hall of Imperial Peace
4 Palace of Earthly Tranquillity
5 Empress and concubines' living quarters
6 Residential palaces
7 Palace of Tranquil Longevity
8 Emperor's living quarters
9 Palace of Heavenly Purity
10 Hall of Imperial Supremacy
11 Palace of Peace and Tranquillity
12 Hall of Preserving Harmony
13 Ghost
14 Offices of the Imperial Household
15 Hall of Central Harmony
16 Archery ground
17 Hall of Supreme Harmony
18 Palaces of the young princes
19 Dragon Pavement
20 Treasury
21 Imperial storehouses
22 Gate of Supreme Harmony
23 Servants' and eunuchs' quarters
24 Secretarial offices
25 Meridian Gate

The Summer Palace

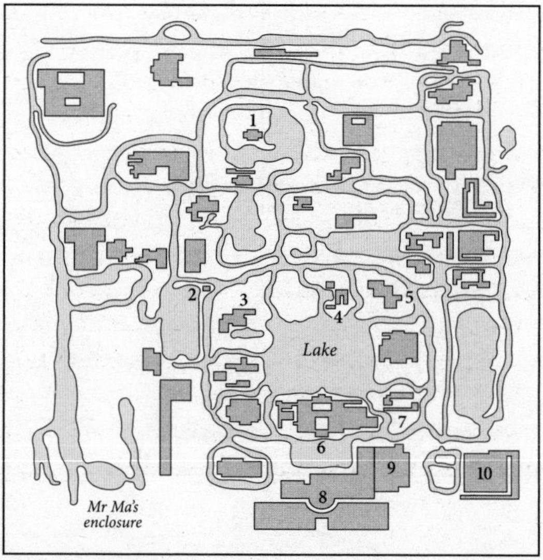

1 Scholar Lianxi's Wonderland
2 Temple of Universal Peace (Swastika House)
3 Apricot Blossom Spring Villa
4 Island of Shrines
5 Green Wutong-Tree Academy
6 Emperor's Private Residence
7 Peony Terrace
8 Audience Hall
9 Hall of Diligent Government
10 The Princes' School

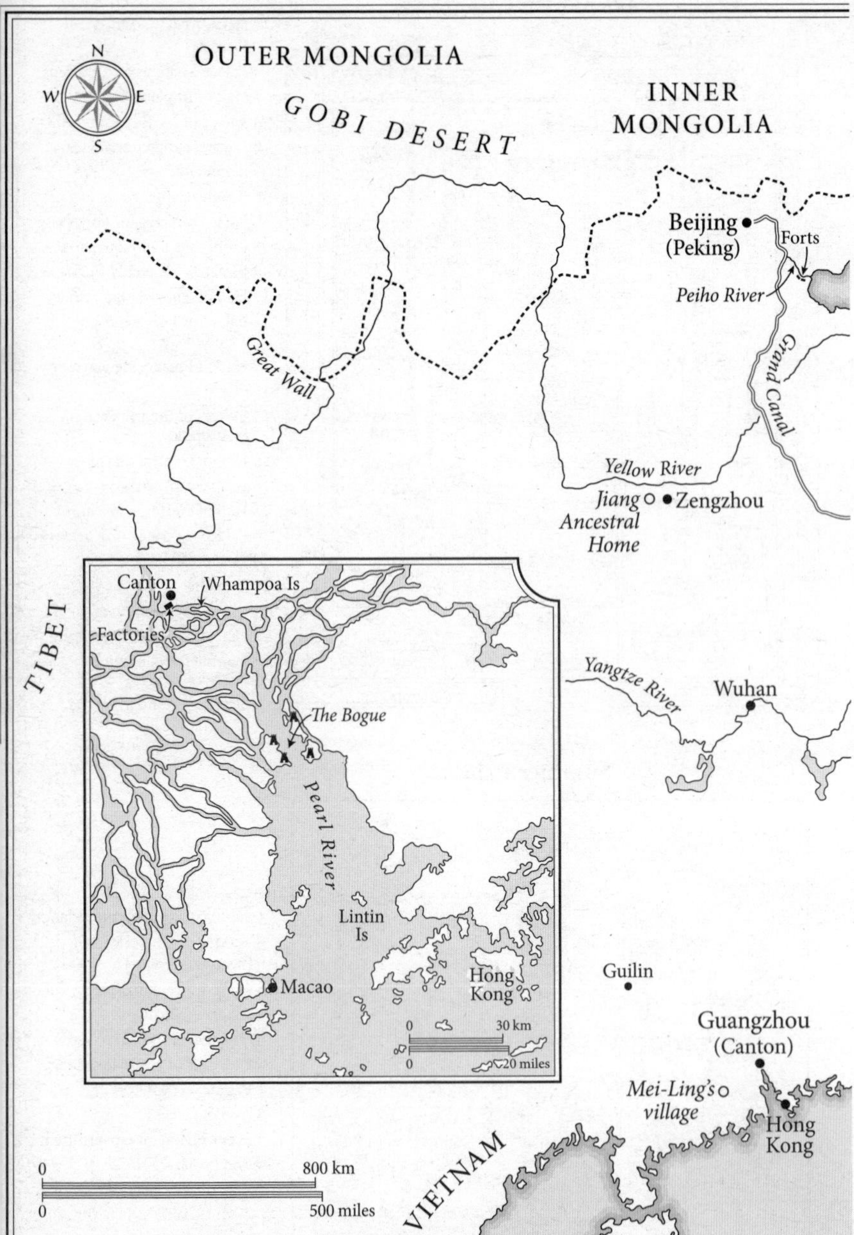
N
W
E
S
OUTER MONGOLIA
GOBI DESERT
INNER MONGOLIA
Beijing
(Peking)
Forts
Peiho River
Grand Canal
Great Wall
Yellow River
Jiang
Ancestral
Home
Zengzhou
Canton
Whampoa Is
Factories
TIBET
The Bogue
Pearl River
Lintin
Is
Macao
Hong
Kong
0
30 km
0
20 miles
Yangtze River
Wuhan
Guilin
Guangzhou
(Canton)
Mei-Ling's
village
Hong
Kong
VIETNAM
0
800 km
0
500 miles

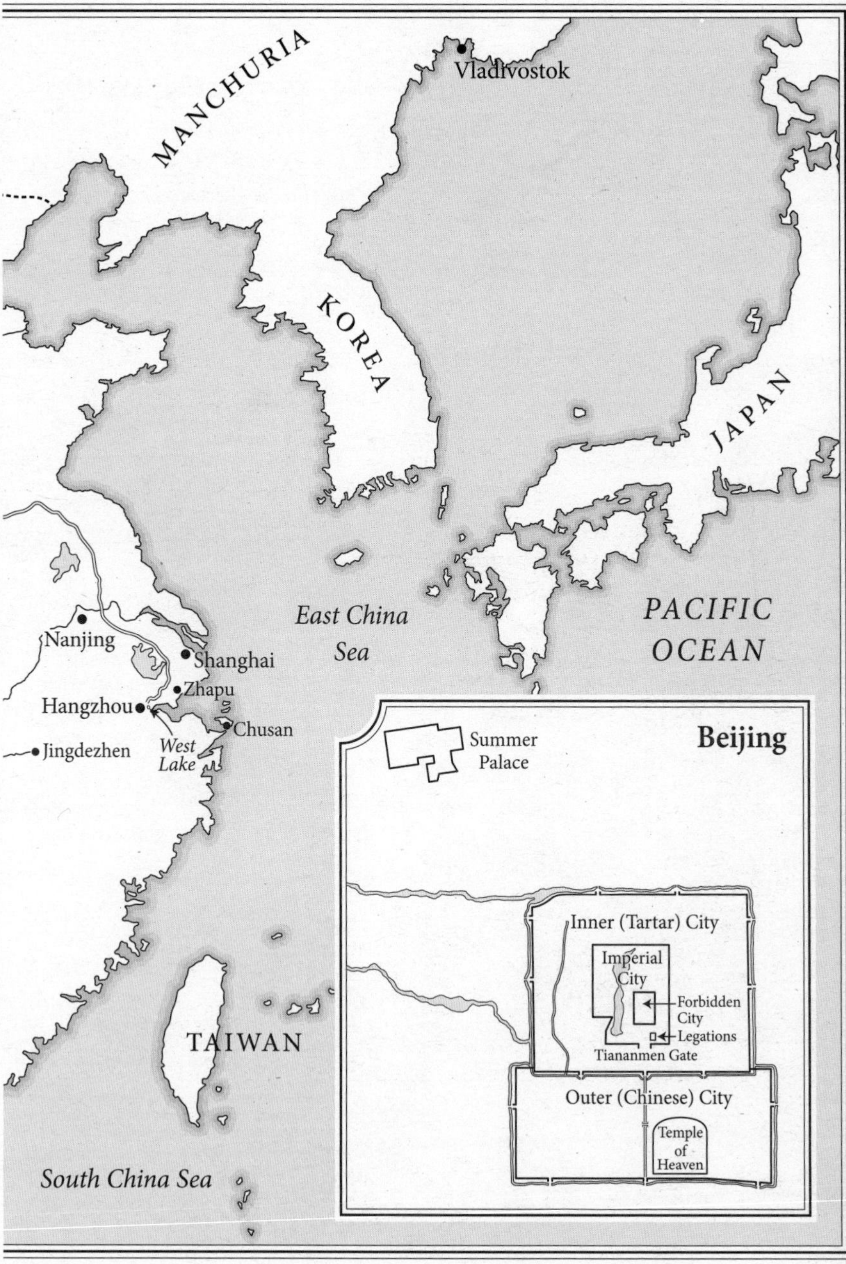
MANCHURIA
Vladivostok
KOREA
JAPAN
Nanjing
Shanghai
Zhapu
Hangzhou
Chusan
Jingdezhen
West Lake
East China Sea
PACIFIC OCEAN
TAIWAN
South China Sea
Beijing
Summer Palace
Inner (Tartar) City
Imperial City
Forbidden City
Legations
Tiananmen Gate
Outer (Chinese) City
Temple of Heaven

AUTHOR'S NOTE

China is first and foremost a novel, but it takes place against a background of real events.

When historical figures appear in the narrative, the depictions are my own, and I hope they are fair. All the principal characters, however – Trader, Charlie Farley, the Odstock brothers, Nio, Shi-Rong, Mei-Ling, Lacquer Nail, Mr Liu, Mr Ma, Guanji, their families and friends – are fictional.

I wish to acknowledge my special debt to the following authors and scholars on whose huge research, often in primary sources, this novel has relied.

GENERAL INTRODUCTIONS: John Keay for the most readable introduction to China's history; Caroline Blunden and Mark Elvin for their *Cultural Atlas of China,* a wonderful resource book; and Marina Warner for her vivid illustrated life of the 'Dragon Empress'.

SPECIALIST WORKS: Julia Lovell for the Opium War of 1839; Peter Ward Fay, for further details of the war and the opium trade; and for the use of opium in China, Zhang Yangwen. Details of a eunuch's life were provided by Jia Yinghua's life of Sun Yaoting, of concubinage and servitude by Hsieh Bao Hua, of a servant's life by Ida Pruitt's account of Ning Lao T'ai-t'ai. For my descriptions of foot-binding I have relied upon the works of Dorothy Ko. For introducing me to the complex subject of the Manchu, I am grateful to Mark C. Elliott, and above all to Pamela Kyle Crossley, whose detailed investigation of three generations of a single Manchu family made it possible for me to create the fictional family of Guanji. For details of the Summer Palace, I owe thanks to Guo

Daiheng, Young-tsu Wong, and especially to Lillian M. Li's work on the Yuanmingyuan. In describing the imperial justice system and the law of torture, I relied upon an excellent monograph by Nancy Park. For the feng shui and characteristics of villages in southern China, I am indebted to an article by Xiaoxin He and Jun Luo. When writing on the Taiping, I drew upon the studies by Stephen R. Platt and by Jonathan Spence. I am especially grateful to Diana Preston for her day-by-day account of the siege of the legations during the Boxer Rebellion that gave me such rich material to work with.

I must add my personal thanks to Julia Lovell for her wise and helpful counsel in setting me on my path; to Dr James Greenbaum, Tess Johnston, and Mai Tsao for helpful conversations; to Sing Tsung-Ling and Hang Liu for their careful cultural readings of my initial drafts; and to Lynn Zhao for her thorough historical vetting of the entire manuscript. Any faults that remain are mine alone.

My many thanks are due to Rodney Paull for preparing maps with such exemplary care and patience.

Once again I thank my editors, William Thomas at Doubleday and Oliver Johnson at Hodder, not only for making such a wonderful team, but for all their great kindness and patience during the long and technically difficult writing of the draft. I also wish to thank Michael Windsor in America and Alasdair Oliver in Britain for their two very different but equally splendid cover jacket designs. My many thanks also to the team of Khari Dawkins, Maria Carella, Rita Madrigal, Michael Goldsmith, Lauren Weber and Kathy Hourigan at Doubleday.

My many thanks, as always, to Cara Jones and the whole team at RCW.

And finally, of course, I thank my agent, Gill Coleridge, to whom for the last thirty-six years I owe an incalculable debt of gratitude.

NAMES: The Chinese place names in this book are mostly given in their modern form, except in a few cases where Western characters use the names Canton and Peking in conversation, as they would have done in the nineteenth century.

CHINA

RED SUN YELLOW RIVER

January 1839

At first he did not hear the voice behind him. The red sun was glaring in his face as he rode across the centre of the world.

Forty miles since dawn. Hundreds to go. And not much time, perhaps no time at all. He did not know.

Soon the huge magenta sun would sink, a melancholy purple dusk would fall, and he would have to rest. Then on again at dawn. And all the time wondering: could he reach his father, whom he loved, and say he was sorry before it was too late? For his aunt's letter had been very clear: his father was dying.

'Mr Jiang!' He heard it this time. 'Jiang Shi-Rong! Wait!'

He turned his head. A single rider was urging his horse along the road. After the glare of the red sun in his eyes, it took Jiang a moment to see that it was Mr Wen's servant, Wong. What could that mean? He reined in his horse.

Wong – a small, plump, bald man who had originally come from the south – ran the house for the ageing scholar, who trusted him completely, and he'd taken young Jiang under his wing as soon as he'd come to stay there. He was perspiring. He must have been riding like an imperial messenger to catch me, the young man thought.

'Is Mr Wen all right?' Jiang asked anxiously.

'Yes, yes. He says you must return to Beijing at once.'

'Return?' Jiang looked at him in dismay. 'But my father's dying. I have to go to him.'

'You have heard of the lord Lin?'

'Of course.' All Beijing had been talking about the modest official, little known before, who had so impressed the emperor that he had been given a mission of great importance.

'He wants to see you. Right away.'

'Me?' He was a nobody. Not even that. An insignificant failure.

'Mr Wen wrote to the lord Lin about you. He knows the lord Lin from when they were students. But Mr Wen did not tell you, did not want to raise your hopes. When the lord Lin did not reply . . .' He made a sad face. 'Then this morning, after you left, Mr Wen received a message. Maybe the lord Lin will take you on his staff. But he needs to see you first. So Mr Wen tells me to ride like a thousand devils to get you back.' He looked at the young man intently. 'This is a big chance for you, Jiang Shi-Rong,' he said quietly. 'If the lord Lin is successful in his mission, and you please him, the emperor himself will hear your name. You will be on the path to fortune again. I am happy for you.' He made a little bow to indicate the young man's future status.

'But my father . . .'

'He may be dead already. You do not know.'

'And he may be alive.' As the young man looked away, his face was a picture of distress. 'I should have gone before,' he muttered to himself. 'I was too ashamed.' He turned to Wong again. 'If I go back now, it will cost me three days. Maybe more.'

'If you want to succeed, you must take chances. Mr Wen says your father would certainly want you to see the lord Lin.' The messenger paused. 'Mr Wen told the lord Lin that you speak Cantonese. Big point in your favour – for this mission.'

Shi-Rong said nothing. They both knew it was thanks to Wong that he could speak the servant's Cantonese dialect. At first it had amused the young mandarin to pick up some everyday expressions from Wong. He'd soon discovered that Cantonese was almost like another language. It also used more tones than Mandarin. But he had a good ear, and over a year or two, chatting to Wong every day, he'd begun to speak enough to get by. His father, who had a low opinion of the people of the south, had been ironically amused when he heard about this achievement. 'Though I suppose it could be useful, one day,' he allowed. But Mr Wen counselled him, 'Don't despise the Cantonese language, young man. It contains many ancient words that have since been lost in the Mandarin we speak.'

Wong was looking at him urgently. 'Mr Wen says you may never get a chance like this again,' he continued.

Jiang Shi-Rong gazed towards the red sun and shook his head miserably.

'I know that,' he said quietly.

For a minute neither of them moved. Then, with a heavy heart, the young man silently began to ride his horse along the road, back to Beijing.

o

By the end of that night, five hundred miles away, in the coastal lands west of the port then known to the outside world as Canton, a mist had drifted in from the South China Sea, shrouding the world in whiteness.

The girl went to the courtyard gate and looked out, thinking herself alone.

Despite the dawn mist, she could sense the presence of the sun, shining somewhere behind the haze; but she still couldn't see the edge of the pond, just thirty paces in front of her, nor the rickety wooden bridge upon which her father-in-law, Mr Lung, liked to watch the full moon and remind himself that he owned the pond and that he was the richest peasant in the hamlet.

She listened in the damp silence. Sometimes one might hear a soft splash as a duck stuck its head in the water and then shook it. But she heard nothing.

'Mei-Ling.' A hiss from somewhere to her right.

She frowned. She could just make out the shape of the bamboo clump that stood beside the path. Cautiously she took a step towards it.

'Who's that?'

'It's me. Nio.' A figure appeared beside the bamboo and came towards her.

'Little Brother!' Her face lit up. Even after the years of absence, there could be no mistaking him. He still bore the telltale scar across his nose and cheek.

Nio wasn't exactly her brother. Hardly a relation at all, one might say. He came from her grandmother's family, on her mother's side, who belonged to the Hakka tribe. After his mother and sisters died in a plague, his father had left him with Mei-Ling's parents for two years before he'd married again and taken the boy back.

His name was Niu, properly speaking. But in the dialect of his native village, it sounded more like Nyok, though one could hardly hear the final *k*. So Mei-Ling had compromised and invented the name Nio, with a short *o*, and so he'd remained ever since.

Long before his father had taken him back, Mei-Ling had adopted Nio as a brother, and she'd been his big sister ever since.

'When did you arrive?' she whispered.

'Two days ago. I came here to see you, but your mother-in-law told me not to come again. Then she came to your parents' house and told them not to let me near you.'

'Why did she do that?'

Although Nio, at fifteen, was only a year younger than Mei-Ling, she noticed that he still looked rather childish. He stared at the ground for a moment before confessing: 'It may have been something that I said.'

'Why are you here, Little Brother?'

'I ran away.' He smiled, as if this were a thing to be proud of.

'Oh, Nio . . .' And she was about to ask for details when he indicated that there was someone watching from the gate behind her.

'Wait at the entrance to the village tomorrow morning,' she told him hurriedly. 'I'll try to come at first light. If I don't, then come again the next day. Run now. Quick, quick.'

As Nio vanished behind the bamboo, she turned.

The oval-faced young woman stood by the gate. Willow was her sister-in-law. They called each other Sister, but all resemblance between them ended there.

Her name signified the graceful willow tree. Without her superior clothes, however, and the makeup she carefully applied to her face, she might have been thought rather plain. Willow came from a rich peasant family in the next county named Wan, and although she had married Mr Lung's elder son, the hamlet people politely referred to her, in the customary manner, as the Woman Wan. In keeping with the Wan family's more leisured status, Willow's feet had been bound when she was a girl, so that she now walked with the fashionable totter that marked her out from the poor peasants like Mei-Ling, whose family laboured in the fields.

Willow was a little taller and affected a slight, elegant droop, as though bowing in a ladylike manner. Mei-Ling was small and stood straight on her natural feet, like the working peasant girl she was. She'd also been known, ever since she was a tiny child, as the prettiest girl in the hamlet.

If her parents hadn't been so poor, they might have bound her feet and dressed her in fine clothes and sold her to a merchant in one of the local towns as a junior wife or concubine. But pretty though she was, no one could ever have imagined she would marry a son of Mr Lung.

In fact, most people thought the marriage was a scandal. Her mother-in-law had been furious.

There was one other difference between them. Willow had given her husband one child already – although, to his parents' displeasure, it was only a girl. Fortunately, however, she was now five months pregnant again.

As they went back into the front courtyard of the Lung house, Willow looked at Mei-Ling languidly.

'I know who that was.'

'Oh?'

'That was your cousin, Nio. I know all about him. You call him Little Brother.' She nodded slowly. 'Everyone in the house knows he's here, but we weren't allowed to tell you.'

'Not even my husband?'

'He wanted to. But he was afraid you might try to see Nio and get into trouble. He was trying to protect you. That's all.'

'Are you going to tell Mother?'

'You can trust me, Sister.'

There was a small orange tree in the courtyard. As Willow reached it, she paused.

'Don't try to see him, Sister. If Mother finds out, she'll whip you. Or something worse.'

o

It was early afternoon in Calcutta that day when a one-horse hackney cab, carrying two young Englishmen, made its way into the pleasant suburb of Chowringhee. The blinds were drawn fully down to keep out the harsh light – for although this was India's cool season, it was still brighter and hotter than most summer days in Britain.

Charlie Farley was a cheerful fellow. At cricket, which he played well, he had enough height to command respect. His face was somewhat round and seemed to be getting rounder as his fair hair receded from his brow. 'I'm not bald yet,' he'd cheerfully remark, 'but I'll be bald in time for tea.' His pale blue, bespectacled eyes were amiable, but by no means stupid. Not only at cricket, but in life generally, he played with a straight bat.

His friend John Trader was slightly taller, his hair the colour of black olives, slim, rather handsome. But his intense cobalt-blue eyes didn't look happy.

'This is all a terrible mistake,' he said in a gloomy voice.

'Nonsense, John,' said Charlie Farley. 'I told the colonel you'd saved my life. He'll be very civil to you.' A few moments later, the wheels of the cab crunched onto the gravel of a short driveway. 'Now, we'll just drop those letters with my aunt Harriet and be on our way. So try and look happy.'

His aunt's house was a typical colonial bungalow of the better sort, with a veranda front and back, whose wide eaves were supported by stout ionic columns painted white. Its airy central hall gave onto a plain but gracious drawing room and a dining room, both furnished in English style. As the two men reached the door, Indian servants, spotlessly dressed in white, seemed to appear from every corner.

Aunt Harriet had obviously heard the cab because she was already in the hall. Charlie loved his aunt. Like his own mother, her sister, she had still kept the wavy golden hair of her youth. She had frank blue eyes, and she and her husband offered any newcomer to British Calcutta the easy-going hospitality that was the hallmark of colonial merchant life.

'What are you doing here, Charlie?' she demanded. 'Shouldn't you boys be working?'

'We have been working, Aunt Harriet,' said Charlie. 'But a packet of letters arrived from England this morning, including one from Mother for you. Thought I'd bring it to you straightaway.'

Aunt Harriet smiled.

'And I suppose now you want to be fed?'

'Not at all. In fact, we can't stop. We're on our way to luncheon with Colonel Lomond.'

'Colonel Lomond? How very grand.'

'Father went to school with him, actually,' Charlie explained. 'So I wangled an invitation for us to lunch at his club. Thought it would amuse John to see the place.'

'Then you boys had better go,' said Aunt Harriet. 'You mustn't be late for Colonel Lomond.'

'We're off,' said Charlie.

It was time to have a man-to-man talk. And since they had ten minutes alone in the cab, Charlie decided to do it now.

'Do you know what's wrong with you, Trader?'

'Tell me.' Trader managed a half-smile.

'You're a good friend. I'd trust you with my life. But you're a moody fellow. Look at you today. All you have to do is observe and enjoy.'

'I know.'

'But it's deeper than that. Your trouble is that you're never satisfied. Whatever you've got, you always dream of more.'

'This may be true.'

'I mean, you were orphaned, which was damn bad luck. But not the end of the world. You went to a decent school. You were left a tidy bit of money. You've got me for a friend. We're in Rattrays, which is one of the best agency houses in India. And though you don't seem to believe it, you're a handsome devil, and half the women in Calcutta are in love with you. What more do you want?'

'I don't know, Charlie,' his friend confessed. 'Tell me about this Colonel Lomond we're to meet. He has a family?'

'A wife. I call on her occasionally. You know, politeness and all that. Gracious lady. His son's in the army, bit older than us. He has a daughter. Met her once or twice at the house. Quite handsome.' Charlie smiled. 'But I keep a distance. The colonel wouldn't like it if I got too pally.'

'Because he's an aristocrat.'

'Old Scottish family. Older brother in the ancestral castle – you know the sort of thing.'

'And we're merchants, Charlie. Tradesmen, dirt beneath his feet.'

'He treats me all right.'

'That's because your father went to school with him.' The dark-haired young man paused, and when his friend didn't reply, he continued: 'You know what annoys me, Charlie?'

'What?'

'Men like Lomond look down on us because we're in business. But what's the British Empire? A huge trading enterprise. Always has been. Who runs India? The East India Company. Who owns the army here? The East India Company. All right, the company nowadays is the British government in all but name, and much of the trade's in the hands of independent merchants like us. But the fact remains, the purpose of the army, in which Colonel Lomond and his class are officers, the reason for its existence, is to protect the trade. You and me. No merchants, no army.'

'You're not going to say that to him, are you?' Charlie asked nervously.

'I might.' Trader looked at him grimly, then smiled. 'Don't worry.'

Charlie pursed his lips, shook his head, and returned to his theme. 'Why can't you just play the game, John? The way things are, you and I have been dealt a pretty good hand. My father spent his life working for the East India Company and retired with a decent fortune, you know. He's got a big house in Bath. Our next-door neighbour's a major-general. Jolly old boy. Plays cards with my father. See what I mean? It'll do for me.'

'It's not to be sneezed at, Charlie.'

'But if I wanted more, here's how the game works. I may get lucky at Rattrays, finish up with enough to buy an estate, set myself up as a landed gentleman. Happens all the time. My son might get into a good regiment and find himself a brother officer of one of the Lomonds.' Farley looked at his friend seriously. 'That's the game of the social classes, Trader, if you want to play it.'

'It takes a long time.'

'Couple of generations, that's all. But you know what they say?' Charlie Farley leaned back and smiled. 'Respectability . . . is just a matter of dates.'

As he entered the stern portals of the Bengal Military Club, John Trader felt all his gloom return. For a start, his black frock coat, suitable only for the cooler British climate – yet which the club's dress code demanded that they wear – made him uncomfortably hot. And then, of course, there was the club itself.

The British were not yet rulers of all India, but they were masters of Bengal. And in Bengal's great city of Calcutta, the evidence was everywhere. At the racetrack. At the golf links. And nowhere more surely than on the Esplanade, where the great classical facade of the Bengal Military Club gazed down, in colonial splendour, at those who passed before its doors.

Who were these passersby? Why, Indians and Anglo-Indians, of course, but British persons, too: merchants, tradesmen, the middle classes and below – all those, that is, who did not rule, but worked.

For the members of the Bengal Military Club were rulers. Army officers, judges, administrators of the British Empire, successors to imperial

Rome – or so they saw themselves. Like the Roman senators they emulated, these warriors and landowners despised both the professions and, above all, tradesmen.

Colonel Lomond was already awaiting them in the big, airy lobby, from whose walls pictures of statesmen and generals stared down upon John, crushingly. He found himself marched into the dining room immediately.

The white linen tablecloth was starched, stiff as a board. Georgian silver, Wedgwood plates, heavy crystal glasses. Sherry served with the soup, to begin. French food might be in fashion, but the colonel disliked it, so honest beef was served with cabbage and potatoes, grown locally in British-run market gardens. The wine was excellent. In short, they might have been at a club in the heart of London.

As for Colonel Lomond himself, he was in uniform that day, a handsome scarlet tunic and black trousers. He was tall, slim; his thinning hair was still dark. His eyebrows turned up at the ends so that he looked like a noble hawk. He was every inch the Scottish chief.

It was clear that he was quite determined to be friendly to young Farley, whom he addressed as 'my boy', referring to Mr Farley senior, now residing in Bath, as 'your dear father'.

'I had a letter from your dear father. He says old General Frobisher's living near him.'

'Did you know him, sir?'

'Yes. A great sportsman. Big game.'

'Tigers?'

'Certainly. When he first came out, you know, they used to hunt on foot. Not the big affairs with elephants, like nowadays.' He gave Charlie an approving nod.

What was it about Charlie Farley that made Colonel Lomond like him? Partly, of course, that he was an amiable fellow, just as his father had been. Straightforward, polite, easy. But something more. He knew where he fitted in, and he was content to be there. Charlie would never overstep the bounds. When he'd told Lomond frankly that he had a friend who'd be interested to see inside the club, but that he'd no way of satisfying his friend's interest, 'unless you were to invite us to lunch, sir', Lomond had invited them at once. 'Cheeky young fellow,' the colonel had later remarked to his wife, with the same approval he would have accorded a daring young officer. But Charlie would never embarrass him by trying to join the club. Not that Colonel Lomond would have minded, particularly, if Charlie Farley was a member. But that, of course, was not the point. As all who governed Britain's empire knew, the point was not the individual case, but what it might lead to.

Which brought the colonel's gaze to John Trader.

There was something about young Trader that Lomond did not like. He wasn't sure what. Naturally, since the dark-haired young man was Farley's friend, he'd be pleasant towards him. But his years of living in India and observing men had developed in Colonel Lomond a sixth sense. And at this moment he was experiencing the same unease he'd once felt just before he discovered a cobra in his house.

'What part of the country do you come from?' he tried. Always a safe question.

'I was brought up in the West Country first, sir,' Trader replied. 'Then just outside London. Blackheath.'

'Blackheath, eh? Used to be highwaymen up there in the old days, what?' Though it was said in a jocular way, was there a subterranean hint that Trader might be a highwayman himself? Of course not. 'You have family there now?'

'I've no family living,' Trader replied.

'Nobody at all?'

'There used to be some distant relations of my father's, generations ago, I believe. But there was a family quarrel, and they never spoke again. I don't even know their names or where they might be.'

'Oh.' The colonel tried another tack. 'You and Farley here weren't at school together, were you?'

'No, sir. Charterhouse.'

'Fine old school.' The colonel took a sip of wine. Not quite Harrow, of course, where he and the Farleys had gone.

'Trader saved my life, sir,' Charlie said hopefully.

Colonel Lomond looked at Charlie noncommittally. They both knew that Charlie had already told him. But the colonel did not wish to grant this dark stranger a triumph.

'Glad to hear it,' he said with a brief nod. 'If we have dinner someday,' he added vaguely to Trader, 'you must tell me the whole story.'

———

The tablecloth was removed for the dessert course. The colonel passed the decanter of port around the table. They had eaten well. If the colonel had not addressed Trader directly during the meal, while he looked fondly at Charlie, it could be taken for absent-mindedness. Now, however, it seemed there was something on his mind.

'Tell me, my boy, your agency house, Rattrays . . .' He leaned towards Charlie just enough to indicate concern. 'They're all right, aren't they?'

'Absolutely, sir. Sound as a bell.' Charlie smiled. 'My father asked me the same thing. After the last crash, sir, Rattrays believes in moderation.'

'Good.' The colonel nodded, relieved. It was only two years since the collapse of the mighty trading house of Palmers – a victim of the excessive greed and debt that periodically returns, like the plague, to every market – had brought down most of the agency houses in Calcutta, ruining countless widows and orphans. 'Of course,' the colonel conceded over his glass of port, 'back in the last century, some of the East India Company nabobs made vast fortunes in just a few years.' A faraway look came into his eyes, indicating that, should chance place it in his path, even a valiant soldier like himself wouldn't take an extra hundred thousand pounds amiss.

'The only fellows who make those quick fortunes at the moment, sir,' Charlie said, 'are the men who go over to Canton, in the China trade.'

'So I hear. Bit of a dirty business, isn't it?' the colonel added quietly.

'Well, we're not in it, sir,' said Charlie, receiving a nod of approval in return.

And now, having remained politely silent for so long, John Trader decided to speak.

'I'm sorry you don't like the China trade, sir,' he remarked. 'It's based on tea, isn't it?' Was there the faintest hint of menace in his tone?

'Tea. Of course,' the colonel grunted.

'The British drink tea, which is imported from China, because that's almost the only place which grows it. The tea is taxed. And the tea tax pays for most of the running costs of the British Navy.'

'I really wouldn't know,' said the colonel.

'So it can't be the tea you object to, sir,' Trader continued. 'Is it the opium we supply to the Chinese in return for the tea that you don't like?'

'It's up to the Chinese what they buy, I daresay,' Colonel Lomond remarked, with a glance at Charlie to indicate that he'd had enough of this.

'The English cup of tea,' Charlie cut in cheerfully. 'You wouldn't believe people could drink so much. It's not as if anyone really needs tea. But they insist on having it. More every year.' He gave Trader a warning look. 'Actually, it's all paid for in silver, you know.' He turned to the colonel. 'I'm afraid, sir, that we must be going. You know, work and all that.'

'Of course, my boy. Always a pleasure to see you,' Lomond said gratefully.

'It's a triangular trade,' Trader went on, quietly but relentlessly. 'Chinese dealers get their hands on opium through our Canton agency men. Those Chinese pay our agency men with silver. The agency men use the silver to buy tea. But where does the opium come from? India. Bengal mostly. Grown by the East India Company. Surely that's right, isn't it, sir?'

Colonel Lomond did not answer. He rose from the table. Taking Charlie by the arm in a friendly manner, but in a way that obliged Trader to walk behind, he led them towards the door.

Moments later, they were all walking down the steps of the club together and would have parted there and then in the street if a voice had not interrupted them.

'Papa!' It came from a covered carriage where, accompanied by her mother, a servant, a coachman and outriders, a young lady dressed in silks and carrying a parasol was being driven along the Esplanade. The carriage stopped.

'Good afternoon, Papa,' said Agnes Lomond. 'Have you had a good lunch?'

Colonel Lomond hadn't expected this encounter, but turned to his daughter with a smile, and to his wife with a look of caution which that lady noted at once.

'You both know young Farley, of course,' he said genially as the two women greeted Charlie. 'And this,' he added vaguely, indicating Trader with a hand that had suddenly gone limp, 'is a friend of his.'

'John Trader,' said Trader, smiling politely at Mrs Lomond before shifting his glance towards her daughter. But once resting on the younger woman, his dark blue eyes did not move.

Agnes Lomond was twenty and already a lady. There was no other word for it. Her mother was a handsome, stately matron. But Agnes was slim, like her father, and a little taller than her mother. Her face, well protected from the sun, showed a wonderful pale complexion. If her nose was too long for her to be called pretty, it served only to make her look more aristocratic. Of her character, it was impossible to guess anything at all.

Perhaps it was this reserve, or her auburn hair, or the fact that she was socially unattainable, or her dark walnut eyes, or a deep desire to steal her from her father – but whatever the causes, John Trader's mouth opened and he stared at Agnes Lomond like a man in a trance.

Her mother saw it and intervened at once. 'Will you go with us?' she asked her husband, who promptly stepped up into the carriage. 'We must let you and your friend get to your work, Mr Farley.' She gave Charlie a nod, to which he returned a bow as the carriage moved off.

But Trader forgot to bow. He only stood and stared.

o

The red sun was setting once again when Jiang Shi-Rong, emerging from the pine groves through which the old road led, came in sight of the city. High above, like a heavenly rib cage, great bars of cloud lay across the sky, catching the orange glow of the sun in the west. As he always did, whenever he gazed upon its mighty walls, its towers, its huge curved roofs of gleaming tiles, Jiang Shi-Rong caught his breath.

Beijing. It was magnificent.

Yet was it his city?

Jiang knew that the people who called themselves the Han – his people – had built a walled city on the site three thousand years ago. But it was only five centuries ago that Kubla Khan, a grandson of Genghis, the mighty Mongol conqueror, had made himself overlord of China and, after building fabulous Xanadu on his summer hunting grounds in the steppes, had chosen this northern town as his Chinese capital.

But after less than a century, a native Han dynasty, the shining Ming, had managed to kick the Mongols out and strengthen the Great Wall to deter other invaders. They'd kept Kubla Khan's capital, however. And for three centuries the Ming had ruled China.

It had been a golden age. Literature and the arts had thrived. Chinese scholars had printed the greatest encyclopaedia of herbal medicine the world had ever seen. Chinese fleets explored westwards to Africa. Ming porcelain was the envy of the world.

But even the shining Ming came to an end. The pattern had been seen in China so many times before: a gradual degeneration, a weak emperor, a peasant revolt, an ambitious general trying to seize power. And in this case, another huge invasion from the north – this time a confederation of clans – the Manchu – from the vast forests and plains northeast of the Great Wall.

The Manchu armies were organised into great companies, known as banners, each led by a prince or trusted chief. As the Ming Empire crumbled and fell under their yoke, its great cities were garrisoned by bannermen, and remained so as the centuries passed.

As for the proud Han Chinese, they were now a subject people. Their men were forced to adopt the Manchu hairstyle, shaving the front of their heads and plaiting the rest of their hair into a single long braid – a pigtail or 'queue' – that hung down their backs.

Yet if the Chinese had succumbed, their culture had not. To be sure, the Manchu were proud of their heroic warrior past, but as masters now of the huge cities, palaces and temples of China, they soon gave themselves a Chinese name – the Qing, or Ch'ing – and ruled more or less as conventional Chinese emperors. The Qing emperors performed the eternal sacrifices to the gods. Some became quite erudite in Chinese literature.

Jiang owed them obedience. Yet even now, like many Han Chinese, he still knew that it was he and his people who were the true inheritors of the millennia of Chinese culture, and that he should have been superior to the overlords he served.

The huge outer wall before him ran four miles across, from east to west, with a mighty gatehouse in the centre. Inside the wall, on the right, raised above the surrounding world on a great mound, he could see the great drumlike pagoda at the Temple of Heaven, before which the emperor performed the ancient ceremonies to ask the gods for good harvests, its three tiers of blue-tiled roofs turning to indigo under the reddening embers of the clouds.

After passing through the gateway, he and Wong continued due north on a raised causeway for another couple of miles towards the even more impressive four-mile-square enclosure of the Inner City, protected by its perimeter wall with mighty guard towers at each corner.

Dusk was falling as they entered, past bannermen guards in their Manchu hats, jerkins and boots. The market stalls on each side of the wide road were closing, their signs being taken down. Refuse collectors, a few in wide-brimmed hats, most in skullcaps, were stooping over their shovels and spooning manure into big earthenware pots. A faint smell of dung, seasoned with soya and ginseng, filled the air.

This Inner City was by no means the centre of Beijing. For within it, behind the colossal Tiananmen Gate, lay another walled citadel, the Imperial City; and within that, across a moat, hidden from almost all eyes by its purple walls, the golden-roofed Forbidden City, the innermost sanctum, the vast palace and grounds of the celestial emperor himself.

Their path this evening took them to the northeastern quarter of the Inner City, to a quiet street where, in a pleasant house beside a small temple, the scholar Mr Wen resided. Jiang was tired and looking forward to a rest.

But no sooner had they entered the little courtyard than the old scholar hurried out.

'At last,' he cried. 'You must go to the lord Lin. He leaves tomorrow. But he will see you tonight if you go at once. At once.' He thrust a written pass to the Imperial City into Jiang's hand. 'Wong will lead you,' he directed. 'He knows the way.'

They entered on foot, not by the great Tiananmen Gate, but by a lesser entrance in the Imperial City's eastern wall; and they soon came to a handsome government guesthouse with wide, sweeping eaves, where the lord Lin was lodging. And a few minutes later Shi-Rong found himself in a small hall where the lord Lin was seated on a big carved rosewood chair.

At first glance, there was nothing so remarkable about him. He might have been any thickset, middle-aged mandarin. His small, pointed beard was greying, his eyes set wide apart. Given his stern reputation, Jiang had expected the High Commissioner's lips to be thin, but in fact they were rather full.

Yet there was something very dignified about him, a stillness. He might have been the abbot of a monastery.

Jiang bowed.

'I had already chosen a young man to join my staff as secretary.' Lord Lin addressed him quietly, without any introduction. 'But then he fell ill. I waited. He grew worse. Meanwhile, I had received a letter about you from Mr Wen, a scholar whom I trust. I took it as a sign. He told me about you. Some good things, some less good.'

'This humble servant is deeply honoured that his teacher Mr Wen should think of him, High Commissioner, and knew nothing of his letter,' Jiang confessed. 'Mr Wen's opinion in all matters is just.'

A slight nod signified that this answer satisfied.

'He has also told me that you were travelling to visit your dying father.'

'Confucius tells us, "Honour thy father", High Commissioner.'

In all the *Analects of Confucius,* there was no more central theme.

'And thy father's fathers,' Lin added quietly. 'Nor would I hinder you in your duty. But I have called you here on a great matter, and my commission is from the emperor himself.' He paused. 'First I must know you better.' He gave Jiang a stern look. 'Your name, Shi-Rong, means "scholarly honour". Your father had high hopes of you. But you failed your exams.'

'This humble servant did.' Jiang hung his head.

'Why? Did you work hard enough?'

'I thought I had. I am ashamed.'

'Your father passed the metropolitan exams at his first attempt. Did you desire to do better than him?'

'No, Excellency. That would be disrespectful. But I felt I had let him down. I wished only to please him.'

'You are his only son?' He looked at Jiang sharply, and when the young man nodded, he remarked: 'That is not an easy burden. Did you find the exams frightening?'

'Yes, High Commissioner.'

That was an understatement. The journey to the capital. The line of little cubicles into which each candidate was locked for the entire three-day duration of the exam. It was said that if you died during the process, they wrapped your body and threw it over the city wall.

'Some candidates smuggle papers in with them. They cheat. Did you?'

Jiang started. An instant flash of anger and pride appeared upon his face before he could control it. He immediately bowed his head respectfully before looking up again. 'Your servant did not, High Commissioner.'

'Your father had a good career, though a modest one. He did not retire a wealthy man.' Lin paused again, looking at Jiang, who was not sure what to make of it. But remembering Lin's reputation for rigid correctness in all his dealings, he answered truthfully.

'I believe, Excellency, that my father never took a bribe in all his life.'

'If he had,' the older man replied quietly, 'you would not be here.'

He gave Jiang another thoughtful look. 'We are measured not only by our triumphs, young man, but by our persistence. If we fail, we must try harder. I also failed the metropolitan exams the first time. Did you know that?'

'No, Commissioner.'

'I took them a second time. I failed again. The third time, I passed.' He let that sink in, then continued sternly. 'If you become my secretary, you will have to be strong. You will have to work hard. If you fail, you will learn from your mistakes and you will do better. You will never give up. Do you understand?'

'Yes, Commissioner.'

'Mr Wen tells me that he thinks you will pass next time. But first you should work for me. Do you agree?'

'Yes, Excellency.'

'Good.' Lin nodded. 'Tell me what you know about opium.'

'People who can afford it like to smoke,' Jiang offered. 'But if they become addicted, they waste all their money. It makes them sick. The emperor has made opium illegal.' He paused, wondering if he dared to say the truth. 'But everyone seems to get it.'

'Correct. In the last generation, the traffic has grown ten times. The numbers of people addicted until they are useless, reduced to poverty, ruined, killed . . . It's terrible. The people cannot pay their taxes. Silver is flowing out of the empire to pay for opium instead.'

'Some opium is grown in China, I believe.'

'Also true. But nearly all of it now is coming from across the seas. Our Chinese smugglers buy it from the barbarian pirates. So what are we to do?'

Did he expect an answer to the question?

'Your servant has heard, Excellency, that it is possible to turn people away from this addiction.'

'We try. But it is very uncertain. The emperor has given me authority to take all steps needed. I shall execute the smugglers. What other problems occur to you?' He watched the young man, saw his awkwardness. 'You are working for me now. You are to tell me the truth at all times.'

Shi-Rong took a deep breath. 'I have heard, Excellency – though I hope it may not be true – that local officials on the coast are paid by the smugglers not to see their activities.'

'We shall catch them and punish them. If necessary, with death.'

'Ah.' It began to dawn upon Jiang that this was not going to be an easy assignment. To refuse bribes oneself was one thing; to earn the enmity of half the officials on the coastland was another. Not good for his career.

'You will have no friends, young man, but the emperor and me.'

Shi-Rong bowed his head. He wondered if he could feign a sudden sickness – as, it now occurred to him, the other young man in line for the post might have done. No, he didn't think so.

'Your servant is greatly honoured.' And then, despite the cold horror that was growing in his mind, he felt a curiosity to ask one further question. 'How will you deal with the pirates, Excellency? The barbarians from over the seas.'

'I have not yet decided. We shall see when we get to the coast.'

Shi-Rong bowed his head again. 'I have one request, Commissioner. May I see my father?'

'Go to him at once. Either to bury him or to bid him farewell. It will please him that you have received such a position. But you must not stay with him. Despite your duty to remain and mourn him, you must continue at once to the coast. You will consider that a command from the emperor himself.'

Shi-Rong hardly knew what to think as he and Wong made their way back to the house of Mr Wen. All he knew was that he needed to sleep, and that he would set out again at dawn.

The following morning, he was surprised to find that Wong was all saddled up and ready to ride with him.

'He will ride with you as far as Zhengzhou,' Mr Wen informed him. 'You must practise speaking Cantonese all the way.'

His old teacher thought of everything.

o

By evening, Mei-Ling was racked with fear. Not that anything had been said. Not yet, at least. She'd performed all the tasks her mother-in-law demanded. During the afternoon the older woman had gone to a neighbour's, and Mei-Ling had breathed a little easier. The men had been out in the bamboo forest on the hill. Willow had been resting, which, considering her condition and her family's wealth, she was allowed to do. So Mei-Ling had been left alone with her thoughts.

Had Sister Willow kept her secret? Or did her mother-in-law know about Nio's visit that morning? Mother usually knew everything. Perhaps some punishment was being prepared for her.

And then there was tomorrow morning to worry about. Mei-Ling cursed her own stupidity. Why had she told Nio she would meet him?

Because she loved him, of course. Because he was her Little Brother. But what had possessed her? She hadn't even talked to her husband about it – her husband, whom she loved even more than Little Brother. Even her husband couldn't protect her from Mother, though. No young Chinese wife disobeyed her mother-in-law.

She'd better not go. She knew it. Nio would understand. But she had given her word. She might be poor, but Mei-Ling prided herself that she never broke her word. Perhaps because she and her family were held of no account in the village, this pride in her word had always been a point of honour with her, ever since she'd been a little girl.

How would she do it, anyway? Even if she slipped out undetected, what were the chances of getting back without her absence being noted? Slim at best. And what then? There was no way to escape a terrible punishment.

Perhaps one. Just perhaps. But she wasn't sure. That was the trouble.

The evening began well enough. Her husband's family owned the best of the peasant farmhouses in the village. Behind the main courtyard was a big central room where, as usual, they had all gathered.

Opposite her on a wide bench, Willow sat with her husband, Elder Son. Despite his rawboned body and his hands, still dirty from his work, too gnarled to match the elegance of Willow, the two of them looked quite comfortable under his mother's gaze. Elder Son drank a little huangjiu rice wine and addressed a remark to his wife from time to time. When Willow's eyes met Mei-Ling's, there was no sign of guilt upon her face, nor of complicity. Lucky Willow. She'd been brought up never to show any expression at all.

Mei-Ling sat beside Second Son on a bench. Left to themselves, they were usually talkative; but they knew better than to have a conversation now. If they did, his mother would shut them up with a peremptory 'You talk too much to your wife, Second Son.' But from where she was sitting, Mother could not quite see that Mei-Ling was discreetly touching his hand.

People thought Second Son was the fool of the family. Hardworking, he was shorter than his older brother and always seemed contented, to the point that he'd soon received the nickname Happy – a name that suggested he might be a bit simple-minded. But Mei-Ling knew better. Certainly he wasn't ambitious or worldly-wise, or he'd never have married her. But he was just as intelligent as the rest of them. And he was kind. They'd only been married six months, and she was in love with him already.

There hadn't been a chance to tell him about Nio since he came in. She was sure he'd beg her not to go, just to keep peace in the family. So what could she do? Sneak out at dawn without telling him?

At the back of the big room, old Mr Lung was playing mah-jong with three of his neighbours.

Mr Lung was always very calm. With his small grey beard, his skull-cap and his long, thin pigtail hanging down his back, he looked like a kindly sage. Now that he had two grown sons, he was content to step back from life and leave most of the hard work to them – though he still supervised his fields and collected all his rents. When he went around the village, he would give sweets to the children, but if their parents owed him money, he'd be sure he got it from them. Mr Lung didn't talk much, but when he did, it was usually to let people know that he was richer and wiser than his neighbours.

'A merchant once told me,' he remarked, 'that he had seen a mah-jong set made of little blocks of ivory.' His set was made of bamboo. Poor people used mah-jong playing cards.

'Oh, Mr Lung,' one of the neighbours politely asked, 'will you buy an ivory set? That would be very elegant.'

'Perhaps. But so far I have never seen such a thing myself.'

They continued to play. His wife watched silently from her chair nearby. Her hair was pulled back tightly over her head, accentuating her high cheekbones. Her hard eyes were turned towards the tiles. Her expression seemed to indicate that if she had been playing, she would have done better.

After a time she turned towards Mei-Ling. 'I saw your mother in the street today.' She stared balefully. 'She had a boy with her. A Hakka boy.' She paused. 'Your mother is a Hakka,' she added unpleasantly.

'Her mother was Hakka,' Mei-Ling said. 'She is only half Hakka.'

'You are the first Hakka in our family,' her mother-in-law continued coldly.

Mei-Ling looked down. The message was clear. Her mother-in-law was telling her she knew about Nio's visit – and waiting for her to confess. Should she do so? Mei-Ling knew she'd better. But a tiny flame of rebellion stirred deep within her. She said nothing. Her mother-in-law continued to stare.

'There are many tribes in southern China,' Mr Lung announced, looking up from his game. 'The Han moved in and dominated them. But the Hakka people are different. The Hakka people are a branch of the Han. They also came here from the north. They have their own customs, but they are like cousins to the Han.'

Mother said nothing. She might rule everyone else, but she could not argue with the head of the house. At least not in public.

'I have always heard so, Mr Lung,' one of the neighbours chimed in.

'The Hakka people are brave,' said Mr Lung. 'They live in big round houses. People say they mixed with tribes from the steppe beyond the Great Wall, people like the Manchu. This is why even the rich Hakka do not bind their women's feet.'

'People say they are very independent,' said the neighbour.

'They are trouble!' Mother suddenly shouted at Mei-Ling. 'This Nio you call your Little Brother is a troublemaker. A criminal.' She paused only to draw breath. 'From the family of your mother's mother. He's not even your relation.' For indeed, in the eyes of the Han Chinese, such a relationship on the female side hardly counted as family at all.

'I don't think Nio has broken the law, Mother,' Mei-Ling said softly. She had to defend him.

The older woman didn't even bother to reply. She turned to her younger son.

'You see what this leads to? Marriage is not a game. That's why parents choose the bride. Different village, different clan; rich girl for rich boy, poor girl for poor boy. Otherwise, only trouble. You know the saying: the doors of the house should match. But no. You are obstinate. The matchmaker finds you a good bride. The families agree. Then you refuse to obey your own father. You disgrace us. And next, suddenly you tell us you want to marry this girl.' She glared at Mei-Ling. 'This pretty girl.'

Pretty. It was almost an accusation. Every peasant family, even an important family like the Lungs, approved the good old adage: the ugly wife is a treasure at home. A rich man might choose a pretty girl as his concubine. But an honest peasant wanted a wife who would work hard, look after him and his parents, too. Pretty girls were suspect. They might be too vain to work. Worse, they might be coveted by other men.

All in all, the village had concluded, Second Son's behaviour had proved that he was a fool.

'She's from a different clan,' he pointed out amiably.

'Clan? There are five clans in this village. You choose the smallest clan and the poorest family. Not only that, her Hakka grandmother was a merchant's concubine. He threw her out when he was passing through the nearest town. She takes up with a plasterer, and they were glad to find a poor peasant to put a roof over their daughter's head. A leaking roof. These are the parents of your bride.'

Mei-Ling bowed her head during this tirade. Though it was hurtful, she wasn't embarrassed. There are no secrets in a village. Everybody knew.

'And now,' her mother-in-law concluded, 'she wants to bring criminals into our house. And you just sit there and smile. No wonder people call you the family fool.'

Mei-Ling glanced at her husband. He was sitting there quite still, not saying a word. But on his face was the quiet, happy smile she knew so well.

That smile was one of the reasons people thought he was simple-minded. It was the same smile he'd worn, week after week, as his parents raged at him about his refusal to take the bride they chose. He'd even smiled when they'd threatened to throw him out of the house.

And that smile had worked. He'd worn them down. Mei-Ling knew it. He'd worn them down because, against all reason, he wanted to marry her.

'You made a good marriage for my older brother. Be content with that.' He said it calmly and quietly.

For a moment his mother was silent. They all knew that her elder son's marriage to Willow would be perfect – as soon as she produced a male child. But not until then. She turned her attention back to Mei-Ling. 'One day this Nio of yours will be executed. The sooner the better. You are not to see him. You understand?'

Everyone looked at Mei-Ling. Nobody spoke.

'Mah-jong,' said Mr Lung calmly, and scooped up all the money on the table.

It was Willow who noticed the figure in the entrance, and she signalled to her mother-in-law, who with both her sons and their wives immediately rose in respect.

Their guest was an old man. His face was thin, his beard long and white as snow. His eyes had narrowed with age and turned down at the corners, as if he were almost asleep. But he was still the elder of the village. Mr Lung went forward to greet him.

'I am honoured that you have come, Elder.'

They served him green tea, and for several minutes they made the customary small talk. Then the old man turned to his host. 'You said you had something to show me, Mr Lung.'

'Indeed.' Mr Lung rose and disappeared through a doorway.

At the back of the big room was an alcove, occupied by a large divan upon which two people might easily recline. The women now set another low table in front of the divan. By the time this was done, Mr Lung re-entered, carrying his prizes, which were wrapped in silk. Carefully he unwrapped the first and handed it to the old man for inspection, while the three neighbours gathered around to watch.

'I bought this when I went to Guangzhou last month,' Mr Lung told the elder. 'If you go to an opium parlour, they are made of bamboo. But I bought this from a dealer.'

It was an opium pipe. The long shaft was made of ebony, the bowl of bronze. Around the section below the bowl, known as the saddle, was a band of highly worked silver. The mouthpiece was made of ivory. The dark pipe gleamed softly. There were murmurs of admiration.

'I hope this pipe will suit you, Elder, if we smoke together this evening,' said Mr Lung. 'It is for my most honoured guests.'

'Most certainly, most certainly,' said the old man.

Then Mr Lung unwrapped the second pipe. And everyone gasped.

Its construction was more complex. An inner bamboo pipe was enclosed in a copper tube and the copper had been coated in Canton enamel painted green and decorated with designs in blue and white and gold. The bowl had been given a red glaze and decorated with little black bats – the Chinese symbol of happiness. The mouthpiece was made of white jade.

'Ah . . . Very costly.' The old man said what everyone was thinking.

'If you recline on the divan, Elder, I will prepare our pipes,' said Mr Lung.

It was the signal for the neighbours to retire. This smoking of opium was a private ceremony to which only the elder had been asked.

Mr Lung brought out a lacquer tray, put it on the low table and began to set out the accoutrements with the same care a woman would use to prepare a tea ceremony. First there was the small brass oil lamp with a glass funnel on top. Then two needles, a pair of spittoons, a ceramic saucer-sized dish and a little glass opium jar, beside which lay a tiny bone spoon.

Taking one of the needles, he first poked in the bowl of each pipe to make sure they were completely clean. Next, he lit the little brass oil lamp. Taking the bone spoon between finger and thumb, he extracted a small quantity of opium from the jar and placed it on the ceramic dish, and using the spoon and the needle, he carefully rolled the opium into a pea-shaped ball.

Now it was time to heat the ball of opium. This required care and skill. Picking it up with the point of the needle, he held it gently over the lamp. Slowly, as the old man watched, the little bud of opium began to swell, and its colour changed, from dark brown to amber.

Then, as the two men watched, the bud of opium turned to gold, and Mr Lung placed it in the bowl of the elder's pipe. The old man adjusted his position so that he was lying on the divan with his head towards the low table and the lamp. Mr Lung showed him how to hold the bowl of his pipe close to the lamp so that the heat would vaporise the golden opium within – but not too close, or the opium would get burned. And after the old man had done this successfully and drawn on the pipe correctly, Mr Lung started to prepare his own pipe.

'Did you know, Elder, that the opium increases a man's sexual staying power?' he asked.

'Ah. That is very interesting,' said the old man, 'very interesting.'

'Though your wife died two years ago,' his host remarked.

'All the same, I might find another,' the elder replied. His face was already wearing a seraphic expression.

Out in the courtyard, Mother sat with her family in silence. Whether she approved of the opium, it was impossible to know. But as a display of the family's wealth that made the other folk in the hamlet more respectful and afraid of her, she was bound to welcome it.

Second Son was tired that night, and Mei-Ling thought he had fallen asleep until he spoke. 'I know you love Nio. I'm sorry about Mother.'

With a little rush of relief, she burst out in an anguished whisper. 'I felt so bad. I promised him I'd go to meet him. But I suppose I can't now. I'd never do anything to upset you.'

'I don't mind if you see Nio. It's Mother who minds.' And he put his arm around her as her tears flowed. By the time she stopped, he was fast asleep.

All things seem possible in the morning. It was only when she awoke, slipped into the courtyard, and saw the morning mist that Mei-Ling realised what she could do. For what she saw, as she peeped out from the gate towards the pond, was not the mist of the day before, but a thick white fog. Impenetrable. Comprehensive. Like a cloak of invisibility sent her by the gods. The sort of fog in which, if you were foolish enough to enter it, you might be lost at once.

So she had an excuse. She'd stepped out and got lost. Just wandered along the path and got lost. Who could possibly prove where she had been? Nobody could see.

She went back into her room. Her dear husband was still asleep. She wanted to kiss him, but she was afraid he might wake. Quickly putting on a pair of loose leggings under her tunic, she stepped into her clogs, took a shawl and slipped out of the room. As she went through the yard, she could hear the village elder snoring from the divan. Obviously he had stayed the night. The door to Willow's room was not quite closed. Was her sister-in-law watching? She hoped not. Moments later, she was outside, enveloped in the fog.

It was lucky she knew exactly where the little footbridge was, because she couldn't see it. After a couple of fumbles she found the handrails and started across. She could smell the reeds in the mud. The wooden boards creaked beneath her feet. Would anyone hear, in the house?

At the far end, she stepped onto the path and turned right. Beside the path, thick green bamboo shoots towered over her. She could hardly see them, but drops of dew from their leaves fell softly on her head as she made her way over the rutted track that led around the edge of the hamlet. A faint tangy scent rose from the ground. She knew, without needing to see it, when she was passing a small grove of banana trees.

And it was just then that she heard the sound. A faint creaking coming across the water behind her. Someone was crossing the little bridge. A cold fear stabbed her. Had Willow seen her go out and told her mother-in-law? She hurried forwards, tripped on a root, almost fell, but recovered herself. If she could get to the meeting place before the older woman caught her, she might be able to hide with Nio in the fog. She listened again. Silence. Either Mother had stopped or she must be on the track.

The path rose up a short incline. At the top it met the dirt road by the entrance to the hamlet. As she reached the road, she could make out the tiny stone shrine, which contained a little wooden figure of a man – though she always thought he looked more like a shrivelled old monkey. The ancestral founder of the hamlet was there to protect his clan, and the hamlet in general. She asked for his blessing, though she wasn't sure she'd get it.

This was where she'd told Nio to meet her. She called his name, softly.

The fog here was more like a thick low mist. It covered the rice fields behind her and the stream where the ducks lived, just ahead on the left; but she could make out the roofs of the huts higher up the road ahead, the modest hill beyond, and the encircling arms of the two small ridges – Blue Dragon and White Tiger, the villagers called them – that protected the hamlet on each side.

Normally the village was a pleasant place. Cool summer breezes came up from the sea in summer; the low sun gave its gentle warmth in winter. The wind and waters – the feng shui – of the hamlet were good. But it would be like one of the eighteen layers of hell if Mother caught her now. She stared into the mist anxiously. She couldn't wait here.

She called Nio's name again. Nothing. There was only one thing to do. If he came out to meet her, even in this mist, she surely couldn't miss him on the narrow road. Muttering a curse, she hurried into the hamlet.

Her parents' house was nothing much to look at. There was no little courtyard in front with a gate onto the street, like the houses on either side. An assortment of wooden boards formed the front of the dwelling, into which an old door, taken years ago from a neighbour's house when it was being pulled down, had been inserted, not quite vertically, so that it seemed to fall rather than swing into the dark interior that was the main room. There was no upper floor to speak of, but an inside ladder allowed her parents to creep up to a low loft space where they could sleep.

As soon as she reached the rickety wooden door, she shoved it open.

'Nio!' she whispered urgently. 'Nio.'

There was a rustling sound from the shadows, then his voice. 'Big Sister. It's you.'

'Of course it's me. Where were you?'

'I didn't think you'd come.'

'I said I would.'

'Daughter.' Her father's head appeared now, upside down, from the top of the ladder. 'Go home. Go home. You shouldn't be here.' Then her mother's voice from the same place: 'You must go back. Quick, quick.' That was all she needed.

She pushed the door closed behind her. 'If anyone comes, say I'm not here,' she called to her parents.

At the back of the house there was a small yard. She stepped into it. Nio was up now, pulling on his shirt. He joined her, dishevelled, but eager to make amends.

'I didn't think you'd get away,' he said, 'and with this fog . . .'

As she stood in the little yard in the morning mist, Mei-Ling looked at him sadly. 'So you ran away from home. Is your family looking for you?'

'No. I told my father I wanted to come and see you all. He gave me money and a present for your parents. I said I'd stay here awhile.'

'But you don't want to go back. Is it your stepmother? Is she unkind?'

'No. She's all right.'

'I heard you've a new little brother and sister. Don't you like them?'

'They're all right.' He looked awkward, then burst out: 'They treat me like a child.'

'We're always children to our parents, Nio,' she said gently. But she could see that she wasn't getting through. There was probably some family quarrel or humiliation that he wasn't telling her about. 'Where will you go?' she asked.

'The big city. Guangzhou.' He smiled. 'You taught me to speak Cantonese.'

Guangzhou, on the Pearl River, the great port that the foreigners called Canton. When he'd first arrived as a little boy, he spoke only the language of the Hakka village where he lived. No one could understand a word he said. It had taken her months to teach him the Cantonese dialect of the village – a rustic version of the tongue spoken in the big city, though intelligible there, at least. But the thought of her Little Brother wandering alone in the great port filled her with fear.

'You don't know anybody there, Nio. You'll be lost. Don't go,' she begged him. 'In any case, what would you do?'

'I can find work. Maybe I can be a smuggler. Make a lot of money.'

The whole coastline around the Pearl River was infested with illegal traffic of every kind. But it was dangerous.

'You don't know any smugglers,' she said firmly. 'They all belong to gangs. And if they're caught, they can be executed.' Not that she really knew about the gangs, but she'd always heard it.

'I know people.' He gave a little smile, as if he had a secret.

'No you don't.'

How could he? She wanted to put the idea out of her mind at once. Except for one thing. Last night, Mother had called him a criminal. She'd said it with conviction. Presumably Nio had let the village know he was running away. That was stupid enough. Now she wondered, had he said something more – some further piece of damaging information that had got back to her mother-in-law?

She gazed at him. She supposed he just wanted to make himself sound mysterious and important. But the thought didn't comfort her. Had he got to know someone in the smuggling business? Possibly. Had he been lured into joining a gang? Had they promised him he'd be a fine fellow and get rich? She had an awful sense that he was about to put himself in danger.

'Nio, you must tell me,' she said urgently, 'have you said anything bad, anything to make people talk about you in the village?'

He hesitated. Her heart sank.

'I had a bit of an argument,' he said. 'I was right.'

'Who with?'

'Just some of the men.'

'What about?'

He didn't answer for a moment. Then he suddenly burst out: 'The Han are not as brave as the Hakka. If they were, they would not have allowed the Manchu to enslave them!'

'What are you saying?'

'The Manchu emperors force everyone to wear a pigtail. The sign of our subjection. The Manchu clans live at ease and the Han have to do all the work. It's shameful.'

She looked at him in horror. Did he want to get arrested? And then an awful thought occurred to her. 'Nio, have you joined the White Lotus?'

There were so many societies a man might join, from respectable town councils to criminal gangs of thugs. It was the same all over China. Scholars created cultural clubs and recited poems to the moon. Rich merchants formed town guilds and built guildhalls like palaces. Craftsmen banded together for self-help.

And then there were the secret societies like the White Lotus. They were huge. One never knew who was a member or what they might be up to. The humble peasant or smiling shopkeeper met by day might be something very different after dark. Sometimes the White Lotus men would set fire to the house of a corrupt official. Sometimes they murdered people. And Mei-Ling had often heard people say the White Lotus would bring the Manchu emperor down one day.

Could her Little Brother have got himself in with such people? He was so obstinate. And he'd always had his own crazy ideas of justice, even as a little boy. That was how he got the scar on his face. Yes, she thought, it was possible.

'Nothing like that, Big Sister,' he said. And then gave a grin. 'Though of course if I had, I wouldn't tell you.'

Half of her wanted to shake him. Half of her wanted to put her arms around him, hold him close, and keep him safe.

'Oh, Nio. We'll talk about this in the days ahead.' Somehow she had to find a way to spend time with him, to make him listen to reason. She didn't know how, but she knew she must.

'I'm leaving today,' he said with a touch of obstinate triumph.

'No, you mustn't,' she cried. 'Wait a little while.' She needed to gather her thoughts. 'Stay a few more days. Don't you want to see me? Will you promise me?'

'All right,' he said reluctantly. And he seemed about to say something more when her father appeared behind them. He looked scared. 'Someone's at the door,' he said.

'Say I'm not here,' she hissed. It could only be Mother. 'Quickly,' she begged. But her father didn't move. Like everyone else, he was afraid of her mother-in-law. 'Father, please.'

But it was too late. The front door swung open unevenly, revealing the outline of a figure in the fog. The figure stepped in.

And then she saw, with joy, that it was her husband.

She had to go with him, of course. He told her right away: 'I guessed you'd be here. But we need to get back.'

'I heard you on the bridge,' she said. 'I thought it was Mother.' She looked at him anxiously. 'Are you angry with me?' He shook his head. 'What will we say to Mother if she's missed us?'

'I'll say I took you for a walk.'

'In the fog?'

'She can't prove anything else.' He smiled. 'Nothing she can do.'

'You are so good to me.'

They passed the little shrine and turned down onto the track.

'Do you know why I made them let me marry you, Mei-Ling?' he suddenly asked. 'Do you think it was because you were the prettiest girl in the village?'

'I don't know.'

'It was because I could see your character – the kind spirit in your face. That is why you are beautiful. That is why I married you. I knew you would try to see your Little Brother, no matter what it cost. Because you love him. Because you are good. So I am happy.'

'And I am lucky to have a husband like you,' said Mei-Ling. And then she told him everything about Nio and her fears for him.

'It's not good,' he agreed.

'He's so obstinate,' she explained. 'You know that scar on his face? He got it here when he was a little boy. One of the older boys in the village was rude about my father. Said he was poor and stupid, and made the other boys laugh at him. And then Nio started fighting him, although the boy was twice his size. And Nio knocked him down, too, until the boy got his hands on a plank of wood and smashed Nio in the face with it. He's still got the scar.'

'Brave.'

'Yes. But if he thinks he's in the right, everything else goes out of his head. I never know what he's going to do next.'

'It will be difficult for you to meet him again,' Second Son said. 'I don't think even I can arrange it.' He brightened. 'But I can talk to him for you. Nobody's forbidden it. Maybe he'll listen to me.'

'You would do that?'

'This afternoon, if you like.'

'Oh, Husband.' She threw her arms around him. One wasn't supposed to show affection, but in the fog no one could see them. They walked on. They were nearly at the little footbridge. 'There's something else I want to tell you,' she said.

'More bad news?'

'Good news. I mean, I'm not certain yet.' She paused a moment. 'Not quite. But I think you're going to be a father.'

A huge grin spread over his face. 'Really?'

'I can't promise it will be a son . . .'

'I don't care, if I can have a daughter like you.'

'Why are you always so kind, Husband?' She didn't believe him, of course. No family in China ever wanted a baby girl. Everyone congratulated the family who had a baby boy. If a girl was born, people just said nothing, or maybe something like 'better luck next time.' Once she heard a man say to the father of a baby girl, 'I'm sorry for your misfortune.'

'No, really, I don't mind. If there are no girls born, then soon there won't be any more children. Obviously. No future mothers. It's stupid the way people only want boys.'

She nodded and then confessed: 'I've always dreamed of having a little girl. But I never told anybody. People would have been so angry.'

They had come to the bridge. The fog was getting thinner. They could see the handrails and the grey water below.

When they entered the house, the village elder was still there, more or less awake now, sitting on the big divan and drinking tea. And so was Mother. She stood in the passageway, glowering at them. She addressed herself directly to Mei-Ling. 'Where have you been?' She seemed ready to explode.

'Walking with my husband, Mother,' Mei-Ling said meekly.

'In the fog? Liar.'

'We had things to discuss, Mother,' said Second Son. He let his mother's angry eyes rest upon him and took his time. 'My wife is going to have a child.'

They both watched the older woman's eyes narrow suspiciously. Did she believe them? If it wasn't true, then they'd made a fool of her. A very dangerous thing to do. But if true . . .

The eyes returned to fasten upon Mei-Ling. Then the voice spoke, with a frightening coldness. 'Make sure, Mei-Ling, that it is a boy.'

It was late afternoon when Second Son returned. He'd been on an errand to the next village. The mist had vanished hours ago. The hamlet, the rice fields, the duck pond and the pleasant protective ridges above were all bathed in the light of the afternoon sun.

Under the broad straw hat he was wearing against the sun, his face was smiling. Ever since that foggy dawn, everything had unfolded wonderfully. And now he had only one task remaining to bring a perfect end to what – it seemed to him – might be one of the best days in his life.

He just had to make his wife happy by persuading this foolish young fellow not to run off to the big city and get himself into trouble. It might not be easy. But he didn't mind the challenge. Indeed, when he thought of the happiness in Mei-Ling's face if he accomplished his task, he welcomed it. He'd been rehearsing sentences of great wisdom all the way along the road.

As he passed the little shrine at the entrance to the hamlet, he reached back over his shoulder to shake any dust from his pigtail. He pulled his tunic straight. He didn't want anything to detract from the impression of quiet authority that was to be his today. As he went up the lane, he greeted several villagers politely, watching to make sure that they were returning his greetings with respect.

When he came to the house of Mei-Ling's parents, he knocked, and the door was immediately opened by her father, who made him a low and somewhat anxious bow.

'I came to see the young man, Nio,' Second Son explained. 'Mei-Ling wants me to talk to him.'

'Oh.' Her father looked distressed. 'I am very sorry. Very sorry.' He bobbed his head again. 'Nio is not here.'

'Will he be back soon?'

'He has left. He went away before midday.' The old man shook his head. 'He went to the big city. Not coming back.' He looked sadly at his son-in-law. 'I think maybe we shall never see him again.'

o

The red sun hung in the evening sky. Leaning on his ebony stick, old Mr Jiang stared down the slope from his family's ancient house, across the great flat sweep of the valley in which the Yellow River ran – almost a mile across – like a huge volcanic flow of gold.

Yellow River. Its waters were clear when it began its journey. But then the river snaked through a region where, for aeons, winds from the Gobi Desert had carried the sandy soil known as loess, depositing it there until a vast orange-brown plateau had formed, through which the river waters churned, emerging as a yellow stream. Here in Henan Province, in the heart of old China, the waters were still yellow, and would remain so for hundreds of miles until they reached the sea.

Four thousand years ago, the legendary Emperor Yu had taught his people how to control the mighty river, dredge it, and irrigate the land. That had been the true beginning of China's greatness, the old man thought.

Of course, as in all things, vigilance was needed. For the river dropped so much silt that it was creating a new riverbed all the time. This was not obvious to the eye because, with the water's seasonal rise and fall, it carved new banks on either side. In fact, the current was now higher than the surrounding land. Dredging and maintenance were needed every decade. Indeed, a new dredging was due in a year or two.

Well, that would be after his time, he thought. And he smiled.

He was glad that the last evening of his life – at least in this incarnation – should be so beautiful.

His plan was quite simple. He'd wait until after dark, when the household was asleep, before he took the poison. It was hidden in his bedroom, in a little Chinese box that only he knew how to open. The poison was carefully chosen. His death would look natural.

He was going to make things easy for his sister and his son, Shi-Rong.

Fifty feet behind him, the narrow gateway to the family compound – its tiled roof elegantly curved and splayed, in the best Chinese manner – seemed ready to welcome a new ancestral owner to the courtyards it protected. Farther up the hill, the wooden cottages of the village clustered beside the track as it made its way into the ravine, past half a dozen small caves in the hillside – some used as storehouses, others as dwellings – until it reached the steeper path that led, like a series of staircases, up the high ridge to an outcrop where a little Buddhist temple nestled among the trees.

As he turned to look westwards at the sun behind the hills, he had only one regret. I wish, he thought, that I could fly. Now, this evening. Just once.

It was more than a thousand miles to the great Tibetan Plateau, that vast rooftop of the world, fringed by the Himalayas, over which the sun seemed to be hovering at this moment. One was nearer to the eternal blue Heaven up there, he supposed, than anywhere on Earth. From those celestial heights came the greatest rivers of Asia: the Ganges, Indus, Irrawaddy, Brahmaputra and Mekong, all flowing to the south; and flowing eastwards, the two mighty rivers of China – the Yangtze, making its stupendous loop down through the valleys and rice fields of southern China, and the Yellow River, moving like a huge serpent across the grain-planted plains of the centre and north.

The Tibetan Plateau: the silent land of frozen lakes and glaciers, the endless plain in the sky where the heavens and the waters met, and from which all life descended.

He'd been there once, when he was a young man. He wished he could go there again, and he envied the red sun that could see it every day. He nodded to himself. Tonight, he thought, that plateau, and nothing else, was what he'd keep in his mind's eye as he sank into the sleep of death.

His sister was sitting at a small table. She was grey-haired now, but still beautiful; and since his own wife and daughter had both departed this life, he'd been lucky to have her for company.

On the table, he saw some piles of *I Ching* sticks. Without looking up at him, she spoke: 'I know about the poison.'

He frowned. 'The *I Ching* told you?'

'No. I opened the box.'

'Ah.' He nodded resignedly. She'd always been clever.

Their father had spotted that at once, when she was a little girl. He'd hired a tutor to teach them both to read and write, along with a peasant boy from the village who had shown talent.

The peasant boy was a respected teacher in the city of Zhengzhou nowadays, with a son of his own who'd passed the provincial exams. It was a noble feature of the empire that peasants could rise to the highest office through the education system – if somebody helped them by paying for their studies. By doing so, his father, who'd been a good Buddhist, had no doubt earned much merit.

His sister had been frighteningly quick. If girls had been allowed to take the imperial exams, he thought wryly, she might have done better than me. As it was, she was one of a small group of highly literate women, perhaps only half a dozen in the province, who were held in high regard even by scholars.

'You have been eating almost nothing for a month, Brother,' she said, 'and you are hiding poison. Please tell me why.'

He paused. He hadn't wanted to tell her. He'd wanted to fade away quickly. Easily.

'You remember our father's death,' he said quietly.

'How could I forget?'

'I believe I have the same condition. Last month, when I made a journey into Zhengzhou, I went to see the apothecary. They say he is the best. He found my chi to be badly out of balance. I also had acupuncture. For a little while I felt better. But since then . . .' He shook his head. 'I do not wish to suffer as my father did. Nor for you to have to watch it, nor my son.'

'Do you fear death?' she asked.

'When I was a young man, though I went to our Buddhist temple and also studied the Taoist sages, I strove above all to obey the precepts of Confucius. I thought of work, family duty, right actions in the world. In my middle years, I increasingly found comfort in Buddhism, and I thought more of the life beyond, hoping that a life well lived would lead to a better reincarnation. But as I grow old, I am increasingly drawn to things that have no proper name, but which we call the Tao. The Way.' He nodded to himself. 'I do not strive for this life or the next, but I desire to surrender to the great flow of all things.' He looked at her benignly. 'Besides,' he added, 'every illiterate peasant knows that we live on in our children.'

'Do not take poison yet,' his sister said. 'Your son may be coming to see you.'

'The *I Ching* tells you this?' He looked at her suspiciously. She nodded. He was not deceived. 'You wrote to him. Do you know that he is coming?'

'He will come if he can. He is a dutiful son.'

The old man nodded and sat down. After a few minutes he closed his eyes, while his sister continued to stare at the *I Ching* hexagrams on the paper in front of her.

And dusk was falling when the silence was interrupted by an old servant hurrying into the house and calling out: 'Mr Jiang. Mr Jiang, sir. Your son is approaching.'

Shi-Rong went down on his knees before his father and bowed his head to the ground. The kowtow. The sign of respect owed to his father and the head of the family. But how thin the old man was.

The sight of his son, however, and the news that he brought seemed to put new life in Mr Jiang. And he nodded vigorously as Shi-Rong outlined his hopes for the future. 'This is good,' he agreed. 'I have heard of the lord Lin. He is a worthy man. One of the few.' He nodded. 'You should sit your exams again, of course. But you are right to take this opportunity. The emperor himself . . .'

'He will hear nothing but good things of me,' Shi-Rong promised.

'I shall make your favourite meal while you are here,' said his aunt with a smile. Of all the dishes of the province's Yu cuisine, it was a fish dish that Shi-Rong had always loved the best, ever since he was a boy: carp from the Yellow River, cooked three ways, to make soup, fried fillet and sweet and sour. And no one made it better than his aunt. But the preparation was complex. It took three days.

'I have to leave in the morning,' Shi-Rong had to confess. He saw her wilt as if she'd been struck by a blow and his father stiffen. But what could he do?

'You must not keep the lord Lin waiting,' his father cried a little hoarsely. And then quickly, to cover his emotion: 'But I am sorry that you have to go down amongst the people of the south, my son.'

Shi-Rong smiled. Even now, his father considered the Han of the Yellow River and the great grain-growing plains of the north as the only true Chinese.

'You still don't admire the people of the rice paddies, Father?'

'Those people think of nothing but money,' his father answered scornfully.

'You say that the lord Lin will be putting a stop to the barbarian pirates,' his aunt said anxiously. 'Does that mean that you will have to go to sea?'

'He will do as the lord Lin commands,' his father interrupted sharply. 'He must be hungry,' he added.

While his aunt went to prepare some food, his father questioned him closely about the mission. 'Are these pirates the red-haired barbarians, or the other bearded devils?' the old man wanted to know.

'I am not sure,' Shi-Rong replied. 'Mr Wen told me that the lord Lin told him that they once sent an embassy here. Also that he has heard they are very hairy and they cannot bend their legs, so that they often fall over.'

'That seems unlikely,' said Mr Jiang. 'But I remember that when I was a young man, an embassy arrived at the court of the present emperor's grandfather. I heard the details from people who were at court. The barbarians came by ship from a distant western land. Their ambassador brought gifts, but he refused to kowtow to the emperor in the proper manner. This had never happened before. The emperor understood that he was an ignorant and stupid man, but still gave him a magnificent piece of jade – though the fellow clearly had no idea of its value. Next the barbarian showed us goods from his country – clocks, telescopes and I don't know what – thinking to impress us. The emperor explained that we had no need for the things he brought, but was too polite to point out that they were inferior to the similar items already given him by embassies from other western lands. Finally this barbarian asked that his wretched people should be allowed to trade with other ports besides Guangzhou – where all the other foreign merchants are content to be allowed – and made all sorts of other foolish demands. He was absurd.' He nodded. 'Perhaps these opium pirates come from the same land.'

'I know almost nothing about the distant lands across the sea,' Shi-Rong remarked.

'Nobody does,' his father said. 'It wasn't always so,' he added. 'About four centuries ago, in the days of the Ming dynasty, we had a great fleet of ships that traded with many western lands. But it became unprofitable. Now the ships come to us. And the empire is so huge . . . There is nothing we cannot produce ourselves. The barbarians need what we have, not the reverse.'

'They certainly want our tea,' Shi-Rong agreed. 'And I have heard that if they cannot obtain enough of our rhubarb herb, they die.'

'It may be so,' his father said. 'But I see your aunt has food for us.'

Soup; dumplings stuffed with pork; noodles, with mutton and vegetables, sprinkled with coriander. Only now, as the rich aromas greeted him, did Shi-Rong realise how hungry he was. To his aunt's obvious joy, his father took a little food also, to keep him company.

As they ate, he ventured to ask his father about his health.

'I am growing old, my son,' his father responded. 'It is to be expected. But even if I died tomorrow – which I shall not – I should be happy to know that our family estate is to pass to a worthy son.'

'I beg you, live many years,' Shi-Rong replied. 'Let me show you my success and give you grandchildren.' He saw his aunt nod approvingly at this.

'I shall do my best,' his father promised with a smile.

'He must eat more,' his aunt said. And Shi-Rong affectionately put a dumpling in his father's bowl.

At the end of the meal, seeing his father looked tired, Shi-Rong asked him if he wanted to rest.

'When do you leave tomorrow?' his father asked. 'At dawn?'

'In the morning. But not at dawn.'

'I am not ready to sleep yet. Say goodnight to your aunt. She wants to go to bed. Then we'll talk a little. I have things to say to you.'

When his aunt had bid him goodnight, the two men sat in silence for a few minutes before Mr Jiang began to speak.

'Your aunt worries too much. But none of us knows when we shall die, so it is time to give you my final commandments.' He looked at his son gravely, and Shi-Rong bowed his head. 'The first is simple enough. In all your actions, Confucius must be your guide. Honour your family, the emperor and tradition. Failure to do so will lead only to disorder.'

'I always try to do so, Father. And I always shall.'

'I never doubted it. But when you are older, especially if you are successful in your career, a great temptation will be placed in your path. You will be tempted to take bribes. Almost all officials do. That is how they retire with great fortunes. Lin does not take bribes. He is a great exception, and I am glad you are to work for him. But when the temptation does arise, you must not fall into it. If you are honest and successful, you will receive sufficient riches. Do you promise me this?'

'Certainly, Father. I promise.'

'There remains one more thing. It concerns the emperor.' His father paused. 'You must always remember that the emperor of China sits at the centre of the world, and he rules by the Mandate of Heaven. It is true that down thousands of years, from time to time, the ruling dynasty has changed. When it is time for a change, the gods have always sent us many signs. By the time that the last Ming emperor hanged himself in despair two centuries ago, it was clear to everyone that the Manchu dynasty from the north was the answer to our needs.'

'Not quite everyone,' his son could not resist inserting.

'Some residual supporters of the Ming who fled to Taiwan. Some rebels like the White Lotus bandits . . .' His father made a dismissive gesture. 'When you serve the emperor, my son, you must always remember that you are obeying the Mandate of Heaven. And this brings me to my last command. You must promise me never to lie to the emperor.'

'Of course not, Father. Why would I do such a thing?'

'Because so many people do. Officials are given instructions to do this thing or that. They have to report. They wish to please the emperor, to get promoted – or at least to stay out of trouble. So they tell the emperor what he wants to hear. Something goes wrong, they fail to meet a quota . . . They send a false report. This is against Confucian principle, and if they are caught, the emperor may be more angry than if they had told him the truth in the first place. But they do it. All over the empire.' He sighed. 'It is our besetting sin.'

'I will not do this.'

'Be truthful for its own sake. Then you will have a good conscience. But it will help you also. If you gain a reputation for reporting truthfully, the emperor will know he can trust you and will promote you.'

'I promise, Father.'

'Then that is all.'

Shi-Rong looked at his father. No wonder the old man approved of Lin. They were both upright men, of the same mould. If the mission had filled him with secret dread at all the enemies he was likely to make, it was no use hoping for any advice from his father as to how to negotiate the dangerous bureaucratic maze. His father was with Lin all the way.

Well, he would just have to hope for success and the emperor's approval.

His father was tired now. It made him look suddenly frail. Was this to be the last time he saw him alive? Shi-Rong was overcome with feelings of gratitude and affection for the old man. And also a feeling of guilt. There must be so many things he could have asked him when he had the chance.

'We shall talk once more in the morning,' the old man promised. 'I have something to show you,' he added, 'before you go upon your way.'

Shi-Rong woke early. His father was still asleep, but as he expected, his aunt was in the kitchen.

'Now you must tell me how my father really is,' he said quietly.

'He believes he is sick. He may be wrong. But he is preparing for death. He wants to die quietly and quickly. He eats nothing.'

'What can I do?'

'You can make him want to live. No one else can.'

'But I do want him to live. I need him to live.'

'Then you may succeed.'

'And you? Are you all right?'

'I shall live a long time,' his aunt said simply. The idea didn't seem to give her much pleasure.

When his father appeared, however, he was in excellent spirits. He took a little food with them, and then, beckoning to Shi-Rong, told him: 'I have a little test for you.'

All through his childhood, from the time when his father himself taught him his first lessons, there had always been these little tests – curiosities, abstruse sayings, ancient tunes – puzzles to tease the mind and teach Shi-Rong something unexpected. They were more like games, really. And no visit home could be complete without something of this kind.

From a drawer Mr Jiang took out a small bag and emptied its contents onto a table. There was a rattling sound, and Shi-Rong saw a tiny pile of shards of broken bone and turtle shell.

'When I was in Zhengzhou last month,' he said, 'I was shopping at the apothecary's when a farmer came in with these.' He smiled. 'He wanted to sell them to the apothecary. "Grind them up," he said. "Sell the powder for a high price. They must be magic of some kind." He had a farm somewhere north of the river. Said he found them in the ground, and that he had more. I expect he hoped the apothecary would sell the powder successfully and pay him handsomely for more. But the apothecary didn't want the stuff, so I persuaded him to sell them to me.'

'And why did you buy them, Father?'

'Ah, that's your puzzle. You have to tell me. Take a look at them.'

At first Shi-Rong couldn't see anything of interest. Just some little bones, grimy with earth. Two of the fragments of turtle shell seemed to fit together, however, and as he placed them side by side, he noticed that there were tiny scratches on their surface. As he searched further among the bones, he found more marks. The scratches were quite neat.

'The bones have some kind of writing on them. Looks a bit primitive.'

'Can you read it?'

'Not at all.'

'They are Chinese characters. I am sure of it. See here' – his father pointed – 'the character for *man;* and here is *horse* and this may be *water.*'

'I think you could be right.'

'I believe this is ancestral Chinese writing, early forms of the characters we know today.'

'If so, they must be very old.'

'We have examples of fully formed writing from a very early period. I'd guess these bones are four thousand years old, perhaps more.'

Shi-Rong was suddenly struck by a beautiful thought. 'Why, Father, you must get more. You must decipher them. This will make you famous.'

His father chuckled. 'You mean I'd have to live for years?'

'Certainly. You must see me win the emperor's favour and become famous amongst all the scholars yourself. It's your duty to the family,' he added cleverly.

His father looked at him fondly. The love of the young is always a little selfish. It cannot be otherwise. But he was touched by his son's affection. 'Well,' he said without much confidence, 'I'll try.'

And now, he knew, it was time for his son to leave. He had a long way to travel. Shi-Rong would follow the river valley to Kaifeng, then take the ancient road until he came to the mighty Yangtze River, three hundred miles to the south. From there, another seven hundred miles down, by road and river to the coast. He'd be lucky to get there in fifty days.

As they parted at the gateway to the house, Shi-Rong begged his father, 'Please live till I return,' and his father ordered him: 'Keep my commandments.'

Then Mr Jiang and his sister watched Shi-Rong until he was out of sight.

Two hours after Shi-Rong had departed, his aunt sat down at her writing desk. Her brother, after going for a short walk, had lain down to rest, and now she returned to the matter that had been occupying her thoughts for several days before Shi-Rong's arrival.

On the desk in front of her, a large sheet of paper displayed a grid of hexagrams. As she had so many times before, she tried to decipher their message.

That was the trouble with the *I Ching*. It seldom gave clear answers. Cryptic words, oracular expressions, mysteries to be solved. Everything lay in the hands of the interpreter. Sometimes the message seemed clear; often it did not.

Had there been a consistency in her readings concerning Shi-Rong? It seemed to her that there had been some. There were indications of danger, but the danger was not close. There were suggestions of death, unexpected but inevitable. Death by water.

It was all so vague.

She had not told her brother. Or Shi-Rong. What was the point?

o

The party for Trader was going splendidly. First of all, they'd given him a present.

'At first we couldn't think what to give you,' they told him. 'Then somebody suggested a picture. Picture of what, though? After much discussion, it was decided that you're such an unconscionably handsome fellow, we'd better give you a picture of yourself!'

'Something to send your ladylove,' a voice called out.

'We should have given you several, for all the girls,' another rejoined. 'But we couldn't afford it.'

'So here it is,' they proudly cried.

It was a miniature, of course. One gave portraits to be hung on walls to senior men when they retired, not to young chaps starting out in life. But they'd done him proud all the same. They'd chosen the usual oval shape. That's what the ladies liked. Painted in oil on ivory. But painted with such striking realism and richness of tone that it might have been by the famous Andrew Robertson himself. It wasn't, but it might have been. They all agreed that with his pale face and darkly brooding good looks, 'Trader's the Byron of the China trade.'

'Remember that artist we had in to make sketches of us all for a group picture?' they cried. 'That was the miniature painter. It was you he was sketching all the time.'

Trader thanked them solemnly. And indeed, he was delighted with the present. Said he'd keep it all his life in memory of the good days spent in their company. And he might have said more if they hadn't shouted, 'Shut up! Shut up! It's time for a song.'

Young Crosbie, a small, sandy-haired Scotsman, was at the piano. He'd made up a song. Well, to be precise, he was making up a song, aided by all the other good fellows there. Garstin, Standish, Swann, Giles, Humphreys – jolly chaps from all the agencies. And Charlie Farley, too, of course.

Ernest Read smiled and took a leisurely puff at his cigar. The American was a barrel of a man. Short-cropped hair, big brown moustache. Twenty-eight years old, but as worldly-wise as a man of forty. A good oarsman. A man's man. A ladies' man, too. He glanced at John Trader. 'They're giving you a pretty good send-off, Trader. When do you leave?'

'Three days.'

'We may meet again, then. I'm taking a trip to Macao before I make my way back home.'

'I'm always glad of good company,' John answered. He didn't ask the American what his own business was. Read seemed the kind of man who would give information if and when he wanted to.

'So you're going into the China trade,' Read continued. 'How do you feel about selling opium?'

'It's a medicine.' Trader shrugged. 'In England, people give laudanum to their children.'

'And if people overindulge . . . it's their problem, right?'

'Same as wine and spirits. Would you prohibit them?'

'No.' Read considered. 'Though they say opium's more addictive. Fact remains, the Chinese emperor doesn't approve. Sale or consumption of the said article is illegal in his domain.'

'Well, I'm not under Chinese law, thank God.' Trader shot a swift glance back at Read. 'Your own countrymen sell opium.'

'Oh yes.' Read grinned. 'Russell, Cushing, Forbes, Delano – some of the best names in old Boston. But American participation in the China trade's nothing compared to you British.' He took another draw on his cigar. 'I hear you've entered into a partnership.'

'Yes. A small firm. Odstock and Sons. It's really two brothers these days. One here, one in Canton.'

'I've heard of them,' said Read with a nod. 'Good operators. I guess you're fortunate you have money to invest.'

'A small inheritance. That's all.'

'And you want to make a fortune in a hurry,' said Read.

John Trader nodded thoughtfully. 'Something like that,' he said quietly.

The next day was Sunday. Charlie usually liked going to his aunt's on Sundays. The main meal was in the early afternoon and was usually followed by a leisurely afternoon stroll to aid the digestion. Often there were guests, but it was only family today.

'Tell me about the party last night,' said Aunt Harriet.

'It was what you'd expect. Jokes about China. Crosbie tried to compose a song. They all teased John about how rich he was going to be.'

'He's not poor now, from what I understand,' said Harriet.

'He needs more.' Charlie gave her a confidential look. 'He's in love.'

'Really? With whom?'

'Agnes Lomond.'

'So tell me about Agnes Lomond. I've met her, but that's all.'

'Nothing to tell, really. I don't know what he sees in her.'

'When did it start?'

'The day we had luncheon with her father. He was struck with a thunderbolt. A few days later I discovered he'd been to call on her mother. He never told me he was going to.'

'Colonel Lomond likes him?'

'Not at all. Hates him. But after he called, Mrs Lomond decided he was charming.' He thought for a moment. 'It's difficult for the colonel, I suppose. Agnes looks well enough, but she's nothing special. Aristocratic, of course, but she ain't rich. So even the colonel has to be careful. Fathers don't want to get a reputation for chasing young men away, you see. Puts people off.'

'So is Trader paying his addresses to Miss Lomond?'

'Hasn't got to that yet. He's allowed to call on her mother and meet her. Sees her at other gatherings, I daresay. But I think he wants to strengthen his hand before he goes further.'

'So he's going to China to make a quick fortune. And while he's away?'

'The colonel will be scouring the British Empire to find a young man he likes better.' He chuckled quietly. 'He must have got the wind up. He even asked me if I'd be interested.'

'I can understand that. He was friendly with your father. He likes you. Any girl would be glad to marry you. Are you interested?'

'Not my type.'

'And do we know what Miss Lomond herself thinks of all this?'

'Not the least idea.' Charlie grinned.

OPIUM

March 1839

China seas. A warm night. A light breeze. Oily slicks of cloud lay along the horizon, and above them, a silver quarter-moon hung among the stars.

The China seas could be treacherous – terrible during the monsoons. But tonight the black water parted, smooth as lacquer, under the clipper's bow.

The cargo, stowed below in five hundred mango-wood chests – a hundred of them Trader's, a large part of his wealth – was also black.

Opium.

John Trader stared from the deck across the water, his face still as a gambler's. He'd made his choices. There was no turning back now.

He'd been lucky the Odstocks had been looking for a junior partner. He'd known the younger brother, Benjamin, for some time before he'd approached him about joining the business. As it happened, he'd chosen a good time.

'My brother Tully's fifty now,' the stocky merchant told him. 'Been in Canton for years. Wants to go back and join our father in London.' He'd smiled. 'Wouldn't be my choice. Father's a crusty old cove. So Tully needs someone to learn the ropes in Canton. Think you could do it?'

'It sounds just what I'm looking for,' Trader had replied.

'We'd be wanting someone who could buy into the business.' Benjamin had looked at him keenly.

'I could be interested – depending on the terms.'

'It's not like being in Calcutta,' Benjamin had cautioned him. 'Not much social life. Only men allowed at Canton itself. They have to stay there for weeks during the trading season. Families live out at Macao, which is not a bad place. Healthy. The Portuguese run it, as you know, but there's an English community. English church. That sort of thing. And a British government representative, by the way. Man named Captain Elliot at present. Quite a good fellow, I daresay.'

'And you retire with a fortune,' Trader added amiably. The fact that he hoped to make his fortune faster was better concealed for the moment.

'With luck.' Benjamin Odstock regarded him thoughtfully while Trader surveyed the tobacco stains on the older gentleman's white waistcoat. 'A man needs enterprise and a steady nerve in this trade. Prices fluctuate. Sometimes there's a glut.'

'The emperor doesn't like the trade.'

'Don't worry about that. The demand's huge, and growing.' Benjamin Odstock puffed out his florid cheeks. 'Just keep a cool head. I wouldn't be surprised,' he said comfortably, 'if the opium trade went on forever.'

The Odstocks knew their business. John thought he could trust them.

It was midnight when they saw the schooner ahead. Three lights. The signal. Trader was still on deck, standing near the captain.

'That'll be McBride, I should think,' said the captain. 'He likes to pick up cargo out here.'

'Why?' The depot was at Lintin, in the gulf.

'McBride prefers the open sea.' A moment later, he gave the order: 'Heave to.' As they drew near, the skipper of the schooner held up a lantern so that they could see his bearded face. 'That's him,' the captain remarked.

Then they heard McBride's voice call across the water. 'Nothing's selling at Lintin. No takers.'

Trader felt his face go pale. Lucky no one could see it in the dark. 'Is he lying?' he asked the captain. 'To get me to sell to him?'

'McBride's honest. Besides, he doesn't buy. He sells on commission.'

My first voyage, John thought, and the cargo in which I've sunk my inheritance is unsalable. Was he going to be ruined?

'I'm going to try up the coast,' McBride shouted. 'Room for a hundred more cases. Are you interested?'

John remembered Benjamin Odstock's words. A steady nerve. A cool head. And enterprise. Yet he was almost surprised to hear his own voice shouting back. 'If you'll take me with you, and bring me into Canton when we're done.'

There was a pause. 'All right,' called McBride.

There were twenty hands on the schooner – English, Dutch, Irish, a couple of Scandinavians and four Indian lascars. It took less than half an hour for them to transfer the hundred chests from the clipper into the schooner's wide hold.

Meanwhile, John discovered that he was not the only passenger. He was pleased to find that Read, his acquaintance from Calcutta, was also on board.

'I was sailing to Macao,' the American told him. 'Then McBride hailed us this afternoon. When I heard he was taking a run up the coast I jumped ship and came along for the ride.' He grinned. 'Glad to have your company, Trader. It should be interesting. We've got a missionary on board, too.' He jerked his finger for'ard to where a figure could be seen sleeping in a hammock. 'Dutchman.'

With his cargo now complete, McBride was anxious to depart. The crew scurried, and they were under way again.

'Use my cabin if you want, gentlemen,' the skipper said. 'Or if you prefer to be on deck, there are blankets aft. I'd get some sleep if I were you.'

Read chose the deck. So did John. If anything happened, he didn't want to miss it. They went forward and settled down. Most of the crew were sitting quietly or sleeping there. The missionary in his hammock, a large, heavy fellow, had never broken his sleep. From time to time, the sound of his snores was added to the faint hiss of the breeze in the rigging.

John fell asleep at once and did not wake until the first hint of dawn was in the sky. Read was also awake, gazing up thoughtfully at the fading stars.

'Good morning,' said John quietly. 'Been awake long?'

'A while.' He turned to look at John. 'You own the cargo you brought aboard?'

'Part of it.' John sat up. A lock of dark hair fell over his forehead. He brushed it away.

'So you've quite a bit riding on this. Did you borrow the money?'

'Some.'

'Brave man.' Read didn't pursue the matter further.

They got up and went to join the skipper at the wheel.

'All quiet?' Read asked.

'Only pirates to watch for now,' McBride replied. 'If we do meet any pirates, sir,' the skipper continued, 'I shall give you a pistol and ask you to use it.'

'I'll shoot.' Read took out a cigar.

'You look like a man,' the skipper ventured, 'that knows the seven seas.'

'I get around.'

'What brings you here, if I may ask?'

'Avoiding my wife.' Read lit his cigar and puffed in silence for a minute or two. 'First time I've smuggled, though.' He grinned. 'Never been a criminal before.'

'Only under Chinese law,' McBride said. 'And we don't count that.'

'Right.' Read glanced towards the missionary, whose snores had just grown loud. 'Tell me,' he asked, 'do you always bring a missionary?'

'Usually. They speak the lingo. Need 'em to translate.'

'And they don't mind . . . the business?'

McBride smiled. 'You'll see.'

They caught sight of the coast an hour after dawn – a small headland to the west that soon vanished again. Then nothing until midmorning, when more coastline began to appear. It was an hour later when Trader saw the square sails coming towards them. He glanced at Captain McBride.

'Pirates?' he asked.

The captain shook his head and handed the wheel to Read for a moment while he went to shake the missionary awake. 'Rise and shine, Van Buskirk. We've got customers.'

Trader watched. The large Dutchman, once awake, moved with surprising speed. From under an awning, he dragged two large wicker baskets and opened them. One contained cheaply bound books; the other was full of pamphlets, in coloured paper wrappers. Then he came to the wheel.

'Bibles?' asked Read.

'Gospels, Mr Read, and Christian tracts. In Chinese, of course. Printed in Macao.'

'To convert the heathen?'

'That is my hope.'

'Strange way to convert people, if I may say so – off the side of an opium vessel.'

'If I could preach the Gospel ashore, sir, without being arrested, I should not be aboard this ship,' the big man replied. He looked at the skipper. 'Which cargo do we sell first?'

McBride indicated Trader. The Dutchman turned to John. 'I have your assurance that the cargo is all Patna and Benares. No loose Malwa cakes.'

'All properly packed, tight in balls,' said John. 'Top quality.'

'Will you trust me to negotiate the prices?' the missionary asked. He saw John hesitate. 'It will be better that way.'

Trader glanced at McBride, who nodded.

A strange fellow, this big Dutchman, John thought. A speaker of many tongues. God knows how many years he'd been out in the East trying to convert the heathen of a land he could not enter.

And now, it seemed, he must place his fortune in the Dutchman's hands.

'All right,' he said.

The smuggling boat was a long, slim, unpainted vessel, with square sails and thirty or forty oarsmen, all armed with knives and cutlasses, at its sides. Scrambling dragons, the Chinese called these boats. From whatever quarter the wind came – or if there was no wind at all – a scrambling dragon could manoeuvre at speed, and it was hard to catch.

The smugglers had no sooner come alongside than a small, tough, barefooted fellow with a pigtail, dressed only in knee-length cotton breeches and an open shirt, climbed quickly aboard and went straight to Van Buskirk.

The negotiation was amazingly brief, conducted in Cantonese, which the Dutchman seemed to speak fluently. After a few words, the smuggler dived down into the hold with the captain and selected a chest, which was carried up on deck by two of the hands. Taking a sharp knife, he cut the gunnysacking from around the wooden chest and prized open the pitch seal. A moment later, the chest was open and he was riffling through the packing filler, removing the matting to reveal the upper layer of twenty compartments containing the spherical cakes of opium, like so many small cannonballs, each tightly wrapped in poppy leaves.

Taking out a ball and scraping back the leaf, the man wiped his knife on his shirt and then worked it a little way into the hard, dark opium cake beneath. Then he placed the blade in his mouth. After closing his eyes for a moment, he nodded sharply and turned to Van Buskirk.

Less than a minute later, after a quick-fire exchange, the deal was done.

'Fifty chests, at six hundred silver dollars each,' the Dutchman announced.

'I'd hoped for a thousand,' said John.

'Not this year. His first offer was five hundred. You're still making a profit.'

Before they had even finished speaking, the crewmen were hurriedly bringing up chests on deck, while others began to lower them over the side to the scrambling dragon. At the same time, a chest of silver was being hauled up. As soon as it was on deck, the Chinese smuggler began to count it out. Bags of coins, ingots of silver, he made a pile on the deck while the captain calmly watched.

Van Buskirk, however, seemed to have lost all interest in the transaction now. Rushing to his wicker baskets, he delved into the first one and pulled out a pile of books. 'Help me, Mr Trader,' he called out. 'It's the least you can do.'

Trader hesitated. The silver was still piling up on the deck. But Read obligingly went to the other basket, scooped up an armful of tracts, and, holding them under his chin, walked to the side of the ship and dropped them into the smugglers' vessel below, while the Dutchman did the same thing with his gospels.

'Read them,' the Dutchman instructed the Chinese oarsmen below, in Cantonese. 'Share the Word of God.'

The business of loading the opium was progressing now with astonishing speed. A human chain had been formed so that the heavy boxes were flowing from hold to deck and from the deck over the side as smoothly as a snake. By the time that Van Buskirk and Read had each collected two more armfuls of literature and distributed them, the loading was complete and the Chinese smuggler was leaving the ship.

'Tell him to wait,' Trader called to the Dutchman. 'I haven't checked the money yet.' But Van Buskirk appeared unconcerned, and to Trader's dismay, the smuggler was over the side and his oarsmen were pushing away. He saw both Read and the captain smile as the missionary calmly closed his wicker baskets before coming over to where the pile of silver lay.

'You think he may have shortchanged you?' Van Buskirk asked. He gently shook his head. 'You will soon learn, young man, that the Chinese never do that. Not even the smugglers. Your silver will be exactly correct, I assure you.'

And as he stowed the money in his strongbox, Trader discovered that this was indeed the case.

For two more hours they continued on their way. It was a fine day, and the sun's rays were dancing cheerfully upon the sea. He and Read stood together by the ship's rail. Several times they saw schools of flying fish skimming over the water.

They'd been enjoying the scene for a while when the American gently observed: 'I've been trying to figure you out, Trader. You seem a nice fellow.'

'Thank you.'

'The men in this trade are a tough crowd, mostly. I'm not saying you couldn't be tough. But you seem a little finer. So I'm wondering what's driving you. Something you're running from, something you're searching for. Sure as hell, something's eating you. So I'm wondering: could it be a woman?'

'Could be,' John said.

'Must be quite a young lady,' Read said with a smile, 'to get you into the opium trade.'

An hour later, when Captain McBride saw the blunt square-rigged vessel slowly approaching, he cursed.

'War junk,' he explained. 'Government ship. Officials aboard.'

'What will they do?'

'Depends. They could impound the cargo.' He glanced at Trader and saw him go very pale. 'We can give up and go home. I can outrun them. Or we can head out to sea and try another approach. But they might still be waiting for us.'

John was silent. He'd chosen to make this run. How was he going to explain the loss of fifty chests of opium to his new partners? He couldn't afford to lose them, in any case. He turned to Read. For once, the worldly American looked doubtful.

To his surprise, it was Van Buskirk who made the decision.

'Proceed, gentlemen,' he said calmly. His fleshy face was impassive. 'Put your trust in me.' He turned to the skipper. 'When we get close, McBride, please heave to, so that the official can board. I shall also require a table placed on deck, two chairs and two wineglasses. Nobody should speak. Just listen politely, even if you have no idea what he is saying. I will do the rest.'

Trader watched as the war junk drew close. Its high wooden sides were certainly impressive. The vessel's masts were huge, as were the sails of bamboo matting. The massive stern was painted like a Chinese mask. On either side of the bow was a staring eye. The deck looked cluttered, but the cannon were plain to see.

Only a single man, a mandarin, came across. He was rowed over to them in a tiny boat, in which he sat, very composed. He was middle-aged, with a long, drooping moustache and he wore a black cylindrical hat. Over his embroidered robes was a blue three-quarter-length surcoat, emblazoned on the chest with a big square, designating his rank. When he came aboard, he looked around him calmly. Obviously he had no fear that these Western barbarians would dare to offer him any violence. Then he took out a scroll and began to read from it. The document was written in the official Mandarin Chinese, which sounded to Trader strangely like birdsong.

'What's he saying?' he whispered to Van Buskirk.

'That the emperor, considering the health and safety of his people, expressly forbids the selling of opium. Should our ship contain any, it will be taken away and destroyed immediately.'

John Trader winced. 'That's it, then.'

'Patience,' the Dutchman murmured.

When the mandarin had concluded his announcement, Van Buskirk stepped forward and made him a low bow. Gesturing to the table that had been set up, he politely asked the mandarin if he would care to sit and talk a little. Once he and the mandarin were seated, he drew from his coat a silver flask and filled both glasses before them with a rich brown cordial. 'Madeira, gentlemen,' he remarked to the onlookers. 'I always keep some with me.'

Ceremoniously he toasted the mandarin, and for some time the two men sipped their drink and conversed politely. At one point, Trader noticed, the missionary looked concerned and seemed to be questioning the mandarin closely. Then he beckoned to Trader.

'I shall require you to give me one thousand silver dollars from your strongbox, Mr Trader,' he remarked blandly. 'McBride will reimburse you for his share later.'

'This is for . . . ?'

'Just bring me the money,' the Dutchman said. 'In a bag.'

A minute or two later, having handed over the bag of silver coins, Trader watched as the Dutchman gravely gave it to the mandarin, who took it and, without being so rude as to count it, rose to depart.

Only when the official was on his way back to the war junk did John speak. 'Did you just bribe a government official?'

'It was not a bribe,' the Dutchman replied. 'It was a present.'

'What did you tell him?'

'The truth, of course. I explained to him that, were he to ask you or the captain or even Read here if there was any opium stowed below, I had every confidence that you would say that there was not. He was courteous enough to agree that, this being the case, your word would suffice. I then gave him a small present. He might have asked for more, but he did not.'

'A thousand silver dollars is small?'

'You got off very lightly. Do you wish me to summon him back to dispute the matter?'

'Certainly not.'

'Then we are free to proceed.' Van Buskirk nodded to the captain to indicate that the ship should get under way again.

'So much,' Trader remarked wryly, 'for Chinese morality.'

'It is you, Mr Trader,' the missionary gently reminded him, 'not he, who is in the drug trade.'

They reached their rendezvous – a small island with a sheltered anchorage – that evening. The receiving ship, flying a pair of red flags, was already there. Half of McBride's original cargo had been presold, paid for with silver at Canton, and the letters of credit were duly passed across. But when the Chinese merchant discovered that they had another hundred, plus Trader's remaining fifty, he paid cash for those as well.

By nightfall, the business of the voyage was therefore complete. Both the ships had dropped anchor and would go their separate ways at dawn.

In the meantime, the Chinese merchant gladly agreed to dine with his new Western friends.

It was a pleasant meal. Simple food, some drinkable wine. A little Madeira supplied by Van Buskirk. Mostly the missionary and the Chinese merchant spoke together in Cantonese, while the others conversed in English. The surprise came at the end of the meal.

'Gentlemen,' the missionary announced, 'you have no need of me now. But our Chinese friend has agreed to take me farther up the coast before he returns here to meet another British opium ship, on which I can make my return. During my days with him, I may even be able to go ashore.'

McBride frowned. 'That's a dangerous thing you're doing, sir. Missionaries normally stick with our ships. You'll have no protection if you get caught. Especially onshore.'

'I know, Captain.' The big Dutchman gave him a smile that was almost apologetic. 'But I am a missionary.' He shrugged. 'I shall hope for protection from . . .' He pointed up to Heaven.

They received this with silence.

'Godspeed, Reverend,' said Read after a pause. 'We shall miss you.'

'I shall go across to the other vessel with my things tonight,' Van Buskirk concluded, 'so as not to delay you in the morning.'

A quarter of an hour later, a leather satchel containing his few possessions over his shoulder and his two big wicker baskets already lowered over the side, Van Buskirk was ready to depart. But before he left, he beckoned to Trader to join him and led him over to the opposite rail, where they would not be heard.

'Mr Trader,' the big man spoke in a low, soft voice, 'would you allow me to give you some advice?'

'Of course.'

'I have been out here many years. You are young, and you are not a bad man. I can see that. But I beg you to leave off this business. Return to your own country, or at least to India, where you may make an honest living. For if you continue in the opium trade, Mr Trader, you will be in danger of losing your immortal soul.'

John did not reply.

'And there is something else you should know,' the older man continued. 'When I was speaking to the mandarin this afternoon, he gave me news which confirmed other rumours I have been hearing.' He dropped his voice to a whisper. 'There is trouble ahead. Big trouble.' He nodded slowly. 'If you enter the opium trade now, I believe you may be ruined. So my advice to you as a man of business – even if you care nothing for your soul – is this: take the money you have made and run.'

'Run?'

'Run for your life.'

o

The following morning, a new thing happened to Mei-Ling. She'd been told to hang out the washing in the yard, and she was already halfway through. Second Son was watching her affectionately. He'd just acquired a new dog, and he was playing with the puppy while he sat on a bench under the orange tree in the middle of the yard.

The sun was shining. Behind the wall on the right, some bamboo fronds were swaying in the breeze. Over the tiled roof on the left, one could see the terraced rice fields on the hill. From the kitchen came the pleasant smell of flatbread, cooking over a wood fire.

But now Second Son saw his wife stagger, as if she was going to faint. He rose anxiously.

Mei-Ling herself hardly knew what had happened. The feeling of nausea was so sudden. Sending a chicken scuttling away, she staggered to the orange tree and put her hand on a branch to steady herself.

At this moment, her mother-in-law chose to come into the yard. 'Bad girl!' she cried. 'Why have you stopped?'

But there was nothing Mei-Ling could do. Before her husband could even support her, she doubled over and retched. The older woman came close, looking at her carefully.

And then, to Mei-Ling's surprise, Mother spoke gently.

'Come.' The older woman pushed her son away and took Mei-Ling's arm. 'Quick, quick.' She helped Mei-Ling towards her room. 'You sit down. Cool place.'

She heard her husband ask what was happening, and his mother tell him sharply to go to work. She sat down on a wooden chair, wondering if she was going to throw up, while her mother-in-law went into the kitchen, returning a few moments later with a cup of ginger tea.

'Drink a little now. Eat later.'

'I'm sorry,' Mei-Ling said. 'I don't know what happened.'

'You don't know?' The older woman was surprised. 'It's morning sickness. Willow is lucky. She doesn't seem to get it. I always did. Nothing wrong.' She smiled encouragingly. 'You will have a fine son.'

The next day, Mei-Ling felt sick again. And the day after that. When she asked her mother-in-law how long she thought it would go on, the older woman was noncommittal. 'Maybe not long,' she said.

In the meantime, however, Mei-Ling was enjoying what seemed to be a change in their relationship. This proof of the vigorous life stirring within her daughter-in-law and memories of her own suffering with morning sickness made her more kind. She would insist that Mei-Ling rest whenever she felt queasy and often sit and chat with her, in a way that she never had before. Naturally, the discussion often turned to the child she was going to have.

'He will be born in the Year of the Pig,' her mother-in-law pointed out. 'And the element for this year is Earth. Earth Pig is not a bad year to be born.'

By the time she was three, Mei-Ling could recite the sequence of animals after whom each Chinese year would be named in turn – Dragon, Snake, Horse, Goat . . . twelve in all, so that an animal came around every dozen years. But that was not all. One had to add, for each animal, one of five elements attached to it: Wood, Fire, Earth, Metal and Water. So the twelve animals, each with its attached element, made a complete cycle of sixty years.

And as every child knew, one's character went with one's birth sign. Some were good, some not so good.

Fire Horse was bad. Fire Horse men brought trouble on their families. Big trouble, sometimes. And if you were a girl born in a Fire Horse year, nobody would marry you. Parents tried not to have a child at all in a Fire Horse year.

Mei-Ling had a general idea of this complex knowledge, but her mother-in-law was an expert.

'The Earth sign can strengthen the Pig,' the older woman explained. 'People say Pig means fat and lazy, but not always. Earth Pig will work hard. Take good care of his wife.'

'Won't he eat a lot?' asked Mei-Ling.

'Yes, but he won't care what he eats.' The older woman laughed. 'Easy for his wife. She won't have to cook so well. If she makes a mistake, he'll forgive her. And people will like him. Trust him.'

'They say that Earth Pig people aren't very bright,' Mei-Ling said a little sadly.

'No need for that here,' Mother pointed out. 'There is another thing about people born in an Earth Pig year,' she continued. 'They are afraid of people laughing at them because they are simple and trusting. You must always encourage him. Make him feel happy. Then he will work well.'

The next day, Mei-Ling dared to ask: 'What if it's a girl, Mother? What will a girl be like?'

The older woman, however, wasn't interested in the idea. 'Don't worry. I went to a fortune-teller. First you will have sons. Daughter later.'

Mei-Ling hardly knew whether she was glad or sorry for this news. But as she looked at her sister-in-law, who was growing big now, it occurred to her that if Willow, as expected, had a boy and she herself had a girl, this friendliness Mother was showing her now might suddenly end.

She was surprised one afternoon to receive a visit. Her father never approached the Lung house normally, but when the servant girl came to say that he was outside and would like a word with his daughter, Mother gave Mei-Ling permission to go out to him and even added, 'Ask your father to come in, if he wishes.'

He was waiting by the little wooden bridge. He looked sheepish. And he was accompanied by a young man Mei-Ling had never seen before.

'This is a friend of Nio,' her father said. 'He has a message from him. But he would not give it to me. Only you.' He backed away.

Mei-Ling looked at the young man. He was maybe twenty-five, slim, handsome. He smiled. But there was something about him she did not like.

'Who are you?' she asked.

'They call me Sea Dragon,' he replied. 'I know your Little Brother. And as I was travelling this way, he gave me a message for you. He wants you to know that he is well.'

'Is he in the big city? In Guangzhou?'

'Near it.'

'What is he doing?'

'He is well paid. One day maybe he will be rich.' The young man smiled again. 'He says he does not want you to call him Little Brother anymore. You should call him Cousin from Guangzhou now.'

Her heart sank. Was her Little Brother telling her he'd become another person? Had he joined a criminal gang?

'Is he armed?' she asked nervously.

'Don't worry. He has a dagger and a cutlass.' He'd misunderstood. 'He is very good with the knife.' He laughed.

'Does he work by land or by sea?'

'By sea.'

Her father came forward again.

'We should go,' he said. And Mei-Ling nodded. She knew all she needed to. Nio was a smuggler or a pirate. It was all the same. She had a terrible feeling that soon he would be dead.

o

Run for your life. John told himself to forget the missionary's warning. Pointless to think about it. He just needed to get to Canton and meet Tully Odstock. He'd know what was going on and what to do.

God knows, he thought, if I can't trust the Odstock brothers better than a Dutch missionary I hardly know, then I shouldn't be in business with them.

If only the Dutchman's words would stop echoing in his mind.

They reached the gulf that was the entrance to the Pearl River system that afternoon.

'See those peaks?' McBride pointed to a distant rocky coastline just visible on the horizon. 'The nearest is Hong Kong island. Nothing there, except a few fishermen. But it's got a fine anchorage. Good place to shelter in a storm.'

Read joined Trader and they gazed towards the rock of Hong Kong for a while.

'They say Odstocks do well,' the American remarked. 'Did you ever meet the old father?'

'No. He retired to England.'

'They tell me he left quite a reputation.' He grinned. 'The devil incarnate, people called him. Sharp as a needle.'

Trader frowned. Was the American giving him a gentle warning about Odstocks? He wasn't sure. 'I've known Benjamin quite a while,' he said. 'He's a good man.'

'And the brother in Canton?'

'Tully Odstock? I haven't met him yet.'

Read looked surprised. 'I'd want to know a man pretty well,' he said quietly, 'before I became his partner.'

'You think I rushed into this business?'

'Most men in love think destiny must be on their side.' The American nodded sadly. 'I've been there myself.'

'I suppose I go with my gut,' said John. 'If a thing feels right . . .' He shrugged. 'It's like being pulled by the current, down the river of life.'

'Maybe.' Read considered. 'In my experience, Trader, life's more like the ocean. Unpredictable. Waves coming from all sides. Chance.'

'Well, I think I'm on the right road,' said John.

It was mid-afternoon when they passed Hong Kong. For several more hours the ship made its way between the small, friendly-looking islands scattered across the entrance of the gulf until, just as evening was beginning, they came in sight of Macao.

Macao island was a very different sort of place. Inhabited by the Portuguese for centuries, it had a shallow bay and steep slopes sprinkled with houses, villas, churches and tiny forts that looked charming in the evening sun.

They dropped anchor in Macao Roads. A jolly boat came out, and Read got into it to go ashore. 'Maybe we'll meet again,' he said as he and Trader shook hands. 'If not, good luck.'

The journey from Macao to Canton started the following dawn and took nearly three slow days. McBride didn't talk much.

The first day they made their way up the gulf. Around noon, Trader saw some sails on the horizon.

'Lintin rock,' McBride grunted. 'Where the opium cutters unload. Out of the Chinese governor's sight.'

During the afternoon, as the gulf began to narrow, Trader could see, away on his left, a distant shoreline of endless mudflats, with the mountains rising behind them. Was it just his imagination, or were they staring down at him ominously?

The second day, they saw a group of headlands ahead. 'The Bogue,' McBride said tersely. 'Entrance to China.'

As they reached the Bogue, the schooner hove to beside a junk moored some distance from the shore, from which a young Chinese official quickly boarded them, collected fees from McBride, and waved them on.

The entrance to China was certainly well guarded. They passed between two huge forts, one on either side of the river, with packed mud walls, thirty feet thick and impressive arrays of cannon trained upon the water. Any unwelcome ship in the channel would surely be blown to bits. A short while later they came to another pair of fearsome forts. Mighty empire, John thought, mighty defences.

The channel became narrower. The men took soundings over the side. 'Sandbanks,' McBride grunted. 'Got to be careful.'

As they proceeded, Trader saw rice fields, villages of wooden huts, more fields of grain and now and then an orchard or a temple with a curving hip roof. Small junks with triangular sails on bamboo frameworks skimmed like winged insects on the shallow waters.

So this was China. Fearsome. Picturesque. Mysterious. Sampans came close enough that he could look down at their occupants – pigtailed Chinese, all of them – and they gazed back at him impassively. He smiled at them, even waved, but they did not respond. What were they thinking? He had no idea.

It was the third morning when they came around a bend in the river and he saw a forest of masts ahead.

'Whampoa,' said McBride. 'I'll be leaving you here.'

'I thought you were taking me to Canton.'

'Ships unload here. You take a chop boat up to Canton. It'll get you there before dark.'

And after the schooner had weaved through the huge network of islands, wharves and anchorages, Trader found himself, his strongbox, and his trunks swiftly unloaded into one of the lighters going upstream. With only a handshake and a bleak 'You're on your own now, Mr Trader,' McBride departed.

He had to wait two hours before the lighter set off. The final miles up the Pearl River were tedious. Since he couldn't communicate with the half-dozen Chinese manning the chop boat, John was left alone with his thoughts.

Like most of the traffic, the lighter was going to collect the tea crop season's final pickings – black tea of the lowest quality – before Canton's trade wound down for the summer months. Perhaps it was his imagination, but there seemed to be an end-of-season lassitude amongst the crew.

During the afternoon, the sky became overcast. The clouds were growing darker. He had begun to wonder whether they would reach Canton before dusk and had just concluded that they probably wouldn't when, as they emerged from another bend, he saw a long, untidy settlement of houseboats up ahead. It looked like a floating shantytown. At the end of the houseboats, a little apart, they passed a big painted vessel, three decks high and moored beside the bank. Servants were lighting lanterns around its decks, and by their lights he saw the painted faces of girls looking over the side.

This must be a Chinese flower boat, the floating brothels he'd heard about. The crew came to life now, grinning at him, pointing the girls out to him, and indicating that they could draw alongside. The girls waved encouragingly, but with a politely regretful smile, Trader shook his head.

And a few minutes later, passing a great gaggle of junks moored in the stream, he caught sight of his destination.

The pictures and prints he'd seen had been accurate. There could be no mistaking the splendid port that the foreigners called Canton.

He'd been told that Portuguese merchants had given the place its Western name. Hearing the Chinese refer to the local province as Guangdong, they'd supposed that this meant the city. And soon Guangdong had become Canton. By the time the outside world learned that the city was actually called Guangzhou – which sounded roughly like *Gwung-Jo* – the name Canton was too well entrenched for foreigners to worry about it.

Come to that, most Western travellers referred to Beijing as Peking, and English speakers said Moscow instead of Moskva and, for some obscure reason, Munich instead of München. A few British diehards even called the French city of Lyon by the splendidly British-sounding name of Lions.

Was it arrogance, ignorance, laziness – or perhaps even the sense that accuracy about foreign names sounded too fussy, intellectual and not quite decent? Probably all of these things.

The ancient city's walls lay some way back from the river. Only Chinese could live in the city. But between the walls and the river, the foreign merchants' quarter had a splendour all its own.

A huge open space, empty apart from a couple of customs booths, ran like an extended parade ground along the waterfront for a quarter of a mile. Behind it, a long line of handsome whitewashed buildings in the Georgian colonial style, many displaying verandas with smart green awnings, stared boldly across the square to the water. These were the offices and warehouses of the foreign merchants and also the living quarters where they dwelt. Each building was occupied by merchants from a different country and had a high flagpole in front of it, on which their national flag could be raised. And since these merchant gentlemen were traditionally known as factors, their splendid quarters were called the factories. British, American, Dutch, German, French, Swedish, Spanish: there were over a dozen factories lining the parade.

As the chop boat came to the jetties, Trader noticed a Chinese porter run across to one of the larger buildings. By the time that his trunks were all onshore, he saw a stout figure bustling towards him. There could be no doubt who it was.

Tully Odstock's cheeks were mottled purple; corpulence had made his eyes grow small; tufts of white hair sprouted from his head. He made Trader think of a turnip.

'Mr Trader? Tully Odstock. Glad you're safe. I heard you went up the coast. Did you sell any opium?'

'Yes, Mr Odstock. Fifty chests at six hundred each.'

'Really?' Tully nodded, surprised. 'You did well. Very well.' He seemed preoccupied.

The porters had already put the strongbox and trunks on a handcart. They started towards the British factory.

'They tell me sales are slow,' said Trader.

Tully gave him a swift look. 'You haven't heard the news, then?' And seeing that Trader looked blank: 'Suppose you couldn't have. Only happened this morning. Not too good, I'm afraid.' He gave a short puff. 'Of course, it'll all blow over. Not to worry.'

'What exactly,' Trader asked suspiciously, 'are we talking about?'

'Chinese playing up a bit about the opium. That's all. I'll tell you over dinner. We eat quite well here, you know.'

Trader stopped. 'Tell me now,' he said, surprised at his own firmness towards the older man. 'How much do we stand to lose?'

'Hard to say. Quite a bit, I should think. Talk about it over dinner.'

'How much?'

'Well' – Tully puffed out his purple cheeks – 'I suppose . . . in theory you understand . . . you might say . . . everything.'

'I could lose everything?'

'It'll all blow over,' said Tully. 'Let's have dinner.'

o

Snow in the mountain passes had added a week to his journey, and Shi-Rong had been afraid he might keep Commissioner Lin waiting. So when he finally reached Guangzhou, he was relieved to discover that the mandarin had still not arrived.

He'd decided to make good use of his time. Whatever Lin might require of him, the more he knew about the locality, the better.

As soon as he'd found temporary lodgings, he set out in search of a guide, and after a few enquiries he found exactly what he needed: a Cantonese student preparing to take the mandarin provincial exams. Fong was a skinny, bright young fellow who was only too pleased to earn a little money in this way.

For three days, they toured the bustling old city, the suburbs and the foreign factories. Young Fong proved to be well informed and a good teacher, too. Under his guidance, Shi-Rong continued to improve his Cantonese, and he soon found that he could understand a good deal of what he heard in the streets. For his part, young Fong would ply Shi-Rong with questions each time they ate together, anxious to know what this important visitor thought of all he saw.

'You like our Cantonese food?' he asked during their first meal. 'Too much rice?'

'The dishes smell so rich. And everything tastes too sweet,' Shi-Rong complained.

'Sweet and sour. That's southern Chinese. Try the white cut chicken. Not so sweet. And spring rolls.'

At the end of the second day, as they sat drinking rice wine together, Fong asked him if Guangzhou was what he'd expected.

'I knew everyone would be in a hurry,' Shi-Rong confessed, 'but the crowds in the market and the alleys . . . You can hardly move.'

'And we all have darker skins.' Young Fong grinned. 'And we only care about money. That's what you say about us in Beijing, isn't it?' And when Shi-Rong couldn't deny it: 'All true!' Fong cried with a laugh.

'And what do the people of Guangzhou say about us?' Shi-Rong asked in return.

'Taller. Paler skin.' Fong was naturally treading carefully. But Shi-Rong coaxed him until the young Cantonese admitted: 'We say the northern peasants just sit around on their haunches all day long.'

Shi-Rong smiled. The peasants of the northern plains would often squat together in this manner when they were resting from their work. 'But they still get the crops in,' he replied.

He was especially interested in what Fong thought about the opium traffic. At first, knowing Shi-Rong's position, Fong was noncommittal. But by the fifth day, he trusted Shi-Rong enough to be honest.

'The orders come from Beijing. Raid the opium dens. Arrest the opium smokers. So they make a big sweep, right out into the countryside. Put a lot of people in gaol. But the people still want opium. Waste of time, really. Even the governor thinks so. Doesn't matter what you do. Wait a year, all back to normal.'

A week had passed before Commissioner Lin arrived. He was pleased to find Shi-Rong already there, and still more so when his young assistant told him how he'd used the time. 'Your diligence is commendable. You will be my secretary, but also my eyes and ears.'

Lin at once commandeered a house in the suburb close to the foreign factories and told Shi-Rong he was to lodge there also. The first evening he outlined his plan of action.

'I have read all the memorials from the province on my journey here. During the next week, we shall talk to the governor of the province, the local mandarins, the merchants of Guangzhou – and their servants, who will tell us more – so that I can make my own assessment. Then we shall smash the opium trade. Who do you think we should strike first?'

Repeating what Fong had told him and other things he had seen for himself, Shi-Rong confessed frankly that he thought it would be a long and difficult task to dissuade people from using the drug.

'I will burn all their opium pipes,' Lin said grimly. 'But you are right. The only way to root out this poison is to stop the supply. So, young Mr Jiang, who is our greatest enemy?'

'The Fan Kuei – the red-haired foreign devils who bring the opium into the kingdom.'

'And what do we know about them?'

'I have been to their factories. It seems they are not all the same. They come from many countries. And only a few of them have red hair.'

'The largest criminals are from a country called Britain. Nobody seems to be sure exactly where it is. Do you know?'

'No, Excellency. Shall I make enquiries?'

'Perhaps. Though it does not really matter where these inferior peoples dwell. I have learned, however, that this country is ruled by a queen. Also that she has sent some kind of official here.'

'Yes, Commissioner. His name is Elliot. From a noble family. At present he is in Macao.'

'Perhaps this queen does not even know what these pirates from her country are doing. Perhaps her servant has not told her.'

'It is possible, Commissioner.'

'I am writing this queen a letter. It is being translated into her own barbarous tongue. When the draft is ready, I shall give her servant the letter to convey to her. I shall reprimand her and give her instructions. If she is a moral ruler, no doubt she will order this Elliot to execute the pirates. The worst is a man named Jardine. He should start with him.' He paused, then looked searchingly at Shi-Rong. 'But the Fan Kuei are not important. It is a small matter for the Celestial Empire to deal with a few pirates. So I ask again: Who is the real enemy, Mr Jiang? Do you know?'

'I am not sure, Excellency.'

'It is our own merchants here in this city: the Hong, the merchant guild – the very group of men the emperor has authorised to deal with these foreigners. They are the traitors, the ones who allow the barbarians to sell opium, and we shall deal with them severely.'

The next few days were busy. Without saying what he intended to do, Lin conducted numerous interviews and collected evidence. Shi-Rong found himself working day and night taking notes, writing reports, and running errands. After a week, Lin gave him a small mission of his own. He was to go to the house of one of the Hong merchants and talk to him.

'Don't give anything away,' Lin told him. 'Be friendly. Talk to him about the foreign merchants and their trade. Find out what he really thinks.'

The following afternoon Shi-Rong made his report.

'The first thing I discovered, Excellency, is that he doesn't believe the opium trade will be stopped. Interrupted, yes. But he thinks that once you have done enough to please the emperor, you will leave. And then things will go back to the way they were before. In the meantime, although he knows your reputation for honesty, he clearly finds it hard to believe you won't be bought off like everyone else.'

'Anything else?'

'Two things, Excellency. His tone suggested that he and the barbarian merchants have become personal friends. More than that, I discovered from his servants that he personally is deeply in debt to one of them, a man named Odstock.'

'You have done well. The emperor was correct to keep these Fan Kuei away from our people. Yet even when we confine them to a single port, in a compound outside the city walls, they still manage to corrupt our Hong merchants, who are supposed to be worthy men.'

'Indeed.'

'You said there was a second thing.'

'Probably of no significance, Excellency. But he told me that this merchant, Odstock, daily expects the arrival of a young scholar who is to be a junior partner in his business. Though it seems strange,' he added, 'that a man of education would become a merchant.'

'Who knows, with these barbarians? When he arrives, I want you to meet him. See if he knows anything useful.'

'As you wish, Excellency.' Shi-Rong bowed his head.

'And now,' Lin said with a grim smile, 'I think we are ready. Summon all the members of the Hong to gather this evening.' He gave Shi-Rong a quick nod. 'We strike tonight.'

o

John Trader gazed at Tully Odstock in horror. They were sitting in his small office, overlooking the narrow alley that ran from the front of the English factory to the Chinese lane at the back. Two oil lamps shed a yellowish glow over the leather chairs in which they were sitting. The atmosphere was warm and stuffy; but to John Trader, it felt cold as the Gobi Desert.

'Happened last night,' Tully explained. 'This Lin fellow called all the Hong merchants in. Told them they were criminals and traitors. Then he says that the factory merchants are to surrender all their opium, and that the Hong must arrange it – they're responsible for all the overseas trade, you see – and that if they don't, he'll start executing them. He's given them three days. In the meantime, none of us are allowed to leave Canton.'

'When he says all our opium . . .'

'Not just the small amounts we have here at the factories. He means all the bulk we keep at the depots downriver and out in the gulf, and the cargoes in ships still coming in. He means everything we have. It's a huge amount.'

'And the opium I bought and paid for?'

'That, too, of course.' Tully nodded sympathetically. 'Rather hard luck that, I must say. But when you invested in the partnership, that immediately became Odstocks' money, you see.' He brightened. 'You're in for ten per cent of future profits, of course.'

'What profits?' Trader asked bitterly. Tully said nothing. 'So I've lost my investment.'

'Wouldn't say that,' Tully replied. 'Daresay it'll all blow over.'

'Are we going to surrender the opium?'

'There's a meeting about that. Day after tomorrow. You'll be there, of course,' Tully added, as though that made things better.

John Trader didn't sleep much that night. Odstocks' quarters in the English factory contained two small bedrooms. Tully's looked into the alley. John's had no window. At midnight, lying in his stuffy box of a room, listening to Tully's snores through the plaster wall, John reached over to the brass oil lamp still burning with a tiny glow and turned up the wick. Then taking a piece of paper, he stared at what he had written. Not that he needed to. He knew all the figures by heart.

Total investment. Debt. Interest due. Cash on hand. Staring dully at the numbers, he calculated once again. Assuming modest expenses, he could pay the interest on his debt and live for a year, but not much more. Fifteen months at best.

The Odstock brothers didn't know about his debt. He'd used the extra investment to negotiate a better deal from the partnership. In normal circumstances, it would have been a good bargain. But now? He was facing ruin.

And why had he done it? To win Agnes, of course. To make a fortune fast. To prove to her father that in time he'd be able to make Agnes the mistress of a Scottish estate. He knew it could be done. The image of her face came before his eyes. Yes. Yes, it could be done. More than that. It was destiny. He felt it with a certainty he could not explain. It was meant to be.

So he'd left the safe mediocrity of Calcutta and gone for broke in China – chosen the high seas and the storms and the sharp rocks, if he failed. Death, if need be, like so many thousand adventurers before him. He had to. It was his nature. And even now, faced with ruin, a little voice told him that, given the choice, he'd do it all again.

But as he stared at those bleak figures in the middle of the night, he was still afraid. And he slept only fitfully in his dark room until the sound of Tully Odstock stirring told him that, outside, it must be morning.

'Time to introduce you around,' Tully had said as they'd set out after breakfast. He'd said it briskly, as though there was nothing to be alarmed about.

John still wasn't sure what to make of Tully. He supposed he was a solid old merchant like his brother. But had the two brothers accepted his money and given him a partnership just a bit too quickly? If he himself had concealed the extent of his borrowings, had they in turn been less than entirely forthcoming with him about the state of the business?

And when Tully said the trouble would all blow over, was he trying to fool a new partner or, perhaps worse, was he fooling himself? For one thing was sure – Trader could almost smell it – Tully Odstock was afraid.

Yet nobody else seemed to be alarmed at all. By noon, they'd been to every factory. He'd met French and Swedish merchants, Danish, Spanish, Dutch. Almost everyone agreed: 'This is just Lin's opening bid. We'll refuse it. Then he'll negotiate.'

'He needs to make a show to impress the emperor so he can get his promotion and move on to somewhere else,' one of the Dutch merchants assured them. 'That's how these mandarins play the game.'

And if this sounded heartening, still further encouragement came when they got to the American factory.

Warren Delano was only thirty, a handsome fellow with a fine moustache and sideburns and a friendly smile – though John did not fail to notice a pair of steely eyes – who'd already made a fortune in the opium trade. He was everything that John hoped to be. And he dismissed Lin's demand easily.

'All the opium I sell is on consignment,' he told them. 'Way I see it, I can't surrender goods that belong to other people. Don't have the legal right. Simple as that.'

'Damn good point,' Tully said. 'A third of our opium's on consignment, too. Belongs to Parsee merchants in Bombay.'

'There you go, then,' said Delano.

By the time they left, it seemed to Trader that his plump partner was covering the ground with a new confidence. 'We'll go back this way,' Tully said, leading him into Old China Street.

Behind their facades, which looked across the waterfront, each of the factories went back, in a series of tiny courts and stairways, for over a hundred yards to a Cantonese thoroughfare known as Thirteen Factory Street, which formed the boundary between the factories' enclosure and the Chinese suburb. Three lanes ran from this thoroughfare through the factory block to the waterfront: Hog Lane, which ran down beside the English factory; Old China Street, beside the Americans' factory; and another between the Spanish and Danish factories. And although they lay within the factory quarter, these lanes were lined with little Chinese stalls selling every delicacy or household goods that their owners imagined the Fan Kuei might buy.

As they walked past the stalls and came out into Thirteen Factory Street, Tully jerked his thumb contemptuously to the left, towards a handsome old Chinese mansion a short distance away. 'That's where Commissioner Lin has based himself.' He snorted. 'Suppose he thinks he can keep an eye on us from there.'

After a brief walk up the bustling street, they turned right into Hog Lane. Tully pointed to a doorway. 'That's our hospital, in case you get sick. There's an excellent doctor, an American missionary called Parker. Nice fella.' He nodded. 'Well, that's given you the lie of the land. Time for lunch, I'd say.'

The English factory had been built in the eighteenth century by the East India Company. At the front on the upper floor, its spacious dining room, flanked by a library on one side and a billiard room on the other, looked out over an English walled garden that extended almost to the waterfront. Oil paintings on the walls, handsome chairs and a platoon of well-trained waiters combined to reproduce all the solid comfort and stability of a London club.

Not all the English merchants resided at the English factory, large though it was. A number lodged in other factories with extra space. But the handsome English factory was their clubhouse, and over a dozen men had gathered there for lunch that day. Jardine himself, the greatest opium trader of them all, had sailed for England not long ago, and so his partner Matheson presided. Several of the men were smaller merchants, one of whom in particular, a fellow named Dent, looked distinctly like a pirate to Trader. By contrast, one of Jardine's nephews had brought along the eminently respectable Dr Parker.

Missionary or buccaneer, they all seemed genial and ready to give good advice. Matheson indicated Trader should sit next to him. Encased between well-tamed whiskers, like a pair of bookends, Matheson's face had a pleasant, rather intellectual look, more like a bookseller, Trader thought, than a ruthless opium merchant.

'The secret to life here, Trader,' he said cordially, 'is to have a first-rate comprador. He's the man who deals with the locals, finds you good Chinese servants, food supplies, anything you want. We've got an excellent man.'

'The servants are all local?'

'Pretty much. They don't give any trouble. The Cantonese are practical people.'

'Should I learn to speak Chinese?' John asked.

'I'd advise not,' his host replied. 'The authorities don't like it. They don't want us getting too close to their people. As I'm sure you know, everyone here speaks pidgin English. The Hong merchants, the servants, the people on the waterfront – they all understand pidgin English. You'll pick it up in no time.' He turned towards the American. 'Dr Parker speaks Chinese, of course, but that's different.'

The American was a short, bespectacled, clean-shaven man. Looked about thirty.

'You see,' the missionary explained with a smile, 'the local people, including the mandarins, come to me for treatment. So they like to be sure we understand each other before I start cutting pieces out of them!'

'I always heard the Chinese were proud of their own medicine,' Trader said.

'Yes. Their acupuncture and herbal cures often work. But when it's a question of surgery, we're far ahead, and they know it. So they come to us.'

'They're nothing but quacks,' said Tully firmly.

'We shouldn't be too proud,' Parker said sensibly. 'Don't forget, sir, it's not so long since surgery in London was performed by barbers.'

Remembering Van Buskirk handing out tracts to the Chinese smugglers, Trader asked Parker if he was able to make any converts in Canton.

'Not yet,' Parker replied. 'But I hope, one day, to earn enough respect as a doctor for them to respect my faith as well. I have to be patient, that's all.'

'Test of faith, eh?' said Tully Odstock.

'You could say that,' Parker replied quietly. Then he gave Trader a kind look. 'Mr Odstock tells me that you have a degree from Oxford University. That's impressive.'

'Ah,' said John Trader. And just for a moment he hesitated.

He knew – he'd taken the trouble to find out – that both Matheson and Jardine had Edinburgh degrees. That of Jardine was in medicine. But for a merchant or a city man to have a university degree was unusual. In the army and navy, it was unheard of. Men with intellectual interests were regarded with suspicion.

There was, however, one way a man could go to Oxford and still show the outside world he was a decent fellow. And that was to take a pass degree.

Clever, studious men took honours degrees. Decent fellows with no intellectual pretensions could opt for a far less rigorous examination, enjoy themselves, and take a humble pass degree, which really signified that they'd been at the place, they could read and write, and they'd learned to drink like a gentleman. John knew one man who swore he'd passed three years at Oxford without ever reading a book.

'My guardian wanted me to go to Oxford,' said John. 'I learned a bit, I suppose, but I only took a pass degree, you know.'

In fact, it wasn't true. He'd taken honours. But he'd thought it wiser to tell people in Calcutta that he'd only taken a pass degree, and he was sticking to his story.

During the meal, the threat from the commissioner was further discussed. Tully told them what Delano had said, which was well received. Everyone agreed that they'd play a waiting game. Dent thumped the table and said that if the commissioner gave any trouble they should all grab the damn fellow and toss him into the river. As the just-arrived new boy, Trader listened without offering any opinions.

But as he silently watched this handful of merchants facing the possibility of massive loss, this small collection of undefended men sitting on a tiny strip of land, while all around them lay a vast empire of millions who could overwhelm them in a minute if they chose, he couldn't help admiring them. They might be arrogant; they certainly didn't occupy any moral high ground; but for all that, as they sat coolly in their club, he found them reassuringly British.

When the dessert was served, however, he did venture to ask a question. 'There is something I don't understand,' he confessed to Matheson. 'In India, we have the East India Company army to protect our trade. We haven't any military force here in China, though there is a British government representative called the superintendent. So my question is, if British trade is at risk and the livelihood of British merchants threatened, what's the superintendent going to do about it?'

'Elliot!' cried Tully Odstock, and snorted. 'Nothing! Useless fella. Won't do a thing.' And there were murmurs of approval at this outburst.

'Captain Elliot,' replied Matheson calmly, 'as you see, is not very popular. He went to Macao the other day, and no doubt he'll return here soon.'

'Why is he disliked?' asked Trader.

'Partly, I think, because he's an aristocrat,' answered Matheson. 'Two of his cousins are lords – one is governor general of India, the other's in the cabinet. At least one of his family's an admiral. We merchants don't feel he likes us much. And he certainly doesn't like the opium trade. Disapproves of it, in fact, and therefore disapproves of us.'

'Why doesn't the damn fella go and work for the emperor of China, then?' Tully interrupted.

'Elliot's obliged to safeguard our interests, of course,' Matheson continued, 'because the tea we import from China is highly valuable to the British government. So is the cotton we sell to China – though despite the eagerness of our mill owners in England, I can assure you that the Chinese market will never absorb enough cotton to pay for all the tea we need to buy.'

'All well and good, Matheson,' said Tully Odstock. 'But if things get rough – and they could – I want a fellow I can trust watching my back. Not a man who's practically on the Chinese side. As for his morals, once a man gets on a moral high horse, you never know what he's going to do. We could lose everything.'

'We must keep cool,' said Matheson.

'I am cool,' said Tully hotly.

'But you are wrong about Elliot if you think he's sympathetic to China,' Matheson continued. 'In fact, I would argue the exact reverse.'

'Damned if I see why.'

'I've observed Elliot carefully. He's an aristocrat, an imperialist, perhaps a diplomatist. Now consider the case of China. A proud empire that sees itself as above all others. If we send an embassy to China, the imperial court sees us as a subject people who have come to pay tribute. They expect the ambassador to kowtow, flat on his face, before the emperor. Merchants like us may not care two hoots about this, so long as we can trade. But to Elliot, it is intolerable, an insult to the British Crown and to his dignity. He's concerned with status.'

'No trade, no money. No money, no status,' said Tully crossly.

'I agree. But even on the subject of trade, Elliot cannot be a friend of China. And why is that? Because China will not allow us to trade with her as we do with other nations. In all this huge empire, we are allowed to trade only at Canton, and we can't even reside in the city. But if we had free access to the cities of China, to offer them our goods – who knows? – we might not even need to trade in opium. Or so Elliot might argue. In short, he hates the status quo. And until the celestial throne recognises the British Empire as an equal and joins the normal trade and intercourse of nations, Elliot will be implacably opposed to it.'

'You know how to talk,' said Odstock grudgingly. He turned to Trader. 'You're an Oxford man. I hope you can give Matheson a run for his money in the talking department.'

But before Trader could respond to this embarrassing proposition, the conversation was interrupted by a servant quickly entering the dining room and announcing:

'Mr Zhou asks Mr Odstock to please come to his house. Bring Mr Trader also. Very urgent.'

Odstock looked at them all in surprise. 'The devil he does.' He turned to Trader. 'Zhou's a member of the Hong. He's the Chinese merchant I deal with, mostly.' He turned back to the servant. 'Why?'

'Commissioner Lin's orders.'

'Me?' said John in horror. And the man nodded.

'How very strange!' exclaimed Matheson. Even he looked slightly alarmed. 'Well,' he said after a pause, 'I suppose you'd better go.'

As Trader walked up Hog Lane with Mr Zhou's servant and Tully Odstock, his partner tried to sound completely calm.

'I call him Joker,' he explained. 'His name sounds like Joe, you see. He doesn't mind.'

They were halfway down Hog Lane when Tully stopped at a stall and bought a couple of almond cookies. Giving one of them to Trader, he slowly began to eat his without moving.

'Mr Zhou says come quick,' that gentleman's servant cried anxiously, but Tully ignored him.

'Never hurry. Never look anxious,' he murmured to Trader, who took the hint and crunched through his almond cookie before taking another step. 'By the way,' Tully continued, 'when we get there, we'll talk, and after a while they'll bring tea. Once you've drunk your tea, you're expected to leave. That's the form here.'

'Anything else I should know?' John asked.

'At the moment, Joker owes us quite a bit of money. But don't worry. Joker's all right. Known him for years. He'll pay.' He nodded. 'As a matter of fact, I haven't seen him for nearly a week. Wonder what he thinks about this Lin nonsense.'

It took only five minutes to reach Mr Zhou's house. It was impressive, with a courtyard, verandas and a handsome garden behind. He received them in a well-furnished room hung with red lanterns.

'Afternoon, Joker,' said Tully. 'Long time no see.'

'Six days,' the Hong merchant answered.

As John Trader gazed at Mr Zhou, it seemed to him that his partner's nickname for the Chinese merchant was very badly chosen. He received them sitting in the most dignified manner, in a chair like a throne. The high polished dome of his head surmounted a long, almost skeletonic face. Over a richly embroidered tunic, he wore a wide-sleeved black silk gown. Around his neck, a long double row of amber beads hung to his waist. He looked to John more like an emperor than a court jester.

'This is Mr Trader,' said Tully. 'Studied at Oxford.'

Mr Zhou inclined his head and smiled.

'How do you do, Mr Zhou,' said John politely.

'You can speak Chinese?' Zhou asked.

'Not yet.'

The Chinese merchant did not look impressed.

'Joker,' asked Tully, 'what's Commissioner Lin want?'

'He wants all the opium,' the Hong merchant answered.

'Why does he want so much?'

'He must get it all or lose face.'

'No can do,' said Tully firmly. He looked at Joker carefully. There was something in the Hong merchant's eyes: a look of real fear. 'Joker's in a funk,' Tully murmured to Trader. He turned back to the Hong merchant. 'Why does Lin ask for Trader?'

But before Joker could answer, there was a sound of voices, and a moment later a servant ushered two men into the room.

o

Jiang Shi-Rong looked at the three men. He already knew Zhou. It was obvious who Odstock was. So the dark-haired young man must be the scholar.

He'd wondered how he might converse with Trader. He didn't want to communicate through Zhou, whom he didn't trust in any case. So he'd brought his own interpreter.

To be precise, the man in question had arrived with Commissioner Lin. He was a curious fellow, small, thin and of indeterminate age. He said he was forty; he might have been fifty. He wore scratched round spectacles with very thick lenses, though Shi-Rong could not detect any sign of magnification in them. And he claimed to speak and write English to an equally advanced degree, having learned it first in the household of a missionary in Macao, before improving his knowledge still further during a sojourn in Singapore. As a result of this last part of his story, he was known to everyone by a nickname: Mr Singapore.

As soon as Mr Zhou had performed the introductions, he observed to Shi-Rong that Odstock had just been asking what the commissioner wished to accomplish in Guangzhou.

Shi-Rong bowed politely and turned to Mr Singapore. 'Tell the barbarian merchant that Commissioner Lin is here to abolish the opium trade forever.' He watched as Mr Singapore, without too much difficulty, conveyed this unequivocal message. He noticed that Odstock looked both cynical and outraged, but that young Trader appeared rather downcast. 'The criminals who engage in this illegal trade will be firmly dealt with,' he continued. 'Some, including Mr Zhou, may be executed.'

Mr Zhou looked very unhappy.

Odstock spoke, and Mr Singapore said, 'The fat barbarian asks if the Celestial Kingdom wants to sell tea.'

'The Celestial Kingdom has no need to sell anything,' said Shi-Rong, 'but the goods it does sell are healthful, such as tea and the rhubarb herb, without which you will die.' He saw the two barbarians look surprised. Obviously they had not realised that he knew that their very lives depended on their getting the rhubarb. 'We will allow barbarian merchants to buy these things for silver,' Shi-Rong concluded firmly. 'That is all.'

Odstock and Zhou were silent. Shi-Rong turned his attention to Trader. 'Ask him, if he is a scholar, why has he become a pirate,' he told Mr Singapore.

'He says he is not a pirate. He is a merchant.'

'Well then, if he is a scholar, why is he a merchant, the lowest form of humanity?'

'He says the merchant is not the lowest form of humanity. Not in his country.'

It seemed to Shi-Rong that this young barbarian had replied hotly to his question, even defiantly, as if his own country were the equal of the Celestial Kingdom. And this when he and his fellow Fan Kuei were busy poisoning people for profit.

'We consider,' Shi-Rong said firmly, 'that to be a peasant, honestly working the land, is a moral occupation. The merchant who takes the work of others and sells it for gain is clearly a person of a lower moral order, and he deserves to be despised. Tell him this.'

Mr Singapore seemed to struggle a bit translating this, but he managed to do so. Trader said nothing.

Shi-Rong returned to the attack. 'In any case, his claim not to be a pirate is false. If he is honest, why is he breaking the law and selling opium to smugglers?'

'He says he is not under Chinese law.'

'He should respect the laws of the Celestial Kingdom, both because he is here and because those laws are benevolent, just, and wise.'

While Mr Singapore tried to convey these ideas, Shi-Rong considered. It seemed to him that Trader's answers did not really add up. 'Is he truly a scholar?' he asked sceptically.

'He says he attended the University of Oxford.'

'I do not know what that is. Ask him where his country is and how big it is.'

'He says it is an island far, far to the west, but that it possesses an empire bigger than the Celestial Kingdom.'

Shi-Rong felt a sense of disappointment. Obviously this young man was not only arrogant, but a liar. Perhaps it was a waste of time talking to him. He kept his face impassive, however, and pressed on. 'Is it true that his kingdom is ruled by women?'

'He says nearly always by kings, but recently his country has a young queen.'

'And does his queen have good morals, or is she a wicked person?'

'He says she is named Queen Victoria and that she has the highest morals.'

'Then why does she permit her merchants to sell opium?'

'His queen does not think opium is bad. She takes it herself. Opium is healthful – only bad if taken to excess.'

'But that is the point,' cried Shi-Rong. 'It *is* taken to excess. People smoke a little. Then they want more. Soon they are unable to stop. They spend all their money. They cannot work. They become like sick shadows. In the end they die. Millions of people in the Celestial Kingdom are being destroyed by this poison. How can he say it is healthful?'

'He says that each man is responsible for his actions.'

'A good ruler should protect his people. He has the same responsibility as a father to his son. Does he know anything of Confucius?'

'He has heard of Confucius.'

The barbarian was not completely ignorant, then.

'Then he will know that all men owe obedience: a son should obey his father; his father should obey the emperor. If the emperor rules wisely and justly, then this flows down through all his people. It is when the chains of proper conduct are broken that evil and chaos ensue. There are millions of people in the Celestial Kingdom. But they are all held together by obedience and right conduct, in service to the emperor, whose justice comes from the Mandate of Heaven. Therefore it is not for you or any barbarian ruler to judge what is right or wrong, but the emperor. Nothing else needs to be said.'

Shi-Rong noticed that Mr Singapore struggled for quite a time in conveying this to Trader. But he was patient. Until this barbarian, whether he was a scholar or not, understood the basic facts of morality, there could be no basis for conversation between them.

'He says that his queen is also anointed by Heaven,' declared Mr Singapore at last.

'In that case,' said Shi-Rong triumphantly, 'I will show him the letter.' And he drew out a document and handed it to Trader. 'You may explain to him that this is a draft, that you have translated into his own tongue, of the letter that Commissioner Lin is going to send to his queen.' And he watched with satisfaction as Trader took the letter and began to read.

It was a good letter. A true mandarin composition. It was reasonable. It was polite.

It pointed out that trade had carried on between their countries for centuries with peace and harmony. But recently, the trade in opium had become huge and destructive. It respectfully suggested that the Way of Heaven was the same for all countries, and that the commissioner was sure Queen Victoria would feel exactly the same about the importation of a poisonous drug into her kingdom as did the emperor. He knew that the opium came only from certain lands under her rule, and that it could not have been sold under her direction. Lin explained that the trade must cease, and asked her to forbid her merchants to continue in it. Lin ended with a veiled warning that neither the emperor nor Heaven itself would look well upon her rule if she failed in this moral duty, but that many blessings would doubtless be granted if she did as the emperor wished.

Indeed, there was nothing wrong with the letter at all, except for Mr Singapore's abominable translation, which was causing Trader to frown as he tried to make sense of it.

After a while, Trader handed it back.

'As a scholar, you will appreciate it,' said Shi-Rong.

'He says it is interesting,' Mr Singapore reported.

'I hope your queen will stop the trade at once,' continued Shi-Rong.

'I cannot speak for Her Majesty, who will make her own decision,' Trader replied carefully.

Tea was brought in. The conversation was fitful and strained. Shi-Rong had delivered the messages that Lin wanted, and since Trader did not seem to be much of a scholar, nothing very useful could be learned from him.

Yet as he watched the dark-haired young man's face, Shi-Rong thought he detected something a little sad in it. Could there be some decency in him? He had no desire to invite intimacy with this barbarian stranger, yet he was curious. And so, rather to his own surprise, he found himself saying: 'My father is a good man. And each day I think of how he would wish me to behave and try to do so. Would your father wish you to engage in the opium trade?'

As Mr Singapore translated, he saw Trader bow his head, as if deep in thought, before he quietly replied: 'You are fortunate. I lost both my parents when I was very young. I was brought up by an elderly relation. He was my guardian.'

'Was he a good man?'

'He is not sure,' Mr Singapore translated. 'He does not know.'

'I think,' said Shi-Rong gently, 'that you know you should not sell opium, and that it troubles you.'

John Trader did not reply. And as the ceremony of tea was over, it was time for them to depart.

'It's all humbug, you know,' Tully Odstock remarked to Trader that evening. They were sitting in the walled garden in front of the English factory. 'You'll see what happens tomorrow, when the real negotiation begins.'

'I'm not so sure,' answered Trader. 'I think Lin means business.'

'He'll collapse tomorrow,' said Odstock. 'As for that stupid letter to the queen . . .'

'It may have been all right in Chinese,' Trader remarked. 'I did manage to get the sense of it in the end. But the English was so garbled it was almost gibberish. Mr Singapore's a complete fraud.'

'There you are,' said Tully. He gave Trader a shrewd look. 'And when that young mandarin started his damn nonsense about you being troubled . . . Bloody cheek, I thought.'

'Quite,' said John.

'They're all heathens, of course, at the end of the day.' Tully took out a cigar, cut and slowly lit it, drew upon it, leaned back, looked up towards the evening sky and exhaled a mouthful of smoke towards the hesitant early stars. 'You know what I'm going to do in a couple of years when I retire, back to England? Get married.' He nodded his head and took another draw on his cigar. 'Find a nice wife. Go to church, I daresay. That sort of thing.'

'Anything else?' Trader asked idly.

'I'm going to found an orphanage. Always wanted to do that.'

'That sounds very worthy.'

'A man with money can do a lot of good, you know,' said Tully. He exhaled again. 'Of course,' he added wisely, 'you've got to have the money first.'

'Absolutely.'

'Think I'll turn in. You?'

'Not tired yet.'

'Goodnight, then.' Tully arose, cigar in hand. 'You'll see I'm right, in the morning.'

John sat in the walled garden. The sky grew darker, the stars more bright. After a while he got up and paced about, but feeling the need for more space, he left the garden and went out onto the great open quayside.

The quay was empty, although there were lanterns in many of the junks out in the stream. He wandered down past the American factory to the end of the quay and sat on an iron mooring post, staring out across the darkened water. And as he sat there and reflected upon the events of the day that had just passed, the truth about the opium came to him, with a terrible, cold clarity.

They'd all been here too long, these merchants. They couldn't believe that things would not continue as they had before. So of course they assumed Lin must be bluffing.

But they were wrong. The more Trader thought about the young mandarin he had just met, the more certain he felt that Jiang Shi-Rong and his master Lin and the emperor himself were indeed all in deadly earnest. It was a moral issue. They had the Mandate of Heaven on their side and hundreds of thousands of troops to call upon. They would end the opium trade, without a doubt.

And God knows, he suddenly thought, if Lin's letter were rendered into decent English and it reached the monarch, it could be that Queen Victoria would agree with him. Elliot, her own representative here, already did.

He'd sunk his money into opium and now – he was sure – he was going to lose it all.

Why had he done it? For love? For ambition? It didn't matter anymore. It was too late. He put his head in his hands and rocked from side to side.

'They're deluding themselves. Odstock, the lot of them. It's all over,' he murmured. 'What have I done? Oh my God. What have I done?'

o

Shi-Rong had been glad he could tell the commissioner that he had watched Trader read the letter and that the barbarian scholar had been impressed.

'At moments he looked thunderstruck,' he reported.

'Let us hope it does some good,' said Lin.

But it didn't. Some forty of the foreign merchants met the following morning. In no time at all, they sent word that they wouldn't surrender any opium at the moment, and that they needed almost a week to think about it.

It was the first time Shi-Rong had seen the commissioner angry. 'Tell them I demand a surrender of opium at once,' he ordered Shi-Rong. 'Take Mr Singapore with you. Make sure they understand that if they do not obey, the consequences will be serious. Go now!'

Having delivered his message at the factories, Shi-Rong had to wait hours before he could return with a reply. 'They offer a thousand chests, Excellency. No more.'

The commissioner's face turned to stone. Shi-Rong wondered if he would start executing them. Lin read his thoughts.

'It would be easy to kill these barbarians. But that is beneath the dignity of the Celestial Kingdom. Or we could expel them all. But the emperor does not wish to destroy all the trade, for some of it is beneficial to his people. The emperor wishes the barbarians to admit their crime and to acknowledge that the Celestial Kingdom is just. Do you understand?'

'Yes, Excellency.'

'Very well. They do not take us seriously. We must ensure that they do.' Lin nodded. 'I will summon one or two of these barbarians, question them, and, if they are not cooperative, arrest them. That may have some effect.'

'Have you particular men in mind, Excellency?'

'There is one Englishman who is particularly insolent. Every report complained about him. His name is Dent. But I need another.'

'What about Odstock, the older merchant I met yesterday?' suggested Shi-Rong. 'We know he has corrupted the merchant Zhou. He showed no sign of remorse, but I did not think he was a brave man. If he is frightened, he may give up his opium. And if one merchant yields, perhaps they will all give in.'

'Good,' said Lin. 'Tomorrow, you will bring me Dent and Odstock.'

o

Trader had gone to stretch his legs on the waterfront the next morning when he noticed a gaggle of men hastily backing out of Hog Lane. A moment later he saw that they were being pushed by Chinese soldiers. The soldiers wore blue tunics and conical hats and carried spears. They filled the entrance to the lane beside the English factory, but did not advance farther. Looking along the waterfront, he could see that Chinese soldiers filled the entrances to the other two lanes as well. The factories and the waterfront were being blocked off.

He'd just finished telling Tully about what had happened, and Tully was just putting on his jacket to come and see for himself, when they heard feet tramping up the stairs. Shi-Rong, flanked by two soldiers, with swords unsheathed, appeared in the narrow doorway, while one of the factory servants ducked in beside Shi-Rong to deliver a message. 'Commissioner Lin wants Mr Odstock to come, please.'

Odstock rose in a dignified manner and bowed politely to Shi-Rong, who returned the bow with equal politeness. If Tully felt fear, he concealed it well. He turned to Trader. 'Suppose I'd better,' he said with a shrug. 'You can stay and hold the fort till I get back.'

'You're going to leave me?' Trader asked in horror.

And Tully would probably have gone that moment if the sound of someone bounding up the stairs hadn't been followed immediately by the appearance of Matheson, who pushed past the soldiers furiously. 'Don't think of going, Odstock,' he cried. 'They just came for Dent as well.'

'Did he agree to go?' Tully asked.

'To be precise, he said he didn't give a damn and he'd be glad to tell the emperor of China what he thought of him.'

'Sounds like Dent.'

'However, I persuaded him not to go. In case he might never come back.'

Trader looked at Shi-Rong, who was standing there impassively, then at Matheson. 'You think they'd . . .'

'Unlikely,' said Matheson. 'But once Dent's in their custody, you can't be certain. And God knows if or when they'd give him back. In any case, it's better if we all stick together. We don't want Lin getting to work on us individually.' He turned to Tully. 'You mustn't go.'

'All right,' said Tully. He turned to Shi-Rong. 'No can do.'

After Shi-Rong and his men had departed, Matheson gave Trader an encouraging smile. 'They could have removed Dent and Odstock by force,' he pointed out. 'This is a good sign.' But Trader wasn't sure he sounded entirely convinced.

Meanwhile, the Chinese soldiers remained in the lanes, keeping the factories sealed off.

And the soldiers were still there the next morning. After a walk along the waterside, Tully and Trader went into the English factory library, where they found Matheson and a dozen others. Tully sank into a deep leather chair.

'Want a book?' asked Trader.

'Certainly not.'

Trader went to the bookshelves. Someone had left a copy of Dickens's *Pickwick Papers* there. As the book had been published only a couple of years ago, he supposed someone had read it on the voyage out from England and obligingly donated it to the library on arrival. Perhaps the delightful comedy would take his mind off his troubles for a while. And so it did, for about twenty minutes, until one of the men gazing out of the window exclaimed: 'Good Lord, look at that!' And a moment later everyone in the library was crowding by the window, looking out on the open space below.

It was a melancholy little procession. Half a dozen Chinese soldiers were leading three members of the Hong. They were all imposing figures. But no man could look dignified with an iron collar around his neck, attached to a chain being dragged by a soldier. One of them was Joker, whose face looked a picture of misery. In the middle of the open space, the procession turned to face the English factory and stopped. The soldier in command had a bamboo rod. Slashing at the back of Joker's leg, he caused the old man to cry out and sink to his knees. He had no need to strike the other two, who took the hint and knelt immediately. Then the soldiers heaped the chains over the shoulders of the three men to weigh them down. Bowed and half crushed, as though about to perform the kowtow, the three merchants knelt there in the sun and the soldiers silently watched them. Nobody moved.

'Are they going to execute them?' asked Trader.

'They're just trying to frighten us,' somebody said.

'Humbug,' said Tully Odstock with a snort. 'Damned humbug.'

'I agree. They're putting on a show,' said Matheson.

'All the same,' said Tully after a pause, 'I hope Joker's going to be all right. He owes me a fortune,' he added quietly.

'And Lin knows that, you may be sure,' said Matheson. 'The only thing to do is take no notice at all.' And he moved away from the window.

But Trader went back to the window again, just before lunch. And again after lunch, when the sun was almost directly over the three men's heads. After that, Tully retired to their quarters to take a nap, and Trader played a desultory game of billiards with Jardine's nephew.

It was mid-afternoon when the Chinese delegation arrived. This time they were not armed. There was a magistrate, attended by two junior mandarins, young Shi-Rong, and Mr Singapore. The magistrate went straight to Dent's quarters. Shi-Rong and Mr Singapore, followed closely by Trader, went to rouse Odstock.

The message, delivered by Mr Singapore, was very simple. 'Mr Jiang is here to accompany Mr Odstock to Commissioner Lin. He will stay here until Mr Odstock comes.'

Odstock gazed at Shi-Rong for a long moment and then indicated a chair. 'Take a seat,' he said, and went back to bed.

Shi-Rong sat, and so did Trader. Mr Singapore explained that he had to go, because Commissioner Lin wanted to make additions to his letter to Queen Victoria. So he left the two young men, sitting together but unable to speak.

It was in that half hour that Trader discovered, for the first time in his life, the frustration of lacking a common language.

Of course, there had been countless millions of people in India whose languages he couldn't speak. But that didn't seem so bad. Many Indian merchants and educated men spoke excellent English. And he often met Englishmen whose knowledge of India was deep and who would gladly explain the local customs, religion and culture for hours at a time.

But China wasn't like that at all. And now here he was, face-to-face with a young man not so unlike himself, who three days ago had tried to understand him and even to offer him friendly advice. They were probably going to spend hours together – hours during which each could have learned so much about the other's world. Yet they couldn't converse. The silence separated them just as effectively as a fortress wall.

He had the urge to pick up an object, any object, and indicate that he wanted to know its name in Chinese. Or he could point: head, hands, feet; sad face, happy face; anything. But Shi-Rong gave no sign that he was inviting conversation, and Trader remembered that the Chinese frowned upon foreigners who wanted to learn their language. So for the rest of the afternoon they sat in the small and stuffy room and learned nothing at all.

At last the light outside the window took on a faintly orange glow, and glancing at his fob watch, Trader realised that the sun was going down. He indicated to Shi-Rong that in a while it might be time to go to sleep. But Shi-Rong indicated in turn that he would be sleeping where he was unless Odstock were to come with him. So Trader showed him the small bedroom where he slept himself and indicated that Shi-Rong should use it. Then he went in to Tully and explained that he'd have the servants from the dining room bring food for Tully and the young mandarin. When he went down the stairs, Shi-Rong did nothing to detain him.

It was half an hour later, when the food had been arranged and Matheson had kindly offered him the use of Jardine's bed, that John Trader looked out of the library window as the red sun sank in the west and saw that out on the waterside, the soldiers were beating and kicking the three Hong merchants to force them to get up. But the three men had been kneeling so long that they could scarcely walk, and one of the soldiers had to carry Joker's chains.

The sunlight was streaming in through the window when Trader awoke in Jardine's comfortable bed. Sunday morning and the sun well up. He clambered quickly out of bed. He ought to go and look after poor old Tully at once. Making his way hurriedly to the big dining room, he thought he would see if there was coffee to be had, and if so, he'd take a pot to his partner. But there was no need. For there at a table sat Tully Odstock himself.

'About time you got up,' Tully remarked cheerfully.

'What happened?'

'My young mandarin has gone. Left before dawn. Dent's fellows have gone, too. And most of the troops. We have a truce for the day.'

'Why?'

'Commissioner Lin seems to think he can show what a good fellow he is by respecting the Christian Sabbath.'

They went for a walk down Hog Lane and made the circuit along Thirteen Factory Street and back to the waterfront. There were still quite a few soldiers about, and not many stallholders, but otherwise one might have thought things were back to normal. An hour later, the two Hong merchants who'd been paraded with Joker in chains appeared at the English factory. They looked tired and somewhat bruised from their ordeal the day before, but accepted some light refreshment. Joker did not appear. They said he had taken to his bed.

It was in the late morning that Trader began to notice something odd. The place seemed to be too quiet. Was it just because of the Sabbath? He met Matheson, who remarked that his comprador had disappeared. In the English factory, there was hardly anyone to serve lunch. 'Bad sign,' Tully said. 'The servants always know things before we do.'

At the start of the afternoon came word that Captain Elliot, the superintendent, was on his way back from Macao. 'It doesn't say when he'll arrive,' Matheson told them, 'even if the Chinese authorities let him through.'

'Why would they stop him?' Trader asked Matheson.

'They may want to keep us isolated.'

'Can't see what use he'll be if he does get here,' grunted Tully, 'unless he brings a battleship.'

The rowing boat appeared on the river about twenty minutes after five – a small clinker-built vessel, hardly twenty feet long, with half a dozen oarsmen. At first no one took any notice of it.

The afternoon had turned cloudy and the river looked grey, but a break in the clouds opened a yellow gash across the water, and it was Trader, standing on the riverbank, who noticed the sunlight catch the blue and gold of a naval tunic in the stern of the rowing boat, guessed what this must mean, and ran to alert Matheson and the others.

It can't be easy, Trader thought, for a single man to look impressive when he's clambering out of a rowing boat. But insofar as it was possible, Elliot achieved it.

He was in full dress naval uniform. His sword hung at his side. He was a good height, and with a plumed hat on his head, he seemed taller. He straightened himself, went across to the group of merchants gathered to meet him, and announced: 'Gentlemen, you are now under my protection.'

And Trader stared at him in surprise.

He knew Charles Elliot was about thirty-five and had risen to the rank of captain in the British Navy. So he'd expected a seasoned, hard-faced commander. In front of him, however, was one of those fair-complexioned Englishmen who continue to look like schoolboys until they are forty. There was even a light down on his cheek. His pale blue eyes, Trader thought, might have belonged to an intelligent clergyman. And when he spoke, it was with a faint lisp.

And this was the man who'd just announced he'd protect them. If Trader had privately thought Tully Odstock was too dismissive of Elliot, at least now he could see why.

'I shall call a general meeting of all the factories this evening,' Elliot announced. 'But first, Matheson, you and your colleagues must tell me exactly what's been happening. In the meantime,' he added as they reached the entrance to the English factory, 'would young Mr Jardine kindly see that the Union Jack is flying on the flagstaff here.'

As Elliot entered, Trader remained outside. He didn't think he'd be required while the superintendent was closeted with Matheson and the other senior men. He preferred to walk alone for a little while and absorb what he'd witnessed.

So he was down at the far end of the quay, sitting on the same iron mooring post where he'd sat so wretchedly three evenings ago, and idly watching a small Chinese chop boat, with lanterns lit, go past, when he realised that the chop boat was turning and heading towards him, to the dock. He stood up and moved away from the mooring post. The chop boat drew alongside.

And in it Trader saw a burly form with a cigar jutting from his mouth. It was Read, the American.

'Evening, Trader,' he called out cheerfully. 'Thought I'd drop by. Didn't want to miss the fun.' He stepped ashore and shook Trader's hand.

'God, I'm pleased to see you,' Trader burst out. 'Have you any idea what's going to happen?'

'Not a clue. I'll take my bag to the American factory, then come across to you fellows. Have you got any whisky in there?'

There were more than forty men gathered in the big room in the English factory: mostly British and Americans, some Parsee merchants from

India, and a few merchants from other nations. The two merchants from the Hong were also present. Trader and Tully Odstock sat in the back row, with the Americans Read and Delano beside them.

Elliot might speak with a slight lisp, but he came to the point tersely. 'Gentlemen, you must all be prepared to leave Canton, with all your possessions, at once. Our trade can be continued, if necessary from the open sea; but the attitude of the Chinese authorities is such that, although no violence has been offered yet, I cannot guarantee your future safety in Canton.'

'As I understand it, they're not allowing anyone to leave here,' Matheson pointed out.

'I shall demand passports straightaway for all those who wish to leave.'

'And if we are threatened with violence?' Matheson pressed him.

'Then we may thank God,' Elliot replied firmly, 'that we have a British man-of-war out past the Bogue. I also know that there are two American warships, the *Columbia* and the *John Adams,* expected any moment at Macao. Naturally our own man-of-war stands ready to protect all our friends here at Canton, and I hope I may count upon assistance from the American warships in turn.'

'That you may!' Read and Delano called out loudly.

The meeting broke up. And perhaps because Elliot had spoken so clearly, with the Americans supporting him, Trader felt a bit more encouraged as he and Odstock were leaving. 'Elliot sounded firm,' he suggested.

But Tully only sniffed. 'That British man-of-war – the one he says will save us. Have you any idea how it's going to get upriver past the Chinese shore batteries?'

'No,' Trader confessed.

'Well, nor has he,' said Tully, and went to bed.

By nine o'clock in the morning, they'd all heard the news. 'No passports. The Chinese have refused. Point-blank. No one's to leave,' Matheson told them in the factory library.

'We're trapped like rats in a barrel,' Tully muttered.

'Our Chinese servants have all disappeared,' somebody called out.

'It's a game of bluff,' Matheson reminded each arrival. 'We just need to stay calm.'

Soon afterwards, they saw Chinese officers riding small sturdy horses issuing from the alleys onto the waterfront. They made for the two little customs booths, where they tethered their mounts. Next, from the mouths of the alleys, men on foot began to emerge. Five, ten, twenty, a constant stream. They wore conical hats and loose dress, and they carried pikes and clubs. 'Local police,' said Tully. 'They're supposed to report to the Hong. Protect the merchant quarter.' He snorted. 'Lin's controlling them now.'

They kept on coming. A hundred. Two hundred. They formed up in lines in front of every factory.

A few minutes passed before Trader saw, from the far end of the factories, a single burly figure emerge and start walking towards them. It was Read.

Trader held his breath. Read walked in front of the police lines. They watched him, but they did not move; and when Read reached the English factory, nobody stopped him from going in.

'Morning, gentlemen,' he remarked cheerfully as he came into the library. 'Got any food?' It was hard not to smile in his cheerful presence. Trader looked at him gratefully. 'I've been watching Delano try to boil an egg,' Read added by way of explanation.

'Can you boil an egg?' Trader asked.

'Yes, but it was more amusing to watch Delano try and fail. Do I see bread and marmalade? And coffee?'

'Help yourself,' said Matheson. 'You seem very calm,' he remarked approvingly.

'No use getting in a flap. Stiff upper lip, and all that.'

An hour passed. The police in front of the factories were doing drill. Was this to intimidate the merchants, or were they preparing for an order to move from Lin?

The men in the English factory took turns keeping watch at the window. Trader, Tully, and Read were all sitting in leather armchairs when Dent came to join them.

'If the police do break in, I suppose it's me and Tully they'll arrest again,' Dent remarked.

'Maybe,' said Read. 'But if Lin decides to cross the line and use force, he might as well arrest all the opium traders.' He considered a moment. 'They might be in a Chinese gaol quite a while.'

'You've assumed Lin's got control of his men,' Tully Odstock observed. 'But it could turn out another way. I've seen riots before. Long hot day. Big crowd. Tempers get short. Then something happens. Who knows what? Anything can set them off.'

'And then?' asked Trader.

'They riot. Burn the factories down.' He nodded grimly. 'With us in 'em.'

Nobody spoke.

The sun beat down that afternoon, burnishing the iron moorings along the water's edge until they were too hot to touch. The police ended their drill and set up bamboo shelters with matting roofs to give them shade. But they gave no sign of leaving, sun or not.

Elliot looked in at the library and they all gathered around. 'There will be a negotiation,' he told them, 'as soon as I meet with the commissioner.'

Matheson introduced Trader to him, explaining that Trader had only recently arrived. Elliot acknowledged Trader's bow very civilly and remarked that he had chosen to come at an interesting time.

They ate salt beef from the larder that evening, with the few fresh vegetables they had left. At least the English factory still had a well-stocked wine cellar.

The sun went down. Through the window, Trader saw the police patrolling the waterfront. No change there. The men were sitting down to play cards, but Trader wasn't in the mood, so he took up his book again and had managed to become quite lost in the riotous comedy of *Pickwick* when a voice interrupted him.

'Stop reading and talk to me,' said Read. He was carrying two glasses of brandy.

'I must say,' Trader remarked, 'I'm glad to have your company, but you must wish you hadn't come.'

'I like to live dangerously.' Read gazed into his brandy meditatively. 'Not that I think we're in that much danger.'

'Why?'

'The Chinese like the tea trade. They've no real interest in destroying the tea merchants. For remember, you fellows may sell opium, but you also buy tea.'

'I have another question.'

'Shoot.'

'The Chinese authorities may not like the opium trade, but it's been going on for years. Now, all of a sudden, the emperor wants to destroy it. I buy the moral crusade story. But is there something else going on here?'

'Good question.' Read took a sip of brandy. 'You could say, Mexico.'

'Mexico?'

'I was drinking with a sea captain in Macao last week. This is how he explained it. What's been the main trading currency all over the world for centuries? Silver dollars. Spanish dollars. Pieces of eight. It's been the only currency everyone trusts. And a lot of the silver came from Mexican mines. But then Mexico becomes independent from Spain. They mint their own silver dollars. Not bad quality. But out on the high seas, everyone still wants Spanish pieces of eight, and trade expands, and there aren't enough of them. People will even pay a premium for them – more than their face value. In short, acceptable silver currency for trading is in short supply. With me so far?'

'I think so.'

'Right. What has always been the problem with the Chinese trade?'

'They sell to us, but they don't buy much in return.'

'Exactly. Half a century ago a Chinese emperor looked at English goods for sale and was not impressed.'

'And nothing's changed.'

'Right. And when the Chinese sell us tea, how do they want to be paid?'

'In silver.'

'When your comprador goes to the local Canton market and buys vegetables, he uses small change, copper coins. But larger transactions, including all government taxes and expenses in China, are paid in silver. So the Chinese government always needed lots of it. They sold us tea, silver flowed in.'

'Right.'

'And when we didn't have enough silver, because pieces of eight are in short supply, we discovered a neat trick: Chinese smugglers will pay us silver if we get them opium. Then the circle was complete. We deal in opium and pay China for tea with their own silver.'

'So China's not getting the silver it wants.'

'Oh, it's much worse than that. Opium's addictive. China's purchases of opium are growing much faster than their sales of tea. Result: more silver is flowing out of China than coming in. Far more. They're bleeding silver.' He shrugged. 'The emperor has to do something.'

'So this is all about silver, then!' Trader exclaimed. 'Nothing else at all.'

'Not so fast, Trader. You asked why the emperor is striking at us. I believe he's got no choice because of the silver problem. But does that mean he isn't concerned about his people? I'll bet he's concerned. Or that the opium trade isn't a dirty business? It is.'

'What's your point?'

'I don't believe in single causes, Trader. Black and white, good versus evil. Real life isn't like that. Historians in the future will find all kinds of things going on here at the same time, some of which may even be random chance. If historians can discern any pattern, it will probably be complex, a system in flux, like the sea.' He smiled. 'God made the universe, Trader, but that doesn't mean He made it simple.'

The placards appeared the next morning, all over the waterfront. They were five feet square, erected on posts, and covered with Chinese characters. Dr Parker went out to read them.

'Lin says he'd rather be patient than resort to violence, but that we've got to surrender the opium. If Elliot can't control the British merchants, then there's no point in him being here. And if he doesn't obey, Heaven may strike him down.' Parker gave them a wry look. 'The threat may be heavenly, but it's real enough.'

'Damn rude,' said Tully.

'The tone is more like a schoolmaster telling off unruly schoolchildren, I'd say,' answered Parker. 'But then, that's probably how Lin sees it.'

Elliot appeared briefly in the library. Matheson accosted him at once. 'This is getting us nowhere,' Matheson said. 'I'm going to offer Lin enough for him to satisfy the emperor and save face. Four, maybe five thousand chests. With luck, that may do the trick.'

'I forbid you to offer him anything,' Elliot replied sharply.

'Do you have a better plan?' Matheson asked angrily.

'Yes.'

'What is it?'

But Elliot turned on his heel and walked out.

It was early evening when he reappeared. Trader, Read, Matheson and most of the British merchants were in the factory, and they gathered around.

'Gentlemen,' he announced calmly, 'it is clear that Lin cannot and will not bargain. I am therefore going to surrender all the opium to him.'

There was a gasp of astonishment.

'All of it?' queried Matheson.

'Everything we have – here, out at the depots, in ships down the gulf. Even the opium on consignment. Every last chest.'

'We're to give it all to Lin?' cried Dent. 'I'll be damned if I will.'

'No. You will give the opium to me. Then I'm going to give it to Lin.'

There was a stunned silence.

Matheson spoke. 'Do you mean that you will take ownership of the opium, as the British government representative?'

'I do.'

'Will the government reimburse us?'

'That is the idea.'

Matheson frowned. 'If you add it all up, there must be over twenty thousand chests of opium to be accounted for.'

'I agree. Forgive me, gentlemen, but I must leave you now.' And Elliot was gone.

'It gets us out of this hole, at least,' said Tully. 'We'll have to wait a devil of a time for our money, assuming we get it, but it's better than what we've got at the moment, which is nothing.' He turned to Trader. 'Don't you agree?

John Trader nodded slowly. Yes, if you had a fortune already, like Tully and Matheson, and you could afford to wait. But if all your money was in the opium chests in question, and you had that much again in debt, it was another story. Since he couldn't admit that, however, he said nothing, nodded to the other men, and went out. But just as he was leaving, Trader overheard Matheson ask Read what he thought. And the American, after coolly exhaling the smoke from his cigar, replied: 'Seems to me, sir, your Captain Elliot is a devious son of a bitch.'

o

On a fine April day, two weeks later, a pair of British vessels passed up the gulf towards the Bogue. From the shallows, half a mile distant, Nio watched them as they passed, on their way to the receiving station. He was alone in a small sampan with Sea Dragon.

Nio saw the pirate turn his eyes down the gulf, and following Sea Dragon's gaze, he could just make out another pair of ships on the horizon. The opium ships had been coming for three days already, bearing their cargoes to Commissioner Lin, who was going to destroy them.

'What a waste,' said Nio wretchedly. 'Do you think Lin will really get twenty thousand chests?'

Sea Dragon allowed his eyes to return to the two ships before them. The opium in either one of them would have been enough to keep him and his men employed and handsomely paid for many months.

But he didn't reply to his young friend. He seemed to have something else on his mind. At last he spoke. 'Would you lie to me, Nio?'

'No.'

'When you first came here, Nio, the men didn't want you in the boat. Did you know that? But I told them: "He is young, he will learn quickly." ' Sea Dragon paused. 'Why did they listen to me?'

'You're the boss.'

'And . . . ?'

'They trust you.'

'Yes.' Sea Dragon gazed across the water. 'They trust me. But they also fear me.' He nodded thoughtfully. 'None of them would lie to me, Nio. Not one. Because if they did, I would kill them. Do you know that?'

'I know that.'

'We were making good money when you came. Trade was down, but we found opium to take along the coast. You were well paid.'

'I owe you everything.'

'And now, thanks to this accursed Lin, up and down the coast they're crying out for opium, and we don't have any. We haven't made any money in a month.' The handsome pirate sighed. 'Maybe we should all go home. So I say, anyone who wants to can leave. But maybe things will get better. We can share our money to buy food, and we can wait. Everyone tells me how much money they have.' He looked at Nio. 'But when you tell me what you have, I ask you, "Why don't you have more?" And you say to me, "I lost money gambling." '

'I did.'

Sea Dragon stared at Nio. 'Do you know why trust is important, Nio?

Because if we get into a fight, our lives depend on one another. I have to know that every one of my men has got my back, and I've got his. If not, he's a danger. He has to die.'

'I owe you everything,' Nio repeated. In his code, that could mean only one thing: he'd defend Sea Dragon with his life. In his loyalties, the pirate came before all people, except for his father and one other person.

'I saw you hide the money,' the pirate said quietly. 'It's in a hole beside a tree. I counted it this morning.' There was a brief silence. 'You lied to me.'

Nio kept very still. Not a muscle in his face moved. His knife was tucked into the red sash around his waist. Sea Dragon was sitting opposite him, but to one side. If the pirate were to lunge at him, he'd be off-balance, just enough to put himself at a disadvantage, and he must know this. Also that Nio would have noticed the fact.

So he's not planning to kill me at this moment, Nio calculated. But he watched carefully, just in case.

'It's not my money,' he said after a pause.

'Yes it is, Nio. What you mean is that you weren't keeping it for yourself. I think you're going to give it to that woman you asked me to visit. The one who calls you Little Brother. But why, Nio? She lives in a big house.'

'She married into a rich family. But her parents are the poorest peasants in the village. She has nothing of her own.'

'So every night, before you go to sleep, you think about how you're going to go and surprise her with a present, and tell her to hide it away and keep it safe for herself. This is the good deed you dream of?'

Nio nodded.

'And you lied to me, even though you knew I would kill you if I found out.' Now Sea Dragon turned to look at him thoughtfully. 'You are a brave young fellow, Nio. You're the best I have.' He sighed. 'But I can't let you lie to me. What are we going to do about that?'

'You tell me,' said Nio. He watched the pirate for the slightest hint of movement, but Sea Dragon was still.

'Keep what you have saved for the woman,' Sea Dragon said quietly. 'But you will give the same amount to me, out of what you earn in the future. And you will not leave me before you have paid. Also, you will never lie to me again.'

'I will never lie to you again.'

'Pray to the gods that the opium trade returns.'

Nio nodded. 'Maybe,' he said quietly, 'we should kill Commissioner Lin.'

o

If John Trader had supposed that the siege was over, he was in for a rude awakening. Elliot might have promised to surrender the opium, but Lin wasn't taking him at his word. 'I'll let you go when I have every last opium chest in my possession,' he told the Englishman. 'Until then, I'm holding you all hostage.'

'It's an outrage,' Tully protested to Matheson.

But the largest opium dealer was more philosophic. 'In his place, Odstock, would you trust us?' He sighed. 'We'll have to empty the cargo of every ship in the gulf – and beyond. It may take weeks.'

It was the season between the cold dry winds of winter and the wet summer monsoon. The days were hot, the waterfront was dusty, and there was absolutely nowhere to go. Now Trader understood why, every April, the men at the factories were so anxious to leave Canton for the hills and sea breezes on the little island of Macao.

The police and troops, if not quite so numerous, continued their siege. Across Thirteen Factory Street, the local Cantonese would amuse themselves by climbing onto their roofs to watch the Western barbarians trapped below. For many days, no servants came in. Fresh food was hard to get. There was a shortage of water. The drains weren't getting flushed out. The stink was sometimes terrible. Only gradually, as the opium chests piled up in their thousands at the receiving station that he had set up downriver, did Commissioner Lin somewhat ease the harsh conditions of his Western hostages.

Early in April he allowed them to send some mail downriver. Trader wrote two personal letters. The first was to Charlie Farley. He gave him some account of what had happened, told him that he felt confident they'd receive compensation from the British government – even though he wasn't really confident at all – and sent friendly greetings to Charlie's aunt.

The second letter was more difficult. He didn't dare write to Agnes Lomond herself, but he could write to her mother.

He struck the right tone: respectful, friendly, frank. As a hostess, Mrs

Lomond would like to show her friends that she had a firsthand account of the China affair, so he made sure to give her precise information. At the same time, he played up the danger of the siege, praising the coolness of Elliot and the merchants – which by implication included himself. Above all, for the colonel's ears, he made clear what an insult this attack was to the British Empire – an insult that couldn't be allowed to stand. He closed his letter with a polite enquiry as to their family's good health and with his good wishes to them all, including Agnes.

Why did he write it? There seemed little chance now that he could ever ask for Agnes's hand. So wasn't the letter a waste of time? He explained it to himself as courtesy. Keep his reputation for impeccable good manners in the British community. But that wasn't the whole truth. A deep survival instinct told him never to give up. Not completely. Not even when the game seemed to be over.

The day John sent his letters, Lin let the servants return. Around the middle of the month, a number of sailors who'd been trapped by the siege were allowed to leave. But the merchants were to remain.

What was going to happen after they finally were permitted to leave? Was the China trade going to end? Would the British government really compensate him for his loss? Nobody could tell him.

One quiet afternoon Trader entered the library of the English factory. Tully had gone back to take an afternoon siesta. Many of the merchants had done the same, and the library was empty except for one elegant figure, fast asleep in a deep armchair.

No less a person than Superintendent Elliot himself.

Taking care not to disturb him, Trader settled down in an armchair on the other side of the room and opened Dickens's *Pickwick Papers.* In a few minutes he was so engrossed in the amusing narrative that he quite forgot he was not alone.

He came to the famous description of the Eatanswill Election. He started to chuckle, then guffaw. Two minutes later he was weeping with laughter.

And was most disconcerted to find Superintendent Elliot by his chair, looking over his shoulder to see what he was reading.

'Ah,' said that gentleman amiably. '*Pickwick.* Excellent.'

'I'm sorry, sir,' said Trader. 'I didn't mean to wake you.'

'That's all right. Time I woke up anyway.' He sat down opposite Trader in a companionable way. 'Glad you're finding something to laugh about at least. This must be a difficult time. Worse for you than the older men, I should think.'

'The big merchants like Jardine and Matheson can ride out the storm, sir. They've got huge resources. I haven't.'

'I know.' Elliot nodded. 'I'm sorry.'

After a moment, Trader said, 'I understand that you need to get us out of here, sir, but may I ask – that is, if you feel you can tell me – do you think I will get the compensation?'

'Eventually, yes. But it will be a long wait.'

'I was afraid you'd say that.'

'If it's any comfort,' Elliot said kindly, 'Jardine must be almost in London by now. And a letter from Matheson will be in his hands the same time my report gets to the British government. Jardine will lobby ministers, including Palmerston himself. The opium lobby in Parliament is strong. And because I took over the opium on the government's behalf, and Lin took it from me, it becomes a government affair. They'll practically have to do something. Do you see?'

'I think so.' It all made sense. Yet for some reason he couldn't quite define, it seemed to Trader that there was still a piece missing from the puzzle. He frowned. 'May I ask another question?'

'Certainly.'

'It's just that I overheard Read say something a bit strange after you announced you were surrendering all the opium and that we'd be compensated.'

'What was that?'

'Well, he said – I'm quoting his words, sir, if you'll forgive me – that you were "a devious son of a bitch." '

'The devil he did!' Elliot looked pleased.

'I did ask him about it once. He said I'd work it out, but I'm not sure that I have.'

Elliot paused, considering Trader thoughtfully. 'If I share a confidence, Trader, will you give me your word that you will not repeat it. Not to your partner Odstock, not to Read, not to anyone?'

'I promise.'

'What value would you place on twenty thousand chests of opium?'

'At least two million pounds sterling. Probably more.'

'And do you suppose that the British government has that much cash lying around?'

'I don't know.'

'They haven't. And if they had, they wouldn't give it. So where must the money come from?'

'I don't know.'

'From the Chinese themselves. We'll have to make them pay.'

'You mean war?'

'*War* is a strong word. China is huge, its people without number. Land war is out of the question. But the shore defences are old; the war junks we have seen are clumsy and poorly armed. Any British naval vessel could pound them to pieces. So that is what we should do. In common parlance, we should knock them about a bit.'

'And then?' asked Trader.

'Those who know something of China's history tell me their normal practice is to buy off foreign trouble if they can. Their empire is ancient and closed. As long as things return to normal, they don't care. But they hate to lose face. It's my belief that rather than lose face and have more of their ships sunk and their shore batteries smashed, they will agree to speedy peace terms. Those will naturally include trade concessions and reparations, which can be used to pay for our military costs and the opium our merchants have lost. Mr Read is perceptive, and correct.' He smiled. 'It's the navy that rules the British Empire.'

So Elliot was engineering a war between his country and China.

Trader was impressed. He was used to the proud military men, the seasoned local administrators, and the cynical merchants of Calcutta, but this was his first real glimpse of the cold, ruthless, diplomatic intelligence that lay behind them all.

But none of this helps me, he thought. My only hope of solvency doesn't lie even with the British government, but in a future war, against a vast empire, which may not take place, and whose outcome, whatever Elliot thinks, must be uncertain.

'I have a last question,' he said. 'You know Commissioner Lin wrote a letter to the queen. It may be written in atrocious English, but his moral case is clear enough. What if Her Majesty agrees and takes the Chinese side?'

Elliot gazed at him and smiled. 'My dear Trader,' he asked gently, 'what on earth makes you suppose that anyone's going to show it to her?'

Early in May, the troops and police withdrew from the waterfront. But Matheson, Dent, Odstock and most of the English merchants were still kept hostage until all the promised opium was surrendered. Only at the start of the fourth week of May did the news come: 'Lin's got his twenty thousand chests.'

But still the commissioner was not quite done. He had one more demand.

'The damn fellow wants us to sign a bond that no cargo we bring to China in the future will contain any opium. Any crew found with opium is to be arrested,' Tully told him.

'It's logical,' Trader said, 'after all the trouble he's been through to destroy this season's opium.'

'Damned if I will,' said Tully. 'For all I know, he'd use it as grounds to arrest me. Execute me as well, I daresay. He's demanded that Elliot sign the bond as well, guaranteeing the whole thing. Elliot refuses even to look at it.'

It came as quite a surprise when, two days later, Matheson casually remarked that he had signed the bond.

'Why the devil did you do that?' Tully demanded.

'To get out of here, Odstock.'

'You intend to keep your word?'

'Certainly not.' Matheson smiled. 'As far as I'm concerned, I signed the bond only under duress, so it doesn't count.'

'Damn fellow,' Tully remarked with grudging admiration.

A few others signed. Elliot did not. Nothing more was said. Perhaps Lin didn't need to bother. In the emperor's eyes, which was what mattered, Lin had won already.

And now the British merchants began to leave. One day Trader saw the portrait of the former king being packed up and carried to the waterfront. On another day he watched a single merchant load forty cases of his own wine into a boat and set off downriver, guarding his precious cargo himself. Yet when Tully told him they'd be leaving the following morning, Trader suggested he should join his partner in Macao somewhat later.

'Read and some of the Americans are staying a few more days. I thought I might follow on with them,' he said. And though Tully looked a bit surprised, he didn't object.

The truth was, John couldn't quite bring himself to go. He had a place to stay in Macao. Tully had offered him a room in his own lodgings for the time being. That wasn't a problem.

It was the secret prospect of bankruptcy hanging over him that held John Trader back. How could he face even the modest social life of Macao? What could he say about himself to the merchants' wives and families that wouldn't be a lie? The fact was, he felt more like hiding from the world than being seen in it.

If I could, I'd sooner swelter alone here in the factories all summer, he thought.

Failing that, he'd even begun to indulge in another dream. What if he absconded? He could write to his creditors, tell them to claim their loan from the government compensation, when it came; and then with good conscience he could take the cash he had in hand and disappear.

The world was a big place. Letters sent from India in the fastest ships still took months to get to England. It could take them years to find him, even if they tried.

And what would he do? Wander the world, like Read perhaps. He could pick up employment here and there. He might go to America. Who knows, he might make a fortune.

How strange: a short time ago he'd been dreaming of settling down with Agnes on a Scottish estate. Now the thought of a rootless life, without ties, almost without identity, suddenly seemed attractive. Free of obligation. Free to do what he liked. Free to find women, come to that, in any corner of the world. Many a young man's dream.

Read seemed to like living that way. Perhaps they could travel together for a while.

Several days passed. The British were all gone now. Dr Parker the missionary was remaining at his makeshift hospital, but the factories were closing down. Finally, Read told Trader that he, too, was off to Macao, and that he'd better come with him.

'But first, young Trader,' he added, 'you're going to join me and some friends for a day out.'

'All right,' said John. 'Where are we going?'

'You'll see.'

o

The sun was shining on the waters of the gulf as Shi-Rong stood proudly beside Commissioner Lin to watch the destruction.

With every day that passed, his admiration for the commissioner had grown greater. It wasn't just his moral strength, for Lin certainly lived up to his reputation for Confucian propriety. Single-handedly, without shedding blood, he had brought the barbarians to surrender. But just as impressive was his thoroughness. He was an awe-inspiring administrator.

'Stopping these barbarian drug dealers is only a first step,' he'd explained to Shi-Rong. 'We must break our people's evil habit.' The opium dens were being raided all over the province. In Guangzhou itself, there were piles of confiscated opium pipes a dozen feet high. 'Even this is not enough,' Lin declared. 'We must find ways to help the addicts lose their desire for the drug. They say there are medicines made with plums or willow and peach blossom that work. Make enquiries,' he ordered, 'and see if you can discover what they are.' Failing that, addicts could be put in prison and denied the drug until they were cured.

Lin's dramatic moves had already reached the ears of the court. One day, Shi-Rong saw a present arrive from Beijing. It came in a magnificent container, and he watched Lin first make the nine kowtows to the container, since it came from the royal hand, and then open it, letting out an '*Ah . . .*' of joy when he saw it.

'It is meat,' he told Shi-Rong. 'Venison. You know what that means.'

The Chinese might write in ideograms, which expressed an idea rather than a sound, but in their spoken language, they made endless puns. In spoken Mandarin, the word for *venison* sounded the same as the word for *promotion*.

'Congratulations, Excellency,' Shi-Rong said quietly. 'Promotion is assured.'

Lin nodded and, just that once, was too overcome to speak.

Lin's arrangements for the destruction of twenty thousand chests of opium were a masterpiece. The site he had chosen was beside a creek that flowed into the Pearl River system. There was already a massive shed there, in which the chests of opium were stacked in long rows. Closer to the waterside, he had begun to build.

Or more precisely, to dig – a huge basin, twenty-five yards by fifty. Then a second and a third. The basins were quite shallow, only a few feet deep. Day after day, a small army of workmen laid flagstones over the bottom of each pit. Then they timbered the sides. There were pipes to carry fresh water from the creek and sluices to allow the contents of each basin to flow out through channels into the river, where each day the tide would carry them out to sea. Across each basin Lin made his men construct broad wooden walkways.

At the same time, carts appeared, laden with sacks of salt and lime, which were stacked under shelters. Lastly he had them make him a small raised platform from which the operation could be supervised. By early June, he was ready to begin.

But before he did, there was one essential duty to perform, which showed so well, Shi-Rong noted, his master's essential piety and reverence. Accompanied by his staff, Lin went to the local temple that the fishermen used and, making his offerings with deep apologies, warned the sea god that he was obliged to empty large quantities of opium waste into the ocean there. He begged the sea god to tell all the fish to leave.

The men had already been at work for an hour that morning when the Americans appeared. They had requested the visit a couple of days ago and it had been granted.

'The American barbarians may come,' Lin had decided. 'With the exception of some, like Delano, they are less engaged in drug smuggling than the English barbarians. They may be less evil.'

Shi-Rong had brought Mr Singapore with him in case the commissioner wished to speak to the visitors.

They were standing on the platform overlooking the basins. Lin was not wearing his official dress and insignia, but was dressed in a simple tunic with a plain conical hat. A servant held a sunshade on a long bamboo pole high over his head.

On the walkways across the basins, the workmen were stamping the black balls of opium to break them down before sweeping the powdery mess into the water below. They had already disposed of the contents of twenty chests, and Lin intended to destroy eight times that amount during this single day.

As the visitors picked their way through the debris of broken chests littering the area, Commissioner Lin frowned. 'I gave permission for three visitors. There are four,' he said sharply.

Shi-Rong looked towards them. For a moment, the glare of the harsh morning light made it difficult to see their faces. Then he recognised Trader. 'Excellency, the fourth man is the English scholar I told you about. Do you wish me to send him away?'

'A scholar?' Lin considered. 'Let him come.'

Having made their low bows, the four men were allowed to stand a few feet away from the commissioner to watch the work. After dumping a mass of opium into the nearest of the huge pits, the workmen began to add lime and salt. As they did so, other workmen jumped down into the pit and began to stir the watery sludge with paddles. A pungent stink arose. Shi-Rong watched with amusement as the visitors covered their noses and puckered their faces. Even the commissioner allowed himself a wry smile. He and his party were used to the smell.

'Now the barbarians wish they hadn't come,' he remarked. And then, as soon as the visitors had started to recover: 'Bring the English scholar to me.'

Mr Singapore translated. Shi-Rong watched. The commissioner was quite kindly. 'Commissioner Lin has heard about you. Although you are a merchant, you have taken your country's examinations. You are a scholar. You know something of Confucius.'

'This is true,' Trader responded with a polite bow.

'The commissioner believes that you are not without morals. You see that the evil drug that your countrymen have brought here to poison our people is being utterly destroyed, and he hopes that they have learned a lesson. The commissioner asks if you feel ashamed of what they have done.'

Trader did not answer at once. He looked thoughtful. 'I am ashamed,' he said at last.

'The commissioner is pleased to hear you say it. It shows that you have a good heart and morals. He asks if you remember the letter he has composed to your queen.'

'I do.'

'The letter is even better now. The commissioner has sent out two copies, but he does not know if they will be given to your queen. He does not have trust.'

'I expect she will see it. But how can I know?'

'The commissioner asks if you know honest scholars in your country.'

'Certainly. My teachers at Oxford are all honest men.'

'The commissioner desires you to take a copy of his letter now, and to send it to honest scholars of your acquaintance, asking them to lay it before your queen. Will you do this?'

Again Trader hesitated a little, but then answered firmly: 'I shall be honoured, and will do all in my power to ensure that it reaches the queen.' Trader bowed his head. 'You have my word.'

Commissioner Lin looked very pleased and indicated to Shi-Rong that he should give Trader a copy of the letter. The interview was over.

After a little time, the barbarians left.

'Do you think he truly repented?' Lin asked Shi-Rong.

'It is hard to tell, Excellency, but I think so.'

Lin nodded. Shi-Rong could see that his master was moved, and he loved him for it.

'It seems,' Lin said reflectively, 'that the Lord of Ten Thousand Years can teach virtue even to barbarians.'

○

The following day, when Trader and Read set out for Macao and their boat passed the place where the opium sludge was being washed into the gulf, Read turned to his young friend and quietly remarked, 'You realise that you gave Lin your word that you'd send that letter.'

'I was afraid that he might not let me out of Canton if I didn't agree to everything he said,' Trader confessed.

'Right. All the same, you gave your word.'

○

One hour later, the baby was born. The village midwife had been in the Lungs' house since the night before. Willow's labour had been long. Mei-Ling and Mother had been helping, and when at last the baby came, the midwife handed it to Mother for inspection. The baby cried, not very loudly. Nobody spoke. Willow, pale with exhaustion, looked up at her mother-in-law and then her head fell back. Her eyes went blank.

Willow had given birth to a second girl.

The household was very quiet that afternoon. No one came by. Everyone in the hamlet knew, of course. People who might have come by on business feared to encounter the wrathful face of the lady of the house. The servants went about their tasks with heads down. Nobody discussed whether or not this was a lucky day; no calculations about the baby's character were made.

Being quite tired herself, Mei-Ling asked Mother if she might rest a little and was told she could. She'd become big with her own pregnancy during the last month, and Mother had been more solicitous than ever, hardly letting her work at all and not even scolding her if she did something wrong.

After resting awhile, Mei-Ling went in to see Willow. Her sister-in-law was awake, but she looked pale and dispirited. The baby, wrapped in the traditional white cloth that Willow's mother had sent, was in a little bamboo cot beside her, sleeping. Mei-Ling inspected the baby. It had a little hair. Perhaps the baby looked like Willow. It was hard to judge.

'You have two days to rest and be quiet, Sister,' she remarked with a smile. After that, it would be time for Willow's mother to arrive with baby clothes and presents.

But her sister-in-law hardly seemed to hear her. 'Now I know what it's like to be you,' Willow said at last.

'What do you mean?'

'When I married into the family, I was treated with honour because my father's rich. They weren't so nice to you.'

'I didn't expect anything else. I was lucky to marry Second Son. He's very good to me.'

'Was I kind to you?'

'You were quite kind.'

'I'm sure I wasn't kind enough. Forgive me, Sister.' She sighed. 'Well, now I know how it feels myself. No son. Two daughters. When Mother came in a little while ago, she hardly even spoke to me. Looked at me as if I were dirt. Once I've recovered, next time I do anything wrong, she'll give me a beating. You'll see.'

After a little while, Willow said she was tired, and Mei-Ling left her.

But something Mei-Ling saw that evening made her think that Willow might be wrong about Mother. The sun was setting when the baby awoke and made some little cries. Mei-Ling was sitting in the shadows just behind the little orange tree when she saw Mother come out with the baby. She walked up and down the yard, gently rocking the baby in her arms, and Mei-Ling heard her murmuring: 'There, my pretty one. Sleep now, poor little thing.'

And it seemed to her that Mother's voice was so tender towards her tiny granddaughter that it wouldn't be long before she'd forgive Willow for having another girl. The baby soon went to sleep, and Mei-Ling saw Mother go back towards Willow's room. Soon after that, she went in to lie beside her husband and sink into sleep herself.

She was surprised when she woke in the early morning to see Second Son standing beside the bed looking distressed. 'The baby died during the night,' he said.

'Died? What do you mean?'

'It must have stopped breathing. It happens sometimes.'

She rose and hurried to Willow. The baby had vanished. There were tears on Willow's cheeks.

'What's happened?' Mei-Ling cried. 'How?'

The look that Willow gave her was so terrible. It was anguished, bitter, helpless, all at once. 'Perhaps Mother will like me better,' she said dully, 'now the baby's dead.'

Mei-Ling had been due to go see her parents that day. She had wondered what she should do, but Mother had said, 'You may as well go.' She'd arrived at her parents at noon and stayed a couple of hours before returning.

When she got back, she found Mother sitting alone on a bench under the orange tree in the middle of the empty courtyard. The older woman looked gloomy. She motioned Mei-Ling to a smaller bench opposite her. Mei-Ling sat down, and Mother gazed at her in silence for a while.

'Tell me what they're saying in the village,' Mother finally asked. Mei-Ling hesitated. 'Tell me the truth,' Mother commanded. 'Everything.'

'They're saying we killed the baby.'

'We?'

'The family.'

Mei-Ling had heard the stories: baby girls born into poor families who couldn't feed them or who had too many girls already. Babies who quietly disappeared. Had they been exposed, drowned, smothered, or just died of natural causes, as babies often did? Who knew? And she supposed that those who knew probably didn't say. She'd never heard of such a thing in her own village. Maybe it was one of those tales that happen in another village or province rather than one's own.

But people still talked about it.

'You mean they're saying I did it,' Mother stated flatly.

Mei-Ling didn't answer. There was no need. Mother sighed. 'They fear me,' she remarked. 'Do you think I did it?'

Mei-Ling thought of the expression she'd seen on Mother's face when she was cradling the baby girl. 'No, Mother,' she said.

'Good.' Mother nodded. 'Well, I didn't.'

And that should have been the end of the matter.

But during the night that followed, Mei-Ling suddenly awoke with such a start that it woke Second Son as well.

'What is it?' he asked.

'A nightmare. It was terrible.'

'Tell me.'

'I had the baby. It wasn't a boy. It was a girl.' She stared ahead in desperation. 'Then Mother took it . . .' She clasped her hands in front of her belly as if she could protect the child within. 'She took it and killed it.'

'She would never do that. You know she wouldn't.'

'I know.' Mei-Ling shook her head. But she didn't know. That was the trouble.

'When people have nightmares,' said Second Son, 'it's often just the worst thing they can think of. It's natural. But it doesn't make it true.'

'Everyone in the village thinks . . .'

'I know. It's stupid. It's just because they're afraid of her.'

'So am I.'

Second Son put his arm protectively around her shoulders. 'I won't let anything happen to our baby. I promise. Go back to sleep.'

But she couldn't.

MACAO

June 1839

Read had a woman in Macao. That's to say, he lodged in her house and there were no other lodgers. Her husband, a Dutch sea captain, had been dead for years.

Read had found his lodgings almost as soon as he arrived. After a while, he'd gone up the coast with McBride and Trader, returned to the widow, then left again to go to Canton. Of course, he hadn't expected to be trapped in Canton for so long, but the widow had not taken any other lodgers, and his berth was still available when he got back.

Just before he'd gone to Canton, a well-meaning but nosy member of the community approached him in the street and suggested it was unseemly to be openly living in sin with a local woman. A moment later, he regretted his words.

Read turned on him. His voice was loud enough for other people in the street to hear. 'Are you suggesting, sir, that an honest widow who to make ends meet lets lodgings to a respectable man is to be accused of lewdness? Do you say that about every landlady?'

'No indeed, sir,' the gentleman protested, 'but you are her only lodger, and you must allow—'

'I allow nothing, sir! If she had six lodgers, would you go about the town saying she'd committed the act of fornication with all six of them?'

'By no means . . .'

'Are you aware of the laws of slander, sir? Must I go to law to defend an innocent woman's name? Or shall I horsewhip you?' Read shouted fiercely.

At this, the well-meaning gentleman hastened away, and within the hour the whole of Macao was laughing. Nobody troubled Read about his woman after that.

Trader heard the story from Tully the very day he arrived on the island.

'All the time we were in Canton,' Trader remarked to Read the next morning, 'you never told me you had a woman here.'

'A good man doesn't talk about his women, Trader.' Read gave him a stern look. 'A lady has to trust a man to be discreet.' Then he smiled. 'You find yourself a good woman of your own. That's what you need.'

The Portuguese island in the China Sea had a Mediterranean air. Tiny antique forts, more picturesque than threatening, dotted its modest hills.

The place had known glory. Two and a half centuries ago, in the shining days of the Ming dynasty, before even the great basilica of St Peter in Rome was completed, the Jesuits had built the magnificent stone church of St Paul on the top of Macao's central hill, to proclaim the Catholic faith's renewed might, even in Asia. It could be seen across the sea from twenty miles away – as could the Jesuit fort with its cannon, which stood just below.

But the glory of Macao was somewhat past. Just recently, the huge church had burned down – all except for its southern facade, which now stood alone on the hilltop like a stupendous stage set, gleaming at the rising and the setting of the sun, but empty nonetheless.

John Trader liked Macao. The lodgings he shared with Tully were in a side street, just behind the Avenue of the Praia Grande that curved along the waterfront of a wide bay. On his first day, he walked with Tully along the esplanade. The long terrace of handsome houses – mostly stuccoed in Portuguese style, some white, others gaily painted red or green or blue – looked cheerfully out across the flagstoned street, the sea wall and a stony little beach towards the square-sailed junks ploughing through the shallows and the masts of sleek European ships anchored out beyond. There was a smell of salt air and seaweed.

'Glad to have my quarters down here,' Tully explained. 'I can take a brisk constitutional along the seafront every day, without puffing up and down hills.'

Above the seafront, covering the slopes, the Portuguese streets gave way to stuccoed villas and British colonial residences.

People still called it an island, though nowadays a narrow sandbar joined it to the mainland. It was an international port, but since its harbours needed dredging, only the shallow local junks could sail there; European vessels usually anchored out in the deeper waters known as the Roads.

What really mattered, however, was that although its Portuguese governors had run Macao for centuries, it still belonged to the emperor of China.

'You've got to understand,' Tully told him, 'that this place is a typical Chinese compromise. If there's opium trading in Macao – and there is a bit – the Portuguese governor keeps it discreet. The Portuguese are Roman Catholic, of course. But you can be damn sure the governor tells the Jesuit missionaries to be careful about preaching to the natives. The Chinese authorities don't like conversions – even in Macao. Still,' he concluded, 'as long as the governor uses a bit of common sense, the Chinese leave Macao alone. So far, it's been a pretty safe haven for us.'

The monsoon season had officially begun, but the weather was still temperate and fine, like the best of an English summer. Trader was glad to enjoy the salty sea air and to be free again.

One small matter did remain, from Canton: the letter from Lin to Queen Victoria.

He'd wondered what he should do with it. Should he give it to Elliot? That would be the simplest thing. He doubted very much that Elliot would forward it, but his own responsibility would end. Of course, if he really meant to honour the spirit of his promise to the commissioner, he'd send it to someone he could trust in England. One of his professors at Oxford had access to the royal court. Or he could burn the letter and forget the business. After a week, he decided just to put it in the strongbox he kept under his bed.

The English-speaking community centred on the merchants' families, with a sprinkling of missionaries, teachers and tradesmen. As a bachelor, he was invited everywhere, and nobody expected him to return the favour. British and American families were good at entertaining themselves with cards, music, amateur theatricals and healthy walks – up the hills where the views were fine, or down in the Campo Plain just north of the city. He was quite enjoying himself and hardly had to spend any money. Once a week he and Read would meet for a drink at a bar Read favoured down at the waterfront.

Despite Read's advice, he'd been cautious about finding himself a woman. Some of the English-speaking families had unattached young ladies. With these, however, Trader was circumspect. After all, he wasn't in a position to court any of them. By letting it be supposed that he was courting a lady in Calcutta, however, he made himself respectable, safe and rather interesting, both to the young ladies and to their mothers, which suited him quite well.

Like any port, Macao had a few bordellos. But he'd always been somewhat fastidious; besides, he had a healthy fear of catching something. Two of the merchants' wives had dropped hints that they'd be interested in getting to know him better. But in a small community such liaisons could mean trouble. The last thing he needed was angry husbands to add to his problems. For the time being, he just had to manage without.

That left only his debts to trouble him. In the midst of all his social activities, he usually managed not to think about them. But he didn't entirely succeed. If he awoke during the night, they came into his mind. As he lay awake, it was as if he could hear the slow drip, drip of the payments leaving his bank account in faraway Calcutta on the first business day of each month, whittling away his substance. And he wouldn't be able to sleep again.

And then one night he had a dream. He was crossing a rope bridge, high over some vast abyss, when he glanced back and saw, to his horror, that the wooden planks upon which he'd just been walking were coming loose and falling away, one by one, behind him. Hurrying forward, he looked back again and realised that the falling planks had almost caught up with him. And then suddenly the planks beneath his feet had gone, and he was falling, falling into the endless void below.

Two nights later, the nightmare came back again, and waking with a cry, he lay there wretchedly till dawn. After that, the sense of fear came to him more and more frequently, and there was nothing he could do about it. Like an addiction, his secret walked beside him, close as a friend, deadly as an enemy. Some days he felt so depressed he had to force himself to get up. But he always managed to put on a cheerful face for the world to see. And in a bleak way, he was even rather proud of himself for concealing his fears.

So the days passed, and with so much on his mind, John Trader scarcely realised he was lonely.

It was the third week of June when he went to the old cemetery. The humid heat of the monsoon season had been slow to arrive that year, but it was making itself felt that day.

He and Tully had taken a stroll down on the Praia Grande, but Trader had felt the need of more exercise. 'Why don't you walk up the hill?' Tully suggested. 'Might be a bit of a breeze up there. And if you want a rest, look in at the Old Protestant Cemetery. It's rather a pleasant spot.'

As he went up the hill, Trader began to sweat. He felt oppressed. If Macao looked pretty from a distance, it was not so lovely up close. And today he noticed its faults.

The painted stucco walls of the houses were mostly cracked. Cornices over doorways were missing pieces. There was dirt everywhere. The dust of the street stuck to his boots. There seemed to be a beggar in every alleyway. He saw a dead cat in a ditch, being stripped by carrion crows.

Halfway up the hill he came to the stuccoed baroque church of St Dominic. Creamy yellow walls, white trim, high green doors. An old woman was sweeping the stone terrace before its entrance, but apart from her, the little square was deserted. There was an inviting bench nearby, but he wasn't ready to rest yet, and he continued on his way, passing the huge open facade of St Paul's and finally walking around the Jesuit cannon emplacement near the hilltop, enjoying the fine views and the breeze. Time now, he thought, to take a little rest.

The Protestants had received permission to build their modest chapel only twenty years ago. It was a small, simple whitewashed building. Its congregation was British and American mostly, though Protestants of any nation were made welcome. And on a level shelf of land just below the chapel, its lawn gently shaded by trees and enclosed by thick stone walls, lay the Old Protestant Cemetery.

It was cooler here than in the street. The faint breeze from the sea touched the higher leaves on the trees, though they made scarcely any sound. The headstones rising from the grass and the tablets set in the walls were larger than he'd expected, some of them six feet high. The engraving, evidently done by a local mason, was a little crude. But all the memorials had this in common: they were the last record of those who had come out to this faraway island and departed life before they could return.

East India Company men, Dutch sea captains, American merchants, their wives, sometimes their children. All gone, all far from home.

John Trader sat on a stone for a while, then walked on the shady grass, reading the gravestones he passed. Set in one wall he noticed a memorial. Lieutenant Frederick Westbury of the British Navy, died after action, mourned by all the ship's crew. Younger than he was himself. The memorial was quite big, so his shipmates must have liked him.

Was there another memorial, he wondered, in some village church in England, set up by the young fellow's grieving family? He decided there was. And then the thought came to him: if I were to die today, would there be a stone for me here? Would Tully arrange it? God knows. One thing was certain. There'd be no stone in any village church in England. There was no one to grieve for him. Only a handful of people even to remember him. Charlie Farley would think of him and want to write a letter of condolence. But there was really no one for Charlie to write to.

And suddenly the shadows of the trees, instead of providing welcome relief from the sun, seemed melancholy. He felt inexpressibly sad and went slowly back to the stone upon which he'd been sitting before. There he sank down and lowered his head. And he was glad he was quite alone, since to his surprise, he found there were tears in his eyes.

He'd been there for twenty minutes and, thank God, his tears were quite dried when he heard a voice say, 'Hello, young Trader,' and looked up to see Read standing before him.

'You look depressed,' said Read.

'No. Not really.'

'This is a good place, isn't it? I often stroll about in here. Funnily enough, I was just thinking about you. Something you said to me when we first met on that boat.'

'What was that?'

'I seem to remember you said you had a bit of debt.'

'Oh. Did I?'

'I should think things might be rather tight, what with the trade being stopped and all the opium destroyed.'

'They say we'll get compensation, as you know.'

'It'll be a helluva long wait. Meantime, you must've got interest payments.'

'True.'

Read gazed at him kindly. 'Why not let me pay the interest for you?'

Trader looked at him in astonishment. 'But my God . . . why? You don't even know what my debts are.'

'I know the scale of your operations. I've got a pretty good idea.' The prospect didn't seem to faze the American in the least. 'You're not such a bad fellow. And it's years since I did anyone a good turn. Pay me back later. When you can. There's no hurry.'

'But, Read, I'm in the opium trade. You've said yourself it's a dirty business.'

'You know what they say, Trader: invest in the man. Perhaps you'll get into some other trade in the future.' He chuckled. 'You may have to.'

'I can't believe your kindness, Read, but I can't let you . . .'

'I have money, my friend,' Read told him quietly. He grinned. 'Enough to have made my wife want to marry me.'

'What if I couldn't repay you?'

'Then' – Read gave him a beautiful smile – 'my wife will get less when I die.'

'I don't know what to say.'

'One other thing, Trader. How about dining at my lodgings tomorrow? My landlady's a wonderful cook.'

Mrs Willems the widow lived in a small blue-stuccoed house, on a quiet lane some fifty yards from the old Jesuit cannon emplacement. The garden behind contained a lily pond. The house belonged to Mrs Willems; the garden belonged to her white cat, whose permission had to be asked if one wanted to visit the lily pond.

Like many Macanese, Mrs Willems looked part Asian, part European. With wide-set almond eyes and fine features, she was attractive, but how old was she? Trader couldn't decide. She might be thirty-five, she might be fifty. When she welcomed him, her English was not quite perfect, but she clearly understood all that was said.

The house was simply furnished in a pleasing mixture of styles: a Chinese table, a handsome old Portuguese cabinet, some Dutch leather armchairs. On the walls, Trader noticed watercolours from many countries. One of them, he saw, depicted the Port of London.

'What fine pictures,' he said politely to his hostess, who seemed pleased.

'My husband give me them,' she said with satisfaction.

'She used to ask her husband to bring her back a picture, whenever he went away on a voyage,' Read explained. 'Proved he was thinking of her, I daresay.' He smiled at Mrs Willems. 'As you see, he had a pretty good eye.'

The two men sat in armchairs, and Mrs Willems served them drinks before disappearing into the kitchen.

'She likes you,' said Read, looking pleased. 'I can tell.'

'Is she mostly Chinese?' Trader asked.

'Depends what you call Chinese,' Read answered. 'Her mother was Asian, part Japanese. Her father was the son of a Portuguese merchant and a local Tanka woman.'

'Tanka?'

'Very ancient people along this coast. Chinese of a kind, I suppose. But their language, which is thousands of years old, isn't like Chinese at all. The Han Chinese despise them because they say the Tanka are not Han. And they didn't treat them well. So the Tanka took to living apart, on boats. Fishermen mostly.'

'Why would a Portuguese merchant marry a Tanka, then?'

'Simple. They were in Macao. They needed wives. And no respectable Han Chinese woman would marry them – to the Han, we're all barbarians, remember. So the Portuguese married Tanka women instead. You can see their descendants in the streets here every day.'

The food was wonderful. Most of the houses he'd visited so far made some attempt at British cooking, with whatever local variation was necessary. But Mrs Willems offered proper Macanese cuisine – that mixture of Portuguese and southern Chinese cooking, fused with Malayan and Indian spices, only to be found on the little island of Macao.

They began with the delicately scented shrimp soup called lacassa, served with white wine, a tangy Portuguese Vinho Verde. Then came a selection of dishes from which to choose. There was chicken baked in the European manner with potatoes and coconut curry sauce. Trader closed his eyes to savour the rich aroma. There was Tchai de Bonzo, a dish of vegetables cooked with noodles. 'They call it Buddha's Delight,' Read informed him with a grin. Minchi, white rice with minced meat and topped with a fried egg. Cod, scallops and black pudding with orange jam, a pig's ear salad, truffled potatoes. Desserts followed in profusion: almond cookies, of course; Portuguese cheeses; a coconut milk custard; a mango pudding. And all this finished off with coffee, rather than Chinese tea.

She might look Chinese, but Mrs Willems sat at the table with the men, as an European woman would. As the meal progressed, extra dishes were brought in by a rather good-looking young Macanese woman whom Trader took to be a servant. Each time she came, she kept her eyes down and quickly disappeared back into the kitchen.

His hostess asked a few polite questions about his family and how he came to Canton. But he sensed that she was not particularly interested in his answers. What she really wanted to know was the date and time of his birth. As for his place of birth, he pointed to the picture of the Port of London on the wall.

Throughout the meal, Read steered the conversation well, like a ship's captain ensuring an easy crossing. Trader made polite conversation with Mrs Willems, asked about her travels, and learned that she had lived in several Asian ports with her husband. But it seemed to him that, although she spoke of the Dutch sea captain's occasional voyages to London, the Netherlands and even Portugal, she was a little vague about the precise location of these places. It was only at the end of the meal that the conversation ran into rough water.

The young serving-woman had brought in the coffee. She lingered a little this time, listening to the conversation, perhaps. Did she understand English? Was she observing him?

She looked more Portuguese than Mrs Willems. She had high Asian cheekbones and almond eyes. But her features were bolder: her hair was dark brown, not black and it was thick. Her mouth was broad, her lips full. A sensual face, he thought. And yes, she was watching him.

Mrs Willems saw it, too, for she suddenly screamed in Macao Portuguese, and the young woman fled.

Then, quite calmly, Mrs Willems turned to him. 'You go to brothels here?'

The question was so unexpected that for a moment he wondered if he'd misheard her. He glanced at Read, but Read only looked amused and said nothing.

'No, Mrs Willems,' he managed to reply. 'I don't.'

She was watching him. He didn't know what she was thinking. He'd told the truth, but did she believe him?

'You go to the flower boats in Canton.' This did not even seem to be a question.

'I was invited,' he said, thinking of the boat he'd passed when he first arrived, 'but I didn't go.'

'Why?'

'Don't want to catch anything.' If she could be blunt, so could he.

'Are you a clean boy?'

'Yes.'

It appeared that she had now lost interest in the subject, because she rose from the table and went into the kitchen, whether to bring something out or to chastise the girl, he had no idea.

Read waited until she'd gone before he spoke. 'You like the look of that girl, Trader?'

'Perhaps. She looks rather interesting, I think. Why?'

'She likes you.'

'The girl? How do you know?'

'I know.' Read paused. 'She's a young cousin of Mrs Willems. She's living with her for a while.'

'Oh.' Trader mulled over these answers. 'Those questions about brothels . . .'

'She was checking you out. I told her you were all right, but she feels responsible for the girl. That's why she asked about your birthday. For your horoscope.'

'I see. What exactly,' Trader asked slowly, 'is on offer here?'

Read's smile broadened. 'Whatever you want.'

Her name was Portuguese: Marissa. In the weeks that followed, Trader saw her every day or two. He would not go to the front door of the house, where he might encounter Mrs Willems, but to the side door, which gave into the kitchen, beside which Marissa had a small bedroom. Sometimes he went in the afternoon, sometimes in the evening. If he stayed the night and returned to his lodgings in the morning, Tully Odstock never asked him where he'd been, though he undoubtedly knew. Nor did the British and American families he visited make any reference to Marissa, though they probably knew about her, too.

As for Read, they continued to meet, go out drinking and sometimes encounter each other on social occasions; but when Trader came to visit Marissa, they kept themselves to themselves in the kitchen corner of the house.

Their affair quickly became passionate. He had only to see her standing at her work in the kitchen or smell the delicate scent of her skin to be possessed by acute desire. She had a strong peasant's body, though paler than he had at first expected; and also, he soon discovered, she was amazingly supple. He couldn't get enough of her, nor she, it seemed, of him. A good part of their time together was spent in her little bedroom. But sometimes they would take a stroll. The nearby gun battery with its fine views over the harbour was a pleasant place to wander in the evening. Or he would enter the Protestant cemetery and walk under the trees with her. It didn't bother her though she was Catholic. More than once he kissed her in that quiet, walled enclosure. Sometimes they would go farther afield, northwards onto the broad open plain of the Campo, or down to the waterside at the southern end of the island, to visit the lovely old Taoist temple of A-Ma, where they would light incense sticks for the goddess Mazu, who protected the fishermen.

He taught her English, and she made rapid progress. She liked to ask him questions about his life. He told her how he'd been orphaned and about his boyhood at school. He gave her vivid descriptions of London and Calcutta. And she told him her own parents were dead, that she had an older sister, married and living on the mainland, where she'd lived herself before coming to Macao to stay with Mrs Willems.

A couple of weeks into their relationship he began to realise that not everything Marissa said was true.

It had been clear from the start of their affair that, sexually, Marissa was very experienced. She taught him things he'd never done before. Their third evening together, after he'd exclaimed, 'Where did you learn to do that?' she'd paused only a moment before replying, 'I was married to a mariner for a year. Then he was lost at sea.'

Yet when, a few days later, he'd remarked to Read that it must have been sad for Marissa to have lost her husband, his friend had looked quite astonished before he recovered himself enough to mumble, a little vaguely, 'I guess so.'

A week later, Marissa referred casually to her mother's being unwell. And when Trader remarked that he thought her parents were dead, she frowned. 'I said that?' Then, after a moment: 'My father died. My mother lives with my sister.' He didn't pursue it.

But he did begin to wonder: did he really know who or what she was? Read and Mrs Willems had set him up with the girl. They must know. Had they made some arrangement with Marissa of which he was ignorant? What kind of arrangement?

'Should I be paying her?' he asked Read one day.

'No. Just give her a present once in a while. Go to the market with her. She'll let you see what she likes.'

A few days later, during one of their walks, she pointed to a bale of silk and remarked that it was beautiful. He took the hint.

And still the weather was kind. Hot and humid, to be sure, but not unbearable. It couldn't last, of course. This was the summer monsoon season.

'Big rains. Got to come soon,' Tully told him. 'Sometimes we get a typhoon.' But the days continued to pass in perfect peace.

Except for one small matter. Starting in June, Elliot had ordered any British merchant ships wishing to remain in the vicinity to use the safe anchorage at Hong Kong. 'Right move,' Tully had remarked. 'Hong Kong may be empty, but it's only just across the gulf, and a ship can survive a typhoon tucked in there.'

Yet it was from sheltered Hong Kong that the trouble had come. Trader heard about it when he returned to his lodgings one evening in early July.

'Stupid business,' Tully explained. 'Sailors got bored. Went over to a Chinese village on the mainland. Got drunk on rice wine. Had a bit of an argument with the locals. Villager killed, I'm afraid.' He shook his head. 'Elliot's going to compensate the family. Hush the whole thing up, you know.'

'The Chinese authorities won't like it if they find out.'

'Quite,' said Tully. 'Daresay it'll all blow over.'

It was three days later, towards the end of the afternoon, that the people of Macao became aware that a vast horde of dark clouds was massing on the southeastern horizon. Soon, like waves of skirmishers, the leading clouds were racing towards them, whipping the waters of the gulf as they came.

Trader and Marissa, out for an evening stroll, had hurried up to where the high, empty facade of St Paul's gazed out across the city. The hill was still bathed in sunlight. As the skirmishing clouds drew close, they felt the first gusts of wind suddenly slap their faces.

'You'd better get home before it starts,' said Marissa.

'Do you want me to go?'

'No, but—'

'I'd rather stay.'

As they went down the broad stone steps from the hilltop, a grey shadow passed over them. And when they reached the end of the steps and looked back, they saw that the soaring facade of the old church was gleaming with an unearthly light, as if it were making a last pale stand in the sky before being engulfed and struck down by the mighty storm.

Trader and Marissa lay together as Macao shook and shuddered under the crash of lightning and thunder and the ceaseless hammering roar of the rain upon the roof. The shutters outside the window rattled. The wind howled. Occasionally, during the brief lulls in the noise, they could hear the water flowing in a torrent down the narrow street.

They clung to each other tightly all through that night as though they were one and scarcely slept until, as the wind began to slacken sometime before dawn, Trader passed into unconsciousness.

But before he did so, an idea came into his mind. What if, after all, the British government did not come to the opium merchants' aid, and despite Read's kind help, he was ruined? What if he chose the alternative he'd imagined once before – to lead another life entirely, wander the world as an adventurer or make a home in some faraway place? Might he take Marissa with him? She wasn't respectable, of course. But would he care about that anymore? She'd be a good housekeeper. As for their nights together, could anything be better than what he was enjoying now? He didn't think so.

By the time they awoke, it was well into the morning. Outside, the clouds were scudding across the sky, but the sun could be discerned behind them. He decided to go down to the Avenue of the Praia Grande to see how Tully had fared in the storm.

When he reached the broad esplanade, he found evidence of the storm's destruction everywhere. The roadway was strewn with broken roof tiles, fronds from the palm trees, and assorted debris. Sadder still was a small cart lying on its side; the traces, still attached, had been torn apart. Had there been an animal in those traces when they broke? A pony, or more likely a donkey?

He went to the edge of the road and looked down into the waters sending up showers of spume as they smacked into the sea wall below.

Was there a floundering animal or a carcass floating in the bay below? None that he could see.

Tully was having breakfast when he arrived. He gave Trader a brief nod.

'Hope you weren't worried about me,' said John cheerfully.

'I knew where you were.'

'Well,' Trader added, with a touch of pride, 'that was my first Chinese typhoon.'

'Storm,' Tully grunted. 'Typhoon's worse. By the way,' he continued, 'there was a fella here looking for you just now. Did he find you?'

'No. Who was he?'

Tully shrugged. 'Never seen him before.'

After changing his clothes, Trader went out on the esplanade to survey the damage further. The grey clouds were still chasing across the sky, but here and there he caught a glimpse of blue. The sharp, salty breeze was invigorating. He felt a pleasant burst of energy and hardly realised that he was increasing his pace. He'd gone half a mile when he heard a sound behind him.

'Mr Trader?' An English voice, slightly nasal. John turned, irritated by this interruption of his exercise. 'Mr John Trader?'

The man looked about his own age. Slim, not quite as tall. He was wearing a tweed overcoat, not well cut, underneath which John thought he could see a white clerical necktie. And for reasons known only to himself, the stranger had wrapped a brown woolen scarf over his narrow head and tied it under his chin. Trader took an instant dislike to him, though naturally he was polite. 'Do you need help?' he asked.

'I came to make myself known to you as soon as I discovered your identity,' the stranger said with a toothy smile.

'Oh. Why was that?'

'I am your cousin, Mr Trader!' he exclaimed. 'Cecil Whiteparish. I feel sure we are going to be friends.'

He gazed at John expectantly. Trader stared back, mystified. And continued to look at him blankly until he frowned.

Whiteparish. Those distant relations of his father's. Wasn't that their name? He'd never known anything much about them. His guardian had mentioned their existence to him once, just before he went up to Oxford. Told him there had been a rift between his father and these people, long ago. Cause unknown. An imprudent marriage, or something of that sort.

'I advise you not to seek them out,' his guardian had said. 'Your parents never did.' That was all John knew. He'd forgotten about them after that.

And judging by the look of Cecil Whiteparish this morning, his father and his guardian had been right. 'I don't believe I've heard of you,' he said cautiously.

'Ah,' said Cecil Whiteparish. 'Allow me to explain. My grandfather and your grandfather were cousins . . .'

'It sounds a bit distant,' John gently interrupted.

If he wasn't being very welcoming, there was good reason. For Cecil Whiteparish was all wrong. The way he dressed, the way he spoke, the way he carried himself. There was only one way to put it: Cecil Whiteparish was not a gentleman. John Trader might not be a gentleman in the eyes of Colonel Lomond, because he didn't come from a gentry family. But he knew how to behave.

If Cecil Whiteparish had been to a decent school, if he'd been to the Inns of Court or university or got himself into a halfway decent regiment, he'd know how to behave. Such things could be learned. But it was obvious he hadn't. He even pronounced his own name the wrong way. The young bloods at Oxford didn't pronounce the aristocratic name of Cecil the way it was written. They said *Sissel.* But Cecil Whiteparish didn't know that. In short, he simply wouldn't do.

As Trader looked at this unwelcome cousin, therefore, he was struck by an awful thought: what if by some miracle he recovered and made his fortune, and courted Agnes Lomond – and the Lomonds discovered that the only family he had was Cecil Whiteparish? How would that make him look? It didn't bear thinking about.

'What brings you here?' Trader asked tonelessly.

'The British and Foreign Bible Society engaged me. I'm a missionary. I'm hoping you'll support our work.'

'Hmm.' Trader wondered how to respond. And then a beautiful thought occurred to him. 'I'm in the opium business,' he said with sudden cheerfulness.

'Not only opium, I hope,' said Cecil Whiteparish with a frown.

'Just opium,' said John. 'That's where the money is.'

'Not anymore, it seems,' Cecil Whiteparish remarked coldly.

'Oh, I'm sure the British government will come through for us.' Trader gave him a robust smile.

Whiteparish was silent. Trader watched him. Things were going better. If he could just shock his missionary cousin enough, the fellow wouldn't want anything more to do with him. Problem solved. He returned to the offensive.

'You'll find Macao's a friendly sort of place,' he continued blandly. 'Some very handsome women here, too, though I don't suppose you'd . . .' He trailed off, as if he were uncertain, then brightened again. 'To tell you the truth, I've got a charming mistress here. She and her mother occupy a little house up on the hill. Pretty little place. My friend Read enjoys the mother, and I, the daughter. Part Portuguese, part Chinese. That's a wonderful combination, you know: beautiful.'

'Mother and daughter? You are all in the house together?'

'Indeed. I've just come from there.' It amused him that he'd made Mrs Willems the mother of Marissa. But then, come to think of it, for all he knew she might be.

'I am very sorry to hear this,' said Cecil Whiteparish gravely. 'I shall pray that you return to the path of virtue.'

'One day perhaps,' Trader acknowledged. 'But I don't plan to yet.'

'True love, the love of God,' the missionary offered, with an effort at kindness in his eyes, 'brings far more joy than the lusts of the flesh.'

'I don't deny it,' said John. 'Have you tried the lusts of the flesh, as a matter of interest?'

'There is no need to mock me, Mr Trader.' Whiteparish gave him a reproachful look.

'I'm afraid there's bad blood in the family,' Trader confessed. And then, with remorseless logic: 'Perhaps we share it.'

Poor Whiteparish was silent. Socially, as in other matters, he was innocent. But he was not a fool; and it was clear to him that, for whatever reason, his cousin had no wish to be his friend. 'I think I should leave you, Mr Trader,' he said with simple dignity. 'Should you ever wish to find me, it will not be difficult.'

Trader watched him go. He was sorry to behave badly – not that he had anything in common with his unwelcome cousin – but he wasn't sorry if Whiteparish had decided to erase him from his life.

If he ever got the chance to pay his addresses to Agnes Lomond, Cecil Whiteparish must never appear. That was certain. A necessity. And then he realised that if, on the contrary, he gave up all ambition and ran away with Marissa, he'd be unlikely to see much of the missionary, either. Which was also a cheering thought.

o

Shi-Rong was overjoyed. He'd done well so far. But his mission today put him on an altogether different level of trust with Commissioner Lin.

When he was so unexpectedly chosen to be the great man's private secretary, Shi-Rong had been granted the lowliest of the nine ranks of the mandarin order. It made his position official and allowed him to wear a silver button in his hat and, on formal occasions, a big square silk brocade badge on his tunic, depicting a paradise flycatcher, which looked very fine and handsome.

As Lin's private secretary, however, he was treated with a wary respect by provincial officials who were older than he and far more senior in rank. For they all knew he had the confidence of the commissioner, who reported to the emperor himself.

Indeed, Lin had kept him so busy that he had even, with the commissioner's permission, engaged his young Cantonese tutor Fong to be his part-time assistant. In particular, Fong could often help him make sure he had understood what the local people said to him, for the people from the countryside often spoke dialects that were hard even for a native of the city to understand.

Three times Shi-Rong had written proudly to his father to let him know of some new task with which Lin had entrusted him. But this present matter was so personal and delicate – proof that the commissioner was sharing his most intimate secrets with him – that he wouldn't even write to his father about it. A letter, after all, could always fall into the wrong hands.

He made his way from Thirteen Factory Street into Hog Lane, glancing behind to make sure he was not being followed. Hog Lane was empty. The stalls had all been boarded up. Even Dr Parker's little missionary hospital had moved into one of the factories. He reached the waterfront, also deserted.

Since the departure of the British for Macao, only a handful of foreigners, mostly Americans, were still using the factories. The place was like a ghost town.

He went along the line of silent factories until he came to a modest doorway and entered.

Dr Parker had just finished treating a Chinese patient. Shi-Rong asked to speak with him privately.

The Chinese never gave Parker any trouble. First, he was American, not English, and had nothing to do with the drug trade. Second, he treated them for ailments that their own doctors did not often cure. And third, they liked him because he was a good and honest man.

'I have come on behalf of Commissioner Lin,' Shi-Rong explained. 'His Excellency does not wish to be seen coming here himself, nor does he wish you to be seen entering his house. This is because he prefers that his malady should not be public knowledge.' He paused and smiled. 'It's nothing shocking. He just wants to keep it to himself.'

'You may assure him of my discretion. May I ask the nature of his trouble?'

'The truth is,' said Shi-Rong, 'that the commissioner has a hernia.'

'Ah. Well, in that case,' said Parker, 'there are various things I can do. One would be to fit him with a truss. But it would be much better if I did it in person, and more comfortable for him.'

'I understand, and I will repeat what you have said. But he hopes you can send him one. Is there something he can adjust?'

Parker mulled over the situation. Then he said, 'I've a fairly good idea of his height and weight. Let me make a proposal. Give me until tomorrow evening, and I'll send over half a dozen trusses. He can try them on, select the one that fits best, and you can bring the others back to me in a day or two. I'll pack them myself and send them tomorrow at dusk. I have a totally reliable messenger. He'll deliver the parcel, and he'll have no idea what's in it.' He smiled. 'But try to persuade him to let me see him.'

Shi-Rong thanked him and left. Commissioner Lin seemed well satisfied with the arrangements. After that, Shi-Rong went out for a meal with Fong.

o

It was night when Nio slipped back into the camp. Though darkness had fallen, he knew the track so well that he'd almost been running, and he was still trembling with excitement when he arrived.

The camp was only ten miles away from Guangzhou, but so far it had remained a safe haven for Sea Dragon and his men. Half the crew came from the nearby village, so no one in the locality was going to give them away. Discreet bribes to the magistrate had ensured that the village was left alone; and even during the crackdown this year, the magistrate had still been able to warn them whenever a police raid was imminent.

But it was still a depressing place. Because there was nothing to do.

Since Lin's destruction of the opium, the drug trade had virtually shut down. They heard of boats pulling into coastal creeks here and there with maybe a dozen chests they'd got their hands on. But out in the gulf, nothing. No smuggling, no income. For the moment, at least, Lin had won. How long could it last?

'Everyone wants opium,' Sea Dragon had declared. 'I could deliver a boatload every day. Every village is crying out for it. Let's hope the emperor gives this accursed Lin a promotion and sends him elsewhere.'

'Wouldn't we get another commissioner, just as bad?' one of his men suggested.

'No,' Sea Dragon told him. 'The emperor can send whom he likes. No other mandarin's going to hold the trade back. Lin's the only one who ever has or ever will. The question is,' he'd remark grimly, 'how long's he going to stay?'

Nio always wanted to kill the commissioner, but Sea Dragon only laughed. 'That's not such an easy thing to do, my young friend,' he'd tell Nio. 'We might surprise him in the street one day. But he won't be by himself, you know. There'll be attendants, troops . . . The difficulty's getting away.'

Sea Dragon had sent Nio into the city several times recently. Using Nio made sense. Not only was he intelligent, but thanks to his accent and dialect – which immediately told any townsman that he came from farther down the coast – nobody would associate him with Sea Dragon and his men. Nio had been glad to go. At least it was a relief from the boredom of the camp. His job was to find out all he could about Commissioner Lin's next plans and to listen for any whisper about opium that might be smuggled in.

He'd known that Shi-Rong was Lin's secretary for months, ever since a stallholder in the market had pointed the young noble out to him. He'd followed Shi-Rong several times to see what he could learn about him, and the last time he was in the city, he'd seen him with young Fong and learned that Fong was working for him. He wondered if he could engage Fong in conversation.

Today, Nio had seen the two men eat a meal together. Then he'd followed Fong to a teahouse, where he'd met some other young fellows. Luck was on his side. He'd found a seat at the next table where he could eavesdrop on their conversation.

And before he'd finished drinking his tea, he'd realised how he could kill Commissioner Lin.

o

Shi-Rong had a sleepless night. Again and again he tossed and turned on his bed. It was all he could do not to cry out aloud. How could he have been so stupid?

The one thing the commissioner had asked of him. Lin, to whom he owed everything. He'd asked for discretion, privacy. And what had he done?

In a moment of foolishness, he'd told young Fong about the truss. Sworn him to secrecy, of course. Of course! But what good was that? If I had a wife, Shi-Rong thought, I'd have told her. But that would have been different. He'd told Fong, a young bachelor who went out with his friends every night. That was always the way of it. You confide a secret to a friend, make him promise not to tell; then he does the same thing; and in an hour everybody knows.

How could he have been so stupid? So weak. If it got back to Lin, then he'd have lost his mentor's trust forever. He'd be finished. His career over, for the rest of his life. And he'd have deserved it. He buried his face in his hands; he rocked his head; he clenched his fists in frustration and agony.

He was up at dawn. He had to find Fong. That was the first thing. But Fong was not at his lodgings, nor was there any sign of him in the streets. And after an hour Shi-Rong had to give up, because Commissioner Lin would be expecting him.

'He's in a bad mood,' a servant warned him as Shi-Rong entered the big building.

Was the commissioner's hernia troubling him? Had Fong already talked? Did Lin know? Inwardly trembling, Shi-Rong went into the office and was greatly relieved when his mentor indicated that he should sit down, and then began: 'Today, Jiang, the British barbarians have shown themselves for what they really are.'

'What is that, Excellency?'

'You remember, before they left Guangzhou, I demanded they sign a guarantee not to ship any more opium to the Celestial Kingdom?'

'Of course, Excellency. Some of them signed, I recall, including Matheson, though Elliot refused to sign.'

'Did you think they meant to keep their word?'

'If you will forgive me, Excellency, I didn't.'

'One should assume a man is honest until he proves he is not. When Elliot refused to sign, I asked myself: *Why does he refuse?* And it occurred to me that perhaps he knows the merchants are lying and he wants no part of a shameful business.'

'If I may say so, Excellency,' Shi-Rong ventured, 'I believe you were imputing your own high virtue to Elliot, who may not be worthy of it.'

'Recently, as you know,' Lin continued, 'we have had the disgraceful case of these British sailors murdering an innocent peasant on Chinese soil. I have rightly demanded the culprit be surrendered to us for justice. Today Elliot has refused. He has declared that he will try his own men, but that I may send an observer.'

'That is an impertinence to the Celestial Kingdom, Excellency.'

'Even more than that, Jiang. I have discovered that according to their own laws, these barbarian countries agree that if an offense like this is committed by one of their people in another country, then he should be tried and punished by the courts of the country where the crime took place. Yet now, in the Celestial Kingdom, which is so much greater, more ancient and more moral than their own country, they refuse to obey even their own law. The merchants, I knew, were no better than pirates. Now I know that their government official has a contempt for all law and justice, even his own. This cannot be tolerated. I may soon have a new mission for you.'

'Whatever you command, Excellency.' A mark of further trust. Good news indeed. Shi-Rong bowed to the great man and was starting to withdraw when the commissioner interrupted him.

'The trusses. They come this evening?'

'They do, Excellency.' He bowed again and went about his work.

It was late afternoon before he could go out in search of Fong again.

Fong was at his lodgings. He didn't look too well. Shi-Rong wasted no time. 'Tell me exactly what you have been doing since we parted yesterday.'

'I met some friends. We went out drinking baijiu,' Fong confessed sheepishly. Baijiu, strong spirits made from grain in the north and from rice down here.

'Then?'

'We went to a teahouse.'

'Were you drunk?'

'Not then. Later.' Fong shook his head sadly. 'I slept until afternoon. My head still hurts.'

'Fool. Think hard: did you tell anyone what I told you about Commissioner Lin?'

'No. Absolutely not. Never . . .'

'You are lying.'

'No.' Plaintively. He was lying.

'If word ever reaches Lin that I told you his secret,' said Shi-Rong, 'then I'll be finished. And if that happens, Fong, I'll take you with me. I'll destroy you. You understand? I may kill you.' He meant it. Fong looked frightened. 'You know the irony?' Shi-Rong went on. 'It turns out Lin didn't have a hernia at all. A Chinese physician gave him acupuncture last night and the pain went away. The trusses are cancelled. If you told anyone, make sure they know that right away.'

It wasn't true, of course. But with luck it would kill the story.

His next errand was to get to Dr Parker. If Parker never sent the messenger with the trusses, no one would see the package leave the hospital or arrive at Lin's headquarters. Extra insurance against the story. He'd take the trusses himself, secrete them on his person and get them in to his chief unnoticed.

Dusk was falling. He had to hurry. He got to Thirteen Factory Street and turned into Hog Lane.

The lane was usually deserted these days, so he was slightly surprised to see a small knot of men gathered halfway down the lane. As they saw him coming, they started to move up the lane towards the main street, bowing very respectfully as he passed.

Parker was still at the hospital. But when Shi-Rong asked him for the trusses, the missionary looked surprised. 'My man just set off with them a couple of minutes ago. You must have met him, I should think.'

'Was he with a group of others?'

'No. Quite alone.'

Shi-Rong frowned and hurried out. He'd be lucky to catch the man now. He almost ran up Hog Lane.

And was halfway up it when, in front of him, a terrible apparition appeared. A figure was emerging from behind one of the boarded-up stalls. The old man was deathly pale. Blood streamed from his head. With one hand he tried to steady himself against the side of the stall. The other clutched his abdomen, from which blood was oozing. He'd been stabbed. Seeing Shi-Rong, he made a croaking sound. 'Help me.'

'Did you come from Dr Parker?' Shi-Rong cried.

'Yes. Please help me.'

But Shi-Rong had guessed it all now, with a horrible flash of clarity. If he was right, there was no time to lose. He turned and ran, panic-stricken, towards the main street.

o

Things hadn't gone the way Nio had planned. His first disappointment had come the night before.

'Your idea may work,' the pirate had said after Nio had told him about the delivery of the trusses. 'Lin expects the delivery. The messenger tells the guards he's come to see the commissioner in private. Lin will say yes, send him in. More discreet. Messenger gives him the package. He takes it. Before he knows what's happening, the messenger's hand is over his mouth, the knife's in his heart. Nobody even knows what happened. Open the door, bow, close the door, leave.' He nodded. 'Dangerous, but worth a try.'

'I can do it,' Nio said excitedly. 'I won't let you down.'

Sea Dragon stared at him in surprise, then shook his head. 'The man who kills Lin will be a hero all along the coast. All over southern China.' He smiled. 'Sea Dragon will be the hero. Not you.'

'But . . .' Nio's face fell. 'I was going . . .' A look from the pirate, however, told him it was more than his life was worth to argue. 'You're the boss,' he said sadly.

'First we have to get the package from the messenger. We take two, maybe three men.' The pirate looked thoughtful. 'Where to do it? If we can be seen, it won't work.'

'I thought of that,' said Nio. 'He'll come up Hog Lane. Lin had the stalls boarded up. It's usually empty.'

'Good.' Sea Dragon gave him a nod of approval. 'You grab the messenger. Knock him out. We push him behind the stalls. I take his place and carry the package to Lin.'

'Do we go with you?'

'No. The messenger is expected alone.' Sea Dragon considered. 'You and the men follow. A little way behind, so nobody thinks you're with me.

Hang about near the gates, but not all together. Everything has to look normal. Wait until I come out.'

'And then?'

'If I walk out, do nothing. Once I'm round the corner, split up. Everyone go in a different direction, and we meet later, outside the city.'

'And if they're chasing you?'

'Run after me. Pretend you're trying to help the guards catch me, but get in their way, fall over, trip them, so I can get away. Then split up and meet later, the same way. Can you do that?'

They'd rehearsed the whole thing, twice, out at the camp in the morning.

'If something goes wrong, do what I say and be ready to scatter,' Sea Dragon ordered. 'But I think it's going to work.'

They got to the city early that afternoon. First they worked out their escape routes. Here, the commissioner's decision to set up his headquarters in Thirteen Factory Street was helpful, since the street lay just outside the city walls, whose eight gates were shut at night. Even if darkness had fallen, they wouldn't be trapped in the city, and there were a dozen paths they could take out into the shantytowns and the waste ground along the river.

Then Nio and Sea Dragon inspected Hog Lane. Halfway down, there was a small alley where three or four men could hide. A few minutes more of discreetly working loose the boards in front of the stall beside it, and they had a space in which to dump the messenger. 'All we need now,' said Sea Dragon, 'is to place the lookouts.' Nio found a spot on the waterfront where he could watch the entrance to Dr Parker's little hospital. Sea Dragon could position himself in a doorway near the foot of Hog Lane. The two other men would wait in the alley. 'You signal me as he leaves the hospital,' the pirate told Nio. 'And I'll slip up the lane.'

They separated after that. Nio went to a teahouse before returning, a little before dusk, to the waterfront.

For the first minutes, everything had gone so smoothly. There wasn't a soul about. Sitting behind a big mooring post by the waterside, Nio had a thick, heavy club, about the length of a rolling pin, on the ground beside him. Just as dusk began, he saw the messenger. There was no mistaking him. He was quite an old man, though he still looked spry. He came out of Hog Lane and went swiftly down the line of empty factories to Parker's door.

He was in there only a few moments. When he came out, he was slightly bent forward, with the package hoisted on his back. It looked bulky rather than heavy. As soon as the old man's back was turned to him, Nio grabbed his club in one hand, stood up, and with his other hand waved a white cloth towards the place where Sea Dragon was waiting. Instantly, he saw the pirate slip like a shadow into the lane. Moving silently, Nio had followed. When the old man turned into the lane, he clutched the club tightly to his chest and started to run, as fast as he could, to catch up with him. He entered the lane. Apart from the old man, it was empty. He raced up the lane. Would the old fellow hear him? He saw him hesitate. Was he going to turn? No. He'd seen Sea Dragon step out in front of him. The pirate was bowing politely. Clever fellow. Only fifteen yards to go. The old man was about to pass. Sea Dragon grabbed his hands. The old man cried out.

He was there. He cracked the club on the side of the old man's head. *Tock!* The sound seemed to fill the lane. But he'd judged it well. The old man went down, smacking into the ground. He was out cold.

The two other men were already out of the alleyway. They tore the package off the old man's back and thrust it at Sea Dragon. They picked up the old man. His body was limp. And they were about to throw him into the stall when Sea Dragon stopped them. 'He saw my face.' He turned to Nio. 'Show me your knife.' Nio pulled it out. 'Good. Kill him.'

'Kill him?' Nio looked up and down the lane. Empty. Nobody even looking in. But he hesitated.

If they were attacked by a war junk when they were smuggling, he wouldn't mind killing. That was the game. Everyone knew it. The thought of killing Lin never worried him, either. Lin was a mandarin from the north, nothing to do with him or his people. And he was trying to destroy a local trade. Let him die. Who cared?

But this old man was harmless. Just an old Cantonese, with children and grandchildren most likely, a poor fellow running an errand. He didn't want to kill him.

'He saw me. Kill him.' Sea Dragon was looking at him. It was an order. No man in his crew could disobey that. And the rest of the crew wouldn't tolerate anyone who did. Sea Dragon was looking at him, and there was death in his eyes.

Nio turned and plunged his knife into the old fellow's body, under the ribs, and twisted it up to strike the heart. He saw one of the men holding the old fellow nod to Sea Dragon. They tossed the old man's body behind the boards and pushed them back in place.

And just then Nio glanced up the alley as Shi-Rong entered it. He did not know that he could move so fast. Reaching across, he scooped up the package containing the trusses and, with a single motion, slung it into the shadows of the alleyway.

'Mandarin,' he hissed. 'Bow when he passes.' Then, taking Sea Dragon's arm, he called out, 'Goodnight, my friends,' to the two other men and walked casually towards Shi-Rong with the pirate beside him.

Shi-Rong was in a hurry. He looked preoccupied. When Nio and Sea Dragon made way for him and bowed, he hardly acknowledged them and scarcely seemed to notice the other two men at all. As soon as Shi-Rong was out of the lane, Nio signalled the other men to bring the package at once and helped Sea Dragon sling it over his back.

'That was Lin's secretary,' he explained. 'He must be making sure the package was sent.'

'Good.' Sea Dragon was walking swiftly. 'Parker will tell him it's on the way. Let's do it.'

There was no problem when they reached Lin's headquarters. From across the street, Nio watched Sea Dragon speak to the guards at the gate, one of whom went to get instructions and soon returned. 'You're to wait inside,' Nio heard him say.

So far, so good. The lanterns were being lit in a big teahouse nearby. There were quite a few people about in the street. It was easy enough for Nio and the other two men to wait around without attracting attention.

Only one thing troubled him. It seemed quite likely that after Shi-Rong had gone to check with Dr Parker that the delivery was being made, the young mandarin would have finished his work for the day. He'd probably meet friends or go to a teahouse. But what if he returned to Lin's headquarters? He might know from Parker that the messenger was an old man. If he saw Sea Dragon inside with the package, he'd smell a rat at once. The game would be up. He cursed himself. Why hadn't he thought of that before?

What could he do if Shi-Rong appeared? Waylay him in the street? How? Could he kill him? He still had his knife, which he suddenly realised he'd never wiped clean.

Difficult, in front of the guards at the gate – and certain death for himself as well.

Should he go back to Hog Lane and try to kill Shi-Rong there? But that would mean deserting his post, when Sea Dragon had told him to wait where he was.

Nio gazed at the gate and prayed: let it be soon. Lin had only to call Sea Dragon in. The whole thing could be over in a moment. If the pirate would just appear. Walk safely out through the gate. Turn down the street.

'Come on,' he whispered to himself. 'Just open,' he silently begged the gates.

And his gaze was so fixed on the gates that he didn't even notice Shi-Rong until it was too late.

Shi-Rong was running at full tilt. He didn't notice Nio, though he passed only feet from him.

'Open the gates! It's Mr Jiang!' he shouted as he reached the entrance. They recognised him and opened immediately, and he burst through. 'Guards, come with me,' he cried. But he didn't look back, so he didn't see that they hesitated. He turned, then ran through the doorway into the inner courtyard and raced across to the main hall.

Behind a door on the right of the main hall was a small library where Lin liked to work. Shi-Rong was just in time to see the door open, a servant come out and a figure carrying a package step in. They hadn't seen him.

Without a word, he went like the wind past the astonished servant, reached the door just as it was almost closed, and hurled himself at it. With a crash, the door burst open, striking the figure on the other side a vicious blow on the back that sent him and his package flying.

'Call the guards!' he cried at the astonished commissioner, and launched himself at the intruder.

The pirate was sprawled on the floor, but he was already reaching for his knife. Even if he'd been carrying a knife himself, Shi-Rong knew that the pirate would have made short work of him, and probably managed to kill the commissioner, too, before anyone could stop him. He threw himself on top of Sea Dragon, wrapped his arms around him, pinning the assassin's arms to his body, and squeezed with all his strength.

If the pirate got a hand loose, he was a dead man. He knew it. But even if it cost him his own life, he had to save Lin. And though Sea Dragon kicked and elbowed and butted the back of his head into his face until blood was pouring from his nose and mouth, Shi-Rong held on like a man possessed. It was a full minute and more until four guards and a sergeant had disarmed the pirate and trussed him up with ropes so that he could not move at all. Only then did Shi-Rong, badly bruised and bleeding, let go and stagger to his feet.

If Lin had been taken by surprise, he quickly recovered. Pointing at the rope-bound figure, he ordered two of the guards: 'Lock him up and watch him.' Then, turning to the chief guard: 'Close the outer gates, lock them and double the guard,' he commanded. 'But do not raise the alarm,' he added. 'There is to be no word of this incident. If other bandits hear I have been attacked, it may encourage them to try.'

Meanwhile, Shi-Rong had done his best to stop the bleeding from his nose and to wipe his face with a cloth.

As soon as the library was cleared, Lin turned to him. 'You have saved my life,' the commissioner said solemnly. 'Are you hurt?'

'It's nothing, Excellency.'

'How did you know?'

Shi-Rong told him he'd gone to make sure the package was sent, and how he had encountered the messenger.

'The poor fellow may be dead by now, Excellency. But I couldn't stay with him. The attack might just have been a robbery, but I feared something worse and had to make sure. So I ran here as fast as I could. Just in time, evidently.'

Lin nodded thoughtfully. 'It seems my assailant knew the messenger was expected here.' He gave Shi-Rong a sharp look. 'Did you tell anyone?'

'No, Excellency.'

'I would be surprised if Dr Parker betrayed a confidence, but he may have let something fall, accidentally.'

'The assailant may have asked the messenger where he was going.'

'That is possible. But I have a feeling that this attack was planned. Were there accomplices? We shall question Parker and the messenger, if he is still alive.' He nodded. 'That leaves the assassin. He surely can tell us everything.' He gave Shi-Rong another careful look. 'Interrogation is not a pleasant business, but it has to be done. The governor has a man who knows how to proceed. He will guide you.'

'Guide me, Excellency?'

'Yes, Jiang. It is you who will interrogate the assassin.'

The use of torture in the Empire of China was strictly regulated. Only certain procedures were allowed. An official who used a method that was not sanctioned was deemed to have committed a crime and might be prosecuted. Numerous persons were excused from torture, including those who had passed the mandarin examinations, the elderly, and pregnant women.

Only high officials like Lin could order the harsher forms of torture. And torturing people to extract confessions was frowned upon, since it was well understood that people would confess to anything in order to stop the pain.

But the case of Sea Dragon admitted no such mitigation. There was no question about his guilt: he'd been caught in the act of trying to assassinate the emperor's commissioner. It was important to know who his confederates might be and whether they were operating under orders from a third party.

The torture chamber was an empty white-walled room with a small, high window and an earth floor. There was an upright post set in the middle of the floor. Against one wall stood a bare wooden table on which Shi-Rong noticed a strange-looking object.

It was made of a dark hardwood and consisted of a handle that was a bit over a foot long, ending in a five-slatted fork, like the fingers of a man's hand. The ends of the slats were pierced and threaded with two lengths of tough twine, tied off at each end. Two stout little pegs had been placed on the table beside this implement.

It looked quite innocuous, Shi-Rong thought.

He'd entered the room with the police sergeant and his assistant, who were both dressed in white cotton tunics and leggings that came to the knee. Their feet were bare.

The sergeant was maybe forty-five, with a round body and face. He looked as if he ran a prosperous teahouse. His assistant was thin and seemed hardly more than a boy.

Two guards brought Sea Dragon in. He didn't look in bad shape.

They made him kneel on the floor and tied his pigtail to the post behind him. Then they stood, one on either side of him.

The sergeant moved forward and told the guards to raise the prisoner's hands above his head. Then he nodded to his assistant, who picked up the instrument of torture from the table.

Together, they fitted the prisoner's fingers between the slats, four fingers from each hand. Pushing the little wooden pegs into the loops at each end made by the tied-off twine, the sergeant began to twist them, tightening the twine, which pulled the wooden slats against the sides of the prisoner's fingers. When all the fingers were held as though clamped in a vise, the sergeant stepped back, while his assistant held the finger pincher by the handle.

The sergeant turned to Shi-Rong. 'Ask him a question,' he said.

'What is your name?' Shi-Rong demanded.

The prisoner stared at the white wall in front of him, but didn't reply.

The sergeant came over and twisted one of the pegs sharply. Shi-Rong saw the prisoner wince and realised that the pressure must be directly on his fingers.

'Ask another question,' said the sergeant as he stepped back again.

'This time,' Shi-Rong said to the pirate, 'you must tell me your name, and the reason you tried to kill the commissioner.'

Sea Dragon seemed to be studying the ceiling with curiosity. He didn't answer.

There was a long silence.

The assistant stretched out one hand. Gazing at the prisoner with a strange cold curiosity, he turned the other peg a full revolution. Shi-Rong saw the prisoner's body tense.

'Just tell me who you are,' said Shi-Rong, 'and I'll stop him.' But the pirate said nothing.

After another minute had passed, the young assistant twisted and shook the finger pincher by the handle. The prisoner gave a terrible grimace, followed by several gasps.

The sergeant tightened the finger pincher some more. Then he struck the pincher sharply.

This time Sea Dragon screamed. He couldn't help it. And Shi-Rong, who up until now had managed to control himself, felt his fists clench and his whole body tense as he squirmed with anguish at what he was witnessing. He saw the sergeant stare at him and quickly moved out of the prisoner's sight. After a moment's pause to collect himself, he spoke again.

'Say something to me,' he proposed to the pirate gently. 'Say anything you like.'

Shi-Rong had already known before they began that unless his accomplices were found, the prisoner was the only person left who could provide the truth about how this business began. The old man he'd found in Hog Lane had died within minutes. Dr Parker declared, to the best of his recollection, that at the start of the day he'd told the old man he'd need him again in the late afternoon, but that he hadn't given him his directions until he set off. There was a small chance that Parker's memory was at fault, but it was unlikely. Nobody imagined he was lying. So that just left the prisoner.

What might the prisoner actually know? Someone must have told him about the private delivery to Lin. Shi-Rong couldn't imagine that Fong had told the assassin himself, but the word had spread until it reached him. Did the prisoner have any idea that the leak could be traced through Fong to the very man interrogating him? He might or he might not.

And here was the irony: the only way to find out was to interrogate him.

If I succeed in breaking him, he thought, I may be signing my own death warrant.

Was there any way he could stop him talking? He didn't see how. Could he kill him? A terrible choice. But not so bad, he thought, as it might seem. After all, if the assassin survived the torture, he was certain to be executed anyway.

He glanced at the sergeant and his assistant. It looked as if they were going to remain there all the time. No doubt they'd be making their own report to Lin about everything that happened. Indeed, it suddenly occurred to him, their job may be not only to torture the prisoner but to watch me, too.

Of course. The realisation hit him with a terrible coldness. I'm a suspect. I'm still the most obvious person to have leaked the information. For all Lin knows, I could even be part of the plot myself. The fact that I rushed in to save him might have been a ruse; or more likely, I'd set up the assassination and had second thoughts, been overcome by fear or guilt, and rushed to stop it at the last minute. How else could I have guessed, even after meeting the old man, that the assassin would be there just then?

And the real truth, indeed, was only a hairsbreadth away: that he'd known the word had got out, that it was all his fault, and that he'd been so full of guilt that he was ready to sacrifice his life to save his master.

And now there was nothing to do except interrogate this man who, if he talked, might destroy him.

'They normally talk,' said the sergeant after a couple of hours. He inspected the prisoner's fingers and showed Shi-Rong. They were reduced to a bloodied mess. The flesh had come away from the joints, and Shi-Rong was staring at bare bones. 'He won't be using them again,' the sergeant remarked.

'What do we do now?' Shi-Rong asked.

'Ankle press,' said the sergeant. 'You'll see.'

It took a little while for them to bring the ankle press. It was nearly six feet long and also made of wood. They laid it on the floor.

'It's big,' said Shi-Rong nervously.

'Same idea,' said the sergeant. 'Only for ankles. This one really breaks 'em up.' Shi-Rong wasn't sure if he meant the ankles or the victims. Both, probably.

The base of the ankle press was thick as a prison door. At one end was a board with two holes to hold the victim's wrists, like a stocks. At the other end, standing vertical to the base, were three boards, like the slats on the finger press, but many times larger and heavier. Instead of rough twine, these were squeezed together near the top by ropes.

They laid Sea Dragon on the wooden base, facedown, imprisoned his wrists in the stocks and placed his ankles in the slots between the heavy upright boards.

The young assistant took a thick rod, like a long truncheon, and began to twist the ropes with it. The press made a creaking sound. He paused, walked around, pushed his narrow face into the prisoner's to see how he was doing, and returned to his work. The press creaked again as the ropes tightened further and the boards seized the ankle bones in their fiendish grip.

Shi-Rong saw the prisoner's mouth clench. Sea Dragon had gone deathly pale.

'Crushes the ankle bones,' remarked the sergeant. 'Turns the joints to mush, given time. We can wait now,' he added.

Shi-Rong did not know it, but he was now as pale as the prisoner. He had never witnessed excruciating agony like this, and it was almost more than he could bear. The minutes passed. Three times, during the next hour, they increased the pressure, and three times he told the prisoner: 'Speak and the pain will be less. Just say your name.'

Nothing. Finally he went over to the sergeant and whispered to him: 'You say they always talk?' The sergeant nodded. 'How long does it take?'

'Maybe hours,' said the sergeant. 'Maybe more.'

'What if he still doesn't talk?'

'We keep going.'

At times, the fellow's torment was so terrible that Shi-Rong almost wished that he would talk – no matter what he said. Anything, just to end the horror.

The assistant was observing him with just the same expression of cold curiosity that he'd bestowed upon the prisoner. What did he know? What was in his mind? Shi-Rong decided he didn't care.

'Why did you want to kill Commissioner Lin?' he demanded.

Silence. Then, to his surprise, he heard the sergeant murmur, 'Stupid question. Half the province wants to kill him.'

It was true. But it showed the sergeant's contempt for him that he would dare to say it. He looked at the prisoner to see if he would react. But the prisoner made no response. Surely he must be close to breaking?

They continued all that night, but still the prisoner gave them nothing. And Shi-Rong was feeling completely drained by the morning, when he went to give Commissioner Lin his report.

Lin was working in the library. He looked up briefly from the papers on his desk. After delivering his report, Shi-Rong wondered if the commissioner would take any pity on the prisoner – or at least give the interrogators some rest. But he said only, 'Continue,' and looked down at his work again.

When he got back, Shi-Rong found that they'd given the assassin water and a little rice, which he'd thrown up. His eyes were sunken.

'We're to go on,' Shi-Rong said to the sergeant. 'Did he say anything?'

The sergeant shook his head. He was tired and irritated. He looked at the man on the dragon bed with fury. 'Time to talk,' he said. And now he took a wedge and a heavy wooden mallet. Forcing the wedge down between the slats, he gave it a sudden vicious blow with the mallet that sent a frightful shock onto the half-shattered ankle bones.

The scream that came from the prisoner was not like anything Shi-Rong had heard from a human being before. Once, camping in a forest at night, he had heard something like this. A wild creature, he did not know what, had uttered a primal scream as it was being attacked – an unearthly scream, echoing through the trees in the darkness. And every man in the little camp had shuddered.

He started in horror. Even the sergeant looked shocked, to conceal which, he shouted angrily at the prisoner: 'Now talk, you son of a dog.' And seizing the rod from his assistant he yanked it around a full turn, as if this would finish the business for good.

The prisoner's gasp of agony and the moan that followed were so piteous that Shi-Rong doubled over. As he forced himself to straighten up, he was trembling. He saw that the assistant was still watching the proceedings with a calm curiosity.

'Ask him a question,' said the sergeant. But Shi-Rong could not.

'Talk, or I'll do it again!' the sergeant snarled at the prisoner with a curse. But the prisoner had lost consciousness. Shi-Rong could only hope he had died.

But he hadn't.

Two hours later, the sergeant went out and came in after a short while carrying a fresh set of boards. Working together, he and the assistant removed the three uprights and inserted the new boards in their place. As they did so, Shi-Rong could see that the pirate's ankle bones were already smashed and that blood was flowing from them freely.

'Why do you change the boards?' he asked the sergeant.

'These ones have been soaked in water. Makes 'em heavier and they grip tighter.' He gave Shi-Rong a bleak look. 'These'll finish the business.'

So they went to work again, the assistant twisting the rope, the sergeant using his wedge and mallet, both occasionally slipping on the darkening pool of blood upon the floor.

Again and again Shi-Rong asked questions: 'What is your name? Who are your accomplices?' He offered mercy, promised more pain. But got nothing. By mid-afternoon, the prisoner was drifting in and out of consciousness. It was hard to tell what he heard and what he did not. The room stank of sweat and urine. Shi-Rong suggested quietly to the sergeant that it might be more productive to pause, let the prisoner rest, and then start again the next day. But the sergeant made it a point of pride, it seemed, to break his victims quickly. And he would not stop.

It was only at the end of the afternoon, when he heard the sergeant curse in frustration, that Shi-Rong discovered that the prisoner was dead.

'I never fail,' the sergeant muttered furiously, and walked out of the room in disgust. His assistant followed him.

But Shi-Rong did not leave. He did not wish to be with them. Let the sergeant tell the commissioner he'd failed. He sat down on the bench and buried his face in his hands.

'I am sorry,' he said to the dead man at last. 'I am so sorry.' Did he want the dead man to forgive him? He had no hope of that. 'Oh,' he moaned, 'it is terrible.'

Silence.

And then the dead man spoke. 'You're lucky.' A faint, rasping whisper.

Shi-Rong started and stared at the dead man, who did not seem to have moved at all. Had he imagined it? He must have. Nothing more likely, given the state he was in. He shook his head, took it in his hands again and gazed miserably at his feet.

'Remember' – the sound was so soft he wasn't even sure he heard it – 'I told them . . . nothing.' A whisper, followed by a sigh.

Was he still alive, then, after all? Shi-Rong leaped up. He stood over the dead man, watching intently. He saw no sign of life.

And there must not be. This business had to end. The prisoner mustn't talk now. Desperately, Shi-Rong looked around for something he could use to suffocate the fellow. He couldn't see anything. He put one hand over the poor devil's mouth, grabbed his nose with the other and stood there while the long seconds passed. He glanced at the door, afraid that someone would come in and see him.

An age seemed to pass before he decided to let go. The fellow was dead, all right. He'd been dead from the start. The whisper? A hallucination. Or perhaps the dead man's ghost had spoken. That must be it.

So long as no one heard.

When Shi-Rong entered the library, Commissioner Lin already knew that the prisoner was dead. He received Shi-Rong calmly. 'You look tired.'

'I am, Excellency.'

'An interrogation is a distressing business. But unfortunately it is necessary. If this man had told us his accomplices, we might have questioned them and learned more.'

'I apologise, Excellency. I thought we should allow him to recover and try again tomorrow, but . . .'

'I am aware of all that. I do not think the prisoner would have talked. I think he wanted to die. For his honour, as he saw it.'

'Do you think he was part of a secret society, Excellency, like the White Lotus?'

'More likely he was just a pirate. These smugglers often come from the same village and clan . . . they'd sooner die than betray their comrades.' He paused a moment and gave Shi-Rong a bleak smile. 'But if I am right, I do not intend to leave his accomplices at large. Tomorrow, I intend to start rounding up all the pirates along these coasts.'

'All of them, Excellency?'

'All that we can find. I expect it will be a large number.' Lin nodded. 'And while I am doing that, I have another important assignment for you. Go and rest now, and report to me tomorrow morning.'

'Thank you, Excellency.' Shi-Rong bowed. And he was about to turn towards the door when Lin interrupted him.

'Before you go, Mr Jiang, there is something I wish to ask you.' The commissioner gazed at him steadily. 'Why do you think I ordered you to conduct the interrogation?'

'I do not know, Excellency.'

'Those who serve the emperor must accept grave responsibilities. A general knows that those following his commands may die in battle. A governor has to mete out punishments, including the sentence of death. And he must order interrogations. These duties are not taken lightly and may be hard to bear. It is important that you learn the bitter meaning of responsibility, Mr Jiang. Do you understand?'

'Yes, Excellency.'

'There is one thing more.' The mandarin was staring at him now in a way that was terrible. 'You must agree, Mr Jiang, that one aspect of this affair remains to be explained: did the assassin have prior knowledge that Dr Parker was going to send me the trusses? If so, was it Parker who gave the secret away? And if not Parker, then who? We cannot exclude the possibility that it was you.' Lin paused. 'Can we?'

It might have been part of an examination essay: those Confucian essays for future government servants that called for logic, completeness, judgement. And justice.

'The possibility cannot be excluded,' Shi-Rong agreed.

'I never doubted your loyalty,' Lin continued. 'But a careless word to a friend. The word repeated. Gossip overheard. This could have been the source.' Lin's eyes remained fixed on him. 'It is fortunate I was not killed. For if you had been the cause of my death, I feel sure you would have experienced a remorse so heavy that it would have weighed upon you like a millstone, perhaps until your death.' Lin paused. 'Instead, you saved my life.'

Was Lin offering him the opportunity to confess? Shi-Rong wanted to. He wanted so much to clear his conscience, to beg forgiveness from this man whom he had come to love and admire.

But what if this was a trap? He could not take the chance.

'I understand, Excellency,' he said, bowing his head.

'Quite so. Assuming you were not the source, as I have already said, the conduct of an interrogation was an unpleasant but valuable experience for you to undergo. But if by chance you were the source, then what better way of letting you understand the gravity of what you had done? And a punishment for your carelessness would have been appropriate. The horror of the interrogation in which you have just participated would have been a just punishment, and a good way of reminding you to be more responsible in future. Do you agree?'

Lin had guessed. No question. The great man had seen straight through him.

'Yes, Excellency,' Shi-Rong murmured, and hung his head.

'Sleep well, Mr Jiang. Tomorrow you will be going on a journey.' The commissioner looked down at the papers on his desk, as a signal that the interview was over.

'A journey, Excellency?' Shi-Rong couldn't help himself. 'Where to?'

Lin looked up again, as if surprised his secretary was still there. 'Macao.'

o

The rumour began at the start of August. John Trader heard it from Tully Odstock. Not that he worried.

The last couple of weeks had been rather pleasant. For a start, Cecil Whiteparish had not appeared again since their awkward encounter. Thank God for that at least. The fellow was still in Macao, of course, but he was keeping his distance. Nor had anyone come up to him and said, 'I hear you have a missionary in the family.' So presumably Whiteparish had lost his desire to have him as a cousin.

He'd enjoyed the usual social round. Marissa was contented. And although there were some war junks anchored off the island, the Celestial Kingdom didn't seem to be taking much interest in the occupants of Macao.

Until the rumours began.

'Lin's got some damned fellow running spies on the island,' Tully told him. 'So be careful what you say.' He nodded. 'Mum's the word, Trader. Watch and ward.'

'Where is he? Do we know who it is?'

'Don't know who. He's operating out of one of the war junks down at the end of the island.'

'Well, I can't think he's going to learn anything of interest. Nothing's happening.'

Tully Odstock gave him a strange look. 'I wouldn't be too sure of that, if I were you,' he said quietly.

'Really? I haven't heard anything.'

'Too busy with that young woman of yours.' Tully's sniff didn't sound too disapproving. 'Fact is, between you and me, the opium trade's started again.'

'Already? We aren't selling any. Who's selling?'

'Matheson.' Tully shook his head. 'The damn fella's so rich he can do things we can't. And behind his gentlemanlike appearance, he's cunning as a barrel-load of monkeys.'

'How's he doing it?'

'He's operating ships out of Manila, other side of the China Sea. They're carrying cargoes of cotton. Piled high with the stuff. Perfectly legal. But he's got chests of opium hidden in the holds. And the clever thing is, there's nothing in writing. Even if spies intercept the letters to his captains, they'll only find instructions about cottons – that's his code, you see. Each kind of opium is called a different sort of cotton. *Cotton Chintz* means Malwa opium, *Whites* are Patna opium, and so on. And with opium being scarce after Lin's confiscation, he's getting high prices for every chest.' He sighed in admiration. 'Of course, if Lin ever does get wind of it, there'll be hell to pay.'

All that day and the next, Trader found himself looking at people in the street with new eyes. Was this spymaster, whoever he might be, using the Chinese to do his bidding? Was he bribing local people? Might he even seek out someone like Mrs Willems, who might get to hear such information? Or Marissa? Could Marissa ever do such a thing? He put the thought from him. All the same, he wouldn't be telling her what he now knew, nor anyone else.

Two days later, coming back to his lodgings at midday, he encountered Tully. His partner was standing by the corner of the seafront, together with Elliot. They were gazing at a large proclamation that had been pasted on a wall. Tully beckoned him over and indicated he should read the poster.

It was from Commissioner Lin. It was in English, quite intelligible. And alarming.

'Remember those sailors who killed a native near Hong Kong last month?' Tully said.

'Yes. But I thought the man's family were paid off. You said the whole thing would blow over.'

'Well, Lin's found out about it. And judging by this poster, he ain't going to let it go. He wants the culprit handed over.'

'Nobody's been found guilty yet,' Elliot said sharply.

'I notice one thing,' Trader remarked. 'Lin says that according to our own laws, a man who commits a crime in another country is tried by the laws of the sovereign state where the crime took place. Is that correct, legally?'

'Do you want our sailors to be tortured and executed?' Tully exploded.

'No.'

'Well then. What I say is, damn the law, if it's not our law. Right, Elliot?'

'We have no treaty with China about such matters,' said Elliot firmly.

'Judging by the tone,' Trader offered, 'I think Lin truly believes we're behaving badly.'

'We have identified six men who took part in the incident,' said Elliot. 'I shall hold a properly constituted trial in ten days. And I have already invited Commissioner Lin to attend or send a representative.'

'Do you think that'll satisfy him?' Tully asked.

But Elliot, with a polite bow, was moving on.

The trial took place ten days later. Elliot conducted it on board ship. It lasted two days. Commissioner Lin did not attend, nor did he send any representative. Trader heard the news from Tully at lunchtime.

'He's found five of the sailors guilty.'

'Of murder?'

'Certainly not. Riot and assault. He fined the lot of them. And they'll be sent back to England to serve time in prison, too. So that's that.'

Trader wasn't so sure. But it was no use worrying about that now. He was due to see Marissa in a few hours. He had lunch with Tully and went for a walk on the seashore afterwards. After that, he took a siesta.

It was early evening. He had climbed the hill and was just below the high facade of St Paul's, and he was thinking that it would be a pleasant thing to turn into the old Jesuit cannon battery for a few minutes and gaze down upon the sea, when he noticed, ahead of him, a pair of figures heading in the same direction – one of whom he could have sworn he knew.

He followed them. And as they stopped beside the first old gun, and the younger turned his head to address his companion, he saw for certain that it was Shi-Rong, the commissioner's secretary.

Insofar as he could judge, the times they'd met before, he'd rather liked the young mandarin. But what the devil was he doing here? Should he speak to him?

And then it suddenly dawned on him: Shi-Rong might be the spymaster.

He'd vaguely supposed it would be some older man. But Shi-Rong was Lin's secretary. If he'd proved himself effective, the commissioner might have entrusted him with such a mission. Did that mean he should avoid him? On the contrary. All the more interesting to talk to him. Try to find out what was going on. He went forward. Shi-Rong glanced his way, recognised him.

And at that moment, Trader remembered: the letter. Lin's letter to

Queen Victoria. The letter he'd promised to forward. He'd completely forgotten about it. Only one thing to do. He bowed, smiled.

'Long time no see,' he offered. 'I sent Commissioner Lin's letter to Oxford. Maybe the queen will see it one day.'

Had they understood? He couldn't be sure. The man with Shi-Rong wasn't Mr Singapore. Short and middle-aged, he looked Malay, though his hair was plaited down his back in the Chinese queue. He might speak English. He might not.

'I was very sorry about the death of the man at Hong Kong,' said Trader politely. 'The guilty men have all been sent to gaol.' He waited. Shi-Rong and his companion looked at each other. 'Did you understand?' Trader asked.

Both men bowed to him politely, but there did not seem to be a trace of understanding on their faces, and neither of them made any reply.

And Trader would no doubt have given up and left them had they not, all three, been surprised by a figure hastening towards them. The figure called out to John.

It was Cecil Whiteparish. He looked furious. He rudely ignored the two Chinese and practically made a run at Trader, as though he meant to knock him to the ground.

'What the devil do you want?' cried John in surprise and some alarm.

'I want to talk to you, sir,' shouted his cousin.

'This is hardly the time and place,' snapped John.

'Is it not, sir? I'll be the judge of that. I sought you at your lodgings. You were not there. So I guessed I might find you up here – no doubt to visit your whore!'

With a supreme effort at self-control, John spoke with icy calm. 'This gentleman' – he indicated Shi-Rong – 'is the private secretary of Commissioner Lin, whom I have the honour to know. I was just expressing to him my regret for the unfortunate death of one of his countrymen, and explaining to him that all the men who took part in the affray have just been sent to gaol.'

Whatever had caused the missionary's tirade, surely this would warn his cousin to be civil until they were alone. Trader glanced at Shi-Rong and his companion. Did they understand what Cecil was saying? He hoped they didn't. But though the two Chinese were impassive, they gave no sign of moving.

'That may be. But I am talking about the foul trade in opium, in which, despite giving promises to the contrary, you and your friends are still engaging at this very moment.'

'No, I am not!' Trader cried. It was true. He might wish he was. But he wasn't. He glanced at Shi-Rong and his companion. Did his wretched cousin have any idea how dangerous it was to say such things in front of these men? 'Our friend here is secretary to the commissioner,' he chided him. 'You should not say such things in front of him. Especially when they are entirely untrue.'

'Do you deny that you are shipping cotton out of Manila, and that those cotton ships are secretly filled with opium?' cried Whiteparish.

How the devil had he come by that information? And why in the name of Heaven was he blurting it out?

'I utterly deny it. I deny it before God.'

'Frankly, Cousin John, I don't believe you. I know it is being done.' Whiteparish looked towards Shi-Rong. 'As for our Chinese friends, when I consider the evil that we do to their people and the duplicity of all our dealings with them, I should prefer that we apologise to them instead of continuing to do them injury.'

'You are mad,' said Trader contemptuously.

'You think I'm not a gentleman,' Whiteparish continued bitterly.

'I never said any such thing.'

'You think it. But in the eyes of God, you "gentlemen" are no better than thieves, a stain upon the honour of your country. I would not wish to be one of you. And as for this man' – he indicated Shi-Rong – 'I'd sooner he knew that not all Englishmen are like you. That there are good men in the British Parliament, honest, moral men, who are going to put a stop to your criminal activities very soon.'

Trader glanced at Shi-Rong and his companion. Their faces were blank.

'You'd better learn to speak Chinese, then,' he observed drily, 'because they don't understand a word you're saying.'

'They won't even need to. Have you heard of young Mr Gladstone? A man of increasing importance. I have it on good authority that he is going to oppose you and your foul trade in Parliament, and that he will carry many members with him.'

Trader gazed at his kinsman. This was the trouble with being unworldly, he thought. Imperfect information. 'You consider Mr Gladstone a moral gentleman?' he asked.

'I do.'

'He occupies the position he does in public life, which allows him to make his moralistic speeches, because his father made a great fortune. Do you know what this family fortune comes from?'

'I do not.'

'The slave trade. His father made his fortune trading slaves. It's illegal now, of course. And it's only a few years since young Mr Gladstone defended the slave trade in Parliament and won a huge monetary compensation for his father when that trade was finally abolished. So I really don't want to hear Gladstone preaching morals to me.'

He watched. Whiteparish sagged, the wind quite taken out of his sails. 'What you do is still evil,' he muttered.

It was just then that Trader noticed something. A fleeting expression on the face of Shi-Rong's companion. What was it: a flash of amusement, a trace of irony? A second later, the face was impassive again. But did it mean that the fellow had understood what they were saying after all?

He couldn't take a chance. For the common good, his tiresome cousin must be sacrificed. 'And now let me tell you something, Whiteparish,' he said fiercely. 'You have already acquired a reputation here in Macao. Your misdeeds in the past – I will not embarrass you by naming them – dishonesty, unnatural vices, they are known to the whole British community. And realising that your past has been uncovered, you seek to revenge yourself upon us all by spreading infamous lies. Yes, sir, your true character is known. You are an unmitigated liar, sir. A liar. And we all know it.' Whiteparish had started by looking stupefied. Now his face was going red with anger. 'Well may you blush, sir,' cried Trader. 'Well may you blush.'

'I have never, in my life . . .' Whiteparish stuttered.

'You are confounded. You are exposed as the villain you are. You have invented this illicit opium dealing just to take revenge upon your betters. I may even report you to Elliot. I shall sue you for slander, and so will anyone else whose reputation you attempt to sully with your lies.'

He turned upon his heel and began to walk away. As he hoped, Whiteparish stuck at his side, protesting and expostulating all the way. He kept him at it until they were halfway down the hill and safely away from the commissioner's secretary. He hoped his ruse had worked.

And he was far out of hearing when Shi-Rong turned to his interpreter and demanded: 'Tell me everything they said.'

o

'Perhaps it'll be a boy,' Second Son reminded Mei-Ling. But she shook her head. 'I'm so afraid it'll be a girl,' she said. How many times had they had this conversation? At least a hundred.

Nobody in the village thought Mother had smothered Willow's baby anymore. Willow never said so. Second Son never imagined such a thing in the first place. Mei-Ling didn't think so, either, and didn't want to. Indeed, Mother had shown her nothing but kindness all through her pregnancy.

Of course, Mei-Ling knew she wouldn't be so popular if she gave birth to a girl. She wouldn't blame Mother for that. It was just the way things were. She could imagine what people in the village would say if, after the eldest son had twice failed to produce a male heir, Second Son had a girl, too. They'd say the Lung family was unlucky. Mr Lung might have money, but the family would surely lose face.

If only Willow's second baby had been a boy. Mei-Ling wished it had been – not only for poor Willow's sake, but because that would have put Mother in such a good mood she mightn't care so much whether Second Son's child was a boy or not.

Meanwhile, her mother-in-law was being nicer to her than ever. Sometimes, while Willow was working about the house, the older woman would sit and talk to Mei-Ling, telling her things about the family in the old days, just as if she were the daughter-in-law she'd always wanted.

'You're the favoured daughter now,' Willow said to her sadly. 'The one who's going to have the baby boy.'

'And if I don't?' asked Mei-Ling.

Willow said nothing.

It was a month before the baby was due that the nightmare returned. It came in the small hours of the morning. It was the same as before. She'd had the baby. It was a girl. Mother had scooped the baby up in her arms and left the room. And then suddenly Mei-Ling was in the courtyard, looking for the baby, going from room to room. The baby had vanished.

She woke with a start. She knew it had been a nightmare, yet she couldn't get free of it. She was shaking, panting . . . She took some deep breaths, made herself calm down, told herself not to be foolish.

Then she turned to look at her husband. She could see Second Son's face by the faint light of the lantern that they kept in their room in case she needed to get up in the night. He was smiling in his sleep. Was her sweet-natured husband dreaming a happy dream, or was it just the natural smile of his kindly face in repose? She wanted to wake him, to tell him her dream and feel his comforting arms around her. But he'd been so tired after his long day's work, she couldn't bring herself to disturb his rest.

So she bided her time as best she could and told him in the morning. And again he assured her that no such thing would happen, and that he would be there to defend the baby in any case.

A week later the dream recurred, and again he comforted her.

But when, some days later, the nightmare afflicted her a third time, she kept it to herself and did not burden Second Son. And she was glad she did, for the panic wore off, and Mother was just as kind to her as ever.

As the time approached, she was getting very big and her back hurt, and she was really looking forward to getting the pregnancy over with. But Mother warned her: 'The first baby's often a bit late.'

Mr Lung had to go over to the local town on business, and he took Second Son with him. They set out in their cart at noon on one day, and promised to be back before noon the day after.

It was in the middle of the night that the terrible cramps began. They made her moan, then cry out.

Then the door opened and Mother entered, carrying a lighted candle. 'What is it, Daughter?'

'I do not know. I have cramps. They're so bad.'

The older woman came over, placed the candle on a table close by, made her lie still, and examined her. Then without a word, she went to the door and called for Willow. A couple of moments later, she heard Mother's voice. 'Go and fetch the midwife. Tell her to come. Now!'

They were kind to her. The midwife gave her a herbal brew to lessen the pain. Her mother-in-law was in the room constantly, reassuring her, soothing her. Again and again Mei-Ling asked her: 'Is it true, do you swear that Second Son will be back in the morning?'

'I promise, little one,' Mother said, her hard, broad face surprisingly tender.

If only she could be sure. She wanted her husband to be there more than anything in the world. If Second Son was there, everything would be all right. For she was sure it was a girl now. She didn't know how, but she was sure.

Dawn came and she was still in labour. Despite all the pain, she had only one desire: to delay the birth. Could she hold out until noon?

Every few minutes she'd cry out to the midwife, 'Is he here? Has my husband come?' To which the puzzled midwife could only reply: 'He'll be here soon enough, I daresay.' And then: 'Don't be silly, child. The baby wants to come out now. Take a breath now . . . Again . . . Push . . .'

'No!'

'The girl's quite mad,' she heard the midwife say to Mother. And she wondered, did Mother guess why she wanted Second Son to be there?

But nature will take its course. Just as the sun was coming over the horizon, her child was born. She saw the little being in the midwife's hands. Moments later, to her horror, she saw the baby in Mother's arms.

And then, to her surprise, her mother-in-law came to her side, her face wreathed in smiles. 'Just as I told you, Daughter. We have a little boy.'

There were many customs to follow after a Chinese birth. Mei-Ling wouldn't be allowed out of the house for a month. She mustn't wash her hair. Or her hands or feet or face. She had nothing to do, really. Her mother-in-law would do everything, including tending to the baby if he woke in the night.

One duty, about an hour after the baby was born, was to breastfeed him. Again, Mother was at her side. As she took the baby and put it to her breast, she was surprised when nothing happened. 'Did I do something wrong?' she asked.

'No. Be patient.' Mother smiled. 'It took your husband a moment or two to work it out when he was born. There now. He's got it.'

Mei-Ling's mother arrived around noon with baby clothes and towels. It was the custom. They were not of high quality, naturally, but her mother-in-law received them as politely as if they had been from the royal court. Mei-Ling was grateful for that.

There was only one time of sadness during that day. Just after noon, Willow came in to see her. She did not look angry, only depressed. 'Aren't you the lucky one?' she said. 'You had a boy.'

'You'll have a boy next time,' said Mei-Ling.

'Perhaps.' She paused. 'I don't hate you. I really don't. I envy you, but I don't hate you.' She gazed at the baby, who was asleep. 'I hate your baby, though.'

'Don't hate my baby, Sister,' Mei-Ling cried. 'Hate me, if you must, but don't hate my baby.'

Willow took a long breath, sighed and shook her head. 'How?'

Second Son arrived an hour later. Mother brought him into the room. He was smiling at her, just exactly the way he had been smiling in his sleep. As he inspected the baby, his smile turned into a huge grin.

○

Sometimes it seemed to John Trader that he was not destined to find any peace in this world. He'd known peace of a kind in Macao, briefly, thanks to Read and Marissa. But if he hoped to steal happiness from China, the Celestial Kingdom was not willing to be cheated for his sake. And now the implacable Commissioner Lin was going to kick him out of Macao, and even perhaps out of the China seas.

Two days after the encounter with Cecil Whiteparish, he heard from Tully Odstock that the Chinese had cut off all food supplies to Macao from the mainland. 'We can manage for a while,' said Tully. But a few days later came more ominous news. 'Lin's moving a lot of soldiers down the coast towards us,' Tully told him. 'Daresay it's just a show of force.'

Was this all a retaliation for Elliot's refusal to hand over any sailors to his justice? Had he got wind of Matheson's latest opium smuggling – thanks to Whiteparish's outburst in front of Shi-Rong, perhaps? Trader didn't know. But whatever the cause, one thing was clear.

'Lin doesn't trust us, and he wants the upper hand,' he said. 'The question is, how far is he prepared to go?'

Macao, after all, still had a Portuguese governor, who was free to rule the place. The governor had some troops as well.

But people were getting nervous. Meeting him in the street one morning, Elliot told him frankly: 'Our friend the Portuguese governor is furious about the supplies and the threatening behaviour. His domain is Portuguese territory, and he's prepared to defend it if he has to. I can't fault his courage. But I have to consider the safety of all our people. We may have to leave.'

'Where would we go?'

'Hong Kong.'

'But there's nothing there except the anchorage. Are we going to camp on the beach?'

'No. We can live on our ships. It won't be enjoyable, but we should be safe. We can stay there a few months and see what happens.'

'So I'd better get ready to leave Macao,' Trader said sadly.

Elliot gave him an understanding smile. Obviously he knew about Marissa.

'I'm afraid so. All good things come to an end,' he added quietly.

'Living bottled up in ships sounds like hell,' Trader said morosely. Elliot didn't contradict him.

And that afternoon, the superintendent made it official, telling the whole community they must prepare to leave. The day after, he set off himself, to prepare the arrangements in the great empty harbour at Hong Kong.

On the twenty-fifth day of August, Commissioner Lin informed the Portuguese governor of Macao that the British people on his island should leave. The Chinese war junks now arriving would not impede their departure. All other nationals might remain, including the Americans, so long as they were not engaged in the opium trade.

John Trader was one of the last to leave the island. His final afternoon, he went for a walk with Read. As he was an American, Read could stay.

'I shall miss your company, Read,' said John.

'We shall meet again.'

'Certainly. I owe you money.'

'You'll pay when you can.'

'What do you think is going to happen?'

'The opium trade will resume. It has to.'

'Why?'

'Because this year's crop is already grown in India. Some of it is on the high seas already. It seems to me that destroying drugs is a waste of time. Lin's just created a pent-up demand for the next supply. And it'll get through – somehow or other. Exactly how remains to be seen.'

'I hope you're right, for both our sakes.' Trader paused. They were standing by the cannon, looking out across the island and the sea. 'I must confess,' he remarked sadly, 'I'm starting to wish I were selling something else. Something that does people good. Something really necessary.' He sighed.

'Trading in something that's not bad is certainly possible. Most people do. But trading in something necessary . . .' Read grinned. 'That's another matter. That's hard to do.'

'Is it?'

'Of course it is, Trader. Do you know how my ancestors made their first money? On the Hudson River in old New York. You know what that trade was? Beaver pelts. Bought from America's Indians. To make felt hats. Felt hats were all the rage in England. Other countries, too. Were they useful? Yes. Were they necessary? Not really. Felt was the fashion. That's all. Yet that's how the great city of New York began. Same with tobacco. Is it necessary? No. Or the mighty trade in sugar? Needed? Only partly. A lot of the sugar crop goes into rum, for the sailors of the British Navy. How did that begin? The men who owned the sugar plantations were producing too much. Prices were falling. So the powerful sugar interest lobbied the British Parliament to give a tot of rum to every British sailor every day. The British Navy drank the rum and kept the price of sugar up.'

'And now we sell tea.'

'Exactly. China tea. No harm in tea at all. And the British consumption of tea is one of the wonders of the modern world. But could the British do without their cup of tea? Of course they could. Very little of what we do, my friend, is necessary.' He nodded. 'It's a humbling thought.'

'But opium's bad.'

'Opium's bad.'

'Yet you're helping me.'

'You're a friend, Trader. Nobody's perfect.' He smiled. 'So there you go.'

'I'm worried about Marissa, Read. I feel bad about leaving her.'

'Sure. Were you going to marry her?'

'No.'

'Did you give her a parting present?'

'Yes. I'm giving it to her in the morning, when I leave.'

'She'll be all right.'

'You really think so?'

'I know so.'

'Will you keep an eye on her, look after her?'

Read gazed at him. Was there something a little strange in his look as he smiled? 'I'll do that,' Read said.

Mrs Willems made them all a meal that evening, and then John Trader spent the night with Marissa, and they made passionate love and he told her he didn't want to go, and she told him she knew he didn't have any choice, and she was sad. But though she looked sad, she wasn't going to cry and she smiled bravely, and they made love again. And he loved and admired her very much, although it seemed to him that even now, maybe, he didn't really know her.

She was pleased with her presents. And if she cried after he was gone, he didn't see it.

Read went with him to his lodgings. Tully had left the day before, but Trader's chests and valises were all ready, and two men put them on a cart and hauled them to the quay.

Then Trader got into the jolly boat with his possessions. He shook Read's hand and was rowed out to the ship anchored in the Macao Roads.

When Trader and his bags were aboard, he found that he was the last passenger to embark, and soon afterwards the ship was ready to weigh anchor.

As he stood by the side of the ship, a friendly sailor addressed him. 'All aboard then, sir?'

'Yes, I suppose so.' John stared across the water at the distant quay.

'Been to Hong Kong before, sir?'

'No.'

'Pity about the water.'

'Water? What water?'

'The drinking water at Hong Kong, sir. Haven't you heard?'

'I've heard nothing. What do you mean?'

'Oh, very nasty, sir. The Chinese have put up signs by all the wells on Hong Kong and the shores around there, to say that they've been poisoned. The wells, I mean. Not a very nice thing to do, is it?'

'Good God! Then what are we going to drink?'

'Couldn't say, sir. Not to worry, eh?'

And so John Trader left Macao. He'd lost his woman. He still didn't know whether he'd lost his fortune, or whether he'd be able to trade with China at all; or whether before long, at Hong Kong, he might die for lack of water.

o

Nio gazed around him. There were at least fifty men in the large cell. He'd been there a week. Others longer. They were all smugglers and pirates, rounded up and brought there.

But once in the cell, nothing had happened. Were they going to be interrogated, tried, executed? Nobody knew. All he knew was that the place stank.

Perhaps if Sea Dragon had been with them, they mightn't have been caught. After that terrible night when he'd failed to come out of Lin's headquarters, Nio and the other men had made their way back to their camp. But the next day, Nio had gone back to the city to find out what he could. For three days he'd stayed there, and not a word had emerged.

But then the story had seeped out – from the sergeant to a friend, then to others. And soon, although nothing official ever appeared, all the gangs and the keepers of teahouses and the policemen, of course – all knew that Sea Dragon had tried to kill Lin and been caught and died under torture and never spoken a word, not so much as his name. Sea Dragon was a hero up and down the coast. In time, no doubt, his name would resonate in legend, all over the China seas.

The crew had stayed together. Partly held by a reverence for his memory, partly because they had no place to go and nothing else to do. And they'd all promised one another that they'd stick together and, when times got better, go out to sea again and ship opium and earn good money just as they had when Sea Dragon the hero had led them.

Then in a dawn raid on their camp, they'd been caught, every one of them, and taken to this place. Perhaps if Sea Dragon had still been there, they'd have posted a better guard. Perhaps they'd have killed the troops who had somehow found them.

It was a disaster. It was probably the end of his life.

He had only one big regret. That cache of money for Big Sister. Did she think of him? Of course she did. And he thought of her, every day.

The money was still in the same hiding place. He'd been intending, the very day the troops came, to tell his companions that he must go to see his family and then secretly take the money to her. He cursed himself for not doing it sooner. And every day he tried to devise ways to escape, not for the sake of his own freedom, but so that he could give that money to Big Sister and see her face.

This morning, he was just in the middle of devising a new way of tricking the guards and breaking out, when he was surprised to see through the cage bars, which ran along one side of the big cell, a small knot of people approaching. Four of them were policemen. But one was a young mandarin.

He heard the young mandarin tell the guards to open the cage door so that he could get into the cell. The guards were arguing with him. They didn't like the idea. But then he heard the young mandarin say something about Commissioner Lin, and a moment later he heard the key turn.

He couldn't see the mandarin's face from where he was, but the man seemed to be very quick at his work. He was selecting prisoners, one by one. They were being taken out of the cell and made to stand in a line.

The mandarin was coming his way. Nio caught sight of his face. And froze.

It was Lin's secretary. He recognised him at once. He even knew his name. It seemed no time at all since they'd been face-to-face in Hog Lane. He was going to be discovered. He tried to hide himself behind another prisoner.

But Shi-Rong detected the movement. In an instant he was in front of Nio, staring at his face. 'This one,' he said.

And Nio was led out of the cell and made to stand in the line – though whether as a prelude to interrogation or execution, he could not guess.

HONG KONG

October 1839

Nio's doubts began on a warm October day.

In the coastal regions by the mouth of the Pearl River, each October, the semitropical heat, humidity and rainstorms of the long summer monsoon come to an end. A new and delightful season begins. The skies are clear and blue; light breezes waft over the waters. It is like a perfect English summer – though more reliable.

Nio was standing on a promontory at the end of the Bogue. Just behind him, four bearers with a silk-curtained mandarin's litter waited patiently; and a short distance in front, just out of earshot, Commissioner Lin and Shi-Rong were gazing across the waters of the gulf, to where twenty war junks were going through their manoeuvres.

Like the two mandarins, Nio also watched the war junks intently. For the exercise would ensure that, if it came to a fight with the barbarians, the gallant sailors of the Celestial Kingdom would destroy the British Navy.

Shi-Rong was excited. If he'd failed Lin in the matter of the pirate, he'd begun to redeem himself with his intelligence gathering in Macao. Today, back on the mainland, he'd prepared a small surprise for the commissioner, which he was hoping the great man would like. First, however, there were the manoeuvres to watch. He'd bought a Dutch spyglass when he was at Macao – a little brass sea captain's telescope of which he was rather proud – through which he could follow the action closely as soon as it began.

But he had one question: 'There are British merchantmen out in the gulf, Excellency. You don't mind them seeing our tactics?'

'I want them to see,' Lin answered. He gazed across the water. 'It is always a good idea, Jiang, to frighten your enemy. Sow doubt and panic in his mind. Destroy his morale. That is what I did when we told the barbarians we'd poisoned the wells at Hong Kong. We were letting them know what we could do if we wanted. Today we shall show them how easily we can crush them at sea.' He pointed to the war junks. 'Look, they are beginning.'

The battle tactics of the Chinese navy were precise and had been perfected over many generations. If the enemy fleet was large, fire ships might be sent in to sow confusion and despair. But the main attack was always the same.

The war junks were not large, like some of the big, clumsy merchant vessels. Mostly they were about a hundred feet, stem to stern. But they manoeuvred well in the coastal waters where they patrolled against the local pirates.

A war junk was a little floating fortress, full of fighting men. It had perhaps a half-dozen cannon on its deck, whose purpose was to damage the enemy's masts and rigging and slow them down. As it closed in, well-trained archers would send volley after volley of arrows to kill the fighting men on the pirate decks. Then they would board.

Today the cannon fired only wadding and the arrow tips were blunted, but Shi-Rong could see that the archers' aim was deadly accurate as the arrows rattled upon their opponents' decks.

'Admiral Guan knows his business,' Lin remarked with satisfaction. 'Every ship exactly in line. Perfect coordination.'

Now Shi-Rong could see the marines snare the enemy's masts with grappling hooks and drag the vessels together. Then – some on boarding planks, others swinging across on ropes – with short swords and knives in hand, they swarmed onto the enemy ships.

'There they go,' Shi-Rong cried. 'Grapple and board. They're like flying squirrels.' He laughed. 'Is it true, Excellency, that the admiral's marines are trained in martial arts?'

'Many of them are,' Lin replied. He nodded with satisfaction. 'The barbarians will be cut to pieces.'

They watched for half an hour. At the end of the performance, the stout figure of Admiral Guan himself could be seen on deck as his ship sent up a firework salute to the commissioner. Lin allowed himself a smile of pleasure.

And now came Shi-Rong's moment. 'With your permission, Excellency,' he said as he stepped forward and raised his brass telescope so that it flashed in the sun. As if from nowhere, three dragon boats that had lain concealed in a nearby creek now appeared, one in front, two behind, their crews paddling furiously, but perfectly synchronised. Red flags fluttered in the sterns. When they drew level with the commissioner, the men gave a loud cheer.

'These are your men?' Lin asked. 'The ones you took from the gaols?'

'Yes, Excellency. We have ten crews now, with more to come. I have them patrolling the coast, as you commanded.'

'And they are effective?'

'Most certainly.'

'This proves two principles I have often enunciated,' Lin declared. 'First, never execute a man who can be useful. What is the second?'

'Set a thief to catch a thief, Excellency.'

'Quite so. These villains know every inlet along the coast and every trick the smugglers use. What better men could we find to use as coastguards?'

'Indeed.'

'By the way' – Lin glanced back towards Nio – 'why isn't that young ruffian with the scar on his face in the boats?'

'It turns out he's not a local man, Excellency. None of the crews wanted him in their boat. So I use him to run errands for me, which he does quite well.'

The answer seemed to satisfy the great man. 'Time to inspect the fort,' he said.

As the bearers carried the commissioner, in his curtained litter, along the bank of the river, Nio and Shi-Rong walked behind.

Nio kept his head respectfully bowed. Everyone knew that Shi-Rong had interrogated Sea Dragon, which made him a man to be feared. That first moment when the young mandarin had picked him out in the prison, he'd thought Shi-Rong must have recognised him. As the days went by, however, it had become clear that the busy nobleman had no idea who he was. To Shi-Rong, Nio was just one more of the nameless multitude; and if he had a scar on his face, so had thousands of others. Nio intended to keep it that way.

When Shi-Rong gave him an order, Nio carried it out at once; if asked a question, he answered as briefly as possible. He spoke only when he was spoken to, and that wasn't too often.

But after the success of his little show, Shi-Rong was in such a good mood that he even deigned to speak to Nio in quite a friendly way. 'So, young man,' he asked pleasantly, 'what do you do with the money you are paid?'

'Your servant saves it, master.'

'And what do you save it for?'

'For my Big Sister, sir. She needs the money.'

'Oh.' Shi-Rong gave him an approving nod. 'Very commendable. Well, we're going to see some of the finest soldiers in the empire now.'

'Bannermen, Lord?'

'Yes. Manchu warriors. Not that our Han soldiers leave anything to be desired,' he added. 'But these are the best Manchu bannermen. Second to none.'

'They say that the Hakka people are also valiant warriors,' Nio offered.

'Really? Nothing like these Manchu bannermen, though.'

Nio did not reply.

And sure enough, as they approached the fort, they saw a guard of about a hundred smartly turned-out Manchu, lined up for Lin to inspect.

There were two groups. The archers, in tightly belted coats with quivers of long arrows at their sides and carrying their mighty composite bows, were still in their dome-shaped rattan summer hats, with a button on top and a feather trailing behind. The musketeers, in soft leather boots and jerkins, were for some reason wearing their cylindrical velvet winter hats, which widened upwards – devilishly smart, Nio had to confess. Each of them held a long, heavy matchlock.

Lin descended from his litter and signalled Shi-Rong to stand just behind his shoulder. Nio stood close to his master. Then the captain of the guard shouted an order, and the archers loosed a flight of arrows, one, two, three times – at amazing speed. Nio was impressed.

'Those are the most powerful bows in the world,' Shi-Rong told him. 'The arrows are so heavy they can go through two men.'

Now it was the turn of the musketeers. The captain shouted the first order. 'Prime your pan!'

Swiftly the men took out small horn flasks and poured a little gunpowder into the small pan on the stock of the musket.

'Close your pan!' They slipped the lid across the pan, shook their musket, then blew any last traces of gunpowder safely away.

'Cast about. And load!' They tipped up the muzzle end, took one of the little packets of powder they carried on their jerkins, and emptied it down the barrel. Then the musket ball was dropped in, followed by a little cotton pad.

'Ram your charge.' Taking the scouring stick from its socket under the barrel, they rammed it down the barrel several times to push the ball and charge firmly into place. 'Return your scouring stick.' The stick was put back in its socket for future use.

During all this complex process, Nio watched intently. Sea Dragon's pirates hadn't used firearms, and he'd never seen this drill before.

Shi-Rong glanced at him and smiled. 'Just like loading a cannon,' he remarked.

'Fix your match!' the captain ordered. And the musketeers took the smouldering cord they carried in their left hands and attached it to the S-shaped metal lock above the firing pan. First they made sure it would come down exactly on the firing pan. Then they blew on the smouldering end to produce a tiny flame.

'Present!' the captain called, and they took aim. 'Open your pan!' With right finger and thumb, each musketeer slipped back the cover of the pan to expose the gunpowder.

'Fire!' the captain shouted. The triggers were pulled, the lock descended onto the open pan, the gunpowder ignited, there was a loud bang, and a narrow flash of flame issued from the barrel of each gun, followed by a great plume of dark blue smoke. All, that is, except for three muskets that had failed to fire.

'Excellent!' cried Lin, and turned to Shi-Rong.

'Splendid,' Shi-Rong agreed, and turned to Nio. 'Well,' he asked, 'what do you think of that?'

Nio frowned. The process, from the first order to the firing of the musket, had actually taken a full minute. 'It seems rather slow, sir,' he murmured hesitantly to Shi-Rong. And thinking of the speed with which

Sea Dragon and the pirates used to move: 'Wouldn't the enemy rush at them before they were ready to fire?'

'What does he say?' Lin demanded.

As Shi-Rong told the great man, Nio cringed. How could he have been so stupid, when all he had to say was 'Wonderful, sir,' or something of that kind? Would the commissioner be enraged and throw him back in gaol?

But he mistook his man. Lin prided himself on knowing how things worked.

'The question is correct,' he announced. 'Explain to him,' he told Shi-Rong, 'the reason that the order of our army is so perfect is because each part supports the others. While our musketeers load, they are protected by a wall of pikemen. But when they fire, not only does the noise and smoke terrify the enemy, but the musket balls, which are made of lead, spread out on impact – and make a huge wound. I have seen a shoulder hit take off a whole arm. Any hit, you probably die.' He nodded grimly. 'For over two hundred years, the world has trembled before our armies.'

As they mounted the huge baked-mud ramparts in front of the granite-walled fort, Shi-Rong looked around admiringly. Every wall had been reinforced. The same was true at the fort on the opposite riverbank. And as they reached the shore battery and gazed at the long line of big cannon set in their granite emplacements, he murmured, 'Magnificent.'

Here again, the commissioner was treated to a demonstration. First, the whole line of cannon fired with a deafening roar. And everyone watched as the cannonballs made a line of splashes far out in the water. A moment later, they saw puffs of smoke, followed by a roar, from the battery almost two miles away on the opposite side. After this little show, the gunnery officer conducted Lin and Shi-Rong along the line of cannon to inspect the gun crews.

Nio waited. But when Lin was halfway along the line, he sidled up to the nearest cannon and looked at it curiously. It was a handsome monster. The outer surface of its mighty barrel was deeply pitted. 'It looks old,' he said to the senior gunner.

'More than a hundred years, but it's good as new,' the sturdy gunner answered.

Nio inspected the great gun more carefully. Its weight must be enormous, but he couldn't see any mechanism for directing its fire.

'How do you point it?' he asked.

'The barrel's fixed. No need to point it. We wait until the ship's in front of us. Then the whole battery fires. So does the battery opposite.'

'It seems a long way to the far bank. Would the cannonballs reach ships out in the middle?'

'Ah, but the channel's narrower between the next pair of forts, farther upriver. Nothing can get past them.'

'What if a dragon boat came in close to the bank, under the line of fire?'

'The troops would take care of them, wouldn't they?'

'I suppose so.' Nio considered. 'What if an enemy ship fires at you with their cannon?'

'Ships' cannon aren't that big. Nothing could get through the rampart walls, anyway. Not a chance.' The gunner laughed. 'We'll smash them to pieces, all right. They'd never get upstream.'

'I see what you mean,' said Nio politely. 'Thank you.'

When the commissioner and Shi-Rong got back, they were looking very pleased.

'Ask him what he thinks of the battery,' said Lin with a smile. 'Is it good enough for him?'

So Shi-Rong asked. And Nio took no chances. 'It is truly wonderful, Lord,' he said.

After Lin got into his litter, he turned to Shi-Rong. 'How is your honourable father? When do you next write to him?'

'I was going to write tonight, Excellency.'

'Come to me when you have finished your letter. I shall add a word myself.'

It was quite late that night when Shi-Rong approached the library where the great man worked. But he could see from the light under the door that his master was still there.

'You told me to report when I had finished the letter to my father, Excellency.'

'Ah, yes. May I see?'

Shi-Rong placed it on the table. It was a good letter. Apart from the usual enquiries after his father's and his aunt's health, he gave a brief report of his recent duties and a vivid account of the events that day. While he used no words of flattery, it was clear that he held his master Lin in the highest regard, and this was no more than the truth.

Lin read it, gave a grunt of approval and laid the letter on the table again. He motioned Shi-Rong to sit down. 'I am considering a private message to Elliot,' the commissioner announced. 'Before I send it, tell me what you think.' After Shi-Rong had bowed, Lin continued. 'The other day, quite accidentally, a British sailor was drowned, and his body has washed up.'

'So I heard, Excellency.'

'It would perhaps be convenient if this corpse was the very man we had demanded for the murder of our unfortunate villager. The case could then be closed without loss of face to ourselves or the British. What do you think?'

'Your Excellency can be devious,' Shi-Rong remarked with a smile.

'The emperor does not require us to be stupid.'

'Elliot would be a fool not to accept your offer,' Shi-Rong replied. 'But may I ask a question?'

Lin gave him a brief nod.

'Our power is overwhelming, and the barbarians must know it. Now you generously offer them a further concession. Yet I cannot help wondering: are you never tempted just to crush the British barbarians once and for all?'

'Personally?' Lin smiled. 'Of course. But you have asked the wrong question. It is the wishes of the emperor that matter, not mine. And what did the emperor tell me to do?'

'To stop the opium smuggling.'

'Correct. Did he tell me to go to war with the barbarians?'

'Not so far, Excellency.'

'There is a large tea trade with the barbarians. Our farmers grow it. Our Hong merchants sell it. Did the emperor tell me to destroy the tea trade?'

'No, Excellency.'

'So the matter is very simple. The British may trade in tea, but they must not smuggle opium, concerning which they must sign our bond promising to submit to our justice. Elliot says their laws forbid them to sign. Then their laws should be changed. I hope that his queen has read my letter by now, and that if she is just, she will forbid the opium trade and tell the British merchants to submit at once. Then the problem is ended and my job is done.' He paused. 'In the meantime, is the tea trade continuing?'

'Yes, Excellency. The American ships are carrying the tea at present.'

'Just so. The Americans and other barbarians who submit to our laws can enter the river and purchase the tea. Meanwhile, the British merchants are not allowed in. The tea gets to Britain, of course, but the British merchants are unable to carry it. Americans and others are commandeering every available vessel, shipping the tea, and taking the profit, leaving the British merchants out in the cold. For this, they have no one to blame but themselves.'

'Is it true, Excellency, that the Americans have been allowed to sign a less stringent bond that doesn't oblige them to submit to our justice?'

'Their bond is in their own language, so I couldn't say.' The cunning bureaucrat allowed himself a faint smile. 'Apart from the villainous Delano, the Americans hardly smuggle opium, so it doesn't really matter what they sign.'

'Do you think the British are so greedy, Excellency, that for this cause they would attack us?'

'Who knows?' Lin answered, this time with genuine perplexity. 'I have yet to understand their morality.'

He picked up Shi-Rong's letter again. Taking a brush and dipping it in the ink, he selected a convenient space on the paper, quickly wrote a few characters and returned the letter to Shi-Rong, who read what he had written.

Fortunate the master, whose secretary is trusted;

Happy the father, whose son is praised.

A perfect Chinese couplet: each sentence a mirror of the other, each word in perfect grammatical balance with its fellows. As for the elegant calligraphy, every brushstroke showed the purity of soul and the sense of justice of the writer. As Shi-Rong gazed at the message and thought of the joy it would bring his father, tears came into his eyes.

He bowed from the waist, both to show his respect and to hide the tears.

o

'Damn Hong Kong!' said Tully as he stood with John Trader on the deck of the ship that for weeks had been their home. He said it every morning. With the steep mountain of the Peak towering just behind it, Hong Kong Harbour presented a magnificent panorama – but not one that gave any pleasure to Tully Odstock.

'At least we can get food from the mainland,' said Trader. 'And they didn't really poison the water.'

'I wish to God they had,' Tully muttered. Eyes bulging, he glared across the waters where the British ships had already been anchored for weeks. 'I'd sooner be dead than go on like this.'

Trader couldn't blame him. Everybody was bored. 'Well, we're safe at least,' he said soothingly.

'Marooned, more like. Chained to that cursed rock.' Odstock nodded towards the Peak. 'Look!' He shot his short arms out furiously towards the anchorage. 'There's seventy British ships at anchor. And not a damned one I can use.'

'We need patience,' Trader ventured.

'We need tea,' Tully growled. He was silent for a moment. 'You saw a letter came aboard for me this morning? It was from my father in London.' He took the letter out of his pocket. 'You'd better read it.'

Ebenezer Odstock's handwriting was still bold, but it seemed that old age was beginning to take its toll.

'I am sorry his teeth are so bad,' said Trader. Tully greeted this with a snort. 'And his leg: he says he can hardly get into the office, even with a stick.' Another snort. Trader started reading aloud. '"And I fear my brain is becoming dull."'

'The old devil,' said Tully.

'"Given the uncertainty of the China trade at present,"' Trader continued to read, '"it is anticipated that tea will be in short supply, and the price may rise very high. I should be grateful, my dear son, if you would send me all the tea you can, at your earliest convenience."'

'And I can't,' Tully almost wailed. It seemed strange to Trader that the gruff middle-aged merchant should still be so afraid of his father. 'The spring harvest from the backcountry, the best damn crop, is coming into Canton as we speak. Joker will sell me as much as I can take. I can pay in silver. I've even got a vessel I could use. But I can't get upriver because I'm not allowed to sign Lin's bond.'

'We can't contract with an American merchant?'

'I've tried. All committed. All loaded to the gills with cotton to sell, and they'll come out with tea. And none of it for me.'

'I suppose we couldn't just sign Lin's damned bond, could we? Promise not to carry opium? I mean, not just at the moment, of course.'

Tully shook his head. 'I don't like Elliot, but he's right about one thing. Got to stick together. We've told Lin that no British merchant can sign any bond that places him under Chinese law. Can't be done. But if so much as one us breaks ranks . . . Case falls to the ground. Not a leg to stand on. And once we submit to Chinese law, we're under their thumb forever. Any Chinese judge can torture and hang us at will.' He shook his head glumly. 'Nothing for it. I'll have to tell the old man I can't get him any tea.'

'I'm sure he'll understand,' Trader offered.

'You don't know him.'

'I think,' said Trader after a brief pause, 'that I may have an idea.'

The little ship, having no cargo, rode high in the water as it emerged the next morning from under the shadow of the soaring Peak of Hong Kong and headed across the gulf.

Halfway across, Trader saw a Chinese war junk in the distance; an hour later a dragon boat appeared. But neither approached his little ship. As he gazed across the waters towards the hills of Macao, he wondered: was he going to see Marissa again?

He remembered the vague awkwardness in his manner when he'd parted from her – a lover who made no promise to return. Perhaps she had another man by now. But if she hadn't? Memories came back: the texture of her skin, her hair in his hands, the smell of her. How would it be if they met again? What would happen?

Before noon, he could see the empty facade of the cathedral, high on top of the hill, gleaming in the sun. He'd have to go up there anyway, to find Read, assuming the American was still on the island – which he surely must be. His kindly friend wouldn't have vanished over the horizon without letting him know.

By the time they anchored in the Macao Roads, a jolly boat was already on its way to greet them. In less than half an hour Trader was on the quay and about to walk up the hill when, to his surprise, he saw the burly American not fifty yards away.

'Why, it's young Trader.' Read came towards him, hand outstretched. 'What brings you here, my friend?'

'I came to see you. I was just going up to Mrs Willems's house.'

'Ah.' Did a tiny shadow pass across Read's face? If so, it was dispelled almost instantly by a big grin. 'Well, you already found me.'

'Is Mrs Willems well?'

'She is.'

'And Marissa?'

'Not on the island just now. She went away to see her family.'

They sat together in a Portuguese taverna while Trader explained what he needed.

'So you want me to act as an American merchant, take over your contracts with this Chinese merchant you call Joker, ship the tea out of Whampoa in that vessel out in the Roads, and bring it to Hong Kong? For which Odstocks will pay me.'

'Generously.'

'You supply the ship, pay for all the goods.'

'Correct.'

Read took a pull on his cigar. 'The fact is,' he said, 'I could do with a little action.' He grinned. 'Macao's a good place. But I was getting a little bored.'

'You should do it, then,' Trader encouraged.

'I could get papers from the governor here, to say I'm a bona fide American merchant. That wouldn't be a problem. I did him a favour the other day. We'd need to fly an American flag, of course. Maybe change the ship's name.' He considered. '*Yankee Lady*. How's that? You got a crew and skipper?'

'A good Chinese crew. The mate can handle the ship. And he knows the waters.'

Read shook his head. 'You need a skipper. But don't worry. I've got one for you.'

'Where?'

'Right here, looking at you.'

'You've actually been a ship's captain?'

'Many times. Pay me the going rate as skipper, in addition to the rest, and you have a deal.'

'Agreed.'

'Let's get those papers from the governor right away, then.'

The governor's offices were on the Praia Grande. It felt good to be walking along the handsome curve of the great esplanade again. Trader half expected Tully Odstock to appear on his afternoon constitutional along the seafront.

When they got to the Portuguese governor's office, Read explained his mission to an assistant, who ushered them into a waiting room. But they didn't have to wait long. Within minutes, the assistant appeared again at the door. 'The governor will see you now, Mr Read.'

A quarter of an hour later, Read reappeared, waving some papers and looking happy. 'Everything we need. Time to go,' he said briskly.

'Are we going up to your lodgings?' Trader asked as they stepped out onto the Praia Grande.

'I am. You aren't,' Read said firmly. 'You'd better go out to the ship right away. Have the men paint the new name on the bow while I get my things together. We'll sail before evening.'

While one of the crew painted in the letters – *Yankee Lady* – that he'd chalked on the bow, Trader stared across the water to Macao, where, high on its hill, the empty cathedral facade gleamed in the sunlight. And he thought about Marissa.

'You're all set now,' Trader said with a nod when Read finally arrived. 'So I'll go ashore. It'll be easy to find a boat to take me from Macao back to Hong Kong.'

Read gave him a curious look. 'I'll need you in Canton, Trader,' he said firmly. 'You know this Chinese merchant, Joker. You tell him it's all right to deal with me. Otherwise I don't sail.' Trader wasn't pleased, though he supposed there wasn't much he could do about it.

As they sailed up the gulf that night, however, he did venture to ask: 'How is Marissa?'

'She's all right.'

'Does she have a new lover?'

'None of your business,' Read answered. A minute went by. 'When you've left a young woman, Trader,' Read said, 'don't go back. You only hurt 'em more.'

In the morning, at the Bogue, Read presented his papers and signed the bond guaranteeing he carried no opium. Two officials quickly inspected the hold and gave Read his pass to proceed. Before noon he and Trader were ashore at Whampoa, and by late afternoon, they were making their way from the Canton factories to the house of old Joker.

The dignified Hong merchant was delighted to see them. 'Mr Trader.' He beamed. 'Long time no see. Your friend wants tea?'

And the next morning he insisted upon coming with them downstream to Whampoa, to ensure that their vessel was properly loaded with all the tea it could carry.

When he inspected their cargo, Tully Odstock was very pleased indeed. He gave a warm grunt of approval, shook hands with Read and patted Trader on the back. 'I never thought you'd be back so soon,' he confessed.

'We left Macao the same day I arrived,' Trader explained. 'And we came straight to Hong Kong from Whampoa.'

Tully was entirely happy with the terms Read and Trader had agreed to and paid Read on the spot.

'Care to go back again for more?' he asked the American.

'Soon as you like.'

That night they all dined together on board Tully's ship. Then Read said he wanted to talk to Odstock alone, so Trader went on deck and watched the sun go down. From where the ship was anchored, he could see out past a scattering of islands to the sea beyond. High above, the dark green heights of the Peak caught the sun's red rays, then slowly turned from orange green to indigo and finally, as Read emerged, to black.

'I'm going back to the ship,' said Read. 'We're transferring the tea to a larger vessel tomorrow. Then I'll go to Whampoa again for more.'

'Will I be coming with you?'

'No, Odstock wants you here. Goodnight.'

After he had gone, Trader remained on deck for a while. The night sky was bright with stars. He thought of Marissa again. He had a great urge to see her. Maybe not to speak to her, but just to look at her. He wondered if perhaps he could slip over to Macao on some pretext.

Finally he went below. Tully was in his hammock, still awake. In the lamplight, it seemed to Trader that the older man gave him a somewhat thoughtful look. But Tully didn't say anything, so Trader closed his eyes and went to sleep.

The next couple of weeks passed quietly enough. Read undertook two more voyages to Whampoa to bring out tea; on the second voyage, he was able to go in with a cargo of cotton as well.

But if Read was busy, Trader was not. Three times he asked Tully if he could visit Macao, and each time Tully refused. So like everyone else, he was obliged to spend most of his time confined on board, though he and Tully would also visit their friends on other ships in search of gossip and amusement. And news, of course; but news was in short supply.

'The fact is, there won't be any news,' said Tully, 'and I'll tell you why. What you have here is a stalemate. It's a simple point of principle. The Chinese are saying: "When in China, obey our laws." We're saying no. All the rest is humbug. Lin says, "Tell you what, we'll forget about that villager you killed if you just agree to obey our laws in the future." Humbug. Elliot's just told Lin: "You can inspect our ships, check there's no opium on board before you let us upriver. But we're not subject to your laws. Won't sign your bond." More humbug.'

'I've heard,' said Trader, 'that some of the British vessels are entering the river so that if Lin were to agree to let them through after inspection, they'll race up to Whampoa and get the best tea first.'

'I know. I call them the Hopeful Boys. They can sit in the river all they like, but Lin isn't going to fall for it. Point of principle. Sign the bond. Obey our law or go to hell.'

'Elliot's just playing for time, isn't he?'

'Waiting for the navy, I'd say.' Tully shrugged. 'If London decides to send it.'

But there was no news from London. Not a word.

It was a clear, sunny day when a party of a dozen young fellows, sick of being cooped up on their ships, set out to climb to the top of the Peak. John Trader was one of them.

Having passed through the scattering of fishermen's huts by the water's edge, they were soon in the thick woods that covered the hill. At first the going was easy. Most of them had walking sticks of some kind. They carried just enough food and wine to have a picnic at the summit.

Gradually the track became steeper. John found that he was sweating a little. He smiled, happy to stretch his legs and get a bit of exercise. They followed a track that circled the big hill, and nearly an hour had passed before, about two-thirds of the way up, they encountered some big outcroppings of rock, where they paused to gaze down at the water, already over a thousand feet below, and feel the breeze on their faces.

During the final part of the climb, the trees thinned and the path broke up into a landscape of scattered rock and tree root. This was hard going, but it didn't take too long before they reached the summit.

They looked down in awe, from eighteen hundred feet above the water, at the great panorama of Hong Kong.

Finally somebody spoke. 'I knew it was a fine harbour, but it's only up here that you really see the hand of the Creator.'

It was true, thought Trader. Even taken alone, the high, rocky island of Hong Kong would have provided a sheltered channel between itself and the Chinese mainland. But when the monsoon gales came hurtling across the gulf's broad entrance, they'd have churned those Hong Kong channel waters into a frenzy, had it not been for a blessed protective barrier.

It lay to the west, just a few miles away, between Hong Kong and the gulf – a long, thin island with its own high mountains, which zigzagged across the waters like a Chinese screen. This was Lantau, which formed the western wall of Hong Kong's huge protected harbour.

But the Creator had done more. Halfway along the Hong Kong channel, China's huge mainland stuck out a dragon's tongue at the island. This tongue was the broad low-lying promontory known as Kowloon, and it divided the channel into two parts, west and east, leaving a narrow passage between them. Ships that threaded eastwards through this passage came into another, smaller harbour, known as the Bay of Kowloon, within whose intimate embrace they could ride out even a typhoon.

So it was hardly surprising that John Trader should remark: 'The Portuguese have got Macao. Perhaps we could take over this place.'

The picnic was over and the party was just preparing to go down the hill again when Trader noticed something strange.

Amongst all the vast collection of vessels at the huge anchorage of Hong Kong, there were just two ships of the Royal Navy. Both were small. The *Volage* carried twenty-eight guns, twelve on each side, plus four more on the quarterdeck, which qualified her to be called a frigate. The *Hyacinth* was only a sloop, armed with sixteen cannon and a couple of nine-pounders in the bow.

What caught Trader's eye was a pinnace carrying somebody out to the *Volage*. Having paused to let its passenger embark, the pinnace went on to the *Hyacinth,* where it remained for a few minutes. While it waited, he saw the *Volage* weighing anchor. The *Hyacinth* shortly followed suit. And then they both began to bear away towards the gulf.

Turning to his companions, Trader pointed. 'Why the devil are those two navy ships going off in such a hurry?' he asked. But nobody had any idea.

A few hours later, Tully told him the news. 'I don't know why,' he moaned, 'but whenever there's a disaster, it always comes out of the blue.'

'You say a British merchant vessel has come in directly from London? And that it ignored Elliot's instructions?'

'Yes. Came by way of Bombay. Goes into the Gulf of Canton. Doesn't stop to ask, just sails through to the Bogue, and when the Chinese tell the captain he has to sign Lin's bond, he signs the accursed thing as if it's no more than a ticket to a play and goes straight in to Whampoa.'

'Perhaps he didn't understand what he was doing.'

'Oh, he knew all right. Didn't give a damn. And now he's cut the ground from under our feet. The entire merchant fleet, Elliot, the British government, the lot of us.'

'We could tell Lin it was a mistake.'

'Nonsense. Lin will say: "You told me that no British vessel can sign the bond. You lied to me. And if this captain, straight from London, can obey Chinese law, then so can you. End of story." In his place, I'd say the same.'

'What'll we do?'

'Elliot's taken the *Volage* and the *Hyacinth* up the gulf. Supposedly to protect the Hopeful Boys up there, but really to make damn sure they don't get the same idea and sign the bond themselves.'

'What will Lin do?'

'Who knows? Tell us to sign or get out. I hope we'll refuse. Then he may cut off our supplies. He can do that. Poison the wells. God knows.'

'Is there going to be a fight?'

Tully considered. 'Quite apart from the fact that Elliot's only got two warships, he doesn't have authority to start a war.' He paused. 'I'm not sure Lin has, either.'

'So no fighting yet.'

'Oh, I didn't say that. Wars are like riots. They can start by mistake.'

o

Nio stood outside Shi-Rong's door. It was evening, and the lamps were lit. For three days they had occupied billets with the artillerymen at the fort, so as to be near at hand. And now it was nearly time.

Nio saw Commissioner Lin approaching and opened the door to announce him. As Lin passed through and Shi-Rong rose respectfully from the table where he was writing, Nio closed the door, but this time he remained inside the room, curious to hear what they said. Neither Shi-Rong nor Lin appeared to notice him.

'Tomorrow morning? You are sure?' Lin asked sharply.

'I am certain, Excellency. Two of my dragon boats have shadowed them all the way. The headwinds are still slowing the barbarian warships, but by dawn we'll see them from the promontory. Captain Smith is the commander, but my men believe Elliot is on board.'

'You have done well.' Lin paused a moment. 'I was wrong to offer Elliot a compromise over the murder. I was wrong to negotiate with him at all. His actions have shown his true nature. He told me that British captains could never sign the bond. And now we know this was a lie. He despises truth. He despises the law. He's just a pirate, and we shall act accordingly.' As he turned to leave, Lin glanced at the table. 'What were you writing?'

'I was copying a poem, Excellency, by the great Yuan Mei.'

'Good.' Lin nodded. 'Whenever possible, in quiet moments, we should attend to calligraphy. This is how a busy servant of the emperor restores his balance and good judgement.' He looked at Shi-Rong thoughtfully. 'After this business is over, you should return to your studies and take the exams again. You are capable of holding high office one day. But the examination system – quite rightly – is the only path that leads there.'

After the commissioner had left, Nio could see that Shi-Rong was moved.

Soon after dawn, with the wind pressing his back, Shi-Rong stood beside Commissioner Lin on the promontory and gazed through his brass telescope at the choppy grey waters of the gulf.

On the left, near the site where the opium had been destroyed, lay Admiral Guan's fleet, ready for action; a little farther away, the convoy of British merchant ships, waiting to be allowed up to Whampoa; and in the distance, he could clearly see the *Volage* and the *Hyacinth* coming slowly up the gulf towards them.

Lin put out his hand for the telescope, gazed through it for a minute, then turned to Shi-Rong.

'Go to Admiral Guan with this message: If the barbarians want to talk, tell them we do not negotiate with criminals. My suggestion about the murderer is nullified. They must hand over the real murderer at once. No British ship will trade until its captain has signed the bond and submitted to our laws. Take Mr Singapore the interpreter with you.' He paused. 'If the barbarians attack, the admiral has permission to destroy them. That is all.'

'Excellency . . .' Shi-Rong gave him a hopeful look. 'May I remain on board the admiral's ship – so he can send me back for more instructions?'

'You wish to join the action.' Lin gave a faint smile. 'You may stay if you are not in the admiral's way.'

Nio was waiting with a small dragon boat. It did not take long to reach the admiral's war junk. Having gone up the side with Mr Singapore, he delivered his message. To his delight, the admiral agreed he could stay aboard.

'Pull into the shore and wait,' Shi-Rong called down to Nio. 'I'll signal when I need you. If there's a battle,' he added, 'you'll have a good view.'

There was no question, Admiral Guan was a splendid figure: a true Chinese warrior of the old school. Still handsome at nearly sixty, holding himself ramrod straight. He had a big strong face with a thin, drooping moustache and his eyes were wise but fearless. His courtesy was well known, and he treated the young mandarin as a fellow gentleman. 'You hope to see a little action, Mr Jiang?'

'If there is action, my lord, I wouldn't want to miss it,' Shi-Rong replied.

'Don't hope for too much. I've sixteen fully armed war junks and a dozen fire boats as well. The British would be foolish to take us on.'

Just then Shi-Rong caught sight of Mr Singapore standing sorrowfully on the deck, farther aft. He looked like a wilting flower. 'Our interpreter is not so eager for battle,' Admiral Guan remarked drily.

It was a couple of hours before the two British naval vessels came close enough to send a cutter, manned by three pairs of oarsmen, across to the admiral's war junk. A young British naval officer came briskly on board and saluted, followed by a large gentleman who clambered up more slowly and who introduced himself, in quite good Chinese, as Van Buskirk, the missionary.

At a nod from the admiral, Mr Singapore then delivered, in his best English, the official message from Lin. The naval officer frowned slightly and replied that it would be difficult to offer any culprit for the unfortunate killing of the Chinese villager, since all the men involved had been sent away to England. 'Nonetheless,' he continued, 'I will return at once with your message and come back to you again with further proposals.' With a polite bow, he then withdrew.

'What do you make of that?' Admiral Guan asked Shi-Rong as the cutter was rowed away. 'Surely there's nothing to talk about.'

'I'm wondering if our interpreter, hoping to keep the peace, may have softened the message.'

Admiral Guan stared bleakly at Mr Singapore, but said nothing.

When the officer and Van Buskirk returned an hour later, the admiral commanded Shi-Rong: 'Tell the missionary exactly what Commissioner Lin said, word for word.'

As Shi-Rong did so, it was clear that Van Buskirk understood him perfectly, while Mr Singapore looked dismayed. The missionary then carefully delivered the message to the officer, in English. The officer winced slightly and then said, 'Oh.'

But now it was Van Buskirk who spoke, in Chinese.

'Will you permit me, Admiral, as an observer, to offer a word? Superintendent Elliot desires to reach an accommodation if he can. But the two naval vessels you see are under the direct command of Captain Smith, a fearless naval commander, like yourself. And if Smith thinks our ships are threatened, he will demand that Elliot permit him to fight.'

'Is he a pirate, like Elliot?' the admiral tersely demanded.

'Elliot is not a pirate, sir.'

'So you say.' Admiral Guan indicated that he would hear no more.

After the delegation left, the remainder of the day passed without any movement from the British ships.

That evening, Mr Singapore approached Shi-Rong. 'The admiral has no confidence in me,' he said sadly. 'And the barbarian missionary speaks Chinese anyway. I should offer my resignation and ask the admiral's permission to withdraw.'

When Shi-Rong gave the message to the admiral, that worthy man only grunted. 'He's afraid there may be a fight,' he said. 'Tell him he's not to leave. Permission denied.'

Later, as they ate together in the admiral's stateroom on board, Shi-Rong asked the old commander what he thought would happen next.

'If your enemy is strong,' Guan answered, 'he attacks. If he hesitates, it means that he is weak. Every Chinese commander knows this. The barbarians hesitate because they know that if there's a battle, they will lose.' He gave a nod. 'But I will tell you something interesting: it is possible to win a battle without fighting.'

'How is that done, Lord?'

'I will show you,' Guan told him, 'in the morning.'

The sun was already up when the admiral made his move. Shi-Rong stood at his side as the entire fleet of twenty-eight vessels, war junks and fire ships combined, sailed out into the gulf towards the British merchantmen.

'We're going to place ourselves between the merchantmen and the naval ships,' Admiral Guan explained. 'From there we can send in our fire ships to burn them any time we want.'

'But you won't actually engage.'

'Correct. The British warships will then be left with only two options. They must either attack us or withdraw themselves and the merchantmen.'

'So you're forcing them either to fight or to be humiliated. You can win a battle without firing a shot.'

'Exactly.'

For the next quarter of an hour, as the Chinese fleet moved slowly down the gulf, neither man spoke. Gazing southwards through his telescope,

Shi-Rong did not detect any movement on the part of the British ships. He did notice a single merchantman in the distance, making its way up the gulf towards them; but he couldn't see what flag it was flying.

He was quite surprised when the admiral suddenly turned to him and remarked: 'The emperor would not consider we are acting irresponsibly. Do you agree?'

It hadn't occurred to Shi-Rong that the tough old admiral might be troubled by such doubts. He understood, of course. In the great bureaucracy of the Empire under Heaven, no man was likely to rise to high rank if he hadn't mastered the gentle art of guessing the emperor's intentions and protecting his back from his friends.

'We are not attacking, Lord,' he offered.

'One could argue we're provoking a fight.'

Shi-Rong thought for a moment and chose his words carefully. 'Commissioner Lin was clear that Elliot has proved himself to be a pirate – and therefore should be treated as such.'

The admiral nodded, then fell silent. Looking through his telescope again, Shi-Rong could now see that the ship in the distance was flying a British ensign. He continued to follow its progress. 'That's interesting,' he muttered. After a while, he turned to the admiral.

'There's a British merchant ship approaching, Lord. But it's not heading for the other merchantmen. I think it's heading straight for the Bogue.' He handed the admiral his telescope.

Guan gazed for some time. 'You're right. So, yet another ship from Britain is ready to respect the law and sign the bond.'

And Shi-Rong was just about to agree when suddenly a puff of smoke was seen from the *Volage,* followed by a distant roar.

'Did you see that?' he exclaimed. 'Elliot just put a shot across the merchant's bow.' He gazed in astonishment. 'The merchant's turning back.'

'Good.' Guan gave a sharp nod. 'If that isn't the act of a pirate, then I don't know what is.' He looked at Shi-Rong for confirmation.

'Elliot is a pirate, Lord. He just proved it.'

They had dropped anchor at their carefully chosen station when the cutter reappeared. As before, it contained the young officer and Van Buskirk. Shi-Rong moved to the side, with Mr Singapore.

The messengers in the boat below didn't even ask to come aboard and ignored Mr Singapore entirely. Van Buskirk called up to Shi-Rong in Chinese. 'Captain Smith requires that you move away directly. You are threatening British merchant vessels.'

'We have done nothing,' Shi-Rong replied.

'Will you move?'

'No.'

Moments later, the oarsmen pulled away, back to the *Volage.*

Half an hour passed. Neither side took any action. Midday was approaching.

'As I thought,' said the admiral. 'They are weak. They are weak.'

But at noon the British warships began to advance. And the admiral gave the order that his line of ships should come out to meet them.

There was nothing much to fear. As the *Volage,* followed by the *Hyacinth,* began to run up the Chinese line, Shi-Rong couldn't imagine they'd get far. Two barbarian ships against sixteen war junks, not counting the fire ships.

The admiral's war junk was larger than the rest. Its broad decks carried six cannon on each side; nearly two hundred mariners, armed to the teeth, waited there also. Above them, from the high deck at the stern, Shi-Rong and the admiral had a good view up and down the line of ships in each direction.

As the *Volage* came level with the first war junk, it was met with fire from the Chinese cannon, one bang after another, aimed at its sails and rigging. Then a huge volley of arrows flew like a swarm of flies into the sky and rained down upon the British decks.

The *Volage* was moving through the water faster than Shi-Rong expected. Evidently the cannonballs had not done enough to slow her down. Through his telescope, he tried to see the casualties from the volley of arrows. But although the *Volage* was going into battle, it seemed that her decks were nearly bare of troops. How did they propose to grapple and board?

Then the *Volage* fired a broadside.

Shi-Rong had never seen a British Navy broadside. It was nothing like the firing of individual cannon from a Chinese war junk. The whole side of the British vessel erupted with a flash, a cloud of smoke and a mighty roar like a thunderclap, as a dozen cannon fired in perfect unison. The guns were not aimed at the Chinese rigging or at the decks, but at the body of the ship and at her bowels, near the waterline.

Even from where he was, he could hear the crash as the Chinese vessel's sides were smashed open and the screams of men torn to shreds by a typhoon of wooden splinters. As he stared in horror, smoke began to issue from the shattered junk.

The *Volage* had moved on; she left the next Chinese vessel, a fire ship, to the *Hyacinth,* who came in to deliver a smaller but perfectly directed broadside at the fire ship's waterline. This time the thunderous crash was followed by a strange silence, during which the fire ship seemed to shudder. Then she began to list. She was foundering.

'She will sink,' said the admiral impassively.

Shi-Rong followed the *Volage*. She was still coming on rapidly, drawing opposite a war junk only a short way downstream of the admiral's flagship. The Chinese ship fired three shots at the *Volage*'s rigging and damaged one of the sails. Yet the British ship came on regardless. The frigate was almost exactly opposite the war junk now. Could the British gunners have reloaded yet? The answer came moments later, as the *Volage* emitted another mighty broadside, with a huge roar.

And then, just for an instant, he thought that the world had come to an end.

The flash was so great it seemed to fill the sky with fire; the bang was deafening. Something, he scarcely knew what, hit him in the chest like a wave and almost knocked him down. The men on the deck below him suddenly turned black against the curtain of flame. Before his eyes, the war junk ahead was exploding like a bursting barrel. Smoke billowed out. Spars, shards, lumps of flesh, began to fall out of the sky and rain down upon the deck.

In the unearthly glare, the admiral's face looked like a fierce Chinese mask. 'Gunpowder,' he growled. 'They hit a magazine.' He turned to Shi-Rong. 'Come with me.'

As they descended onto the main deck, Shi-Rong could see that the mariners were shocked into silence by the explosion. To see men killed in battle was one thing, but to see an entire ship and all the men it carried explode into nothingness before your eyes was another.

'The barbarians got lucky once,' the admiral shouted. 'Now we'll teach them a lesson.' To the gunners he called out: 'Do not aim for the rigging. Aim for the body of the ship. Destroy their guns.' And he placed himself in front of the main mast in the centre of the deck, to put heart into his men. To Shi-Rong he said: 'Go to the first cannon and make sure they aim at the sides. If the first gun gets it right, the others may follow.'

The flagship had a dozen cannon, more than any of the other war junks. But that was still only six on each side, just half the firepower of the frigate. Every shot had to count.

The gunners didn't seem to resent Shi-Rong. They tried their best. 'We always aim at the rigging,' one of them said apologetically. Indeed, they had some difficulty in positioning the cannon to fire at a lower trajectory. But as the prow of the *Volage* came level, they did get off a shot – and knocked off her figurehead. The gun crew let out a cheer. Shi-Rong looked back at the admiral, hoping he had seen. The next Chinese cannon hit the frigate's side. The third crew failed to obey the order and fired high. Shi-Rong wasn't sure where the other three shots went.

And now the British frigate was exactly level. Her length matched the flagship's. She had entered a gentle upward roll, as though she were taking a breath, and now the line of cannon descended, and her guns roared.

The admiral's war junk was stoutly built. But her sides were not made to receive a battering like this. Shi-Rong felt the whole vessel shudder as a dozen cannonballs struck her just above the waterline. He saw the British ship's quarterdeck passing. A double bang from two of the smaller guns mounted there was followed by a huge crack as one of the cannonballs smashed into the main mast, just above the admiral. He ran across to make sure the great man was safe, only to find Admiral Guan, with a splinter wound in his arm that he ignored, coolly assessing the damage.

'The mast's only a little damaged,' he remarked. 'It'll hold. I saw you hit the British ship.' He gave Shi-Rong an approving nod. 'The real question,' he added quietly, 'is how badly we're holed, and how much water we're taking in.'

As if in answer, the big war junk gave a slight but perceptible list towards the side where she'd been holed. The admiral pursed his lips. And he might have gone to inspect the damage himself if just then the *Hyacinth* had not appeared.

Seen from the British vessel, Shi-Rong realised, the exposed deck full of men presented a tempting target. After the shock they'd just received, the flagship's gunners had hardly started to reload. The admiral and his crew could only wait, helplessly. The *Hyacinth* was coming in close. Shi-

Rong saw to his horror that the guns were not pointing at the belly of the ship, but at the deck. One of the guns was pointing straight at him. He saw the flash and hurled himself to the deck as a sound like a thunderclap burst out. A moment later, the screams began. For the *Hyacinth* hadn't fired cannonballs. It had fired grapeshot.

Grape: a canvas bag tightly filled with lead or iron balls, each ball the size of a grape. Fired by the navy at close range. The balls fanned out at once. Any sail, spar, or rigging in the grapeshot's path was torn to shreds. Also humans.

From his lying position, Shi-Rong raised his head to look around. The carnage was terrible. He saw men cut in half. There were probably thirty men down, writhing in agony on the deck. The lucky ones were already dead.

He caught sight of Mr Singapore. The interpreter was tottering by the edge of the deck, one hand gripping the rigging. The other arm had been almost completely torn off and dangled loosely from his shoulder, which was spouting blood. He stared openmouthed towards Shi-Rong with a look of strange sadness before he fell over the side of the ship into the sea.

Admiral Guan was still standing by the big mast, immovable as a statue.

And then Shi-Rong felt ashamed. He hadn't meant to throw himself down on the deck. It had happened without his even thinking. A survival instinct. But the admiral had not moved at all, and he was surveying the awful scene now with a stoic face.

Had the admiral seen him? Did he think him a coward? Had he disgraced himself, his family, shamed his father? Better he should have died than that. In agony of mind, he struggled up and found the admiral watching him calmly.

'I am sorry, Lord . . .' he began, but Guan cut him short.

'Are you wounded?'

'No, Lord.'

'Good. Stand by me.'

And that was all the admiral said to him. As the two British ships continued up the line, their tactics remained the same, and there was nothing the Chinese crews could do about it. All hope of closing and grappling was gone. The British frigate was not a fortress full of men, but a floating gun battery; and the British Navy gunners were the best in the business.

After the shock of seeing the huge explosion so early on, the men on the war junks realised that they were sitting targets. They loosed their arrows and fired their few guns, but always high at the rigging, for that was how they had been trained. And if many dived into the water to save their lives, it was hard to blame them.

But then, having reached the end of the line, the *Volage* and the *Hyacinth* came about and gave the gunners on the other side of their vessels some action. The *Hyacinth,* being smaller and nimbler, weaved her way up the line again, blasting the Chinese ships at point-blank range and sinking several of them.

Twice more the admiral's flagship came under fire, once with cannon at the waterline, once with grapeshot to the deck. Each time Shi-Rong gritted his teeth, braced himself, and, though all colour drained from his face, stood fast beside the admiral. At least, he reasoned, if I am to die, they can tell my father that I died standing firm, beside Admiral Guan himself. And his only fear was that the admiral might also be killed, and no witnesses survive to tell the tale.

At the end of this second run, the British ships did not return, but sailed away down the gulf towards Macao, while the admiral, his flagship almost foundering, led his remaining vessels back to their former anchorage.

By late afternoon Shi-Rong, bearing a note from the admiral, was being conveyed by Nio and his oarsmen upriver to Commissioner Lin.

'The question is,' Lin said to him that night as he sat at his writing table, 'what exactly can I say to the emperor?' He gave Shi-Rong a cautious glance. 'The report from the admiral is very brief, but he says that you will be able to give me a full and accurate account.'

'Yes, Excellency,' said Shi-Rong, 'I can.'

It took him some time to recount all that he saw. And if he was careful to select the most promising information, he said nothing that was not true.

'So, to summarise,' Lin said, going through the list at the end, 'Elliot refused yet again to sign the bond. Not only that, but he shot across the bow of a British ship that was coming, in a proper and lawful manner, to sign the bond and proceed to Whampoa.'

'Thus proving that he is a pirate.'

'Indeed. The admiral did not attack the pirates unprovoked. They attacked him. Their gun ships are formidable – this must be admitted – and they damaged some of our war junks. One junk was blown up.'

'A lucky shot from the pirates, Excellency. They happened to hit a magazine. It was a huge explosion, but the admiral and his men did not flinch and continued to fire.'

'We may say that throughout the engagement our men fought bravely, and that the admiral conducted himself with the utmost skill and coolness.'

'There is no question, Excellency. I saw it all. I was at his side.'

'Not only this, but our ships fired back with success, and even knocked the figurehead off one of the pirate vessels.'

'Correct.' Shi-Rong longed to say that it was he himself who accomplished this, but calculated that it would be even better if, in due course, Commissioner Lin were to learn it from the admiral himself.

'After this, the barbarians retreated down the gulf.'

'They did, Excellency. They seemed to be heading first for Macao.'

'I think that will do.' Lin looked up at him approvingly. 'By the way, the admiral says that you were most helpful to him, and that you are to be commended.'

'I thank him, Excellency.' Shi-Rong bowed deeply. Might this mean that his name would go in the report to the emperor himself? Perhaps. But he knew he mustn't ask.

'I think this means war.' Lin frowned. 'The barbarian ships are fearsome.'

'They fight in a different way, Excellency. They rely on their guns, and they carry many more of them.'

Lin was silent for a few moments. 'Well,' he said finally, 'they'll never get past the forts.'

Shi-Rong slept well that night. Whatever the terrors of the day and the weakness of the Chinese navy they had exposed, he had survived. And it surely had been good for his career.

The next morning, Lin told him to take a message across to the admiral. So he went to summon Nio to bring him a boat. But he couldn't find the young fellow. He searched all over the fort. There was no sign of him. Somehow, in the night, Nio had disappeared.

o

Read arrived in Hong Kong Harbour the day after Elliot. 'I think you British are safe out here,' he told Tully and Trader. 'Lin won't risk a fight with you at sea. But I don't believe he'll ever let you into Canton again. Joker and the Hong merchants think it has to end in war.' He also brought a piece of good news. 'There's a Baltimore clipper sailing from Macao direct to London in three days. The captain's promised me to take all our tea.'

'Excellent.' Tully thanked him. 'I'll send a letter to my father with her.'

Read had a short private conversation with Tully after this, but he didn't dine on the ship, because he wanted to return to Macao at once. Just before leaving, however, he shook Trader by the hand. 'We'll keep in touch, my friend,' he said. 'I wish you well.'

It seemed an odd thing to say, and Trader wondered if it meant the American was going away on his travels again. But as Read was in a hurry, he contented himself with sending greetings to Mrs Willems. 'And to Marissa, of course.'

'I'm sending you to Calcutta for a while,' Tully announced the following afternoon. 'Not much happening here. No point your being cooped up on board for days on end. Stretch your legs for a bit. Work with my brother. Learn more about his side of the business. There's a ship leaving here in two days.'

The prospect of some normal life on land was certainly tempting, but Trader felt guilty about the older man. 'Perhaps you should go,' he suggested.

'Don't like Calcutta,' said Tully. It might have been true.

THE WINDOW

April 1840

They came barrelling up the drive to the bungalow in a two-wheeled gig – a tumtum, as they called it in India – Charlie holding the reins, with John perched precariously beside him.

'You idiots!' Aunt Harriet cried. 'You're lucky you didn't overturn.'

Trader laughed. 'Especially with Charlie driving.'

'Well, you'd better come in for tea,' Aunt Harriet declared.

After tea, while Trader chatted with her husband, Aunt Harriet and Charlie went into the sitting room.

'I've grown quite fond of young Trader during these last few months he's been back,' Aunt Harriet remarked. 'But he looks a bit pale and thin. Peaky.'

'This opium business is taking a toll on him.'

'He's not ruined, is he?'

'I don't think so. But it's bad. Even if the government compensates the opium merchants, it'll be a long wait.'

'Is he still interested in that Lomond girl? She's not taken.'

'He'll have to start making his fortune before he can pay his addresses there.'

'He strikes me as a bit of a loner. Is he selfish?'

'He's a loyal friend. I can tell you that.'

'Ambitious.'

'Certainly. But part of him's a dreamer, I think.'

'Ambitious dreamer. They're the ones that do best of all, quite often.

Or worst, if they don't succeed.' Aunt Harriet considered. 'I've got a feeling Trader's going to be all right. What he needs,' she said decidedly, 'is a nice girl. One of us. Somebody we all like, to steady him and help him fit in.'

'What about the money?'

'Girls are usually brought out here to find rich husbands, of course. But I know one or two who are . . . not short of this world's goods, as they say. Perhaps he should consider one of them. I could introduce him. He's very handsome. And there's something about him . . . a bit of the brooding romantic, the Byron thing . . . you know.'

'Marry rich . . . Trouble is, I'm not sure he'd do it. Too proud, you see. He'd think it dishonourable.' Charlie paused. 'He's not without vanity, either. He wouldn't want to be called an adventurer.'

'You know,' said Aunt Harriet wisely, 'why he wants the Lomond girl? Because he can't have her.'

'Probably.'

Aunt Harriet sighed. 'Well then, I for one can only pray to the Almighty that the opium trade gets back on its feet again.'

Benjamin Odstock always seemed to take life easy. After his midday meal, he'd have a siesta. In the evening, he'd usually look in at one of the Calcutta merchant clubs. He never missed a good day at the racecourse and was quite in demand for dinners. And thanks to his social life and the voluminous correspondence he maintained with contacts in places as far apart as Singapore and London, Benjamin Odstock was extremely well informed.

So it came as quite a shock to John Trader when, as he entered the office the very next morning, that gentleman looked up from the latest pile of letters and grimly informed him: 'The British government isn't going to pay us.'

'Our compensation? For the opium?' Trader's heart sank. 'Do you know this for a fact?'

'No. But it's the only explanation.'

'Tell me,' said Trader in a low voice as he sat down opposite Odstock.

'It begins when Jardine gets to London last autumn. He whips up the opium interest, which is quite large, and they start lobbying Parliament, the merchants, everyone. Soon all London's heard how we've been robbed, how the British flag has been trampled on, and how the Chinese have committed atrocities against the innocent British merchants of Canton.'

'They didn't actually commit atrocities,' Trader interposed.

'They might have. Same thing. Do you want compensation or not?'

'I do,' said Trader.

'Jardine gets an interview with the foreign secretary, Palmerston himself. Tells him the whole story, how we need the navy; gives him maps, everything. Palmerston listens. Then silence. Why is that?'

'Perhaps he wants to verify the story.'

'Nonsense,' Benjamin retorted. 'That's not how governments work. And certainly not how Palmerston thinks.'

'There's opposition in London, then.'

'There is. The bleeding hearts, the missionaries. That humbug Gladstone. Even *The Times* newspaper doesn't approve.' He shook his head. 'But that's not the point. The point is that the government's weak. They may not even have a majority in Parliament. Trouble in the countryside. Bad harvests. And in the cities: Chartists and the like, wanting a vote for every man, God help us. Worse, there are problems around the empire, from Jamaica to Canada. And the threat of hostilities in Syria. Palmerston's got a lot of other things to think about. And what's worst of all?'

'It has to be money.'

'Of course it does. At the end of the day, it always comes down to money. And there, it's very simple. There ain't any. The Chancellor of the Exchequer says so. Baring's been going around London telling anyone who'll listen that there's no money for anything. And although he's a senior member of the government, I think he may be telling the truth.'

'So the navy's not coming, after all?'

'I didn't say that.' Benjamin Odstock paused. 'Something's up. Recently, a British Navy vessel was ordered to leave Bombay for a rendezvous unstated. I'm hearing word of other navy vessels gathering in Ceylon and out at Singapore. And now our governor general, here in India, is quietly gathering regiments for some sort of expedition. No official word as to why.'

'That doesn't prove—'

'Wait. There's more. You know that Elliot and a good many of our people, including my dear brother, have returned to Macao. Lin's threatened to kick them out again, but so far he's done nothing. The emperor's promoted Lin to governor, by the way. The point, however, is Tully writes to me that Elliot received a private letter from Palmerston. Contents secret. But Elliot was overjoyed. And soon after, what does he do? Starts looking for a fast clipper to take him up the China coast. All the way up to the ports that supply Peking. Now why should he – a well-qualified naval officer, remember – want to do that? You tell me.'

'Reconnaissance.'

'Exactly. Ships gathering. Troops. Elliot, in person, wants to inspect the coast without saying why.' Odstock gazed at him. 'Which means . . . ?'

'Good God.' Trader stared at him. 'We're going to blockade the entire Chinese coast. That's far beyond what Elliot planned.'

'Planned?'

'Just something he said to me once, in confidence. Please go on.'

'Well, it's typical Palmerston. You have to understand how his mind works. The man's an imperialist. You think he can tolerate the way the emperor of China wants our ambassador to kowtow to him? Or that we've always been forbidden to trade at any port except Canton? Or – if he ever saw the damn letter – that Lin sends the British monarch a lecture about how to be obedient?'

'Could it work?'

'Oh, I think so. China needs trade. They need all kinds of materials, foodstuffs as well, copper and silver, of course – they're desperate for silver – most of which come from other nations, through the many ports along the coast where we are not admitted. A blockade of all trade would hit them very hard indeed. And if there's one thing the British are good at, it's a blockade.'

'All the same, declaring war on the entire Chinese empire . . . I'm amazed Palmerston could get Parliament to agree to it.'

Benjamin Odstock took a pinch of snuff. 'He hasn't.' The stout merchant watched Trader's look of astonishment. 'Members of Parliament keep asking him what he's up to, but he won't tell 'em.'

'Is such a thing legal?'

'God knows. But he's doing it anyway. The ships and troops are on the way. By the time Parliament finally finds out and complains, it'll be too late.'

'I'm shocked.'

'Do you want your money back?'

'Yes.'

'Palmerston has given no indication to Jardine or anyone that he'll consider making us good. Indeed, if he's unwilling to cough up the money now, still less will he do so after incurring the huge costs of an expedition and blockade. But we'll still get our money back in the end.'

'From China itself.' Trader nodded. Elliot's original plan, but on a bigger scale.

'That's it. From the emperor of China – after he's paid all our military expenses.' He gave a nod of satisfaction. 'Palmerston wants to uphold the dignity of the British Empire. But if he invests in a war with China, he'll expect a financial return.' He smiled. 'After all, if the British Empire isn't profitable, there's not much point in it, is there?'

'So all my hopes depend on the Chinese emperor,' Trader said quietly.

'They depend upon the British Navy,' Odstock corrected him. 'Much better bet.'

'It could take years,' said Trader.

'True. But in the meantime,' Benjamin Odstock continued, 'we can still make money in the opium trade.'

'We can?'

'Is opium still being grown here in India?'

'Yes.'

'Opium's like a river, my boy. A river of black gold. Nothing can stop it. The pent-up demand is huge. You can block one channel, but it will find another.'

'That's what my friend Read said. What channels are we talking about?'

'Tully's already supplying the dragon boats directly.'

'I thought Lin had taken them over. Turned the smugglers into coastguards.'

'And they're turning back to smuggling again just as fast – for the right money. Some of them are probably working both sides of the fence. It doesn't matter – well, not to us – so long as the opium gets through.'

'So we really are pirates, aren't we?' remarked Trader a little sadly.

'Those good old sea dogs back in Shakespeare's day – you know, Sir Francis Drake and all that – they were pirates to a man. That's how it all began. Besides, you forget one thing.' He smiled. 'We're British pirates. That's quite different.' He patted his stomach, chuckled, and took another pinch of snuff. But then suddenly his expression changed. He glared at Trader. 'You don't want to become a missionary, do you?' he asked fiercely.

John Trader thought of his cousin Cecil. 'Absolutely not,' he replied emphatically.

Aunt Harriet was supposed to be coming with them, but as her husband wasn't feeling well that day, she elected to stay with him at the bungalow. So it was just Charlie and John Trader who went to the dance.

The social life of Calcutta was still carrying on at the end of April. By late May it would be getting uncomfortably hot, and most of the British would be leaving for the pleasant hill stations in the Himalayan foothills.

The ball was being held in one of the clubs. Naturally, the women were all resplendent in ball gowns, and the men were in white tie or military evening dress, but this dance was a friendly affair, where military men, government families and the better sort of merchants mixed together.

They'd no sooner arrived than Charlie caught sight of Mrs Lomond and Agnes sitting on one of the many sofas and chairs around the edge of the ballroom. Colonel Lomond was standing behind them. Charlie hadn't known they'd be there, and he certainly wasn't going to be pushy – a greeting later in the evening would have done perfectly well – but Mrs Lomond, seeing not one but two young men who could dance with her daughter, signalled that he should approach at once. The colonel, at the sight of Charlie, gave him a friendly nod. As for Trader, Lomond might have nodded to him, or he might not have. It was impossible to say.

And so they all danced. Charlie and Trader took turns to lead Agnes out. There was a quadrille, then a cotillion. When a waltz began, Colonel Lomond remarked that when he was a young man, no decent man would ask a respectable woman to dance such a thing.

'Not even if she were his wife?' Mrs Lomond asked, giving him the gentlest tap with her fan.

The colonel took the hint and led her out. Trader noticed with amusement that Colonel Lomond actually danced the waltz rather well.

But above all, Trader had to admire Charlie. His friend knew the form, and he was assiduous. He brought a constant stream of young fellows over to be greeted by or introduced to the Lomonds, so that Agnes had fresh partners for almost every dance.

As they all went in to dinner in excellent humour, he heard Colonel Lomond murmur, 'Thank you, Charlie. Well done.'

Halfway through dinner, Charlie decided that, delightful as the evening had been so far, he wasn't quite happy. It was Colonel Lomond's fault. Not that he'd done anything so bad. It was what Lomond *hadn't* done that irked him.

He hadn't addressed a single word to John Trader.

It wasn't obvious. If Trader said something, Colonel Lomond listened politely. If Lomond in turn said anything to the table in general, it could certainly be assumed that Trader was a recipient of the remarks along with everyone else. It was just that he had also addressed particular remarks to his wife, Agnes, and to Charlie himself. But not to John. Towards John Trader, Colonel Lomond maintained an air of coldness that was only just within the bounds of good manners.

Of course, it was partly Trader's fault. He'd deliberately irritated the colonel that first time they'd met at the Bengal Military Club, when, after all, Lomond had been kind enough to give him lunch. He'd behaved badly. But it seemed to Charlie that it was time that there was at least some thaw in their frosty relationship. He owed it to his friend.

So turning to Mrs Lomond, and fully in the hearing of both Agnes and the colonel, he brightly enquired: 'Did I ever tell you how Trader here saved my life?'

'Really?' Mrs Lomond smiled at both the young men. 'You didn't, and you must tell me at once.'

Trader looked embarrassed, and Agnes looked intrigued. The colonel didn't look in the least intrigued, but there was nothing he could do except listen.

'Well,' said Charlie, 'it's how we first met. In London. I'd been dining with my father at his club and stayed quite late. To get to my lodgings, I had to cross Soho. Instead of hailing a cab, like a fool I decided to walk . . . And I was strolling down a street, quite alone, when all of a sudden, out of the shadows step two men, one with a cudgel, the other with a knife. And they demand my money. I hadn't much on me, but I did have my father's watch, a gold hunter that he'd given me when I was twenty-one. I didn't want to part with that.'

'So what did you do?' asked Agnes.

'Shouted for help at the top of my lungs,' said Charlie. 'I thought, if I can just hold them off for a minute, and help comes, I might have a chance. Stupid idea, really. But it was my lucky night. Around the corner a hundred yards ahead, at a run, enters our hero!' He laughed. 'To be precise, a young dandy in evening clothes, including a tall opera hat . . . which fell off as he ran. And carrying an ebony walking cane. Nor,' Charlie continued with delight, 'did our hero hesitate, not for an instant, at the sight of the two armed men. In fact, I'd say it spurred him on.' He turned to Trader. 'There's a rather fierce warrior hiding inside you,' he said. 'Don't think I never noticed.'

'What next?' Agnes wanted to know.

'The men turn to meet the assault. I got my arms around the fellow with the cudgel. And the man with a knife comes at our hero.' He smiled at them all. 'What the villain with a knife doesn't know is that Trader here is a first-rate swordsman. It took only a moment before the brute I was trying to hold threw me off. But by that time, the knife had gone flying through the air and its owner was backing away from Trader. As he saw his friend shake me off, however, he made a great mistake. He made a rush at Trader.'

'Did Mr Trader hit him on the head with his stick?' asked Agnes.

'No, he did something cleverer, though more difficult,' Charlie replied. 'He executed a perfect thrust. It was so fast, I couldn't even see it. The tip of his stick caught the villain precisely between the eyes. It made a crack like a rifle. Next instant, the man was down. Lucky not to be dead, actually. The brute with the cudgel took one more look at Trader and fled. Incidentally,' he added, 'it turned out these same two fellows had robbed and killed another chap like me, just the month before. So I was more than lucky that Trader answered my call.' He stopped and gave them all a big grin. 'That's how we got acquainted.'

'Well,' said Mrs Lomond, 'that was very exciting, I must say.'

'Have you ever fought a duel, Mr Trader?' asked Agnes hopefully.

'No, Miss Lomond,' Trader answered. 'Farley calls me a swordsman, but all I really do – or used to do in London – was a bit of fencing. Just for sport and exercise, you know.'

'Well, time to go back to the dancing,' said Colonel Lomond.

'We're still eating, Papa,' said Agnes.

'So we are.' Colonel Lomond turned and addressed Trader at last. 'You're not one of those fellows who carries a sword stick, are you?'

'No, sir. Never owned one.'

'I have always been of the opinion,' Colonel Lomond continued, 'that deceitfully concealing a weapon is one of the vilest things a man can do. No gentleman would ever walk the streets with a sword stick.'

'He hasn't got a sword stick,' said Mrs Lomond with a trace of irritation.

'Glad to hear it,' said the colonel.

Agnes had just started to dance a waltz with Trader when she suddenly said she felt tired and asked if they might sit the dance out. As the others were all dancing, they had a sofa to themselves. Having sat down, she seemed to recover quite quickly. 'Have you ever been to Scotland, Mr Trader?' she asked.

'Only once, in the summer, while I was up at Oxford. I liked it very much.'

'I love Scotland, Mr Trader. I suppose the nearest I can imagine Heaven would be the family's estate in Scotland. My uncle has it, of course.'

'That's easy for me to understand,' Trader said. 'Several of the merchants in the China trade have acquired estates in Scotland. Both Jardine and Matheson, for a start.'

'And should you like to do that, do you think, Mr Trader?'

'Yes. In fact, I hope to very much.' He smiled. 'But I must sound a note of caution. The prospect may be in my mind, but it is not imminent. I'm really in no position to do more than dream, at present.'

'But you'd like to.'

'I can't think of anything better in the world,' he said in all honesty. 'What is it that you love yourself about Scotland, may I ask, as someone who really knows it well?'

'Oh, the heather, in a way, I suppose. At home – for I do think of it as home – when I walk up onto the wild moors and look back at the old castle set in the trees . . . And there's a stream, a burn, as we say in Scotland – the water's brown, you know, from the peat and it has a soft tangy taste that goes so well with the sweet scent of the heather . . .' And Miss Lomond, to his great surprise, continued on in this vein for nearly five minutes without stopping. He felt the soft breeze; he saw the reddish-brown stone of the old Galloway castle, the sheep and the shaggy little cattle on the high ground; he fished in the Lomond water, as they called the little river; and he talked quietly to the old gillie as her ancestors had talked to his forefathers for centuries . . . And by the time she was done, he was not only in love with Agnes Lomond, but with her home and her land and all the vast, settled security she represented – everything he lacked and all that he desired.

As he thought of his wretched financial condition, he couldn't help looking a little sad. 'Even in the China trade, Miss Lomond, gaining such a fortune takes many years. In the meantime, one lives in places like Macao, and so forth, you know.'

'I understand that.' Her wonderful brown eyes gazed with deep meaning over her fan. 'None of us can have everything at once. But the best things are worth waiting for.'

'I daresay,' he said absently.

'One must never give up hope, Mr Trader. Now that I know you're such a valiant fellow, I don't need to remind you.'

'You think I shouldn't give up hope?' He looked at her earnestly.

'No, Mr Trader.' Again, she looked soulfully at him. 'Please do not give up hope.'

And whether she meant this as a signal to him or just as general encouragement, or whether perhaps she was practising to see what effect she could have upon a young man, it would have been impossible to say. Perhaps she wasn't sure herself. Trader took it as a signal.

'Ah, there you are,' said Mrs Lomond with a smile as she returned.

Charlie and John went back together in the carriage.

'So what did you and Miss Lomond find to talk about?' Charlie asked.

'Scotland,' said John.

'She does like to talk about Scotland,' said Charlie. 'The only thing Agnes Lomond wants,' he continued sleepily, 'is to find a man like her father. With an estate, of course.'

'Is that why she isn't engaged already?' asked Trader.

'Not sure there have been any offers,' Charlie answered. 'The fellows here, you know, they don't really want a wife who thinks she's better than they are. And the wife's got to be able to take to colonial life. Share the rough with the smooth. Roll with the punches. That sort of thing.' He opened his eyes. 'A fellow can be in love and all that. But at the end of the day, if he's thinking about a wife, he needs a pal.'

'I see what you mean,' said Trader.

'Do you know why they say Agnes Lomond is like a Scottish moor?' asked Charlie.

'No,' said John.

'Because she is cold and empty.'

'Oh,' said Trader, and laughed. 'I'm duly warned.'

But he thought he knew better.

o

Shi-Rong stared. It had happened so unexpectedly, he couldn't be sure what he'd seen. Reaching for his spyglass, as they started to give chase, he peered through the small brass telescope for several seconds before he suddenly cried out, at the top of his voice: 'Row faster, faster! As quick as you can.'

Behind him, the round eyes painted on the warship gazed lugubriously after him as though to say, 'You'll never catch them.'

Governor Lin had been so proud when he told Shi-Rong: 'I have bought a British warship. Now that we own a barbarian vessel, we can inspect it thoroughly to see how it works.'

The idea had been sound enough, but the results were disappointing. For when they decommissioned the vessel, the British had been devious. 'It seems that Elliot had all the cannon removed before he let it go,' Lin had reported sadly. And a month later he confessed: 'Our mariners cannot discover how the rigging functions. It is nothing like any boat of ours. I was very angry, but so far they have been quite unable to sail the vessel.'

A use had still been found for the discarded British ship, however. Having loaded it with his own cannon and painted huge eyes on the prow, in the style of a Chinese war junk, Governor Lin had moored it by a sandbar in the Pearl River, just downstream from Whampoa.

'With the shore batteries on either side and this ship in the middle of the river,' he declared, 'it will be utterly impossible for the barbarian warships to threaten Guangzhou.'

Even so, not all was well in the gulf. 'Despite your patrol boats, I hear that opium is being smuggled again in small vessels and even dragon boats,' Lin had told Shi-Rong. 'You must put a stop to it. I am counting on you.'

'I shall redouble my efforts, Excellency,' Shi-Rong had promised.

His boats were out patrolling the waters every day. Frequently he went with them himself. He had spies along the coast. He did everything he could think of. He'd caught a few smugglers, too. But he wasn't satisfied.

And now here was a dragon boat he didn't know, emerging from a creek not half a mile in front of him. Was it a smuggling vessel? It could be. And the fact that, as soon as they saw him giving chase, its occupants started paddling like fury to get away seemed to confirm his suspicion.

But it was what he'd seen through his brass telescope that really gave him a shock. For sitting in the stern of the dragon boat, apparently in charge of it, was Nio. He was sure of it. He'd seen his face, the telltale scar on his cheek. Why, even the way he sat and urged his men on proclaimed it was him.

Nio, his own servant. The one he had chosen, saved from gaol, kept at his side. Trusted. Even grown quite fond of him. Nio, who'd vanished so suddenly, so completely, that he'd wondered if the young fellow might have had an accident or even been murdered.

Well, it seemed he was very much alive. More than that. After all his kindness and trust, Nio had betrayed him. Gone over to the enemy.

Even then, a part of him wanted to greet the young fellow, glad at least that he was alive. But then another thought struck him. How would it look, as he brought the smugglers, bound and in cages, to the governor, if Lin recognised one of them as his secretary's own servant, who'd been in their close company many times?

What will that say about my judgement, Shi-Rong thought, or my ability to control my own people? Disaster. It must not happen. But neither did he want Nio at large, to be recognised or brought in by somebody else. So when he caught up and the smugglers resisted – as they surely would – then Nio must die.

If need be, Shi-Rong thought, I must kill him myself.

o

It was the second week of May. Soon the summer monsoon season would come to Calcutta. Already, people were starting to leave for the hill stations.

As John Trader entered Odstocks' offices, he felt a sense of lassitude at the prospect of a boring day.

He was surprised, therefore, to hear a curious noise coming from Benjamin Odstock's private office. It sounded as if the portly merchant was having a seizure. Alarmed, he rushed into the snug little room.

Benjamin Odstock was sitting at his desk. In his hand was a letter. And the strange gurgling sound Trader had heard was that of a man chortling with laughter. He stared at Trader for a moment as if he hardly saw him. Then, focusing upon him, he cried out: 'The old devil! The old devil!'

'What's happened?' asked John.

'Ebenezer! My father. That's what. The old devil. Look!' He thrust the letter into Trader's hand.

And as Trader began to read, Benjamin Odstock did the strangest thing. Notwithstanding the fact that he was a portly gentleman with snuff stains on his jacket, he placed his two fat little hands together, as if in prayer, and stuffed them between his two fat thighs, and grinned so happily that he looked like a schoolboy.

The letter was terse and to the point. It confirmed that the British government was sending an expedition to China, but that Palmerston still refused to give Parliament any information. Some choice words followed about the humbug of those who objected. As usual, the senior Mr Odstock listed the aches and pains from which he suffered and that made even the smallest conduct of business such a burden for him. And then at the end he added a further piece of information.

> With all the uncertainty in the China trade, the price of tea has fluctuated greatly during recent months. On one day it touched one shilling a pound, on another as high as three shillings. The tea you sent in November has all been sold at close to the highest price. But in addition, acting for the partnership, I made numerous purchases and sales of tea contracts, which have yielded a further profit. I enclose a letter of credit which may be shared between yourself, your brother, and your junior partner also, if you deem that appropriate.

'He's sent us money,' said Trader, trying to sound calm.

'That's right.' Benjamin returned to his usual portly self. He gazed at Trader benignly. 'Seventy-five thousand pounds, to be precise.'

'Seventy-five thousand!' Trader cried.

'We don't call our father an old devil for nothing,' the merchant remarked.

'Do I get some of that?'

'Oh, I think so. As a matter of fact, you get the same as Tully and me. Twenty-five thousand.'

'But . . . my partnership is ten percent. Surely . . .'

'Tully's very pleased with you. As it happened, that ugly business with Lin in Canton was a very good test. Showed us what you're made of. You came through it very well. Steady under fire. Kept a cool head. Then you brought us that American to get our tea in, remember? When you came back from Hong Kong to Calcutta, Tully sent me a private letter, proposing we make you an equal partner, subject to my agreement. Timing left to my discretion. So there you are. I do agree, and this seems an excellent time.'

'I don't know what to say.' Trader was thunderstruck. 'It's more than kind. I never expected . . .'

'Good.' Benjamin Odstock observed him for a moment. 'Will that be enough to pay off your debt?' he asked genially.

'My debt?' Trader went pale for an instant. Then to his embarrassment he began to blush. Had Read told Tully about it? 'How would you know if I had any debt?' he enquired.

'It was obvious right from the start. Tully and I both guessed. Actually,' Benjamin remarked cheerfully, 'we enjoyed watching you sweat.' He took a pinch of snuff. 'Good for you to suffer a bit. Showed you had nerve. It also told us that you were really committed to our business.'

'Oh,' said Trader.

'Is twenty-five thousand enough to clear your debt?'

'Yes.'

'In that case, you're whole again. From now on, you're an equal partner with us in Odstocks. As for the opium we lost, if we get compensated one day, that'll be an extra windfall.' He smiled. 'Something to look forward to.'

'I can't believe it.' Trader shook his head in wonderment.

'Well, I'd say you're out of trouble. As for making your fortune, we'll have to see. If this expedition against the Chinese doesn't work and the opium trade becomes impossible, I daresay Tully and I will take what we've already made and go home. You'll have to trade as best you can.' He gave him a friendly nod. 'Personally, I'm betting on the British.'

'So,' said Trader fervently, 'am I.'

For the next few hours, John Trader answered business letters, checked ledgers, and tried not to think about the future. Shortly after noon, however, he felt the need to stretch his legs and began to walk slowly towards the large nearby park that ran along the bank of the sacred Hooghly River.

Once he was in the park, the trees gave him protection from the midday sun. After a few minutes he came to a shady spot overlooking the wide waters where someone had obligingly set a stone bench. And there he sat down, gazed at the moving river, and allowed himself to think.

What did this sudden change in his circumstances really mean? His debt was gone. He could settle up with Read. His inheritance was intact again. In fact, he was now some thousands richer. And an equal partner in a small but respectable merchant house. Most fellows had to wait many years before they reached that position. He was ahead of the game.

'I suppose,' he remarked to the river, 'that I could marry.'

Plenty of people in Calcutta would have thought him eligible. He'd be seen as a good bet, a 'coming man'.

If I were Charlie, I'd marry a nice girl and be happy, he said to himself. But that was the problem. He wasn't Charlie. Something else drove him on; he wasn't even sure what it was. A quest for the unknown? A dream, perhaps. He continued to sit on the bench staring at the water. 'Why do I always have to want more?' he asked the river. And receiving no reply, he shook his head.

Then, into his mind's eye, came the vision of a wild Scottish moor, a peat-brown burn, and a slim, graceful woman whose face was not clearly defined, but could only be Agnes; and behind her, in the distance, a Scottish castle.

Agnes. She wasn't like the other girls. There was nothing wrong with them, but Agnes was set apart, a soul from another world. Agnes belonged in that mystic land where time was measured in centuries, and people knew who they were, and families were old as the echoing hills. And if he could obtain that for her, and she wanted to place her hand in his and lead him there and give herself to him, why then it seemed to him that he would have reached the holy grail itself.

Yesterday it had been only a dream. But today?

Two things troubled him. The lesser was the almost certain opposition of Colonel Lomond. Agnes might plead his cause. She certainly seemed to have given him the signal that she'd welcome his interest. But while it might be a tough fight with the colonel, he was prepared for that.

The second was more serious. For, as the colonel would no doubt point out, his fortunes still rested on the assumption that one way or another, the opium trade would resume. If it came to an end, he'd surely find a way to make a good living, but not the fortune needed to give Agnes the life she wanted. And above all things in the world, he desired to make her happy. I know the goodness of her soul, he thought. If she makes a commitment to love and cherish me, she'll never let me down. But if I let her down, could I ever forgive myself?

Was it fair to press his suit when things with China were still so uncertain? On the other hand, if he waited too long, would he lose her?

'I need to think some more,' he murmured. He rose to his feet and began to move out of the park.

At the top of the park, he emerged into the district known as Dalhousie Square. It wasn't a single square, but an entire area where the stately British government buildings were set well back from broad streets and open spaces. Few people were about just then. The noonday sun beat down from a clear blue sky on domes, towers, imperial temples. Nothing, it seemed, could disturb the solid peace of the place, as the mighty heart of British India took an afternoon snooze.

He was so occupied with these thoughts that he hardly noticed, until he looked up, that he had reached the Anglican cathedral of St John.

He liked the cathedral. There was something reassuring about its simple classical design, rather like St Martin-in-the-Fields, in London. Handsome, but not too large. Sensible. Anglican.

He hadn't been in the cathedral for quite a while. And – whether to get out of the sun or from some hitherto-unrecognised spiritual impulse – he decided to step inside. It was almost cool within. He noticed an old woman dusting the choir stalls. No one else. He sat down.

For a minute or two he sat there, enjoying the peace. And since thinking about his situation had not yielded any conclusion, it occurred to him that perhaps he had been led to the church for a reason and that he should pray. But if he prayed, what would he ask for? He wasn't sure of that, either.

Then he remembered something the chaplain had said when he was a boy at school. 'It's no good asking God for something you want, you know. Because it's almost certain to be something quite selfish and of no importance to anyone but you. So when you're in a quandary, don't tell God what He needs to do. Just try to empty your mind – don't think about wanting anything – and ask Him to guide you. And with a bit of luck, if you deserve it, He will. And it may turn out to be something you never thought of at all.'

So John Trader closed his eyes and tried to do as the chaplain had said. After all, he reasoned, God had been good to him so far today. He'd led him out of debt. So he placed his future entirely in the Almighty's hands and asked only: 'Send me a sign, Lord, and I shall know what to do.'

And after he had said a prayer or two, he came out into the bright sunlight of Dalhousie Square with a wonderful sense of well-being. I'll go and share the good news with Charlie, he thought.

They stood in the big upstairs room at Rattrays. The big sash windows were open enough to let in some breeze, but not enough to disturb the papers on the desks. The Indian servant in the corner patiently worked the ceiling fan. Charlie's two colleagues busied themselves with their work and pretended they couldn't hear every word.

Not only was Charlie delighted for him, but he said something unexpected. 'Aunt Harriet was right, then!' he exclaimed.

'What do you mean?' Trader asked.

'Just the other day she had a feeling – premonition, you might say – that you were going to be all right.' Charlie shook his head in wonderment. 'Rum thing. Woman's intuition, and all that.'

'Well, God bless her,' said Trader with feeling. 'Have you got anything to drink?'

Charlie grinned and went across to a cabinet at the side of the room. 'We have the water of life, Glenlivet Scotch,' he announced, and taking out a bottle and four glasses, he turned to his colleagues, 'You'll join us, gentlemen?'

The two young merchants rose from their desks and, abandoning all pretence that they hadn't heard every word, congratulated Trader warmly while Charlie poured.

They were all happily toasting the hero of the hour when, from the street outside, came the sound of a band playing. Charlie went to the nearest window and glanced out. 'We've even got a military band to celebrate the occasion,' he announced. And sure enough, the sound grew louder as the small parade approached. 'Last marching band of the season, I should think,' remarked Charlie. 'No parades in the summer monsoon.'

'Take the salute, Trader!' cried the two young merchants.

Trader moved to the window and glanced out. It was a small Indian troop. A couple of platoons and a band. Well turned out, playing well. Made one proud to be British. Some carriages were following patiently behind. No one was in much of a hurry that day.

Charlie turned to fetch the bottle and refill their glasses. Trader continued idly to watch the band.

Then he saw her.

Agnes and her mother were in an open carriage, the third in the little cavalcade behind the marching band. Just the two of them, a coachman, and a groom. No sign of the colonel. They had their parasols up, but he could see their faces clearly. They were talking to each other, smiling. His eyes rested on Agnes. His heart missed a beat.

And suddenly he knew. It was like a blinding flash of light. He'd asked for a sign. This must be it. Within an hour of his prayer, here she was, quite unexpectedly, right in front of him. Agnes was his destiny, the one he was meant to marry.

He'd asked for a sign. But he decided to ask for just one more, a tiny confirmation. The great sash window was not open quite enough. He'd raise it up farther so that he could lean out, call to Agnes and her mother as they passed. Even with the band playing, they should still hear him. He'd wave. And Agnes must wave back. That was all he asked. If she waved, he'd marry her. He was sure she would.

He grasped the bottom of the window and tugged it up. He heard Charlie ask if he needed help. The thing was damnably heavy. But he wanted to open it himself. That, it seemed to him, was part of the deal. He must pull it up himself. He heaved. It came up a little and stuck. He yanked the bottom to the left and right. It gave. He pulled. The big sash began to slide. Their carriage was almost level with him now. He heaved again. The heavy window shot up at last, with a crack he ignored.

And then, with a second crack, it hurtled down. A great eight-foot-high screen of wood and glass, running down without even a rattle, falling free, like a castle portcullis whose ropes have been cut, catching his hands, both of them, before he knew what was happening, and smashing them onto the sill below with such a mighty bang that he did not even hear the bones of his hands breaking.

Nor was he aware that the downward force on his hands had also thrust his head forward into the crashing window, shattering the glass so that shards and splinters flew into his handsome face.

It took Charlie, his two companions, and several servants a full five minutes to lever the window up enough to pull back his broken hands and bloodied face. And John Trader had fainted long before that.

Below, in the street, the band and the Lomond women had long since passed. Agnes had heard the crash, but had seen nothing, except that a sash window in a building had fallen.

Aunt Harriet had been looking forward to going up to the hill station that summer. But she really couldn't leave Trader in the bungalow. Charlie had brought him there, quite rightly of course. That's what friends were for. And the fact was, John Trader was still in a very bad way.

The surgeon had done a good job. Just how good remained to be seen when the bandages and casts were off.

'There will be pain, of course,' the doctor said. 'If it gets too much, give him a little laudanum. Above all, he must rest.'

'Will he make a full recovery?' Aunt Harriet wanted to know.

'With luck,' the doctor replied, 'he'll be able to use his hands again. His face is not as bad as we'd feared. There'll be a few little scars. But he's lost one of his eyes . . .' He shook his head.

'He'll be blind?'

'Just in one eye. He can wear an eye patch. Like Admiral Nelson.'

'I wonder if he'll like doing that,' Harriet said.

'He'd better,' the doctor replied bluntly. 'The surgeon did his best, but I'm afraid it's not a pretty sight. Never will be.'

More alarming, however, was his general state. 'Infection's always the greatest fear,' the doctor said. 'Normally I'd recommend you get him out of the monsoon season and up into the hills as fast as you can. But for the moment, I want to keep an eye on him, and he's not ready to make the journey. I know I can rely on you for that.'

When Aunt Harriet apologised to her husband for their delay in going to the hills, he waved it aside. 'Trader once saved Charlie's life,' he said cheerfully. 'He counts as family.'

John had been installed in the bungalow for only an hour when Benjamin Odstock appeared. The merchant was more than grateful, begged them to let him know if they needed anything, returned the next day with presents for both of them, and called promptly every afternoon thereafter to check on the patient.

More surprising, however, the second morning after Trader's arrival, was the appearance at the bungalow of a carriage containing Mrs Lomond and her daughter.

'Charlie told us about the accident,' Mrs Lomond explained, 'so we thought we'd look in to find out how Trader was – before we go up to the hill station, you know.'

The patient was asleep when they entered the room.

'I can hardly see his face,' observed Mrs Lomond.

'His hands are bandaged, too,' said Agnes.

'Will he be all right?' Mrs Lomond asked.

Aunt Harriet told her what the doctor had said, though she glossed over the grimmer details about Trader's eye.

'I think you're wonderful,' said Mrs Lomond warmly. 'A real friend in need.' She seemed to hesitate. 'I wonder,' she went on, 'as long as we're still in Calcutta, if Agnes and I couldn't come over each day and give you a bit of time off.'

The colonel wasn't very pleased. 'I don't see why it's our business,' he grumbled. 'And I'm not having Agnes left alone with that fella without a chaperone.'

'Of course not,' his wife replied. 'I shall be with Agnes all the time. Harriet doesn't really have to look after Trader, either, you know. She's doing it because Charlie's her nephew and Trader's his friend. Everyone in Calcutta says she's behaving awfully well. So I just think that since people know that you and Charlie's father went to school together, and we like Charlie very much, if we don't rally round and help Harriet before we go up to the hill station . . .' She didn't complete the sentence. 'I'd just like people to say that the Lomonds had behaved awfully well, too.'

'You're quite right, my dear,' the colonel had to concede. 'Just don't leave Agnes alone with Trader, that's all.'

It was clear, from the first afternoon, that they had done the right thing. 'It's our Christian duty, Agnes, don't you think?' her mother had said.

And indeed it was. 'You must do these things even if you're bored,' her mother continued. 'It's very good training for later life.' But Agnes was hardly bored at all.

They weren't really there to nurse the patient, of course. Aunt Harriet had two particularly reliable servants to do the actual nursing, when she wasn't doing it herself. The two Lomonds were there to give Trader a bit of company – and indeed, to provide some conversation and moral support for Harriet, too.

For part of the afternoon, Aunt Harriet took a little nap or walked in the garden. A couple of times she called for the carriage and went on social errands in the town. Meanwhile, the Lomonds chatted with John, if he was awake, or played a game of cards, if Aunt Harriet's husband came in to join them.

When they played cards, Agnes was given a special role. Trader could see perfectly well with his good, uncovered eye, but he had difficulty, fumbling with his thickly bandaged fingers. Her job was therefore to hold his cards for him and play his hand as directed, which everyone agreed she did very competently.

And then there were the visitors: Charlie, Benjamin Odstock, other young men whom Charlie and Trader knew. It was all quite entertaining.

There was something else that Agnes noticed. They'd all come to cheer the patient up, and there were the usual jokes and banter. But, subtle though it was, she detected a hint of deference in their manner. When she asked her mother about it, Mrs Lomond agreed. 'He's a coming man,' she said. 'I was talking to Mr Odstock about him, and he told me that Trader's the best young merchant he's ever seen.'

'So what do you think of John Trader?' her mother asked Agnes that same evening.

'He's very handsome,' Agnes answered.

'Do you think he's interested in you?'

'He says he likes Scotland.' Agnes's face brightened.

When Agnes talked to young men about Scotland, it seemed to her that she was only being practical. It was just to let them know: Scotland was what she wanted. If a young man could get safely past the stern presence of Colonel Lomond – who wasn't such a fool as to be forbidding to possible suitors, so long as he liked them – he still had to reckon with Scotland. Not everyone wanted to finish up on a big estate in the north, even in the event that they could afford it. As one young fellow remarked: 'I'm not riding in that steeplechase. The jumps are too high.' Agnes realised this. But Scotland was what she wanted.

'Scotland isn't everything, you know,' her mother said quietly, but she left it at that.

After a week, the doctor took some of the bandages off Trader's face. 'A few small cuts,' he remarked, 'but give it a month and you'll hardly see they were there.'

He pronounced himself satisfied with the damaged area around the lost eye and rebandaged it. As for Trader's hands, he rebandaged them, too, and said he'd inspect them again in a few days.

Aunt Harriet went out that afternoon, leaving the two Lomonds in charge. Propped up on pillows, Trader talked with them for a while, but then he felt sleepy and decided to nap. So Mrs Lomond went out to take a turn in the garden, leaving Agnes alone, with strict instructions to call her at once if there was any need.

While Trader slept, Agnes sat in a big armchair near the window and read a book. After a while she dozed off herself – she wasn't sure for how long. She woke with a guilty start, went over to the bed, and gazed at Trader. He was still asleep.

His face was in repose, his dark hair falling over the bandage that covered his eye, his lips just open. He looked like a poet, she thought, contemplating some distant landscape in his mind. Scotland, perhaps. She moved a little closer.

His white shirt was partly open. She became aware of the wispy dark hairs on his chest and the scent of his skin. She knew that his body was slim and strong, yet lying in bed like this, hands encased in bandages, he looked strangely vulnerable. He was the patient and she, almost, the nurse. The idea gave her a curious sense of power. She didn't know why.

A few moments later, her mother came back.

It had been a great surprise to John when the Lomonds had appeared at the bungalow. To have Agnes there, keeping him company each afternoon: he could hardly believe it had happened. And every day, it seemed to him, she became more lovely.

He noticed little details about the elegant way she moved or sat, or even how she spoke certain words. Sometimes he would feign sleep and then, through half-closed eyes, gaze at her wonderful hair, or the way the sunlight caught her silhouette against the window. Above all, he was struck by her patience, her kindness. It seemed to him she was an angel.

But why had she come? Of course her mother had brought her. But was there more to it than that? Though he'd fallen in love with Agnes at first sight, she'd given him enough encouragement to make him think he might have a chance. And now here she was, when he'd been knocked about quite badly and lost an eye, visiting him every day and looking after him. Was it an act of charity, like visiting the local hospital, or simply kindness to a friend? Or was she deliberately putting herself in his path – and with her mother's permission? Were these visits a way of giving their friendship a chance to develop into something more? Might she truly care for him already?

Not that she'd show it too much. No girl wants to throw herself at a man. She'd wait for him to make the first move.

And he was ready to make it, but for one thing. It was only fair to her, he thought. He must get well first. Make sure he had the use of his hands. Make sure that, when all the bandages were off, she knew what she'd be getting.

'You are so good to me,' he said before she left that evening. 'Dear Agnes, you've given me a reason to get well.' It was as good as a declaration.

She must have understood that he needed to get well.

When word came that the arrival of the monsoon was imminent, Colonel Lomond announced that they should go up to the hill station immediately.

'I need two days to prepare and pack,' Mrs Lomond told him. In the meantime, at the particular request of Aunt Harriet, who needed to find a replacement, Agnes stayed at the bungalow to help. She arrived to take up her station at noon. Soon afterwards, Aunt Harriet went out to interview two sisters who might be able to take her place.

She read to John for half an hour or so, but he seemed out of sorts and closed his eye to rest. Having nothing else to do, she sat out on the veranda with a book.

It grew hotter during the afternoon. The air felt heavy and humid. Twice Agnes looked in on John and sat with him for a while. The second time he seemed uncomfortable, fretting the bedsheets as he slept; but she put this down to the weather. A little before teatime, a wind arose. It shook the fronds of the trees, but did nothing to cool the garden. She looked up at the sky. It was still blue. The clouds passing swiftly overhead were white.

Aunt Harriet returned. And they were all sitting down to tea when the doctor arrived. Offered tea, he declared that he'd like to see the patient first and disappeared into the bedroom. After a little while, he asked Aunt Harriet to come to help him change the hand bandages and dressing.

When they came down to tea, they both looked grave.

'Infection, I'm afraid.' The doctor pursed his lips. 'You must keep him cool, as far as possible. He may become feverish. If he's really burning up, apply cold compresses. That's really all we can do. I'll return first thing in the morning.'

The monsoon rain arrived with a roar that evening. It beat upon the ground in such a deluge that it turned the garden into a pond within minutes and drummed upon the roof with fury, as if it meant to hammer its way through and drown all the inhabitants within.

Agnes sat in a chair with her shoulders hunched. Aunt Harriet said, 'Just what we need. It'll cool things down.'

Then they both got up and went into the bedroom where John lay. How he could be dozing with the rain making such a mighty din, Agnes didn't know. They agreed that Agnes would watch John that night and Aunt Harriet would take over in the morning.

The rain continued until dawn, when Aunt Harriet relieved her. But Agnes was still awake when the doctor came to dress John's wounds. He had brought an ointment with him. 'It's a remedy against infection,' he announced. 'Iodine and potassium. I developed it myself. Nearly always does the trick.' He smiled. 'Once the fever breaks, he'll be on the mend.'

Agnes slept fitfully that morning. When she finally rose, the wind had died down and the heat was worse. A sickly, humid torpor seemed to have enveloped the house. Aunt Harriet had installed a servant to work the fan in the sickroom.

When Agnes woke late in the afternoon, the doctor had already visited again and gone. A light breeze had arisen, so Aunt Harriet had stopped the servant from working the fan, opened the windows and allowed the air to circulate through the sickroom.

John was lying quite still. He was awake, but he didn't seem to want to talk. As the evening set in and Agnes lit a small lamp on a table in the corner, his face looked gaunt in the soft light it cast. Standing by the window, she could smell the scent of the pale jasmine in the garden. 'Do you smell the jasmine?' she asked, but he did not reply.

It was half an hour later that he gave a little shiver. She went to the bed and felt his brow. It was burning.

Her first thought was to call Aunt Harriet. But she stopped herself. Aunt Harriet had looked so tired when she handed over John's care to her. There was a pitcher of water, still cold from the well, in the corner. She poured some water into a basin and soaked two cloths. Raising John's head, she put one cloth behind the back of his neck. The second she laid on as much of his forehead as she could and held it in place there. It seemed to do some good. But a quarter of an hour later, she had to do it again.

Half an hour after that, she went quietly down to the larder to refill the pitcher. She also got fresh cloths.

And so, for the next several hours, she kept up her lonely vigil. Each time she managed to cool him down a little, he soon seemed more feverish than ever, and she was frightened and wished she was not alone.

It was nearly midnight when he became delirious. He mumbled odd words, of no significance, so far as she could tell. She wondered whether she should wake Aunt Harriet after all.

And she might have done so, if he had not suddenly cried out: 'I've killed him.'

'John? What is it?'

'Killed him . . . Killed him . . . Murder . . . Got to hide.'

'Killed who, John?'

'Run . . . Run . . . Hide.'

'John?'

'I'll be hanged . . . Hide . . .'

She stared at him. What could it mean? She almost forgot about Aunt Harriet. Was it just a nightmare? It must be a nightmare.

Again she cooled him down. She pulled the sheet back to expose his chest and abdomen to the air. She even wished it would rain.

He was really burning up now. There was no point even in calling Aunt Harriet. What could Aunt Harriet possibly do that she couldn't do herself? She knew she mustn't be afraid of the fever, as long as it didn't get too high. But she suspected that high point might be very close. She swabbed his chest with cool water, as well as his brow. He'd fallen silent. Was that a good sign or a bad one?

And then he spoke again. Softly this time. 'Agnes.'

'What is it, John?'

'Agnes!' This time it was a sudden cry. 'Agnes! Oh, Agnes.'

'Yes, John. It's Agnes.'

'Oh.' His eye opened, staring up, but not seeing her. 'Oh, Agnes. Give me your hand.'

So Agnes gave him her hand. 'Everything's all right,' she said. 'I'm here.'

'Ah.' A gentle smile crossed his face, as though he had seen an angel. 'That's all right, then.'

And a few minutes later Agnes realised that the fever had broken.

The following day, as she sat in the carriage with her mother, on their way to the hill station, Agnes was rather sleepy. Even if she had wanted to talk, she wouldn't have raised the subject with her father.

So it wasn't until after breakfast, on their first day up in the hills, when she and her mother were alone, that she told her about the strange way that Trader had cried out in his sleep. 'Could he really have murdered someone, do you think?' she asked.

'Oh, I doubt it very much,' Mrs Lomond said. 'He was just having a nightmare, that's all. When people have nightmares, it's hardly ever about something that actually happened, you know. I should put it out of your mind, if I were you.' She gave her daughter a curious look. 'Does it matter to you, Agnes?'

Agnes didn't answer. She didn't tell her mother about the way Trader had called out her name. For some reason she didn't want to. After all, he had as good as told her that he was in love with her. She was pretty sure that was the truth, not a fantasy like the nightmare. And she wasn't sure what she felt about it.

No man had ever told her he loved her before.

o

It was the start of July. Colonel Lomond was looking forward to a quiet afternoon, undisturbed. He'd arrived at the hill station to join his wife and daughter a week ago, so he'd had several days to unwind. The weather was cooler, the air was clean and a mix of sweet and tangy scents wafted in the breeze.

Lomond loved the cottage – for so the English called their country retreats in the hills. Its architecture was a plain and simple colonial Georgian. Had the walls been clapboard instead of cream-painted stucco, it might have come from any village in New England – with the exception of the roof, of which the colonel was very proud. For this was constructed of the corrugated iron – the colonel called it tin – already in use in Australia and New Zealand, and just now making its appearance in British India. Lomond had supervised the work personally and had ordered the tin roof painted green. It blended pleasantly with the lawn and the rhododendrons, which gave structure to the cottage's hillside garden.

His wife and Agnes were out in the garden now. Colonel Lomond had retired to the small room he called the library, but which was really his private den. He had sat himself in a big chair, stretched out his long legs and lit a pipe when to his irritation the head house servant appeared to announce that a visitor had arrived. His frown relaxed into a smile, however, when he heard, 'It is Mr Farley.' And a few moments later, still holding his pipe in his left hand, he strode outside with his hand outstretched to welcome the young man.

'I hope you don't mind my calling on you without warning, sir,' Charlie said.

'Of course not, my dear boy. Delighted to see you.'

'I just arrived two days ago at my aunt Harriet's cottage, and as you're only a couple of hours away, I thought I'd come over. She sends you her best wishes.'

'Very kind of her. I hope she's well?'

'Absolutely.' Charlie gazed down the slope. 'You really have a splendid view up here, with those waters in the valley.'

'My wife says it reminds her of the English Lake District.'

Charlie nodded, then glanced towards the distant Himalayas. 'Bigger mountains, though.'

'This is true.' Lomond smiled contentedly.

It was just then that Mrs Lomond and Agnes emerged from the lower lawn. But they were not alone. And now Lomond's face fell.

'I brought Trader with me,' Charlie explained. 'He's been convalescing with Aunt Harriet after his accident. I hope it's all right.'

Colonel Lomond did not reply. He stared at Trader.

John was dressed in a short tweed coat. His right hand had evidently recovered, for he held a walking stick. But his left hand was still bandaged and he wore it in a sling. Over his missing eye he wore a large black patch. The effect was rather romantic.

If Trader had been an officer, Lomond would have confessed that he looked rather dashing. But he wasn't an officer, so Lomond was damned if he had to confess any such thing at all. The ladies appeared to find him handsome, though. The colonel closed his eyes, as though this would make the young merchant disappear, and wondered if he could retreat to his lair with Charlie for a smoke. When he opened his eyes, he was horrified to see that Trader had detached himself from the ladies and was advancing straight towards him in a purposeful manner.

'Colonel Lomond,' he began, 'I wonder, sir, if I might speak to you in private.'

Five minutes later, Colonel Lomond stared at Trader bleakly. His great desire, if not to reach for the nearest weapon and shoot him, was to throw Trader out of his house. But the damnable fact was, he really couldn't. Worst of all, the loathsome young man knew it.

Assuming Trader was telling the truth – and Colonel Lomond would most assuredly satisfy himself as to that – the young man actually possessed, at this moment, more money than he had himself. A circumstance the colonel had no intention of letting Trader discover.

The offer therefore was not a bad one. Still more to the point, there hadn't been any others.

'Have you spoken to my daughter about this?' he finally forced himself to enquire.

'Certainly not, sir. I came to ask you first whether I might pay my addresses.'

'I see.' That was proper, at least. If true. 'And have you any reason to think she would welcome your advances?'

'I cannot say. You must understand, sir, that until my circumstances recently changed, as I have explained, I did not feel in any position to marry, and I was most careful not to behave towards your daughter or anyone else in a manner that might suggest such a prospect. In general converse, however, we found so many things in common that I believe she might consider me.'

'I shall speak to her myself. So will her mother. You understand that detailed enquiries will have to be made into your circumstances. And your character,' he added firmly.

'Of course. I believe you will be satisfied. No one has ever impugned my character, sir, and I should defend my honour if they did.'

A swordsman had spoken. They both understood. It could be bluff, of course. Still, at least he talked like a man.

There remained one embarrassing issue. Lomond told himself it would be a test of Trader's sincerity. 'One day Agnes will inherit something. In the meantime' – Lomond was obliged to confess – 'her dowry will not be large.'

'Whatever it is, large or small, it will be received with gratitude,' Trader replied politely.

Colonel Lomond surveyed the battlefield and considered the campaign still before him. 'I have one concern of a more general kind, however,' he continued. 'Even though you have been made an equal partner and cleared your debts, the China trade remains uncertain. I'm speaking not only of the compensation for the lost opium, but of the continuance of the whole business with China. Everything will depend on the outcome of the hostilities which are clearly coming. I should like to see that issue resolved before any marriage. Even if all else is in your favour, therefore, you may have to accept a long engagement.'

A play for time. How would the enemy react?

'For Agnes, sir, I will wait as long as I have to.' It was said with surprising fervour.

The colonel gazed at him. Either the fellow was a devil of an actor or he was actually in love. He hadn't thought of that.

When they emerged, under strict instructions that he was not to reveal his intentions yet, Trader was allowed to rejoin the ladies while the colonel signalled to Charlie that he wanted to talk to him. The moment they were alone in the library, Lomond turned on him. 'Your friend wants to marry my daughter. Did you know?'

'He hasn't said so in so many words, sir, not even on our way up here, but I did suspect it. When he said he wanted to see you alone . . .'

'I'm glad he saved your life and all that, but I don't like him.'

'I know, sir. So does he.'

For a long moment Colonel Lomond was silent. 'If only it was you,' he said at last.

'I should think you wanted something better than me, sir,' Charlie replied amiably.

'Oh, you're all right,' said Lomond affectionately. 'I just wish to God,' he cried plaintively, 'that I could have a son-in-law that I actually liked.'

'He's a strange fellow,' Charlie answered, 'but even if you don't like him, you might come to admire him. I think he's going to succeed, far beyond what I could ever do.'

'I don't like the opium trade.'

'Her Majesty's Government is quite determined it shall continue, sir. We're about to fight for it.' Charlie paused. 'The thing about the opium trade is the amount of money to be made. If I may say so, it's no secret that Agnes likes Scotland. The big opium men are already buying up Scottish land. In ten years' time, I can see Trader setting himself up on a substantial Scottish estate.'

'I know all that,' said Lomond quietly.

'Might I ask what Agnes feels for my friend?' Charlie ventured.

'Don't know yet.' Lomond gazed at him earnestly. 'Is there anything else that I ought, as her father, to know about this man?'

Charlie considered carefully. 'No,' he said finally. 'Nothing important.'

They all had a walk together – except Colonel Lomond, who'd retired to his lair. Mrs Lomond pointed out the many delights of the view. Trader could name some of the mountains in the distance. How the devil did he know that?

When they returned, the servants had set out a table on the lawn, prepared for afternoon tea, under a large parasol.

Mrs Lomond sent word to her husband that tea was ready, but the servant came back with a message that the colonel would join them later.

Over tea, they talked of this and that until Mrs Lomond turned to Trader and in the kindest way enquired, 'I know that you were orphaned at an early age and that you had a guardian. So what was your childhood like?'

John Trader allowed himself to lean back a little in his chair and, as though recalling pleasant days, smiled easily. 'I suppose the loss came so early in my life that I felt it less than I might otherwise have done. It's not very interesting, I'm afraid, but I was fortunate enough to have a very calm and happy childhood.' And he said a few words about his kindly guardian, his happy schools, and that sort of thing, while Charlie Farley watched in silence.

o

John Trader was seven years old when he was sent away to boarding school. Nobody knew he was a murderer. Except his uncle Adalbert, of course.

It was a nice enough school for small boys, in the country. He'd been there only a month, however, when he got into a fight.

There was nothing wrong with that: boys were expected to fight now and then. One of the older fellows had shoved him because he was a new boy, but he'd banged his head against a tree, and it hurt. Fighting back against the bigger boy might have gone against the pecking order, but it showed pluck – anyone would have said so.

When little John Trader squared off against the older boy, he hardly noticed the pain, and he wasn't afraid. He knew only a deep, black rage. And it must have been impressive, for when the other boy saw it in the little fellow's eyes, he was so taken aback that he almost fled, except that he would have lost too much face.

And so they fought and John was knocked down – not once, but many times. Each time he got up to rush at the older boy again. And who knows how long this might have gone on if the headmaster had not suddenly appeared, seized John by the ear, and hauled him to his study.

There was a thin dark cane on the headmaster's desk with a curled handle. When John saw the cane, he trembled a little, because he had never been caned before. But he made up his mind that no matter how much it hurt, he would not cry. And he was just gritting his teeth in preparation when he was told to sit down.

The headmaster was a comfortable man in his fifties. He'd risen to the rank of major in the army of the East India Company, and he'd seen plenty of the world before he'd returned to England, started a family, and bought the school.

'Got yourself into a fight with a bigger boy, eh, Trader?' he said peaceably as he observed the little fellow. 'Now, are you calm enough to listen to me like a sensible fellow?'

'Yes, sir.'

'You have a terrible temper. I saw it. Takes you over. One day it could destroy you. I've seen good men have their careers broken, lose everything, because they couldn't control their tempers. Makes you do things that you wish you hadn't afterwards. But by then it may be too late. Can you understand that?'

'I think so, sir.'

'It's not easy losing your parents. I lost mine years ago. But there's nothing we can do about it.' He paused and saw the boy bow his head. 'All right now. For their sake, young Trader, I want you to make a success of your life. So I want you to promise me that no matter what happens, from this day to the end of your life, you will never lose your temper again. Will you do that?' He paused. 'Well?'

'Yes, sir.'

'Shake my hand. This is a pact between us, Trader, that may never be broken.' He held out his hand, and John shook it.

John Trader had been five when his parents were drowned, returning from a visit to France. His father had no family except the descendants of an aunt who had made an unfortunate marriage, and whom he had never met, nor even corresponded with. Nor was there anyone on his mother's side to take the little boy in, except his mother's widowed uncle.

Uncle Adalbert was a retired lawyer without children of his own. He'd never much cared for Archie Trader, the stockjobber his niece had married.

The stone-gabled house in the west of England to which Uncle Adalbert had retired lay under a bare chalk ridge on its northern side, with miles of dark woodland, into which he never walked, to the west. Along the narrow lane to the east lay a small village, into which he seldom went, either.

Uncle Adalbert had done his best. He'd hired a governess to teach the little boy to read and write and look after him generally – a cheerful, ginger-haired young Scotswoman whose name, which Uncle Adalbert sometimes forgot, was Miss Grant. He'd tried not to show that John's presence in his house was a severe inconvenience to him. Obviously the child was far too young to eat his meals in the dining room, but he'd take him for short walks and talk to him a little, however stiffly; and he began to make enquiries in the neighbourhood to discover if there were any other children of John's age with whom, he supposed, his great-nephew might like to spend some time.

Occasionally, passing along the passage outside the boy's bedroom, he would hear the little fellow softly crying. He did not venture in to comfort the child. Men didn't do that sort of thing, so far as he knew. Tears were natural enough, of course, considering the boy had lost both his parents. But after a time – he couldn't help it – he became somewhat resentful of the fact that the boy did not seem happy in his house.

Once a week Miss Grant would bring John into Uncle Adalbert's small library, where he could show the old man the progress he was making. On the whole these performances went well, and though it wouldn't have been appropriate to spoil the boy with praise, Adalbert would give him an approving nod and thank Miss Grant for her good work. But if occasionally John stumbled on some word or answered his great-uncle's simple questions incorrectly, requiring his guardian to reprove him, Adalbert sometimes noticed a trace of sulkiness or even hostility in the child, which, if he were not so young and orphaned so recently, might have called for severity. Miss Grant had a pleasant way of coaxing John along, however, and rather than risk losing such a good governess and have the trouble of finding another, Adalbert kept his thoughts to himself. He did once ask Miss Grant if she thought the boy might be a little moody, but she assured him that John gave her no trouble at all.

'You may be strict with him, should it be necessary,' he said to her kindly, and left the business in her hands.

He was rather proud of himself when in due course some other children were found with whom, under the eye of the governess, John could play, as children liked to do. And he soon found that these visits could be timed to coincide with one of the long walks he took on the nearby ridges or upon a day when he had to be away.

One of his duties as guardian was to look after the boy's inheritance until he should come of age. This he did assiduously, going up to London every few months to interview the men of business who invested the capital and to inspect the two houses, let to tenants, that the estate also owned. When he first took the inheritance in hand, he had observed that the late Archie Trader had already doubled his niece's dowry and invested very successfully himself as well, so that, given another twenty years, he might have built up quite a handsome fortune for his family – a circumstance that only confirmed the old lawyer in his poor opinion of the stockjobber, that he should have put all this at risk for an unnecessary journey to France.

It was after one of these visits to London, where a tenant in arrears had already put him in a bad temper, that Uncle Adalbert returned home in the evening to be met at the gateway by the kindly Miss Grant, who was looking apologetic. 'I'm afraid,' she confessed, 'that boys will be boys.'

If she thought this was a good opening, however, she had still failed to understand her employer,

'What is the matter, Miss Grant?' he asked tersely.

'Cricket, I'm afraid. The other children were teaching John how to play. I was watching them, and we were well away from the house. It turns out that he has an excellent eye, and he's extraordinarily strong for a little fellow his age. The very first time he was to bat, he was bowled an easy ball, and he hit it, quite magnificently . . .' She looked at him hopefully, hoping this tale of prowess would mitigate the news that was to follow.

'What of it, Miss Grant?' Adalbert cried impatiently.

'I never imagined he could hit it so far, but I'm afraid it went through a window on the second floor,' she added eagerly. 'It's entirely my fault, of course,' she said firmly.

'Where are these children?' he demanded.

'They all went home. There's just me and John here now.'

Perhaps if John had looked penitent, perhaps even if he had smiled, run up to him, and asked forgiveness, Adalbert might have reacted differently. But as the lawyer came across the lawn to where the boy was standing, holding the offending cricket ball, he noticed only that the child was looking at him sullenly.

And it came into the lawyer's mind that he was being put upon. His life had been thrown into disorder, he was being obliged to spend precious days in London dealing with disagreeable and dishonest tenants, and now this boy, who showed no gratitude, no family affection, but only looked upon him, his long-suffering benefactor, with insolent sullenness, was quite content to break the windows of his house like a rioter or a revolutionary.

'Are you sorry for what you have done?' he asked menacingly.

'Yes, Uncle.' He was lying, of course. He was hardly even taking the trouble to look as if he was sorry.

'If this is how you and your friends behave, then they need not come here anymore.' He did not really mean it, but he wanted to shock the boy. He did not understand that to the child, it meant that he was to be denied all his playmates forever.

No words. Only that sullen look again. The lawyer decided to try to shame him.

'What would your dear mother think if only she were here today?' That seemed to have got through. He saw the boy's face pucker up, as if he were about to cry. But still, for Adalbert, it was not enough. 'Neither your behaviour nor your sullen looks come from your mother,' he observed coldly. 'No doubt you get them from your father, whose thoughtlessness has killed your mother and left you an orphan in my unfortunate care.'

'Oh, sir!' Miss Grant's cry of shock might, in a moment, have made the lawyer turn. But he never had time to do so.

What took place happened so fast that it took all three participants by surprise. For suddenly, his little face smitten with pain and then suffused with rage, the boy grasped the cricket ball and hurled it with all his force at his great-uncle. And whether John's aim was devastating, or more likely as the result of sheer chance, the ball struck the old man smack in the middle of his forehead between the eyes. Reeling from the shock of the missile, he fell backwards even before his knees had time to buckle. And there he lay, openmouthed, staring up from the grass at the sky, quite motionless.

Seeing him obviously unconscious, Miss Grant ran into the house crying for water and leaving John alone.

Slowly the boy went forward. His great-uncle's face looked strangely grey. There was no sign of life at all. He had killed him.

And then came the awful realisation. Every child knew what happened to murderers. They will hang me, he thought. He did not wait even for kindly Miss Grant. He turned and ran.

When Miss Grant came back with a pitcher of water and began to mop Adalbert's brow, she noticed that the child had vanished, but assumed he had run into the house. By the time the groom had saddled up and ridden off for the doctor, Adalbert was starting to come around. Miss Grant and the cook helped him to his bedroom, where he lay down with a cold poultice on his head.

Only after this did the governess discover that her charge was nowhere to be found.

She searched in the house and in the grounds, down the lane to the village, and at the houses from which his playmates had come. No one had seen him. The groom arrived back with the doctor, who pronounced that Adalbert would have a large bruise for many days, but that his skull did not appear to be cracked. 'He must have absolute peace and quiet. If there is any change in him, send for me at once. Otherwise I shall come by again in the morning.' When she told the doctor about the boy's disappearance, he instructed her not to trouble Adalbert with this news for the time being. 'There is nothing he can do about it in his present condition,' he pointed out. 'The boy will reappear soon enough, because he will be hungry.'

She sent the groom up onto the ridge and told him to remain on lookout until sunset. Meanwhile, she went into the woods and searched as far as she could. But darkness fell, and John did not appear.

She went out into the woods again that night with a lantern and must have walked two miles and more, calling his name. Unable to sleep, she was up again before dawn, walking through the trees. Soon after breakfast, she went to the village and organised a search party.

It was only at noon, after telling her that the patient was clearly on the mend, that the doctor allowed her, in his presence, to tell the old man about John.

Adalbert received the news coldly. 'The child is evil,' he remarked, his voice suggesting that if the boy disappeared permanently it would be no bad thing. 'The answer, however,' he added with a sniff, 'is simple.'

When the governess heard it, she gave a cry of dismay, for it sounded barbaric. But the doctor was entirely in agreement. 'I know where they can be procured,' he said, 'but they may not be here before tomorrow.' And kindly Miss Grant could only pray that they would not be needed.

At first, the little boy had been very much afraid. He'd heard Miss Grant calling him, even caught sight of her from his hiding place, and he had wanted so much to run into her arms, for the kindly Scotswoman was the nearest thing he had to a mother. But he knew that he must not, for if he did, she would take him back to the house and then he would be hanged for murder. After she had gone, he walked on until he came to a tiny stream, tinkling through the bracken, where he drank some water.

The July night was warm, but it was very dark. He listened for any sound of creatures and heard a soft footfall that, he supposed, might have come from a fox. But after a time he was so tired that he curled up and fell asleep.

At dawn, he realised that he was very hungry. He wondered whether, if he kept on, he might come to any cottages where he could beg some food. But that would be no good. They'd want to know who he was. They might even have been told to look out for him. Could he steal some food? Little chance of that. Most cottagers kept a dog. If he walked for long enough and came to a town where no one would notice him, he could buy something to eat, if he had any money. But he had no money.

All logic told him he must go home. But then, suddenly forced to grow beyond his years, the determined little boy came to a decision. He would rather die out here in the woods, free and on his own terms, than be thrown in prison and hanged by people who had control over him.

So it was, at the age of six, and based upon a childish misunderstanding, that John Trader became the man he would be for the rest of his life.

But he was still very hungry. Hoping that something might turn up, he wandered through the woods, farther and farther from Miss Grant and the gabled house. Early in the afternoon, he came to an orchard where apples were growing, some of which were ripe enough to eat. That put something in his stomach, at least. A little later, he found wild blackberries and gorged himself upon them. By the time he fell asleep that evening, he was seven miles away from his great-uncle's house.

They found him at ten o'clock the next morning. The bloodhounds, that is. He was walking across open ground by a big wheat field, and he was very tired. The baying sound the bloodhounds made as they approached was frightening, but when they reached him, he found himself bowled over by two friendly, floppy-jowled dogs who seemed just as pleased to see him as their handler, a burly fellow with big brown whiskers who told the hounds repeatedly that they were good boys.

Only minutes later he was clasped in the arms of Miss Grant, who hugged him as closely as if she really had been his mother.

He wasn't punished. For several weeks his life resumed exactly as usual, except that Uncle Adalbert was away a good deal and spoke to him little when he was there, and that Miss Grant sometimes looked sad.

Then in September, after parting tearfully from Miss Grant, he was sent away to the little boarding school in the country.

Uncle Adalbert never came to see him there, but parents did not come to see their children in those days, so he felt no deprivation. Nor did he see the old lawyer in the holidays, for Adalbert had found a family with whom he could live in a big house near Blackheath. At least he always supposed that Adalbert had found them, and if the local doctor had obtained their name and if Miss Grant had been sent to inspect them, he never knew of it. They were a jolly family, with a lot of children, and he was happy spending the school holidays there. By the time, at the age of twelve, he went to the big boys' school at Charterhouse, he thought of the Blackheath family as almost his own.

He would have liked to see Miss Grant again, but he never did, though his memory of her remained quite vivid. He did not forget the incident with Uncle Adalbert, either, but he thought about it less each year. As for his parents, they became, in his mind, more like the memory of a memory. And if sometimes, in his bed at night at school, he would have liked to weep, he never did so, even silently, but let his mind drift down into a dark subterranean world, whose hidden streams did service for his tears.

He kept his promise to his first headmaster and never lost his temper again. Sometimes a black mood came over him and he found it difficult to work, but he kept these moods under control.

Uncle Adalbert might still consider that his niece's son was a potential murderer, but he died just before John completed his schooldays, so that young Trader entered the adult world believing, along with everyone else, that he was a pretty decent sort of fellow on the whole.

He also came of age with a tidy fortune. Uncle Adalbert had tended his inheritance with scrupulous care, and though it did not provide more than a decent private income for a bachelor, that was better than most fellows of his age were blessed with. Of his great-uncle's fortune he received not a penny. Adalbert had left everything to his old Oxford college, with the injunction that a fellowship was to be endowed, in his name, for the study of law. He left, together with the accounts concerning his inheritance, a note informing John that his father had some distant cousins, named Whiteparish, resulting from an unfortunate marriage, with whom neither of his parents had wished to have any communication. He advised John to follow their example. That was all.

o

As the months of July and August passed up at the hill station, Agnes Lomond decided that on the whole, she was excited.

Though the family lawyers were in Edinburgh, there was a highly respectable firm of solicitors in Calcutta who had connections with them, and whom her father used from time to time for local matters. As instructed, they had been discreet and assiduous in their enquiries about Trader. And so far at least, the results were promising.

'His bank references are sound. Odstocks gave him a glowing report,' her father told her. 'Everything he told me about his circumstances turns out to be true. That's what really matters.'

'So do you like him better now, Father?'

'You're the one that's got to like him,' he replied. But there was a trace of humour in his voice that told her that he was not totally opposed to the match.

And did she like him? Her father had indicated that Trader might visit once a week; and he'd done so, usually with Charlie.

They were happy afternoons. Trader was handsome. And now with his black eye patch he had a piratical look that was quite exciting. He was charming. Her father did his best to be civil. The cheerful presence of Charlie always made things easier, of course; but even when he wasn't there, Trader made himself not only agreeable but interesting.

Once they talked about Canton and the dangers of the siege.

'The dangers were exaggerated, I'd say,' Trader said, 'mainly to get support from Parliament. If you mean, "Could the Chinese have killed us all?" the answer would be yes. Their numbers are huge. But the fact that we're all alive shows they didn't want to. The danger was from the crowd getting out of control. That could have been the end of us, certainly.'

On that occasion, after tea, her father had taken Trader into the library for a private talk about the military situation. And Agnes was pleased that after Trader had departed, her father had remarked: 'Well, he's no fool. I'll say that for him.'

One day, having tea with Agnes and her mother, he talked about Macao and the pattern of life there. 'It's a pretty place and the climate is kind. But it's small. No big clubs and racecourse like Calcutta. One needs to realise that,' he had said. And Agnes knew that he was gently warning her not to expect too much.

'I quite understand,' said Mrs Lomond firmly. 'Is the English community pleasant?'

'Yes, they are,' Trader replied. 'There's quite a mix: British, American, Portuguese, all sorts of people, really. The social life isn't grand, but it's very agreeable.' And he proceeded to tell some stories – nothing scandalous, but amusing – about the goings-on there.

'I know someone who lives at Macao,' Mrs Lomond remarked suddenly. 'Mrs Barford. I write to her sometimes.' She watched him as she said it.

'Mrs Barford?' His face broke into a smile, and he answered her easily. 'I know her well. She was very kind to me when I first arrived. Please send her my greetings when you write.' He looked her straight in the eye. 'She can tell you all about me, the good and the bad.'

'Will you write to her?' Agnes asked her mother after Trader left.

'I already did,' her mother replied with a smile. 'Months ago, when Trader first returned.'

'Why?'

'One of the duties of a wife and mother is to discover everything she can about the people her family may encounter. You'll do it yourself, if you're wise.'

'Did she write back? What did she tell you?'

'That Trader had a reputation for being handsome, charming, a bit moody, but clever. He also had a mistress in Macao. Half Portuguese, half Chinese, something like that. Rather beautiful, apparently.'

'Oh. How should I feel about that?'

'If you've any sense, you should be glad,' her mother replied. 'I should think your Mr Trader is an accomplished lover – just as your dear father was when I married him, I'm happy to say.'

'You never told me things like that before.'

'I'm telling you now.'

'Is the woman still there?'

'Sensible question. No, she left the island and is not expected to return.'

In these private conversations with her mother, only one thing concerned Agnes a little. 'I wish he were better born. After all, I am a Lomond. And your family's old as the hills. I'd be marrying beneath me.'

'Trader's a gentleman,' her mother said.

'Not the way Father is.'

'One can't have everything, you know. A lot of girls in your position would be very pleased to secure Mr Trader. If you want a big place in Scotland, he's probably your best chance of getting it.' Her mother sighed. 'You may just have to wait, that's all.'

'What will I do in the meantime?'

'Have children,' her mother said firmly. 'With luck you'll have the place in Scotland while they're still at school.'

'Paid for with trade.'

'That's right.'

'The opium trade.'

'Do you want the place in Scotland or not?' her mother asked tartly.

'Oh yes,' Agnes murmured, 'I do.'

She was never entirely alone with him, of course, but when they all went out walking, her mother and Charlie would sometimes go on a little ahead and not look back. And she and John Trader would talk softly of Scotland and the estate they would have one day, God willing. She sensed a gentleness in him and a love of the country that pleased her very much; and she imagined him as the country gentleman she would shape him into once the unfortunate if necessary business of making money in the China trade was done.

It was the end of summer when Trader came to call for a final time before he returned to Calcutta. The Lomonds were also due to return, but ten days later. Trader came alone this time. He was already sitting and chatting to her mother in the garden when Agnes came out to greet him. As she approached, she noticed something different about him. The sling was gone, and his left hand was free of its dressing.

She saw her mother give her a look that seemed to say 'All's well.' Trader rose politely from his chair. Her mother called out: 'John has his other hand back, all healed, thank God!'

And so it was. One could see a scar or two, but that was all.

'I'm so glad,' said Agnes.

She sat down.

'That only leaves the eye,' said Trader. 'Bit of a mess, I'm afraid. But I wear the eye patch, of course.' He smiled apologetically. Agnes noticed he'd gone rather pale.

Then he took the eye patch off.

The doctors had done their best. Perhaps a London surgeon could have made a cleaner job of it. But the shards of glass had done terrible damage as they cut through his eye. One great cicatrix carved its way down from his eyebrow to his cheek. Two others crossed it at different angles. Across the socket where his eye had been, the flaps of skin had been sewn together like crazy paving.

He put the eye patch back on. Agnes stared. She hadn't seen it before.

And received a look from her mother that would have stopped a bolting horse dead in its tracks.

'Of course,' said Mrs Lomond – she sat very straight and calm – 'when one's spent so much of one's life with the army and seen so many people with the most terrible injuries, one realises how grateful one should be to have only one. You have good health, all your limbs, every advantage.' She smiled. 'And the eye patch looks rather dashing, you know. I suppose, to a woman, it's a sign that someone's a man rather than a boy.' She turned to Agnes. 'Don't you agree?'

Agnes bowed her head. There could be no mistaking her mother's meaning. This, she was showing her daughter, is how to be a lady. From a duchess on a great estate in England to a colonel's wife in some remote hill station in India, it was all the same. Grace under pressure. Considering the feelings of others. Good posture was always a great help. That's why girls were taught not to droop.

'I do,' said Agnes, collecting herself as best she could.

'John was telling me that Charlie wants him to take part in a play he and his friends are getting up,' her mother calmly resumed. 'He was asking me what I think.'

'Charlie and I are supposed to be a pair of officers, one always drunk and the other always sober,' Trader explained. 'The trouble is, we both want to be drunk.'

'I really don't know,' said Agnes, and forced a smile.

'Are you good at being drunk?' asked Mrs Lomond.

'Charlie's had much more practice,' he answered promptly.

'Perhaps you should take turns,' Mrs Lomond suggested. 'You could be drunk one night, he the next. Or is there to be only a single performance?'

'What a good idea,' said Trader. 'Why didn't we think of that? There will be two performances, by the way.'

And so they continued, as tea was served, and Agnes pretended to listen.

She understood. He'd known he must show her his eye. He couldn't hide it from her until they were married. But why did he have to wait so long?

Because he hoped that if he waited, she'd come to know him first, come to love him for himself, so that she wouldn't mind the eye. He'd waited in hope that she would love him. Damn him. If only she had loved him, it would all have been all right.

When Colonel Lomond joined them, Trader remarked to him apologetically that he'd showed the ladies his eye. 'Bit of a mess, I'm afraid, sir.'

'Let's have a look,' said the colonel, as if it were a bee sting. So Trader lifted the eye patch again. 'It's healed, I see,' Lomond remarked. 'Won't give you any trouble now. I shouldn't give it a thought, if I were you.'

After Trader had gone, and Agnes and her mother were alone, Mrs Lomond gave her a nod of approval. 'You did very well, Agnes,' she said. 'I was proud of you.'

'Mother, I can't!' her daughter suddenly cried. 'That awful hole where his eye should be. I had no idea. It's hideous.'

For a moment Mrs Lomond was silent. 'You must,' she said firmly. 'It's not so important. And you certainly won't think about it after you've been married a while.'

'How can you say that?' Agnes wailed.

'My child, I'm sorry to say this, but it's time that you grew up. When you marry someone, you commit to love them, honour and cherish them. We love our husbands for their character, including their faults. I don't mean great wickednesses, but the small faults we all have. And we love each other in body as well as soul. And the body isn't perfect, either, but we love it because we love the person. You're really quite fortunate. John Trader is a very handsome man. He has one blemish. Not a very large one, I may say, as these things go.' She paused. 'So you must love that blemish, too. For his sake. That is your gift to him. By doing that, you'll earn his love and his gratitude. It will actually be a bond. If you can't, you will have an unhappy husband. And then you will be unhappy, too. And in my opinion, you won't deserve to be happy.'

A silence fell between them.

'Mother, I don't think I can,' said Agnes finally. She thought, and slowly shook her head. 'It's so . . .' She stopped. 'I don't want him to touch me . . .' she blurted out.

'You've had a shock,' said Mrs Lomond calmly. 'Just wait a few days, take time to get used to the idea, and I promise you it won't seem so terrible after a little while. If you truly cannot get over it, then perhaps you shouldn't marry. It's not fair to him, apart from anything else. But I advise you to consider very carefully. You may not get a better offer. Or any offer.'

'I don't know what to do.'

'For a start,' said her mother frankly, 'you might think about him, instead of yourself.'

'That's easy to say.'

'My child, you've been brought up a Christian. If you were to talk to the vicar about this, I'm sure he'd tell you to pray, and he'd be right. So I suggest you think about what sort of wife you want to be, and then say your prayers.' She gave her daughter a look of admonishment. 'I don't want to hear anything more about this today.'

Agnes went into the house in great unhappiness. Before retiring to her bedroom, however, she passed the door of the library, where her father was writing a letter. And thinking she might get some support from that quarter, she knocked and entered. 'Papa.'

'Yes?' He looked up.

'I know you've always had your doubts about Trader.'

'I'm getting used to him.' He gave her a shrewd look. 'Why?'

'I'm not sure I want to marry him.'

'I see.' He laid down his pen. 'Is it something he's done?'

'No, Papa.'

'Might this have anything to do with his eye?'

'Yes. I can't . . .'

'Can't what?'

'I can't bear the sight of it . . . I can't . . . Oh, Papa . . .' She looked at him beseechingly.

But her father had had enough. 'Am I to understand,' he began quietly, 'that a daughter of mine' – his voice began to rise – 'wants to reject a very fair offer of marriage' – he drew breath before continuing his crescendo – 'just because her future husband happened to lose an eye? Do you suppose,' he fairly shouted, 'if I'd been wounded in action when you were a little girl, lost a limb even, that your dear mother would have taken one look, upped sticks, and bolted? Well?' he roared. 'Do you?' He banged his fist on the table so hard that the pen jumped up as though to stand at attention. And in a voice that might have been heard in the Himalayas along the horizon, he bellowed, 'How dare you, miss? Who the devil do you think you are?'

And greatly frightened, Agnes fled; she threw herself on her bed and wept. And later, as her mother said she should, she tried to pray. And the nights following.

NEMESIS

June 1840

Shi-Rong read his aunt's letter again. There could be no mistaking its meaning.

> Your father wishes me to tell you that he is well. Since he has an indisposition at present, he has asked me to write this letter for him. We are none of us getting any younger, of course. Please come to see us when Commissioner Lin can spare you. I am to say that it is your dutiful service to the emperor and the lord Lin that gives your father his greatest pride and joy.

His father was sinking. Perhaps not fast, but evidently he was too weak to write for himself. His aunt wanted him to come home to bid the old man farewell. His father wouldn't hear of it. And the message the old man had sent was not to remind him of his duty. It was to absolve him. To tell him not to reproach himself if he could not come, for his father would rather he stayed where he was and served the emperor, as his father had always told him to do.

It was correct. But it was also kindly.

He was doubly glad that he'd sent his father a letter just a week ago, full of good news.

For Lin was more pleased with him than ever. His dragon boats had been notably successful. Just recently, they'd intercepted some British longboats on an illegal patrol, out in the gulf. The barbarians had been routed and their leader, an officer named Churchill, apparently from one of their noble families, had been killed.

Might he go to see his father now? He longed to do so. How would Lin take it if he asked? He was just pondering this question when a messenger arrived.

The fellow was trembling. He thrust a report into Shi-Rong's hand. And a minute later Shi-Rong was hurrying to the lord Lin's chamber.

The great man received the report with complete calm.

'You say a fleet of twenty-seven British warships has arrived at Macao? And you believe they have come to blockade us or to attack Guangzhou?'

'Yes, Excellency.'

'These pirate ships may be powerful on the open sea,' Lin remarked, 'but they can't come upriver. Between the sandbanks and the shore forts, they'd all be destroyed. As for blockading us, what would be the point? The reason the barbarians are here is to sell their accursed opium. We know this. Doesn't it occur to you that these ships with guns may also be carrying opium?'

'They could be, I suppose.'

'It may be,' the commissioner continued imperturbably, 'that they will try to smuggle opium in longboats from their ships. But your own dragon boats, my dear Jiang, have shown how easily we can deal with that sort of thing.'

All the same, having experienced the power of British naval gunnery, Shi-Rong wasn't so optimistic. He'd seen what two British warships could do. What kind of havoc would be wreaked by twenty-seven?

'What shall we do then, Excellency?' he asked.

'Nothing,' said Lin. 'Wait.'

The next day the great man was proved correct.

It was mid-afternoon, the Hour of the Monkey, when the fellow from Macao appeared. He was one of the most reliable of the small network of spies Shi-Rong still had on that island. Having questioned the man carefully, Shi-Rong went straight to Lin.

'You were right, Excellency. It seems that Elliot is intending to sail northwards with the warships, up the coast to the island of Chusan. Then they're going to blockade all the shipping to the mouth of the Yangtze River. They could even interrupt the grain supplies up the Grand Canal to the capital.'

'I doubt that is their purpose. The British are ruled by greed, and their only aim is to sell opium.' Lin gazed at Shi-Rong calmly. 'Why is the rich island of Chusan famous for its fine houses and beautiful temples, Jiang? Because the corrupt mandarins on Chusan have never turned down a bribe from the opium smugglers. That's where their money comes from.'

'All the same, since the British ships have so many guns, Excellency, the emperor may want to tell Chusan to prepare,' Shi-Rong suggested. 'He might want to send reinforcements.'

Lin reflected. 'I doubt there'd be time,' he murmured. 'But I shall write to the emperor tonight,' he added, 'and you may see the letter.'

It was the Hour of the Rat, the last hour before midnight, when Lin finally sent for him.

'Kindly read what I have written to the emperor.'

Naturally, the letter followed all the proper forms. Lin referred to himself as 'your slave', 'respectfully beseeching' his ruler's attention. Yet behind these verbal kowtows, Shi-Rong couldn't help noticing, the commissioner's tone was almost smug. Since the barbarians knew they had no hope of fighting their way to Guangzhou, he explained, and that any attempts at smuggling would be thwarted, they seemed to be going northward towards Chusan – presumably in hopes of selling their opium. If the authorities up the coast were equally vigilant, Lin suggested, with a trace of irony, the barbarian smugglers would have no luck there, either.

'And if the barbarians succeed in selling their opium at Chusan?' Shi-Rong asked.

'Perhaps the emperor will send me to investigate the officials at Chusan. There is one honest and worthy man up there: my friend the prefect of Zhenhai. It's a small port on the coast near Chusan. But the rest are criminals.'

'I am still concerned about the British warships, Excellency,' Shi-Rong persisted. 'They could easily destroy any fleet of war junks they encounter and even enter the ports. Shouldn't we warn the emperor more forcefully about this?'

'If the defences of Chusan are inadequate,' said Lin grimly, 'and if they get a bloody nose, that's their problem. Let them explain it to the emperor.'

'I'll arrange for your letter to go by the express messenger, Excellency,' Shi-Rong said.

'No need. Use the ordinary messenger.' Lin smiled blandly. 'As long as it's on record that we informed the emperor.'

In the morning, however, Lin had one further instruction. 'Write unofficially to my friend, the prefect of Zhenhai. Warn him about the warships. And ask him to send word of what's happening up there. It's always good to have information.'

Shi-Rong sent the letter that morning by a private messenger, hoping it would reach its destination quickly.

Over a month passed without any news. Shi-Rong wondered whether to ask Lin if he might visit his father, but decided against it. Still no word came. Finally, in August, a letter arrived from the prefect of Zhenhai.

The news was worse than he could have imagined. He rushed to Lin. 'The British didn't sell opium. They bombarded Chusan. They destroyed the defences in less than an hour. The whole island is theirs.'

'Impossible. There are hundreds of thousands of people in Chusan.'

'They all ran. But there's more, Excellency. Elliot has a letter, from their minister Palmerston to the emperor himself.'

'What impertinence! What's in this letter?'

'Outrageous demands, Excellency. The British want to trade freely with half a dozen ports; their ambassadors are to be treated as though their queen were the equal of the emperor. They demand the island of Hong Kong as their own possession. They say that you have used them very ill and demand compensation for all the opium they say you destroyed. The prefect of Zhenhai writes that they refuse to give back the island of Chusan until all their demands have been met.'

'I can't believe this. Do these pirates imagine they can turn the whole world upside down?'

'The prefect of Zhenhai says they delivered this letter to him, but that it was so outrageous that he refused to forward it to the emperor and gave it back to them.'

'Quite right. What followed?'

'Elliot is continuing northwards. To Beijing itself.'

At this astounding news, Commissioner Lin fell silent, and remained so for some time. 'Then I am destroyed,' he said at last. 'Leave me alone, Mr Jiang.'

Shi-Rong did not see his master until the following night, when he was summoned to join the great man for his evening meal.

'You will wonder why I spoke as I did last night,' Lin began. 'You no doubt think that the emperor will censure me for not warning him sufficiently by express messenger about the strength of the barbarians, and that he will blame me for Chusan.'

'I fear so, Excellency.'

Lin smiled grimly. 'But in fact you are wrong. The emperor does not care about Chusan.'

'Does not care . . . ?' Shi-Rong asked in astonishment.

'Consider the vast size of the territories over which the emperor reigns,' Lin explained. 'Even if he went out every year to inspect his empire for himself, he could never see it all, not in a lifetime. And if there is trouble in a distant province, the empire can always absorb the shock. It can be dealt with at leisure. Sometimes the trouble just goes away.'

'And Chusan?'

'The business of Chusan is shocking. But even Chusan is still a thousand miles away from Beijing. The men in charge there will be dismissed. They may be executed. Then someone will be sent to sort it out. The empire will carry on.'

'But if the trouble gets too close to Beijing . . . ?'

'A totally different matter. The emperor loses face. That cannot be tolerated. The barbarians must be removed at once, whatever the cost. For that, the emperor would sacrifice me, if necessary.'

'But you did everything that the emperor wished in Guangzhou.'

'True. But the barbarians' letter says that they have come because I mistreated them. If sacrificing me will cause them to go away, then the emperor must sacrifice me. And I accept that. It is necessary.'

'I cannot believe the emperor would be so unfair.'

'There is one other factor against me. If the emperor receives Elliot's letter, it will be from the hands of the governor of the Beijing coastal region, to whom Elliot will surely give it next. Do you know that governor?'

'I know he is a Manchu noble.'

'A marquis, to be precise. His ancestors were Mongol – he claims descent from Genghis Khan – and they were given their title a few centuries ago when they joined the Manchu. The marquis was eased through the examinations, like many Manchu nobles. Then he got accelerated promotion. Undereducated and overpromoted, I'm afraid. Some years ago, conducting an investigation, I was obliged to censure him to the emperor – a fact he has not forgotten.'

'So he'll try to get his revenge.'

'I fear he'll succeed. He may be incompetent, but he's cunning.'

'Isn't there anything we can do, Excellency?'

'Not much,' said Lin. He smiled sadly. 'I'll try to save you, Jiang,' he added, 'if I can.'

o

A red December sun hung over the evening water when Nio, standing in the stern of the dragon boat, was rowed towards the big British warship anchored in the Roads of Macao. He was wearing a Chinese archer's hat with a peacock feather stuck in it, which made him easily recognisable to his British merchant friends. Nio the smuggler was a useful fellow. But he wasn't smuggling today.

Nearly six months had passed since the British naval fleet had set off for Chusan in June. Now the British warships were back again. And that was good for him.

As Nio saw it, the only way he could make money now would be if the British could restore the opium trade. Other watermen might have hired themselves out to work for Shi-Rong one day and a British opium merchant the next. But since he'd walked out on the young mandarin – and especially since the day when Shi-Rong had chased him and nearly caught him – Nio had been under no illusion about his choices. There was only one way for him to go at present – the British way.

And today he was going to do more for the British than he had ever done before. He was about to have a private meeting with Elliot himself.

When they reached the British ship, his boat pulled alongside, a rope ladder was thrown down, and Nio went up alone. He was immediately conducted to a large panelled cabin where several men, mostly in naval uniform, were sitting on one side of a long table. In the centre of the men he recognised the tall figure of Elliot. At one end of the table sat a young man in a tight-fitting dark coat and white neckband – a missionary, no doubt, to act as interpreter. For although Nio had picked up some pidgin English by now, the occasion was too important and too formal for that.

They offered him a chair. Elliot smiled, to put him at his ease, then turned to the young missionary: 'Mr Whiteparish, if you please.'

'You are known to us as a reliable person,' Whiteparish began. 'We understand that you worked for Commissioner Lin last year, and that you may have information that could interest us.' His Cantonese was far from perfect, but it was clear enough. 'If we are satisfied with your answers, you will be paid twenty silver dollars. Do you accept?'

'I do.' When he worked for Shi-Rong, Nio had been paid the same as the men employed in the patrol boats: six dollars a month. Twenty dollars was a lot of money for a single day's work.

'Firstly, then, we had understood that Commissioner Lin was dismissed by the emperor in October, and that his place would be taken by the marquis, with whom we have been negotiating in the north. The marquis arrived here ten days ago. Yet we hear that Lin is still in Guangzhou. Do you know if this is true?'

'Certainly.' Anyone in Guangzhou could have answered this. 'Lin received word he was dismissed in mid-October. He packed up his household and vacated his quarters. But then he was told he should stay, to serve the marquis who was taking his place. So Lin took up quarters in the guildhall of the salt merchants. He's still there. The marquis has been to see him, but otherwise Lin keeps himself to himself.'

'What do you know about the patrol boats?'

'I worked for Mr Jiang, the official who organised them.'

'The marquis has told us that, as a sign of good faith, he is disbanding the patrols. Are they being disbanded?'

'They are,' said Nio firmly.

Elliot said something to the missionary, and Whiteparish turned to Nio again. 'What do you know about the shore forts and their defenders?'

'I was present when Mr Jiang and Commissioner Lin inspected them. I saw everything.'

When Whiteparish translated that, the officers at the table all leaned forward keenly. 'Tell us about the defenders.'

'They are the best troops the emperor has. Manchu bannermen, highly trained. Half of them are archers. The others are musketeers.'

'Did you see the musketeers drill? What can you tell us?'

'They are well trained.' Nio hesitated. 'It seemed rather slow . . .'

'Describe the drill as exactly as you can.'

That was easy enough. His memory of that day up at the fort was vivid. He could give them pretty much the entire drill. As Whiteparish translated, Nio heard one of the naval officers exclaim, 'Good

God! Matchlocks. Even the best Manchu bannermen – they're still using matchlocks!'

They asked him more questions: Did the granite forts have roofs? Could they be approached from the landward side? They asked for other details, all of which he was able to answer well enough. They seemed pleased, even delighted. Then came questions about the guns. How many were there in the battery he saw? Were the guns old or new? Did they work? Had he seen them fire?

To all of these, he was able to give accurate answers. The questions came to an end. At a nod from Elliot, one of the officers handed him the silver dollars. Whiteparish expressed their thanks. Nio rose and bowed.

And then he sat down again. 'There is something else I could tell you,' he said calmly.

'What is that?'

'If it is useful information, will you give me another twenty dollars?'

'Bloody cheek!' exclaimed one of the officers. But Elliot motioned him to be silent and nodded to Whiteparish. 'If the information is good,' said the missionary.

'I noticed something about the cannon. I asked the gunners about it, and they said it didn't matter. But I am a smuggler, and I was imagining how I would get past the battery if it was firing at me. I think I could easily do so.'

'Why?'

'Because the guns are all fixed. They cannot be pointed up or down or from side to side. They can only fire directly in front of them, always at the same place.'

Elliot stared at him in disbelief. So did all the officers.

'Are you certain of this?' asked Whiteparish.

'I swear it.'

There was a short silence.

'We could test it,' somebody said.

'If you have lied,' said Whiteparish, 'we shall find out and be very angry.'

'If you assault the fort,' said Nio calmly, 'take me with you. If I lied, shoot me. If I told the truth, give me a third twenty dollars.'

Even the officer who had been angry laughed this time.

'We may do just that,' Whiteparish translated.

But they gave him the second twenty dollars.

o

If Shi-Rong had respected his master when the commissioner was in favour, his admiration became even greater when Lin fell. While he was noble in office, nothing showed the man's dignity more than his manner of leaving it. Having shifted his quarters into the handsome merchants' guildhall, where Shi-Rong was honoured to join him, Lin quietly occupied his time practising his calligraphy, engaging in correspondence with local scholars and writing to his friends in Beijing and other places.

Shi-Rong was glad to join his master in some of these pleasant literary exercises while they both awaited the arrival of the marquis.

'I'd send you home to visit your father,' Lin told him, 'but it's better for you to stay. I have already mentioned to friends in Beijing the good work you've done for me. I can promise you nothing, of course, but if any offers of employment should arise, you'll need to be here on hand.'

So the rest of October passed and most of November.

'The marquis is taking his time to get here,' Shi-Rong once remarked.

'Perhaps we should be glad,' answered Lin.

When the marquis finally did arrive, late in November, he went straight to the governor's house and installed himself there. Though numerous people were summoned for an interview, he didn't ask for Lin at all, making no attempt to see him.

Lin understood at once. 'He's investigating me. Calling witnesses. Gathering evidence. When that's done, he'll interview me. Standard procedure. Then he'll write his report and send it to the emperor.'

'What do we do after that?'

'The marquis will be very busy. He's got to deal with the British. As for me, I wait here and give the marquis any help he wants, as the emperor commanded. In due course, the emperor will decide whether to recall me to Beijing or send me into exile. Or execute me.'

And what, Shi-Rong wondered, in that last event, would happen to him?

The marquis appeared one afternoon without warning. He and Lin were closeted together for over an hour. Then, to Shi-Rong's surprise, they sent for him.

'This is young Mr Jiang,' Lin said easily as Shi-Rong made his lowest bow. 'He's studied the locality, understands Cantonese, and he's the most efficient secretary I've ever had.' He turned to Shi-Rong. 'The marquis needs a secretary who knows the terrain here. You're the obvious choice. You will serve him as you have served me, and do your duty to the emperor.'

The marquis was watching him carefully. He had high Mongol cheekbones, no doubt like those of Genghis Khan, and his eyes were cunning. But there, Shi-Rong guessed, any likeness to his all-conquering ancestor ended. His face was soft. He was running to fat. He looked like a man who lived well and whose principal plan was to keep doing so.

'I represent the emperor here now. You must serve me without question.' His voice was gentle, but Shi-Rong didn't like to think what might happen to him if he disobeyed. 'You will report to me this evening.'

Shi-Rong bowed, and the marquis departed.

As he went to prepare for his removal to the governor's house, Lin told him: 'Leave some of your things here. That will give you a good excuse for coming to see me.' And when, an hour later, Shi-Rong presented himself to bid a temporary farewell to his master, Lin gave him some final instructions.

'You must make yourself useful to the marquis – more than that, indispensable. You must do everything he wishes without question. Make sure he is informed about the local conditions before he takes any action. You may even give him your honest advice, if he asks for it. But be careful. If I am sent away, or worse, he will be the key to your survival and your future career. This is my gift to you.'

'I owe you my life, Excellency.'

'It would appear, my dear Jiang, that I have lost my game with the marquis. But the game may not be over yet. Therefore I ask you to do one more thing for me.'

'Anything, Excellency. Consider it done.'

'Report to me, daily if possible. Tell me everything the marquis does.'

The first thing the marquis had done, the very next morning, was to disband Shi-Rong's patrols. He made Shi-Rong do it himself. It took two days for Shi-Rong to complete the task. The crew were not happy. Each man was losing six dollars a month. Shi-Rong himself was horrified.

But when he looked in on Lin to give him the news, his former master was delighted. 'Splendid, my dear Jiang. He weakens our defences. I shall put this knowledge to good use.'

The next day was worse.

'My report on former governor Lin is complete,' the marquis announced briskly as soon as Shi-Rong appeared. 'But it needs to be organised and written up more elegantly. You have until tonight. Then it will be sent to the emperor by the express courier.'

All day, therefore, Shi-Rong laboured at this miserable task. Was he helping to compose his mentor's death warrant? Dare he alter any of it, soften a word here or there, point out that Lin was, in fact, following the emperor's instructions? And what if it were discovered that he was the one responsible for such an impertinence? There were terrible stories of former emperors executing officials who submitted unwelcome reports. One of the Ming emperors had sawn a man in half for doing so.

It was just as well that he did not tamper with it, for at the end of the afternoon the marquis insisted upon reading the whole report in front of him. Apparently satisfied, he dismissed Shi-Rong for the evening.

But what should he do about informing Lin? His old master would surely want to know exactly what the charges against him were. He wondered whether to go to Lin's lodgings under cover of darkness, but there were always people about in the salt merchants' guildhall who'd see him. Even if the marquis wasn't having him followed, he'd probably hear of the visit and guess. There was nothing to do but wait for a better opportunity.

So he was quite astonished the next morning when the marquis received him kindly, told him to sit down and remarked: 'These must have been disagreeable tasks for you, Jiang.'

Shi-Rong hesitated, saw the shrewdness in the Mongol nobleman's eyes, and decided it was wiser to tell the truth. 'Yes, Excellency.'

'And have you informed Lin of the contents of my report?'

'No, Excellency. I have not.'

'Not yet. But you will. You are aware, however, that apart from the charge that he mishandled the British, which led to all this trouble – a charge he knows all about anyway – I have accused him of nothing else. His honesty and efficiency are not questioned.'

'I noticed, and I am glad of that, Excellency.'

'Make a copy of the report and give it to Lin, when you next see him. With my compliments.'

'Excellency.' Shi-Rong, astonished, rose and bowed low.

'You must be furious about the patrol boats,' the marquis remarked cheerfully.

'You are aware that I built the patrols up, Excellency. It would be foolish to deny that it was painful for me to disband them.'

'An honest answer.' The marquis nodded. 'And you probably think it's a bad idea.'

'I'm sure Your Excellency did it for a reason.'

'I did. Sit down again.' The marquis gazed at him thoughtfully. 'The emperor's immediate object has been to remove the British barbarians from the vicinity of Beijing. After that, we must persuade them to give back the island of Chusan.' He paused a moment. 'So ask yourself: How can we do it? I'm sure you know the ancient tactic known as loose rein.'

'If destroying your adversary is difficult, soothe him instead.'

'We have been using it for two thousand years, ever since the Han dynasty. It's the same technique used to tame a wild animal. Control the barbarians with kindness. Give in to some of their demands, and make them want to be our friends. This is not weakness. It merely requires two qualities that the barbarians seldom possess: patience and intelligence.'

'Your strategy is to coax them to do what we want.'

'Lin affronted the British. We remove the affront. We've already persuaded them to sail most of their warships back to the gulf here. Your dragon boats harassed them, so we've removed the dragon boats, too. Soon we'll offer them more concessions, in return for their vacating Chusan. They won't get everything they want, of course, but they need to trade, and this operation is costing them money.' The marquis smiled. 'Accommodation will be reached.'

A day later, the marquis had offered the British five million dollars for the opium they lost. A week after that, the marquis told Elliot: 'Your queen will be recognised as a sovereign equal in status to the emperor, and her representatives treated as such.' And when Elliot demanded to be given Hong Kong, the marquis mildly stated: 'I can't promise that at this moment. But as our kingdoms become better friends, I could see the emperor giving it to you in the future. What he won't do is give it to you while you occupy Chusan. You must admit, that wouldn't be reasonable.'

All these things Shi-Rong discreetly reported to Lin. But one thing puzzled him, and finally he ventured to ask the marquis: 'Are you sure, Excellency, that the emperor will actually grant the British these concessions?'

'The art of being a negotiator is not only to persuade your adversary to see your master's point of view,' the marquis explained. 'It may also be to persuade your master to be reasonable. If I can show both sides that progress is being made, I can broker an agreement.'

'And if not?'

'The policy of loose rein can lead to two outcomes. One may convert the adversary to sweet reason. But failing that, we lull them into a sense of security, and when their guard is down, we strike.'

'So the emperor expects you to convert the British or . . .'

'Destroy them.'

'Can we do so, Excellency?'

'Patience, Jiang,' the marquis said. 'Patience.'

The following morning they prepared a memorandum to the emperor to bring him up to date with the British talks. 'They've really nowhere to go,' the marquis cheerfully wrote to the emperor. 'A concession or two from us, and we shall wear them down.'

The next afternoon, a curt note came from Elliot. He had waited long enough. British trading must be allowed to resume at once, and he wanted several ports opened to them up the coast as well.

'What shall we do?' asked Shi-Rong.

The marquis smiled. 'There is nothing better to engender good feeling than a banquet,' he replied. 'Send him word that I should like to discuss matters very soon, and I am making preparations for a feast we can all enjoy.'

But days went by, and Elliot did not reply.

At first they didn't see the *Nemesis*. It was hidden behind some sailing ships. Shi-Rong was standing beside old Admiral Guan, on a small hill just upriver, from which they had an excellent view of the first two forts between which the British ships must pass.

Shi-Rong glanced up at the admiral's face. How splendid the old man was. Even the British sailors admired Guan, he'd heard, for his gallantry. 'Some of our local peasants think the admiral's descended from the Chinese war god,' he'd told the marquis. 'He looks the part,' the marquis had agreed.

The marquis had been taken aback, a week into January 1841 as the barbarians reckoned it, when Elliot, having lost patience, had suddenly appeared with his fleet and made straight for the mouth of the Pearl River.

But by the time Shi-Rong asked if he might go to join the admiral to see the action, the new governor had quite recovered himself. 'The pirates can do nothing against the forts,' he said. 'The admiral's battle plan is excellent. The British will be begging for terms by tomorrow.'

Now, looking through his brass telescope at the approaching British ships, Shi-Rong remarked to the admiral: 'You have prepared a trap for them.'

'I try to learn from my mistakes,' Guan replied. 'So tell me what I've done.'

'In the first place, you've run a big chain under the water, at the upstream end of the forts. The British won't be able to see it, but it'll catch them while our battery cannon pound them to bits.'

'Good. What else?'

'You've kept a fleet of war junks up here. But I imagine they're out of range of the British guns.'

'A tempting target, if the British could come close enough. But they can't.'

'Why is that?'

'Shallows. Even if the British finally get past the chain and head towards my ships, they'll enter shallow water, and there they will run aground.'

'Clever.' And Shi-Rong was just thinking how lucky he was to be there when he saw something strange. Two of the leading British ships were peeling apart to reveal, astern of them, a vessel unlike any other he had seen. It had a funnel belching smoke of some kind where the central mast should have been. On either side of the ship were huge paddle wheels. And strangest of all, the entire vessel appeared to be made of iron. 'What in the world is that?' he cried, and handed his spyglass to the admiral.

Guan gazed through the telescope in silence. 'I don't know,' he said at last.

This was the *Nemesis*.

The iron ship didn't make the first move, but one of the two warships in front of it did. Sailing into the entrance of the river, it passed in front of the guns of the nearest fort. At once a cannon roared. Then another, then a third. The first two cannonballs fell just short; the third clipped her rigging. She took no notice at all. Again and again the Chinese cannon fired.

Most of the shots now went over the British vessel. Just before reaching the hidden chain, having established the range of the fixed Chinese cannon, and as if to say, 'Thank you very much,' the ship neatly put about.

'I think the British must know about the chain,' said Shi-Rong.

This was hardly surprising. There were at least a hundred unemployed watermen in the gulf who would gladly have told them for a silver dollar.

Now the other wooden warship took up a safe position farther downstream and fired a trial shot. 'It's shooting at the fort!' the admiral exclaimed in astonishment.

The first ship also fired a trial shot. Both, from their different angles, were aimed at one corner of the battery's granite wall. At their second attempt, the gunners of both ships found their mark. The granite wall was not breached, but Shi-Rong could see that it was damaged.

And then the bombardment began. Steadily, taking their time, with well-trained accuracy, the British smashed the gun embrasures one by one. Other ships, including the iron *Nemesis,* joined in. More than once – Shi-Rong wasn't sure from which ship they came – mortar shells were lobbed over the walls into the battery, where they exploded with devastating effect.

'I didn't know they'd do this,' Admiral Guan said humbly. Shi-Rong could see there were tears in his eyes. But there was nothing the admiral could do. Not now.

Nor was there anything Guan could do when boatloads of British marines pulled rapidly ashore, ran around the sides of the forts, and fell upon their defenders from above. It was a massacre.

They destroyed the fort on the opposite side of the big river in the same way. Then they smashed the pilings that held the great chain across the river and began to move upstream towards the war junks.

'They cannot reach them,' the admiral cried out. 'They cannot!' And he would have been right – if all the British ships were made of wood.

But now, as Shi-Rong watched in horror, the *Nemesis* came into her own. Like a metal monster from another world – a world of iron gods, where even the winds that filled the sails of ships counted for nothing – the *Nemesis* could ignore the riverbed, too. For the iron ship's draught was so shallow that it passed clean over the underwater sandbanks as it headed straight for the war junks moored helplessly ahead.

And then, like a dragon breathing flame, it sent out a thunderbolt.

Neither Shi-Rong nor the admiral had even seen a Congreve rocket.

They had no idea such a thing existed: a rocket carrying explosives. When a Congreve rocket hit its target, it produced an explosion that made the most powerful mortar shell look like a firecracker. And fate had decided that the first rocket the *Nemesis* fired that day should find the war junk's magazine.

The shock of the explosion was so great that even standing on their vantage point onshore, Shi-Rong and the admiral were literally blown off their feet. When the smoke cleared, there was nothing left to see of the war junk or its crew. Hull, masts and men were all gone, atomised. In the place where they had been, there was just a gap.

And it was while Shi-Rong was staring openmouthed at this vision from a new world that two runners came racing across the hillside towards him.

'Mr Jiang,' one of them called. 'You're to come with us to Beijing at once.'

'Beijing? What do you mean? Who says so?'

'The emperor.'

'The emperor? Why? Are you sure? I'll have to prepare.'

'You do not understand,' one of the men cried. 'The emperor wants you at once. You're to leave with us right now. Immediately!'

When Genghis Khan had designed the imperial postal service that his heirs had brought to China, his edicts were carried across the vast empty plains of Eurasia by Mongol messengers. The toughest horsemen who ever lived, they rode night and day without stopping, their bodies tightly bound in cloth to hold them in one piece, throwing themselves onto fresh horses at each staging post, often riding several days without sleeping, before handing over their letter to the next rider in the great relay.

In the southern parts of China, these arrangements had been modified to suit the terrain. Through the lush valleys of rice paddies and in the mountain passes, runners might carry the emperor's letters. But the principle was the same.

And Shi-Rong was to be treated like a piece of urgent mail.

At first, when he left Guangzhou, swift runners carried him in a bamboo litter. That wasn't so bad, except that at each staging post, where new runners were provided, the litter did not rest for longer than it took Shi-Rong to attend to the calls of nature. If he was given a little food, he had to eat it on the road. Day and night he travelled, sleeping as best he could in the litter while it swayed and jerked its way along. Soon he was wretchedly stiff and short of sleep.

And cold. For the mild January weather of the southern Gulf of Canton was a world away from the bitter cold of the northern plains into which they were travelling. After three days winter clothes were found for him at one of the staging posts. With relief, he put on soft fur-trimmed leather boots, a long, padded Manchu coat and a thick felt Manchu hat. Initially these kept out the cold. But a damp snow was falling as they went through the mountain passes, and the snow seemed to cling to him, waiting to seep into any tiny crevice it could find.

It was after they'd crossed into China's northern plains, however, that his torture really began. For now he was expected to ride.

The temperature was now below freezing. The breeze cut into his face like a knife. The ground was hard as iron. The horizon seemed endless. And the Mongol horsemen expected him to keep up with them.

He'd been used to riding since he was a boy. But not long journeys like this. Mongol horsemen covered a hundred and fifty miles in a day. They told him he was slowing them down. By the end of the first day he was badly saddle-sore.

The next day he was in agony and bleeding, and so tired that he twice fell off his horse. When he complained at the next staging post, the official in charge told him: 'We were ordered to bring you with all possible speed.'

'Did they say,' he asked, 'that they wanted me alive?'

He was allowed to sleep for three hours, and when he awoke, he found they had rigged up a sort of hammock for him between two packhorses, into which he was strapped and covered with blankets. This way the couriers could continue their journey day and night, transferring his hammock to fresh horses at the staging posts, and he could sleep or not as he liked.

Finally, after thirteen days of ceaseless travel, haggard, bruised, sore in every joint, with a vicious rash that made him wince when he sat, Shi-Rong saw the mighty walls and towers of Beijing ahead in the distance and knew that this part of his ordeal was about to end.

But what new ordeal lay ahead of him? That was the question. For he still did not know why he was here.

They took him to an official guesthouse just outside the Forbidden City. He was allowed to bathe, was given clean clothes and was fed. The mandarin in charge was polite, but Shi-Rong noticed that there was a guard at the outer gate of the house. Whether he would have been stopped if he tried to go for a walk, he didn't try to find out. He was told that someone from the palace would come to prepare him in the morning. In the meantime, he'd better get some sleep.

And he was about to turn in when his door opened and, to his great surprise, he found himself face-to-face with old Mr Wen, his former tutor. 'Mr Wen! Master.' Shi-Rong bowed low to the old scholar. 'This is such an honour. But how did you know I was here? Or that I was coming?'

'We have all been expecting you,' said Mr Wen.

'We?'

'The lord Lin has many friends and admirers in Beijing. I am proud to be one of them. You do not know why you are here?'

'I know the emperor sent for me, honoured teacher. But I don't know why.'

'Let me explain, then. Ever since he was dismissed, the lord Lin has been writing to his friends here, especially myself. And we have busied ourselves in his cause. We know you have been working for the marquis and reporting to Lin, and that the marquis has been undoing all the good work that the lord Lin – and you yourself – had accomplished. And that the marquis has made promises to the British without authorisation. Frankly, some of us here even wonder if the barbarians are bribing him.'

'I don't think so, honoured teacher.'

'Be that as it may,' Mr Wen continued, 'it does no harm to the lord Lin's cause if such things are whispered.'

Shi-Rong frowned. He was quite surprised to discover the old scholar could stoop to this kind of deviousness. Mr Wen saw it, but was quite unabashed.

'Our words have reached the emperor. He likes the marquis, but he fears that he's misleading him. He wants to find out what is really going on with these barbarians down in Guangzhou. When the lord Lin wrote that you would be the perfect person to give the court an honest account of what is really happening, we were able to arrange that this suggestion was placed before the emperor.'

'I see.'

'You must be pleased to have the chance to repay the lord Lin for his many kindnesses to you.'

'Mr Wen, do you believe that Lin could be reinstated?'

'No. The emperor would lose face. But he could be saved punishment.'

'What am I to do?'

'Tell the truth. It's simple. The marquis has disobeyed the emperor, and he's running our defences down.' Mr Wen paused. 'On my way here,' he continued, 'I heard a rumour that we've just suffered a big defeat in Guangzhou. Do you know anything about that?'

'It's true.'

'There you are, then. This is the marquis's fault.'

'It may not be as simple as that,' said Shi-Rong wearily.

'Just remember where your loyalty lies,' said Mr Wen, and left.

A palace eunuch of about his own age came to collect him in the morning. He tut-tutted over Shi-Rong's condition, treated his saddle sores with ointment and dressed him in the correct court dress for his modest rank.

'Now you must listen very carefully,' he said, 'because etiquette is everything. It can mean success or failure. Even life or death. I am going to tell you everything you need to know – exactly how to enter the emperor's presence, how to kowtow to him, and how to speak to him.'

So Shi-Rong did his best to concentrate as the eunuch told him all that he must do. But the truth was that he heard only half of it.

Then the eunuch led him through huge red gold-studded gates into the Forbidden City, across its vast spaces, and into the golden-roofed palace in the sky where the Son of Heaven dwelt.

The private audience room wasn't nearly as big as he'd imagined, hardly larger than the central hall in his father's house. It contained a throne on which the emperor sat. Shi-Rong was conscious of several officials flanking the throne, but he wasn't sure how many, because his eyes were cast down.

As required, he knelt and bowed down, carefully touching his head on the floor three times. Having slowly risen to his feet, he knelt down and did the same thing again. Again he rose to his feet, and for the third time knelt and knocked his head on the ground three times more. This was the kowtow of the three kneelings and nine head knockings, the ultimate show of respect.

But having done this, he suddenly realised that he couldn't remember what he was supposed to do next. Was he supposed to rise? Or if not, should he look up at the emperor when he answered questions or keep his eyes on the floor? He knew that when the emperor travelled in his yellow carriage, no one was allowed to look at him, upon pain of death. So he decided to play it safe and remain prostrate, facing the floor, until they told him to do otherwise.

They didn't.

'Is it true that the marquis has told the barbarians we will pay them five million dollars for the opium confiscated by Commissioner Lin?' It was one of the officials who addressed him.

'This slave declares that it is true,' he answered respectfully.

'Why did you disband the patrol boats?' The same official.

'It was this slave who set up and organised the patrol boats for Governor Lin. Then I was ordered by the marquis to disband them.'

'Did he say why?'

'He told this slave that it was to show the barbarians that we could be their friends, not their enemies.'

'Did the marquis tell the barbarians that they could have access to other ports besides Guangzhou?'

'He indicated that it could be discussed.'

'Did he say they could have the island of Hong Kong?'

'This slave heard him say that such a thing could not even be discussed.'

'Are you certain?' This was a different, softer voice. It was the emperor, he was sure of it. Shi-Rong hesitated.

'Your slave heard him say that the request was out of the question, that it was against all reason, especially when the barbarians still occupied the island of Chusan.' He was so certain that this was the exact truth that, involuntarily, he gave a tiny nod.

'Not quite the same as a no, is it?' said the emperor. Again Shi-Rong hesitated. He was there to defend Lin, to whom he owed everything. But whatever faults the marquis possessed, he'd treated him well. Shi-Rong actually felt a little sorry for him. It seemed that the emperor sensed what was in his mind. 'You should say what is in your mind,' he continued.

'Your slave believes that the marquis's intention was to keep the barbarians talking. He wished to wear them down, either so they could reach an agreement or so that he could strike them when they did not expect it.' Again he gave a nod.

'That is all very well,' said the emperor, 'but isn't it true that the barbarians continued to insist on their demands?'

'It is true, Majesty.'

'What was the marquis planning to do next?'

'He told your slave that he was inviting them to a banquet.'

There was a silence. Then, presumably at a sign from the emperor, another official addressed him. 'There is a rumour that the barbarians have mounted a new attack. Is it true?'

'It is true.'

'It doesn't seem they wanted to come to the banquet, does it?' The emperor's voice, still soft, but dry.

'Can you tell us what happened?' asked the official.

'Yes. Your slave was present. The barbarians bombarded the two forts at the mouth of the river, then attacked with troops. The forts fell. After that, a strange ship made of iron went upriver a little way. Our war junks lay up there protected by sandbanks, but the iron ship went across the shallows and destroyed most of the war junks with cannon and other projectiles.'

'Perhaps this ship has some sort of armour on its sides. If it was made of iron, surely it wouldn't have floated.' The emperor's voice. 'I am surprised Admiral Guan gave in so easily.'

'Your slave asks permission to comment.'

'Do so.'

'The admiral is most valiant, Majesty. I have been under fire with him. This was not the admiral's fault. He was overwhelmed.'

Nobody said anything for a moment. Then another voice spoke. 'May I make a suggestion, Majesty? Admiral Guan's preparations were extensive. His courage is not in doubt. But it would seem that in his desire to appease the barbarians, the marquis has deliberately weakened our defences. Clearly, Admiral Guan has not been supported. I submit respectfully that it is time for a person with more martial spirit and moral resolution to support the admiral and to teach these pirates a lesson, once and for all.'

Whoever this man was, Shi-Rong thought, it was clear that he was used to speaking his mind before the emperor. What a fine thing it would be to have such a position. The man had even dared to speak up for Lin – for although he had not mentioned Lin by name, it was clear, when he spoke of the need for a man of moral resolution, that he had Lin in mind.

There was only one problem: he was wrong. Shi-Rong was sure of it.

Neither Admiral Guan nor Lin could have stopped the barbarian gunners, let alone the iron ship. Nobody who had witnessed the attack on the forts could fail to see this. The British had better weapons and greater skill. They'd had no difficulty in destroying the forts at all. They could do the same thing to all the forts up the river all the way to Guangzhou.

The emperor spoke. 'First Lin tells me the pirates can do nothing; then they take Chusan. Then the marquis tells me he will control them down in Guangzhou, and they smash his defences to bits.' His soft voice sounded plaintive. 'Does anyone tell the emperor the truth?' Nobody spoke. 'Have you told me the truth?'

It took Shi-Rong a moment to realise that the question was directed at him. He began to look up, then checked himself.

'Your slave has truthfully reported everything he saw and heard,' he said, keeping his eyes on the floor.

The emperor sounded sad. 'Well, I daresay you have. Is there anything else that I should know?'

Was there anything? Just the fact that neither he nor his advisers in the room had any understanding of the situation. The British warships were not a nuisance that could be swept away. Along the entire coastline of his empire, they were a force superior to his own. But did he dare say it?

He thought of Lin, whom he loved and whom he was here to defend. Could he tell the emperor that Lin's moral strength was irrelevant? He thought of the old admiral, whom he respected. Could he tell the emperor that the gallant old warrior was of no use to him? Above all, could he really say to the emperor's face that he and all his counsellors were labouring under a delusion?

'Your humble slave submits that Your Majesty has all the information known.' It was true, in its way.

A light touch on his shoulder told him that he should now withdraw.

Mr Wen came to visit within the hour. Evidently Lin's friends in the meeting had already talked to him. He seemed very happy. 'You made an excellent impression,' he cried. 'The case against Lin is looking much weaker now. And the wind is certainly blowing against the marquis.'

'And the admiral?'

'He'll be told to redeem himself. A small demotion until he does. They liked that you spoke out for him. They thought it courageous. Well done.'

'And what about me?' Shi-Rong asked. 'What happens to me? I work for the marquis, to whom I have to return. He isn't going to be so pleased to see me, is he?' He paused. 'Do you think Lin planned this all along – got me a job with the marquis, made me tell him everything the marquis did, and then wrote to you to suggest I be summoned to the emperor to give evidence?'

'If he did, he had every right. He was owed your loyal service.'

'I'm not complaining,' said Shi-Rong, 'but what shall I do?'

'First you will stay in my house for at least two weeks, because the journey here has made you ill.'

'Has it?'

'That is what I shall tell everyone. Then you will return to Guangzhou. Very slowly. It will take you at least two months. By the time you get there, I suspect that the marquis will be dismissed. If so, Lin and the rest of us will find you employment.' He smiled. 'While you recover in my house, you can study with me for your next exams. My servant Wong will be delighted to look after you again. It will be quite like old times.'

That evening Mr Wen gave Shi-Rong a herbal drink to make him sleep, and it was well into the next morning before he awoke.

There was a dusting of snow around noon that continued for a couple of hours. While it was snowing and Wong busied himself with the housekeeping, the two men played a game of Chinese chess. The old man was skilful in moving his chariots, Shi-Rong perhaps cleverer with his cannon; and though he lost an elephant early on, he was able to hold out until the snow had stopped before Mr Wen finally defeated him. Soon afterwards the sky cleared, and they stepped out into the small courtyard.

Mr Wen's courtyard had many happy memories for Shi-Rong. How often, in summer, they had sat out there, discussed the great poets and practised their calligraphy. Only one thing had changed since he'd gone away. In the north corner there now stood a curious pale stone, taller than a man. It was limestone, of the kind known as karst. Its twisted shape was naturally pierced with openings – some were holes that went clean through; others like curious cave entrances led to who knew what interior worlds within. 'They call them scholar stones, you know,' old Mr Wen said proudly.

'A very fine one, too,' Shi-Rong remarked. 'It must have cost you a fortune.'

'It was a gift.' Mr Wen smiled. 'A pupil of mine from years ago. He has risen quite high and become very rich. He brought it to me as a present, for starting him on his career. He said a wealthy merchant gave it to him. A bribe, I expect.'

'It was good that he showed gratitude.'

'Yes. He might find a job for you, come to think of it.'

The sun was still shining. The sky was crystalline blue. They put on snow boots and went for a walk, just as far as the Tiananmen Gate. The sun was gleaming on the high tiled roofs; the huge snow-covered space was shining white; the red gates looked so cheerful. Not for nothing was it called the Gate of Heavenly Peace.

'There'll be a full moon tonight,' said Mr Wen.

Shi-Rong had already retired to his room before the moon appeared over the courtyard wall. Despite the cold, he opened the door and stood there for some time as it mounted into the clear night sky. In the courtyard the scholar stone gleamed, bone-white in the moonlight, its cavities like sockets in a skull. Whether the stone was friendly or not he couldn't decide, but the silence at least was peaceful. Finally, made sleepy by the cold, he closed the door and lay down on his bed.

It was nearly midnight when the dream began. He was standing just inside the door of his room. Opening it, he looked into the courtyard. Everything seemed to be just as before. Yet he had a feeling that he had heard a sound, very faint, like an echo, though what it was he could not tell.

Then, looking at the moonlit scholar stone, he saw it was his father.

How pale he was, how thin and drawn his face, as though the flesh was already retreating from the bone. But it was his eyes that were truly terrible. For they stared at him with an anger he had never seen before. 'What have you done?'

'Father.' He bowed low, as a son should. And he would have gone forward to receive his blessing, but he was afraid.

'What have you done? Did I not tell you to serve the emperor faithfully?'

'Yes, honoured Father. I have done so.'

'You have not. You have lied to him about the barbarians. You did not warn him of the danger. You are like a scout who deliberately leads his general into an ambush. That is treason.'

'I told him as much as I could.'

'You lied to the Son of Heaven.'

'Everybody lies to the emperor,' Shi-Rong cried.

'Even if that were true, it is no excuse.'

'It was not so easy . . .'

'Of course it was not easy. Virtue is not easy. Honourable conduct is not easy. That is our tradition, the thing for which our education prepares us – to do the thing that is not easy. Have you turned your back upon all the teachings of Confucius?'

'I do not think so.'

'Then you have not understood. When Confucius was asked how to cure the many ills of a corrupt government, what did he say? Perform the sacrifices correctly. What did that mean? That if your conduct is incorrect in small things, it will be incorrect in great things. Honesty and right conduct begin in the home, then in the village, the town, the province, the whole empire. The conduct of the emperor, who makes the great yearly sacrifices to the gods, must also be correct. Otherwise his whole empire will be rotten. Everything must hang together. One weak link breaks the whole chain. This is what Confucius understood. Yet you turn your back on everything I have passed down to you. You have disgraced me. You have disgraced your ancestors.'

Anguished, Shi-Rong fell on his knees and kowtowed to his father. 'Forgive me, Father. I will make amends.'

But his father only shook his head. 'It is too late,' he said in a sad voice. 'Too late.'

'My dear Jiang,' said his old teacher when he saw Shi-Rong's face in the morning, 'you look as if you'd seen a ghost.'

'I slept badly,' said Shi-Rong.

'Go for a walk,' Mr Wen suggested after Wong had served them breakfast. 'It's cold, but it's a beautiful day.'

After breakfast, Shi-Rong took his advice. For an hour he wandered the old city's streets. He came upon a small Confucian temple and went in to meditate awhile. It was nearly noon before he returned.

When he reached Mr Wen's house, he was met by Wong, who told him: 'Mr Wen has received a letter, Mr Jiang. He wants to see you.'

Shi-Rong found his old teacher in the little room where he kept his books. He was looking grave.

'Is there news from the lord Lin?' Shi-Rong asked.

'No.' Wen shook his head. 'From your aunt. She had sent a letter to you in Guangzhou, but it must have arrived after you left.'

Now Shi-Rong knew, with an awful certainty, what the news must be. 'My father.'

'He has died. Almost a month ago, it seems. Peacefully. With words of great affection for you just before he departed. You have been a good son to him. He was proud of you.'

'No. He is not proud of me. Not anymore.'

'I do not understand.'

'I saw his ghost last night. I thought it was only a dream, but it was not. He is very angry with me. I have shamed him and my ancestors. He told me so.'

'You must not say such things.'

'But it is true, Teacher. It is true. And he was right.' Shi-Rong sank to his knees in shame and put his face in his hands.

For a long moment Mr Wen was silent. 'You will have to go home, you know. It is your duty. You cannot work for the marquis anymore, or for anyone, until the period of mourning is over.'

'I know,' said Shi-Rong.

'Perhaps it's just as well,' said Mr Wen. 'It'll keep you out of trouble.'

o

Cecil Whiteparish had been standing on the waterfront at Macao on a quiet day in March in the year of our Lord 1841, looking at the ships in the Roads, when no less a person than Captain Elliot came walking swiftly towards him, and to his surprise hailed him and declared, 'My dear Mr Whiteparish. The very man I was looking for. I need your services as an interpreter again.' Elliot paused. 'How would you like to visit Canton?'

'Is it safe now?'

'The river is clear almost up to the factories at Canton, where I hope British trade will soon resume.'

Since the January day when Elliot's squadron and its iron ship had smashed the Chinese forts at the top of the gulf, the British advance up the Pearl River had continued. The marquis had called for truces, but it was soon obvious that he was only playing for time, and Elliot pressed on regardless. Day after day, mile after mile, the British had destroyed every battery, rampart and garrison. Chinese casualties had been large, British minimal.

'We missionaries act as your interpreters, Captain Elliot, because we're loyal Englishmen. But since this whole business is to support the opium trade, as a man of God, I can't pretend to like it.'

'And you know very well,' Elliot assured him, 'that I hate it, too. But remember, the government's true mission is much larger. We intend to coerce the Chinese to behave like a civilised country – open at least five ports, including Canton, to general trade, with British consuls in each port, perhaps an ambassador at the court. Englishmen will be able to live freely in those places. And there will be Christian churches there, for the Chinese as well. Your desires and mine are the same.'

'That is the end. But the opium trade is the means.'

'I'm afraid so, yes.'

'I must serve the government, I suppose,' Whiteparish said, 'but I hope I shan't be asked to do this again.' He sighed. 'I regret the loss of life,' he said sadly.

'So do I,' said Elliot. 'I was especially sad when that gallant old admiral Guan was killed at one of the forts we stormed. But I'm afraid that's war.' He paused. 'There's been another casualty, of a kind. The marquis has lost the emperor's confidence.'

'Demoted?'

'Carted off to Peking in chains, two days ago, under sentence of death. Lin saw him off, apparently. There's irony for you.'

'Where does that leave negotiations?'

'The marquis ceded Hong Kong to us, evidently without the emperor's authority. But we've occupied it, and we certainly won't give it back. He also promised six million dollars for the lost opium – also probably without authority. But we'll force the Chinese to give it to us, you may be sure.'

'The conflict's not over, then.'

'Not quite.' Elliot nodded. 'And that, my dear Mr Whiteparish, is where Her Majesty's Government needs you. I'm going on a secret expedition. I have a good pilot. You've met the fellow. They call him Nio. He gave us information about the gun batteries – entirely accurate, too. Now I need an interpreter.'

'I see.'

'There may be a little action, but nothing to worry about.' He smiled. 'We'll be on the *Nemesis*.'

They'd entered the great network of waterways that lay west of the gulf, a world of mudflats as far as the eye could see. The *Nemesis,* carrying a contingent of marines as well as its crew, and towing a couple of longboats astern, chugged its way northwards through the watery landscape. Every so often, the channel forked confusingly, but their pilot never hesitated.

'Nio may be a rogue,' Elliot observed, 'but he knows these waterways like the back of his hand.'

'The place seems empty,' Whiteparish remarked.

'According to Nio, it isn't. As well as a town, there's a lot of small forts up here. So I thought I'd better reduce them now. Once we've got control of the whole river, we don't want trouble developing in the rear.'

When they reached the town, Elliot's assertion that they had little to fear seemed to be borne out. This was no mere village. Whiteparish guessed the place might house thirty thousand souls. Archers on the bank loosed arrows at them, though most bounced off the ship's iron sides. But two stout war junks barred their path. The moment the *Nemesis* opened fire with its guns, however, and surged towards them, they fled.

'They've never seen an iron warship before,' Elliot remarked with a chuckle.

'Iron dragon,' said Nio.

'The town's not important,' Elliot explained. 'Exposed on the water like that, we can knock it about whenever we like. It's the forts I'm concerned about.'

They began to encounter these during the afternoon. They were not large. Most had mud walls and batteries of cannon. In each case, the iron ship's cannon soon blasted these defences to bits, and the marines were able to run ashore and spike their guns without suffering casualties. In several places, parties of soldiers appeared and waved antique spears, shouting abuse. But they wisely kept out of the marines' musket range.

At the end of the afternoon they came upon a small fort where the commander asked for a parley. He was quite a young man, with an intelligent face. Coming aboard the *Nemesis,* he explained that his father owned much of the local land. He looked at the ship's armaments with great interest. 'I have heard all about this iron ship,' he explained, 'but I wasn't sure it was true.'

'Tell him he'd better surrender,' said Elliot.

'He says he quite agrees,' Whiteparish reported. 'It would be foolish to do anything else. But he asks you to oblige him so that he and his men can save face. His cannon will fire a few shots at us, but they will be blanks. Could we please do the same? Then he will surrender.'

'Sorry,' said Elliot. 'No time for such nonsense. Surrender at once.'

With a sigh, the young man did so, though he did quietly say one thing, which Whiteparish wasn't going to translate until Elliot insisted on hearing it. 'He says you have better cannon, but a smaller brain.'

'Probably right,' said Elliot cheerfully. 'Spike his guns.'

When the ship anchored a few miles upstream that night, Elliot posted a watch; but nobody disturbed them.

They came upon a bigger fort midway through the morning. It stood on a natural platform of raised ground, commanding a bend in the waterway. It was twice the size of the forts they'd seen the day before, with big ramparts of packed mud.

'I'd say they've twenty cannon in there,' said Elliot, 'and a couple hundred men. Maybe more.' His eyes narrowed. 'If I'm not mistaken, we can station ourselves a quarter of a mile downstream, and their cannon won't be able to hit us.'

He was right. For the next hour the guns of the *Nemesis* methodically pounded the fort. A gaping breach opened up in the wall. They launched a Congreve rocket into the breach, saw it explode, heard the screams that followed. Then, carefully, they proceeded upstream until they were directly opposite the fort. Three of the Chinese guns fired, but their shots went too high. With quick precision, the gunners on the *Nemesis* fired back, and the Chinese guns fell silent. They launched another rocket and again heard awful screams.

'Poor devils,' remarked Elliot. He called the lieutenant of marines, a smart, fair-haired fellow of about thirty. 'Take the sergeant with you.' He indicated a big moustachioed veteran. 'Storm the fort. Offer them quarter, and once they've surrendered, spike their guns.' He turned to Whiteparish. 'Can you tell him what to say?'

In a few words, Whiteparish told the lieutenant how to call for surrender and offer quarter in Cantonese, and made him repeat it back to him twice.

The *Nemesis* was so close to the bank now that they didn't need the longboats. Running out planks, led by the young officer and the big sergeant, the marines raced across them and up the undulating grass slope towards the smoking fort.

The defenders weren't giving up. From the breach and from the damaged walls came a hail of arrows and several musket shots. Fortunately, the uneven ground gave the marines some cover from which to return fire. The cannon on the *Nemesis* roared again. But still the Chinese resisted.

'Plucky fellows,' said Elliot, with a nod of approval.

Some of the marines were peeling off to one side now, working their way unseen towards the breach. At the same time, the lieutenant shouted out the message Whiteparish had given him for the Chinese troops. Twice he shouted. They could not have failed to hear. But it had to be admitted, the message had become horribly garbled.

Whiteparish glanced at Elliot, then at Nio. 'Will they understand that?'

Nio shook his head.

'Damn,' said Elliot. 'I'm afraid this is going to be bloody. But I must have that fort.'

The lieutenant got on top of the grass bank, shouted his incomprehensible message once more, and was rewarded with a musket ball from the wall above that only just missed him.

'Prepare for mortar fire,' Elliot ordered. 'Exploding shells. And get another rocket ready.' He glanced at Whiteparish. 'Can't risk my marines. Too many defenders.'

'What'll you do?'

'Blow the Chinese to bits, I'm afraid.' He turned and called out: 'Ready, Master Gunner?' And he was about to give the order to fire when Cecil Whiteparish did a foolish thing.

He never even thought about it. Almost before he knew what he was doing, he'd run across the plank and was racing up the slope. Reaching the lieutenant, he leaped up onto the grass bank and bellowed in his best Cantonese: 'Surrender now! Our general promises you will not be harmed. Save yourselves!'

And he might have said more, but a huge force struck him in the back and flattened him upon the ground just as, above him, a musket ball hissed by.

Then a voice spoke in his ear. 'Sorry about that, sir. Can't have you getting shot.' It was the burly sergeant. 'Head down, sir.' Another musket ball hissed by.

He allowed himself to be dragged back to relative safety. 'Thank you,' he said.

'Sorry I didn't deliver the message very well,' the lieutenant said cheerfully. 'They heard you all right, though, loud and clear. Maybe it'll work.'

But it didn't. Perhaps the Chinese defenders were too proud. Perhaps they didn't trust the barbarian's word. Whatever their reasons, they continued to shoot, loosing a few arrows and even getting off another cannonball.

Whiteparish saw the marine lieutenant glance back to the ship. Evidently Elliot had sent him a signal. 'Please don't move this time,' the lieutenant said. 'There are going to be a lot of explosions inside the fort. Then we're going to rush them.'

And it happened just as the lieutenant said. And after the great and terrifying noise, the lieutenant and his men left him on the grass, and there were shouts and shots and screaming up ahead. And then it became quieter.

Nobody noticed him as he clambered into the fort. He climbed first over rubble, then over bodies, heaps of them, four or five deep, slippery with blood. Were all the defenders dead already? He did not know. Inside, the scene was terrible. In one corner of the place, a dozen Chinese prisoners were huddled, under guard. They at least would live. But the rest of the space was littered with something far worse than corpses.

The cannonballs and explosives had done their work. So had the hand-to-hand fighting. There were body parts – here a hand, there an arm or leg – from men who had been blown to bits. Then there were the living, men with gaping wounds, several with entrails half out, some screaming, others already sinking into silence. Most of them seemed to be half naked. And in the middle of them all, the lieutenant with a pistol and the large moustachioed sergeant with a cutlass. They moved among the twisted figures on the ground calmly and methodically. Some of the wounded they judged might live; those whose case looked hopeless and whose agony was too great to bear, they killed quickly. It was only common decency that made them do it. He realised that. But he had never seen such horrors before. Soon, he knew, a sickening smell would be added to this terrible scene. He would not wait for that.

Once when he was a boy, he had met a man who had been at the great Battle of Waterloo, and he had asked him what it was like when the battle was over. But the man had only shaken his head. 'Oh no,' he'd said, 'I cannot speak of that.' Now he knew why.

The thought crossed his mind: should he not go and give comfort to the dying? But what comfort could he give to those who did not even know the true and Christian God?

Instead he staggered out of the fort again and, once he was out, bent double and threw up.

It was the sergeant who came upon him. 'Sorry you had to see it, sir. We don't like to leave them like that, you know.'

'I understand.'

'They're only heathens, aren't they, sir? That's a comfort, I suppose.'

Back on the *Nemesis,* Cecil Whiteparish stood, his head bowed. 'It's my fault,' he said to Elliot. 'If I'd gone across with the marines at the start . . .'

'I wouldn't have let you,' Elliot said firmly. 'Besides, when they did get the message, they still ignored it.'

'God forgive me,' said poor Whiteparish.

An hour later, as the *Nemesis* continued northwards through the marshes, Whiteparish, still deep in his own thoughts, was surprised to find himself addressed by the pilot, who had been watching him attentively.

'You are a holy man,' Nio said.

'I suppose so,' Whiteparish replied without conviction.

'I know the British worship a god, but that is all. What is he like, your god?'

For a few moments Whiteparish said nothing. He didn't really want to talk. He didn't feel very worthy. But it was his duty to answer the question. After all, as a missionary, that was what he was there to do. So he told the Chinese smuggler the rudiments of the Christian faith, which made him feel a little better. And when Nio seemed to take an interest and asked him more, he gave him further details. And perhaps grateful to make up for his sense of failure, he found himself telling Nio everything he knew about his loving Lord.

And when he was finally done, Nio looked thoughtful for a while. 'This Jesus, did he have brothers and sisters?'

'Some think he had, others say not.'

'Was Jesus the Son of Heaven? Like the emperor?'

'His father was the King of Heaven. Better by far.'

'I hope so,' Nio said. He thought for a moment. 'Would he have killed all those people in the fort?'

'No,' said Whiteparish firmly. 'He would not.'

Several minutes passed before Nio spoke again. 'You are a good man,' he said.

'I wish I were.'

'I think you are,' said Nio.

Cecil Whiteparish did not answer, but he wondered: had his words about his faith been in the least adequate? Had some seeds fallen on good ground? Might they one day bear fruit?

He could not tell.

o

At first, it seemed to Nio, he was contented enough. If something in his heart troubled him, he ignored it.

He was a free agent. His feelings about the Manchu hadn't changed. He didn't want to go back to the daily uncertainty of the pirate's life. But the British seemed to trust him. They were still prepared to pay him very well. And there was plenty to do.

By the last week of March, the opium trade was in full swing again. The British had returned to their waterfront factory at Canton, though the great walled city overlooking them remained in imperial Chinese hands.

But neither the British nor the emperor intended to leave things as they were – which meant that the British needed spies.

Nio was perfect. Not only did he hear everything in the streets, but he had soon bribed two different servants in the governor's yamen, his administrative office, to give him information. Together with all the news that merchants like Tully Odstock heard through their Chinese counterparts in the Hong, Elliot was well informed.

Each week, Nio went to the missionary hospital beside the factories – supposedly to seek help with a pain in his elbow that Chinese medicine had failed to cure – and made a detailed report to Cecil Whiteparish, who then conveyed the information to Elliot.

After reporting, Nio would usually stay to talk with the missionary – the good man, as Nio thought of him – and Cecil would tell him wonderful stories of Christ's sayings and his miracles. Nio was especially impressed that the Christian Son of God had walked on water. And despite the fact that in the eyes of the law he was just a traitor reporting to his foreign paymaster, Nio drew spiritual nourishment and solace from these talks.

'There's going to be more trouble,' Nio informed Whiteparish the first day he reported. 'The emperor's furious about the loss of Hong Kong. As for the compensation money, he just won't pay. He wants the British trapped in the Gulf of Canton and annihilated.'

'How does he think he'll do it?'

'Extra troops. A lot of them, from several provinces. They're on their way already. And to command them, no less a person than General Yang.'

'Who is he?'

'A hero of the old wars against the steppe barbarians. And the province will be governed by one of the emperor's royal cousins.' A signal that the place was now the court's top priority.

But when the new troops began to arrive in the city, Nio soon reported back: 'They look half starved. Some of the companies are in rags. They're from distant provinces and can't speak a word of Cantonese. Most of them don't even seem to know where they are.'

'And their officers?'

'Drinking and whoring. They only show up on payday. As for General Yang, he's over seventy and deaf as a post.'

'Anything else?'

'Yes. He believes the British are using black magic. If so few of the barbarians can defeat so many Chinese, he says, there can be no other explanation.'

All through April, Nio brought reports of fresh arrivals of troops and cannon. One day in early May, in a secluded inlet near the city, he saw a small fleet of fire ships being prepared. Presumably they could be used against the flotilla of British vessels out in the gulf. This he also reported.

By the third week of May the heat in Canton was growing intolerable. The merchants at the factories, making up for the time lost in the spring, continued their urgent business of selling opium and buying tea, as if the world of trade would never cease. But Nio noticed that the ordinary people of Canton, those who could afford it, were quietly leaving the city.

His informants at the governor's yamen told him that something big was brewing. And then, one afternoon, Nio discovered a cannon hidden in the yard of a disused warehouse near the factories and realised that it could easily be dragged out onto the waterfront to fire at British ships.

The next day he saw Whiteparish. 'Where is Elliot? And where is the iron ship?'

'The iron ship is down at the Bogue. Elliot's on it.'

'They'd better come up fast and take the people in the factories off. I think General Yang's about to attack, and he's going to take over the waterfront.'

Two days later, the *Nemesis* and a flotilla of British warships came up the Pearl River to the factories. Somewhat disgruntled, the merchants allowed themselves to be evacuated.

By nightfall, the flotilla was out in the waters below the city.

So most people were asleep when, at two o'clock in the morning during the ebb tide, all hell broke loose on the Pearl River.

Cannon, dragged onto the waterfront, suddenly roared. Fire ships, chained together in pairs, were floating towards the anchored British vessels. The assault was huge and seemed well organised. The Chinese navy was good at fire ships, after all.

It didn't take Nio long to bribe a guard to let him up on the city wall. The night scene before him was spectacular. The roars and flashes from the cannon, coming from so many directions, were confusing, but Nio could see what the fire ships were doing. The British vessels, tall, ghostly shapes in the half-distance, had been caught unawares. Most were still at anchor or trying to get under way as the flaming hulks bore down upon them. Only the *Nemesis* was moving about and firing its guns. More fire ships were appearing. Some war junks were training their cannon on the

British vessels. He even thought he saw the *Nemesis* take a hit. Were the British going to be defeated for once?

'I believe we've got them,' he cried excitedly. He said it without thinking, and nobody heard.

It was only as the minutes passed that he noticed something odd. Perhaps, he thought, it was the dark. The fire ships were still advancing, but they seemed to be moving more slowly. A couple of the British ships had weighed anchor; one of them had got a grappling hook on to a fire ship and was dragging it off course. He stared into the blackness. And then, as a good waterman, he suddenly realised . . . and let out a groan. 'The fools,' he wailed.

The ebb tide that was supposed to carry the fire ships towards the British was almost over. They'd sent the fire ships out too late.

And so it proved. Through the rest of that short night and as the first hint of dawn appeared, he watched the great fire offensive slowly disintegrate. With the change of tide, some of the fire ships were even carried back to the waterside suburbs of the city, where flames soon broke out amongst the wooden houses. Finally, as dawn sent a faint grey light over the futile remains of the action, Nio made his way down from the wall.

He felt a sense of disgust. Before, when the British attacked the forts, the Chinese weapons were no good, their gun batteries useless. They were bound to lose. But last night, the Chinese could have won. Why did they lose? Because they were foolish. They lost face. And although his own interests lay with the British now, he felt a sense of shame.

So he was glad, two hours later at the governor's yamen, when one of his informants told him: 'It wasn't General Yang who sent in the fire ships last night. He didn't even know. It was his boss. The emperor's cousin. He's the one who gave the order and sent them at the wrong time.' A Manchu. That explained it, Nio thought. No Han Chinese would do anything so stupid.

By chance, Cecil Whiteparish was the first one to recognise Nio in the small sampan coming towards them. There was still so much confusion along the waterfront and in the river that few people would have noticed one vessel more or less. But when he caught sight of Nio, Whiteparish smiled and waved at once. And by the time Nio reached the *Nemesis,* he had Elliot at his side, ready to receive the news.

Nio's report was precise and to the point. The fact that General Yang didn't even know about the plan of attack was interesting.

'It sounds as if their command's in disarray,' Elliot remarked to Whiteparish. 'I believe we can finish this entire business in short order. I shall call on Canton to surrender.'

Whiteparish looked at the city's massive walls. 'But surely, it's not like a fort. We can't knock down and storm those walls. Besides, there may be a million people in there. If it came to house-to-house fighting, we'd just be swallowed up.'

'I didn't say I wished to take the city. And I certainly wouldn't destroy it, even if I could. We came here to trade with Canton, not ruin it. I just want them to surrender.'

'How will you do it?'

'Look over there.' He pointed. 'Do you see that small hill a few miles away, with a pagoda on it? It's right on the city's northern wall. If I could get some cannon up there, they'd command the entire city. We could easily hit the governor's yamen, for instance. And an impressive body of troops as well. Enough to frighten the Chinese. My guess is that if we're bombarding from here, to the south and they see us about to bombard and attack with a first-rate regiment on their north as well, they'll offer terms in no time.'

'But how will you get the cannon to their destination? You can't drag them for miles across the marshes, surely?'

'No. I need to bring the cannon and the troops up close to that hill by ship.' He looked towards Nio. 'Ask him if it can be done. Are there inlets, water channels we could use? I'll wager he knows.'

So Whiteparish asked Nio. And Nio remained silent for a time, apparently thinking, then shook his head.

'Tell him there'll be a big reward,' said Elliot.

But still Nio sadly shook his head. 'I don't know those channels,' he replied.

'I think he's lying,' said Elliot. 'He's always been helpful in the past. Why has he clammed up now? I could have him flogged, I suppose, if I must.'

Whiteparish gazed at Nio. 'Let me talk to him,' he said, and took Nio to one side. 'You think we're going to kill many people, don't you?' he murmured. 'Like we did at that fort. Ordinary Chinese. Your people.'

Nio said nothing.

So Whiteparish explained that Elliot had no intention of killing the people or destroying the city. 'It's just a blockade. We might shoot at the governor's yamen. Something like that. But when the defenders see our cannon and our troops, they'll give up. We've proved it many times. This is Elliot's plan. Nothing else.'

And at last Nio said, 'I know you are a good man. Do you promise me this is true?'

Whiteparish paused for only an instant. After all, he'd said nothing that wasn't true. This was Elliot's plan. 'Yes,' said the missionary earnestly, 'I do.'

'I will be your pilot, then,' said Nio, 'and show you the way to the pagoda hill.' He seemed sad. He didn't ask the price.

Whiteparish could only thank God that the siege of Canton had been over in just a few days. People had lost their lives, of course, but there was no great massacre. Once the cannon began pounding the governor's yamen from the top of the pagoda hill, the governor soon gave in.

Thank God that so many innocent Chinese lives had thus been saved. That was the main thing. But there was something else as well.

He'd given his word to Nio that his people would not be destroyed. And Nio had trusted him.

And what was Nio? A poor Hakka boy. A spy for hire. A drug smuggler. Probably a pirate, too. But he was not without honour. He'd initially refused to take them to the pagoda hill in order to save his people. If I'd betrayed his trust, Whiteparish reflected, I'd never have forgiven myself. Indeed, he realised, I probably care more for his good opinion than I do for that of my own cousin John Trader.

The deal that Elliot had agreed with the governor was very simple. 'I've stopped the bombardment,' he told Cecil, 'and agreed to withdraw all our warships and troops from Canton. In return, Canton will pay us six million silver dollars. At once.'

'So Canton is paying the opium compensation?'

'Certainly not. The emperor has forbidden that. The money is being paid by the city on condition that we cease hostilities and remove our troops. It's an old Chinese practice, you know, paying tiresome barbarians to make them go away.'

'But it's the same amount of money the British demanded for the opium.'

'Mere coincidence.'

'The British merchants will get the money, though.'

'Oh, I daresay. But the point is – from the Chinese point of view – that the emperor's orders have been obeyed. He has not lost face.'

'So our warships and troops will all return home?'

'Oh no. I still have many demands that have not been addressed. I expect to attack up the coast again shortly. But that is not the concern of Canton.'

'What about the opium trade?'

'It was not mentioned at all.'

'It will continue?'

'Nobody has said that it will not.'

Whiteparish thought for a few moments. 'So where does this leave us?'

'It leaves Canton exactly where it was before Lin came to confiscate the opium.' Elliot gave him a seraphic smile. 'Where it leaves China is quite another matter. By the way, I have something for you. For Nio.' He handed Whiteparish a small bag of coins. 'Tell him it's my thanks for showing us the way to the pagoda hill.'

Emptiness. Nio felt only emptiness now. When he'd first run away from home, it had seemed an adventure, a life of freedom with the smugglers in the gulf, a chance to make money. And now he had money, well over a hundred silver dollars. So why should he be depressed?

He was older and wiser. Perhaps that was all. It had been one thing, as a boy, to resent the distant Manchu rulers in Beijing; but it had still been a shock to discover that China's mighty empire could be humiliated by a handful of barbarians. He had only contempt for the Manchu emperor now. And the Han Chinese, and the mandarins like Shi-Rong, were scarcely better.

It seemed to Nio that the best Chinese man he'd met in the gulf was Sea Dragon. A pirate, of course, who'd been quite ready to kill him. But a pirate who never gave the members of his gang away. Died under torture. Kept his honour. A true Chinese hero, in his way. A man in a thousand.

What about the British barbarians? The missionary was a good man. But the British were not his people, and they never would be.

So what was left? What was he? With whom was he to live? I am a Hakka, he reminded himself. I belong with them. But for some reason even this didn't seem enough.

One evening, a couple of days after the settlement was agreed, he heard a commotion outside his lodgings near the factories. The summer monsoon had begun, but there was only a light rain falling as he hurried outside, where he found a small crowd of people. Several of them were shouting angrily, but he couldn't make out what they were saying.

'What's happened?' he asked an older man.

'It's the barbarians,' the man explained. 'Out in the villages. They've raped some women,' he said with disgust.

'That is terrible,' said Nio.

'There is worse,' said the fellow. 'They're attacking the dead.'

'To the cemeteries,' someone cried. 'Protect the ancestors.'

And most likely they'd all have gone out there and then if the monsoon had not chosen that moment to burst and the rain to fall so heavily that it made the expedition impossible.

The storm continued for two days. During that time, Nio learned exactly what had happened. A party of British soldiers, a little drunk, had gone for a walk and blundered into one of the many cemeteries in the surrounding countryside. For some reason, they were curious to see how the Chinese were buried. They ripped open a grave. Then another.

Such a thing would have been sacrilege in Britain, too. But in a land where the entire population visited their ancestral graves for the Qingming Ancestors Day after the spring equinox each year – often travelling great distances to do so – it was a horror past all telling.

The local villagers had seen them and intervened with force. Fighting broke out. A village was attacked. Within the hour, the whole area was up in arms, and only the heavy rain had saved the drunken soldiers' lives.

It was the first clear morning after the rain when Nio heard that an army was approaching the city's northern wall. Along with several hundred others, he went up to see what it meant.

The army – there was no other name by which to call it – was huge, more than ten thousand men. Judging by their dress and the horses they rode, the leaders were mostly members of the local gentry, accompanied by men bearing spears and bows and arrows. These must be the old local militias. But there were also huge crowds of peasants carrying more rudimentary arms – clubs and sickles or no weapons at all.

The army showed its unity in two ways. Throughout its ranks were improvised black flags, whose combined effect was frightening. But more significant to Nio were the banners that every militia contingent seemed to carry. For each banner bore, in bold Chinese characters, the same simple legend: *Righteous People.*

The countryside had risen. And they declared to the people of Guangzhou that they had come to relieve the city from the barbarians who defiled their ancestors and everything that was holy. Having arrived, they waited, ready to fight, but uncertain what to do.

Some time passed. A fellow about his own age, who'd been standing beside Nio, turned to him and remarked: 'We should never have let this happen.'

'What should we have done?'

'Killed the barbarians, of course.'

'They have better weapons,' Nio said.

'I know that. But look at the numbers. All we had to do was let them land, come into the city, make them welcome, then kill them. At night when they're asleep. A million of us, to a few hundred of them.'

'And their ships?'

'Same thing. Row out to them in the dark. Hundreds of sampans. Swarm on board. It's all in the numbers.'

Just then, from the northern city gate, four riders appeared. Three were city prefects. The fourth was a British officer. They rode out to the army. Some of the gentry rode to meet them and confer.

'What do you think they're saying?' asked Nio's companion.

'I should think the prefects are telling them that the barbarian troops are already starting to leave. A few more days and they and all their ships will be gone. They're telling them to disperse.'

'Why's the barbarian officer there?'

'To confirm it's true, I suppose.'

'Or to make sure our prefects do what they're told. They're all traitors.'

'I don't think so.'

'You're on the barbarians' side then, aren't you? Another traitor.'

'No.' Nio gazed across at the peasant army with its banners. 'I'm just a peasant from a village down the coast.' He paused and nodded, as much to himself as his companion. 'I'm one of the Righteous People.'

'I doubt it,' said the other, and moved away.

But I am, thought Nio. He knew it now. That's what he was. Or at least what he wanted to be – whatever form it might take. One of the Righteous People.

o

The marriage was set. It was agreed up at the hill station. With the fall of Canton and the payment of the six million dollars, it seemed clear that John Trader's fortune and the opium trade in general were as secure as such things can ever be. Or perhaps Colonel Lomond was just getting bored by the long engagement. Whatever the reason, the marriage would take place in October.

'As I've no family, I'm afraid the guest list will be rather one-sided,' Trader remarked to Mrs Lomond. Charlie Farley would be his best man, of course. Aunt Harriet and her husband would be coming. Quite a few former colleagues and friends from Rattrays would be on the list. There were a number of people he knew in Macao whom he could invite, though whether any of them would be able to come all the way to Calcutta was another matter. Both the Odstock brothers were coming. That was good. And then there was Read. He'd sent an invitation for Read to Tully Odstock, asking him to give it to the American.

In mid-September, back in Calcutta, he got a letter from Tully telling him that Read's invitation could not be delivered.

> Our friend Read has gone on his travels again. I believe he plans in due course to return to America. But his departure was a little strange in one respect. I don't know if you knew – I certainly did not – but before leaving, he told me that he'd received word in early May that his wife had died in America, leaving him a widower, or perhaps it would be more accurate to say, a free man.
>
> He has taken another wife. I'm not sure where he married. Not in Macao, certainly. But it seems he has married Mrs Willems's niece, the girl called Marissa. Wherever he and his wife may be now, therefore, Read will not be at your wedding. But I look forward to it.

So it seemed he'd been right to wonder about Read and the girl. But he had to admit that as he was going to be living with Agnes Lomond as his wife in the small community of Macao, it was probably just as well that, even if Marissa were ever to return there, she'd be safely married to Read.

On a sunny day in October Trader was walking along the Esplanade. It was only a week to go before he was to be married, and he was in love, and it seemed to him that God was in His Heaven and all was right with the world. He passed the mighty portals of the Bengal Military Club, and even that stern building seemed to look on him with a friendly gaze.

The day before, Agnes had told him about a children's charity that she and her mother favoured, and he was thinking about the contribution he would make, in his name and Agnes's, as a surprise wedding present to her. Something strikingly generous. God knows, he could afford it. And he was so busy with this thought that he did not notice the person coming towards him, who was equally busy with his own thoughts, so that neither of them observed the other until it was too late.

Cecil Whiteparish hesitated, thought rapidly, and then rightly concluded that there was only one decent and Christian thing to do. 'Good morning, Cousin John,' he said politely. Friendly but cautious.

'Morning.' Trader did his best to smile. 'What brings you to Calcutta?'

'I'm spending a month with the London Missionary Society. They have an office here, you know.'

'Ah. Then back to Macao?' He'd realised that at some point, once he and Agnes were living in Macao, she'd become aware of Cecil Whiteparish's existence, but he'd thought he could deal with that when the need arose. Was there any chance, he wondered, that this visit to Calcutta might mean Whiteparish was being sent somewhere else?

'Yes, back to Macao. At least for a while.'

'Ah.'

'I hear that I should congratulate you on your forthcoming marriage.'

'Oh. Thanks.' Trader paused, then said nothing more.

Cecil Whiteparish watched him. His expression seemed quite without rancor, perhaps a little amused. 'Don't worry,' he said quietly. 'I wasn't looking for an invitation. Not my sort of party, you know.' He smiled. 'I wish you every joy in your marriage.' He was quite sincere. Trader could see that. 'Goodbye,' said his cousin, and went on his way.

Early that afternoon, he sat with Mrs Lomond in her private sitting room. 'I'm in a bit of a fix,' he confessed, 'and I don't know what to do.'

'And you've come to me?' Mrs Lomond smiled. 'I'm so pleased. We're family now, you know. Families rally round. Tell me everything.'

So he told her, quite simply and straightforwardly, how Cecil Whiteparish had appeared in his life. 'The only time I'd even seen his family's name was in the note my guardian left me, and I'd actually forgotten it.'

'Did you hate him?'

'No. But we've nothing in common, and I certainly didn't want him as a friend.'

'Not one of us?'

'I'm afraid not.'

'Would you feel embarrassed if he was at the wedding?'

'As the only blood relation I can produce?' He paused. 'I'm afraid your husband wouldn't be too pleased.'

'Funnily enough, you're wrong. He'd roar that the man was a kinsman and that blood is thicker than water. He can get very tribal, you know.' She smiled. 'But I have the feeling that your conscience is telling you you ought to invite him. Am I right?'

'It's mean-spirited of me. I may as well admit it.'

'You judge yourself a bit severely. By the way, you haven't told me this young man's profession. Does he have one?'

'He's a missionary,' said Trader.

'A missionary?' She threw back her head and laughed. 'My dear John, your troubles are over. You should certainly invite him.'

'Really?'

'Of course. Firstly, nobody wants to appear discourteous to a missionary. It's very bad form. The fact you've got one in the family is all to your credit. Secondly, people expect missionaries to be a bit peculiar, you know. I remember one of old Lord Drumossie's sons became a missionary. He was certainly peculiar, not a bit like the rest of the family.' She nodded to herself. 'This is good news, not bad at all.'

'He doesn't approve of the China trade. I just hope he doesn't start in on that.'

'Don't worry. I'll make sure he's kept on a tight rein.'

'Really? How?'

'My friend the vicar. I'll ask him to keep a weather eye. He's very wise.' Her face suddenly lit up. 'My dear, I've just remembered, he's got a young curate. We'll invite him, too. He will be given strict instructions that he is to look after the missionary and never leave his side. We shall all make them welcome. And even if he did tell some of the guests that he didn't approve of the China trade, they'd hardly be surprised. Everyone will be happy,' she concluded blithely.

'Except possibly the curate.'

'He will be doing something useful and good. That,' Mrs Lomond said with firmness, 'is what curates are for.'

So John Trader and Agnes Lomond were married, and it was a most successful event. The groom with his piratical eye patch looked very dashing. The bride was lovely. Later that year, they went to Macao, where they took a pleasant house above the port.

'We won't be here all that long,' Trader told her. 'My guess is that in a couple of years most of the British colony will be settled in Hong Kong. We're starting to build there already.'

For the time being, however, Agnes found herself in a pleasant community where people lived the same sort of way that they did in Calcutta, but with a little less formality and rather more enjoyment. And if people found her a little reserved sometimes, they didn't mind, because they understood that in due course, when John had made his fortune, she would be just what he needed.

They had a charming little villa high up the hill, with a wonderful view over the sea. Agnes had chosen all the furniture and decoration so well that, as she rightly said, 'We might be up at the hill station, except for the sea.'

And those who had access to her boudoir noticed and thought it charming that on her dressing table, just behind the tortoiseshell hairbrushes that her mother had given her as a wedding present, stood the handsome miniature of her beloved husband that his friends had given him before he first left Calcutta for China. It was the last thing she looked at each night before retiring.

Of course, there were the months when John and Tully Odstock were away with all the other merchants in Canton. For trade was busy. But there was plenty of news to talk about.

If Canton was left alone, the British were by no means done with China. Having confirmed, without a doubt, that British arms could obtain what they wanted, the London government had recalled Elliot and sent out a sterner commander to complete the business.

Up the coast he went, in the spring of 1842, from port to port, smashing every defence. Some of the fighting was grim, especially in the summer, when John was back in Macao. On one of his occasional courtesy calls, Cecil Whiteparish brought them an especially significant piece of news.

'We've taken a place called Zhapu. A very pretty little coastal town, I understand, with a fort garrisoned by Manchu bannermen – but these were the real old Manchu warrior clans, you know, who conquered China originally. They fought to the last man. Truly heroic. The point is,' he continued, 'the way is now clear. There are no more garrisons to take until we get to the forts on the coast below Peking itself.'

As Whiteparish was leaving, Trader remarked to him quietly, 'It sounds as if that Zhapu business was pretty frightful.'

'Yes. Women and children, too, though I didn't want to say that in front of your wife.'

'We're fortunate, you and I, that we've never actually seen anything like that,' Trader remarked.

And just for a moment it seemed that Cecil Whiteparish might have said something more. But he didn't.

A few weeks later Agnes Trader gave her husband a healthy baby boy. He invited Cecil Whiteparish round, and they shared a bottle of champagne. It seemed the right thing to do.

And three days after that, Trader was able to tell his wife some joyful news. 'Peking's capitulated. Signed a treaty. We've got everything we wanted. Five ports open to us . . . Well, four, really – they've thrown in a little place called Shanghai to make up the fifth. But that'll do. A British consul in every port. Hong Kong formally ceded, of course. And an indemnity, can you believe it, of twenty-one million dollars!'

'That seems a lot,' Agnes remarked.

'I know.' John gave a wry smile. 'It almost makes one feel guilty.'

ZHAPU

1853

Guanji had been five years old when his mother showed him how to kill himself. All the preceding day, the battle between the Manchu bannermen and the British and Indian troops had raged along the shore. Not until evening had the barbarians dislodged the brave bannermen from the Buddhist temple near the waterfront. But by the next morning, the devils from the sea were advancing on the Zhapu garrison itself, and Guanji's father had gone with the other men to defend the eastern gate.

The walled town of Zhapu formed roughly a square, divided into four by cross streets running north to south and east to west. The northeastern quadrant contained the garrison enclosure where Guanji lived. If the barbarians got through the town's eastern gate, those in the garrison would be trapped with no means of escape.

'Bring me those two knives from the table,' his mother told him. And she had made him hold one of them against his neck, placed her hand over his, and gently guided the blade around his throat. 'Just move the blade like that, and press hard,' she said. 'It won't hurt.'

'Yes, Mother.'

'Now, you know where your Hangzhou uncle's house is. Try to get there if you can. Maybe you'll be safe there. But don't let the barbarians see you. If they catch you, then use the knife and kill yourself right away. Do you promise me?'

'I promise.' His father's elder brother. His name was Salantai – not that it mattered, since Guanji always called him Uncle from Hangzhou, which was where he had his business. The house where his uncle resided, however, was in a suburb outside Zhapu.

'Is Father coming back?'

'If he comes back, he'll find you at your uncle's.'

'I want to stay with you.'

How pale she looked. When the mortar shell exploded, the roof had collapsed, and a falling beam had pinned her to the floor and crushed her leg. He could see a jagged bone poking out through the flesh and the blood forming in a pool beside it.

'No!' she cried. He could see that she was using the last of her strength. 'Go now, Guanji. Before the barbarians get here.'

'Are you going to kill yourself?'

'Don't ask questions. Do as your mother tells you. Go! Quickly, quickly!'

So he turned and ran.

Guanji's memory of that day was like a dream. There were bangs, and shouting from the eastern gate like a distant echo. Yet the street was strangely empty as he ran away from his home. The wall of their neighbours' house had been partly blown down, and between the wall's jagged edges he could see in. They had a well in the middle of their yard.

The head of that family was an old man. Guanji did not know the old man's name, but in his youth he had come to Zhapu from Beijing, so everybody called him Old Man from Beijing. His sons had gone out to fight, but he was standing there with his son's wife and her three little children. The old man saw Guanji and stared at him blankly. He had a broad Mongolian face, but his brow and cheeks were creased with such deep vertical lines that it looked as if the skin had been put in a vice and compressed.

It seemed that the old man had also decided that the garrison was about to fall. For turning his gaze back to his grandchildren, he sadly picked up the first, a boy about Guanji's age and dropped him down the well. Then he picked up a little girl and did the same. Their mother, a pretty young woman, had a baby in her arms. At a nod from her father-in-law, she climbed over the side of the well and they both disappeared.

Guanji stood there, watching. Old Man from Beijing gazed back at him. Guanji suddenly thought that maybe the old man was going to come for him, too, and he prepared to run for his life. But instead, Old

Man from Beijing slowly sat down with his back to the well, and taking out a knife, he calmly drew it across his throat, almost absently, as if he were doing something else. Guanji watched as the red line began to spurt blood. Old Man from Beijing turned his eyes towards Guanji again. They looked sad. Then Guanji heard shouts at the end of the street, so he stopped looking at the old man and bolted.

The way to his uncle's house led through a series of familiar alleys to a small side door in the garrison wall, guarded by half a dozen men. 'We're closing the door in a minute,' one of the guards told him. 'You won't be able to get back.'

'My mother sent me to my uncle's house,' he cried. Nobody tried to stop him.

Running westwards, he soon came to the big north–south street, from which he could see that the northern gate was still open. He ran out quickly before the guards there even had time to question him and took a small lane that led through straggling suburbs. His uncle's house lay a mile away. Fortunately, he didn't see any barbarians on his journey.

Years ago, when his uncle had got permission to live outside the garrison, he'd built up a pleasant family compound of small two-storey houses. The most important building, revered as a temple, though it looked more like a small barn, was the Harmony Hall, which contained the memorial tablets to the family ancestors. In a modest courtyard to one side were some strange little shrines. They were used only occasionally, at deaths and marriages, by the shaman priests – who still at such times would remind the Manchu clans of their ancient ways, when they lived in the northern forests and plains, above the Great Wall of China.

His uncle wasn't home, but his aunt and her children were. Her daughter was fourteen years old, her elder son was twelve. The third child was a girl of about his own age. The baby of the family was a boy of three. When she saw him, his aunt didn't look too pleased, but when he explained what happened, she nodded grimly. Then she noticed the knife he was carrying.

'Give me the knife, little Guanji,' she said. But he shook his head and backed away.

If the barbarians came and they all had to kill themselves, Guanji was going to use the knife the way his mother had shown him. When Old Man from Beijing had slit his throat, it didn't look too bad. He didn't know if his aunt was planning to drown her children. But he was determined about one thing. He didn't want to go down any well. So he clutched the knife tightly and kept out of her reach. His aunt looked angry, but she was too preoccupied to insist upon it.

An hour passed. They saw smoke rising from the garrison. But nobody from the garrison came out their way; neither did the British barbarians. Finally his aunt told them all to go into the house. But she didn't join them. She kept watch at the gate until, at the end of the afternoon, her husband arrived, having ridden as fast as he could from the city of Hangzhou.

There was no more fighting at Zhapu that night. In the morning, his uncle went out to assess the situation. He came back at noon.

'The British have the garrison, and they'll leave a small force to hold it. They're not interested in anything else. Their object is Beijing. They want a treaty from the emperor.'

'And the defenders . . . ?' his wife began before he signalled her not to ask.

He turned to Guanji. 'Little nephew, you can be a very proud boy today. Your father died defending the gate to the last. He died a hero,' he said firmly. 'A Manchu hero!' he cried to them all. 'An honour to our noble clan.'

'And my mother?' Guanji asked.

'She must have been in pain when you left her. You know her leg . . .'

'Yes, Uncle. I saw.'

'I think she ended her life just after you left. Her death would not have been painful.' He glanced at his wife. 'It would have been before the troops came.' He turned back to Guanji. 'The British officer has given me permission to remove both your parents' bodies for proper burial. Everything will be done as it should be.'

And so it was. And little Guanji had this comfort: his mother had not suffered, and his father was a hero.

Not every boy is taught to be a hero. But Guanji was. He didn't mind. It meant they gave him a pony.

Since he'd lost both his parents, his uncle adopted him as an extra son, and certainly no father could have been kinder or taken more trouble to bring him up in the best Manchu tradition. Even before he was six years old, Guanji could answer his uncle's catechism perfectly.

'What is our clan?'

To a Han Chinese, it was his family that mattered, his parents and grandparents who must be honoured; and when asked who he was, he gave the family name first, then his personal name. But for a Manchu, the wider clan, the tribe, was everything. The true Manchu did not have a family name. He went proudly by only a single personal name within his clan.

'We are the Suwan Guwalgiya,' Guanji would answer. 'We can trace our ancestry for seven hundred years.'

'Where is the spirit pole of our clan?'

'In Beijing.'

'Who is the founder of our branch of the clan?'

'Fiongdon, the archer and commander, companion of Khan Nurgaci of the Golden Clan, who brought the Jurchen tribes together and founded our Manchu royal house.'

'How did Khan Nurgaci show his love for Fiongdon?'

'He offered him his own granddaughter as a bride.'

'What happened when Fiongdon died?'

'The sun changed its course, thunder and lightning filled the sky, and Khan Nurgaci himself was chief mourner at his funeral.'

'How many sons had Fiongdon?'

'Twelve, the seventh of whom was Tulai, the great cavalry commander.'

'What did they do?'

'They drove the Ming dynasty from the throne of China.'

'How many generations separate you from Fiongdon?'

'Nine.'

'What ranks did Fiongdon hold?'

'Before his death, Lord of the Bordered Yellow Banner and one of the Five Councillors. After his death, he was made Duke of Unswerving Righteousness. Twice again, as generations passed, his rank was raised higher. A hundred and fifty years after his death, he received the highest rank of all.'

'What is that?'

'Hereditary Duke, First Class.'

'Sometimes, Guanji,' his uncle explained, 'a man may rise high during his life, but after his death, his reputation may fall. He may even be disgraced. But Fiongdon's name and rank have grown over time. That is the proof of his worth.' He smiled. 'One day, little Guanji, you, too, could bring such honour to our clan.'

The pony was a sturdy, shaggy little Manchurian roan, with a big head and a white patch on his face. His name was Wind over Grasses, but little Guanji just called him Wind and loved him very much. One of the old Manchu warriors in the garrison began to teach him to ride in a small field near the house.

After six months the old warrior gave him a toy bow and taught him how to pull it and shoot arrows while he was riding, and before long Guanji could race past the target and hit it every time. The old warrior praised him, and sometimes his uncle came to watch, and Guanji was very proud and happy. After a year they gave him another bow, not quite so small, and soon he was just as accurate with that, too.

Sometimes, after his riding and archery lessons, the old man would take Guanji to the teahouse where he met his Manchu friends, and they'd tell the little boy Manchurian folktales and sing the zidi songs, accompanied with a hand drum, about the glorious deeds of the Manchu past. They'd encourage Guanji to sing along with them, and soon he knew a dozen of the rhythmic songs by heart, and the men were delighted and called him Little Warrior; for there was no other small boy in the Zhapu garrison who knew so much.

'You know what they say,' the old man would declare with a nod, 'a boy who is strong in body will be strong in mind.'

When he was seven, his uncle put him in the garrison's junior school. 'You will learn to read and write Chinese characters,' his uncle told him, 'but you will learn to speak and write Manchu as well. Even many bannermen can't speak our language anymore, but the court in Beijing still uses Manchu in all official documents. If you rise high, therefore, this may be useful to you, and it will certainly please the emperor.'

His uncle was the only person Guanji knew who had ever been to the capital. 'Will you take me to Beijing?' Guanji asked.

'Perhaps,' his uncle said. 'One day.'

Meanwhile, Zhapu itself seemed like a little heaven. The family lived quite well. Like all bannermen, his uncle received a modest stipend in silver from the emperor, and a grain allowance, and some benefits like schooling for his sons. But he supplemented these with the profits of a printing business he owned in the city of Hangzhou.

'Bannermen like us aren't supposed to become merchants and craftsmen,' he explained to Guanji. 'It's demeaning. But preparing and printing fine books the way I do is considered fit for a Manchu gentleman, and so I got permission.' He'd smiled. 'It's just as well, or we couldn't live as well as we do.'

As for his uncle's children – his brothers and sisters now – they'd embraced him so completely that in a year or two he'd almost forgotten they had been his cousins first.

His favourite was Ilha, the elder girl. He admired her with all his heart. She was everything a Manchu girl should be.

Manchu women did not totter on bound feet, like the fashionable Chinese ladies. Their feet were as nature intended. In their platform shoes, wearing the simple, loose qipao dress with the long slits down the sides, they walked tall and straight and free. She was funny, too. Her light-skinned face might be composed and ladylike, but her hazel eyes were often laughing. And she was like a second mother to him.

He loved to walk the streets of Zhapu. For though the British attack had left harsh marks on the garrison quarter, the seaside town was still a charming place, with a winding central canal crossed by nine steep-humped ornamental bridges. Houses, temples, pavilions, whose roof corners curved up into elegant points and high garden walls flanked the canal; here and there, a willow tree hung gracefully over the water.

But most of all, Guanji liked to ride out on Wind. Often they'd skirt the edge of the town and take the trail that led to the end of a long, low spit of land that jutted out into the sea, where there was a small shore battery on a little knoll. The sea, protected by headlands, was often so still that, in his mind's eye, he could imagine it was a vast plain of grassland, like the northern steppe from which his people came. At such times, he liked to think that the spirit of his father, whose face he could scarcely remember, was riding beside him. And this secret company he kept brought him a sense of inner peace and strength.

Since all things come to an end, the time came when Guanji was getting too big to ride his pony. His uncle bought him a small horse, just as sturdy as Wind, but more fleet; and Wind was to be given to another boy.

On the day before Wind's departure, Guanji took him for a final ride by the sea so that his father's spirit also could bid farewell to his pony.

He was on his way back into Zhapu when he saw a boy named Yelu walking along the lane. Yelu was at school with him. He lived in a small house in the garrison and his parents were quite poor. Yelu and he weren't friends; but they weren't enemies, as far as Guanji knew. Sometimes Yelu got angry, and then Guanji used to think he looked like a little pig. But he never said so. He nodded to Yelu politely enough as he drew near. But Yelu stood in his path. 'They say your uncle's bought you a new horse.'

'It's true. This is my last ride on Wind, so I'm feeling really sad.'

'You get everything, don't you? The old men call you Little Warrior.'

'It's because I can sing a lot of zidi songs, I think.'

'And your father's supposed to be a hero.'

'He died in the battle here,' Guanji answered modestly, 'like many others.'

'That's what you think. I heard he ran away. He got killed later. He was hiding in a well. What do you think of that, Little Warrior?'

Guanji was so shocked and surprised that for a moment he didn't know what to say. And before he could even shout that it wasn't true, Yelu ran off.

When he got home, he asked Ilha what she thought.

'Of course he's lying, silly,' she said. 'Isn't it obvious? He's jealous of you. Besides, after his own father escaped alive on the day of the battle, some people said he was a coward, although it was never proved.'

'I didn't know that.'

'People don't talk about it.'

'But how could he make up such a lie about my father?'

'When people make up lies like that, it's often because they're afraid the lie is the very thing people might say about them. It's like transferring an evil spell. You take the ugly spider that's fallen on you and throw it onto someone else.'

The next day, when Guanji told Yelu to be ready to fight him after school, Yelu apologised and confessed he'd made the story up and that he knew it wasn't true. So they didn't fight. But Guanji couldn't help wondering if Yelu had just apologised because he was afraid of getting a beating. So he didn't really feel better. And although he would never disbelieve his uncle, the little episode left a tiny doubt in his mind.

A few days later he went riding on his new horse to the long spit of land by the sea. And as usual, he imagined that the silent water was a great expanse of steppe. But though he waited, the spirit of his father did not come to join him, and he rode out to the end all alone.

A year after this, Ilha got married. 'As nobody's allowed to marry one of their own clan,' she had teased her father, 'I don't see how any husband is going to please you, unless he's one of the royal clan.' But in the end, they found a young man whose ancestors were satisfactory and whose prospects were good. He lived in the great city of Nanjing, on the Yangtze River, a hundred and fifty miles to the north.

Guanji remembered two things about that day. The first was the bride. The beautifully embroidered red marriage qipao she wore seemed fit for a princess. Her platform shoes raised her to the same height as a man. But it was her hair that amazed him. Normally on formal occasions it would be parted in the middle, then wound into two pinwheels, one above each ear. As a bride, however, her hair had been pulled over a big comb, high above her head and decorated with flowers, so that she seemed to be wearing a towering crown. 'You look so tall,' he said in wonderment.

'Be afraid.' She laughed.

The second thing was the shamans. Her father insisted upon them. The two old men set up a curious little shrine and performed ancient rites from the Manchurian forests, in a deep chant that nobody understood except his uncle – and Guanji wasn't even sure that his uncle did, really. It added a strange solemnity to the day.

Guanji was sorry Ilha wasn't living closer, but she promised to come to see him whenever she could.

It wasn't long, in any case, before Guanji himself moved away, at least for part of the year, when the time came for him to enter the Manchu officers school in Hangzhou. As his uncle had a little house beside his printing workshop in the city, Guanji lived there except on holidays, when he returned to Zhapu.

Hangzhou was eighty miles down the coast from Zhapu, at the head of a river estuary. Until that time, Guanji had never been there, and at first he'd been rather overawed. Hangzhou was the capital of the province, one of the oldest cities in China, with mighty thousand-year-old walls and widespread suburbs. On a rise above the river there was a huge pagoda towering into the sky. 'In the old days, they kept a great lamp at the top,' his uncle told him, 'that sailors could steer by from out at sea.' At Hangzhou also, the Grand Canal began, carrying all kinds of goods northwards. 'It's eleven hundred miles long,' his uncle explained. 'If you go up the canal, you'll cross the valley of the mighty Yangtze and then farther north, you'll cross the Yellow River valley, too, until you finish up at Beijing. After the Great Wall, it's the greatest marvel of construction in all China.'

Hangzhou's broad streets contained famous stores, pharmacies and teahouses that had been run by the same families for centuries. As for the vast compound of the Manchu bannermen, it enclosed no less than two hundred and forty acres.

When Guanji entered the big officers' school there, where nearly all the boys were older and already accustomed to this great city, he assumed they would be far more advanced than he was. And in Chinese studies and mathematics he certainly had much to learn. But in Manchu, he discovered that he already knew more than most of them. And to his even greater surprise, there wasn't a single boy in the school who could match him in the traditional martial arts. Many of the pupils couldn't ride at all.

'If the emperor gives them an allowance for horses,' said his uncle sadly, 'they just spend the money on themselves.'

It was during the years at Hangzhou that Guanji came to know and understand his uncle better. Since he was being raised as a bannerman soldier, he'd never taken much interest in his uncle's printing business. So he was quite surprised to discover how much of a tradesman his uncle was and how hard he worked.

He liked the printing workshop. Beside the big wooden presses and the paper stacked on shelves, there was a long table where a line of craftsmen sat, diligently carving. For the books were not printed using metal type, but little woodblocks, each bearing a character, fitted into sets of page frames.

His uncle handled all kinds of projects. 'Here's a fine book of poems on the presses,' he might explain. 'We're copying characters from an old Ming dynasty text for this printing. Here's a mandarin, good friend of mine, wants his essays printed. And this' – he pointed to a pile of thick papers, covered in untidy writing – 'will be the genealogy of a certain nobleman, going back three thousand years. Partly invented, of course, but he's paying me handsomely.' He smiled. 'I may not be a scholar, but

I know how to write an introduction – you know, gracefully flattering, that sort of thing.'

None of this would have been possible, Guanji came to realise, if his uncle hadn't developed a huge network of contacts. There wasn't a cultivated person in the province he didn't know. These were his patrons and his audience.

Some lived in the city. But the favourite meeting place was outside, at the lovely West Lake, where emperors went to relax, writers and artists to contemplate nature and mandarins to retire. From time to time his uncle would take Guanji to some rich man's villa on the lakefront or some scholar's retreat in the encircling hills. And Guanji enjoyed these visits.

But though he admired his uncle, he wouldn't have wanted such a life himself. He had far too much energy. He wanted action, not to be cooped up all day in a library or printing house.

During these years at the officers' school, Guanji did well at his work. He grasped ideas quickly; his memory was excellent. As for his physical prowess, there were hardly any big open spaces where one could gallop in Hangzhou, so his horsemanship did not improve. But archery practice was another matter. As Guanji entered adolescence, he grew far more muscular and exceedingly strong. Before he was fifteen, he could draw a more powerful bow and shoot farther and with more deadly accuracy than any other boy at the school. His face also began to change. It became rounder, more Mongolian; a wispy dark brown mustache began to droop from the sides of his mouth. One day his uncle, looking through some drawings, pulled out an ancient picture of a warrior prince. 'You're getting to look just like that,' he remarked with a smile. And though this was a slight exaggeration, there was a certain resemblance. Whenever the school was putting on one of the plays the Manchus loved, Guanji was always picked to be the warrior prince.

Only two small clouds appeared on the horizon of his life during these years. The first was the death of the emperor. He was succeeded by his son, quite a young man. But this dynastic business hardly affected Guanji's daily life, except for the need to observe the official mourning.

The second was a revolt that had broken out in one of the southern provinces.

'It's the usual story,' his uncle posited. 'The empire's so huge there's always a revolt somewhere. The White Lotus wanting to restore the Ming dynasty, the Muslims on the western border, Triad gangs trying to take over the ports, minority tribes giving trouble in the outer provinces. We've seen it all before.'

'Who's behind this one?'

'The leader is a Hakka called Hong.'

'What do they want?'

'To throw out the Manchu. Once we're gone, apparently, all the troubles of the world will be over.' He sighed. 'They're even promising their own heavenly kingdom – a Taiping, as they call it. Good luck with that!'

'They say the Hakka are good fighters. Could the revolt grow?'

'I doubt it.' His uncle shook his head. 'They've already made one huge mistake. Their leader follows the barbarians' Christian god. Our country people won't like that.'

'I don't really know what Christians are,' Guanji confessed.

'They have one chief god and two lesser gods. One of those is called Jesus.'

'I've heard the name.'

'Well,' said his uncle, 'this Hakka, the Taiping leader, says he's Jesus's younger brother.' He laughed. 'Nothing will come of them.'

It was a year later that Ilha returned to Zhapu on a visit with her husband and their infant son. They had come for an important occasion. In fact, it was for a family triumph.

If her father's career had been a series of modest successes – printing a prestigious book, securing an extra pension for a member of the family – each one designed to add in some small way to his family's advancement, this time he'd outdone himself.

'The emperor himself is honouring our family,' he told them. And not just with the usual written memorial. 'We have permission to erect a ceremonial arch,' he announced triumphantly, 'by the garrison gate in Zhapu.'

It was all on account of a virtuous woman, the kind the Chinese most admired – the loyal widow.

'My father had several children,' his uncle would relate, 'but only one son lived long enough to marry. Soon after marrying, however, and before producing an heir, he died. His widow was young and beautiful. Many men wanted her. Her duty was to look after her father-in-law, who was getting to be an old man. But she went further. Refusing to let her husband's family die out, she found her old father-in-law a young wife and persuaded him to marry her. Thanks to that, Guanji, your father and I were born. When the old man died, the two widows brought us up at first. Then my young mother became sick and died, which left only that loyal daughter-in-law, whom we always called Grandmother. She looked after us. She slaved for us. She was the rock on which this family is founded. She died the year you were born. The most virtuous woman I have ever known. And now the emperor himself is honouring her.'

The celebrations for the arch were attended by the local magistrate, numerous officials and all the family. In the evening there were fireworks. Then the family returned to their compound.

Guanji knew that Ilha was going to tease her father that night. He could see the mischievous glint in her eye. It was done with affection, of course. She started as soon as they'd all sat down. 'Well, Father,' she inquired, 'are you satisfied now?'

Her father gave her a cautious look. 'Aren't you?'

'Yes, but I'm puzzled.' She smiled. 'That's all.'

'Why are you puzzled?' he asked suspiciously.

'The virtuous widow. Preserving the family so that the ancestors will have descendants to remember them. It's all very Confucian. Very Han Chinese.'

'That is true.'

'Yet you're always reminding us that we're Manchu. We're not supposed to worry about the smaller family so much. It's the clan that matters. And the clan's plentiful. The spirit pole of the clan is well cared for in Beijing. The noble Fiongdon has plenty of descendants.'

Her father gazed at her. He knew he was being teased, but he wasn't going to let her get away with it. 'Treat your father and your family with more respect,' he said firmly.

Ilha wasn't deterred at all. 'I'm a Manchu lady, Father, not Han Chinese. Manchu girls walk tall and straight. We don't bind our feet. And we say what we think. Even the great khans of old used to take advice from their wives and mothers. It's well recorded.'

'I doubt they took any cheek from their daughters,' her father retorted. 'In any case, there are many things that are noble in Chinese tradition.

Confucian loyalty and correct behaviour, in particular. We Manchu are the guardians of China, so the emperor is encouraging us to celebrate virtuous women.' He gave her an admonishing look. 'And if it's good enough for the emperor, it's good enough for you.'

'Yes, Father,' she said obediently.

But she wasn't quite done. Maybe she'd drunk a little more rice wine than she should have. It was always the men who drank most of the wine, but everyone was celebrating that night. Whatever the cause, at the very end of the evening, she turned to her family with a big smile and addressed them all.

'Say thank you to Father,' she cried, 'for all he has done for you. He's raised the family yet again. Every rich man and mandarin in Hangzhou owes him gratitude. Every scholar at the West Lake is his friend. Now the emperor himself honours us with a family arch in Zhapu. And you know what? This is only the beginning. He has plans for us all. I had the easiest task. All I had to do was marry a worthy man.' She beamed at her husband. 'I've no complaints. Thank you, Father.' She turned to her brothers. 'But he has plans for every one of you. You're going to be rich and powerful. And Guanji's going to be a general, aren't you, Guanji?' She laughed. 'He doesn't know it yet, but Father will arrange that, too, I'm sure. We're all part of his great scheme. His wonderful plan for the glory of our family.'

'Be quiet, Ilha,' said her mother. 'It's time to go to bed.'

So the evening ended. Only Guanji was frowning a little.

When Guanji woke at the first hint of dawn, he decided to go for a ride. Nobody else was up. He wanted to think, all by himself.

He was just saddling his horse when his uncle appeared, seemingly from nowhere, and asked, 'May I join you?' And although Guanji didn't really want company, he could hardly refuse.

There was enough light in the eastern sky to see their way as they rode together, enjoying the coolness of the morning and the faint damp breeze coming from the sea. They skirted the walls of Zhapu and started out onto the long spit of land. It was quite empty. The sun had not yet risen out of the blue-grey sea.

'You've always liked to ride out here, ever since you were a little boy,' his uncle said at last.

'Yes,' said Guanji absently. 'On Wind.'

They rode on awhile before his uncle spoke again. 'Ilha's wrong, you know,' he said. 'She thinks I try to decide all the children's fates. That is not correct. I try to *discover* what it is they are fated to do. That is quite different.'

Guanji didn't reply at once. His observant uncle had guessed correctly: Ilha's words had been on his mind when he'd set out for his ride. Had the older man been waiting for him that morning so that he could talk to him? Probably.

Guanji didn't question his duty to serve the clan or the obedience he owed his uncle. That wasn't the problem. But Ilha's words had sowed a tiny doubt in his mind. Was it possible that his own belief in his destiny, one he'd held since his earliest childhood, was somehow an illusion – a falsehood created, with whatever good intention, by his uncle?

'How did you discover my destiny, Uncle?' he asked finally.

'I considered your horoscope,' his uncle replied. 'And the fact that your father was a hero – which he was,' he added quickly. 'But what really showed me the way was something else.'

'What was that?'

'The old Manchu who taught you to ride and draw a bow. *He* was the one.'

'I know he liked me . . .' Guanji began.

'Oh, it was more than that.' His uncle smiled. 'I knew it was my duty to put you on a horse. Your father would have wished me to. But I didn't know if you'd take to it. I put my own sons on a pony, too, you know. And they liked to ride well enough. But that was all. The old man took no interest in them.'

'And he did with me?'

'After your third lesson, I asked him how it was going. But he would not say. He told me to ask him in a month. So I waited a month and asked him again. And this is what he said: "I've taught plenty of boys to ride, but never one like this. Boys like this are born, not made. He is a Manchu warrior. It's not just his talent. It is his spirit. Give me this boy." So I did. But I never forced you, Guanji. You loved it. That's why the old man and his friends adopted you and taught you all their songs. They knew you were one of them.' He paused and nodded. 'That's how I knew it was your destiny.'

'I was certainly happy,' said Guanji.

'I'm annoyed with Ilha. She was foolish. She made a joke about something that is sacred. So if you want the truth about what you are, all I can tell you is to search your own heart. There's no other way.'

They reached the battery on the knoll. A line of golden light was gleaming along the horizon. They waited and watched in silence as the sun slowly emerged from the sea. Then they wheeled their horses and started back.

'I think I am a Manchu,' Guanji said. 'It is what I feel.'

'Very well.' The older man seemed pleased. They rode on a little way. But then his uncle reined in his horse and they both stopped. 'And now, Guanji, I have some more news for you to hear.'

'Good or bad?'

'Bad.' His uncle sighed. 'But it is time.' He considered a few moments. 'You have known only two places in your life so far: Zhapu and Hangzhou. Both towns with garrisons of Manchu bannermen. And while it's true that most of our bannermen don't practise horsemanship as they should, our Manchu tradition is respected here.'

'Of course.'

'What you do not know is that, outside Beijing itself, these two towns are almost the only places where that is the case.' He smiled regretfully. 'I never told you.'

'I don't understand.'

'The Manchu bannermen are broken, Guanji. In most of China, we're a laughing stock. Even the emperor has nearly given up on us.'

'But the emperor's a Manchu. The Manchus rule China.'

'Two hundred years ago,' said his uncle, 'when we drove the Ming dynasty from China, a bannerman would say proudly that he was the slave of the emperor. Why was he proud? Because to be the slave of the emperor was to be above all other men.' He nodded. 'Our garrisons, all over China, were to remind the Han that we were in charge. Bannermen were well paid – the silver stipend, the rice allowance and all sorts of other benefits besides. And we weren't allowed to engage in menial trades that were beneath a Manchu. We held our heads high. But then something happened.'

'What?'

'The march of generations. It took time, of course, but our numbers grew. Revolts, bad harvests, piracy, not to speak of the recent war with the barbarians and their evil opium, put great stress on the treasury. The emperor couldn't pay so many bannermen. The payments got smaller, and the bannermen still weren't supposed to take other work. Do you know what happens when you pay men just for existing? They become demoralised. Many forgot how to fight. But they still expected their stipends and their rice. Some even rioted when they didn't get enough. There are cities where half the bannermen are beggars now – still proud of being Manchus, of course, because they've nothing else to be proud of, poor devils. If there's trouble in one of the provinces, the emperor often uses banners of Han Chinese or even local militias instead of us.'

'Then why do you want me to be a Manchu warrior?'

'Good question. Because it's your only hope.' His uncle paused. 'There are four ways to succeed in China. One, if you're a Han, is to be a merchant. They're despised, unless they become so rich they can buy their way into the gentry. In reality I am a small merchant, though we don't call it that. But I and my sons will never get rich on our little printing press. The second way is to be a mandarin. The exams are very hard, but the rewards can be high. For the Han, there is a third way. That's to cut your balls off and become a eunuch at the royal court, where the pickings can be excellent.'

'Glad I'm not a Han.' Guanji allowed himself a smile.

'But the fourth is to be a Manchu.'

'Not from what you just said . . .'

'Wait. There is more to come. Remember: the Mandate of Heaven was granted to the Manchu dynasty. Now put yourself in the emperor's place. What does it mean to be emperor of China? What must you do?'

'The emperor must perform the ancient sacrifices to the gods to ask for good harvests.'

'Certainly. He is the Son of Heaven. He must also embody the culture of the people he rules: the Han. And for generations our Manchu dynasty has done so. The last emperor could write quite passable Chinese poetry and was proud of his calligraphy. I've heard that he even liked to correct the Chinese grammar of the memoranda he received – in red ink, of course! Above all, in order to show that his dynasty continues to hold the Mandate of Heaven, he cannot afford to let the Manchu clans lose face.'

'How does this help me?'

'Precisely because of the poor condition of so many bannermen, he is in desperate need of worthy Manchus. Men who can show both that they are literate Chinese and that they have something more – the ancient Manchu virtues that set us apart from the people we rule.'

'And that would be me?'

'I could not give you great wealth or high position, Guanji, but because of your own natural talent you have received a Manchu upbringing that is rare. Your father is recorded as a hero. The emperor himself has honoured us with an arch. And I have friends amongst the mandarins and scholars who will speak in your support. The emperor will be eager to advance your career.'

'You have done so much.'

'But you yourself can do far more. As the son of a bannerman, in the officers' school, you are already in line to become an officer. And even today, an officer gets a handsome salary. Beyond that, Guanji, you should take the provincial exams.'

'I'm not a scholar.'

'You don't need to be. Remember, you won't have to compete against the Han Chinese entrants. There is a quota of pass grades reserved for Manchu bannermen. You'll have to work hard, of course. But I'll arrange coaching, and you'll only have to make a modest showing to get through. Once you have the juren provincial degree, the doors of the administration are open to you. There's really no position you couldn't reach.'

'So I'm lucky to be a Manchu after all.'

'In this life, Guanji, you must use every advantage you have. In another generation, these privileges may not even exist. Who knows? But now you have to choose. Do you want to finish up a poor Manchu like the rest, or are you ready to fight?'

'I'm ready to fight,' said Guanji.

In the months that followed, he redoubled his efforts at school. He liked the challenge. So far, he realised, everything he'd done had been because he wanted to follow in the footsteps of his father, the hero he scarcely remembered. The idea had spurred him on, given him comfort, and brought him joy. But now he saw that his future was no longer a birthright, a natural progression, and that he'd have to fight for survival. His future was his to make – with his uncle's help, certainly – but his to lose as well.

By the time Guanji was fifteen, he'd discovered what it was to rely upon himself.

And yet it was at this time that a strange new feeling entered Guanji's life. It would come upon him suddenly, for no reason: a sense that something was missing, though he couldn't say what it was.

He'd try to shake the mood off, tell himself it was foolish. The things his uncle had said were reasonable and wise. The new realities of his life made sense. Why then should this vexatious little voice intrude itself, asking him: 'Is this truly what you want?' Of course it was, he'd answer. But the voice would persist: 'What is your life for? Is it only about the wind across the steppe, the whispers of your ancestors and the emperor's smile? Or is there something more?' And this Guanji could not answer. He wished that he could talk to Ilha about it. But Ilha was far away in Nanjing.

His teachers were delighted when Guanji and his best friends formed their little group. Their plan was to sing the old zidi songs and to practise archery, and they did it for fun. But they were also assiduous. Guanji was the best archer in the school anyway, but by practising together on their free afternoons, they all became quite outstanding. As for the songs, the group was soon much in demand at parties in Hangzhou, and they studiously added to their repertoire. When someone laughingly called them the Five Heroes, they immediately adopted the name for their musical group.

But behind their little enterprise there was a more serious intent. They did mean to be heroes. Manchu heroes. The teachers at the school understood this very well, and that was the real reason they were so delighted. Guanji's class was proving to be, as they say in schools, a very good year. Word of these young idealists even reached the court itself.

But heroes need adventures; warriors need enemies. Who was there for the Five Heroes to fight and vanquish?

The barbarians from the West were not at war with China now. They were bleeding them dry with their reparations, but neither side could afford another conflict with the other. Not yet, anyway.

The only revolt of consequence was that of the Taiping rebels in the south – and that was only sporadic.

The character of these Hakka rebels – the God Worshippers, they were calling themselves now – was quite striking. Shocking, even. They said that the Buddhists and Confucians were idolaters. They'd go into the Buddhist temples and smash every statue in them, however beautiful. 'Not only have these criminals no respect for religion and tradition,' his teacher declared to Guanji's class one day, 'but they defy the emperor himself. They've stopped shaving their heads and wearing the Manchu pigtail. They leave their hair uncut and grow it long without even combing it, so they look like the wild animals they truly are!'

'We'll fight them,' said Guanji.

The teacher replied approvingly, 'I'm afraid you won't get the chance. We've got them trapped in a town northwest of Guangzhou. I daresay they'll all be dead in a month.'

During that summer, word came that the Taiping had escaped into the hills and that they were heading north. Forty thousand of them. They'd come to a town and massacred the inhabitants. In July, his teacher proudly announced to the class that Manchu forces had skilfully ambushed the rebels by a river. Ten thousand of them were killed or drowned. A month later, however, news came that the Taiping were still operating, and that the peasants were flocking to them.

'They promise to take from the rich and give to the poor,' the class teacher explained. 'They tell the peasants that they'll set up a Christian kingdom where all the people will be free and happy – except for Manchu people, of course, who will all be killed. They'll start with the emperor, whom they call a Tartar dog, and replace him with Hong – the Hakka fellow who says he's the brother of Jesus. He's already calling himself the True Sovereign of China.'

This sounded like an enemy worth fighting. The Five Heroes went to the school authorities and asked permission to join the army. But it was refused, and the next thing Guanji knew, his uncle had been summoned to the school, where he and the principal informed the five that the emperor himself commanded them to remain at school.

Towards the end of that summer, the Taiping reached a fortified town on the great Yangtze River. But the government troops there were ready for them. A month went by, two months, three. The Taiping couldn't take the place. Towards the end of the year, the garrison at Hangzhou heard: 'The rebels have given up.'

News came slowly, for that section of the Yangtze River was nearly a thousand miles away. All Guanji heard were vague reports of Taiping columns foraging along the Yangtze, dragging boats and barges with them, looking for food.

The Chinese New Year came and went.

So Guanji was surprised to learn that the Taiping had managed to take a modest provincial town along the Yangtze. The rebels had got lucky this time, for the town contained a government treasury with a lot of silver in it. But they were still quite out of the way. The nearest major city was Nanjing, and that was six hundred miles downriver. The next report, a month later, was that they had decided to stay where they were.

It was a morning in late March when Guanji and his uncle went for a ride by the sea again. They'd returned to Zhapu ten days before, but it was nearly time for them to go back to Hangzhou. There were just a few clouds drifting in from the bay, and the air felt damp. As they had before, they rode in silence to the end of the point and waited for the sun to appear.

'I was so proud of you and your friends for wanting to fight,' his uncle said softly after a while. 'The emperor said you brought honour to the Suwan Guwalgiya clan.'

Guanji smiled. 'Dear uncle, I wish Ilha could hear you.'

'To laugh at me, you mean. I wish she were here, too.'

They rode back quietly together as the sun cast a golden light on the coarse grass. They crossed under the looming walls of the small garrison. Then as they passed the southern gate of Zhapu, a man came running out. 'Have you heard the news?' he cried. 'A messenger just came from Hangzhou. He's ridden all night. Nanjing has fallen.'

'What are you talking about?'

'The Taiping rebels. They've taken it.'

'They're six hundred miles away from Nanjing.'

'Not anymore. They've slaughtered every Manchu in the city. Men, women, children – the lot of them.'

The older man spoke first. 'The report may be incorrect.'

'Perhaps Ilha got away,' said Guanji.

o

Cecil Whiteparish was only ten miles from Nanjing when the Taiping patrol found him. They clearly thought he was a spy, so they'd brought him through the defensive checkpoints, and now he was in sight of the city gates. In a few minutes those gates would be opening. Whether he got out again remained to be seen.

Six months had passed since the huge Taiping horde had taken the place. They'd streamed down the Yangtze, their troops on the banks, their cannon and supplies in ships and barges collected along the way.

Better organised than anyone expected, they covered an astounding six hundred miles in thirty days, taking the great city of Nanjing by surprise.

Perhaps it was because the rebels had moved so fast, Cecil thought, that the countryside he'd passed through didn't look devastated. Close to the city, of course, there were untidy earth and stone ramparts and ground cleared to allow easy cannon fire. But that was all. On his right, a pale porcelain pagoda soared into the sky. It looked as if the Taiping had gutted the inside of the pagoda, but its lovely outer shell was still untouched.

The shaggy-haired Taiping troops were prodding him with spears. He rode slowly forward. They supposed he was obeying them, and in a way he was. But in truth, he was obeying the will of the Lord. At least he hoped so.

Everyone had told him not to make this journey. 'Even if you reach the place,' they said, 'you may not get out alive.' All, that is, except one. 'Trust in the Lord,' she had told him. 'I will wait for you.'

Minnie Ross had been educated by her father, who was a minister in Dundee. She'd come to Hong Kong as a governess. She was small, under five feet tall. She hadn't a penny to her name. But she was very neat in her person, and the light of the Lord was in her eye. And she was going to marry Cecil Whiteparish.

They had known each other for a year before their courtship began. It was initiated by Minnie. And it was brief.

Whiteparish had been politely walking her home from a meeting at the London Missionary Society's chapel in Hong Kong's Lower Bazaar. The chapel had been built almost as soon as victory in the Opium War put Hong Kong in British hands. The modest colonial building with its plain portico had looked rather incongruous at first, in the untidy Chinese fishing village that looked across the water to Kowloon. But recently, a fire had burned most of the Chinese village, and now British builders were tidying the area up. It was all part of the expanding occupation, which brought not only the British and their dependents to the steep slopes of Hong Kong, but all manner of Chinese from Kowloon and Canton to service the new colony.

In British Hong Kong, the missionaries had at last been able to make some Chinese converts. The London Mission was already running a medical centre and a thriving little school by the Lower Bazaar chapel.

'Tell me, Mr Whiteparish,' Minnie Ross had enquired, 'do you still hope to make converts on the mainland of China?'

'I do,' Cecil replied.

'But so far you have not.'

'Hardly anyone has,' he answered with a sigh. 'After the Opium War, when the Chinese guaranteed British entry into five ports, we thought we'd be able to preach the Word freely. But in practice, the local governors still make it almost impossible even to trade in those ports, let alone have consuls and a British community. Canton is somewhat open. The only other place is Shanghai, much farther up the coast – which is curious, really. For Shanghai was only a very minor place at the time, you know, almost an afterthought, really – though it's growing rapidly now.'

'But you still have faith in your mission?'

'Let us say that I am ten years older and a little wiser.' Cecil Whiteparish smiled. 'The life of a missionary to China is dispiriting, Miss Ross. Many of the missionaries I knew when I first came have given up and returned home. One of them may even have lost his faith. I suppose I'm still here because I put so much effort into learning Chinese, so there's more chance I might be useful in China than anywhere else. But I've no illusions. I'm a single Christian. If during my life I could bring even two others into the faith, especially if they have families, that would be a small numerical advance.'

'I'm sure you hope for more. Is it true that you are thinking of going into China illegally very soon?'

He stared at her and frowned. 'That is supposed to be a secret.'

'I don't think there are many secrets in Hong Kong, Mr Whiteparish. They say you want to go to Nanjing.'

'This rebel army, the Taiping or whatever we are to call them, say they are Christians. Nobody knows quite what they are, but they number in the tens of thousands, and they may soon control an entire province. If they are truly Christians or can be made so, it could be of huge importance. Somebody has to go and find out.'

'A dangerous mission.'

'I'm a missionary. And I know something of the Chinese by now. If I can elude the Manchu authorities along the way and reach the rebels, I doubt they will harm me.'

'You'll trust in the Lord.'

'It's what I usually do.'

'You must go,' she said, as though she had decided the matter herself.

He gazed at her. What a strange little person she was. Apart from her smallness, there was nothing really noticeable about her. Mousy hair, nose thin and pointed, eyes small, cobalt blue – that was unusual. There was something quiet but very determined about the way she set about her tasks. He'd noticed that and assumed that she had a great certainty in herself. Not surprising, really, in a daughter of the manse. One had to respect her; and if sometimes he felt a desire to laugh – though he never did so – it would have been a laugh of affection.

He was quite unprepared for what came next.

'Isn't it time you married, Mr Whiteparish?'

'I don't know about that,' he said. 'Not many women would want to share the life of a missionary; and my means are very modest. I've never considered myself in a position to marry.'

'I would marry you,' she said simply.

'Good heavens.' He hardly knew what to say. 'Why?'

'Because you are a good man. What other reason could there be to marry?'

He stared down at her and realised that she was entirely serious. This was how she thought. Without meaning to, he burst out laughing.

'Why do you laugh, Mr Whiteparish? Are you mocking me?' She looked hurt.

'No, Miss Ross. I was laughing with pleasure. At your goodness. Would you marry me, then?'

'Why, yes. I already said so.'

He gazed at her, then across the water. Then back at her again. 'Well then,' he said, 'it seems you know your mind, Miss Ross. I suggest we marry when I get back from Nanjing.'

'Not before?'

'Better that you should become a wife,' he said gently, 'than a widow.'

Yet now that the gates of Nanjing were in front of him, and he was about to meet his destiny, what most impressed Cecil Whiteparish was not the danger he might be in. Indeed, he almost forgot to be afraid.

For to his surprise, the main sensation he felt was one of wonder. Wonder at the beauty of the place.

Most of China's great cities were ancient. Nanjing was over two thousand years old. Cecil didn't know exactly, but he was sure the walls of Nanjing must be nearly twenty miles in circuit and so thick that an entire army could have marched on top of them. The city's position was excellent, at the centre of China's rich heartland in the Yangtze River valley. For the three hundred years before the Manchu invaded, the Ming dynasty had made it their capital.

But each great city also had its own particular feature, one that came into the imagination the moment the place was mentioned. And this was what he gazed at now.

The Purple Mountain.

One couldn't miss the Purple Mountain. It began to rise outside the walls of the city's northeastern quadrant, where the old Ming emperor's palace lay. It continued northwards for miles, in a sweeping slope to its final ridge, which seemed to be in close communion with the heavens. And for some reason – the atmosphere, the angle of the light filtering through the blue-grey clouds that formed over it, or other natural causes, whatever they might be – the great green hill was often bathed in a magical glow, tinged with violet and reds, that caused it to seem not green, but purple.

The Purple Mountain was a holy place. The tombs of the Ming emperors were still to be found upon it.

Yet as Cecil Whiteparish gazed at this Chinese hill, it seemed to him that although the landscape might be dotted with Buddhist and Taoist monasteries, Confucian temples and heathen graves, it would be hard, in such beauty, not to see the Creator's hand. Could it be that the true God was indeed being worshipped here by these Taiping rebels? What a wonderful thing that would be.

He was about to find out – if they didn't kill him.

As soon as his captors reported at the gates, he was delivered to a sergeant with a platoon of soldiers who conducted him up the main central street for about a thousand yards. Then they turned eastwards, towards the old Ming palace, but hardly went more than a quarter mile when they entered a big complex of buildings, like a barracks.

Five minutes later he had discovered that it was a prison – and that he was locked inside it.

Not that he had been thrown into a vile cell. The room was a good size, and he was the only occupant. It contained a chair and a table. But the windows, which looked out onto a small blank courtyard, were heavily barred.

During the next few hours several people came in. One was a gaoler who gave him water and a little rice before leaving in silence and locking the door. Three others came at intervals. Though with their long hair they looked to him like wild men, they were probably officers of some kind. Each of them asked him the same questions about who he was and why he had come there, before departing. Hours passed. He sat and read his Bible. Evening came. He wondered if they would give him a lamp. They did not. Darkness fell. He felt hungry. He found three grains of rice he had missed in the bowl he'd been given. He did not see them, but felt them with his fingers and ate them.

He had not been able to make out the face of the stout fob watch he carried, so he did not know what time it was when the door of his prison opened and two figures came in. One of them was evidently a gaoler, who carried a lamp on a pole. The other was an officer, and Cecil had a feeling that this might be a man of some importance. He murmured to the gaoler, who brought the lamp close to Cecil's face so that the officer could inspect it. Another order followed, and the lamp was held high so that all three men were illumined.

The officer had long hair, but it was neatly combed and brushed. He wore a simple tunic, spotlessly clean, with a sash. He looked to be maybe thirty, but the lines on his face suggested that he had the experience of a man ten years older. He had a scar on his cheek. 'You know me,' he said in Cantonese.

It was Nio.

'When they described this strange spy to me, I thought it might be you. So I came to see.'

'Not a spy, Nio. A British missionary, just as I was before. I came because I heard that the Taiping were Christian. I wanted to know. Is it true?'

'We follow the One True God.'

'Do you yourself?'

'Of course.'

'I wonder . . .' Cecil ventured. 'Do you remember when I used to speak to you about our Lord and our faith?'

'I remember it well. You are wondering if your words affected me.'

'I should be glad if perhaps—'

'Your words did not affect me.'

'Oh.'

'But I thought that you were a good man, and this may save your life. Nobody here knows what to do with you.'

'I see.' Cecil frowned. 'Please tell me, for people say different things, what caused the Taiping to be Christian?'

'Years ago, our leader, the One True King, was given some Christian tracts. Perhaps they came from an American missionary on one of the opium smuggling boats. I do not know. But wherever they came from, our leader put them away and forgot about them. Sometime later, however, he chanced to read them and immediately received a divine revelation. He began to preach. People gathered around him, and the movement was born.'

'The Heavenly Kingdom.'

'Nanjing is about to become the Heavenly Capital.'

'Your One True King says he is the younger brother of Jesus?'

'That is so. We call Jesus Heavenly Elder Brother.'

'But Jesus lived a long time ago.'

'All things are possible to God.'

'Perhaps we can discuss that later. And you believe in brotherly love, goodness and kindness to all mankind?'

'Certainly.'

'I have heard that many Manchu were killed here.'

'It is true. They lived in the quarter around the old Ming palace. The Manchu are not true Chinese. They have trampled upon our people. And they are idolaters, too. When they fought us, we killed them all.'

'The women and children, too?'

'God told His people to kill all the idolaters.'

'It is better to love and convert them.'

'They weren't willing.' Nio paused. 'You missionaries used the evil opium trade to spread the Gospel. And we're killing some Manchus to establish God's Heavenly Kingdom. That's all.'

'What will the Heavenly Kingdom be like?'

'It is here,' said Nio. 'I will show you tomorrow.'

They gave Cecil a good breakfast in the morning. Then Nio arrived and took him out into the street. It was a sunny day. They went westwards.

There were plenty of people about. The stores were open. Everything seemed normal. And yet, Cecil thought, something felt strange – as if this wasn't China, but some other land.

And then he realised: none of the men were wearing the queue, the pigtail down their back, the sign of their servitude to the Manchu. Chinese men had worn the queue for so many generations now that foreigners supposed it was how the Chinese looked. But no man in China had worn a pigtail during the centuries of the Ming dynasty or the Tang or the Han or any dynasty before. He'd observed the Taiping warriors with their long hair on his way to Nanjing. But now he saw a whole population in their natural state. No wonder it seemed strange.

They passed a small Buddhist temple. The statues in the courtyard had been smashed. He frowned. Why did it offend him? Because they were perhaps works of art? Or was it the destructive anger he sensed in the deed?

'Soon,' Nio remarked, 'that will be a church to the One True God.'

They passed a weaving works, then a large storehouse.

'What's that?' Cecil asked.

'The main granary,' Nio replied. 'It's for all the people now. No more merchants profiteering on the people's food. This is the Earthly Paradise. All men are equal. No private property. Everything is shared in common. Nobody goes hungry. To each according to his need.' He looked at Whiteparish questioningly. 'This is how the followers of Jesus lived after he rose into the sky, is it not?'

'It wasn't quite that simple,' said Cecil, but he didn't argue.

They came to what might have been a barracks, though Cecil saw no soldiers there.

'Women's quarters,' Nio explained. 'The single men and women are not allowed to mix. No immorality.'

'And if any should stray from the path of chastity . . . ?'

'They are executed,' Nio answered firmly. He pointed up the street. 'That is the palace of the East King. It was a prince's palace before, I think.'

'Tell me about the East King.'

'The Heavenly Kingdom will be ruled by the Heavenly King, whom we also call Lord of Ten Thousand Years. But he will have four lesser kings.'

'That has been done in many empires before. Genghis Khan's empire, for instance. And ancient Ireland.'

'I know nothing of that.'

'Tell me more about the Heavenly King. I know he is a Hakka, but what was his story?'

'He was a poor student. He worked hard and passed first in the local examinations. But though he tried four times, he could not pass the provincial examination in Canton. They say many candidates pass by bribing the examiners, but he did not. God sent him a vision and told him he was His younger son. But for a long time he did not understand the vision. At last he read the tracts and understood his mission. He began to preach. Followers came to him. That is how the Heavenly Kingdom began.'

'He truly believes he is the second son of God?'

'He does.'

They followed the broad street until they came in sight of a large palace behind a high wall. 'That is where the Heavenly King lives,' said Nio.

'I should like to meet him,' Cecil remarked.

'That will not be possible.'

'Does he know I'm here?'

'Of course.'

They advanced towards the palace gates. And they had nearly reached them when a little procession emerged – a line of brightly coloured carriages and sedan chairs, well guarded, and through whose windows Cecil could see what appeared to be richly dressed court ladies. 'Is he coming out?' he asked.

'No.'

'Who are they, then?'

'Those are the wives of the Heavenly King.'

'How many wives does he have?'

'Seventeen.' Nio glanced at the missionary and saw his surprise. 'It is necessary for the Heavenly King to have many wives, like the emperor,' he explained. 'Otherwise he would not be regarded as a king.'

'I hardly think . . .' Cecil began.

'Your rulers do not have wives and concubines?'

'Well . . .' Cecil wanted to refute it, but a need for honesty prevented him. Who could deny that, from King Solomon in Jerusalem to the most

Christian monarchs of even his own time, the rulers of the West had usually had many women? Only in the United States in modern times was the case otherwise – and he was not quite sure even about that. He decided to change the subject. 'Tell me,' he asked, 'what is it that you yourself desire to find in the Heavenly Kingdom?'

'An end to oppression. An end to corruption. Justice. Truth. The rule of the good people.'

'Did you always seek this?'

'Since I was a boy. But I did many bad and foolish things along the way.'

'Many people, hurt or disappointed by the world and its imperfection, seek purity. That desire is not unusual.'

'It is what we seek.'

'But you seek it here on Earth.' Cecil Whiteparish sighed. 'And Christians understand that a perfect world is not possible on Earth. We say it was lost when Adam and Eve were expelled from the Garden of Eden. The purity you seek can be found only in Heaven.'

'We shall make Heaven here.'

'It cannot be done on Earth.'

'Why?'

'Human nature.'

'Then we shall change human nature.'

'A noble desire, Nio. But history shows this path leads to tyranny.'

'You are supposed to be a missionary.'

'Yes. These are the lessons that missionaries learn.'

Nio was silent for a few moments. 'You should not stay here,' he finally said.

'Why?'

'You argue too much. But I will arrange a safe conduct for you.'

'When must I leave?' Cecil asked.

'Today.'

'Can I go up the Purple Mountain? It looks beautiful.'

'No.' Nio walked a few paces in silence. 'I have a message for you. From the Heavenly King.'

'I am listening.'

'Tell your rulers that we worship the One True God. The Manchu are idolaters and they will never give you what you want. You should help us destroy them. That is all.'

Cecil Whiteparish left that afternoon with a guard of six horsemen. His parting from Nio was polite. Perhaps each of them wanted to show more warmth. Cecil knew that he did; and he thought the same was true of Nio, but it was hard to tell.

o

It was the second of December when John Trader reached Hong Kong. He didn't plan to stay there long. He meant to see Cecil Whiteparish before he left, of course. Indeed, he had already prepared a short note to make the missionary aware of his presence.

But since he bumped into him on the dock, while the men were still unloading his travelling trunks, there was no need to send it.

'Cousin John!' cried Whiteparish. 'Welcome back. I didn't know you were coming.'

'I've written you a note to tell you. But here you are, which is better.'

'It's been more than a year. Did you find your estate in Scotland?'

'We did. Just twenty miles from the Lomond estate, where the general and my mother-in-law rent the dower house now. My wife is overjoyed. And the children love the place.'

'And you?'

'It's everything I always dreamed of.'

'You'll reside in Scotland?'

'Yes.' Trader nodded. 'As you may know, I bought out the Odstocks a while ago. Now I've sold two-thirds of the firm, which will continue here under new partners. I'm retaining a third for myself, and I shall manage the business in Britain.'

'You'll still have to go to London, I suppose.'

'Every so often. But with the new railway, one can make the entire journey from Glasgow to London in only twelve and a half hours. That's four hundred miles. Thirty-two miles an hour!'

'Astounding. Unimaginable when we were boys.' Whiteparish shook his head in wonderment. 'So you've come to sell your house in Hong Kong.'

'I have.'

'Will you stay there meanwhile?'

'No. It's too much trouble. I have lodgings in the lower town.' He glanced up towards the Peak above. 'My wife never liked it up there.'

'She wasn't alone,' Whiteparish agreed. 'Almost all the big merchants that built places up on the Peak seem to have had problems – cracking walls, leaking roofs . . . something's always going wrong.'

'She was quite right to take the children back to Macao. Young children and all that.'

'She always came here to keep you company, though.'

'A week every month, without fail. She was very good about that.'

'We were glad to see her, too. She took a great interest in the mission. As did you, of course,' Cecil added quickly.

Trader gave a wry smile. My wife's enthusiasm, he thought, and my money. But he didn't say so.

Cecil Whiteparish had his own views about Agnes Trader. In the early days of her marriage, when she and John had lived in their charming hillside villa in Macao, they'd certainly been busy. John was making a fortune. Agnes gave birth to four children. And he himself had been busy enough with his missionary work. A couple of times a year, however, they'd ask him up to the villa for dinner, and these were always pleasant occasions.

Gradually, however, the British community was moving across to Hong Kong. As yet, the place was more spartan and lacked the Mediterranean charm of Macao. He'd set up the mission there. Some time afterwards, the Trader family had followed.

And Agnes hadn't liked Hong Kong. Cecil could understand, but he thought that for John's sake she should have shown it less. And when she'd taken the children back to Macao, he'd felt disappointed in her. She might have been scrupulous about spending a week with her husband each month, but when one considered that John often had to be away at the factories in Canton, it had seemed to Cecil that his cousin was getting a raw deal.

Whenever she was in Hong Kong, Agnes made a point of visiting the mission, sometimes having quite long conversations with him, and ensuring that John made a handsome contribution to the mission's work each year. This was all very well, and he was grateful for the money, of course. But he still thought privately that she could have behaved better.

She'd got what she wanted, anyway. The estate in Scotland.

'Agnes has become very religious recently,' Trader suddenly said.

'Indeed?' Whiteparish wasn't sure how to respond. 'By the way,' he remarked, 'I am about to get married myself. Next week, in fact. Would you come to my wedding?'

'My dear fellow!' Trader shook him by the hand. 'How splendid. I had no idea.'

'It happened rather suddenly.'

'You were kind enough to come to my wedding. I certainly wouldn't miss yours.'

Whiteparish glanced towards the ship and saw two men bringing Trader's bags.

'Will you dine with me tomorrow?' he asked. 'Simple fare. But I can introduce you to my fiancée.'

'Delighted,' said John Trader. And indeed, he had to admit, he was quite curious to see the lady.

He liked her at once. How could he not? After all, he thought, if someone is so obviously good and at the same time matter-of-fact and friendly, one would have to be a strange kind of person to dislike them.

He also noticed, with amusement, that this neat little Scottish lady had already made some changes to Cecil's spartan quarters near the mission chapel. A vase of flowers, a perfectly laid table: small signs of a woman's hand that his bachelor cousin would probably never have thought of.

He wondered, though, how much Cecil had told her about him.

He didn't imagine she approved of his business any more than Cecil did. On the other hand, since most of the small British community on Hong Kong were connected with the opium trade in one way or another, he supposed she'd decided it wiser to keep her thoughts to herself. As for his past love life, it was long ago and hardly scandalous, he thought, even to a puritan.

She asked him about his children.

'We have four, Miss Ross. James is the eldest. He's at boarding school with his brother, Murdo; he'll go to Eton in a couple of years. My daughters, Emily and Constance, are at home with a governess.' He noticed Whiteparish give his fiancée a glance suggesting that even if he disapproved of the source of the Trader family wealth, his missionary cousin was still just a little bit pleased to have such aristocratic-seeming connections. 'So like my own wife, Miss Ross, you are Scots, but from the east coast rather than the west, I think?'

'Indeed, sir, my father is a minister in Montrose.'

'And what brought you to Hong Kong?'

'The family by whom I was employed in Edinburgh asked me to

accompany them here. When I consulted my father, he told me that I should go and see the world, if I wished.'

'What an adventurous soul you have, Miss Ross, and what a wise father.' Trader smiled.

This seemed to please her. But she wanted to draw something else to his attention. 'Has your cousin told you about his own recent adventure on the mainland?' she asked. And when Trader looked uncertain, she turned to her fiancé.

'Ah,' said Cecil. 'Indeed. This might be of interest to you. I have been to Nanjing, to see the Taiping.'

'That's a dangerous undertaking.' Trader looked at Whiteparish with a new respect. Then he glanced at Minnie Ross. 'Weren't you worried?'

'No,' she replied simply. 'Whatever happened to him, it would be God's will.'

'Oh,' said Trader.

'I'll tell you about it over dinner,' said Cecil with a smile.

They had completed the main course by the time he'd finished. Trader was fascinated and thanked him warmly.

'Would you say they were Christian?' he asked his missionary cousin.

'I'd hoped, of course. Perhaps they can be made into Christians. But many things concern me. Their leader, by claiming to be the brother of Jesus, is trying to make a cult of himself. That is never good.'

'You don't think he could mean it in a general sense, as we might speak of "brothers and sisters in Christ"?'

'I think he means it literally. As for having seventeen wives . . .'

Trader glanced at Minnie Ross.

'These Taiping speak of their Heavenly Kingdom,' Minnie said, 'yet they killed every Manchu in Nanjing – women and children, too.'

'It's true,' said Cecil. 'I asked.'

'I don't much care for their idea that all private property should be abolished, either,' Trader remarked. 'There is, however, another consideration. Namely, that whether these people are genuine or not, it may not really matter. At least to the British government.'

Minnie Ross looked puzzled, but Whiteparish nodded. 'I was afraid you'd say that,' he murmured sadly.

'The British government is unhappy, Miss Ross,' Trader explained. 'The treaty of 1842 promised our merchants access to five ports, consuls in those ports as well – all the usual things that we, and other nations, expect in other countries. Apart from Canton and Shanghai, it hasn't happened, and even in those places there have been difficulties.'

'The Chinese feel those concessions were made under duress,' Cecil added. 'And the reparations we demanded were crushing.'

'All treaties following a defeat are made under duress. History's full of them,' Trader countered. 'Though I agree about the reparations. But the fact remains that we, the French, even the Americans, are growing impatient with a regime we see as corrupt and obstructive.'

'And the Taiping are seen as a possible alternative?'

'Back in London, a Christian government in China looks an attractive proposition.'

'You remember, Cousin John,' the missionary said, 'how we all learned in school the ancient doctrine that the enemy of my enemy is my friend. For centuries, Britain preserved itself by pitting the great continental powers of Europe against each other, and it worked pretty well. But I believe there are two potential fallacies in the doctrine.'

'Expound.'

'The first fallacy is simple. Your enemy's enemy may seem to be your friend today, but not tomorrow. Say you help him to victory, and then, being more powerful, he may turn on you. We may help the Taiping gain power, but as soon as they've got it, they may treat us worse than the Manchu did.'

'The idea was to keep rebalancing the powers. But I agree, there's a danger in changing any regime. Better the devil you know. What's the other fallacy?'

'It is more insidious, I think,' said Whiteparish. 'It is the moral fallacy. Consider: your enemy is a bad man. You know without a doubt that he is evil. The man who opposes him, therefore, the man who can strike him down, must be good. But it's not so. There is no reason at all to suppose he is good. Very likely, he is just another bad man.' He paused. 'So you try to find out if your enemy's enemy is good or bad, and he tells you that he is good. For this will bring you and others to his cause. And this pleases you.' He paused again, then shook his head. 'But he is lying. He is just another bad man, perhaps worse than the first.'

'And the Taiping?'

'They say they are Christian. So we think they must be good. We want to think them good. We may even close our eyes to their evil, because we do not wish to see it. A man puts on a coat like mine, so I think he must be like me. But he is not.'

'A wolf in sheep's clothing.'

'Exactly so. As my dear Minnie has just pointed out, the Taiping say they are Christian and that they mean to build a kindly Heavenly Kingdom; yet their first act has been to slaughter an entire population of innocent women and children. I will work to convert them into better Christians; but you certainly shouldn't give them any guns.'

'I thought missionaries were supposed to be more idealistic,' Trader said with a smile.

'They may be idealistic until they get into the field. Then they see real life, and it's not pretty.'

'They carry on, though.'

'That's the test of faith.'

'You're a good man, Cousin Cecil,' said Trader warmly. 'I admire you. And when I get back to London I shall repeat what you say. I just hope,' he continued quietly, 'that they listen.'

When their meal was over, the two men walked Minnie Ross back to the house where she was governess. 'A few more days, and you will not have to do this anymore,' she remarked to him with a smile as he kissed her on the cheek at the door. Then the two men made their way slowly towards Trader's lodgings.

'Tell me,' Whiteparish ventured, 'are you keeping a third share of the business for your son to manage one day?'

'One of them, perhaps. If either of them is interested.' Trader smiled. 'That's a long way off. I just like to keep my hand in. I'm far too young to retire, even though I can afford to.'

'You'll keep yourself busy in Scotland. I'm sure you'll be a model landlord.' Cecil paused. 'I thought that perhaps the next generation . . .'

'Would prefer to avoid the dirty old opium trade. You can say it.' Trader walked on a few steps. 'In ten, fifteen years' time, the opium trade may not even be important. It's ironic, but I suspect that if China became less defensive and opened her ports up to more general trade – in other words, if we could sell her more – the problem would disappear. The country is so huge and potentially rich. I'm not alone in thinking this.

The men at Jardine Matheson, whose operations dwarf the rest of us, anticipate a far more general trade in the future.'

'I hope you're right.'

They came in sight of Trader's lodgings.

'There is one thing I'd like to ask you,' Trader said. 'It's a private matter.'

'Then it will remain so.'

'Thank you.' Trader nodded slowly. 'It concerns Agnes. She has always shown a proper respect for the church. But in recent years her religion has become' – he hesitated – 'more intense. Had you ever noticed?'

'That's rather hard to say. She's been very good to the mission, of course.'

'Has she ever discussed matters of faith with you?'

'Now and then, as far as I recall.'

'Has she ever discussed the question of marriage and children?'

'Let me see.' Cecil thought a moment. 'I think I remember one conversation. This was quite a long time ago, you know. We spoke about it in a general way.'

'Did she discuss Saint Paul or Saint Augustine, might I ask?'

Whiteparish took another moment to consider. 'I believe,' he answered slowly, 'she asked me about Saint Paul and marriage. The saint was celibate himself, of course, which was unusual amongst the Jews. Along with his strictures against lust, he recommended celibacy – if it could be managed. One has to remember that in those early days, the Christian community expected the world to end within their lifetime.'

'And after Paul?'

'You really come to Saint Augustine, over three centuries later. People still awaited the end of the world, but its date was unclear. Augustine thought that devout Christians could marry, but that the act of procreation should be for the purpose of having children. Otherwise, he argued, it became lust and was therefore sinful. That was generally the doctrine of the early church.'

'Have your children. Then abstain.'

'Yes.' The missionary smiled. 'I'm not saying it was adhered to.'

'And nowadays?'

'The marriage service, as you know, speaks only of regulating the natural affections. Not many clergymen would want to go further than that.'

'You told this to my wife?'

'Yes. As doctrinal history.'

'You did not . . . recommend?'

'Oh.' Cecil stared at his cousin in surprise. 'No, I did not. I would not.' He frowned, then gave his kinsman a curious look. 'I should be happy to write to your wife to clarify the subject, if you wish.'

'No. I just wondered. Don't write. Goodnight.' After all, Trader thought, if celibacy was what his wife desired, he had no wish to make demands that were repugnant to her.

o

The first time Shi-Rong saw Mei-Ling was in the autumn of that year. As magistrate for the area, he was making a tour of inspection when he came to the hamlet where she lived. The villagers had seen his cavalcade approaching and they were clustered in the lane to watch him pass. The headman had welcomed him and offered refreshment, but it was only mid-morning and there was no reason to stop, so Shi-Rong thanked him but proceeded on his way.

He caught sight of Mei-Ling just as he was leaving. She was standing beside the lane with a thickset friendly-looking peasant – her husband, perhaps – and three or four others. Peasants, certainly. None of the women had bound feet. But they appeared a little better dressed than most villagers.

He turned to his secretary, Sun, who was riding beside him. 'Did you notice that pretty woman? Rich peasant, would you say?'

'Yes, Lord.' Sun had been with him for five years now. He still didn't know Sun's age, exactly. Maybe he was forty-five. It didn't matter. Tall, almost cadaverous, silent, trustworthy Sun had no ambition. His presence was restful. 'One of the headman's family, perhaps.'

'Did you notice her complexion?'

Whether one was in a great city or the depths of the country, nearly everyone had some physical flaw. Most adults past a certain age had missing teeth, of course. They might have a squint, a mole on their face, a damaged arm or leg. Accidents and disease were the common lot of the people in every land, he imagined. Yet so far as he could see, this peasant woman was perfect in every way. Beautiful. Flawless. He almost stopped the cavalcade. He wanted to linger. At the least, he wished to ascertain if she was truly as perfect as she seemed.

'We have business to attend to elsewhere, Lord,' said Sun.

'I know.' Shi-Rong sighed. 'I've been away from my wife too long. You know,' he continued, 'if I hadn't been told this was only a temporary appointment and that I'd soon be sent elsewhere, I would have brought my family here. I thought it was less disruptive to leave them at home until I had a better establishment to receive them.'

'I understand, Lord.'

'All the same . . . Perhaps I should send for them.' He paused. 'I thought I'd get something better than this by now,' he murmured.

After his father's death, he'd used his time pretty well. First he'd studied at the family estate; then he'd gone back to old Mr Wen in Beijing. He'd passed his exams – not with outstanding honours, but well enough to put him in line for a good career. And he'd married. The daughter of the prefect of a province. An appropriate marriage. They were happy enough.

'It's a pity that Commissioner Lin has died,' said Sun.

'It was he who first got me a job as a magistrate,' Shi-Rong acknowledged. 'But I doubt he could do more for me now, even if he were alive.'

Lin had regained his good name. To some, he was a hero. He'd even been made governor of a province again, though not an important one. But he'd never advanced beyond that point.

'The fact is, anyone connected with the Opium War is under a cloud at court,' Shi-Rong remarked. 'The emperor thought quite well of me, but he's dead, too, and the new emperor doesn't know me at all.'

'At least, Lord, you have a fine family estate on the Yellow River to go back to. Few magistrates have such good fortune.'

'Which is why they take bribes. You know I have never taken a bribe.'

'I do, Lord. You are greatly to be commended.'

'Good fortune may be a blessing. It may also be a curse. Perhaps, if I were a poorer man, I might strive harder. I do not know. What do you think?'

'I cannot say, Lord. But I am glad I am not ambitious. It never seems to make people happy.'

'Tell me, Sun – I know you are a Buddhist – what do you expect to be in your next incarnation?'

'Something peaceful, I hope, Lord.'

'Well, you deserve it.' Shi-Rong nodded. 'I think I should go back for that pretty woman we just saw.' He glanced at his secretary, saw the look of concern on his face, and laughed. 'Don't worry,' he said, 'I won't.'

Nor did Shi-Rong pass through the hamlet again during the course of that year or the year after.

o

Mei-Ling remembered that day, but not because of Shi-Rong. She'd hardly even seen his face. She remembered it because that night her sister-in-law had gone into labour for the eighth time. And by morning poor Willow was dead. She left four living children, the youngest a boy.

Willow's life had not been very happy and would have been worse if it hadn't been for Mei-Ling. This wasn't so much because Mei-Ling tried to be kind to her, though she did. But the fact that every time poor Willow produced another daughter, Mei-Ling had produced another son seemed to deflect the rage that Mother would otherwise have felt towards her elder daughter-in-law. The family matriarch came to regard Willow as a lost cause, an unfortunate fact of nature, like bad weather. When at last Willow did produce a son, she was treated in the same manner as a useless employee who finally does something right, but cannot be relied upon to do so again. And now she was dead. What did it signify?

As it happened, a turning point.

Old Mr Lung had been so proud of his little opium ceremonies and furious when Commissioner Lin's campaign stopped his supplies. When in due course the opium had become available again, he'd laid in a considerable quantity. He could afford it. Indeed, guests were treated to a visit to the storeroom where his cases of opium were kept, which greatly impressed them.

'If any interfering mandarin starts throwing opium into the sea again, he won't worry me,' the old man would declare.

'No, Mr Lung,' his guest would agree respectfully.

But the British opium trade had continued, so there was an excess available in the house. Old Mr Lung's sessions became more frequent. He attended less to his business, and in due course bought more opium than he had before. Sometimes Elder Son would join him in these sessions. Second Son never did. He was offered the chance, but he always smiled and said he was happy as he was. He just went about his tasks on the land as usual, and old Mr Lung and his elder brother attended to the loans and the collection of rents and the other business.

So when one night old Mr Lung slipped into unconsciousness after his usual evening smoke and never awoke, it came as a shock to discover that there wasn't much money left. There were all kinds of loans due to him and other complex arrangements that Elder Son declared were all safely in his head, but somehow the loans were never collected, and though his mother demanded to know who owed what, so she could go and collect the money herself, Elder Son proved surprisingly obstinate about supplying the information.

'I am the head of the family now,' he reminded her, as if that solved anything. And though Second Son did try to get some sense out of him, as he truly said to Mei-Ling, 'If he isn't going to tell Mother, he certainly isn't going to tell me.' They even tried to enlist the help of Willow, but she only bowed gracefully to her husband's authority, which was no use at all.

So the rents were paid in arrears, if at all. Several of the villagers bought their rented fields from him, at reduced prices. Even the family house was beginning to show some signs of neglect, although Second Son attended to all the repairs himself.

And then, that night after the magistrate passed through, Willow had died.

Elder Son seemed to have lost his desire to do anything much after that. He smoked more opium. His raw-boned body became thin and wasted. He hardly had energy to attend to any business at all. And if he did manage to bestir himself to collect some of the remaining rents, for instance, his tenants treated him almost as if he were a vagrant seeking charity, instead of their landlord. Mother did manage to transact some of the family business, but even her fierce spirit was becoming tired.

One day Mei-Ling went to the secret place where the silver Nio had given her was buried. She took a little of it and gave it to Mother. 'It's for the house,' she said. 'Not for opium.' A few months later she had to go to the secret place again. A few visits more and all the silver was gone.

A sense of torpor and neglect descended upon the Lung family house after that. People didn't come there anymore.

It was two and a half years after Willow's death when the Americans arrived.

The three men had set out from Canton a week ago. Now they sat drinking together after their meal at the small town's only inn. Read was smoking a cigar. He looked just as big, hard and burly as he had almost twenty years ago. Some grey hairs, some deeper lines. Few other changes. His son, Franklin, was a dark-haired, handsome young fellow of eighteen or so. The third was Cecil Whiteparish.

When Read had turned up in Hong Kong and asked if there was a merchant called Trader there, it was natural enough that he should have been directed to the mission house, where he found Cecil Whiteparish.

'Mr Trader is a kinsman of mine,' Cecil explained. 'But I'm afraid he lives with his family in Scotland now – I can give you his address if you want to write to him.' He'd smiled. 'I'm rather busy at this moment, but if you'd care to come to my house this evening, my wife will feed us, and I can give you all the news about my cousin John.'

It had been a very pleasant evening. Read had been delighted to hear about Trader's good fortune and his burgeoning family. The Whiteparishes had given him some account of the activities of the mission and its converts. And then Minnie had asked: 'What has brought you to Hong Kong just now, Mr Read?'

'Railways, ma'am,' Read answered easily. 'Or to be precise, railway workers. I mean to find them in the villages down the coast from Canton and take them to America.'

'Will they wish to go so far?' she asked.

'They already have.' And seeing her look surprised: 'During the California Gold Rush, back in '48 and the years following, quite a few adventuresome fellows from the Cantonese coastland heard about it from Western sailors and thought they'd try their luck. I shipped a few of them across the Pacific myself. Sailors. Smugglers, I daresay. All kinds of good fellows.'

'What do you think impelled them?' asked Whiteparish.

'I'd probably have done the same in their place,' Read answered. 'You remember how it was here, after the Opium War. The government was broke. The men along the coast heard about the Gum Shan, the American mountain of gold. They went to the Klondike like everyone else, and most came out empty-handed. Plenty of them are still in California – running small restaurants, laundries, that sort of thing. But now we're looking for something different. That's why we're going inland.'

'Men to build railways.'

'Yes. Local railways, in California first. But soon there'll be a railway stretching right across America, from California to New England. It's got to come. They'll need a lot of labour.'

'Don't the Irish supply that?' Cecil asked.

'They do. But my guess is the railway men want to give the Irish a little competition. Keep them in line, you know.'

'Why Chinese?'

'They aren't as strong as the Irish, but they're very steady. They drink tea instead of alcohol. They give no trouble. I'm not looking for gold diggers,' Read said. 'I want honest farming men who've fallen on hard times. Men who'll work hard and send money back to their families. I believe we'll find them in the villages.'

'When do you set off?' asked Cecil.

'Any day. I just need to find a couple of porters, a local guide and an interpreter. I speak a bit of Cantonese, but not enough.' A thought struck him. 'I wonder if you've got any converts who might act as interpreter with the locals. Any suggestions?'

Cecil considered. 'Let me think. Come by the mission tomorrow afternoon, and I'll let you know if I've got anyone.'

Young Franklin looked at his father and the missionary. Then he glanced across to where the two local men who acted as porters and guides were sitting apart with the owner of the inn, talking quietly in the local dialect.

It was exciting to be on an adventure with his father in this hinterland. He wondered what the next day would bring.

It had been such a surprise when Whiteparish had volunteered himself as their interpreter. His first thought had been that the missionary might not be up to the physical challenges of the business. But although his hair was thinning, Whiteparish seemed quite a tough, wiry sort of man, so Franklin assumed he'd be all right.

His father had raised another sort of question. 'How does your lady wife feel about your travelling with us?'

'She says that a man needs an adventure now and then.' Cecil had smiled. 'Glad to get me out of the house for a bit, I expect.'

'And the mission?'

'Ah. That's just the point. Besides Hong Kong, we now have a small subsidiary mission outside Canton. The Chinese don't much like it, though they turn a blind eye. I was due to visit that mission soon in any case. But I've been thinking for a while that I should also venture out into the backcountry, talk to the local people, that sort of thing. Not easy to do by oneself. So when you turned up with your plan for an expedition, I thought: this might be the perfect opportunity.'

'Do you mean to bring tracts?' Read had wanted to know.

'No. If the local authorities stop and search us, that might get everyone in trouble.' He gave them a wry smile. 'One gets more cautious with time. I prefer talking to people, telling them what I believe and why. You never know where that may lead.' He nodded. 'There's another factor as well.'

'The Taiping?'

'Exactly. I've been to Nanjing. The Taiping are not really Christians. I'm certain of that. They've imbibed a few ideas that are Christian. Before they moved north, there were quite a few Taiping in this region, and I'm wondering if they may have left behind some notions that we could correct and build upon. This little expedition may allow me to find out.'

'You're a spy, then,' young Franklin had cried, then glanced at his father, who gave him a look that said, 'You're on your own now, son.'

'A spy for God,' Cecil replied. 'Though the Almighty already knows everything,' he'd added cheerfully.

'Indeed,' said Franklin.

Before they turned in, however, Whiteparish insisted on going over the order of business a final time. He addressed himself to Read. 'You'll take these men, these volunteers, from Canton to America. And the Chinese volunteers won't pay you for their passage, the railway bosses will.'

'Correct. I charge 'em up to a hundred dollars a head, delivered and guaranteed. I carry other cargo as well, to make it worth my while.'

'Effectively then, these Chinese will be indentured servants until they've worked off the cost of their voyage. And history tells us that in practice, an indentured man can become a slave.'

'It's true.' Read drew on his cigar. 'And I know of Chinese servants in California who are in exactly that position.'

'I'm not sure I like it, Read.'

'Nor do I. So I made a deal with the railway men. I'll take back any of my Chinese that aren't satisfactory after a month; and if any of the Chinese want to leave, I'll take them back, too, and refund the fare.'

'That could be an expensive proposition for you.'

'I doubt it. These Chinese are going to make pretty good money. They all live together. They form little teams and gangs of their own. It comes naturally to them. My guess is that as soon as the big coast-to-coast railway starts building, I'll be filling my ships every season with Chinese as eager to go as the railway men are to have them. Half of them will probably settle in America.'

'Well, I hope you're right.'

'And I hope you trust me.'

'Oh yes.' The missionary smiled. 'I trust you.'

When they came to the little hamlet the next day, they asked for the headman, and Whiteparish explained what they were looking for. The headman was uncertain. 'I have heard of men from the big city going to this land across the ocean to work,' he said. 'But I don't know what happens to them when they arrive, or if they ever return.'

'They are well paid,' said Whiteparish. 'Some stay there and some return.'

'What is this iron road you speak of? And this engine like a dragon that races along it? Have we such a thing in China?'

'No.'

'Does it work?'

'Yes.'

'Does the emperor or the governor allow men to leave like this?'

'We shall not ask them.'

'There are men here who need money,' the headman confessed. 'I will call the village together.'

And so Cecil Whiteparish explained Read's offer to the assembled village, and after that, for an hour, he interpreted the many questions the villagers had and Read's answers. And when they were finished, around noon, he and the Reads went on towards the next hamlet, promising to return the next day to collect any men who wished to go to America.

That night was warm, and the moon was riding high in the clear sky over the hamlet when Mei-Ling and Second Son walked down from the house to the pond, and they stood on the little bridge together, talking quietly.

'I don't want you to go,' Mei-Ling said.

'I was thinking that if I go with one of our boys, maybe we can come back in a year or two with a lot of money.'

'You want to take one of our sons?'

'Two men, twice the wages.' He considered. 'I could take Ka-Fai.

He's the eldest. But I think he should stay here in my place. I'll take our second boy. He's sixteen and he's strong. He wants to go. He thinks it's a big adventure.'

'You talked to him already?'

'This afternoon.'

'I didn't know.'

'We're getting poorer every year. Last time my brother went to town he spent a lot of money. Even Mother can't control him. I have to do something.'

'You should be head of the family.'

'I'm not.'

'I wish he would die,' she cried wretchedly.

'Don't say such a thing.' He paused. 'It'll be all right. You and Mother can keep things going.'

Mei-Ling started to cry. 'I shall be so lonely.'

'I, too.'

'The moon's nearly full,' she said dully.

'Two more nights,' he said.

She looked down at the moon's reflection in the pond. The water was smooth as glass, but the moon's outline was blurred by her tears.

'We should go back in,' her husband said. 'Everyone's asleep.'

She took his hand in the dark. 'Come,' she said.

Cecil Whiteparish was in quite a good mood the next day. The evening before he'd been able to have a long talk with the headman of the second hamlet, a kindly old man. He knew about the Taiping's god, but he thought the rebels were more bent on destroying the Manchu than performing acts of kindness. Cecil had been able to explain many things about the true God to him, and the old man had seemed to be quite impressed. It was a small beginning, but it gave the missionary hope.

The Reads had also picked up five volunteers, who accompanied them now as they returned to the first hamlet.

Five more men awaited them there. One was a thickset fellow accompanied by his son. Read liked the look of him. 'Exactly the sort of honest farmer we're looking for,' he remarked.

It was sad to see the fellow's wife, though. The best-looking woman he'd ever encountered in that region. The Chinese didn't like to show their emotion. When she parted from her husband, they hardly touched each other. But tears were running down her face. She stood in the lane at the end of the village, watching them until they were out of sight.

Normally Shi-Rong would have ignored the reports, which were entirely confused. Strangers had been seen, heading for the hinterland. One report said they were barbarians. Another said Taiping. No doubt the messages had become altered in transmission. They came from a scattering of villages by the coast that were normally quiet. He hadn't even been down there for a couple of years.

Two considerations, however, had made him set off with a party of armed riders. One was that he had nothing else to do. The other was that if he wanted promotion from his humble magistracy, he needed some public displays of vigilance – something the governor might mention in his dispatches to the royal court – to bring himself to the emperor's notice.

And there might be something in the business. He doubted that the Taiping were involved. All the Taiping action these days was far to the north, around Nanjing. A local triad? Triads had attacked the unpopular Manchu authorities near Guangzhou several times in recent years. Triads didn't usually push far into the hinterland, but he supposed it was possible. Or could it be something to do with the Hakka people? There was always a bit of jealousy and bad blood between the Hakka villages with their big round houses and the neighbouring Han peasantry. Any kind of trouble could be brewing these days.

One thing was certain. If there was trouble and he failed to investigate and was afterwards blamed, he could probably forget the rest of his career.

For the truth was that his career hadn't been going anywhere. He was still only a county magistrate – at the top of the humble seventh rank, but below even a deputy sub-prefect of a province. He'd been moved three times already, but never promoted. Nor did the provincial governor have any particular interest in him. Even his loyal servant Sun had recently retired to a life of Buddhist peace.

The position had many duties. Not only did he preside over a law court, but he was responsible for every aspect of government in the county. He toured the towns and villages. He had to know the merchants and the village headmen. 'Remember, you are the Parent of the People,' the governor had told him when they first met. In other words, if anything went wrong, it was his fault.

He'd hoped to be a sub-prefect in the fifth rank by now. But he wasn't even in contention. He felt alone. He wasn't in disgrace, just forgotten.

He knew it. And his wife knew it, too. He'd brought her and the children down to the region a year ago. But it had not been a success. She had disliked the humid climate, despised the Cantonese, whose language she refused to learn, insisted on being served noodles instead of rice in her home and generally made it clear to him and to their children that she didn't think they should be there. 'I don't know why you can't get a better posting. I'm sure that when he was your age, my father was at least in the sixth rank,' she once remarked.

A month ago he'd suggested it might be better if they returned to the family estate. 'My aunt is getting very frail now. She really can't cope. And it's probably healthier for the children,' he said. His little son and daughter were upset to leave him; his wife made a good show of pretending to be. He promised he'd see them soon. And he fully intended to.

For he was no happier with his situation than his wife was. And there was a way out. It wouldn't please her if he gave up his career, but he was tempted to retire to the family estate nonetheless. He could devote himself to improving the place and to educating his son. He'd been thinking about it increasingly during the last month.

Today, however, he was fully engaged in his work. And he was making rapid progress with his men. They'd ridden through half a dozen villages so far, and nobody had reported anything about the strangers, but there were still plenty of little settlements to visit.

He remembered he'd seen a beautiful woman in one of these hamlets, a couple of years ago.

Mei-Ling slept badly that night. The house seemed strangely empty without her husband and their younger son. Her brother-in-law was no help. Soon after the Americans had departed, he'd gone to his room, taken out his opium pipe and soon retired into oblivion. Mother had looked grim and said little to anyone. Mei-Ling felt sorry for her, and towards the end of the afternoon she even went to her side and said softly: 'Don't blame yourself, Mother. None of this is your fault. It's you that keeps us all together.'

Mother had touched her arm, as though to say thank you, but she had shaken her head and gone outside, and Mei-Ling had thought it better not to follow her.

As for the children, her elder son looked so like his father, it was almost laughable. He had a similar character, too – solid, hardworking, kindly. In the months ahead, she hoped that might be some comfort to her – almost as if his father were still there. As for Willow's children, two of her girls were married now; her third was still in the house, a rather sad, skinny girl, a willow without its leaves, Mei-Ling used to think. And the young boy, her one success.

Years ago there would have been several servants to think of as well. But only one remained, an old woman who had lived with the family all her life. She couldn't do much, but her presence was like a talisman, a reminder of the house in those better days to which, who knew, it might one day return. She, too, was a kind of comfort.

But for herself, that night, Mei-Ling felt only a sense of desolation. She kept thinking about her dear husband and her son. Where were they now? In some other hamlet? Camping out on a hillside? She tried to send her husband messages of love – like little presents, carefully wrapped. In her imagination she saw them fly through the night sky under the watchful moon, magically floating until they alighted, to be opened by her husband's hands. Did he sense her messages? Was he awake? Did he receive them in his dreams?

Once or twice a terrible cold fear came to her. He was in danger. Something had happened to him. But with all her strength and will, she drove that evil spirit out of her mind, lest it should bring him bad luck.

She must have slept fitfully. When she awoke, she thought it might be dawn, but she was not sure. Leaving her room, she stepped into the courtyard – and found that she could scarcely see across it. The walls were invisible. Even the small tree in the centre was only an indistinct shape, enveloped in the mist. Somewhere above the mist, there was light, or she would not be able to see even the little she could. But whether it was the faint light of daybreak or the brightness of the moon, almost full now, she could not tell.

She moved through the hushed glimmer to the gate, unbolted and opened it. She looked down towards the pond. But she couldn't see even ten feet into the dense damp whiteness. A world without form. All life, all thought, dispersed in white nothingness.

She was going to step out. The ground, at least, would be solid under her feet. But a strange sense of fear held her back, as though the white nothingness were like a death. If she went blindly down towards the pond and missed the bridge, she might even slip into the water and drown. She stood in the entrance, therefore, one hand on the gatepost to steady her.

And then, somewhere close by, she thought she heard a horse's cough.

She frowned. It couldn't be. It must be one of the ducks that lived on the bank of the pond.

Then came a whisper, on her right, close by. Very close. 'Mei-Ling.' Was it a spirit voice?

She turned her head and stared, saw nothing for a second, until a shadow began to coalesce in the faint unearthly light of the mist and a shape emerged.

'Nio! Little Brother.'

He was standing right beside her now. She could see the scar on his face. His long hair was held in place by a yellow silk scarf tied around his head. He wore a loose tunic, a red sash and soft leather boots. He was leading a fine horse with a flowing mane. And something else was obvious.

He wasn't her Little Brother anymore.

How long was it since he'd been there? Half a dozen years. He'd come through the hamlet briefly, told her he was joining the Taiping. Then the Taiping had moved away. There had been much fighting. They ruled a big area centred on Nanjing, but she never heard a word from Little Brother, and she'd wondered if he might be dead.

And now here he was, alive. He must be about thirty-five. To judge from his long hair, still a Taiping. An officer, too. It wasn't only the clothes and the horse that made her think so. The way he held himself, every line of his face, proclaimed he was now a man of authority.

'Are you alone?' she asked, and he nodded. 'How long can you stay?'

'Until this evening. I need to rest during the day. It's safer to travel at night.'

She had to tell Mother. To her relief, the older woman took the news calmly. But she was firm. 'He mustn't stay in the house. We've enough troubles without being accused of harbouring a Taiping. Take him and his horse to the barn at the back.'

The barn lay a short distance behind the house. It consisted of a store-room above, under the roof and an open bamboo area below with plenty of room for his horse as well as the plough and other farm implements kept there. It was enclosed, together with some low sheds, in a small yard of its own.

'The boys will be out in the bamboo grove today,' Mother said. 'Nobody will be going to the storeroom. You and I could always say he must have hidden there without our knowing.'

Nio agreed with the plan at once, and long before the mist had lifted, he was fast asleep.

It was mid-afternoon when Mei-Ling brought him food. And as he ate, they talked. She wanted to know so much about his life. He explained that he was an officer, with many men under his command. Had he a wife? she asked. 'I have women.' He said this without feeling. 'I'll marry when the war is over.'

'You still believe the Manchu must be overthrown?' she asked. 'Just like the Little Brother I remember.'

'That hasn't changed.'

'And you think the Taiping army can overcome them?'

'We've been fighting for years now. Sometimes we advance towards Beijing. Other times they push us back. An awful lot of people have been killed. But we have more troops in Nanjing than the emperor's armies opposing us. And our men are better trained.'

'Is it worth it, all the killing?'

'For a Heavenly Kingdom, yes.' He paused. He saw her look doubtful. 'When you've killed so many, Big Sister,' he said quietly, 'it has to be worth it. One couldn't have done all that for nothing.'

'And the Heavenly King himself? They all believe in him still?'

Nio paused for a moment. 'The Eastern King rebelled against him a while ago. That's all over now,' he added with finality. He was silent for a few moments. 'Where is your husband?' he suddenly asked.

And now it was her turn to be silent. She didn't want to tell him what had happened, how bad things were. Was her husband dead? he demanded. She shook her head. 'I'll ask your mother-in-law,' he suggested.

So there was nothing for it but to tell him the truth. When she had finished, he did not look shocked, but only sad. 'It's the opium,' he said with a sigh. 'It ruins every man who touches it.'

'It's the British barbarians—' she began, but he cut her off.

'They sold it. They are to blame, without a doubt. And we bought it. I smuggled it myself.' He nodded grimly. 'Black gold. Though the poppy flower is white – the colour of death.'

'Do the Taiping also use it?'

'Some do. It's everywhere.' He gazed at her. 'You have used all the money I gave you, I'm sure.'

'I am ashamed. But I had to.'

'I know. I will give you more before I leave. But you must keep it hidden. Your husband's brother will never stop smoking now. Never let him find your money. Otherwise there will be nothing left. Nothing at all.'

'I cannot take from you again . . .'

'I have money.'

It was night. Mei-Ling and Mother had hidden the money in a safe place where the head of the family would never find it. And the full moon was in the sky to light him on his way when Nio led his horse out from the little barn. Mei-Ling walked beside him.

She was wondering if she would ever see him again, but she did not say so. Before he mounted, she looked down at the still water of the pond, in which she could see the gleaming reflection of the moon. 'Stand on the bridge and let's look at the moon before you go,' she said.

'Like when we were young and I was still Little Brother.'

'Something like that.'

She thinks she may never see me again, he thought, and she wants to remember me as I used to be. 'Why not?' He smiled and nodded. There was nobody about. They wouldn't be seen.

It was dusk when Shi-Rong and his men reached the hamlet. Though their approach had been rapid, the headman was already out in the village street awaiting them. The villagers they passed had looked at them a bit apprehensively, but that was normal enough. As he gazed at the wizened old headman, however, Shi-Rong thought that even in the falling light, he detected something shifty in the fellow's manner.

He wasted no time. 'I am looking for Taiping. Have any come this way?'

'Taiping?' Unless the headman was a consummate actor, he was genuinely astonished. 'No Taiping came here.'

'Any other rebels? Triads? Hakka? Troublemakers?'

'No, Lord. None at all. We don't see those people here. Not for many years.'

He was telling the truth. Shi-Rong was certain of it. But the headman was also looking relieved. Did that mean there had been something else he'd been afraid this magistrate might ask?

'Have you seen any strangers at all?'

The old fellow frowned, as if trying to remember. That was absurd. He must be hiding something. The other villagers were standing around, listening.

Shi-Rong cursed his own stupidity. He'd been too eager. He should have talked to the man alone, then cross-questioned the others one by one. As it was, they were all going to take their cue from the headman and give him the same story.

'What sort of strangers, Lord?'

'Missionaries!' Shi-Rong cried angrily, darting a sharp look around the other men to see if there was any reaction. But there was none.

'No missionaries, Lord.'

'British soldiers?' A shaking of heads. 'Opium sellers?' They, after all, were everywhere.

'None recently, Lord. Not in the last month.'

There really wasn't any other kind of stranger the authorities would have been interested in, so Shi-Rong gave up.

'We'll stop here the night. We shall need food, fodder for the horses . . .'

'Everything, Lord.' The headman smiled. 'Everything you desire.'

It was while Shi-Rong was eating in the headman's house that he thought to ask about the beautiful woman he had seen on his previous visit. Here at least he got some information. She lived in a big house with her extended family, on the outer edge of the hamlet by a pond. Did she have a husband? She did, and several children. Was the husband there?

The headman seemed to hesitate. Why was that?

'I suppose so, Lord. Sometimes he or his brother goes to the local town. But even then, he'd normally be back by nightfall.'

Why did Shi-Rong have a feeling this wasn't quite true? Perhaps the woman was without a husband for some reason, and the headman was trying to protect her from a magistrate and soldiers who, for all he knew, might try to take advantage of her.

But after he'd finished eating, he went outside and began to stroll along the lane. There was a full moon. He did his best to remember the woman. Had she really been so beautiful? The vision in his mind was incomplete, imperfect, like an old silken garment that has become frayed. He wanted to know.

At the entrance to the village, by a little shrine, he noticed a path on his left that led through woodland. Was that the way to the woman's house? He turned into it.

There was enough moonlight through the trees to pick his way along the uneven path, though he stumbled on tree roots once or twice. After a while, as the path wound through a bamboo grove and then back into the woods again, he decided he must have made the wrong choice. And he was just about to turn back when he thought he saw a glimmer of water ahead on the left. So he pressed on until he reached a place where, looking between two trees, he found himself staring across a moonlit pond.

The farmhouse lay on the far side of the pond. Below the farmhouse, a narrow wooden bridge stretched across the water, and obviously led to the very path on which he was standing. He saw a horse tethered to the end of the bridge. And close to the middle of the bridge, two people were standing in the moonlight. Everything was still. There was not a sound. It was like a dream.

The two figures clearly had no idea he was there. Even if they'd looked his way, they probably wouldn't have seen him in the shadow of the trees. Their faces were turned down, towards the pond below them. Of course, he realised, they were looking at the moon's reflection in the water.

Who were they? Was it the beautiful woman? If so, was the man her husband, just arrived back from the town? He was slightly behind the woman, so it was hard to make him out. The horse was too good for a peasant to own.

Now the woman turned to look up at the sky, and her face was caught in the moonlight. He saw the face so clearly it almost took his breath away. It was the woman he'd seen before. No question. But she was even more beautiful than he remembered.

She must be about the same age as his own wife, he supposed. But whereas his wife, who came from a gentry family, with her bound feet and rich dresses, looked highborn but commonplace, this simple peasant woman was like a princess from ancient legend, a celestial being of some kind. It must be the moonlight, he told himself, that produced the strange spirit of grace that emanated from her – ageless, timeless.

A soft sound, between a whisper and a murmur, came across the water. She must have spoken to the man, who pulled slightly away from her, straightened, and looked boldly up at the moon.

Shi-Rong stared. He could see every detail now – the long hair of the Taiping, the face etched with lines of authority, the scar down his cheek. He knew that face. It was older, of course, but he was almost sure. It was Nio. Without meaning to, he let out a gasp of surprise.

Nio heard it. His senses must be sharp as a wild animal's. His eyes searched the trees by the water's edge. Could Nio spy him in the shadows?

Shi-Rong saw Nio glance past the end of the bridge. That must be where the path came out. Then Nio spoke. 'Whoever you are, come out onto the bridge where I can see you.' His voice was very calm, his tone that of a commander who is used to being obeyed. He drew out a long knife. 'If you do not, I shall come into the woods. I shall find you easily, and I will kill you.'

Shi-Rong hadn't brought his sword with him when he set out on his walk. He suspected that even if he had, he wouldn't have been a match for the former bandit. He had no wish to die ignominiously on some obscure path in the woods. He'd rather meet Nio face-to-face.

'Wait,' he said, with what he hoped was equal authority. It took him only a few moments to follow the path to where it led onto the bridge. He stepped onto it, keeping his head down. When he was about a dozen paces from Nio, he stopped and looked up.

'Good evening, Nio,' he said. 'Do you remember me?'

The look of astonishment on Nio's face was very satisfying. 'Mr Jiang!'

'Last time we met you were running away from me in a dragon boat. My question is, what in the world are you doing here? I see you're a Taiping bandit now, but I didn't think they were operating in these parts.'

'They're not. I went home to see my family. I'm on my way back.'

'And I'm the magistrate. We're looking for rebels. I'll have to arrest you.'

'I can't allow that.' Nio's hand went back to his knife. 'I don't want to kill you, Mr Jiang, but if you try to arrest me, I'll have to.'

'No, Little Brother!' the woman cried out in terror. 'Do not bring that upon us.'

'She's right,' said Shi-Rong. And turning to the beautiful woman: 'Are you harbouring this man? Why do you call him Little Brother?'

The woman looked lost, but Nio intervened. 'When I was a boy, Mr Jiang, I ran away from home. Her family took me in, saved my life.

She was like a sister to me. Whenever I make a journey this way, I look in to see that she's all right.' He gestured to his horse. 'I just arrived a few moments ago, as you see.' He smiled. 'We're out on the bridge because her family won't have me in the house.'

Shi-Rong watched the woman. She loved Nio. He could see that. He was also pretty sure Nio was telling the truth. 'She appears to be doing well enough,' Shi-Rong said drily. He indicated the farm. 'Big house.'

'But falling apart,' said Nio. 'The family's ruined.' He gave Shi-Rong a bleak look. 'The usual story. Opium.'

'Which I tried to stop,' Shi-Rong reminded him.

And which I helped to smuggle, Nio thought sadly. They looked at each other in silence for a moment. 'The woman and her family have no part in this, I promise you,' he said.

Shi-Rong nodded. 'We have no interest in them.'

'I'm going to ride away.'

'I shall ride after you.'

Nio allowed himself a faint smile. 'You didn't catch me last time.'

'I shall catch you.'

'Then one of us will die.' Nio gave a wry grimace. 'Perhaps both of us.' He turned to the woman. 'Goodbye, Big Sister. Take care of yourself.' Then without another word he strode towards his horse, mounted and rode away towards the lane.

Shi-Rong watched him go. 'That lane up there,' he asked the woman, 'it leads to the village?' She nodded. He might as well return that way then, he thought. No point in taking the dark path through the woods again,

But he did not move.

Should he set out after Nio at once? He calculated. His riders were probably asleep already. He'd have to rouse them. They wouldn't like that. And their horses needed rest in any case. It would probably be better to wake the men at dawn, tell them a Taiping warrior had been seen during the night, and set off then, with men and horses that were fresh.

No doubt Nio would make detours to give them the slip, but there were only certain roads he could take to get him back to Nanjing.

Truth to tell, if the task of capturing Nio fell to someone else, he wouldn't be sorry.

But the woman standing before him did not know that. 'He did not want to kill you, Lord,' she said in a low voice. 'Were you friends?'

'We knew each other.'

'Do you want to kill him?'

'He's a traitor. I serve the emperor.'

'Do you want money, Lord?'

She was trying to bribe him. What else could she do? Many officials, no doubt, would have taken the money.

'I thought you had no money.'

'He gave me money,' she said dully.

He nodded slowly. Of course. Nio had given her money. Money she needed for her family. And she was going to give it up to save his life. 'I have no need of money,' he said.

She made a little gesture of despair. 'What will they do to him?' she asked in a whisper.

He didn't answer. Put him in chains, for a start. Then they'd ask him questions. They'd want to know everything about the Taiping, the state of affairs in Nanjing, the future plans of the Heavenly King.

If they were intelligent, they might even try to persuade Nio to turn informant, return to Nanjing and act as a government agent. After all, that was usually the way with these pirates and smugglers. They'd work for any side so long as you paid them.

The question was, would Nio cooperate? Would he talk at all?

Shi-Rong had a feeling he would not. In the years gone by, he would have. But there was something about the fellow now, a maturity, a firmness. As if he'd found a purpose in life. If he did break, he probably wouldn't tell them anything of much use.

For they were sure to torture him. They'd do to Nio just what he himself had done to that pirate who'd tried to kill Commissioner Lin, all those years ago in Guangzhou.

The woman might have some idea about torture, but he wasn't going to tell her.

And as the horror of that torture and death suddenly came back to him with an appalling vividness, he knew he did not want that for Nio. I'm not sending him to that, he thought, not even for the emperor.

His father would surely have told him that he must. But he wasn't going to.

How beautiful the woman was. Perfect. Spotless. How extraordinary to find such a beauty in a humble village. A precious pearl in the wilderness.

'Have you wine?' he asked. She nodded. 'Bring me wine and I shall look at the moon,' he said.

While she went to get the wine, he remained on the little bridge over the pond and gazed at the moon's reflection in the water. When she came back again, he told her, 'I am not going after Nio, on one condition. You must never tell anyone that I met him and let him go. Otherwise, it is I who will be arrested. Do you understand?'

She bowed. 'I swear, Lord,' she said. And she was about to retire to the house when he motioned to her to sit down on the bank, a few feet away from him. He saw her look alarmed.

It was hardly proper for a married woman to remain out there with him. But who was going to see? She was certainly in his power. Some men, military commanders on campaign, he supposed, might have tried to take advantage of her.

He gazed at her. I would not touch her, he thought. But I can enjoy her beauty in the moonlight. 'I shall remain here until dawn,' he remarked. 'You are going to entertain me.' He smiled. 'You will have to tell me a long story.'

'A story, Lord? There are many famous tales.'

'No. I want something different. Tell me the story of your life. It must be truthful. You must leave nothing out.'

'It's not very interesting,' she said.

He smiled. 'Then I shall fall asleep.'

But he did not fall asleep, and the peasant woman told him her story until dawn.

The morning passed quietly. She helped Mother as if everything were normal. In the afternoon, they both rested a little.

That evening the sky was clear as darkness fell. Nobody stayed up late. Mother was ready to turn in. Her elder boy, Ka-Fai, was tired from his work. Even her brother-in-law had been out in the fields that day and had already gone to lie down.

Only Mei-Ling was still awake. From the courtyard she could see the moon, almost full, rising over the wall, but she had no desire to go outside and look at the glimmering pond. She stayed sitting by the tree, with the gate shut. She could feel her eyes drooping, and she was about to go to her bed when a sound at the gate caused her to start, then frown.

Someone was trying to get in. Who could it possibly be at this hour? Surely Nio was far away by now. Then with a sinking feeling, she thought of the magistrate. Had he changed his mind? Had he caught Nio and returned to arrest the family for harbouring him? Was it an intruder? The gate was closed fast by a stout wooden crossbar. It would take more than a single man to break it down. Just wait, she told herself, and the intruder would go away. But he didn't. Now Mother appeared, woken by the noise. They looked at each other uncertainly.

And then came a voice calling for someone to let him in. A voice she could not mistake.

'I had to come back,' Second Son explained when they were all sitting together. 'I just had this feeling something was wrong, that you needed me.'

'What did the American say?' Mei-Ling asked.

'He was all right.' Her husband smiled. 'He said: "You gotta do what you gotta do."' So he and their son had hurried back. They'd been travelling since before dawn. 'But now that you're all well,' he continued, 'I wonder if I should go back and join the American again. I'm sure we could catch him up. We still need the money.'

'There's no need,' Mother told him. 'I found money today that your father must have hidden away.' She glanced at Mei-Ling, who nodded at once and said that it was most fortunate. 'Enough to keep us going for quite a while.'

'Really?' said Second Son. 'Well then, it was fate that brought me back.'

'It was,' said Mei-Ling.

And tired though they were, they made love that night.

It was just a few days later that Mei-Ling began to have a strange feeling. She could not say exactly why. Was it an instinct? A memory of how she had felt before? Or was it her imagination? Whatever the cause, the suspicion came and would not go away. A suspicion that a new life had begun within her.

Three weeks later, the suspicion grew much stronger. A month after that, she was almost sure. She told Mother, who nodded and made no comment.

That evening, when Second Son came in, Mother told him: 'Good news. You're going to be a father again.' And Second Son was overjoyed.

'It must have been the night before I left,' he said to Mei-Ling when they were alone later.

'It could have been the night you came back,' she replied.

'No, I don't think so,' he said. 'Don't you see? That's why I had the message, telling me I needed to return.' He beamed at her excitedly. 'It all makes sense. The ancestors were watching over us.'

'I hadn't thought of that,' Mei-Ling said. It could be so.

But although she was happy at the turn events had taken, there was still something else that Mei-Ling would need in order to complete her happiness.

A few days later, without telling Mother, she went to a small Buddhist temple a few miles away. Taking great care, making sure to step with her right foot over the entrance and not to do anything to offend the spirits of the place, she offered two lighted candles to the Buddha. Then, kneeling before him and pressing her forehead three times to the ground, she prayed most fervently that the life within her should be a girl.

As she returned home, she felt the warm light of the afternoon sun falling so kindly on her face that she took it for a blessing.

When the baby was born seven months later, Second Son was overjoyed. 'Our first daughter,' he cried in delight. 'You always wanted one. And she looks just like you!'

It was true. The baby was tiny, delicately featured and looked just like Mei-Ling.

Even Mother was pleased. 'You are a good daughter,' she told Mei-Ling with a smile. 'If the baby has your character as well as your looks, we shall be fortunate indeed.' All the astrological signs were promising as well.

But what should they call her? It was Second Son who provided the answer.

'She must have been conceived just around the time of the full moon,' he said. 'We shall name her Bright Moon. As long as you don't mind,' he added, looking at Mei-Ling, who smiled and agreed.

THE PALACE

Everyone calls me Lacquer Nail. Ever since I was a young man. But I had to find my way into the palace of the emperor himself to get my name. So I'd better explain how that came about. It's quite a strange tale, really. I don't know anyone else who has a story as interesting as mine.

The village where I was born lies about fifteen miles south of Beijing. My parents had nine children, but just three of us lived beyond infancy – my two sisters and me. So it was up to me to carry on the family line.

My father was a carpenter, but I don't think he was very good at it, because sometimes he wasn't employed at all. He was a bit of a dreamer, really. 'My grandfather was the son of a merchant with money,' he'd say, 'but money's not important to me.' When he said that, my mother would cry: 'That's only because you haven't got any.' She was impatient with him sometimes, although I think they loved each other.

The only time I remember him trying to get money was when I was seven years old. The time he took me to Beijing.

My grandfather's brother had left for Beijing long before my father was even born. But he used to come to our village every spring for the Qingming Ancestors Day, to pay his respects at the family graves. He'd given that up a couple of years before I was born, on account of his age, so I'd never met him. He must have been almost eighty when we went to Beijing.

Of course, as the oldest living member of my father's family he was a person of consequence. I remember my father instructing me how I should address him, because I didn't know the correct term for a paternal grandfather's elder brother. On my mother's side, of course it would have been completely different. And even little children have to be exact about such relationships. 'If he was my father's younger brother, you'd call him *shu gong,*' my father told me. 'But he's an older brother, so you call him *bo gong.*' Once I'd learned how to address him right, my mother said, 'After you've spent some time with him, you could try calling him Granddad in an affectionate way, as if he were your grandfather. Maybe that will please him and make him like you.'

It made me happy to imagine being loved by such a venerable member of the family. That night, however, I heard my mother say to my father: 'If the old man's got any money, he really ought to leave it to us now that he sees we have a healthy son to carry things on. I mean, he has no children of his own. Who else would he leave it to?'

Whatever the motives behind our visit, I was excited to be going to Beijing. It was the autumn season, which was very dry that year, and I remember that the leaves falling from the trees beside the road were all brown and crisp, as though they'd been baked.

We walked the whole way. Every so often my father would pick me up and put me on his shoulders, but I must have walked about half the distance myself. At noon we stopped and ate the food my mother had given us for the journey. We arrived in Beijing in the evening.

The old man had owned a place that sold noodles. My father knew where it was, but it was already getting dark and the lamps were being lit when we reached it. Grandfather's brother wasn't there. The people who were running the noodle place then told us the old man had retired, but that he still lived in the next street. So off we went.

We found his house quite easily, though it didn't look big at all. In fact it was tiny. After my father knocked softly on the door, there was a long pause before somebody opened it cautiously.

People shrink when they get old, and Grandfather's brother was tiny. He seemed hardly bigger than me. But he looked quite sprightly all the same. He held up a lamp in his hand to inspect us, and I remember thinking he looked like an inquisitive bird. I knew at once that this was Grandfather's brother because he had a little face just like my father's. I had supposed he would be wrinkled, like the old men in the village, but his skin was rather smooth. He might have been a monk.

'Nephew,' he said to my father. 'You look a little older than when I last saw you. Who is the boy?'

'My son,' Father replied.

'*Bo gong,*' I murmured, and bowed very low.

The old man looked at me. I could see in the lamplight that his eyes were still quite clear and sharp. 'He's quite good-looking,' he remarked. Then he led us into his house. It was just a single room, really, with a tiny kitchen behind. In the main room there was a broad kang to sit on, which extended through the dividing wall to the kitchen fire, which heated it. There was also a small wooden table, one wooden bench and a chest in which I suppose he kept his clothes and other possessions.

He asked my father if he had a place to stay, and Father shook his head.

'Well then,' he said, 'you can sleep here.' He didn't seem to mind. 'There is room for me and the boy on the kang, and if you sleep on the floor beside the kang, you'll be quite warm.' He looked at my father appraisingly. 'I hope you've eaten,' he said, 'because I haven't any food.'

'We brought you a present,' said my father, and handed it to him.

My mother had gone to great trouble over that present. Eight little mung bean cakes she'd made herself – she was a good cook and could make a meal out of almost anything. Each cake was beautifully wrapped in red paper. And all neatly set in a little bamboo box.

Grandfather's Elder Brother put the box on the table and inspected it in the lamplight.

'This looks very beautiful. Did your wife make it? How lucky you are to have such a good wife. What does the box contain, may I ask?'

'Cakes,' said my father.

'Well then,' he said, 'normally one doesn't open a present in front of the giver, but as it's cakes, let's open it now.' He turned to me. 'Would you like a cake?' As I had not eaten since the middle of the day, I was very hungry, so I thanked him and said that I would. 'We'll all have some, then,' said Grandfather's Elder Brother.

While my father and I each ate a cake, the old man made a pot of tea and put three cups on the table. Nobody said very much, because we were so tired.

'If you need it,' Grandfather's Elder Brother said to my father, 'there's a latrine just along the street.' My father went out, but I didn't want to go, too. Seeing this, the old man said to me: 'If you have to go in the night, there's a chamber pot over there, under that cloth. You can use that. It's quite clean.'

I saw it in the corner. Even by lamplight I could see the dusty cloth. So I thanked him and lay down on the warm kang, and before my father even got back, I had fallen asleep.

In the morning I went to that latrine along the street with my father. I had never been in a place like that before. In our village, the richer peasants with courtyard houses had their own latrine, usually in the southern corner of the courtyard, which could be emptied from the lane outside. Some of the farms had little covered sheds, and the waste fell down into an open pit from which it could be carted for manure or fed to the pigs. But we didn't have a latrine. We went to the communal place, where there were holes in the ground and you did what you did in the open air. You tried not to go when it was raining. But I still prefer those open-air latrines because the wind carries a lot of the smell away.

Whereas when I went to that public latrine in Beijing, which was in a closed shed, the smell was so bad that I almost fainted.

After that, we washed and went with Grandfather's Elder Brother to the noodle shop he used to own. And we ate noodles for breakfast.

'I still come here and work an hour or two,' the old man explained. 'Then they give me free noodles. So as long as I can manage that, I shall never starve.' Father didn't look too happy when he said that, but I noticed how friendly the people at the noodle place were towards him, and that made me feel the old man was honoured.

Then he took us to a small Taoist temple close by, and he lit three incense sticks in there. One of the priests, dressed all in dark blue, came by and greeted him, and the old man explained who we were, and the priest smiled and told my father that his uncle had progressed far along the spiritual path. The next day, when we were on our way home, my father said his uncle must have given money to the temple to be so well thought of. I remember being sad when he said that. And in fact, even now that I'm an old man myself, I still believe that priest was being sincere. You never know in life. Sometimes people can mean what they say.

But the highlight of that visit – the little event that opened my eyes to the world – had nothing to do with my family at all.

Late in the morning we'd gone for a walk. Grandfather's Elder Brother said he was going to show me the great Tiananmen Gate. He and my father were walking side by side, with me just behind, and the old man was telling my father stories about the family in the past when suddenly we heard the noise of drums and gongs coming down the street towards us.

'Someone important must be coming,' said my father, and we moved quickly to the side of the street to let this great person pass.

'Are we going to see the emperor?' I asked. Grandfather's Elder Brother laughed when I said that.

'He hardly ever comes out of the palace, but if he should, you certainly won't see him – unless you want your head cut off. He'll be inside a carriage, and we're not allowed to look at him. So you keep your eyes on the ground.'

'I heard,' said my father, 'that in some barbarian countries, the people are allowed to look at their kings.'

'Which just shows how inferior their kings must be,' the old man replied instantly. And I remember feeling proud to think that the emperor of my country was so like a god that we couldn't look at him.

It wasn't the emperor anyway. It was some court official, important enough to be preceded by a retinue of people, some of whom were wearing conical hats and dressed in rich embroidered silks. Show me an embroidered silk nowadays, of course, and I can probably tell you straight off who made it and if they've dropped a single stitch. But that was the first day in my life I'd ever seen such gorgeous things. I realised they must be heavy and wondered if that was why these men walked in such a slow and stately way.

But most important of all, the moment I saw those silk gowns, I knew my destiny. How does a migrating bird know which way to fly? You tell me. It just does. By instinct, I suppose. Well, it was the same for me, that day in Beijing. The first time I'd seen the finer things of life, and I knew that's where I belonged. Simple as that.

'Who are those men?' I asked.

'We call them "palace persons",' my great-uncle said.

'That's what I want to be,' I said. This made him laugh, and my father shook his head. But I didn't know why until, a few minutes later, we sat down in a teahouse.

'Did you notice those men you saw had very soft skins?' Grandfather's Elder Brother asked me. But I really hadn't. 'They have soft voices as well,' he said. 'That's because they are eunuchs. Do you know what a eunuch is?' I had to shake my head. 'A eunuch is a male who has had his balls and penis cut off so that he can't have any children. It's called castration. Eunuchs are employed in the palace because there's no chance of them interfering with any of the royal wives and concubines.'

'I thought,' said my father, 'that sometimes they just cut their balls off and left the penis so they can pee.'

'It used to be so,' said Grandfather's Elder Brother. 'But then they discovered that some of the eunuchs could still get it up, even though they had no balls. So you can just imagine the goings-on there were between them and all those women with nothing to do in the palace.'

'Oh,' said my father. 'Well, I never.' And he laughed.

'So now everything gets chopped,' the old man continued. 'Usually when they're still young boys. It's not so dangerous then.'

'So they pee like a woman?' asked my father.

'More or less. They don't have so much control, usually. They have to wash a lot.' The old man turned to me. 'It's true that some of them make a fortune in the palace. Though many die poor. But you want to have a wife and children, don't you?'

'Yes, he does,' said my father.

'I do,' I said.

'Then you'll have to find another way to get rich,' said Grandfather's Elder Brother, 'though I've no idea what that might be.'

So that was the task I set myself, from that very day. How to get rich and have a family, too.

When we returned to the little house, the old man wanted to rest, and we were quite tired, too. I suppose I may have slept an hour or two, but when I awoke, I found the old man looking at me thoughtfully. My father also opened his eyes, but when Grandfather's Elder Brother spoke, he addressed himself to me rather than my father.

'You are quite wrong if you think that riches will make you happy,' he said. 'In fact, the reverse is the case. The more possessions you have, the more there is to worry about. They are nothing but a burden on your shoulders. The wise man concerns himself only with what he needs. Nothing more. Then your life will be simple and you will be free. That is how I have learned to live.' He smiled and made a gesture with his arm. 'Look around this room. What is the most important thing you see?'

I looked at the bench, the table, the chest and the chamber pot under the clean cloth.

'The chamber pot,' I said, thinking of the smell of that awful latrine.

'Nearly right,' he said, 'but not quite. It is the kang on which you are sitting. Think how simple our traditional bed-stove is. Instead of wasting the heat from the kitchen fire by letting the smoke go up a chimney, we let it come out sideways through the duct in the middle of the kang, where it warms the bricks before it leaves through the vent at the other end. Even after the fire goes out, the bricks will stay warm all night. So we can sit on our kang by day and sleep on it at night. What could be more efficient? Even the imperial family sit on kangs in the palace.' He smiled serenely. 'And yet down in the south, in places like Guangzhou, they don't have kangs. Why's that?'

'I don't know,' I said.

'Because it's hot down there. They don't need them. The circumstances are different. So the needs are different.'

'I have heard,' my father said, 'that the Russian people have something similar in their land, which is cold.'

'They must have learned it from us,' the old man said.

'Perhaps we learned it from them,' I suggested, thinking how clever I was being.

But the old man shook his head. 'That is most unlikely,' he answered.

'Why?'

'Because the Chinese are more intelligent,' he replied, as if it was obvious. I have always remembered that. He was right, of course.

And I must say that his wisdom made a great impression upon me. It was clear that he was truly at peace with himself. Children sense these things, even if they don't fully understand them. 'I see that you have everything you need and nothing else,' I said.

'Yet even so,' he told me, 'we can always do better. At the start of every new year, I try to find one more thing I can do without. It isn't always easy, but in the end, I always find something I don't really need and get rid of it.'

'What will you get rid of this year, Granddad?' I asked. And I used the affectionate form of address this time, as my mother had told me to.

He looked at me for a moment. Whether he was pleased by my little show of affection, I don't know, but I think he was. Then he smiled.

'Why, you have brought me the very thing,' he said. 'The beautiful wrappings your mother used for the cakes you've given me. There are many people who would be delighted to have them and would make good use of them. So I shall keep them and enjoy them, and think kind thoughts of your dear mother until the new year, and then I shall give them away. It's made my task much easier, because to tell the truth, I really didn't know what I had left that I didn't need at present.'

'Then we did a good thing by coming here,' I said happily.

'You did. And now I am going to give you a present in return,' he answered. And getting up from the kang, he went over to the chest, opened it, took out a little leather purse and extracted a copper coin. It was just the ordinary little coin, with a square hole in it. Even then I knew that it took a string of a thousand of those to make a single silver tael. 'Here,' he said. 'This is for you. I want you to keep it, to remember your visit here, and say a prayer for me, from time to time.'

'I will,' I said. I was quite overjoyed.

'You know, Uncle,' my father said, 'if you want to return to live in the village at any time, you can always come to live with us.' He didn't sound all that happy, but I was very pleased, because I really liked the old man.

'Oh yes,' I cried. 'That would be wonderful.'

Grandfather's Elder Brother sat on the kang and smiled at us. He looked so serene.

'That is very kind of you,' he replied. 'But you are there to tend to the ancestors. That's the important thing. I think I shall stay in Beijing, and one of these days I'll die quietly here without being a bother to anybody. The Taoist priests at the temple will know what to do when the time comes. One never knows,' he added cheerfully, 'it might come tomorrow or not for years.'

'Will you have enough money to live?' my father asked.

'I manage. My needs are small,' he replied. 'But if I think it's time to go, for whatever reason, it's quite easy to depart this life, you know.'

'Really,' I said. 'How do you do that?'

'You just stop eating and drinking. It's not even painful, really. You just get very weak and sleepy. You mustn't drink. That's the difficult bit, but quite essential. Then you die.'

'You're telling my seven-year-old son how to kill himself?' my father burst out.

'He asked,' said the old man.

I didn't mind. I just thought it was interesting.

My father went for a walk after that. Grandfather's Elder Brother and

I sat together in the house and ate two more of my mother's cakes. He told me about how he and my grandfather lived in the village when they were boys. Apparently their father really had been a merchant with some money, but he'd lost it. 'He was very unhappy about losing his money,' the old man told me. 'That's what taught me not to get too attached to things.'

'Why did you come to Beijing?' I asked.

'I was bored,' he said.

Early the next morning we left. My father parted from the old man politely, but when I made my low bow, the old man gave me such a lovely smile. And I showed him I had the copper coin he gave me clasped safely in my hand.

My father was quite disgusted that the copper coin was the only thing Grandfather's Elder Brother had given me. 'A single copper coin. You realise that's almost worthless, don't you?' he said.

But actually it was very clever of the old man to give me a copper coin. If he'd given me a silver coin, I'd surely have spent it, whereas I had no temptation to spend the copper coin. I still have it to this day. It's probably why I can remember everything about that visit.

The rest of my childhood was quite boring. There were certainly none of the finer things of life. Not that our village was cut off from the world. It was only four miles across the fields to the Grand Canal that runs up from the coast to Beijing; and I often used to walk over there to watch the ships.

On its way north from the port, sections of the Grand Canal are actually the Peiho River – though in places the muddy banks of the old stream have been so packed into mud walls that they look more like a canal than a river. The final stretch into Beijing is all man-made, however, and it goes through several locks. Beside the first of these locks, there's a little inn where the boatmen often pause for refreshment and gossip with the innkeeper.

I used to love to go to that lock. For some reason I felt drawn to it. They say that we Chinese mastered the art of building them a thousand years ago. Or maybe earlier, for the oldest canals go back to the Han dynasty, twenty centuries ago.

The main cargo was grain, but all sorts of other goods went by. And though they were usually in crates, I'd sometimes get a glimpse of a bale of silk or a great standing jar of painted porcelain. I used to dream of being on those ships, you can be sure.

Anyway, I was standing by the lock when I heard a conversation that made a great impression on me.

A merchant and his son – a boy of about my own age – were on the side of the canal, stretching their legs while their vessel went through. 'You may not like it,' I heard the merchant say to his son, 'but you must study all the same. You can't get anywhere in life if you don't learn how to read and write. It's the key to everything.'

I'd never heard that it was so important before. There were a few people in our village who knew how to read and write, but none of the poor men like my father could. So it didn't take me long to make the connection. If I wanted the finer things of life, I had to learn to read.

From that day I pestered my father to find me a teacher. There was one old man who gave lessons to the half-dozen sons of the richer peasants and master craftsmen; but teachers have to be paid, so that was no good. If you want to make money, I thought, you need a teacher; but to hire a teacher, you need money. There didn't seem a way out of that conundrum.

Then my father had a good idea. He went to see the old man and asked if he would accept payment in kind for those lessons. The old man certainly didn't want any of my father's carpentry.

'What I really need is a pair of leather boots, like the Manchu wear, for the winter. Do you think you could make those for me?'

'Certainly,' said my father. 'I'll make you the best leather boots you ever saw.' So it was agreed.

When he got home, he asked my mother, 'Can you make a pair of leather boots?' Because making shoes was really a woman's occupation.

'I have no idea how to do such a thing,' she replied.

'Oh well then, I'll just have to do it myself,' said my father. He was quite cheerful about it. So I started on my lessons.

Most of the boys went to be taught by the old man because they had to. But I loved the lessons. Before long I could recognise about two hundred characters. As for writing, I soon got the hang of the basic brush-strokes that you have to learn to construct each character. The old man wouldn't let his pupils be careless and make the strokes quickly, which most boys want to, because they're thoughtless and impatient. But I thought the brushstrokes were beautiful. For me, each stroke belonged to the finer things in life. I wanted to linger on every one of them. And I think the old man saw this, because sometimes he would talk to me. He had a funny way of talking because he hadn't any teeth, but once you got used to it he was quite easy to understand.

'Writing is like playing a musical instrument, you know,' he said. 'It takes enormous practice and attention to the rules. A bad hand is painful to look at. It exhibits all the stupidity and vulgarity of the writer. But a fine hand is a pleasure to see. Scholars can identify the great masters by their hand, which we do not only look at but study. For that calligraphy is the pure emanation of the writer's soul.'

'So the scholars work very hard to express their souls,' I said.

'Oh no,' he replied. 'In fact, quite the reverse. They study the character as if it were a landscape, practise it endlessly, always trying to express the thing they see before them. Gradually they lose their sense of self entirely. It's the Tao, if you like. Their soul, as we like to say, is something they are not conscious of at all. It's a sort of nothingness. Every attempt to describe it, funnily enough, destroys it.' He smiled. 'Even I, a poor old man in a village with a few stupid pupils, understand this – a little at least.'

'I don't understand what you are saying at all,' I said. I wasn't being rude. I just didn't know what he meant. It didn't sound like the finer things of life to me.

'I know,' he answered. 'Perhaps you will one day.'

'Really?' I asked.

'No, not really,' he told me. 'But one never knows.' He seemed to find this funny.

I did love the characters, though, and within weeks I could write quite a few in a manner that seemed to satisfy him.

The problem was the boots. My father had been able to get the leather from the workshop where he was employed at that time. And my mother had found him cloth and other things. But of course, he'd never made a pair of boots in his life. 'It turns out,' he told my mother, 'that it's quite difficult.'

'You'd better get help,' my mother said. There was a shoemaker in the next village, and my mother knew her and went to ask her. But it didn't do any good: the shoemaker said my father had no business making boots, and she wouldn't help at all.

'Not to worry,' my father said. 'I'll get the hang of it.'

And finally he presented the old man with the boots, which seemed to fit all right. This was the early autumn season, and so my lessons continued. But then winter came. And one cold, wet morning, the old man came around to our house, very angry, and called out to my father so all the neighbours could hear: 'Look at these boots. They're letting in all the water, and my feet are freezing.'

'I'll fix them,' said my father.

'No, you won't,' the old man shouted. 'If you knew what you were doing they wouldn't be leaking in the first place. I'm not getting chilblains so that your son can learn to read and write.'

So that was the end of my lessons. I wanted to try to earn money myself to pay for the lessons, but whenever I did, my mother told me the family needed it. My father seemed to be depressed, and my mother told me not to talk to him about the lessons anymore, because it made him unhappy.

But I didn't give up. If I saw a sign anywhere – in a temple, for instance – I'd copy it down on any scrap of paper I could find and try to work out what it meant. As you know, most of our Chinese characters are made up of little pictures of elements – a man, a house, the sun, water and so forth – that combined together produce a meaning. As the years went by, I got to figure out a lot of them. But whenever I couldn't, I'd go to my old master and ask him. The first time I did this he was rather angry. But when I told him what I thought a particular character meant and why, he burst out laughing and explained it. And after that, if he saw me in the village street, he'd call out, 'Have you a new character for me?' Sometimes I guessed quite difficult meanings correctly, and once he looked at what I'd written and remarked: 'Your writing isn't all that bad, considering you have no idea what you're doing.' I was so proud that he said that to me. But he still wouldn't teach me because I couldn't pay.

When I was fourteen years old, a message came from the Taoist monastery that Grandfather's Elder Brother was dying, so my father and I walked back to Beijing. We found him in his house with one of the monks looking after him, and I could see that he must be close to the end. The monks had the coffin already in the house, as you're supposed to do before someone dies. I looked around to make sure there wasn't a mirror on any of the walls. I knew that if you saw a coffin in a mirror it means someone else in the family is going to die, and I didn't want it to be me. I don't believe Grandfather's Elder Brother had a mirror, actually.

He'd have thought it was superfluous. But if there was one, the monks had removed it.

He looked so frail and tiny. I remembered what he'd told me about how to die by starving oneself, but the monk assured me that the old man was still taking food and liquid. 'He's just very old,' he said.

When Grandfather's Elder Brother saw me, he managed a weak smile and tried to raise his hand. So I held it, and I could just feel him give my hand a little squeeze. Then he saw my father.

'All gone,' he whispered. 'All gone.' Though whether he was talking about his life or the fact that all the money was used up, I wasn't sure. He didn't say anything after that. He seemed to be dozing. During the night he was restless for a while; then he was still. He slipped away just before dawn.

He had no children to organise the funeral, of course. Fortunately the monks said that the old man had given them enough money to take care of the funeral, and they arranged everything, which was just as well, as I don't think my father would have been a lot of use. They gave him a poor man's wake – only three days instead of seven. But honestly that was enough.

Everything was in proper order. They placed a small gong on the left of the doorway and hung a white cloth from the lintel. They wrapped the old man's body in a blue sheet, laid a yellow napkin over his face and put him in the coffin. We set up a little altar at the foot of the coffin. My father stood a white candle on it, and the monks placed an incense burner there. We all wore white. The monks also left a little box near the door so that people could leave contributions for the cost of the burial.

I was amazed by how many friends Grandfather's Elder Brother had. Everyone from the nearby streets seemed to know him. While the monks chanted the prayers, these friends all came by. People are supposed to make a lot of noise to show their grief, but he was so old and he'd gone so peacefully that it didn't seem appropriate somehow. People just came in and told us nice stories about him, talking about what a kind and simple nature he had and that sort of thing. There was plenty for everybody to eat. The monks had seen to that, too.

That night some of the local men came and played card games like mah-jong with my father to help him keep awake through the vigil. If they hadn't, I'm sure he would have disgraced us by falling asleep instead of standing guard over the body. I felt sorry for him, mind you, with all the walking he'd had to do and no inheritance to claim at the end of it all.

I was allowed to sleep for a few hours, though.

The second day went all right except for two things. First, a little boy came into the yard wearing a red shirt – which as everyone knows is a fine colour for a wedding, but terribly bad luck at a funeral. He didn't get through the door, though, so the monks said it didn't count. I hoped they were right. Sometimes, when I think about the way our lives developed, I've wondered if that little boy brought us all bad luck after all. But there's no way of telling, really, is there?

In the afternoon, my father and the priest went through Grandfather's Elder Brother's chest. He had only a few clothes. You know it's the custom to burn the clothes of the dead, and the monks had already burned the shreds he had on when he died. So now they took the other clothes to burn them, too. But my father kept rummaging around in the chest looking for some money, and when he found none, he got quite upset. I thought this was a bit unfeeling of him; but I'd forgotten that you're supposed to give a little bit of money wrapped in paper to each guest at a funeral. And my poor father was upset because he was ashamed he hadn't got any money to give. When the priest realised that, he told us the old man had already taken care of it, and sure enough the presents appeared at the right time. Whether Grandfather's Elder Brother had really made these provisions, I don't know. He might have. He was quite thorough.

The only time my father lost his composure was that moment after they put the lid on the coffin, when the senior family member has to take a hammer and drive in the nail that holds the lid down. But my father made a mess of it and the nail bent, and even the Taoist priest looked angry. My father just threw the hammer down and cried, 'I can't do anything right!' Then he picked the hammer up and gave it to me, saying, 'You'd better do it. He liked you better than me.' Then he started crying, which wasn't a very good idea.

Apart from that, everything went off all right. When we came to take the coffin to the slope where the old man was to be buried, I was allowed to be one of the bearers, which pleased me very much, because it's an honour that brings good luck. There were two little bridges along the way where we crossed streams, and each time my father was careful to tell the corpse in the coffin that we were passing over water. So he got that right. After the burial and the prayers, we all went back to the house. The next day the monks put a little sign by the entrance of the house with red writing on it, to tell the old man's ghost that this was his house. Why do we think that ghosts will get lost on their way home? I wonder. The idea is that the ghost will find its way home by the seventh day, and people often put powder across the threshold hoping that the ghost will disturb it in passing, so they'll know it got safely back. Not that there's much you can do about it, I suppose, if it didn't. I don't know if the monks put any powder across the threshold. We started for home the same day as the burial.

I remember wondering if anyone would really care whether a poor man's ghost got home or not.

Father was quite depressed on the way back, but I wasn't. 'The old man lived just the way he wanted,' I said to cheer him up, 'and he even died when he meant to, as well.'

'I suppose you're right,' my father replied. 'It's more than you can say for most people.' But he didn't look any happier.

Actually, Grandfather's Elder Brother chose a good time to die. Because it was only months after we buried him that the Taiping appeared on the horizon.

One thing about living where we did, we always got all the news. In the back of beyond, up in the mountain villages, an emperor can die in the Forbidden City, and they may not hear about it for years. But we were only a day's walk from Beijing. And because we were almost on the Grand Canal, there was constant news coming up from the port as well. The canal lock-keepers always knew everything.

The Taiping came up from the remote southwest. By the time they swept along the Yangtze River, they were like an invading Mongol horde, besieging towns and fighting huge battles with the emperor's troops. Nobody knows how many people were killed at that time.

It's amazing how people can just disappear and be forgotten after a single generation.

In any case, they kept advancing along the Yangtze, and more and more people joined them as they went. Of course, they were still a thousand miles away from us. And the hill country along the Yangtze has always seemed like another world to people on the great northern plains. So we just told ourselves not to worry.

Until they took Nanjing.

It happened so suddenly. One month they were deep in the Yangtze valley; then before we knew it, they'd raced hundreds of miles north, almost to the Yangtze delta and had come to the walls of Nanjing.

Nanjing may be six hundred miles away, but it's linked by the waterway of the Grand Canal that runs all the way to Beijing. We'd often see cargo vessels that had begun their journey in Nanjing. We felt as if the rebels were on our doorstep.

No one had believed the Taiping could take Nanjing – a huge walled city like that. Yet it fell in no time, and they killed every Manchu family in the place.

And now the old Ming capital, the sacred City of the Purple Mountain, which controlled the whole Yangtze valley and half the river trade of China, was in the hands of these shaggy-haired vagrants, who told the world that it was the capital of their Heavenly Kingdom. And the emperor couldn't do a thing about it.

I wonder how Grandfather's Elder Brother, for all his serenity, would have felt about that. Would he have been so philosophical then? That's what I mean when I say he died at the right time.

Well, having set up their Heavenly Kingdom, the Taiping stayed there for a while. And I had to get on with my life.

I was fifteen, so naturally I was anxious to find steady employment. I wanted to learn a craft, but there were only a few craftsmen in our village, and they had sons of their own to employ. Besides, they weren't anxious to employ me, because they didn't have much respect for my father.

It was my mother who came to the rescue. She was friendly with another woman in the village where the bootmaker lived, who was married to quite an important man who made lacquer goods, which were sold in Beijing and to foreign merchants down at the coast as well. My mother told me to go to this lady and her husband, and perhaps something would come of it.

But I didn't do that. Not at first.

One sees it all the time: people being asked to give jobs to young fellows they don't really need or want. Then they have to think of tactful ways of saying no, without giving offense. So I decided on another plan.

First, I told my mother that I wasn't interested. She was quite upset, but that couldn't be helped. Then, a few days later, I walked to the next village to take a look at the lacquer workshop.

The works consisted of a broad yard with open sheds on one side and closed sheds on the other. The open sheds had bamboo blinds that could be rolled down if the breeze blew in too much dust. But there was no wind that day, so the men were sitting at a long table in the open shed, because most craftsmen prefer to work by natural light. There was nothing to stop people entering the yard, so I went in, chose a place opposite a thin, sad-looking man with thinning hair who seemed to be engaged in the simplest task – applying a layer of lacquer to a plain wooden tray – and began to watch.

I wasn't just idly staring. The first thing I noticed was that the tray was made of two pieces of wood glued together with opposing grains. This, I guessed, must be to make the tray more rigid, so it wouldn't warp. He was quietly coating the tray with red lacquer, using a small brush. I took note of the tiniest details: the way he held the brush, how he moved it. And I'd been watching like this for half an hour when a big middle-aged man emerged from one of the closed sheds and came towards me. He had a broad bony head with deep eye sockets and a jutting brow that reminded me of a rock face. I felt sure he must be the owner.

'What are you doing?' he said.

'I was watching the craftsman, sir,' I said with a low bow. 'Just to see how it's done.'

He looked at me suspiciously. He probably wondered if I was planning to steal something. He turned to the craftsman. 'Is this boy annoying you?' he asked. The thin man shook his head. 'Well, throw him out if he gives any trouble,' he said, and went into the street.

When the craftsman had finished the thin coating of lacquer, he took the tray over to another shed, but this one was closed. As he went through the door, however, I could see that there was a pot hanging over a lamp in there, and a little steam was coming from the pot. As it was a warm day, but rather dry outside, I supposed that this arrangement must make the room more humid. I took note of that, but I didn't say anything.

Then the thin man took up another piece of work. This one had already been coated with lacquer. But as he started brushing a new coat on it in exactly the same way, I realised that each piece of lacquer work had probably been coated several times.

I was still there two hours later when the owner came back. He looked very surprised, which was just what I wanted. For a moment I thought he might throw me out, but he decided to ignore me and disappeared back into the closed shed. I stayed there another hour and then left.

Now by this time I'd committed to memory every hand movement the craftsman made, and when I got home I took out my ink stone and brushes and some of the scraps of paper I had saved, and I made strokes just like his, again and again, until I thought I really had the feel of it.

The next day I took my writing equipment with me. This time I stationed myself opposite another of the craftsmen. This was a placid fat man, a bit younger than the first. And he was doing something different. The lacquer box he was working on had a design of two figures in a bamboo garden on it, and the lacquer had been built up so thickly that I realised it must have dozens of coatings, perhaps more than a hundred layers. With infinite care, he was carving into it, using several implements – razor-sharp little knives, a gimlet almost as thin as a needle and other curious instruments I'd never seen before. It was such intricate work that I imagine he might have taken weeks to complete it. I was quite fascinated, and I almost forgot about the master and why I'd come there.

At the end of the morning, I sat down on the ground in the yard, and taking out my brushes and my ink stone and a tiny bottle of water, I started to make a rough approximation of the design I'd seen on one of my scraps of paper. Then using the ink, I tried to do the same process, but in reverse, forming the design by building up a layer of ink, waiting for the ink to dry, which it does quite quickly, and then adding another layer. It was very clumsy, of course, but it helped me get the feel of the process. I continued like that, getting up to watch the fat craftsman, then sitting down to play with my brush and ink, all afternoon. There was no sign of the master that day. But at the end of the afternoon, the fat craftsman indicated that I should come over to him. And he put a brush in my hand and showed me how to hold it for lacquer work, which, despite my observation, I still hadn't got quite right. So then I bowed very deep and thanked him and went home.

Well, the next day I was back again. I was afraid they'd probably send me away as soon as they saw me, because craftsmen don't like young people hanging around. But they didn't say anything. So I watched another of the craftsmen, who was carving. It was exciting to watch him, but I couldn't copy that, so in the afternoon I went back to copy some more of the fat man's work. After a while the master came out again, and this time he came straight to me angrily and said, 'Why are you still hanging around here? What do you think you're doing?'

'If you please, sir,' I said respectfully, 'I had the idea that I might like to work in lacquer. But I thought that I should learn all I could about it first, to discover whether I might have any talent for it.'

'A master tells a pupil whether he has aptitude,' he replied sharply.

'I did not dare waste the time of any master until I had taken the trouble to find out all I could for myself,' I replied. 'And I had to consider whether it was a craft to which I could dedicate the rest of my life.'

'Why do you have an ink stone and brushes? Are you a young scholar?'

'Oh no, sir,' I said. 'I did have some lessons. But I am poor, and so I've had to teach myself to read and write as best I could.'

'Can your father not teach you?'

'My esteemed father, unfortunately, cannot read and write.'

'Write something,' he commanded. So I wrote a few characters in my best hand, and he looked at them and said, 'Not bad.'

'I thought, master,' I ventured, 'that since I could learn to use a brush to write, perhaps I could also learn to use a brush applying lacquer.'

He glanced at the fat craftsman, then turned back to me. 'Well, I've nothing for you,' he said firmly. 'The way these Taiping devils are ruining all the trade, we'll be lucky to keep the people we have, let alone take on an apprentice.' He frowned. 'Who are you, anyway, and how did you get here?'

I try never to lie, but I didn't want him to know about my father yet, so I just invented a name, said I came from Beijing, and that we were staying with relations in the area for a month. He looked a bit cynical. 'Well, don't bother anyone,' he said. Then he left.

But the next day, when I turned up, the thin man beckoned me over, told me to sit beside him, gave me a brush, and showed me how to use it properly. Then he gave me some splinters of wood and a tiny pot of lacquer and told me to try. It was quite difficult, because the lacquer is sticky and not like ink at all, but I began to get the feel of it. I spent the rest of the day doing that.

The following day, the same thing happened, and the day after. I'd really have liked to work with the fat man, because what he was doing was much more interesting. But that would have been rude to the thin man and would have made me look ill-mannered. Besides, I'd already realised that this was a kind of test, to see if I was hardworking and obedient.

Another three days went by. Now and then the thin man would show me something I was doing wrong, so I was all the more glad that I had been patient. I'd been there ten days when the master appeared around noon and said to me severely: 'I've let you learn here. But I'm quite sure you lied to me about who you are. So you'd better tell me the truth now, or you can get out and never come back.'

I was really glad that he gave me a chance like that. I confessed everything. I told him who my family was, how I'd wanted to learn to read, how my father had made the boots for my teacher and got me thrown out, and how I'd gone on learning for myself and bothering the teacher as much as I dared.

'But wait,' he said, 'you're the boy whose mother knows my wife. You were supposed to come and see me.'

'Yes, master,' I said, 'but how could I expect you to take an interest when I had nothing to recommend me?'

'It's quite true that your father's reputation goes against you,' he said. 'He's not a good worker. Never takes enough trouble.'

'I honour my father,' I said quietly, with a low bow.

'Very proper. But you're determined not to be like him, all the same. You want to be a real craftsman. Isn't that true?'

I nodded.

'Well then, you can start here tomorrow,' he said suddenly. 'An apprentice gets paid only a pittance, you know.'

I didn't care about that. Not then. I was so excited.

I worked hard and learned fast. In less than two years I was as good as the thin man, and I worked with the fat man, too. But I was still the apprentice and I was always deferential to everyone. People should know their place.

I also came to understand how lucky I was. They say that the art of lacquer-making goes back to the days of the Han dynasty. For a long time lacquer goods came mostly from the southern provinces, where the ingredients for the lacquer are to be found and the climate is suitably humid. But gradually the craftsmen came north, and in the reign of the great Manchu emperor Qianlong, there was a huge royal works in Beijing. But with the troubles from the barbarians and the Taiping, and the court's being so short of money, the art and industry were in decline. My master was one of the few small works still going, supplying a little to the court and any other rich persons he could find – for the lacquer takes so long to make that it cannot possibly be sold at a price any modest person can afford. My master could have found any number of out-of-work craftsmen in the capital. But hardly any young persons wanted to enter the craft. That was why he had been intrigued by me. That, and my persistence.

I loved that lacquer works. The finished stock was stored on racks in one of the closed sheds. I'd go in there and look at the rows of boxes, bowls and vases. Sometimes we even produced furniture, too. Some of the work was in black lacquer, but mostly it was red. There were beautiful fans of lacquered bamboo, and a big black screen, with a flying stork and a distant mountain painted on it, that was going to the port to be sold to a rich barbarian. The master would hire in artists to do the painting.

I could have gazed at them for hours. Sometimes I'd let my fingers gently touch the intricate carving on the boxes. The patterns were so deep and tight, it was like feeling a little world under your hand.

One day – it was the start of my second winter there – the master found me in the storeroom. I was still a bit afraid of him. He hardly ever smiled, and that great cliff face of a head he had was quite intimidating. 'You love the goods we sell, don't you?' he said to me.

'Yes, master,' I answered. 'I've always liked the finer things in life.'

'Well, you'll never be rich enough to own most of the things in here,' he told me, 'but the joy of the craftsman is greater than the pleasure of the owner.'

That impressed me very much, I have to say.

Then he smiled and gave me my pay packet and told me to check it.

'I think there's a mistake, master,' I said. 'There seems to be too much.'

'Those last two little boxes you lacquered, they were plain but perfect,' he said. 'So I'm paying you for those at the full rate – for a junior craftsman, of course.'

I bowed very low. The truth was, I couldn't speak for a moment.

It was a month later that we thought we were going to die.

We'd become used to the Taiping ruling down in Nanjing. But one morning I arrived at work and found everyone with long faces, and the master told me, 'Those devils are on the move again. They're sending a great horde up here to take Beijing.' And we were right in their path, of course. 'If this Taiping Brother of Jesus were a real king, it mightn't be so bad,' the master said. 'Real kings don't kill craftsmen. We're too valuable. But with this rabble, who knows?'

That night in our village, everyone was discussing: should we stay put and hope for the best? Or should we put our possessions in a cart and get behind the great walls of Beijing? Surely the Taiping couldn't get into Beijing, people said. But I wasn't so sure. No one had thought they could take Nanjing, either.

Then word came that the horde was camped by the mouth of the Peiho River, about sixty miles down the canal to the south. I daresay they could have reached us in three days.

If I saw clouds on the southern horizon, I'd think: they could be on the move under those clouds right now. Once, on a clear winter night, I remember gazing down the canal to see if I could make out any faint glow from the horde's campfires in the distance. But all I could see was the reflection of the stars in the cold water.

We watched the emperor's troops heading south, of course – Manchu bannermen, Chinese troops, cavalry – a lot of them. But to tell the truth, we weren't very confident.

So you can imagine that I was a bit surprised when, in the middle of all this worry and uncertainty, my father announced one evening, 'I've found you a wife.'

'What are you talking about?' I turned to my mother. 'Do you know about this?'

'She's a girl from the village where you work,' she told me.

'Don't tell me,' I said, 'you know her mother.' But apparently she didn't.

'I found her. She's perfect,' my father cried with a big smile.

'Why's that?' I asked. 'Is she rich?'

'No.' My father looked at me as if I were stupid. 'Her family are respectable people like us.'

'I see. Is she pretty?' I wanted to know.

'Pretty women are trouble. She's not too bad.'

'Well, thank you very much,' I said. 'And why now? I'm too young to marry.'

'That's the thing,' said my father. 'Her father's got three other daughters. The marriage broker discovered that he'd be prepared to part with her if she comes to live in our house now, like a daughter, until you're both older. Then we wouldn't need to pay a bride price.' Which of course he didn't have.

'Perhaps,' I said, 'in a few years I can earn enough to afford a bride price myself. We might do better. Are there any other reasons for all this hurry?'

'The girl could help your mother,' my father said. He looked thoughtful. 'And with all these troubles in the world, she might come in useful.' I'm still not sure what he meant by that.

'I want to see her,' I said.

This wasn't difficult. Once I knew who she was and where her family lived, I found a good place where I could catch sight of her without her seeing me and hung about there after work.

She was a year or two younger than me. I'd have preferred more years between us, but you can't have everything.

'I will obey you, Father,' I said, 'but let's just wait and see what the Taiping do.'

It turned out the emperor's armies were better than we thought. Although they couldn't break the Taiping, they managed to push them back across the plain to Nanjing. That certainly gave us heart.

But in my opinion, it was the old Yellow River that really saved us.

For in 1855, when the river broke its banks just above that plain, the water came down like a great tidal wave, right across the landscape. You wouldn't think water from even a great river could do so much damage, but the impact destroyed entire sections of the Grand Canal between Nanjing and the Peiho River. That southern extension became unusable. It took a generation to repair the damage.

But if it was a disaster for the people living there, that flood was also a warning to the Taiping. That's how I saw it – a warning from the ancient gods. If they ever returned to that plain, the old yellow serpent would strike them with another flood and drown them all.

And whether they were mainly afraid of the river or of the emperor's armies, I don't know, but the Taiping never came near us again.

The next year, the wretches were quarrelling amongst themselves. One of their generals had become too popular, it seemed, with the Taiping troops, and their Heavenly King didn't like that. So he killed the general, all his family, and twenty thousand of the general's men as well. Just like that. It's strange how people can preach brotherly love one day and tear you to bits the next.

And so I got married. Her parents had named her Rose – because the rose is the flower of Beijing – though she was rather pale to be called that, I thought. I must say, she didn't give any trouble. She helped my mother and was very respectful to my father, which I thought was a good sign for the future. And although mothers-in-law are supposed to be like dragons, my mother was always kindness itself to Rose.

Rose and I would talk a bit in the evenings. I'd ask her how she'd spent the day, and she'd ask if I liked the food. If I said I liked the noodles, for instance, my mother would tell me, 'Rose cooked them,' and give the girl a smile. That seemed to please Rose very much. She'd been living in our house only a year or so when we got married. And I have to say we were very happy together. Soon after that my master gave me full craftsman's wages.

Our life just then was quite uneventful. The Taiping were safely down in Nanjing. We heard there'd been a Muslim revolt out in the far western provinces, but to tell the truth, ordinary peasants like us hardly knew anything about those faraway provinces – except that the empire had taken in all sorts of tribes at one time or another, and some of these people were Muslim. My father got very angry about it: 'These barbarian religions are nothing but trouble,' he cried. 'First the Taiping Christians, now the Muslims, they're all the same. The emperor should forbid them all.'

As they didn't come our way, though, we didn't worry much.

But the British were another matter.

The first we heard, there had been trouble down in Guangzhou. The barbarians were still complaining because they hadn't got everything in the shameful treaty their pirates had forced on us after the Opium War. Consulates in our ports weren't enough for them. The British wanted an ambassador in Beijing, who could come barging into the emperor's presence without even performing the kowtow, as though he were the equal of the Son of Heaven. I don't think such a thing had happened in a thousand years, maybe two thousand.

And the barbarians wonder why we say they have no manners.

It was in the winter after my marriage that the British got into a fight with the governor of Guangzhou, who wouldn't let them into the city. Suddenly we heard that they'd seized him and taken over that city.

Actually, some people in Beijing were quite amused, because that governor was known to be a most objectionable character. All the same, such behaviour couldn't be tolerated.

Next, the watermen sailing up the canal were telling us, 'The British are coming.' They came right up the coast. And then we heard: 'They've taken the forts at the mouth of the Peiho River. They control the canal.' But what really frightened us was when people started saying, 'They'll join up with the Taiping rebels in a Christian army and sweep up to Beijing.' Would anyone be able to stop them? We didn't think so. Would they turn out the emperor? What would that mean?

My father got very depressed. 'The Mandate of Heaven is being withdrawn,' he said. 'There'll be chaos. There always is when that happens. We'll all be killed. Then there'll be a British emperor or a Taiping one. We may even be forced to be Christians, whatever that means.'

'It won't happen,' I said. I don't know how I was so sure, but I was.

I believed it then, and despite all I've seen in my life, I still believe it now: our kingdom is eternal. When you think of the thousands of years of our history, the wisdom we've learned, our arts and inventions . . . Why, even our writing's a miracle: every character is like a little world. And when it comes to the finer things of life, everything's made to last.

Those lacquer boxes I love to hold – the ones with the deep patterns cut into them and the many layers of lacquer hardened like a stone – they'll last as long as the Grand Canal or the Great Wall. Sometimes, when I look at those boxes, I think they're how a great city must look, seen from the eye of Heaven. Walls within walls, streets and avenues, palaces and temples, houses and courtyards, all packed tight as a geometric pattern on a box. Dynasties come and go, war and disease, famine and flood. But Nanjing and Beijing are still standing; and even if they weren't, the idea of them would still be there, preserved like a garden, in every lacquer box.

You can't destroy a great idea. That's what I believe.

Patience is the key. And that's what the emperor's servants showed now. Just as they had before, they negotiated with the British, promised enough to satisfy them, and persuaded them to go back to Guangzhou. They also granted one new concession.

It seemed the British were hurt that all our official documents called them barbarians. We had to promise not to call them barbarians anymore.

Of course they are. So we went on calling them barbarians amongst ourselves. And since they couldn't speak Chinese, they didn't even know, which shows how foolish their request was in the first place!

That autumn my son was born. I think it was the best day of my life. You might say it changed everything.

The first time I held the baby in my arms, I remember I started to count his fingers and toes, and Rose looked at me and said, 'What are you doing?' And I replied, 'I'm just making sure he has the right number of fingers and toes.' And she said, 'What will you do if he hasn't?' and I said, 'I don't know.' 'Well,' she asked, 'has he?' 'Yes,' I said proudly, as if this were a great achievement. 'He's perfect.'

Then I looked down at his little face, and he looked just like my father. So I walked outside where nobody could hear, and I whispered to my son, 'You may look like your grandfather, but you're going to work hard and be a big success.' That's the first thing I ever said to him. He may not have understood, but I thought it was important to say it right away.

We called him Zi-Hao, which means Heroic Son.

I loved being a father. Sometimes the baby would cry in the night because he needed to burp, and if I woke up and Rose was asleep, I'd pick him up and rock him in my arms until he felt better. Several times my mother appeared and told me, 'You shouldn't be doing that. It's woman's work.' And she'd make me go back to sleep while she rocked the baby. But I didn't mind doing it at all. I think those were some of the happiest moments I ever knew.

One day I had just taken a piece of work I had completed to the storeroom when the master appeared. He asked in a friendly way after my family and then told me that he was awarding me a small pay raise. 'I'm now paying you the top rate for what you do,' he said, 'and you have earned it. In due course, as you master more complex work, you'll be paid accordingly.'

Naturally, I bowed deeply and thanked him.

'Is the baby letting you get any sleep?' he asked with a smile.

'Enough, master,' I said, and I told him how my mother made sure of this, and how I liked holding my son, even in the middle of the night. 'You know how I love the finer things in life, like these,' I said, indicating the work all around us, 'but I never realised I'd love my child even more.'

'It was the same with me,' he replied with a nod. Then he gave me a strange look. 'But you must take care,' he said. 'However attached you are to a child, you will lose some of them. We all do. Just treasure them all the more while they are here.'

I understood what he said, of course, but I didn't really listen. I mean, you don't, do you?

Another good thing about the birth of Zi-Hao was the effect it had on my wife. She put on a little weight, and it suited her. I don't mean she was plump, but I suppose you might say she changed from a girl to a perfectly formed young woman. I was very happy about it. A year after Zi-Hao was born, Rose was pregnant again.

There was some more good news that summer. The British barbarians came back again and stormed the forts down at the mouth of the Peiho. But this time we were better prepared and our men drove them back to Guangzhou. Even my father was triumphant. 'I told you that one day the emperor would teach the barbarians a lesson,' he cried – which was quite untrue, of course. All the same, it did seem to be a good sign.

My little boy had started to walk. I would put him between my legs and hold his two tiny hands above his head, teaching him to put one foot in front of the other. By summer's end he could walk a few paces by himself. And he could speak some words as well. I felt as if everything was right with the world.

So it came as quite a shock when he fell sick. It began in early autumn. One day he suddenly threw up. We didn't think much about it. These things happen all the time with little children. But the next day it happened again, and afterwards he seemed very listless, which wasn't like him at all. The day after that, he just lay on the kang covered with a shawl and didn't want to move. We didn't know what was the matter with him. He looked awfully pale.

My mother, the midwife and a woman from the next village who knew many cures all took a hand, but nothing did any good. I became so worried I could hardly work.

It was my master who came up with a suggestion. 'I know a physician in Beijing,' he told me. 'If anyone can cure your son, he can. Take the baby to Beijing and come back as soon as you can.'

That was an act of great kindness on his part. Not many masters would have done it. I almost broke down when I thanked him.

So I took Rose and the baby to Beijing. My father insisted on coming, too. 'You never know, I might be useful,' he said. And in fact he was, because he persuaded the master of one of the ships on the canal to take us there for nothing.

The apothecary's where the doctor was to be found turned out to be a huge emporium. The main hall was like a temple. Behind the dark wood of the high counters were rows and rows of glass jars and baskets of herbs. The doctor himself was a tiny old man, sitting on a chair in one corner of the place, so small that only his toes touched the floor. He looked up at me curiously as I told him who'd sent me, but he was very courteous. He asked us a lot of questions and examined the baby.

I'd heard about how the best physicians examine the tongue and the pulse. Each wrist has three pulses, from just above the thumb to farther up the arm. There are all sorts of descriptions for what doctors feel – floating, surging, hard, soft, hollow, irregular and so many combinations it makes the mind spin. I couldn't believe the old man would be able to perform all these tests on a tiny child, and I don't know how many he did, but it took a long time. Finally he delivered his verdict. 'Your son is very sick,' he told us. 'He may die. But I think I can cure him. However, the medicine will be expensive,' he warned me.

I'd have paid everything I had.

We waited patiently by the counter while the assistants collected the ingredients in a wooden bowl. Then they ground it into a powder. It all took some time.

Rose was looking exhausted. I had my little boy in my arms, and I was so busy whispering to him how the medicine was going to make him feel better – although he didn't know what I was saying, the sound of my voice seemed to soothe him – that I hardly noticed that my father had gone off.

When I did realise, I started to look around, and finally I saw him deep in conversation with the tiny old doctor. My father was busy talking, and the old man nodded and said a word from time to time, though I couldn't tell whether he was interested in what my father was saying or not. And I was just wondering how long this would be going on when

Rose nudged me and pointed towards the counter. The medicine was ready. They gave me a slip of paper to take to the desk where you pay. I hardly looked at it. I had the money ready. I gave the slip of paper to the man at the desk, and I saw him look a bit surprised.

I don't think I heard him at first. I'd put silver on the desk, but he was shaking his head and pointing at the slip of paper. Then I read it.

I still had my little boy in my arms, but I must have staggered and nearly dropped him, because suddenly Rose was at my side, and she had her hands out to take the baby from me. I stood there and stared at the cashier dumbly, like a man who's just been struck dead but doesn't know it. For the cost of the medicine was more than I'd brought to Beijing. In fact, it was more money than I possessed in the world. I couldn't pay.

So what was to become of my little boy?

Just then I saw my father moving towards me. He was looking pleased with himself.

'Do you know who the old doctor is?' he said excitedly.

'No,' I mumbled. I was so wretched I was hardly listening.

'He owns the whole store,' my father said. 'And you'll never guess: his father came from our village. He knew my grandfather, the merchant, who had all the money.'

'Well,' I said sourly, 'you can tell him we can't pay.' I wasn't sure he even heard me. 'The medicine's too expensive,' I shouted at him. 'Your grandson's going to die!'

He heard that all right. He blinked at me. But he hardly even paused. 'I'll talk to him,' he said.

I watched my father speak to the old man. Then I saw the old man shake his head.

'He said he's sorry. He told us it was expensive. The herbs are very rare. He can't give them away. He says there's another apothecary not far away.'

So we went outside, and half an hour later we were at the other apothecary. It was much smaller and the doctor there was a younger man. After listening to our case he said: 'I can give you a different medicine that does almost the same thing.' And he named the price, which was a third of what the old man had wanted. When we agreed to that, he went and attended to the order himself, making the assistants bring every ingredient for his inspection.

'It had better work,' I said, 'because it's still all the money we've got.'

'It'll work,' said my father.

We'd been back at home only two days when my little boy started to show signs of improvement. At work, every time I saw my master, I thanked him again for sending us to Beijing. And though he didn't show it, I'm sure this made him happy.

It was on the tenth day that my father showed up at the workshop. He came by at noon, when we were all eating and having a rest. 'I had an errand in the village, so I thought I'd look in,' he told me cheerfully. After bowing politely and greeting the other craftsmen, he asked me what I was working on. As it happened, the piece on my table wasn't that interesting, though he examined it admiringly. 'Can I see some of your finished work?' he asked.

'I suppose so,' I said, and I took him over to the storeroom.

I always loved showing people the shelves of finished work. You're just so proud of what you produce when you work in a place like that. Sure enough, when my father saw the rows and rows of beautiful treasures, he was quite amazed. I showed him a few small things I'd done, which weren't too bad. 'You really are a craftsman,' he said, and he looked so pleased and proud. Then he asked some questions that weren't at all stupid about some of the more complex and valuable pieces and the skill that went into them. And I was feeling really pleased that he'd come when he suddenly turned to me with a serious face.

'I didn't come in here to look at the lacquer work,' he said. And while I stared at him, he went on. 'I needed us to be alone.'

'What's all this about?' I asked.

'I didn't want the other men to hear us. I didn't want them to know – especially after your master gave you time off to go to Beijing.'

'What are you talking about?' I said.

'You've got to ask your boss a big favour.' He gave me a wise nod. 'Never ask a man for a favour in public – because if he does it for you, then everyone else will want the same from him. So if ever you need to ask a favour, son, always do it in private.'

'What favour?' I asked. I didn't like the sound of this.

'He needs to lend you some money,' he says. He gazed at me sadly. 'It's Zi-Hao. Our little boy.'

'What are you saying?' I felt my heart sink.

'It happened soon after you left this morning. He was sick, the same way as before. And then he just lay there. He didn't move all morning. He's pale as a ghost.' My father looked so wretched. 'I don't think the medicine's working anymore,' he said.

'What do we do?' I cried.

'That's exactly why I came,' he said. He sounded quite eager. 'All your master has to do is lend you the money for the right medicine – the one from the old man that we couldn't afford. Go to him right away. Tell him what's happened and ask for the loan. He'll trust you. You're a good worker. You'll pay it back over time.'

'He wouldn't like it,' I said. 'I don't think I can.'

'You've no choice,' he told me, 'if you want to save your son's life.' For once he was right. 'Go and see him now. I'll wait for you here.'

So I did as he said. My master was in his house. When I went to the door and asked to speak to him, he saw me at once. He gave me a friendly welcome, but I saw a trace of caution in his eyes.

I'd never told him the detail about our buying the cheaper medicine from the other doctor. But now I had to tell him about that and about what was happening to my son.

'Have you any suggestion about what I should do, master?' I asked. Because I thought perhaps he might offer something, and if he did, it would be better than my asking for a loan. Perhaps I was wrong to go about it that way. I don't know.

He didn't keep me waiting long. 'You should go to the temple and make an offering,' he said. 'Sometimes that works.'

'I was thinking,' I said in desperation, 'that if he had the expensive medicine, it might cure him. If you could give me a loan, you know I'd pay it back. I'd do extra work. Anything you want.'

He looked at me silently for a few moments. 'Do you remember,' he said, 'what I told you about children? You must be prepared to lose a few. We all do. It's very sad' – he sighed – 'but that's the way of things.'

'I have to try to save him,' I said.

'Sometimes,' he answered me, 'we just have to let go.'

So I knew he wasn't going to lend me any money.

'It's no good,' I told my father when I got back to him. He looked very depressed. Then he left and I went back to work.

——

I didn't know what to expect when I returned home that night. My son was lying there so quietly. He'd eaten less than half the tiny bowl of soft noodles my wife had been feeding him. She'd given him some of the medicine, but there was no sign it was doing him any good. I didn't know what to say. More important, I didn't know what to do.

'I'm going to Beijing tomorrow,' my father suddenly said.

'What for?' I asked. 'We've no money.'

'I'm going to talk to the old man at the big pharmacy.'

'But he already refused when we hadn't enough money. And now we haven't even got that.'

'I'll tell him what happened. His father knew my grandfather. And people can be good-hearted. You never know.' He stopped. 'Have you got a better plan?'

So you can imagine how amazed I was, four days later, when he came back with the medicine.

If he'd come the day after, it might have been too late. My little boy had been getting weaker and weaker. The night before, I'd looked into his eyes, and I could see he was giving up. I've often noticed that children don't really have the life force until they're five or six. I remember picking him up and hugging him to me and telling him, 'You've got to fight, little fellow. You've got to fight.' And I think he may have sensed what I was saying to him, even if he couldn't understand the words. Maybe he did try to fight a bit longer, but I'm not sure he would have lasted another day.

'How did you get the old man to give you the medicine?' I asked my father.

'I reminded him that this was where he came from. I said my grandson's life was in his hands. Perhaps he was ashamed, or kindness intervened. Who knows?' He smiled. 'It doesn't really matter why people do things, does it, as long as they do them?'

So we gave my son the medicine, and by the next day, he started to get better. He's still alive today, I'm glad to say.

A few days later my master told me he'd heard my son was getting better and that he was glad to hear it. 'How did it happen?' he said.

So I told him about my father and the old man and the medicine. When he heard it, he looked a bit thoughtful. I supposed he might be feeling guilty that the old doctor behaved more kindly than he did. In any case, he didn't say anything. A few days later, he had to go to Beijing himself.

It was the morning after he returned that he called me into his house. 'Did you know that your father paid the doctor for the medicine he received?' he asked me.

I was completely astonished. 'But that's impossible, master,' I said. 'We have no money.'

'I assure you he did,' he replied. 'I spoke to the doctor myself.'

'Could it be that he doesn't want to admit his kindness?' I suggested. 'He may be afraid that if people knew about his generosity, they'll all come asking for favours.'

'I don't think so,' my master replied. He was watching me carefully. 'There's a piece missing out of the storeroom,' he went on. 'Small, but quite valuable.'

I stared at him. It took me a moment to understand. 'Oh, master,' I cried, 'you don't think I would steal from you, do you?'

'Who knows what any of us would do to save our child?' he answered.

It was true, I suppose. I'd have thought the same in his place. But I knew that I hadn't. And then I realised what had happened. 'I did not take it, master.' I shook my head. I couldn't think what more to say.

'I know you didn't,' he quietly replied. 'Your father did. When you left him in the storeroom and came to speak to me.'

'I can't believe . . .' I started.

'It's obvious,' he said. 'But he didn't tell you.'

'I wouldn't have let him,' I cried.

'I know that, too.' He paused. 'I'm not going to do anything about the missing piece,' he continued. 'But I'm afraid you'll have to go. I can't have you here anymore.'

'Master,' I pleaded, 'you know I'm a good worker, and I love it here. I'll do anything . . .'

He waved my words aside. 'While I was in Beijing,' he said, 'I spoke to the owner of a fine little lacquer workshop that I know. He used to be in the imperial works. I told him that I had a good worker, a young fellow with talent, who was forced by family circumstances to move to the city. On my recommendation, he'll take you on – as a pieceworker at first, but in time you may get a permanent position. Just don't ever let your father go near the place, or you'll disgrace me.' He nodded. 'I'm the only one that knows about this theft, and it will stay that way. But you must go to Beijing. There's nothing else to say.'

When I got home that evening and accosted my father, he admitted the theft, but he didn't even apologise. 'You do what you have to. I saved your son's life,' he told me.

'But you've disgraced our family,' I shouted.

'Not if nobody knows.' He sounded quite happy about it.

'I've lost my job,' I reminded him. 'How's that going to help the family?'

'Fine,' he said. 'Ask for your job back if I plead guilty. Let the magistrate punish me. At least I'll have done something for my family.'

'He won't give me my job back, even if you get a hundred strokes of the heavy bamboo,' I said. 'Anyway, he doesn't want to prosecute.'

'He feels guilty, that's why,' my father said triumphantly.

We all went to Beijing together: my two parents, my pregnant wife and my little boy, who, with the correct medicine, was soon nearly himself again. The owner of the lacquer workshop gave me piecework, but for the time being there wasn't enough to support a family, and I wasn't sure there ever would be. My mother found part-time work as a servant in a merchant's house. The only one of the family who was really happy was my father.

The city seemed to suit him. Not that he found regular employment. But wandering the streets, he seemed to make friends with astonishing speed. Perhaps it was because he was always talking to people and asking about their business. In no time he became a well-known figure around our lodgings, and people began to employ him on all kinds of errands. They'd always give him something for his time and trouble, and though it wasn't much, he made enough to pay for our food and part of the rent. For the first time I realised that my father wasn't actually lazy – it was just that he hated repetitive work. There wasn't much scope for a man like that in a village; but in a big city, he could survive quite well.

When my second child was born, he turned out to be a healthy son. You might think that would have made me happy, and in a way it did. But it also made me anxious.

With my family growing, I was looking for ways to earn more money for my wife and children. As for my parents, my mother could be paid as a servant and my father might pick up a sort of living hustling in the streets, but one day that would end and I'd have to look after them, too. Everything fell to me. Getting paid for piecework was all very well, but I needed a permanent position – not only for the money today, but so that I could work with more advanced craftsmen, improve my skills and earn more in the future.

I'd already discovered that the master owner of the lacquer store employed very few craftsmen on-site. He mostly farmed the work out to people like me. There were other lacquer workshops in the capital, of course, though I had no introduction to them. I did visit several, all the same, to ask if they had any piecework for me, but had no luck; and nobody was offering a permanent position at that time.

So every day, you can imagine, there was a nagging fear in my mind. What if my little boy got sick again, or the new baby? What was I going to do then?

My father had done quite well when he'd sold the lacquer piece he'd stolen, and he still had some money left over. That was our reserve in case of emergencies. After that, there was nothing.

It was a month before the new year when I brought a piece of finished work to the lacquer store. This little box was a bit more complex than anything I'd done before. There was a pattern on the lid that had needed to be carefully carved, and I was quite proud of the result.

When the owner of the store examined it, he nodded in appreciation. 'This is beautiful work,' he said. 'I'm going to pay you double what we agreed.' I was quite overwhelmed. But only for a moment. 'I'm afraid I won't be needing you anymore,' he went on. 'If I do, I'll let you know. But don't expect anything.'

'But surely, my work . . .'

'Oh, your work is excellent. The trouble is, I've a fellow who's been supplying me for years who wants more commissions. So I'm giving him the work that you do. I'm sorry, but I'm afraid he comes before you do.' He gave me a kindly look. 'That's partly why I'm paying you double now, to help tide you over.'

There was no point in arguing. I said thank you and went on my way.

It was still early morning. I didn't go home. I remember walking through the streets for hours in a kind of daze. I began to imagine terrible things – my father stealing again and getting caught, my children dying for want of medicine . . . I scarcely even noticed where I was going until I found myself not far from the Tiananmen Gate and opposite a large teahouse. This won't do, I thought. I need to stop having nightmares, drink some tea, calm down and think about what I can do to make a living. So I went into the teahouse. And once I had my tea, I tried to be logical.

It seemed to me that, whether I liked it or not, there wasn't much hope of getting employment practising the one craft for which I had any skill. And I couldn't afford to start again as an apprentice in a new trade. Perhaps I could be a servant in a merchant's house. But the pay isn't much. I started to go through all the trades and occupations I could think of. And I'd been doing that for a little while when I heard the sound of drums.

It was a small procession, like the one I'd seen the time I came to visit Grandfather's Elder Brother when I was a boy. A magnificent company of palace eunuchs solemnly led the way, flanked by drummers and men beating gongs. And the moment I saw them I felt a thrill of pleasure. The silks the eunuchs wore were so richly embroidered, so splendid, just to see them was like a glimpse of Heaven. I could almost forget my own troubles for a moment.

They were followed by a closely guarded sedan chair, no doubt containing some high palace official. They passed the teahouse and came to a big mansion where the sedan chair entered. Some of the eunuchs disappeared into the courtyard of the mansion or were brought chairs and sat by the gateway. Three decided to go for a walk. And to my surprise, one came into the teahouse.

The manager of the teahouse almost fell over himself as he rushed forward to make a low bow before the eunuch. I must say, in his splendid silk robes and conical hat, he was a stately figure. But he smiled very pleasantly, and when asked where he would care to sit, nodded easily at the table next to mine, which happened to be empty. I heard him say softly that he desired only tea, nothing to eat. 'Have you Lushan cloud tea?' he asked.

'Certainly, certainly,' the manager said, and hurried away.

Right from the moment he sat down, I couldn't help admiring his elegance. This is a man, I thought, who knows how to live. There is no better or more lustrous variety of mountain green tea than Lushan. But it wasn't just his choice of tea. He was in his forties, I guessed, but the way he sat, very straight and still, made me think of an older man. There was a grace in every movement he made. He might have been a priest. I'd always heard that most of the eunuchs were from the poorest class, but whether it was innate in the man himself or the result of years spent in the imperial palace, this eunuch exhibited nothing of the crudeness of the common folk.

I realised that I was staring at him and, ashamed of my bad manners, forced myself to stop. I gazed out of the window and told myself: think about what to do next, instead of staring at this palace eunuch who can't do you any good.

I did notice, however, that when the woman served his tea, she brought him little delicacies to eat, which he ignored.

I'd been staring out of the window thinking of my sorrows for a little while when I was interrupted by a quiet voice. 'You look unhappy, young man.'

I turned and saw to my surprise that it was the eunuch who had spoken to me. The flesh of his face was soft, his mouth was kind but not weak and his expression was one of genuine concern.

'I daresay every man has troubles, sir,' I answered politely. 'I don't suppose mine would seem very interesting to a distinguished gentleman like yourself.'

'Perhaps not,' he said pleasantly. 'But as I have to wait here for an hour, which is quite boring anyway, I should like to hear your life story, if you would tell it to me.' And he offered me some of the food on his table.

So begging him to stop me as soon as he'd heard enough, I gave him a brief outline of the story. He seemed to observe me quite carefully while I talked, and at the end he nodded. 'It wasn't boring at all,' he said. 'So what are you going to do?'

'I don't know, honoured sir,' I replied. 'I wish I did.'

'I couldn't help noticing,' he continued, 'that while you were talking, you kept glancing at my robe. May I ask what interested you about it?'

'As a craftsman, sir,' I said, 'I always notice beautiful workmanship of any kind. In fact,' I told him, 'ever since I was a boy I've been drawn to the finer things of life – even though I can't have them myself,' I added with a smile.

To my surprise, he stretched out his arm. 'Would you like to feel the silk?' he offered.

Well, I did. The embroidered silk was even stiffer than I'd expected, almost like brocade, and was finely sewn with tiny beads that made it almost scratchy. I couldn't stop myself leaning forward to inspect the stitching, which was so tight I could scarcely believe it. 'This is made to last a thousand years!' I said.

'Perhaps it will,' he said, and laughed. Then he drew back his arm and gazed at me thoughtfully. 'You know,' he remarked quietly, 'there may be a way for you to get what you want, though it is not without risk and would entail great sacrifice.'

'Please tell me about it, sir,' I said.

'You could become one of the palace people, as they call us. A eunuch.'

'A eunuch?' I stared at him, astounded. 'But I'm a married man, sir,' I protested. 'I'd have had to become a eunuch when I was a boy.'

'That's what most people think,' he said, 'but they are not correct. It is true,' he explained, 'that by far the majority of eunuchs are castrated when they are still boys. But there are a number in the palace who were castrated after they became men, had married and had families. They use the money they make in the palace to support their wives and children.'

'I never heard of such a thing!' I exclaimed.

'I assure you it is so. I am in the palace, and I know such men.'

'And their wives . . . ?'

'They live better than they might have done otherwise. Their children are cared for and fed. The eunuchs are often allowed out of the palace at night, you know. Some of these men go home at night to be with their families.'

'But they cannot . . .'

He raised his hand. 'Such arrangements do not mean that the woman can receive no pleasure at all. We need not speak of all the possibilities.' He nodded. 'Indeed, I daresay there are women married to ordinary men in Beijing who would gladly trade places with these wives.'

'I don't know what to say, sir,' I stuttered. I was quite flabbergasted.

'All eunuchs receive a modest pay,' he went on. 'But if one is lucky, there are plenty of ways of making money on the side. A few eunuchs even become rich.' He paused. 'My impression of you is that you would make friends easily and do quite well. And of course,' he said, smiling, 'you would be surrounded by the finer things of life.'

I was silent. He glanced out of the window.

'I must be off,' he said suddenly. 'Should you ever wish to take this further – but only if you are truly sure that you are ready for such a drastic step – then there is a merchant in the city that I recommend you visit. You should go to his house discreetly, in the evening, without telling anyone the true nature of your business. But once alone with him, tell him why you have come, and he can be very helpful to you, both in arranging the operation and in getting you accepted by the palace – without which, of course, the operation would be a most unfortunate waste of time and money. This is the name of the street where he lives in the Inner City. Ask for Mr Chen, the merchant.' He got up. 'Good luck.'

'Thank you, sir,' I said.

When I got home, I didn't say a word about this conversation. But I had to tell them, of course, that I'd lost my work. I saw my mother's whole body sag with shock, though she quickly tried to hide it.

Rose put on a very brave face. 'I'm sure I can take in work of some kind,' she said calmly. 'And I know you will find a position soon.'

As for my father, he didn't even seem to think there was a problem. 'I'll think of something,' he told us all airily.

'That,' I muttered, 'is what worries me.'

You'd think in a huge city like Beijing that there would be plenty of opportunities for work, but after ten days of looking, I soon discovered a simple fact: a city is a vast collection of villages. And just like in any village, a craftsman employs his own family or the son of a friend. Nor does a rich man looking for a servant want to employ a stranger who may rob him. He'll more likely ask a trusted servant he already has, 'Do you know of anyone?' And that servant probably has a cousin or a friend he can recommend. In short, most of the good jobs were already spoken for, and strangers could pick up only casual work, the way my father did – which is to say, jobs with no prospects at all.

I also discovered something else: poor people. They were in every street. I'd seen them ever since the first day I came to see Grandfather's Elder Brother when I was a boy. But I hadn't really seen them. They were just in the background, nothing to do with me.

Starving people, dressed in rags, barefoot in winter. Sick people with dying children. Once you looked, you saw them everywhere, leaning against walls or peering out from narrow doorways. They reminded me of skinny birds, stripped of their feathers. As for their children, they made me think of fledglings that've fallen from their nest to the ground. If they weren't dead already, you knew they soon would be.

And by the end of the tenth day, I was thinking, What lies between me and them? Not much. The money left from my father's theft. Whatever work we could find as a family, so long as we kept our health. But with one more sickness – why, even if my father had an accident – we could be begging in the streets like those poor folk. And I'd be standing there, holding my little boy by the hand, watching him get thinner and thinner . . .

It was as if I were walking along the edge of a great dark abyss into which the whole family could fall. One bit of bad luck – that's all it would take.

Sometimes I used to watch my father scurrying about the streets, looking so cheerful. Didn't he realise the danger we were in? Was he just acting cheerful to keep our spirits up? Or maybe he couldn't face the truth at all. I was never sure.

On the tenth day, I told him: 'It's no good, I'm not finding anything.'

I suppose I was expecting him to tell me to be patient, that something would turn up. But he didn't say that. He was quiet for a minute. He seemed to be working out a solution of some kind. 'You know,' he remarked as if he was sharing a secret, 'the best thing one can do is save a rich man's life.'

'I'm sorry,' I said. 'What does that mean?'

'Well,' he said, 'if you see a rich man in trouble, especially if you get the chance to save his life, he's so grateful he'll do anything for you. Quite a lot of people have come to fame and fortune that way.'

'You've lost your mind!' I shouted, which was no way to talk to one's father.

'No, really,' he replied, looking offended. 'It sometimes happens. You hear all kinds of stories.'

'I'll keep an eye out,' I said.

The next day, dusk had fallen when I reached the street the eunuch had told me about and asked for Mr Chen the merchant. This hutong, as such streets are called, was on the western side of the Inner City, quite a respectable area where a lot of rich merchants and tradespeople lived.

Chen's place looked like a typical merchant's courtyard house – with a doorway up a few stone steps, by the southeast corner of the wall on the street.

I'd already learned how to tell somebody's status in Beijing by the doorway of their house. Royalty and nobles had gateways flanked by stone lions – and you could tell their exact rank by the size of gate they were allowed. As a commoner, Mr Chen's doorway was far more modest. Instead of lions, he had a thick disc like a millstone on either side of the double doors, which were dark red. The heavy lintel above the doors, however, suggested his wealth was pretty solid.

A servant came to the doorway. I gave my name and said I'd come to see his master on private business. It took him only a few moments to return and usher me in.

I stepped carefully over the threshold into the open passageway that ran across the house from right to left. In many houses, the blank wall in front of me would have been enough to stop evil spirits getting into the house, for everyone knows that spirits have difficulty turning corners. Some people have fierce gods painted on their doors as well, to scare off the bad spirits. But in Mr Chen's entrance, one had to pass between a pair of door-god statues, fully armed and looking as if they'd destroy anything, body or spirit, that dared enter without permission. They were so impressive, they almost belonged in a bigger mansion. I suppose he'd got a good deal on them.

But the message was clear enough. Mr Chen showed a modest face to the world, but he'd kill you if you tried to hurt his family. I followed the servant, first left along the passageway, then right into the courtyard.

The first thing I noticed in the courtyard was the stone beneath my feet. Not a speck of dust. It must have been swept a dozen times a day. The wooden pillars and panels on the walls glowed in the soft light from the tasselled red lamps that hung around them. At the far end stood a pair of beautiful Ming vases with plants in them. Valuable. Then I was ushered into an office where the merchant awaited me.

Mr Chen was sitting on a square-framed wooden armchair behind a carved rosewood table. He was dressed in a long grey silk gown, very simple, best quality and wearing a black skullcap. I bowed low. He indicated I should take a chair on the other side of the table. I sat down. Then I stared in surprise.

Mr Chen was the eunuch I'd met.

'You are Mr Chen?' I asked stupidly.

'I am,' he acknowledged. 'You had not guessed?'

I shook my head.

'Well, I'll tell you something,' he continued. 'Neither have any of my neighbours. They only know Mr Chen, the merchant, and my wife and children.'

'They don't know you're a palace person?'

'They have no idea. They see me come and go, dressed as a merchant, but they're not sure what my business is. I change my clothes at the palace, you see. Only one of our servants, a woman, is aware of the truth. She's known me all my life, and she will never tell.'

He rose from the table, indicated I should follow him and led the way into a handsome room where a lady was sitting on a wide sofa. There was a girl – about seventeen, I thought – sitting beside her, who was reading aloud, but paused as we entered. At a writing desk on the other side of the room, a young man of about twenty was making notes.

'This is my wife, and these are my two children,' said Mr Chen, as I bowed low. 'What are you reading, my child?' he asked the girl.

'*Journey to the West,* Father,' she replied.

'My daughter reads well,' Mr Chen said to me with pride. 'Her mother does not read, but she likes to listen. *Journey to the West* is a great classic and an entertaining story, but it's awfully long, and my daughter's to be married in a few months. She won't possibly finish it before she leaves us. Do you know the book? Could you read it?'

Journey to the West was very famous, so I knew a bit about it. The huge tale of how Monkey helps a priest on his journey to find the Buddhist Scriptures, and the demons and dangers they encounter along the way, would certainly have taken months to get through.

'I can read a bit, Mr Chen,' I answered honestly, 'but not nearly well enough for that.'

'I couldn't do it, either,' Mr Chen replied. 'And my son is too busy working for a distinguished merchant to spend his time reading novels.' He smiled kindly at his wife. 'So when our daughter's left the home, I suppose I shall have to engage a poor young student to read us the rest of it.'

After this little exchange, telling his family that we had business to complete, he led me back into his office. 'So you have seen my family and how I live. I work in the catering department in charge of buying all the groceries for the palace. I am allowed to take a small cut from every purchase, so you can imagine, I make a lot of money from my position. It took me over fifteen years before I got this house. But you could work in the palace for thirty years and have nothing. There's no way of knowing. Some men are lucky. It's their destiny. Some are not.'

'Do you think I'm lucky, Mr Chen?'

'I had a feeling that you were from the moment that I met you. Your karma, if you like. I wouldn't have suggested that you came here otherwise. Also,' he said, smiling, 'you are quite good-looking. They don't want ugly people in the palace, you know.'

I don't believe I answered at first. But I do remember thinking about the scene I'd just witnessed with his children, and realising that what this man had was everything I desired in the world. I wasn't sure about being lucky. Losing my job didn't seem like good luck. But then again, it might have been fate's way of taking me from my humble village to the imperial palace in Beijing. You can never tell.

But I did know one thing. I knew it so completely that I think I must have been a rich person in a former life: a house like this, with all the finer things in life it contained, was where I belonged.

'I'll do it,' I said.

'You must wait three days,' he told me. 'During that time, I shall make the necessary arrangements. Strictly speaking, to get employment as a palace person, you should supply forms from your family, your relatives, and the chief of your village, which has to be notarised by the local authorities. However, I have some influence, and I can take care of all that. But you must take care never, at any time, to speak of any dishonesty on your father's part. The operation itself is not without danger, especially for a grown man. The surgeons in the establishment run by a gentleman named Mr Bi are the best, and Mr Bi supplies more eunuchs to the palace than anyone. You will remain at his place for some time after the operation to make sure that everything heals safely. The charge for the operation is considerable, and I shall be happy to advance you the money, at a small rate of interest, which you can repay me at your leisure. For your loyalty and friendship, I assure you, are worth more to me than the repayment of the loan.'

I was starting to thank him, but he raised his hand to stop me.

'There are two other things you must know,' he went on. 'As a eunuch, you can't be buried with your family in holy ground, as self-mutilation is considered a sin. You'll be buried in the eunuchs' graveyard outside the city. However, there is a way around this. The surgeon at Mr Bi's will keep the parts of you he removed in a sealed jar. Those jars are well guarded, I can promise you. One day, if you have the money, your son can buy them back and then your body will be considered complete again, and they can be buried with you in your family graveyard. Most eunuchs, of course, don't have a son and thus they adopt one for this purpose. But you've got a real son, so you won't have to go to that trouble.'

That was a comfort to me, I must say.

His final words were very clear. 'During these coming days,' he said, 'you must discuss this with your family. You're free to change your mind. Indeed, if you're in any doubt at the end of that time, I urge you: do not proceed. Remember, once you have gone to Mr Bi, it'll be too late.'

I told my family that evening. My mother sat down and burst into tears. 'To think this should happen to my only son,' she kept wailing.

'You've got your grandchildren,' I reminded her. 'That's all that matters now.' But it didn't seem to comfort her.

As for my father, he didn't say anything for about a minute. Then he looked up at me so sadly. 'I'm sorry about the boots.' He shook his head.

'What are you talking about?' I said.

'The boots I made for your teacher,' he says. 'If he'd liked the boots he'd have gone on teaching you, and you might be a schoolmaster by now. Or even a government official. It's all my fault.'

I just didn't reply. I mean, what can you say?

As for my wife, poor Rose wasn't pleased at all. 'That's not very nice for me, is it?' she said.

'Well, it isn't very nice for me, either.' I may have snapped at her a bit when I said that. 'We've got to think of the children, Rose,' I said. 'I wish you could have seen Mr Chen's house. You would have been amazed. And his wife seemed to be quite happy. She's got every comfort. And the life their children are going to have . . . It's beyond anything you and I ever dreamed of.' I was trying to comfort her. 'If I could do the same thing for all of you . . .' I said. But I wasn't sure she was even listening.

'Even if you don't care about me,' she blurted out, 'aren't you ashamed?'

'I'll be more ashamed if we all starve and die,' I cried. I was getting a little desperate myself, I suppose. Nobody seemed to be giving me any support, and I was the one making the biggest sacrifice.

'What will it cost?' my father suddenly wanted to know.

'Don't worry,' I said. 'The money we've still got saved will cover it.' I just said it to hurt him, I daresay. I didn't tell him Mr Chen would lend me the money. I wanted him to suffer, too.

Well, nobody said anything to me after that. Not that evening or the next morning. Not a word. That was worse than if they'd kept arguing with me. Or perhaps they'd seen I was right – except that none of them wanted to say thank you.

The second evening, my mother sat beside me and begged me to think about it some more. 'Perhaps something will turn up,' she said. 'I went to the Buddhist temple today. I'm going to the Taoist one tomorrow.' Then she started crying again.

As for Rose, after refusing to speak to me all day, she was cold to me at night as well.

'You may as well get some while it's still there,' I said when we got into bed. But she turned her back to me.

It was noon of the following day when my father returned to our lodgings looking pleased with himself. 'Good news,' he told me. 'There's no need to spend all that money.'

'What do you mean?' I said.

'I've been speaking to a man whose nephew was castrated when he was a boy. It turns out it's not that difficult. His family performed the operation themselves. All you need is to make sure you have a really sharp razor, plenty of paper, sesame oil and some prickly ash pepper. He gave me all the details. It takes a couple of months for everything to heal, but I'll be there all the time, or if I'm not, Rose can always bandage you.' He looked quite happy about it all.

'Forget it,' I said. 'I'm going to the professional.'

'You could save money,' he said. He sounded quite reproachful.

The house of Mr Bi was built of brick, at the corner of an alley in the Tartar City, as they sometimes call the Manchu Inner City. When Mr Chen took me there, he seemed in a cheerful mood. He made me carry a chicken and a bottle of rice wine, as presents for the surgeon, and kept up a running commentary all the way.

'As suppliers of eunuchs to the palace,' he explained, 'the Bi family are granted quite a high rank amongst the Manchu bannermen. Even their surgeons are seventh grade officials, which is higher than a local county magistrate.' It all sounded quite impressive. 'After your recovery, as soon as you start work,' he went on, 'you'll get a monthly stipend, which is quite handsome, even at the start. You'll be assigned a mentor and be taught all kinds of things, from court etiquette to skills that make you useful. After six years, if you do well, you may get lucky and be chosen to serve one of the imperial family. You could even find yourself in the emperor's company every day.'

He kept me so busy listening to all these wonderful things that I hardly had time to think of what was about to happen to me.

You have to fast for two days. Only liquids, no food. The third day they washed my body and gave me a potion brewed from the hemp plant they call cannabis.

The surgeon came in to see me and asked how I felt. 'Good,' I said. 'I feel good.' And gave him a smile.

It was strange, really. I remember feeling quite relaxed and calm. Very mellow. But it was better than that. A sense of peace, you might say. I just knew for certain that I was doing the right thing.

'I thought you'd give me opium to take away the pain,' I said.

'Sorry. No opium.' He shook his head. 'Opium's very bad. The cannabis won't take away the pain,' he added, 'but it helps with inflammation. And you won't vomit so much, either.' He seemed only a bit older than I was, but he had the quiet confidence of a man who knows his business. 'This way,' he said, and he led me into a room where I hadn't been before.

There was a raised bench in the middle of the room, made of dark wood. His assistant, an old man, was standing beside it. He was wearing a grey cotton apron that made him look like a butcher. They had to help me onto the bench. I realised I was moving a bit slowly. 'We strap you down now,' the surgeon said, 'so that you won't move. Things go more smoothly that way.'

'I'm glad to hear it,' I said, trying to sound cheerful. You can't help being a bit frightened.

So they strapped my arms and body to the bench, and opened my legs wide and strapped them to the sides of the bench, too, so that I couldn't move at all. Then the surgeon put a black cloth over my eyes and tied it tight. I didn't know he was going to do that, and I started to protest, but he said not to worry, they always did that.

At first, when he made the cuts on either side of my abdomen, I didn't feel all that much. But then I began to cry out.

'Take a deep breath, then close your mouth and push down as if you're trying to shit,' he said. 'Good. Again. Again. Open your mouth.' And the assistant popped something in. It felt like a hard-boiled egg – because that's exactly what it was. 'Close your mouth. That's it. Now hold still. This is going to hurt.'

Hurt? It felt as if everything between my legs was suddenly on fire. I tried to scream, but the assistant had his hand over my mouth, and my mouth was full of the hard-boiled egg, so all I could do was make a sound like a horse whinnying in my throat. Then I felt another fire from down there. And then I blacked out.

They use pig's gall to control the bleeding. I don't know why, but that's what they told me.

Actually, the worst thing wasn't even the day of the operation. It was afterwards. I was strapped to that wooden bench for a month.

It just ached and burned, day after day. I kept taking the cannabis drink for three days, which helped a bit, and they made me drink rice soup through a wheat straw. Three times a day the assistant would help me move my legs – I was still strapped to the bench, of course – because otherwise you probably couldn't walk when you got up. But it's so uncomfortable, being tied to a hard bench like that. Torture, really.

And it's so boring. Just lying there, staring at the ceiling, for thirty days. I didn't know the true meaning of boredom until that time.

The only other thing I remember happening was, a day after the operation, the surgeon came in with a jar and let me look inside it. And there were all the vital bits he'd cut off me – pickled, you might say, in lime. I suppose I was glad to see them and to know they were safe. But honestly, they looked so shrivelled, so completely separate from me, that I could have wept.

My father came to see me. 'Rose wasn't sure if she should come,' he said, and I told him not to bring her. I didn't want my wife to see me strapped to the bench. 'We may need to use a little of the money I have,' he went on sheepishly, 'with you not bringing any in just yet.'

'That's all right,' I said. 'I won't need it all.' I still hadn't told him about the loan from Mr Chen, and I wasn't going to.

A month later, when I was able to walk, I sent word to the family to come and see me, but it wasn't a great success. Rose asked me if I was all right, and I said yes, and she said, 'That's good.' It didn't sound as though she really meant it. My mother started to cry, so my father said he'd better take her home, and Rose went with them.

They'll cheer up when I bring them some money, I thought.

Mr Chen looked in several times to see how I was getting along, but apart from that I had no visitors.

I wasn't the only person undergoing the operation at the house of Mr Bi. There were half a dozen others, but they were all boys. I was the only adult. Normally it took a patient three months from the operation until the day he was ready to go to the palace, but I made such unusual progress that I was fit to leave after only two. I was told I should go with three of the boys who were to leave next. They were nice enough, and I took care to be friendly to them. We'd sit and talk, and they'd ask me all sorts of questions, assuming that because I was older I must know everything. They were simple country boys, and none of them could read or write. So I was able to tell them a good deal they didn't know about the palace and Beijing. I had a feeling they were destined for quite lowly careers. Certainly none of them had any feeling for the finer things of life.

On the day we were due to be collected, however, we were told we'd have to wait, on account of a yellow wind.

That's the only thing I hate about our northern springs: they always seem to end with a yellow wind.

For four days the yellow dust filled the sky, so that if I ventured into the street, I could hardly see my hand in front of my face. I'd wrap a piece of silk or cotton across my nose and mouth, but the dust was so fine it seemed to get through, encrust itself on my lips and block my nose until I could scarcely breathe.

But at last it was over. A palace eunuch arrived to escort us. And Mr Chen also turned up to keep me company, which was very good of him.

The sky overhead was a clear pale blue that morning, but there was a sandy-coloured haze hanging over the horizon, and the sun came through it with a strange, harsh light. It almost felt like a dream. The street was still thick with dust, and we left our footprints as we went. 'I hate this dust,' I said to Mr Chen; but he only laughed.

'You shouldn't,' he told me. 'This is the dust that turns the waters of the Yellow River into gold.'

'It still gets up my nose,' I said.

'And it enriches the great northern plain,' he went on, 'where all our wheat grows. Tell me,' he asked, 'are the roof tiles in the Forbidden City a different colour from those in the rest of Beijing?'

'Yes,' I said. 'Yellow.'

'What colour is worn only by the emperor?' he continued.

'Yellow,' I replied.

'Learn to love yellow, then,' he ordered. 'Yellow River, yellow earth, yellow roofs, yellow silks . . .'

'I get the point,' I said.

As we approached the red walls of the Imperial City in that harsh sunlight, with a sullen glare coming from the huge roofs of the Tiananmen Gate, I noticed the three boys cowering nervously. I didn't blame them. The closer one gets, the higher those great red walls and towers seem. And remember, the circuit of those walls is six miles and more. Six miles. No wonder people are frightened. But I wasn't afraid.

Because walls have two purposes: they keep strangers out, of course; but they also protect the fortunate within. That's what I was thinking as we entered the tunnel of the smaller gateway. This was the safest place in the world. I'd be protected. Well paid. Most of the people on the outside were losers; but I was a winner now. It was true I'd paid a price to get there. But you usually do pay a price for things, don't you?

And as we came out of the tunnel, there it was before us: the Forbidden City itself, the Son of Heaven's Palace, the centre of the world. I was so excited. I'd never seen it before.

There was a broad moat all the way around it. The walls were purple. We crossed the moat by a beautiful bridge and entered by a modest gateway in the western wall, where the eunuch showed our passes to the Manchu guards. Then, after passing through a little park of trees, we made our way down a short alley until we came to a low building.

'I'll leave you now,' said Mr Chen. 'Just do everything you're told. They'll give you all sorts of training about palace rules and so forth, which I know you'll learn easily. I'll come by in ten days to find out how you're getting on.'

Well, naturally, I didn't know what to expect. But I must say, I spent a very agreeable day.

They gave us all a medical check first. It might have been embarrassing, but since both we and all the people inspecting us had been castrated, it wasn't so bad.

Then we got our uniforms – simple cotton top and bottoms, blue underwear, a broad black belt and short boots. That's what you got when you started. The beautiful silks I'd seen were only for the eunuchs who'd attained high rank.

After that, we got to meet our mentors. These were eunuchs with some years of service who would teach us the basics. Though my mentor was older than the others, he evidently hadn't been picked out for any promotion yet. He was like a rather solemn family dog, moving slowly and speaking in a soft, mournful voice, but he wasn't unfriendly. 'Did you know I'm supposed to hit you with a bamboo cane if you don't learn your lessons?' he asked me sadly. 'Some of the eunuchs like whipping the new boys. But I hate it.'

'I'll try not to give you cause,' I reassured him, which seemed to cheer him up a little.

'By the way,' he said, 'as I'm your mentor, you've got to call me master.'

'Yes, master,' I said, and bowed.

'You don't really need to if we're alone,' he went on, 'but I suppose you'd better, because otherwise you might forget when we're in front of an official, and then I'd get into trouble for not teaching you to be respectful.'

'Yes, master,' I said, 'that's very wise.'

The first thing he explained to me was how to identify the senior eunuchs. 'There are about two thousand eunuchs altogether,' he said, 'though there used to be more. And two hundred of them are officials – from the eighth mandarin rank up to the third. That's normally as high as a palace person can go.'

'And each rank has a different uniform and insignia?' I suggested.

'Exactly. I'll tell them to you now,' he said.

'I have an idea,' I said. 'Is there a wardrobe room where we could look at the robes? I'd remember them a lot more easily if I could see them.'

'Well . . .' He looked a bit doubtful. 'I suppose we could.'

The wardrobe was next to the eunuchs' laundry. It was like a treasure trove to me: rows of silk coats – blue, red, purple and other colours. Some were plain silk with a big square patch on the chest, embroidered with the bird belonging to their rank. Others were covered with embroidery, with the bird worked into the rich design. The third rank was a gorgeous peacock, then a wild goose, then a silver pheasant, an egret and for the seventh rank a mandarin duck. The humblest clerk of the lowly ninth rank wore a little bird called a paradise flycatcher. There were hats as well, with feathers in jade holders and various grades of tassels. After we'd studied these for a while, I said: 'Will you please test me, master?' And of course I got them all right. He was quite amazed.

He didn't realise that this wasn't work to me at all. The moment I saw each beautiful design, I had it in my mind. These were the finer things of life – everything I loved. I could have stayed in there all day. I couldn't wait to come back.

'I expect I'll forget some of them by tomorrow, master,' I said. 'But if we come in here for a few minutes each day, I'm sure I'll get them all fixed in my head, so that I won't let you down.'

The next morning, he taught me about the rooftops. For like everything else in the Forbidden City, each building belonged to a particular rank. 'You know how every government building has at least three little figures on each corner of the roof,' my mentor began. 'On the outer point is a tiny man riding a bird. That's the emperor's servant running his errands. Behind him is at least one other animal, watching over him, and behind them both is an imperial dragon – he's a bit bigger – who'll eat them up if they don't get on with it.'

'A minimum of three figures,' I said.

'That's right. But a more important building will have another two figures, making a total of five. More important still, another two, making seven; and most important of all, two more again, making nine. Always an odd number, you'll notice, in a little procession down the roof's ridge-line. There's a bird, a lion, a seahorse, a bull, a figure that's half goat and half bull, a young dragon and a fish. You'll have to learn them all, their individual significance and exactly what all the combinations tell you about the building or gateway in question. Here in the Forbidden City you'll find examples of every kind.'

'All right,' I said.

'But there's still one more figure. It's only on a single building in the whole kingdom. Do you know what that is?' I didn't. 'It's a figure of a walking man,' he told me. 'He's holding a sword as if it were a stick. He goes at the back, just in front of the dragon, to oversee all the other figures. And he's to be found only on the roof of the Hall of Supreme Harmony, here in the Forbidden City, because that's where the emperor's throne is.'

'Will I ever go in there?' I asked.

'I doubt it,' he said, 'but you may see the roof.'

The next day he took out a scroll and unrolled it on the table. It was a map of the Forbidden City, beautifully illustrated with little pictures of every building with their names written beside them, as well as the number of figures on each roof. We studied this closely for a couple of hours and I made good progress. When we paused in the middle of the day, my master asked if I had any questions.

'I have noticed one thing, master, which you haven't yet discussed.'

'What is that?' he enquired.

'The names of the buildings,' I said. 'Every palace, every hall, has a beautiful name. Going north from the Hall of Supreme Harmony, for instance, I see the Hall of Preserving Harmony, then the Gate and the Palace of Heavenly Purity, the Palace of Earthly Tranquillity and the Hall of Imperial Peace. In the east there is the Gate of Tranquil Longevity. To the west there's the Palace of Everlasting Spring. The list goes on and on. Everything is about heavenly peace, harmony, absence of discord.'

This pleased my master very much.

'You are exactly correct,' he replied. 'And how could it be otherwise when the rule of the emperor is dedicated entirely to the maintenance of harmony, justice, and peace within the kingdom?'

'Can the emperor really be so wise all the time?' The moment I said it I cursed myself for being such a fool. Now I'll be in trouble, I thought. But my master only smiled.

'That was all thought of centuries ago,' he said. 'Everyone in the palace, including the emperor himself, is watched all the time. All his memoranda and all his actions, no matter how small, are recorded. Not only does he have counsellors, but there are officers who will inform him of the precedents for every action, going back into previous dynasties. Everything he does has to be according to law and custom. Not only that, there is always at hand at least one Confucian philosopher called a censor, who acts like a tutor and who is required to warn him if any action he is considering would be unjust. The censor may speak freely, without any fear, and the emperor is obliged to listen.

'So you see,' he concluded, 'all this attention to order is part of a larger theme. If the palace isn't perfectly ordered, with everything in its proper place and rank, and morally correct, how can we expect the kingdom to be ordered?'

'I understand, master,' I said. 'And I think it's wonderful.' I still do, as a matter of fact.

Learning deportment took much longer. How to walk, how to bow, how to address everybody respectfully. There were so many little mistakes you could make, and even the smallest one could land you in deep trouble.

'You can be grateful that we're not as strictly treated as the serving-women,' my mentor told me.

There were scores of these, from the humblest cleaner who polished the floor on her hands and knees, to the women who tended personally to the empress. These last were usually from high-ranking Manchu families, and it was supposed to be a great honour. 'I can't imagine the Manchu ladies waiting on the empress have a bad time,' I said.

'Actually, it's the reverse,' he said. 'They have to keep terrible hours. If a member of the imperial family wants one of these women, nobody cares if she's sleeping after a long day, she has to get up and run at once. The closer you are to the royal family, the greater your danger. They say that one poor girl dropped a piece of burning ash onto the empress's gown once – by accident, of course – and it caught light. They put it out, but all the same . . . Bad mistake. What do you think happened to the girl?'

'I don't know.'

'Beheaded. Straightaway. So were most of her family, though it was hardly their fault, was it?'

'And if a eunuch had done it?'

'Oh, punished, demoted. But not beheaded – unless they thought you'd done it on purpose. They trust us more, you see. We're just poor boys who owe everything to the court, so we're not going to do anything against our masters.'

You can be sure I devoted myself to learning everything I could, and my master never even had to strike me once, though I often heard the other recruits catching it. In fact, by the time Mr Chen came to see me after ten days, word had already reached him that I was the best pupil they'd had for over a year, and that I was a paragon of virtue.

I'd just had my first pay packet, but when I offered to make a payment towards what I owed him, he wouldn't hear of it.

'Don't even think of it yet,' he told me, 'your family needs the money.' He smiled. 'You've done me far more good already, by impressing everybody. I've been busy reminding them that it's all thanks to me you came here.' He made me tell him everything I'd been doing, and nodded approvingly. 'Later on,' he told me, 'after you've completed your training and got a position, there's a nice little job we'll try to get you for extra money.'

'What's that?' I asked.

'Carrying a sedan chair for members of the royal family,' he told me. 'You're one of a team and you aren't often needed, but it would give you a second salary.' He laughed. 'It was an honour reserved for elderly eunuchs of long service, but after they'd nearly dropped one of the princes a few times, it was given to younger fellows like you.'

When I got home and gave my family my pay and told them all the good news, they were very happy to see me. I played with my little children, and that night I lay with my wife and made her quite happy, one way and another.

So you can imagine what a good mood I was in when I returned to the palace early in the morning.

My mentor was waiting for me, but instead of going with me into the schoolroom we often used for our lessons, he told me to go in alone and whispered: 'Mr Liu wants to see you. He's a head eunuch. Remember to bow low.'

The only person in the room was sitting in a chair. From the peacock on his silk robe I knew at once that this must be one of the few eunuchs in the third grade. The sleeves of his robe had long white extensions that flapped down to his knees – which told me he served the emperor personally. I bowed very low indeed. As I raised myself back to a respectful attention, I saw there were some papers on the small table at his side.

His face was smooth and still as a statue's. 'Did you know your papers are not in order?' he asked me.

'Your unworthy servant did not, honoured sir,' I said.

'I daresay Mr Chen arranged them for you,' he remarked. I nodded, since this was indeed the case. 'Mr Chen is an important person,' he went on. 'If Mr Chen tells the clerks in my department – for I am in complete charge of all the palace eunuchs, you see – that an applicant's papers are good enough to be stamped and sealed, they will do as he says. I have the power to countermand him, of course.'

I trembled. He watched me.

'I shall not countermand his orders, however. You will remain here – for the time being, at least.' He paused. 'Why do you suppose I am doing that? Do you think it's because you are an exemplary student, one who shows outstanding talent for this kind of work?'

'I hope so, honoured sir,' I said uncertainly.

'Well, it's true that if you were useless, I'd throw you out at once. I might express surprise that Mr Chen introduced such an unworthy person. I might even question his judgement. But of course that's not the case. Mr Chen has excellent judgement. The reports from your mentor, and others who are watching you – for one is always watched in the palace, you know – are really outstanding. You are considered very promising indeed.'

'I am grateful, honoured sir, and strive to please,' I murmured.

'Yet that is not why I am keeping you.' He gazed at me. 'So how can we explain this puzzle?'

'Your foolish servant cannot say,' I answered.

'Normally, after their basic training, we sort the new recruits into two categories. Those who show little talent are sent out to be servants in the houses of nobles and high officials in the city. Those who show promise receive further training and education for all kinds of special tasks – anything from keeping accounts to becoming musicians. They may work in any of several dozen departments. Mr Chen, for instance, has made his career in food procurement. Once allocated, everyone's performance is reviewed after three years, and again at six years. At the six-year review, a few may be selected to work in the household of a member of the royal family. Most eunuchs remain in quite humble jobs. About one in ten rises to official rank, as Mr Chen has done. Long service and seniority also mean – minus some heinous crime – that the eunuch has a position for life.' He paused a moment. 'I assume that you are hoping for both security and promotion to official rank. Is that correct?'

'If I am found worthy,' I said softly, and bowed very low.

'Well, the reason I'm keeping you here is to deny your hopes. You will remain under my eye so I can ensure that you receive no promotion and no rewards of any kind. You'll be assigned menial tasks, in obscure corners of the Forbidden City – places where you'll never even catch a glimpse of the emperor's family. You'll have to stay here as a drudge as long as you live, and when you die, you'll be buried in the poor eunuchs' cemetery. Because you'll certainly never earn enough to buy your balls back. What do you think of that?'

I stared at him in horror. I couldn't believe my ears. 'But why?' I cried.

'Can't you guess?' He gave me a bland smile. And then I began to understand.

'Since I have given satisfaction, honoured sir,' I said slowly, 'I am wondering if this has something to do with Mr Chen.'

'You are correct. You have a quick brain.' He nodded. 'Were the circumstances otherwise, you might go far. It's really a pity, but there it is.'

'Honoured sir,' I ventured, 'if you intend to ruin my life, would you graciously tell your servant why he is to be destroyed.'

'I detest Mr Chen and all persons like him.'

'Because we were not castrated until after we had families?'

'Exactly. You think you can have it both ways. The rest of us were denied everything you enjoyed. In compensation, we receive the protection and opportunities of service in this palace. But then interlopers like you and Mr Chen, who've paid none of the penalty, come in and steal our rewards for yourselves.'

'Do most of the palace people feel the same about us?' I asked.

'Probably. But what matters is what I feel. Although I outrank Mr Chen, I can't touch him because he has tenure. But thanks to your presence, I can humiliate him. He brings in a talented protégé. He boasts about him. Excellent. I watch. Then I see to it that you get no favour or promotion of any kind. There will be nothing he can do about it. For he has no say over any department outside his own, you see. You are completely in my power.'

'And you're going to sacrifice me.'

'Yes, I am. By sacrificing you, I show that his scheme to infiltrate more of his own kind into the palace will never work. Everyone will know. I shall make sure they do. Mr Chen is going to lose face. And that will please me. More important still, married men are hardly likely to apply in the future, once they hear what happened to you.'

It made sense. I couldn't deny it. So everything I had gone through was for nothing. Both I and my family were destroyed. I looked at him with hatred. I couldn't help it.

'Don't look at me like that,' he said sharply.

'Why not?' I said. 'You're going to destroy me anyway.' I had nothing to lose. ‘Do you know why I came here?’ I said. ‘My little boy was sick. We thought he was going to die. We saved him, but the medicine cost us everything we had. So I said to myself, what if he gets sick again? And then I met Mr Chen. What would you have done in my place?’

‘This isn’t going to do you any good, you know,’ he replied. I noticed he was watching me, but I couldn’t make out what he was thinking. Was there just a hint of sympathy in his eyes when I told him about my son? Did he respect me for standing up for myself? Or was he just waiting, like a cat playing with a mouse? I couldn’t guess which. Looking back on it, I daresay it could have been all three things at the same time.

‘You’re going to have a very unhappy life,’ he said. ‘Now get out.’

And I thought to myself: now what am I going to do?

TAIPING

1858

In the spring of 1858, Cecil Whiteparish had taken a chance. Of course he couldn't be certain. It was a shot in the dark.

'It's never worked before,' he said to Minnie, 'but it just might, this time.'

Since the expedition with Read, Cecil's life in Hong Kong had been pretty good. His marriage to Minnie was happy. He had three children now.

The Hong Kong missions were all thriving. As well as tracts and Bibles, their printing presses were turning out all kinds of lively Christian works. *The Pilgrim's Progress* was a particular favourite. And missionary scholars were translating Chinese classics into English. 'We must help our people understand this country better,' Cecil liked to say. 'That's part of our task, too.'

Mr Legge, the Scots Congregationalist minister, had started a seminary where Chinese converts were training to become missionaries themselves. And some of these converts were showing great promise.

Perhaps the best of them was Hong. Hong was a Hakka. As a young village schoolmaster, he'd been attracted to the Taiping, then given that up and worked for several missions before finding Legge. 'I've taught him well,' the Scotsman observed. 'Doctrinally, he's sound. A few more years, and he'll make converts of his own.'

When Hong attended the Bible classes that Cecil gave at his house, the Whiteparish family soon adopted him. In his mid-thirties, strongly built, friendly, always glad to play with the children, he became like their favourite uncle. The family even gave him a private nickname – Daniel – after the Old Testament hero. Everyone was delighted when he married one of the Chinese converts, a lovely young woman, and they had a baby son.

'I believe our Daniel has got everything a man could want,' Cecil remarked to Minnie at the time. But Minnie was not so sure.

'I have a feeling,' she replied, 'that there's something we don't know about him. Something in his past.'

'I'm sure it's nothing bad,' said Cecil.

Another pleasure in Cecil's life had been the development of a new relationship with his cousin Trader. Naturally, this had all been done by letter. And so interesting did the two men find each other's letters that as time went on, the social differences that had divided them in the past were practically forgotten. More than once Cecil had remarked to Minnie: 'We haven't seen John since he came to our wedding. I'd be so glad if he came to see us here again.'

Most surprising to John Trader had been how well informed his missionary cousin had become about all matters relating to trade. Yet it wasn't really so surprising. For as the Hong Kong colony grew and living conditions got better, not only Western merchants gathered there, but the big Chinese operators of Canton had been coming to the island to live beside them. Missionaries, merchants and professional men from many nations were living side by side, and an intelligent fellow like Whiteparish could not fail to be well informed about most of the things that were passing in that world.

Cecil had been especially flattered to receive a letter from John asking for his opinion: 'My two partners are suggesting,' he wrote, 'that we should take on a fourth, a junior partner who might in due course be based in the port of Shanghai. What do you think?'

He'd replied at once:

> As it happens, I visited Shanghai recently. At the time of the Opium War, it was only a walled fishing village, near the mouth of the Yangtze River, with a little fort to protect it from pirates. But now it's growing fast. Some Triad gangs got control of the place for a while, but they've been kicked out. The local Chinese mandarins and the British get along rather well – we help the

Chinese keep order and collect the taxes. Outside the old walled town, new French and British quarters are building fast. Quite handsome.

The Taiping have devastated the Yangtze valley. Since their advance on Peking failed, however, they've been contained by the emperor's army in the Nanjing area. But they still disrupt the river trade. They'd like to break out of Nanjing; and the emperor's men would like to break in. But this stalemate can't last forever. And once China is at peace and open for trade, I predict the huge wealth of the Yangtze will flow through Shanghai.

So the South China trade will be conducted in Hong Kong, the Yangtze trade in Shanghai. You'll need a man in each.

With so much progress already evident in Hong Kong, and more to be hoped for, at least in China's future, why should Whiteparish, a thoughtful missionary, be troubled by a sense of foreboding?

He didn't like to say it, but the truth was that he had misgivings about his own countrymen and their friends.

For the West was growing impatient with the East. The reports he received from Trader confirmed the fact. The treaties made after the end of the Opium War – not only with Britain but with France and America, too – were not eternal. They came up for renewal during the following decade, and those renewals were now overdue.

'The politicians say they want free trade and Christianity,' he remarked to Minnie.

'By which they mean free trade,' she replied.

British merchants still believed, correctly or not, that they could sell huge quantities of cotton goods to the vast population of China – which might be four hundred million people, though nobody knew.

But it was the profounder issue that really made the men of the West impatient. It was time China entered the modern world, they insisted. Time to stop treating other countries as ignorant barbarians and servants; time to live in a world of free men and equals. They wanted change, and they wanted it now. History was on their side. The Chinese had had a whole decade to think about it. What was wrong with them?

The new treaties would end all this nonsense. British, French and American representatives were ready. British troops had been earmarked to accompany the diplomats. They might not be used, but they would show that the envoys meant business. The British delegation was led by Lord Elgin, a seasoned diplomat.

Before they could go to Beijing, there were two interruptions. The first came in 1857, the sudden outbreak of violence in India against insensitive British domination, known as the Mutiny, which almost threatened Calcutta itself. The troops due to come to China had to deal with this first.

'The one salutary result of this bloodletting,' Cecil wrote to Trader, 'is that the British Empire has learnt it must seek a better understanding of the customs and religions of the local people. A useful lesson in humility.'

The second had been the local dispute down in Canton over illegal shipping between the British and the cantankerous Chinese governor of Guangzhou, which resulted in the governor being booted out and the British, French and Americans, for the moment at least, running the city themselves. No one showed any humility in this affair. A sense of tension remained.

But after these interruptions the West was ready, the troops were available, and the envoys had been about to sail up the coast from Hong Kong to the mouth of the Peiho River that led up to Beijing.

It was ten days before Lord Elgin was due to leave Hong Kong that Cecil, finding a chance to be alone with the envoy at a dinner, had raised his fears. 'May I speak frankly to you, Lord Elgin?'

'You certainly may.' Middle-aged, balding, his intelligent eyes set wide apart, the noble diplomat was known as a good listener.

'You have seen how our missions are thriving here on the island, and how we and the Chinese get along. I am hopeful that, with patience, this kind of cooperation could spread throughout the Chinese empire.'

'The sentiment for patience is lacking in London.'

'I am aware. But here's the thing. If we again impose our will by force of arms, then not only do we create enmity, but the only thing the Chinese will see is that our arms are better. They will therefore acquire similar arms, which is surely not our objective.'

'I'm hoping not to use arms.' Elgin paused. 'I may have another card up my sleeve. Tell me your opinion of the Taiping and their so-called Heavenly King. Are they Christians?'

'They might become Christians in the future; but at present they are a cult, ruled by a man who claims to be the brother of Jesus, but who is certainly moody and possibly mad.'

'The Chinese, however, may suppose that we and the Taiping worship the same god.'

'They shouldn't. But they may.'

'So if I indicate that we might consider joining forces with the Taiping, it'll frighten the emperor. Make him more amenable.'

'You are devious.'

'That is my job.'

'Will you demand that our ambassador present his credentials to the emperor without performing the kowtow, face on the ground?'

'Of course. No kowtow. Not appropriate in the modern age.'

'I have a suggestion. Let the ambassador meet with a minister or a royal prince. Both men will be the representative of their monarch, but no kowtow would be called for.'

'Intelligent. But impossible. London won't hear of it. Question of principle.'

'Damn the principle.'

'I didn't think missionaries talked like that!' Elgin smiled.

'This one does.'

Elgin sighed. 'I'm not sure,' he said quietly, 'I can do that.'

It was a week after Lord Elgin and his party had departed, that early one morning, Cecil and Minnie heard someone hammering at the door – and were surprised to find Daniel there, apparently beside himself. 'You've got to help me!' he cried as soon as they let him in.

'What's the matter?' Minnie asked.

'I must go to Nanjing. I have to see the Heavenly King.'

'Nanjing's surrounded by the emperor's army,' Cecil had pointed out. 'You'll never reach it. And even if you did, whatever makes you think the Heavenly King will see you?'

Daniel looked at him, a little wildly, then shook his head. 'You don't understand, dear friend,' he said. 'You see' – he took a deep breath – 'the Heavenly King is my cousin.'

It did not take him long to tell his story. He hadn't seen the Heavenly King for many years, since they had studied the Bible together. But they had been close. Legge knew about this, but thought it best for Hong to keep the matter secret.

And now Daniel had had a dream. A powerful dream, in which he'd been instructed to go to the Heavenly King, correct the errors in his cousin's understanding and bring the Taiping truly within the Christian fold.

'It's my destiny,' he cried. 'Suddenly my whole life makes sense.' He looked at Minnie earnestly. 'I must do it. I must.'

By noon, Cecil had spoken to Legge, who confirmed the story. But the Scottish minister was dismissive. 'If the imperial army doesn't kill him, his own cousin will. The Heavenly King has built his rule on the basis of his own warped ideas of Christianity. D'you think he's going to like it if his long-lost cousin appears and tells him it's all wrong? He'll murder him.'

'Hong understands that,' Cecil replied. 'But he thinks it's his mission, and he's prepared to risk his life. What if he were to bring all those people to the true Christian faith? It's not impossible. Who are we to tell him he's wrong?'

'I'll take no part in this,' Legge replied. 'I'd restrain the man by force, if the law allowed.' He nodded grimly. 'He'll be needing money for his journey, which I'll not give him. Not a penny.'

And so it was that Cecil Whiteparish took his chance. He knew it was a shot in the dark. Of course it might fail. One couldn't be certain. 'No one has put the Taiping on the right path before. But as a missionary, I cannot say that such a thing cannot be done. Perhaps Daniel is the one man who could pull it off.'

It took Cecil a week to get the money together. Many of the community supported Legge. Even those who contributed to the fund that Cecil raised – even these friends – mostly asked Cecil not to reveal that they'd contributed.

But what about Daniel's wife and baby son? He could not possibly take them with him on such a dangerous journey.

'My wife insists she'll look after the lass and the bairn,' Legge announced. 'But don't forget, Whiteparish, you're sending the man to his doom.'

After Daniel set out, months passed. And nobody knew whether he had reached Nanjing, or even if he was alive.

Lord Elgin had done a good job that summer. His gunboats knocked the shore forts guarding the Grand Canal to bits; and after some brutal negotiations, he got everything he wanted.

A British ambassador would meet the emperor without making the kowtow. The opium trade was made legal. There was to be free trade. Christian missionaries could make converts all over China; the emperor would protect them. And the British, French, Americans and other foreigners were not to be called barbarians anymore – at least officially!

Lord Elgin, praised by his countrymen, departed for his home in Scotland.

All that remained was for the treaty to be formally ratified, when ambassadors from Britain, France and America came to the Chinese capital the following summer.

And so it might have come to pass without further ado, had it not been for Lord Elgin's younger brother, who, arriving as ambassador the following year, came with troops rather than tact, got embroiled in a dispute down at the forts, decided to barge through like the bully he was, and this time found that the Chinese had repaired the forts and learned to defend them better, and they gave him the drubbing he deserved and sent him packing. So all Lord Elgin's work was brought to naught.

> Can you believe it, my dear cousin? Poor Elgin was staying with the royal family at Balmoral when news of the catastrophe arrived. He's mortified. What words he will say to his younger brother when they next meet doesn't bear thinking about. He's being asked to go back and sort out the mess. You may be sure he has no wish to go, but feels duty bound. I imagine he'll set out in the new year. It's possible that I may encounter him before he departs. If so, I'll write you word of our meeting.
>
> Yr affectionate cousin,
> John Trader.

o

On a February morning, in the year of our Lord 1860, a single slim middle-aged Chinese man in a long robe might have been observed making his way swiftly up the lane from the waterfront towards the house of Cecil Whiteparish. There was nothing about him to attract attention.

Nobody would have suspected that the plaited queue that hung from his hat down the centre of his back was false, and that a few months ago the hair on his head, though grey, had been thick and free. In short, no one would have taken him for a Taiping warrior.

Nio hurried up the lane. Hong Kong was bigger than he'd expected, with building sites everywhere. Down at the dock, they'd given him directions to the missionary's house, but twice he'd had to pause to ask the way.

He could hardly believe that he'd made it to the British island alive. Getting past the Manchu camps and patrols between Nanjing and the coast had been the hardest. He might have been killed or captured a dozen times. But it seemed the Heavenly King had been right when he'd assured him, 'My Elder Brother, Jesus, has promised me: you are under divine protection.' And therefore the Heavenly King might also have been right when he ordered: 'First, you must get the support of Cecil Whiteparish. He is the key to everything. He may be the man upon whom our entire future depends.'

Sometimes it had seemed to Nio that the Heavenly King, with his strange moods, when he'd hardly speak for days, and his religious visions, might be going a little mad. But there was nothing mad about the plan. The plan could work.

Nio had seen many things. Things that haunted him, things he'd like to forget. But if the plan worked, they might have been worthwhile.

Just before Cecil Whiteparish left his house, he kissed his wife. Minnie was pregnant again, with only two months to go before the baby was due. This would be their fourth.

He went to the door and opened it. A bright morning. Small white clouds scudded busily across a pale blue sky. He closed the door and was about to step into the lane when he saw the lone figure coming towards him. 'Good Heavens,' said Cecil. There was no mistaking Nio. He hardly needed to notice the scar on his cheek.

The two men had been closeted together in the dining room for half an hour before Minnie Whiteparish made her appearance.

'Sit down, my dear,' said Cecil, 'and let me tell you the remarkable news my friend here has brought. You remember how Daniel left last year, hoping to get to Nanjing?'

'How could I forget?'

'Well, not only did he reach Nanjing. It seems the only people the Taiping Heavenly King trusts now are his own family; so when his cousin and childhood companion turned up, he was overjoyed. He's made our friend Hong his closest adviser.'

'I hope Daniel will be a good influence on him,' said Minnie calmly.

'That's just the point,' replied Whiteparish. 'It seems he put his plan into effect with notable success. He sends us assurances that the community at Nanjing is, if not perfect in every particular of doctrine and behaviour, so hugely reformed that we should have no hesitation in pronouncing them Christian.'

'Does the Heavenly King still believe he is the brother of Christ?'

'Hong particularly sends me word that the king and the Taiping now believe themselves to be brothers and sisters in Christ, just as all good Christians do.'

'Let us hope so,' said his wife.

'I don't think we need quibble too much on every point.'

'Has our visitor been to see Daniel's poor wife and child? They've been waiting up at the mission here for a year without any word from him, not knowing if he is alive or dead.'

'He is going there directly, as soon as we have finished,' Cecil answered.

'I'll leave you, then, so that you can conclude your business quickly,' said Minnie, with a nod to Nio as she withdrew.

Once she was gone, the two men resumed their conversation in Cantonese.

'You said when you arrived that you had come to me for help,' said Whiteparish. 'What can I do for you?'

'I have a message for the British government's highest representative. It is of greatest importance.'

'I see.' Whiteparish was thoughtful. 'There's no one really senior in Hong Kong at this moment. But someone's probably on the way.'

'Whom do you think they will send?'

'Well' – Whiteparish hesitated only a moment – 'the word is that it's Lord Elgin.'

'It will be Lord Elgin,' Nio said with certainty, though how he could know such a thing Cecil had no idea.

'Then you'd better wait and deliver your message to him.'

But Nio shook his head. 'It is not I whom the Heavenly King wishes to deliver the message. It is you.'

'Me?' Whiteparish stared at him in astonishment.

'Yes. The Heavenly King cannot come himself. He must remain in Nanjing. Nor can his cousin, whom you call Daniel, be spared. But Daniel has told the Heavenly King that he trusts you entirely. The British respect you. No one would doubt your word. And you know Lord Elgin personally. You are the perfect person to explain to Lord Elgin what we ask and what we offer. The only reason the Heavenly King sent me was because I know you. I am to tell you everything, then leave. All our lives depend on you.'

'Oh,' said Cecil.

'I am to reveal to you the Taiping strategy and battle plan.'

'Isn't that supposed to be secret?'

'We trust you.'

Whiteparish considered. 'You understand I cannot hide anything from Lord Elgin?'

'I understand.'

'You may tell me, then,' said Whiteparish.

'The emperor's forces have almost surrounded Nanjing. They hope to throttle us.'

'Can they?'

'Maybe. If they don't give up. And as long as they keep getting supplied.'

'Where do the supplies come from?'

'Through Hangzhou city, from the coast at Zhapu.'

'Have you forces outside who can relieve you?'

'No need. We have General Li.' Nio smiled. 'The only Taiping leader who wears spectacles. Looks like a schoolmaster. But the men worship him. Very cunning.'

'What is his plan?'

'We break out. A few thousand men, very fast. Attack Hangzhou, maybe Zhapu. The emperor's army will chase us, leaving not so many troops around Nanjing. We double back and the whole Taiping force attacks the emperor's men left at Nanjing.'

'Split the enemy and then smash the divided parts. You think it will work?'

'Yes.' Nio nodded. 'General Li is very good at this.'

'And then?'

'Another breakout. This one strikes north, up the Grand Canal. But not far. Just enough to protect our flank. Then cut across to the coast at Shanghai. Two days' march.'

'You want to take Shanghai?'

'We want the harbour. The Chinese defences at Shanghai are nothing. Easy to take.'

'Aren't you forgetting something? Shanghai's not an old fort and a fishing village anymore. It's the one treaty port that's really open, and it's grown. There are foreign concessions outside the fort now, not just merchant factories, but whole communities – British, French, American. What are you going to do about them?'

'We only want the fort. Not the concessions. This is the message for Lord Elgin: tell the Western communities to fly a yellow flag over every building – house, church, store. Our troops will know: touch any foreigner under a yellow flag and you'll be executed. Tell your people: just stay indoors until the fighting's over. It won't take long.'

'And then?'

'Business as usual.'

Whiteparish wondered: was this the whole story?

'What else do the Taiping want from us?' he asked.

'Only what I've said.'

'You mean, don't interfere between the Taiping and the emperor. Remain neutral, as we call it.'

'Of course.'

On the face of it, the message made sense. When Lord Elgin came, it would be to settle the relationship with the emperor of China and open up trade. Cecil didn't imagine Elgin would wish to involve his troops in a sideshow battle between the emperor and the Taiping.

'What about arms?' Once or twice he'd heard rumours of British merchants discreetly running arms up to Nanjing for the Taiping.

'You can always buy arms,' Nio answered. He smiled. 'When it comes to selling arms, there are no nations on the high seas.'

'So that's everything?'

'No. Did you notice, when you spoke of Lord Elgin, that I already knew it was he who would come?'

'Yes. But it made no sense.'

'I will tell you why. Some time ago, the Heavenly King had a vision, in which he was told that God was sending a great man to help him.

After praying further, the Heavenly King was certain that this great man is Lord Elgin.'

'I see. How curious.' Cecil frowned. 'We'll have to see, won't we?'

'So this is the further message from the Heavenly King to Lord Elgin. The Taiping are friends of the British. We share the same religion. The old Manchu dynasty is corrupt and crumbling. It is God's will that we should replace it with a Christian kingdom, where the British and other Christian people will be welcome to send missionaries – for we know what good people you are – and also to trade freely. We shall open the doors of the new kingdom to you.'

'It is a powerful message.'

'Daniel told me to say to you that you may trust this message.'

'We can have consuls in the ports? An ambassador in Beijing?'

'Why not?'

'And the trade will be free? Our merchants can go up the Yangtze River and sell cotton?'

'Of course. The only items the Heavenly King cannot approve are alcohol and tobacco. He believes they are bad.'

'I don't think that would be a problem.'

'And opium, of course. But all the Christian missionaries are against the wicked opium trade. Daniel was able to assure the Heavenly King about that.'

'Ah,' said Whiteparish, and fell silent. 'We must go step by step,' he said at last.

'That is all my message,' said Nio. 'Will you deliver it?'

'I promise,' said Cecil. 'How long will you stay?'

'One day at the mission with Daniel's family. Then I have another duty to perform.'

'What's that?'

'I am going to see my Big Sister.'

It was not until his children were tucked up in bed that night, and he and Minnie were dining quietly together, that Cecil was able to share his thoughts.

'You know, my dear,' he said after telling her everything that Nio had proposed, 'Nio may be deluding himself. The Taiping king may be using him cynically. But if the message is genuine, the implications of all this could be very great. The prospect of our missions having free access to the whole of China . . . it's what we've always dreamed of.'

Minnie was a little tired. Her back was hurting. 'If it's God's will,' she said quietly.

'There are some,' he mused, 'who believe that a Christian China is prophesied in the Book of Isaiah. The prophet speaks of a great gathering of those who believe in the Lord God, from the north and the west and from the "land of Sinim". It could be that Sinim is China. I heard an excellent sermon on that very subject a year ago.' He paused. 'I must confess, the responsibility of conveying the message to Lord Elgin – assuming it's he who will come – weighs heavily upon me.'

'If you think you may forget something, dear, you should write it down while it's fresh in your mind.'

'I don't mean that. It's the import of the message that is so grave.'

She smiled gently. 'Fortunately, that will be for Lord Elgin to worry about, Cecil, and not you.'

'He may ask for my assessment of the message, what it means. He may ask for my advice.'

'He may not.'

'And then what should I say? That is what troubles me.'

'God will tell you what to say,' she replied, hoping he was done.

o

There was nothing special about the day. As she often did in the early afternoon, Mei-Ling had crossed the little bridge and was walking along the path that led through the trees by the edge of the pond when she thought she heard a faint rustle to her left. She stopped, and so did the sound – a small animal among the leaves, no doubt. But she'd gone only a few more steps when she heard the snap of a breaking twig upon the track behind her and turned.

'Little Brother,' she cried. And seeing him glance down the path quickly: 'There's no one about. How did you get here?'

'My horse has been tethered in the woods since early morning. I watched the village wake up, saw your husband leave the house. He must have returned from America.'

'You're being careful.'

'I wasn't careful enough last time. Remember?'

She gazed at him. Her Little Brother was looking older, greyer, she thought. 'My husband never went to America. He came back.'

They found a log to sit on, hidden from the path.

'What are you doing here?' she asked. 'I have thought about you so often, wondering what had become of you. I want to know everything.'

'I will tell you. But first you must tell me: how is your family? Are things any better?'

'The same, I suppose.' She smiled sadly. 'My husband is well, but his brother is useless. Even with our sons, who are good workers, there's only so much we can do. My husband's brother has sold most of the land. The house is falling apart. They say the Americans are looking for workers again, and the pay is good. Maybe my husband and one of the boys will go. Maybe not. But we survive, Little Brother. We are not starving.'

'I brought you money.'

'There is no need, Little Brother. I still have some of what you gave me before. Keep it for yourself.'

'I brought it for you. I have money for myself. We'll hide it before I go.'

She sighed. She supposed he could afford it.

He told her about his mission, just as he had told Whiteparish. 'But there was one thing I did not tell the British,' he added.

'What's that?'

'We still have a lot of silver from the towns we captured. I mean, a lot. And there's more stored in the fort at Shanghai.'

'What will you do with it?' She smiled. 'Retire rich?'

'No. Once we have Shanghai harbour, we're going to buy iron warships, steamships, like the British have. Maybe a dozen, maybe more. Then we'll take them upriver to Nanjing, blast the emperor's camps outside the city and completely cut off their supplies. The whole Yangtze River will be ours.'

'You really think you will overcome the emperor?'

'And drive the Manchu out? Yes. Especially if the British cooperate. It's in their interest to do so.'

Mei-Ling thought for a moment. 'I know it's what you've always wanted,' she said softly. She paused. 'Can I ask you something?'

'Of course.'

'Is the Heavenly King insane?'

She noticed that Nio hesitated. 'I don't know,' he replied slowly. 'I think maybe great men often seem a little mad. They see things we don't.

You have to look at what he's achieved. He has a kingdom. He may yet take the whole empire. It's ready to fall.'

'You say that because you want it to be true.'

'I know.'

'He could win and still be crazy.'

Nio was considering this proposition when, glancing across the water, he gave a small start and pointed. 'Who's the child?'

Across the pond, Mei-Ling's mother-in-law could be seen emerging from the gate of the house, leading a small girl by the hand.

'That's our daughter,' she said. 'She came less than a year after your last visit.' She smiled. 'I'd always wanted a girl.'

'You must be happy.'

'Yes.'

'Your husband doesn't mind having a girl?'

'He dotes on her.'

The old woman and the little girl had stepped onto the bridge.

'She looks just like you!' Nio exclaimed.

'So people say,' Mei-Ling answered. 'Mother says that when she's a little older, we should have her feet bound. She could make a fine marriage.'

'Hakka women don't bind their feet,' said Nio with a frown.

'Nor do the Manchu women. But it's the only way she can have a better life than ours.'

The answer didn't seem to satisfy Nio. 'When we take over, things will be different,' he said.

But even while her eyes rested on her daughter, Mei-Ling's mind had moved elsewhere. 'Are you going to marry, Little Brother?' she suddenly asked.

'Some time ago, I did take a wife. The Heavenly King gave her to me.'

'That is good. Have you children?'

'There was a child, but it died at birth. My wife died, too.'

'I am sorry. Did you love her?'

'We weren't together long.' He gave her a sad smile. 'Not like I love you, Big Sister.'

'That's different.' She shook her head. Her Little Brother was a middle-aged man, yet just for a moment he had sounded almost like a child.

'When this is over,' he said, 'I shall retire and settle down. Take a wife. Have a family. The Heavenly King has promised me.'

'Good. I hope it is soon.' She was still staring across the water, but now she turned to him. 'Does it haunt you? All that you've seen. The men you have killed.'

'I am a soldier.'

She nodded slowly. He could not speak of it. She understood.

They buried the silver he had brought. Then they went to where his horse was tethered, and he said goodbye and rode away through the trees. And Mei-Ling gazed after him, feeling as helpless as a mother parted from her child.

o

By the time this reaches you, Cousin Cecil, Lord Elgin will already be close. I had the opportunity to converse with him for some time just hours ago, and hasten to share what I learned while it is still fresh in my mind.

He's doing his duty by going back, but hopes he won't be in China long. His object, he confirmed to me, is quite simply to ratify the treaty he already made, by whatever means are necessary. Whether that proves easy or difficult remains to be seen. He will be accompanied by the French envoy, Baron Gros. The two will support each other.

But it was when we touched upon the larger issues that I found him most interesting. Would we be content, I asked him, to let the crumbling old Manchu dynasty collapse? What about the Taiping, nominally Christian as they may be? Would he want the foreign powers to take over, as we recently did in Canton? He was careful not to be specific, but he did make a general point, which I share with you.

We need a Chinese government, he said, that is strong enough to make treaties and keep order. But no stronger than that. Perhaps a government that can rule only if we help them. That may be ideal. But on no account do we want a China that is powerful enough to inconvenience us. Remember what Napoleon said: China is a sleeping giant. When she awakes, the world will tremble.

I wonder what you think.

MOMENT OF TRUTH

March 1860

Guanji was nearer thirty than twenty, and it was the first time that anyone hadn't been impressed with him. Unfortunately, the person in question held the key to his future career.

There was no doubt about it: the Mongolian brigade general who had arrived to command the Zhapu garrison didn't think much of him or his attainments. He told him so.

When he saw Guanji ride his horse, he remarked, 'A boy of seven from the steppe would outlast you.' When he saw him shoot his bow and arrow, he merely said, 'Pretty.' As for the fact that Guanji had assiduously studied and achieved his juren status in the imperial exams, the Mongolian's eyes narrowed to a slit, thin as a knife to cut a throat, while from his mouth came a snort of contempt.

'He's an oaf, a vulgarian,' Uncle remarked. 'You know his nickname, don't you? Genghis. Because he seems to think he's Genghis Khan. All the same,' he cautioned Guanji, 'he's your commander, he belongs to the Mongol Plain White Banner, which gives him prestige, and he has influence, so you need a good report from him.'

'What can I do?' Guanji had asked.

'Keep your head down and do your duty. Don't try to ingratiate yourself. He'll despise you for it. But be absolutely thorough.'

The Mongolian was thickset and strongly built, with a wide, intelligent face. He always smelled of snuff, which he took from a small cylindrical snuffbox with an ivory spoon. He never wasted words, but his orders were always clear, and for three months Guanji carried them out quickly, efficiently, and to the letter.

At the end of that time, Genghis had rewarded him with one remark. 'You know the trouble with you? You've never been face-to-face with death. To see another man in front of you, looking straight into your eyes, and know that only one of you is going to live. That's the moment of truth.'

Guanji carried the thought with him and wondered what he could do about it.

He might have grown up as the pet of the old warriors in the garrison and been made to understand that the development of his Manchu identity was his only chance of success in life, but it had been the news that his cousin and big sister Ilha had been killed with all her family at Nanjing, back in 1853, that had finally decided the course of his life.

That had been the shock. That had been the rage. That had been the sense of loss that could not be assuaged. That had been the memory that came to him late in the night, when his shoulders hunched in hatred and he stared ahead into the dark and conjured up dreams of vengeance in time to come.

A grim determination had gathered, set, and hardened within him, like a lodestone. He'd focused himself entirely. Everything he did was in pursuit of twin goals: to reach high office under the Manchu emperor; and to destroy the Taiping rebels.

The intimations that something spiritual might be lacking in his life, which had come to him from time to time during his schooldays, were not entirely snuffed out. In the course of his studies for the imperial exams, aided by his uncle and his scholar friends, he had been able to drink a little at the great fountain of Chinese culture. Indeed, after he took the exams, the examiners told him privately that had he studied for a few more years, he might well have earned this degree that as a Manchu bannerman he was entitled to, and which it was now their pleasure to bestow.

By the time he reached his mid-twenties, therefore, as a rising young Manchu officer in the Bordered Yellow Banner, he was taken very seriously in his native garrison of Zhapu.

'In a while,' his uncle said, 'it may be time to find you a wife. I'd like to see you receive a promotion first, though.'

Guanji agreed. All he needed, he thought, as the emperor's army slowly tightened its circle around the Taiping's Heavenly Kingdom, was a chance to join the army outside Nanjing and to distinguish himself. He made applications, but had so far been refused.

'No job is more important than keeping the supplies coming through Zhapu to Hangzhou,' he was told. And he knew this was true.

When the terse Mongolian brigade general had arrived to take charge, Guanji had hoped that it might be a prelude to action. He answered directly to Genghis, so the opportunity was excellent, if only he could impress him.

If he could just encounter a moment of truth.

The orders arrived without warning. Guanji was talking to old bannerman friends in the Zhapu garrison one morning when the brigade general suddenly appeared and beckoned him.

'The Taiping rebels have broken out of Nanjing. They're headed for Hangzhou. Seven thousand men under General Li. We're to reinforce the garrison defending the place. I want four hundred riflemen, fully equipped, ready to march in two hours.'

'At once, sir.' Guanji hesitated, just a moment. Did he dare ask?

'You're coming, too.'

They followed the line of the canal leading from Zhapu to the northern edge of Hangzhou. The men with their smart uniforms and pigtails looked sharp and eager. They were well drilled.

Guanji rode beside the Mongolian. 'I'd have thought,' he ventured, 'that the Taiping might come in larger numbers.'

'Seven thousand good troops could take Hangzhou,' Genghis grunted.

'They say that their General Li wears spectacles.'

'Don't underestimate Li. He knows his business.'

Guanji didn't interrupt the brigade general's thoughts after that, until they made their bivouac for the first night of the eighty-mile march.

It was on the fourth evening that they came to the great city of Hangzhou. An officer with half a dozen mounted men met them upon the road and led them to the first of the two gates in the northern wall of the city, which opened to receive them and immediately closed again once they were in. To their right they saw the inside wall of the garrison quarter. Guanji smiled.

Genghis noticed. 'Why smile?'

'My old school, sir.'

The Mongolian said nothing.

Inside the garrison, to Guanji's pleasure, they were allocated quarters in the school hall. The men were fed and soon asleep. Guanji also was ready to turn in. But Genghis was not. 'Take me up on the city wall,' he demanded.

While the garrison enclave was separated from the rest of the city on its northern, southern and eastern sides by a strong, high curtain wall, with small gates giving access to the city streets, its western border was the city wall itself. And this section of wall contained a single stout gateway that gave onto a broad stretch of open ground, dotted with trees, beyond which lay the placid waters of the great West Lake. The gateway contained a staircase up onto the ramparts.

They mounted together in the darkness and looked over the battlements.

The entire space from the gate to the lakeshore had been occupied. A hundred campfires were burning there. One could even see shadowy figures by the glow of the fires.

'Taiping,' said the Mongolian. 'A detachment of 'em, anyway.'

'It looks as if they mean to assault this gate and take the garrison.'

'They may try,' agreed Genghis. 'They'll have to kill you and me first,' he added.

Guanji awoke at dawn to the sound of gunfire. A lot of guns – though it seemed to be coming from down at the southern end of the city. He'd hardly leaped up before the brigade general appeared.

'It's begun. There's a council of war. Assemble the men and wait till I return.'

An hour passed. When the brigade general finally got back, he was looking grim. He told Guanji to stand his men down and then to follow him. A few minutes later they were back on the wall where they'd been the night before.

The Taiping, whose fires they had seen in the darkness, were drawn up in formation two hundred yards away. There were about a thousand of them. With their long hair down to their shoulders, swords and guns at the ready, they looked fearsome. Their red-bordered yellow war banners were streaming in the wind.

Genghis looked at them impassively. He put a little snuff on the back of his hand and sniffed. 'The commanders here are fools,' he remarked. He didn't say why. Then he turned to study the view to his left.

Below the garrison quarter there was a broad thoroughfare leading to the next western gate. On the other side of the thoroughfare was the big yamen of the city prefect, a collection of buildings and courts surrounded by a brick-and-plaster barrier, built for privacy rather than defence and with a parade ground in front of it. Immediately after the prefect's yamen lay a maze of streets, where merchants' mansions, craftsmen's workshops, temple precincts and great labyrinths of poor folks' hovels clustered and bustled and crumbled all together in the typical tightly pressed chaos of an ancient Chinese city. This continued about a mile until the southern rampart.

'The Taiping have breached the wall in the southwest corner.' He pointed. Guanji could see troops and Taiping banners on the West Lake shoreline at the end of the city wall. 'They've been pouring in. Of course, the local militia was there to oppose them. What do you suppose happened?'

'Hard fighting I should think, sir.'

'Most of the militiamen started running away.' The brigade general nodded thoughtfully. 'Maybe they panicked. Maybe the Taiping had already infiltrated them. Probably both. Care to guess the next move?'

'I suppose the Taiping are working their way towards us.'

'The townspeople are furious. They've filled the streets. Told the militia if they don't fight, they'll string 'em up. And they've started attacking the Taiping themselves, with their bare hands if necessary. Quite a lot of Manchu in this city.'

'The Manchu will fight,' said Guanji proudly.

'Hmm. Seems the women are fiercest. They've already hanged a dozen militiamen, and they're hacking at the Taiping with chopping knives.' He nodded with amused satisfaction, then turned to Guanji. 'Why are Manchu women better street fighters than Han Chinese women?'

'It's the warrior spirit in our blood,' said Guanji proudly.

'You've had too much education. Rots the brain. Keep it simple.'

'I'm not sure, sir.'

'Feet! In any city, more than half the Han women have got bound feet. They can only hobble about. Manchu women don't bind their feet. So they move ten times as fast.'

'You're right, sir,' Guanji acknowledged. 'I'm a fool.'

'They won't be able to stop them, you know. It'll be a bloody business down there. First thing they'll do is kill every civilian they find – men, women and children. Spreads terror. Then they'll tell the rest: "Join us or be massacred." Ever seen anything like that?'

'Once, at Zhapu, when I was a little boy. I'm afraid thousands of people are going to die.'

'Not thousands. Tens of thousands. Think about it. There must be well over half a million people crowded into this city. Say they kill only one in ten. That's fifty thousand. It's not the open battles where most of the lives are lost. It's in the cities.'

'Are we going to help them?'

'The fools at the council wanted me to. I managed to hold 'em off.'

'You don't think we should, sir?'

'I've got four hundred riflemen. What's their best terrain?'

'Open field of fire, sir. From behind cover, if possible.'

'And what do you see down there? An anthill. House-to-house fighting. The worst kind of battle there is. I could lose half my men in a morning. The local people will do better sneaking up on them, because they know every nook and cranny of the place.' He smiled grimly. 'Let the Manchu women slit the Taiping throats at night.'

Guanji pondered. 'If we made a sudden sally out of the garrison gate, we could hit those Taiping in front of us, on the open ground, and then retreat inside the garrison.'

'We could. There may not be much point.'

'You don't think they mean to attack the garrison, sir?'

'When General Li shows you his men, it's for a reason. You have to ask, why does he do it? What does he want me to think? What does he want me to do? Yesterday he showed us his men threatening the garrison. Then he attacked the other end of the town. His men are still outside the garrison. All that tells you is that he wants us to think they'll attack it.'

'Do you have an idea what his game really is, sir?'

The Mongolian grunted, took some more snuff, and didn't reply.

But even Genghis couldn't keep his men out of a street fight that day. At noon, he was overruled. By that time the southern part of Hangzhou was under Taiping control, and the rebels were feeling their way northwards. 'What would the emperor say if we do nothing?' the gathered commanders asked themselves. A show of force was called for. At the very least, the rebels must be stopped before they reached the prefect's yamen and the Manchu garrison.

About a thousand men, Manchu bannermen of the Hangzhou garrison and the four hundred rifles from Zhapu, were ordered forward. The Mongolian drew his men up in a long line, on the space in front of the yamen, where he also erected a stout barricade, but he was obliged to sacrifice a company of fifty men to form one of the columns that were to march into the narrow streets of the city to probe and engage the enemy.

'You command them,' he ordered Guanji.

'Yes, sir,' Guanji replied.

As he led his men southward down the long street, Guanji assumed he was probably going to die. He imagined the Mongolian thought so, too. He felt no resentment. Genghis was doing his job.

And to his own surprise he found that, at this moment, he had only one desire himself. To do the same. His job. As he focused on the present necessity, his childhood dreams of bringing honour to his clan with a great career faded into the background. I should like, he thought, to perform just one professional action before I die. That would be enough. One good performance.

With this in mind, he led his men forward.

There were only a few people in the streets. He questioned them as he passed. Any sign of Taiping? Not yet. Was he going to fight them? he was asked. And when he said yes, he was met with smiles and encouragement.

After a quarter of a mile, the street veered left in front of a little temple, then resumed its path southward again. There were fewer people now. Then the street reached a small open square into which three other streets, all from the south, debouched. Guanji raised his hand for his troops to stop.

The square was silent, empty. Except for one figure. On the opposite side, a rope was hanging from the wooden balcony of one of the houses. At the end of the rope was a dead militiaman. His body was slowly swaying in the wind. Were his executioners concealed in the houses in the square? Impossible to tell.

He listened attentively. From a street at the far corner of the square he could hear sounds of shouting, then the beat of a drum, distant, but slowly getting closer. He turned to the sergeant.

'Take a dozen men, break into the houses and grab anything you can to make a barricade. And send a scout across the square to see who's coming.'

The position was excellent. If he placed his barricade across the end of the street here, his men would have a clear view of the whole square. He could also retreat up the street the way he came.

The barricade was soon built. Tables, chairs, benches, chests, wooden screens – good cover for his men, tough for any assailant to climb over.

'I found one old woman, sir,' the sergeant reported. 'The Taiping were here. Killed a few people before they moved on. But they said they'd be occupying the place and told all the people to get out in the meantime. The old woman says she isn't moving. And something else.'

'What's that?'

'She wants her furniture back.'

Moments later, their scout came running across the square. 'Taiping. At least a hundred, maybe more. They'll reach the square in a few minutes.'

Guanji thought fast. 'Divide the men, Sergeant. They must all be primed and ready to fire. Send ten back up the street behind us, a hundred paces. Form a line across the street. If we have to retreat, they'll cover us and pick the enemy off as they climb the barricade. The other forty in four lines of ten across. The first line at the barricade. Three more lines to replace them. As soon as we've fired the first volley, the front line goes to the back and reloads. And so in turn, until I order the retreat.'

The men were well drilled, and in moments all was ready. Guanji stationed himself at one end of the barricade where he had a good view of the street at the far corner of the square. He told the men to keep their heads down so they'd be invisible to the enemy until he gave the order.

A minute passed. Another. Then he saw three men enter the square. Tough-looking fellows with ragged hair halfway down their backs. Taiping, certainly. They glanced around. One of them caught sight of the barricade, stared, and pointed it out to his fellows. Guanji kept very still. They had not seen him. With luck they'd think it was abandoned. They started forward, clearly intending to inspect it. Guanji silently cursed. He wanted more than three men to shoot. But they'd only gone a few paces when a crowd of Taiping issued from the street behind them. One carried a yellow Taiping banner. Then more, including two drummers, who obligingly made a rat-a-tat. The whole column was piling in behind them now. There must be fifty men, densely crowded, in the line of fire. A perfect target.

'Now,' he told his men. 'Fire!'

There was a roar. The first three Taiping all went down. Another half dozen went down behind them. An easy target, but good shooting. He heard the sergeant behind him call out: 'Back. Reload. Next line forward.'

The Taiping, taken completely by surprise, had stopped in their tracks. Those who hadn't seen the barricade would see the smoke, but could have no idea what size of force they were up against.

'See the target?' he called out, and received several nods. 'Fire!'

Again, the volley did its work. There were screams of agony coming from across the square now. Thanks to the smoke, he could only see imperfectly. It looked as if, under such rapid and withering fire, the Taiping were trying to retreat from the square. But they couldn't, because of the column of men still pushing forward from the street behind them.

The third line of his riflemen were in place. He indicated where they should aim through the smoke. 'Fire!'

More screams. How many had they brought down so far? Twenty? Maybe more? He had two lines of riflemen left. The line covering them up the street at the rear, and the ten men taking their position at the barricade. He glanced back to see whether the first group had reloaded yet. Almost. 'Hold your fire,' he ordered the men at the barricade. Let the smoke clear.

But before he had a clear view across the square again, a group of a dozen Taiping came charging through the smoke towards the barricade. Whatever else they might be, these Taiping warriors were no cowards. They carried guns and long knives. With their hair streaming out, they looked like demons.

'Mark your man and fire at will,' he cried as he drew his sword.

A series of bangs. He saw five, six of the Taiping go down. The rest had reached the barricade. One was scrambling over right in front of him. He thrust, hard, caught the fellow in the neck, saw him fall back, his hand still gripped around the leg of a wooden chair. Two more were almost over, and he could see more figures running across the square.

'Fall back!' he called to his men.

But it was too late for one of them. A couple of Taiping were almost upon him. Guanji threw himself at them. He caught the first with a sword thrust from behind, into the kidney. As he did so, the second swung at him. He felt something in his left arm, nothing much. He slashed and saw a red line open into a gash on the fellow's neck. The man staggered. Guanji didn't wait, but grabbed his rifleman by the belt and jerked him up. 'Come!' he cried as together they ran unevenly back up the street.

He looked back. Any other men down? It didn't look like it. But Taiping warriors were scrambling over the barrier. He heard his sergeant shout, 'Go to the side,' and understood. Of course. His fifth line of men, ready to fire. He dragged the rifleman with him against the wall of a house. There was a crash as the fusillade was delivered. Screams came from the barricade. He didn't even look back, but plunged forward. Moments later he passed the line of riflemen. 'Go on, sir,' the sergeant cried. 'Keep going.'

Fifty yards ahead, the sergeant already had another line of men, ready to fire. Good work, he thought. He'd recommend the sergeant for that.

By the time they all assembled behind the second line, it didn't seem that the Taiping were going to follow them past the barricade. All the same, better to be safe. 'Reload,' he called out. 'Every man reload.'

As soon as this was done, Guanji had the sergeant tell the men to fall in. 'Have we lost anyone?' he asked.

'Not one, sir.'

'Anybody wounded?'

'Only you, sir.'

'Me?' He'd forgotten feeling something in his arm.

'Often happens in the heat of battle, sir. Man gets wounded, doesn't feel it.' The sergeant smiled. 'With permission, sir.' He drew out one of several lengths of white cotton cloth wrapped around his belt. 'I always carry a few of these.' He took hold of Guanji's arm, from which a quantity of blood was now flowing. 'I'll just bind that up,' he said cheerfully. 'You'll be wanting to march the men back, I should think, sir,' he suggested as soon as he was done.

When they reached the brigade general, Guanji gave his report. Brief but precise, including a commendation of the sergeant for good order and initiative. 'We inflicted casualties,' he concluded. 'I'm pretty confident of twenty. None of us hurt, except for a few bruises and this nick on my arm.'

'You didn't hold your position.'

'No, sir. I had no backup and every reason to believe there were large numbers of Taiping to come. I might have killed another twenty, but then lost all my men.'

'Good. Correct decision.' A hint of a smile appeared on the Mongolian's face. 'Some of the other parties have taken quite a mauling.' He turned and called the sergeant over. 'Twenty enemy casualties?' he asked.

'Maybe more, sir. They were very nicely grouped. And we had a good position.'

'How are the men?'

'In very good heart, sir. They'll always trust a good officer.'

'I'll see to his wound. Bring me a bucket of water. And a warm knife.' He turned to Guanji and indicated a crate of ammunition. 'Sit on that.'

It was several minutes before the sergeant returned. Putting the bucket of water on the ground, he unwrapped the bandage from Guanji's arm. The Mongolian poured some of the water onto the wound, inspected it carefully, then poured some more.

'It's clean,' he said with a nod, and turned to the sergeant. 'Knife?'

It was a short dagger. Guanji glanced at it. The blade seemed to be glowing. He felt the sergeant's arm go around his chest.

'I'll just hold you now, sir,' the sergeant said calmly.

Guanji saw the brigade general dip the dagger into the water. It made a loud hiss. Then Guanji heard the Mongolian's voice, very soft, just behind his ear.

'I'm going to cauterise the wound. Grit your teeth, put your tongue on the roof of your mouth, and don't let your mouth open. If you make any sound at all, I'll send you back to Zhapu with a bad report.' Then he laid the dagger on Guanji's arm.

The pain was unlike anything he'd felt before. A blazing, searing shock that would have thrown his whole body upwards if the sergeant's arm had not held him in place, like a hoop of iron around his chest. He might have fainted, except that he was too afraid of annoying the Mongolian. And he did make a sound.

It did not come from his mouth. It came from somewhere between his chest and his throat, so suddenly and so violently that there was nothing he could do about it.

There was a silence.

'Did you hear a sound, sergeant?' the Mongolian enquired.

'Came from the town.'

Genghis grunted. 'That must've been it.'

Suddenly Guanji found he was shivering.

'I'll give you some water, sir,' said the sergeant.

The Taiping did not try to attack the Mongolian's big barricade that afternoon. The prefect's yamen remained untouched. At dusk, leaving a watch of forty men to guard the barricade, the rest of the Manchu troops went back inside the walls of the garrison. Guanji went with them.

And there he remained. Days passed. The Zhapu riflemen continued to man the barricade, but they were not sent down into the city streets again. Instead, the Hangzhou command adopted a different policy, sending a stream of squads with gunpowder and ammunition to supply the Manchu partisans who were harassing the Taiping troops wherever they could. The Manchu women had shown a talent for making small bombs and delivered them effectively. Every hour, Guanji would hear the rattle of musketry or the sound of an explosion coming from somewhere in the town.

But though they lost dozens of men, the Taiping continued to make progress, advancing several blocks a day, taking their revenge on each troublesome enclave as it came. After three days, they were nearly at the yamen. And by that time, the Hangzhou military council had already sent an urgent plea to the imperial forces besieging Nanjing, begging for reinforcements.

Guanji was optimistic. 'If they send us enough men,' he suggested to the Mongolian, 'General Li could be trapped here. His Taiping troops could be wiped out.'

'Perhaps,' Genghis replied.

Meanwhile, a stalemate seemed to prevail.

Each night, Guanji would go up on the wall. It was quiet up there, and he liked to be alone. Despite the campfires of the Taiping, he could see the great West Lake clearly and could make out the gentle curves of the hills around it in the moonlight.

A few days before his sudden departure from Zhapu, his uncle had gone to visit an old friend, a scholar who lived in a house on one of the lakeside hills. Was his uncle there now? he wondered. Was he safe? He thought of his uncle's printing press in the city and hoped the old man hadn't gone there. Had the Taiping ransacked the place? There was no way of finding out at the moment. He'd try to go and inspect it himself as soon as this business was over.

It was strange to think of these two worlds side by side – the quiet, poetic world of the scholars and the angry banners of the Taiping – both sharing the lakeside space in the moonlight. But the moon was waning. A few more days, and he wouldn't be able to see the water at all, unless the stars were very bright.

The Taiping struck suddenly, hours after Guanji had gone down from the wall, on the night of the waning crescent moon. A thousand men, moving silently and carrying knives, raced to the barricade in front of the yamen and overpowered the watch. Forty sleepy Manchu riflemen were slaughtered in the darkness in less than a minute, and their bodies tossed in a heap at the eastern side of the open space, for the garrison to collect if they chose. Then, before the dawn, they dismantled the barricade and re-erected it so that it ran from the yamen across the street to the garrison wall, sealing off the city gate. As though to proclaim their dominance, they ran their Taiping flags and banners up all around the walls of the areas they occupied, including the prefect's yamen and the adjoining western gate, as if to say: 'All this is our precinct, our fortress.' This left only the garrison and the northernmost part of the city in imperial hands.

Their plan of action became clear, even before the dawn. It was signalled by the sound of picks and shovels striking the ground. Guanji and the brigade general looked down from the garrison wall. The rebels had erected a protective roof to cover them while they worked, but there could be no doubt about what they were doing. 'They're tunnelling under the garrison wall, sir,' said Guanji. 'What'll they do then?'

'Fill it with gunpowder and blow it up, most likely. That'll make a breach they can get through.'

'What can we do?'

'Try a countermine. Dig underneath them and collapse the floor of their tunnel. That's the usual procedure. Of course, they may dig a counter to our countermine, and so on.' Genghis nodded. 'Tedious business.'

By the next day, the Taiping were digging four mines, and it was hard to be sure where they were all going. And there was still the big Taiping force outside the garrison's western gate to consider. Would the Taiping launch two attacks at the same time, one from the south and the other from outside the western gate? Guanji supposed so.

There was talk that day of a big Manchu assault on the yamen, but there were so many well-armed Taiping in there that the Hangzhou command was nervous of losing too many men. 'Let's wait for the reinforcements from Nanjing,' they agreed.

So the Taiping continued their preparations; and the emperor's men waited for help.

Help came. The day of the new moon. A huge contingent from the emperor's Southern Grand Battalion had broken off its siege of the Heavenly Kingdom to relieve Hangzhou. Thousands of troops were massed outside the city's northern gates.

Guanji was expecting them to enter at once, but the brigade general explained, 'Not enough room in the city at the moment. They'll camp outside tonight.' It seemed to make sense. Only later, when they were out of earshot of anyone else, did his commander tell him in a low voice: 'They may be full of Taiping spies. We want to keep them out there until the moment we fight.'

'Can I trust anyone, sir?' Guanji asked sadly.

'No. Except me. D'you know why?'

'You're my commander.'

'Because I'm Mongolian. We're the only trustworthy people.' It seemed to amuse him, because he laughed. 'Every Mongolian will tell you that.'

Guanji didn't go up on the wall that night. First thing in the morning, the brigade general went to a war council. Guanji made sure that all the Zhapu riflemen were ready for action and awaited his chief's return eagerly. But hours passed and there was no sign of him.

It was late morning when the sergeant brought the woman to him. She'd come to a small side gate of the garrison, asking to speak to an officer. One of the sentries knew her as a trustworthy Manchu and had summoned the sergeant.

She was a tough, stout woman, about forty, he guessed. Her story was simple. The rebels had killed her husband a week ago. She hated them. The evening before, a lot of the Taiping in the southern part of the town had started moving towards the garrison. Word was, they were preparing a big assault. They were going to smash their way into the garrison soon. Very soon. So she'd made her way cautiously from the southern part of the town and come to warn them.

It made sense. Seeing the emperor's reinforcements arrive, the Taiping were clearly going to throw everything they had at the garrison, to take it quickly. Then let the Manchu break in if they could.

Guanji didn't hesitate. Sending a man to tell the brigade general, he immediately split his riflemen into two parties: a hundred and fifty in formation, to deliver volley after volley at any Taiping force that broke in through the garrison's west gate; the other two hundred and fifty to be ready to repel whatever attack might come through a breach in the wall from the southern side.

He didn't have to wait long until Genghis appeared. The Mongolian approved his actions, listened carefully to the Manchu woman, and told Guanji to accompany him up onto the wall.

'Will this affect the battle plan, sir?' Guanji asked.

'There is no battle plan,' the Mongolian replied drily. 'The war council still can't make up their minds.'

They gazed out at the Taiping troops opposite the west gate. The rebels had dug a trench and thrown up a rampart that stretched from the city wall to the lake. If the men of the Southern Grand Battalion came around the city to attack them, they obviously meant to put up a strong defence.

The Mongolian turned to look down the length of the city wall. There seemed to be a Taiping flag flying every few yards. Guanji stared at the prefect's yamen. The roofs of the buildings and the numerous Taiping banners obstructed much of the view, but it was evident that the rebels were still busily undermining the garrison wall. He could see men adding to the piles of excavated earth.

'They were mining last night as well,' Guanji volunteered. 'I stood at the foot of the wall, and I could hear them digging underground. They were still at it when I turned in – and that was after midnight.'

'Did you go up on top of the wall?'

'Not last night, sir. I didn't think I'd see much, as there was no moon.'

'No moon.' The Mongolian nodded thoughtfully. 'Of course. It's been waning for days.' He was silent for a moment. And then suddenly he slapped his thigh. 'No moon,' he cried. 'What a fool I've been!'

'Sir?'

'That's what Li's been up to. The cunning devil.'

'General Li?'

'This . . .' The Mongolian waved towards the activity in the yamen below. 'It's a bluff. He's not trying to take the garrison at all. He doesn't want Hangzhou. He's just been waiting for our relief force to show up. That was his game. Draw troops away from Nanjing, split the Southern Grand Battalion.'

'And now they're here, sir, what'll he do?'

'Do? He's already done it. Why would he wait? He's gone. He must have sneaked his troops out by the western gate last night. Right under our noses, in the dark. Made a night march. They're on their way back to Nanjing.'

'Where they'll fall upon the remaining besiegers.'

'That's right.'

'And the Taiping troops burrowing under the garrison wall, and the Taiping camp outside?'

'Decoys. Like those flags on the walls. To make us think he's still there. Every day he can fool us, he puts more distance between himself and any troops we send after him.'

'What'll you do, sir?'

'If I'm right, there's probably no more than three hundred men in the yamen. We can take care of them and the Taiping camp ourselves, and send the Southern Grand Battalion troops straight back to Nanjing.' Genghis shook his head. 'Trouble is, I can't prove it. The only thing the war council will do is prepare for the possible enemy attack. Strictly defensive. That's all.'

Guanji considered.

'If I can get into the yamen, I should be able to see at once. There's either six thousand men in there, or a few hundred. Would the war council accept a report from me?'

'They might. How would you get in?'

'Maybe,' said Guanji, 'the Manchu woman could guide me.'

She'd looked at him appraisingly. 'If you want to get into the yamen, you'll have to go dressed as a rebel. I have Taiping clothes that would fit you, at my house.'

'How did you get them?'

'Killed a Taiping.'

Even getting to her house, they had to be careful. He couldn't go through the rebel-occupied city dressed as a Manchu officer and risk being arrested by a Taiping patrol. By the time they set out, he'd changed into poor man's clothes. If anyone asked, he was her brother.

It was mid-afternoon by the time they got to her house, near the southern gate. Time to change again. Two of her children and an old woman he assumed was her mother-in-law watched as he tried on the loose smock with its red Taiping badge and the dead man's leather belt.

'Do you want his sword?' she asked. 'He had a sword.'

It was a typical Chinese soldier's sword, straight and pointed, with sharpened sides, about the same length as his own, though not as good. Guanji tried it. 'I may as well,' he said. 'What about my hair?'

'Turn around.' She carefully undid his plaited Manchu pigtail, wet his hair and spread it across his shoulders. She tried the dead man's hat on Guanji's head. It fitted, near enough.

'Could I pass for a rebel now?' he asked with a grin.

'Not in daylight,' she said. 'Better wait for dusk.'

It was nearly two hours before they set off. Even going through the southern part of the city, they had to be careful. For now that he was dressed as a rebel, he had to watch out for the townsfolk. There were still plenty of local people, Han or Manchu, who'd willingly slit the throat of a lone Taiping rebel if they saw one. Hiding his Taiping clothing under an old Chinese coat, and with his hair loosely bound into a temporary pigtail with twine, Guanji shuffled along beside the Manchu woman as they made their way northwards up quiet streets and alleys.

If the streets were strangely deserted, he soon realised that the houses were mostly occupied. Uncertain what was going to happen next, people were staying indoors for safety. When she did meet someone in the street, the Manchu woman would ask them, 'Where are the Taiping?' And each time the answer was similar: either that they had left the day before, or that a patrol had been seen an hour or two ago, but not since.

Once they came to a Buddhist temple. The door had been broken in, but someone, out of devotion presumably, had placed a lamp inside and lit a few candles. They paused for a moment to look in. The Taiping had smashed the tables, the statues, everything. As they continued working their way northwards, the situation remained the same: people hiding, Taiping gone.

When they came to the square where he and his riflemen had ambushed the Taiping, however, the woman put her hand on his arm and told him to stop. 'This is where you must be Taiping,' she whispered. She took his coat and quickly untied his hair, letting it fall loose to his shoulders. 'Yesterday, all these houses were full of them.'

He surveyed the square. A wood fire had been lit in the centre. It was still burning with a low flame, but there was no sign of anyone to tend it. A few remains of the barricade he'd thrown up could be seen in one corner of the square. They'd been using it for firewood. The houses stared blankly. He couldn't see a lamp in any of them, or any indication of human presence. But looking northwards up a street that must lead to the yamen, he could see lights a quarter mile ahead.

'I'll go on alone,' he said quietly. 'Wait for me.'

She nodded.

He was almost certain already. The Mongolian was right. The Taiping had fooled the defenders of Hangzhou, and they'd gone. But he had to be sure. Totally sure. Otherwise, if the Taiping breached the wall and came rushing into a garrison who believed the threat was over, thousands of his people were going to die. He walked slowly, the Taiping sword hanging from his belt. He was conscious of the beating of his heart.

He'd gone a couple hundred yards when he saw some Taiping at last. A small group, two of them carrying torches, crossed the street ahead of him and disappeared into an alley. Several of them glanced at him, but without interest.

So far, so good. The houses he passed appeared to be empty. He saw no lights within, nor did he hear any voices. Twice he pushed open a street door and stepped into the courtyard of a house. The first was empty. In the second, a single old man, squatting in a corner under a lamp, looked at him sadly, probably wondering if this intruder was going to hurt him. His confidence growing, Guanji walked towards the lights ahead.

Banners. There were red-and-yellow Taiping banners everywhere. That was the first thing he noticed as he came to the yamen quarter's open spaces. Banners, but not in the hands of Taiping warriors. Some were stuck in the ground; others were tied to posts or fastened to the overhanging roofs of the buildings. A field of banners, rippling in the wind. Campfires and lamps hanging from the buildings completed the effect.

Seen from above – from the garrison wall, for instance – anyone would have thought the place was full of troops.

There were some troops: a couple of men by each fire, rows of men sitting or lying on the broad steps in front of the larger buildings. Strangely, when he boldly entered the big prefect's mansion in the centre of the yamen, he encountered only half a dozen warriors playing checkers in the big hall. They looked up at him idly. He glanced around as if he'd been expecting to find someone there, shook his head and walked out. At the north end of the yamen he saw several big heaps of earth, obviously quarried from the tunnelling under the wall, and realised that these, too, had been carefully sited so as to be visible from the garrison.

So how many men were in the quarter? He estimated he'd seen about a hundred. Double it, and double that again: it still didn't amount to five hundred. Certainly not five thousand.

Just to be certain, he worked his way back through the streets under the western wall. It was the same story. Almost empty.

He was done. The mission had been easier than expected. With a sense of relief, he made his way back towards the empty square.

It was just as he had left it. The small fire was still glowing in the middle, the houses silent. Where was the Manchu woman? He stepped into the square and started to walk towards the fire so that she'd see him. He looked from side to side. Was she hiding? Had something happened to her? Did she know something he didn't?

He heard a hiss from somewhere directly on his left, and was just turning to look, when something else caught his eye: torchlight ahead, by the remnants of the barricade in the corner. Two torches, three, four. And before he could take evasive action, a small patrol swung briskly into the square. Four torchbearers and six fully armed Taiping, led by an officer. They came straight towards him.

He froze. No good running. Better bluff it out.

'You're going the wrong way,' the officer called. 'Fall in behind.'

Obviously the patrol was making a final roundup in the town, to collect all their men. It probably meant they were leaving tonight.

He waited for them to draw level. If he fell into step at the back, he might be able to make a run for it as they left the square. The officer was only ten feet from him.

'Halt!' the officer cried. He stared at Guanji.

He looked to be about forty. His hair was grey. His bearing suggested years of authority. He had a scar down one cheek. His eyes were fixed on Guanji's long hair, so recently released from a pigtail. Seen close up, even by torchlight, it might not look very convincing. 'I don't know you,' he said. 'What's your name?'

'Zhang, sir.' It was the first common name Guanji could think of.

'What's my name?'

Guanji saw the trap at once. If this was a senior officer, every Taiping in the city would know his name. But what could he say? He hesitated.

'You're a spy,' said the officer calmly. He drew out a long knife.

Guanji pulled out his sword. A useless gesture, of course. The patrol could easily overpower him. It was just instinctive.

Two of the Taiping soldiers started towards him, but the officer raised his hand and signalled them to stand back. 'Are you an officer?' asked the man with the scar on his face.

'Yes.'

'Good.' He nodded. 'Prepare to die.' It wasn't a threat. Just a statement of fact.

Understanding what was required, two of the torchbearers stationed themselves on one side of the space between their officer and Guanji, and two on the other. The little killing ground needed light.

Guanji held his sword firmly. The straight blade glimmered in the torchlight. He felt its weight, made sure that he was well balanced, and kept his eyes on his man. There were two things to watch: the point of your opponent's weapon and his feet.

The words of the Mongolian suddenly came into his mind: 'You know the trouble with you? You've never been face-to-face with death. To see another man in front of you, looking straight into your eyes, and know that only one of you is going to live. That's the moment of truth.'

So this was it. The moment of truth.

Guanji did not feel fear, exactly. He was too concentrated on the business in hand. He was not a bad swordsman. He bent his knees a little, testing his balance again. The point of his sword was up, trained upon the throat of his opponent, fixed. His arm might move, but the point of his sword would not.

And then the Taiping officer with the scar began to move, and it was not like the way Guanji moved at all. He seemed to rock from side to side, as though transforming himself into another animal. Maybe a cat? If so, a feral cat. Or something else, still more deadly, a creature that Guanji did not know. A serpent cat, perhaps.

The Taiping was passing his long knife between his hands, from side to side, rhythmically. It was almost hypnotic to watch.

Guanji's sword was longer that the Taiping's knife. That should give him the advantage. But as the Taiping moved in a swaying crouch towards him, he knew it did not. This was no ordinary soldier. This was a pirate, a street brigand, who had killed many men.

Then Guanji knew that he was going to die. He kept his sword up, but he took a step back.

Was the Taiping smiling? No, he might have been, but he was not. He knew he was going to kill his man. It would be quick, clean.

Guanji took one more step back. The torchbearers did not move. The Taiping was fully in the torchlight, Guanji almost in shadow. But it made no difference. Guanji saw the Taiping's feet twitch. He was about to spring. Guanji tensed, gripped his sword.

The woman came from the shadows so suddenly that no one even saw her. She barrelled into the torchbearer nearest the Taiping officer, seizing his torch, which she thrust towards the officer's face.

But there was no need. The Taiping officer had been distracted. Not for long. Not even for a second. But long enough for Guanji.

Instinctively, he leaped forward and lunged with his sword into the Taiping's chest. The man's knees buckled. With all his strength, Guanji ripped the sword down, to open the wound, and out.

He heard the woman cry: 'Run. This way. Quick!' He felt her grabbing his arm.

The torchbearers and the half-dozen troops were so surprised they hadn't even started to move as Guanji and the woman fled into the shadows.

At the edge of the square she pushed him into an alley and commanded again, 'Run,' as she flung the torch back at the pursuing soldiers.

He couldn't see where he was going, but she was right behind him. He stumbled, felt her strong arm under his, and righted himself. There were shouts behind them. They were still being pursued.

'To the end, turn left, then turn right,' the woman's voice said. 'Keep running. I'll catch up with you.'

At the end of the alley he made the turn and suddenly realised that she was no longer with him. Ten yards farther, as he turned right, he heard a scream behind him. A woman's scream. She screamed again. He paused. Should he go back? He had to help her. But he also had to get away. He had to report. By the sound of it, the woman might already be dead. He ran on. He could hear the sound of running steps behind him. It must be one of the Taiping troops. Ahead, he could just see that the alley ended in a dimly lit street. He got to the street. Empty, except for a single lamp hanging from a house. He threw himself to one side and gripped his sword. He'd kill his Taiping pursuer as he came out of the alley.

And was in the act of lunging when he saw that it was the Manchu woman.

'Come,' she said, turning up the street. 'The garrison's this way.'

'I thought you were dead,' he said. 'I heard you scream twice.'

'That's because there were two of them.' She glanced at him and gave a grim smile. 'I scream when I kill.'

'Thank you,' he said.

The brigade general was pleased with them both, for Guanji told him exactly what happened, including how the woman had saved his life.

The Mongolian gave her a small bag of silver.

'You don't have to pay me,' she said.

'You have children?'

'Yes.'

'Then take the money,' said the Mongolian.

'Everything you said was right,' said Guanji as soon as she was gone. 'We can take the Taiping camp tonight, and the ones in the yamen, too.'

'We can, but we can't,' the Mongolian answered. 'I spoke to the army council while you were gone. They won't risk anything at night. But we can attack in the morning.'

'The Taiping may have gone by then, sir,' Guanji protested.

'Probably.'

'Then my mission was for nothing.'

'Don't say that. You had your moment of truth.' He smiled. 'And you may have killed a senior Taiping officer.'

'Thanks to the woman,' Guanji reminded him.

'If you're going to be a general,' said Genghis, 'you'd better learn something. Never miss a chance to claim a victory for yourself. It's the only thing people want to hear.'

'I'll remember that, sir. Though I doubt I'll ever be a general.'

'Why not? You've proved that you possess the one thing a general needs.'

'Really, sir? What's that?'

The Mongolian grinned and put a little snuff on the back of his hand. 'Luck.'

°

It was in August of that year that the bespectacled General Li and his Taiping army finally came to Shanghai. They were confident of success.

During the last six months, all the clever plans of General Li had worked. The feint up to Hangzhou had fooled the emperor's men entirely. The huge detachment of the Southern Grand Battalion that had gone to relieve Hangzhou had left the remaining army outside Nanjing severely weakened. Slipping back from Hangzhou by night marches, the Taiping had taken the emperor's men completely by surprise and devastated them.

Even better – and this General Li had not foreseen – the Southern Grand Battalion troops, having discovered their mistake, didn't race back to Nanjing to see if they could save the situation. When they discovered that even the rear guard of the Taiping had given them the slip in the night, they went into Hangzhou and looted the town. Raped, killed, and pillaged their own side – Han Chinese and Manchu alike. Not a way to make the emperor's government popular with his people.

Hangzhou had been a success for General Li, no question. Except for one sadness. He'd lost his best commander. Nio.

Well, not quite lost him. Badly wounded, arresting a spy. His men wouldn't leave him for dead. They'd carried his body back and brought him with them out of the town that night. Then carried him all the way back to Nanjing.

He should have died, with the great wound that he had. But Nio was tough.

And so General Li, his commander, had made it his personal mission to bring Nio back to life.

For many weeks, Nio had lain in the Heavenly Kingdom, being tended by the best physicians the city had. His wound had slowly healed without infection. But he was very weak. He couldn't walk. He didn't even seem to want to talk. He just lay on his bed like a pale ghost.

And General Li wasn't having it. If Nio had lost heart, then he was going to get it back for him. 'You know,' he remarked as he sat by Nio's bed one day, 'everything's going our way. Lord Elgin has arrived in Hong Kong. He'll certainly have got the message you left. And he's on the way to Beijing with eighteen thousand men. Even if he doesn't join forces with us yet, he's going to humiliate the emperor. That's what we need. Meanwhile, I'm going to strike up to Shanghai. Do exactly what we planned. The garrison's not large. The barbarians will stand aside. We'll take the port, buy those iron ships, and this rotting old empire will fall to bits. Would you like to see that?'

He stared through his glasses at Nio's face and thought he detected a faint smile. 'I'll tell you what,' he cried, 'I'll bring you with me to Shanghai. You can watch us take the place. That'll put heart into you. We'll enter Shanghai together.'

And so it was that, on a sunny August day, Nio was brought on a stretcher, with General Li's Taiping army, to the walls of Shanghai.

'Put him in a chair,' said General Li. 'Let him watch.' The day was not too hot. 'A little sun will do him good.' He put an orderly in charge of him. 'Put a hat on him if the sun's too much.'

'Yes, sir,' the orderly said.

General Li had taken every precaution. Though he had no doubt that the message would have been given to the foreign communities months ago, by the British authorities at Hong Kong, he had caused fresh instructions to be printed in both Chinese and English and delivered to the gates of the foreign concessions this very last night. They knew they had only to put yellow flags on their buildings and they would not be harmed. He wasn't even going to enter the foreign quarters for the time being. Just the old Chinese fort.

And there it was, in plain view. A modest enclosure near the broad water's edge.

Would the Chinese troops even fight? Not if they had any sense.

So with their red-and-yellow banners streaming, to the sound of gongs and drums, the Taiping troops marched towards the gate of the old Chinese fort. The wall of the British concession lay on one side of them. It was only eight or ten feet high.

The Chinese defenders of the old fort had thrown up an emplacement for cannon in front of their gates. But Chinese gunnery held few fears for the seasoned Taiping troops. They'd probably fire a token volley and give up.

General Li went forward with his men. He glanced back once, towards Nio in his chair. When Nio saw Shanghai as a Taiping port; when he witnessed the foreign merchants living cheerfully under the rule of their Taiping fellow Christians; above all, when those iron ships, which would smash the Manchu forces and bring the emperor down, were moored off the Shanghai waterfront, then Nio would come back into the land of the living.

The thought pleased General Li very much.

It was just at that moment that the firing began. First, a salvo from the cannon by the gates. A deadly salvo of grapeshot that ripped great red gashes in the lines of fluttering yellow flags.

General Li frowned. Those did not sound like Chinese cannon.

A perfectly directed second salvo, canister shot this time, punched through the advancing Taiping column.

Those were British guns and gunners. Li was sure of it. What were they doing there?

Before he could even work it out, all along the British concession wall appeared lines of men armed with modern British rifles pouring a terrible fusillade onto the Taiping flank. Now firing started from the Chinese fortress wall as well. Flintlocks mostly. But when they did hit, they did awful damage.

The Taiping troops were so astonished that they stopped. They'd been given strict instructions to respect the British, who were on their side. Even cunning General Li stopped and stared in horror.

'Retreat!' he ordered. They were sitting ducks where they were. Few of the men heard the command. They hesitated. Another volley of canister shot from the cannon battery. The British were pouring their fire from the walls. Shots were coming from the other concessions, too.

The Taiping troops, realising they were in a horrible trap, began to fall back. General Li fell back with them.

But why had the British turned suddenly into enemies? It made no sense. They were making war on the emperor, too. Was there something they still didn't like about the Taiping version of Christianity? Nothing wrong with it as far as General Li knew. Was this to do with opium? Had they cut a deal with the emperor?

He had no idea. But he must regroup the men and call off the assault. That was the first thing. He must save his men.

For the next half hour he had no time to think of anything else.

Neither the British nor the Chinese came out from behind their walls. That was something. He was able to draw up his men at a safe distance.

But if he did not know how or why, one thing was certain: the game had changed. All his hopes and plans were in ruins. And those of the Heavenly King.

And of Nio, of course.

Nio. Was he still sitting in his chair, out in front of them, now? Had they retreated past him?

They had.

At least none of the British had tried a shot at him from their walls.

But when General Li came to Nio, he saw that his best commander was very far away by now, in another place entirely, leaving, in death, a look of inexpressible sadness on his face.

SUMMER PALACE

You can imagine how I felt. Mr Liu was a head eunuch in charge of the palace household. He had the power. I had none. And he was going to destroy me.

He didn't waste any time.

The next morning, when I arrived for work at the eunuchs' quarters and went to my mentor, he told me, 'I'm sorry, but I'm not your mentor anymore. You're to report to the laundry next door.'

The laundry was a big rectangular workroom, with vats you could have drowned in. Along one side there were the mangles and the racks where the clothes were hung to dry. Apart from a faint scent of pine resin from the wooden scrubbing boards, the space was pervaded by the acrid smell of lye laundry soap. The eunuch in charge was a tall man who looked as if he'd had the life scrubbed out of him long ago. And I remember looking around and thinking, This is going to be so boring.

But I needn't have worried about that.

'The orders have been changed,' the laundryman said. He pointed to a shrivelled old eunuch in blue cotton overalls – none too clean, I might add – standing by the door. 'You're to go with him,' he told me.

'You can call me Stinker,' the old man said. 'Most people do.' He looked at me curiously. 'What was your crime?'

'Does it matter?' I asked.

'No,' he said. 'But usually people get sent to work with me for a month, to punish them for something. And I was just told you'll be working with me for the rest of your life. So I wondered what you could have done.'

'There's plenty of time to tell you,' I said. 'Where are we going?'

'Up to the kitchens,' he answered.

The eunuchs' quarters were tucked away in the corner of the southern wall, just below the side gate. The kitchens were all the way up in the northwestern corner. So we had to walk the entire length of the Forbidden City to reach them.

Our path took us by long alleyways, past the walls of all kinds of enclosures: the Garden of Benevolent Tranquillity, the Palace of Longevity and Health, the Pavilion of Rain and Flowers.

There were gardens and alleys into which we could look. Once we passed a small, rather dark alley. 'What's in there?' I asked.

'A ghost,' Stinker told me. 'She's been haunting that alley for three hundred years, and she can be really mean. People avoid it.'

'Oh,' I said. 'I won't go in there, then.'

The kitchens occupied a long range of buildings inside the northern wall. Nearby gateways gave access to the courtyards of the imperial quarters.

'Welcome to your new home,' said Stinker.

'Are we going to cook?' I asked.

'No. We are in charge of the waste,' he replied.

The Forbidden City's plumbing arrangements were impressive. The drinking water was brought through pipes and channels that went all the way out to the Jade Spring in the Western Hills. It was healthy and sweet to the taste.

The sewage system dated back centuries, to the start of the Ming dynasty, with tunnels deep underground where streams carried the waste away.

So every morning, the junior eunuchs took the chamber pots and emptied them into these deep drains, and that took care of that business.

But the solid waste from the kitchens was another matter. It all had to be carried away by carters, who could come as far as the Forbidden City's western gate, but not enter. The eunuchs had to bring the kitchen waste to them in handcarts, and this was normally done every other day.

Stinker's job, therefore, was to collect the scraps, bones, entrails, carcasses, slops, blood, dirt and any other waste from the kitchen workers, put it in barrels, cart the barrels to the gate, and keep the kitchen area clean. Every ten days or so, he also had to clean out the barrels. That, of course, is how he got his name.

The worst thing for me, that first day, was when Stinker told me: 'As it happens, today's the day we clean out the barrels. We always strip naked for that,' he added. I didn't want to. I was still embarrassed about being a eunuch. Some people imagine being castrated makes you look like a woman, but it really doesn't. No matter how well the operation's been done, it's not a pretty sight.

'Why?' I wailed.

'Because by the time we're done, if we're wearing our overalls, the laundry can never get the stink out of them. And even if they could, they don't want to handle them.'

I have to say they were right. It took hours to scrub and wash down those barrels and somehow get the smell out of the wood. When we were done and had cleaned the handcarts as well, we washed ourselves with laundry soap and scrubbing brushes – especially our pigtails, you can imagine. Then we put on the clean overalls we'd been given in the morning, stacked the clean barrels in the storeroom, lit the incense burners to fumigate them during the night, and closed the door. We took the dirty overalls we'd worn during the day to the laundry and then went home.

There was a delicious smell coming from the kitchen when I got home. Someone had paid my father for running errands by giving him a duck to roast. Rose had been preparing a little feast all afternoon: Beijing duck, noodles, stir-fry vegetables, dumplings.

So I played with my little children, and then they were put to bed while my father and I sat down to our meal.

'It's a pleasure to see how much you love your little boy,' my father said to me quietly.

'I do,' I admitted.

'One day he will thank you for saving his life,' he went on. 'He'll understand the sacrifices you've made.'

'I hope so,' I said. But I was thinking that, the way things were going, my son mightn't have much to thank me for. As for my sacrifices, it looked as if they'd all been for nothing.

The night before, I hadn't told my family anything about my

troubles, and I certainly wasn't going to tell them anything now. I suppose I was just praying that something would turn up to end the nightmare I was in.

'So did anything good happen today?' he wanted to know. 'Did you make any friends?'

'Yes,' I said. 'An old palace servant. He told me all sorts of things about the palace, going back to the Ming dynasty.'

'That's good,' he agreed. 'You should always listen to old people. They know so much. What did you do today?'

'Well, actually,' I said, 'we worked in the emperor's kitchen.'

'You saw the emperor?'

'Oh no.' I laughed. He nodded as though he understood, but he looked impressed. 'Don't go boasting to the neighbours,' I said. 'We don't want anyone to know what I do.'

'Of course not,' he said.

After the meal, we all went to bed. My parents and our children all slept on the kang in the main room, but Rose and I had a tiny room to one side that was more private. When I lay beside her, I felt such a surge of gratitude and affection, I wished there was more I could do for her; but at least I could caress her. And she had just started moaning softly with pleasure when suddenly she stopped and sat up.

'What's the matter?' I asked.

'There's a smell,' she said, and she wrinkled up her nose. 'Ugh,' she said, 'it's your hands. They smell like waste.'

'There was an accident at the palace,' I told her. 'We had to clean it up.'

'Oh,' she said. And she turned her back to me, which wasn't very nice, but I couldn't blame her when I thought of the barrels she must be smelling. So I just lay there feeling ashamed and wondered what I could do.

The next time we cleaned the barrels, I scrubbed my fingers over and under my nails until they almost bled. Rose didn't say anything more that night.

My fingers soon got so raw that I had to bandage them. Next I started wearing leather gloves. The gloves smelled terrible, but they helped a bit.

The next time I was paid, of course, I got only the bare minimum, which was a pittance, and when I brought it home, my father took me to one side and asked me, 'Is that really all you got?' And I said, 'Things will get better. We just have to be patient.' But the truth was, I had no idea how to get anything more.

Since I had been sent to work with Old Stinker, I had never set eyes on Mr Chen. I could understand it. He'd been humiliated. There was nothing he could do. I was just an embarrassment to him, and I daresay he wished everyone would forget he had anything to do with me.

But I was growing so desperate that I decided to go to see him all the same. After all, he knew everything there was to know about the palace. Perhaps together we could think of some way out of the mess I was in. So I went to his house one evening and knocked at the big door on the street. A servant appeared and took my name. But then he came back and said that his master wasn't there; then he closed the door in my face.

I wasn't surprised. But I wasn't giving up, either. The next day I managed to get away early and I waited by the corner of the street. And after a while, sure enough, I saw him coming.

He wasn't at all pleased to see me, I can tell you, but I stuck to him like glue, and I could see that he was afraid I'd make a scene, so he hurried me into his house just to get me out of people's sight.

'I can't do anything for you,' he said. 'If I'd realised Mr Liu hated me so much, I'd never have helped you in the first place. But I didn't.'

'Have you got anything on him, sir?' I asked. 'Something I could use to blackmail him.'

'No,' he answered. 'He's taken bribes, of course, but then . . .' He spread his hands as though to say, *Haven't we all?*

'That's a pity,' I said.

'You owe me a lot of money,' he suddenly declared.

'Which I can't pay,' I replied. But he was just saying that to get rid of me, so I left.

After a while I began to think about killing myself. Was I really going to spend the rest of my life with the old man – day after day, month after month, year after year – and then turn into the next Old Stinker? I'd never have enough money to repay Mr Chen or buy my private parts back. So I'd go into the poor eunuchs' graveyard, incomplete.

In the meantime, how was I going to keep my family on the pittance I was getting? And once my father was gone, would my little boys even survive?

Everything I'd done had been for nothing. And sooner or later my family was going to discover the truth about what I did at the palace. I didn't know if I could face the shame of that. I'd sooner have died, to tell the truth and come back in my next life as a worm.

So that was the choice: a lifetime of shame ahead of me, and maybe not even save my boys; or death, and turn my back on every duty I had.

Head eunuch Liu appeared to inspect the kitchen without any warning. One morning I came in to get my overalls, and there he was, just as I remembered him, in his peacock robes, looking serenely into the cooking pots. Everyone was terrified, of course. And so was I for a moment or two. But then something else occurred to me.

I daresay he inspects the kitchen once in a while, I thought, but he's also come to look at me, just to make sure that I'm suffering and that he has really humiliated Mr Chen.

One thing was sure: I wasn't going to pass up a chance to confront him.

So I went up to him, made a low bow, and said, 'Mr Liu, may your humble servant speak with you for a moment, after your inspection?' And I must have been right, because after staring at me blankly for a moment, he said, 'Tell Old Stinker to start without you.'

He led me to the little office and sat down behind the table, leaving me standing in front of it. Then he just watched me, waiting for me to speak.

'Mr Chen is very humiliated,' I began.

'So I hear,' he answered.

'It's terrible, what you've done to me, Mr Liu,' I said. 'My family still don't know what I do, but they'll find out. I can't get the smell off my hands. And I get so little pay . . . I can't support them on it. Will you ever show me any mercy?'

'No. It would make me look weak.'

'Then may this foolish servant ask your advice?' I said.

He looked a bit surprised. 'My advice?'

'Yes, Mr Liu. Should I kill myself?'

'Are you serious?' he asked.

'Your lowly servant is very serious,' I said.

'How would you do it?' he asked. He seemed quite curious.

'When the last Ming emperor lost his kingdom to the Manchu invaders, he went up a hill and hanged himself for shame,' I said. 'If that was good enough for him, it's got to be good enough for me. But I thought I should ask you first.'

'Why?'

'You might not want me to.'

'Oh?' He glared at me. 'Why not?'

'Well, sir,' I said, 'everyone knows that my suffering is to embarrass Mr Chen. So if it drives me to kill myself, people might say bad things about you.'

After a pause, he nodded. 'You're quite intelligent,' he replied. 'But you're mistaken. People don't value life as much as you think. You've heard the story of the lady-in-waiting who spilled hot ash on an empress, and how she was executed. Unlike you, she came from a noble family. But nobody complained. So don't think anybody's going to be shocked by your death. Or even interested.' He considered. 'And you're overlooking something else. There are dozens of people in this palace whom I've helped and promoted down the years, who owe their lives and fortunes to me. If I drive you to your death, it will only add fear to their gratitude, which is quite useful to me, you know.'

'I see what you mean, Mr Liu,' I said.

'On the whole,' he continued easily, 'I'd be quite agreeable to your killing yourself.'

You had to admire his logic.

'Well, that's it, then,' I said.

'You were unlucky in having Mr Chen for a friend.'

'I don't believe in friendship anymore,' I cried. 'I don't think it exists.'

'No,' he corrected me, 'it does. But I grant you it is rare.' He seemed to be meditating. 'You know,' he said, 'you could have taken another line of argument.'

'May your humble servant ask what that would have been?' I enquired.

'That for the time being, I might prefer to have you alive. As long as you're with Old Stinker, you're a constant humiliation to Mr Chen. Once you are dead, people will soon forget. Though Mr Chen certainly won't try to promote any more of his kind in the palace – which was my goal – I'd like to rub his nose in it for a few more years.' He nodded to himself. 'So I will make you this offer. I shall give you a present that will allow you to keep your family for a year. A private present from me to you. On no account may you tell anyone about it. Above all, you must not pay Mr Chen a single copper coin of the money you owe him. If he asks for anything, you will tell him you have no money. Do you agree to this?'

'But I have to go on with Old Stinker?' I forgot even to address him politely.

'Exactly so.'

I had to think of my family. 'You've got me there, honourable sir,' I said.

'In a year's time, if I still wish to humiliate Mr Chen, and if you have done nothing to displease me, then I may give you another present.' He looked at me. 'Well?'

'Your servant thanks you, Mr Liu,' I said.

'On your way home tonight, you will see me in the street, and I shall slip you the money.'

And sure enough, he did. A small bag of silver, far more than I expected. It was nothing to him, of course, but it would more than feed my family for a year.

'Don't tell your family about the money,' he warned me, 'or they'll spend it all. Keep it hidden and give them only a little at a time.'

He was right, of course. The moment I produced a silver dollar that night and told my family I'd been given a tip for my good work in the palace, I saw my father's face light up.

'Well done, my son,' he cried. 'At this rate, I shan't need to work anymore.' And although he was laughing, I could tell he meant it. In my experience, the minute someone thinks they don't have to work, you can never get the notion out of their head again.

'Don't stop working, Father,' I said. 'This could be the last tip I ever get.'

The next problem was: where to hide the money?

I still kept all my lacquer work brushes and other implements in a box. So I stowed the silver in that for the night. But it was no use leaving it there. Sooner or later, someone would be sure to open the box and find it. By the morning, though, I'd had an idea.

After work that day, instead of hurrying home at once, I walked slowly past the alley that Old Stinker had told me was haunted. It appeared to be empty, and nobody saw me turn into it. The alley ended in a little yard with a door a few feet away on the left and a garden beyond. It was very quiet, and the moss on the cobblestones suggested to me that no one ever came there. I gently tried the door. It was locked.

I looked about. The alley walls were topped with little tile roofs, but they were too high to reach. The cobblestones under my feet seemed more promising. And sure enough, a couple of feet from the door, against the wall, I saw a cobblestone that seemed to be loose. I had a short knife with me. In a few minutes, I'd managed to prize the cobblestone out. Underneath it was just beaten earth. I carved out a little pocket in the middle, just big enough to receive the silver coins, leaving a rectangle of hard earth around it. Then I replaced the cobblestone. One would never have guessed there was a tiny hiding place beneath it.

During this time, I wasn't troubled by the ghost at all.

The next day, early in the morning, I visited that place again. I easily prized up the stone and deposited the silver. Everything fitted perfectly. But just to be safe, I had made a little paste using dust and lacquer to bind it, and this I worked in around the cobblestone like a thin cement. It would hold the stone perfectly, but I could easily loosen it whenever I needed to open my little store again. By the time I'd carefully cut and transplanted some pieces of the moss growing on the neighbouring stones, no one would ever have imagined the place had been disturbed.

I was still kneeling on the ground when I had the sensation of something behind me. It felt like the shade of a passing cloud. It was rather cold.

I didn't look back or move at all. I just said, 'Thank you, Honoured Lady, for guarding my silver. It's all I've got.'

There was no sound, but the sense of coldness seemed to melt away. And when I got up and looked around, there was nobody there.

As it happened, a month later, head eunuch Liu was sent on a mission by the emperor to inspect the coastal defences to the south of Beijing. This showed how much the emperor trusted him, because normally eunuchs were not allowed to leave the capital. But it meant that Liu was away for nearly a month, and during that time his deputy took his place. This eunuch was rather frail. His name was Mr Yuan, but behind his back everyone called him Shaking Leaf because he was always worried something would go wrong, which is probably why his arrangements were actually rather thorough.

To make matters worse for Mr Yuan, the emperor returned to the Forbidden City for that month. People told me that everything was more formal in the Forbidden City than up at the Summer Palace; nobody wanted to be there, and all the courtiers were in a bad temper.

Old Stinker and I had far more work to do because of all the extra chamber pots, so we weren't happy. As for poor Shaking Leaf, there were so many little things that could go wrong each day that he was in a constant state of anxiety.

He was certainly in quite a flap the day that changed my fortune.

They say that we're all made by our previous lives. Our affinities for each other were made in the deep past, and when we meet people who become important in our lives, it may seem like a chance accident – no more significant than the flapping of a butterfly's wing – but in fact a hidden force is drawing us together across the surface of the stream of life. *Yuanfen,* they call it.

So you might say that the head eunuch's being away on the day that the emperor's favourite concubine broke her fingernail was just a coincidence. Random chance. But I don't think so. It was *yuanfen,* drawing us together.

I was in the kitchen at the end of the afternoon, all cleaned up and ready to go home, when Shaking Leaf suddenly appeared. 'Does anyone here know how to reattach a lady's broken fingernail?' he cried out.

Now the moment he said that, I was all ears. I knew what he must be talking about. Fashionable Manchu ladies at that time often had fingernails whole inches long. Proof they didn't have to work, I suppose. But if the most important eunuch in the palace was so concerned about it, then the owner of the fingernail must be someone important. Very important. And why was he asking in the kitchen, of all places?

Obviously, he'd tried everywhere else. So why hadn't anyone volunteered? I mean, it was hardly likely that none of the palace ladies or the servants on duty could have fixed a broken fingernail, was it?

They don't want the job, I thought. This means danger. But also opportunity. And what did I have to lose? Nothing. As a matter of fact, if he'd asked if anyone knew how to catch a tiger, I daresay I'd have volunteered for that, too.

'I can help you, Mr Yuan,' I said.

'You? Why?' he demanded.

'I was a lacquer craftsman, sir,' I answered. 'I did the finest work. With lacquer and varnish I'm sure I could fix any broken nail.'

'Well, you're all I've got,' he said irritably. 'I hope you can.'

'May your foolish servant ask,' I ventured, as he led me along a passage, 'whose fingernail has been broken?'

'The emperor's favourite concubine. The Noble Consort Yi.'

That was her name just then. Later she'd be known as Cixi. People often change their names several times as they move up in rank. But she was already important.

If the empress, his official wife, had been able to give the Son of Heaven children, things would have been different. But for some reason the empress, who was a gentle, rather timid young woman, seemed unable to have them. So it was up to the concubines.

I'd heard that, like most of the palace concubines, the Noble Consort Yi came from a noble Manchu clan – the Yehe Nara, in her case – though her father hadn't amounted to much. 'She isn't beautiful,' people said, 'but she's clever.' When her father hadn't troubled to get her a teacher, she'd taught herself to read and write. The emperor liked to talk to her. And most important of all, she'd given him a son.

'I hear she is a charming lady,' I said softly.

'Yes,' he answered. 'When she wants to be. Just don't cross her, that's all.' As we hurried along, he told me more. 'The servant who does her nails broke one. So she's had the girl beaten.' He frowned. 'Unfortunately, the girl wasn't strong enough to take it.' He shook his head. But then he brightened. 'Don't worry,' he added, 'you'll be all right.'

No wonder no one wanted to take the girl's place.

'How do I address her?' I asked him. 'Am I supposed to kowtow?'

'Just call yourself her slave and bow low.' He gave me a nod. 'She won't be testing your etiquette. All she wants is her nail fixed.'

The concubines lived in a compound of several little palaces, each with its own courtyard, on the west side of the emperor's private apartments. Shaking Leaf led the way. He knew all the shortcuts. We went through corridors with gilded walls and heavy-beamed ceilings, down open passageways with red walls and golden gateways, through courtyards where curving yellow-tiled roofs gracefully overhung their sides. I noticed ornamental trees in many of them. They say the huge central spaces of the Forbidden City are treeless because the emperors were afraid of assassins hiding behind tree trunks. But there were all manner of fragrant and flowering trees in the smaller palaces.

Finally we came through a gateway with a green lintel and found ourselves in a long rectangular courtyard, with apartments to the left and right. Some of the doors were open, and I could see silk-covered beds in curtained alcoves inside.

There were half a dozen ladies in the courtyard, attended by a couple of eunuchs. The ladies were all dressed in long silk Manchu gowns, with slits down the sides and Manchu platform shoes that made them look even more tall and elegant. I noticed several Pekinese palace dogs waddling around. But the ladies were looking nervous. There was a swing hanging from a tree bough. No one was sitting in it.

Shaking Leaf led me towards the hall at the end. The central doorway was open. On either side of it stood one of the big bronze water tubs they keep in every palace in case of fire. Shaking Leaf stepped into the hall in front of me. I watched him bow low and murmur a few words. Then it was my turn.

'Your slave attends you, Highness,' I said quietly. Then I knelt. He'd told me only to bow, but I wanted to kneel.

'Get up and let me look at you,' said a voice – very clear; quite pleasant in fact. So I stood and raised my eyes towards the Noble Consort Yi.

I've met only a few people in my life whom I'd call superior beings. Even in palaces most of them aren't. But she was. I could see it at once. And I could see how she'd done it.

Most women try to make themselves look pretty with makeup. They want small features and doe eyes. They smile. They haven't a thought in their heads. It's what the men want, so you can't really blame them. Please the men – and your mother-in-law – and you'll survive. But this young woman was different. She was sitting bolt upright on a wooden armchair, still as a Buddha. I could see the square white platforms under her embroidered shoes, and then I realised something else. Her feet were tiny. You'd have thought they were bound, except that she was a Manchu, so they couldn't have been.

Her gown was the colour of plum blossom, which signifies inner strength. As well as the borders, which were a shade darker, the gown had a pattern of stripes and open squares, each side matching the other. And this bold effect was continued above. For while her hair was parted in the middle and pulled tightly back, in the usual Manchu manner, it wasn't wound around a big fan-shaped comb on the back of her head, as with the other ladies, but around a single horizontal wooden bar above her head, which she hadn't even decorated with flowers.

Instead of trying to look pretty, the Noble Consort Yi had created an ensemble like a perfectly constructed Chinese character: complex yet strong. And she was perfectly controlled, her emotions contained. Every gardener knows: contain a space inside a wall and it seems larger. Contain a character, and its symmetry grows fearsome. Clearly she understood all this. She knew how to look at herself from the outside, to create a design of which she was only a part. That is style, and art.

People said her face was plain. What did they know? Her face was oval. Her features were certainly too heavy to be called pretty, but they were perfectly regular. She wore long heavy earrings. Her chin was firm. She knew her own mind. Did something in her mouth suggest she might like to be kind? Perhaps. But her dark amber eyes belonged to an older woman – cautious, watchful. This woman is brave, I thought, but careful.

Her eyes took me in. 'Have you experience with manicure?'

'Your slave is not a manicurist, Highness,' I replied. 'But I am skilled in all kinds of lacquer work. I am sure I could apply manicurist's lacquer well enough to hold your broken nail.'

She gazed at me. 'The stupid girl's things are on that table over there.'

The cutters, files, brushes and little lacquer pots were jumbled in a shallow box as if they had been thrown there.

'Perhaps if we had some glue . . .' Shaking Leaf began.

'No glue,' she said sharply. 'I hate glue.' She was quite right, by the way. Glue's more trouble than it's worth. Sometimes it's poisonous. Worse, it's often stronger than the nail, which means the nail may tear again.

So I gathered what I needed and knelt in front of her. Her hand was resting on the arm of the chair, with the fingers pointing downwards, level with my eyes. The fingernails were certainly long. The nail of the third finger was the longest, a good three inches and curved. It was wonderfully decorated. I don't just mean the red lacquer – which, I soon learned, only the royal women are allowed to wear – but the droplets of gold and the tiny diamonds embedded in the lacquer. I'd never seen such a fingernail before.

It was the index finger that had the broken nail. A nasty tear. No wonder she was angry. 'Do we have the broken end?' I asked.

One of the ladies brought it to me on a little cushion. I put it back in place on the finger to see if it fitted cleanly. It did. The tear might help me, because there was some overhang between the broken-off bit and the rest. If I put a little lacquer between the top of the existing nail and the underside of the torn section, that would act as a glue to hold the two together. Then it would be a question of lacquering both the underside and the top of the nail.

'Your slave will need you to rest your hand on the arm of the chair and not move it, Highness,' I said to her. 'I shall apply some coats of lacquer, but it will take time to dry.'

She said nothing, but put her hand where I wanted.

I must say, she was very good. I worked for an hour and she never moved at all. Not a flicker. She had wonderful control.

'Your slave thinks that is enough for today,' I said finally. While I was working, I'd noticed that as well as the diamond inlay on her index fingernail, she had a beautifully worked silver nail guard on her fourth. 'Is there perhaps a nail guard Your Highness could wear to protect the broken nail for the night?' I asked. 'The lacquer will continue to strengthen during that time.' She had a painted wooden one that I was able to fit nicely over my work.

I'd just put that in place when I heard Shaking Leaf's soft voice. 'We shall find a proper manicurist by the morning, Noble Consort,' he murmured, 'and bring her to you.'

Well, that didn't suit me at all. I knew exactly what he was thinking. He'd brought me there because she was throwing a tantrum and he was in a panic. But he also knew how furious head eunuch Liu would be when he discovered I'd got in there.

'May your slave speak?' I asked. She nodded. 'What your slave has done will last until tomorrow,' I said, 'but if I may bring my own lacquer and brushes in the morning, I can make something so strong it will last until the nail has grown at least another inch.'

Shaking Leaf started to object, but she cut him short. 'Let him finish,' she said. 'There's no point in doing it otherwise.'

The next morning she had changed her gown. A pale cream colour, with a softer pattern. She wore the same head comb as the day before, but this time she had dressed it with artificial flowers, peony and plum blossom, made of pearl and coral. I told myself she'd done it for me. Not that she had, of course.

I set to work straightaway. It felt so good, having my own brushes in my hand.

She didn't say a word at first, but I could sense that she was watching me closely. 'You really know what you're doing,' she said finally.

'Yes, Highness,' I replied. 'I do.'

Shaking Leaf had already told me that, as she wasn't actually a princess, I shouldn't address her as 'Highness'. 'You should say "Noble Consort" instead,' he'd instructed. But I think she liked 'Highness', so I pretended I didn't know any better and went on doing it.

She didn't say anything more for a bit, but then she turned to Shaking Leaf, who was watching morosely. 'What happened to that stupid girl I told you to beat?' she demanded.

'I'm afraid she died, Noble Consort,' he said softly.

'Really? They must have beaten her too hard.' She didn't sound upset. But people with privilege and power are often cold. They have to be. A minute later, she tapped me on the head with one of the fingernails of her free hand. I looked up. 'You like the finer things of life, don't you?'

She'd seen that in me! I don't know how, but she'd seen it. 'Your slave does,' I murmured, and bowed my head.

And then she smiled at me. 'Tell me about yourself,' she ordered. I don't suppose she was truly interested, but it was a way of passing the time. 'What age were you when you had the operation?'

'Just recently, Highness, a few months ago,' I told her.

'Recently? What do you mean?' Now she was really curious. 'Explain.'

So while I worked on her nail, I told her my life story – well, some of it, anyway. And how I had the operation to become a palace person on account of my little boy.

'So you have a wife and family?'

'Your slave does.'

'How extraordinary.' Then she frowned. 'When they did the operation, did they take everything off?' She was looking at me suspiciously now.

'Yes, Highness,' I assured her. 'Everything. I promise.'

'It was all done according to the regulations,' Shaking Leaf said nervously.

'Show me,' she said.

It was one of the worst moments in my life. I know I blushed. It was so humiliating. 'Oh, please, Highness,' I begged her.

She pointed to a screen in a corner of the room. 'Go behind that,' she told me. Then she turned to one of her ladies. 'Look, and tell me.'

So I did as I was told and stripped down. It was bad enough having one of the court ladies look at me, but at least it wasn't all of them, and particularly the Noble Consort Yi.

'All gone,' the lady called out in a singsong voice.

'You can't be too careful,' the Noble Consort remarked to me when I was back at my work. 'You certainly made a sacrifice.'

'It is worth it to serve you, Highness,' I said, and I went on with my work. I could see Shaking Leaf fidgeting, but I took my time. 'Your slave has done all he can for now,' I said finally. I saw Shaking Leaf look relieved.

So this'll be it, I thought. Back to the chamber pots for me tomorrow.

'You seem to have done a good job,' the Noble Consort said. I saw her nod to the lady who'd inspected me. I understood what was coming: a silver coin or two, thank you very much. Goodbye. Unless I could pull off one more trick.

'May your slave speak?' I said. Shaking Leaf gave me a warning look. I ignored it. The Noble Consort nodded, so I pressed on. 'Often the palace people are given training in all manner of skills and arts. Your slave believes, with the skills he already has, that he could quickly learn the arts of manicure and serve you in that capacity.'

She gazed at me. 'Cheeky monkey,' she remarked. She seemed to be thinking.

'Such training is provided only to trainees who show great aptitude, after several years,' Shaking Leaf reminded her. 'And then more years of proof are necessary before a palace person may be considered to serve a member of the royal family.' He spoke softly, but I could see he was terrified.

'Well,' she replied tartly, 'so far you've provided me with a servant who broke my nail, and then you beat her to death, which nobody told you to do.'

'It was not I who beat her, Noble Consort,' he said nervously.

'You're in charge while Mr Liu is away,' she retorted. 'So it's your responsibility.'

I felt quite sorry for him, actually, because I knew what a pickle he was in. And what he said about the employment rules was true, of course.

'Your slave meant no disrespect.' I made a low bow first to her, then to Shaking Leaf. 'Your slave was so eager to serve that he forgot himself. It is true that it is far too early for me to think of such an honour. I only beg that in the years ahead Your Highness may remember me, if I am worthy.'

She might remember me, I thought. You never know. She might.

'There are also certain objections to this person,' said Shaking Leaf.

Looking back, I've often thought that if he hadn't said that, she probably would have given me up – for it wasn't of any consequence to her, really. I'd have been dismissed.

But anxiousness had made him overplay his hand, and she'd picked up on it at once. Her instincts were excellent. 'Objections to him? Then why did you bring him here?' she demanded.

'It was an emergency, Noble Consort. I wished to serve you quickly.'

'What objections?'

'It would be best to ask Mr Liu when he returns,' he murmured.

'Did his mentor complain of him?'

Shaking Leaf was in a bind now. He didn't like to lie. I could see that. Dangerous to lie, too. She'd be furious if she found out – and he was already in trouble.

'No, Noble Consort.'

'How was his mentor's report? Good, poor, or indifferent?' She wouldn't let go.

I looked at him – not as if I'd contradict him, and not an imploring look, either. I just looked at him.

'Good,' he said reluctantly.

'How good?' She was like a cat with a rat.

'Very good, Noble Consort.'

'So I should speak to Mr Liu?'

'It would be best,' he said miserably.

'Then I shall. It's settled.' He looked relieved. 'In the meantime, however,' she continued, 'he is to be trained in manicure at once. And he will attend to my nails each day so that we can see if he is learning anything.'

'Noble Consort . . .' Shaking Leaf tried to interrupt her. He was in agony.

'Just until Mr Liu returns,' she said with a smile, and dismissed us both.

He was away for fifteen days. Fifteen blessed days. Every morning I went to the palace to attend to her nails, but the rest of the day I spent with a manicurist in Beijing. 'Find me the best manicurist in the city,' I'd told my father, and sure enough he had: an old man who'd been amazed how fast I learned. For if you have talent and your entire existence is focused on a single object, you can learn ten times as fast as a normal student will.

I paid for that apprenticeship myself, using some of the money I'd hidden. I could have asked the palace to pay, but I didn't want to. I wanted to surprise them. And I did. By the end of the fifteen days, the Noble Consort said I was the best manicurist she'd ever had.

'It's because your slave was a lacquer craftsman first,' I told her.

'I'm giving you a new name: Lacquer Nail,' she said. 'Do you like it?' Not that it would have made a difference if I didn't.

'Your slave is honoured,' I said, and bowed low. I did like it, in fact.

So that is how I got the name of Lacquer Nail.

She usually talked to me as I worked. And she was always curious. Naturally, one of her first questions was about the head eunuch. What had he got against me? Why didn't Shaking Leaf want to tell her? I'd known she'd ask, and I'd prepared my answer.

'Highness,' I said, 'you know your slave wants to obey you. How could it be otherwise? But if Mr Liu thinks that I have told you, it will make him so angry that I don't know what will happen to me.' I paused and looked into her eyes. 'Perhaps I would disappear.' I said it quietly. I saw her take it in. She didn't contradict me. 'However,' I continued, 'all the eunuchs know the story. Any of your ladies could find it out from one of them.'

She said nothing, but the next day she gave me a funny look. 'I heard about Mr Chen,' she said.

'Not from me, Highness,' I said anxiously.

'No. Not from you.'

She didn't mention it again. But then she got curious about another thing, which was much more personal and quite embarrassing. 'So what's it like for a eunuch to be married?' she asked me one day.

I realised what she was after, but I pretended I didn't. 'As your slave expects you know, Highness, some of the palace people – if they've been fortunate in their careers and are able to buy back their missing parts – adopt sons to inherit from them, whose duty is to make sure they are buried in the proper manner with their ancestors. And your slave has heard that some of these older palace people also take wives.'

'I know,' she said. 'But can their wives be happy?'

'Your slave supposes each case is different,' I replied. 'The wives are well provided for.'

She gave me a look, and I was afraid she was going to interrogate me further. But I suppose she felt it was beneath her dignity.

Two days later, as I was leaving through the courtyard, one of her ladies who was alone out there asked me to push her in the swing. After we'd done that for a little while and she'd engaged me in conversation in a friendly manner, she casually remarked: 'It's nice to talk to someone. We're quite lonely here, you know.' I bowed politely but said nothing. 'Some concubines have been here for years,' she went on, 'and scarcely seen the emperor, let alone spent time with him.'

'I suppose it's no worse than being an unmarried spinster,' I suggested. 'And still a great honour for the lady and her family.'

'They'd rather be married,' she said. 'At least they get to make love and have children.' Again, I remained silent. She glanced around, to make sure there was no one else in the courtyard. 'I want to ask you something,' she whispered.

I already guessed what was coming and who was behind this little game. But there was nothing to do except play along.

'I don't mean to pry,' she said, 'but is it like that for your wife?'

'My wife?' I pretended to misunderstand. 'My wife has children.'

'I know. But now that you've been castrated . . . when you're with her at night, I mean . . . what do you do?'

I'd known it was coming. I knew who wanted to know. And I had prepared for it. But I still had to be awfully careful. It was so dangerous.

If I said a word about my intimate life with my wife, it would be all around the palace in no time. And people would think I might want or might be persuaded to do the same for the emperor's women. It would be just the excuse Mr Liu was looking for to forbid any more people like me from being admitted again. He'd have me thrown out at once. If anyone suspected I'd even tried anything, I'd probably be executed.

'My wife is a good woman,' I said. 'She looks after my parents and the children. She asks for nothing. Naturally, now I can only be her friend.

She is like a sister. But there are many married couples who live in this way. She is dutiful and quite content.'

'Oh,' she said. She didn't bother me again.

And so the fifteen days passed. I may not have satisfied the Noble Consort's curiosity, but she continued to be happy with my manicures, which was all that mattered. I met her little boy a few times. He was four, I think. He seemed to be a nice child.

The emperor was in the palace, and the Noble Consort Yi was often with him, but I did not see him myself at that time.

Then head eunuch Liu returned.

He gazed at me. If I hadn't known better, I'd have said he looked benevolent. 'Well, I didn't foresee this,' he remarked.

'Nor did I, Mr Liu,' I said.

'You needn't bother to explain,' he said, raising his hand. 'I know everything that happened.' He shook his head. 'I thought I couldn't be surprised.' He sighed. 'But one can always learn something new.' That was typical of him, I must say. People who get to the top always want to keep learning. The question was, what would he do?

'I hear the Noble Consort Yi has given you a new name,' he went on drily. 'Lacquer Nail.'

'It is true, Mr Liu,' I said, and bowed my head.

'Well, if she wants you to do her nails, I suppose you'd better.' The look he gave me said it all. He'd bide his time, but he'd still destroy me. 'Rejoice while you can,' he said bleakly.

'Your unworthy servant can only accept his fate,' I mumbled.

'You haven't accepted your fate at all,' he snapped. 'You volunteered for the job, and then you asked her for a position.'

'Your foolish servant was so surprised, he acted impulsively,' I said. 'You were not there to guide me.' That got a snort. 'May your servant speak?' I ventured.

'What?' He glared at me.

'Your servant has been drawn to the finer things in life, ever since he was a boy,' I said. 'It made me become a lacquer worker. And the day I first saw a retinue of the palace people, I knew this was where I belonged. So I have dared to wonder if these extraordinary circumstances, which I certainly didn't foresee, might be the result of some hidden force at work. Could it be the operation of *yuanfen*?'

I've never seen a more cynical expression on any man's face. 'I see. You think you're someone special. It's a common delusion.' He sighed. 'Any fool who wins a game of mah-jong believes it was destiny.'

'I suppose, sir,' I suggested, 'that if something happens, it must have been destined.'

'Don't try to be clever,' he said. 'Do you realise you're making a lot of enemies? How do you imagine the other palace people feel? They'd have to wait six years for such a chance. But you, a new arrival, insinuate yourself with the emperor's consort and get promoted over all their heads. You think they like that?'

'No, Mr Liu,' I replied.

'You haven't a friend in the palace,' he said. 'Except one: the Noble Consort Yi. And how long will that last? Until you make a mistake and she throws you out.' He paused a moment. 'Or she gets thrown out herself.'

He said those last words very softly, but I heard them well enough, and I felt a stab of fear. What did that mean? What did he know that I didn't? I must have looked shocked.

'I've seen them come,' he went on. 'I've seen them go.' He considered for a moment. 'She's got some things in her favour. At least the emperor manages to perform with her. Most of the time he can't, you know.'

I stared at him in disbelief. He was talking about the Son of Heaven! To me, the lowest of all the eunuchs.

'It's no secret,' he said blandly. 'Not here in the palace. When he was a very young man he used to sneak out and visit whores in the city. That was his main adventure. But since then . . . He's had a child with one of the other concubines. But only a daughter. The empress herself, poor lady, seems to be barren. Only the Noble Consort Yi has given him a son.'

'Doesn't that make her position secure, sir?' I dared to ask.

'Not entirely. Legally, her son could be given to another mother. The empress, for instance. The son might still be the heir. But the Noble Consort Yi could find herself out in the cold.'

'Your servant hears that the emperor likes her company,' I said.

'Yes. He even discusses state affairs with her. It's against the rules for concubines to meddle in such things, but he doesn't seem to care. He asks her advice, and she gives it.'

'Her advice is bad?' I asked.

'No. She may be ignorant, but her judgement is rather good.' He sighed. 'The kingdom's in a terrible state. I suppose you realise that? The

Taiping have ruined most of the Yangtze valley. That's where the Noble Consort Yi spent her childhood, by the way. She hates the Taiping with a passion. We had them boxed in, but they broke out again this spring, went up to Hangzhou and back, then mauled our troops outside Nanjing. Who knows what their next move will be? The emperor is terrified of them. The last time the Taiping got anywhere near Beijing, he wanted to desert his capital and run away beyond the Great Wall. Did you know that?'

'No, sir,' I said, 'I didn't.' I remembered the Taiping advance all too well, but I didn't know about the emperor. I was quite shocked.

'She's the one who persuaded him to stay, before the news of his cowardice leaked out.'

'Why north of the Great Wall, sir?' I asked.

'Centuries ago, before the Ming dynasty, the Mongol emperors, the family of Genghis Khan, had a huge hunting palace called Xanadu up on the steppe. I suppose because they wanted to be like them, the present Manchu dynasty built a similar place, though not as far north, on their ancestral hunting grounds. Until a generation ago they used to go up there for a huge hunt every summer. But it got so expensive they gave it up. The place is slowly falling apart. But he feels safer up in those endless plains, I suppose. I daresay he'd run all the way into the forests of Manchuria if he had to.'

I was quite astonished that Mr Liu was saying these things to me. Looking back on it, I'm sure he must have felt frustrated by the emperor. I like to think that however angry he was with me, he allowed himself to share his thoughts because he knew I was intelligent. Naturally, I wanted to know more.

'Is the emperor afraid of the barbarians, too, sir?' I prompted.

'The pirates? We're still not sure what they want. There's always the worry they could combine with the Taiping, of course.'

'And the Noble Consort Yi?'

'Despises all barbarians. Says we should destroy them. They may have better ships and guns, but their numbers are small. Do you know how many people the emperor rules?'

'Your servant does not,' I said.

'About four hundred million. Think of it. In a land battle, if the pirates fired every musket and every cannon they have, how many could they kill before they were swamped? Twenty thousand? I doubt it. Moreover, though it's true that they've smashed our ships and forts in the past, when they came to the coastal forts last year, we were better prepared and we defeated them. That put the Noble Consort Yi in high favour. Even the emperor pretends not to be afraid.'

'Is it believed the barbarians will come again?' I asked.

'They may. But we're even better prepared now. I have seen for myself.'

This sounded well. But it raised a question in my mind. 'All this would seem to support the strong position of the Noble Consort Yi,' I suggested. 'Yet your servant had the impression that you thought she might fall from favour.'

'Yes. It must worry you a great deal.' I noticed the satisfaction in his voice. 'You'll have to discover that for yourself, won't you? By the way,' he continued, 'the court's moving to the Summer Palace in two days. You'll like it there.' He gazed at me. 'Enjoy it,' he said softly, 'while you can.'

As the long cortege left the Forbidden City, I was sitting in a covered wagon with a dozen other eunuchs. The morning was overcast but warm. As we rumbled slowly through the northwestern suburbs, I wasn't really paying much attention to the scene. I was too busy wondering why Mr Liu seemed so confident that the Noble Consort Yi would fall.

'This is the road to paradise,' the fellow sitting next to me cried, and several of the other eunuchs nodded and smiled.

Despite what Mr Liu had said about everyone's hating me, the other palace people in the cart had all been very friendly. I suppose I might have wondered why, but I didn't.

The narrowing road wound between wooded slopes. The distance from the suburbs to the Summer Palace was only a few miles. Although we travelled at a snail's pace, we still passed through the gateway before noon. And I found that the fellow's words had been true: we were in paradise.

How can I describe it, the most beautiful place in the history of the world? People call it the old Summer Palace now, but the palace itself, the emperor's residence, was just one compound in the Yuanmingyuan – the Garden of Perfect Brightness. And when we say *garden,* we don't mean a walled enclosure, but a huge park, a landscape with lakes, islands, and wooded hills, sprinkled with temples, villas, pagodas – everything to delight the eye and calm the soul. Nor was the Yuanmingyuan the only garden. There were two or three other great parks adjoining it so that the emperor's paradise went on for miles.

That first day when we entered, I felt as if I'd walked inside a landscape painting – the kind where mountains rise out of the mists into the silent sky, curved bridges hang over the empty void, and scholars contemplate in tiny hermitages, perched high on distant rocks.

People talk about yin and yang as the two forces of the universe. We say that yang is the male force, the bright sun, the blue heavens and so forth, while yin is the female, the earth, the moon, shadow. Like man and wife, yang and yin complement each other; each needs the other to exist. And our sages showed great wisdom when they also declared that there is a little yin in yang and a little yang in yin. For inside the famous yin-yang circle, we see that each of the two interlocking shapes contains a dot of the opposite colour. Yang and yin must be in balance, or there can be no harmony in the world.

So it didn't take me long, once I came to know the Yuanmingyuan, to understand its purpose. For it was nothing less than to be the yin to the yang of the Forbidden City.

The mighty symmetry of the vast fortress was all about the emperor's power, which shines, golden as the sun; the huge round temple, with its blue roof, where the Son of Heaven made sacrifices to the gods; the animals and figures on the corners of every roof that showed the exact status of the building in the city's perfect Confucian order. All these were tokens of the manly yang, which belongs to the sky.

But the paradise of the Summer Palace evoked the spirit of the yin. This wasn't a walled fortress, but nature's landscape. The various buildings were dotted here and there, sometimes half hidden in the trees in the most picturesque manner. Nor was each building strictly regular. The different parts seemed to have grown up together in the most informal way, almost by chance.

There was art in all this. One might say the hand of man arranges the chaos of nature, and that this is the yang within the yin. Indeed, it's true that some of the hills and lakes in the Yuanmingyuan were artificial. But it wasn't so simple. Like the painter and the calligrapher, the landscape designer must sense the spirit of the place and allow that spirit to permeate and fill his mind. This is the negative capability of the yin. Then, almost without positive thought, he allows the spirit to guide his hand.

She sent for me the next morning. The emperor and his family lived in a waterside compound by what they call the Front Lake. This was just like a rich man's summer villa, really, but more spread out, with a lot of courtyards.

After I'd done her nails, she asked me, 'Are the other palace people treating you kindly?' I said that they were. She looked a bit surprised, but she didn't make any comment. Then one of the older eunuchs appeared and asked if she wished to walk outside with her ladies, and she said yes. So I assumed I should withdraw. But she motioned me to follow them.

The royal compound faced the Front Lake, which was a large body of water. Behind the compound, however, lay the Back Lake, which was also a good size. This being my first day on duty, I hadn't had a chance to look at this lake, and so as we walked towards it, I was quite curious.

'Lacquer Nail's never seen the Back Lake,' the Noble Consort said to the old eunuch. 'Tell him about it, and we shall all listen.' So after bowing low and clearing his throat, the old man began.

'The Back Lake has for many generations been the delight of the Son of Heaven.' He called the words out in a high singsong voice, as if he were reading out a royal proclamation. I noticed several of the ladies looking amused, but nobody interrupted him. 'As well as its waters, which contain many golden carp and other fish of great rarity, the lake is blessed with nine islands, which are reached by footbridges of wonderful beauty. Each island, some small, others larger, has its own particular character. Over there' – he indicated an island not far off – 'you see the Island of the Peony Terrace, where there are over a hundred kinds of peony and where many of the emperors have composed notable poems. Over there' – he pointed to another – 'is the Island of the Green Wutong Tree Academy, where the emperor likes to listen to the sound of falling rain. Farther off you can see a steep hill, the top of which is the highest point in the Yuanmingyuan. That hill is in fact on another island. At the base of the hill is the lovely Apricot Blossom Spring Villa, a favourite place in the spring. Of great importance also is the Island of Shrines, where there are temples to all the important religions.'

And so he went on until he had described the nine islands. And all the time he was speaking I, who truly love the finer things of life, was gazing in rapture across the lake at this silent, watery stillness, in the heart of the paradise at the centre of the world.

'Thank you,' said the Noble Consort Yi when he was done. 'Very good.' She turned to me. 'Some women,' she remarked, 'use red paint on their lower lip, in the middle and smear it down into a little red square towards their chin. I hardly ever do that. Do you think I should? What's your opinion?'

I stared at her in amazement. 'My opinion, Noble Consort?' I asked. I didn't know why she was asking me. What did it mean? And what on earth was I supposed to say?

'It's quite a simple question,' she said. 'And if you don't answer at once, it will be disobedient.'

I hoped this was some kind of joke, but I couldn't be sure. 'Your servant thinks the Noble Consort's face has a perfect elegance and can hardly imagine it could be bettered,' I replied. Now as it happens, I've never liked that fashion of smearing the lower lip red. So what I really wanted to say was: don't do it for me. But of course I couldn't say that.

'So you're telling me not to,' she said with a smile.

'Your humble servant could never do such a thing,' I replied.

'Oh well,' she said, 'you can go now. Come back tomorrow.'

The next morning she was waiting for me with several of her ladies. Her little son the prince was there, too. And the first thing I noticed was that she had painted her lower lip with a red square. I bowed low and didn't say anything. Nor did she.

Had she done it to tease me? I wondered. Or to remind me that my opinion counted for nothing? Be careful, I told myself. This may have nothing to do with you at all. She'd probably been asking everybody before deciding to give the red lipstick a try. Whatever her reasons, it wasn't for me to say a word unless she asked me, which she didn't. But I had the feeling, all the same, that she was teasing me for her private amusement.

When I had done her nails, which didn't take long, she called one of her ladies and told me to attend to her nails as well.

I'd just finished this second task when everyone in the room suddenly turned towards the door and bowed. So I turned, too.

I'd caught sight of the empress once or twice in the Forbidden City, but I'd never been in her presence before, so I immediately went on my knees and knocked my head on the floor in the kowtow.

'Just bow,' I heard her say softly. So I scrambled to my feet and bowed low.

'Bow lower,' called the Noble Consort Yi. So I tried to do that and nearly fell on my face. Then I realised that both she and the empress were laughing. Not maliciously. They were just having a little fun with me. 'This is Lacquer Nail, the one I told you about,' said the Noble Consort.

'I have heard only good things about you, Lacquer Nail,' said the empress. And she smiled at me.

I knew she was pretty, of course. But I must say, seeing her close up for the first time, I was really amazed. Dainty features, flawless skin: she looked like a painting on a vase.

So how was it possible that she hadn't given the emperor a child? Mr Liu had said she was barren. It might be the case. Or was the emperor not attracted?

I'm not impressed by conventional prettiness. If she'd been a painted doll with a cold heart, I suppose her character might have put him off. But she wasn't like that at all. A sweet gentleness radiated from her. She was a lovely person in every way. Any man would want to take her in his arms. And if you feel affection, then it's going to be all right on the night, I always think. I could remember that, even if I had been chopped myself.

And I felt sorry for her, because she must have felt that she'd failed the Son of Heaven and the whole empire, not to mention her own clan, who were losing a lot of face when they might have expected all kinds of riches, if only she'd produced an heir. And every day the poor girl had to walk around the palace and know that people were looking at her and thinking: there goes the pretty wife who was a failure in the bedroom.

So I wondered how she felt about the concubine who'd done so much better and given the emperor a son. Was she jealous? However nice a person she was, I thought, it would be hard for her not to hate the Noble Consort Yi.

Yet this didn't appear to be the case. Not that day or any time afterwards. Quite the contrary. As far as I could see, the empress loved the Noble Consort Yi like a sister.

How had the concubine done it? I still don't know. Perhaps she saw the empress was lonely and needed a friend. Was it possible the empress didn't really like being intimate with her husband and wasn't sorry if someone else performed that duty? As for discussing state affairs with His Imperial Majesty like the Noble Consort did, I can't imagine the empress had the desire or the ability to do such a thing. I daresay she never had any wish to be empress in the first place. It's not as if anyone would have asked her what she wanted.

They stayed in the room chatting for a while, talking about what they should wear and how they might do their hair and whether they should visit one of the nine islands that afternoon. Then the Noble Consort gave me a sign that I should go, and I didn't see her again that day.

But where was the emperor? That's what I wanted to know. If I could just observe him and the Noble Consort together, then I might get some idea of how things stood between them – and therefore what my own fate was likely to be. Was he getting bored with her? How long had I got before she fell out of favour and I was cast out of paradise?

I soon learned where he was physically. Close by the residential compound was the Audience Hall, where the emperor might receive ministers, provincial governors, or even the envoys of subject peoples from faraway lands; and a short distance from that was a courtyard complex called the Hall of Diligent Government, where palace people conducted the imperial administration. When the emperor was not secluded in his private apartment, he was usually in one or the other of these business places.

Over ten days or so, I saw a governor, several ministers, and other great men making their way into the Audience Hall. But although people went about quite freely in the open grounds of the Summer Palace, I never once in that time caught a glimpse of the Son of Heaven.

Until I made a new friend. Though the other palace people were all pleasant in their manner towards me, they all knew I shouldn't be there, so I couldn't expect any of them suddenly to become my new best friend. But Mr Ma was different.

I discovered him by accident when I was walking by myself one afternoon and noticed a fenced enclosure. Being inquisitive, I looked in.

The space reminded me of the lacquer workshop where I'd first gone as an apprentice. Along each side were long, low sheds. The middle was filled with tables upon which stood dozens of miniature trees in shallow pots. And when I say miniature, I mean that many were hardly two feet high. But they'd been bound with ropes, to constrict their growth and twist them into curious shapes.

I'd found the nursery of the penzai trees. And Mr Ma was their keeper.

He was very old and bent. He'd been a gardener all his life. His face was rather hollow and his eyes watered, but when they peered up at you, they were surprisingly clear.

Since I like the finer things of life and always want to know how works of art are made, it wasn't long before I got to talking to Mr Ma. I don't think he welcomed visitors to his domain, but once he saw I was genuinely interested, he decided to tolerate me.

'You've heard of the land of Japan, across the sea?' he asked, and I said I had. 'Well, they have trees like this. They call them bonsai. But they didn't think of the idea themselves, you know. They stole the idea from us. Almost everything those people have comes from us.'

'Of course,' I said. 'We're the centre of the world.' This answer seemed to satisfy him.

'I put the trees out on tables during the summer, and they go into the sheds for the winter. All the penzai trees in the Summer Palace and the Forbidden City come from my nursery.'

'May I return?' I asked, and he didn't say no.

A few days later I looked in there again. Mr Ma was busy adjusting the ropes on one of the trees. I watched him from a distance but didn't interrupt him.

When he'd finished, he beckoned me over. 'What do you notice about this tree?' he asked me.

'You have made the branches grow horizontally,' I answered.

'What else?'

'The crown of the tree spreads out like a fan,' I said.

'Good. That is the Beijing style.' He nodded. 'When we bind the penzai tree with ropes, we do not stop it growing, but we compress the tree's growth into a small space. As a result, the tree looks delicate, but it is very strong. All its essence, all its energy, is held contained.'

'That is like a work of art,' I told him. 'All the natural energy is forced into a pattern from which it can never escape.'

He'd just started to nod his approval when something else caught his eye. His thin hand grabbed my arm and dragged me down with him as he fell to his knees. Looking towards the entrance, I saw that a single man was standing there, accompanied by two eunuchs. Mr Ma began the kowtow, so I knew who it must be.

I suppose I'd expected the emperor to be richly dressed in imperial yellow, the way one sees emperors in official portraits; but he wasn't dressed like that at all. Actually, he was in a loose brown robe tied with a girdle, like a monk or scholar, with a simple red conical hat on his head, the same as the two eunuchs accompanying him. He was still quite a young man, not even thirty, but his face looked strained, his eyes hollow. Was there a nervous tic by one eye? I wasn't sure. I've seen similar expressions on ragged poor people in the street. But to see a youthful emperor in such a state? That was a bit of a shock.

As soon as we were on our feet, I drew back while the emperor addressed himself to the old gardener.

'We need three or four more trees in the apartments, Mr Ma,' he said very pleasantly. 'Will you help me choose them?'

They spent several minutes selecting the trees, the emperor asking questions, and old Mr Ma answering in a soft voice. I heard the old man say, 'They'll be delivered directly, Majesty.'

Then I heard the emperor sigh. 'It's so peaceful in here,' he said. 'I always feel better when I come to see you.'

It seemed a strange thing to say when, as far as I was concerned, the entire paradise of the Yuanmingyuan was a haven of peace. But I suppose it wasn't the same for him.

The emperor left, and after waiting until he was well out of the way, I scurried off myself.

The next day, for the first time since I'd been at the Summer Palace, just as I was entering the eunuchs' quarters beside the imperial residence, I found myself face-to-face with head eunuch Liu. I really didn't want to encounter him, but there was nothing I could do, so I bowed low.

'Ah,' he said. 'Are the palace people being nice to you?'

'Yes, Mr Liu,' I answered. 'It's very kind of you to ask.'

'Have you made any friends?'

'Your servant has only just arrived,' I said. 'But I have had the honour of making the acquaintance of Mr Ma. He is good enough to talk to me when I visit his tree nursery.'

'You always find the interesting people, don't you?' he remarked. He sounded almost friendly. 'Have you seen the emperor yet?'

'Your humble servant saw the emperor yesterday, when he was visiting Mr Ma,' I replied.

'And what did you think of him?'

Was it a trap? Was he hoping I'd say something bad about the Son of Heaven that he could report?

'His Majesty was very kind to Mr Ma,' I said carefully. 'Your servant had the impression that he was fond of the old gentleman.' After all, it was true.

And just for a moment Mr Liu's face seemed to soften. 'He is. Ma's a dear old man, no question. What else did you notice?'

'His Majesty said he felt at peace there. Was His Majesty tired, perhaps?'

'He's a wreck. He's still young, of course. I suppose he might live for years.' As on previous occasions, I wasn't quite sure if Mr Liu was talking to me or to himself. 'Well, I must go,' he said briskly, and left me.

So now I had another thing to worry about. Not only did my life depend on the Noble Consort Yi, but on whether the Son of Heaven continued to live. And it didn't sound as if the prospects were too good.

What would happen to me if he died? I had no idea.

Several days later I went to see Mr Ma again. I followed him around in silence, leaving it to him to speak to me if he wished. After a while he showed me an unusually complex little tree and told me it was the same age as he was. I didn't like to ask what age that might be, so I just nodded politely.

'They can grow to be centuries old, you know,' he remarked. Then he turned and looked up at me with his watery eyes. 'I am not yet centuries old,' he added.

I laughed and bowed. 'Not yet, master,' I said. I was pleased that he had shared a little joke with me, and I called him master because, to me, that's what he was. He noticed the compliment and silently accepted it.

This emboldened me, a few minutes later, to venture a question concerning myself. 'I am so happy to be in this place, master,' I told him. 'But I am only here because of the favour of the Noble Consort Yi. Without that favour, Mr Liu would send me away at once.'

'So I have heard,' he said.

'Yet sometimes I think that despite his opposition, Mr Liu likes me,' I went on. 'I've also noticed that all the palace people have been very kind to me, and I don't think they would be without his instructions. Can you tell me what all this means? Is it possible that one day, even if I lost the Noble Consort's patronage, he might change his mind and be my friend?' One might say I was grasping at straws, but I was so anxious to find some way of staying in that paradise.

The old man didn't answer at once. After I'd waited a bit, I thought he wasn't going to answer at all.

But in the end, he asked me a question. 'Why would Mr Liu tell the palace people to be nice to you?' When I couldn't answer, he continued: 'If the palace people were unfriendly towards you, the Noble Consort would hear about it, wouldn't she?'

'I suppose so,' I said. 'Actually, she asked me if they were being kind to me.'

'Exactly. And if they weren't nice to you, she'd blame Mr Liu and be angry with him. And powerful though he is, he'd avoid that. But there's another reason he wants everyone to be kind to you. Can you guess why?'

'No,' I confessed.

'He wants you to be happy.'

'You mean he likes me?'

'You're intelligent, so he may. But that's got nothing to do with it. He wants you to be happy so that one day, when he sends you away, your pain and humiliation will be greater.'

'Why?'

'To show his power.' He paused to let that sink in. 'No one will have driven you out. For fear of him, all the palace people have smiled at you so that, when the day comes, you will fall by his hand alone, while they all watch. It's like a ritual. He has to sacrifice you to save his own face, even if he does like you.'

'I've been very foolish,' I said.

'It's a palace. You rose too fast. If you want to rise in the world, you need a lot of friends.'

'Has anything like this ever happened to you?' I asked him.

'No, I stuck to gardening.' He gave a wry smile. 'Only my trees obey me.'

People sometimes complain about the summer weather in Beijing. I never do. First, in the month of May, as the barbarians call it, comes the fifteen-day period we know as Summer's Coming. Then Full Grain; then Ear of Grain; then Summer Solstice. Some sixty days in all – mostly calm and clear. Is the heat uncomfortable? Is it too humid? Not up in Beijing.

After the fifteen days of the Summer Solstice come the Lesser and then the Greater Heat. Here, I grant you, it's hot and humid. A few thunderstorms at first, downpours later. Our clothes stick to our skin. But we shouldn't complain. The land needs the water.

For just as the Winter Solstice is the male season of the yang – when the emperor must be in the Forbidden City to make the sacrifices for the return of the sun to the sky – so the Summer Solstice is the time of the female yin, when the earth brings forth her fruits and is nourished by the rain.

In fact, out in the hills and lakes of the Summer Palace, I hardly felt the humidity. And when the thunder did come rolling in and the curtains of rain drew across the sky and the flashes of lightning lit up the nine islands in the lake . . . those were some of the most exciting moments I ever experienced in my life.

As for the outside world, by the Solstice that year, I'd almost forgotten about it. The Taiping were far away. There was no sign of the barbarians returning. After my duties tending to the nails of the Noble Consort Yi and her ladies, she often told me to remain in attendance, and I'd find myself one of a party visiting the islands in the afternoon or evening. Sometimes the eunuchs put on little plays to amuse everybody. Several were notable musicians. One old man was a master of the twenty-one-string guzheng zither; another of the bamboo flute; another of the lute. Though the most magical moments of all, for me, were listening to the mournful song of the two-string erhu drifting over the lake as the sun went down.

I discovered another thing about the Summer Palace, too. It wasn't only the most beautiful park in the world. It was a gigantic treasure house.

Every villa, every temple, was full of the most wonderful objects – porcelain, lacquer, statues of gold, furniture inlaid with mother-of-pearl and precious gems, gorgeous silk tapestries, jade stones, paintings . . . collections built up over centuries. Even in the eunuchs' quarters there were beautiful old beds and chairs and carpets. In the passage by the main entrance there was a gleaming antique sword, its hilt encrusted with rubies, just hanging on the wall within easy reach. I should think it was priceless. I daresay someone, maybe a hundred years ago, had hung it there temporarily and then forgotten about it.

At Summer's Coming, the Noble Consort Yi had told me I should go to see my family for a day or two. This was very thoughtful of her. I informed Mr Liu, who gave me my wages.

My little family was pleased to see me. I'd bought presents for my parents and the two children and a beautiful painted fan for Rose. Naturally, they wanted to know all about the Summer Palace, and I gave them detailed descriptions of everything I'd seen. My father was especially amazed at all the treasures I told him about.

'They must have a lot of soldiers to guard everything,' he said, 'or it'll get stolen.'

'First of all,' I reminded him, 'though there are a few soldiers at the guard post by the outer gates, they can't enter the Summer Palace precincts because they aren't eunuchs. Secondly, none of us would ever steal anything. It's unthinkable.'

'What are you talking about?' he said. 'What about the eunuchs who take bribes? Or the people like Mr Chen who take a cut out of every contract? Isn't that what you want to do?'

'That's totally different,' I told him. 'Those are the perquisites that go with the job. Everyone knows that.'

'I don't see much difference,' he said. 'It's still grabbing something for yourself.'

'You think I'd steal a work of art from the palace?' I cried. 'I'd sooner be dead.'

Of course, that's what he'd done, really, when he stole the lacquer box that got me in trouble in the first place. And he knew it. So perhaps I shouldn't have said it. That was disrespectful. But I didn't care.

'Well, we won't quarrel,' he said.

'No,' I said. 'We won't.' But that was the only unpleasantness during my visit home, I'm glad to say. I played with my little children; I spent a delightful night with my wife; and she said she hoped I would come back again soon.

I began to see the emperor and the Noble Consort Yi together quite often during those summer months. Perhaps because there was less business to occupy him, he quite often joined the parties on the nine islands, together with the empress, the Noble Consort Yi, and the other women of the court. He never spoke to me in person, but I could tell he knew who I was, and he even gave me a smile one evening while we were listening to music.

So was there trouble brewing between him and the Noble Consort?

Naturally, I watched them whenever I got the chance, but the Solstice came and went and I didn't see any sign of it. They seemed happy in each other's company, and I heard they quite often shared a bed.

As for his health, it was hard to say. Some days he looked a little better, some days he didn't. I wanted to ask how the state would be governed if something happened to him, but that's a dangerous question inside a palace, so I kept my curiosity to myself.

The only clue I did get came from old Mr Ma one morning. We were walking back from his tree nursery towards the eunuchs' quarters when a carriage drew up by the entrance to the Audience Hall. We bowed low when we saw the four figures that got out of it.

Every so often, some prince of the royal clan would come to see the emperor. Sometimes they'd join the evening party and stay overnight at one of the guest villas. There were quite a number of these princes, mostly the descendants of former emperors' brothers. Some of these cousinships went back centuries. Their exact rank depended on what great deeds their ancestors had done and their present importance in the office they held themselves.

The first two to get out of the carriage were the tall figure of Prince Sushun and his brother Prince Zheng, both royal clansmen and advisers of the emperor.

The second pair were two of the emperor's half-brothers, the princes Chun and Gong. For the emperor had several half-brothers by various concubines, all younger than he was.

Prince Chun was a very handsome young military officer, only twenty years old, I think, but just married to the Noble Consort Yi's sister – probably a shrewd career move on his part, though the young couple were already devoted to each other. He was mostly busy with his military duties and did not often come to court.

The one who counted was Prince Gong, who was nearly the same age as the emperor, though he had a different mother. He wasn't impressive to look at, and he had a little cicatrix on his cheek, from a boil that had been badly lanced, I believe. He had a high domed forehead, his eyes were set very wide apart, and he was wise for his years.

I'd seen Prince Gong a few times before. Not only was he close to the emperor, but there was a retired lady of the court he often came to visit who had quarters in a villa near the lake. She was yet another of his late father's imperial concubines, and when his own mother had died young, this lady had become like a second mother to him. He called her Auntie and was quite devoted to her.

Old Mr Ma wasn't looking at Prince Gong, though, but at Sushun and his brother. 'Here come the vultures,' he murmured. I think it was just a trick of the light, but Prince Sushun and his brother did look strangely like birds of prey just then.

'Are they so bad?' I whispered.

'Sushun's enormously rich,' said the old gardener, 'but he always wants more money. That's why he got himself put in charge of the treasury. People hate him.' He waited until they'd disappeared inside. 'It's a pity the last emperor died so early in life. Each emperor's quite free to choose his successor from amongst his sons, you know. Prince Gong, even as a boy, showed great promise as a future soldier and administrator. But his elder brother was a better scholar, so his father chose him. If he'd lived longer, he might have discovered the weakness of the elder boy's character and chosen Prince Gong instead.'

'If the emperor dies,' I ventured, for we were quite alone, 'could Prince Gong . . . ?'

'No. They made the rule a long time ago: the throne must always pass down a generation. Otherwise the royal brothers will start fighting each other. It's happened in the past.' He nodded. 'We must always learn from history.'

'Why did you call them vultures?'

'They all want power. The weaker the emperor, the more power they have over him. Rule by council, that's the trick. In that respect, even Prince Gong's no different. Did you know that he's taken a motto for himself? "No Private Heart." He means that he seeks only to serve, with no thought for himself.' He smiled. 'Do you believe that?'

'I don't know,' I said.

'He wants to rule from behind the throne. Actually, it might be a good thing if he did.'

'So if the emperor died, who'd be on the throne?' I whispered.

'Depends whom the emperor designates as his heir. Normally, he could select a grown-up nephew. But there aren't any yet. He could turn to a son of one of his royal cousins, I suppose, as long as it's the right generation. With all their consorts and concubines, most emperors produced lots of sons and grandsons, you know. Someone could be found.'

'What about the Noble Consort Yi's little boy?' I asked.

'Too young, wouldn't you say?'

I didn't answer. I was thinking, If the emperor dies and another prince is chosen, the Noble Consort Yi will be lucky to get a room in one of the villas. Perhaps something worse might happen to her. Either way, not good for me.

The Solstice came. In the old days it used to be a three-day holiday. It's just one day now. But it was very pleasant. The court ladies gave one another coloured fans and little sweet-scented sachets. The sachets, actually, were most useful in that residence between the lakes, since their smell kept the mosquitoes off.

And we all ate noodles. Down in the south, at the Solstice, they eat dog meat and lychees, both of which I dislike – another good reason not to live in the south, in my opinion.

Eight days after the Solstice, the Noble Consort Yi sent me home again for three whole days. When I returned, there was a full moon, and all of us, including the emperor, went out onto the bridges to the islands and gazed at the moon in the water as the twilight slowly turned to darkness. The best musician went out onto the lake in a boat and played the erhu. And although the crickets were making quite a noise, there was no wind, and we could hear every note. I shall always remember that.

The Solstice season was followed by twenty days of peace. Everyone seemed to be happy. The Lesser Heat was quite mild. But when the Greater Heat began, the humid air became oppressive. A storm was due, and we looked forward to the sense of release when it came.

The messenger who brought the bad news arrived an hour after dawn. The emperor and his family were supposed to visit the Island of Shrines that afternoon, and when we heard the news, we assumed the outing would be cancelled. But it wasn't. Perhaps the emperor wants to pray at the shrines, I thought.

Prince Gong was already at the Summer Palace, visiting the lady he called Auntie. So he was on hand. Prince Sushun and his brother were summoned from the city, together with three or four ministers. Mr Liu was also of the party. It looked as if the emperor meant to hold a council on the island.

As I say, the empress, several court ladies, and the Noble Consort Yi and her son had been expecting to go to the island. Whether the emperor forgot to change the order or he wanted them there, I do not know. But when they all appeared, just as he was setting off, he didn't send them away. And since the Noble Consort Yi had told me to be in attendance on her, I'd turned up, too. So I tagged along behind with the servants and tried not to attract the attention of Mr Liu. He soon saw me, of course, and shook his head in disbelief; but he didn't say anything.

The Island of Shrines lay in a cove at the north end of the lake. There was a Buddhist temple and a Taoist shrine there, and another handsome house for the Dragon King, sea lord and bringer of rain. The shrines were very beautiful, full of golden ornament, and the emperor visited them all and made offerings before any business was discussed.

But one other building on the island was rather odd. This was a bell-tower pagoda, three storeys high. Nothing strange about that, of course, except that one side of the second storey was entirely covered by a big round white clock face. I'd never seen such a thing on a building. It looked most peculiar, especially in a temple complex. And I was just staring at it when I found Mr Liu at my side.

'Ugly, isn't it?' he said.

'It's unusual, Mr Liu,' I said carefully.

'I will tell you how it got there,' he went on. 'Over a century ago, the Qianlong Emperor allowed a few of the barbarian priests to attend his court. These priests were called Jesuits. They had no wives, but they were quite well behaved and obedient. And they were surprisingly skilled in mathematics and painting – after their own fashion – and they knew a lot about geography. We've lost interest in geography since then, because it hardly seems relevant to our lives. But the Qianlong Emperor, who was a very great man, was always intrigued by every kind of knowledge. He even let the Jesuits visit the Summer Palace, and they made some paintings of him and his family.'

'I never knew that, Mr Liu,' I said.

'I daresay the Jesuits hoped the Qianlong Emperor would let them make converts in his empire. And since they worship Jesus, like the Taiping do, it's a good thing he didn't, because look at the trouble the Taiping have caused.'

'Your servant is very glad he didn't,' I replied warmly.

'He knew how to handle them.' Mr Liu gave a nod.

'How was that, sir?' I asked.

'With Chinese diplomacy. Rule number one: flatter the barbarian. Rule two: give him hope. Rule three: keep him waiting. Now the emperor admired some of their skills. Their clocks, for instance. So rather than let them erect a shrine to their god on the island here, he let them put a clock on the pagoda. Apparently it gave them great pleasure.'

'I think I can imagine it, sir,' I said with a laugh. 'Each time the emperor saw the priest he would say, "I was just out at the Island of Shrines, my dear fellow, and I can tell you that your excellent clock is still keeping perfect time." '

He gazed at me. 'You're quite amusing,' he remarked. 'I'll give you that.'

'May your humble servant ask,' I enquired, 'if the barbarian priests ever became impatient?'

'Perhaps. But the art is to be polite and treat them well so they have nothing to complain of. Then gradually, like a man in love with an unattainable woman, hope deferred acquires a beauty all its own.' He smiled. 'Our diplomacy towards the Jesuits worked just as efficiently as their clocks – though their clocks mark only the hours, while our diplomacy is told in centuries.'

'There are no Jesuits at the court now?'

'Not for a long time. They sneak into the kingdom occasionally, without permission, and try to convert the peasants in the hinterland; but usually we catch them and execute them. They've broken the law, after all.'

'Of course,' I agreed. 'They deserve it.'

Once the emperor had finished his devotions at the temples, everyone was told to attend upon him. There was a patch of ground in front of the pagoda, with a small pond just behind, which made a pretty setting, if you kept your eyes off the clock. The servants had placed a big chair for the emperor and some covered benches for the members of his court. When the Noble Consort Yi sat on her bench, I knelt on the ground just behind. Nobody really noticed me, though I could see most of them and hear everything.

It's strange: when the great lords of the world are discussing weighty matters, they never seem to worry about the servants being present. Maybe they trust us. Maybe they forget that we exist or think we're just part of the furniture. Or maybe they like an audience. Of course, if the emperor was thinking of killing his brother or something bad, I suppose he'd be private about it. But generally it's amazing what one can hear at court. I certainly heard everything that afternoon.

Though the emperor looked tired, he opened the discussion in quite a dignified voice. 'You have all heard the news. The British barbarian Lord Elgin is back. He comes with the French envoy, Baron Gros, who was also here before.' He turned to Prince Sushun. 'They are still at Hong Kong?'

'So we believe, Majesty. We imagine they will come north again.'

'How many troops did they bring?' the emperor wanted to know.

'British and French together, nearly twenty thousand.'

'That's quite a lot,' the emperor remarked. He seemed to wince when he said it – though whether it was on account of some pain in his body or the thought of the barbarian troops, I couldn't say. 'Could they breach our defences?'

'The best person to ask would be Mr Liu,' Prince Sushun said. And they all looked at the head eunuch.

I'd never seen Mr Liu put on the spot before, but I must say he handled it well. 'I can't claim to be a military expert,' he said in a decided manner, 'but as Your Majesty knows, I carried out a thorough inspection. Last year, when the barbarians attacked the forts, they were beaten back. Since then, the defences have been enlarged. There are miles of mud and barriers to cross. Even the barbarians' cannon will be of little use to them. Our officers would rather die than give way, and the troops are well under control. Any attempt on the forts will take a terrible toll on the barbarians – surely more than they can sustain.'

It was clever: he didn't actually promise victory, but you couldn't fault his facts.

The emperor nodded wearily. 'I wish someone would explain to me the true nature of these barbarians. Letters have been written to the British queen, but there has never been any reply. Are they trying to destroy our kingdom?' He looked around the circle of advisers. Neither Prince Sushun nor his brother answered. Mr Liu gazed at his feet. The faces of the other ministers were blank. None of them wished to commit himself. The emperor turned to Prince Gong. 'Well, Brother?'

Prince Gong wasn't afraid. Was there a hint of contempt in his eyes as he, too, gazed at his fellow counsellors? Perhaps. I wasn't sure.

'Your Majesty, I've spoken to everyone who has dealt with these people,' he answered firmly, 'and I am convinced: the barbarians from the West are interested in only one thing, and that is money. They want to trade. The ships and troops their rulers have provided are there only to smash anything or anyone that stands in the way of their making money.'

'Can their governments be so base?' the emperor asked.

'I have discovered something about their navies – especially the British, who are the most warlike. It seems that beyond a pittance to keep them alive, the sailors are paid by giving each a share of the value of the ships and treasure they can capture. That is their livelihood, from the greatest admiral to the humblest seaman.'

'So even their governments are pirates!'

'Exactly. It has been so for centuries. Consider also,' his brother went on, 'that each time we've tried to stop their evil opium trade, they've sent in gunboats, forced treaties on us, and demanded reparations so huge that even our treasury is sinking under the burden. Is this any different from the criminal gangs who, regrettably, exist in our own cities and who extort protection money from the townspeople?'

'It's the same,' said the emperor.

'Everything makes sense if we understand that their sole aims are trade, piracy and extortion.' Prince Gong paused. 'Yet strangely enough, this may be good news.'

'How so?'

'Because if money is their only interest, then they have no reason to destroy or take over our kingdom. And beyond the extortion that is the result of their greed, there has been no sign that their object is conquest. We have been afraid, for instance, that they will join with the Taiping. Yet despite the fact that they apparently share the Taiping's religion, they have made no attempt to form a joint army.' He looked around them with some satisfaction. 'I would even go further, Your Majesty. Since they worship nothing but money, I suspect we might be able to make the British serve us.'

'In what way?'

'Pay them to turn their cannon on the Taiping.'

'Well.' The emperor turned back to the others. 'What do you think of that?'

I wondered what they did think. There was a daring intelligence in what Prince Gong said. It was clear they didn't like that.

'I think we have to wait and see what the barbarians do,' Prince Sushun said.

'Wait and see,' said his brother.

'Wait and see,' said all the ministers.

Then the emperor turned to his wife the empress and asked her what she thought. I was surprised he did that, with all those men there.

'I'm sure I don't know,' the empress said sweetly. Actually, she'd have said that to almost any question you asked her. She was just telling the truth: she had no idea.

Then the emperor turned to the Noble Consort Yi, and I realised what he was doing. He'd asked the empress only out of politeness. It was the concubine he really wanted to hear.

From where I was kneeling, I could see her in profile. Her face was very calm. She bowed her head modestly. 'I venture an opinion only at Your Majesty's command,' she said quietly, and inclined her head again. She really was admirable. 'No one could doubt the wisdom of Prince Gong,' she began, 'but given all he has just said about the greed of the barbarians and how they will wage war to satisfy their lust for money, have we not also seen that this same quest leads the barbarians to take territory? They took Hong Kong. When they quarrelled with the governor down at Guangzhou, they threw him out and ruled the city – a major Chinese city! – as if they owned it. In the ports where we've allowed them to trade, they refuse to obey our laws. They want to set up alien states within our kingdom. So I ask myself, where will this lead? They may not want conquest, but they mean to take bites out of the empire wherever and whenever they please. And surely this is not desirable.'

I noticed several people were nodding. The emperor turned to Prince Gong. 'Well, Brother?' he said.

Prince Gong didn't look annoyed at all. I think he admired the Noble Consort Yi. 'I agree the barbarians will take all they can. But they can be controlled.'

The emperor considered for a moment. Then he sighed. 'I still think they may join the Taiping,' he said gloomily. We all waited. 'It's always the same. A dynasty rules for centuries, then things start to go wrong. Barbarians trouble the borders. Provincial generals rebel . . . The peasants revolt. There are famines and floods as the gods show their disapproval . . .'

'Many emperors face challenges,' said Prince Gong. 'But they can be overcome.'

'Everybody lies to me,' cried the emperor.

'I am not lying to you,' said Prince Gong quietly.

'My ancestors are looking down on me.'

'We must give them cause to be proud.'

There was a silence. We were all watching the emperor, but I'm not sure he cared.

'I am nothing to be proud of.' He sounded so sad. But it wasn't the sadness of wisdom. More childish, really. Nobody said anything. Then he started weeping.

This was the emperor of China. I stole a glance at the face of the Noble Consort Yi. She didn't even blink. Had she seen him cry before? I wondered if she felt pity for him. Perhaps she had at one time, but not by then, I suspect. She'd tried to make him more of a man and failed. Does a woman blame herself when her man ceases to be a man?

Not for long. She cannot. 'Your Majesty has held firm on the most critical matter of all,' she suddenly declared. They all looked at her. 'The kowtow! That is the most important thing.'

'Ah. Indeed.' Prince Gong was the first to react. She'd thrown them all a lifeline, to get out of their embarrassment. Prince Sushun and his brother saw it, too. 'Indeed,' they echoed.

'At least I haven't given way on that,' said the emperor, recovering himself.

Her timing was always wonderful. And taking advantage of the tide, so to speak, she rowed her boat forward. 'Your Majesty has never wavered. The kowtow is the symbol of the emperor's authority that not only your subjects but the envoys of all other kingdoms use in your presence. Abandon the kowtow, and we as good as say that our authority is at an end.'

'This cannot be denied.' The emperor nodded.

'Will Your Majesty allow me to say, then,' she gently pursued, 'that one of the reasons I believe that the Western barbarians – even the American barbarians, who generally seem to be more courteous and less immoral than the others – want to undermine and destroy our empire is that they steadfastly refuse this sign of respect that has been given to emperors since time began. It is a deliberate insult that all the world will come to hear about. All the subject kingdoms. All our own people. It effectively says that the authority of the emperor is denied. That truly will be the beginning of the end. And these barbarians must know it. Therefore I say they have come here to destroy us.'

She has to be right, I thought. What else could it mean? I think everyone who heard her thought so, too, even Prince Gong.

'They must kowtow,' the emperor said firmly. 'They must come peacefully, without arms, up to Beijing and be received in the usual way. If they refuse to behave, they will be stopped at the forts.'

The conference ended. I'm not sure any action had really been decided, but the emperor had made it sound as if it had. I noticed that above us, grey clouds were moving in, with shafts of yellow light falling between them. And I remember looking at the emperor. He'd turned his eyes up towards the sky, and the yellow light showed all the lines of strain on his pale face. He just kept staring upwards, for so long that I could even detect the movement of the minute hand on that stupid barbarian clock on the pagoda.

I didn't see him again for almost a month. Some days he'd be closeted with officials in the Audience Hall. He'd also taken to visiting the islands alone. But I knew he was still spending time with the Noble Consort Yi, and that was all that mattered to me.

It was very quiet at the Summer Palace. Everyone was sleepy in the humid weather.

As for the barbarians, they didn't seem to be making much progress. One morning, on my way to the Noble Consort, I met Mr Liu. He was feeling so pleased with himself that he even smiled at me. 'The barbarians are stuck in the mud,' he announced, 'just as I predicted.'

'You were right, sir,' I said with a bow. 'Your humble servant rejoices.'

But a day later, I heard that they were still advancing on the forts. Slowly and painfully, but they weren't giving up.

Not long after this, I was with the Noble Consort Yi when Prince Gong looked in. 'Two of the smaller coastal forts have fallen,' he said glumly.

'Our men ran away?' Her face was anxious.

'No, they fought like fiends. It wasn't the men. It's their guns. The barbarians' rifles load so much faster, and they're so much more accurate, that before our poor fellows can get off a volley, half of them have been mown down. I'm off to tell the emperor now.'

The next morning I asked the Noble Consort how the emperor had taken the news.

'With perfect calmness,' she said. But I didn't really believe her.

And we had to wait only a few days before we heard: the barbarians had smashed all the forts, and the road to Beijing was open before them.

How could it have happened? That's what everyone wanted to know. How had the barbarians been able to get through the miles of mud and bamboo spikes and walls and all the rest? Naturally, all eyes were on Mr Liu. He'd told the emperor it couldn't happen.

I almost felt sorry for him. But I must say, he knew how to fight with his back to the wall.

During the main battle, it seemed, a shot from the barbarian cannon had blown up one of our gunpowder magazines. The damage had been catastrophic. Mr Liu seized on this. 'It's nobody's fault,' he cried to anyone who'd listen. 'Who could have foreseen such a thing?' He even told me: 'You should explain this to the Noble Consort Yi.' He must be scared, I thought, if he's coming to me for help. When I told her, she just nodded, and I told Mr Liu.

'Good,' he said. 'Good.' I could see the *thank you* forming on his lips, but he thought better of it and just said, 'You did right.'

He wasn't much blamed, as it happened. I think everyone wanted to believe him.

I asked the Noble Consort Yi about the emperor again.

This time she answered: 'He is very upset.'

'Not with you, I hope,' I blurted out.

'With everybody,' she said.

At first Lord Elgin and Baron Gros, with the main British and French forces, stayed down at the forts they'd captured and sent patrol boats up to the depot at the head of the canal – which was only a dozen miles from the walls of Beijing. Meanwhile, the emperor's envoys went to Elgin. But instead of receiving them politely, he told them: 'Give us everything we want, including compensation, or it's war.'

At the Summer Palace, ministers were arriving every day with memorials telling the emperor how to destroy the barbarians, but they always came out of the Audience Hall muttering the same thing: 'The emperor's dithering.'

Then, one morning, I arrived as usual to find the Noble Consort in a sunny mood. Except for a single servant, kneeling in a corner, she was alone, sitting at a table inlaid with mother-of-pearl and sipping tea. She was dressed in green silk, I remember, with a flowered hair comb. Her face was serene, and she smiled at me as I bowed.

'You look happy today, my lady,' I said.

'I am, Lacquer Nail,' she replied.

'May your lowly servant enquire the reason?' I asked.

'His Majesty has made a great decision,' she told me. 'The orders are going out this very moment. Since the barbarians have no manners and understand nothing but brute force, there will be no more talk. The emperor is ordering our armies to exterminate them.'

'That is wonderful news,' I said.

'I think so, too.' She inclined her head. 'I was most pleased when the emperor told me.'

And it was probably you, my lady, who made him do it, I thought to myself.

The decree was sent out to all the provinces. It was excellent. Firm government action at last. It also offered rewards: fifty taels for the head of one of the dark-skinned troops the British had brought from India, and a hundred for the head of a white barbarian. That should bring Lord Elgin to his senses, I supposed.

But it didn't. The next thing we heard, he was marching up to Beijing himself, saying he'd knock down the walls.

I was due to pay a visit to my family just then, and with twenty thousand barbarians approaching Beijing, I was anxious we should discuss what they should do. Permission was granted, as long as I stayed away only one night.

They were pleased to see me. I brought them money. And while my mother and Rose prepared the evening meal, I had a talk with my father. 'Maybe you should get out of the city,' I said.

But he shook his head. 'We're safer inside,' he answered.

'Lord Elgin's threatening to knock the walls down,' I told him.

'He's bluffing,' said my father. 'They've left their heavy cannon downriver. They're only bringing light field pieces up here. You couldn't make a dent in the walls with those.'

'How do you know they've left the big guns behind?'

'Every sailor and barge man on the canal knows it. I've been talking to them.'

'Assuming you're right, what then?'

'Let them come. We've ten men to every one of theirs. We've got our own cannon, and the walls here are much bigger. They'll be stuck outside, in the middle of enemy territory. In two months it'll be winter. If they don't starve, they'll freeze.'

'Why have they come then? Are they stupid?'

'They're gambling that if they race up to Beijing, we'll panic. If we don't, they'll pull back.'

Just for once, I thought the old man might be right. At least, I hoped so. The next morning I went back to the Summer Palace, and who should I see but Mr Liu. He was quite friendly, and I told him what my father had said.

'Your father is a wise man. That is exactly what I think. We should let Elgin and his troops get as close as they like, then trap them. They'll never get home alive.'

As the British and French drew closer and closer to Beijing, couriers were still arriving at the Summer Palace every hour with messages from prefects, magistrates and governors urging the emperor to stand firm. All this advice seemed to have affected the emperor, because he suddenly announced he was planning to lead the troops himself.

There was a whole division of bannermen, our best men, just below the city, right across the barbarians' path, and with orders to annihilate them. Some were infantry with muskets. But the main force were the best of the Manchu cavalry. It might be old-fashioned warfare, but these mounted bowmen could loose their arrows so fast you could hardly believe it; and those arrows had a longer range than a musket ball. The barbarian troops had never faced this sort of cavalry on open ground before. They were in for a shock. Meanwhile, their patrols and ours were edging closer to each other every day. There was sure to be some kind of fight soon. We all thought so.

I was with the Noble Consort Yi when one of the court ladies came rushing in. 'We've captured thirty or forty barbarians – in a skirmish,' she told us excitedly.

'What sort of barbarians?' the Noble Consort demanded.

'At least one of their negotiators. A dozen are being sent here for us to see.'

They arrived at the Summer Palace that afternoon. We all turned out to look at them, of course. It wouldn't have been dignified for the emperor to appear, but there's a little pagoda beside his quarters, and the Noble Consort told me that he'd gone up there and watched them from a distance with a telescope.

I've always had difficulty telling one barbarian from another. Some are tall, some are short. They're all hairy. But it was very gratifying to see these arrogant villains in chains. After we'd all had a chance to laugh at them, they were carted off to gaol in the House of Corrections. They wouldn't have had a very good time there. The dungeons are full of rats and lice, and there's a poisonous maggot that can kill you. Serve them right, I thought.

Soon after this, we heard that a force of French and British troops was moving on the city and that they were furious we'd got the hostages. But in order to reach the city they'd have to cross a bridge and come face-to-face with that Manchu division drawn up there.

'That's where we'll destroy them,' everyone agreed. 'There's no way they'll get through. We outnumber them five to one.'

With all this encouraging news, I wasn't surprised that the emperor decided he'd go out to the lake islands that evening.

He chose the small, sheltered island that contained the Temple of Universal Peace – on the principle, I suppose, that as soon as Elgin was crushed, peace should be the order of the day. The temple, which stood in a pond, had a very unusual shape – for its floor plan was in the form of a cross with an extension at a right angle on the end of each arm. This was the character we call 'wan,' which signifies the peaceful Heart of Buddha. I've heard that the Western barbarians call this sort of cross a swastika, though I believe in their lands the extensions point the other way. In any case, the Temple of Universal Peace was a pleasant place to relax and watch the moon at any time of year.

Naturally, I wanted to be one of the party if I could. So I stood at a spot where I knew the emperor and his entourage would pass. If the Noble Consort saw me and gave me a nod, I could fall in behind. And sure enough she did.

Besides the empress, the Noble Consort Yi, her son, and several court ladies, Prince Sushun and his brother were in the company; also a few officials, who'd come out to the Summer Palace to urge the emperor to stand fast; and Mr Liu, together with a dozen other eunuchs, including me. One of the court ladies, I remember, was Prince Gong's auntie. Prince

Gong himself wasn't there, because he'd gone down to keep an eye on the barbarians at the bridge.

The long corridors of the temple had spaces for many shrines, looked after by a few elderly monks. In the central crossing, the bodhisattva Guanyin, made of precious woods plated with gold, sat on a lotus throne. She had more than forty hands and eyes. They say Guanyin hears all the sounds of the world. And if she does, then you might think it would make her angry or despairing; but the priests say her compassion knows no end.

After we had prayed before her and lit candles, we gathered in one of the temple's outer arms, and a lady musician played the pipa to entertain us. She played an ancient piece called 'Ambushed from Ten Sides', which was a good choice, considering what was going on just a few miles to the south, and the emperor told her to play it again. When she finished, we sat in the warm silence. Outside, the evening sky was still pale blue and pink, and I caught sight of the half-moon. Everything seemed so perfect at this temple on the water that you could quite imagine the whole world was at peace. And I remember that, just at that moment, everyone was smiling – including even the emperor.

So nobody even noticed that Prince Gong had quietly entered the room until he spoke. 'Majesty, the barbarians have broken through.'

Prince Gong was visibly shaken. And he blamed himself. 'We'd seen what happened downriver at the forts,' he said. 'But they had heavier cannon down there, and I thought that with our best cavalry, who are highly mobile, waiting for them on open ground, as well as the infantry with muskets, they'd take so many casualties that they'd retreat. Now I know better. Bravery is useless. Our men never wavered. But the French rifles and British guns cut them to pieces. It was terrible to see.'

'With your permission, Majesty,' one of the mandarins quietly offered, 'a skirmish on open ground is one thing, but the walls of Beijing are another.'

We all looked at the emperor. He was staring into the middle distance, as if he were in another world. 'If they took the forts, why wouldn't they take Beijing?' His voice was dull, almost mechanical.

'Their rifles won't help them against the city walls,' said Prince Gong. 'And if they did get in, no general would risk his army inside a huge city where every man, woman and child could slit their throats. Now they're at Beijing, they'll want to negotiate.'

'If we negotiate,' asked Prince Sushun bleakly, 'what other cards have we in our hands?'

'The forty men we have hostage,' said Prince Gong. 'Both British and French. They'll want them safely back.'

'They'll bargain for forty prisoners?' Prince Sushun frowned in disbelief.

'I think so. The barbarians care more about their men's lives than their countries' honour.'

'Doesn't that show they are weak?' the Noble Consort Yi demanded.

'Perhaps,' said Prince Gong. 'But it helps us.'

I was sitting on a low bench just behind the Noble Consort. I could smell the jasmine scent she'd used that day. She was sitting very straight, wearing a pale green silk dress.

I heard an owl outside. The owls at the Summer Palace often used to cry before the sun went down. It was a mournful sound.

Then the emperor turned to Mr Liu. 'We shall go to the Hunting Palace. Make it ready.'

'The Hunting Palace, Sire?' Mr Liu was taken aback. 'North of the Wall?'

'Is there another?'

'Sire, it needs repair . . .'

'We can repair it when we get there.'

'Brother,' Prince Gong burst out, 'you promised to lead the troops in person. Not that you actually need to do it. But if you leave Beijing now, you'll start a panic.' Prince Gong was always so careful to address his brother with deference when there were other people around; so it just showed how shocked he must have been to forget himself like that.

'You have failed to understand,' said the emperor. It was meant to be dignified. 'It is beneath the emperor's dignity to take notice of these insolent barbarians. Tell Lord Elgin it is the custom for the emperor to hunt at this time of year. The court arrangements cannot be altered for a bandit like himself. Tell him also that at my hunting lodge I often welcome my friends, the forty-eight Mongol princes of the steppe. I have only to raise my hand and they will bring three hundred thousand Mongol horsemen down to Beijing and slaughter every Frenchman and Englishman they find. Elgin should mind his manners.'

I could see from the expression on Prince Gong's face that this was all nonsense. 'You wish me to remain here?' he said grimly.

'Since you are so confident you can handle these barbarians, you will remain in charge of Beijing. No doubt by the time I return you will have settled everything.'

That's strange, I thought to myself. Our ancestors built the Great Wall to protect us from the north, and now the emperor's running to the other side of it to hide from barbarians coming from the south. Everything's topsy-turvy.

I looked around the emperor's party. Apart from the empress, whose face was blank because I don't suppose the dear creature was thinking anything, they all seemed horrified.

Except Prince Sushun. He still looked like a bird of prey, but he smiled.

'Your Majesty is right,' he said smoothly. 'Let us wear the barbarians down. The added distance between the Son of Heaven and Beijing will provide a useful excuse whenever Prince Gong wishes to delay negotiations.'

The emperor nodded gratefully and looked quite pleased with himself.

But it was the Noble Consort I was watching now. She had wonderful self-control. If she was angry and hiding it, people would never guess. But I could tell.

There were two little giveaways. First, a tiny vein would start to throb on her right temple. That meant she was getting annoyed. The second was a faint flush around the back of her neck. Once I saw that, I knew she was really angry.

I'd noticed the vein when the emperor first mentioned the hunting lodge. But by the time he'd finished his excuses for running away, the back of her neck was red.

'I do not understand,' she began coldly. The moment I heard her tone of voice, I knew we were in for trouble. 'If you run away in front of all your people, they'll say you care nothing for your empire.' The fact it was true only made it worse. Everyone heard. A few glanced at her, but it was the emperor their eyes were fixed upon.

She's got to stop, I thought. Because I saw where this was going. A wife can be angry with her husband in public and it can all blow over. Even a weak man like the emperor can forgive a fit of rage. But if she humiliates him in front of others, she'll live to regret it.

I couldn't speak, of course, so I did the only thing I could think of. I leaned forward and tugged the side of her robe. Nobody saw, but she felt it. She twitched her head, just the smallest bit, to let me know she was aware of the interruption, and her hand reached down and jerked the robe back up, to let me know to stop.

The emperor had given a little start when she spoke. But he forced a smile.

'The Noble Consort Yi has the true warrior spirit of the Manchu. But an emperor has to be wise as well. And she must learn discretion.'

I couldn't fault his reply. It just showed, if circumstances had been different, he might have had the makings of a ruler.

But she wasn't having it. I've often wondered since if perhaps she'd had some private disagreement with him earlier in the day that she was still brooding about. Who knows? Whatever the reason, she wasn't going to take any more from him.

'Have you no shame? Have you no pride? Do you care nothing for your ancestors or the royal house?'

'We have heard enough!' the emperor cried. 'The Noble Consort will be silent.'

I wanted to whisper to her. I'd have gladly shouted: 'Keep your mouth shut! Save yourself – if it's not too late!' But I couldn't. So I did the only thing left. I reached forward and tugged at her robe again, really hard this time. I saw her shoulders go up in rage. Her head turned sharply. Then she slapped her hand down, hard as she could, on mine. I felt her fingernails cut like knives into the flesh on the back of my hand.

And I heard the brittle crack, loud as a pair of woodblocks clapped together, as her long lacquered nails snapped. She raised her hand and saw the broken fingernails. I glanced at my own hand and saw the thin red lines of blood. She turned right around to stare at me, and I saw a look of venomous rage that I had never seen before. It was terrifying. It was not hatred, mind you. Not hatred, only rage.

'Look at what you've made me do!' she screamed. 'Get out! Get out!'

I didn't know how to move. You can't withdraw from the emperor's presence without his permission. I half rose in obedience to her, but looked at him for a sign. In the awful silence I stayed like that, in a stooped position, like an idiot.

Then the emperor solved my problem for me. He turned to Mr Liu. 'That eunuch is to be taken away and flogged at once,' he said.

Mr Liu did it himself. He took his time. Two other eunuchs stripped my bottom naked and held me spread-eagled on the ground. Then he laid into me with the broad split bamboo we call the *banzi*. If it hadn't been Mr Liu I should have screamed with the pain. But I would not give him the satisfaction, though I did think I might faint.

Actually, the punishment could have been worse. It was the standard beating any eunuch might receive for bad behaviour. After all, they wanted you to be able to get back to work in a few days. My humiliation was terrible, of course. It must have given Mr Liu a great deal of pleasure. The whole palace would have known about it by the following day. My sponsor, Mr Chen. Everybody. 'Lacquer Nail broke the Noble Consort's fingernails. In front of the emperor! Who told Mr Liu to flog him. What a comedown.' How they'd mock me. 'Lacquer Nail's finished,' they'd say. And I supposed they were probably right.

I stayed in my little room all the next day. I didn't feel up to leaving it. An old orderly arrived during the morning to give me a washdown and apply some lotions to my backside. A junior eunuch came in at midday and again in the evening to bring me food. Neither of them spoke more than a few words, and I didn't try to engage them in conversation. I just spent most of the time lying facedown on my bed and resting.

But the next morning I decided I really had to face the general mockery and find out what was going on. Had the Noble Consort Yi dismissed me forever? Was she herself in disgrace? Where were the barbarians and what were they doing? And I was all ready to leave my room when the door opened, and in walked Mr Liu. He seemed quite friendly.

'I've good news and bad,' he announced. 'I'll give you the bad news first. The Noble Consort Yi is finished. The emperor won't let her in the room with him.'

'You said it would happen,' I answered.

'True. But her fall is not quite as complete as I expected. The emperor feels that she should continue to look after the boy – who could still become the future emperor. Therefore she is to travel with the rest of the court to the hunting grounds.'

'So he's still running away, north of the Great Wall?'

'Of course. Prince Gong will remain here.'

'May I ask you something, sir?' I said. 'I was very shocked when Prince Sushun encouraged the emperor to make a run for it. Can he really have believed it was the right course of action?'

'Certainly he did,' Mr Liu replied. 'It's true, of course, that Prince Sushun means to keep close with the emperor. He's delighted that Prince Gong is left here to negotiate. If Prince Gong fails, regrettable though that would be, then his star will fade – and that of Prince Sushun will shine more brightly. If, on the other hand, Prince Gong succeeds, it will be good for the empire, but the emperor will secretly hate Prince Gong for showing him up. That's good for Prince Sushun, too.' He paused. 'There is, however, a further consideration. Prince Sushun is a patriot. And he is convinced that there will only be chaos here in Beijing unless we can get the emperor as far away as possible. He told me so himself.'

'So whatever happens,' I remarked, 'he looks good.'

'The greatest and most difficult art in government,' said Mr Liu with satisfaction, 'is to keep a clear conscience.'

'I see,' I mumbled.

'You have not asked for the good news,' he continued. 'Which is that you are to go to the hunting lodge yourself. With the Noble Consort Yi.'

'She has forgiven me?' I cried.

'She is distressed about what happened to you. Says it's her fault.'

'Perhaps I can fix her broken nails,' I said eagerly.

'You'll have to wait for them to grow again. She already had them cut short.' He smiled. 'Not even you could have repaired them.'

'And what about the barbarians, sir?'

'Still south of the city. Threatening. We hold their hostages. I expect there'll be more fighting and more negotiating. It may go on for weeks. But we shall both be north of the Great Wall.' He gazed at me steadily. 'Which brings me to your orders. They come directly from the Noble Consort and must be obeyed exactly.'

'Of course,' I said.

'You are to go home this evening and spend three days with your family. You may not see them for some time to come. Here are your wages and a little more, which you should give them. After that time, and not before, you are to report back here. Some of the baggage will be leaving in the next few days, and I shouldn't be surprised if the emperor leaves, too. But the Noble Consort Yi and her son will not be departing until later, and she wishes you to accompany them in person. Is that clearly understood?'

I made a small grimace.

'What's the matter?' he asked sharply.

'I was wondering how to explain the state of my backside to my wife,' I told him.

'Please don't bother me with details,' he replied.

At home, I spent happy hours with my children; and although I winced a few times when I was sitting down, I told them I had twisted my back, and no one thought anything about it. As for Rose, I pretended I wasn't feeling well, so we just slept, and I was able to hide my condition from her. I noticed she was putting on a little more weight. Eating too much, I daresay.

The second day, my father went out for a while, and when he got back, he said, 'The emperor left town yesterday.'

'I expect he did,' I said.

'I heard the whole court went with him,' he went on. 'Are you sure the Noble Consort didn't go, too?'

'You don't understand,' I told him. 'The emperor doesn't want her anywhere near him.'

'Is it such a good idea for you to serve her, then?' he asked me.

'It would be a worse idea if I didn't,' I replied.

'Well,' he said, 'if Prince Gong's in charge, he's going to have a difficult time. Everyone's panicking because the emperor's run off. The troops are saying they haven't been paid. Not even their rice rations. I wouldn't be surprised if they deserted.'

'Perhaps we should get you away from Beijing,' I said.

'Where would we go?' my father replied. 'And even if twenty thousand barbarian troops did get into Beijing, the population's so huge, I doubt they'd be much of a danger to us.'

Come to that, I thought, my father would be sure to find some way to make himself useful to the barbarians, just as he did with everyone else.

I was up before dawn on the day I was due back, and though I was sorry to leave my family, I was quite excited by the thought of the adventure north of the Great Wall.

The city gates were open. The guards seemed half asleep. One would never have guessed there was a barbarian army just a few miles away as I made my way along the lane that led to the Summer Palace. When I finally reached the entrance, I could hear the sentry in the guardhouse snoring, which I didn't think much of, because the sky was getting light.

But I walked in and made my way around the Front Lake towards the eunuchs' quarters, passing the enclosure where Mr Ma kept his penzai trees. He wasn't there yet.

I don't know what I'd expected to find at that hour: a few early risers; a line of carts loaded up and ready to leave? Something, anyway. But all I saw were the silent pavilions. They were beautiful, of course, with their curving roofs floating over the mist on the lake behind. But somehow they looked sad and empty.

I went straight to the entrance of the eunuchs' quarters and turned into the main passage. The first thing I saw was the big ornamental sword in its usual place on the wall, with its hilt gleaming on account of all the rubies. That cheered me up.

And then what should I see but Mr Ma coming up the passage towards me. 'I wondered where you were,' he said.

'With my family,' I answered. 'I'm going north with the Noble Consort Yi today.'

'I don't think you are,' he said. 'She left three days ago with the emperor.'

'How can that be?' I said. 'Where's Mr Liu? I need to speak to him.'

'He left three days ago with all the rest,' said Mr Ma. 'They all went together. He left Shaking Leaf in charge. Everyone was looking for you,' he added. 'Mr Liu said you must have deserted. The Noble Consort was furious. She told him she never wanted to see you again.'

'But he told me she wouldn't be leaving until today,' I protested, 'and that I was to go and see my family in the meantime.'

The old man stared at me silently. 'So he's had his revenge,' he said quietly. 'I told you he would. Got your hopes up and then destroyed you.'

I realised it even before he finished. You had to admire Mr Liu. He could mask his feelings completely and bide his time. But when he struck, he was implacable.

'I'll go after them,' I said.

'That won't do you any good,' Mr Ma told me. 'They're already three days away.'

'Yes, but with all the baggage carts, they won't be going very fast,' I pointed out. 'Maybe I can catch them up.'

'And then what?'

'I'll tell the Noble Consort what really happened.'

He thought for a moment. 'Did anyone see you arrive?' he asked. I told him no. ‘Then come with me quickly,’ he said. ‘We’ve got to get you out of sight.’

It didn’t take long before we were inside the enclosure where he kept his trees.

‘What’s all this about?’ I asked.

‘Mr Liu’s given orders that as soon as you arrive, you’re to be arrested.’

‘For what?’

‘Absconding. Desertion. You’ll be kept in gaol until the court returns. That could be months. And he’s put out orders that you’re to be arrested if you’re seen on the road or in the city.’

‘What shall I do?’ I asked.

‘I suggest, at this moment, that you hide in the park here. Don’t let a soul see you. Wait until dark, then come back here, and we’ll make a plan.’

As I didn’t see any other option, I did as he said. It wasn’t too difficult to hide. The park was huge and hardly anyone was about. After darkness fell, I made my way back to Mr Ma’s enclosure. He had plenty of news.

‘Poor Shaking Leaf. When you didn’t appear this morning, he sent three eunuchs to your house to find you. Naturally, they learned that you’d gone to the Summer Palace. So he looked around and couldn’t find you. He was in a terrible flap. “Where can he be?” he says to me. I should think it’s obvious, I told him. He probably discovered on his way that none of the court is left here, so he’s gone racing up the road to the Great Wall to try and catch them. “But he’ll be arrested,” Shaking Leaf protests. But he doesn’t know that, I reminded him. I bet you that’s where he’s gone.’

‘That’s what I was going to do,’ I said.

‘Exactly. And he looked quite relieved, because he wouldn’t have to arrest you and guard you for months himself. He told me something else, too. When the royal party reaches the Great Wall, Mr Liu is going to order the guards to arrest you at once if you show up there.’

‘He thinks of everything,’ I muttered.

‘Well,’ Mr Ma continued, ‘I’ll tell you where I think you could hide.’

‘Where’s that?’

‘Here at the Summer Palace.’ His old eyes gleamed at me. ‘When you think about it: most of the court’s gone. One or two of the old palace ladies are left behind, and a small staff of eunuchs, including me and the gardeners. But that's all. There's no business being done here. No entertaining, no concerts. We've got the whole park almost to ourselves.'

'I'd like a roof over my head,' I replied.

'You could install yourself on one of the islands. Not the Island of Shrines – there are some priests on it. But most of the islands are deserted. I'd let you know if the gardeners were coming your way. And I can bring you food every day or two. There's plenty of food.' He smiled at me. 'You can live like a scholar hermit for a while. Perhaps it will suit you.'

We discussed the islands. I liked the Apricot Blossom Spring Villa, with its orchard and steep hill; and I could see myself in one of the little villas around the lotus pond on the curious island known as Lianxi's Wonderland. Both of them were quiet, out-of-the-way places where you could hide. But it was the Peony Terrace, the closest island of all, almost opposite the emperor's private residence, that we finally decided upon.

'It's really a spring and summer retreat,' Mr Ma explained, 'and with the emperor away, the gardeners don't bother with it for the moment.' I also liked the fact it was easy for Mr Ma to get to, when he wanted to bring me food or news.

So after sharing a little food with me, he led me through the darkness to the Peony Terrace.

I believe the period that followed was one of the happiest of my life. Partly it was the beauty of the place. The peonies had already been trimmed back for autumn by the time I got there, and I must say I was glad it wasn't summer, since if you were actually living out there, the heady fragrance of some of those rich, double-globed flowers might have been altogether too much of a good thing.

The fact remained, here I was, the sole inhabitant of the emperor's most gorgeous garden in the paradise of the Yuanmingyuan, in perfect peace and safety. It has to be fate, I thought, that no matter what disasters befall me, I am lifted up and surrounded, time and again, with the finer things of life. The sixth emperor of the Manchu dynasty, the present emperor's glorious forebear, used to retire to the Peony Terrace to write poetry – for which he had great talent. I wondered whether, had my education proceeded further, I might have done the same. But I'd probably have been too busy smelling the peonies.

Each time Mr Ma came, he'd bring me news. 'The barbarians are still camped just to the south,' he told me on the second day. 'They say the

French are a bit closer, with the British farther behind them, waiting for reinforcements. It's easy to tell which is which. The French uniforms are blue and the British red. There have been a few skirmishes, nothing more.'

A couple of days later, he explained that the French were angry on account of one of their priests who'd been killed in a skirmish and thrown in the canal.

Meanwhile, Lord Elgin wanted the hostages back and Prince Gong wouldn't give them up unless Elgin promised to go away. Some days it seemed like a stalemate, but on other days there were signs that the situation couldn't go on. Our troops were close to mutiny, the old man told me. People were starting to flee the city. I was sure my father wouldn't be one of them.

I'd been there some time when Mr Ma turned up chuckling. 'I have good news today,' he announced. 'You're dead.'

'I am?' I said.

'Shaking Leaf's had a couple of palace people making enquiries after you – just to protect himself from Mr Liu, I should think. When nobody could find you and you never turned up at the Great Wall, one of the searchers told Shaking Leaf that he thought you were dead. I expect he said it because he was bored with looking for you. But Shaking Leaf wants to believe it. So now the word is that you're dead, and I've no doubt that in another day or two Shaking Leaf will believe it himself. You know how these things go.'

'Well,' I replied with a laugh, 'it's better being dead in the Peony Terrace than it ever was being alive in the kitchens.'

Shortly after that, Lord Elgin declared he was going to knock down the walls of the city and destroy it. 'I doubt he could do that, Mr Ma,' I said.

'Perhaps not,' he agreed, 'but it's frightening the inhabitants. Even more of them are leaving.'

One evening, Mr Ma told me that two of the more important hostages had been transferred to better quarters. 'I hear that most of the hostages are in terrible shape after starving with the rats in prison,' Mr Ma said. 'It looks to me as if Prince Gong's fattening these two up before returning them.'

'It must mean he wants to talk,' I suggested. 'Where are the British now?' I asked.

'In the same place.'

'And the French?'

'Wandering about. Bored. Looking for loot, I should think.'

And during all these days, from the emperor and his court north of the Great Wall, we heard not a word.

It began so quietly. The first thing I heard, coming from beside the emperor's residence, was a low voice laughing and another speaking, just like two people having a quiet conversation. I supposed they were gardeners and hoped they wouldn't discover me. But the sound of their voices retreated, and for a few moments there was silence.

Then there were shouts, farther off. Not angry shouts. More like cries of joy. Next I heard something breaking, quite nearby. It had to be in the emperor's residence. What could be going on?

I started across the footbridge that led from the island to the shore.

You may wonder why I didn't hide. I couldn't say for certain. Curiosity, as far as I remember. Like most people, I always go towards the action.

They were scattered all over the place: small knots of men. French troops. I could tell by their uniforms. Every moment more were streaming in from the entrance. They may have wandered into the Yuanmingyuan without even knowing what it was. Whatever officers came with them were doing nothing to hold the men back. I don't suppose they could have. Their men had scented loot. And there were still two hours of daylight left.

As I ran along the side of the emperor's residence, some of the barbarians were already coming out, carrying jewellery, watches, bronze figures, even a small golden Buddha.

You can imagine how I felt: how dare these savages smash their way into paradise, commit sacrilege, and lay their hands on the treasures of the Celestial Kingdom?

Those who appreciate the finer things of life need our own army. We'd know what to do with vermin of this kind. That's what I was thinking.

I could see a group of palace people gathered at the main entrance to the residence trying to keep the hooligans out. One of them had got a pike from somewhere; another had a garden fork. The rest had only brooms or kitchen knives. But they were fighting.

It's important to remember that. People often think of the palace eunuchs as simpering weaklings, but it's not true. The palace people fought as bravely as any soldiers.

I must get a weapon, I thought, and I was wondering where to find one when I suddenly remembered that jewelled sword inside the entrance to the eunuchs' quarters. So I ran across and I took it down. It was quite heavy, and the rubies on the hilt bit into my hand, but the blade was sharp. So back I went with it.

I wasn't afraid. It was pretty obvious the barbarians had only one idea in their minds – grab as much loot as they could and make off with it. So if we made it too hot for them in one place, there was a good chance they'd move on and try another. With luck, we might be able to keep them out of the emperor's quarters.

And I was only fifty yards from those brave fellows defending the doorway when I saw a sight that almost made my heart stop. A single figure running out from another pavilion. With one arm he was carrying a rich plum-coloured robe; in his other hand he held a splendid head comb encrusted with gems. Even at a distance I couldn't fail to recognise them. They belonged to the Noble Consort Yi herself. The robe was the very one she'd been wearing the first time I ever came into her presence.

I forgot everything. I wasn't even thinking. I was just running, so fast it felt as if I were flying. Blind rage, fury, yes, love, carried me forward, and when I got to him, I plunged that ceremonial sword into his belly. He let out a scream. I pulled the sword out and drove it in again with all my force as he went down. I did it for the Noble Consort and the Celestial Kingdom.

Then I tore her robe and the comb from his hands, seized the sword again, and left him quivering in his death throes as I ran towards the Noble Consort's quarters. I half expected some of the barbarians to chase after me. But if they did, they'd given up before I got to her rooms.

And who should I find there but Shaking Leaf.

I think he'd just walked in there. I'm not sure he even realised what was going on. So when he saw me burst in there with a bloody sword, it must have been a shock.

He blinked, his mouth fell open, and he went deathly pale. He stared at me in terror. Did he think I was going to attack him?

'I am sorry, Lacquer Nail,' he cried. 'I'm sorry for all the bad things that were done to you. It wasn't my fault. You know that. It was all Mr Liu.' I didn't say anything. I was just staring at him. 'Zhong Kui, protect me,' he suddenly cried.

And then I understood. Since Zhong Kui is the demon who frightens off evil spirits, Shaking Leaf must have thought I was a ghost. A hungry ghost, as they're the only ones who can take on human form.

'The only hungry ghosts are the barbarians who are looting the place,' I cried. But he wasn't taking it in. Let him believe I'm a ghost, then, I thought. 'Grab all the valuables that belong to Noble Consort Yi,' I told him, 'and hide them. Quick, quick.'

'At once,' he said, and started gathering things up.

'Hide them well,' I shouted.

It's amazing that I was ordering the senior eunuch around like that, but I felt I had the right to. After all, I'd just killed a man for stealing her robe.

I left Shaking Leaf to his work and went back outside. The French looters were fanning out all over the place. Obviously I couldn't fight them all. I didn't want to go back to Shaking Leaf, who at some point would figure out I wasn't a ghost. I thought of old Mr Ma. I didn't imagine the barbarians wanted to run off with his trees. The best thing's to stay where I am, I decided, and guard the way into the Noble Consort's quarters. So I stood there with my bloodied sword and looked threatening. Some of the French troops glanced in my direction, but none of them came at me.

I'd been there a few minutes when I noticed a small party of them heading towards a group of pavilions that housed the older ladies of the court. But I wasn't paying much attention until I noticed a single figure emerging from the back. She was too far away for me to see her face, moving hesitantly, peeping around the corner of the building, then pulling back and obviously wondering where she could flee.

Would the barbarians harm her? Even a lady of the court could get attacked on a day like this. I cursed under my breath. I really didn't want to quit my post. But I couldn't just leave her. So skirting behind some bushes where the looters wouldn't catch sight of me, I bent low and ran towards her.

I was already close before the lady saw me, and at the sight of my bloodied sword she started with fear. But she could see from my dress that

I was a palace person, so she quickly collected herself and waited. She was quite simply dressed, but she had a fine necklace of pearls and gemstones. I was sure I'd seen her before.

Then I realised: It was the lady Prince Gong called Auntie. I bowed low as I reached her.

'Princess,' I said, 'I am Lacquer Nail. I serve the Noble Consort Yi.'

'Yes, yes. I recognise you now. You have been fighting?'

'Your slave has been fighting,' I acknowledged.

'Prince Gong was supposed to be here this afternoon,' she said. 'I sent my servant girl to find him, but I don't know where she is now.'

'I don't think we can wait here,' I said. 'Are there other noble ladies inside?'

'There's only me,' she replied.

'Perhaps we could hide on one of the far islands,' I suggested.

She seemed to like this idea.

'You know the Apricot Blossom Spring Villa,' she said. 'The pavilions are mostly down by the waterfront. But the wooded hill behind is quite wild. We could hide up there, I think.'

'It's a steep climb, my lady,' I cautioned her.

'I am a Manchu, Lacquer Nail,' she reminded me with a smile. 'No bound feet. But I'm like the Noble Consort Yi. My feet are so dainty, you might think they were bound.'

We followed the path around the edge of the lake as quickly as we could. The French barbarians were still busy looting all the pavilions near the emperor's residence, so they hadn't come this way yet. We passed across two deserted islands. As we came towards the Apricot Blossom Spring Island, there wasn't a soul in sight.

There was a pretty humpbacked stone footbridge ahead that crossed over the water to the island. We'd reached the top of it when the princess, who was just behind me, spoke.

'Stop, Lacquer Nail, and hide your sword.' Her voice was quiet but urgent.

I stopped and held my sword with one hand just behind me. For a moment I didn't understand. Then I saw what she had seen. Her eyes were sharper than mine.

A single barbarian was stepping out from the bushes about twenty paces away, directly in our path. He seemed to be alone. He had a rifle in his hands. He grinned at us.

I have seen many villainous barbarians in my life, but never one as ugly as this one. He was huge, with a bushy black beard and a nose that seemed to dip down to his chin. One of his fiery eyes squinted to the right, but the other was fixed on me. He pointed his gun, but he did not take aim. If he'd seen my sword he probably would have shot me.

'What do you think he wants?' the princess asked me quietly. She was wonderfully calm.

'Loot, I think,' I answered. And then it came to me why he might be there alone. 'Perhaps he ran here ahead of his friends to grab the best bits of loot for himself,' I said.

Nobody moved. But I saw the barbarian's eye shift to the princess. My hand tightened on my hidden sword. If he tried to harm her, I'd surely kill him or die in the attempt.

I remember thinking that if I was going to die, at least it would be defending a member of the imperial family. Even if we were both found dead, everyone would get to hear of it. My name would be honoured for generations. I wondered if Prince Gong would buy my missing parts back so that I might be buried with them as a whole man. That would be a good recompense. But would he think of it?

The hideous creature's hand went up to his neck, then pointed at the princess. I understood at once. 'He wants your pearls,' I said.

'How dare he?' There speaks a noblewoman! I thought. The loss of her pearls was nothing. Her concern was for her dignity. 'Certainly not,' she said firmly.

The bearded savage made a motion towards me with his gun.

'He means to shoot me and take the pearls from you,' I translated.

'If he touches me with his hands, I shall have to drown myself,' she remarked.

She still wasn't thinking of giving her pearls away. As for drowning herself . . . If a lady of her rank – born a noble, consort of an emperor – should be defiled by the touch of the disgusting barbarian before us, she'd certainly be right to take her own life.

So it didn't look as if there was any honourable way for us to survive.

But then I had a moment of inspiration. Remember, always put yourself in the place of your enemy. Try to think as he does.

'Trust me, Princess,' I said. I knew she'd understand at once. Then I gave him my most servile bow. And with my free hand I indicated he should come forward and take the pearls for himself, as though to say: 'I can't take them, but I won't stop you.'

He smirked scornfully. A palace eunuch, he was thinking. Just what I've always heard: weak, effeminate, disloyal.

He strode up onto the bridge and started to walk past me as I made way for him. And I don't think he even saw my sword as I whipped it from behind my back and plunged it under his rib cage and up into his heart.

He gave a grunt, stood stock-still with the sword sticking out of him, and sank onto his knees. I put my foot on his chest, yanked the sword left and right to make sure the point had torn up everything within, and pulled it out. The rifle dropped from his hand and clattered on the stone bridge, but he remained on his knees. I glanced back at Prince Gong's auntie.

Her face was absolutely still, betraying no emotion of any kind. She had, as I say, the highest breeding.

Then the monster suddenly vomited blood and fell face forward onto the bridge and was convulsed by two or three huge spasms. As soon as that stopped, I picked up his rifle.

I looked at the princess. Her face was the same. She glanced around the lake as though the death of the barbarian was of no concern or interest to her at all. And I was just wondering whether we should still hide on that island or go to another one, when she suddenly called to me: 'Look over there, Lacquer Nail. Here he comes.' And I looked, and there, from farther up the lake, came a dozen soldiers at a run, with four more men carrying a sedan chair. 'I wonder if he's seen us,' she said. And she started waving at the sedan chair like an excited girl.

I could hardly believe the transformation from the dignified lady to the happy girl. But then of course he was another member of the royal family.

He was with us in no time. He surveyed the scene. There was already a pool of blood around the bearded barbarian's head. 'Are you all right?' he asked her. 'I came as soon as I could.'

'Yes,' she cried. 'Thanks to him.' And she pointed at me.

'Do I know you?' he said.

I made a low bow.

'It's Lacquer Nail,' she interrupted. 'He was fighting the barbarians with his sword. Then he saw me and rescued me. He killed this one, too. He saved my life.'

'Oh,' said Prince Gong. I noticed the soldiers were giving me looks of respect, which was very gratifying. 'Weren't you in trouble?' he said. 'I heard you were dead.'

'Not yet, Highness,' I replied, and made a brave smile. 'But your slave must tell you the barbarians may be here any minute. And they're at the main entrance.'

'We're going out another way,' he said briskly. He helped his auntie into the sedan chair. He looked at me again and at my sword. 'That's a ceremonial sword. Where did you get it?'

I told him. He indicated I should give it to him. But as I started to do so, I suddenly winced with pain. And I discovered the rubies on the hilt had bitten into my hand and it had been bleeding for quite a while. In all the excitement I'd never felt the pain at all.

He got into the sedan chair with his auntie. 'Go!' he ordered his men.

'He saved my life,' I heard the princess say again as they raised the sedan chair.

Prince Gong stuck his head out. 'You come, too,' he told me. So off we went.

It was as we left the Yuanmingyuan that I suddenly remembered my father's advice: the best way to make your fortune, he'd told me, is to save a rich man's life. And now I'd done even better: I'd saved the life of one of the imperial family. I had to laugh.

I was in clover. For a start, I was safe in Prince Gong's well-guarded mansion inside the city walls. Everything in it was magnificent. One of Prince Gong's eunuchs showed me the servants' bathhouse, gave me fresh clothes and balm for my hand. I asked for some extra balm, which I applied to my backside. Then I was given a good meal and a little room all to myself. That night I slept nearly ten hours.

When I finally awoke, the same eunuch gave me breakfast and told me that I should attend upon the princess as soon as I was ready.

She was in a small receiving room, sitting very upright in a big polished chair. She was wearing a flowered dress and a simple tortoiseshell comb in her hair. She looked very royal and dignified, but she smiled at me and told me to sit down on a wooden stool before her.

'First, I wish to thank you again for saving my life,' she said.

'It was your slave's honour,' I answered, and bowed my head.

'And now I wish to hear your whole story, Lacquer Nail, ever since you first decided to become a palace person.'

'I am afraid you will find it very boring, Princess,' I replied.

'I'm sure I shan't,' she said. 'And as Prince Gong is out all day attending to the city defences, I've no one else to entertain me, so I may as well listen to you.'

It crossed my mind that Prince Gong could have asked her to find out how I'd suddenly turned up again when I was supposed to be dead and what I'd been up to. If I hadn't saved his auntie's life, someone might be asking questions in quite a different way.

So I told her everything: about my wife and children, my little boy being sick, how Mr Chen got me into the palace, Mr Liu's dislike of me – the whole tale, right up to the trick Mr Liu had played on me and how I'd hidden in the Peony Terrace. I knew this might make Mr Liu angry if it got back to him, but I needed to defend myself, and she'd know that it would have been madness on my part to make such a thing up if it wasn't true. The only thing I left out was about my money and where I'd hidden it. It's always a good rule in life to be as honest with people as you can, but never tell them where the money is.

'Well,' she said, 'isn't that just like Mr Liu? What an awful person he is.'

'Your slave admires him, Princess,' I said. 'He thinks of everything. I just wish he didn't dislike me.' Which was all true.

'You shall stay with us, Lacquer Nail,' she said. 'I'm sure Prince Gong can use a person of your abilities.'

When Prince Gong came back in the early evening, he was looking quite grim. It wasn't long before the servants all knew what was happening. He had protested to both the French and the British barbarians about the disgraceful looting of the Summer Palace. But he'd got nothing from them except demands that he return their hostages. Worse still, the envoys he'd sent to Lord Elgin got the impression the British soldiers were angry that only the French had been given the chance to loot. And other spies reported that the French officers had been showing the British officers around the Yuanmingyuan that very day.

After he'd eaten his evening meal, Prince Gong sent for me. He gave me a curt nod. 'I've been told about your adventures. Is it all true? I shall have you thrown in gaol if you've lied.'

'Your slave swears on his life it is all true,' I answered.

'She wants me to employ you.' He gazed at me for a moment. 'At least you can take out the chamber pots!' he suddenly cried, with a shout of laughter. Then he waved me away.

I didn't mind. I was just glad that he was in a good mood and that I could stay there.

I was going to bed that evening when I was told the princess wanted me again. She received me in the same room, but her maid was already undoing her hair.

'Lacquer Nail,' she said, 'I want you to perform a great service for me. In all the confusion yesterday, I left something in the Summer Palace to which I am very attached. And if it is still there and if the British barbarians come to loot the place again, I fear it may be lost forever. It is a beautiful jadeite pendant that the emperor himself gave me. It is of great sentimental value.'

'Of course, Princess,' I said with a low bow. 'Your lowly servant would be honoured.' And I gave her a smile to show that I really meant it.

'The pendant is on a ribbon,' she explained, 'and it's hidden inside a secret compartment in a cabinet.' And she told me where the cabinet was and explained exactly how to get the compartment open. 'It takes a few moments,' she said. 'You'd never know the compartment's there. Just so long as the barbarians didn't start breaking up the furniture.'

I couldn't imagine even the British barbarians would start smashing the palace furniture.

'I suggest that I go at first light, before anyone goes out there,' I said.

'Do you want any soldiers to protect you?' she asked.

'I don't think so,' I said. 'If the British were to turn up early, a few soldiers wouldn't be able to help me much. It's probably best if I just slip in and out before anyone sees.'

It was early dawn when I went out of the western city gate. Before sunrise I passed through the main entrance of the Yuanmingyuan. There were no guards on duty.

I had just one task to perform: find the princess's jadeite pendant and return.

All the same, I did make one small detour on my way in from the entrance. I walked across to look into Mr Ma's enclosure of penzai trees.

I didn't expect to find him there so early; and indeed, I couldn't have stopped to talk to him if I had. But I wanted to make sure that no one had damaged his precious trees.

Mr Ma was in the entrance to the enclosure, lying on his back. His jaw was hanging open and his blue cheeks had drawn in so that his mouth made a meaningless little O. His eyes stared blankly up at the sky. There was a circle of blackened blood in the middle of his small chest where someone had shot him. I wondered why. A few of his penzai trees had had their ropes cut, as if the French troops had meant to liberate them from their bondage. But I didn't think any of the trees had been taken to a new home. I expect he'd tried to prevent the looters from coming into the enclosure, and they'd shot him because he was in the way.

I suppose that's how it is with war. Some people are killed for a good reason, some for a bad reason, and others for no reason at all.

The cabinet was just as the princess had described it – beautiful double-doored, dark rosewood – standing against one wall. There was no sign that the cabinet had been tampered with. It should be easy enough to open, I thought. I went across, opened the right-hand door, and felt inside for a little sliding panel, exactly as the princess had told me to.

Ten minutes later, I was still flummoxed. Five steps: slide the panel, press the wood behind, slip one's fingers into the cavity, reach up to a small lever and pull down.

I couldn't find the lever. Was there another panel to slide? Had she mistaken the cabinet door? Patiently I tried every different alternative I could think of. Nothing.

Had she got the sequence wrong? I spent nearly an hour trying one thing after another. Once, having opened the door on the other side, I thought I had found the lever, but though I pulled down, then up, and side to side, the cabinet remained impregnable, refusing to yield up its secret. If only I could speak to the old lady, maybe she could tell me what I was doing wrong; but obviously I couldn't.

It occurred to me that if I'd come there with a single assistant and a cart, we could have carried the cabinet out and hauled it away in far less time than I'd already spent trying to open it. But it was too late to think of that now.

What was I to do? Time was going on. Were the British going to arrive? In the worst case, I supposed, I might leave the pavilion and come back after the British had gone. After all, if I couldn't find the pendant, it wasn't very likely they would. But I didn't want to fail in my mission. The princess might not care for me so much. Love is conditional in palaces.

There was only one thing I could think of: break the cabinet open. But how? With an axe? What kind of damage was that going to do to the cabinet, which was a work of art itself? How would I explain it? I suppose I could say the barbarians did it.

I started to hunt around the adjoining rooms to see if there was any implement I could use. I couldn't find a thing. And I was just about to go over to the palace kitchens to see what I could find there when outside I heard the sound of voices. Loud voices. Barbarian voices. I looked out from a doorway and saw red uniforms, a hundred yards away.

The British had come.

I rushed back to the cabinet. In one last attempt I reached in, slid the panel I'd tried first, pushed . . . And this time, lo and behold, I found the lever. I pulled it down.

And nothing happened. I couldn't believe it. With a howl of rage and frustration, forgetting I'd wounded it, I slammed the flat of my hand against the side of the cabinet as hard as I could. I felt a huge shock of pain in my hand. I cursed the rosewood cabinet.

And from somewhere inside it, I heard a faint click.

I reached in. The secret compartment was open. A moment later, the jadeite pendant was in my hand, and I was gazing at it. I couldn't help myself. The jadeite was so beautifully carved, with birds and bats, for luck. Yet it retained the watery purity of this most lovely of all the jades. Such stones are not to be found within the entire Celestial Kingdom. They are brought by merchants from Burma. Soft as a reflecting pool, yet tougher than a diamond. You can carve it, and it will never break. The gift of an emperor to his love. And I was about to carry this wonder, resting against my own unworthy body.

For there was only one thing to do: I hung the pendant around my neck. It was quite invisible under my clothes. The question was, could I get out of there without being captured or killed by the British? Cautiously, I went to the door.

The British barbarians were already fanning out around that end of the lake. A second column of troops had just arrived from the entrance. In front of my eyes they peeled off to the left and right, going to the islands by the look of it. Then I noticed something else. They were laughing, as if they were at a festival.

Of course, I realised: their officers had brought them there as a reward. A big treat. A day in paradise, looting the emperor's vast treasure house to their hearts' content. All they could carry. No wonder they were happy.

I started to walk away from the pavilion. They saw me, but nobody made a move towards me. I suppose if I'd carried a gun or brandished a knife someone might have taken me down. Or if I'd been pushing a handcart full of gold, they'd have had that off me. But all they saw was a lone palace eunuch, unarmed and carrying nothing, trying to get out of their way. I kept going, towards the main entrance.

I was only twenty paces from Mr Ma's enclosure when things went wrong.

I may have difficulty telling one barbarian from another, but this one was an exception. His uniform wasn't quite the same as the other men's, and he had a sword. He was standing alone, watching the troops as they fanned out.

He was average height for a barbarian, I think, but strongly built. He had a short light brown mustache. He face was regular, broad of brow, intelligent. And he had the bluest eyes that I have ever seen. They gave me a keen look, but not unfriendly, as if he'd let me pass.

He didn't. He drew his sword and made a gesture that I should stop. He surveyed me thoughtfully. Then, with the tip of his sword, he raised my robe, to see if I was hiding anything between my legs. He didn't find anything, but he wasn't satisfied.

Just then, I heard a voice calling him. 'Goh-Dun!' He took no notice, but kept his eyes on me. 'Goh-Dun!' the voice called out again. I supposed this must be the officer's name. Then the voice said something in his barbarian tongue that sounded like: 'Wat yur gat dare?'

Goh-Dun half turned. I did the same. It was another officer, dressed the same way and walking towards us. Goh-Dun waited for him to arrive and said something to him. The officer nodded and patted me down: legs, arms, my crotch. He turned back to Goh-Dun and shook his head.

But Goh-Dun still wasn't satisfied. His bold blue eyes gazed at me, like an engineer inspecting a bridge. He said something, and the other officer opened the top of my tunic. Goh-Dun let the blade of his sword rest lightly against my neck. Then he started tracing the blade along my collarbone. I kept very still, but I tried to lower my collarbone imperceptibly so that the sword blade would slide easily over the ribbon. It nearly worked, but not quite. I saw him give a tiny frown, then a half-smile. He drew the blade back a few inches, inserted the point under the ribbon, and pulled it up.

A moment later, the jadeite pendant was hanging down my front for all to see.

'Aha,' said Goh-Dun.

The two officers inspected it. They were talking and nodding. It was obvious that they thought the pendant was very fine. Then Goh-Dun took it in his hand and cut the ribbon.

'No,' I cried, and tried to cling on to the pendant.

But he only smiled and put it in his pocket.

I shook my head and tried to explain that it belonged to Prince Gong himself, so he'd better not touch it. But of course he didn't understand a word I said. I fell to my knees and begged him. I was almost weeping.

The other officer said something and laughed. As for Goh-Dun, he gestured towards the pavilion, pointed to me, and made a grabbing motion. Then he pointed to himself, made another grabbing motion, and pointed to his pocket. His meaning was clear: I'd looted the pendant from the pavilion; and now he'd looted it from me.

After all, he and his men were there to loot. So he assumed that I was looting, too. When I remained on my knees, shaking my head and protesting, he took me by the arm, pulled me up, gave me a friendly whack on the backside with the flat of his sword, which hurt more than he knew, and then indicated that if I didn't run off, he'd give me another.

It was humiliating, of course. Far worse was the thought that this jadeite pendant should be polluted by the touch of his barbarian hands. And worst of all, I was wondering: what was I going to say to Prince Gong and his auntie?

It didn't go well. The princess was kind to me. She believed me, or said she did. But she looked so sad and disappointed I could hardly bear to see it. As for Prince Gong, I discovered what he thought that evening. I happened to be near the door of her room after he'd gone in to speak to her. So I listened to what they were saying.

'First he deserts instead of going north with the rest of the court,' I heard him say. 'Then he fakes his own death. Then he steals a sword that's worth a small fortune.'

'He was fighting. I saw the blood on it.'

'For all we know he stuck it into one of our own people who was trying to prevent him stealing it. Or a barbarian who tried to get it off him.'

'He saved my life.'

'If you say so, Auntie. It's the only reason I haven't thrown him in gaol. But now he goes off to fetch your jadeite pendant and returns with a story that a British officer took it. Don't we see a pattern here? He goes from one story to another, each more improbable than the last. I bet he's hidden the pendant somewhere.'

'I believe him,' she replied. Then I heard footsteps coming towards the door, and I ran.

The next morning Prince Gong went to the Yuanmingyuan to inspect the damage. To my surprise, I was ordered to go with him. I suppose he wanted to keep an eye on me. We went up there with twenty bodyguards. He was carried in a sedan chair. I had to run behind it.

There were still no sentries at the entrance. When we got to old Mr Ma's enclosure, we stopped and Prince Gong got out.

Mr Ma's corpse was bloated and putrid now. The prince turned to me. 'That's him?' Seeing me nod, he asked me: 'You knew him well?'

'He was very kind to me, Highness,' I answered.

'He shouldn't be left like that,' the prince said. But we moved on.

We seemed to have the entire Summer Palace to ourselves. It was quite amazing. I saw no corpses at the entrance to the emperor's residence, nor any sign of Shaking Leaf in the Noble Consort's apartment, so I supposed that most of the palace people had got away.

We went from one pavilion to another, from island to island. Had I not seen with my own eyes what I saw that day, I do not think I would have believed it.

They had not taken everything. They had taken gold and silver, jewellery and pearls; they had taken paintings and religious statues and silken dresses by the hundreds. I have heard that some of the soldiers put on the silk dresses – whether to carry them more easily or in the spirit of some festival of their own, I cannot say. But they had not taken everything for the simple reason that there was too much for even an army of thousands to carry away.

It was not the loss that shocked me most. It was the destruction.

Silken robes torn, priceless scroll paintings unrolled just to see how long they were and left on the ground to be trampled on. Lacquer boxes broken, mother-of-pearl smashed, temple ornaments torn down. This was not done in revenge or anger. Not at all. They were just enjoying themselves on their holiday. They had no respect for the Celestial Kingdom, its rulers, its scholars and artists, or any of the finer things of life.

I'd lingered behind the rest of the party for a few moments, and I was alone, kneeling in one of the temples on the far side of the lake, picking up the pieces of a cloisonné box that had been crushed under some barbarian's boot and silently weeping, when I realised I was being watched. Was it one of the soldiers? I turned, brushing away my tears, and saw it was Prince Gong. I struggled to my feet and bowed. But my cheeks were wet.

'So what do you think, Lacquer Nail?' he asked me quietly.

'Truly, Highness,' I blurted out, 'your slave thinks that these barbarians are animals. No,' I cried, 'not animals. Lower than the beasts! I'd execute them, every one.' And I meant it. I meant it with all my heart.

He didn't say anything, just turned and left, and I followed him out.

But as we came to the enclosure where Mr Ma's bloated little corpse lay, he stopped the cortege and called me.

'Lacquer Nail,' he said, 'as soon as we get back to Beijing, go to the palace and see if you can find Shaking Leaf.' I noticed that he used Mr Yuan's palace nickname. 'If you can't, then you are to act yourself, on my authority. Discover whether Mr Ma had any family. It shouldn't be too difficult. Everything in the palace is recorded. I want Mr Ma's body properly buried as he would have wished. Everything's to be done well. Bring me any bills. Take this.' He gave me a piece of paper stamped with his seal. 'Show that wherever you need to. It carries my authority. Let me know your progress.'

I found Shaking Leaf in the Forbidden City palace. He was quite astonished when I showed him Prince Gong's seal, and he looked a bit embarrassed about our last encounter. 'I thought you were a ghost,' he said.

'I could have been, Mr Yuan,' I answered. I was very respectful. 'I almost died.'

'And now you have Prince Gong's seal of authority?'

'I saved his auntie's life,' I explained. He shook his head in amazement. 'We came looking for you in the Summer Palace today,' I said. 'We were worried about you and the other palace people up there.'

'Most of us got out,' he replied. 'But we had to run.'

'Mr Ma's dead,' I told him. 'Prince Gong sent me to ask if he had any family.'

'A nephew, I think, who's got his private parts for his burial.'

'If you could send some people up to the Summer Palace to collect Mr Ma's body, I can inform the nephew. Prince Gong wants everything done correctly. He's even offered to pay.'

'I'm glad he's done that,' said Shaking Leaf. 'You can hardly imagine how scared the palace people are. Prince Gong taking such care of old Mr Ma will put heart into them.'

He soon found the nephew's address, and I was on my way.

That evening I made my report to Prince Gong. He was looking preoccupied. Then I went to see the princess. She was alone and obviously longing to talk to someone.

'What a time we've had, Lacquer Nail. Poor Prince Gong. Have you heard about the British barbarians and the loot? They gathered all the loot from the Summer Palace and had a big auction. I don't know how it works, but at the end every soldier and officer gets a share, depending on their rank.' She paused. 'I expect you found the prince very tired.'

'He must have a lot on his mind, Princess,' I ventured.

'A messenger arrived from the emperor today. Had the barbarians been driven out? If not, why not? It's all very well for them. What do they know? They're not here.'

'They aren't,' I agreed.

'I don't blame the emperor,' she remarked sadly. 'I brought him up, you know, after his mother died. He was a nice little boy, always wanting to please. And then his father chose him to be the next emperor. So he was supposed to be perfect, which nobody is.'

'It must be very difficult to be emperor,' I echoed.

'It's impossible,' she said. 'At least nowadays. But I don't believe it's the emperor sending these stupid messages. It's Prince Sushun and his gang. They've got him in their clutches. And they want to undermine Prince Gong.'

'Does the emperor know about the Summer Palace being looted?' I asked.

'He will very soon. And they'll blame Prince Gong for that, too. I don't know what will become of us,' she cried. Or what'll become of me, I thought. For if Prince Gong falls, then I've no protector left. 'The barbarians have got to leave,' the princess suddenly burst out. 'No matter what the cost.'

The British terms were simple. They'd go away, but first they wanted all their original demands met, including the kowtow, and the hostages back, and a huge indemnity payment, of course. And they promised not to attack Beijing upon one condition: that they and the French should be given the southern gate, the main entrance to the city, where they could garrison their own troops.

Could one imagine anything more humiliating? The emperor has to give the keys of his capital to barbarian pirates. What was to stop them deciding who came in and out?

In the morning, Prince Gong had a meeting with all the senior officers at his house. Then several other important persons came to call. I was with the princess, but he came in to us afterwards. He was looking depressed.

'We can hold the city,' he said. 'Lord Elgin would lose so many men taking it that I don't think he'll try. But a lot of troops have deserted, and we're short of ammunition for even the wretched guns we've got. We can't risk any open engagement.'

'So you'll have to agree to Elgin's terms,' said the princess.

'I fear so.'

'You know I believe the barbarians must leave,' she went on. 'But whenever they do, they always seem to come back later with new demands. How do we ensure that this agreement is final?'

'Ah.' The prince nodded. 'There has been a new development. The Russians have approached me. They say they want to be our friends. They're offering to guarantee any agreement. If the British and French don't stick to it, Russia will give us arms and send in troops. That will make the British think twice.'

'They'll want something in return.'

'No doubt. We'll see.'

His auntie didn't press him further.

That still left the matter of the hostages. I happened to be in attendance upon the prince the next morning when the chief gaoler was summoned to his office. He was a big, corpulent Manchu who looked as if he always ate a huge breakfast.

'We're returning the hostages,' the prince told him. 'Show me the list of them.'

The gaoler gave him a sheet of paper. 'That includes the two you wanted fattened up, Highness,' he said.

Prince Gong frowned. 'There should be more,' he said.

'Well, we lost a few,' said the gaoler.

'Lost? You mean they're dead? How did you let that happen?'

The gaoler looked puzzled. 'Nobody told me the prisoners had to be kept alive, Highness,' he replied. 'I never thought about it . . .'

'The barbarians want the bodies of the dead as well as the living. How do the prisoners look?'

'Like men who've been in gaol, Highness. But they can mostly walk.'

'And the corpses?'

'Oh, you don't have to worry about that, Highness. I buried them in quicklime. Nobody'll see a thing.'

'You are a fool,' the prince told him curtly. 'You should know that quicklime does not eat away flesh and bone. It preserves them. Any marks on the skin will be clearly visible.'

'Oh,' said the chief gaoler. 'That's a pity.'

'Go away and make them as decent as you can,' Prince Gong ordered.

I did not see the prince in person after he came back that evening. I did see the bearded Russian envoy arrive. He was with Prince Gong for quite a time. The meeting ended about an hour before midnight. Prince Gong had been alone in his office for another half hour when, to my surprise, he sent for me. 'Lacquer Nail,' he said, 'I need your help.'

'Your slave is honoured,' I answered.

'I want you to do something for me. But if you are ever discovered, I shall deny all knowledge of the matter. I shall say that you are a thief who escaped death by lying. You will be executed, and I shall not raise a finger to save you.'

I bowed low. 'Knowing your honourable character, Highness,' I replied, 'it must be important.'

'I have received a private message this evening, from north of the Wall. Prince Sushun and his friends have persuaded the emperor to order the immediate execution of the barbarian hostages. The emperor's messenger is on his way. He could arrive tomorrow. If I receive that message, I must obey it or lose my own head. But if I execute the hostages, the barbarian negotiations will break down, and I don't know what will happen then. I need another two days to complete the negotiations and transfer the hostages. After that, the emperor's message will be too late.'

'If the messenger is killed . . . ?'

'It might arouse suspicion. I want him delayed. But there must be no connection to me. Nobody in the palace, no official, must know. Can you think of anything?'

It made sense that he would ask me. I had no position to protect. My life depended entirely upon him. And he knew I had courage. I considered. He waited.

'The emperor's messenger will come down the main road from the north?'

'Certain to. There's an imperial posthouse about a dozen miles above the city limits. He'll want to change horses there. Then it's open road to the suburbs.'

'I have a request, Highness,' I said. 'I became a eunuch to save my little boy's life. If I die or if I am executed, I should like to be buried with my missing parts and to know that my family is provided for. Perhaps the princess could give orders for this, because I had saved her life?'

'Something will be arranged.' He nodded.

'I shall need money, Highness, to engage some men.'

'Of course. But wouldn't they know you're a palace person?'

'Even my own hand will be concealed, Highness,' I told him. 'For I know just the man who can do this.'

It was the middle of the night when I got to my family's lodgings. I was wearing an old silk merchant's robe. The gate to the courtyard where we lodged was not locked, and I knew where my father slept. I crept in, put my hand over his mouth and woke him. Within minutes we were moving up the street together.

Once I'd showed him the bag of silver Prince Gong had given me and explained my plan, he seemed quite delighted. 'No problem,' he said happily. That made me nervous.

'You said that about the boots you made, and that didn't turn out so well,' I told him. 'We have to be very careful. And remember, we mustn't kill the messenger.'

'I've never forgiven myself for those boots,' he said sadly. Then he brightened. 'But this is different. Do you realise how many thousand soldiers there are roaming about looking for food and money? They don't care about the emperor or his laws – not since he ran off. They'll do anything, and no questions asked. I can find half a dozen before dawn. You go up the road. Find a good place where we can ambush the messenger. And if you can, a place where I can hide him for a day or two. Give me a little money and keep the rest for the moment. I'll join you a couple of hours after dawn. I've got to visit an apothecary.'

I waited by the road. I'd found a spot. There was an outcrop of rocks by the side of the road with some trees behind it. Good cover. A couple of anxious hours had passed. What was I going to do if the messenger arrived before my backup? Try to stop him myself, I thought. I'd get a heavy stone. Grab the reins, tip him off and hit him over the head with the stone. That was my only hope. But I wasn't sure it would work.

One cart passed by. That was all. Not many people wanted to be on the road just then, when you never knew if the barbarians were going to come your way.

Then at last, three hours after dawn, I saw my father. He was alone. He signalled me to step off the road so that we'd be out of sight. 'You chose a good place,' he said. 'My men are waiting down the road, but I don't want them to see you. They think the horseman's carrying money. So give me the rest of the silver now, and I shall tell them I found it on him. Then we share it together.'

'And the messenger?'

'I'll knock him out with this.' He pulled out a short, heavy club. 'Then I'll tie him up in the trees here. When he starts to come around, I'll give him some of this to drink.' He pulled out a flask. 'The apothecary made it for me. Hemlock, opium. Sends you unconscious for hours. I'll keep my face covered – not that he'll even remember anyway. I'll keep him doped until you come to tell me all's well. Just give a whistle from the road, and I'll whistle back. He'll wake up with a sore head and walk into Beijing with his message.'

'What about his horse?'

'The boys get that as extra payment.'

'Selling a horse from the imperial posthouse could be dangerous,' I said. 'People might ask questions.'

'The horse will be cut up into meat within hours,' he told me.

'I thought horsemeat was bad for you,' I said. I'd often heard so.

'Plenty of people like it. That horse'll be eaten before anyone even knows it's missing.' He grinned. 'Now, walk on up the road. Keep walking at least a couple of miles. When you see the messenger go by, wait a while, then you can come back. Don't look for me, but if everything goes well, I'll leave three stones in a little triangle here by the roadside.'

At noon I saw the messenger ride by. Two hours later, when I came to the rock and the trees, I saw three stones neatly arranged at the side of the road.

Prince Gong was busy with correspondence when I arrived back. He glanced up and I gave him an almost imperceptible nod. 'Tell me,' he said.

'He never knew what hit him. Horse and money stolen, so he'll think he was robbed. He's unconscious now, Highness, and he'll be kept drugged as long as you need.'

The prince nodded. 'Not long, I hope,' he said.

All the next day the negotiations continued. Prince Gong really didn't want to yield the southern gate, but when the barbarians saw the state of the hostages and the corpses, they were so angry that he was afraid the deal would fall through. So after an all-night session, he gave them the gate, and the treaty was signed early the next day. The Russians guaranteed it.

When he came back to catch some sleep early that morning, he told me: 'That messenger can wake up now.' He smiled. 'Go and spend some days with your family, Lacquer Nail. You've earned it.'

My heart was full as I set off up the road towards my father again. It was a perfect autumn morning, pleasantly warm, the sky clear blue. In my mind, I went over the events of the past few days. They'd been full of anxiousness, but how could I not feel grateful that fate had allowed me to be at the centre of great events, and even play a part?

The only mystery was the identity of the person at the Hunting Palace who had warned Prince Gong about the messenger. Someone close to the emperor? One of the princes? Well, I thought to myself, there are some things you're never going to know.

When I reached the rock, the three stones at the roadside were still in place, and there wasn't a soul to be seen in either direction. So I disobeyed my father, and instead of whistling, I crept around the rock.

He was sitting very peaceably on a small outcrop of stone. The messenger was lying on one side, gently snoring. I whistled softly. The messenger went right on snoring, but my father gave quite a start. Then he looked at me. 'I hope nobody saw you,' he said.

'Nobody saw me, Father,' I told him. 'The road's quite empty.'

'All the same . . .' he said. 'Did everything work out?'

'Yes, Father.' I pointed at the unconscious man. 'He can wake up now.'

'Well, he won't for a while yet. You're sure everything's all right?'

'You saved the day, Father, for everyone. Especially me.'

'It wasn't anything much, really,' he said.

'Yes, it was. You saved my life, Father,' I told him.

'Really?' He looked at me uncertainly. Then he gave a beautiful smile. 'That's good,' he said. 'So I did something right for once.' He looked so happy. He might have started crying. I'm not sure. 'I never forgave myself about the boots,' he whispered.

'Forget the boots,' I said. 'You saved my life. Prince Gong says I'm to spend time with my family, so I'll see you at home. But not a word to them about any of this business.'

He nodded, and I left him. I was so happy knowing I'd made things right for my father.

I spent four days with my family. I told them that instead of going north with the emperor, I'd been ordered to serve Prince Gong. 'There's been so much going on,' I said, 'that this is the first time he could let me take some leave.' My father kept his mouth shut. As for my mother and wife, they had no reason to disbelieve me. I told my children about the prince's house and that I'd saved his auntie's life, all of which greatly pleased them.

'Prince Gong can make you rich,' my father said.

'I wouldn't count on it,' I replied. 'What with the Taiping Revolt and the huge payments the barbarians have extorted from us, money's been short for years. And now the treasures of the Summer Palace have all been looted as well. Prince Gong's quite careful with his money, but the fact is, I don't think he's got much to throw around.'

'Well, at least get paid in silver,' my father said. 'No paper money.'

While Prince Sushun was in charge of the treasury, he'd tried issuing paper money. In no time at all, the paper was worthless. When his carriage went through the city, the street vendors used to throw the paper money at him. It especially enraged them that he was so wealthy himself.

'Don't worry,' I said, 'I'll get silver.'

So after those days spent happily with my children, and nights with my wife, who was quite affectionate, I set off happily to the mansion of Prince Gong.

I was more than halfway there when I saw the smoke. Just a single column. It was coming from somewhere a few miles away to the north of the city. It was probably a barn out in the country, I thought. And I was just continuing on my way when a second column of smoke started to rise up, next to the first.

I stopped and thought. It was impossible to gauge accurately from inside the city's walls, but the smoke did seem to be coming from the direction of the Summer Palace. And then, with a sinking feeling, I suddenly realised: it could be. Since the looting, the Yuanmingyuan would have been pretty much deserted. If something caught light in one of the pavilions, no one would have seen. A fire could have smouldered for hours until the building finally caught light. And then the flames could easily spread from one tinder-dry wooden roof to another.

So I ran. I ran as fast as my legs would carry me to Prince Gong's mansion. He was there. I told him breathlessly what I'd just seen and we went outside to look. A third column of smoke had already appeared.

The prince cursed. 'That barbarian Elgin told me there would have to be punishment – that's what he called it, punishment – for our treatment of the hostages. But he didn't say what.'

'He would burn the Yuanmingyuan?' I asked incredulously.

'Who knows? Who knows what these creatures would do?'

'Your slave begs you, let me go there,' I cried.

He looked at me. 'You are not to kill anybody, especially Lord Elgin,' he said drily. 'That is an order. I've enough trouble on my hands.'

'Your slave swears,' I replied fervently.

'Try not to get yourself killed, either,' he remarked.

We both knew there was nothing I could do. But he knew I had to go. They were burning China's treasures. You might as well tell a mother not to run to where her children are being burned. If I could just save something. Anything.

The sun was high in the morning sky, but I couldn't see it. Under the huge black cloud that hung over the park, day had turned into night. A night lit by fires.

The Yuanmingyuan was like an infernal region: the emperor's residence was already a charred wreck, swept by little whirlwinds of glowing cinders. A nearby temple had become a roaring wall of fire. As I looked, a pagoda began to spout a column of oily smoke. Everywhere, figures like demons ran about, silhouetted by the crackling flames.

And the demons wore red uniforms.

They weren't only burning the pavilions in front of the lake. They'd started to move around it, from island to island. The Peony Terrace had been wrecked and its buildings set alight. I do not know how many British soldiers were at work in that huge park. They say four thousand. But one thing is certain: they were determined to destroy the imperial paradise as if it had never been.

I had started to make my way around the lake when I saw a party of British barbarians just ahead. The officer in charge glanced at me, but he obviously wasn't interested. If some foolish palace person wanted to watch, let him.

He clearly didn't know who I was, but I recognised him. It was Goh-Dun. He and his men had encountered that prettily carved stone bridge that led onto the Apricot Blossom Spring Island. They were hauling with ropes and pulleys. But the little bridge was holding firm. I was glad that our bridge wasn't giving in to them. They paused and Goh-Dun consulted with the sergeant. They were probably thinking: let's get some gunpowder so we can blow it up.

Then Goh-Dun turned and stared at me. So I stared back. And I'm not certain, because it's hard to know with a barbarian, but I think he looked ashamed – though whether that was because he was embarrassed by his vandalism or because he'd failed to knock it down, I couldn't say. Then they gave up and moved on.

There was nothing I could do. I had such a sense of helplessness. And strangely – this I can't explain – watching so much wickedness without lifting a finger, I felt as if I were guilty myself. After that, I could not bear to stay there anymore, and I departed.

The British didn't finish their work that day, or the next. They continued smashing, burning down, and looting anything they had missed before. The Apricot Blossom Spring Villa, the Temple of Universal Peace, the Island of Shrines: every single haven of peace and beauty in the paradise of the Yuanmingyuan was destroyed forever. They even went beyond the Yuanmingyuan into the outer parks and destroyed most of them, too. On the third day they stopped. Perhaps they were tired.

I have heard that a big group of palace people and maidservants who were hiding in one of the outer pavilions were burned alive when their retreat was set on fire. It might have been so, or it might not. But even without that horror, the crime was great enough.

Why did the British burn down the Summer Palace? Lord Elgin put up a big sign, written in Chinese, to say that it was to punish us for our cruelty and treachery over the hostages. The death of the hostages was to be regretted, certainly. But is that a just cause for the destruction of one of the wonders of the world?

Some say it was just an excuse, and that he really just wanted to cover up the looting his men had done in the days before. But he had publicly allowed the looting, and all the soldiers had received their share, so he could not hide that business. In any case, the destruction of the outer parks went far beyond the original looting sites of the Yuanmingyuan – and I bet his men pocketed any other valuables they found out there.

This much is certain. In their victory, if such it may be called, the barbarians showed abundantly how well they deserved that name. And they showed not only their barbarism but also their contempt for the Celestial Kingdom, our heritage, our arts and our religions. It also seems to me that they showed their stupidity. For it is not wise to tell a vanquished enemy that you despise him and everything he loves. He will not forgive it. In the Celestial Empire, as I still call it, the rape and burning of our paradise and the contempt it showed will never be forgiven or forgotten. Not in a thousand years.

I spent a lot of time with Prince Gong in the months that followed. He paid me only a pittance, but I was just glad to be alive and in his favour. When I wasn't waiting upon him, I was often with the princess. I did her nails and those of her friends. She liked my company, and would talk to me and slip me a little money now and then.

I think he trusted me more than most people. He had numerous eunuchs in his household, but they were house servants to whom he rarely spoke. One was trained as a secretary, so he was highly literate. But his duties were writing letters and preparing documents. I don't believe the prince ever asked his opinion. Whereas I was special, glad to serve him in any way he chose, and to be discreet and enterprising, and to see a mission through.

He also discovered that if he wanted to know what people in the streets were saying, I was a reliable source. That's because I went and asked my father, of course.

And during those months, I have to say, I came to admire Prince Gong very much. There he was, holding the fort in Beijing, keeping the whole empire together really, while the emperor, Prince Sushun, and the rest of the court stayed safely north of the Great Wall and criticised him from a distance. The weight on his shoulders must have been unbearable.

For instance, during those hectic days when he was negotiating the treaty with the British, the Russian envoy had put him in a horrible position. 'Our empire extends across the whole of Siberia to the Pacific Ocean,' the envoy said, 'but our Siberian coastline is frozen all winter. What we need is a Pacific port farther south. If you'll give us just a piece of your huge territory in Manchuria – which is empty anyway – and let us move a few of our Siberian settlers there, they can build a little trading post by a natural harbour you've got there – just for our local needs. This will cost you nothing,' he'd pointed out. 'But it will greatly please the tsar.'

But would it please the Son of Heaven?

'Prince Gong knew all the emperor's people would blame him,' the princess told me. 'But at that moment, it seemed the only thing to do.'

That little trading post is now the mighty Russian port of Vladivostok.

But even if he wasn't always right, there's no doubt that Prince Gong did what he thought was best for his country, at risk of his own life. I admired him for that, and I always shall.

At this time he also got his hands on a quantity of modern rifles and ammunition. Then he formed some of the best troops we had into a brigade to police Beijing and gave them the rifles. They'd lost to the barbarians again and again, seen their comrades helplessly mown down – not through any lack of courage or discipline, but because the barbarians were so much better armed. Now they could look any enemy in the eye. Deserters started coming back. People looked at them with new respect. And the prince restored order to Beijing.

If we consider the career of Prince Gong, both at this time and in the years that followed, I would say that part of his genius lay in his pragmatism.

Having understood the simple greed of the British, he made good use of them, just as he had suggested to the emperor. With the trading rights they wanted, they now supported the imperial government, and if the Taiping were going to cause chaos, they'd help the emperor smash them. Simple as that. And so Prince Gong was able to build up a new army, trained and commanded by British officers, with British rifles and cannon, that could be used against the Taiping rebels. It did so well that it was soon known as the Ever-Victorious Army. And thanks to this force, within a few years, the Taiping rebels were finally broken forever.

At first this army was commanded by an American named Ward. But after a time, command passed to a British officer who was to make a great name for himself. And I was to meet him in interesting circumstances.

This was a few years after the treaty. So successful had the Ever-Victorious Army been that there was talk of awarding this British commander the Yellow Jacket, which is the highest honour that can be given to a Chinese general, and which he was most desirous of receiving – for like many military commanders, he was not without vanity.

Now I'd heard enough about this British servant of China to make me curious, but I hadn't seen him in person. So when I heard that he'd been summoned to an official audience with Prince Gong in the Forbidden City, I hung about to get a look and saw him just as he was arriving at the outer gate.

Minutes later I was at the door of the prince's office. He was just on his way to the audience himself, but he gave me a friendly nod and asked what I wanted.

'Highness,' I said, 'you are about to meet General Gordon.'

'I am,' he said. 'What of it?'

'Do you remember I told you that a British officer had taken the jadeite pendant from me at the looting of the Summer Palace?' He said nothing, so I continued. 'At the time I had thought his name was Goh-Dun. When I heard of this General Gordon I wondered if I had misheard the name, and they might possibly be of the same family. But, Highness, this morning your slave has just caught sight of General Gordon. And it is the same man! It is General Gordon who took the pendant.'

'You are sure of this?' the prince demanded. 'You could not be mistaken?'

'I am sure, Highness. I never saw eyes like that on any man. I swear it upon my life.'

'Never mind your life,' he replied with a smile. 'But I trust your judgement.' He considered. 'After the official audience, I shall tell Gordon I want a private word with him, in one of the antechambers. I want you there, in respectful attendance – silent, of course, but where he can't fail to see you. Do you think he'll recognise you?'

'Probably not, Highness. But if the subject of the pendant is raised, he might.'

'Good,' he said. 'Be there.'

I must say, Goh-Dun looked every inch a general by now. His eyes were even more piercing than I'd remembered, and he had an unmistakable air of command.

'My dear Gordon,' said Prince Gong. 'I wanted the chance to thank you and congratulate you in private. You know there is talk of awarding you a Yellow Jacket. I can't promise, of course, but I'm much inclined to recommend it.'

'Your Highness is too kind,' Gordon replied with a bow. I could see he was pleased.

'I wonder,' said the prince most politely, 'if I might ask you a personal favour. It concerns my dear aunt.'

'If I can be of help, of course,' said Gordon, looking a little puzzled.

'At the time that British troops first went to the Summer Palace, where my aunt had been living, she unfortunately lost a jadeite pendant. It was of great sentimental value because my father the emperor had given it to her. I have often wondered if it might have been picked up. It would give great joy to our family if it could ever be found.'

'I see,' said Gordon.

'I can describe it for you,' said Prince Gong. And he did so, precisely.

Gordon frowned. Then he looked at me, as if he was trying to remember something.

The next day the jade pendant arrived. It came with a note from Gordon; and Prince Gong was good enough to send for me so that I might hear it.

When the valuables had all been gathered together, Gordon explained, the best of the small pieces had been reserved to go into museums in his country that would exhibit the wondrous arts of the Celestial Kingdom. This pendant – which he was sure from the description must be the one in question – had been reserved in this way. If, however, this was not the one, he would gladly institute further searches.

'Let us compose a reply,' said Prince Gong, and he called in his secretary. 'My dear Gordon,' he dictated, 'this is indeed the lost pendant, and my aunt is overjoyed. Both she and I thank you for going to so much trouble. My memory is bad, I forget things constantly, but I can assure you that your kindness in this matter will never be forgotten by either my aunt or me.' He gave a wry smile. 'Well, Lacquer Nail, what do you think of that reply?'

'It seems to me like a work of art, Highness,' I answered, 'because of its symmetry.'

'Explain.'

'It is implied, Highness, that you will remember the return of the pendant, yet forget the original theft. Therefore your reply seems to me to be perfectly balanced, like a poem or a work of art.'

'Excellent, Lacquer Nail. You could have been a scholar.'

I bowed low. 'May your slave ask, Highness, if there is a name for communications of this kind?' I ventured.

'Certainly,' he said. 'It's called diplomacy.'

Yet here is a curious thing. Months after this, when the Taiping had been finally destroyed and Gordon, his work done, was preparing to leave China, the imperial court not only honoured him with the Yellow Jacket, but gave him a large gift of money to show their appreciation. This was entirely proper. Indeed, I have heard that the British Parliament votes large gifts of money to successful commanders.

And Gordon refused the money. Wouldn't take it. The imperial court was quite offended, for it is great rudeness to refuse a gift. And given the looting of the Summer Palace, in which he had participated, his refusal hardly seemed consistent. So why did he do it? Was looting against his religion? It didn't seem to affect the other Christian soldiers. Was he punishing himself for having looted before? Or did he think refusing the gift would make him look finer and more heroic than his fellow men? That would be vanity.

Much later he was to die heroically in Egypt, and the whole of Britain mourned him. I should think he'd have liked that.

But what of the emperor, north of the Wall, and the Noble Consort Yi?

As soon as Prince Gong had restored order, he begged his brother to return. 'The emperor belongs on his throne in Beijing,' he said. That would tell the world that the Son of Heaven was ruling his empire again, and natural order had been restored.

The emperor wouldn't come. I suppose he must have been ashamed of showing his face in Beijing again. And he may have been afraid of failing if he did take control.

But his staying away didn't do him any good, either. In all the chaos, the rice harvests were down. The city's reserves had been used to feed the troops. And when people found only musty rice on sale in the markets, they said the good rice had all been shipped north to feed the court – and blamed the emperor.

Worst of all, when the time came to make the sacrifices to the gods for good harvests, the emperor sent word he couldn't come and told Prince Gong to perform the sacrifices for him.

'If the Son of Heaven won't speak to the gods for us, then what's the good of him?' my father said. That was the general feeling.

So it wasn't surprising that Prince Gong was becoming more popular by the day. Food was still scarce; silver money was in short supply. But he'd given us peace and some order. Things were slowly getting better. The mandarins knew he was trying his best, and the ordinary people knew it, too. And he was here in Beijing, sharing our hardships, not skulking north of the Great Wall. 'At least he behaves like a king,' people said.

But I learned other qualities of kingship from the prince also. One day an old scholar visited him. I came in just after the old man had left and found the prince looking thoughtful. 'I've learned something new today,

Lacquer Nail,' he said to me. 'You have heard of the old Silk Road across the desert and steppes to the west?'

'Your slave has heard the caravans still come,' I said.

'In the days of the Ming, they came all the time. The barbarians of the West were not so strange to us then. The old man also told me that we had a great fleet of ships that sailed to other western lands far to the south, where men have dark skins. All kinds of treasures and spices came from there. But those fleets were broken up and even the records of them were destroyed or lost. I had never heard of this until today.'

'It is very strange, Highness,' I agreed.

'We have been wrong to cut ourselves off from the world. It has made us ignorant.'

A few days later I brought in refreshments to him when he had granted an audience to a young British barbarian whom he employed to organise the customs collections in the ports.

Now I was always pleased that the prince encouraged the employment of skilled barbarians in matters of finance and trade. For together with the use of men like Gordon in our army, it let all the people see that the barbarians of the West were being tamed and becoming obedient servants of the empire. So I had expected the barbarian to be kneeling respectfully before him. But to my surprise I found the two men sitting at a table side by side.

Seeing my astonishment, the prince laughed. 'This fellow has been teaching me the arithmetics of trade,' he said. 'It's quite shocking how little I know. I'm like a child. I was educated in all the things a mandarin should know,' he went on. 'Confucius, the classics, how to write an elegant essay. Yet I was never taught anything of these practical affairs. Our system of education is clearly deficient.'

At the time I was unhappy that he should say such a thing in front of a barbarian. But now I realise that the prince was showing his kingly nature in the highest degree. For a great king must constantly desire to improve his kingdom by learning new things. And to learn, he must be curious and also humble. For a proud man never learns anything.

I heard only one person speak against Prince Gong. And that was my father. 'Prince Gong has one great weakness,' he told me.

'Oh,' I said. 'What's that?'

'He should kill the emperor,' he replied, 'and rule in his place.' He wasn't joking.

'Don't say such a thing,' I begged him. 'You could get us all in trouble.'

'Who was the greatest of all the emperors of the mighty Tang dynasty?' he asked.

'The Emperor Taizong,' I replied, 'called by history the Emperor Wen.' Though twelve hundred years had passed, he was still a legend.

'And how did he come to power? By killing his two brothers and persuading the emperor his father to step down. That's breaking every Confucian principle. Yet he did it, and it was the right thing to do.'

'I don't know about right,' I said. 'Anyway, the emperor has a son, by the Noble Consort Yi, who should succeed him.'

'We need a strong ruler, not a boy who'll be just as useless as his father.'

'Prince Gong will behave correctly,' I said stiffly.

'That's what's wrong with him,' my father replied.

'If you want the emperor dead,' I said next time I saw him, 'you may not have long to wait.'

It was absurd. The man was only approaching his thirtieth birthday. He'd looked terrible before he'd skulked off to the north, but by spring we heard from the Hunting Palace that he was falling apart. They were bringing girls in to him for orgies, they said. He was drinking and taking opium; his legs were so swollen he couldn't stand. Was he deliberately trying to debauch himself to death?

Summer came. A great comet appeared in the sky. Some people said that the comet was a sign of hope, but most thought it meant the emperor was about to depart.

'The Mandate of Heaven is being withdrawn,' my father said. 'End of the dynasty.'

I remember the moment I knew the emperor had died. It was a sweltering day in August. I'd been to see my family, and I was walking back to Prince Gong's mansion. A heavy downpour of rain had just ended. The dust in the streets was still sodden.

A wedding procession came by. There had been a lot of weddings that summer, because the rule was that when an emperor died, the nation had to go into mourning, and nobody in the capital could marry for a hundred days. So anyone who wanted to get married just then was in a hurry.

There was the bride, a pretty girl all dressed in red for her wedding and carried in a gilded litter. Her brightly dressed escorts were looking full of themselves. People were smiling and applauding as they passed. And then suddenly I saw a man come hurrying towards them and say something to the escorts. Next thing, the little procession was running down the street with the bride as fast as they could, with the poor girl clinging on to the sides of the chair for dear life. I looked quickly up at the sky to see if there was a cloudburst coming, but the sky was clear blue. So then I realised what it must mean. The emperor had died, and they were running to start the wedding before anyone forbade them. I hope they made it.

By the time I reached Prince Gong's mansion, everyone was already dressed in white for imperial mourning. Mandarins, officers, and relations were coming in and out of the house all day and the next. His handsome young brother Prince Chun arrived with his wife. She somewhat resembled her sister the Noble Consort Yi, though not quite so fine, I thought. Then a messenger from north of the Wall rode in and Prince Gong spoke with him alone.

I just kept quiet and remained in the main hall to listen to what people were saying. It wasn't long before I learned what was going on.

We had a new emperor. That was the first thing. The Noble Consort Yi had been excluded from the emperor's presence. But when she'd realised that he was on the point of death, she'd taken matters into her own hands, grabbed her little son, forced her way into the emperor's chamber, woken him up, shown him the boy and asked if he was the heir. And the emperor had stirred himself, declared that the throne must pass to the child, and said there must be a regency council. That was all-important, because once the emperor chooses an heir in the correct line of succession, then the court must obey his decision.

Some people had wondered whether Prince Sushun wanted to seize the throne for himself; but he really couldn't now. Everyone in Beijing was full of praise for the Noble Consort Yi.

But who was on the council? Who, as they say, would hold the seals?

There were twenty-five great seals with which imperial decrees were stamped. The regents would hold the seals, therefore, until the boy emperor came of age. As for the council, there was plenty of precedent. First, the new emperor's uncles. That meant Prince Gong obviously, and at least some of his brothers. People even wondered whether dashing young Prince Chun might be included. It was not unknown for the late emperor's widow to hold one of the seals also. Then there would be some senior mandarins and other wise men. We had to wait another day for this news.

When it came, it was devastating. None of the uncles, not even Prince Gong, was on the council. All the places had gone to Prince Sushun and his gang. It was against all precedent. It was an outrage. In an attempt, perhaps, to make the thing look more legitimate, the empress and the Noble Consort Yi, because she was the new emperor's mother, had each been given a seal. The empress, obviously, wouldn't give any trouble; and the Noble Consort Yi, so recently in disgrace, wasn't in a position to thwart the council even if she wanted to.

'We don't believe the late emperor made these provisions at all, whatever state he was in.' That's what most of the people who came to Prince Gong's house said. 'This is all Prince Sushun's doing.' And I was expecting Prince Gong to denounce the whole business.

But to my surprise, Prince Gong said nothing at all. Neither that day nor in the days that followed. He quietly continued to maintain order in Beijing and let it be known that he would perform his duties there until such time as the regency council decided otherwise.

Prince Gong did also receive private news from the Hunting Palace. He never confided any of this to me, but the princess did.

'The mandarins at the court up there aren't at all happy with Prince Sushun,' she told me one day. 'One of the censors – you know the censors are allowed to say whatever they wish – anyway, one of the censors has told Prince Sushun that the regency council is illegal and that he should hand all the seals to the empress. Though I don't know what good that would do, since she hasn't got an idea in her head.'

'How did Prince Sushun take that?' I asked.

'He was furious. He'd like to get rid of the censor and the empress, and the Noble Consort Yi as well.'

'Could he do it?' I asked anxiously.

'He's got to be careful. Even some of his own council won't let him go that far.'

Then we heard Prince Sushun had backed down and that the council had raised both women to the rank of dowager empress, which was a status higher than any of the other regents – at least in theory. But with the regents up in the north while Prince Gong was running Beijing, China was in suspense. No one knew what would happen next.

And there was one other big problem: the dead emperor's body. It had to be brought to Beijing for official burial. Prince Sushun and his gang would have to come with it. And the weather was still warm. The corpse wasn't getting any younger. They must have embalmed it, but even so . . .

Nearly a month passed, and nobody moved. Then Prince Gong and Prince Chun went up together to the Hunting Palace to see the regents there.

The princess was in a terrible state. 'I'm just afraid Prince Sushun might poison them,' she said.

'He wouldn't dare do that,' I reassured her. Not that I had the faintest idea, really.

We heard that Prince Sushun received Prince Gong and Prince Chun very coldly. Almost insulting. But it was agreed Prince Gong should continue to maintain order in the capital for the moment, and he did manage to see the dowager empresses.

When Prince Gong got back here, the word went out: 'Prince Gong remains steadfast to his motto: "No Private Heart." He serves at the pleasure of the Regency.' A lot of people were disappointed and criticised him for not standing up to Prince Sushun. But he was firm.

A little while after this, Prince Chun went north again and saw the empresses before returning. Arrangements were made for the emperor's body to travel south as soon as possible. The whole court would accompany the body – the boy emperor, the dowager empresses, the regents, the lot of them.

'And that'll be the end of your friend Prince Gong,' my father told me. 'Once the regents take over in Peking, he'll be out. If not something worse.'

The corpse was forty-four days old before it began its journey, in a golden carriage down the mountain passes towards the Great Wall. Within days, the rains had begun, and the cortege slowed its pace to a crawl. Everyone knew there were bandits up in that wild country.

'I must say,' the princess remarked to me, two days running, 'I'm glad Prince Gong isn't with them. Anything could happen to you in a storm up there and no one would be any the wiser.'

I thought of the Noble Consort Yi.

One evening I entered the chamber where Prince Gong liked to work, made a low bow and asked if I might speak to him. He stared at me. 'Well?'

'Your slave dares to wonder whether the young emperor and his party are safe as they travel through the mountains in this weather,' I said. 'Might your slave enquire if Your Highness has any news?'

'You are wondering if the Noble Consort Yi is safe?'

'Your slave was concerned for all the party,' I said.

But he laughed. 'Do you want me to give you a sword and tell you to go and defend her?'

My face must have given away the fact that this was my heart's desire.

'I've just sent two of the best cavalry squadrons from my Beijing brigade to escort them,' he told me. 'They're on their way.'

It wasn't until they'd been on the road for twenty-seven days that the imperial cortege came to the gates of Beijing. Even then, the heavy golden carriage containing the corpse was still a day's journey in the rear. Prince Sushun himself rode with the late emperor's body. Because he was the senior member of the regency council, this was the correct procedure.

But the boy emperor, the two empresses, the rest of the regents, and the court all came to the city gates that day. The weather was fine. The roofs of the city shone in the sunlight. The long street from the outer southern gate, which led through gateway after gateway until it reached the moated purple walls and golden roofs of the Forbidden City itself, had been covered half an inch deep in golden sand that made a gleaming path. On either side, all the way from the southern gate to the entrance of the Imperial City, blue screens had been set up to keep the boy emperor from being stared at.

And Prince Gong had summoned all twenty thousand of his new Beijing brigade, beautifully turned out to line the last part of the route and salute the emperor and the regents as they passed.

I was allowed to be in attendance on Prince Gong as he waited to receive the boy emperor at the gate of the Imperial City – an act of great kindness and thoughtfulness on his part. It was a splendid sight. The boy emperor and his mother were carried in a magnificent yellow chair. Prince Gong advanced to make the kowtow and then conducted the imperial party and the regents, in the most friendly manner, into the Forbidden City. I was walking just behind with some of the mandarins, who were all looking with great admiration at the splendid Beijing brigade guards who surrounded us.

It was just after we'd entered the Forbidden City that I noticed something a little strange.

The imperial party, the regents, and other members of the princely families were all going into a chamber where refreshments were to be served. The Beijing brigade guards were formed up by the doorway. Handsome young Prince Chun was with the imperial party, of course, but instead of entering with the rest, he hung back by the door. He seemed to be watching for a signal. I saw him give a slight nod. Then he stepped outside, as the guards closed the doors, and I saw him walking swiftly away.

Well, I hung about with the other people. And after a few minutes an extraordinary thing happened. The doors burst open. A company of guards marched out. And in their custody were the regents, Prince Sushun's gang, the lot of them.

They'd been arrested.

The whole business took only seven days. Prince Chun and a squadron of cavalry arrested Prince Sushun within hours. They say he was found in bed with one of his concubines only yards from the dead emperor's golden catafalque, which he was supposed to be guarding and respecting. It may be true or not. But there was no need to make up any bad stories about him. The mandarins hated him; the people hated him; the military were all against him. The Imperial Clan Court immediately found him and his gang guilty of crimes against the state. His brother and another royal regent were allowed to hang themselves. As for Sushun himself, he was beheaded like a common criminal.

But there was no vengeance against those who'd gone along with Sushun. I think Prince Gong was very wise. A new regents council headed by Prince Gong and including both the dowager empresses was soon in place. And life went on again.

As I look back on it now, I have to say that I think Prince Sushun was exceedingly foolish. Firstly, by excluding the royal uncles, he went against all precedent, so that put all the mandarins against him. Secondly, he tried to start a coup from a distant place, cut off from the power centre of Beijing. For you need to be on the spot where all the players are.

Above all, he had no military force to make his enemies submit to him.

Power comes from the barrel of a gun – the barbarians had shown us that. Our huge numbers had been useless against their superior arms. And Prince Gong had twenty thousand well-trained men with modern rifles. It was never any contest. Even the twenty-five seals of the Celestial Empire count for nothing against the barrel of a gun.

The only puzzle, one might say, is why Prince Sushun was so foolish. In my opinion, Prince Sushun was arrogant, where Prince Gong was humble – and the humble man has an advantage over the arrogant man. And why was Prince Sushun so arrogant? It may have been because he was so rich. Rich people are used to getting their own way all the time. So they get arrogant and make mistakes. Prince Sushun made a mistake and lost his head.

It was two days after the arrest of Prince Sushun that Mr Liu came to Prince Gong's house. The two of them were closeted together for some time. Then Mr Liu came out and started towards the quarters of the princess. I was standing just outside her receiving room in the passageway, so Mr Liu and I came face-to-face.

I hadn't seen him since the day he tricked me into missing the court's departure for the Great Wall. And as he'd only just come back from there himself, I thought he might not even know that I was still alive. I really wasn't sure what to say to him. So I just bowed low.

But he didn't look surprised to see me at all. His face lit up with a big smile. 'Ah, Lacquer Nail, there you are,' he says. 'I've heard all about your exploits. You've turned into a warrior since we last met. A slayer of barbarians. A rescuer of princesses. Splendid, splendid.' You'd have thought he was my greatest benefactor.

'Your humble servant, Mr Liu,' I answered quietly.

'I've come to call on the princess,' he went on. 'Would you go in and ask if she will receive me?'

Not with any pleasure, she won't, I thought to myself, remembering how she'd once told me he was an awful man. But moments later I was holding the door open for him. And I was quite astonished when I heard her say, in the friendliest voice: 'My dear Mr Liu. How can we thank you for all you have done for us?' And then to me: 'Close the door, Lacquer Nail.' By which she meant that I should be on the outside of it. So I heard no more.

Later that day, after Mr Liu had gone, I did venture to say to the princess that I'd been quite surprised at how pleased she was to see him. For a moment she didn't reply.

'You're clever, Lacquer Nail,' she remarked finally. 'But you have a lot to learn.'

It took me a while to realise what she meant: it must have been Mr Liu who was in secret communication with Prince Gong from above the Great Wall, Mr Liu who had warned him of the order on its way to execute the British hostages. And no doubt he'd been sending messages to Prince Gong in this last crisis. No wonder the princess was grateful to him. Of course, she wasn't going to tell me all this.

To this day, I can't be quite sure. But I do know one thing: Mr Liu always seemed to come out on the winning side.

My greatest joy, however, was yet to come.

The new regime was quite ingenious. The boy emperor became the official ruler of China right away. The decrees all went out in his name, and he received the officials himself in person. Naturally the little fellow couldn't yet know what to say, so the two dowager empresses remained in the room with him. But they sat behind the throne, hidden by a yellow curtain. A mandarin would deliver his report, and the empresses would whisper to the little boy what he should say – which usually meant that his mother would do the whispering, since the dear empress herself had hardly more idea what to say than the boy.

But everyone understood that this was a formality, so that was all right.

The real power lay with a small advisory council. There were no troublemakers, just long-standing, reliable men whom all the mandarins and officials knew and respected, and with Prince Gong as their head. The idea was to restore calm and follow precedent in the good old-fashioned way. But Prince Gong was also expected to add some judicious modernising, just as he had when he formed the Beijing brigade.

And to emphasise the stability of the regime, the position of the two dowager empresses was ratified by granting them new honours and titles. The title given to the empress meant 'Motherly and Restful' – which was a tactful way of putting it! As for my former mistress, her title was Cixi – which meant 'Motherly and Auspicious.' And that's how she was officially known for the rest of her life: Cixi.

But Prince Gong, in his wisdom, arranged one other kindness for the two women. It was clever also, I suspect, in that it prevented anyone claiming that he himself had profited from the destruction of the former regents. The entire vast fortune of the executed Prince Sushun was confiscated and given to the two dowager empresses, half each.

After all her tribulations, my former mistress was now suddenly one of the richest persons in the empire.

There had been a light dusting of snow over Beijing on the day I was told by Prince Gong that I was to report to the palace. The sky was a crystalline blue. The huge all-white expanse in front of the Hall of Supreme Harmony shone so brightly in the sun that I had to blink. Its vast roof, however, since the snow was so thin, gleamed white in the furrows, with myriad ribs of gold where the yellow tiles showed through.

It was, I think, the most magical thing I ever saw.

I was shown into the presence of the Dowager Empress Cixi in a small throne room, where to my astonishment, she received me quite alone. She was dressed in white. But I smelled the familiar jasmine scent she had worn before.

'Well, Lacquer Nail,' she said after I had performed the kowtow, 'look what has happened to us both. I have heard all about your adventures from Prince Gong. He and the princess speak very highly of you.'

'Your slave is honoured,' I said.

'I was very sad when you deserted me before we went north of the Wall,' she said.

'Highness,' I cried in agony, 'that was not of my doing . . .' But then I saw that she was laughing.

'Mr Liu was very naughty,' she said.

It was more than that. He'd deliberately countermanded her orders by giving me the wrong instructions. He should have been demoted and punished, at least. But of course, with Mr Liu, that was never going to happen.

'Yes, Highness,' I said.

'The problem is,' she went on, 'that now I have no one I trust to look after my nails. Do you think you could do it?'

And she smiled at me.

'Oh yes, Highness,' I cried. And I performed the kowtow again, so close this time that I could almost have kissed her dainty feet.

IN DUTY BOUND

1865

Would she ever see her husband again? Mei-Ling did not know. But she had an instinct – she could not say why – that he had gone forever. Perhaps it was just her fear.

They had spoken about America so many times down the years. As a possibility. No more than that. But when the handsome son of the big, bluff American who had come before – when the son came again and offered a generous payment in advance – how could they turn it down, things being as they were?

There'd been no good news in the hamlet for so long, or anywhere else. If the Taiping's Heavenly Kingdom had ruined the great Yangtze valley for a decade, the barbarians' destruction of the Summer Palace in Beijing had humiliated the entire empire. Now the emperor who'd run away was dead, a child was upon the throne, and in essence the kingdom was being ruled by a pair of unschooled women.

Was this the whimpering end of an age? Was the Mandate of Heaven being withdrawn?

Along the coast, from Shanghai to Hong Kong, the barbarians had their ports, ruled like separate kingdoms under their own laws. Up in Manchuria, the Russians had taken a huge territory. As for the Taiping rebels and their Heavenly Kingdom, they'd been kicked out of Nanjing only a year ago, and not even by an imperial army, but by Chinese troops equipped and trained by Gordon and his British officers.

The message was clear enough: the barbarians had decided to keep the imperial court in power because Beijing would give them whatever they wanted. Everybody knew.

The empire was humiliated and its treasury exhausted.

Mei-Ling hadn't any money, either. The last silver she'd held in her hands had come from Nio, when he'd been on his way to take Shanghai, and that had been spent long since.

What had become of Nio? She had never heard from him again. The Shanghai campaign had been a disaster. By the time that Nanjing had fallen, she feared he must be dead. But she couldn't be certain. He'd turned up after huge absences before. Sometimes she'd be down at the pond, and if the breeze made a rustle in the trees by the path, she'd start and glance quickly towards the sound, half expecting that Nio would appear. But he never did. Time passed and her rational mind told her he must be dead and that she must accept it.

If only she knew for sure, she could weep and mourn him properly. But without that certainty, she felt she would be giving up on him, deserting him instead of keeping the flame of hope alive.

Her husband understood. At times he used to wish that someone would arrive with news of Nio's death, if only to release Mei-Ling from the endless pain of not knowing.

Finally, as they were walking one morning, he suddenly said to her: 'Nio's dead. You must accept it.' And she nodded and said: 'I know.' Then she clung to him and wept.

At least her family wasn't starving. But that was almost all that could be said.

Elder Son of course was still nominally head of the family. But if he'd been weak before, he was little more than a walking shadow now. He seldom smoked opium, but only because he hadn't the money to buy it. And alas, it hardly seemed to improve his health.

Three years ago, to everyone's surprise, his skinny daughter had been found a husband, quite an old man from a neighbouring village, who just wanted her as a housekeeper. But he was a husband. So she was gone. And perhaps Elder Son might have found strength to be a man for the sake of his one remaining child, poor Willow's little boy. But three years ago, in one of those plagues that swept through the countryside every few years, the child had succumbed.

For Elder Son, that had been the end. From then on, he roused himself only enough to declare from time to time that he was the head of the family and must make the decisions, but never to do anything about it.

A sort of lethargy had descended upon the house. The bridge over the pond needed repairing. Second Son was ready to do the work, but his brother always insisted that he'd attend to it, although he never did. 'It's not worth quarrelling about it,' Second Son told Mei-Ling, which was probably true. So nobody stepped onto the bridge anymore, because it wasn't safe. When Mei-Ling went out to look at the full moon, she gazed at it from the bank.

Even Mother was affected. Instead of ruling the household and the kitchen nowadays, she let Mei-Ling make all the arrangements and sat in the courtyard. When Elder Son stopped collecting the rents, she did it herself, but with surprisingly little success. Sometimes she'd come back with nothing.

So effectively, Mei-Ling and Second Son kept the place going. He and their two grown boys worked the land. The family ate and was clothed. But they had little money to spare.

There was one ray of hope, though: one person who might be able to achieve the good life and, with a bit of luck, help them all. Her little girl: Bright Moon.

'She'll be as beautiful as you,' Second Son often declared.

'She is more beautiful,' Mei-Ling would reply.

'Not possible,' he'd say, and perhaps he really thought so. But Mei-Ling knew better.

It was extraordinary how perfect the child was: her skin was so pale, pure white, the hallmark of a Chinese beauty. And Bright Moon's eyes were large, and her nose and eyebrows were straight, like those of a noble lady of the court from the days of the shining Ming.

Second Son doted on the little girl. As soon as he got home from work each evening, he'd sit and play with her.

Sometimes, if there was a wind, he and Bright Moon would go up to a place where they could watch the forest of tall bamboos swaying in the wind. The bamboo made beautiful clicking sounds as they knocked against one another, and if the wind was strong enough they sighed as well. 'Their music is even more lovely than the erhu,' Second Son would happily declare. 'And do you see along the forest fringe how their heads and shoulders droop so gracefully? Yet in a storm, even the tallest heads can touch the ground without the bamboo breaking.'

'Don't they ever break?' the little girl once asked.

'If a bamboo is beside a wall, or even other bamboo canes that prevent it from bending the way it wants to,' he answered, 'then sometimes it can snap.'

'Does it die?'

'No. The best thing is to cut it just above the ground, and by the next year another cane will grow up just as tall as the one before.'

'You love the bamboo, don't you, Papa?' the little girl cried.

'Almost as much as I love your mother and you,' he answered, and the little girl knew that it was true.

Bright Moon was three years old when Second Son and Mother began to talk about her feet.

'She could become a rich man's wife,' Mother said.

'And live the good life,' Second Son agreed.

'We need to bind her feet,' Mother said. 'She can't get a rich man otherwise.'

'I want her to have a good husband like I did,' said Mei-Ling. 'And my feet weren't bound.'

'She could do much better than me,' said Second Son. 'I want her to have the best.'

'But would she be happy?' Mei-Ling asked.

'Why not?' her husband reasonably asked. 'Being rich doesn't make you unhappy. And it's better than being poor, as we are now.' He gestured to the house and the broken bridge in the pond. 'She's been given so much beauty. We have to respect that, not waste it.'

'Perhaps she could marry a rich Hakka man,' Mei-Ling suggested. 'Some Hakka are rich. And their women don't bind their feet.'

'No Hakka,' said Mother.

'Or a Manchu, even. Their women don't bind their feet, either.'

'The rich Manchu usually marry other Manchu. And their Han Chinese concubines all have bound feet,' said Mother. 'You can be sure of that.'

'It's painful,' Mei-Ling cried. 'Everyone says it is.'

'It's not so bad,' said Mother.

'Do you know how to do it?' asked Mei-Ling.

'There's a woman in the town who has bound lots of girls' feet. She'll come and show us.'

Mei-Ling was still unhappy, though Second Son tried to comfort her.

'It's all for the best. She'll thank us one day,' he promised. 'And being born with such beauty, she'd never forgive us if we didn't give her the chance to make use of it.'

'I still can't bear to think about it,' Mei-Ling confessed.

'Then don't,' said Second Son. 'She's only three. We wouldn't start until she's six.'

So they didn't talk about the foot-binding, not for the time being. And the only thing Bright Moon knew was that she had to carry a sunshade whenever the sky was blue.

The rumours from the coast began when Bright Moon was five years old. American merchants had been going around the towns and fishing villages again, offering good money to men who'd come out to California to build a railway.

Of the three men who had gone to America from the hamlet when Read had come before, two had remained there, but one had returned. He'd come back with money.

And stories of the huge continent in the West: its temperate climate, beautiful bays, soaring mountains. And of course, the railway: the endless iron tracks the barbarians were laying across the land, and the engine with the fiery furnace inside, belching steam and sparks, that raced along the tracks. Some people in the hamlet thought it was wonderful, though to Mei-Ling it sounded like a terrible and evil thing.

But the iron dragon on rails did not frighten her as much as the effect all this information had on her husband.

'I've heard they're giving good money to people before they go. An advance payment. A lot more than I could ever earn around here.' He looked at her seriously. 'You could use that money for the farm and for Bright Moon. And then, if I could come back with another pile of money . . .' He looked at her sadly. 'I'd be away from you.'

'Please don't go.'

He sighed. 'I don't know what to do. We have to think of the family.'

She thought of the run-down farm and the poor hamlet. It was hard for anyone in that area to make a living. If the Americans came offering well-paid work and cash down, they'd have no shortage of takers.

As for Second Son: she knew her beloved husband. If he decided a thing was right, nothing would stop him. He'd shown the same obstinacy when he'd insisted on marrying her. Wonderful then; terrible now.

'How long would you go for?' she asked.

'I don't know. Two or three years, I suppose. I'd take our younger boy with me.'

'I'd be lonely,' she said simply.

'So would I. But if we need the money . . .'

'You're not going down to the coast to look for the Americans, are you?'

'No,' he answered, 'but if they came here . . .'

She understood. If they came all the way up here, that would be fate. That's what he was telling her. If the Americans came, he'd go. She could only pray they wouldn't. After all, if the money was so good, the Americans would find all the men they needed on the coast. And time had passed, and nobody came.

It was a sunny autumn day when the handsome young American appeared. He'd remembered the hamlet from the time he'd come with his father years before. He was offering a bag of silver in advance, so long as the men promised to stay three years.

But he remembered Second Son, too. And when her husband offered himself and his son, the handsome young American shook his head. 'You changed your mind last time, after only a day,' he told him.

'I won't do it again,' Second Son said.

'Sorry. Can't take the chance,' the American replied. 'I need men who really want to go.'

Mei-Ling was standing beside her husband when the American said that, and she felt such a rush of joy and relief. They'd get by without the money, she told herself.

'I'll promise four years instead of three,' said Second Son.

She stared at him in horror. What was he saying? The young American looked at him thoughtfully. 'You swear?' he said.

'I promise,' said her husband. 'For both of us.' He didn't look at her.

Afterwards, she asked him, 'Why did you say that?'

'Because he wasn't going to take me otherwise,' he answered. 'It was obvious.'

So the American gave her the bag of silver, and her husband and her younger son left straightaway. Second Son promised that the time would soon pass and tried to pretend that everything was all right. Her boy said he'd think of her every day, but he couldn't help looking a little excited to be going on such an adventure.

That night there was a quarter-moon and a sprinkling of stars. And as she had when he left before, Mei-Ling sent messages of love after her husband. But this time clouds filled the sky, snuffed out the stars and hid the moon; and she wasn't sure that the messages reached her husband. She wasn't even sure they left the valley where the hamlet was.

Bright Moon's father had been away for two years when they began to bind her feet.

The autumn season was the time to begin. Summer's heat and humidity, which caused the feet to sweat and swell, was past. So the pain was less.

They told the little girl she should be grateful.

Even down here in the south, plenty of women in the towns had bound feet. But out in the countryside bound feet were not so common, and in their poor little hamlet Bright Moon was the first girl to be so lucky for years.

She was doubly lucky, because the woman who came from the local town to supervise the procedure was well known throughout the area for her skill. People called her the Binder. 'She has bound feet in some of the finest houses in the region,' Mother told them all. 'It's got to be done right, no matter what it costs.'

A propitious date was carefully chosen: the twenty-fourth day of the eighth moon. But before that, there was much to be done. Weeks ago, Mei-Ling had made a journey to the town with a pair of tiny silk-and-cotton shoes that she had made, hardly two inches tall, but embroidered with a prayer, and placed them on the incense burner in the Buddhist Goddess of Mercy's temple.

On that journey she had also bought some of the items that would be needed in the months and years ahead: dozens of rolls of narrow binding cloth, a small bamboo receptacle for fuming the cloth to make it smell sweet, and several kinds of foot powder. Mother had supplied the money for all this, though Mei-Ling wondered where the money had come from. But when she asked, Mother told her. 'I managed to collect some of the rents, but I didn't tell you. I've been saving for years.'

Together she and Mother tried to make a pair of quilted cotton shoes that the child could wear when her feet were initially bound. 'I hope we got it right,' said Mother. And the day before the Binder was due, they prepared the kitchen so that they could make balls of sticky rice and red beans. But in spite of all these preparations, Mei-Ling noticed that Mother was quite nervous and ill at ease on the morning the Binder arrived.

Not that the Binder was so impressive to look at. She was just a peasant woman, aged about fifty, quite short and simply dressed. But her feet were bound, and her face, thanks to the application of lotions, was smooth. Mei-Ling thought that the Binder's eyes were sharp, like a market woman who knows the price of everything.

'You must not think that we are unfamiliar with binding feet,' Mother told her. 'My elder son's wife had bound feet, but sadly she has died.'

'I see you have a big house,' the Binder replied. 'Your daughters have no need to work.' She glanced at Mother's feet.

'My sister's feet were bound, and my parents could well afford to bind mine, but for some reason they didn't,' Mother explained. Mei-Ling had never heard Mother say this before. Then the Binder looked at her feet. 'Her parents were poor,' said Mother apologetically.

'I have known even the poorest parents who borrow money to bind the feet of their eldest daughter,' said the Binder, 'especially if she is beautiful. But it can be hard for them, because such girls are supposed to come to their husbands with at least four pairs of silk shoes, one for each season, and often a dozen or more.'

'The child will have all the shoes she needs,' Mother assured her.

'She is fortunate then,' said the Binder. 'May I see her?'

'Of course,' cried Mother. 'Of course. I'll fetch her.'

While Mother was gone, Mei-Ling asked the Binder, 'Does it hurt a lot?'

'There is pain. But it's worth the result.'

'Is it true you break the bones in the foot?'

'Only the toes. The tiny bones in the toes will snap as they are folded under the foot. But they're so small and soft at that age that it doesn't hurt much. Hardly counts as a break, really. The rest of the bones are forced to grow a certain way, but we don't break them.' She paused for a moment. 'Have you ever seen the miniature trees that rich people have in their houses? They call them penzai trees. It's just the same idea. They bind the baby tree with ropes to keep it small. All the energy of the tree, its inner essence, goes into miniature form. The skill of the binder and the force of nature pushing against each other. That's what we do when we bind a girl's foot. We make a lily foot. A work of art. They are so beautiful, and when the girl wears her embroidered slippers, people call them golden lotus feet.'

'I see,' said Mei-Ling unhappily.

Then Mother came back with the child.

Mei-Ling did not know what reaction she'd expected when the Binder saw Bright Moon. She'd supposed the Binder would say something. But the Binder didn't say a word. She just stared. Then she walked slowly around the little girl, peered closely at the skin on her neck, stood back, gazed at Bright Moon's eyes, looked for a chair, and sat down. 'I shall need to stay here some time,' she announced. 'Maybe a month.'

'A month?' Mother looked alarmed. What would that cost?

'A month,' said the Binder firmly. 'My fee remains the same, but you'll have to feed me.'

'Of course,' said Mother. 'Of course.'

The Binder gazed at Bright Moon. 'A work of art,' she murmured. She wasn't talking to them. She was talking to herself.

When she was ready to begin, the Binder asked the men in the house to go out until the evening. 'This is women's work,' she explained. 'No men in the house.'

Then she instructed Mei-Ling and Mother to prepare a small tub of warm water in the kitchen, and made the little girl sit on a stool with her feet in the water.

'Do I have to stay here for long?' the little girl asked.

'We'll keep the water nice and warm,' the Binder reassured her.

'What happens next?'

'I trim your toenails.'

'Does that hurt?'

'Of course not. You've had your nails cut lots of times. Did it ever hurt?'

'No.'

'There you are, then.'

Bright Moon looked at the two older women doubtfully, then at her mother.

'That won't hurt,' said Mei-Ling, and smiled. At least it was true, so far.

'You'll have such pretty feet when it's all done,' said Mother.

'So tell me,' said the Binder, 'what sort of little girl are you, besides being beautiful? Are you a good girl? Do you try to please your family as you should?'

Bright Moon nodded cautiously.

'She's a very sweet-natured child,' said Mei-Ling. 'Though she has a mind of her own. She learned that from you,' she remarked to Mother.

'That could be,' said Mother, looking quite pleased.

'You are seven years old now,' the Binder told the little girl. 'You know what that means, don't you? It means you become a woman. Not in your body, not yet, but in your mind. You are old enough to understand the things that belong to women. Your hair will be tied in tufts on your head so that everyone will know that you have completed the first seven-year cycle of your life. They will treat you as a responsible person. Do you understand?'

'Yes,' said Bright Moon. She didn't sound very happy about it.

'We women grow up faster than boys. That is why a boy's second cycle of life doesn't begin until he's eight. Once you're thirteen, if you're going to be a young lady, you'll have to remain in the house all the time and never be seen by any man outside the family, not even your neighbours. Because you'll be considered a bride by then. And by the time you complete your second cycle, you'll be two years more advanced in your understanding than a boy of your age. Did you know that?'

Bright Moon shook her head.

'Well, it's so,' said the Binder. 'The men grow wiser than we are only when they're older, which is why we obey them.'

Mei-Ling glanced at Mother, whose face suggested that this last wisdom might be open to doubt, though of course she didn't say so.

After half an hour the Binder took a pair of scissors and carefully trimmed Bright Moon's toenails as short as possible, inspecting each toe and the underside of her feet carefully as she did so. Then she put fresh hot water in the tub. 'You'll have to wait an hour or two,' she said, 'to make your feet as soft as can be.'

So to pass the time, she told her the story of Yexian, the good little peasant girl with a cruel stepmother. Yexian was befriended by a magic fish who provided all the clothes she'd need to go to a party with the king. And how she lost her dainty slipper, and the king searched all over the land to find the owner and found Yexian and married her.

'You see,' said the Binder after she'd finished her story, 'it was Yexian's beauty and tiny feet that the king liked so much. And that is why all the pretty girls in China bind their feet. Because the fine husbands want wives with lily feet.'

'Maybe you could marry a prince,' Mother chimed in. 'Or a great official or a rich man.'

'You're just as pretty as they are,' the Binder explained. 'But without tiny feet as well, nobody will look at you.' She smiled. 'And I'm like the magic fish, to make it all possible.'

'Couldn't I have a plain husband, like Father?' the little girl asked.

'Your father married me despite my feet,' said Mei-Ling, with a glance at Mother, 'but you might not be so lucky.'

'You can help your father and all your family by marrying a rich man,' said Mother. 'Then he wouldn't have to go away to work.'

'Really?' asked Bright Moon.

'Yes,' said Mother quickly. 'You're doing it for him and all your family. Then he will come back and say you were a dutiful daughter who loved him.'

'Oh,' said Bright Moon.

'And you will have a rich husband who loves you, and beautiful clothes, and all your family will be grateful.'

'Is it so good to be rich?' the little girl asked Mei-Ling.

'It is not good to be poor,' Mother answered for her.

Then they put some more hot water in the tub, and the Binder massaged the little girl's feet for a while. Bright Moon was sleepy, so Mother sat beside her and let the girl's head rest on her, and Bright Moon slept for another hour while her feet continued to soften in the tub.

'She's the most beautiful child I have ever seen,' the Binder told Mei-Ling, as they drank tea together. 'That's why I'm staying for so long. I want to give her special care. She was born in the Year of the Horse, wasn't she?'

'Yes,' said Mei-Ling.

'They are always the most beautiful ones. But she is truly exceptional.

You will do very well with her. And she'll be a credit to me, too, I don't mind saying.'

When the Binder began that afternoon, she first put a powder on the little girl's feet to protect against infection. Then she took a long strip of binding cloth that had been soaked in water, and leaving the big toe free, she wrapped it around the four small toes of Bright Moon's left foot, folding them carefully under the pad. When she was satisfied that they were correctly and neatly in place, she pulled the cloth tighter, quickly wrapped it around the sole of the girl's foot, and gave it a sharp tug. Bright Moon uttered a little cry, but the Binder said soothingly, 'That's all right. That's all right.'

Then she drew the binding cloth around the big toe again, and then right around the little girl's instep, then back around the ankle, then around the back of the heel, then to the front of the foot, under the instep and around the heel again – embalming the foot, as it were. Then she pulled harder and harder until the little girl screamed. 'That's all right,' said the Binder, and wrapped the cloth around her ankle and tied it off.

Then she did the same thing with the right foot.

'Rest now, my little princess,' she said.

So they took Bright Moon and let her rest on her bed, and Mei-Ling remained with her while Mother and the Binder sat down together in the yard in the autumn sun.

They had been chatting for a while when Mei-Ling came out and said the girl was crying. 'It's the bandages,' said the Binder. 'I put them on wet. As they dry, they get tighter.'

'I think her toe bones may have broken,' said Mei-Ling.

'That could be,' said the Binder.

So they all went in to look at Bright Moon, and the Binder felt her feet and Bright Moon cried out.

'Don't worry, my sweet,' said the Binder. 'There's pain in everything that's good.' She smiled. 'One day you'll have a baby, and that pain will be greater than this, but we all go through it. And we do it gladly.' She turned to Mother. 'That's our lot, being a woman, isn't it?'

'It is,' Mother agreed.

'I'll unwrap the bandages in the morning,' the Binder said. 'Then we'll see. Everything's as it should be,' she assured them.

'One thing I forgot to ask,' Mother said to the Binder when the two of them were outside again. 'Is it true that sometimes the toes develop gangrene and drop off?'

'It is true,' said the Binder. 'And some people think that is better, because then the foot will be even smaller. But often those girls get infected and die. So I don't let that happen. Not a single girl whose feet I have bound has died. Not even one.'

'That is good.' Mother nodded. 'That is good.'

'Will the pain be over soon?' Mei-Ling asked as the three women ate together in the early evening. As her mouth was full of rice and beans, their visitor couldn't answer, but Mother did. She was glad to show that she knew about these things.

'You must be patient,' Mother said. 'You don't only bind the toes. You have to rotate the heel bone until the back of the heel is flat on the ground. That's a much bigger task. Takes longer.'

'So the whole foot gets completely distorted by the binding.'

'Of course. The foot gets squeezed heel to toe, breaking the arch under the foot until it's like a little hoof. That takes two or three years.' Mother turned to the Binder. 'Am I right?'

'It's not only the bandages that do it,' the Binder answered. 'Tomorrow I'll show you how to make training shoes. It's a bit like our flat platform shoes – which raise the foot above the mud – except that the platform is only under the heel. So the girls get used to walking with their feet pointing down into their toes. High heels are very helpful in crushing the toes and in breaking down the arch of the foot.'

'And the pain continues all those years?'

Mother looked at the Binder.

'Maybe not all the time,' said the Binder.

'My poor little girl,' moaned Mei-Ling.

'Don't encourage her to complain,' said Mother. 'You'll only make it worse.'

The two men returned at dusk. They were hungry. Mei-Ling could see that her brother-in-law had drunk a little wine in the village. Not too much, but enough to give him a slightly absent air.

Had her son also been drinking? Hardly at all. He never did. He smiled at them all in his usual quiet way. He looked so exactly like his father at the same age. Kind, even-tempered, thinking of others. But there was something else, a tension in him, that he hid.

He should have been married years ago. They'd had offers. But like his father before him, he'd been strangely obstinate about the whole business. She had an idea why.

'How's my little sister?' he wanted to know at once. 'Can I see her?'

'Not now,' Mei-Ling said. 'She's asleep.'

'Did everything go all right?'

'No problems at all,' Mother cut in. 'Sit down and eat.'

After the two men had eaten, Elder Son went to fetch his father's best opium pipe and prepared to smoke it.

The Binder stared at it. 'That's a fine pipe,' she said.

'My late husband's. Cost a lot of money,' said Mother.

'Most of the opium pipes in the town were confiscated and destroyed back in the time of Commissioner Lin,' the Binder remarked. 'You were lucky.'

'We hid it. He had another one, too,' Mother added with satisfaction. 'But Lin's men never came here.'

The Binder looked pensive. She's probably thinking she should have charged us more money, Mei-Ling thought.

'You know,' said the Binder after a pause, 'if you're going to secure a fine husband for Bright Moon – and I think you can – you need to make sure that she's expert at embroidery. Before she marries, besides making her trousseau, she'll be expected to make presents of embroidered shoes and other things for every one of the bridegroom's family. The satin and silk will cost money, of course, but most important of all will be the quality of her embroidery. She'll be judged by her future family entirely on that. If she wants to be respected, her needlework will need to be of the highest quality. Otherwise, she'll have a bad time.'

'Ah,' said Mother a little uncertainly.

'There's a woman in the town, a cousin of mine, who could teach her what she needs to know.'

'I'll remember that,' said Mother.

The next day, when they unbound Bright Moon's feet, they discovered the four small toes of each foot were already neatly broken. 'That's a very good start,' said the Binder. She started to wash the little girl's feet.

'Everyone needs to wash their feet to keep them clean and smelling nice,' she said, 'but you have to be especially careful with bound feet because of all the crevices. The big crevice will be between the folded heel and the ball of the foot. Sweat and dirt can start infections in there, which can smell bad.' She smiled at the little girl. 'Your lily feet will be your greatest asset in life, so you must take care of them and always keep them clean.'

When she'd dried and powdered Bright Moon's feet, she began to bind them again, a little more tightly this time. And Bright Moon began to cry out and complain.

'There there, my dear, I know it hurts,' the Binder said to her kindly. 'But just think how proud your father will be when he comes home and finds you've become such a fine young lady.'

'When is he coming back?' asked the girl miserably.

'Not until you've got some lily feet to show him,' said Mother firmly.

There was one question Mei-Ling wanted to ask. She could have asked her own sister-in-law years ago. But strangely, when poor Willow was alive, they never discussed such things. At first as the poor peasant girl in the family, she hadn't dared raise the subject with the elegant wife of the senior son. And later, with Willow trying to produce a boy and being sickly, it hadn't seemed appropriate.

Once she'd asked her husband, but he'd only grinned and told her: 'I'm sure I don't know, but I'm glad your feet aren't bound. I love you exactly the way you are.'

So that afternoon, when they happened to be alone, she asked the Binder: 'Why is it that men like women with bound feet so much?'

'Why do you think?'

'Well, it shows that the family has money. The woman doesn't have to work in the fields like a peasant.'

'That's true. It doesn't actually prevent your working in the fields, by the way. But it makes it harder, and you can't walk very far.'

'And men think that tiny bound feet are more beautiful than natural feet?'

'Some men are fascinated by the naked lily foot,' said the Binder. 'They like to kiss it and caress it. But mostly women keep their feet bound when they sleep with their husbands, and they wear tiny scented silk and satin slippers. Men find the slippers arousing.' She looked thoughtful. 'I suppose they like seeing the slippered feet waving about in the air, and that sort of thing. Like little boots, you know.'

The moon was nearly full that night. The house was silent. Her little girl had fallen asleep, but Mei-Ling lay awake.

After a time, she got up and went out into the courtyard. The moonlight was so bright that it made her blink. Most of the yard was gleaming, but part was in shadow. She sat on a bench at the shadow's edge. In front of her feet, in the moonlight, she could see a little pile of crinkled autumn leaves.

She'd been sitting there a minute or two when she became aware of a shape in the dark corner of the courtyard wall off to her right. She peered at it.

'You couldn't sleep, either,' said the shape.

'Oh, it's you,' she said as her son came out of the corner and sat beside her.

'I'd come out here when our little one was crying,' he said. 'Couldn't bear it.'

'She fell asleep an hour ago,' Mei-Ling said.

'I know. I just stayed here, watching the moon.' They were both silent for a while. 'I feel so bad.'

'Why?'

'The little girl having to suffer like this so she can have tiny feet and get a rich man and help us, when we should be helping ourselves. And what am I doing? I ask myself.'

'You're doing your best. You're a good worker. You keep the place going.'

'You know, there's a piece of land we could buy on the other side of the village. Maybe I could borrow the money. If Elder Uncle would do some work, we could farm it. But I can't take it on by myself.'

'Maybe when your father and your brother get back . . .'

'Yes.' He nodded. 'They haven't sent us any money yet, have they?'

'It's a long way. They will.'

'I don't even know where California is.' He fell silent again.

'Far away,' she said absently.

'When my little sister gets married, she'll need to have all sorts of things. Embroidered shoes and I don't know what. That all costs money. Do you suppose we'll have enough?'

'Mother and I have thought of that,' said Mei-Ling.

'What are you going to do?'

'Sell your uncle's opium pipe.'

'He won't like that.' A slow smile crept over her son's face. 'He'll have a fit.'

Mei-Ling nodded slowly, but her thoughts seemed to have moved on to another subject. 'Do you know what else worries me?' she asked.

'No.'

'You should be married. We should have made you marry long ago.'

'Like father, like son, I suppose.' He smiled. 'My father was obstinate when he made his parents let him marry you.'

She sighed. He looked so like his father just then that it almost gave her pain. 'What sort of girl do you want?'

'Someone like you.'

'I'm sure you could do better. My family had nothing, remember.'

'I'm not ambitious. I'm a peasant. I work the land. I like it that way.'

'Then we'll find you a nice girl like me.'

'Not yet.'

'Why?'

'The house is too sad.'

'Maybe it would be happier if you had a wife and children.'

'Maybe.' He paused. 'Nothing feels right. What with Elder Uncle being the way he is, and Father not here and . . . I don't know.'

'Things are never completely right.'

'When Father gets back, and my brother, and they bring more money . . .'

'You'll marry then? You promise?'

'All right.' He nodded. 'I promise.'

When Father gets back. But when might that be? In another two years?

There was not a day when Mei-Ling did not think of Second Son. Not a night when she did not long for him. But there had been no word. Soon, perhaps, they might hear something. If the American came again, he would bring news and money, too, perhaps. But so far, nothing.

And still that little voice spoke to her and told her: 'You will not see him again.'

The Binder was as good as her word, and it had to be said she was thorough. By the time the month was up, she had taught both Mei-Ling and Mother how to tie the bandages, wrapping them a little tighter each time; how to sew them in place so that they didn't need to be changed every day; how to wash and powder each foot. She also taught them how to lift the little girl up and drop her onto a narrow block of wood laid on the ground – a most useful exercise that helped to break down the arches of her feet. Though she still had to reprove Mei-Ling from time to time for weeping when Bright Moon screamed – which, as she pointed out, was no help to the little girl at all.

'When will I stop wearing bandages?' Bright Moon asked her one day.

'Never, my dear,' the Binder explained. 'You'll always have a light binding for the rest of your life, just to keep everything in place.'

She left on a sunny morning, promising to return a month later.

Around noon that day, the weather changed. Grey clouds, trailing skirts of mist, came into the valley from the coast. A dull humidity settled over the hamlet. Bright Moon was subdued. Mother had sat down indoors and closed her eyes.

Mei-Ling went out through the gate and stared down at the pond. The water was grey as the sky. The reeds by the bank hung their heads – in boredom, perhaps. The flock of ducks at the foot of the bridge made no sound.

She stood there for a quarter of an hour before she saw the single figure emerge from the trees at the far end of the bridge. The figure paused, as if debating whether to cross the bridge, so she supposed it wasn't someone from the hamlet. And she was about to call out that the wood was rotten and that it wasn't safe when the person evidently came to the same conclusion and disappeared back onto the path through the woods. She wondered idly who the stranger might be. But since the track led to the village lane in one direction, or into a network of fields some way behind the house in the other, she didn't expect to see him again.

She was taken by surprise, five minutes later, when the figure came from behind the barn and made its way towards her, and she realised that it was her younger son.

'Mother.' He had grown a little taller, thickened, turned into a powerful young workingman during his absence. He carried a bag on his back, a stick in his hand. He didn't smile at the sight of her. He looked very tired.

'You are back,' she cried. How could he be back already? 'You came from America?'

'Yes.'

'Where is your father?'

But with a sinking heart she guessed, even before he said it.

'Father's dead.'

After he told her what had happened, he said he needed to lie down. Then he slept.

Mei-Ling told Mother first, asked her to tell the others and to ensure no one disturbed her sleeping son. 'We'll get the whole story when he wakes up tomorrow,' she promised.

But first, she thought, she'd better prepare her poor little daughter. So she went in to Bright Moon and sat on the bed and gently told her: 'There is bad news. Your father had an accident. He was killed, in America.'

The little girl didn't say anything for a moment. She just stared in shock.

'I'm here, my little one, and so is all your family, and your brother is back from America, too. We're all here. But your father won't be back.' And she put her arms around the child.

'I'll never see him again?'

'You can think of him. I'm sure he's watching over you.'

Then Bright Moon started to cry. And Mei-Ling cried with her. And stayed with her for an hour until she had fallen asleep.

But she herself lay awake for a long time afterwards. And she thought of all the good things about her husband and wished she could speak to him just one more time, at least to say goodbye.

And then she felt anger towards him for leaving her like this, as the living often do towards the dead.

Her son slept and she would not let anyone disturb him. He slept through the evening, all through the night, and into the next morning. At noon he woke. Mei-Ling brought him a little food; and she made him go for a long walk in the afternoon. It wasn't until the evening that he faced the rest of the family, who gathered to hear his story.

Elder Son presided. It was strange to see him sitting in old Mr Lung's chair, trying to look important. As long as her husband was alive, Elder Son knew that however little he did, there was someone else to take over control. But now Second Son was suddenly gone. Until Mei-Ling's boys were older, there was no one to be head of the Lung family. Perhaps Elder Son meant to do his duty after all, though she wondered how long that would last.

'Tell us how it happened,' he said gravely.

'It was an accident,' his nephew explained. 'No one's fault, really. Laying the tracks is hard work, but it isn't difficult. The work's always the same. Clear the land, build the foundation, place the wooden sleepers, then the iron rails on top of them. You have to be careful because the timber and iron are all so heavy, but it's all routine and we knew what we were doing. Everything was all right until we went up into the mountains.'

'What mountains?'

'A range they call the Sierra Nevada. Runs parallel to the coast. The mountains are high, but the railway has to cross them to go east. It can be dangerous working in the passes.'

'How did he die?'

'An avalanche. No one saw it coming. The foreman had sent me down the line to order extra gravel. I'd gone just a quarter of a mile when I turned and saw a section of cliff high above the tracks split from the mountain and come sliding down. It was almost silent for a moment, and it seemed to be moving quite slowly. Then there was a rumble, and a sort of gravelly hiss and then a roar. I could see rocks bouncing down the mountainside, and the earthslide was so fast it was almost like a waterfall. Then a huge cloud of dust at the bottom.' He paused. 'We all started working with shovels or anything we could use to dig the men out. There were twenty or thirty. A lot of them were quite badly hurt and two or three suffocated. But we didn't find Father.'

'He didn't escape?'

'I thought he might have and I kept calling his name, but there was no sign of him. So I just kept digging with some of the other fellows. And after an hour I found him. Well, what was left of him. A big boulder hit him. It must have killed him at once.' He glanced at his mother and little sister, then at his brother. 'I'm sure he didn't feel any pain.'

'When was this?'

'About a year ago.'

'Then why,' asked Elder Son, 'did you return? You should have completed your contract.' Mei-Ling looked at him furiously, but Elder Son shook his head and continued sternly: 'You must have given up a lot of money, and that's what you went there for.'

'I know. I thought of all that,' said the young man. 'And I didn't leave. They gave me what was due to Father, and I went on working.'

'Then why are you here now?' Elder Son pursued relentlessly.

'The young American came by. He checks on all the people he transports. I believe he's the only one who does that. So he knew about Father before he even got to me. Then he said, "Do you know there's smallpox in the next work camp?" Well, I'd heard a rumour that some of the rail workers were sick, but since I was under contract, I didn't see much point in worrying about it. "You're to get out of here," he told me. "I watch out for my Chinese fellows, and I'm not losing you as well as your father." '

'That's all very well . . .' Elder Son started, but his nephew hurried on.

'I was going to refuse. But he said he did a lot of business with the railways and he'd take care of it. And before I knew it, he'd got them to pay out my full contract and Father's as well; and I was on my way back home.'

'Let me see the money you brought,' said Elder Son.

'It's in a safe place,' said Mother firmly. 'I'll show you tomorrow.'

All this time, Mei-Ling was watching her daughter, who'd been listening, wide-eyed but silent. Then Bright Moon closed her eyes, as though she was trying to shut the news out. When the little girl opened her eyes again, her look was so blank that Mei-Ling had the feeling that her daughter was retreating, closing herself off from them all, like a person folding their arms across their chest. She hoped it would pass.

'Where is your father buried?' she asked her son.

'Farther down the valley. It's a proper grave. I'd know where to find it.'

She nodded slowly. Would she ever tend her husband's grave? She didn't imagine so.

'What is this place like, this California?' asked Elder Son.

'The weather's mild, drier than here. America's big, but not many people.'

'They don't have big cities like ours?' Elder Son asked.

'Not in California. Not yet, anyway. There are big cities in other parts of America. But mostly they don't have walls around them.'

'How can you have a city without walls?' said Mother. 'What if you're attacked?'

'I don't know. They just had a big war there. Fighting each other. A lot of people killed. Like the Taiping. The fighting never came near California.'

'How did the railway bosses treat you?' Mei-Ling asked.

'They like the Chinese. We work hard. We don't give any trouble. There's a lot of Chinese working on the California railway already, and more coming all the time. It used to be mostly Irishmen doing the manual work out there,' he added proudly. 'Big, strong men. But when the Irish complained about us taking their jobs, the railway boss told them that if they didn't stop complaining, he'd replace them all with Chinese.'

'What's Irish?' asked Mother.

'A barbarian tribe. There are many barbarian tribes in America.'

Elder Son seemed satisfied with all he'd heard. 'Perhaps we should all go to America,' he said.

'You have to work there,' Mother murmured softly, but Elder Son didn't hear. That night he smoked his father's opium pipe.

In the morning, while Elder Son was still asleep, Mother, Mei-Ling and her two sons held a family conference. By now, both in the family and in the village, her younger son had acquired a new name: California Brother.

The first question was what her two sons should do. California Brother offered to return to America, but before Mei-Ling could even voice her anguish at the thought, Mother told him firmly: 'No. We need you both here.'

'In that case,' Ka-Fai said, turning to Mei-Ling, 'what about the land I told you about that's for sale on the other side of the village? Do we have enough money to buy it now? I'm sure the two of us could work it.'

Mei-Ling looked at Mother, who pursed her lips. 'I know the price of that land. If we use the money from America and sell the opium pipe, we might have enough. But then we won't have the money we need to spend on Bright Moon so she can get a rich husband. And now that we've already bound her feet . . .'

'We could borrow the money for the land,' California Brother suggested.

'No debt,' said Mother firmly.

'I think . . .' Mei-Ling spoke slowly, weighing her words. 'I think that you should buy the land. After all, as soon as you work it, that'll bring in extra money. We don't have to find a husband for Bright Moon for years yet. Something might turn up in the meantime.' She saw Mother give her a long look.

'As you wish,' said Mother. 'We'll sell the opium pipe.'

'You're going to sell Grandfather's opium pipe?' California Brother asked in surprise. 'What will Elder Uncle say?'

'He can smoke through a bamboo pipe instead,' Mother said dourly. 'The opium will keep him quiet.'

Nobody spoke. She had just deposed her own son as the nominal head of the family. They all heard it. Things weren't supposed to be that way. But they knew she was right.

As her two boys went out together, Mei-Ling heard California Brother say, 'The first thing I'm going to do is rebuild the bridge over the pond.'

'We'll do it together,' his brother Ka-Fai agreed.

The incident happened in the middle of the day. It took Mei-Ling by surprise. She and little Bright Moon and Mother were all sitting on a bench, watching the two brothers who were already waist-high in the pond pulling rotten timbers from the bridge.

A few minutes earlier, she'd gone down and whispered to her younger son: 'You've had so much to think about since you got back, but when you finish, just pay some attention to your little sister, because you've hardly said a word to her yet.'

He'd given her a nod. And sure enough, as he came out of the water and squelched his way up the slope to the bench with a big friendly grin on his face, he looked down at Bright Moon and said, 'How's my beautiful little sister today?'

When Bright Moon didn't reply, but stared at the ground, they thought she must be shy.

'She's not used to you,' said Mother.

'Once I'm dry,' he said to the girl, 'we'll sit and have a talk together.' And he went inside.

Everyone was back in the courtyard when he reappeared. Elder Son, unaware of the family conference earlier on, had also joined them. Bright Moon was sitting under the tree with Mei-Ling, who got up and indicated to California Brother that he should take her place. He'd just sat down when Elder Son decided to address them.

'Since my dear brother died almost a year ago, in a far country, none of the usual funeral rules apply. But we shall mourn him for two days.' It was said in a simple and dignified manner, and nobody argued. Mother nodded her approval. After that, conversation resumed.

'You look so grown-up already, with your dainty feet,' California Brother remarked to Bright Moon in a kindly way. 'Father often talked of you when we were working on the railway, you know. He'd be so proud to see you now.'

Bright Moon didn't reply.

'I'm sorry I brought bad news,' he went on. 'You must be very sad.'

It seemed that she might be about to speak to him now, so he waited. 'Everyone says that,' she suddenly burst out. She was still staring at the ground.

'Says what?'

'That Father would be proud. It's not true.'

'Oh?' He frowned. 'Why?'

'I hate my bound feet,' she burst out. 'I hate them. They're not dainty. They're all squashed and the bones are broken, and they hurt all the time. It hurts!' she screamed out.

'Well, I know it hurts for a while . . .' he ventured. But she cut him short.

'What do you know? Did they bind your feet? No, I'm a cripple now.'

'Don't speak that way,' said Mother sharply. 'You should be beaten.'

'I don't care,' the little girl shouted back. 'It can't hurt more than my feet.'

'What a temper she has,' cried Mother. But she didn't do anything.

'It's for your own good,' said Elder Son firmly, not because he'd really been involved, but because he thought he was head of the family.

'If you and Father hadn't gone away' – she turned on California Brother – 'I wouldn't be like this. Father would never have let them bind my feet. He loved me.'

'It's for your own good,' said Mei-Ling.

'No, it isn't,' her daughter replied sorrowfully. 'You just want me to marry someone rich so I can get money for you.'

'Where did she learn to talk like that at such an age?' Mother demanded.

'Actually, you know . . .' California Brother began gently, but Mei-Ling gave him such a look that he stopped.

'Go to your room,' Mei-Ling ordered her daughter. She watched the child hobble painfully across the courtyard. When Bright Moon had gone, Mei-Ling turned back to her younger son. 'You were going to say your father agreed her feet should be bound.'

'He said so in California many times.'

'But the child has got it into her head that her father would have stopped it.' And perhaps, if he'd seen the pain, he might have, she thought. 'And now,' she went on, 'her father's dead. And she remembers how kind he was and how he held her hand, and so she believes he would have saved her from the foot-binding. It's the only thing she has.'

'Who's she going to blame, then?' asked California Brother. 'Me? My brother? You?'

'Me and Mother, I should think,' said Mei-Ling.

'But it's still a lie,' said Mother.

Mei-Ling looked at Mother. 'We know that Second Son doted on his daughter,' she said. 'And if the only way Bright Moon can know that big truth is to believe a little lie, then let her believe.'

Mother nodded. 'You may be right, my daughter. Besides, she is angry because she is so hurt by her father's death.'

The rest of the day passed peacefully. The two brothers went over to inspect the fields on the other side of the village. Elder Son went with them. On their return, California Brother sat and talked to Bright Moon without further incident. And after they had eaten that night, California Brother said he was sleepy, and everyone turned in.

But Mei-Ling didn't feel sleepy. She took a small lantern and went out into the courtyard.

She wanted to be alone with her thoughts for a while, to mourn alone. And for some time she sat there. But mourning does not always come so easily. The sky was overcast, opaque.

And she had been there for some time when her older son appeared.

'Not tired?' Ka-Fai asked. She shook her head. 'I'm tired, but I still can't sleep.' He sat beside her. 'The moon must be almost full,' he said, jutting his jaw up at the clouds, 'if we could only see it.'

'Full tomorrow,' she replied. 'Perhaps the sky will be clear.'

He yawned. She watched. His face was just like his father's. She felt a sudden bittersweet rush of love.

'Do you remember what you promised to do when your father came home?' she asked. He nodded. 'Your brother's home,' she went on. 'That counts as the same thing.'

'I know.'

'So you'll marry?' Again he nodded. 'Have you anyone in mind?' she wanted to know. He shook his head. 'Do you want to think about it?'

'Families are supposed to decide these things,' Ka-Fai said, 'not the bridegroom.'

'I know. But you're so obstinate, I thought . . .'

'You choose.' He gave her a smile.

'Oh,' she said. She felt rather pleased.

They were quiet for a little while. Then he said, 'I'm sleepy now,' and went to bed.

Mei-Ling stayed there alone. She was pleased about the marriage. As she considered her son's strengths and limitations, she couldn't immediately think of any particular girl for him, or even a type of girl. But she felt sure she'd recognise the right girl when she found her.

And after the misery she had endured watching Bright Moon suffer so much, the idea of arranging a happy marriage for her son was like balm on a wound.

As the minutes passed, her thoughts turned to her husband. How was it she'd sensed that Second Son would not return? She couldn't say. Had something happened that first cloudy night after he'd left, when her little messages of love, so carefully wrapped, had never seemed to reach him? Had he turned away from her? Surely not. She had continued to send her thoughts after him as the months went by; and several times it had seemed to her that she could feel him thinking of her in return. But she wasn't sure, if truth be told.

She'd always thought she'd know it if he died. It was just an assumption, an article of faith, almost.

But she hadn't. She knew now when it must have happened. Yet at that time she'd felt nothing. Nothing at all.

As she sat in the courtyard now, in the dark, she remembered all the good things about him, all the moments they had shared. She thought of his kindly ways. Surely, she supposed, these things would bring her comfort and warmth. She wanted to open a door in the sky, through which his spirit might enter and be with her again.

But the sky was blank. His spirit did not come. As if she were inside a box whose lid had been locked, she waited in silence. Her love was lost. And she felt nothing.

Nothing at all.

o

It was the following spring when Shi-Rong made his journey to Guilin Prefecture. He was accompanied only by two servants and his secretary, a tall young man named Peng. The journey took two months.

At the end of the first month Peng asked him: 'Isn't this the wrong way, master?' To which he replied: 'You ask too many questions.' He'd taken Peng as a favour to the young man's father, an important man, a friend of Prince Gong. The young man was Mr Peng's third son, and his father didn't quite know what to do with him.

The understanding between Shi-Rong and Peng's father was simple. 'We both know you should have had a promotion years ago, my dear fellow,' Mr Peng had declared. 'There's a job open down in Guilin. Sub-prefect. Fifth rank. Go down there. Avoid trouble. Play it safe. In another year or two there will be a number of appointments coming up, and I think I can get you one which carries both promotion and profit.'

'Guilin?' Shi-Rong had pursed his lips. It wasn't just a backwater. The Miao people, a big ethnic tribe who'd been giving trouble for centuries, had been in a state of rebellion for the last decade. True, the insurrections had all been in the next province to the north. But there were plenty of Miao folk in the area around Guilin. It might be uncomfortable, even dangerous. 'You've really nothing else to suggest?' he asked.

'If you're worrying about the Miao, I just had a letter from the prefect there. He's a splendid fellow. He assures me it's all right. It's poor but quite beautiful. Put a little time in there, and you'll be rewarded, I promise you.'

It was a chance, at least, the best hope he'd had for quite a while. So he'd accepted it gratefully. And when his patron mentioned that his third son needed a job, Shi-Rong had taken the hint at once.

'Is there anything I need to know about the young man?' he asked.

'You'll have to tell him to stop talking.' Peng's father gave him an apologetic smile. 'Frequently.'

During the first month Peng asked quite a lot of questions about the administration of a prefecture and his duties. The questions weren't stupid, and Shi-Rong was content to answer them. He also taught the young man some Cantonese. It passed the time, after all. And he soon evolved ways of shutting the young man up, without being unkind.

'Will your wife and family be joining us?' Peng asked on the second day.

'Not at present. My daughter, sadly, is not in good health. Not well enough to travel. My dear wife will remain with her at our family home until she is stronger.'

'I see. Shall we have the pleasure of seeing your sons?'

'Perhaps. My elder boy is busy with his studies at present. But it may do him good to come to Guilin for a rest in a few months.'

'It must be difficult to be parted from one's wife,' Peng ventured.

'Indeed,' said Shi-Rong. Not as difficult as you suppose, he could have added. Instead he said solemnly: 'Our duty to the emperor comes first.'

'Oh. Of course, master. Duty first.'

'And now I should like to enjoy the view in silence, my dear Peng,' Shi-Rong said firmly, 'if you would be so kind.'

'Is it true,' Peng asked another time, 'that you were with the great Lord Lin as his private secretary during his time in Guangzhou?'

'It is true.'

'My father says that Lord Lin was a great hero, and the most honest servant of the emperor who ever lived,' Peng continued.

'He was certainly honest,' Shi-Rong replied. 'As you know, he was temporarily disgraced and then reinstated, but his career never quite recovered. I am glad that after his death his memory has been held in ever higher esteem.'

'My father says most mandarins are just out to line their pockets.'

'Nobody's perfect,' Shi-Rong said cautiously.

'My father says you're like the lord Lin.'

'He is too kind. I am undeserving.'

'I know I shall see nothing but the utmost correctness in all your actions in Guilin, master,' Peng went on enthusiastically. 'I shall study all you do.'

Shi-Rong did not reply. He seemed to be considering something.

In fact, young Peng's enthusiasm was not entirely misplaced. By the standards of many men in his position, Shi-Rong had been a model of probity. But it wasn't as if his reputation for probity had brought him any promotion. It hadn't. He was in his fifties now, and he hadn't risen very far. If he was going to do something for his family, earn the respect of his children at least, then he needed to put some money by and add to the family fortune. Not that he would stoop to evil conduct. If a man was rightly accused of a crime and the family tried to bribe him to find the fellow innocent, he wouldn't even consider it. But there might be other, more harmless ways to come by extra money. And if these came his way, then perhaps occasionally he might avail himself of the opportunity in future. If he was sure he wouldn't be caught.

Anyway, it was time for Peng to shut up again. 'Do you know the little poem "Silent Night" by the poet Li Bai of the Tang dynasty?' he suddenly asked.

'Of course, master. Every child knows it.'

'Recite the poem to me.'

Peng did so:

Moonlight makes my bed board gleam
Like the ground frost's silver sheen
Look up to see the moon so bright
Look down, and see your childhood home

'Excellent,' said Shi-Rong. 'Li Bai wrote over a thousand poems, you know, and another of them has just come into my mind. I should like to contemplate it now, uninterrupted,' he added pleasantly, 'for the rest of the day.'

So they continued into the second month. And Shi-Rong was pleased to note that never, not even once, did Peng again ask him why they were going so far to the south.

o

The sun was sinking in the west when Mei-Ling saw the four horsemen approaching. She was standing at the gate with Elder Son admiring the newly completed bridge over the pond below.

The head of the household was in a cheerful mood. He'd even managed to collect some rent from a tenant that day. 'Look at what a good job we've made of that bridge,' he had just remarked, quite as if he'd done some of the work himself.

One of the horsemen, a tall young man, dismounted and approached them. 'My master is an important official,' he told Elder Son in halting Cantonese. 'We need shelter for the night. We'd pay you well.'

The young man certainly looked like an official. Mei-Ling's gaze travelled to the other riders: two servants, obviously and a mandarin. The mandarin was walking his horse closer.

But when she saw his face, Mei-Ling went very pale. Her mind began to race. Why had he come? Could it be about Nio? Had he heard something? Was it possible?

'Of course, by all means, we should be honoured,' she heard Elder Son saying. 'We were about to eat, if you will join us.'

The men sat around the table: Shi-Rong, young Peng, Elder Son, and her two boys. She and Mother served them. Her son's new wife, a cheerful peasant girl they all liked, was looking after Shi-Rong's two servants, who were to be housed in the barn. Bright Moon had been told to stay in her room.

Shi-Rong was treating Elder Son with a friendly courtesy that he certainly didn't deserve. California Son was telling Peng about America, while Ka-Fai was smiling amiably at everyone.

'It's him, isn't it?' Mother whispered when they were in the kitchen together. When Mei-Ling silently nodded, Mother explained: 'I never really got a good look at him that time before. Not enough to recognise him. But when I saw your face just now . . .'

'Why is he here, Mother? Could it have something to do with Nio?'

'It might be Nio, if he's alive.'

Bright Moon appeared, just as they were finishing the meal. Curiosity got the better of the young girl, and she came out of her room to see what was going on.

Shi-Rong stared at her in surprise. 'Who is this beautiful young lady?'

'My daughter,' Mei-Ling said.

'I see.' He gazed at them both. 'She looks just like you.'

'Her father's pride and joy,' said Mother. 'My younger son, sir. He adored the child.'

'Adored?'

'He died a year and a half ago.'

'I am sorry to hear it.' Shi-Rong bowed his head, but he continued to look at Bright Moon. 'You are binding her feet, I see,' he remarked.

'Beauty like this shouldn't go to waste,' said Mother.

'Certainly not.' Shi-Rong nodded his approval.

The girl opened her mouth as if to speak. She still complained about her feet, almost every day. Was she about to embarrass them by venting her feelings to a mandarin? Mother gave her such a look that even Bright Moon wisely decided to remain silent.

'An excellent meal,' Shi-Rong said politely. 'And now I shall stroll by the pond for a little while.' He turned to Mei-Ling. 'Perhaps the mother of this lovely child would accompany me.'

Shredded clouds, high in the sky, caught the light of the third quarter moon as they walked down to the bridge in silence.

What did he want? Mei-Ling wondered.

They stepped onto the bridge and walked towards the middle, where he paused. He pointed down at the reflection of the moon in the water. She nodded, to signify that she had seen it.

'Tell me,' he said quietly, 'have you heard anything from Nio?'

So that was it. He was after Nio again.

'Nothing.' She looked at him sadly. 'You want to arrest him?'

'No. I just wondered what happened to him. We were not always enemies, you know.'

'I have heard nothing in five years.'

'Then he's dead. Maybe at Nanjing.'

She knew how the Taiping had at last been broken. The Ever-Victorious Army, as they were called – armed with barbarian rifles and cannon – had smashed them. Finally Nanjing had been taken. The Heavenly King was dead. The slaughter had been terrible.

'I know he loved you,' Shi-Rong continued. 'If he were alive, I think he would have come by now.' He smiled sadly. 'The Taiping will never be a threat again. So I wouldn't arrest him if I did see him, unless he forced me to. Actually, it was you I came to see,' he continued quietly.

'Me?' She looked astonished. 'Why?'

It was fate, he thought. It had to be fate. When he set out on his journey, he had known only one thing: he needed a change. A couple of years away from a not-very-happy marriage until he got a promotion that might put his wife in a more affectionate temper. A time to reflect, live for himself a little.

And perhaps find some companionship.

From time to time he'd wondered whether to take a concubine. Law and custom allowed it. People almost expected it of a man in his position. Many a respectable family down on their luck would have been happy to supply him with one of their daughters – well brought up, with bound feet and a smattering of culture – on reasonable terms.

Sometimes concubines and wives got along quite well. But he couldn't see it working with his own wife. It would cause her pain. There would be anger. Endless anger. He might not feel that he was loved, but he had no wish to cause his wife more pain.

The solution was to take a temporary concubine, just for the period he was away. This, too, was perfectly acceptable. Any middle-aged mandarin might be expected to regain his youth with a pretty girl. And there were plenty of pretty and elegant women in the big cities who were well trained to fill such a role.

So why had he turned south and made a detour, which added two hundred and fifty miles to his journey, to reach an obscure hamlet that might or might not contain a peasant woman with unbound feet with whom, years ago, he had spent a moonlit night sitting by a pond while she told him the story of her life?

Her beauty. Her honesty. That had impressed him. Her intelligence. And something else, something magical that he couldn't define. Maybe it was just the moonlight, but he didn't think so. It had haunted him.

And now that he had this little period of freedom, he had just wanted to find her again, to see if she was how he remembered. He was quite ready to find her changed or find her magic gone in the broad daylight, so to speak. Most likely of all, to find that she was unavailable.

But he had almost gasped when he saw her just now. She was everything he remembered. Perhaps more.

And she was widowed. And therefore, presumably, available. It had to be fate.

He paused a moment. 'I am sorry that you lost your husband. But you have two fine sons at home and your little girl. She has your beauty. And with bound feet, she could find a rich husband.'

'We hope she will find a good husband,' she said quietly.

'You should also teach her embroidery and so forth, and some of the other arts that belong to a young lady. She should learn to recite a few poems. That sort of thing.'

Why was he telling her this? She had no idea. But in order to say something and because it was so much in her mind, she heard herself respond: 'You have to spend money to get a rich husband. I've learned that much already.'

'Ah.' He placed his hands on the rail of the bridge and stared at them. 'I may be able to help you there.' He turned to her. 'If you like.' He saw her look suspicious. 'I shall be in Guilin Prefecture for a year, maybe a year and a half,' he went on quickly. 'I want you to accompany me.'

'Accompany?' She frowned. 'You mean as a concubine?'

'Yes.'

'Why don't you get a concubine there?'

'You have haunted me ever since we met that night with Nio. I have thought of you ever since. I came two hundred and fifty miles out of the way to find you.'

'Have you a wife?'

'She will not be there. You can bring your little girl, if you want. She would learn much that way, about how a man like me lives. It could be useful to her.'

Have her child living in this man's house where she was a concubine? It was not what she wanted.

But she couldn't deny that what he'd said was true. She knew almost nothing about the sophisticated lifestyle of a rich man or a mandarin. The habits, the conversation, the social rituals. Nor did anyone in her family or in the hamlet, if truth were told. If Bright Moon wanted to find a rich husband, a year or two in a mandarin's house would be the perfect education for her.

A year or two – or until he gets tired of me, she thought, and kicks me out. She didn't want her little girl to see that.

'My daughter stays here at home,' she said.

'As you wish. Does that mean that you might consider my proposition?'

'I would be free to leave in a year and a half?'

'Yes.'

Mei-Ling thought. Buy the land, she'd told her sons. The money for Bright Moon would turn up. She'd believed it was the right thing to do. But the truth was she had no idea where that extra money would come from. And now, suddenly, here was an opportunity for her to earn the money herself. However little she liked it, her duty was clear. As long as the money was enough and she was sure of getting it.

There were risks, of course. This mandarin might mistreat her. She supposed she could endure a beating or two. If it got worse, she could always run away. Or maybe kill him, she thought, and then kill myself. So long as the money was secure.

'You'd have to pay me in advance,' she said. 'You'd have to pay me now.'

'And trust you?'

'Yes.'

'I thought you might say that.'

He took out a small bag full of coins, put it in her hands and opened it. She looked inside. She could see the silver coins by the moonlight. She didn't take them out to count them, but it was quite a lot of money.

'I need two bags like this,' she said.

He looked impressed. And to her surprise, pulled out another bag. She looked inside that one, too.

'The same,' he said. 'You have my word.'

Mei-Ling calculated quickly. If she gave the bags of silver to Mother at once, the older woman could hide them where no one would find them, not even her own two sons.

She looked at this man she hardly knew. What would Second Son say? That she was doing what she had to, she supposed, since he was not there to help her. Yes, she told herself, he'd say something like that. And just for a moment, the first time since she'd heard of his death, it seemed to Mei-Ling that she felt her husband's presence.

'We shall have to ask the head of the family,' she said.

o

Mei-Ling liked Guilin. Shi-Rong could see she did. It had been a long journey, some three hundred miles north of the hamlet, but when they got there, they both agreed: the place was quite remarkable. Millennia of rains and flowing waters had sculpted the soft karst stone of the region into a landscape of miniature mountains, steep as anthills, hundreds of feet high and covered with green trees, except for the grey cliffs on their sides, here and there, where even mountain trees couldn't find their footing. A pleasant river, called the Li, flowed beside the town.

On sunny days the hills gathered around the intimate plateaus of pastures and rice fields, like giant green dolmens protecting a sanctuary. But when the mists filled the river valleys, then the onlooker seemed to be witnessing an army of hooded gods moving slowly through a world of clouds. Shi-Rong had seen such landscapes in paintings and supposed they must be imaginary. Now he discovered that this paradise was real.

She liked the subtropical climate, rather hot and humid for his own taste, and she liked the people, too.

Some of the local tribes had lived around Guilin since before China was a state. Each tribe seemed to have its own language or dialect – often as not incomprehensible to its neighbours. The servants in Shi-Rong's official residence were all from the Zhuang tribe, which was the largest. And somehow, within a month, Mei-Ling was freely conversing with them, and even enjoying their sour pickled cabbage and the tea leaves fried in oil that they seemed to eat with rice every day. 'You can eat it for me,' Shi-Rong told her with a laugh.

But he couldn't help being impressed by how adaptable this peasant woman from her little hamlet showed herself to be. 'How do you do it?' he asked.

'I don't know,' she said. 'But my mother was half Hakka, so I was used to having family in two worlds from the start of my life. Perhaps that helps me.'

He soon realised that her intelligence went far beyond talking to the Zhuang servants.

When he first arrived, he'd wondered what to do with Mei-Ling as regards the prefect and the other officials. Of course, he could keep her secluded in the house. But then people would talk and make up stories. So after a month, when he had got to know the prefect, who turned out to be a kindly and easygoing man, he told him frankly about his charming concubine. 'She's just a peasant, part Hakka. But she's intelligent and very beautiful. What should I do with her?'

'My dear Jiang,' the genial grey-bearded prefect said, smiling, 'rumours of her beauty had reached me. I was wondering if I'd get to see her.'

'I must warn you that her feet aren't even bound.'

'I'll start a rumour that she's half Manchu.' The older man grinned. 'We're so far from Beijing down here, you know, and surrounded by all these curious tribes, that we don't worry about all that. Bring her to see my wife. She's always glad of fresh company.'

Shi-Rong did as bid. The two women met for an hour. Afterwards, Mei-Ling told him that the prefect's wife wanted her to return the next day. And to his astonishment, this invitation was repeated a dozen times in the course of a month. Any doubts he might have had about these visits were soon dispelled when the prefect remarked: 'My wife enjoys Mei-Ling's company so much. They chatter away all afternoon.'

'How do you talk to each other?' he once asked Mei-Ling. 'I suppose she speaks Cantonese.'

'Yes, she speaks Cantonese. But she's teaching me to speak Mandarin.'

'What do you talk about?'

'She's quite curious about my little hamlet and our simple life. She's always lived in towns. And I have many questions for her.'

'Oh,' he said, wondering what those might be. He was to discover a month later, when she announced one day that she was going to serve him tea. Nothing unusual in that, of course. It was a normal ritual in any household in the land. He was surprised, however, to find a beautiful new tea set laid out in the most elegant manner, and still more so when Mei-Ling ministered to him in a rich silk dress and with her hair coiffed as elaborately as a Beijing lady's. Not only did she make polite conversation in Mandarin, but she even dropped appropriate poetic quotations into the conversation.

How in the world had she learned such things? Obviously, from the prefect's wife. And as time passed, her accomplishments increased. She began to hold herself in a different way. Her Mandarin improved so much that in a year, he supposed, it would be quite elegant.

What was her purpose? To please him? To show what she could do? Or might it be that after enjoying the life of a sub-prefect's household, she might not want to go back to her poor hamlet. She might be thinking that after they parted she could become the concubine of another official, or even the wife of a merchant, perhaps.

A new suspicion came to him when he noticed something else.

At first he had observed that she gently avoided his attentions at the time of the month when she might conceive, and he did not complain.

But then she gave that up. She was not too old to have a child. Was it possible that she was now calculating that she could make her position permanent if she gave him a child? And come to that, if such an event had occurred, what would he do? So one evening he asked her outright: 'Are you risking having a child?'

'No,' she said calmly. 'There's an herbal drink you can take. It's made from dandelion roots and the thunder-god vine. It's very effective. The apothecary gives it to me.'

'I didn't know that,' he confessed.

'Neither did I. The prefect's wife told me about it.'

Shi-Rong wasn't sure how he felt about the prefect's wife intruding quite so far into his private life, but there wasn't much he could do about it.

The idea of keeping her for the longer term still remained. It was tempting. As a lover, she gave him everything a man could wish for. He constantly looked at her with a sense of wonder. While they were making love, there were moments when he would ask himself: how can it be that I feel this strange magic? She was like that southern region's rose, with its never-fading colour, repeatedly blooming. Or like the lotus, China's symbol of purity, which rises out of the common mud to flower.

Whether Mei-Ling's own emotions were engaged was another matter.

Did he know how she felt? Not really.

'You do so many things to please me,' he said to her kindly one day. 'I hope you know that I am grateful that you learn so much.'

'I am glad you are pleased,' she said politely. She seemed to pause for a moment. 'And I am grateful to you in turn, that I can learn such things for my daughter.'

For her daughter. Of course. How could I have been so vain, he thought and so foolish? She is learning so that she can teach all this to her little girl, whose feet are being bound, to make her a lady. And though he might have liked it if she had been seeking to please only him, he couldn't help admiring her.

Soon afterwards, she started learning to read and write, and curious to discover more about her mind, he even began to teach her a little himself.

She learned fast. 'Another skill you'll be able to teach your little girl,' he remarked laughingly.

But she shook her head. 'I can get her started, but she'll need a proper teacher. I'll need money for that.'

Shi-Rong said nothing. But he got the message.

She was curious about everything. She wanted to know about Beijing and the Forbidden City, and how things were done there. She asked about the great rivers and the city of Nanjing, the Grand Canal and the Great Wall. All these things she had heard of, but never seen. She wanted to know about the emperor, too.

'He was only six when his father died,' he explained, 'so he's still a young boy. He's taken the name of Tongzhi for his reign. It means "Union for Order" – which is certainly what we need. He's advised by a regency council headed by his father's senior wife – who's very nice and quiet and doesn't know much – and his mother, who used to be called the Noble Consort Yi, but who's now known as Dowager Empress Cixi, a very strong character. They have the imperial seals used to authenticate royal documents. They're advised by Prince Gong.'

'So is this Cixi really allowed a say in the government?'

'In practice, yes. In fact, just recently she's become even more important than Prince Gong.'

'Has China ever been ruled by an empress?'

'Only once, by a very wicked woman they call the Empress Wu, during the Tang dynasty, twelve hundred years ago. She killed so many of her family to get power that after she died her gravestone was left blank.'

'Oh.' Mei-Ling sounded a bit disappointed.

'Funnily enough,' Shi-Rong went on pleasantly, 'here in this region, in ancient times, the tribes were ruled by women.' He smiled. 'Confucius would not have approved at all.' He noticed with amusement that when he said this, she kept silent.

She was also curious about the barbarians and the world outside the Celestial Empire. He explained how wise Prince Gong and others had discovered how to turn the barbarians to good use, as mercenaries, customs officials, and so forth.

'We have acquired their arms, and soon we shall buy their iron ships. We are even sending scholars to inspect their universities,' he told her proudly.

'I have one other question,' she said one day. 'You spoke of buying the barbarians' ships and guns. But what about their railways?'

'Railways?' He had heard the term, but was still a little vague as to what they were. The previous year, one of the barbarians had set up a few hundred yards of track with a small engine to demonstrate this invention in Beijing. Shi-Rong hadn't seen it himself, but the authorities, having inspected the devilish contraption, had ordered it dismantled at once. 'How did you hear of railways?'

'One of my sons went to California, in America, and worked on the railways. Thousands from our province have done the same.' And she told him all about the railway: how it was constructed, what the engines and rolling stock were like, how much noise they made, and how these trains could carry people and goods for hundreds of miles, faster than any horse and cart. When she had finished speaking, Shi-Rong could only gaze at her in horror.

'This invention you describe sounds loathsome. We need to acquire arms from the barbarians to protect our civilisation, not foul engines to destroy it. If the man we are sending to the West should encounter such a monstrous machine and report upon it, I am sure the emperor will continue to forbid its appearance here.'

Mei-Ling nodded respectfully.

But how strange it was, he thought, that an illiterate peasant woman from an obscure hamlet should know about such things when he, a highly educated mandarin, did not. And it seemed that thousands of other peasants must know about it, too.

Only one thing caused him unease at this time. It concerned Mei-Ling and young Peng. What did Peng think of his mistress?

The young fellow did his job well, he was respectful, and Shi-Rong had trained him not to talk too much. But he seemed rather straitlaced, and there'd been no sign of his taking up with any local women. Well, that was his business. But given that Peng's father has told him I'm such a paragon of virtue, he thought, he may secretly disapprove of Mei-Ling. What if he were to tell his father about his feelings in a letter?

Shi-Rong knew what letters went from the prefecture to Beijing and the young man didn't seem to have written home – a fact that rather surprised him. If this somewhat solemn young man was to tell his father that his new master's domestic arrangements left something to be desired, Mr Peng Senior would probably just laugh. But he might not.

Avoid trouble, Mr Peng had advised. Play it safe. Would he think having a concubine from a country village was inappropriate behaviour?

'You get along with my concubine, Mei-Ling, I think, don't you?' he'd asked young Peng casually one morning.

'Yes, master. She's very intelligent,' Peng added respectfully.

'Quite. And she thinks well of you.' He paused a moment. 'It's a pity that she is only a country peasant, with unbound feet, of course. She'll return to her village when my tour of duty here is done. But I confess that I shall be sorry to part from her.'

'You will part from her?'

'Naturally.' He gave the young man a serious look. 'It is very important in one's career, Peng, to observe all the proper conventions. It's one thing to have a concubine like Mei-Ling down here – and you may be sure that I discussed the matter with the prefect. But up in Beijing, for instance, no matter how charming and intelligent she is, it wouldn't do. I'm sure you understand.'

'I understand, master.'

'Good. That's all, Peng. I'll let you get on with your work.'

This conversation should have set Shi-Rong's mind at rest. But it didn't. Within days he was cursing himself. I shouldn't have raised the subject at all, he thought. All I've done is put it in his mind. He wondered what he could do about it.

When he'd first arrived at the sub-prefect's residence at Guilin, he'd been pleased to find that it was well furnished, but not in an ostentatious manner. Much of the furniture was wooden, some carved with pleasing fretwork, and other pieces in the Ming dynasty's simplest style, with hardly any ornament at all. Together with its enclosed philosopher's garden and fishpond, his home was a tranquil retreat, which both he and Mei-Ling enjoyed.

It contained a few small treasures, some of which rested unobtrusively on a plain wooden side table in the hall. His favourite was a little jade figure, not even three inches high, that was normally placed towards the back.

'You'd hardly notice it, would you?' he'd remarked to Mei-Ling one day. For not only was the figure, of a bald musician like a Buddha, very small, but its creamy brown colour blended into the pale wood of the table on which it stood. 'People think of jade as being green or some other bright colour. But it's not always so. And this little fellow is jade and quite valuable.'

'I think it brings the house good luck,' she said. And he smiled and agreed that it probably did.

So he was rather shocked one morning when she silently led him over to the table and pointed to the spot where the tiny musician usually lived.

'Oh,' he said. 'Perhaps one of the servants is cleaning it.'

But Mei-Ling shook her head. 'I'm afraid someone will think I stole it,' she murmured.

He frowned. But they might. It was true. He wondered what to do.

'I know who took it,' she went on quietly.

'You do? Tell me.'

'I don't want anyone to know I told you. That would make trouble for me. Bad for me. Bad for you.'

'I'll protect you.'

'It was Peng. He didn't see me, but I saw him.'

'Peng?' How strange. He didn't disbelieve her. But why should Peng, the son of a rich and powerful man, need to steal?

'Please don't tell him I told you.'

'I won't.'

He thought about it all that day. He'd seen such cases before. He slept on it, and by the next morning he knew what to do.

'Tell me, Peng,' he said amiably when he was alone with his secretary in the office, 'are you happy in your work here?'

'Yes, master. Very much.' He seemed to mean it.

'It's very important, Peng, when a young fellow serves a master – just like a son who obeys his father – that he should feel that he is valued and appreciated. Fathers must take care how they treat their sons, for if they do not, then the son, in his unhappiness, may do something foolish in order to retaliate or simply to comfort himself. Confucius is stern against such things, but that does not mean they do not happen. So if as a master I have made you unhappy in any way, you may tell me now.'

'Oh no, master. Not at all,' said the solemn young man fervently.

'Good.' Shi-Rong smiled. 'Now to another, entirely unrelated matter. A small thing. I haven't told anyone yet. I want to share it with you. Maybe you can solve it.'

'Certainly, master.' Peng was studiously attentive.

'There was a little figure of a musician – pale brown jade – on the table in my hall. I particularly like it. It's actually rather good. And it's disappeared. You didn't by any chance borrow it, did you? Used it to decorate your own room, perhaps? I'd quite understand your liking it, but I'm afraid I want it on my own table. So if you borrowed it, would you please return it now?'

Did young Peng hesitate for just a second? Shi-Rong thought so.

'I know nothing of this, master,' he said.

'Peng.' Shi-Rong looked at the young man. 'You've done this sort of thing before.'

'No, master.'

'Peng, I know you have.'

There was an awful silence. Peng looked wretched. 'My father promised he would not tell you,' he cried in vexation.

So his guess was right, and the young man had fallen into the trap. 'I ought to inform your father, and the prefect, too,' Shi-Rong continued. 'But I fear that if I do, it might enrage your father and also end your career – which would be a pity, when you are so young.'

'Yes, master.'

'Go and get it, and bring it here.'

A few minutes later Peng reappeared with the jade figure. Shi-Rong put the little musician in the palm of his hand and gazed at him affectionately. 'You must promise never to do this again.'

'I promise, master.'

'No, Peng. It's yourself you must promise, not me. You do your job well. You should take pride in it. You will make your father proud. Then you will have no need to steal.' He paused. 'And now I am going to write to your father, and I shall give him a good report of you. Tell me, have you written to your father since you were here?'

'No, master.'

'He will think it rather hurtful if he receives a letter from me, but none from his own son. Go and write to him now, then bring me your letter to inspect.'

In an hour the whole business was done. Shi-Rong's letter was craftily composed. The young man was working hard, a credit to his family, and well liked by the prefect, by his wife, and by the members of Shi-Rong's own household. He was most grateful to Mr Peng Senior for the gift of his son, for whom he predicted a fine career. He cheerfully passed the letter to his secretary to read when the young man came in again.

As for Peng's letter, it expressed all his duties to his father in the most correct manner. It then provided a brief account of his work, of the beautiful scenery, of the prefect's wise administration. But when it came to Shi-Rong, young Peng outdid himself. His master's wisdom, his rectitude and his kindness were described with such obvious gratitude and sincerity that, if it hadn't been exactly what he had all along intended, Shi-Rong might have blushed.

'Seal your letter,' he instructed, 'and I shall seal mine.' He smiled at Peng. 'I hope you will look back on this day as a happy turning point in your life, and for that reason it has been a good day for me, too.'

o

As the months went by, Shi-Rong had to confess that although Guilin might have seemed a backwater as far as his career was concerned, he had never been happier in his life. And in terms of his career, it hadn't been wasted time, either. For he'd soon come to realise that behind the prefect's genial manner lay a great shrewdness as well as kindness.

He was also a great teacher. He showed Shi-Rong how to deal with the different tribes and avoid conflict. He taught him not just how to administer the law, but how to manage the magistrates. By the end of a year Shi-Rong realised he was learning more from him than he had from anyone since Commissioner Lin.

So when a letter came from Mr Peng to inform him that, if he would just be patient an extra six months, he was confident he could secure him a most remunerative appointment nearer the capital, he was quite content.

Except for one thing. Mei-Ling would be leaving. Her year and a half would be up.

Half a year without her. He asked her to stay a few months longer, but she refused.

'It has been, still is, the most astounding thing that ever happened to me in my life. I am full of gratitude,' she said. She was too honest to lie to him about such a thing.

'Stay the extra months then,' he begged.

'My girl's expecting me. I told her a year and a half. Do you think she hasn't got the days all counted?'

It so happened that just at that time a letter had come from Shi-Rong's wife. It was quite friendly, but it told him that his son Ru-Hai, who was due for a rest from his studies soon, would dearly like it if his father invited him to see the beauties of Guilin for a month.

'I am due to leave a month after the end of the summer monsoon,' Mei-Ling pointed out. 'Why don't you summon him to arrive just after that? It's a delightful time of the year, and you'll have him for company. You'll be so busy you'll hardly notice I've gone.'

'It won't be the same.' He smiled ruefully. 'But you're right. It's what I ought to do.' And he sent instructions to that effect.

o

The summer rains had come to an end a few days ago, and Shi-Rong had just begun to plan how he might amuse the boy. He hardly knew what he'd expected their meeting would be like. It had been nearly two years since they'd last seen each other. Ru-Hai must now be in his eighteenth year and quite a young man, he supposed, no longer the boy he remembered.

So he was quite astonished one afternoon when Ru-Hai turned up at the house. 'We weren't expecting you for a month,' he cried.

'I came early,' said Ru-Hai. 'Are you not pleased to see me?'

'Of course I'm pleased. Delighted,' Shi-Rong assured him. 'Just surprised. You look taller,' he said. 'Have you been studying hard?'

'Yes, Father,' said Ru-Hai, and bowed respectfully.

'Well, well, come in,' his father said cheerfully, 'and tell me all the news.'

Ru-Hai recited the news from home. His mother was well. 'Excellent,' cried Shi-Rong. 'I shall write to your dear mother at once to let her know you've arrived safely.' His younger brother was also well and attending to his schoolbooks assiduously. 'Good, good,' said Shi-Rong with a smile. But his sister was still sickly and really couldn't travel far from the family home. 'I wish it were otherwise,' Shi-Rong said sadly. 'Your mother is quite right to remain with her, but I wish it were otherwise.'

Leading him to his office, Shi-Rong introduced his son to Peng, told him about the kindly prefect and his wife, and gave him some account of the area and its beauties. A servant brought them tea.

The boy seemed happy enough. Being tired from his journey, he went to rest for a while before joining his father and Peng for the evening meal.

'What do I do?' Shi-Rong asked Mei-Ling.

'Do you want me to leave?'

'No.'

'Then do nothing.'

When Mei-Ling entered to serve them, Shi-Rong introduced her by name, and Ru-Hai acknowledged her politely; but it wasn't clear he'd realised who she was. After the meal, Peng had to attend to some correspondence, so father and son were left alone.

'The housekeeper's rather beautiful,' Ru-Hai remarked. 'Did she come with the residence?'

'No, she didn't come with the residence,' his father said. 'Actually, she is my concubine. I forgot to mention it when I introduced you.'

'You have a concubine?' Ru-Hai looked at his father in consternation.

'Just one,' his father replied.

'Does my mother know?'

'No. I only acquired her when I got here, you see.'

Ru-Hai was silent for a moment. 'You have another woman, and my poor mother doesn't even know?'

'It's perfectly proper for a man in my position to have a concubine.'

'My mother was right,' Ru-Hai burst out. 'You think only of yourself.' And he rushed out of the room.

Shi-Rong waited an hour. He wondered what else his wife had said about him behind his back. He wasn't angry with the boy for wanting to defend his mother. But he couldn't have him insulting his father, either. When the hour was up, he summoned Peng and told him to find Ru-Hai and bring him back.

When Ru-Hai returned, still looking sulky, Shi-Rong was firm. 'You are not to insult your father. Whatever your feelings are, you must show respect to me. That is your duty. Kindly remember it.' He paused. 'As far as Mei-Ling is concerned, she will probably never meet your mother, because when I leave here, she will return to her family. I shall be sorry to lose her, but that is what will happen. In the meantime, you will find her a charming person.'

'She's just a poor peasant from a village in the middle of nowhere. She hasn't even got bound feet.'

'She is part Hakka. As you will know, the Hakka, like the Manchu, do not bind their feet. Though as it happens, her daughter's feet are being bound. As for her family, they have a big farm and a great deal of land. They live off the rents.' It had been true in the past, he thought. It might be true in the future. The present, therefore, could be overlooked.

'She's still a Cantonese peasant,' Ru-Hai muttered.

Shi-Rong should have rebuked him at once for being rude, but he decided to reason with him instead. 'You will find that her manners are elegant, she can read and write a little, which is as much as many well-born ladies can manage, and she speaks enough Mandarin to recite poetry.' He sent a silent prayer of thanks to the prefect's wife for these accomplishments, and as he did so, he realised that he had another card in his hand. 'You had better be careful what you say about her to the prefect, by the way,' he added, 'because she is also a close friend of his wife.'

That struck home. His son looked up in surprise and then fell silent.

Shi-Rong had seen such things before. A merchant, for instance, takes a second wife, his children inspect her, and the thing they care about most is whether she will enhance the family's status or not. It was natural enough, he thought. It's the instinct for survival. The children hate the new wife not because she is pretty when their own mother is ceasing to be so, but because firstly, if she has children, their own inheritance will be diluted, and secondly, they consider the younger woman comes from a lower class. Of course, if she is rich and brings money into the family, that may be another matter.

Ru-Hai said nothing more. But later that evening, as Mei-Ling passed quietly through the courtyard, Shi-Rong noticed his son look at her curiously.

The next day they all went to see the prefect. Mei-Ling and the prefect's wife retired together while the prefect and Shi-Rong took Ru-Hai on a tour of the area.

The setting, with the river Li flowing past the houses and winding its way through rice fields, under the gaze of the soaring green hills, was so lovely it made one gasp. The boy was also impressed by the different tribes he saw in the street. He admired the Zhuang men in their severe dark blue costumes, and their women, also in dark blue, but with brightly embroidered aprons. By contrast, the women of the Yao tribe wore gorgeous flowery robes, so covered with silver trinkets that he thought it a wonder they could walk. He counted at least five tribal communities all mixing in the streets in the easiest way.

He saw tall wooden houses that began as hay barns, turned into dwellings higher up, and then into storerooms in the roof. 'So high that even the rats can't get at them,' the prefect informed him with a laugh.

They went down to the river and saw the fishermen in their boats. 'It's probably the best-stocked river in the whole empire,' his father said. 'There are two hundred different kinds of fish in these waters.'

'Are they all edible?' Ru-Hai asked. His father didn't know and passed the question on to the prefect.

'The Cantonese will eat almost anything,' that worthy gentleman answered with a smile.

In the marketplace they saw magnificent embroidered cloths for sale, each tribe having their own rich style. They watched a crowd listening to a pair of musicians, one with a flute, the other a horn, accompanied by an old fellow beating a big copper drum. 'The drum's probably hundreds of years old,' Shi-Rong explained. A group of singers came down the street. 'They won't perform for an hour or two, but you can hang around to listen if you want,' the prefect said. 'If you stay here a year, you'll see all kinds of festivals. They even have a bullfight, you know.'

In short, by the time they came back to the prefect's residence at noon, young Ru-Hai had almost forgotten his anger of the day before, having decided that Guilin was the most exotic and romantic place he had ever seen in his life.

It was afternoon, still quite warm. Ru-Hai had gone into the town again. Mei-Ling had returned home, and she was sitting on a stone bench in the garden, half hidden from the path by a sweet osmanthus tree. She'd brought a small piece of embroidery with her, hoping to improve her skill. But she hadn't yet begun when she became aware of someone coming along the path.

She was surprised to see Ru-Hai. She'd assumed he was still down in the marketplace listening to the singers.

She got a glimpse of his face before he saw her. He looked preoccupied. Not unhappy, but thoughtful. He's probably come into the garden to be alone, she thought, and she was about to rise so he could have the place to himself.

But when he saw her, he seemed quite pleased and sat down on the bench beside her. 'Can I ask you a question?' he said.

She bowed her head politely. 'Of course.'

'How did you become my father's concubine?'

'Oh.' She hadn't expected quite such a blunt question. 'Your father was very kind to my family,' she said after a slight pause. 'But if I tell you how, you must promise not to repeat it to anyone – because it might embarrass your father.'

'All right.' He frowned. 'I promise.'

'Some years ago, a cousin of mine got into trouble,' said Mei-Ling. 'He was very close to me. My family had virtually adopted him. I called him Little Brother. Officially, your father should have arrested him, but Little Brother was young and your father let him get away. So I owed your father a debt of kindness that I thought I could never repay. After that, I didn't see your father for years. But a few months ago, as he happened to find himself near our village, he came to call on us. My dear husband had died a year and a half before. Your father and I talked. I suppose I was lonely, and to tell you the truth, it seemed to me that he was lonely, too. And one thing led to another. And here I am.'

'I didn't know he had it in him,' Ru-Hai said. He looked impressed.

'We none of us know everything, do we?' she suggested.

'I suppose not.' He nodded sadly. 'I felt angry with him because of Mother. I'd been thinking I'd go home tomorrow, unless Father stopped me.'

'I don't think your father would stop you,' she said. 'But although he might not show it, he'd be very hurt.'

'He's hurting my mother.'

'Does she know?'

'No.'

'Then, forgive me for saying this – you may think very badly of me – but do you have to tell her? You know I shall be going home myself in a while.'

'You don't think he'll take you to the next place?'

'Oh no, I have to return to my family,' she replied. 'I believe your father will reunite with your mother.'

'Maybe.' Ru-Hai considered for a moment. 'Mother complains a lot,' he said gloomily. 'She thinks my father should have been more successful.'

'He seems successful to me.'

'Maybe. Not to her, though.'

He stared at the ground. He seemed to be ruminating, so she didn't interrupt him. Suddenly he turned to her. 'Do you think my father is a good man?'

She stared at him, taken aback. What a question for a son to ask. Or for her to answer.

'When we're young,' she said carefully, 'we expect people to be good or bad. But they aren't, you know. We're all just somewhere in between.' She thought of Nio. How many people had Little Brother killed, even before he went to fight for the Taiping? She didn't want to know. 'Not many people are good all of the time,' she went on. 'More like *some* of the time. You just have to hope a person performs more good actions than bad ones. I think,' she concluded, 'that one has to look for what is best in people.'

'And that's all?'

'Well, you can try to change the things that aren't so good in another person. I think we women try to change our men more than the other way round.'

'Really?'

'And one has to be careful. If you nag a man too much or hurt his pride, he'll walk away. Most of the time it's wiser to accept him as he is.' She gave a wry smile. Did he realise she was telling him about his mother? Probably. But he gave no sign. He seemed to be done with the subject, anyway.

'So you think I should stay here?'

'I do. It's a beautiful place. I think you should enjoy your holiday.' She smiled. 'I'm sure a handsome boy like you could make friends with the local girls.'

He looked doubtful. 'All the respectable girls are hidden indoors,' he pointed out. 'Nobody's allowed to see them until they marry.'

'There may be others,' she said. She stood up. 'I should go to see your father now. If you quarrel with him because of me, I shall feel bad. But if you don't quarrel, I think you will be glad later.' She wondered if he'd take her advice.

For Shi-Rong, that month was a happy period. He took Mei-Ling's advice and spent as much time with his son as possible. They made tours of the area, and he was able to tell Ru-Hai all sorts of useful things about life in imperial service. They visited tribal villages, climbed up a couple of mountains, and even went fishing on the river together.

The boy was also a great success with the prefect and his wife. They thought he was charming. The prefect's wife said he was very handsome; and the prefect wrote about Ru-Hai in glowing terms to one or two friends who might be useful to him in later life.

Peng also played his part. 'Take the boy out in the evening a bit, if you would,' Shi-Rong had asked him. 'He should have fun with someone closer to his own age.' They'd gone out drinking several times. 'Though I doubt, with Peng for company, that he got into much trouble,' Shi-Rong confided to Mei-Ling.

Halfway through the month, Shi-Rong told Mei-Ling: 'I've had a letter. When he leaves here, Ru-Hai should go to visit his mother's relations in Beijing. So I wonder, as you are going downriver to Guangzhou yourself on your way home, would you mind if he accompanies you to the port? Then he can take a ship up the coast and the Grand Canal to Beijing.'

Mei-Ling had been looking forward to her journey. River travel was both quicker and more pleasant than travelling by road. The weather should be warm and mild and the scenery was beautiful. It would be the first time in her life, really, that she'd ever had a period of time without any responsibilities and completely to herself.

But it would have been ungracious to him and unkind to the boy not to go along with such a sensible request, so of course she said she would.

It was the prefect, a few days before Ru-Hai was due to leave, who suggested the visit to the caves. As was to be expected in a landscape of karst hills, there were quite a few caves in the region. The nearest was only a short walk from their house. Ru-Hai and his father had gone in a couple of times with lanterns to inspect the graceful curtains of stalactites hanging from its high roof. But it was quite small.

'There's an old musician working here,' the prefect said, 'who told me that once his father showed him a deserted place, all overgrown with reeds, which he used to cut and make into flutes. His father told him there used to be a big cave in there, but he'd never seen the entrance and didn't know anyone who had. It could be the roof fell in or something like that. But I'd be curious to know. I think it's only about three miles away. Why not send your son with Peng to try to find it? That'd give them something to do. If they discover anything worth seeing, we'll make an expedition to look at it.'

Peng and Ru-Hai were delighted with the adventure and set off eagerly with the old musician the next morning.

They came back that night flushed and excited. 'It's only three miles away, but it's quite deserted. We had to cut a path through the reeds and dig around a bit, but we found the cave. And it's huge!' cried Ru-Hai.

'It is impressive,' Peng confirmed. 'If the prefect wants to inspect it, master, we'd need some workmen, and two days to prepare.'

'And lanterns,' said Ru-Hai. 'Coloured lanterns. A lot of them. A thousand.'

'Certainly not,' said his father. 'You'll be lucky to get a hundred.'

But when he told the prefect the next morning, that worthy gentleman laughed aloud. 'Give him a thousand,' he commanded.

It was quite a cavalcade. The first sedan chair contained the prefect, the second Shi-Rong; the next two, somewhat smaller, carried the prefect's wife and Mei-Ling. After these came various lesser officials and local gentlemen, followed by a small company of guards and a retinue of servants all on foot.

They made their way along the path that had been cut through the reeds until they came to a level clearing beside the rock face where Peng and Ru-Hai were waiting. The two young men greeted the prefect with low bows, but Shi-Rong could see that his son was grinning.

As soon as all the party had gathered, they proceeded on foot up a steep track where the workmen had made some wooden steps to help them. It wasn't far, not even fifty yards, before they came to the entrance, where a lamplit passageway led into the limestone rock. With Peng and Ru-Hai leading the way, they all filed down the glowing passage until suddenly they emerged into the great, cavernous hall.

Shi-Rong stood beside the prefect, who was quietly chuckling. 'I've never seen anything like it,' the worthy gentleman remarked. 'I believe your boy has used every lamp we gave him.'

It was a remarkable sight. The cave extended nearly three hundred yards, but it was divided into several sections. The largest was a huge curved chamber where stalagmites, like miniatures of the steep karst hills above ground, ranged themselves along the far side of a central underground lake. Cleverly, Ru-Hai had placed lanterns – blue, red, and green

– amongst the stalagmites so that they were reflected in the water. It looked like a magical city. Having noticed that the ceiling of the chamber contained areas of mottled stone, he had placed white lamps just below so that it seemed as though the stone cityscape by the water was lying under gleaming, billowing clouds. For several minutes everyone stood motionless and silent, gazing at the beauty of this secret world.

'May we lead the way, Lord?' Ru-Hai asked the prefect at last.

'By all means.'

The workmen had made a stony path that wound between little pools of water and stalagmites. From the ceiling long stalactites descended like fingers seeking to touch them in a friendly way. Here, too, the men had done a good job, alternating lantern light and deep shadow so that the fingers seemed to descend from ghostly forms unseen. They came to a jutting wall where the gnarled formations looked like a collection of stone waterfalls, and to another place where a single pitted limestone figure stood alone, as though it had come from a Chinese garden. 'This has been a good idea,' the prefect said cheerfully.

'It's very beautiful. Quite wonderful,' said his wife. She turned to Mei-Ling. 'Don't you agree, my dear?'

'It's one of the loveliest things I ever saw in my life. Thank you, Lord.'

'We should all thank the young men,' the prefect announced. 'I only told them where the cave might be. They did the rest.'

'With your permission, Lord,' said Peng, 'there is something else we wish to show you, as a scholar.'

'As a scholar, eh? Come along, Shi-Rong,' the prefect called, 'we'd better both see this.'

So the prefect, Shi-Rong, and several mandarins followed as Peng led them deeper into the cave, into a section less brightly lit. Half a dozen workmen, holding lanterns on long poles, were waiting beside a particular section of wall. At a nod from Peng, they raised the lanterns high, close to the stone.

'Well, I never,' said the prefect.

Inscriptions. Dozens of them, apparently made with big brushes directly onto the porous stone in ink. The script was archaic, but the characters were entirely readable. Shi-Rong and the prefect peered at them intently.

'What do you think?' the prefect asked.

'Tang dynasty. Early Tang, I'd say,' Shi-Rong replied.

'I agree. This place must have been in use a thousand years ago.'

'And by mandarin scholars, it seems.'

'How many inscriptions are there?' the prefect asked Peng.

'I have found seventy so far, Lord.'

'We ought to have them copied,' said the prefect.

'Peng,' said Shi-Rong, 'you will copy them. You may take a month.'

'Yes, master.' Peng bowed his head, whether in gladness or sadness, it was hard to tell.

Only at this moment did Shi-Rong realise his son was not one of the party. He frowned. Ru-Hai should have been there to witness this demonstration of scholarship. He should have shown the prefect that he took an interest. He might have listened to his father explain why he could so easily identify the period from which the writing came. But he wasn't there. Where was he?

The prefect's wife gazed around the cavern. When her husband and Shi-Rong had gone to look at the inscriptions, she and Mei-Ling had stayed in there with the rest of the party. And while Mei-Ling remained by the water, the prefect's wife had moved to one side to survey the scene.

With the guards and servants, there must have been twenty or thirty figures standing here and there on the floor of the great cave, some in shadow, some partly lit by the glow from the lamps, and two or three in black silhouette.

Mei-Ling was standing alone by the side of the lake. The reflection of the coloured lights on the water softly lit her face. She was staring across at the shimmering cityscape, oblivious to anything else in that subterranean womb.

How lovely her friend looked, her face lifted slightly, unearthly pale in the blue light. Her childbearing years must be near their close, the prefect's wife thought, yet at that moment she seemed eternally young. What a pity Mei-Ling and Shi-Rong couldn't marry. They'd have been happy together.

But there it was. She turned her head. And then she saw the boy.

Ru-Hai was standing by the wall. A red lantern illumined his face. And he, too, was staring with rapt attention towards the water. She tried to work out what the boy was watching so intently. It took her a moment to realise.

The boy was staring at Mei-Ling.

Just then Ru-Hai left the wall and moved across until he was standing beside Mei-Ling. He must have spoken, because she turned in surprise. He seemed to say something else, and Mei-Ling nodded, turning her gaze across the lake again. He'd probably made some remark about the panorama, the prefect's wife thought. She waited a little longer, then walked over to them. As Ru-Hai saw her, he moved back from Mei-Ling's side, though Mei-Ling remained quite still.

Afterwards, as she and Mei-Ling were walking to their sedan chairs, the prefect's wife remarked, 'Young Ru-Hai's in love with you. Did you notice?'

'With me?' No woman could entirely object to such a proposition. 'I hardly think so,' said Mei-Ling. 'I'm old enough to be his mother.'

'Such loves are well known.' Her friend smiled. 'Besides, you hardly look more than thirty. I admire his choice.'

Mei-Ling shook her head. 'This is nonsense,' she said.

'It was probably half in his mind, because you're beautiful and you were kind to him. But I think it hit him suddenly in the cave.'

'Oh. The cave.'

'It was magical in there, you know.'

'Well,' Mei-Ling said drily, 'I'm sure he'll get over it.'

But if she thought her friend had finished with the subject, Mei-Ling was wrong.

The next morning, while Ru-Hai was out with his father, the prefect's wife came around for a chat. 'You know,' she remarked, 'I'm sure Ru-Hai is still a virgin.'

'I daresay he is,' Mei-Ling replied.

'You hadn't thought about it?'

'No. Why should I?'

'You might have.'

'I didn't.'

'Well, some nice woman ought to look after him. Better than his finding out by himself with a whore down an alley in the city, and with all the risks that entails.'

Mei-Ling stared straight ahead. She knew from their many talks that the prefect's wife, in private, could be surprisingly crude. And that she was not above a little intrigue.

'I'm sure somebody could arrange something,' Mei-Ling said drily.

'No doubt. But wouldn't it be nice for him to be a bit in love, to have a magical memory, something to treasure for the rest of his life?'

Mei-Ling said nothing.

'You like him, don't you?'

Whatever her thoughts, Mei-Ling kept them to herself.

On the eve of her departure, Shi-Rong spoke gently to Mei-Ling. 'I am truly sorry you are leaving,' he said. 'I have already told you my feelings. As far as our bargain is concerned, you have kept your part. Far more than that. Before you came, I trusted you and paid in full. Now I am giving you the same again. You will need it for the education of Bright Moon.' He smiled. 'I hope I have treated you well.'

'You could not have treated me better.' She paused. 'But since you really wish to help, I will tell you that I need something more. We are peasants in a hamlet. We know a few people with money in the local town. But that's all. We've no way to find her the husband she deserves. Her beauty shouldn't be wasted.'

'It should not.'

'But you could find her a worthy husband. There is plenty of time.'

'Yes.' He nodded slowly. 'I'll see what I can do.'

The next morning, Mei-Ling and Ru-Hai took their leave. They were travelling in luxury, for the prefect had insisted that they use his personal riverboat – a large sampan with a sail, and a covered seating area like a tent containing upholstered benches and divans with silken cushions, where they could sit, sleep and dine in the greatest comfort. There was a serving girl and a crew of six boatmen.

The prefect himself saw them off at the jetty, together with Shi-Rong, who parted from her with the most friendly affection. So did the prefect's wife, who whispered a loving message to her as she boarded.

Ru-Hai was obviously excited by the adventure of the river journey ahead, but Mei-Ling was pleased to see that he bade his father farewell with every sign of filial devotion; she was glad to think she might have played her part in that.

And so they were off, waving back to the little group on the jetty until a bend in the river slowly nudged them out of sight.

She leaned back against the cushions and looked out at the scenery. The weather was perfect. She could feel the faint touch of a breeze on her cheek. The morning sun glinted on the river. The steep karst mountains soared into the clear blue sky above.

The journey would take several days. There were two famous inns at which they might spend the night along the way. But they could certainly sleep on the boat as well. Slow days of perfect peace.

It occurred to her that, perhaps in all her life, she had never known any days during which she had no duties to perform, no responsibilities of any kind at all. She'd fulfilled all obligations under her agreement with Shi-Rong, and it would be half a month before she entered her family duties again.

This was a magical interlude, just for herself: a time apart, a place apart. She felt a little thrill.

She looked at Ru-Hai. He had been watching her. He smiled, then, perhaps embarrassed, glanced away and pretended to gaze at the mountains.

She thought about her friend the prefect's wife. What was it she'd whispered as they parted? 'Don't forget to look after the boy.'

Mei-Ling shook her head. Silly woman. To think of such a thing, at her age. She felt maternal towards him. Certainly. A pleasant feeling.

She closed her eyes and allowed herself to ponder.

He was certainly a handsome boy. Almost a young man, really.

If one did such a thing, would anybody know? And would they care if they did? What would Shi-Rong think about it? she wondered. She didn't know. Could the boy be trusted to be discreet? That was a good question. Unlikely, she supposed. But not impossible.

She'd never done anything like that before. There might be no great harm in it now, in such a magical place.

She opened her eyes to find him looking at her again.

Well, she thought, she really didn't know. Perhaps she would, perhaps she wouldn't. But if she did, one thing was certain: she'd like it to be her own little secret.

THE MISSIONARY

1875

John Trader took a shortcut. Cantered his horse across open ground. The stupid meeting he'd promised to attend at a neighbouring estate hadn't ended until half past noon, and now he was late.

Late for Emily. His favourite daughter.

It had been three years since Agnes had died, rather unexpectedly, mourned by the whole county. And though Emily looked just like her mother, she had a sweetness that was all her own. Even when she was a child, if he was depressed for some reason, his wife would calmly pray; but little Emily would come into the estate office where he was usually to be found and sit beside him and hold his hand and say, 'Don't be sad, Papa.' And then she'd say, 'Shall we go for a walk?' And even though he didn't want to, he'd get up and take her hand and they'd go out into the garden. He'd feel better after that. And sure enough, before long, Emily would appear in the office again with a little painting she'd just made for him, which he would pin to a board propped up on his rolltop desk where he could see it all the time.

Today, she and her husband, Henry, were due to arrive at noon. They could stay only two days. And then? Who could tell?

The big house at Drumlomond came in sight. Built of red sandstone, it was typical of the region: large and square. 'It's a bit of a barracks,' Trader would say fondly. But with its ample spaces, its conservatory, where there was a parrot in a cage, its stables, fishing and rough shooting, not to mention the barn and the beasts of the home farm, it had been a paradise for his growing children.

The house looked so solid and serene in the autumn sun. They'd renamed the estate using Agnes's family name, which had pleased everyone very much and reminded the county that its occupants belonged there since ancient times. And if John Trader had bought it with the profits from the opium trade, even the origins of his ownership were fading gradually away into the background. For since British planters had recently learned to grow tea in India and the British public had acquired a taste for the darker Darjeeling brew, the need for tea from China had become less urgent. His eldest son had taken his place in the partnership now, and the business was making far more money importing Indian tea than it was in selling opium to the Chinese.

But Drumlomond wasn't solid and serene for John Trader. Not anymore. Not since Henry Whiteparish had come into his life and stolen his daughter away.

He'd tried to reason with her, that first terrible day when Henry's letter had arrived. 'Do you remember,' he'd asked, 'the time you went to Paris?'

'Yes, Papa.' Young ladies were supposed to speak French, but the rudimentary conversation they'd learned from their English governess had been so inadequate that when they tried it out on a young Frenchman who was visiting, he had burst out laughing. Very rude of him. But it was a signal that something had to be done.

Emily had gone. First time she'd been abroad. She'd loved it. Even learned some French. She'd said she wanted to travel again.

'I'm just so afraid you may suppose that going off to China with a missionary is going to be the same sort of thing,' he'd said. 'And it really isn't.'

'Do you think Henry's unsuitable?'

'Yes.'

'He's my cousin.'

'I know.'

'I love you, Papa, and I wouldn't want to do this, but I could elope with him.'

'Elope?' Trader looked at her in astonishment. He'd never heard of anyone eloping with a missionary before. Were missionaries allowed to elope?

———

His strongest support had come from a completely unexpected quarter. The day after his conversation with Emily, Trader was sitting in the library when, a few minutes past noon, a hansom cab rolled up the drive, from which emerged, under a large brimmed hat, and in urgent haste, the unhappy figure of Cecil Whiteparish.

'My dear cousin,' he cried, as soon as the butler had announced him, 'forgive me for appearing without warning, but I left Salisbury for London the instant I heard this terrible news and took the train straight to Dumfries.'

Trader led him into the library. 'What's your view of this business?' he asked before they even sat down.

'Why, it must be stopped, of course,' Whiteparish cried. 'It must be stopped at once!' He fell back in the leather armchair. 'I think,' he confessed, 'I need a drink.' And having gratefully received a heavy lead crystal tumbler of the local Bladnoch malt, well filled, he took a large sip, shook his head, and declared: 'I blame myself.'

'I don't know about that,' said Trader mildly. 'You could say it was my fault. I invited him here.'

'No. You invited me and Minnie to stay – almost the moment I retired to Salisbury, which was exceedingly good of you. But as Henry was just home from China and I was proud of him – and because, I confess, I wanted my son to see what a fine estate my cousin had – I asked if he could come, too, and you said yes. Little did I imagine what it would lead to.'

In fact the visit had gone rather well. They'd all spent a week together, enjoying family meals and country walks. They'd gone to church, where the missionary and his wife had been welcomed with deep respect. John had even asked a couple of his more religious-minded neighbours to dinner one evening, and they had questioned Cecil closely about China and the Christian work there and thought him a splendid fellow.

And truth to tell, during that whole week, no one had really noticed that Henry and Emily were often together.

'Did you know that Henry and your daughter started corresponding after that?' Cecil asked.

'Not at the time.'

'He wrote from the mission's headquarters in London, of course, so it didn't look like a personal letter. What I resent is that he never told me.'

'He was nearly thirty. He didn't have to.'

'He didn't tell me because he knew what I'd have said. And then Emily and her sister went to Edinburgh for a week, so he went there and met them, and made it look as if it were quite by chance. Deceitful.'

'All's fair in love and war, they say.'

'Not if you're a missionary!' Cecil retorted furiously. 'My son has treated you abominably.'

'Have you told him so?'

'I most certainly have. I have told him that he has been underhanded, selfish, and irresponsible.'

'What does he say?'

'Oh, the usual. He respects me, but in this case he must trust his own judgement. You know the sort of thing.'

'She told me she's prepared to elope with him.'

'Elope?' Cecil blinked his eyes. 'Elope?'

'She's of age. It may not be illegal. What would the mission do if they eloped and then turned up in China? Assuming they were married, of course.'

'Send them back at once, I trust,' said Cecil firmly. Then he paused. 'They might not,' he conceded. 'They're always short of hands.' He shook his head in puzzlement. 'What does she see in him? He's not a tall, handsome fellow like her brothers. He's hardly better looking than I am.'

'He's got a sort of magnetic force,' said Trader thoughtfully. 'Knows what he wants. Won't take no for an answer. Women like that. Whether it's gone further . . . Though she's always been chaperoned.'

'Heaven forfend! Please don't tell me so.'

'I don't think he's seduced her. Or she him. I think she's in love with the idea of being a missionary's wife. You know, romantic and all that.'

'There is absolutely nothing romantic about being a missionary's wife,' Cecil said firmly. 'Nothing.' He took an angry sip at his whisky, ruminated silently for a few moments, and continued. 'A good deal of my life,' he said slowly, 'is spent asking people for funds to support the missions.' He smiled wanly. 'There are tricks to that trade, and I've learned most of them. It helps, of course, that I honestly believe it's a good cause.' He paused. 'But I never suggest to anybody that they should become a missionary.'

'What if they ask if they should? You surely don't discourage them?'

'In almost all cases that's exactly what I do. Even if they insist that they want to.'

'Why?'

'Because as with a lot of difficult callings – in my observation – the good people are not the ones who desire the career. It's the people who just find they have to do it. They can't help themselves. In the church, the best priests often didn't want to follow the stony path at all. But something led them to it. So my guess is that you're right. She's in love with the idea of the missionary life – which is exactly why she shouldn't do it.'

'Will you tell her this?'

'In words of one syllable.'

He did, the following evening. He explained to her kindly but firmly what the life of a missionary was really like. 'One of the worst things,' he informed her, 'is that you never really know whom you can trust. And just when you think you may at last be securing a genuine convert, they let you down.' He outlined the constant lack of money, the worries about one's children, and the stress that can arise between husband and wife in such difficult conditions. 'You'll be lonely, too. You'll yearn for home. In short, to put the matter frankly, you won't find it's what you imagined at all. You'll find you've made a huge mistake.'

To which, after smiling and nodding gently, she answered: 'You sound just like Henry.'

'I do?'

'Those are all the things he keeps telling me.'

It was time to get tough. 'You seem to think that everything's going to be all right just because you'll be with Henry. But I must tell you that in my opinion, you are not only unprepared, but unsuited for this life. You have never known anything except comfort, whereas life in a Chinese mission is harsh. We often have to work with our hands. You won't like it, and frankly you won't be any good at it.'

'We may live in the big house, Mr Whiteparish, but this is the countryside. I know the farmworkers. I've grown up with their children. I know exactly how they live and how to work with my hands.'

'But China is nothing like Galloway. You'll be surrounded by people who speak no English. None.'

'Some of the old people in Galloway still don't speak English. They speak Gaelic. I can even speak a little myself.'

'Had it ever occurred to you that, without wishing it, you may be a hindrance to your husband?'

A shadow seemed to pass across her face. 'You really think so?'

'I'm afraid I do.'

Emily was silent, frowning. Had he got through to her? Was this a ray of hope? And all credit to the girl, he thought, it appeared that the idea that she might be letting Henry down meant more than anything else.

'Henry says that he has faith in me,' she said uncertainly. 'He says that God will give me the strength I need.' She looked at him earnestly. 'Do you think he is mistaken? And that perhaps because he loves me, he is deceiving himself?'

Cecil Whiteparish gazed at her. What should he say? The truth, he supposed. What else? 'I do not know,' he answered. 'But I can see why he loves you.'

The marriage went off well, thanks to Colonel Lomond. His speech was short.

'Our lovely bride is marrying a kinsman – which is usually a sensible thing to do. After all, if you marry a kinsman, at least you know what you're getting.' Murmurs of approval. No member of the Scots gentry would ever disagree with that. 'And this kinsman of hers is a man who's decided to put his service to our religion first, as I daresay we all should. More than that – I'm speaking as an old soldier here – he's prepared to face discomfort and possible danger to do it. And he's found a wife, from my own family, I'm proud to say, who's prepared to share that mission with him. So I ask you to raise your glasses in our old Scottish toast: good health.' He paused, and then firmly: 'Long life.'

They got the point. Only good words could be said after that.

There were three of them at the big dining room table. As today was Thursday, that meant cold beef and pickle for lunch. Trader liked it served with a local French wine his vintner had discovered, one nobody else at that time had ever heard of. 'They call it Beaujolais; it's red but you serve it cold,' the vintner told him. So at Drumlomond, alone in all Scotland, this wine was served on Thursdays with the beef and pickle.

They talked of family matters first, and friends, and general things. The meat course was cleared.

In most houses of any consequence, the cook had her special dishes. At Drumlomond, Mrs Ives was adept at every kind of pastry. Depending on the season she would produce a salmon en croûte or a beef Wellington that guests would remember for years. And at all seasons, both at dinner and after the meat course at lunch, she would bring forth two flans, one fruit and one savoury. In Emily's honour, knowing it was her favourite, the savoury flan was mushroom.

There was a cry of pleasure from Emily. Mrs Ives was summoned forth, beaming, from the kitchen and duly thanked.

Then John Trader finally addressed the matter in hand. 'Well, my dear,' he said, 'you and Henry have been in London quite a few months before setting forth. Have you had to make a lot of preparations?'

'Quite a lot, Papa, yes.'

'I'm happy to tell you that as well as everything else, Emily has been learning to read Chinese,' said Henry, 'and made impressive progress, I may add.'

'Well done, my dear.' Trader gave Emily a nod of approval. He mightn't have wanted her to marry a missionary, but if you were going to take a thing on, you should do it properly. 'Proud of you,' he said. 'Tell me, do you and Henry yet know exactly where you'll be stationed?'

'Not yet, Papa.'

'We go to Hong Kong first, of course,' Henry explained. 'We might be sent to Shanghai, which would be quite agreeable. But we might be going to any of the treaty ports, or possibly farther into the interior.'

'I saw some photographs the other day,' Trader remarked. 'The caption said they were Protestant missionaries in China. But as far as I could judge, they were dressed as Chinese merchants. Was the caption wrong, or are you going to dress up like that? And if so, why?'

'Ah.' Henry nodded. 'The caption was probably correct. As for myself, I'm not sure, but I may dress like a merchant, at least some of the time.'

'Why's that?'

'Imagine you're Chinese. Put yourself in their place. Think of what's happened in the last thirty years: the Opium Wars; the burning of the Summer Palace. Acts of huge disrespect. You might well be suspicious of the British. And of their religion – especially when you remember the appalling death and devastation caused by the Taiping rebels, who, so far as most Chinese understand, worshipped the same deity that we do.' He paused. 'You may win a war quickly, but earning trust takes far longer. And one way to make a start is to show respect for local customs – as long as they're not against our faith. Wearing local dress seems an obvious choice. It's also well adapted to the climate.'

'Sensible,' Trader agreed. 'Gordon used to wear a Chinese uniform.' He paused. 'I'm glad it's safer to be a missionary nowadays than it used to be.'

Henry pursed his lips. 'Some things have changed,' he acknowledged cautiously.

'You sound a bit doubtful.'

'One should never discount the possibility of danger,' Henry answered. It was against his nature to lie.

'What concerns you most?' Trader wanted to know.

'Let me assure you first,' Henry said, 'before I answer, that this is not religious rivalry, let alone dislike. Their priests include some of the best men I know. But I think the Catholic Church is making a mistake.'

'How so?'

'It's their churches, really. They keep building these huge churches on important and cherished sites, where they can only give offense. There's one on the site of an old temple, another in the grounds of a governor's yamen. Churches that dominate the landscape for miles around.'

'That's hardly new, is it?' Trader asked. 'The church has made a point of building over pagan temples ever since the early centuries of Christianity. It took over the old pagan festivals as well. Midsummer solstice, Halloween . . . you name it. The Church Triumphant.'

'True, but they usually did something else first. They converted the king. Then his people would follow. For three centuries the Jesuits hoped to convert the Chinese emperors, but they never succeeded. And I certainly can't see them getting anywhere with the Dowager Empress Cixi. In short, the Catholics don't have a strong enough hand to be triumphant.'

'So,' Trader summarised, 'the alien barbarians beat the Chinese in battle, then they insult them, and then they trumpet their superiority by dominating the landscape in a country they don't control. Not a good idea.'

'I have complete faith, obviously, or I wouldn't be there,' Henry continued. 'But it's a question of judgement. I suspect triumphalism is always unwise. It's asking for trouble. Also I might add, as a Christian, that I think it's better to be humble.'

'Are there any signs of trouble yet?'

'A few popular tracts and broadsheets have appeared in the streets,' Henry answered. 'Aimed at the Catholics, really – though whether ordinary people distinguish Catholic from Protestant is another matter. They accuse the Christians of kidnapping Chinese children and drinking their blood. That sort of thing. Complete nonsense, of course. In fact, it's exactly what the Christians used to say about the Jews in the Middle Ages. In any case,' Henry went on calmly, 'if at some time in the future, God forbid, things got too bad, there should be time to get Emily out quickly, together with any children we might have. Emily and I have already discussed it.'

John Trader was silent. At the far end of the room there was a painting of a Highland sunset. It glowed sadly, like a lament.

'So you could get them out in time?' Trader said slowly. 'You're sure of that?'

'Oh yes,' said Henry, 'I think so.'

JINGDEZHEN

1875

On the southern bank of the mighty Yangtze River, about a hundred and fifty miles upstream from the ancient city of Nanjing, the great stream was joined by tributaries descending from the hills above. A day's journey up one of these tributaries, in a spacious, protected valley, lay a town – a peaceful place, though important enough for the prefect to have his residence there.

Yet there was something out of the ordinary about its suburbs. Instead of the usual scattering of workshops with yards and storehouses, there were hundreds of them; and above their roofs, amongst the treetops, a forest of squat brick chimneys could be seen.

For this was Jingdezhen, porcelain capital of China, where the pottery made from local clay was shaped, painted, glazed and fired in the town's kilns – of which, if one counted even the smallest, there were more than nine thousand. The potters of Jingdezhen had been making porcelain since the Han dynasty, more than fifteen hundred years ago. There were many varieties, but the most famous was the blue and white.

The finest work was all reserved for the imperial court.

In recent years, most people in Jingdezhen would have agreed, they had been fortunate in the prefect who resided there. For he was a man of unusual probity.

In particular, his administration of justice was impeccable. The poorer folk especially were grateful to him. Woe betide any local magistrate who took a bribe to convict some poor but innocent man. If punishment was called for, he chose leniency. He showed a marked aversion to the use of torture. In short, he was kindly but fair.

And if there were occasions when, in a spirit of understanding and friendship, he was able to help a local business avoid some restriction, and the owner of the business showed him some gratitude, that was a private matter between them. Such arrangements were usually to benefit trade and were therefore welcomed by everyone in Jingdezhen. The only person who might not profit was the emperor. But the emperor was far away, and not so many people cared about him nowadays.

Timing was everything. Shi-Rong looked across the town from the balcony of the prefect's residence and smiled. A perfect autumn day. Some way down the long street he saw his quarry approaching. He was confident of success. He had everything planned.

He'd been a widower now for five years. Though he and his wife had hardly been close, he'd been sorry for her nonetheless. The cancer that claimed her had taken its time, and he had suffered with her.

He hadn't taken another wife after that. Whether he had come to prefer limited engagements, such as the one with Mei-Ling, or whether he had a residual fear that any woman he married might turn into a nagging wife like his first, he hardly knew himself.

He'd parted from his last concubine a few months ago. No doubt he'd take another before long. But not a wife.

A perfect autumn day: the monsoon season past. The heat of the sun in the pale blue sky was moderated by a breeze that dispersed the shimmer from the kilns and the wisps of smoke from their chimneys before it brushed the trees and flowers in the prefect's garden.

Shi-Rong liked Jingdezhen. Its combination of commerce, art, and quiet peace was pleasing to him.

Some years before he arrived, that peace had been disturbed. The Taiping zealots had come from their Heavenly Kingdom downriver at Nanjing, swarmed up the valley, entered the town and destroyed the kilns, all nine thousand of them.

Why had they done it? Who could say? As far as he was concerned, for all practical purposes, a zealot and a hooligan were one and the same. But a decade had passed since their Heavenly Kingdom had fallen, and the busy potters and merchants of Jingdezhen had restored the kilns with such skilful speed that one would hardly guess they'd ever been smashed.

All being well, Shi-Rong intended to leave town tomorrow on a visit to Beijing. An interview or two. A bribe to pay, naturally, but he had the money. And after that he could look forward to a few years of semi-retirement, during which, with a bit of luck, he might even double his fortune. Done discreetly, this would be the crowning achievement of his life.

He'd see his son as well, while he was in Beijing. That was a happy prospect. I might not have risen to the greatest heights, he thought, but having a father who's a prefect isn't so bad. The lower fourth rank. Not to be sneezed at. The mandarin square on a prefect's chest depicted a wild goose. He wore a solid blue button on his hat. That was something for the young man's friends to see.

First, however, there was the girl to look after. Bright Moon. His new daughter.

He'd promised Mei-Ling he'd find the girl a good husband, and today he was going to make good on his promise. He was quite surprised at his own delight in the business.

Now, in the street below him, his quarry had reached the residence gate. Shi-Rong turned and made his way down to greet him.

'I can hardly believe, Mr Yao,' he said as soon as they were sitting down, 'that a whole year has passed since we buried your dear wife.' He sighed. 'I know how it feels. It is only a few years since I lost my own.' He nodded sadly. 'How are your two daughters?'

'They are well, I thank you, and a great comfort to me,' the merchant replied. 'If only my poor little son had not been sickly . . . His death was a great sadness to me and my wife.'

'I know how devoted you were to each other,' Shi-Rong said.

'She was the only wife I ever had. Most merchants in my position take junior wives, but I never did.'

'You were an exceptional husband,' Shi-Rong agreed. He seemed to hesitate for a moment. 'But I wonder – I speak as a friend – if the time might not come when your duty compels you to provide a male heir. You owe it to your ancestors, after all. Who else will tend their graves?'

'It is true. Life must go on.'

According to Shi-Rong's spies, the life force had already begun to assert itself. During the last three months, Mr Yao had paid several visits to the best of the local houses of pleasure.

Besides being rich, Yao wasn't a bad-looking fellow. Still in his forties, he was sturdily built. With his flared nose, his broad moustache turned down at the ends, and his bulbous head thrust slightly forward, he reminded Shi-Rong of a bull about to charge. Certainly not a man to be trifled with. But he'd proved himself a kindly and devoted husband. No question. And he was subtler than he looked.

For instance when, each year, he showed his friendship to Shi-Rong, he always found the most creative ways to do it. Once he'd pointed to an antique vase he'd recently acquired, one of a collection he'd bought, and remarked, 'My wife doesn't like it; I suppose you wouldn't care to take it off my hands?' And he'd named a trifling sum as a price. Sure enough, when Shi-Rong had shown the vase to a dealer, he'd found that it was worth twenty times what he'd paid. On another occasion, Yao had recommended that Shi-Rong purchase the house of a deceased merchant. 'They say the old man hoarded silver in there. I looked around the place, and I couldn't find any. But who knows, you may be luckier.' And of course, after buying the house, Shi-Rong had discovered a crate of silver dollars most imperfectly concealed under the floor.

Thanks to these discreet favours, Mr Yao, who owned two of the town's finest potteries – where production was exclusively reserved for the imperial court – was able to run an illicit business in export porcelain on the side. The profits were large, the gifts in proportion. After taking care of various local officials, Shi-Rong still retained a handsome share for himself.

As it happened, history had done Shi-Rong another favour. Three years after he'd come to Jingdezhen, at the very time when he might have expected to be moved on to another post, a significant event had taken place in the court at Beijing.

For the decade that her son was still a minor, the Dowager Empress Cixi and the late emperor's widow had continued their rule from behind the throne.

Last year, however, the time had come for the youth to rule in person. And it didn't go well. The boy took after his useless father. Neither his mother nor the finest tutors nor the wisest counsellors could do anything with him. All he knew about his empire and his people was what he'd learned by escaping from the palace into the city whorehouses. He'd been found a suitable wife, but he wasn't interested in her. He didn't seem to be interested in anything really, except debauchery – and the fastest way to ruin his health.

And then he died. Was he poisoned? Nobody knew. Did his own mother have a hand in it? Cixi said no. He was her only son, after all. And since his departure was obviously for the best, no one wanted to probe too deeply. So another boy emperor was found.

He was the son of Prince Chun, who'd married Cixi's sister. Strictly speaking, since he was the same generation as the emperor who'd died, this was breaking the laws of succession. But Cixi wanted it, and she got her way. She adopted the little boy as her own and resumed her role as the imperial mother behind the curtain.

With so many things going on, nobody at court had remembered to move the prefect at Jingdezhen to a new post. Shi-Rong certainly hadn't reminded them. He just kept his head down and continued to enjoy Mr Yao's friendship – as a result of which, by the autumn of 1875, he had considerably increased the modest fortune his father had left him.

'Normally, of course,' Shi-Rong continued, 'it is for the family of the bridegroom to find a suitable wife for him, and to put the entire matter in the hands of a matchmaker. But given our friendship, I hope you will not mind if I make a suggestion to you. Should you wish to marry again, my dear Yao, I think I might have a bride for you.'

'Really?' The merchant was interested. 'May I ask who?'

'This girl.' Shi-Rong went to a side table, opened a drawer and took out a framed photograph. 'The lady she's standing beside is her mother.'

He'd gone to a lot of trouble over that picture. The photographer, who'd been trained in Macao, had been sent all the way down to the hamlet. He'd understood his mission perfectly. The picture was taken in the courtyard of the house, which he'd improved with several exotic plants in pots. Both Mei-Ling and the girl were elegantly dressed and made up like fashionable ladies. The photograph had even been tinted in the latest manner. Cleverly, he'd also taken a photograph of the farmhouse from across the pond. The little footbridge, nowadays beautifully restored, was reflected in a pond pleasantly strewn with patches of water lilies. The whole effect was one of modest provincial wealth.

Mr Yao examined both photographs carefully. 'The girl is beautiful. So is her mother,' he said admiringly. Then he frowned. 'The mother's feet . . .'

'Are not bound. Her own mother came from a rich Hakka family. Her father's family did not wish to annoy them by binding their granddaughter's feet.'

'The Hakka family were important, then.'

'Exactly so,' Shi-Rong lied. 'But Bright Moon – that is the girl's name – has bound feet, as you can see.'

'You have known this family a long time?'

'I have. After the girl's mother was widowed, she accompanied me down to Guilin and stayed with me there for some time. Despite her feet, she is a most elegant and accomplished lady. She and the prefect's wife became best friends.'

Mr Yao was looking at him curiously now. 'You take a particular interest in her daughter, it seems.'

'I do. In fact, I have adopted her as my own.' He'd done it just a year ago, explaining to her family that it would help her find a good husband – which indeed was true.

'The mother is beautiful, but there is something finer, perhaps, in the young lady,' Mr Yao ventured.

Shi-Rong inclined his head slightly, as though accepting a compliment. 'She looks very like my late father's sister, as it happens,' he acknowledged.

'Ah.' The merchant gave him a knowing look, which Shi-Rong pretended to ignore.

It was going exactly as he hoped. He hadn't actually said that Bright Moon was his own, which of course she wasn't. But Yao was free to believe it – as he certainly wanted to. For a merchant like Yao, the idea of marrying the daughter, legitimate or not, of a prefect from an old gentry family like Shi-Rong's was something to boast about.

'It may interest you,' said Yao, 'that I am soon to enter the gentry myself.'

'Indeed?'

'The negotiations are almost concluded.'

They were all doing it, these merchants – at least, those who could afford to. For a suitable fee, the imperial court would give them gentry rank. It allowed them to display the symbols of their social rank in their houses. They were, at least officially, no longer the despised, money-grubbing merchants they had been before.

Personally, Shi-Rong regarded this as a debasement of the nobility, a lack of respect for Confucian order. But in these troubled times, what could you expect? In this case it would clearly be to the advantage of his adopted daughter.

'I congratulate you,' he said. 'There are many men, my dear Yao,' he went on blandly, 'who would be glad to marry my adopted daughter. I should like a rich man, certainly, but not too old. You are still vigorous. I want a man who would treat her kindly. I know you will. In return, she is young, she is healthy; and until she was born, her own mother had produced nothing but sons.'

'That is very good,' said Yao.

'Before speaking to you about the matter,' Shi-Rong continued, 'I thought it wise to consult a marriage broker. She looked at your birth dates and consulted the calendar, and I am happy to tell you that if a marriage were to take place this year, there are no bad auguries. So we have some months. I can send the broker to you, or of course you may wish to consult your own.'

'Please send her to me,' said Yao eagerly. 'I shall be glad to take her advice.'

'Naturally,' Shi-Rong continued, 'Bright Moon's trousseau is in order, and she would send all the usual gifts to your family. But I thought you might like to see these.' And returning to the drawer he'd opened before, he took out some pieces of embroidery and showed them to the merchant.

'Very fine.' Yao was deeply impressed. 'Very fine indeed.'

'All by her own hand. She is most accomplished. She performs the tea ceremony elegantly. She is versed in poetry . . .' He noticed Yao look a little nervous. 'I mean only to the extent,' he assured him, 'that a new member of the gentry would wish.'

'Of course,' said Yao. 'Very proper.'

'I have to make a visit to Beijing,' Shi-Rong announced. 'Meanwhile, I shall send word that Bright Moon and her mother should travel to Jingdezhen, where they will stay at my residence. I expect to get back from Beijing before they arrive. Would that be agreeable to you?'

'Most certainly,' said Yao. 'Most certainly.'

He sailed down the Yangtze with the current to Nanjing, then to Hangzhou and the coast, where he found a swift ship at Zhapu. Eighteen days later, from the coast below Beijing, he came easily by the Grand Canal to the capital and quickly found suitable lodgings. He sent word to Ru-Hai that he must attend to business the first day, but would call upon him the next.

It was his old friend Mr Peng Senior who had suggested this visit.

Besides taking young Peng under his wing at Guilin, Shi-Rong had helped the young man with numerous testimonials, and his father was not a man to forget favours. If everything in his letter worked out, he'd have more than repaid any debts of gratitude.

As you know, my friend, no state office has been more profitable to the holder than the collection and distribution of the salt tax. Hitherto, there was one man in charge, who, by taking a cut of the enormous volume, could make a huge fortune.

In recent years, the business has been less tightly controlled. Quite a number of men can get a share, and still do very well. So these posts are much sought after.

I've just heard that one of these positions will be available before long, and I thought you might be interested. Hardly anyone knows about this yet, so if you move quickly, you might be able to secure it. Normally I'd have asked Prince Gong to put in a word for you – and that would probably have done the trick. But as you will have heard, during this recent succession crisis at court, Dowager Empress Cixi not only adopted her nephew and made him the new boy emperor, but she has reduced the power and influence of Prince Gong, alas. So for the time being, his support mightn't do you much good.

However, there's another fellow I happen to know who has the ear of Cixi. He's a strange chap. I'll tell you all about him if you come to Beijing. You'll have to bribe him, of course.

So it was, after a pleasant midday meal with Mr Peng, that Shi-Rong made his way to a prosperous street in the merchant quarter and came to a handsome doorway, where a servant let him in.

Given all that Mr Peng had told him about his host, Shi-Rong was quite curious. As soon as the door closed, he found himself between the two fearsome warrior gods who guarded the hallway, stared at his reflection in the big mottled mirror in front of him, which repelled all evil spirits, and followed the servant to the left and then to the right into the courtyard.

He was impressed. This was the house of a rich man. He wondered how his host could have accumulated so much in only a dozen years. Was the bribe Peng had recommended going to be enough to satisfy such a person?

As they entered the courtyard, he noticed a youth of sixteen or seventeen, slipping quietly into a doorway in the far corner. Was this the son of his host? Glancing to one side, through the latticework screen of an open window, he caught a glimpse of a lady sitting on a brocade-covered divan; she appeared to be smoking an opium pipe. The boy's mother, perhaps?

Ushered into a small but pleasant office, he was informed that the master of the house would be with him directly. And indeed, it was only moments before a faint rustle of silk outside the door announced his host.

So this was the married eunuch known as Lacquer Nail. A strange chap, Peng had called him. Certainly he wasn't like any eunuch Shi-Rong had seen before.

He wore a simple but costly grey robe. On his head, a plain round cap of the same material. He looked exactly like a rich merchant. But there was a hint of the servile eunuch about him as well, Shi-Rong thought, as Lacquer Nail bowed low and sat down opposite his guest.

'My friend Mr Peng has explained your requirements in detail, honoured sir.' His voice was soft, but not as high as many eunuchs'. Did he detect, behind the respectful politeness, a hint of an impatient mind? Shi-Rong wondered.

Though it was hardly customary to compliment a stranger on first meeting him, Shi-Rong couldn't help remarking: 'I must congratulate you on your fine house.'

'It is not mine, sir,' his host replied. 'This house belongs to my esteemed friend Mr Chen. Since his retirement to the country, I rent it from him, on the understanding that it is his to use whenever he wishes. He comes to stay with us for a month, twice a year.'

'An admirable arrangement.'

'Mr Chen was an early mentor of mine. Like me, he became a eunuch after he had married and had a family. Here he lived as a merchant, as I do. The neighbours are not even aware of my position in the palace.'

'Remarkable.'

For the next few minutes the two men exchanged the usual courtesies.

Shi-Rong asked whether it was the eunuch's son whom he'd caught a glimpse of, and Lacquer Nail said that it was. Shi-Rong thought it better not to ask after his wife.

'My own son is nearly thirty now,' he offered. 'He's in the Bureau of Foreign Affairs, here in Beijing.'

'An interesting place to be,' his host politely remarked. 'I believe this generation is the first to take an interest in the lands beyond our borders since the days of the Ming dynasty. No doubt you are proud of him.'

Shi-Rong acknowledged this with a slight bow of his head.

'Mr Peng has spoken to you of my requirements?' Lacquer Nail continued. Evidently he was done with the pleasantries now.

'He has. Everything is in order. He suggested I should leave this small gift with you' – Shi-Rong produced a bag of silver – 'to cover any expenses you might incur, with the balance to be made upon my securing the appointment.'

'Quite so. It will require patience, you know. Timing is everything.' Lacquer Nail gazed at the mandarin thoughtfully. 'May I speak frankly and without reservation?'

'Of course.'

'Then I must tell you, honoured sir, that while I am a devoted slave to the Dowager Empress Cixi – I owe her everything and I would die for her – that doesn't mean she's without fault.'

'Few of us are.'

'She has a remarkable instinct. Even her most exasperating decisions often turn out to be good – at least for her. But she's changeable. You never know what mood she'll be in from one day to the next. Someone like me, trusted for many years, is fairly safe. I'm only the eunuch who does her nails, and it amuses her to talk to me. But you know how she recently turned upon Prince Gong himself.'

'Of course.'

'She didn't try to destroy him. For she's not without gratitude. But for the present, his influence is uncertain.'

'So I have heard.'

'In short, honoured sir, I must tread carefully. First, I must wait until the post is officially under consideration. To raise the matter beforehand might seem impertinent.'

'I understand.'

'Then I have to catch her on a good day. I can always tell her mood as soon as I come into her presence. On a bad day, she'll take a delight in telling me no. On a good day, she'll smile and ask me how much I'm being bribed.'

'She will?' Shi-Rong asked, alarmed.

'Of course. Everyone in the palace is bribed. It will amuse her.'

'But then she'll know it's me who bribed you.'

'I doubt she'll care. I don't suppose she's ever heard of you.'

Shi-Rong sighed. It was painful to hear such a thing from this eunuch, but it was probably true.

'The Dowager Empress was born quite poor,' the eunuch went on. 'She still had nothing when her son was born, or even when his father died. Her existence was uncertain. You may have heard that Prince Sushun wanted to kick her out. He may even have planned to kill her. But then, as we all know, Prince Gong triumphed, Sushun was executed, and his huge estate was given to Cixi and the widowed empress. Suddenly, for the first time in her life, Cixi had a lot of money. And like many people so blessed, she's generous. By fits and starts, of course. But she loves it when her servants get rich, too. It makes her happy.'

'I am glad to hear it.'

'Of course, your getting one of the salt inspector positions won't actually cost her anything. Once you have the post, you'll take your cut of all the salt tax that belongs to the state – which is theft, really. But then so would anyone else who got the job, so it makes no difference. And I will have received a bribe from you, and she likes me, so that's all right.'

'You have a charming way of putting things,' said Shi-Rong. He was starting to resent Lacquer Nail, and the eunuch knew it, but it didn't seem to worry him. Shi-Rong imagined Lacquer Nail was quite enjoying the spectacle of a man so superior to himself being forced to look at the uncomfortable truth. Instead of being angry, therefore, he took the opportunity to ask something he'd often wondered about. 'Tell me,' he enquired, 'what does the dowager empress really want from her position these days? What else makes her happy?'

'Ah.' Lacquer Nail nodded. It seemed he liked this question, for he thought for a few moments before replying. 'First,' he replied, 'I think she just wants to survive. A dozen years ago, as we've just said, she nearly didn't.'

'That is understandable.'

'Second, she'd like to enjoy herself a bit, as any person would. But in her position, that is not easy. She's just turning forty. She may not be conventionally pretty, but she has the same needs as any woman of her age. Her whole position, however, depends on her being the official mother of the boy emperor. So she probably can't risk taking lovers.' He paused reflectively. 'If she wasn't so strong-minded she might have taken to opium. But she loves the theatre. She can afford troupes of actors and dancers. In court, the parts are mostly played by eunuchs, you know. So we all have fun at that.'

'They say she's extravagant: wanting to rebuild the Summer Palace when we still haven't recovered from the Taiping and the Opium Wars. They call her a spendthrift.'

'They call her all kinds of names. Officials who get on the wrong side of her say she's a dragon lady. I know palace people who call her Old Buddha – which seems a bit premature – because they think she's inscrutable. But in my opinion, they've all missed the point. To understand what the dowager empress does, one has to forget the person and look at the situation.'

'Which is that the empire's ruined.'

'Yes. And it'll take us years to recover. But what's she to do in the meantime? She has to give her people hope.' Lacquer Nail paused. 'What was the greatest single catastrophe, would you say, during the Opium Wars?'

'The burning of the Summer Palace, certainly.'

'Indeed. And it wasn't only the destruction; it was the humiliation. A blackened ruin at the heart of our empire.' He paused. 'I was there, you know, and saw the whole thing. I even fought the barbarians myself with a sword, killed two of them.'

'You fought?' Despite himself, Shi-Rong couldn't quite keep the incredulity out of his voice.

Lacquer Nail observed him coldly. 'You do not believe me.'

'I didn't say that.'

'It doesn't matter. Today,' the eunuch went on, 'the barbarian powers still encircle us like hungry rats, trying to steal whatever they can. Cixi hates it. She also knows that we can't do much about it. Not yet. Not until we get stronger. But at least she can start rebuilding a part of the Summer Palace to show that the empire means to get its dignity back.'

The eunuch was no fool, Shi-Rong thought. Yet something was missing from this explanation. And because he felt at such an uncomfortable disadvantage in the interview so far, he pressed on when he should have remained silent. 'But the Summer Palace was still, at the end of the day, a private pleasure ground,' he pointed out. 'It's not as if the emperor performed the ritual sacrifices there, if you see what I mean. It's more about art and display than about the serious business of the state.'

Did he realise that he was indirectly suggesting the eunuch was frivolous? Or was he so busy constructing his proposition that he hadn't considered the bricks of which it was built?

'The ritual sacrifices are ceremonies,' Lacquer Nail replied coolly, 'with a correct procedure. That's a display, of a kind. If the emperor goes through the streets, there are finely dressed attendants, soldiers, drummers. Display again. For how do the people know there's order in the empire? Only by ceremony. Because ceremony is what they see. Wouldn't you agree?' He stared at Shi-Rong until the mandarin bowed his head in acknowledgment. 'Anyway,' Lacquer Nail went on blandly, 'people like parades. They like the emperor and his servants to make a fine show – just as they like their temples to be full of beauty and scented candles and gleaming gold. It makes them feel good. The emperor shows them their land is great; the temples bring them closer to the heavens.'

'And if the people are poor?'

'The peasants like to dress up, too. Even in the poorest hill villages. Look at the colourful tribal costumes they put on at festivals. It's amazing how they manage it all, but they do. It's just human nature.' He paused. 'And they like to be entertained. That's part of the art of ruling. You mustn't let the people starve, but they'll forgive you almost anything else if you keep them entertained.'

'They respect justice and good morals,' Shi-Rong declared.

'When they need them,' Lacquer Nail replied. 'But mostly they want to be entertained.'

'Perhaps you are too cynical about the people,' said Shi-Rong stiffly.

'I come from the people,' the eunuch riposted. 'We were dirt poor when I was a boy.' He let his gaze rest for a moment on a fine piece of porcelain standing on a table by the wall. 'Perhaps that's why I like the finer things of life so much.'

'I was brought up to respect Confucian order,' Shi-Rong observed.

'Ah yes,' said Lacquer Nail. 'So shall we call our arrangement a Confucian bribe?'

Shi-Rong winced as if he had been punched. He couldn't help it.

He thought of his father. He looked helplessly at Lacquer Nail, but the eunuch seemed suddenly weary.

'I believe our business is done for today,' Lacquer Nail said. 'I'll send word as soon as I have news. Please just be patient.'

The two men rose.

'It has been my privilege to meet you, honoured sir,' the eunuch murmured, his manner disconcertingly servile again as he conducted Shi-Rong towards the entrance.

And Shi-Rong was just about to pass between the two warrior gods in the doorway and out into the street when he stopped for a moment.

He felt the need to speak again. Not to have the last word. Just to speak again. To say something, anything, that might allow him to quit the field of battle with his colours still flying. 'Forgive my asking,' he said, 'but I am curious. To what use will you put the money I give you? Towards buying this splendid house, perhaps?'

'No,' Lacquer Nail replied calmly. 'I have another matter to attend to before that. I need to buy back my private parts, so that when the time comes, I can be buried as a complete man. Often eunuchs do not accomplish this until late in life, and sometimes never. Naturally, it is a point of honour – both for me and for my family.'

'Ah,' said Shi-Rong. 'I hadn't thought of that.'

The entrance to the Tsungli Yamen, the Bureau of Foreign Affairs, was just wide enough to allow a carriage through. It resided inconspicuously amongst the larger ministries in the Imperial City. For despite the vigorous advocacy of Prince Gong over a period of a dozen years, many mandarins still saw the bureau as only a temporary department. Many of the officials who worked there also held positions in other parts of the government.

Some thought otherwise. Young Ru-Hai certainly did. 'We're going to be more important as time goes by,' he told his father. 'This could be a quick way to the top.'

As a good father, Shi-Rong always spoke respectfully of the Tsungli Yamen to anyone who would listen, even if in private he wasn't so sure his son was right.

Be that as it may, he'd been delighted when Ru-Hai suggested they meet there. I daresay my son's proud of his father, he thought. Wants his friends to meet me. It would be interesting to talk to the boy's colleagues and find out what these young fellows thought.

He'd woken that morning in a cheerful mood. He almost forgot the humiliation of his meeting with Lacquer Nail. All he remembered was that the eunuch knew how to handle the Dragon Empress, and that soon the salt inspector's post would be his.

In centuries to come, his descendants, when they tended the family graves on Ancestors Day, might speak in awe of the achievements of others, even of his own son Ru-Hai perhaps – he certainly hoped so – but at least when they came to his own grave, they'd be able to say: 'He was a prefect, he attained the honourable fourth rank, and he left the family richer than it had ever been before.'

So he arrived at the gateway of the bureau with a smiling face.

One cannot always assume, because one is in a happy mood oneself, that other people will be, too. As his son greeted him and led him towards his office, Shi-Rong noticed that they were passing through the ministry kitchens. Like many such places, they were none too clean.

'I don't think much of this, I must say,' he said jovially. 'Taking your old father through the kitchens. Who gets to come through the front door?'

Ru-Hai didn't smile. 'This is the only way in,' he said tensely. 'When the bureau was created, they divided up an old building to house us.'

'You mean you bring foreign ambassadors in through the kitchens?'

'If they're having a formal audience, they go to the Imperial Palace. But private meetings between officials take place here in the bureau.' It was clear he was embarrassed. 'I daresay we'll get rehoused one of these days.'

Shi-Rong frowned. Such lack of ceremony hardly signified that the court thought much of the foreign ambassadors – or of the mandarins they were to meet, for that matter. Personally, he didn't care about the barbarian ambassadors. But he cared about Ru-Hai's career. His cheerful mood was somewhat muted, therefore, as he entered his son's office.

It was a long, narrow, dusty room with tall windows that looked into a silent yard containing one stone lion and a tree with a broken branch. There were three desks. At the far end, a large map hung on the wall.

Ru-Hai introduced his two colleagues. Neither of them looked over thirty. The first, a Han Chinese, was a thin, nervous fellow with round eyeglasses. He was called Gao. The other was a short, plump Manchu, whose broad face was puckered as if he were looking into the wind. He didn't seem to say much. But they both seemed friendly enough and showed proper respect for his rank.

'We thought you might like to know what we do here,' Ru-Hai said when the pleasantries were over.

'By all means,' said Shi-Rong.

They moved down the room towards the map on the wall. The Manchu stood on one side of it with a long pointer. Gao stood on the other. Ru-Hai nodded to him. Evidently this was a routine they'd rehearsed.

'We are here,' said Gao, 'to save the empire.'

'Well,' said Shi-Rong with a smile, 'I suppose somebody's got to do it.'

None of the three young men thought this was funny.

'For centuries,' Gao went on, 'the Celestial Empire had little need of anything from beyond its borders. Envoys from other lands came to pay tribute and to learn from us, since our power, our wealth, our civilisation, was superior to theirs.' He paused for a moment. 'Then came the British pirates from the West, corrupting our people with their opium. We told them to desist. They attacked us. Their ships, cannon and rifles were superior. And now look where they are.'

On cue, the Manchu took his long pointer and rapped the map on one place after another, along the coast and on the Yangtze River.

'Treaty ports where the barbarians live under their own laws. Little kingdoms within our own empire. Why? Because, while we ignored them for two hundred years, they had improved their weapons. The world had changed, but we didn't know it.'

'The mission of the Tsungli Yamen,' Ru-Hai said, taking up the theme, 'is to contain the barbarians, to learn from them, and to protect our land. But it hasn't been easy. We find, for instance, that to their credit, they will abide by the treaties they make. Recently therefore we renegotiated the agreements concerning the ports and the trade tariffs. The new treaty was fair to both sides. But when the unhappy British envoy sent it to his own government, they refused to ratify. Whatever we give, they always seem to want more.'

'They have no respect for our traditions,' said Gao, 'and they want everything done their own way.'

'Ten years ago,' Ru-Hai said to his father, 'we tried to buy warships from the West. Yet we still can't get them. We suspect the British prefer us to be weak.'

'And whether this is a deliberate policy or not,' Gao continued, 'the fact is that other countries still perceive us as defenceless, so they take advantage.'

'Russia,' announced Ru-Hai. And the Manchu tapped the map on the wall again. 'They have Vladivostok. But we know very well that they're after another huge territory up in Manchuria. They've already got troops there. Will we be able to make them withdraw? It remains to be seen.' He turned to the Manchu. 'France,' he called out.

The Manchu tapped the map up and down the long coastline south-west of China's border. 'Tonkin, Annam, Vietnam – call these lands what you like – they have either been part of our empire or paid us tribute for two thousand years. But last year the French moved in and made themselves overlords of the region.'

'The French despise us,' said Gao. 'First they build huge churches to dominate the landscape and convert our people to their religion. Now they're calmly taking over our tributary kingdoms.'

'So what are you suggesting we do?' Shi-Rong asked him. 'Go to war with the French?'

'When we're strong enough, maybe yes,' Gao answered.

'Here's the thing, Father,' said Ru-Hai. 'A generation ago we underestimated the British Navy. We have come to terms with Britain now, but our own navy is weak and our land forces far behind. Now we're making the same mistake with all these other barbarian powers. We still haven't learned our lesson. And there's one power that is far more dangerous than either the Russians or the French, because it's right on our doorstep.'

'Japan!' cried Gao.

And now the Manchu banged his pointer repeatedly on the country of Japan, so violently that he seemed to be trying to drive Mount Fuji down into the ocean.

'Twenty-five years ago,' Gao went on, 'Japan was closed to the world. Then the American, Commodore Perry, came with modern warships and smashed the Japanese navy. Forced them to open their ports to trade, but with unequal treaties, to America's advantage. Just like the British did with us. What happened next? The Japanese woke up. They have a new emperor, Meiji, who's taken power, and Japan is changing as never before.

They're taking all the knowledge they can from the Western barbarians, developing a new, modern army. Not only that, they know that if they want to defend themselves in the future, they need to expand their control across the seaways.'

'You mean the Ryukyu Islands,' Shi-Rong cut in. The Ryukyu Islands might be small, but they stretched all the way from the shores of Japan to the island of Formosa, as the barbarians liked to call Taiwan. Three years ago, the Japanese had landed on those little islands and taken them over. He'd been quite shocked. But nothing had been done about it.

'Of course. *Our* Ryukyu Islands,' his son responded. 'And like the weak fools we are, we let them. Next thing, they'll want Taiwan, which has been ours for two hundred years.'

'I suppose I'm a bit out of touch down in Jingdezhen,' said Shi-Rong, 'but as far as I could discover, it was the Tsungli Yamen – you fellows here – that let them do it.'

'Not us,' the three young men cried. 'The old idiots that are still in charge and don't even work here full-time.'

'I see.' Shi-Rong grimaced. 'And Prince Gong?'

'Prince Gong should never have let this happen,' said Ru-Hai sadly. 'But the dowager empress wasn't listening to him.'

'And still isn't now,' said Shi-Rong, remembering the eunuch's words from the day before, 'from what I hear.'

'In any case,' said Gao, 'Japan's big game isn't the islands, even Taiwan.'

'It isn't?' Shi-Rong frowned. 'Then what is?'

Gao hesitated a moment and glanced at the other two. Ru-Hai nodded. 'This is,' said Gao. And the Manchu rapped his pointer on the great peninsula of Korea.

'Japan hasn't gone near the peninsula,' said Shi-Rong.

'They're going to,' said his son.

'How do you know?'

'We know.' Ru-Hai looked seriously at his father. 'Any day. They could be there at this very moment, as we speak.'

'I find that hard to believe,' said Shi-Rong. He paused. 'It's our most important vassal kingdom.'

'More than that,' said Gao. 'For centuries the great peninsula has been like a protective arm, shielding our northern coast, including access to Beijing from the Sea of Japan. The tribute payments and the loyalty of their people have never been in question.'

'The Japanese would like to change that,' said Ru-Hai.

'You think they'll invade?'

'No, not yet. They're not ready. But they'll infiltrate. They'll tempt them with foreign trade, new ideas. They'll try to separate them from us.'

'And what are we supposed to do?'

'Get back in the game,' said Gao. 'We have to do what the Japanese are doing. Engage fully with the Western barbarians. Learn everything possible about not only their arms but also their ships, their factories – everything that makes them strong and leaves us weak if we do not have them.'

'Just so long as we don't have their railways,' said Shi-Rong. 'They are monstrous. Life would not be worth living with such foul machines.' He said it as though in jest, but he really meant it, and Ru-Hai and his friends knew he did. The young men looked at each other in silence, then politely ignored his remark.

'Father,' said Ru-Hai very seriously, 'we are all proud to be Chinese. But being Chinese alone isn't enough anymore. Put another way, if we want things to stay the same, we must change. We've sent an envoy to the British in London to learn all he can. And a few students have already gone to America to attend the universities there. We used to be ahead, but now we're deficient in mathematics and engineering and the science of money, all of which they can learn there. And our leaders must understand these things, too.'

'I'm well aware of all these expeditions,' Shi-Rong replied. 'But be careful. We still need mandarins learned in morals and philosophy. You cannot have an empire run by money-grubbers and mechanics.' He paused. 'But there is one thing that concerns me.'

'What's that?' asked Ru-Hai.

'Even if I don't like all of it, I admire you for trying to save the Celestial Empire in this way. Your sincerity and your courage are clear. But it's also clear that the court and your own superiors are not yet persuaded and – forgive me if I say it – you are very young, too junior to take such a burden upon yourselves.'

'We know,' said Ru-Hai. 'That's why we're trying to convert our elders – people like you, Father. If you and others like you speak up for us, then the court will take more notice. The matter is urgent: that's what the court needs to understand.'

'I can talk to Peng about it,' said Shi-Rong, 'and some others I know – prefects, a few governors, people with influence.'

'Thank you, Father,' said Ru-Hai. 'I suppose you don't know anyone who has the ear of the Empress Cixi?'

'Not really.' Shi-Rong was sorry to disappoint his son. He'd like to have cut a more important figure in front of his friends. Then a thought occurred to him. 'The only fellow I know who claims to have her ear' – he smiled with amusement at the idea – 'is a eunuch who does her nails. I don't suppose that would be much use to you.'

His son's mouth fell open. 'You know the eunuch who does her nails?' he cried in amazement.

'That's wonderful,' cried Gao in chorus.

'How do you know him?' Ru-Hai asked eagerly.

'Mr Peng knows him, really. This eunuch is also a merchant, and I'm transacting a small piece of business with him.' He didn't say what. 'I daresay I'll see him quite soon.'

'Please speak to him, Father. That would be magnificent.'

'If there's any further information we can provide for you, sir, please let us know,' said Gao.

Even the Manchu nodded fervently.

And Shi-Rong realised with sorrow that in the eyes of his son and his son's colleagues, he, a prefect of the fourth rank, was a very insignificant person compared with the eunuch who cut and polished the dowager empress's nails.

He ate at his lodgings with his son that night. It was a handsome hostel, often used by mandarins like himself who were visiting the capital. The servants were attentive, the meal excellent, and by the end of it, Shi-Rong was in quite a good humour. The meeting in the Tsungli Yamen might have damaged his amour propre a little, but not too much. He hadn't cut such a bad figure. It had certainly been interesting. And now here he was, at the end of a good meal, looking with affection at his boy.

'You know,' he remarked, 'it might be time for you to get married. What do you think?'

'I'd like to be further along in my career first, Father.'

'I understand that,' said Shi-Rong. 'But the path you're following in the Tsungli Yamen is quite uncertain.' He saw his son frown. 'Don't misunderstand me. I admire you. And it could lead to great things. But it's risky.' He paused. 'Your grandfather left the estate in pretty good shape. And I've been able to save money myself. So as far as marriage is concerned, whatever happens at the bureau, you're quite a good catch. We can probably find you a rich wife as well, with a bit of luck.'

Ru-Hai nodded slowly. He seemed to be considering. 'Can I ask you something, Father?' he said at last.

'Of course, my boy.'

'Why are you meeting with the eunuch? The one who does Cixi's nails?'

Shi-Rong hesitated for a second. He didn't want to mention the salt inspector's position, even to his son, until the deal was done. Firstly, it was confidential; and secondly, he always felt that announcing things in advance would bring bad luck.

'Just a piece of private business,' he said firmly, to head him off. But by the look on his son's face, this wasn't going to be enough. Very well, then: irrelevant information, obfuscation. He knew how to do that. 'He's a rather strange fellow,' he said easily. 'He had a wife and children of his own before he got chopped. Better pickings in the palace, I suppose. He lives in a merchant's house. His neighbours don't even know he's a eunuch. I never knew it before, but it turns out there are several of these married eunuchs at court.' He hoped that would do the trick. He certainly wasn't prepared for what came next.

Ru-Hai was staring down at his food. Suddenly he looked up. 'Are you bribing him?'

That was impertinence. It was also dangerous. 'And why would you think that?' Shi-Rong's voice was cold.

'People say you accept bribes.'

'What people? Your colleagues in the office?'

'No. Other people.'

'You realise, don't you, that there's hardly a public official in the empire who hasn't been accused of that, at one time or another?'

'No doubt.'

Shi-Rong paused for a moment. He was angry, but he kept calm. 'When I was about your age,' he said reflectively, 'my father made me promise him not to take bribes. He needn't have worried, as I was going to work for the most incorruptible official ever recorded. I am speaking of course of the great Commissioner Lin.' He nodded. 'Lin liked me. He trusted me. He was right to trust me. I am sad that my own son cannot extend me the same courtesy.'

It was a big rebuke. But Ru-Hai did not bow his head in shame, as he should have. 'I only mean that I have no desire to benefit, Father, even indirectly, from any bribes,' he said quietly.

Shi-Rong was silent. How long had his son been waiting to spring this on him? It was almost a year since they'd spent time with each other, and he'd supposed the boy would be pleased to see him. Indeed, he'd still imagined so in the bureau, just hours ago. Yet apparently not. The lack of respect struck him like a blow.

The boy takes after his mother, he thought angrily. As for his show of self-righteousness, I see his game. He's absolving himself, just in case I get caught.

Clearly he would have to treat his son like any other dangerous person, with caution. And cunning. He knew how to do that.

'Your attitude is quite correct. I am glad to hear it,' he said. 'Now I think this matter is closed.' And then a thought occurred to him. 'By the way,' he asked, 'do you remember Mei-Ling, whom you met in Guilin?'

'Of course.'

'Did you know that she had a daughter?'

'I remember hearing it.'

'A beautiful girl. She is to be married soon, to a merchant I know in Jingdezhen.' He smiled. 'Since she has no father of her own, I decided to adopt her. It was an act of kindness to the girl and her mother – she's marrying into a rich family, you see.'

'She is fortunate.' Ru-Hai inclined his head politely, but his father could see he was taken aback. 'You did not tell me.'

'I was intending to tell you when I saw you. It was not a matter of great importance.'

'When is this happy event to take place?'

'As soon as I have returned to Jingdezhen.'

'So I have a new sister.'

'An adopted sister, yes.' And now, Shi-Rong thought, with grim satisfaction, my self-righteous son is wondering if I'm going to give his new sister any of the money he claims to despise. He smiled again. 'In the meantime,' he continued blandly, 'while I remain here in Beijing I shall do what I can to further the cause you spoke about today.'

He was as good as his word. He soon found that there were quite a number of mandarins he knew in Beijing who were happy to discuss the Tsungli Yamen with him. Most of them seemed to agree that the military must modernise with Western arms and methods. 'We call this the Doctrine of Self-Strengthening,' a former governor told him. But when it came to matters like trade and education, there was far less agreement. Some were with the young men. Others held to the old rule: 'Keep the barbarians at a distance.'

An unexpected event helped him. Just two days after his meeting with the young men in the bureau, news came that a Japanese warship had raided the coast of the Korean peninsula – exactly as Ru-Hai and his friends had predicted. 'That raid has shaken up the mandarins,' he reported to Ru-Hai. 'When I tell them your mission is urgent, they listen.'

'Perhaps your eunuch will listen, too,' his son reminded him.

'I've got to see him first,' Shi-Rong replied.

Unfortunately, this was proving a problem. Lacquer Nail had told him to be patient. But after ten days had passed with no word from him, Shi-Rong decided to call at his house. The eunuch was there. He was polite, though Shi-Rong detected a hint of irritation in his voice when he assured him: 'Nothing has changed, honoured sir. I am still waiting for the vacancy to become official. I am confident that we shall succeed.' And seeing that Shi-Rong still didn't look satisfied: 'I have just as much interest in the matter as you.'

'I understand,' said Shi-Rong. And since it was clear that Lacquer Nail was waiting for him to leave, he went away without broaching the matter of the Tsungli Yamen.

The days that followed grew ever more frustrating. His lobbying for the bureau's cause began to wind down, because he was running out of people he knew. Most of the time he had nothing to do all day, except wait for the news from Lacquer Nail, which never came. Twice more he ate with his son, and these encounters went off without incident. The question of bribery was never raised again.

But time was getting on. Mei-Ling and her daughter must be well on their way up to Jingdezhen by now. He must get back for the wedding.

After a further ten days he could bear it no more. He knew he shouldn't do it, but he went back to the eunuch's house.

Dusk was falling. The servant who opened the street door looked surprised and told him that his master was not at home. 'He may not be back tonight,' he said.

Was he lying? Probably not. There might well be some play or concert in the palace that Cixi had told the eunuch to attend, in which case he'd probably sleep there. But then again, he might just come home late.

Shi-Rong turned away. Having come this far, he didn't want to miss Lacquer Nail if he should return. On the other hand, he thought, I can't just stand around on the street corner. It was undignified. So he began to walk slowly towards the Imperial City.

It wasn't difficult to work out the route that Lacquer Nail would be most likely to take. This would lead him to the Tiananmen Gate. If he encountered the eunuch on the way, well and good. As for the open space in front of the gate, it was well lit by lanterns, and a prefect could stroll there as he pleased without guards asking him what he was doing.

He reached the square. It was getting chilly. There were not many people about. He took a turn around it, pausing for a few moments to look up at the great gate. He walked around once more and again paused quite close to the gateway this time. And he was just wondering whether to go around or return to his lodgings when he noticed a tall, stately figure come out and make his way towards him. As the figure came close, Shi-Rong saw that it was a eunuch, and judging by his dress and insignia, one of the highest rank.

Should he ask him? He might just as well. If he was discreet, there was nothing to lose. Pausing in a place where the lamplight plainly revealed the insignia of the fourth rank on his chest, he let the tall eunuch draw a little closer and then addressed him. 'Excuse me, but I wonder if I might ask you. I was hoping to catch a word with a friend before I leave Beijing. He is known in the palace as Lacquer Nail. Would you know whether he is on duty in the palace this evening, or if he may be coming out?'

The tall figure paused, took in his rank at once, and in a soft voice replied: 'Good evening, sir. My name is Mr Liu. Might I ask whom I have the honour of addressing.'

'I am the prefect of Jingdezhen.'

'Ah.' Mr Liu smiled. 'Well, I can tell you that he will not be coming out tonight. This I know for a fact. Is there anything I can do to be of help?'

'Not really, thank you, Mr Liu. You have already helped me.'

'I am so glad.' Mr Liu seemed to be regarding him with interest. 'I should explain that I am one of your friend's greatest admirers. I was instrumental in setting him on the road to success right at the start of his career.'

'Indeed?' Shi-Rong was delighted. He wondered if this Mr Liu could help him discover the best time and place to waylay his elusive partner.

'I was just going to a teahouse I like to frequent,' said Mr Liu. 'Would you give me the pleasure of your company?'

'Why certainly,' Shi-Rong said.

What a charming and intelligent person Mr Liu was. It was soon evident that he and Lacquer Nail were very old friends. He told Shi-Rong stories of their times together, of delightful evenings spent on the lake islands at the Summer Palace, of scandals they had witnessed in the Forbidden City – these were told in strict confidence, of course – and having expressed the opinion that Lacquer Nail was probably the best friend he had in all the world, he earnestly assured Shi-Rong: 'You can absolutely trust him with your business. He's honest, and he'll never let you down.'

'That is good to know,' said Shi-Rong.

'Without being indiscreet,' Mr Liu confessed, 'he may have told me a little about your business already – only because he can trust me, you understand. He and I share such things from time to time.'

'He told you about the salt inspector's position?'

'Ah.' Mr Liu smiled. 'He did indeed.'

'The trouble is, it's taking so long. He says we have to wait until it's announced officially.'

'And he's absolutely right,' Mr Liu assured him. 'Do nothing until then. Who is putting your name forward officially?'

'My friend Mr Peng and people he knows in the ministry.'

'Excellent. As soon as they've done so, Lacquer Nail will whisper in Cixi's ear. That should do the trick. Timing is the key.'

'I went to see him the other day, and he told me to be patient. But I can't wait here much longer.' And Shi-Rong explained about Mei-Ling and the wedding.

'There is no need to wait around in Beijing,' Liu told him. 'It's not as if Cixi will want to see you in person. Go to the wedding with confidence. The position is as good as yours.' He paused. 'If it will put your mind at rest, I'll speak to Lacquer Nail about it myself. My word carries some weight in the palace. And having met you, I should be glad to add my advocacy to his. Your application will sail through.'

'It is very kind of you, Mr Liu.' Shi-Rong hesitated. 'The thing is, my arrangements were already made . . .'

'I understand what's in your mind.' Mr Liu slightly raised his hand and smiled. 'Please do not concern yourself, my dear sir. You would owe me nothing for this little favour. Indeed, you cannot imagine how much pleasure it gives me to involve myself in this affair.'

'Should I leave him word that I spoke to you?'

'What for? I shall speak to him myself. Whereas if you try to contact him again when he has asked you to be patient, he might feel a little insulted. He'll know how to reach you in Jingdezhen, as will the estimable Mr Peng, no doubt. Travel back there as soon as you like.'

So he did. The very next day.

o

As the wedding drew near, Mr Yao's family were all delighted with Bright Moon. His elderly mother, his sisters, his aunt, his nieces and nephews and cousins. The needlework she had sent was exquisite. The women had all met her face-to-face and declared that she was beautiful, and charming, and respectful, and good. And even if some of them found her accomplishments a bit too far above their own, they all agreed that, since Mr Yao was about to become a gentleman, this was the girl they needed.

The only person of consequence in Jingdezhen who had not met the bride was the bridegroom. Nor would he, until they were married. That was tradition, and everything was being done correctly.

For Shi-Rong, these were happy days. He enjoyed having this beautiful young woman in his house. And the fact that Mr Yao had circulated the rumour that Bright Moon might be more than his adopted daughter added to his local reputation in an agreeable way. The beauty of the girl's mother, who was known as his former concubine, was taken as further proof that the prefect of Jingdezhen was a man whose taste matched his rank.

Since the bridal party should include another male relation, Mei-Ling had brought California Brother with her. Though his manners were somewhat rustic compared with those of his mother and sister, he was quiet and friendly. And if asked, he was happy to give an account of the strange wonders of America.

Only one thing irked Shi-Rong. Mei-Ling and her daughter shared a room, and the mother insisted that she should remain with her daughter every night. He had secretly hoped that Mei-Ling would make herself more available to him. But as she did not offer, he said nothing.

The wedding was a great success. Of course, Bright Moon wept as she was carried to the bridegroom's house. A girl was supposed to show grief at being parted from her loving parents. She didn't look overjoyed when she met her husband. But no doubt with a little time, and her husband's careful attention, she'd be happy enough.

The toasts were made, the presents given. Bright Moon served the guests. Both her husband and, equally important, his family were well satisfied.

It had cost him money, Shi-Rong reflected, but it was the right thing to do. He was glad he'd done it. All was right with his world.

Almost all. But not quite.

He was surprised the next day when Mei-Ling came to him, looking rather concerned. 'May I sit down?' she asked. 'There is something I need to discuss with you.' He nodded. She sat opposite him. 'I have come to ask a favour,' she said.

'Another?'

'I had a bad dream last night.' She paused for a moment. 'Many years ago, Nio gave me some money. It was the only money I ever had in my life. I kept it hidden. And it helped me through difficult times.'

He frowned. 'Your family is not so poor now, though.'

'That is true. My bad dream was about Bright Moon.'

'Bright Moon?' What could she be talking about? 'I have just found her a rich husband,' he pointed out. 'She'll never want for anything in her life.'

'I know.' She hesitated. 'But in my dream, something had gone wrong. Her husband had divorced her. Sent her home.'

'Why?'

'My dream did not explain. But she had nothing.'

'If she does something bad, if she were unfaithful, her husband could throw her out and keep her dowry. But not otherwise. You're surely not suggesting she would do that?'

'No. Of course not. But that's how it was in my dream.'

'This was a foolish dream. If it happened, she would be greatly to blame. She would be disgraced. Though her family might look after her, I suppose.'

'We spent so much giving her the education and all that she would need to make such a marriage, I do not think her brothers would want to help her.'

'I would not blame them.'

'And I could not help her, because I have no money at all. You gave me money before, but I have spent it by now. But if you could just give me a little, as Nio did, I would keep it secretly, so that if I ever had to, I could help her.'

Shi-Rong stared at her. Was she trying to extract something for herself? No, he thought, that was not her way. She was telling the truth, however foolish her fear might be. He felt angry, given all the expense he'd just incurred; but he was touched as well. She was in distress and she'd come to him for help.

And the truth was, he could afford it. Indeed, the moment he heard the good news from Beijing, his fortune would be so assured that he'd hardly even notice any amount of money he was likely to give her.

So he smiled. 'I'll see what I can do,' he said. 'There'll be something.'

'Thank you.' She bowed her head. 'This means a great deal to me.'

It was the custom on the third day for the bride and bridegroom to visit her parents' house. They were welcomed with warm smiles and celebrations. With a big smile, Mr Yao presented Shi-Rong and Mei-Ling with the customary gifts and addressed them as Father and Mother. Everybody seemed happy. The ritual of wedding was now complete.

The messenger from Beijing arrived at the prefect's house at noon the following day. Along with various packages and official dispatches, he brought a personal letter from Lacquer Nail. Eagerly, before even opening the business documents, Shi-Rong went into his study to read the eunuch's message.

> It is with great distress, honoured sir, that I must inform you that a disaster has occurred. Our plans are ruined.
>
> I flatter myself that I have few enemies. But one enemy, who formerly tried to destroy me, and who has never ceased since then to place every obstacle in my path that he can, is a certain Mr Liu, a palace person of great power and importance.

Somehow, by what means I have been unable to discover, he came to know in advance of the salt inspector's position and of my interest in the matter. The very night before I was going to mention it to the empress, he obtained an audience with her and secured the post for a candidate of his own. When I spoke to her the next morning, she laughed and said, 'Bad luck, Lacquer Nail. I just gave it away to a friend of Mr Liu's. You're too late.'

There is nothing I can do, honoured sir. If I hear of something else, I shall endeavour to let you know. But there's nothing on the horizon at the moment. Accordingly, I am returning the down payment with this same messenger.

This is a heavy blow for both of us, and I can only express my deep regret.

Shi-Rong let out a great cry of anguish. His chance of riches gone. The wedding of Bright Moon a great hole in his purse. As for the extra gift of money for Mei-Ling, it was not even to be thought of.

WEST LAKE

1887

Guanji didn't have a plan. He'd generally found that in matters of the heart, it was better not to make plans. If something was meant to happen, it would, one way or another. If not, not.

If there was a woman he was interested in, he'd be charming, he'd let her know he admired her, but that was all. The next move was hers – if and only if she chose to make it. That was the challenge and the art.

Normally, widows were his game. Much safer. But this case was different. He wasn't sure what to make of it yet. There were difficulties to be overcome, danger, uncertainty. It would require patience. But he had plenty of time. At least he thought he had.

He was still in his fifties, a widower in robust good health with two handsome grown-up sons and a daughter already well married. That gave him freedom. As a Manchu, he was given the respect that came from his great clan and his high rank. He had all the money he required and a delightful house in one of the most beautiful and fashionable places in the world.

His neighbours in West Lake called him the general. It was true that he'd briefly held a general command, and he might have gone further. He might even have been granted a title if he'd won a great battle. But seven years ago, he'd chosen to retire with a comfortable pension, and since then he'd enjoyed a very pleasant life.

It might be supposed that his nickname, the general, carried with it a hint of mockery. Soldiers, after all, were considered crude fellows, far below scholars in status. But amongst the Chinese literati – the poets and scholars who liked to gather in the delightful region around Hangzhou – he found himself well regarded. His cultivated uncle was still remembered; many of the local gentlemen and scholars had been aware of Guanji since he was a boy and knew that he'd shown literary promise as a student. If now, in his retirement, he chose to live the life of a cultivated gentleman in West Lake, they were glad to welcome him.

Mr Yao had only just acquired his lakeside villa. His business in Jingdezhen had continued to flourish. His twelve-year marriage to the lovely Bright Moon had produced three fine sons and a daughter. The family succession was assured. He had to wait only another fifteen years or so before handing the potteries over to his oldest son; and in the meantime, he had a nephew who was perfectly competent to run the business day to day.

So he could afford to take two or three months off each year, to live the leisured life of the gentleman he had become. What better way of doing so than setting himself up in a fine villa in the fashionable West Lake, a good ten days journey away from the smoking chimneys of his potteries in Jingdezhen?

And if he wasn't quite sure what to do in this aristocratic place once he'd got there, the merchant meant to find out.

He'd been glad therefore, on a visit with his wife and children to a famous nearby temple, to be introduced by the temple priest to a distinguished neighbour, the general, who had politely expressed his pleasure that the villa, which had been left empty and neglected for some years, now had an owner at last. Would the general care to visit, Mr Yao had asked, and perhaps suggest improvements he could make? The general had been delighted. He had business to attend to in Hangzhou, but a date for his visit had been fixed for ten days after his return.

And now here he was.

'The setting is really excellent,' Guanji remarked as the two men toured the grounds. They were right on the waterfront.

'I've ordered a boat so that we can go out on the lake,' Mr Yao said.

'There are particular places on the water recommended for viewing the moon, sunsets behind the pagoda on the hill, and so forth,' Guanji told him. 'I'd be glad to show you when the boat arrives.' And your pretty wife, too, he thought to himself. He'd met her only briefly at the temple, but had seen enough to make him accept the invitation to visit the merchant's villa with pleasure.

'Thank you, General,' Mr Yao replied.

Like many Chinese gardens, the grounds of the waterside villa were divided into numerous smaller spaces, which provided both intimacy and constant surprise, making the place as a whole seem an even larger domain than it was.

They passed over a miniature humpbacked bridge that crossed an empty pond. 'Red carp for the fishpond, I thought,' Yao remarked.

'Excellent.'

The path led them to a walled garden, entered through a circular moon gate. The garden had been cleared, but not yet planted. 'You've thought about plants?' Guanji asked.

'A lot of peonies,' Mr Yao replied.

Guanji paused. 'May I suggest you don't make peonies your main statement,' he said. 'I'll tell you why. At least two of the lake villas are already famous for their peonies. I'd advise you to consult a professional and devise something unique, all your own.'

'Thank you.' Yao was appreciative. 'That sounds wise. Just a few peonies then, to please my wife.'

'Of course.' Guanji smiled. 'One should always please one's wife.'

'My wife can be wilful,' Mr Yao remarked with a laugh, 'but I count myself a fortunate man.'

'Ah,' said Guanji. 'You might try some plum blossom trees,' he remarked casually, 'to complement the cypresses you have in here.'

Having left the walled garden, they followed the path, which led up a few steps. At the top of the steps, Guanji suddenly stopped, struck by a thought. 'What about a philosopher's stone?' he said, pointing to a site just ahead.

The karst limestone rocks with their exotic shapes and mysterious cavities remained as popular as ever with the rich who could afford them.

Mr Yao gave a wry smile. 'You mean, General, that there's no point in my pretending to be poor.'

'None at all.' Guanji laughed. He rather liked this intelligent merchant.

He learned more about his host when they went inside. The villa had already been comfortably furnished, with solid, excellent-quality tables and chairs and divans covered with expensive silk brocade. Some lacquerware. But he noticed several more interesting items.

The first, by the entrance, appeared to be a very fine blue-and-white Ming vase on a table. Or was it?

'You are wondering,' remarked Mr Yao, 'whether that is a Ming vase or a copy.'

'No copy, surely, could be so fine,' Guanji replied politely.

'At one of my potteries in Jingdezhen, we make a copy of that vase which even experts, at first glance, have mistaken for the genuine article. This, however, is the Ming original.'

They went down a passageway past other treasures.

Entering the room where they were to be served tea, Guanji noticed a cloisonné pot. Modern cloisonné was plentiful enough, but with time, it disintegrates. Ancient cloisonné, therefore, was greatly prized. Some jade figures caught his eye. Han, two thousand years old. 'You are a connoisseur, Mr Yao,' he said.

'Not really, General.' Yao gave a self-deprecating smile. 'Just well advised.'

Guanji bowed his head. His host might be a newly made gentleman indulging his vanity, but he knew what he was doing.

'You may be acquainted with them already,' Guanji offered, 'but thanks to my late uncle I know most of the antique dealers in Hangzhou personally, and I should be happy to share my thoughts as to which ones best merit your trust.'

'You are most kind,' said Yao. 'Ah.' He looked up. 'Here is my wife.'

She was perfect. Can one really say that of anybody? Perhaps one can, he thought. If he'd been struck by her beauty when he briefly met her at the temple, that was only enhanced by what he was experiencing now. She was serving them tea.

There was nothing stiff or formal about the Chinese ritual of serving tea. The aim was to make the guest feel welcome, at home, at peace. Every move was simple and practical. The warming of the teapot and the wide, bowl-shaped cups with hot water; the gentle tipping of the dark twists of tea leaf into the teapot. The scenting cup offered to each guest to sniff the tea's aroma; the first infusion in the teapot; then the pouring of the tea, straining the leaves, into a jug, from which the cups were carefully half filled, no more, with the clear, delicately scented liquid.

Only one detail of the tea ritual was not strictly practical. This was when the guest gently tapped two knuckles on the table to say thank you – referring to the charming tale of how once, centuries ago, a certain emperor who was travelling incognito and staying at an inn poured tea for his own servant, who, so as not to give the emperor's identity away, made this almost invisible gesture, to indicate the kowtow.

What made Bright Moon so special, then? She served the tea flawlessly, but so did the serving girls in the teahouses. No, it was the grace with which she did the whole thing. It was almost magical.

And how did she achieve that? Guanji tried to analyse it. Her posture, the way she held herself perhaps. For she sat very correctly, with her back slightly arched – but only so far as nature intended. She was perfectly centred, her face in repose.

He noticed that her breasts had a beautiful curve, not large, yet womanly.

And suddenly he desired her. It wasn't the usual mixture of curiosity and lust he experienced with most pretty women. This was something more. I may be falling in love, he thought.

'I have told my wife,' said Mr Yao, 'that you know more about this area than anyone on the lake.' This was clearly an invitation to him to say some words to her.

'Your husband gives me too much credit,' he said politely. 'But it is true I was born in the garrison at Zhapu, up the coast here, and my uncle was a well-known printer and literary figure down the road in Hangzhou. So I suppose it was natural I should come to the West Lake to retire.' He smiled. 'I am sure you know the charming legend of how the West Lake was formed.'

'I do, sir,' she said. 'The Sky Empress tried to steal the magical White Jade Stone that the Jade Dragon and the Golden Phoenix guarded, and finally, during a battle with her army, the Jade Stone fell to earth and created the West Lake, which is guarded to this day by the Phoenix Mountain.'

'Exactly. And there are lots of other stories concerning the lake, you know – mostly stories of lost love, of course. The tale of the White Snake, for instance.'

'"The White Lady is imprisoned in the pagoda by the lake,"' Bright Moon said quietly.

Guanji looked at her in surprise. There were endless versions of the tale. The most popular modern ones twisted what was really quite a grim old story into a more conventional romance. But the line she had quoted came from an older, lesser-known poem that he wouldn't have expected her to know.

'"Her lover will die when he finds a white snake,"' he quoted back at her. He turned to Mr Yao. 'Your wife has an unusual knowledge of poetry,' he remarked admiringly.

'She has. She has,' Yao cried with a laugh. 'She can quote all sorts of stuff.'

Bright Moon inclined her head towards Guanji, accepting his compliment. Then she raised her eyes and gave him a little look. It was brief and Mr Yao didn't see it, but the message was clear: my husband's crude. But what can we do?

Guanji turned to Mr Yao. 'Have you been up to the Leifeng Pagoda yet?' The curious old ruin was nine centuries old. Long ago, Japanese pirates had burned down the wooden top storeys of the great eight-sided tower, but the stone trunk still stood like a ghostly old guardian on its low hill above the waters. 'Some scholars believe, you know, that there's a hidden tomb under the tower that contains a lock of the Buddha's hair.'

He continued to talk easily in this fashion about past emperors who'd visited the lake and some of the notable residents at present. He was addressing them both, but he was careful to make eye contact only with the merchant, not with his young wife.

'Your mother should hear this,' Yao suddenly cried to Bright Moon. 'Go and fetch her.'

'You know my mother was not feeling well,' she gently reminded him. 'And I am still serving tea.'

'Never mind, never mind,' he said. 'Your mother is only a little tired. Tell her I asked her to come. This will brighten her up.'

Bright Moon said nothing as she rose to go, but her resentment was obvious, and Guanji could hardly blame her. Mr Yao, however, was unrepentant.

'It does her good to be contradicted sometimes,' he remarked cheerfully as soon as she'd left. 'Her mother came to visit us just after we first met you at the temple,' he continued. 'A most beautiful woman. From a rich peasant family, but unusually refined. She was the concubine of a senior mandarin of an ancient and distinguished family, after she was widowed. My wife was a late child, with grown-up brothers when she was born.'

'I see.'

'Bright Moon looks like her mother, but she also bears a close resemblance to some of the mandarin's family. Indeed, he adopted her as his own daughter, if you take my meaning.'

'I believe I do.'

'It may surprise you that Bright Moon's mother, unlike the rest of her family, has unbound feet. That is because her own mother came from a rich Hakka family and it was to please them that her father did not bind her feet.'

'As a Manchu, of course,' Guanji replied easily, 'none of the women in my family, including my own wife, had bound feet.' Although from time to time he had slept with Han women whose feet had been bound, Guanji had never found the fabled lotus feet erotic. In fact, on these occasions, he'd tried to ignore them.

'I hope she is well enough to join us,' Mr Yao said. 'I think you will like her.'

A few minutes later, the lady in question appeared.

And Guanji stared. What age must this woman be? From the information he'd been given, she had to be in her sixties. Older than he was. Yet she looked like a woman of fifty at most – an exceptionally beautiful one, too.

It suddenly crossed his mind that Mr Yao might have an ulterior motive in making this introduction. He smiled to himself. Did Yao want him to take the woman into his own household? It would create a social bond between the newly made gentleman and his distinguished neighbour. It might also, he shrewdly guessed, keep a mother's steadying hand closer to his young wife.

Well, I'm free to do whatever I please, Guanji thought.

'The general has kindly said,' Mr Yao told her, 'that when the new boat arrives, he will take us all out and show us the best beauty spots on the lake.'

'There will be a full moon in three days,' Guanji reminded them. 'Might your boat have arrived by then, Mr Yao? I should be at your service.'

'Alas, I don't think it'll come so soon,' Yao replied.

'The next full moon, then,' Guanji said cheerfully.

'It will have to be without me,' Mei-Ling said. 'I must return to my family before long.'

'Stay at least until then,' Yao encouraged her.

'You are very kind, though I'm afraid it's not possible,' she replied. And turning to Guanji, she added, 'You will say I am "hurrying like a traveller with far to go." '

A famous quote, from *Nineteen Old Poems.* It referred to the short time between life and death – with the implication that one must seize the day. Was it a signal that she was interested in him? Or was she just showing that she was literate, like her daughter, because she knew this would please the vanity of her daughter's husband?

'Perhaps the boat will arrive in time,' said Bright Moon.

A momentary silence fell, and the girl's mother stepped in to keep the conversation going. 'I have heard, General, that you retired early to pursue the literary life. If it is not an impertinent question: was that a sudden decision, or one you had contemplated a long time?'

Mei-Ling did not really care, but men of rank, in her experience, liked to talk about themselves.

'Ah.' Guanji paused and considered. He did not really need to consider at all, for he had given this little speech many times. But people like to think they have asked an original question. 'When I was an orphaned boy,' he began, 'I was told it was my duty to become a warrior like my father, who died a hero. He was a member of the Suwan Guwalgiya clan, whose spirit pole is in Beijing. I am the ninth-generation descendant of Fiongdon, Lord of the Bordered Yellow Banner, close companion of the founder of the Manchu royal house. Fiongdon was made Duke of Unswerving Righteousness, and in the centuries after his death was raised still further, finally becoming a Hereditary Duke, First Class.'

'Outside royalty, there is no higher rank,' said Mr Yao, with a nod to his wife and her mother, to make sure they understood what a fine guest he had been able to invite to his house.

'My uncle in Hangzhou, who brought me up, was a figure in the literary world. He printed many fine books and often wrote memoirs and dedications. But he impressed upon me that my duty and destiny were to become a great warrior in the service of the emperor. And as he was a man of some fortune he was able to ensure that I had the best horses, arms, and teachers, as well as a good education in both the Manchu and Chinese languages to fit me for such a role. As you know, there are not so many Manchu warriors nowadays who are trained in the old ways, and he hoped I would stand out.'

'Which you surely did,' said Yao politely.

'Up to a point, Mr Yao. The bannermen treated me as one of their own. They taught me their songs and all the old stories. I rode with them. I shot the bow and arrow. I knew the freedom of the open steppe. I loved it. I also enjoyed my studies at school. But I never wanted to be a scholar. I think I had too much energy and high spirits.' He looked at the two women. 'And yet something was missing from my life. I found it in poetry, perhaps. I sensed it on visits to the temple.' He stopped, as if he could not find the words. 'I even secretly wondered if I should become a priest. Boys of a certain age often have these feelings, if they are at all sensitive. I felt it was a weakness. I stuck to my duty. I fought against the Taiping. I willingly risked my life, as every soldier must. I rose to command men.' He stopped.

'But your sense that something was missing did not entirely leave you?' Bright Moon asked.

'I was fortunate in my marriage. I often told my dear wife that she was too good for me, but she was kind enough to pretend that she was not.' He gave a self-deprecating smile. 'I think I may say that we were both very happy, and I miss her every day. When my dear daughter was ready to marry, we went to great trouble to find her a husband with whom we believed she would be equally happy. And I'm glad to say she is.' He paused a moment. 'To answer your question, as long as my wife was living, I felt spiritually complete. But after I lost her, then . . . I longed for Hangzhou and the West Lake. It is perhaps a weakness for a soldier to admit that he is vulnerable. But I suspect that I may have had more of the character of my uncle than of my father, really.'

'It is not a weakness,' said Bright Moon with feeling.

'Well, you are kind to say so,' Guanji replied. Then he suddenly brightened. 'I have two fine sons who've been bred to the military life and have no such doubts at all. Handsome young devils.' He turned to Mr Yao. 'They say the Dowager Empress Cixi likes handsome young Manchu warriors and promotes them.' He laughed and gave the merchant a knowing look. 'So I have high hopes for their careers!'

Mr Yao laughed, too. But it was the two women Guanji was watching.

Most women liked a manly man. But a general who showed such respect for his wife, who could admit he was sensitive, even vulnerable . . . This little speech of his nearly always seemed to interest them.

Indeed, Bright Moon was looking distinctly thoughtful. Her mother's face, however, gave nothing away.

They talked a little more, of recent events at court, of the new railway that had finally, alas, been established at Beijing. They all agreed that such a horror must never come near the West Lake. Then, the tea ritual having been completed, Guanji politely indicated that he should go.

His hostess graciously hoped he would honour them with another visit before too long, and Guanji was on the point of rising. But it seemed that his host was not quite ready to let him depart.

'The general has been too discreet to mention the fact,' he said to the two ladies, 'but you should know that he is also a notable collector.'

Clearly the merchant had been making enquiries about him. Guanji bowed his head. 'It is true, Mr Yao,' he answered, 'that I collect historical seals – though my collection is very modest.'

The collection was not old. Before retiring to the West Lake, Guanji had decided that it would be pleasant to secure some sort of position for himself in the culture of the place. He hadn't the literary attainments to emulate the essays of his Hangzhou uncle. But it had occurred to him that he could become an expert in some not-too-demanding field. 'Why don't you start a collection?' a scholar friend had suggested. 'What about seals? They're not too expensive.'

It had proved to be an inspired choice. Sealstones, after all, had been in use since the dawn of Chinese civilisation. The underside, carved with Chinese characters that were often primitive but always artfully geometric, would be dipped in ink and then used to stamp documents or, as time went by, paintings and works of calligraphy. The stamps of collectors' seals were considered validation of a work of art and even became considered part of its value as time passed. Sometimes the upper part of the sealstone, which the user held when he applied the stamp, might be a simple rectangular block, or any shape. But in recent centuries especially, the upper part was often carved and polished into a beautiful little sculpture that might rest in the palm of one's hand – so that the seal became a double work of art.

What suited Guanji especially was that the art of making sealstones had reached its apogee under the Ming dynasty and continued through the Manchu as well, so that by embracing this art form he, a Manchu, was associating himself both with his own ancestry and also with the Han culture of which he wished to be a part.

It hadn't taken him long, with the help of dealers, to build up quite an impressive collection; and by applying his mind, he had soon become expert at explaining the origin of each seal, the historical documents and works of art to which it might have been applied, and thereby seemed far more cultured than he really was. The literati of the West Lake were always glad to visit his house, especially when there was another rare old seal from antiquity to be inspected.

If this social strategy had worked well, Guanji had augmented the effect by his skill in tactics. For invitations were not so easy to come by. A visitor to the lake who was lucky enough to be introduced to the general needn't expect to receive one. Only a favoured few were so honoured. If a new arrival asked to see the collection, the general would not seem to hear him, and he might have to wait a year or two, and become the general's friend, before an invitation was proffered. Some people were never asked. So the community around the lake was already divided into two classes: those who had seen the seal collection and those who had not.

'I'm sure,' said Mr Yao, 'that my wife and her mother would be most interested to see the collection, though alas, since she is not here for long, my wife's mother may not have the chance.'

Guanji gazed at him. Nice try, he thought. Pushy, but a nice try. 'I'm afraid they'd find my collection of musty old sealstones terribly boring,' he countered.

'I have heard it's most intriguing,' said Bright Moon. 'My mother and I would love to see them.'

Had the merchant put her up to it? Guanji wondered. Probably. This merchant was a wily adversary. He's tempting me with the women to make sure he gets to see the collection quicker than anyone else has. Very well, he'd concede the point. 'Why don't all three of you come, if you really think it wouldn't bore you,' he suggested. 'Tomorrow is not good for me, but would you be free the day after?'

'Most certainly we should,' said Mr Yao at once.

It was the following afternoon that Mei-Ling and her daughter had a little talk. They were standing in the walled garden. The sky was grey, and the floor of the empty enclosure was a colourless expanse of bare stalks and stripped weeds. The walls looked raw, their unwanted creepers torn away. Was there a chill in the air? Mei-Ling couldn't tell. It seemed to her that it was neither warm nor cold nor anything. The moon gate stared at them emptily as Mei-Ling spoke: 'You were making eyes at the general yesterday. You think nobody noticed, but I saw.'

'I think it's you he's interested in, Mother,' Bright Moon replied.

'I've seen his sort before.'

'So have I. They usually go after widows. Wives are too much trouble.'

'You must not even think of being unfaithful.'

'Who says I have?'

'You were taken with him.'

'He's unusual. He knows how to treat a woman.'

'He knows how to seduce a woman. All that talk about being a warrior with a sensitive soul. How could you fall for such stuff?'

'It makes a change from my husband. You brought me up to know a little about the world of cultivated people. You know you did. So you can hardly blame me if I'm attracted to an educated man.'

'A little culture is expected if you want to make a good marriage.'

'Like binding one's feet. You never suffered that. But you forced me to. I still wish I'd kept my feet the way nature made them and married a peasant from the village.'

'You don't know what you're talking about,' her mother cried. 'You've never known . . .'

'Never known what?'

'What it's like to be powerless, short of money, even short of food. There is no comfort for the soul, no dignity in that, I promise you. Do you think I was happy that my husband had to go all the way to America so he could send us the money we needed? And we were better off than most people in the village.'

'When a bride is carried in the red-and-gold litter from her parents' house to the wedding, she has to pretend to weep all the way to show how sorry she is to leave her home. But I wept real tears.'

'You have children, a family, a beautiful home.' Mei-Ling made a gesture towards the villa. 'Your husband's rich. He's a good man. Hardly one bride in a thousand gets all that. Surely he doesn't mistreat you.'

'No, he doesn't mistreat me.' Bright Moon made a little gesture of irritation.

'Then do your duty.' Her mother paused. 'Do you understand what will happen to you if you are unfaithful?'

'Perhaps we can agree to part. The law allows it.'

'Only if your husband wishes. He can throw you out and keep the children. Think of them. And if he prosecutes you, the law is very clear. You'll get ninety strokes of the cane.'

'The wife and her lover are both caned.'

'Wrong. You forget. As well as his rank, the general has juren status. He's exempt from corporal punishment. He'd get off, free as a bird. But you'll be destroyed.' Mei-Ling took a deep breath. 'Promise me, my child, you must promise me that you will never, ever be unfaithful. I couldn't bear to see you destroy yourself. Not after all I've been through.'

'I don't know that you've been through so much.'

'There are many things you don't know,' her mother replied. For although Bright Moon was over thirty and had a family of her own, it seemed to Mei-Ling sometimes that her daughter was still in some ways a child.

Had she really understood the terrible danger she could be in?

Bright Moon didn't respond. She seemed to be pondering. 'Mother,' she said at last, 'can I ask you a question?'

'I suppose so. What?'

'Were you unfaithful to my father?'

'What a thing to ask your mother!' she cried. 'We were a very happy couple.'

'My husband tells people that my adopted father is my real father. It pleases him to have them think his wife is descended from high-ranking gentry. But I wondered if it might be true.'

'I met your adoptive father long after I became a widow. He came through our village on his way to Guilin. He caught sight of me, made enquiries, and then he asked me to become his concubine. I said I would go with him for a year or two if he would pay me the money we needed for your training and education. That's how it happened.' She might have left a small piece of information out, but everything she had just said was true. 'You were already a little girl by then. I did it for you and left you with Mother at home, but it wasn't long before I was back.'

'So why did he adopt me?'

'When I parted from him, I asked him to help me by finding you a good husband. His adopting you made that easier. He didn't tell Yao that you were actually his, but Yao jumped to that conclusion, and there wasn't much point in having a dispute about it.'

'So you got me a rich husband under false pretenses.'

'Nobody ever said it was so. He just chose to believe it. He may not even think it himself, but he probably likes it if others do.'

'So where does that leave me?'

'Married to a good husband. Be grateful,' said Mei-Ling firmly. 'He'd have married you anyway, you know. And I'm sure he's very glad he did.'

'Why does everything have to be a lie?'

'Your kind husband is not a lie. Your children are not a lie. Your home is not a lie. We must build on all the things that are true in our lives. And you have more to build on than most people. That's how we go forward.'

'Perhaps I don't want to go forward.'

'You must.'

Bright Moon didn't answer.

Then Mr Yao appeared at the far gate of the garden, and their conversation ended.

The stranger arrived at the general's house the following morning. Guanji was in his small library, reading a letter from a collector in Hangzhou, when a servant told him: 'There is a man to see you, sir, who says he is your kinsman.'

'You don't look very certain about it,' Guanji remarked.

'No, sir.'

The Suwan Guwalgiya had grown many branches down the centuries, and as a public man the general always made a point of treating clansmen kindly, even if he wasn't quite sure who they were. 'Show him in, and let's take a look at him,' he said amiably.

And almost immediately wished he hadn't.

The fellow was about his own age and height – or would have been if he didn't stoop so much. But there the resemblance ended. His face was sallow. His clothes were not in tatters, but worn through, which was strangely depressing. An opium addict, Guanji guessed.

'We have something in common, General,' he said.

'Oh?' said Guanji.

'You are ninth generation in descent from our great ancestor Fiongdon; and so am I.'

Was he? Who knew? No doubt he was ready for a detailed rehearsal of their ancestry, but Guanji didn't want to hear it. 'Where do you live?' he asked, hoping it was far away.

'Xi'an.'

Xi'an, one of the four ancient capitals of China. Built and rebuilt on nearby sites, carrying other names – Chang'an, Daxing – the place had once been the entrance to the Silk Road to the west. Also a fort with a big garrison of Manchu bannermen.

And over eight hundred miles away.

'Why are you here?'

'I came to visit Beijing, to see the spirit pole of our clan – just once in my life.'

'A journey in a good cause.'

'It cost me all I have.' So that was it. He'd come for money.

'But then you came here.'

'To see the West Lake. And to call upon you.'

'I am honoured,' Guanji said drily.

'I have followed your glorious career for many years.'

And no doubt those of other kinsmen you hope to sponge off, Guanji thought.

'What do you do for a living?' he mildly enquired.

'My father was a bannerman, a soldier,' his visitor replied.

'Mine too. But what about you yourself?'

'Alas, the emperor employs fewer of us now.'

'That's true. Han Chinese troops have often proved themselves better. I have commanded them myself.' Guanji let that sink in. 'So you rely upon the rice and silver to which, as hereditary bannermen, we are entitled,' he went on.

'Which has shamefully been growing less all my life!' the fellow cried indignantly.

'Don't be absurd,' Guanji told him. 'You know as well as I do, the money's not there. The Taiping revolt ruined the whole Yangtze valley, and the barbarian reparations exhausted the treasury. Besides, there are more Manchu mouths to feed every generation. You know the empire can't afford the old stipends.'

'Then what are we supposed to do?'

'People sometimes forget, but when the Manchu first conquered China and drove out the Ming, there were huge numbers of bannermen to be looked after. Were they given stipends? No. Most of them were given land and told to farm it, just like the humble Han peasants. They weren't very good at it, unfortunately, but that was their reward.'

'But the Suwan Guwalgiya were the chosen few, above the others.'

'It is true that we and other clans were the chosen bannermen who manned the garrisons in the great cities and who were given stipends to reward us for military service.'

'And we're not allowed to do anything else.'

'At first that was so. But not anymore. Times change. Garrison bannermen are even allowed to engage in commerce now. My esteemed uncle ran a printing press,' Guanji reminded him. 'A gentlemanly occupation, but still commerce.' He gazed with distaste at his kinsman – if that's what this fellow really was. 'You think,' he remarked, 'that you are entitled to something.'

'Of course,' came the reply.

Guanji nodded to himself. He'd seen it all so many times before, seen bannermen beg in the streets of Hangzhou sooner than work, because they thought that work was beneath them. They were worthless, really, these clansmen of his. Secretly, he despised them just as much as the Han Chinese did.

Only one uncomfortable thought niggled his mind: was he any better? How much of his own success was thanks to his uncle's skill in making use of whatever Manchu entitlements were left? Certainly he'd been waved through the imperial examination system and become juren because he was a Manchu. Yes, he'd worked hard and risen by merit. But what if he hadn't had his uncle behind him? Might he have turned out just like this useless kinsman? He told himself no, a thousand times no. The thought was so infuriating that he suddenly realised he was clenching his hands with rage. And so instead of giving the fellow some money and sending him on his way, he suddenly decided to punish him first.

'I'm afraid I can't help you,' he said. 'If I give you money, you'll only spend it on opium. You'll have to find someone else to sponge off.'

His kinsman looked at him in disbelief. Then his face creased into a look of fury. 'Is this how you treat a member of the House of Fiongdon?' he cried.

'It appears to be,' said Guanji.

'Screw you!' It was screamed so loudly that the servant looked in from the doorway. 'You think you can look down on me? You sit in your fine house and everyone calls you general, and you think you're better than me? I'm a nobleman. I've got a better line of descent from Fiongdon than you have, if you really want to know.'

'I don't.'

'Screw your mother!'

'You're making a fool of yourself.'

'You don't impress me. Not one little bit.'

'Be quiet,' said Guanji. The servant was still watching nervously in the doorway. 'If you want me to give you money to go home,' Guanji continued calmly, 'I think you should be more polite.'

'Pervert! Bitch!'

Guanji eyed him impassively, then turned to the servant. 'Go and get help,' he said.

'I demand,' the fellow shouted grandiosely, 'to be shown proper respect in this house.'

'Me too.' Guanji got up, went to a cabinet, opened a drawer, and took out a small bag of coins. He removed some of the coins, put them back in the drawer, returned with the little bag, and sat down again as the servant reappeared with two others.

Guanji addressed his visitor. 'Here is some money. Enough for your journey back. But that is all I can give you. Please do not think that there will ever be any more. There will not.' He handed him the bag. He wondered if his visitor would make a show, flinging the bag and its contents back at him. He noticed, however, that his kinsman's hand closed over the bag as tight as a hawk's talons. He turned to the three servants. 'Show him out, and never let him in again.'

'Keep your hands off me,' the fellow ordered the servants as they grabbed him. 'You'll be sorry for this,' he cried to Guanji as they hustled him out. 'More sorry than you dream.'

'I'm sorry already,' said Guanji, and went back to reading his letter.

But the truth was that the interview had shaken him, and he was glad that afternoon when the visit of Mr Yao and the two ladies obliged him to put it out of his mind.

It took Mei-Ling a little while to realise how perfect the general's house was – and to understand why. It was set on rising ground above the lake.

Seen from a distance one might have supposed it was a little monastery with a bell tower in the grounds.

As they arrived at the outer gate, she saw that the main building was essentially a Chinese courtyard house, not unlike her own family's farmhouse in the south. The courtyard was about the same size, but seemed grander – perhaps because the walls were higher and the central hall taller and more spacious – almost like a mansion in a provincial town.

The general greeted them affably and led them to a doorway on the left side of the yard. Here, in what would normally have been family bedrooms, he had created a single long gallery to house his collection.

Against the wall at one end of the gallery stood a big cabinet. Paintings on silk, in protective frames, hung on the walls. But there was no other furniture or decoration. All the rest of the space was given over to the seals.

She had to admit, he'd done it beautifully. Right at the start, rather than let his little museum grow in a piecemeal fashion, he'd ordered first-rate craftsmen to construct a showcase that ran the entire way down the centre of the gallery, with glass doors on either side and two broad shelves between.

'I was lucky,' he explained to them. 'A good collection, the life's work of an old scholar, came up for sale just as I was starting. It contained work from almost every period. So I bought the lot, and that formed what I call the spine of my collection. All I've had to do since is take good advice and add flesh and bones, so to speak.'

Mei-Ling eyed the display. It was already handsome. Some of the seals lay on the shelf with their stamp face outward. Others, whose backs were elaborately sculpted, were displayed facedown so that one could admire the carving. The majority of the seals were wood and stone, but some were bronze or other metals, or even jade. In every case, the item was accompanied by a little square of thick paper displaying the stamp in red ink.

She noticed something else. Though both the shelves had been used, the seals were widely spaced, with the lower shelf reserved for the most special articles. Given that one could view from both sides, it was obvious that there was room for the collection to grow to two or three times its present size inside the existing case without its looking crowded.

The general had made his battle dispositions well. They were thorough, but also flexible.

Mei-Ling heard a grunt of admiration from Mr Yao. The porcelain merchant knew a good display when he saw one.

The general was an excellent guide. He took them on a journey through time, showing how the seals had developed while often retaining elements of primitive Chinese characters from thousands of years ago. Several times he also paused in front of paintings on the wall. Some were mountain landscapes. Others depicted people or animals. In each case, the painting was graced with a few vertical lines of calligraphy, to which collectors had added their red stamps.

'Whenever I acquire a new seal,' the general explained, 'I try to obtain a piece of work – a painting or a book – that bears the same stamp. A great collector's stamp often adds value to a work of art, and it may add beauty, too. Of course I'm just a beginner, but the real connoisseur builds up a huge knowledge. He comes to see into the mind of both the artist and the collector. It starts like a game and becomes like a drug.' He smiled. 'A good drug.'

At the end of his presentation he led them to the cabinet at the end of the room. He opened it and Mei-Ling saw a dozen of the long, handsome, leather-bound boxes that contained scrolls and also a number of flat books bound with silk ribbon. He took one of the books out and pointed to its title page.

'This book dates from the Ming dynasty. It's about the conquest of China by the Mongol descendants of Genghis Khan more than five centuries ago. As you can see, it has been stamped with a fine collector's seal just beside the title.'

'We saw that on a painting,' said Bright Moon. 'I recognise it.'

'You have an excellent eye.' The general bowed, and Bright Moon looked pleased. 'But there's something wrong with the title. I wonder if anyone can see what it is.'

They all looked.

'A character seems to be missing,' said Mr Yao.

'Indeed. We can see the gap where it was.'

'So it's been erased,' said Yao, 'yet I can't see any sign of the erasure.'

'Nor can I, my dear sir. It must have been done with great skill. And now I'll tell you the missing word: *Barbarian.*' He beamed at them all. 'Although the Mongols – the Yuan dynasty, as we call them – were all-conquering warriors, the Han Chinese still considered them barbarians.

When the native Ming dynasty came to rule our land once more, they usually referred to the Yuan as "the Barbarian Yuan". And that's what was written here: the Barbarian Yuan. But after some centuries the Ming were kicked out by our present dynasty, the Manchu – who I need hardly tell you were another group of barbarians from the north, part Mongol themselves. My people!' He gave a big grin. 'We didn't like the epithet *barbarian* being applied to the Yuan, because then it might just as well be applied to us.'

'Was the word forbidden then, throughout the empire?'

'An attempt at censorship was made, though never with much conviction. Funnily enough, it was some of the Manchu emperors themselves – as you know, they were quite scholarly – who got bored with it first. But the collector whose red stamp we're looking at now, having acquired the book in Manchu times, wasn't taking any chances. So he erased the word from the title page. Then he started to erase it from the text, but it must have been too much trouble, because I discovered that after a few pages he gave up.'

'You certainly do your homework,' said Mr Yao.

'It's my hobby,' the general replied easily. He turned to Bright Moon and Mei-Ling. 'But I want you to know, ladies, that I understand my place. At the end of the day, I'm still just a humble barbarian from the north.'

It was nicely done. An exercise in self-deprecation by a Manchu noble to the family of an upstart Chinese gentleman – not to be taken seriously, but charming. Even Mei-Ling had to smile.

And she continued to smile, until she saw her daughter's face.

Admiration. Suppressed excitement. It was understandable. Here was a man of a type she had not met before. A Manchu noble. A soldier-scholar. A man who showed her respect. A man of experience, a man of the world, a man who had the self-assurance to laugh at himself. A superior man. Younger than her husband.

It was just as she'd feared. Her daughter was about to fall in love with the general and destroy herself, and Mei-Ling didn't know what she could do about it.

'Is there anything more to see?' Bright Moon asked.

'The only other seals I have are the most recent acquisitions. I keep them with me and study them in my private room upstairs until I've learned all I can about them. Then I put them in the showcase down here.' He turned to Mr Yao. 'I've never taken anyone up there before, but I can show you if you like.'

'By all means,' said Mr Yao.

'There's a nice view,' said Guanji to the ladies.

They went through a small garden beside the house, then out by a gate onto the wooded slope. A curving, stepped pathway led them up about fifteen feet to a ledge overlooking the house, where a charming little pavilion with a Chinese roof had been constructed. So this, Mei-Ling realised, was what she'd mistaken for a bell tower from a distance. 'My little hermitage,' Guanji explained.

It was very simple. A good-sized single room. Against the far wall was a desk with a chair and some open shelves on the wall above it, on which she could see a dozen sealstones awaiting their owner's attention. Some papers on the desk and a tray with writing equipment suggested that the general had been working there earlier in the day. A small cabinet beside the desk, a clothes chest in one corner and a handsome divan directly opposite the window completed the furnishings.

Mei-Ling looked at the divan. 'You sleep up here?'

'Usually.' The general smiled. 'I am just "a hermit with a bed full of books".'

She caught the reference – to a famous poem about the onset of winter and old age. She glanced at him cynically. 'I am sure you find ways of keeping warm, General,' she said, then inwardly cursed herself. It might sound as if she were flirting with him.

If so, he courteously ignored it. 'There's no fire up here, as you see. But as a soldier I grew used to sleeping in tents or even in the open.' He gestured to the window. 'I like the fresh air. Normally I sleep here until well into the autumn. Then I go back into the house for the winter.'

Bright Moon had already gone to the window to look out. It was a wide window, without any hangings, but with big wooden shutters to keep out the rain and the wind. The shutters were wide open now, and there was a wonderful view over the house and garden below and across the lovely waters of the West Lake. Mei-Ling joined her, and mother and daughter remained there in silence while, behind them, the two men talked.

The general was showing Mr Yao one of his new purchases. Mei-Ling couldn't hear exactly what the general was telling him, but she heard the merchant reply, 'Ah. Most interesting.'

Bright Moon was whispering to her. 'I could stay up here forever.' And she sighed. The remark itself was quite artless: she was just admiring the view.

But Mei-Ling didn't like the sound of it. 'Well, you can't,' she replied in a stern mutter.

'I must look at this view,' she heard Yao say, and she moved back to make room for him to join his wife.

Meanwhile, a thought had occurred to her. 'Tell me, General,' she began, 'I noticed on our way up here, we left the enclosure around your house. Doesn't that mean that anyone could walk up here from the road?'

'I suppose so. No one ever has.'

'You're not afraid of a robber getting in one night?'

'The West Lake's very quiet. I've never heard of anyone being robbed.' He smiled. 'But I can defend myself.' He indicated something resting against the bedpost, something that hadn't caught her eye before. It was a sword, a Chinese sabre. 'An old soldier's habit,' he confessed with a laugh.

'Oh, look,' called Bright Moon, who had just glanced back towards her mother. 'He keeps a sword by his bed.'

'It's to keep the other collectors away,' the general told her.

And now Mei-Ling saw it all. She saw how his seductions worked. His rank, the collection, his sympathetic ways, his secret lair overlooking the most beautiful lake in all of China, the military sword, the hint of danger, the adventure . . . That was how he did it.

And there, standing beside her husband, Bright Moon was imagining just such an encounter. Mei-Ling could see it in her eyes.

The general had led them down the path again. Bright Moon had walked with him. Mei-Ling had followed, as she supposed, with Mr Yao. But reaching the bottom of the steps, she'd looked behind her and realised that, for some reason, the merchant had gone back to linger by the window, from which he was still gazing over the lake. Not wanting to seem to leave him behind, she paused and waited for him to come down so they could go together through the half-open gate into the garden.

And because she was standing there alone, in silence, she could overhear the words that passed between the general and her daughter.

'You were very quick about recognising the seal on that book,' he remarked. 'You could be a collector.'

'I don't think so, General,' Bright Moon replied. 'You see, I'd never really looked at any seals before – at the design, I mean. So the few I'd seen were very fresh in my mind. Children are the same. They notice everything, because it's all fresh. But adults are so used to the daily things of life that we hardly notice them at all.'

'Perhaps. But I think you're observant.' He paused. 'There's something very fine about you,' he said suddenly. 'Your husband is a fortunate man.'

'I'm not sure he knows it.'

'Confucius says that a wife should obey her husband, but he forgot to say that none of us husbands are good enough for our wives.' He hadn't quite said it, thought Mei-Ling, but he'd as good as said it, those words that every discontented wife wants to hear: *You are too fine for your husband.*

'I shall look forward to showing you all the beauty spots on the lake,' the general said, 'when your boat arrives.'

'When the boat arrives.'

Mei-Ling turned. Mr Yao was descending. He reached her.

'Here we are at last,' she said as they came through the gate.

The general did not, like the emperor in the story, pour the tea himself. An elderly woman servant performed the ceremony as they sat in the main hall.

They talked of this and that. The general told them that although they mightn't think it, given the pleasant autumn weather today, he expected bad weather ahead. 'I can always read the weather,' he remarked. 'You'll see tomorrow.'

'I hope,' said Mr Yao politely, 'that the next time we meet, General, you might tell us something of your distinguished military career. I know that you were engaged in the great struggle against the Taiping.'

'It is true that I fought the Taiping,' Guanji acknowledged, 'but many others had far more interesting stories to tell than I have.'

'Were you ever in great danger?' Bright Moon asked.

'Any soldier is in danger,' Guanji said mildly, 'because you never know what's going to happen. You could be killed by a stray musket ball just as well as in hand-to-hand fighting. As for notable deeds, I don't think I performed any.' He smiled. 'I will tell you this: the only time I really thought I was going to lose my life, I won a single combat fight by sheer luck, which didn't reflect any credit upon me at all.'

'Do tell us, General,' begged Bright Moon, 'before we go.'

'Well,' said Guanji, 'it was like this.' And he briefly told them of the fierce, snuff-taking general he had met when he was a young officer, and how they had gone from Zhapu to Hangzhou. He didn't bother to tell them about the action and how he'd been wounded. He went straight to the moment of truth, when he'd come face-to-face with the Taiping officer.

'He was certainly quite a senior fellow in their army. But he looked more like a pirate, and he moved like a cat. I had a sword and he only had a knife. I'm not a bad swordsman, by the way. But from the way he handled that long knife of his, I knew I hadn't a chance. "Prepare to die," he said. And as he came towards me, crouching and swaying from side to side, I thought, Yes, I'm going to die. Though I kept the point of my sword up, just in case. And then an extraordinary thing happened. The woman who'd been guiding me, who had hidden in the shadows, rushed out at him. It was just enough to distract him. So I lunged and I got him.' He grinned. 'Then I ran away. I'm good at doing that, too.'

Mr Yao laughed. 'I think you're far too modest.'

'But you killed him?' asked Bright Moon.

'Oh yes, I killed him.'

Mei-Ling was looking thoughtful. 'What was the name of this senior officer?'

'I never discovered.'

'What did he look like?'

'Forty, perhaps. Going grey, but very lithe. And he had a scar.' Guanji traced a line on his cheek. 'Like that. Why, could you have known him?'

'How would I know an officer in the Taiping?' Mei-Ling replied. 'But I've seen pictures of some of them. None with a scar like that, though.'

'Well, whoever he was, the fellow I killed certainly had a scar.'

Soon after that, when they took their leave, the general was particularly gracious in saying how much he hoped to see Mei-Ling again while she was staying at the West Lake.

'I think,' Mr Yao said to her on the way home, 'that the general's taken rather a fancy to you.'

Mr Yao's new boat arrived in the morning. It was very handsome. The beam was broad, with an awning over the midsection, and there were benches covered with cushions where ladies could sit in great comfort. Mr Yao called Bright Moon and their children to inspect it. The children wanted to go out in the boat at once, but Mr Yao would not let them onto the lake yet because, as the general had warned the day before, the sky was overcast, and there was enough wind to make the water choppy.

Mei-Ling felt tired and rested that morning; and it was noon before she came to the little jetty where the boat was moored. She saw that Bright Moon was there alone, staring out across the water. She could see at once why Mr Yao would not let the family go out in the boat that day. It was flat-bottomed, capacious certainly, but with a shallow draught. A pleasure boat, good for fine weather only.

She came and stood beside her daughter. For a little while, neither spoke.

'You must not think of him,' she said quietly. 'It's all a game to him.'

'What is?'

'You. Even me. The other women he's doubtless had. We are a hobby, like his collection.'

'He takes his collection seriously.'

'He studies us, too, just as he studies the seals. He discovers their patterns, their complexity. And you may be sure, they go to him willingly. I daresay that sometimes they think that it's they who have seduced him. Yet in the end, to him, we are only good for a single purpose. Another stamp for private display in his collection. You are taken with him now, but it will pass.'

'Everything will pass.'

'Don't let him destroy you – and your children.'

Her daughter was silent for a few moments. Then she remarked, 'There will be a full moon tonight.'

'We shan't see it.'

'If the clouds cleared and the wind dropped, we could go out on the lake.'

'No.'

'Was there something else about him, Mother?'

'What do you mean?'

'I don't know. When he was telling us about his fight with the Tai-ping officer, I caught sight of your face. I saw something. I don't know what.'

'You saw nothing.'

'I am going in now,' said Bright Moon.

But Mei-Ling did not go in with her. She remained alone on the jetty, staring over the water. She thought of Nio. It was Nio whom the general had killed. She was quite sure of it. All the circumstances fitted into place. All her instincts told her. Nio had died at the hand of this charming old seducer, who was threatening to destroy her daughter next.

Later that afternoon, the wind became stronger. The clouds were dark, thick as ever. Not a hint of the full moon, not even where it might be. By nightfall the wind was whipping the surface of the lake into a fury and rushing in under the awning on the shallow boat, which no one had thought to remove, making it flap and bang and shaking the pleasure boat to and fro.

They all went to bed early.

No one saw Mei-Ling slip out of the house into the dark. She was carrying a small bag.

Guanji was half dozing on the divan. He had not decided: now I will sleep. But he might slip into unconsciousness at any moment; and if he did, he thought, he wouldn't mind. He wouldn't mind one way or the other.

On the desk a small brass oil lamp – one he'd taken on campaign many times – provided just enough light so that, if he did sleep and wake again, he'd be able to see where he was.

Outside, the wind rattled the shutters. He liked the rattle of the wind, just as he loved the rain and thunder. They had never seemed threatening. They reminded him of the endless open plains he used to dream of as a child.

And perhaps he would have started dreaming then, except that he became conscious of a soft click that did not come from the shuttered window, but from his left. The door was being opened.

Instantly, he was fully awake. His right hand reached across to the sword beside his bed and grasped the hilt. But he kept his eyes almost closed, as though he were asleep.

Slowly, almost silently, the intruder moved across the floor and reached the foot of the bed. And then, by the lamplight, he saw: it was the woman, Mei-Ling.

'Good evening,' he said.

'Ah.' She gave a little involuntary gasp. 'I thought you were asleep.'

'I'm awake now.' He opened his eyes and smiled. 'There's quite a storm out there.'

'Just a little wind.'

'You came here by yourself?'

'Whom would I bring with me?'

'And what can I do for you?'

Mei-Ling had come with two possible plans: one if he was asleep; the other if he wasn't. She would have preferred it if he had been asleep, but he wasn't. Going over to the clothes chest, she laid the little bag on it and began to undress.

She had kept her figure. The soft light was kind to her, but even in a harsher light she could have passed for a healthy woman ten years younger than she was. Then she turned to face him. He was smiling. She joined him on the divan.

Over the years, Guanji had formed a theory. The Chinese moon festivals might be about the completeness of the family, but many people also found the full moon to be conducive to the act of love. Guanji's theory was that women were more affected by the moon than men.

That evening, however, a further idea occurred to him. Could it be that the full moon had drawn this woman to him, even though it was invisible behind the clouds? While he'd considered the thought that he might be able to seduce Mei-Ling before she left for the south again, he really hadn't expected the older woman to make the first move, and to make it at once. It must be the moon, he thought, even though we can't see it. Unless it's the storm that excites her.

Whatever the reasons for her presence in his bed, he certainly had no complaints that night.

It was an hour after midnight when Mei-Ling very carefully stepped off the divan. The wind was still rattling the shutters almost as loudly as before. The general was lying on his back, fast asleep, his lips slightly parted, his face at peace. Exactly what she needed.

She didn't waste any time. She didn't want him to wake. She reached for the sword at the side of the bed and carefully drew it from its scabbard. The blade shone in the lamplight. She quickly tested it, just to make sure it was sharp. Then, balancing herself with her feet comfortably apart, she raised the Chinese sabre high over her head and brought it down with a smooth, flowing swing. 'Let the blade do the work,' she'd heard the men in the village say when they chopped down a tree. So that's what she did.

The general's eyes started wide open. He opened his mouth, but no sound came out. She pulled up the sword, wondering whether to strike again. She could see that she had cut clean through everything down to the neck bone. Did she need to sever the bone? His throat was opening in a great V. There was a gurgling sound, not very loud. Blood was pumping out. She stepped back.

She put the sword down over by the window. There was no need to put it out of the general's reach, but she felt more comfortable doing so. Taking the small bag she'd brought with her, she opened the drawers of the desk. There was a little money in one of them. She took the money and tossed it into the bag. Then she took the seals off the shelves over the desk and put them in the bag, too. She looked around for anything else a robber might take and saw a small jade ornament. That also went in the bag.

She quickly got dressed. She saw that there was blood all over the bed now. That was good. If there were any signs of the evening's activity, they'd be covered by the blackened blood.

She made sure she had left nothing behind other than the general's sword and let herself out again.

It was pitch-dark, but she'd taken careful note of every inch of the way, and she knew how to move through the country. At one point, the lane passed directly beside the waters of the lake. Reaching into the bag, she tossed the contents – the coins and the seals and the little jade ornament – one by one out into the water, as far as she could.

Inside the hour, she was back in her bed. No one had seen her leave or return.

In the morning, Mr Yao went to see a neighbour about a mile away. At noon he came back, looking shocked. 'Have you heard? The general's been killed by a robber, during the storm last night. Killed with his own sword. Who would do such a thing?'

By afternoon, however, a rumour was buzzing around the lake. The general's servants were saying that the general had had a terrible quarrel with a distant kinsman who'd come to get money from him. The fellow had threatened to do the general harm.

Two days later, news came from Hangzhou. The man had been found in an opium den in the city. Couldn't account for his movements.

'It's an open-and-shut case,' said Mr Yao. 'He did it, all right.'

'He should be executed,' said Bright Moon with feeling.

'He will be. Don't worry about that,' said her husband.

Mei-Ling said nothing.

Ten days afterwards, she returned to her home.

YELLOW RIVER

September 1887

Shi-Rong smiled. This time, at last, he was going to get it right. He'd redeem his reputation – not only with his son, but with his late father too. He might even be remembered in the history books. But he had to be careful. He needed to talk to his son. Not that he was going to tell Ru-Hai exactly what his plan was. Better keep that a secret. But he needed to talk to him all the same.

He pulled the last weed from beside his father's grave. He liked tending his ancestors' tombs. It gave him a sense of peace. The modest graveyard in which they rested, on a ledge overlooking the wide plain of the Yellow River, was in perfect order. So was the small Buddhist monastery higher up the hill. He'd paid for its restoration just a few years ago. So was the estate. Everything was in order.

The huge orb of the sun had broken free of the eastern horizon, and the gleaming river, its waters choked with rich yellow dust from the vast Asiatic plateau through which it had carved its way, snaked heavily across the land.

Perhaps Ru-Hai will arrive today, he thought. My son and his little boy. He was sure they would come.

They had not come for Qingming that spring or the year before. The festival when all the world returned to their families' ancestral graves, to meet relations, tend the tombs, and show respect to those who had given them life. All, that was, who could. But it wasn't easy for Ru-Hai. Beijing was over four hundred miles away. A month's journey. He couldn't do that each year. Shi-Rong had swept the graves and prayed alone.

But Ru-Hai would make the journey now. He couldn't fail to, after the message Shi-Rong had sent.

> It has been too long since I have seen you. Your father asks you to come now, since there are matters concerning the estate I need to tell you. Please also bring your son, so that he will have a memory of his grandfather.
>
> I suggest you spend perhaps two days at the house, then take your son up to the great monastery of Shaolin in the hills, where you can see the Zen masters of the martial arts, which no doubt he will enjoy, before you return to Beijing.

Shi-Rong had hardly been to Beijing in the last decade. He'd made one visit to the court when he retired; another to arrange the wedding of his son – quite a good marriage, as it happened, to the daughter of a third-rank mandarin; and a third to see Ru-Hai and his family three years ago. That was all. But he'd kept abreast of events.

Looking back over the last two decades, it seemed to Shi-Rong that China's affairs could be summed up in two words: *stagnation* and *corruption.* He should know. He'd been part of it.

The treasury was still empty. One province after another had suffered famines. There were beggars in the streets of every city. The planned rebuilding of the Summer Palace had been postponed so many times for lack of funds that he'd lost count.

In his own neighbourhood, most people whom Shi-Rong knew just wanted to return to the old life as it was a generation ago. And who could blame them? If ageing mandarins took bribes and clung to their office, what of it? If governors lied to the imperial court about conditions in the provinces – they always had. Better stagnation than chaos.

The military reforms had slowed down; the colonial powers were circling like wolves. In the northeast, Russia had continued to steal territory at every chance she got. In the southwest, the Burmese no longer took their orders from China, but the British. France was now master of Vietnam, and her warships were patrolling the waters around Taiwan. So far, the Japanese had been stopped from actually taking over the Korean peninsula – but only just. And for how long?

How had it all happened?

Shi-Rong knew what his father would have said: if the king follows the rules of Confucian morality, his kingdom will be ordered. If not, anarchy will follow.

Look what happened a quarter of a century ago, he would have pointed out, when the emperor disgracefully abandoned his post and ran away to the north. The barbarians had destroyed the Summer Palace and humiliated the Celestial Empire.

When the first regency was set up, the rules had been followed. The boy emperor had been the old emperor's son. The empress was a regent – that was correct procedure. Including the boy's mother, Cixi, in the circumstances, had made sense. And there had been a council, led by Prince Gong.

But when the young heir had died and they'd had to set up a second regency, it was a different story. Who had chosen the new boy emperor? Cixi. Why? Because he was her sister's son, and his father, Prince Chun, was on her side. Was it proper? No. The rules of succession had not been followed. Therefore, Shi-Rong's father would have said, no good could come of it. Yet no one had stood up to the dowager empress.

Except one man. One heroic mandarin: Wu the Censor. He alone had behaved like a true Confucian and made a formal protest. Wu the Martyr, some people called him. For he had sacrificed his life.

And what did I do that same year? Shi-Rong thought ruefully. Failed to get the salt inspector's position and was accused by my own son of taking bribes. The year of my humiliation and my shame.

As for Cixi, it seemed to him she'd achieved nothing in the first few years except to outmanoeuvre Prince Gong, the one man the empire really needed, and to reduce his role from head of her council to a mere adviser.

Then something strange had happened. Cixi had suddenly fallen ill. Word came she was close to death. For months no one saw her. She sent messages to the council from time to time; but it was the docile empress who conducted business. This went on for about a year.

What was wrong with Cixi? Nobody seemed to know. What was she hiding? Ru-Hai had made a brief visit home at this time and Shi-Rong had asked him: 'Is it possible she got herself pregnant and wants to hide it?'

'I doubt it, Father,' he replied. 'She's a bit old for that.'

'There are no rumours?'

'Might be smallpox, but we don't think so.' Ru-Hai had smiled. 'Say what you like, the Forbidden City knows how to keep a secret.'

'Perhaps she's being punished by the gods for her sins,' Shi-Rong remarked sourly. But he was never able to learn anything more.

A year later, she appeared again as though nothing had happened. Some said she looked older. More people started calling her Venerable Buddha after this. The two empresses resumed their regency. Shi-Rong imagined it would last another five or six years until the new boy emperor came of age.

So how was it, he asked himself, that the kindly little empress, who'd never done anyone any harm, should suddenly drop down dead a year later? Ru-Hai wrote that she'd had a stroke. At forty-four? Or had she been poisoned? And if so, by whom? Might Cixi have concluded, since the empress had managed the business of government well enough without her while she'd been ill, that people might say that she, Cixi, was not really needed, and therefore decided to poison her little friend?

The idea was not so outlandish. Everyone knew the story of the only female emperor of China, twelve hundred years ago, who'd begun her life in a similar way to Cixi. She'd been the concubine of one emperor. When he died, she'd become the concubine of his son. She'd murdered two legal empresses, two other concubines, and probably four of her own children before making herself sole ruler of the empire.

Was Cixi cut from the same cloth? It seemed to Shi-Rong that she might be.

For the facts alone about Cixi's court were enough to invite censure. And now the events of the last three years had confirmed all his fears.

She'd dismissed her entire council. Prince Gong, still her best adviser, she'd sent packing. Told him to retire from public life. Then she'd made the boy emperor's father, Prince Chun, head of the council. Quite apart from the fact that the once gallant prince had degenerated into a toady who'd do anything Cixi wanted, it was also against palace law for the boy emperor's father to be his official councillor. Finally, when the boy emperor reached his majority, when he was supposed to take the reins of government, she got her new council to say he wasn't ready, leaving her in charge. Would she ever give up power? Shi-Rong doubted it.

And so he had formed his secret plan.

Once the plan was settled, he'd be free. His Confucian duty to his family and his country would be completed. Nothing more to hold him back from other things. From the meditative life. And beyond.

Shi-Rong couldn't say exactly when he had begun to withdraw from active life. It was certainly after he had retired from Jingdezhen. The following year he'd been busy with Ru-Hai's marriage. Then there had been the excitement of his grandson's birth. Young Bao-Yu would be ten next birthday.

After he'd left Jingdezhen without the salt inspector's post, he'd retired to the family estate. His friend Mr Peng had come up with one other suggestion – a lucrative position, down in the south – but after the humiliation of his failure the last time, Shi-Rong wasn't anxious to go through anything like it again. Besides, the estate needed his full attention just then. So he'd decided to devote himself to handing on the home of his ancestors in the best shape he could and content himself with that.

Thanks to these efforts, the estate was now in better shape than it had ever been before. Everything was in good repair; the storehouses were full. His duty to his family being accomplished therefore, Shi-Rong had felt free to devote himself to the things of the mind.

Whenever the weather was fine, he had fallen into the habit of walking through the village before dawn and taking the narrow path that led up the steep hillside to the family graveyard. Or sometimes he would continue to the little Buddhist temple higher up. And from these high vantage points he would gaze down the great sweep of the Yellow River valley while the dawn chorus began. Often he would remain up on the hill from before even the first hint of light appeared on the eastern horizon until long after the sun was up.

At these times when the whole world as far as the eye could see was filled with the sound of the birds' grand salutation to the sun, he would so lose his sense of self that he felt as if he had dissolved into the great space of the morning. Some days he'd return to the same place to watch the sunset and then, for an hour or more, stare up at the stars.

Over time, these sessions became as important to him as prayer to a monk, so that he could hardly imagine living without them anymore.

He'd also made a new friend – an old scholar who lived a few miles away, up in the hills overlooking a village called Huayuankou, where, since time out of mind, there had been a ferry across the Yellow River.

Mr Gu was nearly a decade older than Shi-Rong. It was hard to be sure of his original height, since he was almost bent double now. His little face was wizened, but his eyes remained very bright, and he still kept up a busy correspondence with scholars all over the kingdom.

He lived in a modest farmhouse with a small garden, where he liked to tend the plants. Sometimes Shi-Rong worried because the house was in disrepair, and he'd offered to build a new house for the old scholar on his own property. 'I shouldn't bother you with visits,' he assured him. 'At least, no more than I do now.'

But Mr Gu shook his head. 'These are the lands that the Zhou kings gave to my family,' he reminded Shi-Rong. 'That was over two thousand years ago. Where else should I live?' His bright eyes twinkled with amusement.

'Tell me if you change your mind,' Shi-Rong replied. But it was obvious his friend had no intention of moving.

Shi-Rong would go over to Mr Gu's house about twice a month, and they would discuss all manner of things. The old scholar would lend him books, and they would read together. It was like becoming a student again, Shi-Rong used to think – only without the exams.

These visits were never complete without their taking a walk to the river. It was over a mile down a long, steep path, but the old man was remarkably spry. 'I can go up the hill easily by myself,' he'd explain, 'as long as I have a good stick to lean on. But getting down is harder. I need your arm for that.' Shi-Rong was happy to oblige, though he'd warned Mr Gu that he might not be able to manage this himself for much longer.

But the thing he loved best of all in these visits was when they practised calligraphy.

Shi-Rong had always been rather proud of his writing. As a mandarin, he had been known for his elegant letters and memorials. Shi-Rong's brushstrokes were always well balanced, firm and flowing. So the first time that the older man had suggested they might each take the same poem and write it out, he'd gladly complied. It was an ancient poem about a scholar in the mountains, and Shi-Rong's version expertly reproduced the style of calligraphy from the period when the poem had been written. When he handed it, not without some pride, to the scholar, Mr Gu nodded thoughtfully.

'This would impress the national examiners very much,' he said.

'Thank you.'

'One can see at once that you are a bureaucrat.'

'Ah.' Shi-Rong frowned. Was that a compliment?

Without a word the older man passed across his own copy. It was not just different. It came from another world. Each character had a mysterious life of its own – merging with, commenting upon, sometimes opposing the next – until the last but one, which, having a long tail, seemed almost to dissolve into the mountain mist until the final character acted as a kind of seal to hold the whole together.

'In calligraphy and painting, which are almost the same thing, both the yin and the yang must be present,' said Mr Gu. 'You know this. But you do not practise it. You think too much. You impose. This is the yang. You must let go, not try to form your thought. Forget yourself. Allow the negative, the yin, to enter. Contemplate in silence and then, with much practice, without your seeking any form at all, your hand will unconsciously become the thought.'

As the old man said, Shi-Rong knew all this in theory; but he was surprised, after so many years as an administrator, to find how hard it was to do it in practice.

Almost every day after that, he would spend an hour or two working on his calligraphy. Sometimes he would write only a single character and ponder its meaning. Quite often, he would copy a poem. Occasionally he would compose a short poem of his own and then try to write it, perhaps many times, closing his eyes as he wrote the characters so that he would not correct them at all. And sometimes, when he did this, the results had a beauty quite beyond what he would have thought of himself. And when he shared these efforts with the older man, Mr Gu would say: 'Better. You have far to go, but you are on the path.'

One winter afternoon, after he'd been applying himself in this way for some three years, Shi-Rong made a confession to his mentor. 'I have noticed something recently. But I am not sure what it means.'

'Tell me.'

'I hardly know how to describe it,' said Shi-Rong. 'A feeling of separation. Things that were always important to me – my rank, my family honour, even my ancestors – no longer seem to be so. It is a terrible thing, surely, not to care about one's ancestors.'

'As we grow older, we become more aware of the larger flow of life,' said Mr Gu. 'This is part of what the Taoists practise. Our individual lives become less large in our minds.'

'Even the rules of Confucius, by which I have tried to live, no longer seem so important.'

'In my opinion,' said Mr Gu, 'Confucius is important for the young. He gives them moral rules by which to live, without which society falls apart. Young people need to believe. If they don't believe in Confucius, they'll only believe in something worse.'

'You don't think the young should seek enlightenment?'

'A little, but not too much,' the scholar replied cheerfully. 'If they become too enlightened, they won't do any work.' He smiled. 'Enlightenment is for old men like us.'

In the months that followed, as Shi-Rong's calligraphy continued to improve, his sense of detachment also seemed to grow, and generally this was accompanied by a sense of peace. But he still attended to the business of the estate. And the small things of life – a difficult tenant, a leaking roof – were just as irritating as they had been before.

During this last year, however, he had begun to notice a further change in himself. It was insidious, hardly noticeable from one day to another, but it was there. He was losing the desire to attend to things. He walked up the hill at dawn less often. His studies were becoming more desultory. He wished he could turn the estate over to his son.

Ru-Hai and the boy did not come that day, but they came the next, arriving at noon, Ru-Hai riding a strong horse and his son a sturdy pony, which the groom took care of. The little gaggle of servants had all known Ru-Hai since he was a boy, so there were many greetings before the three of them sat down to eat a meal together, and Shi-Rong had a chance to observe his grandson. He wanted to like the boy and to be liked by him.

It had to be said, his grandson was not quite what he had expected. Of course, he reminded himself, it had been some years since he'd seen Bao-Yu, and naturally the child had grown a lot. All the men of the mother's family were large, so it really wasn't surprising if, already, one could see young Bao-Yu was going to be a big, flat-faced sort of fellow when he grew up. But he was very polite and respectful. Shi-Rong was grateful his father had seen to that – even if the boy did wolf his food.

During the meal Shi-Rong asked Ru-Hai for news about his wife and two daughters, and received a promise that the entire family would come for Qingming the following spring. Then, so as not to leave him out of the conversation, Shi-Rong asked his grandson about his studies at school. How far had he progressed with Confucius?

'He does all right,' Ru-Hai answered for him, a little too quickly perhaps. 'He has a good head for mathematics,' he added.

'Ah,' said Shi-Rong a little absently. 'I am glad to hear it.' And he gave the boy an encouraging nod.

If Shi-Rong was slightly puzzled by his grandson so far, he was entirely disconcerted when, after the meal was over and they were about to walk up the hill to visit the ancestral tombs, Bao-Yu suddenly lay down on his back in the courtyard and invited his grandfather to stand on his stomach.

'What does he want?' Shi-Rong asked Ru-Hai.

'He wants you to stand on his stomach,' his son replied with a smile. 'He's always asking people to do that.'

'He can jump on it if he wants,' the boy cried proudly.

'Certainly not. Tell him to get up at once,' said Shi-Rong crossly.

'It's all right, Father,' said Ru-Hai, 'he just wants to impress you with how strong he is.' It seemed to Shi-Rong that both Ru-Hai and his son had taken leave of their senses. Was this any way to show respect to a grandfather?

'He can lie there all day,' he said, 'but I've got better things to do than jump up and down on him.' And taking his son firmly by the arm, he started to leave the courtyard. If the boy was crestfallen, however, he didn't show it. He just bounced up and trotted after them.

'It's all right, you know, Father,' said Ru-Hai. 'Remember what they say: strong in body, strong in mind.'

'He needs exercise,' Shi-Rong replied drily.

It was a fine afternoon. The view from the tombs across the huge valley was magnificent.

'You have been here before,' Shi-Rong said to the boy, who looked uncertain.

'He doesn't remember,' said Ru-Hai.

Quietly Shi-Rong showed the boy the tombs. 'This is my father, your great-grandfather. Here is his father and his . . .' For several minutes he went reverently from tomb to tomb, saying a few words about each. Then he and Ru-Hai and the boy prayed for all their ancestors. Bao-Yu behaved very properly, and Shi-Rong told him: 'You must remember this day for the rest of your life, when you and your father and your grandfather prayed together at the tombs of our ancestors. Will you promise me to do that?'

'Yes, Grandfather,' he said.

'He will remember this time,' said Ru-Hai.

'Good. Let us look at the view. It will be fine today.' Indeed, Shi-Rong could scarcely remember a day when it had been clearer. 'You like the view?' he asked Bao-Yu.

'I do, Grandfather.' The boy nodded vigorously.

'Our family's been looking at this view for hundreds of years,' Shi-Rong said. 'This river valley is where Chinese history began. We don't even know when we first came here, it's so long ago. And whatever we do in life, we always finally come home and look over the river. My father did. So will your father, I daresay.' He glanced at Ru-Hai.

'Of course,' said Ru-Hai.

'And me too?' asked the boy.

'I can't see any point in moving, can you?'

'Oh no,' said his grandson, 'I can't.'

'Well then, we agree,' said Shi-Rong. 'What else do you know about the river?'

'It runs within its banks because of the irrigation works of Yu the Great.'

'The civilisation of the Yellow River owes everything to him. When did he live?'

'Legend says four thousand years ago.'

'Good boy. And did he have illustrious ancestors?'

'He was tenth generation in descent from the Yellow Emperor, who may have been a god.'

'Well,' Shi-Rong remarked to Ru-Hai, 'my grandson knows the most important things.' He gave the boy a smile of approval. 'Perhaps I'll jump on his stomach after all.'

'It needs dredging again,' said the boy unexpectedly.

'Yes, it probably does,' Shi-Rong agreed, but with some surprise.

'He wants to dredge it,' his father explained.

'I want to be like Yu the Great,' Bao-Yu declared.

'He wants to be an emperor?' Shi-Rong asked in astonishment.

'No, Father.' Ru-Hai laughed. 'He wants to be an engineer.'

'An engineer?' Shi-Rong frowned. 'That sounds rather mechanical.

We don't become engineers in this family,' he told the boy, 'though you can employ engineers, of course.'

'You forget, Father,' Ru-Hai interposed, 'Yu the Great was not too proud to work with his hands alongside his labourers when they were building and dredging. So they say.'

'That was a long time ago,' his father muttered. He turned to the boy. 'I'll show you an even better view,' he said, and led them up the path towards the little Buddhist temple.

There was nobody there. But the view of the valley was breathtaking.

'It's beautiful,' said the boy. 'Has the temple been here long?'

'About three hundred years. We gave the money to build it, on our land.'

'Where are the monks?'

'They come from a big monastery about three miles away. Every few days one of them comes.'

'Are they Zen monks?'

'No.'

'Father's taking me to a big Zen monastery where they practise martial arts,' said Bao-Yu. He punched his arms in the air. 'Bam, bam . . . Hai . . . Za-bam.'

'I know,' said Shi-Rong. 'It was my idea.'

'Really?' The boy looked at his grandfather in surprise. 'That was a really good idea,' he said artlessly.

After a while, they returned to the house, where Shi-Rong showed them around, talking about his scholarly father and his old aunt. 'She could have been a scholar or a musician herself,' he told them. 'Here' – he showed them – 'are the *I Ching* sticks she used.'

His grandson listened attentively to everything, though whether he was really interested, Shi-Rong couldn't tell. It was Ru-Hai who finally suggested that, as they were both tired from the journey, they might like to rest a little.

About an hour had passed before, sitting in the room he used as a library and office, Shi-Rong suddenly became aware of his grandson standing in the doorway. He looked a bit sleepy, uncertain whether to disturb his grandfather.

'Come in,' said Shi-Rong. 'They just brought me some tea. Would you like some?' The boy nodded, and Shi-Rong poured him a cup.

'It's nice and quiet here,' the boy said.

'Yes, isn't it?' I've lectured him enough for today, he thought. So he said nothing as the boy started to wander about the room, looking at things.

'What are these?' Bao-Yu asked, taking a bowl off a shelf. The bowl was full of little bones and broken shells.

'My father bought them in an apothecary's. A farmer had found them on his land, thought they might be magical, and wanted the apothecary to grind them up to make a magic potion.'

'Oh.' His grandson sat down with the bowl in his lap and started turning the bones over. '*Man,*' he said suddenly.

'Man?'

'The writing on the bones. *Man. House.*' He turned a bone over, then inspected another. '*Sun. River. Horse.* It's writing, isn't it – on the bones?'

'That's what my father thought. Very old writing. Thousands of years. The characters aren't like ours today. They look primitive, you might say.' Shi-Rong paused. 'Where did you find the character for *horse*?'

Bao-Yu showed him a splintered bone and pointed to a tiny scratching. 'It looks sort of skinny and incomplete,' he said, 'but the idea's the same.'

'So it is,' said Shi-Rong. 'I never noticed that before.'

They ate early that evening. Bao-Yu was getting tired and Ru-Hai told him to go to his room and sleep. Only when the two men were alone did Ru-Hai turn to his father to address the issue that was really on his mind. 'I came at once when I got your letter.'

'You are a good son.'

'Are you unwell, Father?'

'I am getting old.'

'Not so old. You do not look ill.'

'Perhaps. But I believe the end is near. I feel a strange weakness. Other things also. Something similar happened to my father. I am certain this winter will be my last.'

'I hope you may be wrong.'

'I would not have sent for you otherwise,' Shi-Rong went on calmly. He gave a wry smile. 'I want my grandson to remember me as I am now.'

Shi-Rong gazed at him. They hadn't seen much of each other over the last ten years. It was nobody's fault. Ru-Hai had been busy in Beijing.

On the one occasion since Ru-Hai's marriage when Shi-Rong had gone to the capital, his son's wife and little children had received him respectfully and kindly, exactly as they should treat an honoured grandfather. His daughter-in-law had several times said how much she wished they could spend more time at the family estate so that his grandchildren should know him better.

'The house awaits. I'm keeping it warm until you come,' he had told her with a smile.

Did his son respect him? He hoped so, but he wasn't sure. That accusation, about the bribes he took, had been made a dozen years ago. But it still hung, silently between them, like a swinging pendulum in a clock.

He led the way into his small library, went to a cabinet, took out a big book of flat sheets bound together with silk and put it on the table.

'You need not fear,' he said, 'if that is still in your mind, that there are boxes of illicit silver, bags of bribes. If there had been, I might be a rich man. But these are the estate accounts. Everything is recorded, as it should be. You should really thank your grandfather, though I have continued his work. Two generations of good management and frugality have brought this estate into an excellent condition. I told you this a dozen years ago. Follow through the accounts and you will see exactly how, since then, I have through wise and honest work increased the size and value of our holdings much further.' He paused. 'Here is a spare key to this cabinet. Please keep it and do not lose it.'

Was his little speech true? Judging by the accounts, it certainly was. Nor was there anything, anywhere, that would ever give the lie to what he said.

If there had been cash that could not be explained, it had been spent long ago in places that had absorbed it without trace: Bright Moon's wedding, for instance; or the refurbishment of the little Buddhist temple on the hill. True, there were valuable objects in the house that he had bought. But he had documented every one of them as belonging to some ancestor or other, and nobody in the world could deny these attributions. The land purchases had been financed with debt that had been paid off swiftly with more of the bribes he'd taken. Some of these lands had then been sold at a handsome profit, and other lands had been purchased with the proceeds. By now it would be almost impossible to disentangle these transactions. The bribes had vanished.

'You will also find a lot of family documents in this cabinet, going back centuries,' Shi-Rong continued. 'And others more recent, including calligraphy and poems of my own.'

He paused. Was Ru-Hai going to challenge him about the bribes again? It seemed not. His son only bowed his head.

'That is enough for now,' Shi-Rong continued. 'You should get some sleep. Tomorrow we can spend some time in the village. But then we must have a further conversation, of great importance, about you yourself.'

When his son had retired, Shi-Rong continued to sit in the library. He didn't feel sleepy. After a while, he took the big book of estate accounts and put it back in the cabinet. Reaching into one of the small drawers, he pulled out two little scrolls, read them over, checking that they were identical, grunted with satisfaction and returned them to the drawer.

So far, everything was going according to his plan.

But he still felt restless. He went into the courtyard. The stars were bright and a waning quarter-moon lit the sky. Letting himself out of the entrance gate, he crossed the level grassy area in front of it to the top of the slope where there was a fine view of the valley – not as good as the view from the tombs farther up the hill, but handsome enough. He could see the huge waters of the Yellow River gleaming in the partial moonlight for mile after mile downstream until they dissolved into a silvery vagueness. He turned to look upstream.

And then he saw it – far away in the west – a flicker and flash above the horizon. Flashes that must come from lightning.

It must be a big storm, he thought. Very big. But how far away? Too far for any sound of thunder to reach him, certainly.

A band of blackness stretched all the way along the western horizon, blotting out the stars. But he quickly realised that what he was seeing were not lightning bolts, but their reflections on the massive cloud columns that soared high above the storm, which itself was hidden out of sight, below the horizon. It must be far away then, perhaps a hundred miles upriver.

He was up at dawn the next morning. Grey clouds covered the whole sky now. But it wasn't raining yet. The storm remained on the horizon, and the wind, so far as he could judge, was coming more from the south than the west.

They spent the morning pleasantly, touring the village and the estate, a chance for Ru-Hai to pick up old acquaintances again. As for young Bao-Yu, the villagers were curious about him. The boys of his age were told to show him around. They soon discovered he was strong and friendly, so that was satisfactory. Inevitably, before Bao-Yu returned to the house, they had taken turns standing on his stomach. So had some of the little girls. This was not quite what Shi-Rong would have wished, but it was clear they thought well of his grandson, and that was the main thing.

They were finishing their midday meal when they heard the patter of raindrops outside. 'If the storm comes here, it'll be almost impossible to get up to the Zen monastery,' Shi-Rong remarked. 'You'll have to delay a few days.'

'We can always give it a miss,' said Ru-Hai. 'We can go another time.'

'No,' said his father. He needed them to go up there. It was part of his plan. 'The boy's looking forward to it,' he said.

As the rain drummed steadily on the roof that afternoon, he was glad Ru-Hai had suggested he play a game of Chinese chess with the boy. It took his attention off the rain and allowed him to probe his grandson's mind gently, without seeming to interrogate the boy.

'Some people,' he remarked easily, 'like the other kind of chess, the Persian one the barbarians play. But I prefer our own. It allows for more variation. Besides,' he continued, smiling, 'as a good Confucian, I can hardly wish to abandon a game my ancestors have been playing for four thousand years.'

'I'm a Confucian, too,' said Bao-Yu, making a move.

'Watch your game, Father,' said Ru-Hai.

'Tell me about being a Confucian,' said Shi-Rong to his grandson.

To his surprise and pleasure, Bao-Yu proceeded to give him an excellent account of the main precepts of the sage. Not only that, he had memorised a number of apt quotations and even a couple of anecdotes about the great master. Not bad for a boy of his age. Not bad at all. With this sort of foundation, Shi-Rong could see young Bao-Yu sailing through the first provincial examination when the time came.

'If our conduct is not correct,' he observed, 'then sooner or later society will collapse into primitive chaos. This has happened many times, in the ages of chaos between the dynasties.'

'It's like engineering,' the boy said. 'If a building isn't soundly constructed, it'll fall down. The state has to have order to be strong.'

Shi-Rong frowned. 'What you say is true, but not quite correct,' he cautioned. 'Correct conduct derives from good morals.'

'Yes, Grandfather. I will remember.'

'Tell me,' Shi-Rong continued, 'do you know the story of Wu the Censor?'

'No, Grandfather.'

'I'm not sure it's a good idea to tell the boy this,' Ru-Hai intervened. But his father ignored him.

'It happened just eight years ago,' Shi-Rong told Bao-Yu, 'not long after you were born. Do you know what a censor does?'

'Not really, Grandfather.'

'For many centuries there were certain men, carefully chosen for their scholarship and moral rectitude, who were given the post of censor. They were like guardians of the government. If they saw an official doing something that was against law, custom, or morals, they could impeach the official to the emperor. Even if the emperor himself acted improperly, they would tell him so to his face, and they could not be punished for doing it.'

'That's amazing,' said the boy.

'It is Confucian,' his grandfather responded. 'The true Confucian order rests not upon power but upon morals. During the last century or so, however' – Shi-Rong saw Ru-Hai shaking his head, but went on regardless – 'the role of censor has somewhat changed. Nowadays it is officials who are censured for misconduct. Emperors have become less tolerant of criticism.'

'Would the emperor punish a censor?' Bao-Yu asked.

'He would hesitate. But he would be unlikely to ask that censor's advice again. To all intents and purposes, the old function of the office has gone.' He paused. 'But that does not mean it is forgotten.'

'Did Wu censor the emperor?'

'The present emperor was chosen as a boy according to the wishes of the Dowager Empress Cixi. The way he was chosen was improper. Wu told the dowager empress that this was so. But Cixi brushed the objection aside. So what do you think Wu did? He committed suicide.'

'What good would that do?'

'It is called body-shaming. He shamed her by showing that he was prepared to take his life rather than agree to her improper action. He was a true Confucian, you see.'

'Did she change her mind?'

'No. But mandarins and scholars all over the empire knew what he had done and why. His name is spoken with reverence, as an example to us all.'

'Do you think he was right, Grandfather?'

'When I was a young man,' Shi-Rong told him, 'my father made me promise always to serve the emperor loyally. But in this case he would certainly have agreed that Wu was correct. Confucius himself always, as the expression is, spoke truth to power.'

'He's a little young to hear these things,' Ru-Hai warned quietly.

'He will learn it soon enough,' his father replied. 'There may come a time,' he said to the boy, 'when we need another Wu the Censor.'

'I don't want him to repeat this,' Ru-Hai intervened again. 'Not back in Beijing.'

'You're right.' Shi-Rong turned to his grandson. 'You are not to repeat what I have said to you. It will be a secret between you and me. Do you understand?'

'Yes, Grandfather.'

'You promise?'

'Yes, Grandfather.'

'Good. Let's continue our game of chess.'

They did until, ten minutes later, Shi-Rong discovered that his grandson had beaten him.

The rain was ending. Bao-Yu asked if he could go outside, and they told him yes.

It was time for Shi-Rong to have that last, all-important conversation with his son. He proceeded carefully.

'My dear son,' he began, 'I have told you that I believe this year will be my last. If I am right, then certain decisions will have to be taken, and I want to make them with you. For the big question is this: after the period of mourning, would you want to remain here permanently to run the estate, or would your career keep you in the capital – perhaps for many years? If the latter, then I need to take steps straightaway to appoint a steward and make local arrangements so that everything will go smoothly.' He gave Ru-Hai a searching look. 'Your career is of paramount importance.

On no account give up any prospects for advancement; there's no need for you to do so.'

Ru-Hai shook his head sadly. 'I wish I could say my career was going anywhere, Father,' he said. 'It's not just me, either. Do you remember those two young fellows who worked with me when you came to my office?'

'Of course.'

'They've both gone. So have four of the most senior officials. The Tsungli Yamen is just a shell these days. The colonial powers are all eating away at us.'

'We held off Japan.'

'For the moment, yes. But in the long term, Japan is a huge threat. And for the same reason I said a dozen years ago. Because she is modernising.' He sighed. 'It's no good ordering Western ships, for instance, if none of our sailors are trained to operate them. Only one city in China is connected to Beijing by telegraph, and that's Shanghai. And I know you don't approve, but it's absurd that we've almost no railway system. The old mandarins think the colonial powers would use the railway to oppress us.' He shook his head. 'They're all afraid of change, including Cixi.'

'Cixi knows only one thing,' said his father, 'which is how to survive.'

'I daresay she's lonely and afraid,' Ru-Hai went on. 'But the empire is drifting, and I don't feel as if there's anything to keep me at the ministry anymore.'

Shi-Rong nodded. He was sorry for Ru-Hai, of course. But this news at least made everything simpler. One other thought occurred to him. 'Your boy, my grandson. He seems intelligent. What do you think he'll do in life?'

'I'm not sure.'

'He could do well at the exams.'

'I agree. Did you hear that the exams are changing, by the way?'

'Changing? How?'

'They're going to add a modern component. Commercial. More practical. I expect you'll disapprove.'

'No,' Shi-Rong considered. 'This may be a good idea. But the Confucian foundation must remain. Commercial knowledge, any knowledge, without a moral foundation is useless. Worse than useless. Dangerous. Even engineers need a philosophy.'

'But an engineer may not need so much archaic Chinese.'

'Classical studies are good for the brain.' Shi-Rong paused. 'I suppose he'll serve the emperor in some way or other. He'll have to if he wants to build bridges or canals or anything like that.'

'If there is even an emperor to serve.'

'People have been saying the Mandate of Heaven is being withdrawn all my life,' his father remarked, 'but despite the wretched conduct of the court, it hasn't happened.'

'And if the court has its way, nothing will ever happen,' said his son. 'But when things finally fall apart, some people think there'll have to be a complete change of regime, though nobody seems to know what that would be.'

'Well,' his father said, 'I'm glad I shan't be there to see it.'

It was after the evening meal that they heard the thunder. Darkness had fallen some time before. The boy wanted to go outside to see, so he and Shi-Rong went into the courtyard. As they did so, they saw a flash of lightning in the west.

'Look, Grandfather.' Bao-Yu pointed up. 'Stars.'

He was right. The thunderstorm was closer than the one before, but it hadn't reached this part of the Yellow River valley yet. The sky above was clear and full of stars.

Shi-Rong went to the gate and stepped through it. From out there, looking across the valley, he could see the whole weather system.

It was a strange sight. A line of blackness stretched right across the sky from south to north like a great curtain. And from within it came great rumblings and flashes and roars. The storm was ten, maybe a dozen miles away, he thought.

'Grandfather.' Bao-Yu was at his side. 'Can we go up the hill to watch?'

Shi-Rong looked down at him. 'You think we should?'

'Oh yes.'

'What a good idea.' He turned to Ru-Hai, who had appeared just behind him. 'You and I can each take a lamp. Not that I need one, really, I know the path so well.'

'What if the rain reaches us?' Ru-Hai objected. 'We'll get soaked. And it'll be slippery.'

Shi-Rong and his grandson looked at each other. 'We don't care,' they said.

So they took lanterns and made their way through the village, whose occupants, thinking this must be a ritual of some kind, watched from their doorways with interest. And as they moved up the path, the only person who tripped was Ru-Hai, who wasn't very pleased about it.

When they finally reached the ledge where the ancestral graves were, Shi-Rong put the lamps behind one of the graves, so that their light wouldn't distract from the view, and for a quarter of an hour they gazed out at the huge storm as it advanced towards them. Now and then came a huge flash, a bang, and a roar that seemed as if it meant to rip the firmament apart.

Then Ru-Hai looked up at the sky and noticed that there were not so many stars to be seen. He said they'd better go back. But Shi-Rong caught a glimpse of his grandson's face in a big lightning flash and said: 'We could have a last look from up at the temple if we're quick.' And before anyone could say anything, the boy was running to retrieve the lamps. Shi-Rong turned to Ru-Hai. 'Only for a minute or two,' he promised.

And indeed, they had been up by the temple only a few moments when their view was obscured by a film of rain not far away, and they felt the damp breeze on their faces.

'Time to go down,' said Shi-Rong to his grandson. 'Did you enjoy it?'

'Oh yes, Grandfather.'

'It was quite a sight,' said Ru-Hai, with slightly less enthusiasm.

So they went down, and the rain did not start to fall until they had reached the village street. The rain was quite light as it pattered on the path and splashed the tops of the lamps, so they were only a little wet when they got home.

Then they all retired, to sleep until the morning.

The storm was kind to them that night, veering northwards so that only its outskirts passed over the village in a series of light rains and showers, dying to nothing before the dawn.

By the time they had breakfasted and the horse and pony had been brought to the gate, the sky was a clear pale blue.

'There's no need to take the valley road into the town and then go all the way back up again into the hills,' Shi-Rong pointed out to his son. 'Just go through the village here and take the path across the high ground. You know the way. You'll be at the Shaolin Monastery by late afternoon.'

Ru-Hai agreed and bade his father farewell. 'We shall all meet for Qingming in the spring,' he told his father firmly.

Shi-Rong nodded without replying. Then he turned to the boy. 'I have something for you,' he said, and gave Bao-Yu a tiny box. 'Do you remember the little bone where you spotted the character for *horse* was scratched?'

'I do, Grandfather.'

'Well, that's what's in there. I want you to keep it as a present from me in memory of this visit.'

'Thank you, Grandfather.' The boy looked overjoyed.

'You must keep that always,' said his father.

'I will,' Bao-Yu promised.

'Goodbye then,' said Shi-Rong. And he stayed by the gate and watched them go up the lane until they were out of sight.

An hour later, he sat at the table in his small library. The two scrolls he had prepared were in front of him. No need to change them. Everything had worked out exactly as he'd hoped. He was almost ready to walk over to Mr Gu's house.

But there was one small duty that perhaps he should perform. He'd been thinking about it for some time.

Mei-Ling. That money she'd asked him for at Bright Moon's wedding.

He'd been so shocked by the turn of events just then, so shaken by the loss of all that money he'd expected to make, that having spent enough already on the wedding, he'd told himself he couldn't part with anything more. Looking back now, he realised that it would have made no difference to him at all.

He could so easily have rectified the business. But having refused at the time, he had thought for no good reason that it would make him look weak if he relented. So he'd done nothing. Almost forgotten it. And he realised to his shame that he didn't even know for certain whether Mei-Ling was still alive. He imagined she probably was.

Those about to die, he thought, should keep good accounts.

He went to the cabinet and took out a small square box, tightly packed with silver. It was more than Mei-Ling had asked for. Closing the box and sealing it, he wrapped it carefully in a piece of silk brocade, tied it and sealed the knot. Then he placed it in a leather bag.

After this he sat down at his desk again and wrote a letter to Bright Moon, letting her know that, if her mother was still alive, she should apply to Mr Gu, who was holding a package for her. Then he gave orders for the groom to attend on him directly.

The sun was already high in the clear blue sky as they walked to Mr Gu's house. Shi-Rong carried the two scrolls and the letter in a satchel; the groom had the leather bag slung over his shoulder. When they reached the scholar's little hill farm, Shi-Rong took the leather bag and told the groom he could return home.

Old Mr Gu was delighted to see him. He was in a cheerful mood. 'Look at this perfect autumn day. Did you see the big storms they had upriver? And we got nothing but a shower or two. I was composing a poem just before you arrived. Would you like to help me? Shall we do it together?'

'I really want to talk to you,' said Shi-Rong. 'I have a favour to ask.'

'Of course. Of course. Let's sit down then and you can tell me all about it.'

'The fact is,' said Shi-Rong, 'that I'm going to kill myself today.'

'Really? That is a surprise. Are you sure? Why do you want to do that? It's not at all a Confucian thing to do, you know. It's really allowed only in special circumstances.'

'I know. I want you to read this.' And Shi-Rong gave him one of the two scrolls.

Mr Gu read in silence for a minute or two.

'Your criticism of the goings-on at court is exactly right, I must say. Whether the country can be saved by the emperor taking charge, I'm not so sure. But I'm sure Confucius would endorse your message entirely. So are you trying to be another Wu the Censor? Do you want to body-shame Cixi? Wu actually wrote his protest in a poem, as you know.'

'Not exactly. That's where you come in. Firstly, Wu the Censor's magnificent effort should not be copied. It stands alone. I'm not worthy to imitate him. Secondly, I am not addressing this to the court. It's addressed to the community of scholars. I'm blaming them for not uniting to advise the court.'

'You don't want to attack Cixi directly.'

'Exactly. Partly because I don't want to bring down her wrath upon my son. In fact, I was ready to delay the whole thing if it would damage his career. But he says he has no chance of getting anywhere, and he wants to retire.'

'That is understandable.'

'And also because I think that, in the long run, agitating the scholars will be far more effective.'

'And you take your life to show them your commitment.'

'Exactly. I want you to wait until my son – who knows nothing of this, of course – is safely retired on the estate, and then circulate my protest to a small group of scholars. Not too widely. Just let it seep out.'

'That's clever. Your name will live on. You'll be honoured.'

'In a small way. Quietly. That's all I want.'

'You made two copies.'

'Yes. I'd like you to give one to my son. But not yet. In a year or two, perhaps.'

'You've thought it all out. What's in the leather bag?'

'Ah. A second and unrelated favour. Would you send this letter to my adopted daughter and hold the box in the leather bag until she or her mother makes arrangements to collect it?'

'I don't see why not. How will you kill yourself?'

'Hanging is the normally approved method in these circumstances. It does less violence to the body than other methods.'

'That's true. You should probably hang yourself. Shall we go down and have a look at the river? Then we can have tea, and you can help me with my poem before you go.'

They stood on the towpath just above the water, gazing at the huge yellow-brown expanse before them. The rains had certainly swollen the river. Instead of its usual placid flow, the vast stream had become a torrent, or rather, a moving sea with roiling waves.

'Look at that!' cried the old man. 'The mighty Yellow River in all its majesty and power. The soul of our ancient land. How lucky we are to live here.'

'We certainly are,' Shi-Rong agreed.

They watched it in silence for a minute or two, then turned to go back.

'I'm not sure that it's really necessary for you to kill yourself,' Mr Gu remarked. 'Why not delay a bit? I could still send out the letter, you know.'

'It's better this way,' said Shi-Rong. 'It completes everything.'

'You could work on your calligraphy.'

'I know. By the way, could you send someone up to the Shaolin Monastery tomorrow? Ask the abbot to give my son a message that his father died. He and my grandson are visiting there.'

'As you wish. You're going to do it tonight?'

'Yes.'

'I shall miss you. Perhaps you'll change your mind later today. Come and see me in the morning if you do.'

'I will. If I do.'

They descended from the towpath together. Shi-Rong offered to accompany the old man home, but Mr Gu said there was no need and set off with his stick along the path that led across the big expanse of open ground before it began its steep ascent up the hill towards his home.

Shi-Rong didn't want to go home yet himself. It was quite exciting to watch the huge waters of the Yellow River in full spate, and he wouldn't be seeing them again. So he went back onto the towpath. Several times he turned to watch Mr Gu's progress. From the high bank he could see him quite well. After a time the old man was just a little dot in the distance, but he could make out his tiny form slowly mounting the track that rose from the valley floor. He caught his last glimpse of him just as he neared his little farm, tucked into the trees some three hundred feet above the valley.

For another half hour he watched the big river, which was carrying away all kinds of branches and other detritus that had fallen into its churning waves.

Everything in nature was flux, he thought. And if the Yellow River was anything to go by, the great flux had no end.

At last, it seemed to him, it was time to go. He'd seen all he needed. Descending from the towpath, he took the track that would take him in a more westerly direction, towards his own home.

He walked slowly. There was no hurry. The plan was complete. Perfect.

And he had gone a quarter of a mile across the valley floor when, behind him, he heard the strangest roar.

Then Jiang Shi-Rong turned, looked back in terror, and began to run.

But the waters of the Yellow River were swifter and infinitely greater than he as they swept all before them.

The great flood of the Yellow River, when it broke its banks at Huayuankou and rushed across the broad valley, sweeping farms, villages, and towns before it, was worse than any tsunami from the sea because, being one of the greatest rivers on the earth, and flowing as it did above the surrounding land, it kept coming on. And on. And continued without ceasing.

It is estimated that nine hundred thousand people lost their lives.

The ancestral home of Shi-Rong's family, being well above the valley, was not touched. Neither of course was the Shaolin Monastery high in the mountains. Nor Mr Gu's little hill farm.

But of Mr Gu's neighbour and pupil Shi-Rong, there was no sign at all.

BOXERS

February 1900

Dr Cunningham looked at old Trader. He had two lady patients in their nineties; after them came John Trader of Drumlomond. He was the type, of course. Tall, athletic, no fat on him. They were the men who lasted longest, in his experience.

'I cannot answer for you if you undertake this journey,' he declared.

'You can't answer for me if I don't,' Trader replied cheerfully. 'I'm nearly ninety.'

'Take your medicine and avoid stress. Can you do that?'

'I should think so. A long voyage. Good ship. I may get bored, but not stressed, I imagine. All I have to do then is take the train up to Peking. I'll be staying with my daughter in the mission, which is safely inside the Inner City. Can't see much stress there.'

'You're determined to go?'

'I'd like to see Emily again before it's too late. I haven't met her youngest boy yet, either. It's about ten years since she and her husband last came back.' He smiled. 'Not sure I can wait much longer.'

'Well then, I suppose you'd better go.' Dr Cunningham put away his stethoscope. 'What's going on in China, anyway? I read the papers, but I can't make head nor tail of the place. Do you understand it?'

'I think so. They tried to modernise, but never got very far with it. So everybody's been taking advantage – especially the Japanese. You know the Japanese smashed the Chinese navy, just five years ago. Now they've got control of the Korean peninsula as well. To add insult to injury, they also grabbed the island of Taiwan.'

'That's Formosa, isn't it?'

'Different name, same place. Right off the Chinese coast, between Shanghai and Hong Kong. Absolutely humiliating.'

'I can never make out if China's a rich or a poor country.'

'Both, really. Agricultural of course. Not much industry yet. But wealth underground. I've heard there's a young American prospector called Herbert Hoover who's looking for anthracite in north China. Gold as well, I believe. So all kinds of possibilities in the future, you might say – when they wake up.'

'What about the palace coup I read about?'

'Part and parcel of this business – whether to modernise or not. After the Japanese humiliation, the young Chinese emperor, who'd finally got the old dowager Cixi to retire, announced a sweeping set of reforms. Tried to modernise his empire overnight. Bit naive, I'm afraid. The conservative establishment wasn't having it. Next thing you know, Cixi's back in control and the young emperor's a prisoner in his own palace. Still is, I believe.' He paused. 'Not that you ever really know what's going on in the Forbidden City. It's the most secretive place on earth.'

'The old woman's been ruling through emperors who are boys or weak young men for about forty years, hasn't she?'

'Pretty much.'

'One last question: Who are these people wearing red sashes and turbans who've started stirring up trouble? Boxers, they call them. Is it a secret society? Are they like the Taiping?'

'A sort of nationalist sect. Not the first. You know, get the foreigners and their religion out of China. That sort of thing. And they practise some kind of magical martial arts – that's why our people call them Boxers. Makes them immune even to bullets, they claim.'

'Good luck with that,' said the doctor.

'Popular with the peasants, but only in a few northern provinces. They wear red shirts and turbans. That's all I know.'

'Are you worried about your daughter?'

'I did go to the Foreign Office and have a talk with them. Our man in Peking – minister, as we call him – reports that everything's quiet enough.'

'Do you believe it?'

'Have to see when I get there.'

Dr Cunningham looked at his patient quizzically. 'I have a feeling this may not be such a quiet holiday as you're telling me.'

'Nonsense.'

'You want to persuade them to come back, don't you? That's what you're really up to.'

'Not at all,' said Trader. 'Just a little holiday in the sun.'

o

It was a May morning in Beijing. Yesterday a wind from the Gobi Desert had swept in like a tsunami, carrying black dust this time, and Emily couldn't get it out of her hair, which only added to her feeling of discomfort and unease.

Her father was coming. He might arrive any day. She would have stopped him – except that by the time she got his letter, he was already on his way. She longed to see him, of course; but how was she to look after an old man of nearly ninety, with everything else that was going on?

The spacious yard of the Anglican mission was dusty. The mission building ran along one side; there were dormitories on two of the other sides. The fourth side was a high wall with a gateway onto the street.

There were usually a few Chinese converts – men, women, children – squatting or walking about in the yard. But during the last three days there had been a constant trickle of families coming to find shelter there. Before long, the dormitories would be full. What had they seen to frighten them?

She knew of one thing, of course: the red balloons.

They'd appeared about ten days ago: first clusters, then great clouds of them, floating up into the sky over Peking. They were a signal from the Boxers, to let the people of the capital know that they'd arrived there. The balloons were an invitation to all good Chinese to join the Boxers; perhaps a warning of trouble if you didn't. But to the foreigners and those Chinese foolish and disloyal enough to have converted to the barbarians' religion, the balloons were clearly a threat.

To be taken seriously? All that most of the converts arriving at the mission would say was: 'Better here.'

The Anglican mission was safely tucked in behind the huge walls of the protected Inner City – the Tartar City, as the foreigners called it – and only a five-minute walk from the Tiananmen Gate.

Emily saw some new arrivals, a young family who'd turned up with a little handcart piled with their few possessions. But they hadn't come from the outer Chinese city. She knew they lodged only half a mile away, inside the Tartar quarter. Why were they coming here for sanctuary?

Then she noticed they were looking towards the gateway of the mission. She followed their gaze and saw a young woman – hardly more than a girl, really – in the street outside. She was wearing a red sash, with a red scarf tied around her head, and she was attaching a poster to the open gate.

Emily hastened towards the girl in red. 'What do you want?' she cried. But the girl took no notice of her at all. Emily reached her and stared at the poster. The message, scrawled in big Chinese characters, was easy enough to understand.

BARBARIANS OUT. TRAITORS DIE.

Traitors. That meant the converts. The girl must be a member of one of the brigades of women the Boxers were using now. The Red Lanterns, they were called. She'd heard of them, but this was the first time she'd seen one.

'Go away!' Emily cried. But the girl in red just stared at her with contempt. Then, taking her time, she walked to the end of the mission wall and calmly pasted another, identical poster there before turning the corner and walking away. Furiously, Emily tore the poster off the gate. The one at the corner proved harder to remove, but she managed to shred it using her fingernails. The Red Lantern girl had vanished – for the time being, at least.

Having returned to the yard and said a few words to the newly arrived family, Emily went back indoors.

The night before, Henry had told her there was a rumour that the Boxers had attacked a mission out in the back country and killed all the Chinese converts. Was it true? Were the Boxers planning to do the same thing even here, in the middle of the capital? Surely it couldn't come to that.

She thought of her son Tom. Most families like theirs sent their boys back to England to boarding school by the age of seven or eight. But Tom was their last. They'd kept him with them as long as they felt they could. He was nearly eleven now, and they'd been preparing to part with him at the end of the year. Should Tom go straightaway? Was it right to keep him here if there was so much danger?

She'd been turning the problem over in her mind for a quarter of an hour when she heard a sound at the front door. 'Tom?' she called out. 'Henry?'

She got up and went into the hall, to find the tall, only slightly bent figure of her father, smiling down at her.

Trader was in rather a good mood. He stooped to kiss her. 'I stopped at the British legation to get directions,' he said. 'You're not far away.'

'Quite near,' said Emily. 'You look very well, Papa.'

'They told me there's a party this evening. Queen's birthday. Hope we're going.'

'If you're not feeling too tired.'

'Why should I be tired? I've only been sitting on a ship for the last three months. Wouldn't miss the party for worlds. Catch up on news, and so forth.'

'Talking of news,' said Emily, 'did you see any signs of trouble on your way up from the coast?'

'I suppose you mean these Boxer fellows. Didn't see any of them. We saw a lot of troops as we got near Peking, but I was told they were Kansu.'

'Really?' Emily smiled. 'That's good news. Those troops are part of the regular imperial army. They don't like the Boxers much.'

And Trader might have questioned her about the Boxers more if a slim, handsome boy with dark, tousled hair hadn't suddenly appeared.

'Here's Tom,' said Emily. 'Your grandson.' And she smiled as her father stared in surprise. 'He looks exactly like you.'

'So he does,' said Trader. 'Is he moody?'

'Not at all.'

'I don't seem to have passed that on to anyone, then.' Trader smiled and shook the boy's hand. 'Glad to have met you at last.'

Young Tom looked at him appraisingly. 'Grandfather?' he asked hopefully. 'Do you play cricket?'

The British legation party obeyed the traditional protocol: a formal dinner for the great and good, followed by a reception with dancing for a larger company.

'I'm afraid Henry and I don't quite make the cut for the dinner,' Emily explained to her father, 'but we go along afterwards.'

Her father had come well prepared. No gentleman of the Victorian age travelled without a good supply of formal evening clothes, and Trader's were pressed tight in the great-ribbed trunk that two servants had staggered to bring into the mission. With his tall frame, black eye patch, perfectly cut evening dress, and courtly manners, he made a distinguished figure. Indeed, he might have been taken for a former ambassador himself. So Emily felt rather proud to introduce him to Sir Claude and Lady MacDonald as they received their later guests.

'You are Emily's father?' Lady MacDonald couldn't quite conceal her surprise. 'I heard you'd arrived today.'

'I did,' Trader said, with a slight bow and a charming smile.

'Did you come from far?' Sir Claude wanted to know.

'Galloway. Quite a way south of MacDonald country, of course,' Trader added pleasantly. For the lands of that great clan lay in the Highlands and on the Isle of Skye.

'I wonder if you know some people called Lomond down there,' Sir Claude ventured, seeing if he could gauge Trader's position in the scheme of things.

'My wife's family,' Trader replied easily. 'Our place is called Drumlomond.'

'Pity you didn't get here earlier in the month,' said MacDonald in the most friendly way. 'We set up a little racecourse just outside the city. It all went like clockwork, but the season ended three weeks ago.'

'I thought I noticed some good-looking ponies on my way into the legation,' Trader remarked.

'Well, we're so delighted you've come,' said Lady MacDonald warmly. 'I do hope we shall be seeing more of you.' And it was hardly five minutes before she was at Emily's side. 'We didn't know your mother was a Lomond. I suppose we just associated you with the Anglican mission.'

'Well, I am part of the mission,' said Emily. 'Henry's a cousin of ours, you know.'

'Oh. And does your family farm the land at Drumlomond . . . ?'

'We keep some in hand. But most of the farms are tenanted. It's not huge. A few thousand acres.'

'Ah,' said Lady MacDonald. 'My husband and I were wondering if your father would let us give a dinner party in his honour while he's here. Do you think he'd like it, and would you and your husband bring him?'

'How very kind of you, Lady MacDonald,' said Emily. 'I'm sure he would.'

'I'm so glad,' said her hostess, and touched Emily's arm before she swept away.

The Legation Quarter lay just inside the Imperial City walls, a little to the east of the central Tiananmen Gate. The British compound was the largest. There was a handsome residence with stables and numerous other buildings, including a theatre, which was being used for the dinner that night, spacious lawns, tall trees to provide graceful shade, and even a tennis court.

While Emily had her encounter with their hostess, Trader and Henry stood under a tree and surveyed the scene.

'Those are mostly diplomats from the other colonial powers,' Henry observed, indicating a group of gentlemen chatting amongst themselves. 'French, Germans, Austrians, Russians, Japanese.' He nodded. 'You might think they were here to learn everything they can about China. But in fact they spend their entire time watching one another, making sure no one's getting more out of China than they are. Same story in Africa, of course. Every European nation trying to grab as much as they can.'

'You left out the Americans.'

'They're a bit different. See the young man with a face like a Roman general over there? That's Herbert Hoover. American. Just married a nice girl, by the way. She's called Lou.'

'I hear he's prospecting for minerals.'

'He's found anthracite. Hoover will do a deal with the Chinese. But that's all. Strictly business. He's not a colonist – though the Americans do have missionaries.'

'Who are the best people to talk to, if one wants to find out what's really going on in China?' Trader asked him.

'The missionaries, generally, because we spend our lives with the ordinary people. You have to know someone pretty well to convert them.' Henry looked around, then smiled to himself. 'I see a couple of fellows over there who might interest you: Morrison of the London *Times* and a man called Backhouse, who speaks Chinese. I'd better warn you that Backhouse is a bit of an odd fish. Full of gossip. Would you like to meet them?'

'Absolutely.'

Morrison looked exactly what he was: an intelligent, widely travelled Australian Scot, nearing forty, a professional observer who meant business. Backhouse, still in his late twenties, looked eccentric. Might he be a little mad?

'Unusual name,' Trader remarked. 'I believe you pronounce it *Bacchus*. Isn't there a Backhouse baronetcy?'

'My father, sir.'

That made sense, Trader thought. Young Backhouse might not be a mad baronet yet; but no doubt he would be, given time.

Having had his own conversation interrupted, to talk to an ancient visitor he'd never heard of, the *Times* man couldn't have been overjoyed. But he greeted Trader politely. 'Your first time in China, sir?' he enquired.

'Not exactly.' Trader smiled amiably. 'I was in Canton during the first Opium War – caught in the siege, as a matter of fact.'

'Really?' Morrison's face completely changed. 'Are you staying here awhile? May I come and talk to you? I'd love to hear your story.'

'Whenever you like.'

'Sir Claude's going to speak,' Henry broke in. Sir Claude MacDonald's tall figure was moving towards a low grassy bank on one side of the lawn.

'Do you know how MacDonald got his appointment here?' Backhouse whispered to Trader. 'It is *said* that he had unimpeachable evidence that Lord Salisbury – in his private life, as we might say – was none other than Jack the Ripper. Confronted the great man and told him the price of his silence was to be made minister to Peking.'

The idea of Britain's massively respectable prime minister as the infamous serial killer was certainly preposterous. 'Are your stories always so improbable?' Trader enquired.

A glass was loudly tapped. Britain's envoy began to speak. 'Excellencies, ladies and gentlemen, we are delighted to welcome you on this happy occasion. But before I propose the loyal toast, I would like to say a word about the situation here in Peking.

'We have all learned with deep shock of the recent atrocities committed against missions and their Chinese converts. Our thoughts go out to all those who have suffered.

'I must stress, however, that there is no indication that these Boxer outrages have spread beyond a few northern provinces. In South China, the Boxers are unknown. The Chinese government, through the Tsungli Yamen, has given us assurances that an edict is being issued for the total suppression of the Boxers. The leaders of all the legations have met, and we have told the Chinese that if they do not at once make good on their promise, we shall summon our troops from the coast, where we already have warships in place. I have every reason to believe, therefore, that this regrettable business will soon be put behind us.'

There was applause. And then came the loyal toast to Victoria, Britain's queen and India's empress, on the joyous occasion of her eighty-first birthday, sixty-three years on the throne with, God willing, many more to come. Long may she reign. And the British all cheered, and everyone clapped, on the legation's broad and sunlit lawn.

'So what do you really think?' said John Trader to Morrison.

'The Boxers may not be so easy to stop. It's not really surprising if nationalist groups resent the foreigners who keep humiliating them. And I'm afraid' – Morrison glanced at Henry – 'our missionaries, though they mean for the best, may not have helped.'

'For example?' Trader asked

'Telling the Chinese they shouldn't worship their ancestors. Theologically correct, but perhaps not wise. Venerating the dead is central to the Confucian idea of moral family life.'

Trader nodded. 'On Scottish hills,' he remarked, 'they still build cairns of stones for the dead. Pagan practice, old as time. But nobody thinks there's any harm in it.' He gave Henry a mischievous look. 'Perhaps my children will do it for me.'

'I'll add a stone to your cairn,' Henry replied cheerfully. 'And Christians tend family graves in every churchyard. Just don't ask me to worship you or think you can send me help from the afterlife.' He turned to Morrison. 'I don't make an issue of all this myself. If I can bring my converts the spiritual benefit of Christianity, they'll gradually understand that everything comes from God and pray to Him for the souls of their ancestors. But it's true that some Chinese claim we're attacking their traditions.'

Emily returned, bringing the two Hoovers with her, and introduced them to her father.

'Morrison was just telling us what we missionaries have done to offend the Chinese,' Henry explained. 'Go on, Morrison. What else?'

'In recent years, our attempts to discourage foot-binding.'

'But it's such a terrible custom,' cried Lou Hoover.

'And very painful,' said Emily. 'All the women tell me that.'

'I can never see,' said Lou Hoover, 'why people would do such a thing.' She turned. 'What do you think, Mr Trader?'

'Strange, isn't it,' he replied, 'how all over the world, people want to distort the bodies God gave them. In some parts of Africa, I've been told, the women stretch their necks with metal rings so that if you took the rings away, their necks could no longer support their heads. The ancient Maya in Central America used to lengthen babies' skulls by squeezing them between two boards. But you could argue that the worst custom of all is our very own – on both sides of the Atlantic, I may say.'

'What's that?' asked Hoover.

'To lace our women into whalebone corsets so tight that, doctors assure us, it damages their health far more than if we bound their feet like the Chinese.' He shook his head. 'As for why human beings do these things, I have no idea.'

'What does the Chinese government say about foot-binding?' Hoover asked.

'The ruling Manchu don't bind their women's feet,' Morrison answered. 'So I don't think they care much one way or the other. It's a Han Chinese custom. There's social prestige involved, and naturally, they don't like it when outsiders tell them how to live.'

'You've left one thing out,' Backhouse butted in. 'It's a fetish. The men get excited by the tiny feet, like little hooves, in silk and satin slippers.'

There was an awkward silence.

'I'm afraid it's true,' said Emily.

'No need to say it,' growled her father.

'None at all,' said Mr Hoover very firmly, giving Backhouse a furious look.

'The other thing the Boxers have going for them,' Morrison went on, 'is their mystique. They've persuaded themselves and many of the people that they have magical powers. You know how superstitious the Chinese can be. I mean, we've had telegraph wires here for some years now, but many Chinese still think it's some kind of black magic.'

'Henry's got a telescope at the mission,' said Emily with a smile. 'You know, on a tripod. Most of the converts won't go near it because they think it's a magical weapon of some kind.'

'You'll find almost as much superstition in Gaelic Scotland, actually,' Trader reminded them. 'And when you consider all the horrors we've brought here – like the iron gun ship in the Opium War, which they'd never seen before – if I were Chinese and I saw a barbarian with a strange tube on a tripod, I daresay I'd be pretty leery of it.'

'Chinese superstition may help us, strangely enough,' Morrison continued. 'I was talking to Sir Robert Hart – who's run the Chinese customs for forty years and knows more than anyone – and he told me that according to Chinese folklore, there's a day coming up this September when cataclysms are supposed to occur. If the Boxers are going to stage something big, he says, that's the day they'll choose – which gives us nearly four months to prepare.'

'So, sir, are you reassured?' Trader asked Hoover.

'Not really. I've pulled my fellows out. Can't risk their lives. The anthracite will have to wait. Lou and I leave for the coast tomorrow.'

'MacDonald says he's had assurances from the Tsungli Yamen,' Trader said. 'But here's my question. Who makes the final decisions in China now?'

'The old lady. The dowager empress,' Morrison replied.

'Cixi,' Backhouse echoed. 'The Old Buddha.'

'And where does she stand on the Boxers?'

'She may love them. She may fear them. Hard to know,' said Morrison.

'Oh no, it isn't,' Backhouse cried. 'Cixi has hated the West ever since the Opium Wars. She's always wanted to kick us out, but she's never been able to do it, for fear of the West's reprisals. But if the Boxers rise and do her dirty work for her, she'd be delighted.'

'How do you know?' Hoover demanded.

'Because she told me so,' said Backhouse with a little smile of triumph. 'I happen to be a friend of hers.'

'I don't believe a word of this,' said the American.

'You are quite wrong, sir. First, I speak Chinese. Second, I made the acquaintance of Lacquer Nail, one of the palace eunuchs who is close to her. Third, I am neither a missionary nor an employee of the British government. Fourth, my eunuch friend knows the empress is curious about foreigners and thought I might amuse her. As a result, I have already spoken with her on numerous occasions.'

'I always heard only eunuchs could get into the palace,' said Trader.

'Generally you are correct, though foreigners, princes and ministers have always been received there for audiences. But for years now, Cixi has pretty much done what she wants. Especially out at the Summer Palace, where she likes to reside.'

'But we destroyed the Summer Palace,' said Trader.

'Cixi always wanted to restore it, but there were never the funds. Finally they rebuilt one of the smaller parks, and they constructed a huge pleasure boat in the lake. At least it looks like a boat, though it's actually made of stone. Cixi loves to have festive parties on that stone boat – *very* festive.'

'I imagined the Dragon Empress was rather severe,' Trader remarked.

'Not in private. In fact, her most trusted eunuchs are allowed to take intimate liberties that might astonish you. And so am I.'

'You are preposterous,' said Hoover in disgust. 'Let's go, Lou.' And they left. Mercifully, a moment later, Lady MacDonald appeared.

'The dancing is beginning. I just suggested to Sir Robert Hart that he should claim the first dance, and he says he's too old. So I have come to you, Mr Trader.'

'But, Lady MacDonald, I'm much older than he is,' Trader pointed out.

'Don't you think we should show him up?' she rejoined.

Trader grinned. 'Absolutely,' he said.

So to the general pleasure, the oldest man present led his hostess onto the dance floor, namely the tennis court, where they gave a very good account of themselves, and everybody clapped. They even took a second turn. Emily felt so proud. And though Henry invited her to dance, she asked him to wait until the next, so that she could watch them because, as she said to Henry, she'd like to remember her father this way.

Meanwhile, Trader and his partner were chatting pleasantly.

'You really should stay with your daughter for as long as you can,' Lady MacDonald said. 'We're so fond of her. We like to have a tennis tournament here for the people who are still in Peking during the summer,' she went on blithely.

'I hope you're not expecting me to play.'

'You can give out the prizes.'

'You'll need to roll the courts a bit after this dancing,' he remarked.

'Of course. Though given our standard of tennis, it may not really matter.'

'When I was in India,' he said, 'we went up to the hill stations in the hot season.'

'It's the same here. People go into the mountains. Not as nice as the

Indian hill stations, but quite picturesque. Some of the mountain houses used to be temples. Those are very quaint. If you stay, I promise you shall visit some.'

'You think it'll be all right, with the Boxers and all that?'

'The French minister has just told me that we're all going to be massacred,' she said easily. 'But we can't have the French knowing better than we do, can we?'

The next morning Emily counted another thirty converts seeking refuge in the mission. All the beds in the dormitories were now taken. She started piling up blankets that could be laid on the floor. At noon Mrs Reid, the wife of one of the British doctors, arrived and told her that several British families had found their servants gone. Warned off. Then Henry went over to the legation and returned with confusing news.

'There's been a skirmish between a party of Boxers and some imperial troops. The Boxers won. It doesn't look as if Cixi's in control of the Boxers.'

Henry didn't say anything more just then. But the following evening, when they were alone, he returned to the subject. 'You know,' he said, 'whether Cixi controls the Boxers or she doesn't, the fact is that the Boxers could cut us off in Peking. Any day.' He paused and looked at her bleakly. 'We shouldn't keep Tom here anymore. Or your father. They'd better go down to the coast while they still can, and your father should take Tom to England.'

'If you think so.' She sighed. 'I shall miss them both so much. But I've had Tom longer than most mothers do. He's nearly eleven.' She smiled affectionately at her husband. 'It'll just be the two of us, then.'

Henry was silent for a moment. Then he said: 'I think you should go, too.'

'Me?' She looked horrified. 'You're not getting rid of me.' She watched him. He was shaking his head. 'When we married, Henry, you warned me about the dangers. I signed up for the duration: richer, poorer, in sickness and in health, as long as we both shall live. I'm not leaving you now.'

'Perhaps I should order you, then. When we married, you also took an oath to love, honour – and obey.' He was looking at her with great affection, but she knew he wasn't joking.

'In any case, Henry,' she went on, 'if you really believe things could get so bad, there is another solution: you should come, too. Hardly anyone's served here as long as you.'

'I can't desert the converts.' He shook his head. 'I'm responsible for converting them. I can't abandon them now. So if, God forbid, the worst were to happen, let's not leave our children without either parent.'

'I'm just as responsible for the converts as you, Henry,' she replied. 'You know it's true. As for the children, both our girls are married. My brothers would always look after the boys. They'd have a home at Drumlomond. Once Tom goes to school, he's not going to see us for years anyway – just the same as hundreds of children with parents serving all over the British Empire, who spend the holidays with relations in England and probably never see their parents until after they've finished school. Perhaps not even then.'

'We'll wait a day or two,' he said, 'and see.'

He was over at the legation all the following morning and came back soon after noon. 'Word is that the Boxers have sworn allegiance to Cixi,' he reported. 'They've been going through some kind of martial arts drill inside the Imperial City. I don't know what it means,' he confessed, 'and nor does anyone at the legation. How's your father?'

'Oh,' she said, 'Father's being an absolute brick. He's keeping Tom occupied.'

'What are they doing?'

'Playing cricket.'

Trader was quite enjoying himself. His grandson wasn't complicated. Young Tom was just anxious not to make a fool of himself when he got to England.

'The other fellows will have been at school for three or four years already,' he explained. 'I don't know why my parents held me back for so long. So I want to make sure I'm good at something that matters, like cricket, so that I don't look like a duffer. One thing'll do for a start, I hope. What do you think, Grandfather?'

'Do one thing well. That's all you need at school. All you need in life, really.'

'I've got a cricket bat. And a cricket ball. Could you bowl at me?'

'Net practice without a net, eh? All right.' Trader didn't like to think how long it was since he'd held a cricket ball in his hand, but they took over one end of the mission's yard and started. He didn't try to bowl overarm, but by throwing the ball with a short arm he could be pretty accurate. He could also put all kinds of spin on the ball. 'Keep your bat straight,' he'd call. 'Step forward and block those ones . . .' He hadn't been in his school first eleven, but he'd been a useful all-rounder and he knew enough to coach young Tom quite effectively. When he grew tired of this net practice, he was quite happy to play catch with his grandson for half an hour, in front of the curious converts, until Emily rescued him.

'You're a very good grandfather,' she told him.

'Enjoyed it, actually.'

'Can we play again tomorrow?' Tom asked.

'Of course we can,' said Trader.

'Can I ask you something, Grandfather?'

'I should think so.'

'At school, will they all wear white flannels for cricket? Father says I can perfectly well play in the grey flannels I have.'

'Well, of course your father's quite right.' And also on a missionary's salary, Trader thought. 'I daresay we'll sort all that out when the time comes,' he went on blandly. 'It'll be nearly a year before the next cricket season begins. You'll be taller by then.'

'Thank you, Father,' said Emily as soon as Tom had trotted off. Trader smiled. The boy would have white flannels, the same as everybody else. He'd see to that.

Inside, she brought him lemonade and a glass for herself, too. 'Father,' she resumed finally, 'Henry and I are worried about Tom.'

'He seems all right to me.'

'It's the Boxers. We don't know what's going to happen, but we think he ought to go to England at once. Just in case.'

'I see. What about you and Henry? Shouldn't you get out, too?'

'Henry won't desert the converts. And I won't desert Henry.'

'I understand. But I don't agree about you. You must think of your children.'

'Please don't you start. Henry's already . . .' She trailed off. 'I'd love to see you for longer. It's been so wonderful. But will you please take Tom home?'

'When?'

'Tomorrow. Or the next day at latest.'

'You know,' he said, 'I came all the way out here to see you, spend a bit of time with you before it's too late. But I was a bit concerned about these Boxers. So I'd thought, if things look bad, I'll try to get you all to come back to England. Might be the last important thing I could do for the family.'

'So you came across half the world for us.'

'Not as if I didn't know the way.'

'Well, Henry's trying to force me, but he won't succeed. And nor will you. So I'm afraid you'll just have to take Tom. He'll be very pleased. You're his hero.'

'The boy doesn't really need me on the boat, you know. Just put him on board. The captain will keep an eye on him. Give instructions for where he's to be sent at the other end. He can go to Drumlomond. Easy enough with the trains.'

'Like a parcel with a label?'

'That's how children are being sent about, all over the British Empire.'

'If Tom goes to England, where are you going to go?'

'If you leave, I shall leave with you and Tom. But if you stay, I'd rather stay with you. If you don't mind, that is.' He smiled. 'It was really you I came to see.'

'You'd be putting your life at risk.'

'Not much life to risk when you're nearly ninety.'

'You'd stand there, sword in hand?'

'I used to be rather good with a sword, you know.'

'Oh, Father.' She got up and kissed him. 'Will you get Tom on a ship, at least?'

He nodded. 'All right.'

The feathery clouds in the east were gleaming red the following morning, and she wondered if it meant a storm. But by the time Tom and his grandfather went out into the yard with bat and ball after breakfast, the sky overhead was clear.

She hadn't told Tom he was leaving yet. Now he was out of the house, she was busy packing his trunk. By mid-morning she closed the lid. That's it then, she thought. From now on, Tom's childhood would be closed to her. Closed like the padlocked trunk. He'd wave goodbye, and quite possibly, they'd never see each other again. She mightn't even be alive herself by the time he reached England.

She sat down on the trunk. Faint sounds came from the yard outside. She suddenly wanted to open the trunk again, put something inside for

Tom to remember her by. But what? People used to have miniature portraits painted for their loved ones to carry. Those miniatures were mostly photographs now. Such an easy thing to do.

Yet she never had. Not in all these years. Somehow there always seemed to be too much of God's work each day for her to attend to such a thing. And now she had nothing to give her son. She searched her mind. A little prayer book perhaps, except that he had one already. There must be something. Her mind was a blank. She felt so helpless, such a failure. She started to cry. And she was still sitting in a state of desolation on the trunk when she heard the door of the house open.

A moment later Henry hurried in. 'The Boxers have started tearing up railway lines. They've set a station on fire. Everyone's summoning troops from the coastal garrisons. The French and Russians already have. The Americans, too.'

'Is the line to Peking open? Will the troops be able to get to us?'

'We'll have to wait and see. Either way, your father and Tom can't travel today.'

'Oh,' she said. And against all common sense and concern for Tom's safety, she felt glad. Perhaps in that time she'd at least find a keepsake to give him.

All the next day they waited. The Boxers paraded in the streets. Was the court controlling them? Would they suddenly strike and burn the mission down? That night she and Henry heard the Boxers singing war songs by their campfires.

The messenger arrived at the mission soon after dawn. He brought a note from MacDonald. They were to evacuate, discreetly, and make their way to the legation. They could bring their converts. But they must be out of the mission that day, the British minister urged, because he could not guarantee their safety.

Henry called the family together. 'The converts are all Chinese. Tell them to remove any crucifixes,' he instructed, 'any sign that they might be Christian. Then they should filter out a few at a time, vanish into the crowds and make their way by different routes across to the Legation Quarter. Tell them to take their time. It's only a mile or so. We must get them out first.'

There were plenty of people about in the street. Fortunately the

Boxers, who were all openly wearing their red turbans and sashes, didn't seem to be hanging around the mission just then. They were too busy parading about elsewhere. So it was easy enough for the converts to slip out in small groups. By late morning they were all gone.

'What can we do about you?' Henry asked Emily. 'I don't think you can try to pass as a Han Chinese townswoman, because your feet aren't bound.'

'Do you remember when Dr Smith's wife and I went as Manchu women to that fancy dress party at the legation?' said Emily. 'I've still got the costumes. They were real Manchu dresses, actually.'

'Perfect. You and Tom can use them. The Boxers insist they're supporting the regime, so they shouldn't give you any trouble.'

Tom started to protest at putting on women's clothes, but his grandfather told him firmly to do as he was asked. 'And you'd better make a decent job of it,' he added. 'You don't want to put your mother's life in danger.'

While Emily and Tom were busy getting dressed indoors, Henry and the three most trusted mission servants started loading an open donkey cart with clothes, blankets, and provisions – everything that they thought could be of use in the legation.

'You're far too tall to disguise as any kind of Chinese man,' Henry said. 'I suppose the best thing might be for you to lie down in the cart and we'll cover you with blankets.' Trader didn't much like the idea, but he didn't say anything.

The last item they loaded was Henry's telescope and tripod. 'I suppose it might come in useful if we're under attack,' Henry said. 'The truth is, I don't want to part with it.' But by the time both the telescope and tripod were installed, there was no room to conceal his father-in-law.

'I've got it,' Trader said suddenly. 'Set the tripod up in the cart and mount the telescope on it. That's it. Emily,' he called, 'I need a white sheet and a few minutes of your time with a needle and thread.'

And sure enough, ten minutes later, his tall figure appeared in the yard again, completely draped in a long white cloak that reached down to his feet. When he got up and stood in the cart beside the tripod, holding the telescope in his hand and swivelling it to point this way and that, he looked like a figure of death or a magician at a ghost festival, to which his tall, thin frame and his black eye patch lent an effect that was truly terrifying. 'That should frighten 'em off,' he remarked with satisfaction.

'You certainly frighten me,' said Henry.

It was agreed that first the cart, driven by a servant and guarded by Trader and his magic telescope, should drive out into the street and make its way eastwards, past the Tiananmen Gate. While all eyes were on the cart, the two Manchu women could slip out with two servants and cross the city towards Legation Street.

'But what do you plan to do yourself, Henry?' Emily asked him.

'Stay here until nightfall to stow away whatever I can and to deal with any converts who come this way. After that, when everything's quieter at dusk, I'll lock up, make my way across the city and rejoin you.'

So Emily did as asked. After she and Tom had been in the street a few moments, she saw a ruffian try to climb onto the cart. But when her father swung the telescope and pointed it right into his face, the man fell off the cart in terror and disappeared.

Not long afterwards, crossing in front of the huge Tiananmen Gate, she saw her father's cart again, in the distance this time, like a small sailing ship ploughing through the sea of people. She caught her breath when she noticed a party of Boxers with red turbans only a hundred yards away from him. But they kept their distance, seemingly uncertain whether they could rely upon the power of their spirit warriors against the magic weapon of the tall white one-eyed wizard.

What troubled Trader most, all that summer, was a simple concern: how to make himself useful. Otherwise, what was he? An old man getting in the way. A mouth to feed when food supplies were dwindling. A danger to others, even. He had to contribute something. But what?

Only a couple of hours after his own arrival, the advance troops from the coast had also reached the legation. They'd all come together in the train, and everyone was happy to see them. But they warned that the Boxers were giving all kinds of trouble down the line, so that it might be a little while before the main military body could clear them away and march up to the capital.

Trader watched the troops with interest. There were between three and four hundred men – British troops, Americans, French, German, Russian, Japanese. The Americans looked the most seasoned. The British boys looked awfully young and raw. But at least their arrival would show that the foreign powers meant business, and he assumed that their arms would be superior to any Chinese weapons.

When, to Emily's great relief, Henry arrived that evening, Trader asked him about the Chinese arms.

'It's quite odd, actually,' Henry told him. 'The Boxers don't only rely on their swords and magic spirits. Some of them have guns. The imperial troops quite often have modern rifles, and a few Krupp field guns, too. But then you'll still suddenly come upon a troop armed with bows and arrows. Why do you ask?'

'Just wondered.'

The Legation Quarter was big, nearly half a mile square. From north to south down the middle ran a waterway called the Imperial Jade Canal – though in the dry season it was hardly more than a big ditch – before it disappeared under the city wall through a water gate.

One thoroughfare, Legation Street, crossed the lower part of the enclave from west to east, just a few hundred feet above the southern wall. Between Legation Street and the looming city wall lay the Dutch, American, and German compounds, together with the Hong Kong Bank and the offices of Jardine Matheson. On the northern side of the street were the compounds of the Russians, Japanese, French and Italians.

Almost the whole of the Legation Quarter's upper part was taken up by just two large enclosures. On the east side of the canal lay a palace with acres of walled grounds that belonged to a friendly Chinese prince. This enclave was known as the Fu. 'We've asked the prince to let us put the converts in the Fu,' Henry told him. 'In case of trouble, the troops should be able to defend them there.'

'More space than we need, isn't it?' asked Trader.

'Remember, it's not just the converts that we've brought. There are the other Protestant missions, especially the Methodists, and a much larger group over at the Catholic cathedral. If things get rough, we'll need all of it.'

Across the canal the big British compound, with its gracious garden acres, took up the whole northwestern corner of the Legation Quarter. Outside the compound's western wall lay an open square, where a small Mongol market would often appear. North of the compound was an ancient Chinese library, over whose roof one could see the purple wall of the Forbidden City a few hundred yards away.

For about a week the legations were quiet. True, news came of Boxer outrages: more of the railway line had been ripped up; the grandstand at the little racecourse had been burned, which annoyed everyone very much. They heard that the Empress Cixi had arrived in the Forbidden City from the Summer Palace with a large body of Kansu troops. Could this be hopeful? When some of the European envoys called at the Tsungli Yamen, however, they got a shock. 'Normally they're polite enough,' they reported back. 'But this time, they wouldn't even speak to us.'

'Keep calm,' MacDonald told them. 'And wait for more troops.'

Trader kept Tom occupied, for which his parents were grateful. The boy was so keen that he wandered around with the cricket ball in his pocket all the time. Emily wanted to stop him doing this, but Trader dissuaded her. 'I think it's like a talisman,' he pointed out. 'A sort of promise that everything's going to be all right and that he'll go to school safely and play cricket when he gets there.'

'Oh,' she said. 'Shouldn't he be praying about that, rather than relying on a talisman?'

'Of course he should pray. But let him keep the ball. It can't do any harm.'

To provide some variation, as well as rest for himself, Trader rigged up a big piece of netting in a secluded corner of the gardens. On this he had a patch of canvas strongly sewn with twine. And on the canvas, exactly to size, a wicket and bails were painted in white. Above the wicket, also painted white, he placed an old pair of leather gloves, donated by MacDonald, which were more loosely attached with twine. 'Those are the wicketkeeper's gloves, you see,' he explained to Tom, 'waiting to receive the ball. So when you're fielding, your object is always to return the ball into his hands, either directly or after a single bounce. You'll see the gloves move if you hit them.'

This was a great success. Tom had a natural throwing arm, and his grandfather taught him technique, so that he wouldn't damage his elbow; and before long, throwing from five yards to over fifty yards, Tom was hitting the gloves over ninety percent of the time and getting better every day. MacDonald himself came to take a look at him and remarked that at this rate, they'd be needing another pair of gloves before long.

'Can you spare them?' asked Trader.

'I thought we might use a pair of my wife's,' MacDonald replied with a smile.

Trader also organised a cricket game for all the boys and girls on the tennis court, using a tennis ball – though young Tom didn't think much of this.

In the evenings, after eating, he usually had a drink and a cigar with Henry, telling him stories about the Opium War and India in the old days, to take his mind off the present for a little and help him unwind.

And if it seemed to Trader that the legations' leading men were being awfully slow to organise their defences, he kept his thoughts to himself.

On the tenth of June, as Trader and Tom were doing a little net practice, MacDonald came out of the residence and hailed him. 'Good news. I've just had a telegraph message from Admiral Seymour, the British commander down at the coast. A large relief force will shortly be on the way.'

They were just finishing their cricket practice when MacDonald came by again. This time he was frowning.

'Everything all right?' Trader quietly asked him.

'Not entirely. The telegraph line's been cut. I'm afraid we may be without news for a bit.'

Two days later, John Trader had a good idea. The nearest boy in age to Tom was the fifteen-year-old son of one of the American missionaries, a bright, rumbustious young fellow who rejoiced in the name of Fargo. Being so far his junior, Tom had been a little shy of him, and Fargo, though civil enough, wasn't much interested in Tom. But when Trader approached Fargo and said, 'You know, I haven't got the energy to toss a cricket ball to Tom for as long as he wants; is there a chance you could give me a helping hand?' the young American grinned and replied, 'If I can throw a baseball, I guess I could throw a cricket ball.'

And he came and joined them within the hour. And came again several times in the days ahead.

The shouting began after dark. The people in the legations heard the Boxers shouting as they burst into the Inner City through the eastern gate. They came with torches, many torches, that cast red glows and leaping shadows on the high buildings. It was hard to know how many there were. Hundreds, certainly.

From the garden of the residence, Trader and Henry watched the glow from the torches moving northwards and westwards. 'They're going towards our mission, I think,' said Henry. 'They won't find anyone there, thank God. They may be heading for the Catholic cathedral as well.'

'How many Catholic converts have the French got up there?' Trader asked.

'More than three thousand, I believe. Mind you, it's built like a fortress.'

Then the screams began. They heard someone frantically ringing a bell. They could see bigger flames and billowing smoke in the darkness.

The flames did not begin to subside until nearly dawn, when the two men went in to sleep.

It was well into the morning when Trader was awoken by Emily.

'They attacked all the missions,' she told him. 'A lot of people were killed. We've had converts straggling into the Legation Quarter all morning. We're putting them in the Fu. Some of the men were tortured. As for the women . . . what you'd expect.' She looked at him sadly. 'Father, would you do something for me?'

'If I can.'

'I want a pistol. Not too heavy. Something I can handle easily. And some ammunition. Just to defend myself, if I have to. Can you get one from somewhere?'

He looked at her searchingly. 'If you're sure that's what you want.'

'Don't tell Henry. There's no need.'

During that day, the Boxers were out in the streets, looking for anyone who might be a convert. The day after, they went into the western quarter of the outer city and burned down the houses of rich Chinese merchants who'd done business with the Christians.

MacDonald called a council. Both Henry and Trader went.

'The court has just ordered every foreign mission to leave Peking at once,' MacDonald announced. 'I suspect that, knowing the relief force is on its way, Cixi's making a last attempt to get us to leave. Whether we should is another matter. Does anyone have any thoughts?'

'Backhouse came to see me an hour ago,' said Morrison. 'His eunuch friend at the palace told him that the British admiral down at the coast has declared war on the entire Chinese empire, and Cixi's so enraged that she's vowed to throw all the foreign diplomats out for good.'

'Admiral Seymour declared war?' MacDonald cried. 'I don't believe it.'

'You're right. It isn't true. The eunuch told Backhouse that the report was concocted by some of the nobles and eunuchs who want to see us gone. But Cixi believes it.'

'God help us. Where's Backhouse now?'

'Disappeared again. But the story makes sense.' He paused a moment. 'There's one other thing. He says the relief force may be delayed. Quite a lot of Boxers down at the port. Got to get through them first. I don't suppose it'll take long.'

MacDonald went around to the other heads of legation. Most of them suggested playing for time. Finally he turned to Trader. 'You were in the siege of Canton,' he said with a smile. 'Any advice?'

'Just this,' said Trader. 'Once you've got huge crowds out in the street, it doesn't matter who's in charge, they may not be able to control 'em. And whoever leaves the protection of the Legation Quarter will be utterly defenceless. If the Boxers kill us, with or without Cixi's orders, she can always claim that it wasn't her fault. Our only hope is to barricade ourselves in here until the relief force arrives.'

This seemed to strengthen the resolve of the diplomats to wait and see. So that was what they did.

It was the next day that Trader privately intervened in the business of the legations. Not that many people knew it. He asked Henry to gather as many of the missionaries as possible on the tennis court for a prayer meeting. When they were gathered, he discreetly joined them.

Then, asked by Henry to say a few words before they prayed, he spoke simply and to the point. 'If we want to survive this,' he told them, 'we may need more than your prayers. We need your skills. For as far as I can see,' he went on frankly, 'these diplomats can't seem to agree with one another about anything much. And they couldn't organise a beer-fest in a brewery. There's no central organisation in the Legation Quarter, no coordination of medicine, food, supplies, anything. You fellows have all run missions. If you don't take over this place, we'll never get anywhere.'

'The heads of the legations may object,' Henry pointed out.

'I'd give you ten to one against. Because none of them knows what to do.'

'What about the defences, barricades, that sort of thing?' Henry asked, looking around.

'As it happens,' an American Methodist confessed, 'I'm a qualified engineer.'

From then on it was plain sailing. Within hours, effective barricades were up and emergency accommodations allocated. The missionaries had set up a food committee, a laundry, a sheepfold, a yard for the milking cows, and an infirmary staffed with two doctors and five nurses.

Which was just as well since, at four o'clock that day, with a single shot from the back of a Chinese store nearby, the siege of the legations began.

Many things surprised John Trader in the weeks that followed. The first was that they were still alive at all.

They'd prepared their defences pretty well. The big city wall overlooking them was manned, with barricades at each end of their section. If the wall was lost to the enemy, they were finished.

The smaller outlying legations – the Austrians, Belgians and Dutch – were abandoned as too difficult to defend. Even the Americans, nearest to the western barrier on Legation Street, had been brought into the safer British compound. If the American troops were the best marksmen, the Japanese were the most disciplined and reliable, and they were guarding the swollen numbers of converts across the canal in the Fu.

Besides the sniping, there was bombardment from the small Chinese field guns, every day and most of the nights.

The converts in the Fu were pressed into service as general labourers and were kept constantly busy repairing the damage and building new barricades.

The greatest fear was fire. Aside from the fire watch, a chain of fire buckets was kept constantly at the ready, for one never knew when the Boxers would lob another bundle of flaming rags soaked in kerosene over the walls. One terrible night the red-turbaned Boxers set fire to the old Chinese library by the compound's northern wall. 'They've just burned some of their own greatest national treasures in the hope of setting fire to us,' Henry remarked in disgust.

'War and intelligence never march together,' Trader remarked.

For the family, however, there was one welcome relief. With all the hundreds of extra folk crowding into the British compound, dormitory space was at a premium, and they had been sleeping, with many others, on mattresses in the compound's chapel, until Lady MacDonald quietly came up to Emily one day.

'I hate to think of your father having to sleep on the chapel floor at his age,' she said. 'We have one spare room in our house. And if my two daughters share, we'll have two. We wondered if you and your husband would like to use one of them and your father the other. They have beds.'

'I'm sure . . .' Emily began, then hesitated. 'I'll ask Henry right away.'

'Take them,' said Henry when she told him.

'You don't feel it's unfair for us to be getting special treatment?'

'Take them.'

Later, when she informed her father, he was delighted. 'You and Henry have one room,' he said. 'Tom can sleep with me.'

'I'm sure she only offered because you own Drumlomond,' Emily said.

Trader smiled. 'I knew there must be some reason I bought the place.'

A less happy surprise came a few days later. Trader and Henry were just out near the tennis court when they suddenly heard a fusillade of shots coming from the west end of Legation Street, and a few moments later a whooping noise as a little cart, piled high with provisions and driven by a fifteen-year-old boy in a cowboy hat, came bouncing into the compound. As it drew up, the body of one of the converts fell off the back of the cart and lay motionless upon the ground.

Trader recognised the youth in the hat at once. It was young Fargo. Knowing the general store that lay on the Chinese side of the now-vacated American legation was full of good things, he'd secretly commandeered a cart and two Chinese converts, run the gauntlet of sniper fire, and filled up the cart with provisions.

Fargo had been lucky: he returned without a scratch. The two Chinese had not been so fortunate. One was wounded; the other, whose body had fallen off the cart, was dead. He was given a good funeral, as a mark of respect. But Fargo was taken to task only slightly for risking the fellow's life, and his mother was told to keep most of the food. After all, she was an excellent cook; and whenever the family had food, they always shared it.

'What worries me,' Trader remarked to Emily, 'is Tom. He already sees Fargo as an older boy to look up to. But now he idolises him. I'm just afraid that if Fargo starts some other damn fool escapade, Tom might try to join him – or worse, go and do something by himself.'

'Henry will talk to him, severely,' said Emily. 'And perhaps you can talk to Fargo.'

The strange silence began two evenings later. Trader was just watching the sun go down when he noticed that the Boxers' sniper fire, which normally continued through twilight, was petering out. He waited a few minutes. The firing had stopped. The red sun hung, apparently motionless, over the roof tiles of a nearby Chinese gateway as if it, too, was surprised by the eerie silence below. What could it mean? Had a truce been called? Were the Boxers breaking off their siege because the relief force had arrived from the coast?

There was a courtyard near the centre of the compound where a small Chinese bell tower, protected from sniper fire by the surrounding buildings, was being used as an information point. He strolled over to it and found a gaggle of people already gathered there. But no notice had been posted that might explain the silence.

An hour later, still without any explanation, the Chinese started shooting again and went on well into the night.

The next morning Trader, MacDonald and Morrison set up Henry's telescope in the garret at the top of the residence. The room was small, but it had two windows, one looking east across the canal to the Fu, the other looking west. They placed the telescope by the eastern window. 'You go first,' said MacDonald to Trader.

The view was excellent. He could see the faces of the converts down in the Fu and the Japanese guards at their barricades. He tilted the telescope up a little, found the Chinese houses beyond and began to scan their upper windows and roofs. The snipers were concealed, but after a few moments he saw one fire from a window.

He frowned. That was odd. He scanned the roofline, saw another sniper and stepped back. 'All yours,' he said to MacDonald and the *Times* man.

The British envoy searched, glanced at Trader and motioned Morrison to take his turn.

'No red turbans,' said the journalist after a moment. 'Those are imperial troops, not Boxers.'

'That's what we thought,' the other two men confirmed.

The western window provided a view of the Mongol marketplace. Morrison spent two minutes surveying the buildings around the open space. 'Imperial troops,' he stated flatly. 'Not a Boxer in sight.'

'So what do you think it means?' asked the British minister.

'The Boxers have all been pulled back. Whether to rest them or send them south to block our relief force, I couldn't say. But the troops around us are now, indisputably, under the direct control of the Dragon Empress in the Forbidden City.' He grimaced. 'And it would seem that she wants us dead.'

The last days of June were terrible. The sniping had taken its toll on the defending troops. Every evening a few more bodies, wrapped only in sacking for a winding sheet, were given a makeshift burial. But worse were the bodies of the Chinese attackers, who often fell in places where they could not be safely recovered. As the daily temperatures rose to tropical highs, the smell of death pervaded the place.

Then came the rain, in tropical torrents; then thunder and lightning, banging and crashing over the legation as if the Dragon Empress herself had commanded the lightning to destroy the impious intruders and all their works. Henry went over into the Fu to be with the converts for an hour and came back drenched.

'This is harder for them than for us,' he explained to Trader. 'When Cixi's troops hear the thunder, they think the gods are signalling their approval. And the converts may wonder, too.' He smiled wryly. 'Not every conversion is perfect.'

That evening, though the thunderstorm was still raging, the attack on the Legation Quarter began to rise to a new crescendo. From east, west and north, with rifles and cannon, the Chinese troops were pouring in their fire at a tremendous rate. With bullets tearing into the roof and smacking against the walls, the Whiteparishes and Trader came downstairs to the hallway. The MacDonalds were in the drawing room with their girls. Emily and Henry decided not to intrude, but to stay discreetly in the hall.

They'd been there only a few minutes when, despite the great thunderclaps and the accompanying barrage, they became aware of another sound. It was coming from a storeroom behind the hall into which the residence's piano had been put for safety. One had to clamber over packing cases to reach this piano, but it was a formidable instrument, a Bösendorfer, no less, with a big, rich tone. When a young fellow at the German legation had asked MacDonald if he might practise on it, the British envoy, not wanting to be churlish at such a time, told him that he might play it whenever he pleased. And if, in this steaming hot weather, the instrument was a little out of tune, the young German didn't seem to mind.

He had just started to play it now.

Could he have been sleeping in there? Was he unaware of the attack? Was he trying to give himself courage? Or maybe, in all the heat and noise and fear, he was a little out of his mind. Whatever the reason, he was playing 'Ride of the Valkyries'. He thumped it out on the piano, as loudly as he could. In the drawing room, the MacDonalds must have heard it, too. When he was done, he paused, and Trader wondered what he would play next. The answer soon came. He was playing 'Ride of the Valkyries' again.

Just then, a young officer burst in through the front door. 'Where is the minister?' he called.

Before Henry could even direct him, MacDonald strode out of the drawing room. 'Well? What news?'

'The Chinese have been firing into the Fu with a Krupp cannon, sir. Now they're advancing and the Japanese commander can't hold them back. He has a second line of defence, sir, but if he can't hold them there . . .'

'I must go to the Fu,' said Henry.

'Don't go,' said Emily. 'It's too late. Stay with us.'

Henry shook his head. Emily looked beseechingly at MacDonald.

'You can't do any good there, Whiteparish,' MacDonald said firmly. 'Not at the moment. The Japanese commander knows his business. You're to stay here. That's an order,' he added.

'But my converts . . .'

'Later. Not now. Stay with your family, as I'm doing.'

MacDonald glanced at Trader. If the Japanese held their second line, then Henry could comfort the converts later. If the Chinese overran it, there would be nobody left to comfort.

MacDonald turned back to the young officer. 'What about the west side?' he demanded.

'The Chinese are in the Mongol market, sir,' the young officer replied. 'They haven't broken into the legation yet.'

'And the city wall?'

'They're trying to get up there. Our barricades are holding so far.'

'Keep me informed.' MacDonald nodded to the young man, who left. Then he went back into the drawing room.

So the Whiteparish family stood together in the hall, Tom between Henry and Emily, who each had an arm around him, and Trader beside Emily.

Trader wasn't sure how much Tom understood. But his parents did. If any one of the three lines of defence fell – the Mongol market, the Fu, or the high wall overlooking the legations – then it was all over.

He glanced at Emily. Was she carrying the small revolver he'd procured for her? He felt sure she was. He had a Webley service revolver himself. He could see, by the bulge in his pocket, that Tom had his cricket ball. Trader wasn't sure if Henry was carrying a weapon.

Now the noise of firing outside was growing louder than ever. He tried to count the speed of fire. About five rounds a second, he thought. Three hundred or more a minute. That would be twenty thousand bullets an hour. And it wasn't letting up. Surely nothing could withstand an assault like that. They must be about to break in, he thought, any moment. As if to counter the terrible din, the German pianist was playing the Wagnerian tune louder and louder, in a sort of delirium.

Suddenly MacDonald appeared and rushed down the passage to the storeroom door. They heard him shouting furiously, 'Shut up! Shut up!' then slam the door. A moment later he strode back through the hall to the drawing room, throwing up his hands as he went.

And the piano still continued, more wildly and louder than ever.

Trader felt something touching the back of his wrist and glanced down. Emily spoke in a little voice. 'Hold my hand.' So he did, and squeezed it once or twice when the angry roar outside became so deafening that not even 'Ride of the Valkyries' could be heard.

It was after one of these huge outbursts that they noticed the piano had stopped. A minute passed; then MacDonald reappeared, looking a little calmer now.

'Did one of you shoot the pianist, by any chance?' he enquired. They shook their heads. He went down the passage and soon returned. 'He must have gone out the back.' He paused and gazed at Henry, then at

Trader. 'Well,' he said slowly, 'as a military man, I can tell you this, for what it's worth: our friends outside are shooting too high.'

During all the turmoil since his arrival, Trader had failed to realise one thing about his son-in-law. There was no reason, he thought afterwards, why he should have guessed. There had been no sign.

During the terrible night of the storm and the day that followed, the legation compound survived, but only just. Up on the wall, the Chinese had managed to take one of the defenders' positions, but not the other; and having got it, they were pinned against their own barricade and couldn't do much. In the Fu, they had made a big advance. The legation's line of defence was now a barrier stretching diagonally across the open space and enclosing only two-thirds of the total. But it was solidly constructed and expertly manned by the Japanese troops. Moreover, to reach this barricade, the Chinese now had to come across open ground, where they would be subject to withering fire.

It was a few days after the storm that Trader accompanied Henry and Emily on one of their daily visits into the Fu.

It was a shock. He'd realised that the converts must be having a bad time. But he hadn't imagined it was as terrible as this. The place looked and smelled like a shantytown that had been flooded or a camp that had been bombarded. That wasn't surprising. But as they began to move among the occupants, Trader blanched visibly. He couldn't help it.

'I shouldn't have let you come, Father,' Emily said apologetically.

Half the converts seemed to have dysentery. Trader had expected that. More frightening were the cases of smallpox. 'It started a little while ago,' said Henry. 'People are going down with it every day, mostly the children.' But worst of all was the fact that the converts were close to starving.

'What can we do? We've got to feed the people in the legations enough to keep their strength up, especially the troops,' explained Emily. 'That just leaves a few eggs and scraps and musty rice for the converts.' She shook her head. 'The troops expect the converts to repair the defences, but they're so weak. I try to feed them more, if I can find the food. But when I do, they just take it and give it to their families. That's why they all look like skeletons, and I feel so guilty.'

They spent nearly half an hour in the Fu. Trader saw all kinds of good people, Catholic priests and nuns, Presbyterian ministers and Anglicans, each attending patiently to their own flock. But no one had any food to give. Henry and Emily selected four of their converts for a visit to the infirmary, and then they all trooped back together. As they left the Fu, a sniper sent a bullet over their heads, just to remind them who was boss.

It was after Emily had gone with the converts to the infirmary that Henry turned to Trader and asked if they might have a private word.

They found a protected corner of the garden where there was a bench by some trees, and they sat down. Henry was silent for a moment or two. Then he asked, 'Can I tell you something in confidence?'

'I should think so.'

'I don't want you to tell Emily.'

'All right,' said Trader. 'As long as it isn't something I feel I have to tell her.'

'It isn't.' Again Henry hesitated. 'It helps to talk sometimes,' he said.

'Talk away.'

'It's funny, you know, my father always warned me it was an occupational hazard for missionaries. But it never happened to me. Not in all these years.' He paused. 'I suppose,' he went on, 'I thought it would be an agonising thing. You know, a dark night of the soul.'

'What would be?'

'Oh. Sorry. To lose my faith.'

'Ah. Well, I've heard of that, of course. What brought it on?'

'It may have been brewing for some time. I'm not sure. But it's been this last month. The converts in the Fu.'

'It's enough to shake anybody up. I was pretty shaken myself, to tell you the truth.'

'Yes, but don't you see, it's my fault. I look at these poor people, starving, their children dying, and I think to myself, It's my fault you're here. If I hadn't converted you, the Boxers wouldn't be trying to kill you.'

'Christians have suffered persecution down the ages.'

'Yes, but these wretched Chinese didn't take up the cross to be martyred. They just believed all the good things I told them. Now the bullets are flying, they're probably going to die, and it's my fault.'

'You've brought them to Christ. Saved their souls, perhaps.'

'That's what I'm supposed to feel.'

'And what do you feel?'

'Nothing. I feel nothing. Just an awful blankness.'

'As I understand it, the point is to have faith.'

'That's right. And it's gone, flown away, vanished over the horizon.'

'I'm no theologian, but isn't this the dilemma they call the problem of evil? That's to say, if God is loving and all-powerful, then why would He create a world that is so full of cruelty and pain? Why do bad people triumph while good people are destroyed?'

'That's right. And religion has many ways of explaining the conundrum. God is testing us. God has a purpose we do not know. There are other arguments. But suddenly I found I didn't believe any of them. They all seemed a lot of nonsense.'

'Christianity preaches kindness to others. That can't be bad.'

'It's good. The Sermon on the Mount is wonderful. I could have come to China to be a doctor, for instance, or to help the poor, and done no harm at all.'

'You know,' said Trader thoughtfully, 'years ago I was at a dinner party in London, and there was a Jesuit priest there. And when we were sitting with the port, we got onto the subject of saints, and canonising new ones. And someone asked him whether there had ever been a case of a candidate for beatification who was discovered to have lost their faith. And he told us something that surprised us all. "As a matter of fact," he said, "that would strengthen their case. Loss of faith can be a part, a very testing part, of the spiritual journey." And I remember thinking afterwards that although I'm not a Catholic myself, one can't deny that the Catholic Church knows a lot about the secrets of the human heart.'

'You're trying to comfort me, and it's very good of you,' Henry replied. 'I'm sorry that I've brought your daughter into all this.'

'Nonsense. She chose it. Stop blaming yourself for everything.' Trader smiled at him kindly. 'I can tell you one thing, though, if it's any help: something I've been thinking in the last couple of days. I believe there's some kind of influence at work that's protecting us. Now whether it's the hand of God or something more mundane, I can't begin to guess. But something's keeping us alive.'

'How do you mean?' asked Henry.

'The Chinese could have taken the legations the other night. But they didn't. Something's holding them back.'

'You don't think the Dragon Empress wants to destroy us?'

'My guess is that she does. But maybe there are two factions at court. Something like that. Her orders are being obeyed, but not completely followed through on. Personally, although I can't prove it, I like to think that the hand of God is operating through those people. And you might find comfort in that thought. But whatever is holding them back, it's only got to do so long enough for the relief force to reach us. So even if you've lost your faith at this moment, there's a good reason to carry on regardless and hang on.'

'I shall,' Henry promised. 'You're the only one I could share this with, you know.'

'I know,' said Trader.

It was early that evening that he received supporting evidence for his theory about the Chinese attacks. He'd just gone over to the bell tower to scan the notices when he encountered Morrison.

'I saw our friend Backhouse today,' the *Times* man said. 'I'd gone up to the barrier by the old library that burned down. Thought I'd just check that the Chinese weren't trying to sneak in that way again. No sign of any Chinese, but I could hear someone rummaging about in there. It turned out to be Backhouse. He's been hiding out somewhere in the city – God knows how he does it – and he'd come to see if there were any books he could salvage.'

'Did he have news of what's going on out there?'

'He did. The Catholics are holding out in their cathedral, but there have been some awful massacres. Our relief force is on the way, but it's still got to break through some big lines of Boxers. We'll have to wait. I've told MacDonald, but he's unwilling to announce the news. Bad for morale. And in any case, he doesn't trust the source.'

'He's probably right on both counts.'

'Agreed. But Backhouse did say some things that make sense. He says the Chinese court is split. Cixi's party wants to wipe us out and close the city to foreigners once and for all. The other party fears retribution from our governments. Our own telegraph's cut off, but the court's getting threatening cables from Western capitals now.'

'So, two parties in the Forbidden City. I was wondering about that.'

'It goes further. Cixi sent messages to her provincial governors demanding troops.'

'And?'

'Deafening silence. They're ignoring her. She's furious, but there isn't a lot she can do.'

'Interesting. Let's hope,' said Trader, 'that for once Backhouse is telling the truth.'

Emily had always known her father was a good man. And the sweltering first half of July saw Trader at his best. Each day he maintained a calm routine. In the morning, dressed in a long linen jacket with big patch pockets, he'd usually spend time with Tom. They'd take a little light exercise, after which he'd turn his grandson over to young Fargo, who'd run about with him and engage in some fielding practice.

In the afternoon, sitting in a wicker chair, he'd draw a book from one of his big pockets and read to the two boys and anyone else who cared to join them. It might be a humourous tale by Mark Twain, or a Sherlock Holmes mystery, or a funny scene from his old favourite, *The Pickwick Papers* – something to take their minds off the uncomfortable facts of the siege for an hour or two. After the evening meal, when it was a little cooler, and if the firing had died down, he'd walk with her, and they'd talk about family or times past or places far away.

He seemed to have a good effect on Henry, too. Of course, Henry had always been steady as a rock. But she thought he'd been a little strange lately. It was hardly surprising, with all the stress he was under. One moment he'd seem tense – too tense for her even to be able to comfort him at night – but a few hours later she might come upon her husband humming to himself, which was a thing he'd never done before. With her father, however, Henry always became calm and quiet, like his old self again.

The British minister might be under siege, but he still kept up his social obligations. So Emily wasn't surprised when Lady MacDonald informed her: 'We haven't forgotten about giving a dinner in your father's honour. Would the day after tomorrow suit, do you think?'

The day of the dinner got off to a bad start. The Chinese began firing a Krupp gun directly at the roof of the MacDonald residence to see if they could bring down the flag flying over it. Emily had wondered if the dinner would take place, but her father reassured her: 'The gunners are just bored, my dear. They'll give it up long before sundown.' Which indeed they did.

Then came a visit from Lady MacDonald. 'I was just wondering, my dear, what your father would be wearing. The Italian minister always wears full evening dress, and so can my husband. But with all this going on, some of the men may not be able to. As your father is the guest of honour, I thought I'd better find out what he'd be doing.'

'White tie, unless he's told not to.'

'Oh, good. And you and your husband?'

'Long dress for me. Henry likes to wear an old black frock coat – it's quite presentable – and a clerical collar.'

'Yes, there are two other clergymen coming. I'm sure they'll do something similar. Dressing for dinner's so easy for clergymen, isn't it?' She smiled. 'Perhaps Henry will be a bishop one day. I do so like those violet clerical shirts they wear, don't you?'

'I happen to know that Father has worn white tie only once since he came,' Emily informed her, 'so his shirt will be all starched and ironed, just as it was when he unpacked his trunk.'

Lady MacDonald's eyes opened wide. The little laundry they'd set up in the legation was doing a wonderful job keeping everyone's shirts clean, but there were no facilities for ironing them. A starched shirt had become a rarity indeed. 'I am so looking forward to this,' she declared.

And that evening her father played his part perfectly. None of the men looked so handsome. And although the Italian minister was wearing white tie and all his medals, Trader allowed his one eye to rest upon the diplomat's unpressed shirt just long enough to cause the MacDonalds much amusement.

It had to be said, the British legation did things with style. They dined twenty people. The table was beautifully set, for the legation had still preserved its handsome dinner service, glass, and all the rest.

As for the food . . . it represented everything that ingenuity could contrive.

They began with soup, made with vegetable extract; then fish paste on toast, curried sparrows and rissoles. The main course was meat, and this was eaten with solemnity, for it was, after all, one of the precious racing ponies, of which there were only a few left. It was accompanied by tinned peas and potatoes – all washed down, of course, with excellent claret.

It was at this point that MacDonald himself, who had been suffering from dysentery, was obliged to leave the party.

But the rest of them carried on, and Trader had just asked Lady MacDonald what was coming next, and she had said, 'I hope you like pancakes,' and he had just replied, 'I do, very much,' when a Chinese explosive shell burst into the house somewhere over their heads, and there was a great bang, and the entire ceiling seemed to give way over their heads. As plaster rained down, those who could dived under the table – though Lady MacDonald, who was sitting in a tall wooden chair with arms, and Trader, who was a little too old to move so fast, remained in their places. For a moment, after the dust had settled, there was silence. Then, with a sound of scraping chairs, people reappeared and started dusting themselves off. Fortunately, it seemed, nobody in the dining room had been much hurt. But the table looked like the aftermath of a battle, a long field of broken plates and glasses.

In the doorway, the pale face of Sir Claude MacDonald appeared. Young Tom was beside him.

'Are there any casualties upstairs?' his wife enquired.

'Nobody there except myself and young Tom here. Our girls are in the downstairs sitting room. They're all right. No damage in the kitchens.' The minister indicated his empty chair and told Tom to sit in it. 'I'm going back to bed,' he announced.

'This is most unfortunate,' said Lady MacDonald calmly. And she rang the bell for the servants, who were mostly Catholic converts that night, to clear the table.

While they were at work, she turned to Trader. 'What do you think we should do now?' she asked.

'Have you more glasses, back there?' Trader indicated the butler's pantry.

'Certainly.'

'In that case, Lady MacDonald,' he said, 'I think this calls for a bumper of champagne!'

Later, as they were retiring, Lady MacDonald took Emily to one side. 'You know, my dear,' she said, 'if I hadn't met my husband, then I'd like to have married your father.' She smiled. 'I do like a man who knows how to behave.'

But the hot days dragged on, and there was still no news of the relief force. Each day the Chinese snipers seemed to be improving their aim. British, French, German, Japanese troops: their numbers were gradually dwindling. Emily wondered how long things could go on.

She discovered one evening.

There were two kinds of sewing inside the besieged legations. The first was making sandbags for the walls and barricades. The women used whatever cloth they could get their hands on – sacking, old shirts, pantaloons – anything that could be fashioned into a small sack the size of a pillowcase, filled with earth, and sewn up with tough thread. In the rain, these makeshift sandbags tended to leak a grey sludge onto the ground; and they often burst. A fresh supply was always needed, and Emily would often help the women make them.

There was another, grimmer kind of sewing to be done, however: the winding sheets in which the bodies must be buried. There were no coffins, just winding sheets, which were often made in a hurry, using whatever material there was to hand. Since the burials were carried out after dark, when it was cooler, the shortcomings of the winding sheets weren't so visible.

There had been two men to bury that night. She and Henry attended at the makeshift grave. One was a small fellow, neatly enclosed in his shroud, which made her think of the sandbags of earth she'd been making. But the other man was tall, and the winding sheet she'd made was too short, and his bare feet stuck out in such an ungainly way. And try as she might, she kept thinking of her father, wondering if she would soon be burying him, and what she could do to cover his feet if the shroud was too short, and it made her want to cry.

When they got back, she went to make sure that Tom was asleep. And she had just come from Tom's room onto the upstairs landing when she heard her father speaking in a low voice in the hall below.

'How long do you give it?'

It was MacDonald who answered. 'At the present rate of attrition, there won't be any troops left by the end of the month.'

'And ammunition?'

'About the same. End of the month.'

'Well, that still leaves the relief force a bit of time. By the way,' her father went on, 'I heard something underground by the French legation this afternoon. Thought I'd better mention it.'

'You think the Chinese are digging mines?'

'Wouldn't surprise me.'

'Nor me. Goodnight.'

Emily tiptoed quickly to her room. She wondered whether to tell Henry. Not now, anyway. He seemed to be asleep. But then he opened one eye.

'What's the matter?' he asked.

'Nothing,' she said, hoping he'd go to sleep again.

'Emily.' He sat up. 'Please tell me.'

So she did. 'We can only pray,' she said when she'd finished.

'God will not desert us.' He said it with such a sweet smile. 'And one thing I know for certain,' he added firmly. 'The only thing that really matters is that God's will be done.'

That comforted her a little. At least she supposed it did.

Trader had prepared his family for what was to come. 'The relief force is on the way,' he told them. 'The closer they get, the more desperate Cixi will be to kick us out. Her hope will be that if we've departed or been killed, she can close the city gates and tell the relief force that there's nobody left to rescue. I'm saying this,' Trader continued, 'so that when the next big attack comes, you'll understand clearly what it means. It'll be desperate – their last attempt to dislodge us before the siege is lifted. If we can just hold out, the relief will arrive, and we'll all be saved – including the converts, God willing.'

Ten days passed, the Chinese edged a little closer, the sniper fire went back and forth, and from time to time they could hear the faint sound of picks and shovels in the tunnels underground. Although they had no definite news, Trader felt sure the relief force could not be far away.

So when, at dawn on Friday the thirteenth of July, a huge bombardment began, he told Emily: 'This is it. We're almost home. One last stand, and our boys will come through.'

All day the Krupp guns rained shells upon the Fu. Around the converts, the low buildings with their tiled roofs were catching fire and collapsing in upon themselves. To the south, the positions on the city wall were just holding. To the north, the Chinese were trying to break into the British compound through the ruined library.

At four in the afternoon, the bell in the little tower where the message boards were began to ring wildly – the signal that the legations were under general attack on every side, and that everyone must defend themselves as best they could.

Despite Emily's begging him not to, Henry had gone to the Fu. She and her father were standing with Tom in the hall of the MacDonald residence. Lady MacDonald and her daughters were in the back parlour inside. Trader had his Webley revolver in his hand. He glanced at Emily. She nodded and drew out the little pistol he'd got for her.

'You've got six shots. Use the first five of them,' he said quietly. He looked down at his grandson. 'Don't you worry, boy,' he said. 'They won't get this far, but if any of them do, we'll deal with 'em.' Tom was pale, both frightened and excited by the look of it, but facing forward bravely. 'Good lad,' said Trader approvingly. 'Well done.'

And now they heard a new sound. A chant taken up by a thousand throats, seemingly all around them.

'*Sha!*' Kill. '*Sha! Sha! Sha!*'

There were roars of Krupp guns and small cannon, fusillades, screams. God knows how many men were fighting – hand to hand, by the sound of it. A German soldier rushed in, calling for MacDonald.

'Out by the bell tower,' shouted Trader, and the German disappeared.

The terrible racket continued. They could hear bullets banging and rattling on the roof above. The chanting seemed to be getting louder. Was it closer? Hard to tell.

MacDonald appeared.

'Did the German find you?' Trader called.

'Yes. The Russians are helping them. They're holding the line.' He went down the passage to check on his family, then emerged again. 'The Japanese in the Fu have a new line of defence. They've halted the Chinese advance for the moment.'

'My husband?' asked Emily.

'Don't know. Can't say. But there's a new attack coming just south of the Fu. Through the French legation.'

He hurried out. Minutes passed.

Then came the thunderclap. The ground under their feet shook. And moments later, as though a tornado had just passed, objects began falling from the sky. Bits of masonry were crashing onto rooftops. Other things, softer things, were falling, too, with bangs and bumps and thuds. And as they rushed to the doorway they saw a thick, dirty cloud peppered with red cinders rising like some demonic spirit over the Fu and heard screams, terrible screams.

'It's a mine,' said Trader. Was it under the Fu? Close to it? He couldn't be sure. Was this the final moment? Were the Chinese about to come streaming in? 'Back indoors,' he ordered Tom and Emily. God knew if Henry was still alive. 'Back indoors.'

So they waited in the hallway. They waited and listened for the shouts of '*Sha! Sha!*' from the approaching Chinese troops.

But no shouts came. Indeed, as the minutes passed, the firing seemed to falter. And soon after that, to their astonishment, the figure of Henry appeared – his face sooty, his clothes covered with grime, but still recognisably Henry and very much alive.

'Did you hear the mine go off?' he asked them.

'Of course we did,' cried Emily. 'I thought you were dead.'

'That's why I came back. To let you know.'

'Are the Chinese coming?' Trader demanded.

'I don't think so. They blew themselves to bits with their own mine. There's a huge crater where the French legation was. The Chinese were advancing. I suppose they knew the mine was going off, but didn't understand the power of the thing. It must have killed scores of them. Anyway, they've pulled back.'

'I bet that wasn't the only mine,' said Trader. 'They probably planned to let off several. Now they're wondering what to do.'

As the hours passed, this seemed to be the case. MacDonald came in and confirmed: 'Assault's paused on all fronts.' Henry went back to comfort the converts in the Fu. Emily took Tom upstairs and put him to bed.

Trader poured himself a glass of brandy, went out onto the veranda that overlooked the garden, sat down in a wicker armchair and gazed at the lawn bathed in the pale moonlight. Even the sniping had ceased. Only the faint crackling of fires from around the smoking crater broke the silence.

He'd been sitting there for a little while when he became aware of Emily, in a pale gown, coming towards him. She also had a glass of brandy. He rose and offered her his chair, but she shook her head.

'You sit in the chair, Father. I'd rather sit on the stool beside you. It's quite comfortable.'

'Is Tom asleep?'

'Yes. I think all the excitement wore him out.'

'Henry's not back?'

'No. Which makes it rather a good moment to talk to you.' She paused and he waited. 'Do you remember,' she went on after a moment, 'when we thought they were about to break in, you told me I had six rounds and to use five of them on the enemy?'

'I do.'

'That would have left me with one shot to use on myself.'

'I'd assumed that's what you wanted the pistol for.'

'It was. But I realised this evening that I could only fire four shots at the enemy. I needed another two, you see.'

'Two?'

'One for Tom, one for me.' She looked up at him sadly. 'What do you think they'd do to him? Bayonet him, at best. Isn't that right?'

'I don't know.' He didn't want to think about it.

'Well, I do. So I needed two bullets. But that's the problem. I realised I couldn't trust myself. I knew I should do it, but I didn't think I could. I was just so afraid I'd hesitate, and then it might have been too late.'

'Well, thank God there was no need. It's all over now.'

'What about the next time?'

'There won't be a next time.'

'There might.' She sighed. 'If there is, I'm awfully sorry, but you'll have to do it.'

'You're asking me to shoot my grandson?' He looked at her in horror. 'Talk to your husband, Emily, not to me.'

'Henry's man enough to do it, but I'm afraid he might refuse. His faith might prevent him, you see.'

'His faith?'

'Henry's faith is very strong, you know.'

Trader said nothing.

'Will you promise me?'

Trader paused. He thought of Tom. He thought of the bayonets.

'I might be killed first,' he pointed out.

'Please don't be,' she said.

'Cixi wants a truce,' said MacDonald the next day. 'We've had a message from the Tsungli Yamen: all a misunderstanding. My eye. Cixi herself sends her regrets.'

'She's got the wind up,' said Trader. 'Was it the mine blowing them up, or is there something more behind it?'

'I've just heard that the relief force has broken through and is already on its way up the canal. Eleven thousand men. She probably knew last night.'

'That was the last try, then, as I thought.'

'Probably,' said MacDonald. 'Let's hope they get here soon.'

It felt strange to walk about the legation again without having to duck one's head and watch for sniper fire. On the second day of the truce, Trader even went up on the wall. He watched some Chinese collecting their dead from outside the legation barricades. Looking across the quarter towards the Imperial City, he could see into the open square of the Mongol market on the western side of the British legation. To his amazement, there were already a few stalls there selling food again. He saw an old Chinese fellow, a crate of eggs on his back, making his way across the market to the British barricade. Turning to look east across the canal to the Fu, he caught sight of Emily moving amongst the converts there.

He was on his way down from the wall when he tripped. He wasn't hurt. Nothing to worry about. But to be sensible, he went over to the infirmary.

The infirmary was quite impressive. It had been enlarged to include a couple of old storerooms. There were two doctors, aided during the emergency by several women nurses, two of whom were fully qualified doctors themselves – a higher level of care, Henry had pointed out, than one could ever get under normal conditions. The two doctor-nurses had checked him thoroughly, diagnosed a bad sprain and let him go. They'd given him a crutch and told him to use it. But he'd soon exchanged this for a silver-topped ebony stick that MacDonald lent him and that he thought looked better.

'I'm so glad, Father,' said Emily with a smile, 'that you haven't lost your vanity.'

The truce seemed to be holding in the days that followed. There were occasional shots fired at the Catholic cathedral in the distance, but nothing more.

And it was one day at this time that, awaking from an afternoon siesta on the veranda, Trader found himself looking into the face of his grandson Tom.

'Are you asleep, Grandfather?' Tom said.

'Not anymore.'

'Can I ask you a question?'

'Fire away.'

'Fargo says that all this trouble with the Chinese is our fault because we sold them opium, which makes people sick. Is that true?'

'Well . . .' Trader hesitated. 'It wasn't as simple as that. They had their own opium, you know. But it's true they bought quite a bit of opium from us. Trouble was, we wanted to sell them all sorts of things – cotton goods, manufactured things – but the only thing the Chinese people wanted was opium.'

'Is opium bad for you?'

'It's like a lot of things, I suppose. It's a medicine, actually. And people here liked to smoke a bit, the same way we might take a glass of brandy. But if you smoke too much, then you can get a craving for it and that can make you sick. Same with drinking brandy, come to that.' He nodded wisely. 'Moderation in all things, Tom. Moderation. That's the secret of life.'

'Mother says that the Chinese kept everybody out, including the missionaries, and that they'd still like to.'

'That's true as well. Sometimes a country can keep itself cut off from the outside world for centuries. But then one day the world will come knocking at the door, and something has to change. That's what happened with Japan. There was no opium involved there at all.'

'So it was the Chinese who were in the wrong then, and we were in the right?'

'I wouldn't put it that way. In practice, you'll find as you go through life, it's really all about how you manage things.'

'Oh.' Tom looked a bit doubtful. Then a new idea seemed to strike him. 'Grandfather.'

'Yes.'

'If you had your life again, would you go to China and sell opium?'

Trader was silent. He thought about Canton and then Macao, but not for long. Then his mind went back to Calcutta.

'I daresay,' he said, 'I'd have stayed in India.' He nodded slowly, then smiled at his grandson. 'That's where I met your dear grandmother, you know,' he added. The statement was perfectly true, in its way.

'So if you'd stayed in India, what would you have done?'

'I expect I'd have been dealing in tea. That's the business I'd be in nowadays. My son, your uncle, is in that business, as a matter of fact. Indian tea. But there wasn't any then, you see.'

'If you hadn't sold opium, would anybody else have?'

'Oh, some people would have. No doubt about that.' Trader paused.

'It's all a question of time, you see,' he offered. 'It's a question of what you can do, and what you can't do, and when you can do it.' The boy still looked puzzled. 'Now,' said Trader, 'you come along with me.'

He got up, not without discomfort, and made his way stiffly across the lawn. Taking his ebony stick, he pushed the ferrule into the turf so that the stick stood upright. 'We'll say that's the wicket,' he said. 'I want you to throw the ball so that it bounces once and passes just over the top of the stick.'

And for half an hour he watched as Tom threw the ball – which he did with remarkable accuracy – went and picked it up, then threw it again and again, which was good exercise for the boy, and stopped him from asking any more questions.

As July merged into August, the days passed slowly. For Trader, it was a strange, almost unreal time.

The truce held, but it seemed uneasy. Everybody repaired their defences. He noticed, however, that on the eastern side of the legation, beyond the Fu, the Chinese soldiers patched up their barricades without much conviction; whereas on the western side, beyond the Mongol market, the imperial soldiers were busy strengthening their redoubts as though they expected fighting to break out any day, and their surly looks suggested that they'd be glad if it did.

Did this reflect the two different factions within the Forbidden City? Perhaps.

They had definite news of the relief force now. It was making its way up the canal towards the city. But the soldiers brought cannon, and they were short of boats, so the going was slow. All the same, they'd be there in a week, ten days at most.

The main problem was food. The Tsungli Yamen might send baskets of fruit, small traders came across the open ground with eggs and chickens; but supplies of basic food inside the legations were beginning to dwindle.

'We've just got to keep body and soul together until they arrive,' Emily remarked.

Because they were bored, people were starting to take a few potshots across the barriers. Nothing too much, Trader thought.

It was a sunny morning in August when he and Tom decided to go for a walk together. 'We'll make an inspection of the defences,' he told Emily with a smile.

'Be careful,' she warned.

'Of course we will,' he answered.

Trader was feeling rather pleased with himself that day. Though he was still walking with the ebony cane, his leg seemed to be better. He could almost put his full weight on it. As they set off, he noticed with amusement that, as usual, his grandson had his cricket ball in his pocket. 'We won't be playing any cricket, you know,' he remarked. But when this failed to elicit any response, he smiled indulgently, told himself it really didn't matter anyway, and led the way towards their first objective.

He took care as he mounted the stone steps up to the broad parapet of the city wall. He didn't want to trip and fall as he had so recently before. But he made it easily enough; and if he winced once or twice, Tom didn't see.

They admired the views for a few minutes. After that, they made their way back into the British legation and walked through the grounds until they reached the northern end. The wall between the legation and the burned-out Chinese library had been thickly reinforced from the legation side since the truce began. 'They'll have a job to get through that,' Trader remarked, 'if they try again.'

Indeed, the space they were standing in had almost become like a peaceful walled garden, he thought, and they were just about to move on when Tom pulled at his sleeve. 'Grandfather,' he whispered, 'did you hear that?'

'What?' For a man of his age Trader had good hearing, but he had to confess: 'I didn't hear a thing.'

Tom stood still, concentrating, while his grandfather waited. 'It's very faint. It's underground. Like scraping.'

'Are you sure?'

'Yes.' Tom nodded.

'Damn,' said Trader. 'They must be mining. So much for the truce.'

'Should we report it, Grandfather?'

'Absolutely. I'll tell MacDonald as soon as we get back.'

And they might have gone straight to the residence except that, as they returned along the western wall of the legation, they met a soldier carrying a small chicken.

'Where did you get that?' Trader enquired.

'The Mongol market. There's a few stalls open today.'

'Oh, Grandfather, let's get something for Mother,' cried Tom.

'I don't know,' Trader replied. 'We're not supposed to do that. The food committee's asked everyone to pool their food until the siege is over.'

'Maybe just some eggs?' suggested Tom.

Trader said nothing. But they went to the little alley that gave access to the Mongol market and looked in.

There were only half a dozen stalls clustered in the middle of the little square. The broad, weather-beaten faces of the Mongol traders looked strangely incurious, as if to say: 'We belong to the steppe. Your quarrels have nothing to do with us.' They appeared to be selling eggs, chickens, sweetmeats of some kind, nothing very appetising. But it was food.

Trader's eyes searched the low buildings on the far side of the market. Could there be snipers hidden there? The man with the chicken hadn't mentioned any trouble. Trader just wished there were some other people in the place.

An old Mongol woman caught sight of them. Picking up a basket, she came across, tilting the basket to show them the eggs it contained. She stopped a few feet away and indicated that, if they would follow her, she could show them other, better things. Back at the stall a middle-aged man, her son perhaps, held up a scrawny chicken by its neck, while it feebly flapped its wings. He beckoned, and the old woman motioned to them to walk beside her, as though she could provide a safe conduct to the stall.

Tom looked up eagerly. 'Can't we go, Grandfather?' he begged.

'I suppose so,' Trader muttered.

So they made their way across the empty marketplace and reached the stall. They looked at the scrawny chickens and the other goods on offer.

The Mongol was inspecting Trader with interest. It seemed he had correctly concluded that this tall figure with his ebony cane and black eye patch must be a rich man. For suddenly he seized the basket of eggs, stuffed three live chickens into an open wooden box, and presented them to Trader with a simple word: 'Yuan.'

'Yuan? You want a yuan for this?' Trader exclaimed in astonishment. Then he laughed. In its most recent efforts to strengthen its economy, the Chinese government had issued this new and valuable silver coin. Trader held up the fingers of one hand. 'Five fen,' he said. Five cents. A twentieth of a yuan. And a good price at that, even in wartime.

The Mongol looked disappointed, offered half a dozen eggs instead, and indicated this was what five fen would buy. Trader shook his head and pointed to a chicken that would need to be added. He gave Tom a quick glance as though to say: observe the gentle art of bargaining. The Mongol considered. But whether he would have accepted the offer they never discovered. For suddenly he stared over Tom's head at something behind the boy. And Trader turned.

The man was dressed in red. A Boxer, obviously. He was crouched in a kung fu tiger stance, with a light jian sword in his hand, and he had positioned himself directly between Trader and the alley through which they'd entered the market, so that there was no escape.

Where the devil had he sprung from? He must have slipped over one of the barriers. And how did he come to be in that part of the city at all? The Boxers had all been withdrawn.

Maintaining his crouch, the Boxer began to come closer. Trader shot a glance back at the Mongols, but they were watching impassively. Clearly they weren't going to interfere.

There was only one thing to do. Keeping his eyes on the Boxer, he called softly to Tom. 'Stay behind me until I give the word. The moment I do, run for the alley. You understand? Don't ask any questions. Do exactly as I say. All right?'

'Yes, Grandfather.'

'Good.' Trader began to move slowly towards the Boxer, raising his ebony stick as he did so. It had been a long time since he'd done any fencing, but he should be able to keep the fellow occupied for a few moments. Long enough for the boy to escape. And if he was going to die, as he supposed he probably was, it wouldn't be such a bad way to go.

Of course, he might be lucky. If he could just poke the point of his stick into the fellow's eye, he and Tom might both get away. 'So, my red friend,' he muttered, 'let's find out how good a swordsman you are.'

He was en garde now, edging forward, the point of his stick up, always on target. 'Get ready, boy,' he called to Tom. Then he made a feint.

The Boxer was deceived, swung at the stick that was not there, left himself open, and quick as a flash, Trader lunged.

Except that he did not. He'd overestimated the strength of his leg. The ankle gave way, his leg collapsed, and before he even knew what was happening, he fell facedown. Looking up helplessly, he saw the Boxer smile and raise his sword.

'Run, Tom,' he shouted. 'Run for your life!' He couldn't see the boy, but he tried to swing at the Boxer's ankles with his stick, just to keep him in place while Tom got away. He tensed, knowing the Boxer's sword was coming. Would it be a thrust or slash?

And then, to his astonishment, he heard a crack like a pistol shot. The Boxer's body jerked violently, fell backwards, and crashed to the ground like a man knocked clean unconscious.

Turning his head, he saw young Tom, with a look of triumph, already at his side and trying to help him up. 'What happened?' he mumbled.

'I got him with my cricket ball,' Tom cried. 'Right between the eyes!'

'By Jove, so you did.' Trader was up on one knee now. He could see that the unconscious man's sword was lying on the ground beside him. The Boxer emitted a low groan. 'Grab his sword, Tom, quick, before he comes round!' he ordered.

Tom did so and brandished the sword in his hand. The Boxer was dazed, but coming to, struggling to get up.

'Shall I kill him, Grandfather?' Tom cried eagerly. 'I can chop his head. Easy.' He was beside himself with excitement.

'Not now. Keep the sword and help me up.'

A moment later, with one arm around Tom's shoulders, he was hobbling towards the alley. The Boxer had managed to stand up groggily, but then fallen down again. They got to the alley and made their escape.

'I wish you'd let me kill him, Grandfather,' said Tom.

'I know, my boy,' said Trader. 'But your mother wouldn't have liked it.'

They were safely inside the legation and making their way towards the residence when Tom suddenly let out a schoolboy curse.

'What's the matter?' asked his grandfather.

'I left my cricket ball in the market. Can I go back for it?'

'No,' said Trader. 'I'm afraid you cannot.'

When they reached the residence, they found both Emily and Henry at home. Their story was quickly told. Though delighted to have them both back alive, Emily looked at her father a little reproachfully.

'What were you doing in the Mongol market?' she wanted to know.

'We were buying chicken and eggs,' said Tom. 'For you.'

'I see,' said Emily, staring at him. 'Well, I'm glad you're safe.'

'I shouldn't have gone in there,' Trader said with shame. 'And Tom saved my life by throwing that cricket ball in his face.'

'He's got a powerful throw,' said Henry.

'Yes.' Trader nodded slowly. 'Runs in our family.'

'Does it?' said Emily.

'I threw something at somebody once. Old story from long ago. I'll tell you some other time.'

'Well, I'm very proud of you, Tom, for saving your grandfather's life,' said Henry firmly.

Tom beamed. 'Before that, we were up by the old Chinese library wall,' he went on. 'And we heard something Grandfather says we have to tell Sir Claude right away.'

As he was speaking, there was a tap at the door and the head of that worthy gentleman himself appeared. 'Is my name being taken in vain?' MacDonald enquired with a smile.

'We heard something you should know about,' said Trader. 'At least I didn't hear it, but young Tom here's got sharper ears. Tell Sir Claude what you heard, Tom.'

So Tom described the scraping sound underground, and MacDonald nodded and said it probably meant the Chinese were mining again, and Trader said he'd thought so, too.

'Well done,' said MacDonald to Tom. 'By the way, the reason I came to your quarters was because a certain item has just been thrown over the legation wall from the Mongol market. I had a feeling it might be yours.' And to the boy's delight, the minister handed him his cricket ball. 'Very sporting of those Mongols, I must say,' MacDonald remarked. 'Perhaps we should teach them to play cricket.'

The next morning MacDonald met Trader by the front door. 'I've got three men up by the old Chinese library. Also one of the infirmary doctors laid a sounding board on the ground and is listening with a stethoscope. Rather ingenious, I thought.

'I've a favour to ask now,' the minister went on briskly. 'I need to borrow Henry's telescope. Something's come up.'

He returned at noon, looking serious. 'You were right. They're mining under the old library. Now we're trying to find out where else they may be burrowing. But there's another piece of news. Not good. I've been up on the wall with Henry's telescope. Troops with new banners have arrived in Peking. I could see them clearly. So it seems that one of the governors, at least, has answered Cixi's call for extra troops. But there's more. The Boxers are back as well. A lot of them.'

'That's why that damned fellow showed up in the Mongol market then,' said Trader.

'Evidently. The latest report is that our own relief force is about five days away. But frankly, I've given up placing any reliance on these messages. I suppose Cixi must know where they are, but I don't. So the question is, will the moderates in the Forbidden City or the militants prevail? If the latter, we have to expect another big attack any day.'

What irony, Trader thought. If all the efforts that had been made, the fighting, the hunger, the sickness and sacrifice – his own poor attempts to bolster Henry's faith, young Tom's saving his own life – if all these things had been for nothing. The relief force would arrive only to find that every soul in the legations – soldiers, women, children, and converts alike – had all been slaughtered, every one, perhaps only hours before they got there.

He didn't share his thought, of course. No point in doing that. He hobbled about trying to look cheerful and thought he'd succeeded pretty well until Emily came up to him one day, put her arm through his, and said, 'Poor Father. You look so sad.'

'No,' he assured her. 'Just this damned leg giving me a bit of gyp, that's all.'

She squeezed his arm, though whether she believed him was another matter.

A week passed. People didn't want to discuss the threat from the Chinese bannermen and the Boxers. They preferred to share whatever news came through about the approach of the relief force. And one might indeed draw comfort from the fact that each day that passed without a major assault meant that there was less and less time in which it could be attempted.

But the mining continued. The sniping grew more insistent each day so that the truce, for all practical purposes, no longer existed.

As for Trader, he counted each night and each day, just like everyone else, but with this one difference: his promise to Emily about Tom.

If only Emily hadn't been right. That was the trouble. He could imagine those Boxers with their jian swords and the imperial troops with their bayonets. He knew what they'd do to Tom. Of course the boy should be saved from that.

But he couldn't do it. The thought haunted him. The boy's even saved my life, he thought, yet I haven't the guts to grant him a merciful death. He told himself he must. But he feared in his heart that he might fail him. He prayed to God that the relief column would come quickly.

Once when he was reading an adventure story to Tom in the afternoon, his voice almost broke and he couldn't go on. And Tom was concerned and puzzled until he explained that it was just his leg playing up again.

And though he did not do so, of course, he almost wept with relief when MacDonald finally told him: 'This time we know for certain. Our troops will be here tomorrow.'

It was pitch-black that night. There was a strange silence and electricity in the air, as if a thunderstorm was brewing. And sure enough it came – a deep roll that spread into a growl all along the horizon. Somewhere there was a flash of lightning.

And then, as if they had only been waiting for this heavenly sign, the thousands of bannermen and Boxers surrounding the legations erupted together in the terrible cry, which drowned out even the thunder.

'*Sha! Sha!*' Kill. '*Sha!*' Kill.

MacDonald was at the door of the residence in seconds. Soldiers were running in from every defence post reporting that they were under attack. 'Sound the alarm!' MacDonald cried, and moments later the bell in its little tower could be heard jangling wildly.

So it had come to this. Trader stood with his pistol in his hand as the rain poured down in front of him. An hour had passed since the alarm had sounded and a drenching rainstorm had burst over the legations. MacDonald had gone out long ago and not returned. Every other able-bodied man was out on the barricades, including Henry; and if it wasn't for his leg, Trader would have been there, too. Instead, he was mounting guard in the porch by the front door of the residence, inside which Lady MacDonald and her girls were in the back parlour, while Emily and Tom huddled together in a protected corner of the hall.

Thunderstorm or not, this was the last chance for the Chinese. One night left to destroy the foreigners and their traitor-converts. One night left to seal the capital off from the outside world and tell the relief force: 'You've no one to rescue anymore.'

Trader wished he could make out what was going on. Sometimes the Chinese war chant sounded louder; sometimes it died down a little. He wished he could leave his post to go and see.

Then, to his surprise, Henry appeared. He was drenched but unhurt. 'What news?' he asked.

'We're holding them,' said Henry, and disappeared inside. Five minutes later, he came out again.

'What did you tell Emily and Tom?' Trader asked.

'The same as I told you. We're holding them.' Henry paused, then gave his father-in-law a sad look. 'Between you and me, I'm not sure we can hold them much longer.' He shook Trader's hand with emotion before going on his way.

Trader understood: Henry had come for a last look at his wife and son and to bid him goodbye.

Glancing in through the door, he could just see the hem of Emily's skirt. Tom he couldn't see. He would have liked to go in there himself, but he stayed at his post, and the minutes passed.

He lost track of time. He felt as if he had entered a nightmare world where time and space were shaped by rain, cries, screams, and the bangs of countless bullets and shells all around. Sometimes the screams sounded close and getting nearer; at other times they were quieter, though whether that meant that they were farther away he could not tell. The only time the night offered him any solid, static forms was when a flash of lightning would suddenly illumine the scene, and he'd see the sharply curved tile roofs of nearby buildings glistening in the rain like swords and knives.

It couldn't go on for many hours now, he thought. And when the Chinese broke through, he knew what he would do. He'd keep firing, where he was, until they cut him down.

He didn't want to see his daughter's end, nor Tom's. Was that selfish? Not really. Not if there was no hope. Emily would have to do whatever she thought best, and despite her trying to unload the business onto him, he believed he knew what that would be, whatever she said.

As for himself, he'd just as soon a bullet took him out any time now, rather than prolong the agony of waiting.

They were starting to shell the garden in front of him with a Krupp gun. Explosive shells. Did they know where the shells were falling? Would they adjust their aim and hit the residence instead? Despite the rain, he began to move forward onto the lawn, into the line of fire. He wasn't even conscious he was doing so. An explosive shell hit a tree only twenty feet away.

It was a moment later that he noticed that someone else was hastening to the residence door. He stared and frowned. 'What the devil are you doing here?' he demanded.

It was Backhouse.

'I thought I'd come by.'

'Go and fight on the barricades like everyone else.'

'I was. Then MacDonald arrived. He may have thought I was getting in the way. I really don't know. But he sent me here to help you.'

'Don't go inside. You'll disturb people. You can stand in the rain.'

'If we stand in the porch, we'll be outside, but we won't be in the rain.'

Trader said nothing.

'If you stay where you are at this moment, you will be in the line of fire,' Backhouse observed.

Still Trader said nothing, but he reluctantly moved back to the porch. The two men stood in silence for a couple of minutes. A shell from the Krupp gun exploded on the lawn, in the place where Trader had been standing.

'There you are,' said Backhouse. 'MacDonald was right to send me here. I just saved your life.'

'Damn your eyes.'

After a little while, Backhouse spoke again. 'I think you have a death wish, Mr Trader. Do you have a death wish?'

'No.'

'If the Chinese break in – and they very well may – we're the first line of defence for the residence.'

'Obviously. I assume you have a gun.'

'Oh yes. In fact, I'm quite a good shot. We may be able to keep them at bay for a while. But we can't really stop them from getting into the residence. Who's in there?'

'Lady MacDonald and her daughters. My daughter, Mrs Whiteparish, and her son.'

'Has Lady MacDonald got a gun?'

'Don't know. My daughter's got a pistol.'

'If the Chinese do get through, your daughter should use the pistol on herself. And her son, of course.'

'Mind your own business.'

'Are you going to do it, then – assuming you get the chance?'

'None of your affair.'

'I can do it, if you want.'

'You?' Trader looked at Backhouse in horror. This loathsome creature shoot Emily and Tom? Trader pulled out his Webley and pointed it at Backhouse's chest. 'Get out of here!' he shouted. 'Get out of here, or I swear by God I'll kill you.'

And Backhouse, seeing the older man really meant it, gracefully but speedily retired.

So Trader stayed there, half in and half out of the rain, while the thunder and the barrage of shots and shells continued, standing like a tall old rock on a Scottish hillside, bleak and dour and without any hope of salvation.

Then, in the darkest time of the night before the dawn, he heard another deep rumble of thunder in the east, and soon after that, he heard cheering. Supposing that the Chinese must have broken through, he took out his gun and prepared to shoot the first Boxer or bannerman who approached.

And sure enough, a figure did come running in, but he cried out as he came, 'It's me, Henry.' And Trader felt a surge of joy that the two of them could go down fighting side by side. 'Did you hear the big guns in the east?' Henry cried as he reached him.

'Guns? I thought it was thunder.'

'No. Our guns. The relief's arrived. We're saved!'

Emily had many memories of the months that followed. The arrival of the relief force had been a joy indeed: British troops, American, Russian, French, German, Japanese; perhaps most magnificent to behold, the splendid Sikhs from India. But the moment she cherished above all was when a single officer, the first man they saw, walked onto the British legation lawn, wondering where exactly he was, to be greeted by Lady

MacDonald herself, together with a bevy of wives, all dressed formally as though for a diplomatic reception, with the immortal words: 'I don't know who you are, but we are *very* pleased to see you.'

A close second had to be the reaction of her dear father, who on being told that the Dowager Empress Cixi had managed to disappear from the Forbidden City overnight and could not be found, delightedly remarked: 'She's done a bunk. A moonlight flit. You'd think she couldn't pay the rent!'

A third was more moving.

For the day after these events, a discovery was made, of two mines that the Chinese had dug – not the mine that Tom had detected on the northern side of the legation, but two others that no one had known anything about. Inside the mines were found huge quantities of explosive, all primed and ready to be detonated. Why had they not been used? Nobody ever found out. She was with her father, her husband and Tom when MacDonald came in with the news.

'Had those gone off,' MacDonald told them, 'there'd have been nothing left of the legations. We should, all of us, have been blown to smithereens.'

And she saw her father put his hand on Henry's shoulder and quietly say, 'Well, if that isn't a sign of God's providence, then I don't know what is.' And Henry suddenly broke down and wept, though she didn't quite know why.

The following months were relatively quiet for Emily. The Boxer Rebellion was not completely over. Though the Christians in the Legation Quarter and up at the Catholic cathedral had been rescued, there were terrible massacres, of Catholics especially, in the northern prefectures that continued for almost a year until the movement came to an end.

During that time, the Empress Cixi, having got clean away in disguise, had reemerged in the central provinces, where she made a diplomatic tour of ancient cities until terms were finally agreed for her safe return, with the support of the Western powers, to the capital.

In the legation, however, the rebuilding of life began right away. In the autumn, Tom was sent to England with another family who were making the voyage. Henry was busy with the mission, which had to be rebuilt. Emily took it upon herself to write a long letter giving the family a full account of everything that had passed, including a glowing account of her father's gallant role in the whole business.

The surprise had been her father. She'd supposed he'd probably go back to England with Tom. But instead he'd announced that there was something he wanted to do before he left, and that it might take a month or two.

She and Henry were perfectly happy about it and glad of his company. But she'd been amazed at how busy he'd been. There had been calls upon diplomats and long discussions with Morrison, old Sir Robert Hart, and others knowledgeable in the conduct of affairs. And finally, after two months, he had completed his project.

His report, entitled *The Folly of Reparations in China,* was never published, but it was widely read. And admired. For it was a masterpiece.

'You see,' he told her, 'what I came to suspect, over some decades involved with China in one way or another, was that we'd all been making a great mistake. Every time there was a conflict – and of course we always insisted that each war was started by the other side and not by us – we would claim compensation. Both to cover our own expenses and to deter the other side from starting any trouble again. And I came to see that this policy has many problems. In the first place, since the argument is presented as a moral one – that the whole thing's the other fellow's fault – it means that you're simply increasing the enmity between the parties. Secondly, to substantiate your claim to the moral high ground, you'll probably need to tell a pack of lies, which is bad for you. Thirdly, it encourages an attitude of self-righteousness in the party who's on the winning side, which means he doesn't listen to the views and needs of the other party.'

'Shouldn't one be in the right?' she asked. 'Surely we should.'

'Not if it makes you a bully. For here's the thing. I've been over all the figures most carefully. I've made tables of them. All we've done is ruin China. Every time. Think of it: we want China to be open and to trade with us. When they won't, because however foolishly they closed themselves off from the outside world, we come in and ruin them. Is that going to induce them to welcome us? Is that even going to make it possible for them to increase their trade? No. The first thing you've got to do in all business – or diplomacy – is discover the other fellow's point of view and what he needs. Then you've got to find a way to make it in his self-interest to act as you wish. It takes patience, but any other course of action will be counterproductive in the long run. We need to help the Chinese, not punish them. Call it enlightened self-interest, call it anything you like. But that's what we should do.'

'You really have strong feelings about this, don't you?'

'Yes, I do, now that I've understood it. And this report backs it up with chapter and verse, all the way.'

'And you wanted to write it before you left.'

'Yes, while it was fresh in my mind, and I had access to people like Hart who had a lot of hard information. I also wanted to get it out there before we indulge ourselves in another round of reparations for this latest affair.'

She'd been so proud of the old man. And although the foreign powers had, once again, demanded reparations, she'd watched with pleasure as, over quite a short period of time, starting with the Americans, one by one, every participant had returned the money to China, sometimes in charitable form, sometimes as investment, but returned the money all the same.

Of course, her father had gone away long before then.

He'd departed on a ship that was going to pass by Macao. That had given her the chance to tease him a little, just as he was leaving. 'You'll have time to go onshore and look at some old haunts in Macao,' she said. 'Romantic memories, I daresay.'

'Oh. With your mother, you mean?'

'No. There was the lady before her. Half Oriental, wasn't she?'

'How the devil do you know about that?'

'Grandmother told me. She found out. Mother knew, too. Didn't Mother ever tease you about it?'

'No. Never mentioned it, actually.'

'Well, good for you, anyway. Safe journey. Happy memories.'

The ship ploughed its way towards Macao. Most of the passengers were on deck, for it was a sunny day and the view across to the island, with the gleaming facade of St Paul's high on its hill, was splendid indeed. But John Trader wasn't on deck.

He'd been getting sick before he got on the boat, and he'd known it. But it didn't matter. Everybody was safe. His report was done. It was the right time to leave. Right for Emily and Henry, too. They'd all enjoyed one another's company, but it was better to leave before people were glad to see you go.

The ship's doctor came into his cabin. He was a good, sensible man, in his forties. An Irishman, O'Grady by name. He looked at Trader seriously. 'I've got to put you off, you know.'

'Why?'

'You've got pneumonia.'

'I know that.'

'Fresh air and sun in Macao may save you.'

'I want to stay here.'

'I can't answer for you.'

'No. But you can bury me.'

'At sea? That's what you want?'

'Yes.'

'I'm not supposed to.'

'Write a note to cover yourself. I'll sign it. Not that anyone will ever ask to see it.'

'Probably not.'

'How long shall we be here at Macao?'

'Two days.'

'I'll sit on deck in the sun for one of them, if it's fine.'

And it was fine, and he did, and then the ship left on the evening of the second day, after dark, and he made his way with difficulty back to his cabin and collapsed on his bed.

As he lay there, he thought: if I hadn't come down with pneumonia, I'd be buried in Scotland. But he didn't want that. Leave Drumlomond to the Lomonds. He wasn't really one of them. He'd got the Scottish estate he'd always wanted, acted the part of landowner well enough all these years, but it was time to move on.

Where would he have chosen to be buried, then, if on land? He couldn't think of anywhere. Not with the life he'd had. There was no turning back now. I am a man at sea, he thought. Let the sea have me.

He began to sink late that night, and continued to sink, watched by Dr O'Grady, while the night grew blacker. Black as opium.

THE MANDATE OF HEAVEN

It was me. I did it. She foresaw everything. And she was in control up to her last breath. But she needed me. And I did it.

I caught my first glimpse of her secret plan – for I am sure that is what it was – about two years after she'd returned to Beijing following the Boxer Rebellion. The day before, she'd been out to the Eastern Tombs to inspect her mausoleum, and she'd returned in a very good temper. The mausoleum was magnificent. When the time came, she'd be buried in splendour. And people would look upon her tomb with awe for centuries to come.

That day, however, she was to receive a group of Western ladies, Americans mostly, who were coming to pay her a courtesy visit.

Such visits had become rather a feature of her life at this time. I believe she talked to these women for several reasons. She'd clearly decided that, since she couldn't get rid of the Western barbarians, it would be best to make friends with them, and she could still be very charming when she wanted. The Western women loved these meetings, and they seemed to amuse Cixi; though whether she was really amused, it was hard to tell.

But I'm sure that she was also curious, for if there was anything they could tell her about their customs that might be useful to China, she wanted to find it out.

The meeting that day was typical. The Western women wanted to talk about foot-binding, and Cixi explained: 'As a Manchu, I am no more in favour of the custom than you are. Indeed, I'm going to take steps to end it.' They liked hearing this very much. Several of the women, at the urging of their husbands, I expect, told her about the wonders of the great railways that the Western powers could build for her in China if she granted them concessions. The dowager empress always said to me in private that she hated trains, but she smiled and said that, no doubt, there would be many more railways in China in the future. Actually, I rode in a train with her once, and she seemed rather to enjoy it.

But that day, what she really wanted to talk about was their form of government. 'In your country,' she asked the American women, 'the people elect assemblies to represent them, and also a president who rules – but only for a few years. Is that not so?'

'It is,' one of them replied.

'All the men elect?'

'Most. Not all.'

'And the women?'

'Not yet.'

'Is it not disruptive that you have to go through such a process so frequently?'

'Perhaps. But it means that if we do not like a government, we can soon change it.'

'Your Majesty might think our system is better,' a young English lady suggested. 'We have a monarch who rules with the advice of our Parliament. We think that makes our government wiser and more stable.'

'I have outlived your queen,' said Cixi with some satisfaction. She frowned. 'There is a man called Sun Yat-sen who was partly educated by you British in Hong Kong. He produced a big plan for an elected assembly for China. He wants a revolution. In the end he had to leave the country. But there are many people with progressive views, as his ideas are called, in our southern provinces. They are quite troublesome.'

'We think our constitutional monarchy is stable and respectful of tradition,' the English lady replied.

The empress did not say anything, but I noticed that she looked thoughtful. 'I must remind you,' she said quietly, 'that the British have not always been respectful of our traditions. Did you know that at this moment a British force is encroaching on Tibet?'

'I do not know that,' said the lady, looking awkward.

'I daresay you do not. But it is so.' Cixi pursed her lips. 'I have been fortunate these last few years to have an excellent general who can keep order in this huge land and also defend our borderlands if necessary. I am speaking of General Yuan.'

'We have met him,' said several of the ladies. 'A splendid soldier,' said one. 'A man of the old school!' exclaimed another. 'You are fortunate indeed, Majesty,' said a third.

'I am so glad you agree,' said my mistress.

After they had gone, the empress turned to me. 'What do you think of General Yuan, Lacquer Nail?'

I thought for a moment. I knew I could say whatever I wanted and she would not mind. She trusted me. 'An old warlord who's out for himself, my lady.'

'Of course. But we need him. And what about our visitors?'

'They seem to think that their forms of government are superior to ours,' I said. 'Of course,' I added, 'we always felt ours was superior to theirs.'

'Certainly,' she replied. 'I will tell you something, Lacquer Nail. You will remember how, when the foreign troops came to relieve the legations, I had to leave the capital in a hurry.'

'How could I forget?' I said.

'It was chaos. I was glad I had you with me. And we all wandered from city to city, province to province, until I was sure it was safe to return. A tour of inspection, we called it. But in doing this, you know, I discovered who my friends were – the prefects and governors who took us in – and I also got to see the country more than I had in many years. And to talk to people, mandarins and scholars who had no idea if I'd get back to power or not, and who told me what they really thought. I learned so much about my country and about its history.' She paused. 'We need to change, Lacquer Nail. I know that now. That's why I like listening to these Western ladies, to discover more about them.'

'Do you know how we should change the Celestial Kingdom, my lady?'

'Not exactly. Not yet. But I've realised something else. It's all a question of timing. You remember how the present emperor tried to turn the whole kingdom upside down?'

'I always suspected, my lady, that they were all his tutors' ideas.'

'Setting up the university was all right. But all his other reforms . . . Nobody – none of the mandarins or the nobles and gentry – was ready for it. He had no support. I had to come back and lock him up.'

'You did what you had to, my lady.'

'But you see, Lacquer Nail, the same is true of Sun Yat-sen and his progressive friends. They think that because something is a good idea, it will work. And it's not true. In both cases, they came too suddenly and too soon. It's all about timing. That's the thing.' She smiled sadly. 'And you know the other thing?'

'No, my lady.'

'There's never enough time.'

Cixi might not have been certain what changes the empire needed, but those years saw a lot of activity.

They made plans for electing a National Assembly, and they finally abolished the old Confucian exams for mandarins and designed a new syllabus in science and foreign languages. And they abolished torture. Just imagine it. You'd have been executed for proposing such things a few years before.

As for the railway concessions, in no time the British and French, the Russians, the Japanese and the Germans were all setting up railways to suit themselves.

I continued to serve the empress in the usual way. She also encouraged me to see the young emperor every little while. Although he was waited on hand and foot by the eunuchs, he was quite lonely in his pavilion, and he always seemed pleased to see me. He knew my story, and that I was a bit different from the run-of-the-mill palace people, and I think he trusted me.

After my visit, Cixi would ask me, 'How did you find him? Is he all right?' She saw him herself, of course, but she seemed to want to know how other people found him. I think she cared for him, in her way.

The truth was that sometimes I hardly knew what to tell her. I don't mean his physical condition – though he always seemed to have a lot of ailments. I mean his state of mind. With his long, pale, fleshy face, he always looked sad. And some days he was moody. But once or twice I'd arrive and find him sitting alone and happily tinkering with a clock, almost like a child. Some people thought he wasn't quite right in the head. But gradually I began to wonder if he wasn't doing it on purpose – acting like a simpleton, to make people think he was harmless. Perhaps he should have acted that way all the time.

Almost five years passed in this way. I could have retired, of course. I had years ago acquired the fine house of Mr Chen. I had a considerable fortune. And I had bought back my balls, of course. I spent the majority of my time living as my other self, the merchant. But I could not desert the empress. A day or two every week I became Lacquer Nail again and waited upon her. Sometimes we'd be out at the Summer Palace, but mostly in the Forbidden City. There were still theatricals and other amusements for Cixi, but these gradually grew fewer and fewer. One thing she enjoyed particularly was being photographed. I think it was the Western women who got her to like it. For they wanted to be photographed with her. She always took the greatest care of her appearance right to the end, but even more than usual if there was a chance she might be photographed.

Though we often talked during those years, she usually kept her designs hidden, even from me – except for one small occasion on which she said something that came back into my mind many times in the years to come. 'You know, Lacquer Nail,' she said, 'I have told you of the need for change, and that change must come only when the time is ready.'

'Yes, my lady,' I said.

'But our history is so long that if we study it, we shall discover that nothing is new. It may seem new, but it isn't. Therefore, we can usually foretell, in a general way, what is to come.' I'm sure she meant me to remember that.

But what her plans for the future were, or whether she had even worked them out in detail, I did not discover.

At the same time, the clouds were darkening. Japan and Russia went to war. Japan smashed the Russians, took over most of their Manchurian lands, and now dominated the Korean peninsula as well. The emperor's health was deteriorating, and so was Cixi's. She suffered a slight stroke. Her face drooped a little on one side. Her mental acuity, however, as far as I could judge, remained as sharp as ever. And I wondered: what was the plan for the empire?

I knew that the Empress Cixi was ready to die before she did herself. She hadn't been well for some time, but she had remarkable powers of recovery. Above all, she had a will of iron. It was only when her will began to falter that I knew she was on the way out.

It began one morning when I was doing her nails. She was looking downcast. If there had been anyone else in the room, I wouldn't have said a word, because you must never imply that a ruler has any weakness. But we were all by ourselves.

'You look sad today, Majesty,' I said.

'I am, Lacquer Nail,' she answered me. 'I feel very disappointed with my life.'

'You've had the most remarkable career of any woman in history,' I told her.

'Perhaps,' she said. 'And yet I have failed. At first I thought I had succeeded. I had given the emperor a son. What greater thing could a woman do for the Celestial Kingdom or for her own family? I had to fight for him. I was nearly killed. But my son became emperor.' She sighed. 'But to what end? He was not fit to rule. I blamed myself.'

'It was not your fault, my lady,' I said. 'His father hardly helped.'

'All the men in my life have been weak. But I hoped that my stronger blood . . .'

'Your blood is very strong,' I said.

'Is it? I thought so. That is why I chose Prince Chun's son to succeed, when there were other candidates. Because his mother was my sister. He seemed more promising. Yet when he finally came to power, what did he do? Tried to overturn four thousand years of history – overnight! He was a fool.'

'One needs a sense of timing,' I agreed.

'There, Lacquer Nail,' she cried. 'You, a poor eunuch, would have done better.'

Yes, I thought, but I had to fight for my life, and so did you. That's how one learns. I didn't say it, of course.

There was a long pause after that. I put some finishing touches on her nails.

'I am tired, Lacquer Nail,' she said at last. 'I know the world must change. But I don't want to live in it. I don't want to live in a world with trains and people's assemblies.'

'Your body and mind are strong,' I said.

'The Mandate of Heaven is being withdrawn,' she went on quietly.

Now that really knocked me sideways. To be exact, I froze. I had her hand in mine at that moment and I didn't dare make even the tiniest motion, in case it should be interpreted as any kind of comment.

What did she mean? That the dynasty was coming to an end? Or did she mean that her own life was ebbing away? I thought it was just herself she meant.

But then, when she spoke the next words, I wasn't so sure. 'After I die, Lacquer Nail, what will happen?'

'The emperor will rule, I suppose,' I ventured.

She didn't say anything. Not a word.

I got up and made ready to leave.

'General Yuan thinks the emperor will have him killed,' she said.

'Oh,' I said. 'I never heard the emperor say that,' I added.

'The emperor may not like General Yuan,' she went on quietly, 'but that is not the point. He is by far the best general we have at present, and the army follows him.'

She was right about that. Killing Yuan would be really stupid. I was pretty sure what she wanted me to say next. 'Perhaps I might pay a visit to the emperor, to see how he is,' I said.

'That is a good idea, Lacquer Nail,' she answered. 'I have been concerned about his health lately.'

Well, I had just reached the anteroom when whom should I see but General Yuan, waiting for an audience with Cixi.

He was a gruff, bluff man, not tall, but round as a barrel, with a huge grey moustache like a water buffalo's horns. He was quite frightening, really, but he was always friendly with me. I bowed low.

'Where are you off to, Lacquer Nail?' he asked.

'I thought I might call upon the emperor, sir,' I said.

'He's planning to kill me, you know,' he remarked.

'I've never heard him say it,' I replied.

'Well, perhaps you can persuade him not to,' he suggested cheerfully.

Then I left.

It was a couple of hours later when I went along the corridor and over the narrow bridge that led to the emperor's pavilion. The bridge was always guarded, to see he didn't get out, really; but the guards let me through without a word.

I found him lying on a divan. Though he was still only in his thirties, he seemed like a man in decline. His hair was thinning. His face looked a little blue, and I noticed that there were telltale white bands across his fingernails. From arsenic, I guessed.

'I came to see if Your Majesty wanted any company,' I said softly.

'Not really,' he said. But then he sat up. 'Is anything happening out there, Lacquer Nail?'

'I wouldn't say a lot,' I replied. 'I was with the dowager empress earlier today, doing her nails. I thought she was tired.'

'Is she unwell?'

'She's got such a spirit,' I said, 'that it's very hard to know. She's not getting any younger. She worries about you, I think.'

'She sent you to spy on me?'

'No.' I smiled. 'She's got half the eunuchs in the palace to do that. You know how it is.'

He laughed when I said that. 'They're not cleaning my rooms properly,' he said with a frown.

'I can tell her that,' I said. 'She'll have them whipped.'

'Good. You do that,' he said. Then he dropped his voice. 'How do I look to you?'

'You don't look well,' I said. 'As if you haven't been eating properly or taking any exercise, if you'll forgive my saying so.'

'I think they're trying to poison me. Do you think they are?'

'I don't know why they would be,' I replied. 'I always thought they needed you there. Everything has to be done in your name, after all.'

'Yes, it does, doesn't it?' The thought seemed to please him. 'Tell me more about Cixi.'

'She was complaining about the railways,' I said. 'Though she's been in a train, I know for a fact.'

'What's new?' He gave a small laugh. 'Did you see anyone else?'

'Yes,' I said. 'General Yuan was waiting for an audience with her when I was leaving.'

'Did he say anything?'

'Only that he thinks you're planning to kill him.'

'Hmm.' He pursed his lips and looked thoughtful. 'Well, he got that right, anyway,' he said. 'Too big for his boots. And if Cixi dies and I'm incapacitated, I've written instructions that he's to be beheaded.' And he nodded with satisfaction.

And then I understood. Cixi was right. If he was rash enough to kill Yuan, he shouldn't be ruling. And worse still, if he was stupid enough to tell me, then he was never going to learn anything.

'Shall we play a game of checkers?' I suggested. And for an hour or so we amused ourselves with that.

'I'm tired now,' he said finally. 'Will you come back again and see me soon?'

'Whatever Your Majesty desires,' I replied. 'Sometimes,' I said gently,

'I smoke an opium pipe, to calm my nerves. Would Your Majesty like it if I brought pipes for us both another time?'

'Can you do that?' he asked.

'Oh, I think so,' I replied.

Cixi sent word that I should come to see her the next day. She was clearly going downhill, but her mind was still clear as a bell.

'You know, Lacquer Nail,' she said, 'if the emperor were unable to resume his duties after my death, it would be necessary to make other arrangements for the succession.'

'I suppose it would.' I didn't say anything else. Just that.

'The father of the emperor, Prince Chun, has another son, not by my sister.'

'Of course,' I said. 'The young Prince Chun.'

'The young Prince Chun is the same generation as the emperor,' she went on, 'so he is not supposed to succeed him.'

That's exactly the rule you broke when you selected your sister's son to be emperor last time, I thought. But all I said was: 'These things are complex.'

'But the young Prince Chun has a son, by a woman I personally selected for him.'

And whom he hates, I might have said.

'You mean the boy they call Puyi?' I asked.

'Puyi could be the heir. His father could be regent.'

The child was not even three years old. I stared at her in amazement. What was she thinking of?

And then I thought I understood. The two times she'd seen an emperor actually ruling, it had been a disaster. The first emperor had deserted his post and run away to the north; the second had nearly brought down the administration. The only governments she knew that worked – however badly – in nearly fifty years were regencies. Perhaps she'd come to think that this was a natural state. With Puyi on the throne, she'd guarantee another dozen years of regency, at least.

And what then? Perhaps a wise emperor. There had been wise emperors in the past.

But then I thought about all she'd said to me about change and timing. The final arrangements for the assembly they'd been talking about had been pretty much agreed just weeks before. It was to begin functioning after a period of eleven years. Just about the time little Puyi would reach his majority. Of course, that would all make sense. The new National Assembly would rule and Puyi, in all likelihood, could be a constitutional monarch. I cannot prove this was her plan, but if it was, it might be a pretty good one.

So she did have a plan. A gradual transition. It seemed to me that people might even support it. After all, I'd always supported the Confucian ideal of moral government by a good emperor. But having observed emperors for half a century I had to ask: where do you find this good emperor? I'd never seen one.

Knowing Cixi as I did, I'm nearly certain of one other thing, too. She suspected the dynasty was doomed, and she wanted it to end with her.

Think of it. She'd ruled for half a century. She'd been the one to defend the old order – braver and bolder than any of the men. And more cunning. And now she was ushering in the new world. No more emperors after her. She'd be the last to rule. A heroine, perhaps. The most extraordinary woman, certainly. An enigma: ah, she'd built a splendid tomb for herself, and so have many rulers; but if you want to fascinate historians, then you must be an enigma.

The art of the thing. The symmetry. How I admired her.

But she still took me by surprise by what she said next.

'So, Lacquer Nail, what do you think I should do?'

'About?'

'The emperor.'

'You are asking me, my lady? Your humble servant?'

'I've known you fifty years, Lacquer Nail. You're intelligent. I trust you. And you're not an interested party. You've nothing at stake one way or the other. And the truth is that I hardly know what to do myself. I am so old and tired. But I would trust you to do the right thing.'

I stared at her. And I thought very hard. 'You know I am loyal to you, my lady,' I said. 'I've never been anything else in my life. And I think you understand things better than anyone else.'

She was listening to me carefully. 'And?'

'Are you sure, my lady, that you want me to express an opinion? Personally,' I went on, 'if I have understood you correctly, I don't think anyone should say anything at all.'

She looked me in the eye and nodded slowly, and I knew that she had just left the fate of the Celestial Kingdom in my hands. Think of it. In my hands.

'I am tired now,' she said. 'You have things to attend to. Come and do my nails in the morning.'

It was early evening when I went across the little bridge to see the emperor. There were lamps lit in the corridor and on the narrow bridge. They made shiny little reflections in the ice-covered water of the pond.

He was looking very low. 'My stomach's been hurting all day,' he said. 'I'm awfully tired, but the pain won't let me sleep.'

'May I prepare a pipe for Your Majesty?' I asked. 'I brought a little opium. It will take the pain away.'

'All right,' he said.

'May I also smoke?'

He nodded, and I prepared two pipes. After we had smoked for a little while I asked him if the pain had eased, and he said, 'Yes, but it's still there.'

'I believe,' I said, 'it would help if you also drank a little tea. It's good for the bowels. Would Your Majesty allow me to pour a little tea for myself also?' I dared to ask.

He indicated that I should prepare the tea, so I did. He was quite drowsy, so I had to prop him up with one arm as I gave him the tea, which I naturally did before taking any myself.

'Drink it all,' I said. And he emptied the cup.

It was quite a big cup, with enough arsenic in it to kill two horses.

People say that the Empress Cixi herself went to see the emperor on his deathbed and watched him die. But it's not true. I was the one with him. Only me. It was me who took the life of the last reigning emperor of China.

Two hours later, after I had cleaned everything up, I went back across the bridge, leaving word with the eunuch on duty that the emperor was asleep, but that he didn't seem very well.

'He's been like that all day,' he said.

When I came to see Cixi the next morning, she was already up and busy dealing with the death of the emperor the evening before. The infant Puyi had already been sent for.

I was still there when his father brought him in to present him to Cixi. She was having a rest at that moment and the child did nothing but scream, so I don't think anybody enjoyed the meeting.

But the succession was decided. Puyi was the infant boy emperor and his father was regent.

Before I withdrew, Cixi called me to her side. 'Is there anything you need, Lacquer Nail?'

She had so much money. She'd have given me anything I asked for. But I was already well set up by then. So I was glad to be able to ask her for nothing, and I'm sure she was pleased.

But I did have one bright idea. 'Your Majesty,' I said, 'I should like a few books for my house. It would add distinction, and there are many in the palace. Might I take a dozen or so?'

'What an extraordinary request. You are full of surprises. Take whatever you want, but let me see them before you go.'

So I went to the private library and selected a dozen books I believed to be valuable and brought them to her. She was quite tired, drained by all the events of the day I'm sure, and she hardly glanced at them. But she managed a smile at me.

'I don't think we shall meet again, Lacquer Nail,' she said.

'Please don't say that, Majesty,' I muttered.

'You are unlike the other palace people,' she went on, 'because you used to be a man. And I have often thought that you had feelings for me.'

I bowed my head. 'It is true, my lady,' I said softly. I was very moved.

'Here,' she said, 'take this in memory of me.' And she pulled off one of the beautiful jewelled nail guards she wore and gave it to me.

I have it still.

That very evening, she laid herself out in the correct posture, with her face turned towards the south, and died. She willed it.

There was never any woman like her.

That day was my last in the palace. I retired with honour. I ceased forever to be Lacquer Nail the eunuch. From that day, I lived only as my other self, the rich merchant with a fine house and children and grandchildren.

But before I left the Forbidden City, I walked down towards the western side gate and turned into the little haunted alley. I hadn't been in there for a long time, but down the years I had always kept my secret store of silver under the stone there, just in case I should ever have need of it. Indeed, I'd added to it from time to time.

'Good evening, my lady,' I said to the ghost, just in case she should be there. Then I prized up the stone and removed the little cache of silver coins. But before putting the stone back, I placed a single coin under it.

'Thank you for protecting my fortune, honoured lady,' I said. 'I have left you a coin just in case you should ever have need of it.'

Then I went on my way. And I think she was pleased, for had she thought it was not enough, I'm sure she would have let me know.

○

In the years that followed, one might have said that the arrangements Cixi made for the succession collapsed. At the time of what we now call the revolution, the little boy king was removed from the throne and Dr Sun Yat-sen was elected president. But that didn't last long, either. Then General Yuan took over and tried to found a new dynasty. But no one wanted that, and soon the republic dissolved into scores of little territories under the control of local warlords.

That was when I remembered Cixi's words to me about history. 'Nothing is new.' China's history is long. The pattern takes new forms, but in essence it is always the same. A dynasty slowly degenerates. Outsiders encroach. Insiders rebel. The Mandate of Heaven is withdrawn. The dynasty falls. A period of chaos and warlords follows. Finally order is restored by a new dynasty, usually from inside. The old empire rises again for a few more centuries.

She might not have been pleased by the course of events, but she would have hardly been surprised.

○

For me personally, there still remained one small piece of business to attend to. It was for this business I needed those books from the emperor's palace.

For shortly before the Boxer Rebellion I had made the acquaintance of a rather strange Englishman, a Chinese scholar, who would do anything for books, if they were rare and valuable. And I needed him to do something for me.

His name was Edmund Backhouse.

When I asked him to visit me and showed him the books I'd taken, he was very pleased.

'I should very much like them for my collection,' he said. 'What do you want for them?'

'No money,' I said. 'A service.' And I told him what I needed. 'Do you think you can do it?' I asked.

'There's only one way to find out,' he said. I think he was quite amused by the challenge. 'Where do I find him?'

The Temple of Prosperity was an old monastery dating back to the Ming dynasty, just outside the walls of the Forbidden City. It was really the nicest place you could end your days if you were a palace person. You could come and go as you liked, but you had comfortable quarters and the monks looked after you. The other residents were former eunuchs like yourself, so everyone felt comfortable in one another's company. But you had to be rich to get in there.

They lived a very dignified life, I must say. I'd have been glad to go there myself, if I didn't have another life.

'He's in the Temple of Prosperity,' I told Backhouse. 'But that's all I know. You'll have to do the rest. I suppose you could say you're compiling a history or something like that, and ask if he'd talk to you.'

'I often do that sort of thing,' he replied.

'Well, good luck, then,' I said. 'When you've something to tell me, come here after dark, and make sure you're not followed.'

I had to wait only ten days before Backhouse arrived at my house one night.

'Any luck?' I asked.

'Yes,' he said. 'I'd have come sooner, but he was such a mine of information that I visited seven times before I did the deed. Then I said my final goodbye and gave him a present as thanks, and we parted as friends. With a bit of luck he may not even realise what's missing for a while.'

'You've got them, then?'

'Of course.' He produced a jar.

And I found myself looking at the tiny sexual organs of the boy who became Mr Liu.

'It took me a while to discover where he kept them, but it just came out naturally when he was discussing the whole procedure he went through. They were on a shelf behind a little votive Buddha.'

'Here are the books,' I said. 'Can you take them now? And after this, we'd better not meet for a while.'

It took a couple of days for Mr Liu to discover his terrible loss. Naturally, he supposed it must be someone in the monastery, and he tried to think of anyone who might be his enemy there. It turned out there were quite a few. It's always like that in monasteries, I think.

It was only gradually that his thoughts turned to Backhouse. But why would Backhouse want to do such a thing? That was what Backhouse himself asked the police when they came to see him.

'You're most welcome to search my little house,' he said. 'But I don't think my stealing Mr Liu's balls, especially when we had such cordial and interesting conversations, makes much sense.' And although the police did look around his rooms, it was pretty clear that they couldn't see why he'd have done such a thing, either.

Meanwhile, I waited. I waited three months. I suppose he went from one person he'd bullied or cheated after another, but even so, I was surprised he took so long to come to me.

But there he was, one afternoon, speaking to a servant at the street door, asking to be admitted to my presence. I made sure he had to wait in the outer yard some time. I watched him, actually, from behind a screen. I could see he was impressed by the house.

Finally he was admitted to my presence.

'Why, Mr Liu,' I said, 'what brings you here?'

I must say, he was looking very old and tired and bent, and really quite beaten. Not at all the old Mr Liu I remembered.

'I thought you might know,' he said. I wonder how many people he'd already been forced to say that to.

'There's a rumour going around that you have suffered a great loss,' I told him. 'A terrible loss.'

'Terrible, indeed. I do not need to tell you what it means.'

'Quite,' I said. 'But I don't see how I can help you.'

He looked at me. His eyes were pleading. 'If there is anything . . .' he offered. 'I would pay . . .'

'When I heard about this,' I said, 'I was curious. Either someone bears him a grudge, I thought, or there is ransom money involved. Has anyone asked for ransom money?'

'Nobody. I thought of that. But there has been no demand.'

'All the same,' I continued, 'that doesn't mean that someone wouldn't be prepared to part with your balls – having made you suffer – for a sum of money.'

'How should I go about finding them?'

'Inside the palace, you knew everything. Outside, you know very little. But I am a merchant. Give me a little time and I will make some enquiries. I promise nothing, but come back in a month.' Then I dismissed him.

He came back in a month. The moment I was told he was waiting outside, I sent a servant with a message to a certain young fellow whom I trusted to run discreet errands for me. Before Mr Liu was ushered in, the young fellow was on his way to the Temple of Prosperity, where he left the package containing the jar with Mr Liu's private parts with the abbot, to be given to Mr Liu on his return. Before they even had time to ask who he was, he'd disappeared into the street.

Mr Liu looked quite unwell, I must say. He was all in. He gazed sadly at my face, and seeing no encouragement, he seemed quite to shrivel up.

'No news, then?' he said, as if he knew the answer.

'There is news,' I answered. 'I believe your jar will be returned.'

'You do?' He brightened. 'Truly?'

'I hope so. It will cost money.'

'Tell me how much.'

I shook my head. 'You can't afford it.'

He didn't like that.

'I assure you . . .' he started.

'I know you have money, Mr Liu. But I am a merchant and a rich man. Your problem and its price are not significant to me.'

'If there is anything I can do . . .' he began again.

'Yes,' I said. 'There is. For old times' sake.' I savoured the moment. 'Get down on your knees and kowtow.'

'Kowtow?'

'You remember how to, I'm sure. As you did to the emperor. Kowtow.'

'This is sacrilege,' he cried.

'Do you want your balls back? Yes or no? Kowtow.'

Slowly he went down on his knees. He looked up. There was a flash of the old Mr Liu in his eyes now. 'You want to humiliate me,' he hissed.

'There is no one to see,' I answered blandly.

He made the first kowtow.

'It was you,' he cried. 'You all along.' His instincts were still good.

'No, it wasn't,' I replied calmly. 'I have no idea how I could have accomplished such a thing if I'd even thought of it. This is an opportunity that fate has unexpectedly thrown in my way. But when I think,' I went on, 'of all you have done to me in the past, it's a very small penalty that I'm exacting. Had I actually planned all this,' I added for good measure, 'you'd never have got your balls back at all.'

That shut him up.

'Kowtow again,' I said.

AFTERWORD

Students of Chinese history will be aware of a problem: what was really going on in the court during the long years of Cixi's effective rule? The confusion has been made worse by one man in particular. I refer of course to Edmund Backhouse. His accounts of the court and his scandalous memoirs make vivid reading, and were used in popular histories for decades. But are they total inventions of his imagination, gossip from the city street, or partly reliable? Nobody knows. He was an extraordinary linguist and bibliophile, certainly. Some of his stories I personally do not believe. But as a novelist with a sense of duty to history, what was I to do?

My solution was technical: I employed a third person, my character Lacquer Nail, to be the narrator of the Forbidden City and Summer Palace sections of the story. A narrator who had his own distinctive point of view and who might or might not be totally reliable. I had fun with this most useful character, and I hope that both general readers and students of China's history will feel that my efforts were worthwhile.

And since Edmund Backhouse was indeed present during the siege of the legations, I gave him a part to play as well, based on things he actually did, together with a few imagined interactions with my fictional characters. I also could not resist giving him a small, entirely fictitious part in my final chapter. After all, I thought, if he can invent things, then I can invent things, too!

There remain a pair of mysteries. How did the emperor, Cixi's nephew, die? There seems to be a general consensus nowadays that he was probably poisoned by palace eunuchs. I have allowed my fictional eunuch, Lacquer Nail, to claim the honour for himself.

And what of Cixi during her final years: had she a plan? What was she trying to achieve? There has been some controversy recently, following the publication of Jung Chang's biography of Cixi. Through the mouth of my narrator, Lacquer Nail, I have offered my own best guess, for what it is worth.

ABOUT THE AUTHOR

Edward Rutherfurd is the internationally bestselling author of eight novels, including *Paris, London, The Princes of Ireland, The Rebels of Ireland* and *New York*.